AN ENCYCLOPEDIA

OF

FREEMASONRY

AND

ITS KINDRED SCIENCES

COMPRISING

THE WHOLE RANGE OF ARTS, SCIENCES AND LITERATURE
AS CONNECTED WITH THE INSTITUTION

BY

ALBERT G. MACKEY, M.D., 33°

THIS NEW AND REVISED EDITION

PREPARED UNDER THE DIRECTION, AND WITH
THE ASSISTANCE, OF THE LATE

WILLIAM J. HUGHAN, 32°

BY

EDWARD L. HAWKINS, M.A., 30°

FOREWORD BY

MICHAEL R. POLL, FPS, FMS

PHOTOGRAPHIC REPRODUCTION OF THE 1916 EDITION
REPUBLISH IN 2015

BY

CORNERSTONE BOOK PUBLISHERS
NEW ORLEANS, LA

VOLUME I

Encyclopedia of Freemasonry
Volume One
by Albert G. Mackey
Revised by William J. Hughan and
Edward L. Hawkins
Foreword by Michael R. Poll

A Cornerstone Book
Published by Cornerstone Book Publishers
An imprint of Michael Poll Publishing

Cornerstone Book Publishers
New Orleans, LA
www.cornerstonepublishers.com

Photographic Reproduction of the 1916 Edition

First Cornerstone Edition - 2015

ISBN:1613422520
ISBN-13:978-1-61342-252-6

MADE IN THE USA

PREFACE

I ONCE delivered an address before a Lodge on the subject of the external changes which Freemasonry had undergone since the period of its revival in the commencement of the eighteenth century. The proper treatment of the topic required a reference to German, to French, and to English authorities, with some of which I am afraid that many of my auditors were not familiar. At the close of the address, a young and intelligent brother inquired of me how he could obtain access to the works which I had cited, and of many of which he confessed, as well as of the facts that they detailed, he now heard for the first time. It is probable that my reply was not altogether satisfactory; for I told him that I knew of no course that he could adopt to attain that knowledge except the one that had been pursued by myself, namely, to spend his means in the purchase of Masonic books and his time in reading them.

But there are few men who have the means, the time, and the inclination for the purchase of numerous books, some of them costly and difficult to be obtained, and for the close and attentive reading of them which is necessary to master any given subject.

It was this thought that, years ago, suggested to me the task of collecting materials for a work which would furnish every Freemason who might consult its pages the means of acquiring a knowledge of all matters connected with the science, the philosophy, and the history of his Order.

But I was also led to the prosecution of this work by a higher consideration. I had myself learned, from the experience of my early Masonic life, that the character of the Institution was elevated in every one's opinion just in proportion to the amount of knowledge that he had acquired of its symbolism, philosophy, and history.

If Freemasonry was not at one time patronized by the learned, it was because the depths of its symbolic science and philosophy had not been sounded. If it is now becoming elevated and popular in the estimation of scholars, it owes that elevation and that popularity to the labors of those who have studied its intellectual system and given the result of their studies to the world. The scholar will rise from the perusal of Webb's *Monitor*, or the *Hieroglyphic Chart* of Cross, with no very exalted appreciation of the literary character of the Institution of which such works profess to be an exponent. But should he have met with even Hutchinson's *Spirit of Masonry,* or Town's *Speculative Masonry,* which are among the earlier products of Masonic literature, he will be conscious that the system which could afford material for such works must be worthy of investigation.

Oliver is not alone in the belief that the higher elevation of the Order is to be attributed " almost solely to the judicious publications on the subject of Freemasonry which have appeared during the present and the end of the last century." It is the press that is elevating the Order; it is the labor of its scholars that is placing it in the rank of sciences. The more that is published by scholarly pens on its principles, the more will other scholars be attracted to its investigation.

At no time, indeed, has its intellectual character been more justly appreciated than at the present day. At no time have its members generally cultivated its science with more assiduity. At no time have they been more zealous in the endeavor to obtain a due enlightenment on all the topics which its system comprehends.

It was the desire to give my contribution toward the elevation of the Order, by aiding in the dissemination of some of that light and knowledge which are not so easy of access, that impelled me years ago to commence the preparation of this work—a task which I have steadily toiled to accomplish, and at which, for several years, I have wrought with unintermitted labor that has permitted but little time for other occupation, and none for recreation.

And now I present to my brethren the result not only of those years of toil, but of more than thirty years of study and research—a work which will, I trust, or at least I hope, supply them with the materials for acquiring a knowledge of much that is required to make a Masonic scholar. Encyclopedic learning is not usually considered as more than elementary. But knowing that but few Freemasons can afford time to become learned scholars in our art by an entire devotion to its study, I have in important articles endeavored to treat the subject exhaustively, and in all to give that amount of information that must make future ignorance altogether the result of disinclination to learn.

I do not present this work as perfect, for I well know that the culminating point of perfection can never be attained by human effort. But, under many adverse circumstances, I have sought to make it as perfect as I could. Encyclopedias are, for the most part, the result of the conjoined labor of many writers. In this work I have had no help. Every article was written by myself. I say this not to excuse my errors—for I hold that no author should wilfully permit an error to pollute his pages—but rather to account for those that may exist. I have endeavored to commit none. Doubtless there are some. If I knew them, I would correct them; but let him who discovers them remember that they have been unwittingly committed in the course of an exhaustive and unaided task.

For twelve months, too, of the time in which I have been occupied upon this work, I suffered from an affection of the sight, which forbade all use of the eyes for purposes of study. During that period, now happily passed, all authorities were consulted under my direction by the willing eyes of my daughters—all writing was done under my dictation by their hands. I realized for a time the picture so often painted of the blind bard dictating his sublime verses to his daughters. It was a time of sorrow for the student who could not labor with his own organs in his vocation; but it was a time of gladness to the father who felt that he had those who, with willing hearts, could come to his assistance. To the world this is of no import; but I could not conscientiously close this prefatory address without referring to this circumstance so gratifying to a parent's heart. Were I to dedicate this work at all, my dedication should be—To FILIAL AFFECTION.

ALBERT G. MACKEY, M. D.

REVISER'S PREFACE

THE revision of this most comprehensive Encyclopedia has been a most anxious and laborious task. I have endeavored to preserve as much as possible of Dr. Mackey's work untouched, but at the same time to correct statements which later investigations have shown to be unfounded; thus I have left all of Dr. Mackey's opinions and theories unaltered.

All completely new articles, or old ones with many alterations, I have marked with my initials and I must take all responsibility for them, though as far as possible they were submitted to Bro. Hughan for his approval.

I have to return hearty thanks for kind aid to the late Bro. Henry Sadler, Librarian of the Grand Lodge of England; to Bro. W. J. Songhurst, Secretary of the Quatuor Coronati Lodge, No. 2076, London, England, for valuable advice and assistance on many points; to Bro. the Rev. M. Rosenbaum, P. Prov. G. Chaplain of Northumberland, for help with Hebrew words; to Bro. John Yarker, P. G. Warden of Greece, for information about the Antient and Primitive Rite; and to Bro. A. C. Powell, P. Prov. G. Sup. of Works of Bristol, for the article on the Baldwyn Encampment.

EDWARD L. HAWKINS, M. A.

St. Leonards-on-Sea, England, 1912.

FOREWORD TO THE
CORNERSTONE EDITION

The ultimate success of Masonry depends on the intelligence of her disciples.
~ Albert Mackey

Read the above words a few times. They are important. We often hear of the need for education in Masonry, but is education the same as intelligence? No, it's not. The two do not perform the same service to mankind. Intelligence guides us in the proper use of education. Education provides us with a foundation, but it is intelligence which allows us to apply what we have learned so that we may better construct our chosen spiritual or physical castles.

Freemasonry will not survive with members who do not understand or know the basics of Freemasonry. Masons who do not understand Masonry do not benefit us. Uneducated leaders can destroy us. Our goal is not to be a civil club or charitable organization. We are part of society and we do charitable work *because* we are part of society. But, our goal is a basic alchemical formula; to take something good, but less, and make it better. While *better* is a subjective word, we can see it as meaning improved. We improve through learning - through education.

Mackey's *An Encyclopedia of Freemasonry* provides sound, valuable Masonic education. No one should think for a second that it is a work of perfection or that it will answer every question that could be asked, but it is a classic educational tool. This work is, without question, a stone in the foundation of any Masonic education program. What a Mason does with that education, however, is up to him and the depth of his intelligence and dedication.

Cornerstone is proud to republish this indispensable work for the general Masonic public. It is our hope that it can help guide you to a richer and more blessed Masonic life.

Michael R. Poll
July, 2015

Eng.d by A.H.Ritchie

Yours paternally
Albert G Mackey

A

A. (א, *Aleph*.) In the Accadian, Greek, Etruscan, Pelasgian, Gallic, Samaritan, and Egyptian or Coptic, of nearly the same formation as the English letter. It originally meant *with* or *together*, but at present signifies *one*. In most languages it is the initial letter of the alphabet; not so, however, in the Ethiopian, where it is the thirteenth. The sacred Aleph has the numerical value of one, and is composed of two Yods, one on either side of an inclined Vau. It is said to typify the Trinity in Unity. The word *Aleph* signifies " ox," from the resemblance to the head and horns of that animal. The Divine name in Hebrew connected with this letter is אהיה, A H I H.

Aaron. Hebrew אהרן, Aharon, a word of doubtful etymology, but generally supposed to signify *a mountaineer*. He was the brother of Moses, and the first high priest under the Mosaic dispensation, whence the priesthood established by that lawgiver is known as the " Aaronic." He is alluded to in the English lectures of the second degree, in reference to a certain sign which is said to have taken its origin from the fact that Aaron and Hur were present on the hill from which Moses surveyed the battle which Joshua was waging with the Amalekites, when these two supported the weary arms of Moses in an upright posture, because upon his uplifted hands the fate of the battle depended. See Exodus xvii. 10–12. Aaron is also referred to in the latter section of the Royal Arch degree in connection with the memorials that were deposited in the ark of the covenant. In the degree of " Chief of the Tabernacle," which is the 23d of the Ancient and Accepted Rite, the presiding officer represents Aaron, and is styled " Most Excellent High Priest." In the 24th degree of the same Rite, or " Prince of the Tabernacle," the second officer or Senior Warden also personates Aaron.

Aaron's Band. A degree instituted in 1824, in New York City, mainly for social purposes, and conferred in an independent body. Its ceremonies were not dissimilar to those of High Priesthood, which caused the Grand Royal Arch Chapter of the State to take umbrage, and the small gathering dispersed.

Aaron's Rod. The method by which Moses caused a miraculous judgment as to which tribe should be invested with the priesthood, is detailed in the Book of Numbers (ch. xvii.). He directed that twelve rods should be laid up in the Holy of Holies of the Tabernacle, one for each tribe; that of Aaron, of course, represented the tribe of Levi. On the next day these rods were brought out and exhibited to the people, and while all the rest remained dry and withered, that of Aaron alone budded and blossomed and yielded fruit. There is no mention in the Pentateuch of this rod having been placed in the ark, but only that it was put before it. But as St. Paul, or the author of the Epistle to the Hebrews (Hebrews ix. 4), asserts that the rod and the pot of manna were both within the ark, Royal Arch Masons have followed this later authority. Hence the rod of Aaron is found in the ark; but its import is only historical, as if to identify the substitute ark as a true copy of the original, which had been lost. No symbolical instruction accompanies its discovery.

Ab. אב. 1. The 11th month of the Hebrew civil year and corresponding to the months July and August, beginning with the new moon of the former. 2. It is also a Hebrew word, signifying *father*, and will be readily recognized by every Mason as a compo-

1

nent part of the name *Hiram Abif*, which literally means *Hiram his father*. (See *Abif*.)

Abaciscus. The diminutive of Abacus, and, in architecture, refers to the squares of the tessellated pavement or checkered flooring of the ground floor of the Solomonian Temple.

Abacus. A term which has been erroneously used to designate the official staff of the Grand Master of the Templars. The word has no such meaning; for an abacus is either a table used for facilitating arithmetical calculations, or is in architecture the crowning plate of a column and its capital. The Grand Master's staff was a *baculus*, which see.

Abaddon. A Hebrew word אֲבַדּוֹן, signifying *destruction*. By the Rabbis it is interpreted as the *place of destruction*, and is the second of the seven names given by them to the region of the dead. In the Apocalypse (ix. 11) it is rendered by the Greek word Ἀπολλύων, *Apollyon*, and means the destroyer. In this sense it is used as a significant word in the high degrees.

Abazar. The title given to the Master of Ceremonies in the Sixth Degree of the Modern French Rite.

Abbreviations. Abbreviations of technical terms or of official titles are of very extensive use in Masonry. They were, however, but rarely employed in the earlier Masonic publications. For instance, not one is to be found in the first edition of Anderson's *Constitutions*. Within a comparatively recent period they have greatly increased, especially among French writers, and a familiarity with them is therefore essentially necessary to the Masonic student. Frequently, among English and always among French authors, a Masonic abbreviation is distinguished by three points, ∴, in a triangular form following the letter, which peculiar mark was first used, according to Ragon, on the 12th of August, 1774, by the Grand Orient of France, in an address to its subordinates. No authoritative explanation of the meaning of these points has been given, but they may be supposed to refer to the three lights around the altar, or perhaps more generally to the number three, and to the triangle, both important symbols in the Masonic system.

Before proceeding to give a list of the principal abbreviations, it may be observed that the doubling of a letter is intended to express the plural of that word of which the single letter is the abbreviation. Thus, in French, F∴ signifies " Frère," or " Brother," and FF∴ " Frères," or " Brothers." And in English, L∴ is sometimes used to denote " Lodge," and LL∴ to denote " Lodges." This remark is made once for all, because I have not deemed it necessary to augment the size of the list of abbreviations by inserting these plurals. If the reader finds S∴ G∴ I∴ to signify " Sovereign Grand Inspector," he will be at no loss to know that SS∴ GG∴ II∴ must denote " Sovereign Grand Inspectors."

A∴ Dep∴ *Anno Depositionis*. In the Year of the Deposit. The date used by Royal and Select Masters.

A∴ and A∴ Ancient and Accepted.

A∴ and A∴ S∴ R∴ Ancient and Accepted Scottish Rite.

A∴ and A∴ R∴ Ancient and Accepted Rite as used in England.

A∴ F∴ M∴ Ancient Freemasons.

A∴ F∴ and A∴ M∴ Ancient Free and Accepted Masons.

A∴ Inv∴ *Anno Inventionis*. In the Year of the Discovery. The date used by Royal Arch Masons.

A∴ L∴ *Anno Lucis*. In the Year of Light. The date used by Ancient Craft Masons.

A∴ L∴ G∴ D∴ G∴ A∴ D∴ L'U∴ *A la Gloire du Grand Architecte de l' Univers*. To the Glory of the Grand Architect of the Universe. (French.) The usual caption of French Masonic documents.

A∴ L'O∴ *A l'Orient*. At the East. (French.) The seat of the Lodge.

A∴ M∴ *Anno Mundi*. In the Year of the World. The date used in the Ancient and Accepted Rite.

A∴ O∴ *Anno Ordinis*. In the Year of the Order. The date used by Knights Templars.

A∴ Y∴ M∴ Ancient York Mason.

B∴ A∴ *Buisson Ardente*. Burning Bush.

B∴ *Bruder*. (German for Brother.)

B∴ B∴ Burning Bush.

B'n∴ *Brudern*. (German for Brethren.)

C∴ C∴ Celestial Canopy.

C∴ H∴ Captain of the Host.

D∴ Deputy.

D∴ G∴ G∴ H∴ P∴ Deputy General Grand High Priest.

D∴ G∴ H∴ P∴ Deputy Grand High Priest.

D∴ G∴ M∴ Deputy Grand Master.

D∴ Prov∴ G∴ M∴ Deputy Prov. Grand Master.

Dis∴ D∴ G∴ M∴ District Deputy Grand Master. (England.)

D. D. G. M. (America.)

E∴ Eminent; Excellent.

E∴ A∴ Entered Apprentice or E∴ A∴ P∴

E∴ C∴ Excellent Companion.

Ec∴ *Ecossaise*. (French.) Scottish; belonging to the Scottish Rite.

E∴ G∴ C∴ Eminent Grand Commander.

E∴ V∴ *Ere Vulgaire*. (French.) Vulgar Era; Year of the Lord.

F∴ *Frère*. Brother. (French.)

F∴ C∴ Fellow-Craft.

F∴ M∴ Freemason. Old Style.

G∴ Grand.

G∴ A∴ S∴ Grand Annual Sojourner.

G∴ A∴ O∴ T∴ U∴ Great Architect of the Universe.

G∴ C∴ Grand Chapter; Grand Council.

G∴ Com∴ Grand Commandery; Grand Commander.

G∴ D∴ Grand Deacon.

G∴ D∴ C∴ Grand Director of Ceremonies.

G∴ E∴ Grand Encampment; Grand East.

G∴ G∴ C∴ General Grand Chapter.

G∴ G∴ H∴ P∴ General Grand High Priest.

G∴ H∴ P∴ Grand High Priest.
G∴ L∴ Grand Lodge.
G∴ M∴ Grand Master.
G∴ N∴ Grand Nehemiah.
G∴ O∴ Grand Orient; Grand Organist.
G∴ P∴ Grand Pursuivant.
G∴ P∴ S∴ Grand Past Sojourner.
G∴ R∴ Grand Registrar.
G∴ R∴ A∴ C∴ Grand Royal Arch Chapter.
G∴ S∴ Grand Scribe; Grand Secretary.
G∴ S∴ B∴ Grand Sword Bearer; Grand Standard Bearer.
G∴ T∴ Grand Treasurer.
H∴ A∴ B∴ Hiram Abif.
H∴ E∴ Holy Empire.
H∴ K∴ T∴ Hiram, King of Tyre.
H∴ R∴ D∴ M∴ Heredom.
Ill∴ Illustrious.
I∴ N∴ R∴ I∴ *Iesus Nazarenus, Rex Iudæorum.* (Latin.) Jesus of Nazareth, King of the Jews.
I∴ P∴ M∴ Immediate Past Master. (English.)
I∴ T∴ N∴ O∴ T∴ G∴ A∴ O∴ T∴ U∴ In the Name of the Great Architect of the Universe. Often forming the caption of Masonic documents.
J∴ W∴ Junior Warden.
K∴ King.
K—H∴ Kadosh, Knight of Kadosh.
K∴ H∴ S∴ Knight of the Holy Sepulcher.
K∴ M∴ Knight of Malta.
K∴ S∴ King Solomon.
K∴ T∴ Knights Templar.
L∴ Lodge.
LL∴ Lodges.
L∴ R∴ London Rank. A distinction introduced in England in 1908.
M∴ Mason.
M∴ C∴ Middle Chamber.
M∴ E∴ Most Eminent; Most Excellent.
M∴ E∴ G∴ H∴ P∴ Most Excellent Grand High Priest.
M∴ E∴ G∴ M∴ Most Eminent Grand Master (of Knights Templar).
M∴ L∴ *Mère Loge.* (French.) Mother Lodge.
M∴ M∴ Master Mason.
M∴ M∴ *Mois Maçonnique.* (French.) Masonic Month. March is the first Masonic month among French Masons.
M∴ W∴ Most Worshipful.
M∴ W∴ S∴ Most Wise Sovereign.
O∴ Orient.
OB∴ Obligation.
P∴ Past.
P∴ G∴ M∴ Past Grand Master.
P∴ M∴ Past Master.
Prov∴ Provincial.
Pro∴ G∴ M∴ Pro-Grand Master.
Prov∴ G∴ M∴ Provincial Grand Master.
P∴ S∴ Principal Sojourner.
R∴ A∴ Royal Arch.
R∴ C∴ or R∴ †∴ Rose Croix. Appended to the signature of one having that degree.
R∴ E∴ Right Eminent.
R∴ F∴ *Respectable Frère.* (French.) Worshipful Brother.

R∴ L∴ or R∴ ☐ ∴ *Respectable Loge.* (French.) Worshipful Lodge.
R∴ S∴ Y∴ C∴ S∴ Rosy Cross (in the Royal Order of Scotland).
R∴ W∴ Right Worshipful.
S∴ Scribe.
S∴ C∴ Supreme Council.
S∴ G∴ I∴ G∴ Sovereign Grand Inspector General.
S∴ P∴ R∴ S∴ Sublime Prince of the Royal Secret.
S∴ S∴ Sanctum Sanctorum or Holy of Holies.
S∴ S∴ S∴ *Trois fois Salut.* (French.) Thrice greeting. A common caption to French Masonic circulars or letters.
S∴ W∴ Senior Warden.
T∴ C∴ F∴ *Très Chère Frère.* (French.) Very Dear Brother.
T∴ G∴ A∴ O∴ T∴ U∴ The Great Architect of the Universe.
V∴ or Ven∴ *Venerable.* (French.) Worshipful.
V∴ D∴ B∴ Very Dear Brother.
V∴ D∴ S∴ A∴ Veut Dieu Saint Amour, *or* Vult Dei Sanctus Animus. A formula used by Knights Templar.
V∴ L∴ *Vraie lumière.* (French.) True light.
V∴ W∴ Very Worshipful.
W∴ Worshipful.
W∴ M∴ Worshipful Master.
☐ ∴ Lodge.
⌗ ∴ Lodges.
✝ Prefixed to the signature of a Knights Templar or a member of the A. and A. Scottish Rite below the Thirty-third Degree.
✝ Prefixed to the signature of a Grand or Past Grand Commander of Knights Templar or a Mason of the Thirty-third Degree in the Scottish Rite.
✝ Prefixed to the signature of a Grand or Past Grand Master of Knights Templar and the Grand Commander of the Supreme Council of the Ancient and Accepted Scottish Rite.

Abda. A word used in some of the high degrees. He was the father of Adoniram. (See 1 Kings iv. 6.) Lenning is wrong in saying that he is represented by one of the officers in the degree of Master in Israel. He has confounded Abda with his son. (*Encyc. der Freimaur.*)

Abdamon. The name of the orator in the Fourteenth Degree of the Rite of Perfection, or the Sacred Vault of James VI. It means a servant, from *abad*, "to serve," although somewhat corrupted in its transmission into the rituals. Lenning says it is the Hebrew *Habdamon*, "a servant"; but there is no such word in Hebrew.

Abdiel. (Heb., Servant of God.) The name of an angel mentioned by the Jewish Kabbalists. He is represented in Milton's *Paradise Lost*, Book V., as one of the seraphim, who, when Satan tried to stir up a revolt among the angels subordinate to his authority, alone and boldly withstood his traitorous designs:

Among the faithless, faithful only he;
Among innumerable false, unmoved,
Unshaken, unseduced, unterrified,
His loyalty he kept, his love, his zeal.   (894-7.)

The name *Abdiel* became the synonym of honor and faithfulness.

Abditorium. A secret place for the deposit of records—a Tabularium.

Abelites. A secret Order which existed about the middle of the 18th century in Germany, called also "the Order of Abel." The organization was in possession of peculiar signs, words, and ceremonies of initiation, but, according to Gädicke (*Freimaurer Lexicon*), it had no connection with Freemasonry. According to Clavel the order was founded at Griefswald in 1745.

Abercorn, Earl of. James Hamilton, Lord Paisley, was named Grand Master of England by the retiring G. Master, the Duke of Richmond, in 1725. He was at that time the Master of a Lodge, and had served on the Committee of Charity during that year. He succeeded his father as Earl of Abercorn in 1734.

Abercorn, Duke of. Grand Master of Ireland 1874–85.

Aberdour, Lord. Grand Master of Scotland, 1755–6. Also of England 1757–61.

Abib. The original name of the Hebrew month Nisan, nearly corresponding to the month of March, the first of the ecclesiastical year. Abib is frequently mentioned in the Sacred Scriptures, and signifies green ears of corn or fresh fruits.

Abibale. The name of the first Assassin in the Elu of the Modern French Rite.

Derived most probably from the Hebrew *abi* and *balah*, אבי and בלע, which mean *father of destruction,* though it is said to mean "*le meurtrier du Père.*"

Abide by. See *Stand to and abide by.*

Abif (or **Abiff,** *or perhaps more correctly* **Abiv**). An epithet which has been applied in Scripture to that celebrated builder who was sent to Jerusalem by King Hiram, of Tyre, to superintend the construction of the Temple. The word, which in the original Hebrew is אביו, and which may be pronounced *Abiv* or *Abif,* is compounded of the noun in the construct-state אבי, *Abi,* meaning "father," and the pronominal suffix ו, which, with the preceding vowel sound, is to be sounded as *iv* or *if,* and which means "his"; so that the word thus compounded *Abif* literally and grammatically signifies "his father." The word is found in 2 Chronicles iv. 16, in the following sentence: "The pots also, and the shovels, and the flesh hooks, and all their instruments, did Huram his father make to King Solomon." The latter part of this verse is in the original as follows:

שלמה   למלך   אביו   חורם   עשה
Shelomoh   lamelech   Abif   Huram   gnasah

Luther has been more literal in his version of this passage than the English translators, and appearing to suppose that the word *Abif*

is to be considered simply as an appellative or surname, he preserves the Hebrew form, his translation being as follows: "Machte Huram Abif dem Könige Salomo." The Swedish version is equally exact, and, instead of "Hiram his father," gives us "Hyram Abiv." In the Latin Vulgate, as in the English version, the words are rendered "Hiram pater ejus." I have little doubt that Luther and the Swedish translator were correct in treating the word *Abif* as an appellative. In Hebrew, the word *ab,* or "father," is often used, *honoris causa,* as a title of respect, and may then signify *friend, counselor, wise man,* or something else of equivalent character. Thus, Dr. Clarke, commenting on the word *abrech,* in Genesis xli. 43, says: "Father seems to have been a name of office, and probably *father of the king* or *father of Pharaoh* might signify the same as the *king's minister* among us." And on the very passage in which this word *Abif* is used, he says: "אב, *father,* is often used in Hebrew to signify *master, inventor, chief operator.*" Gesenius, the distinguished Hebrew lexicographer, gives to this word similar significations, such as *benefactor, master, teacher,* and says that in the Arabic and the Ethiopic it is spoken of one who excels in anything. This idiomatic custom was pursued by the later Hebrews, for Buxtorf tells us, in his "Talmudic Lexicon," that "among the Talmudists *abba,* father, was always a title of honor," and he quotes the following remarks from a treatise of the celebrated Maimonides, who, when speaking of the grades or ranks into which the Rabbinical doctors were divided, says: "The first class consists of those each of whom bears his own name, without any title of honor; the second, of those who are called *Rabbanim;* and the third, of those who are called *Rabbi,* and the men of this class also receive the cognomen of *Abba,* Father."

Again, in 2 Chronicles ii. 13, Hiram, the King of Tyre, referring to the same Hiram, the widow's son, who is spoken of subsequently in reference to King Solomon as "his father," or *Abif* in the passage already cited, writes to Solomon: "And now I have sent a cunning man, endued with understanding, of Huram my father's." The only difficulty in this sentence is to be found in the prefixing of the letter *lamed* ל, before *Huram,* which has caused our translators, by a strange blunder, to render the words *l'Huram abi,* as meaning "of Huram my father's," * instead of "Huram my father." Luther has again taken the correct view of this subject, and translates the word as an appellative: "So sende ich nun einen weisen Mann, der Berstand hat, Huram Abif"; that is, "So now I send you a wise man who has understanding, Huram Abif." The truth, I suspect, is, although it has escaped all the commentators, that the *lamed* in this passage is a Chaldaism which is sometimes used by the later Hebrew writers, who

---

* It may be remarked that this could not be the true meaning, for the father of King Hiram was not another Hiram, but Abibal.

incorrectly employ ל, the sign of the dative for the accusative after transitive verbs. Thus, in Jeremiah (xl. 2), we have such a construction: *vayikach rab tabachim l'Yremyahu;* that is, literally, "and the captain of the guards took *for* Jeremiah," where the ל, *l*, or *for*, is a Chaldaism and redundant, the true rendering being, "and the captain of the guards took Jeremiah." Other similar passages are to be found in Lamentations iv. 5, Job v. 2, etc. In like manner I suppose the ל before Huram, which the English translators have rendered by the preposition "of," to be redundant and a Chaldaic form, the sentence should be read thus: "I have sent a cunning man, endued with understanding, Huram my father"; or, if considered as an appellative, as it should be, "Huram Abi."

From all this I conclude that the word *Ab*, with its different suffixes, is always used in the Books of Kings and Chronicles, in reference to Hiram the Builder, as a title of respect. When King Hiram speaks of him he calls him "my father Hiram," *Hiram Abi;* and when the writer of the Book of Chronicles is speaking of him and King Solomon in the same passage, he calls him "Solomon's father"—"his father," *Hiram Abif.* The only difference is made by the different appellation of the pronouns *my* and *his* in Hebrew. To both the kings of Tyre and of Judah he bore the honorable relation of *Ab*, or "father," equivalent to *friend, counselor,* or *minister.* He was "Father Hiram." The Masons are therefore perfectly correct in refusing to adopt the translation of the English version, and in preserving, after the example of Luther, the word *Abif* as an appellative, surname, or title of honor and distinction bestowed upon the chief builder of the Temple, as Dr. James Anderson suggests in his note on the subject in the first edition (1723) of the *Constitutions of the Freemasons.*   [E. L. H.]

Abiram. One of the traitorous craftsmen, whose act of perfidy forms so important a part of the Third Degree, receives in some of the high degrees the name of *Abiram Akirop.* These words certainly have a Hebrew look; but the significant words of Masonry have, in the lapse of time and in their transmission through ignorant teachers, become so corrupted in form that it is almost impossible to trace them to any intelligent root. They may be Hebrew or they may be anagrammatized (see *Anagram*); but it is only chance that can give us the true meaning which they undoubtedly have. The word "Abiram" means "father of loftiness," and may have been chosen as the name of the traitorous craftsman with allusion to the Biblical story of Korah, Dathan and Abiram who conspired against Moses and Aaron. (Numbers xvi.) In the French ritual of the Second Elu it is said to mean *murderer* or *assassin*, but this would not seem to be correct etymologically.

Able. There is an archaic use of the word able to signify *suitable.* Thus, Chaucer says of a monk that "he was able to ben an abbot," that is, suitable to be an abbot. In this sense the old manuscript *Constitutions* constantly employ the word, as when they say that the apprentice should be "able of Birth that is ffree borne." (*Lansdowne MS.*)

Ablution. A ceremonial purification by washing, much used in the Ancient Mysteries and under the Mosaic dispensation. It is also employed in some of the high degrees of Masonry. The better technical term for this ceremony is *lustration*, which see.

Abnet. The band or apron, made of fine linen, variously wrought, and worn by the Jewish priesthood. It seems to have been borrowed directly from the Egyptians, upon the representations of all of whose gods is to be found a similar girdle. Like the zennaar, or sacred cord of the Brahmans, and the white shield of the Scandinavians, it is the analogue of the Masonic apron.

Aborigines. A secret society which existed in England about the year 1783, and of whose ceremony of initiation the following account is contained in the *British Magazine* of that date. The presiding officer, who was styled the Original, thus addressed the candidate:

Original. Have you faith enough to be made an Original?

Candidate. I have.

Original. Will you be conformable to all honest rules which may support steadily the honor, reputation, welfare, and dignity of our ancient undertaking?

Candidate. I will.

Original. Then, friend, promise me that you will never stray from the paths of Honor, Freedom, Honesty, Sincerity, Prudence, Modesty, Reputation, Sobriety, and True Friendship.

Candidate. I do.

Which done, the crier of the court commanded silence, and the new member, being uncovered, and dropping on his right knee, had the following oath administered to him by the servant, the new member laying his right hand on the Cap of Honor, and Nimrod holding a staff over his head:

"You swear by the Cap of Honor, by the Collar of Freedom, by the Coat of Honesty, by the Jacket of Sincerity, by the Shirt of Prudence, by the Breeches of Modesty, by the Garters of Reputation, by the Stockings of Sobriety, and by the Steps of True Friendship, never to depart from these laws."

Then rising, with the staff resting on his head, he received a copy of the laws from the hands of the Grand Original, with these words, "Enjoy the benefits hereof."

He then delivered the copy of the laws to the care of the servant, after which the word was given by the secretary to the new member, viz.: *Eden,* signifying the garden where ADAM, the great aboriginal, was formed.

Then the secretary invested him with the sign, viz.: resting his right hand on his left side, signifying the first conjunction of harmony.

It had no connection with Freemasonry, but was simply one of those numerous imitative societies to which that Institution has given rise.

Abrac. In the Leland MS. it is said that the Masons conceal "the wey of wynninge the facultye of Abrac." Mr. Locke (if it was he who wrote a commentary on the manuscript) says, "Here I am utterly in the dark." It means simply "the way of acquiring the science of Abrac." The science of Abrac is the knowledge of the power and use of the mystical *abraxas*, which see; or very likely "Abrac" is merely an abbreviation of Abracadabra.

Abracadabra. A term of incantation which was formerly worn about the neck as an amulet against several diseases, especially the tertian ague. It was to be written on a triangular piece of parchment in the following form:

ABRACADABRA
ABRACADABR
ABRACADAB
ABRACADA
ABRACAD
ABRACA
ABRAC
ABRA
ABR
AB
A

It is said that it first occurs in the *Carmen de Morbis et Remediis* of Q. Serenus Sammonicus, a favorite of the Emperor Severus in the 2d and 3d centuries, and is generally supposed to be derived from the word *abraxas*.

Abraham. The founder of the Hebrew nation. The patriarch Abraham is personated in the degree or Order of High Priesthood, which refers in some of its ceremonies to an interesting incident in his life. After the amicable separation of Lot and Abraham, when the former was dwelling in the plain in which Sodom and its neighboring towns were situated, and the latter in the valley of Mamre near Hebron, a king from beyond the Euphrates, whose name was Chedorlaomer, invaded lower Palestine, and brought several of the smaller states into a tributary condition. Among these were the five cities of the plain, to which Lot had retired. As the yoke was borne with impatience by these cities, Chedorlaomer, accompanied by four other kings, who were probably his tributaries, attacked and defeated the kings of the plain, plundered their towns, and carried their people away as slaves. Among those who suffered on this occasion was Lot. As soon as Abraham heard of these events, he armed three hundred and eighteen of his slaves, and, with the assistance of Aner, Eshcol, and Mamre, three Amoritish chiefs, he pursued the retiring invaders, and having attacked them near the Jordan, put them to flight, and then returned with all the men and goods that had been recovered from the enemy. On his way back he was met by the King of Sodom, and also by Melchizedek, King of Salem, who was, like Abraham, a worshiper of the true God. Melchizedek refreshed Abraham and his peo-

ple with bread and wine, and blessed him. The King of Sodom wished Abraham to give up the persons, but retain the goods that he had recovered; however, Abraham positively refused to retain any of the spoils, although, by the customs of the age, he was entitled to them, and declared that he had sworn that he would not take "from a thread even to a shoe-latchet." (Genesis xdv.) Although the conduct of Abraham in this whole transaction was of the most honorable and conscientious character, the incidents do not appear to have been introduced into the ritual of the High Priesthood for any other reason except that of their connection with Melchizedek, who was the founder of an Order of Priesthood.

Abraham, Antoine Firmin. A Mason who made himself notorious at Paris, in the beginning of the present century, by the manufacture and sale of false Masonic diplomas and by trading in the higher degrees, from which traffic he reaped for some time a plentiful harvest. The Supreme Council of France declared, in 1811, all his diplomas and charters void and deceptive. He is the author of *L'Art du Tuileur, dedié à tous les Maçons des deux hémisphères*, a small volume of 20 pages, 8vo, printed at Paris in 1803, and he published from 1800 to 1808 a periodical work entitled *Le Miroir de la vérité, dedié à tous les Maçons*, 3 vols., 8vo. This contains many interesting details concerning the history of Masonry in France. In 1811 there was published at Paris a *Circulaire du Suprême Conseil du 33e degré, etc., relative à la vente, par le Sieur Abraham de grades et cahiers Maçonniques* (8vo, 15 pp.), from which it is evident that Abraham was nothing else but a Masonic charlatan.

Abraxas. Basilides, the head of the Egyptian sect of Gnostics, taught that there were seven emanations, or æons, from the Supreme God; that these emanations engendered the angels of the highest order; that these angels formed a heaven for their habitation, and brought forth other angels of a nature inferior to their own; that in time other heavens were formed and other angels created, until the whole number of angels and their respective heavens amounted to 365, which were thus equal to the number of days in a year; and, finally, that over all these an omnipotent Lord—inferior, however, to the Supreme God—presided, whose name was Abraxas. Now this word Abraxas, in the numerical force of its letters when written in Greek, ΑΒΡΑΞΑΣ, amounts to 365, the number of worlds in the Basilidean system, as well as the number of days in the year, thus: Α, 1.., Β, 2.., Ρ, 100.., Α, 1.., Ξ, 60.., Α, 1.., Σ 200 = 365. The god Abraxas was therefore a type or symbol of the year, or of the revolution of the earth around the sun. This mystical reference of the name of a god to the annual period was familiar to the ancients, and is to be found in at least two other instances. Thus, among the Persians the letters of the name of the god Mithras, and of Belenus among the Gauls, amounted each to 365.

M	= 40	B	= 2
E	= 5	H	= 8
I	= 10	A	= 30
Θ	= 9	E	= 5
P	= 100	N	= 50
A	= 1	O	= 70
Σ	= 200 = 365	Σ	= 200 = 365

The word Abraxas, therefore, from this mystical value of the letters of which it was composed, became talismanic, and was frequently inscribed, sometimes with and sometimes without other superstitious inscriptions, on stones or gems as amulets, many of which have been preserved or are continually being discovered, and are to be found in the cabinets of the curious.

There have been many conjectures among the learned as to the derivation of the word Abraxas. Beausobre (*Histoire du Maniche-isme*, vol. ii.) derives it from the Greek, 'Αβρος Σαω, signifying "the magnificent Saviour, he who heals and preserves." Bellermann (*Essay on the Gems of the Ancients*) supposed it to be compounded of three Coptic words signifying "the holy word of bliss." Pignorius and Vandelin think it is composed of four Hebrew and three Greek letters, whose numerical value is 365, and which are the initials of the sentence: "saving men by wood, *i. e.* the cross."

Abraxas Stones. Stones on which the word Abraxas and other devices are engraved, and which were used by the Egyptian Gnostics as amulets.

Absence. Attendance on the communications of his Lodge, on all convenient occasions, is considered as one of the duties of every Mason, and hence the old charges of 1722 (ch. iii.) say that " in ancient Times no Master or Fellow could be absent from it [the Lodge] especially when warn'd to appear at it, without incurring a severe censure, until it appear'd to the Master and Wardens that pure Necessity hinder'd him." At one time it was usual to enforce attendance by fines, and the By-Laws of the early Lodges contain lists of fines to be imposed for absence, swearing and drunkenness, but that usage is now discontinued, so that attendance on ordinary communications is no longer enforced by any sanction of law. It is a duty the discharge of which must be left to the conscientious convictions of each Mason. In the case, however, of a positive summons for any express purpose, such as to stand trial, to show cause, etc., the neglect or refusal to attend might be construed into a contempt, to be dealt with according to its magnitude or character in each particular case.

Acacia. An interesting and important symbol in Freemasonry. Botanically, it is the *acacia vera* of Tournefort, and the *mimosa nilotica* of Linnæus, called *babul tree* in India. It grew abundantly in the vicinity of Jerusalem, where it is still to be found, and is familiar in its modern use as the tree from which the gum arabic of commerce is derived.

Oliver, it is true, says that " there is not the

smallest trace of any tree of the kind growing so far north as Jerusalem " (*Landm.*, ii., 149); but this statement is refuted by the authority of Lieutenant Lynch, who saw it growing in great abundance in Jericho, and still farther north. (*Exped. to Dead Sea*, p. 262.) The Rabbi Joseph Schwarz, who is excellent authority, says:  " The Acacia (Shittim) tree, Al Sunt, is found in Palestine of different varieties; it looks like the Mulberry tree, attains a great height, and has a hard wood. The gum which is obtained from it is the gum arabic." (*Descriptive Geography and Historical Sketch of Palestine*, p. 308, *Leeser's translation. Phila.*, 1850.) Schwarz was for sixteen years a resident of Palestine, and wrote from personal observation. The testimony of Lynch and Schwarz should, therefore, forever settle the question of the existence of the acacia in Palestine.

The acacia is called in the Bible *Shittim*, which is really the plural of *Shittah*, which last form occurs once only in Isaiah xli. 19. It was esteemed a sacred wood among the Hebrews, and of it Moses was ordered to make the tabernacle, the ark of the covenant, the table for the shewbread, and the rest of the sacred furniture. (Exodus xxv.– xxvii.) Isaiah (*l. c.*) in recounting the promises of God's mercy to the Israelites on their return from the captivity, tells them that, among other things, he will plant in the wilderness, for their relief and refreshment, the cedar, the acacia (or, as it is rendered in our common version, the *shittah*), the fir, and other trees.

The first thing, then, that we notice in this symbol of the acacia, is that it had been always consecrated from among the other trees of the forest by the sacred purposes to which it was devoted. By the Jew, the tree from whose wood the sanctuary of the tabernacle and the holy ark had been constructed would ever be viewed as more sacred than ordinary trees. The early Masons, therefore, very naturally appropriated this hallowed plant to the equally sacred purpose of a symbol, which was to teach an important divine truth in all ages to come.

Having thus briefly disposed of the natural history of this plant, we may now proceed to examine it in its symbolic relations.

First. The acacia, in the mythic system of Freemasonry, is preeminently the symbol of the IMMORTALITY OF THE SOUL—that important doctrine which it is the great design of the Institution to teach. As the evanescent nature of the flower, which " cometh forth and is cut down," reminds us of the transitory nature of human life, so the perpetual renovation of the evergreen plant, which uninterruptedly presents the appearance of youth and vigor, is aptly compared to that spiritual life in which the soul, freed from the corruptible companionship of the body, shall enjoy an eternal spring and an immortal youth. Hence, in

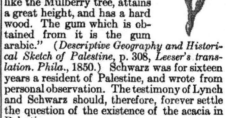

the impressive funeral service of our Order, it is said that " this evergreen is an emblem of our faith in the immortality of the soul. By this we are reminded that we have an immortal part within us, which shall survive the grave, and which shall never, never, never die." And again, in the closing sentences of the monitorial lecture of the Third Degree, the same sentiment is repeated, and we are told that by " the ever-green and ever-living sprig " the Mason is strengthened " with confidence and composure to look forward to a blessed immortality." Such an interpretation of the symbol is an easy and a natural one; it suggests itself at once to the least reflective mind; and consequently, in some one form or another, is to be found existing in all ages and nations. It was an ancient custom—which is not, even now, altogether disused—for mourners to carry in their hands at funerals a sprig of some evergreen, generally the cedar or the cypress, and to deposit it in the grave of the deceased. According to Dalcho,* the Hebrews always planted a sprig of the acacia at the head of the grave of a departed friend. Potter tells us that the ancient Greeks " had a custom of bedecking tombs with herbs and flowers." † All sorts of purple and white flowers were acceptable to the dead, but principally the amaranth and the myrtle. The very name of the former of these plants, which signifies " never fading," would seem to indicate the true symbolic meaning of the usage, although archeologists have generally supposed it to be simply an exhibition of love on the part of the survivors. Ragon says that the ancients substituted the acacia for all other plants because they believed it to be incorruptible, and not liable to injury from the attacks of any kind of insect or other animal—thus symbolizing the incorruptible nature of the soul.

Hence we see the propriety of placing the sprig of acacia, as an emblem of immortality, among the symbols of that degree, all of whose ceremonies are intended to teach us the great truth that " the life of man, regulated by morality, faith, and justice, will be rewarded at its

closing hour by the prospect of Eternal Bliss." * So, therefore, says Dr. Oliver, when the Master Mason exclaims " my name is Acacia," it is equivalent to saying, " I have been in the grave—I have triumphed over it by rising from the dead—and being regenerated in the process, I have a claim to life everlasting." (See *Landmarks*, ii.,151, *note* 27.)

The sprig of acacia, then, in its most ordinary signification, presents itself to the Master Mason as a symbol of the immortality of the soul, being intended to remind him, by its ever-green and unchanging nature, of that better and spiritual part within us, which, as an emanation from the Great Architect of the Universe, can never die. And as this is the most ordinary, the most generally accepted signification, so also is it the most important; for thus, as the peculiar symbol of immortality, it becomes the most appropriate to an Order all of whose teachings are intended to inculcate the great lesson that " life rises out of the grave." But incidental to this the acacia has two other interpretations which are well worthy of investigation.

Secondly, then, the acacia is a symbol of INNOCENCE. The symbolism here is of a peculiar and unusual character, depending not on any real analogy in the form or use of the symbol to the idea symbolized, but simply on a double or compound meaning of the word. For ἀκακία, in the Greek language, signifies both the plant in question and the moral quality of innocence or purity of life. In this sense the symbol refers, primarily, to him over whose solitary grave the acacia was planted, and whose virtuous conduct, whose integrity of life and fidelity to his trusts have ever been presented as patterns to the craft, and consequently to all Master Masons, who, by this interpretation of the symbol, are invited to emulate his example.

Hutchinson, indulging in his favorite theory of Christianizing Masonry, when he comes to this signification of the symbol, thus enlarges on the interpretation: " We Masons, describing the deplorable estate of religion under the Jewish law, speak in figures:—' Her tomb was in the rubbish and filth cast forth of the temple, and ACACIA wove its branches over her monument; ' ἀκακία being the Greek word for innocence, or being free from sin; implying that the sins and corruptions of the old law, and devotees of the Jewish altar, had hid religion from those who sought her, and she was only to be found where INNOCENCE survived, and under the banner of the divine Lamb; and as to ourselves professing that we were to be distinguished by our ACACY, or as true ACACIANS in our religious faith and tenets." †

But, lastly, the acacia is to be considered as the symbol of INITIATION. This is by far the most interesting of its interpretations, and was, we have every reason to believe, the primary and original; the others being but incidental.

---

* " This custom among the Hebrews arose from this circumstance. Agreeably to their laws, no dead bodies were allowed to be interred within the walls of the City; and as the Cohens, or Priests, were prohibited from crossing a grave, it was necessary to place marks thereon, that they might avoid them. For this purpose the Acasia was used." (Dalcho, *2nd Oration*, p. 23, *note*.) I object to the reason assigned by Dalcho, but of the existence of the custom there can be no question, notwithstanding the denial or doubt of Dr. Oliver. Blount (*Travels in the Levant*, p. 197) says, speaking of the Jewish burial customs, " those who bestow a marble stone over any [grave] have a hole a yard long and a foot broad, in which *they plant an evergreen*, which seems to grow from the body and is carefully watched." Hasselquist (*Travels*, p. 28) confirms his testimony. I borrow the citations from Brown (*Antiquities of the Jews*, vol. ii., p. 356), but have verified the reference to Hasselquist. The work of Blount I have not been enabled to consult.

† *Antiquities of Greece*, p. 569.

* Dr. Crucefix, MS. quoted by Oliver. *Landmarks*, ii., 2.

† Hutchinson's *Spirit of Masonry*, Lect. IX., p. 160, ed. 1775.

It leads us at once to the investigation of the significant fact that in all the ancient initiations and religious mysteries there was some plant peculiar to each, which was consecrated by its own esoteric meaning, and which occupied an important position in the celebration of the rites, so that the plant, whatever it might be, from its constant and prominent use in the ceremonies of initiation, came at length to be adopted as the symbol of that initiation.

Thus, the *lettuce* was the sacred plant which assumed the place of the acacia in the mysteries of Adonis. (See *Lettuce.*) The *lotus* was that of the Brahmanical rites of India, and from them adopted by the Egyptians. (See *Lotus.*) The Egyptians also revered the *erica* or heath; and the mistletoe was a mystical plant among the Druids. (See *Erica* and *Misletoe.*) And, lastly, the myrtle performed the same office of symbolism in the mysteries of Greece that the lotus did in Egypt or the mistletoe among the Druids. (See *Myrtle.*)

In all of these ancient mysteries, while the sacred plant was a symbol of initiation, the initiation itself was symbolic of the resurrection to a future life, and of the immortality of the soul. In this view, Freemasonry is to us now in the place of the ancient initiations, and the acacia is substituted for the lotus, the erica, the ivy, the mistletoe, and the myrtle. The lesson of wisdom is the same—the medium of imparting it is all that has been changed.

Returning, then, to the acacia, we find that it is capable of three explanations. It is a symbol of immortality, of innocence, and of initiation. But these three significations are closely connected, and that connection must be observed, if we desire to obtain a just interpretation of the symbol. Thus, in this one symbol, we are taught that in the initiation of life, of which the initiation in the Third Degree is simply emblematic, innocence must for a time lie in the grave, at length, however, to be called, by the word of the Great Master of the Universe, to a blissful immortality. Combine with this the recollection of the place where the sprig of acacia was planted—Mount Calvary—the place of sepulture of him who "brought life and immortality to light," and who, in Christian Masonry, is designated, as he is in Scripture, as "the lion of the tribe of Judah"; and remember, too, that in the mystery of his death, the wood of the cross takes the place of the acacia, and in this little and apparently insignificant symbol, but which is really and truly the most important and significant one in Masonic science, we have a beautiful suggestion of all the mysteries of life and death, of time and eternity, of the present and of the future.

Acacian. A word introduced by Hutchinson, in his *Spirit of Masonry*, to designate a Freemason in reference to the *akakia*, or innocence with which he was to be distinguished, from the Greek word ακακια. (See the preceding article.) The Acacians constituted an heretical sect in the primitive Christian Church, who derived their name from Acacius, Bishop of Cæsarea; and there was sub-

sequently another sect of the same name Acacius, Patriarch of Constantinople. But it is needless to say that the Hutchinsonian application of the word Acacian to signify a Freemason has nothing to do with the theological reference of the term.

Académie des Illumines d'Avignon. A Hermetic system of philosophy, created in 1785.

Academy. The Fourth Degree of the Rectified Rose Croix of Schroeder.

Academy of Ancients or of Secrets. (*Academie des Secrets.*) A society instituted at Warsaw, in 1767, by M. Thoux de Salverte, and founded on the principles of another which bore the same name, and which had been established at Rome, about the end of the 16th century, by John Baptiste Porta. The object of the institution was the advancement of the natural sciences and their application to the occult philosophy.

Academy of Sages. An order which existed in Sweden in 1770, deriving its origin from that founded in London by Elias Ashmole, on the doctrines of the *New Atlantis* of Bacon. A few similar societies were subsequently founded in Russia and France, one especially noted by Thory (*Act. Lat.*) as having been established in 1776 by the mother Lodge of Avignon.

Academy of Secrets. See *Academy of Ancients.*

Academy of Sublime Masters of the Luminous Ring. Founded in France, in 1780, by Baron Blaerfindy, one of the Grand Officers of the Philosophic Scotch Rite. The Academy of the Luminous Ring was dedicated to the philosophy of Pythagoras, and was divided into three degrees. The first and second were principally occupied with the history of Freemasonry, and the last with the dogmas of the Pythagorean school, and their application to the highest grades of science. The historical hypothesis which was sought to be developed in this Academy was that Pythagoras was the founder of Freemasonry.

Academy of True Masons. Founded at Montpelier, in France, by Dom Pernetty in 1778, and occupied with instructions in hermetic science, which were developed in six degrees, viz.: 1. The True Mason; 2. The True Mason in the Right Way; 3. Knight of the Golden Key; 4. Knight of Iris; 5. Knight of the Argonauts; 6. Knight of the Golden Fleece. The degrees thus conferred constituted the Philosophic Scotch Rite, which was the system adopted by the Academy. It afterward changed its name to that of Russo-Swedish Academy, which circumstance leads Thory to believe that it was connected with the Alchemical Chapters which at that time existed in Russia and Sweden. The entirely hermetic character of the Academy of True Masons may readily be perceived in a few paragraphs cited by Clavel (p. 172, 3d ed., 1844) from a discourse by Goyer de Jumilly at the installation of an Academy in Martinique. "To seize," says the orator, "the graver of Hermes to engrave the doctrines of natural philosophy on your columns; to call Flamel, the Philalete, the Cosmopolite, and our other masters to my aid for the purpose of unveiling the mysterious principles of the occult sciences,—these, illustrious knights, appear to be the duties imposed on me by the ceremony of your installation. The fountain of Count Trevisan, the pontifical water, the peacock's tail, are phenomena with which you are familiar."

Academy, Platonic. Founded in 1480 by Marsilius Ficinus, at Florence, under the patronage of Lorenzo de Medicis. It is said by the Masons of Tuscany to have been a secret society, and is supposed to have had a Masonic character, because in the hall where its members held their meetings, and which still remains, many Masonic symbols are to be found. Clavel (p. 85, 3d ed., 1844) supposes it to have been a society founded by some of the honorary members and patrons of the fraternity of Freemasons who existed in the Middle Ages, and who, having abandoned the material design of the institution, confined themselves to its mystic character. If his suggestion be correct, this is one of the earliest instances of the separation of Speculative from Operative Masonry.

Acanthus. A plant, described by Dioscorides, with broad, flexible, prickly leaves, which perish in the winter and sprout again at the return of spring. It is found in the Grecian islands on the borders of cultivated fields or gardens, and is common in moist, rocky situations. It is memorable for the tradition which assigns to it the origin of the foliage carved on the capitals of Corinthian and Composite columns. Hence, in architecture, that part of the Corinthian capital is called the *Acanthus* which is situated below the abacus, and which, having the form of a vase or bell, is surrounded by two rows of leaves of the acanthus plant. Callimachus, who invented this ornament, is said to have had the idea suggested to him by the following incident. A Corinthian maiden who was betrothed, fell ill, and died just before the appointed time of her marriage. Her faithful and grieving nurse placed on her tomb a basket containing many of her toys and jewels, and covered it with a flat tile. It so happened that the basket was placed immediately over an acanthus root, which afterward grew up around the basket and curled over under the superincumbent resistance of the tile, thus exhibiting a form of foliage which was, on its being seen by the architect, adopted as a model for the capital of a new order; so that the story of affection was perpetuated in marble. Dudley (*Naology*, p. 164) thinks the tale puerile, and supposes that the acanthus is really the lotus of the Indians and Egyptians, and is symbolic of laborious but effectual effort applied to the support of the world. With him, the symbolism of the acanthus and the lotus are identical. See *Lotus.*

Accepted. The Worshipful Company of Masons of the City of London—a flourishing Guild at the present day—possesses as its earliest document now existing an account book headed

"1620.

The Accompte of James Gilder Mr (Master) William Ward & John Abraham wardens of the Company of ffremasons w^thin the Citie of London beginninge the first day of Julie 1619 And endinge the   day of Julie 1620 of all receite & payment for & to the use the same company as ffolloweth, viz."

From the entries in this book it appears that besides the ordinary Freemen and Liverymen of this Company there were other members who are termed in the books the "Accepted Masons," and that they belonged to a body known as the "Accepcon," or Acception, which was an Inner Fraternity of Speculative Masons.

Thus in the year 1620 the following entry is found:

"They charge themselves also wth Money Receyued of the Psons hereafter named for theyr gratuitie at theyr acceptance into the Lyvery viz" (here follow six names); and among the accounts for the next year (1621) there is an entry showing sums received from several persons, of whom two are mentioned in the entry of 1620, "Att the making masons," and as all these mentioned were already members of the Company something further must be meant by this.

In 1631 the following entry of the Clerk's expenses occurs: "Pd in goeing abroad & att a meeteing att the hall about ye Masons yt were to bee accepted VI^s VI^d."

Now the Company never *accepted* its members; they were always *admitted* to the freedom either by apprenticeship, patrimony, or redemption. Thus the above entries suggest that persons who were neither connected with the trade nor otherwise qualified were required, before being eligible for election on the livery of the Company, to become "Accepted Masons," that is, to join the Lodge of Speculative Masonry that was held for that purpose in the Company's Hall.

Thus in the accounts for 1650, payments are entered as made by several persons "for coming on the Liuerie & admission uppon Acceptance of Masonry," and it is entered that Mr. Andrew Marvin, the present warden, and another paid 20 shillings each "for coming on the Accepcon"; while two others are entered as paying 40 shillings each "for the like," and as the names of the last two cannot be found among the members of the Masons Company it would seem as if it was possible for strangers to join "the Accepcon" on paying double fees.

Unfortunately no books connected with this Acception, or Lodge, as it may be called, have been preserved: but there are references to it in several places in the account books which show that the payments made by newly accepted Masons were paid into the funds of the Company, that some or all of this amount was spent on a banquet and the attendant expenses, and that any further sum required was paid out of the ordinary funds of the Company, proving that the Company had entire control of the Lodge and its funds.

Further evidence of the existence of this

Symbolical Lodge within the Masons Company is given by the following entry in an inventory of the Company's property made in 1665:

"*Item.* The names of the Accepted Masons in a faire inclosed frame with lock and key"; and in an inventory of 1676 is found:

"*Item.* One book of the Constitutions of the Accepted Masons.*

"A faire large table of the Accepted Masons." And proof positive of its existence is derived from an entry in the diary of Elias Ashmole—the famous antiquary—who writes:

"March 10th. 1682. About 5 p.m. I received a summons to appear at a Lodge to be held next day at Masons Hall London.

March 11th. Accordingly I went and about noon were admitted into the Fellowship of Free Masons: Sir William Wilson Knight, Capt. Rich Borthwick, Mr Will Woodman, Mr Wm Grey, Mr Samuell Taylour, and Mr William Wise.†

I was the Senior Fellow among them (it being 35 years since I was admitted)."

He then mentions the names of nine others who were present and concludes: "We all dyned at the halfe Moone Taverne in Cheapeside, at a noble dinner prepaired at the charge of the New-Accepted Masons."

All present were members of the Masons Company except Ashmole himself, Sir W. Wilson and Capt. Borthwick, and this entry proves conclusively that side by side with the Masons Company there existed another organization to which non-members of the Company were admitted and the members of which were known as "Accepted Masons."

It may here be mentioned that Ashmole has recorded in his diary that he was made a Freemason at Warrington in Lancashire on October 16, 1646. In that entry the word "Accepted" does not occur.

No mention is made of the Accepted Masons in the accounts of the Masons Company after 1677, when £6—the balance remaining of the last Accepted Masons' money—was ordered to be laid out for a new banner; and it would seem that from that time onward the Lodge kept separate accounts, for from the evidence of Ashmole's diary we know it was at work in 1682; but when and why it finally ceased no evidence is forthcoming to show. However, it may fairly be assumed that this Masons Hall Lodge had ceased to exist before the Revival of Freemasonry in 1717, or else Anderson would not have said in the *Constitutions* of 1723 (p. 82): "It is generally believ'd that the said Company (i.e. the London Company of Freemen Masons) is descended of the ancient Fraternity; and that in former Times no Man was made Free of that Company until he was install'd in some Lodge of Free and Accepted Masons, as a necessary Qualification. But that laudable Practice seems to have been long in Desuetude," which passage would indicate that he was aware of some tradition of such a Lodge as has been described attached to the Masons Company admitting persons in no way operatively connected with the craft, who were called "Accepted Masons" to distinguish them from the Operative or Free Masons. (Conder's *Hole Craft and Fellowship of Masonry and Ars Quatuor Coronatorum*, vol. ix.)

Anderson in the 1738 *Constitutions* quotes from a copy of the old *Constitutions* some regulations which he says were made in 1663, and in which the phrases *accepted a Free Mason* and *Acceptation* occur several times. These regulations are found in what is known as the Grand Lodge MS. No. 2, which is supposed to have been written about the middle of the 17th century, so that Anderson's date in which he follows the *Roberts Old Constitutions* printed in 1722 as to the year, though he changes the day from December 8th to December 27th, may quite possibly be correct. And Bro. Conder (*Hole Craft*, p. 11) calls special attention to these regulations on account of the singular resemblance that one of them bears to the rules that govern the Masons Company.

The extracts given above from the books of the Masons Company, the 1663 Regulations (if that date be accepted), and the quotation from Ashmole's diary, are the earliest known instances of the term "Accepted" Masons, for although the Inigo Jones MS. is headed "The Antient Constitutions of the Free and Accepted Masons 1607," yet there is a consensus of opinion among experts that such date is impossible and that the MS. is really to be referred to the end of the 17th century or even the beginning of the 18th; and the next instance of the use of the term is in 1686 when Dr. Plot in *The Natural History of Staffordshire* wrote with reference to the secret signs used by the Freemasons of his time "if any man appear, though altogether unknown, that can shew any of these signes to a Fellow of the Society, whom they otherwise call an Accepted Mason, he is obliged presently to come to him from what company or place soever he be in, nay, though from the top of steeple."

Further, in 1691, John Aubrey, author of *The Natural History of Wiltshire*, made a note in his MS. "This day (May 18, 1691) is a great convention at St. Pauls Church of the fraternity of the free Masons," in which he has erased the word *free* and substituted *accepted*, which, however, he changed into *adopted* in his fair copy.

In the "Orders to be observed by the Company and Fellowship of Freemasons att a Lodge held at Alnwick, Septr. 29, 1701, being the Genll Head Meeting Day," we find: "There shall noe apprentice after he have served seaven years be admitted or accepted but upon the Feast of St. Michael the Archangell."

* No doubt this was a copy of one of the *Old Charges*.

† In the edition of Ashmole's diary published in 1774 this was changed into "I went, and about noon was admitted . . . *by* Sir William Wilson &c." an error which has misled many Masonic historians. See *Ars Quatuor Coronatorum*, vol. xi., p. 6, for a facsimile of the entry as in the original diary.

And from that time onward the term *Accepted Masons* becomes common, usually in connection with *Free*: the term *Free and Accepted Masons* thus signifying both the Operative members who were *free* of their guild and the Speculative members who had been *accepted* as outsiders. Thus the Roberts Print of 1722 is headed, "The Old Constitutions belonging to the Ancient and Honourable Society of Free and Accepted Masons," and in the *Constitutions* of 1723 Anderson speaks of wearing " the Badges of a Free and Accepted Mason " (p. 48) and uses the phrase in Rule 27, though he does not use the phrase so frequently as in the 1738 edition in which " the Charges of a Free-Mason " become " the old Charges of the Free and Accepted Masons," the " General Regulations " become " The General Regulations of the Free and Accepted Masons, and regulation No. 5." " No man can be made or admitted a Member " becomes " No man can be accepted a Member," while the title of the book is " The new book of Constitutions of the Antient and Honourable Fraternity of Free and Accepted Masons " instead of " The Constitutions of the Free-Masons," as in the earlier edition.

[E. L. H.]

Acclamation. A certain form of words used in connection with the battery. In the Scottish rite it is *hoshea;* in the French *vivat;* in Adoptive Masonry it was *Eva;* and in the rite of Misraim, *hallelujah.* (See *Battery.*)

Accolade. From the Latin *ad* and *collum,* around the neck. It is generally but incorrectly supposed that the accolade means the blow given on the neck of a newly created knight with the flat of the sword. The best authorities define it to be the embrace, accompanied with the kiss of peace, by which the new knight was at his creation welcomed into the Order of Knighthood by the sovereign or lord who created him. (See *Knighthood.*)

Accord. We get this word from the two Latin ones *ad cor,* to the heart, and hence it means *hearty consent.* Thus in Wiclif's translation we find the phrase in Philippians, which in the Authorized Version is " with one accord," rendered " with one will, with one heart." Such is its signification in the Masonic formula, " free will and accord," that is, " free will and hearty consent." (See *Free Will and Accord.*)

Accuser. In every trial in a Lodge for an offense against the laws and regulations or the principles of Masonry any Master Mason may be the accuser of another, but a profane cannot be permitted to prefer charges against a Mason. Yet, if circumstances are known to a profane upon which charges ought to be predicated, a Master Mason may avail himself of that information, and out of it frame an accusation to be presented to the Lodge. And such accusation will be received and investigated, although remotely derived from one who is not a member of the Order.

It is not necessary that the accuser should be a member of the same Lodge. It is sufficient if he is an affiliated Mason; but it is generally held that an unaffiliated Mason is no more competent to prefer charges than a profane.

In consequence of the Junior Warden being placed over the Craft during the hours of refreshment, and of his being charged at the time of his installation to see " that none of the Craft be suffered to convert the purposes of refreshment into those of intemperance and excess," it has been very generally supposed that it is his duty, as the prosecuting officer of the Lodge, to prefer charges against any member who, by his conduct, has made himself amenable to the penal jurisdiction of the Lodge. We know of no ancient regulation which imposes this unpleasant duty upon the Junior Warden; but it does seem to be a very natural deduction, from his peculiar prerogative as the *custos morum* or guardian of the conduct of the Craft, that in all cases of violation of the law he should, after due efforts toward producing a reform, be the proper officer to bring the conduct of the offending brother to the notice of the Lodge.

Aceldama, from the Syro-Chaldaic, meaning *field of blood,* so called because it was purchased with the blood-money which was paid to Judas Iscariot for betraying his Lord. It is situated on the slope of the hills beyond the valley of Hinnom and to the south of Mount Zion. The earth there was believed, by early writers, to have possessed a corrosive quality, by means of which bodies deposited in it were quickly consumed; and hence it was used by the Crusaders, then by the Knights Hospitalers, and afterward by the Armenians, as a place of sepulture, and the Empress Helena is said to have built a charnel-house in its midst. Dr. Robinson (*Biblical Researches,* i., p. 524) says that the field is not now marked by any boundary to distinguish it from the rest of the field, and the former charnel-house is now a ruin. The field of Aceldama is referred to in the ritual of the Knights Templars.

Acerrellos, R. S. A *nom de plume* assumed by Carl Rössler, a German Masonic writer. (See *Rössler.*)

Achad. One of the names of God. The word אחד, *Achad,* in Hebrew signifies *one* or *unity.* It has been adopted by the Masons as one of the appellations of the Deity from the passage in Deuteronomy (vi. 4): " Hear, O Israel: the Lord our God is (*Achad*) one Lord"; which the Jews wear on their phylacteries, and pronounce with great fervor as a confession of their faith in the unity of God. Speaking of God as *Achad,* the Rabbis say, " God is one (*Achad*) and man is one (*Achad*). Man, however, is not purely one, because he is made up of elements and has another like himself; but the oneness of God is a oneness that has no boundary."

Acharon Schilton. In Hebrew אחרון שלטן, signifying *the new kingdom.* Significant words in some of the high degrees.

Achias. A corruption of the Hebrew *Achijah,* the brother of Jah; a significant word in some of the high degrees.

Achishar. Mentioned in 1 Kings (iv. 6)

under the name of *Ahishar*, and there described as being "over the household" of King Solomon. This was a situation of great importance in the East, and equivalent to the modern office of Chamberlain. The Steward in a Council of Select Masters is said to represent *Achishar*.

Achtariel. A Kabbalistic name of God belonging to the Crown or first of the ten sephiroth; and hence signifying the Crown or God.

Acknowledged. When one is initiated into the degree of Most Excellent Ma ter, he is technically said to be "received and acknowledged" as a Most Excellent Master. This expression refers to the tradition of the degree which states that when the Temple had been completed and dedicated, King Solomon received and acknowledged the most expert of the craftsmen as Most Excellent Masters. That is, he *received* them into the exalted rank of perfect and acknowledged workmen, and *acknowledged* their right to that title. The verb *to acknowledge* here means to own or admit, to belong to, as, to acknowledge a son.

Acousmatici. The primary class of the disciples of Pythagoras, who served a five years' probation of silence, and were hence called *acousmatici* or *hearers*. According to Porphyry, they received only the elements of intellectual and moral instruction, and, after the expiration of their term of probation, they were advanced to the rank of Mathematici. (See *Pythagoras*.)

Acquittal. Under this head it may be proper to discuss two questions of Masonic law. 1. Can a Mason, having been acquitted by the courts of the country of an offense with which he has been charged, be tried by his Lodge for the same offense? And, 2. Can a Mason, having been acquitted by his Lodge on insufficient evidence, be subjected, on the discovery and production of new and more complete evidence, to a second trial for the same offense? To both of these questions the correct answer would seem to be in the affirmative.

1. An acquittal of a crime by a temporal court does not relieve a Mason from an inquisition into the same offense by his Lodge; for acquittals may be the result of some technicality of law, or other cause, where, although the party is relieved from legal punishment, his guilt is still manifest in the eyes of the community; and if the Order were to be controlled by the action of the courts, the character of the Institution might be injuriously affected by its permitting a man, who had escaped without honor from the punishment of the law, to remain a member of the Fraternity. In the language of the Grand Lodge of Texas, "an acquittal by a jury, while it may, and should, in some circumstances, have its influence in deciding on the course to be pursued, yet has no binding force in Masonry. We decide on our own rules, and our own view of the facts." (*Proc. G. L. Tex.*, vol. ii., p. 273.)

2. To come to a correct apprehension of the second question, we must remember that it is a long-settled principle of Masonic law, that every offense which a Mason commits is an injury to the whole Fraternity, inasmuch as the bad conduct of a single member reflects discredit on the whole Institution. This is a very old and well-established principle of the Institution; and hence we find the *Old Constitutions* declaring that Masons "should never be thieves nor thieves' maintainers." (*Cooke MS.*, 1. 916.) The safety of the Institution requires that no evil-disposed member should be tolerated with impunity in bringing disgrace on the Craft. And, therefore, although it is a well-known maxim of the common law— *nemo debet bis puniri pro uno delicto*—that is, "that no one should be twice placed in peril of punishment for the same crime," yet we must also remember that other and fundamental maxim—*salus populi suprema lex*—which may, in its application to Masonry, be well translated, "the well-being of the Order is the first great law." To this everything else must yield; and, therefore, if a member, having been accused of a heinous offense and tried, shall, on his trial, for want of sufficient evidence, be acquitted, or, being convicted, shall, for the same reason, be punished by an inadequate penalty—and if he shall thus be permitted to remain in the Institution with the stigma of the crime upon him, "whereby the Craft comes to shame," then, if new and more sufficient evidence shall be subsequently discovered, it is just and right that a new trial shall be had, so that he may, on this newer evidence, receive that punishment which will vindicate the reputation of the Order. No technicalities of law, no plea of *autrefois acquit*, nor mere verbal exception, should be allowed for the escape of a guilty member; for so long as he lives in the Order, every man is subject to its discipline. A hundred wrongful acquittals of a bad member, who still bears with him the reproach of his evil life, can never discharge the Order from its paramount duty of protecting its own good fame and removing the delinquent member from its fold. To this great duty all private and individual rights and privileges must succumb, for *the well-being of the Order is the first great law in Masonry.*

Acta Latomorum, ou Chronologie de l'Histoire de la Franche-Maçonnerie française et étrangère, etc. That is: "The Acts of the Freemasons, or a chronological history of French and Foreign Freemasonry, etc." This work, written or compiled by Claude Antoine Thory, was published at Paris, in 2 vols., 8vo, in 1815. It contains the most remarkable facts in the history of the Institution from obscure times to the year 1814; the succession of Grand Masters; a nomenclature of rites, degrees, and secret associations in all the countries of the world; a bibliography of the principal works on Freemasonry published since 1723; and a supplement in which the author has collected a variety of rare and important Masonic documents. Of this work, which has never been translated into English, Lenning says (*Encycl. der Freimaurerei*) that it is, without dispute, the most scientific work on Freemasonry that French literature has ever produced. It must, however, be confessed that in the historical portion Thory has committed many errors in respect to English and American Freemasonry, and therefore, if ever translated, the work will require much emendation. (See *Thory.*)

Acting Grand Master. The Duke of Cumberland (grandson of George II., brother of George III.) having in April, 1782, been elected Grand Master of England, it was resolved by the Grand Lodge "that whenever a prince of the blood did the society the honour to accept the office of Grand Master, he should be at liberty to nominate any peer of the realm to be the acting Grand Master." (*Constitutions of G. L. of England*, ed. 1784, p. 341.) The officer thus provided to be appointed was subsequently called in the Constitutions of the G. Lodge of England, ed. 1841, and is now called the *Pro Grand Master.*

In the American system, the officer who performs the duties of Grand Master in case of the removal, death, or inability of that officer, is known as the Acting Grand Master. For the regulations which prescribe the proper person to perform these duties see *Grand Master.*

Active Lodge. A Lodge is said to be active when it is neither dormant nor suspended, but regularly meets and is occupied in the labors of Masonry.

Active Member. An active member of a Lodge is one who, in contradistinction to an honorary member, assumes all the burdens of membership, such as contributions, arrears, and participation in its labors, and is invested with all the rights of membership, such as speaking, voting, and holding office.

Actual Past Masters. This term is sometimes applied to those who have actually served as Master of a Craft Lodge in order to distinguish them from those who have been made "Virtual Past Masters," in Chapters of the United States, or "Past Masters of Arts and Sciences," in English Chapters, as a preliminary to receiving the Royal Arch degree. (See *Past Master.*)

Adad. The name of the principal god among the Syrians, and who, as representing the sun, had, according to Macrobius (*Saturnal*, i., 23), an image surrounded by rays. Macrobius, however, is wrong, as Selden has shown (*De Diis Syris*, i., 6), in confounding Adad with the Hebrew *Achad*, or one—a name, from its signification of unity, applied to the Great Architect of the Universe. The error of Macrobius, however, has been perpetuated by the inventors of the high degrees of Masonry, who have incorporated Adad, as a name of God, among their significant words.

Adam. The name of the first man. The Hebrew word אדם, ADaM, signifies man in a generic sense, the human species collectively, and is said to be derived from אדמה, ADaMaH, *the ground*, because the first man was made out of the dust of the earth, or from ADaM, to be red, in reference to his ruddy complexion. It is most probably in this collective sense, as the representative of the whole

human race, and, therefore, the type of humanity, that the presiding officer in a Council of Knights of the Sun, the Twenty-eighth Degree of the Ancient and Accepted Scottish Rite, is called Father Adam, and is occupied in the investigation of the great truths which so much concern the interests of the race. Adam, in that degree, is man seeking after divine truth. The Kabbalists and Talmudists have invented many things concerning the first Adam, none of which are, however, worthy of preservation. (See *Knight of the Sun.*)

Adam. * The Entered Apprentice degree symbolizes the creation of man and his first perception of light. In the Elohist form of the Creation we read, " Elohim said, ' Let us make man in our image, according to our likeness, and let him have dominion over the fishes of the sea, over the fowls of the air, over the cattle, and over all the earth, and over every reptile that creeps upon the earth!' And Elohim created man in his image; in the image of Elohim he created him; male and female he created them. . . . And Yahveh Elohim formed man of the dust of the ground, and breathed in his nostrils the breath of life, and man was made a living being." Without giving more than a passing reference to the speculative origin and production of man and to his spontaneous generation (*Principe Generateur*) as set forth by the Egyptians, when we are told that " the fertilizing mud left by the Nile, and exposed to the vivifying action of heat induced by the sun's rays, brought forth germs which spring up as the bodies of men," accepted cosmogonies only will be hereinafter mentioned; thus in that of Peru, the first man, created by the Divine Omnipotence, is called *Alpa Camasca*, " Animated earth." The Mandans, one of the North American tribes, relate that the Great Spirit molded two figures of clay, which he dried and animated with the breath of his mouth, one receiving the name of First Man, and the other that of Companion. Taeroa, the god of Tahiti, formed man of the red earth, say the inhabitants; and so we might continue. But as François Lenormant remarks in the *Beginnings of History*, let us confine ourselves to the cosmogony offered by the sacred traditions of the great civilized nations of antiquity. " The Chaldeans call Adam the man whom the earth produced. And he lay without movement, without life, and without breath, just like an image of the heavenly Adam, until his soul had been given him by the latter." The cosmogonic account peculiar to Babylon, as given by Berossus, says: " Belos, seeing that the earth was uninhabited, though fertile, cut off his own head, and the other gods, after kneading with earth the blood that flowed from it, formed men, who therefore are endowed with intelligence, and share in the divine thought," etc. The term employed to designate " man," in his connection with his Creator, is *admu*, the Assyrian counterpart of the Hebrew Adam. (G. Smith, *Chaldean Account of Genesis*.)

---

* This article is by C. T. McClenachan.

Lenormant further says, that the fragments of Berossus give Adoros as the name of the first patriarch, and Adiuru has been discovered on the cuneiform inscriptions.

Zoroaster makes the creation of man the voluntary act of a personal god, distinct from primordial matter, and his theory stands alone among the learned religions of the ancient world.

According to Jewish tradition in the Targumim and the Talmud, as also to Moses Maimonides, Adam was created man and woman at the same time, having two faces, turned in two opposite directions, and that during a stupor the Creator separated Havvah, his feminine half, from him, in order to make of her a distinct person. Thus were separated the primordial androgyn.

With Shemites and Mohammedans Adam was symbolized in the Lingam, whilst with the Jews Seth was their Adam or Lingam, and successively Noah took the place of Seth, and so followed Abraham and Moses. The worship of Adam as the God-like idea, succeeded by Seth, Noah, Abraham, and Moses, through the symbolism of pillars, monoliths, obelisks, or Matsebas (images), gave rise to other symbolic images, as where Noah was adored under the emblems of a man, ark, and serpent, signifying heat, fire, or passion.

Upon the death of Adam, says traditional history, the pious Gregory declared that the " dead body *should be kept above ground*, till a fulness of time should come to commit it to the middle of the earth by a priest of the most high God." This traditional prophecy was fulfilled, it is said, by the body of Adam having been preserved in a chest until about 1800 B.C., when "Melchizedek buried the body in Salem (formerly the name of Jerusalem), which might very well be the middle of the habitable world."

The Sethites used to say their prayers daily in the Ark *before the body of Adam.* J. G. R. Forlong, in his *Rivers of Life*, tells us that " It appears from both the *Sabid Aben Batric* and the Arabic *Catena*, that there existed the following 'short litany, said to have been conceived by Noah.' Then follows the prayer of Noah, which was used for so long a period by the Jewish Freemasons at the opening of the Lodge:

" ' O Lord, excellent art thou in thy truth, and there is nothing great in comparison of thee. Look upon us with the eye of mercy and compassion. Deliver us from this deluge of waters, and set our feet in a large room. By the sorrows of Adam, the first made man; by the blood of *Abel*, thy holy one; by the righteousness of *Seth*, in whom thou art well pleased; number us not amongst those who have transgressed thy statutes, but take us into thy merciful care, for thou art our *Deliverer*, and thine is the praise for all the works of thy hand for evermore. And the sons of Noah said, *Amen, Lord.*' "

The Master of the Lodge would omit the reference to the deluge and add the following to the prayer: " But grant, we beseech thee,

that the ruler of this lodge may be endued with knowledge and wisdom to instruct us and explain his secret mysteries, as our holy brother Moses did (in his lodge) to Aaron, to Eleazar, and to Ithamar (the sons of Aaron), and the several elders of Israel."

Adam Kadmon. In the Kabbalistic doctrine, the name given to the first emanation from the Eternal Fountain. It signifies the first man, or the first production of divine energy, or the son of God, and to it the other and inferior emanations are subordinate.

Adams, John Quincy, the sixth President of the United States, who served from 1825 to 1829. Mr. Adams, who has been very properly described as " a man of strong points and weak ones, of vast reading and wonderful memory, of great credulity and strong prejudices," became notorious in the latter years of his life for his virulent opposition to Freemasonry. The writer already quoted, who had an excellent opportunity of seeing intimately the workings of the spirit of anti-Masonry, says of Mr. Adams: " He hated Freemasonry, as he did many other things, not from any harm that he had received from it or personally knew respecting it, but because his credulity had been wrought upon and his prejudices excited against it by dishonest and selfish politicians, who were anxious, at any sacrifice to him, to avail themselves of the influence of his commanding talents and position in public life to sustain them in the disreputable work in which they were enlisted. In his weakness, he lent himself to them. He united his energies to theirs in an impracticable and unworthy cause." (C. W. Moore, *Freemasons' Mag.*, vol. vii., p. 314.) The result was a series of letters abusive of Freemasonry, directed to leading politicians, and published in the public journals from 1831 to 1833. A year before his death they were collected and published under the title of *Letters on the Masonic Institution, by John Quincy Adams.* (Boston, 1847, 8vo, pp. 284.) Some explanation of the cause of the virulence with which Mr. Adams attacked the Masonic Institution in these letters may be found in the following paragraph contained in an anti-Masonic work written by one Henry Gassett, and affixed to his *Catalogue of Books on the Masonic Institution.* (Boston, 1852.) "It had been asserted in a newspaper in Boston, edited by a Masonic dignitary, that John Q. Adams was a Mason. In answer to an inquiry from a person in New York State, whether he was so, Mr. Adams replied that 'he was not, and never should be.' *These few words, undoubtedly, prevented his election a second time as President of the United States. His competitor, Andrew Jackson, a Freemason, was elected.*" Whether the statement contained in the italicized words be true or not, is not the question. It is sufficient that Mr. Adams was led to believe it, and hence his ill-will to an association which had, as he supposed, inflicted this political evil on him, and baffled his ambitious views.

Adar. Hebrew, אדר; the sixth month of

the civil and the twelfth of the ecclesiastical year of the Jews. It corresponds to a part of February and of March.

Adarel. Angel of Fire. Referred to in the Hermetic degree of Knight of the Sun. Probably from אדר, *Adr*, splendor, and אל, *El*, God, i. e., the splendor of God or Divine splendor.

Addresses, Masonic. Dr. Oliver, speaking of the Masonic discourses which began to be published soon after the reorganization of Masonry, in the commencement of the eighteenth century, and which he thinks were instigated by the attacks made on the Order, to which they were intended to be replies, says: " Charges and addresses were therefore delivered by brethren in authority on the fundamental principles of the Order, and they were printed to show that its morality was sound, and not in the slightest degree repugnant to the precepts of our most holy religion. These were of sufficient merit to insure a wide circulation among the Fraternity, from whence they spread into the world at large, and proved decisive in fixing the credit of the Institution for solemnities of character and a taste for serious and profitable investigations."

There can be no doubt that these addresses, periodically delivered and widely published, have continued to exert an excellent effect in behalf of the Institution, by explaining and defending the principles on which it is founded.

The first Masonic address of which we have any notice was delivered on the 24th of June, 1721, before the Grand Lodge of England, by the celebrated John Theophilus Desaguliers, LL.D. and F.R.S. The *Book of Constitutions* (ed. 1738, p. 113), under that date, says " Bro. Desaguliers made an eloquent oration about Masons and Masonry." Dr. Oliver (*Revelations of a Square*, p. 22) states that this address was issued in a printed form, but no copy of it now remains—at least it has escaped the researches of the most diligent Masonic bibliographers.

On the 20th of May, 1725, Martin Folkes, then Deputy Grand Master, delivered an address before the Grand Lodge of England, which is cited in the *Freemason's Pocket Companion* for 1759, but no entire copy of the address is now extant.

The third Masonic address of which we have any knowledge is one entitled " A Speech delivered to the Worshipful and Ancient Society of Free and Accepted Masons, at a Grand Lodge held at Merchants' Hall, in the city of York, on St. John's Day, Dec. 27, 1726, the Right Worshipful Charles Bathurst, Esq., Grand Master. By the Junior Grand Warden. *Olim meminisse juvabit.* York: Printed by Thomas Gent, for the benefit of the Lodge." The author was Francis Drake, M.D., F.R.S., who was appointed Junior Grand Warden of the Grand Lodge of All England at York on December 27, 1725. (See *Drake, Francis.*) The first edition of the speech bears no date, but was probably issued in 1727, and it was again published at London in 1729, and a second London edition was published in 1734, which has been reprinted in Hughan's *Masonic Sketches and Reprints* (American edition, p. 106). This is, therefore, the earliest Masonic address to which we have access. It contains a brief sketch of the history of Masonry, written as Masonic history was then written. It is, however, remarkable for advancing the claim of the Grand Lodge of York to a superiority over that of London, and for containing a very early reference to the three degrees of Craft Masonry.

The fourth Masonic address of whose existence we have any knowledge is " a Speech Deliver'd to the Worshipful Society of Free and Accepted Masons, at a Lodge, held at the Carpenters Arms in Silver-Street, Golden Square, the 31st of December, 1728. By the Right Worshipful Edw. Oakley, Architect, M.M., late Provincial Senior Grand Warden in Carmarthen, South Wales." This speech was reprinted by Cole in his *Ancient Constitutions* at London in 1731.

America has the honor of presenting the next attempt at Masonic oratory. The fifth address, and the first American, which is extant, is one delivered in Boston, Mass., on June 24, 1734. It is entitled " A Dissertation upon Masonry, delivered to a Lodge in America, June 24th, 1734. Christ's Regm." It was discovered by Bro. C. W. Moore in the archives of the Grand Lodge of Massachusetts, and published by him in his magazine in 1849. This address is well written, and of a symbolic character, as the author allegorizes the Lodge as a type of heaven.

And, sixthly, we have " An Address made to the body of Free and Accepted Masons assembled at a Quarterly Communication, held near Temple Bar, December 11, 1735, by Martin Clare, Junior Grand Warden." Martin Clare was distinguished in his times as a Mason, and his address, which Dr. Oliver has inserted in his *Golden Remains*, has been considered of value enough to be translated into the French and German languages.

Next, on March 21, 1737, the Chevalier Ramsay delivered an oration before the Grand Lodge of France, in which he attributed the origin of Freemasonry to the Crusaders and traced an imaginary history of its course through Scotland and England into France. which was to become the center of the reformed Order. The best report of this speech is to be found in the *Histoire &c. de la tr. ven. Confraternité des F. M. &c. Traduit par le Fr. de la Tierce. Francfort, 1742;* and an English version of it is given in Gould's *History of Freemasonry* (iii., 84–9). (See *Ramsay.*)

After this period, Masonic addresses rapidly multiplied, so that it would be impossible to record their titles or even the names of their authors.

What Martial (i., 17) says of his own epigrams, that some were good, some bad, and a great many middling, may, with equal propriety and justice, be said of Masonic addresses. Of the thousands that have been de livered, many have been worth neither printing nor preservation.

One thing, however, is to be remarked: that within a few years the literary character of these productions has greatly improved. Formerly, a Masonic address on some festal occasion of the Order was little more than a homily on brotherly love or some other Masonic virtue. Often the orator was a clergyman, selected by the Lodge on account of his moral character or his professional ability. These clergymen were frequently among the youngest members of the Lodge, and men who had no opportunity to study the esoteric construction of Masonry. In such cases we will find that the addresses were generally neither more nor less than sermons under another name. They contain excellent general axioms of conduct, and sometimes encomiums on the laudable design of our Institution. But we look in vain in them for any ideas which refer to the history or to the occult philosophy of Masonry. They accept the definition that "Freemasonry is a science of morality, veiled in allegory and illustrated by symbols," only in part. They expatiate on the science of morality, but they say nothing of the symbols or the allegories. But, as has been already said, there has been an evident improvement within a few years, in America especially, for the reform has not equally extended to England. Many of the addresses now delivered are of a higher order of Masonic literature. The subjects of Masonic history, of the origin of the Institution, of its gradual development from an operative art to a speculative science, of its symbols, and of its peculiar features which distinguish it from all other associations, have been ably discussed in many recent Masonic addresses, and thus have the efforts to entertain an audience for an hour become not only the means of interesting instruction to the hearers, but also valuable contributions to the literature of Freemasonry.

It is in this way that Masonic addresses should be written. All platitudes and old truisms should be avoided; sermonizing, which is good in its place, is out of place here. No one should undertake to deliver a Masonic address unless he knows something of the subject on which he is about to speak, and unless he is capable of saying what will make every Mason who hears him a wiser as well as a better man, or at least what will afford him the opportunity of becoming so.

Adelph. From the Greek ἀδελφός (a brother). The first degree of the order of the Palladium (q. v.). Reghellini says that there exists in the Masonic archives of Douai the ritual of a Masonic Society, called Adelphs, which has been communicated to the Grand Orient, but which he thinks is the same as the Primitive Rite of Narbonne.

Adept. One fully skilled or well versed in any art; from the Latin word "Adeptus," having obtained, because the Adept claimed to be in the possession of all the secrets of his peculiar mystery. The Alchemists or Hermetic philosophers assumed the title of Adepts.

(See Alchemy.) Of the Hermetic Adepts, who were also sometimes called Rosicrucians, Spence thus writes, in 1740, to his mother: "Have you ever heard of the people called Adepts? They are a set of philosophers superior to whatever appeared among the Greeks and Romans. The three great points they drive at, are, to be free from poverty, distempers, and death; and, if you believe them, they have found out one secret that is capable of freeing them from all three. There are never more than twelve of these men in the whole world at a time; and we have the happiness of having one of the twelve at this time in Turin. I am very well acquainted with him, and have often talked with him of their secrets, as far as he is allowed to talk to a common mortal of them." (Spence's Letter to his Mother, in Singer's Anecdotes, p. 403.) In a similar allusion to the possession of abstruse knowledge, the word is applied to some of the high degrees of Masonry.

Adept, Prince. One of the names of the 28th degree of the Ancient and Accepted Scottish Rite. (See Knight of the Sun.) It was the 23d degree of the System of the Chapter of Emperors of the East and West of Clermont.

Adept, the. A Hermetic degree of the collection of A. Viany (q. v.). It is also the 4th degree of the Rite of Relaxed Observance, and the 1st of the high degrees of the Rite of Elects of Truth. "It has much analogy," says Thory, "with the degree of Knight of the Sun." It is also called "Chaos disentangled."

Adeptus Adoptatus. The 7th degree of the Rite of Zinnendorf, consisting of a kind of chemical and pharmaceutical instruction.

Adeptus Coronatus. Called also Templar Master of the Key. The 7th degree of the Swedish Rite (q. v.).

Adeptus Exemptus. The 7th degree of the system adopted by those German Rosicrucians who were known as the "Gold und Rosenkreutzer," or the Gold and Rosy Cross, and whom Lenning supposes to have been the first who engrafted Rosicrucianism on Masonry.

Adhering Mason. Those Masons who, during the anti-Masonic excitement in America, on account of the supposed abduction of Morgan, refused to leave their Lodges and renounce Masonry, were so called. They embraced among their number some of the wisest, best, and most influential men of the country.

Adjournment. C. W. Moore (Freemasons' Mag., xii., p. 290) says: "We suppose it to be generally conceded that Lodges cannot properly be adjourned. It has been so decided by a large proportion of the Grand Lodges in America, and tacitly, at least, concurred in by all. We are not aware that there is a dissenting voice among them. It is, therefore, safe to assume that the settled policy is against adjournment." The reason which he assigns for this rule, is that adjournment is a method used only in deliberative bodies, such as legislatures and courts, and as Lodges do not partake of the character of either of these, adjournments are not applicable to them. The rule which Bro. Moore lays down is undoubtedly correct, but the reason which he assigns for it is not sufficient. If a Lodge were permitted to adjourn by the vote of a majority of its members, the control of the labor would be placed in their hands. But according to the whole spirit of the Masonic system, the Master alone controls and directs the hours of labor. In the 5th of the Old Charges, approved in 1722, it is declared that "All Masons shall meekly receive their Wages without murmuring or mutiny, *and not desert the Master till the Lord's work is finish'd*." Now as the Master alone can know when "the work is finished," the selection of the time of closing must be vested in him. He is the sole judge of the proper period at which the labors of the Lodge should be terminated, and he may suspend business even in the middle of a debate, if he supposes that it is expedient to close the Lodge. Hence no motion for adjournment can ever be admitted in a Masonic Lodge. Such a motion would be an interference with the prerogative of the Master, and could not therefore be entertained.

The Earl of Zetland, when Grand Master of England, ruled on November 19, 1856, that a Lodge has no power to adjourn except to the next regular day of meeting. He said: "I may . . . say that Private Lodges are governed by much the same laws as Grand Lodges, and that no meeting of a Private Lodge can be adjourned; but the Master of a Private Lodge may, and does, convene Lodges of Emergency." (*Freemasons' Magazine*, 1856, p. 848.)

This prerogative of opening and closing his Lodge is necessarily vested in the Master, because, by the nature of our Institution, he is responsible to the Grand Lodge for the good conduct of the body over which he presides. He is charged, in those questions to which he is required to give his assent at his installation, to hold the Landmarks in veneration, and to conform to every edict of the Grand Lodge; and for any violation of the one or disobedience of the other by the Lodge, in his presence, he would be answerable to the supreme Masonic authority. Hence the necessity that an arbitrary power should be conferred upon him, by the exercise of which he may at any time be enabled to prevent the adoption of resolutions, or the commission of any act which would be subversive of, or contrary to, those ancient laws and usages which he has sworn to maintain and preserve.

Admiration, Sign of. A mode of recognition alluded to in the Most Excellent Master's Degree, or the Sixth of the American Rite. Its introduction in that place is referred to a Masonic legend in connection with the visit of the Queen of Sheba to King Solomon, which states that, moved by the wide-spread reputation of the Israelitish monarch, she had repaired to Jerusalem to inspect the magnificent works of which she had heard so many encomiums. Upon arriving there, and beholding for the first time the Temple, which glittered with gold, and which was so accurately adjusted in all its parts as to seem to be composed of but a single piece of marble, she raised her hands and eyes to heaven in an attitude of admiration, and at the same time exclaimed, "Rabboni!" equivalent to saying, "A most excellent master hath done this!" This action has since been perpetuated in the ceremonies of the degree of Most Excellent Master. The legend is, however, no doubt apocryphal, and is really to be considered only as allegorical, like so many other of the legends of Masonry. (See *Sheba, Queen of.*)

Admission. Although the Old Charges, approved in 1722, use the word *admitted* as applicable to those who are *initiated* into the mysteries of Freemasonry, yet the General Regulations of 1721 employ the term *admission* in a sense different from that of *initiation*. By the word *making* they imply the reception of a profane into the Order, but by *admission* they designate the election of a Mason into a Lodge. Thus we find such expressions as these clearly indicating a difference in the meaning of the two words. In Reg. v.—"No man can be made or admitted a member of a particular Lodge." In Reg. vi.—"But no man can be entered a brother in any particular Lodge, or admitted to be a member thereof." And more distinctly in Reg. viii.—"No set or number of brethren shall withdraw or separate themselves from the Lodge in which they were made brethren or were afterwards admitted members." This distinction has not always been rigidly preserved by recent writers; but it is evident that, correctly speaking, we should always say of a profane who has been initiated that he has been *made* a Mason, and of a Mason who has been affiliated with a Lodge, that he has been *admitted* a member. The true definition of *admission* is, then, the reception of an unaffiliated brother into membership. (See *Affiliated Mason.*)

Admonition. According to the ethics of Freemasonry, it is made a duty obligatory upon every member of the Order to conceal the faults of a brother, that is, not to blazon forth his errors and infirmities, to let them be learned by the world from some other tongue than his, and to admonish him of them in private. So there is another but a like duty or obligation, which instructs him to whisper good counsel in his brother's ear and to warn him of approaching danger. And this refers not more to the danger that is without and around him than to that which is within him; not more to the peril that springs from the concealed foe who would waylay him and covertly injure him, than to that deeper peril of those faults and infirmities which lie within his own heart, and which, if not timely crushed by good and earnest resolution of amendment, will, like the ungrateful serpent in the fable, become warm with life only to sting the bosom that has nourished them.

Admonition of a brother's fault is, then, the duty of every Mason, and no true one will, for either fear or favor, neglect its performance.

But as the duty is Masonic, so is there a Masonic way in which that duty should be discharged. We must admonish not with self-sufficient pride in our own reputed goodness—not in imperious tones, as though we looked down in scorn upon the degraded offender—not in language that, by its harshness, will wound rather than win, will irritate more than it will reform; but with that persuasive gentleness that gains the heart—with the all-subduing influences of "mercy unrestrained"—with the magic might of love—with the language and the accents of affection, which mingle grave displeasure for the offense with grief and pity for the offender.

This, and this alone, is Masonic admonition. I am not to rebuke my brother in anger, for I, too, have my faults, and I dare not draw around me the folds of my garment lest they should be polluted by my neighbor's touch; but I am to admonish in private, not before the world, for that would degrade him; and I am to warn him, perhaps from my own example, how vice ever should be followed by sorrow, for that goodly sorrow leads to repentance, and repentance to amendment, and amendment to joy.

Adonai. In Hebrew, אֲדֹנָי, being the plural of excellence for *Adon*, and signifying *the Lord*. The Jews, who reverently avoided the pronunciation of the sacred name JEHOVAH, were accustomed, whenever that name occurred, to substitute for it the word *Adonai* in reading. As to the use of the plural form instead of the singular, the Rabbis say, "Every word indicative of dominion, though singular in meaning, is made plural in form." This is called the "pluralis excellentiæ." The Talmudists also say (Buxtroff, *Lex. Talm.*) that the tetragrammaton is called *Shem hamphorash*, the name that is explained, because it is explained, uttered, and set forth by the word *Adonai*. (See *Jehovah* and *Shem Hamphorasch*.) Adonai is used as a significant word in several of the high degrees of Masonry, and may almost always be considered as allusive to or symbolic of the True Word.

Adonhiram. This has been adopted by the disciples of Adonhiramite Masonry as the spelling of the name of the person known in Scripture and in other Masonic systems as *Adoniram* (which see). They correctly derive the word from the Hebrew *Adon* and *hiram*, signifying the *master who is exalted*, which is the true meaning of Adoniram, the ה or *h* being omitted in the Hebrew by the coalescence of the two words. Hiram Abif has also sometimes been called Adonhiram, the Adon having been bestowed on him by Solomon, it is said, as a title of honor.

Adonhiramite Masonry. Of the numerous controversies which arose from the middle to near the end of the eighteenth century on the Continent of Europe, and especially in France, among the students of Masonic philosophy, and which so frequently resulted in the invention of new degrees and the establishment of new rites, not the least prominent was that which related to the person and character of the Temple Builder. The question, Who was the architect of King Solomon's Temple? was answered differently by different theorists, and each answer gave rise to a new system, a fact by no means surprising in those times, so fertile in the production of new Masonic systems. The general theory was then, as it is now, that this architect was Hiram Abif, the widow's son, who had been sent to King Solomon by Hiram, King of Tyre, as a precious gift, and "a curious and cunning workman." This theory was sustained by the statements of the Jewish Scriptures, so far as they threw any light on the Masonic legend. It was the theory of the English Masons from the earliest times; was enunciated as historically correct in the first edition of the *Book of Constitutions*, published in 1723 (p. 11); has continued ever since to be the opinion of all English and American Masons; and is, at this day, the only theory entertained by any Mason in the two countries who has a theory at all on the subject. This, therefore, is the orthodox faith of Masonry.

But such was not the case in the last century on the Continent of Europe. At first the controversy arose not as to the man himself, but as to his proper appellation. All parties agreed that the architect of the Temple was that Hiram, the widow's son, who is described in the 1st Book of Kings, chapter vii., verses 13 and 14, and in the 2d Book of Chronicles, chapter ii., verses 13 and 14, as having come out of Tyre with the other workmen of the Temple who had been sent by King Hiram to Solomon. But one party called him *Hiram Abif*, and the other, admitting that his original name was Hiram, supposed that, in consequence of the skill he had displayed in the construction of the Temple, he had received the honorable affix of *Adon*, signifying *Lord* or *Master*, whence his name became *Adonhiram*.

There was, however, at the Temple another Adoniram, of whom it will be necessary in passing to say a few words, for the better understanding of the present subject.

The first notice that we have of this Adoniram in Scripture is in the 2d Book of Samuel, chapter xx., verse 24, where, in the abbreviated form of his name, *Adoram*, he is said to have been "over the tribute" in the house of David; or, as Gesenius translates it, "prefect over the tribute service," or, as we might say in modern phrase, principal collector of the taxes. Seven years afterward, we find him exercising the same office in the household of Solomon; for it is said in 1 Kings iv. 6 that Adoniram, "the son of Abda, was over the tribute." And lastly, we hear of him still occupying the same station in the household of King Rehoboam, the successor of Solomon. Forty-seven years after he is first mentioned in the Book of Samuel, he is stated under the name of Adoram (1 Kings xii. 18), or Hadoram (2 Chron. x. 18), to have been stoned to death, while in the discharge of his duty, by the people, who were justly indignant at the oppressions of his master.

The legends and traditions of Masonry

which connect this Adoniram with the Temple at Jerusalem derive their support from a single passage in the 1st Book of Kings (v. 14), where it is said that Solomon made a levy of thirty thousand workmen from among the Israelites; that he sent these in courses of ten thousand a month to labor on Mount Lebanon, and that he placed Adoniram over these as their superintendent.

The ritual-makers of France, who were not all Hebrew scholars, nor well versed in Biblical history, seem, at times, to have confounded two important personages, and to have lost all distinction between Hiram the Builder, who had been sent from the court of the King of Tyre, and Adoniram, who had always been an officer in the court of King Solomon. And this error was extended and facilitated when they had prefixed the title *Adon*, that is to say, lord or master, to the name of the former, making him *Adon Hiram*, or the Lord Hiram.

Thus, in the year 1744, one Louis Travenol published at Paris, under the pseudonym of Leonard Gabanon, a work entitled *Catechisme des Francs Maçons, ou Le Secret des Maçons*, in which he says: " Besides the cedars of Lebanon, Hiram made a much more valuable gift to Solomon, in the person of Adonhiram, of his own race, the son of a widow of the tribe of Naphtali. His father, who was named Hur, was an excellent architect and worker in metals. Solomon, knowing his virtues, his merit, and his talents, distinguished him by the most eminent position, intrusting to him the construction of the Temple and the superintendence of all the workmen." (*Recueil Precieux*, p. 76.)

From the language of this extract, and from the reference in the title of the book to Adoram, which we know was one of the names of Solomon's tax-collector, it is evident that the author of the catechism has confounded Hiram Abif, who came out of Tyre, with Adoniram, the son of Abda, who had always lived at Jerusalem; that is to say, with unpardonable ignorance of Scripture history and Masonic tradition, he has supposed the two to be one and the same person. Notwithstanding this literary blunder, the catechism became popular with many Masons of that day, and thus arose the first schism or error in relation to the legend of the Third Degree. In *Solomon in all His Glory*, an English exposure published in 1766, Adoniram takes the place of Hiram, but this work is a translation from a similar French one, and so it must not be argued that English Masons ever held this view.

At length, other ritualists, seeing the inconsistency of referring the character of Hiram, the widow's son, to Adoniram, the receiver of taxes, and the impossibility of reconciling the discordant facts in the life of both, resolved to cut the Gordian knot by refusing any Masonic position to the former, and making the latter, alone, the architect of the Temple. It cannot be denied that Josephus (viii. 2) states that Adoniram, or, as he calls him, Adoram, was, at the very beginning of the labor, placed over the workmen who prepared the materials on Mount Lebanon, and that he speaks of Hiram, the widow's son, simply as a skilful artisan, especially in metals, who had only made all the mechanical works about the Temple according to the will of Solomon. (viii. 3.) This apparent color of authority for their opinions was readily claimed by the Adoniramites, and hence one of their most prominent ritualists, Guillemain de St. Victor (*Recueil Precieux de la Maçonnerie Adonhiramite*, pp. 77, 78), propounds their theory thus: " We all agree that the Master's degree is founded on the architect of the Temple. Now, Scripture says very positively, in the 14th verse of the 5th chapter of the 3d Book of Kings,* that the person was Adonhiram. Josephus and all the sacred writers say the same thing, and undoubtedly distinguish him from Hiram the Tyrian, the worker in metals. So that it is Adonhiram, then, whom we are bound to honor."

There were, therefore, in the eighteenth century, from about the middle to near the end of it, three schools among the Masonic ritualists, the members of which were divided in opinion as to the proper identity of this Temple Builder:

1. Those who supposed him to be Hiram, the son of a widow of the tribe of Naphtali, whom the King of Tyre had sent to King Solomon, and whom they designated as Hiram Abif. This was the original and most popular school, and which we now suppose to have been the orthodox one.

2. Those who believed this Hiram that came out of Tyre to have been the architect, but who supposed that, in consequence of his excellence of character, Solomon had bestowed upon him the appellation of *Adon*, " Lord " or " Master," calling him Adonhiram. As this theory was wholly unsustained by Scripture history or previous Masonic tradition, the school which supported it never became prominent or popular, and soon ceased to exist, although the error on which it is based is repeated at intervals in the blunder of some modern French ritualists.

3. Those who, treating this Hiram, the widow's son, as a subordinate and unimportant character, entirely ignored him in their ritual, and asserted that Adoram, or Adoniram, or Adonhiram, as the name was spelled by these ritualists, the son of Abda, the collector of tribute and the superintendent of the levy on Mount Lebanon, was the true architect of the Temple, and the one to whom all the legendary incidents of the Third Degree of Masonry were to be referred. This school, in consequence of the boldness with which, unlike the second school, it refused all compromise with the orthodox party and assumed a wholly independent theory, became, for a time, a prominent schism in Masonry. Its disciples bestowed upon the believers in Hiram Abif the name of *Hiramite Masons*, adopted as their own distinctive appellation that of

---

* In the LXX the two books of Samuel are called the 1st and 2d of Kings.

Adonhiramites, and, having developed the system which they practised into a peculiar rite, called it *Adonhiramite Masonry.*

Who was the original founder of the rite of Adonhiramite Masonry, and at what precise time it was first established, are questions that cannot now be answered with any certainty. Thory does not attempt to reply to either in his *Nomenclature of Rites,* where, if anything was known on the subject, we would be most likely to find it. Ragon, it is true, in his *Orthodoxie Maçonnique,* attributes the rite to the Baron de Tschoudy. But as he also assigns the authorship of the *Recueil Precieux* (a work of which we shall directly speak more fully) to the same person, in which statement he is known to be mistaken, there can be but little doubt that he is wrong in the former as well as in the latter opinion. The Chevalier de Lussy, better known as the Baron de Tschoudy, was, it is true, a distinguished ritualist. He founded the Order of the Blazing Star, and took an active part in the operations of the Council of Emperors of the East and West; but we have met with no evidence, outside of Ragon's assertion, that he established or had anything to do with the Adonhiramite Rite.

We are disposed to attribute the development into a settled system, if not the actual creation, of the rite of Adonhiramite Masonry to Louis Guillemain de St. Victor, who published at Paris, in the year 1781, a work entitled *Recueil Precieux de la Maçonnerie Adonhiramite, etc.*

As this volume contained only the ritual of the first four degrees, it was followed, in 1785, by another, which embraced the higher degrees of the rite. No one who peruses these volumes can fail to perceive that the author writes like one who has invented, or, at least, materially modified the rite which is the subject of his labors. At all events, this work furnishes the only authentic account that we possess of the organization of the Adonhiramite system of Masonry.

The rite of Adonhiramite Masonry consisted of twelve degrees, which were as follows, the names being given in French as well as in English:

1. Apprentice—*Apprentif.*
2. Fellow-Craft—*Compagnon.*
3. Master Mason—*Maître.*
4. Perfect Master—*Maître Parfait.*
5. Elect of Nine—*Premier Elu, ou L'Elu des Neuf.*
6. Elect of Perignan—*Second Elu nommé Elu de Pérignan.*
7. Elect of Fifteen—*Troisieme Elu nommé Elu des Quinze.*
8. Minor Architect—*Petit Architecte.*
9. Grand Architect, or Scottish Fellow-Craft—*Grand Architecte, ou Compagnon Ecossois.*
10. Scottish Master—*Maître Ecossois.*
11. Knight of the Sword, Knight of the East, or of the Eagle—*Chevalier de l'Épée surnommé Chevalier de l'Orient ou de l'Aigle.*
12. Knight of Rose Croix—*Chevalier Rose Croix.*

This is the entire list of Adonhiramite degrees. Thory and Ragon have both erred in giving a thirteenth degree, namely, the Noachite, or Prussian Knight. They have fallen into this mistake because Guillemain has inserted this degree at the end of his second volume, but simply as a Masonic curiosity, having been translated, as he says, from the German by M. de Bérage. It has no connection with the preceding series of degrees, and Guillemain positively declares that the Rose Croix is the *ne plus ultra* (*2nde Ptie,* p. 118), the summit and termination, of his rite.

Of these twelve degrees, the first ten are occupied with the transactions of the first Temple; the eleventh with matters relating to the construction of the second Temple; and the twelfth with that Christian symbolism of Freemasonry which is peculiar to the Rose Croix of every rite. All of the degrees have been borrowed from the Ancient and Accepted Rite, with slight modifications, which have seldom improved their character. On the whole, the extinction of the Adonhiramite Rite can scarcely be considered as a loss to Masonry.

Before concluding, a few words may be said on the orthography of the title. As the rite derives its peculiar characteristic from the fact that it founds the Third Degree on the assumed legend that Adoniram, the son of Abda and the receiver of tribute, was the true architect of the Temple, and not Hiram, the widow's son, it should properly have been styled the *Adoniramite* Rite, and not the *Adonhiramite;* and so it would probably have been called if Guillemain, who gave it form, had been acquainted with the Hebrew language, for he would then have known that the name of his hero was *Adoniram* and not *Adonhiram.* The term Adonhiramite Masons should really have been applied to the second school described in this article, whose disciples admitted that Hiram Abif was the architect of the Temple, but who supposed that Solomon had bestowed the prefix *Adon* upon him as a mark of honor, calling him Adonhiram. But Guillemain having committed the blunder in the name of his Rite, it continued to be repeated by his successors, and it would perhaps now be inconvenient to correct the error. Ragon, however, and a few other recent writers, have ventured to take this step, and in their works the system is called Adoniramite Masonry.

Adoniram. The first notice that we have of Adoniram in Scripture is in the 2d Book of Samuel (xx. 24), where, in the abbreviated form of his name Adoram, he is said to have been "over the tribute" in the house of David, or, as Gesenius translates it, "prefect over the tribute service, tribute master," that is to say, in modern phrase, he was the chief receiver of the taxes. Clarke calls him "Chancellor of the Exchequer." Seven years afterward we find him exercising the same office in the household of Solomon, for it is said (1 Kings iv. 6) that "Adoniram the son of Abda was over the tribute." And lastly, we hear of him still occupying the same station in the household of King Rehoboam, the successor of Solomon. Forty-seven years after he is first mentioned in the Book of Samuel, he is stated under the name of Adoram (1 Kings xii. 18), or Hadoram (2 Chron. x. 18), to have been stoned to death, while in the discharge of his duty, by the people, who were justly indignant at the oppressions of his master. Although commentators have been at a loss to determine whether the tax-receiver under David, under Solomon, and under Rehoboam was the same person, there seems to be no reason to doubt it; for, as Kitto says, " It appears very unlikely that even two persons of the same name should successively bear the same office, in an age when no example occurs of the father's name being given to his son. We find, also, that not more than forty-seven years elapse between the first and last mention of the Adoniram who was ' over the tribute'; and as this, although a long term of service, is not too long for one life, and as the person who held the office in the beginning of Rehoboam's reign had served in it long enough to make himself odious to the people, it appears, on the whole, most probable that one and the same person is intended throughout." (*Encyc. Bib. Lit.*)

Adoniram plays an important *rôle* in the Masonic system, especially in the high degrees, but the time of action in which he appears is confined to the period occupied in the construction of the Temple. The legends and traditions which connect him with that edifice derive their support from a single passage in the 1st Book of Kings (v. 14), where it is said that Solomon made a levy of thirty thousand workmen from among the Israelites; that he sent these in courses of ten thousand a month to labor on Mount Lebanon, and that he placed Adoniram over these as their superintendent. From this brief statement the Adoniramite Masons have deduced the theory, as may be seen in the preceding article, that Adoniram was the architect of the Temple; while the Hiramites, assigning this important office to Hiram Abif, still believe that Adoniram occupied an important part in the construction of that edifice. He has been called " the first of the Fellow Crafts"; is said in one tradition to have been the brother-in-law of Hiram Abif, the latter having demanded of Solomon the hand of Adoniram's sister in marriage; and that the nuptials were honored by the kings of Israel and Tyre with a public celebration; and another tradition, preserved in the Royal Master's degree, informs us that he was the one to whom the three Grand Masters had intended first to communicate that knowledge which they had reserved as a fitting reward to be bestowed upon all meritorious craftsmen at the completion of the Temple. It is scarcely necessary to say that these and many other Adoniramic legends, often fanciful, and without any historical authority, are but the outward clothing of abstruse symbols, some of which have been preserved, and others lost in the lapse of time and the ignorance and corruptions of modern ritualists.

Adoniram, in Hebrew, אדנירם, compounded of אדן, ADON, *Lord*, and הרם, HiRaM, *altitude*, signifies the *Lord of altitude*. It is a word of great importance, and frequently used among the sacred words of the high degrees in all the Rites.

Adoniramite Masonry. See *Adonhiramite Masonry.*

Adonis, Mysteries of. An investigation of the mysteries of Adonis peculiarly claims the attention of the Masonic student: first, because, in their symbolism and in their esoteric doctrine, the religious object for which they were instituted, and the mode in which that object is attained, they bear a nearer analogical resemblance to the Institution of Freemasonry than do any of the other mysteries or systems of initiation of the ancient world; and, secondly, because their chief locality brings them into a very close connection with the early history and reputed origin of Freemasonry. For they were principally celebrated at Byblos, a city of Phœnicia, whose Scriptural name was Gebal, and whose inhabitants were the Giblites or Gebalites, who are referred to in the 1st Book of Kings (chap. v. 18) as being the " stone-squarers " employed by King Solomon in building the Temple. See *Gebal* and *Giblim*. Hence there must have evidently been a very intimate connection, or at least certainly a very frequent intercommunication, between the workmen of the first Temple and the inhabitants of Byblos, the seat of the Adonisian mysteries, and the place whence the worshipers of that rite were disseminated over other regions of country.

These historical circumstances invite us to an examination of the system of initiation which was practised at Byblos, because we may find in it something that was probably suggestive of the symbolic system of instruction which was subsequently so prominent a feature in the system of Freemasonry.

Let us first examine the myth on which the Adonisiac initiation was founded. The mythological legend of Adonis is, that he was the son of Myrrha and Cinyras, King of Cyprus. Adonis was possessed of such surpassing beauty, that Venus became enamored of him, and adopted him as her favorite. Subsequently Adonis, who was a great hunter, died from a wound inflicted by a wild boar on Mount Lebanon. Venus flew to the succor of her favorite, but she came too late. Adonis was dead. On his descent to the infernal regions, Proserpine became, like Venus, so attracted by his beauty, that, notwithstanding the entreaties of the goddess of love, she refused to restore him to earth. At length the prayers of the desponding Venus were listened to with favor by Jupiter, who reconciled the dispute between the two goddesses, and by whose decree Proserpine was compelled to consent that Adonis should spend six months of each year alternately with herself and Venus.

This is the story on which the Greek poet Bion founded his exquisite idyll entitled the *Epitaph of Adonis*, the beginning of which has been thus rather inefficiently " aone into English ":

"I and the Loves Adonis dead deplore:
The beautiful Adonis is indeed
Departed, parted from us. Sleep no more
In purple, Cypris! but in watchet weed,
All wretched! beat thy breast and all aread—
'Adonis is no more.' The Loves and I
Lament him. 'Oh! her grief to see him bleed,
Smitten by white tooth on whiter thigh,
Out-breathing life's faint sigh upon the mountain high.'"

It is evident that Bion referred the contest of Venus and Proserpine for Adonis to a period subsequent to his death, from the concluding lines, in which he says: " The Muses, too, lament the son of Cinyras, and invoke him in their song; but he does not heed them, not because he does not wish, but because Proserpine will not release him." This was, indeed, the favorite form of the myth, and on it was framed the symbolism of the ancient mystery.

But there are other Grecian mythologues that relate the tale of Adonis differently. According to these, he was the product of the incestuous connection of Cinyras and his daughter Myrrha. Cinyras subsequently, on discovering the crime of his daughter, pursued her with a drawn sword, intending to kill her. Myrrha entreated the gods to make her invisible, and they changed her into a myrrh tree. Ten months after the myrrh tree opened, and the young Adonis was born. This is the form of the myth that has been adopted by Ovid, who gives it with all its moral horrors in the tenth book (298–559) of his *Metamorphoses*.

Venus, who was delighted with the extraordinary beauty of the boy, put him in a coffer, unknown to all the gods, and gave him to Proserpine to keep and to nurture in the under world. But Proserpine had no sooner beheld him than she became enamored of him and refused, when Venus applied for him, to surrender him to her rival. The subject was then referred to Jupiter, who decreed that Adonis should have one-third of the year to himself, should be another third with Venus, and the remainder of the time with Proserpine. Adonis gave his own portion to Venus, and lived happily with her till, having offended Diana, he was killed by a wild boar.

The mythographer Pharnutus gives a still different story, and says that Adonis was the grandson of Cinyras, and fled with his father, Ammon, into Egypt, whose people he civilized, taught them agriculture, and enacted many wise laws for their government. He subsequently passed over into Syria, and was wounded in the thigh by a wild boar while hunting on Mount Lebanon. His wife, Isis, or Astarte, and the people of Phœnicia and Egypt, supposing that the wound was mortal, profoundly deplored his death. But he afterward recovered, and their grief was replaced by transports of joy. All the myths, it will be seen, agree in his actual or supposed death by violence, in the grief for his loss, in his recovery or restoration to life, and in the conse-

quent joy thereon. And on these facts are founded the Adonisian mysteries which were established in his honor.

While, therefore, we may grant the possibility that there was originally some connection between the Sabean worship of the sun and the celebration of the Adonisian festival, we cannot forget that these mysteries, in common with all the other sacred initiations of the ancient world, had been originally established to promulgate among the initiates the once hidden doctrine of a future life. The myth of Adonis in Syria, like that of Osiris in Egypt, of Atys in Samothrace, or of Dionysus in Greece, presented, symbolically, the two great ideas of decay and restoration: sometimes figured as darkness and light, sometimes as winter and summer, sometimes as death and life, but always maintaining, no matter what was the framework of the allegory, the inseparable ideas of something that was lost and afterward recovered, as its interpretation, and so teaching, as does Freemasonry at this day, by a similar system of allegorizing, that after the death of the body comes the eternal life of the soul. The inquiring Freemason will thus readily see the analogy in the symbolism that exists between Adonis in the mysteries of the Gebalites at Byblos and Hiram the Builder in his own institution.

Adoption, Masonic. The adoption by the Lodge of the child of a Mason is practised, with peculiar ceremonies, in some of the French and German Lodges, and has been recently introduced, but not with the general approbation of the Craft, into one or two Lodges of this country. Clavel, in his *Histoire Pittoresque de la Franc-Maçonnerie* (p. 40, 3d ed.), gives the following account of the ceremonies of adoption.

" It is a custom, in many Lodges, when the wife of a Mason is near the period of her confinement, for the Hospitaller, if he is a physician, and if not, for some other brother who is, to visit her, inquire after her health, in the name of the Lodge, and to offer her his professional services, and even pecuniary aid if he thinks she needs it. Nine days after the birth of her child, the Master and Wardens call upon her to congratulate her on the happy event. If the infant is a boy, a special communication of the Lodge is convened for the purpose of proceeding to its adoption. The hall is decorated with flowers and foliage, and censers are prepared for burning incense. Before the commencement of labor, the child and its nurse are introduced into an anteroom. The Lodge is then opened, and the Wardens, who are to act as godfathers, repair to the infant at the head of a deputation of five brethren. The chief of the deputation, then addressing the nurse, exhorts her not only to watch over the health of the child that has been intrusted to her care, but also to cultivate his youthful intellect, and to instruct him with truthful and sensible conversation. The child is then taken from the nurse, placed by its father upon a cushion, and carried by the deputation into the Lodge room. The procession advances beneath an arch of foliage to the pedestal of the east, where it stops.

" ' Whom bring you here, my brethren? ' says the Master to the godfathers.

" ' The son of one of our brethren whom the Lodge is desirous of adopting,' is the reply of the Senior Warden.

" ' What are his names, and what Masonic name will you give him? '

" The Warden replies, adding to the baptismal and surname of the child a characteristic name, such as *Truth, Devotion, Benevolence,* or some other of a similar nature.

" The Master then descends from his seat, approaches the louveteau or lewis (for such is the appellation given to the son of a Mason), and extending his hands over its head, offers up a prayer that the child may render itself worthy of the love and care which the Lodge intends to bestow upon it. He then casts incense into the censers, and pronounces the Apprentice's obligation, which the godfathers repeat after him in the name of the louveteau. Afterwards he puts a white apron on the infant, proclaiming it to be the adopted child of the Lodge, and causes this proclamation to be received with the honors.

"As soon as this ceremony has been performed, the Master returns to his seat, and having caused the Wardens with the child to be placed in front of the north column, he recounts to the former the duties which they have assumed as godfathers. After the Wardens have made a suitable response, the deputation which had brought the child into the Lodge room is again formed, carries it out, and restores it to its nurse in the anteroom.

" The adoption of a louveteau binds all the members of the Lodge to watch over his education, and subsequently to aid him, if it be necessary, in establishing himself in life. A circumstantial account of the ceremony is drawn up, which having been signed by all the members is delivered to the father of the child. This document serves as a dispensation, which relieves him from the necessity of passing through the ordinary preliminary examinations when, at the proper age, he is desirous of participating in the labors of Masonry. He is then only required to renew his obligations."

In the United States, the ceremony has been recently practised by a few Lodges, the earliest instance being that of Foyer Maçonnique Lodge of New Orleans, in 1859. The Supreme Council for the Southern Jurisdiction, Ancient and Accepted Scottish Rite, has published the ritual of Masonic Adoption for the use of the members of that rite. This ritual under the title of " Offices of Masonic Baptism, Reception of a Louveteau and Adoption," is a very beautiful one, and is the composition of Brother Albert Pike. It is scarcely necessary to say that the word *Baptism* there used has not the slightest reference to the Christian sacrament of the same name. (See *Lewis.*)

Adoptive Masonry. An organization which bears a very imperfect resemblance to Freemasonry in its forms and ceremonies, and which was established in France for the initiation of females, has been called by the French " *Maçonnerie d'Adoption,* " or *Adoptive Masonry,* and the societies in which the initiations take place have received the name of " *Loges d'Adoption,* " or *Adoptive Lodges.* This appellation is derived from the fact that every female or Adoptive Lodge is obliged, by the regulations of the association, to be, as it were, adopted by, and thus placed under the guardianship of, some regular Lodge of Freemasons.

As to the exact date which we are to assign for the first introduction of this system of female Masonry, there have been several theories, some of which, undoubtedly, are wholly untenable, since they have been founded, as Masonic historical theories too often are, on an unwarrantable mixture of facts and fictions— of positive statements and problematic conjectures. Mons. J. S. Boubee, a distinguished French Mason, in his *Études Maçonniques,* places the origin of Adoptive Masonry in the 17th century, and ascribes its authorship to Queen Henrietta Maria, the widow of Charles I. of England; and he states that on her return to France, after the execution of her husband, she took pleasure in recounting the secret efforts made by the Freemasons of England to restore her family to their position and to establish her son on the throne of his ancestors. This, it will be recollected, was once a prevalent theory, now exploded, of the origin of Freemasonry—that it was established by the Cavaliers, as a secret political organization, in the times of the English civil war between the king and the Parliament, and as an engine for the support of the former. M. Boubee adds, that the queen made known to the ladies of her court, in her exile, the words and signs employed by her Masonic friends in England as their modes of recognition, and by this means instructed them in some of the mysteries of the Institution, of which, he says, she had been made the protectress after the death of the king. This theory is so full of absurdity, and its statements so flatly contradicted by well-known historical facts, that we may at once reject it as wholly apocryphal.

Others have claimed Russia as the birthplace of Adoptive Masonry; but in assigning that country and the year 1712 as the place and time of its origin, they have undoubtedly confounded it with the chivalric Order of Saint Catharine, which was instituted by the Czar, Peter the Great, in honor of the Czarina Catharine, and which, although at first it consisted of persons of both sexes, was subsequently confined exclusively to females. But the Order of Saint Catharine was in no manner connected with that of Freemasonry. It was simply a Russian order of female knighthood.

The truth seems to be that the regular Lodges of Adoption owed their existence to those secret associations of men and women which sprang up in France before the middle of the 18th century, and which attempted in all of their organization, except the admission of female members, to imitate the Institution of Freemasonry. Clavel, who, in his *Histoire Pittoresque de la Franc-Maçon-nerie,* an interesting but not always a trust-worthy work, adopts this theory, says that female Masonry was instituted about the year 1730) p. iii., 3d ed.) ; that it made its first ap-pearance in France, and that it was evidently a product of the French mind. No one will be disposed to doubt the truth of this last senti-ment. The proverbial gallantry of the French Masons was most ready and willing to extend to women some of the blessings of that Insti-tution, from which the churlishness, as they would call it, of their Anglo-Saxon brethren had excluded them.

But the Masonry of Adoption did not at once and in its very beginning assume that pe-culiarly imitative form of Freemasonry which it subsequently presented, nor was it recog-nized as having any connection with our own Order until more than thirty years after its first establishment. Its progress was slow and gradual. In the course of this progress it affected various names and rituals, many of which have not been handed down to us. It was evidently convivial and gallant in its na-ture, and at first seems to have been only an imitation of Freemasonry, inasmuch as that it was a secret society, having a form of initia-tion and modes of recognition. A specimen of one or two of these secret female associations may not be uninteresting.

One of the earliest of these societies was that which was established in the year 1743, at Paris, under the name of the "*Ordre des Félicitaires,*" which we might very appropri-ately translate as the "Order of Happy Folks." The vocabulary and all the em-blems of the order were nautical. The sisters made symbolically a voyage from the island of Felicity, in ships navigated by the brethren. There were four degrees, namely, those of *Cabin-boy, Captain, Commodore,* and *Vice-Admiral,* and the Grand Master, or presiding officer, was called the *Admiral.* Out of this society there sprang in 1745 another, which was called the "Knights and Ladies of the Anchor," which is said to have been somewhat more refined in its character, although for the most part it preserved the same formulary of reception.

Two years afterward, in 1747, the Cheva-lier Beauchaine, a very zealous Masonic ad-venturer, and the Master for life of a Parisian Lodge, instituted an androgynous system under the name of the "*Ordre des Fendeurs,*" or the "Order of Wood-Cutters," whose cere-monies were borrowed from those of the well-known political society of the Carbonari. All parts of the ritual had a reference to the sylvan vocation of wood-cutting, just as that of the Carbonari referred to coal-burning. The place of meeting was called a *wood-yard,* and was supposed to be situated in a forest; the presiding officer was styled *Père Maître,* which might be idiomatically interpreted as *Goodman Master;* and the members were designated as *cousins,* a practise evidently bor-rowed from the Carbonari. The reunions of the "Wood-Cutters" enjoyed the prestige of the highest fashion in Paris; and the society became so popular that ladies and gentlemen of the highest distinction in France united with it, and membership was considered an honor which no rank, however exalted, need disdain. It was consequently succeeded by the institution of many other and similar an-drogynous societies, the very names of which it would be tedious to enumerate. (Clavel, pp. 111, 112.)

Out of all these societies—which resembled Freemasonry only in their secrecy, their be-nevolence, and a sort of rude imitation of a symbolic ceremonial—at last arose the true Lodges of Adoption, which so far claimed a connection with and a dependence on Masonry as that Freemasons alone were admitted among their male members—a regulation which did not prevail in the earlier organiza-tions.

It was about the middle of the 18th cen-tury that the Lodges of Adoption began to attract attention in France, whence they speedily spread into other countries of Europe —into Germany, Poland, and even Russia; England alone, always conservative to a fault, steadily refusing to take any cognizance of them. The Masons, says Clavel (p. 112), embraced them with enthusiasm as a prac-ticable means of giving to their wives and daughters some share of the pleasures which they themselves enjoyed in their mystical as-semblies. And this, at least, may be said of them, that they practised with commendable fidelity and diligence the greatest of the Masonic virtues, and that the banquets and balls which always formed an important part of their ceremonial were distinguished by numerous acts of charity.

The first of these Lodges of which we have any notice was that established in Paris, in the year 1760, by the Count de Bernouville. Another was instituted at Nimeguen, in Hol-land, in 1774, over which the Prince of Wal-deck and the Princess of Orange presided. In 1775, the Lodge of Saint Antoine, at Paris, organized a dependent Lodge of Adoption, of which the Duchess of Bourbon was installed as Grand Mistress and the Duke of Chartres, then Grand Master of French Masonry, con-ducted the business. In 1777, there was an Adoptive Lodge of *La Candeur,* over which the Duchess of Bourbon presided, assisted by such noble ladies as the Duchess of Chartres, the Princess Lamballe, and the Marchioness de Genlis; and we hear of another governed by Madame Helvetius, the wife of the illustrious philosopher; so that it will be perceived that fashion, wealth, and literature combined to give splendor and influence to this new order of female Masonry.

At first the Grand Orient of France appears to have been unfavorably disposed to these pseudo-Masonic and androgynous associa-tions, but at length they became so numerous and so popular that a persistence in opposi-tion would have evidently been impolitic, if it did not actually threaten to be fatal to the interests and permanence of the Masonic Institution. The Grand Orient, therefore, yielded its objections, and resolved to avail itself of that which it could not suppress. Accordingly, on the 10th of June, 1774, it issued an edict by which it assumed the protection and control of the Lodges of Adoption. Rules and regulations were provided for their government, among which were two: first, that no males except regular Freemasons should be permitted to attend them; and, secondly, that each Lodge should be placed under the charge and held under the sanction of some regularly constituted Lodge of Masons, whose Master, or, in his absence, his deputy, should be the presiding officer, assisted by a female President or Mistress; and such has since been the organization of all Lodges of Adoption.

A Lodge of Adoption, under the regulations established in 1774, consists of the following officers: a Grand Master, a Grand Mistress, an Orator (dressed as a Capuchin), an Inspector, an Inspectress, a Male and Female Guardian, a Mistress of Ceremonies. All of these officers wear a blue watered ribbon over the shoulder, to which is suspended a golden trowel, and all the brothers and sisters have aprons and white gloves.

The Rite of Adoption consists of four degrees, whose names in French and English are as follows:

1. *Apprentice,* or Female Apprentice.
2. *Compagnone,* or Craftswoman.
3. *Maîtresse,* or Mistress.
4. *Parfaite Maçonne,* or Perfect Mason.

It will be seen that the degrees of Adoption, in their names and their apparent reference to the gradations of employment in an operative art, are assimilated to those of legitimate Freemasonry; but it is in those respects only that the resemblance holds good. In the details of the ritual there is a vast difference between the two Institutions.

There was a fifth degree added in 1817—by some modern writers called " Female elect " —*Sublime Dame Ecossaise,* or Sovereign Illustrious Dame Ecossaise; but it seems to be a recent and not generally adopted innovation. At all events, it constituted no part of the original Rite of Adoption.

The first, or Female Apprentice's degree, is simply preliminary in its character, and is intended to prepare the candidate for the more important lessons which she is to receive in the succeeding degrees. She is presented with an apron and a pair of white kid gloves. The apron is given with the following charge, in which, as in all the other ceremonies of the Order, the Masonic system of teaching by symbolism is followed:

" Permit me to decorate you with this apron; kings, princes, and the most illustrious princesses have esteemed, and will ever esteem it an honor to wear it, as being the symbol of virtue."

On receiving the gloves, the candidate is thus addressed:

" The color of these gloves will admonish you that candor and truth are virtues inseparable from the character of a true Mason. Take your place among us, and be pleased to listen to the instructions which we are about to communicate to you."

The following charge is then addressed to the members by the Orator:

" MY DEAR SISTERS:—Nothing is better calculated to assure you of the high esteem our society entertains for you, than your admission as a member. The common herd, always unmannerly, full of the most ridiculous prejudices, has dared to sprinkle on us the black poison of calumny; but what judgment could it form when deprived of the light of truth, and unable to feel all the blessings which result from its perfect knowledge?

" You alone, my dear sisters, having been repulsed from our meetings, would have the right to think us unjust; but with what satisfaction do you learn to-day that Masonry is the school of propriety and of virtue, and that by its laws we restrain the weaknesses that degrade an honourable man, in order to return to your side more worthy of your confidence and of your sincerity. However whatever pleasure these sentiments have enabled us to taste, we have not been able to fill the void that your absence left in our midst; and I confess, to your glory, that it was time to invite into our societies some sisters who, while rendering them more respectable will ever make of them pleasures and delights. We call our Lodges Temples of Virtue, because we endeavor to practise it. The mysteries which we celebrate therein are the grand art of conquering the passions and the oath that we take to reveal nothing is to prevent self-love and pride from entering at all into the good which we ought to do.

" The beloved name of Adoption tells you sufficiently that we choose you to share the happiness that we enjoy, in cultivating honour and charity; it is only after a careful examination that we have wished to share it with you, now that you know it we are convinced that the light of wisdom will illumine all the actions of your life, and that you will never forget that the more valuable things are the greater is the need to preserve them; it is the principle of silence that we observe, it should be inviolable. May the God of the Universe who hears us vouchsafe to give us strength to render it so."

It will be seen that throughout this charge there runs a vein of gallantry, which gives the true secret of the motives which led to the organization of the society, and which, however appropriate to a Lodge of Adoption, would scarcely be in place in a Lodge of the legitimate Order.

In the second degree, or that of *Compagnone,* or " Craftswoman," corresponding to our Fellow-Craft, the Lodge is made the symbol of the Garden of Eden, and the candidate passes through a mimic representation of the temptation of Eve, the fatal effects of which, culminating in the deluge and the destruction of the human race, are impressed upon her in the lecture or catechism.

Here we have a scenic representation of the circumstances connected with that event, as recorded in Genesis. The candidate plays the *rôle* of our common mother. In the center of the Lodge, which represents the garden, is placed the tree of life, from which ruddy apples are suspended. The serpent, made with theatrical skill to represent a living reptile, embraces in its coils the trunk. An apple plucked from the tree is presented to the recipient, who is persuaded to eat it by the promise that thus alone can she prepare herself for receiving a knowledge of the sublime mysteries of Freemasonry. She receives the fruit from the tempter, but no sooner has she attempted to bite it, than she is startled by the sound of thunder; a curtain which has separated her from the members of the Lodge is suddenly withdrawn, and she is detected in the commission of the act of disobedience. She is sharply reprimanded by the Orator, who conducts her before the Grand Master. This dignitary reproaches her with her fault, but finally, with the consent of the brethren and sisters present, he pardons her in the merciful spirit of the Institution, on the condition that she will take a vow to extend hereafter the same clemency to the faults of others.

All of this is allegorical and very pretty, and it cannot be denied that on the sensitive imaginations of females such ceremonies must produce a manifest impression. But it is needless to say that it is nothing like Masonry.

There is less ceremony, but more symbolism, in the third degree, or that of " Mistress." Here are introduced, as parts of the ceremony, the tower of Babel and the theological ladder of Jacob. Its rounds, however, differ from those peculiar to true Masonry, and are said to equal the virtues in number. The lecture or catechism is very long, and contains some very good points in its explanations of the symbols of the degree. Thus, the tower of Babel is said to signify the pride of man—its base, his folly—the stones of which it was composed, his passions—the cement which united them, the poison of discord—and its spiral form, the devious and crooked ways of the human heart. In this manner there is an imitation, not of the letter and substance of legitimate Freemasonry, for nothing can in these respects be more dissimilar, but of that mode of teaching by symbols and allegories which is its peculiar characteristic.

The fourth degree, or that of " Perfect Mistress," corresponds to no degree in legitimate Masonry. It is simply the summit of the Rite of Adoption, and hence is also called the " Degree of Perfection." Although the Lodge, in this degree, is supposed to represent the Mosaic tabernacle in the wilderness, yet the ceremonies do not have the same reference. In one of them, however, the liberation, by the candidate, of a bird from the vase in which it had been confined is said to symbolize the liberation of man from the dominion of his passions; and thus a far-fetched reference is made to the liberation of the Jews from Egyptian bondage. On the whole, the ceremonies are very disconnected, but the lecture or catechism contains some excellent lessons. Especially does it furnish us with the official definition of Adoptive Masonry, which is in these words:

" It is a virtuous amusement by which we recall a part of the mysteries of our religion;

and the better to reconcile humanity with the knowledge of its Creator, after we have inculcated the duties of virtue, we deliver ourselves up to the sentiments of a pure and delightful friendship by enjoying in our Lodges the pleasures of society—pleasures which among us are always founded on reason, honor, and innocence."

Apt and appropriate description of an association, secret or otherwise, of agreeable and virtuous well-bred men and women, but having not the slightest application to the design or form of true Freemasonry.

Guillemain de St. Victor, the author of *Manuel des Franches-Maçonnes, ou La Vraie Maçonnerie d'Adoption* (which forms the 3d part of the *Recueil Precieux*), who has given the best ritual of the Rite and from whom the preceding account has been taken, thus briefly sums up the objects of the Institution:

" The first degree contains only, as it ought, moral ideas of Masonry; the second is the initiation into the first mysteries, commencing with the sin of Adam, and concluding with the Ark of Noah as the first favor which God granted to men; the third and fourth are merely a series of types and figures drawn from the Holy Scriptures, by which we explain to the candidate the virtues which she ought to practise." (P. 13, ed. 1785.)

The fourth degree, being the summit of the Rite of Adoption, is furnished with a " tablelodge," or the ceremony of a banquet, which immediately succeeds the closing of the Lodge, and which, of course, adds much to the social pleasure and nothing to the instructive character of the Rite. Here, also, there is a continued imitation of the ceremonies of the Masonic Institution as they are practised in France, where the ceremoniously conducted banquet, at which Masons only are present, is always an accompaniment of the Master's Lodge. Thus, as in the banquets of the regular Lodges of the French Rite, the members always use a symbolical language by which they designate the various implements of the table and the different articles of food and drink, calling, for instance, the knives " swords," the forks " pickaxes," the dishes " materials," and bread a " rough ashlar"; * so, in imitation of this custom, the Rite of Adoption has established in its banquets a technical vocabulary, to be used only at the table. Thus the Lodge room is called " Eden," the doors " barriers," the minutes a " ladder," a wineglass is styled a " lamp," and its contents " oil"—water being " white oil " and wine " red oil." To fill your glass is " to trim your lamp," to drink is " to extinguish your lamp," with many other eccentric expressions. †

Much taste, and in some instances, magnificence, are displayed in the decorations of the Lodge rooms of the Adoptive Rite. The apartment is separated by curtains into different divisions, and contains ornaments and decorations which of course vary in the differ-

---

* Clavel, *Hist. Pitt.*, p. 30.   † Clavel, p. 34.

ent degrees. The orthodox Masonic idea that the Lodge is a symbol of the world is here retained, and the four sides of the hall are said to represent the four continents—the entrance being called "Europe," the right side "Africa," the left "America," and the extremity, in which the Grand Master and Grand Mistress are seated, "Asia." There are statues representing Wisdom, Prudence, Strength, Temperance, Honor, Charity, Justice, and Truth. The members are seated along the sides in two rows, the ladies occupying the front one, and the whole is rendered as beautiful and attractive as the taste can make it.*

The Lodges of Adoption flourished greatly in France after their recognition by the Grand Orient. The Duchess of Bourbon, who was the first that received the title of Grand Mistress, was installed with great pomp and splendor, in May, 1775, in the *Lodge of St. Antoine*, in Paris. She presided over the Adoptive Lodge *Le Candeur* until 1780, when it was dissolved. Attached to the celebrated *Lodge of the Nine Sisters*, which had so many distinguished men of letters among its members, was a Lodge of Adoption bearing the same name, which in 1778 held a meeting at the residence of Madame Helvetius in honor of Benjamin Franklin, then our ambassador at the French court. During the reign of terror of the French Revolution, Lodges of Adoption, like everything that was gentle or humane, almost entirely disappeared. But with the accession of a regular government they were resuscitated, and the Empress Josephine presided at the meeting of one at Strasburg in the year 1805. They continued to flourish under the imperial dynasty, and although less popular, or less fashionable, under the Restoration, they subsequently recovered their popularity, and are still in existence in France.

As interesting appendages to this article, it may not be improper to insert two accounts, one, of the installation of Madame Cesar Moreau, as Grand Mistress of Adoptive Masonry, in the Lodge connected with the regular Lodge *La Jerusalem des Vallées Egyptiennes*, on the 8th of July, 1854, and the other, of the reception of the celebrated Lady Morgan, in 1819, in the Lodge *La Belle et Bonne*, as described by her in her *Diary*.

The account of the installation of Madame Moreau, which is abridged from the *Franc-Maçon*, a Parisian periodical, is as follows:

The fête was most interesting and admirably arranged. After the introduction in due form of a number of brethren and sisters, the Grand Mistress elect was announced, and she entered, preceded by the five lights of the Lodge and escorted by the Inspectress, Depositress, Oratrix, and Mistress of Ceremonies. Mons. J. S. Boubee, the Master of the Lodge *La Jerusalem des Vallées Egyptiennes*, conducted her to the altar, where, having installed her into office and handed her a mallet as the symbol of authority, he addressed her in a copy of verses, whose merit will hardly claim for them a repetition. To this she made a suitable reply, and the Lodge then proceeded to the reception of a young lady, a part of the ceremony of which is thus described:

"Of the various trials of virtue and fortitude to which she was subjected, there was one which made a deep impression, not only on the fair recipient, but on the whole assembled company. Four boxes were placed, one before each of the male officers; the candidate was told to open them, which she did, and from the first and second drew faded flowers, and soiled ribbons and laces, which being placed in an open vessel were instantly consumed by fire, as an emblem of the brief duration of such objects; from the third she drew an apron, a blue silk scarf, and a pair of gloves; and from the fourth a basket containing the working tools in silver gilt. She was then conducted to the altar, where, on opening a fifth box, several birds which had been confined in it escaped, which was intended to teach her that liberty is a condition to which all men are entitled, and of which no one can be deprived without injustice. After having taken the vow, she was instructed in the modes of recognition, and having been clothed with the apron, scarf, and gloves, and presented with the implements of the Order, she received from the Grand Mistress an esoteric explanation of all these emblems and ceremonies. Addresses were subsequently delivered by the Orator and Oratrix, an ode was sung, the poor or alms box was handed round, and the labors of the Lodge were then closed."

Madame Moreau lived only six months to enjoy the honors of presiding officer of the Adoptive Rite, for she died of a pulmonary affection at an early age, on the 11th of the succeeding January.

The Lodge of Adoption in which Lady Morgan received the degrees at Paris, in the year 1819, was called *La Belle et Bonne*. This was the pet name which long before had been bestowed by Voltaire on his favorite, the Marchioness de Villette,† under whose presidency and at whose residence in the Faubourg St. Germaine the Lodge was held, and hence the name with which all France, or at least all Paris, was familiarly acquainted as the popular designation of Madame de Villette.

Lady Morgan, in her description of the Masonic fête, says that when she arrived at the Hotel la Villette, where the Lodge was held, she found a large concourse of distinguished persons ready to take part in the ceremonies. Among these were Prince Paul of Wurtemberg, the Count de Cazes, elsewhere distinguished in Masonry, the celebrated Denon, the Bishop of Jerusalem, and the illustrious actor Talma. The business of the evening commenced with an installation of the officers of a sister Lodge, after which the candidates were admitted. Lady Morgan describes the arrangements as presenting, when the doors were opened, a spectacle of great magnificence. A profusion of crimson and

---

Recueil Precieux, p. 24.   † Clavel, p. 114.

gold, marble busts, a decorated throne and altar, an abundance of flowers, and incense of the finest odor which filled the air, gave to the whole a most dramatic and scenic effect. Music of the grandest character mingled its harmony with the mysteries of initiation, which lasted for two hours, and when the Lodge was closed there was an adjournment to the hall of refreshment, where the ball was opened by the Grand Mistress with Prince Paul of Wurtemberg. Lady Morgan, upon whose mind the ceremony appears to have made an impression, makes one remark worthy of consideration: " That so many women," she says, " young and beautiful and worldly, should never have revealed the secret, is among the miracles which the much distrusted sex are capable of working." In fidelity to the vow of secrecy, the female Masons of the Adoptive Rite have proved themselves fully equal to their brethren of the legitimate Order.

Notwithstanding that Adoptive Masonry has found an advocate in no less distinguished a writer than Chemin Dupontès, who, in the *Encyclopédie Maçonnique,** calls it " a luxury in Masonry, and a pleasant relaxation which cannot do any harm to the true mysteries which are practised by men alone," it has been very generally condemned by the most celebrated French, German, English, and American Masons.

Gaedicke, in the *Freimaurer Lexicon,* speaks slightingly of it as established on insufficient grounds, and expresses his gratification that the system no longer exists in Germany.

Thory, in his *History of the Foundation of the Grand Orient* (p. 361), says that the introduction of Adoptive Lodges was a consequence of the relaxation of Masonic discipline; and he asserts that the permitting of women to share in mysteries which should exclusively belong to men is not in accordance with the essential principles of the Masonic Order. The Abbé Robin, the author of an able work entitled *Recherches sur les Initiations Anciennes et Modernes,* maintains (p. 15) that the custom of admitting women into Masonic assemblies will perhaps be, at some future period, the cause of the decline of Masonry in France. The prediction is not, however, likely to come to pass; for while legitimate Masonry has never been more popular or prosperous in France than it is at this day, it is the Lodges of Adoption that appear to have declined.

Other writers in other countries have spoken in similar terms, so that it is beyond a doubt that the general sentiment of the Fraternity is against this system of female Masonry.

Lenning is, however, more qualified in his condemnation, and says, in his *Encyclopädie der Freimaurerei,* that while leaving it undecided whether it is prudent to hold assemblies of women with ceremonies which are called Masonic, yet it is not to be denied that in these female Lodges a large amount of charity has been done.

<hr />

* Published in Paris in 4 vols., 1819–25.

Adoptive Masonry has its literature, although neither extensive nor important, as it comprises only books of songs, addresses, and rituals. Of the latter the most valuable are: 1. *La Maçonnerie des Femmes,* published in 1775, and containing only the first three degrees, for such was the system when recognized by the Grand Orient of France in that year. 2. *La Vraie Maçonnerie d'Adoption,* printed in 1787. This work, which is by Guillemain de St. Victor, is perhaps the best that has been published on the subject of the Adoptive Rite, and is the first that introduces the Fourth Degree, of which Guillemain is supposed to have been the inventor, since all previous rituals include only the three degrees. 3. *Maçonnerie d'Adoption pour les Femmes,* contained in the second part of E. J. Chappron's *Necessaire Maçonnique,* and printed at Paris in 1817. This is valuable because it is the first ritual that contains the Fifth Degree. 4. *La Franc-Maçonnerie des Femmes.* This work, which is by Charles Monselet, is of no value as a ritual, being simply a tale founded on circumstances connected with Adoptive Masonry.

In Italy, the Carbonari, or " Wood-Burners," a secret political society, imitated the Freemasons of France in instituting an Adoptive Rite, attached to their own association. Hence, an Adoptive Lodge was founded at Naples in the beginning of this century, over which presided that friend of Masonry, Queen Caroline, the wife of Ferdinand II. The members were styled *Giardiniere,* or Female Gardeners; and they called each other *Cugine,* or Female Cousins, in imitation of the Carbonari, who were recognized as *Buoni Cugini,* or Good Cousins. The Lodges of *Giardiniere* flourished as long as the Grand Lodge of Carbonari existed at Naples.

Adoptive Masonry, American. The Rite of Adoption as practised on the continent of Europe, and especially in France, has never been introduced into America. The system does not accord with the manners or habits of the people, and undoubtedly never would become popular. But Rob. Morris attempted, in 1855, to introduce an imitation of it, which he had invented, under the name of the " American Adoptive Rite." It consisted of a ceremony of initiation, which was intended as a preliminary trial of the candidate, and of five degrees, named as follows: 1. Jephthah's Daughter, or the daughter's degree. 2. Ruth, or the widow's degree. 3. Esther, or the wife's degree. 4. Martha, or the sister's degree. 5. Electa, or the Christian Martyr's degree. The whole assemblage of the five degrees was called the Eastern Star.

The objects of this Rite, as expressed by the framer, were " to associate in one common bond the worthy wives, widows, daughters, and sisters of Freemasons, so as to make their adoptive privileges available for all the purposes contemplated in Masonry; to secure to them the advantages of their claim in a moral, social, and charitable point of view, and from them the performance of corresponding duties." Hence, no females but those holding the above recited relations to Freemasons were eligible for admission. The male members were called "Protectors"; the female, "Stellæ"; the reunions of these members were styled "Constellations"; and the Rite was presided over and governed by a "Supreme Constellation." There is some ingenuity and even beauty in many of the ceremonies, although it is by no means equal in this respect to the French Adoptive system. Much dissatisfaction was, however, expressed by the leading Masons of the country at the time of its attempted organization; and therefore, notwithstanding very strenuous efforts were made by its founder and his friends to establish it in some of the Western States, it was slow in winning popularity. It has, however, within a few years past, gained much growth under the name of "The Eastern Star." Bro. Albert Pike has also recently printed, for the use of Scottish Rite Masons, *The Masonry of Adoption*. It is in seven degrees, and is a translation from the French system, but greatly enlarged, and is far superior to the original.

The last phase of this female Masonry to which our attention is directed is the system of androgynous degrees which are practised to some extent in the United States. This term "androgynous" is derived from two Greek words, ἀνήρ (ἄνδρος), a man, and γυνή, a woman, and it is equivalent to the English compound, *masculo-feminine*. It is applied to those "side degrees" which are conferred on both males and females. The essential regulation prevailing in these degrees, is that they can be conferred only on Master Masons (and in some instances only on Royal Arch Masons) and on their female relatives, the peculiar relationship differing in the different degrees.

Thus there is a degree generally called the "Mason's Wife," which can be conferred only on Master Masons, their wives, unmarried daughters and sisters, and their widowed mothers. Another degree, called the "Heroine of Jericho," is conferred only on the wives and daughters of Royal Arch Masons; and the third, the only one that has much pretension of ceremony or ritual, is the "Good Samaritan," whose privileges are confined to Royal Arch Masons and their wives.

In some parts of the United States these degrees are very popular, while in other places they are never practised, and are strongly condemned as modern innovations. The fact is, that by their friends as well as their enemies these so-called degrees have been greatly misrepresented. When females are told that in receiving these degrees they are admitted into the Masonic Order, and are obtaining Masonic information, under the name of "Ladies' Masonry," they are simply deceived. When a woman is informed that, by passing through the brief and unimpressive ceremony of any one of these degrees, she has become a Mason, the deception is still more gross and inexcusable. But it is true that every woman

who is related by ties of consanguinity to a Master Mason is at all times and under all circumstances peculiarly entitled to Masonic protection and assistance. Now, if the recipient of an androgynous degree is candidly instructed that, by the use of these degrees, the female relatives of Masons are put in possession of the means of making their claims known by what may be called a sort of oral testimony, which, unlike a written certificate, can be neither lost nor destroyed; but that, by her initiation as a "Mason's Wife" or as a "Heroine of Jericho," she is brought no nearer to the inner portal of Masonry than she was before—if she is honestly told all this, then there can hardly be any harm, and there may be some good in these forms if prudently bestowed. But all attempts to make Masonry of them, and especially that anomalous thing called "Female Masonry," are reprehensible, and are well calculated to produce opposition among the well-informed and cautious members of the Fraternity.

Adoptive Masonry, Egyptian. A system invented by Cagliostro. (See *Cagliostro*.)

Adoration. The act of paying divine worship. The Latin word *adorare* is derived from *ad*, "to," and *os, oris*, "the mouth," and we thus etymologically learn that the primitive and most general method of adoration was by the application of the fingers to the mouth. Hence we read in Job (xxxi. 26): "If I beheld the sun when it shined, or the moon walking in brightness, and my heart hath been secretly enticed, or *my mouth hath kissed my hand*, this also were an iniquity to be punished by the judges; for I should have denied the God that is above." Here the mouth kissing the hand is an equipollent expression to adoration, as if he had said, "If I have adored the sun or the moon." This mode of adoration is said to have originated among the Persians, who, as worshipers of the sun, always turned their faces to the east and kissed their hands to that luminary. The gesture was first used as a token of respect to their monarchs, and was easily transferred to objects of worship. Other additional forms of adoration were used in various countries, but in almost all of them this reference to kissing was in some degree preserved. It is yet a practice of quite common usage for Orientals to kiss what they deem sacred or that which they wish to adore—example, Wailing Place of the Jews at Jerusalem. The marble toes of the statue of St. Peter in the Cathedral of St. Peter's at Rome have been worn away by the kissings of Catholics and have been replaced by bronze. Among the ancient Romans the act of adoration was thus performed: The worshiper, having his head covered, applied his right hand to his lips, thumb erect, and the forefinger resting on it, and then, bowing his head, he turned round from right to left. And hence Apuleius (*Apolog.*) uses the expression "to apply the hand to the lips," *manum labris admovere*, to express the act of adoration. The Grecian mode of adoration differed from the Roman in having the head uncovered, which practise was adopted by the Christians. The Oriental nations cover the head, but uncover the feet. They also express the act of adoration by prostrating themselves on their faces and applying their foreheads to the ground. The ancient Jews adored by kneeling, sometimes by prostration of the whole body, and by kissing the hand. This act, therefore, of kissing the hand was an early and a very general symbol of adoration. But we must not be led into the error of supposing that a somewhat similar gesture used in some of the high degrees of Freemasonry has any allusion to an act of worship. It refers to that symbol of silence and secrecy which is figured in the statues of Harpocrates, the god of silence. The Masonic idea of adoration has been well depicted by the medieval Christian painters, who represented the act by angels *prostrated before a luminous triangle.*

Advanced. This word has two technical meanings in Masonry.

1. We speak of a candidate as being advanced when he has passed from a lower to a higher degree; as we say that a candidate is qualified for advancement from the Entered Apprentice's degree to that of a Fellow-Craft when he has made that "suitable proficiency in the former which, by the regulations of the Order, entitle him to receive the initiation into and the instructions of the latter." And when the Apprentice has thus been promoted to the Second Degree he is said to have advanced in Masonry.

2. However, this use of the term is by no means universal, and the word is peculiarly applied to the initiation of a candidate into the Mark Degree, which is the fourth in the modification of the American Rite. The Master Mason is thus said to be "advanced to the honorary degree of a Mark Master," to indicate either that he has now been promoted one step beyond the degrees of Ancient Craft Masonry on his way to the Royal Arch, or to express the fact that he has been elevated from the common class of Fellow-Crafts to that higher and more select one which, according to the traditions of Masonry, constituted, at the first Temple, the class of Mark Masters. (See *Mark Master.*)

Advancement Hurried. Nothing can be more certain than that the proper qualifications of a candidate for admission into the mysteries of Freemasonry, and the necessary proficiency of a Mason who seeks advancement to a higher degree, are the two great bulwarks which are to protect the purity and integrity of our Institution. Indeed, we know not which is the more hurtful—to admit an applicant who is unworthy, or to promote a candidate who is ignorant of his first lessons. The one affects the external, the other the internal character of the Institution. The one brings discredit upon the Order among the profane, who already regard us, too often, with suspicion and dislike; the other introduces ignorance and incapacity into our ranks, and dishonors the science of Masonry in our own eyes. The one covers our walls with imperfect and worthless stones, which mar the outward beauty and impair the strength of our temple; the other fills our interior apartments with confusion and disorder, and leaves the edifice, though externally strong, both inefficient and inappropriate for its destined uses.

But, to the candidate himself, a too hurried advancement is often attended with the most disastrous effects. As in geometry, so in Masonry, there is no "royal road" to perfection. A knowledge of its principles and its science, and consequently an acquaintance with its beauties, can only be acquired by long and diligent study. To the careless observer it seldom offers, at a hasty glance, much to attract his attention or secure his interest. The gold must be deprived, by careful manipulation, of the dark and worthless ore which surrounds and envelops it, before its metallic luster and value can be seen and appreciated.

Hence, the candidate who hurriedly passes through his degrees without a due examination of the moral and intellectual purposes of each, arrives at the summit of our edifice without a due and necessary appreciation of the general symmetry and connection that pervade the whole system. The candidate, thus hurried through the elements of our science, and unprepared, by a knowledge of its fundamental principles, for the reception and comprehension of the corollaries which are to be deduced from them, is apt to view the whole system as "a rude and indigested mass" of frivolous ceremonies and puerile conceits, whose intrinsic value will not adequately pay him for the time, the trouble, and expense that he has incurred in his forced initiation. To him, Masonry is as incomprehensible as was the veiled statue of Isis to its blind worshipers, and he becomes, in consequence, either a useless drone in our hive, or speedily retires in disgust from all participation in our labors.

But the candidate who by slow and painful steps has proceeded through each apartment of our mystic Temple, from its porch to its sanctuary, pausing in his progress to admire the beauties and to study the uses of each, learning, as he advances, "line upon line, and precept upon precept," is gradually and almost imperceptibly imbued with so much admiration of the Institution, so much love for its principles, so much just appreciation of its design as a conservator of divine truth, and an agent of human civilization, that he is inclined, on beholding, at last, the whole beauty of the finished building, to exclaim, as did the wondering Queen of Sheba: "A Most Excellent Master must have done all this!"

The usage in many jurisdictions of the United States, when the question is asked in the ritual whether the candidate has made suitable proficiency in his preceding degree, is to reply, "Such as time and circumstances would permit." We have no doubt that this was an innovation originally invented to evade the law, which has always required a due proficiency. To such a question no other answer ought to be given than the positive and unequivocal one that "he has." Neither "time nor circumstances" should be permitted to interfere with his attainment of the necessary knowledge, nor excuse its absence. This, with the wholesome rule, very generally existing, which requires an interval between the conferring of the degrees, would go far to remedy the evil of too hurried and unqualified advancement, of which all intelligent Masons are now complaining.

After these views of the necessity of a careful examination of the claims of a candidate for advancement in Masonry, and the necessity, for his own good as well as that of the Order, that each one should fully prepare himself for this promotion, it is proper that we should next inquire into the laws of Masonry, by which the wisdom and experience of our predecessors have thought proper to guard as well the rights of those who claim advancement as the interests of the Lodge which is called upon to grant it. This subject has been so fully treated in Mackey's *Text Book of Masonic Jurisprudence* (b. iii., ch. i., p. 165 *et seq.*) that we shall not hesitate to incorporate the views in that work into the present article.

The subject of the petition of a candidate for advancement involves three questions of great importance: First, how soon, after receiving the First Degree, can he apply for the Second? Secondly, what number of black balls is necessary to constitute a rejection? And thirdly, what time must elapse, after a first rejection, before the Apprentice can renew his application for advancement?

1. *How soon, after receiving a former degree, can a candidate apply for advancement to the next?* The necessity of a full comprehension of the mysteries of one degree, before any attempt is made to acquire those of a second, seems to have been thoroughly appreciated from the earliest times; thus the 13th Article in the Regius MS., which is the oldest Masonic document now extant, provides that " if the master a prentice have, he shall teach him thoroughly and tell him measurable points, that he may know the craft ably, wherever he goes under the sun." Similar direction is found in most all the MS. But if there be an obligation on the part of the Master to instruct his Apprentice, there must be, of course, a correlative obligation on the part of the latter to receive and profit by those instructions. Accordingly, unless this obligation is discharged, and the Apprentice makes himself acquainted with the mysteries of the degree that he has already received, it is, by general consent, admitted that he has no right to be entrusted with further and more important information. The modern ritual sustains this doctrine, by requiring that the candidate, as a qualification in passing onward, shall have made " suitable proficiency in the preceding degree." This is all that the general law prescribes. Suitable proficiency must have been attained, and the period in which that condition will be acquired must necessarily depend on the mental capacity of the candidate. Some men will become proficient in a shorter time than others, and of this fact the

Master and the Lodge are to be the judges. An examination should therefore take place in open Lodge, and a ballot immediately following will express the opinion of the Lodge on the result of that examination, and the qualification of the candidate. [Such ballot, however, is not usual in Lodges under the English Constitution.]

Several modern Grand Lodges, looking with disapprobation on the rapidity with which the degrees are sometimes conferred upon candidates wholly incompetent, have adopted special regulations, prescribing a determinate period of probation for each degree. [Thus the Grand Lodge of England requires an interval of not less than four weeks before a higher degree can be conferred.] This, however, is a local law, to be obeyed only in those jurisdictions in which it is in force. The general law of Masonry makes no such determinate provision of time, and demands only that the candidate shall give evidence of " suitable proficiency."

2. *What number of black balls is necessary to constitute a rejection?* Here we are entirely without the guidance of any express law, as all the Ancient Constitutions are completely silent upon the subject. It would seem, however, that in the advancement of an Apprentice or Fellow-Craft, as well as in the election of a profane, the ballot should be unanimous. This is strictly in accordance with the principles of Masonry, which require unanimity in admission, lest improper persons be intruded, and harmony impaired. Greater qualifications are certainly not required of a profane applying for initiation than of an initiate seeking advancement; nor can there be any reason why the test of those qualifications should not be as rigid in the one case as in the other. It may be laid down as a rule, therefore, that in all cases of balloting for advancement in any of the degrees of Masonry, a single black ball will reject.

3. *What time must elapse, after a first rejection, before the Apprentice or Fellow-Craft can renew his application for advancement to a higher degree?* Here, too, the Ancient Constitutions are silent, and we are left to deduce our opinions from the general principles and analogies of Masonic law. As the application for advancement to a higher degree is founded on a right enuring to the Apprentice or Fellow-Craft by virtue of his reception into the previous degree—that is to say, as the Apprentice, so soon as he has been initiated, becomes invested with the right of applying for advancement to the Second—it seems evident that, as long as he remains an Apprentice " in good standing," he continues to be invested with that right. Now, the rejection of his petition for advancement by the Lodge does not impair his right to apply again, because it does not affect his rights and standing as an Apprentice; it is simply the expression of the opinion that the Lodge does not at present deem him qualified for further progress in Masonry. We must never forget the difference between the right of applying for advance-

ment and the right of advancement. Every Apprentice possesses the former, but no one can claim the latter until it is given to him by the unanimous vote of the Lodge. And as, therefore, this right of application or petition is not impaired by its rejection at a particular time, and as the Apprentice remains precisely in the same position in his own degree, after the rejection, as he did before, it seems to follow, as an irresistible deduction, that he may again apply at the next regular communication, and, if a second time rejected, repeat his applications at all future meetings. The Entered Apprentices of a Lodge are competent, at all regular communications of their Lodge, to petition for advancement. Whether that petition shall be granted or rejected is quite another thing, and depends altogether on the favor of the Lodge. And what is here said of an Apprentice, in relation to advancement to the Second Degree, may be equally said of a Fellow-Craft in reference to advancement to the Third.

This opinion has not, it is true, been universally adopted, though no force of authority, short of an opposing landmark, could make one doubt its correctness. For instance, the Grand Lodge of California decided, in 1857, that " the application of Apprentices or Fellow Crafts for advancement should, after they have been once rejected by ballot, be governed by the same principles which regulate the ballot on petitions for initiation, and which require a probation of one year."

This appears to be a singular decision of Masonic law. If the reasons which prevent the advancement of an Apprentice or Fellow-Craft to a higher degree are of such a nature as to warrant the delay of one year, it is far better to prefer charges against the petitioner, and to give him the opportunity of a fair and impartial trial. In many cases, a candidate for advancement is retarded in his progress from an opinion, on the part of the Lodge, that he is not yet sufficiently prepared for promotion by a knowledge of the preceding degree—an objection which may sometimes be removed before the recurrence of the next monthly meeting. In such a case, a decision like that of the Grand Lodge of California would be productive of manifest injustice. It is, therefore, a more consistent rule, that the candidate for advancement has a right to apply at every regular meeting, and that whenever any moral objections exist to his taking a higher degree, these objections should be made in the form of charges, and their truth tested by an impartial trial. To this, too, the candidate is undoubtedly entitled, on all the principles of justice and equity.

Adytum. The most retired and secret part of the ancient temples, into which the people were not permitted to enter, but which was accessible to the priests only, was called the adytum. And hence the derivation of the word from the Greek privative prefix α, and δύειν, *to enter = that which is not to be entered.* In the adytum was generally to be found a Τάφος, or tomb, or some relics or sa-

cred images of the god to whom the temple was consecrated. It being supposed that temples owed their origin to the superstitious reverence paid by the ancients to their deceased friends, and as most of the gods were men who had been deified on account of their virtues, temples were, perhaps, at first only stately monuments erected in honor of the dead. Hence the interior of the temple was originally nothing more than a cavity regarded as a place for the reception of a person interred, and in it was to be found the σορός, or coffin, the Τάφος, or tomb, or, among the Scandinavians, the *barrow* or mound grave. In time, the statue or image of a god took the place of the coffin; but the reverence for the spot as one of peculiar sanctity remained, and this interior part of the temple became, among the Greeks, the σηκός, or chapel, among the Romans the *adytum*, or forbidden place, and among the Jews the *kodesh hakodashim,* the Holy of Holies. (See *Holy of Holies.*) "The sanctity thus acquired," says Dudley (*Naology*, p. 393), " by the cell of interment might readily and with propriety be assigned to any fabric capable of containing the body of the departed friend, or the relic, or even the symbol, of the presence or existence of a divine personage." And thus it has happened that there was in every ancient temple an adytum or most holy place. The adytum of the small temple of Pompeii is still in excellent preservation. It is carried some steps above the level of the main building, and, like the Jewish sanctuary, is without light.

Æneid. Bishop Warburton (*Div. Leg.*) has contended, and his opinion has been sustained by the great majority of subsequent commentators, that Virgil, in the sixth book of his immortal Epic, has, under the figure of the descent of Æneas into the infernal regions, described the ceremony of initiation into the Ancient Mysteries.

Æon. This word, in its original Greek, αἰών, signifies the age or duration of anything. The Gnostics, however, used it in a peculiar mode to designate the intelligent, intellectual, and material powers or natures which flowed as emanations from the Βυθός, or Infinite Abyss of Deity, and which were connected with their divine fountain as rays of light are with the sun. (See *Gnostics.*)

Æra Architectonica. This is used in some modern Masonic lapidary inscriptions to designate the date more commonly known as *annus lucis,* the year of light.

Affiliate, Free. The French gave the name of " free affiliates " to those members of a Lodge who are exempted from the payment of dues, and neither hold office nor vote. Known among English-speaking Masons as " honorary members."

There is a quite common use of affiliate in Lodges of the United States to designate one who has joined a Lodge by demit.

Affiliated Mason. A Mason who holds membership in some Lodge. The word *affiliation* is derived from the French *affilier,* which Richelet (*Dict. de la langue Française*) defines,

" to communicate to any one a participation in the spiritual benefits of a religious order," and he says that such a communication is called an " affiliation." The word, as a technical term, is not found in any of the old Masonic writers, who always use *admission* instead of affiliation. There is no precept more explicitly expressed in the Ancient Constitutions than that every Mason should belong to a Lodge. The foundation of the law which imposes this duty is to be traced as far back as the Regius MS., which is the oldest Masonic document now extant, and of which the " Secunde poynt " requires that the Mason work upon the workday as truly as he can in order to deserve his hire for the holiday, and that he shall " truly labour on his deed that he may well deserve to have his meed." (Lines 269–274.) The obligation that every Mason should thus labor is implied in all the subsequent Constitutions, which always speak of Masons as *working members* of the Fraternity, until we come to the Charges approved in 1722, which explicitly state that " every Brother ought to belong to a Lodge, and to be subject to its By-Laws and the General Regulations."

Affirmation. The question has been mooted whether a Quaker, or other person having peculiar religious scruples in reference to taking oaths, can receive the degrees of Masonry by taking an affirmation. Now, as the obligations of Masonry are symbolic in their character, and the forms in which they are administered constitute the essence of the symbolism, there cannot be a doubt that the prescribed mode is the only one that ought to be used, and that affirmations are entirely inadmissible. The *London Freemason's Quarterly* (1828, p. 286) says that " a Quaker's affirmation is binding." This is not denied: the only question is whether it is admissible. Can the obligations be assumed in any but one way, unless the ritual be entirely changed? And can any " man or body of men " at this time make such a change without affecting the universality of Masonry? Bro. Chase (*Masonic Digest*, p. 448) says that " conferring the degrees on affirmation is no violation of the spirit of Freemasonry, and neither overthrows nor affects a landmark." And in this he is sustained by the Grand Lodge of Maine (1823); but the only other Grand Lodges which have expressed an opinion on this subject—namely, those of Missouri, Tennessee, Kentucky, Delaware, Virginia, and Pennsylvania—have made an opposite decision. The entire practise of Lodges in America is also against the use of an affirmation. But in England Quakers have been initiated after affirmation, the principle being that a form of O B∴ which the candidate accepts as binding will suffice.

Africa. Anderson (*Constitutions*, 1738, p. 195) has recorded that in 1735 Richard Hull, Esq., was appointed " Provincial Grand Master at Gambay in West Africa," that in 1736 David Creighton, M.D., was appointed " Provincial Grand Master at Cape Coast Castle in Africa," and that in 1737 Capt. William Douglas was appointed " Provincial

Grand Master on the Coast of Africa and in the Islands of America, excepting such places where a Provincial Grand Master is already deputed." However, in spite of these appointments having been made by the Grand Lodge of England, there is no trace of the establishment of any Lodges in West Africa until 1792, in which year a Lodge numbered 586 was constituted at Bulam, followed in 1810 by the Torridzonian Lodge at Cape Coast Castle. There are now on the West Coast of Africa fourteen Lodges warranted by the Grand Lodge of England, one holding an Irish warrant, one under the Grand Lodge of Scotland and two German Lodges; and in the Negro Republic of Liberia a Grand Lodge was constituted in 1867, with nine daughter Lodges subordinate to it.

In the North of Africa there is the Grand Lodge of Egypt at Cairo with 47 subordinate Lodges; both England and Scotland have established District Grand Lodges in Egypt by consent of the former, while Italy, France and Germany have Lodges at Alexandria and Cairo. In Algeria and Morocco French influence is predominant, but in Tunis there is an independent Grand Lodge, established in 1881.

Masonry was introduced into South Africa by the erection of a Dutch Lodge (" De Goede Hoop ") at Cape Town in 1772, followed by another under the same jurisdiction in 1802, and it was not until nine years later that the first English Lodge was established there, which was gradually followed by others, the Dutch and English Masons working side by side with such harmony that the English Provincial Grand Master for the District who was appointed in 1829 was also Deputy Grand Master for the Netherlands. In 1860 a Scotch Lodge was set up at Cape Town, and 35 years later one was erected at Johannesburg under the Grand Lodge of Ireland, so that there are four different Masonic bodies exercising jurisdiction and working amicably together in South Africa, viz., the Grand Lodges of England, Ireland and Scotland, and the Grand Orient of the Netherlands. Under the Grand Lodge of England there were at the last issue of the Masonic Year-Book, 155 subordinate Lodges arranged in 5 Districts, viz., Central, Eastern and Western South Africa, Natal and the Transvaal. At the same time there were 16 Lodges owing allegiance to the Grand Lodge of Ireland, 76 under the Scotch Constitution, divided among the Districts of Cape Colony, Cape Colony Western Province, Natal, Orange River Colony, Rhodesia and the Transvaal, and 28 under the jurisdiction of the Grand Orient of the Netherlands, besides two German Lodges at Johannesburg.

On the East Coast of the Dark Continent there are two Lodges at Nairobi, one of them being English and the other Scotch, and there is also an English Lodge at Zanzibar.

[E. L. H.]

Africa. In the French Rite of Adoption, the south of the Lodge is called *Africa.*

African Architects, Order of. Sometimes called *African Builders;* French, *Architectes de l'Afrique;* German, *Africanische Bauherren.*

Of all the new sects and modern degrees of Freemasonry which sprang up on the continent of Europe during the eighteenth century, there was none which, for the time, maintained so high an intellectual position as the Order of African Architects, called by the French *Architectes de l'Afrique,* and by the Germans *Africanische Bauherren.* A Masonic sect of this name had originally been established in Germany in the year 1756, but it does not appear to have attracted much attention, or indeed to have deserved it; and hence, amid the multitude of Masonic innovations to which almost every day was giving birth and ephemeral existence, it soon disappeared. But the society which is the subject of the present article, although it assumed the name of the original African Architects, was of a very different character. It may, however, be considered, as it was established only eleven years afterward, as a remodification of it.

They admitted to membership those possessing high intellectual attainments rather than those possessing wealth or preferment.

There was probably no real connection between this order and Freemasonry of Germany, even if they did profess kindly feelings for it. They based their order on the degrees of Masonry, as the list of degrees shows, but their work began in the Second Temple. While they had a quasi-connection with Freemasonry, we cannot call them a Masonic body according to the present day standards.

The degrees were named and classified as follows:

FIRST TEMPLE

1. Apprentice.
2. Fellow-Craft.
3. Master Mason.

SECOND TEMPLE

4. Architect, or Apprentice of Egyptian secrets [or Bosonien (*Acta Latomorum,* i., 297)].
5. Initiate into Egyptian secrets [or Alethophilote (*Acta Latomorum,* i., 292)].
6. Cosmopolitan Brother.
7. Christian Philosopher [Thory calls this the Fourth Degree (*A. L.,* i., 332)].
8. Master of Egyptian secrets.
9. Squire of the Order.
10. Soldier of the Order.
11. Knight of the Order.

The last three were called superior degrees, and were conferred only as a second or higher class, with great discrimination, upon those who had proved their worthiness of promotion.

The assemblies of the brethren were called Chapters. The central or superintending power was styled a Grand Chapter, and it was governed by the following twelve officers:

1. Grand Master.
2. Deputy Grand Master.
3. Senior Grand Warden.
4. Junior Grand Warden.
5. Drapier.
6. Almoner.
7. Tricoplerius, or Treasurer.
8. Graphiarius, or Secretary.
9. Seneschal.
10. Standard-Bearer.
11. Marshal.
12. Conductor.

The African Architects was not the only society which in the eighteenth century sought to rescue Masonry from the impure hands of the charlatans into which it had well-nigh fallen.

African Brother. One of the degrees of the Rite of the Clerks of Strict Observance, according to Thory (*Acta Latomorum,* i., 291); but it is not mentioned in other lists of the degrees of that Rite.

African Brothers. One of the titles given to the *African Architects,* which see.

African Builders. (See *African Architects.*)

African Lodge. (See *Negro Lodges.*)

Agapæ. The agapæ, or love-feasts, were banquets held during the first three centuries in the Christian Church. They were called "love-feasts," because, after partaking of the Sacrament, they met, both rich and poor, at a common feast—the former furnishing the provisions, and the latter, who had nothing, being relieved and refreshed by their more opulent brethren. Tertullian (*Apologia,* cap. xxxix.) thus describes these banquets: "We do not sit down before we have first offered up prayers to God; we eat and drink only to satisfy hunger and thirst, remembering still that we are to worship God by night: we discourse as in the presence of God, knowing that He hears us: then, after water to wash our hands, and lights brought in, every one is moved to sing some hymn to God, either out of the Scripture, or, as he is able, of his own composing. Prayer again concludes our feast, and we depart, not to fight and quarrel, or to abuse those we meet, but to pursue the same care of modesty and chastity, as men that have fed at a supper of philosophy and discipline, rather than a corporeal feast."

Dr. August Kestner, Professor of Theology, published in Jena, in 1819, a work in which he maintains that the agapæ, established at Rome by Clemens, in the reign of Domitian, were mysteries which partook of a Masonic, symbolic, and religious character.

In the Rosicrucian degrees of Masonry we find an imitation of these love-feasts of the primitive Christians; and the ceremonies of the banquet in the degree of Rose Croix of the Ancient and Accepted Rite, especially as practised by French Chapters, are arranged with reference to the ancient agapæ. Reghellini, indeed, finds an analogy between the table-lodges of modern Masonry and these love-feasts of the primitive Christians.

Agate. A stone varying in color, but of great hardness, being a variety of the flint. The agate, in Hebrew שְׁבוֹ, SHeBO, was the center stone of the third row in the breastplate of the high priest. Agates often contain representations of leaves, mosses, etc., depicted by the hand of nature. Some of the representations on these are exceedingly singular. Thus, on one side of one in the possession of Velschius was a half moon, and on the other a star. Kircher mentions one which had a representation of an armed heroine; another, in the church of St. Mark in Venice, which had a representation of a king's head, adorned with a diadem; and a third which contained the letters I. N. R. I. (Oliver's *Historical Landmarks*, ii., 522.) In the collections of antiquaries are also to be found many gems of agate on which mystical inscriptions have been engraved, the significations of which are, for the most part, no longer understood.

Agate, Stone of. Among the Masonic traditions is one which asserts that the stone of foundation was formed of agate. This, like everything connected with the legend of the stone, is to be mystically interpreted. In this view, agate is a symbol of strength and beauty, a symbolism derived from the peculiar character of the agate, which is distinguished for its compact formation and the ornamental character of its surface. (See *Stone of Foundation*.)

Agathopades. A liberal ecclesiastical order founded in Brussels in the sixteenth century. Revived and revised by Schayes in 1846. It had for its sacred sign the penta-stigma • • •

Age, Lawful. One of the qualifications for candidates is that they shall be of "lawful age." What that age must be is not settled by any universal law or landmark of the Order. The Ancient Regulations do not express any determinate number of years at the expiration of which a candidate becomes legally entitled to apply for admission. The language used is, that he must be of "mature and discreet age." But the usage of the Craft has differed in various countries as to the construction of the time when this period of maturity and discretion is supposed to have arrived. The sixth of the Regulations, which are said to have been made in 1663, prescribes that " no person shall be accepted a Freemason unless he be one and twenty years old or more "; but the subsequent Regulations are less explicit. At Frankfort-on-the-Main, the age required is twenty; in the Lodges of Switzerland, it has been fixed at twenty-one. The Grand Lodge of Hanover prescribes the age of twenty-five, but permits the son of a Mason to be admitted at eighteen. (See *Lewis*.) The Grand Lodge of Hamburg decrees that the lawful age for initiation shall be that which in any country has been determined by the laws of the land to be the age of majority. The Grand Orient of France requires the candidate to be twenty-one, unless he be the son of a Mason who has performed some important service to the Order, or unless he be a young man who has served six months in the army, when the initiation may take place at the age of eighteen. In Prussia the required age is twenty-five.

Under the Grand Lodge of England the Constitutions of 1723 provided that no man should be made a Mason under the age of twenty-five unless by dispensation from the Grand Master, and this remained the necessary age until it was lowered in the Constitutions of 1784 to twenty-one years, as at present, though the " Ancient " Masons still retained the requirement of twenty-five until the Union of 1813. Under the Scotch Constitution the age was eighteen until 1891, when it was raised to twenty-one. Under the Irish Constitution the age was twenty-one until 1741, when it was raised to twenty-five and so remained until 1817, when it was lowered again to twenty-one. In the United States, the usage is general that the candidate shall not be less than twenty-one years of age at the time of his initiation, and no dispensation can issue for conferring the degrees at an earlier period.

Age, Masonic. In some Masonic Rites a mystical age is appropriated to each degree, and the initiate who has received the degree is said to be of such an age. Thus, the age of an Entered Apprentice is said to be three years; that of a Fellow-Craft, five; and that of a Master Mason, seven. These ages are not arbitrarily selected, but have a reference to the mystical value of numbers and their relation to the different degrees. Thus, *three* is the symbol of peace and concord, and has been called in the Pythagorean system the number of perfect harmony, and is appropriated to that degree, which is the initiation into an Order whose fundamental principles are harmony and brotherly love. *Five* is the symbol of active life, the union of the female principle *two* and the male principle *three*, and refers in this way to the active duties of man as a denizen of the world, which constitutes the symbolism of the Fellow-Craft's degree; and *seven*, as a venerable and perfect number, is symbolic of that perfection which is supposed to be attained in the Master's degree. In a way similar to this, all the ages of the other degrees are symbolically and mystically explained.

The Masonic ages are—and it will thus be seen that they are all mystic numbers—3, 5, 7, 9, 15, 27, 63, 81.

Agenda. A Latin word meaning " things to be done." Thus an " Agenda Paper " is a list of the matters to be brought before a meeting.

Agla. One of the Kabbalistic names of God, which is composed of the initials of the words of the following sentence: אתה גבר לעלם אדני, *Atah Gibor Lolam Adonai*, " thou art mighty forever, O Lord." This name the Kabbalists arranged seven times in the center and at the intersecting points of two interlacing triangles, which figure they called the *Shield of David*, and used as a talisman, believing that it would cure wounds, extinguish fires, and perform other wonders. (See *Shield of David*.)

Agnostus, Irenæus. This is supposed by Kloss (*Bibliog.*, Nos. 2442, 2497, etc.) to have been a *nom de plume* of Gotthardus Arthusius, a co-rector in the Gymnasium of Frankfort-on-the-Main, and a writer of some local celebrity in the beginning of the seventeenth century. (See *Arthusius*.) Under this assumed name of Irenæus Agnostus, he published, between the years 1617 and 1620, many works on the subject of the Rosicrucian Fraternity, which John Valentine Andrea had about that time established in Germany. Among those works were the *Fortalicium Scientiæ*, 1617; *Clypeum Veritatis*, 1618; *Speculum Constantiæ*, 1618; *Fons Gratiæ*, 1619; *Frater non Frater*, 1619; *Thesaurus Fidei*, 1619; *Portus Tranquillitatis*, 1620, and several others of a similar character and equally quaint title.

Agnus Dei. The Agnus Dei, Lamb of God, also called the Paschal Lamb, or the Lamb offered in the paschal sacrifice, is one of the jewels of a Commandery of Knights Templar in America, and is worn by the Generalissimo.

The lamb is one of the earliest symbols of Christ in the iconography of the Church, and as such was a representation of the Savior, derived from that expression of St. John the Baptist (John i. 29), who, on beholding Christ, exclaimed, "Behold the Lamb of God." "Christ," says Didron (*Christ. Iconog.*, i., 318), "shedding his blood for our redemption, is the Lamb slain by the children of Israel, and with the blood of which the houses to be preserved from the wrath of God were marked with the celestial *tau*. The Paschal Lamb eaten by the Israelites on the night preceding their departure from Egypt is the type of that other divine Lamb of whom Christians are to partake at Easter, in order thereby to free themselves from the bondage in which they are held by vice."

The earliest representation that is found in Didron of the Agnus Dei is of the sixth century, and consists of a lamb supporting in his right foot a cross. In the eleventh century we find a banneret attached to this cross, and the lamb is then said to support "the banner of the resurrection." This is the modern form in which the Agnus Dei is represented.

Ahabath Olam. Two Hebrew words signifying *eternal love*. The name of a prayer which was used by the Jews dispersed over the whole Roman Empire during the times of Christ. It was inserted by Dermott in his *Ahiman Rezon* (p. 45, ed. 1764) and copied into several others, with the title of "A Prayer repeated in the Royal Arch Lodge at Jerusalem." The prayer was most probably adopted by Dermott and attributed to a Royal Arch Lodge in consequence of the allusion in it to the "holy, great, mighty, and terrible name of God."

Ahiah. So spelled in the common version of the Bible (1 Kings iv. 3), but according to the Hebrew orthography the word should be spelled and pronounced *Achiah*. He and Elihoreph (or Elichoreph) were the *sopherim*, scribes or secretaries of King Solomon. In the ritual of the Seventh Degree of the Ancient and Accepted Rite, according to the modern American ritual, these personages are represented by the two Wardens.

Ahiman Rezon. The title given by Dermott to the *Book of Constitutions* of the Grand Lodge of "Ancient" Masons in England, which was established about the middle of the eighteenth century in opposition to the legitimate Grand Lodge and its adherents, who were called the "Moderns," and whose code of laws was contained in Anderson's work known as the *Book of Constitutions*. Many attempts have been made to explain the significance of this title; thus, according to Dr. Mackey, it is derived from three Hebrew words, אחים, *ahim*, "brothers"; מנה, *manah*, "to appoint," or "to select" (in the sense of being placed in a peculiar class, see Isaiah liii. 12); and רצון, *ratzon*, "the will, pleasure, or meaning"; and hence the combination of the three words in the title, Ahiman Rezon, signifies "the will of selected brethren"—the law of a class or society of men who are chosen or selected from the rest of the world as brethren. Dr. Dalcho (*Ahim. Rez. of South Carolina*, p. 159, 2d ed.) derives it from *ahi*, "a brother," *manah*, "to prepare," and *rezon*, "secret"; so that, as he says, "Ahiman Rezon literally means *the secrets of a prepared brother*." But the best meaning of *manah* is that which conveys the idea of being placed in or appointed to a certain, exclusive class, as we find in Isaiah (liii. 12) "he was numbered (*nimenah*) with the transgressors," placed in that class, being taken out of every other order of men. And although *rezon* may come from *ratzon*, "a will or law," it can hardly be elicited by any rules of etymology out of the Chaldee word *raz*, "a secret," the termination in *on* being wanting; and besides the book called the *Ahiman Rezon* does not contain the *secrets*, but only the public laws of Masonry. The derivation of Dalcho seems therefore inadmissible. Not less so is that of Bro. W. S. Rockwell, who (*Ahim. Rez. of Georgia*, 1859, p. 3) thinks the derivation may be found in the Hebrew, אמון, *amun*, "a builder" or "architect," and רזן, *rezon*, as a noun, "prince," and as an adjective, "royal," and hence, Ahiman Rezon, according to this etymology, will signify the "royal builder," or, symbolically, the "Freemason." But to derive *ahiman* from *amun*, or rather *amon*, which is the masoretic pronunciation, is to place all known laws of etymology at defiance. Rockwell himself, however, furnishes the best argument against his strained derivation, when he admits that its correctness will depend on the antiquity of the phrase, which he acknowledges that he doubts. In this, he is right. The phrase is altogether a modern one, and has Dermott, the author of the first work bearing the title, for its inventor. Rockwell's conjectural derivation is, therefore, for this reason still more inadmissible than Dalcho's.

But the most satisfactory explanation is as follows: In his prefatory address to the reader, Dermott narrates a dream of his in which the four men appointed by Solomon to be porters at the Temple (1 Chron. ix. 17) appear to him as sojourners from Jerusalem, and he tells them that he is writing a history of Masonry;

upon which, one of the four, named Ahiman, says that no such history has ever yet been composed and suggests that it never can be. It is clear, therefore, that the first word of the title is the name of this personage. What then does "Rezon" signify? Now the Geneva or "Breeches" Bible, published in 1560, contains a table giving the meanings of the Bible names and explains *Ahiman* as "a prepared brother" or "brother of the right hand" and *Rezon* as "a secretary," so that the title of the book would mean "Brother Secretary." That Dermott used the Geneva Bible is plain from the fact that he quotes from it in his Address to the reader, and therefore it may fairly be assumed that he selected these names to suit his purpose from the list given in it, especially as he styles himself on his title-page merely "Secretary."

But the history of the origin of the book is more important and more interesting than the history of the derivation of its title.

The premier Grand Lodge of England was established in 1717 and ruled the Masons of London and the South of England without opposition until in 1751 when some Irish Masons established another body in London, who professed to work "according to the old institutions," and called themselves "Antient" Masons and the members of the older Grand Lodge "Moderns," maintaining that they alone preserved the ancient usages of Masonry.

The former of these contending bodies, the Grand Lodge of England, had, in the year 1722, caused Dr. James Anderson to collect and compile all the statutes and regulations by which the Fraternity had in former times been governed; and these, after having been submitted to due revision, were published in 1723, by Anderson, with the title of *The Constitutions of the Freemasons.* This work, of which several other editions subsequently appeared, has always been called the *Book of Constitutions,* and contains the foundations of the written law by which the Grand Lodge of England and the Lodges deriving from it, both in that country and in America, are governed. But when the Irish Masons established their rival Grand Lodge, they found it necessary, also, to have a *Book of Constitutions;* and accordingly, Laurence Dermott, who was at one time their Grand Secretary, and afterward their Deputy Grand Master, compiled such a work, the first edition of which was published by James Bedford, at London, in 1756, with the following title: *Ahiman Rezon: or a Help to a Brother; showing the Excellency of Secrecy, and the first cause or motive of the Institution of Masonry; the Principles of the Craft; and the Benefits from a strict Observance thereof, etc., etc.; also the Old and New Regulations, etc. To which is added the greatest collection of Masons' Songs, etc. By Bro. Laurence Dermott, Secretary.* 8vo, 209 pp.

A second edition was published in 1764 with this title: *Ahiman Rezon: or a help to all that are or would be Free and Accepted Masons; containing the Quintessence of all that has been published on the Subject of Freemasonry, with many Additions, which renders this Work more useful than any other Book of Constitution now extant. By Lau. Dermott, Secretary.* London, 1764. 8vo. 224 pp.

A third edition was published in 1778, with the following title: *Ahiman Rezon: or a Help to all that are or would be Free and Accepted Masons, (with many Additions.) By Lau. Dermott, D.G.M. Printed for James Jones, Grand Secretary; and Sold by Peter Shatwell, in the Strand. London, 1778.* 8vo, 232 pp.

Five other editions were published: the 4th, in 1778; the 5th in 1787; the 6th in 1800; the 7th in 1801; the 8th in 1807, and the 9th in 1813. In this year, the Ancient Grand Lodge was dissolved by the union of the two Grand Lodges of England, and a new *Book of Constitutions* having been adopted for the united body, the *Ahiman Rezon* became useless, and no subsequent edition was ever published.

The earlier editions of this work are among the rarest of Masonic publications, and are highly prized by collectors.

In the year 1855, Mr. Leon Hyneman, of Philadelphia, who was engaged in a reprint of old standard Masonic works (an enterprise which should have received better patronage than it did), republished the second edition, with a few explanatory notes.

As this book contains those principles of Masonic law by which, for three-fourths of a century, a large and intelligent portion of the Craft was governed; and as it is now becoming rare and, to the generality of readers, inaccessible, some brief review of its contents may not be uninteresting.

In the Preface or Address to the reader, Dermott pokes fun at the History of Freemasonry as written by Dr. Anderson and others, and wittily explains the reason why he has not published a history of Freemasonry.

There is next a "Philacteria for such Gentlemen as may be inclined to become Freemasons." This article, which was not in the first edition, but appeared for the first time in the second, consists of directions as to the method to be pursued by one who desires to be made a Freemason. This is followed by an account of what Dermott calls "Modern Masonry," that is, the system pursued by the original Grand Lodge of England, and of the differences existing between it and "Ancient Masonry," or the system of his own Grand Lodge. He contends that there are material differences between the two systems; that of the Ancients being universal, and that of the Moderns not; a Modern being able with safety to communicate all his secrets to an Ancient, while an Ancient cannot communicate his to a Modern; a Modern having no right to be called free and accepted; all of which, in his opinion, show that the Ancients have secrets which are not in the possession of the Moderns. This, he considers, a convincing proof that the Modern Masons were innovators upon the established system, and had instituted their Lodges and framed their ritual without a sufficient knowledge of the arcana of the Craft. But the Modern Masons with more semblance of truth, thought that the additional secrets of the Ancients were only innovations that they had made upon the true body of Masonry; and hence, they considered their ignorance of these newly invented secrets was the best evidence of their own superior antiquity.

In the later editions Dermott has published the famous Leland MS., together with the commentaries of Locke; also the resolutions adopted in 1772, by which the Grand Lodges of Ireland and Scotland agreed to maintain a " Brotherly Connexion and Correspondence " with the Grand Lodge of England (Ancients). The *Ahiman Rezon* proper, then, begins with twenty-three pages of an encomium on Masonry, and an explanation of its principles. Many a modern Masonic address is better written, and contains more important and instructive matter than this prefatory discourse.

Then follow " The Old Charges of the Free and Accepted Masons," taken from the 1738 Edition of Anderson's *Constitutions.* Next come " A short charge to a new admitted Mason," " The Ancient manner of constituting a Lodge," a few prayers, and then the "General Regulations of the Free and Accepted Masons." These are borrowed mainly from the second edition of Anderson with a few alterations and additions. After a comparison of the Dublin and London " Regulations for Charity," the rest of the book, comprising more than a hundred pages, consists of " A Collection of Masons' Songs," of the poetical merits of which the less said the better for the literary reputation of the writers.

Imperfect, however, as was this work, it for a long time constituted the statute book of the " Ancient Masons"; and hence those Lodges in America which derived their authority from the Dermott or Ancient Grand Lodge of England, accepted its contents as a true exposition of Masonic law; and several of their Grand Lodges caused similar works to be compiled for their own government, adopting the title of *Ahiman Rezon,* which thus became the peculiar designation of the volume which contained the fundamental law of the "Ancients," while the original title of *Book of Constitutions* continued to be retained by the "Moderns," to designate the volume used by them for the same purpose.

Of the *Ahiman Rezons* compiled and published in America, the following are the principal:

1. *Ahiman Rezon abridged and digested; as a help to all that are or would be Free and Accepted Masons, etc. Published by order of the Grand Lodge of Pennsylvania; by William Smith, D.D.* Philadelphia, 1783. A new *Ahiman Rezon* was published by the Grand Lodge of Pennsylvania in 1825.

2. *Charges and Regulations of the Ancient and Honorable Society of Free and Accepted Masons, extracted from the Ahiman Rezon, etc. Published by the consent and direction of the Grand Lodge of Nova Scotia.* Halifax, 1786.

3. *The New Ahiman Rezon, containing the Laws and Constitution of Virginia, etc. By John K. Reade, present Deputy Grand Master of Virginia, etc.* Richmond, 1791. Another edition was published in 1818, by James Henderson.

4. *The Maryland Ahiman Rezon of Free and Accepted Masons, containing the History of Masonry from the establishment of the Grand Lodge to the present time; with their Ancient Charges, Addresses, Prayers, Lectures, Prologues, Epilogues, Songs, etc., collected from the Old Records, Faithful Traditions and Lodge Books; by G. Keating. Compiled by order of the Grand Lodge of Maryland.* Baltimore, 1797.

5. *The Ahiman Rezon and Masonic Ritual, published by the order of the Grand Lodge of North Carolina and Tennessee.* Newbern, N. C., 1805.

6. *An Ahiman Rezon, for the use of the Grand Lodge of South Carolina, Ancient York Masons, and the Lodges under the Register and Masonic Jurisdiction thereof. Compiled and arranged with considerable additions, at the request of the Grand Lodge, and published by their authority. By Brother Frederick Dalcho, M.D., etc.* Charleston, S. C., 1807. A second edition was published by the same author, in 1822, and a third, in 1852, by Dr. Albert G. Mackey. In this third edition, the title was changed to that of *The Ahiman Rezon, or Book of Constitutions, etc.* And the work was in a great measure expurgated of the peculiarities of Dermott, and made to conform more closely to the Andersonian *Constitutions.* A fourth edition was published by the same editor, in 1871, in which everything antagonistic to the original *Book of Constitutions* has been omitted.

7. *The Freemason's Library and General Ahiman Rezon; containing a delineation of the true principles of Freemasonry, etc.; by Samuel Cole.* Baltimore, 1817. 8vo, 332 + 92 pp. There was a second edition in 1826.

8. *Ahiman Rezon; prepared under the direction of the Grand Lodge of Georgia; by Wm. S. Rockwell, Grand Master of Masons of Georgia.* Savannah, 1859. 4to and 8vo, 404 pp. But neither this work nor the third and fourth editions of the *Ahiman Rezon* of South Carolina have any connection in principle or theory with the *Ahiman Rezon* of Dermott. They have borrowed the name from the " Ancient Masons," but they derive all their law and their authorities from the " Moderns," or the legal Masons of the last century.

9. *The General Ahiman Rezon and Freemason's Guide, by Daniel Sickles.* New York, 1866. 8vo, pp. 408. This book, like Rockwell's, has no other connection with the archetypal work of Dermott but the name.

Many of the Grand Lodges of the United States having derived their existence and authority from the Dermott Grand Lodge, the influence of his *Ahiman Rezon* was for a long time exercised over the Lodges of this country; and, indeed, it is only within a comparatively recent period that the true principles of Masonic law, as expounded in the first editions of Anderson's *Constitutions*, have been universally adopted among American Masons.

It must, however, be observed, in justice to Dermott, who has been rather too grossly abused by Mitchell and a few other writers, that the innovations upon the old laws of Masonry, which are to be found in the *Ahiman Rezon*, are for the most part not to be charged upon him, but upon Dr. Anderson himself, who, for the first time, introduced them into the second edition of the *Book of Constitutions*, published in 1738. It is surprising, and accountable only on the ground of sheer carelessness on the part of the supervising committee, that the Grand Lodge should, in 1738, have approved of these alterations made by Anderson, and still more surprising that it was not until 1756 that a new or third edition of the *Constitutions* should have been published, in which these alterations of 1738 were expunged, and the old regulations and the old language restored. But whatever may have been the causes of this oversight, it is not to be doubted that, at the time of the formation of the Grand Lodge of the Ancients, the edition of the *Book of Constitutions* of 1738 was considered as the authorized exponent of Masonic law by the original or regular Grand Lodge of England, and was adopted, with but little change, by Dermott as the basis of his *Ahiman Rezon*. How much this edition of 1738 differed from that of 1723, which is now considered the only true authority for ancient law, and how much it agreed with Dermott's *Ahiman Rezon*, will be evident from the following specimens of the first of the Old Charges, correctly taken from each of the three works:

First of the Old Charges in the *Book of Constitutions*, edit., 1723.

" A Mason is obliged by his tenure to obey the moral law; and if he rightly understands the Art, he will never be a stupid Atheist, nor an irreligious libertine. But though in ancient times Masons were charged, in every country, to be of the religion of that country or nation, whatever it was, yet it is now thought more expedient only to oblige them to that religion in which all men agree, leaving their particular opinions to themselves; that is to be good men and true, or men of honour and honesty, by whatever denominations or persuasions they may be distinguished; whereby Masonry becomes the centre of union, and the means of conciliating true friendship among persons that must have remained at a perpetual distance."

First of the Old Charges in the *Book of Constitutions*, edit., 1738.

" A Mason is obliged by his tenure to *observe* the moral law, *as a true Noachida;* and if he rightly understands the *Craft*, he will

never be a stupid Atheist, nor an irreligious libertine, *nor act against conscience.*

" In antient times, *the Christian* Masons were charged to comply with *the Christian usages* of each country *where they travelled or worked. But Masonry being found in all nations, even of divers religions*, they are now only charged to adhere to that religion in which all men agree, (leaving each brother to his own particular opinions;) that is, to be good men and true, men of honour and honesty, by whatever *names, religions,* or persuasions they may be distinguished; *for they all agree in the three great articles of Noah enough to preserve the cement of the Lodge.* Thus, Masonry is the center of *their* union, and the *happy* means of conciliating persons that *otherwise* must have remained at a perpetual distance."

First of the Old Charges in Dermott's *Ahiman Rezon.*

" A Mason is obliged by his tenure to *observe* the moral law, *as a true Noachida;* and if he rightly understands the *Craft*, he will never be a stupid Atheist, nor an irreligious libertine, *nor act against conscience.*

" In ancient times, *the Christian* Masons were charged to comply with *the Christian usages* of each country *where they travelled or worked; being found in all nations, even of divers religions.*

" They are *generally* charged to adhere to that religion in which all men agree, (leaving each brother to his own particular opinions;) that is, to be good men and true, men of honour and honesty, by whatever *names, religions,* or persuasions they may be distinguished; *for they all agree in the three great articles of Noah enough to preserve the cement of the Lodge.*

" Thus, Masonry is the center of *their* union, and the *happy* means of conciliating persons that *otherwise* must have remained at a perpetual distance."

The italics in the second and third extracts will show what innovations Anderson made, in 1738, on the Charges as originally published in 1723, and how closely Dermott followed him in adopting these innovations. There is, in fact, much less difference between the *Ahiman Rezon* of Dermott and Anderson's edition of the *Book of Constitutions*, printed in 1738, than there is between the latter and the first edition of the *Constitutions*, printed in 1723. But the great points of difference between the " Ancients " and the " Moderns," points which kept them apart for so many years, are to be found in their work and ritual, for an account of which the reader is referred to the article *Ancient Masons.* [E. L. H.]

Ahisar. See *Achishar.*

Aholiab. A skilful artificer of the tribe of Dan, who was appointed, together with Bezaleel, to construct the tabernacle in the wilderness and the ark of the covenant. (Exodus xxxi. 6.) He is referred to in the Royal Arch degree of the English and American systems.

Aid and Assistance. The duty of aiding and assisting, not only all worthy distressed

Master Masons, but their widows and orphans also, "wheresoever dispersed over the face of the globe," is one of the most important obligations that is imposed upon every brother of the "mystic tie" by the whole scope and tenor of the Masonic Institution. The regulations for the exercise of this duty are few, but rational. In the first place, a Master Mason who is in distress has a greater claim, under equal circumstances, to the aid and assistance of his brother, than one who, being in the Order, has not attained that degree, or who is altogether a profane. This is strictly in accordance with the natural instincts of the human heart, which will always prefer a friend to a stranger, or, as it is rather energetically expressed in the language of Long Tom Coffin, " a messmate before a shipmate, a shipmate before a stranger, and a stranger before a dog "; and it is also strictly in accordance with the teaching of the Apostle of the Gentiles, who has said: " As we have therefore opportunity, let us do good unto all men, especially unto them who are of the household of faith." (Galatians vi. 10.)

But this exclusiveness is only to be practised under circumstances which make a selection imperatively necessary. Where the granting of relief to the profane would incapacitate us from granting similar relief to our brother, then must the preference be given to him who is " of the household." But the earliest symbolic lessons of the ritual teach the Mason not to restrict his benevolence within the narrow limits of the Fraternity, but to acknowledge the claims of all men who need it, to assistance. Inwood has beautifully said: " The humble condition both of property and dress, of penury and want, in which you were received into the Lodge, should make you at all times sensible of the distresses of poverty, and all you can spare from the call of nature and the due care of your families, should only remain in your possessions as a ready sacrifice to the necessities of an unfortunate, distressed brother. Let the distressed cottage feel the warmth of your Masonic zeal, and, if possible, exceed even the unabating ardour of Christian charity. At your approach let the orphan cease to weep, and in the sound of your voice let the widow forget her sorrow." (*Sermons*, p. 18.)

Another restriction laid upon this duty of aid and assistance by the obligations of Masonry is, that the giver shall not be lavish beyond his means in the disposition of his benevolence. What he bestows must be such as he can give " without material injury to himself or family." No man should wrong his wife or children that he may do a benefit to a stranger, or even to a brother. The obligations laid on a Mason to grant aid and assistance to the needy and distressed seem to be in the following gradations: first, to his family; next, to his brethren; and, lastly, to the world at large.

So far this subject has been viewed in a general reference to that spirit of kindness which should actuate all men, and which it

is the object of Masonic teaching to impress on the mind of every Mason as a common duty of humanity, and whose disposition Masonry only seeks to direct and guide. But there is another aspect in which this subject may be considered, namely, in that peculiar and technical one of Masonic aid and assistance due from one Mason to another. Here there is a duty declared, and a correlative right inferred; for if it is the duty of one Mason to assist another, it follows that every Mason has the right to claim that assistance from his brother. It is this duty that the obligations of Masonry are especially intended to enforce; it is this right that they are intended to sustain. The symbolic ritual of Masonry which refers, as, for instance, in the First Degree, to the virtue of benevolence, refers to it in the general sense of a virtue which all men should practise. But when the Mason reaches the Third Degree, he discovers new obligations which restrict and define the exercise of this duty of aid and assistance. So far as his obligations control him, the Mason, *as a Mason*, is not legally bound to extend his aid beyond the just claimants in his own Fraternity. To do good to all men is, of course, inculcated and recommended; to do good to the household is enforced and made compulsory by legal enactment and sanction.

Now, as there is here, on one side, a duty, and on the other side a right, it is proper to inquire what are the regulations or laws by which this duty is controlled and this right maintained.

The duty to grant and the right to claim relief Masonically is recognized in the following passage of the Old Charges of 1722:

" But if you discover him to be a true and genuine Brother, you are to respect him accordingly; and if he is in want, you must relieve him if you can, or else direct him how he may be relieved. You must employ him some days, or else recommend him to be employed. But you are not charged to do beyond your ability; only to prefer a poor brother, that is a good man and true, before any other poor people in the same circumstances."

This written law agrees in its conditions and directions, so far as it goes, with the unwritten law of the Order, and from the two we may deduce the following principles:

1. The applicant must be a Master Mason. In 1722, the charitable benefits of Masonry were extended, it is true, to Entered Apprentices, and an Apprentice was recognized, in the language of the law, as " a true and genuine brother." But this was because at that time only the First Degree was conferred in subordinate Lodges, Fellow-Crafts and Master Masons being made in the Grand Lodge. Hence the great mass of the Fraternity consisted of Apprentices, and many Masons never proceeded any further. But the Second and Third Degrees are now always conferred in subordinate Lodges, and very few initiates voluntarily stop short of the Master's Degree. Hence the mass of the Fraternity now consists of Master Masons, and the law which

formerly applied to Apprentices is, under our present organization, made applicable only to those who have become Master Masons.

2. The applicant must be worthy. We are to presume that every Mason is " a good man and true " until a Lodge has pronounced to the contrary. Every Mason who is " in good standing," that is, who is a regularly contributing member of a Lodge, is to be considered as " worthy," in the technical sense of the term. An expelled, a suspended, or a non-affiliated Mason does not meet the required condition of " a regularly contributing member." Such a Mason is therefore not " worthy," and is not entitled to Masonic assistance.

3. The giver is not expected to exceed his ability in the amount of relief. The written law says, " you are not charged to do beyond your ability "; the ritual says, that your relief must be " without material injury to yourself or family." The principle is the same in both.

4. The widow and orphans of a Master Mason have the claim of the husband and father extended to them. The written law says nothing explicitly on this point, but the unwritten or ritualistic law expressly declares that it is our duty " to contribute to the relief of a worthy, distressed brother, his widow and orphans."

5. And lastly, in granting relief or assistance, the Mason is to be preferred to the profane. He must be placed " before any other poor people in the same circumstances."

These are the laws which regulate the doctrine of Masonic aid and assistance. They are often charged by the enemies of Masonry with a spirit of exclusiveness. But it has been shown that they are in accordance with the exhortation of the Apostle, who would do good " especially to those who are of the household," and they have the warrant of the law of nature; for everyone will be ready to say, with that kindest-hearted of men, Charles Lamb, " I can feel for all indifferently, but I cannot feel for all alike. I can be a friend to a worthy man, who, upon another account, cannot be my mate or fellow. I cannot like all people alike." And so as Masons, while we should be charitable to all persons in need or in distress, there are only certain ones who can claim the aid and assistance of the Order, or of its disciples, under the positive sanction of Masonic law.

Aitchison's - Haven Lodge (*also spelled* **Atcheson, Achison**). This was one of the oldest Operative Lodges consenting to the formation of the Grand Lodge of Scotland in 1736. The age of this Lodge, like many or most of the oldest Lodges of Scotland, is not known. Some of its members signed the St. Clair Charters in 1600–1601. The place of its meeting (Aitchison-Haven) is no longer on the map, but was in the county of Midlothian. The origin of the town was from a charter of James V., dated 1526, and probably the Lodge dated near that period. Aitchison's-Haven was probably the first meeting-place, but they seem to have met at Musselburgh at a later period.

Lyon, in his *History of the Lodge of Edinburgh*, speaks of trouble in the Grand Quarterly communication respecting representatives from this Lodge when (May, 1737) it was " agreed that Atcheson's Haven be deleted out of the books of the Grand Lodge, and no more called on the rolls of the Clerk's highest peril." It was restored to the roll in 1814, but becoming dormant, it was finally cut off in 1866. The Lodge of Edinburgh has long enjoyed the distinction of having the oldest preserved Lodge minute, which dated July, 1599.

Just recently Bro. R. E. Wallace-James has brought to light a minute-book bearing this title: *The Buik of the Actis and Ordinans of the Nobile Maisteris and fellows of Craft of the Ludg of Aitchison's heavine*, and contains a *catalogue of the names of the fellows of Craft that are presently in the Zeir of God* 1598.

The first page of this rare book bears in a bold hand the date, " 1598."

The minute is as follows:

The IX day of Januerie the Zeir of God upon ye quhilk day Robert Widderspone was maid fellow of Craft in ye presens of Wilzam Aytone Elder, Johne Fender being Warden, Johne Pedden Thomas Pettencrief John Crafurd George Aytone Wilzame Aytone younger Hendrie Petticrief all fellowis of Craft upon ye quhilk day he chois George Aytone Johne Pedden to be his intenders and instructouris and also ye said Robert hes payit his xx sh. and his gluffis to everie Maister as efferis. See vol. xxiv., Trans. Quat. Cor. Lodge.

[E. E. C.]

Aitchison's-Haven Manuscript. One of the " Old Charges," or records of Masonry now in the custody of the Grand Lodge of Scotland, formerly preserved in the archives of the Aitchison-Haven Lodge, which met at Musselburgh in Scotland. The MS. is engrossed in the minute-book of Aitchison-Haven Lodge. The writer attests to his transcription in the following manner: " Insert by me undersub and the 19" of May, 1666, Jo. Auchinleck, clerk to the Masones of Achisones Lodge."

It has been reproduced (with 24 lines in facsimile) by D. Murray Lyon in his *History of the Lodge of Edinburgh*.

Aix-la-Chapelle. (In German, *Aachen*.) A city of Germany, remarkable in Masonic history for a persecution which took place in the eighteenth century, and of which Gädicke (*Freimaur. Lex.*) gives the following account: In the year 1779, Ludwig Grienemann, a Dominican monk, delivered a course of Lenten sermons, in which he attempted to prove that the Jews who crucified Christ were Freemasons, that Pilate and Herod were Wardens in a Mason's Lodge, that Judas, previous to his betrayal of his Master, was initiated into the Order, and that the thirty pieces of silver, which he is said to have returned, was only the fee which he paid for his initiation. Aix-la-Chapelle being a Roman Catholic city, the magistrates were induced, by the influence of

Grienemann, to issue a decree, in which they declared that anyone who should permit a meeting of the Freemasons in his house should, for the first offense, be fined 100 florins, for the second 200, and for the third, be banished from the city. The mob became highly incensed against the Masons, and insulted all whom they suspected to be members of the Order. At length Peter Schuff, a Capuchin, jealous of the influence which the Dominican Grienemann was exerting, began also, with augmented fervor, to preach against Freemasonry, and still more to excite the popular commotion. In this state of affairs, the Lodge at Aix-la-Chapelle applied to the princes and Masonic Lodges in the neighboring territories for assistance and protection, which were immediately rendered. A letter in French was received by both priests, in which the writer, who stated that he was one of the former dignitaries of the Order, strongly reminded them of their duties, and, among other things, said that "many priests, a pope, several cardinals, bishops, and even Dominican and Capuchin monks, had been, and still were, members of the Order." Although this remonstrance had some effect, peace was not altogether restored until the neighboring free imperial states threatened that they would prohibit the monks from collecting alms in their territories unless they ceased to excite the popular commotion against the Freemasons.

Akirop. The name given, in the ritual of the Ancient and Accepted Rite, to one of the ruffians celebrated in the legend of the Third Degree. The word is said in the ritual to signify an assassin. It might probably be derived from קרב, KaRaB, *to assault* or *join battle;* but is just as probably a word so corrupted by long oral transmission that its etymology can no longer be traced. (See *Abiram.*)

Alabama. On August 29, 1811, while Alabama was yet a part of Mississippi Territory, the Grand Lodge of Kentucky granted a dispensation for Madison Lodge, No. 21, in Madison County. On August 28, 1812, a Charter was granted to this Lodge, locating it at Huntsville, and was issued the same day, and the Master was installed in Grand Lodge. When the Territory was divided and Mississippi admitted into the Union in 1817, the Grand Lodge of Mississippi had not been organized, so that it never claimed jurisdiction outside of that State, and this Lodge remained under the jurisdiction of the Grand Lodge of Kentucky until the Grand Lodge of Alabama was formed.

The Grand Master of the Grand Lodge of Tennessee granted dispensations for Lodges in Alabama, as follows: Alabama Lodge, No. 21, at Huntsville, April 6, 1818; Washington Lodge at Hazel Green, in 1818; Rising Virtue Lodge at Tuscaloosa, in 1819; Halo Lodge at Cahawba, April 4, 1820; Moulton Lodge at Moulton, May 4, 1820; Franklin Lodge at Russellville, October 3, 1820; Tuscumbia Lodge at Courtland, March 3, 1821; and Farrar Lodge at Elyton, March 5, 1821. Charters were granted to Alabama and Washington Lodges, October 6, 1818; to Rising Virtue Lodge, October 5, 1819; and to Moulton, October 3, 1820.

A convention to organize a Grand Lodge was held at Cahawba, June 1, 1821, and was in session five days.

The constitution, dated June 14, 1821, was published by itself; it was signed by the Grand Officers and the Representatives of nine Lodges, viz.: Madison Lodge, Alabama Lodge at Huntsville, Alabama Lodge at Claiborne, Rising Virtue Lodge, Halo Lodge, Moulton Lodge, Russellville Lodge, U. D., Farrar Lodge, U. D., and St. Stephen's Lodge.

Thomas W. Farrar was elected Grand Master and Thomas A. Rogers Grand Secretary.

The Grand Chapter of Alabama was organized on the 2d of June, 1827, at the town of Tuscaloosa, and at the same time and place a Grand Council of Royal and Select Masters was established.

On the 27th of October, 1860, Sir Knt. B. B. French, Grand Master of the Grand Encampment of the United States, issued his mandate for the formation of a Grand Commandery of Alabama.

Alapa. A Latin word signifying "a blow on the cheek with the open hand." Such a blow was given by the master to his manumitted slave as a symbol of manumission, and as a reminder that it was the last unrequited indignity which he was to receive. Hence, in medieval times, the same word was applied to the blow inflicted on the cheek of the newly created knight by the sovereign who created him, with the same symbolic signification. This was sometimes represented by the blow on the shoulder with the flat of a sword, which has erroneously been called the *accolade.* (See *Knighthood.*)

Alarm. The verb "to alarm" signifies, in Freemasonry, "to give notice of the approach of some one desiring admission." Thus, "to alarm the Lodge" is to inform the Lodge that there is some one without who is seeking entrance. As a noun, the word "alarm" has two significations. 1. An alarm is a warning given by the Tiler, or other appropriate officer, by which he seeks to communicate with the interior of the Lodge or Chapter. In this sense the expression so often used, "an alarm at the door," simply signifies that the officer outside has given notice of his desire to communicate with the Lodge. 2. An alarm is also the peculiar mode in which this notice is to be given. In modern Masonic works, the number of knocks given in an alarm is generally expressed by musical notes. Thus, three distinct knocks would be designated thus, ♪♪♪; two rapid and two slow ones thus, ♪♪♩♩; and three knocks three times repeated thus, ♪♪♪ ♪♪♪ ♪♪♪, etc. The word comes from the French "alarme," which in turn comes from the Italian "all'arme," literally a cry "to arms," uttered by sentinels surprised by the enemy. The legal meaning of *to alarm* is not *to frighten,* but to make one aware of the necessity of defense or protection. And this is precisely the Masonic signification of the word.

Alaska. Masonry in regular form was introduced into Alaska by the establishment of Gastineaux Lodge, No. 124, at Douglass, late in 1904, under a warrant from the Grand Lodge of Washington. This was followed by Anvil Lodge, No. 140, at Nome; Mount Tuneau, No. 147, at Tuneau; Tanan, No. 162, at Fairbanks; Valdez, No. 168, at Valdez; and Mount McKinley, No. 183, at Cordova; all under warrants from the same Grand Lodge.

[W. J. A.]

Alban, St. (See *Saint Alban.*)

Alberta (Canada). This Grand Lodge was established in 1905, and in 1910 had 34 Lodges and 2,380 brethren under its jurisdiction.

Albertus Magnus. A scholastic philosopher of the Middle Ages, of great erudition, but who had among the vulgar the reputation of being a magician. He was born at Lauingen, in Swabia, in 1205, of an illustrious family, his subtitle being that of Count of Bollstadt. He studied at Padua, and in 1223 entered the Order of the Dominicans. In 1249, he became head-master of the school at Cologne. In 1260, Pope Alexander VI. conferred upon him the bishopric of Ratisbon. In 1262, he resigned the episcopate and returned to Cologne, and, devoting himself to philosophic pursuits for the remainder of his life, died there in 1280. His writings were very voluminous, the edition published at Lyons, in 1651, amounting to twenty-one large folio volumes. Albertus has been connected with the Operative Masonry of the Middle Ages because he has been supposed by many to have been the real inventor of the German Gothic style of architecture. Heidcloff, in his *Bauhütte des Mittelalters,* says that " he recalled into life the symbolic language of the ancients, which had so long lain dormant, and adapted it to suit architectural forms." The Masons accepted his instructions, and adopted in consequence that system of symbols which was secretly communicated only to the members of their own body, and served even as a medium of intercommunication. He is asserted to have designed the plan for the construction of the Cathedral of Cologne, and to have altered the Constitution of the Masons, and to have given to them a new set of laws.

Albrecht, Heinrich Christoph. A German author, who published at Hamburg, in 1792, the first and only part of a work entitled *Materialen zu einer critischen Geschichte der Freimaurerei,* i. e., Collections towards a Critical History of Freemasonry. Kloss says that this was one of the first attempts at a clear and rational history of the Order. Unfortunately, the author never completed his task, and only the first part of the work ever appeared. Albrecht was the author also of another work entitled *GeheimeGeschichte eines Rosenkreuzers,* or Secret History of a Rosicrucian, and of a series of papers which appeared in the *Berlin Archiv. der Zeit,* containing " Notices of Free-

masonry in the first half of the Sixteenth Century." Albrecht adopted the theory first advanced by the Abbé Grandidier, that Freemasonry owes its origin to the Steinmetzen of Germany.

Alchemy. The Neo-Platonicians introduced at an early period of the Christian era an apparently new science, which they called ἐπιστήμη ἱερά, or the Sacred Science, which materially influenced the subsequent condition of the arts and sciences. In the fifth century arose, as the name of the science, *alchemia,* derived from the Arabic definite article *al* being added to *chemia,* a Greek word used in Diocletian's decree against Egyptian works treating of the χημία or transmutation of metals; the word seems simply to mean " the Egyptian Art," χημία, or *the land of black earth,* being the Egyptian name for Egypt, and Julius Firmicius, in a work *On the Influence of the Stars upon the Fate of Man,* uses the phrase " scientia alchemiæ." From this time the study of alchemy was openly followed. In the Middle Ages, and up to the end of the seventeenth century, it was an important science, studied by some of the most distinguished philosophers, such as Avicenna, Albertus Magnus, Raymond Lulli, Roger Bacon, Elias Ashmole, and many others.

Alchemy—called also the Hermetic Philosophy, because it is said to have been first taught in Egypt by Hermes Trismegistus.

Freemasonry and alchemy have sought the same results (the lesson of Divine Truth and the doctrine of immortal life), and they have both sought it by the same method of symbolism. It is not, therefore, strange that in the eighteenth century, and perhaps before, we find an incorporation of much of the science of alchemy into that of Freemasonry. Hermetic rites and Hermetic degrees were common, and their relics are still to be found existing in degrees which do not absolutely trace their origin to alchemy, but which show some of its traces in their rituals. The Twenty-eighth Degree of the Scottish Rite, or the Knight of the Sun, is entirely a Hermetic degree, and claims its parentage in the title of " Adept of Masonry," by which it is sometimes known.

Aldworth, the Hon. Mrs. This lady, who is well known as " the Lady Freemason," was the Hon. Elizabeth St. Leger, daughter of Lord Doneraile of Doneraile Court, Co. Cork, Ireland. She was born in 1693, and married in 1713 to Richard Aldworth, Esq., of Newmarket Court, Co. Cork. There appears to be no doubt that while a girl she received the First and Second degrees of Freemasonry in Ireland, but of the actual circumstances of her initiation several different accounts have been given.

Of these the most authentic appears to be one issued at Cork, with the authority of the family, in 1811, and afterward republished in London.

From this it appears that her father, Viscount Doneraile, together with his sons and a few friends, was accustomed to open a Lodge and carry on the ordinary ceremonies at Doneraile Court, and it was during one of these meetings that the occurrence took place which is thus related:

" It happened on this particular occasion that the Lodge was held in a room separated from another, as is often the case, by stud and brickwork. The young lady, being giddy and thoughtless, and determined to gratify her curiosity, made her arrangements accordingly, and, with a pair of scissors, (as she herself related to the mother of our informant,) removed a portion of a brick from the wall, and placed herself so as to command a full view of everything which occurred in the next room; so placed, she witnessed the *two* first degrees in Masonry, which was the extent of the proceedings of the Lodge on that night. Becoming aware, from what she heard, that the brethren were about to separate, for the first time she felt tremblingly alive to the awkwardness and danger of her situation, and began to consider how she could retire without observation. She became nervous and agitated, and nearly fainted, but so far recovered herself as to be fully aware of the necessity of withdrawing as quickly as possible; in the act of doing so, being in the dark, she stumbled against and overthrew something, said to be a chair or some ornamental piece of furniture. The crash was loud; and the Tiler, who was on the lobby or landing on which the doors both of the Lodge room and that where the Honorable Miss St. Leger was, opened, gave the alarm, burst open the door and, with a light in one hand and a drawn sword in the other, appeared to the now terrified and fainting lady. He was soon joined by the members of the Lodge present, and luckily; for it is asserted that but for the prompt appearance of her brother,* Lord Doneraile, and other steady members, her life would have fallen a sacrifice to what was then esteemed her crime. The first care of his Lordship was to resuscitate the unfortunate lady without alarming the house, and endeavor to learn from her an explanation of what had occurred; having done so, many of the members being furious at the transaction, she was placed under guard of the Tiler and a member, in the room where she was found. The members reassembled and deliberated as to what, under the circumstances, was to be done, and over two long hours she could hear the angry discussion and her death deliberately proposed and seconded. At length the good sense of the majority succeeded in calming, in some measure, the angry and irritated feelings of the rest of the members, when, after much had been said and many things proposed, it was resolved to give her the option of submitting to the Masonic ordeal to the extent she had witnessed, (Fellow Craft,) and if she refused, the brethren were again to consult. Being waited on to decide, Miss St. Leger, exhausted and terrified by the storminess of the debate, which she could not avoid

---

* This is a mistake; her father, the first Lord Doneraile, did not die until 1727, when his daughter had been married for fourteen years.

partially hearing, and yet, notwithstanding all, with a secret pleasure, gladly and unhesitatingly accepted the offer. She was accordingly initiated."

A very different account is given in the *Freemason's Quarterly Review* for 1839 (p. 322), being reprinted from the Cork *Standard* of May 29, 1839.

According to this story Mrs. Aldworth was seized with curiosity about the mysteries of Freemasonry and set herself to discover them; so she made friends with the landlady of an inn in Cork in which a Lodge used to meet, and with her connivance was concealed in a clockcase which was placed in the Lodge room; however, she was unable to endure the discomfort of her confinement in such narrow quarters and betrayed herself by a scream, on which she was discovered by the members of the Lodge and then and there initiated.

It will be observed that according to this version the lady was already married before she was initiated. The story is said to be supported by the testimony of two members of Lodge 71, at Cork, in which Lodge the initiation is said to have taken place; this, however, can hardly be correct, for that Lodge did not meet at Cork until 1777, whereas, Mrs. Aldworth died in 1773.

If, however, the commoner version of the story is preferred, according to which Miss St. Leger was initiated as a young girl, then the occurrence must have taken place before her marriage in 1713, and therefore before the establishment of Grand Lodges and the introduction of warranted and numbered Lodges, and it is therefore a proof of the existence of at least one Lodge of Speculative Masons in Ireland at an early period.

After her marriage Mrs. Aldworth seems to have kept up her connection with the Craft, for her portrait in Masonic clothing, her apron and jewels, are still in existence, and her name occurs among the subscribers to Dassigny's *Enquiry* of 1744; and it has even been stated that she presided as Master of her Lodge.

The story has been fully discussed by Bros. Conder, Crawley, and others in the eighth volume (1895) of the *Transactions of the Quatuor Coronati Lodge of London*, to which the curious are referred for further information.

[E. L. H.]

Alethophilote, Lover of Truth. Given by Thory as the Fifth Degree of the Order of African Architects. (*Acta Latomorum*, i., 292.)

Alexander I., Emperor of Russia. Alexander I. succeeded Paul I. in the year 1801, and immediately after his accession renewed the severe prohibitions of his predecessor against all secret societies, and especially Freemasonry. In 1803, M. Boeber, counselor of state and director of the military school at St. Petersburg, resolved to remove, if possible, from the mind of the Emperor the prejudices which he had conceived against the Order. Accordingly, in an audience which he had solicited and obtained, he described the object of the Institution and the doctrine of its mysteries in such a way as to lead the Emperor to rescind the obnoxious decrees, and to add these words: "What you have told me of the Institution not only induces me to grant it my protection and patronage, but even to ask for initiation into its mysteries. Is this possible to be obtained?" M. Boeber replied: "Sire, I cannot myself reply to the question. But I will call together the Masons of your capital, and make your Majesty's desire known; and I have no doubt that they will be eager to comply with your wishes." Accordingly Alexander was soon after initiated, and the Grand Orient of all the Russias was in consequence established, of which M. Boeber was elected Grand Master. (*Acta Latomorum*, i., 218.)

Alexandria, School of. When Alexander built the city of Alexandria in Egypt, with the intention of making it the seat of his empire, he invited thither learned men from all nations, who brought with them their peculiar notions. The Alexandria School of Philosophy which was thus established, by the commingling of Orientalists, Jews, Egyptians, and Greeks, became eclectic in character, and exhibited a heterogeneous mixture of the opinions of the Egyptian priests, of the Jewish Rabbis, of Arabic teachers, and of the disciples of Plato and Pythagoras. From this school we derive Gnosticism and the Kabbala, and, above all, the system of symbolism and allegory which lay at the foundation of the Masonic philosophy. To no ancient sect, indeed, except perhaps the Pythagoreans, have the Masonic teachers been so much indebted for the substance of their doctrines, as well as the esoteric method of communicating them, as to that of the School of Alexandria. Both Aristobulus and Philo, the two most celebrated chiefs of this school, taught, although a century intervened between their births, the same theory, that the sacred writings of the Hebrews were, by their system of allegories, the true source of all religious and philosophic doctrine, the literal meaning of which alone was for the common people, the esoteric or hidden meaning being kept for the initiated. Freemasonry still carries into practise the same theory.

Alincourt, François d'. A French gentleman, who, in the year 1776, was sent with Don Oyres de Ornellas Praçaõ, a Portuguese nobleman, to prison, by the governor of the island of Madeira, for being Freemasons. They were afterward sent to Lisbon, and confined in a common jail for fourteen months, where they would have perished had not the Masons of Lisbon supported them, through whose intercession with Don Martinio de Mello they were at last released. (Smith, *Use and Abuse of Freemasonry*, p. 206.)

Allah. (Assyrian (Fig. 1), *ilu;* Aramaic, אלה, *elah;* Hebrew, אלוה, *elôah*.) The Arabic name of God, derived from (Fig. 2) *ilâh*, god, and the article (Fig. 3) *al*, expressing the God by way of eminence. In the great profession of the Unity, on which is founded the religion of Islam, both terms are used, as, pronounced " Lá iláha ill' Alláh," there is no god but God, the real meaning of the expression being, " There is only one God." Mohammed relates

that in his night journey from Mecca to Jerusalem, on ascending through the seven heavens, he beheld above the throne of God this formula; and the green standard of the

(Fig. 1.)   (Fig. 2.)   (Fig. 3.)

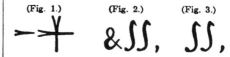

Prophet was adorned with the mystic sentence. It is the first phrase lisped by the infant, and the devout Moslem utters the profession of the faith at all times, in joy, in sorrow, in praise, in prayer, in battle, and with his departing

breath the words are wafted to heaven; for among the peculiar virtues of these words is that they may be spoken without any motion of the lips. The mourners on their way to the grave continue the strain in melancholy tones. Around the supreme name is clustered the masbaha, or rosary, of the ninety-nine beautiful names of God, which are often repeated by the Mohammedan in his devotions.

[W. S. Paterson.]

Allegiance. Every Mason owes allegiance to the Lodge, Chapter, or other body of which he is a member, and also to the Grand Lodge, Grand Chapter or other supreme authority from which that body has received its charter. But this is not a divided allegiance. If, for instance, the edicts of a Grand and a Subordinate Lodge conflict, there is no question which is to be obeyed. Supreme or governing bodies in Masonry claim and must receive a paramount allegiance.

Allegory. A discourse or narrative in which there is a literal and a figurative sense, a patent and a concealed meaning; the literal or patent sense being intended, by analogy or comparison, to indicate the figurative or concealed one. Its derivation from the Greek, ἄλλος and ἀγορεύειν, *to say something different,* that is, to say something where the language is one thing and the true meaning another, exactly expresses the character of an allegory. It has been said that there is no essential difference between an allegory and a symbol. There is not in design, but there is in their character. An allegory may be interpreted without any previous conventional agreement, but a symbol cannot. Thus, the legend of the Third Degree is an allegory, evidently to be interpreted as teaching a restoration to life; and this we learn from the legend itself, without any previous understanding. The sprig of acacia is a symbol of the immortality of the soul. But this we know only because such meaning had been conventionally determined when the symbol was first established. It is evident, then, that an allegory whose meaning is obscure is imperfect. The enigmatical meaning should be easy of interpretation; and hence

Lemière, a French poet, has said: "L'allegorie habite un palais diaphane"—*Allegory lives in a transparent palace*. All the legends of Freemasonry are more or less allegorical, and whatever truth there may be in some of them in an historical point of view, it is only as allegories or legendary symbols that they are of importance. The English lectures have therefore very properly defined Freemasonry to be " a system of morality veiled in allegory and illustrated by symbols."

The allegory was a favorite figure among the ancients, and to the allegorizing spirit are we to trace the construction of the entire Greek and Roman mythology. Not less did it prevail among the older Aryan nations, and its abundant use is exhibited in the religions of Brahma and Zoroaster. The Jewish Rabbis were greatly addicted to it, and carried its employment, as Maimonides intimates (*More Nevochim*, III., xliii.), sometimes to an excess. Their *Midrash*, or system of commentaries on the sacred book, is almost altogether allegorical. Aben Ezra, a learned Rabbi of the twelfth century, says, " The Scriptures are like bodies, and allegories are like the garments with which they are clothed. Some are thin like fine silk, and others are coarse and thick like sackcloth." Our Lord, to whom this spirit of the Jewish teachers in his day was familiar, inculcated many truths in parables, all of which were allegories. The primitive Fathers of the Christian Church were thus infected; and Origen (*Epist. ad Dam.*), who was especially addicted to the habit, tells us that all the Pagan philosophers should be read in this spirit: " hoc facere solemus quando philosophos legimus." Of modern allegorizing writers, the most interesting to Masons are Lee, the author of *The Temple of Solomon portrayed by Scripture Light*, and John Bunyan, who wrote *Solomon's Temple Spiritualized*.

Alliance, Sacred. An organization of twenty-one brethren possessing the ultimate degree of the Scottish Rite formed in New York, September 19, 1872, who assemble annually on that day. One by one, in the due course of time, this Assembly is to decrease until the sad duty will devolve on some one to banquet alone with twenty draped chairs and covers occupied by the imaginary presence of his fellows. It was instituted to commemorate the breaking of a dead-lock in the close corporation of the Supreme Council by the admission of four very prominent members of the Fraternity.

Allied Masonic Degrees. A body has been formed in England called the Grand Council of the Allied Masonic Degrees, in order to govern various Degrees or Orders having no central authority of their own. The principal degrees controlled by it are those of St. Lawrence the Martyr, Knight of Constantinople, Grand Tiler of King Solomon, Secret Monitor, Red Cross of Babylon, and Grand High Priest, besides a large number, perhaps about fifty, of "side degrees," of which some are actively worked and some are not.

Allocution. The address of the presiding officer of a Supreme Council of the Ancient and Accepted Scottish Rite is sometimes so called. It was first used by the Council for the Southern Jurisdiction of the United States, and is derived from the usage of the Roman Church, where certain addresses of the Pope to the Cardinals are called allocutions, and this is to be traced to the customs of Pagan Rome, where the harangues of the Generals to their soldiers were called *allocutions*.

Allowed. In the old manuscript Constitutions, this word is found in the now unusual sense of " accepted." Thus, " Every Mason of the Craft that is Mason *allowed*, ye shall do to him as ye would be done unto yourself." (Lansdowne MS., *circa* 1600.) *Mason allowed* means *Mason accepted*, that is, *approved*. Phillips, in his *New World of Words* (1690), defines the verb *allow*, " to give or grant; to approve of; to permit or suffer." Latimer, in one of his sermons, uses it in this sense of approving or accepting, thus: " St. Peter, in forsaking his old boat and nets, was *allowed* as much before God as if he had forsaken all the riches in the world." In a similar sense is the word used in the Office of Public Baptism of Infants, in the Common Prayer-Book of the Church of England.

All-Seeing Eye. An important symbol of the Supreme Being, borrowed by the Freemasons from the nations of antiquity. Both the Hebrews and the Egyptians appear to have derived its use from that natural inclination of figurative minds to select an organ as the symbol of the function which it is intended peculiarly to discharge. Thus, the foot was often adopted as the symbol of swiftness, the arm of strength, and the hand of fidelity. On the same principle, the open eye was selected as the symbol of watchfulness, and the eye of God as the symbol of Divine watchfulness and care of the universe. The use of the symbol in this sense is repeatedly to be found in the Hebrew writers. Thus, the Psalmist says (Ps. xxxiv. 15): " The eyes of the Lord are upon the righteous, and his ears are open unto their cry," which explains a subsequent passage (Ps. cxxi. 4), in which it is said: " Behold, he that keepeth Israel shall neither slumber nor sleep."

In the Apocryphal *Book of the Conversation of God with Moses on Mount Sinai*, translated by the Rev. W. Cureton from an Arabic MS. of the fifteenth century, and published by the Philobiblon Society of London, the idea of the eternal watchfulness of God is thus beautifully allegorized:

" Then Moses said to the Lord, O Lord, dost thou sleep or not? The Lord said unto Moses, I never sleep: but take a cup and fill it with water. Then Moses took a cup and filled it with water, as the Lord commanded him. Then the Lord cast into the heart of Moses the breath of slumber; so he slept, and the cup fell from his hand, and the water which was therein was spilled. Then Moses awoke from his sleep. Then said God to Moses, I declare by my power, and by my glory, that if I were to withdraw my providence from the heavens and the earth, for no longer a space of time than thou hast slept, they would at once fall to ruin and confusion, like as the cup fell from thy hand."

On the same principle, the Egyptians represented Osiris, their chief deity, by the symbol of an open eye, and placed this hieroglyphic of him in all their temples. His symbolic name, on the monuments, was represented by the eye accompanying a throne, to which was sometimes added an abbreviated figure of the god, and sometimes what has been called a hatchet, but which may as correctly be supposed to be a representation of a square.

The All-Seeing Eye may then be considered as a symbol of God manifested in his omnipresence—his guardian and preserving character—to which Solomon alludes in the Book of Proverbs (xv. 3) when he says: "The eyes of the Lord are in every place, beholding (or, as in the Revised Version, keeping watch upon) the evil and the good." It is a symbol of the Omnipresent Deity.

All-Souls' Day. The 2d of November. A festival in the Romish Church for prayers in behalf of all the faithful dead. It is kept as a feast day by Chapters of Rose Croix.

Almanac, Masonic. Almanacs for the special use of the Fraternity are annually published in many countries of Europe, but the custom has not extended to America. As early as 1752, we find an *Almanach des Francs-Maçons en Écosse* published at The Hague. This, or a similar work, was continued to be published annually at the same place until the year 1778. (Kloss, *Bibliographie*, Nos. 107–9.) The first English work of the kind appeared in 1775, under the title of *The Freemason's Calendar, or an Almanac for the year 1775, containing, besides an accurate and useful Calendar of all remarkable occurrences for the year, many useful and curious particulars relating to Masonry. Inscribed to Lord Petre, G. M., by a Society of Brethren. London, printed for the Society of Stationers.* This work was without any official authority, but two years after the *Freemason's Calendar for 1777* was published "under the sanction of the Grand Lodge of England." A *Masonic Year Book* is now issued annually by the Grand Lodge of England, and most of the English Provinces publish Masonic Almanacs.

Almighty. In Hebrew אל שדי, *El Shaddai.* The name by which God was known to the patriarchs before he announced himself to Moses by his tetragrammatonic name of Jehovah. (See Exodus vi. 3.) It refers to his power and might as the Creator and Ruler of the universe, and hence is translated in the Septuagint by παντοκράτωρ, and in the Vulgate by *omnipotens.*

Almond-Tree. When it is said in the passage of Scripture from the twelfth chapter of Ecclesiastes, sometimes read during the ceremonies of the Third Degree, "the almond-tree shall flourish," reference is made to the white flowers of that tree, and the allegoric signification is to old age, when the hairs of the head shall become gray.

Almoner. An officer elected or appointed in the continental Lodges of Europe to take charge of the contents of the alms-box, to carry into effect the charitable resolutions of the Lodge, and to visit sick and needy brethren. A physician is usually selected in preference to any other member for this office. An almoner may also be appointed among the officers of an English Lodge. In the United States the officer does not exist, his duties being performed by a committee of charity. It is an important office in all bodies of the Scottish Rite.

Alms-Box. A box which, toward the close of the Lodge, is handed around by an appropriate officer for the reception of such donations for general objects of charity as the brethren may feel disposed to bestow. This laudable custom is very generally practised in the Lodges of England, Scotland, and Ireland, and universally in those of the Continent. The newly initiated candidate is expected to contribute more liberally than the other members. Bro. Hyde Clarke says (*Lon. Freem. Mag.*, 1859, p. 1166) that "some brethren are in the habit, on an occasion of thanksgiving with them, to contribute to the box of the Lodge more than on other occasions." This custom has not been adopted in the Lodges of America, except in those of French origin and in those of the Ancient and Accepted Scottish Rite.

Almsgiving. Although almsgiving, or the pecuniary relief of the destitute, was not one of the original objects for which the Institution of Freemasonry was established, yet, as in every society of men bound together by a common tie, it becomes incidentally, yet necessarily, a duty to be practised by all its members in their individual as well as in their corporate capacity. In fact, this virtue is intimately interwoven with the whole superstructure of the Institution, and its practise is a necessary corollary from all its principles. At an early period in his initiation the candidate is instructed in the beauty of charity by the most impressive ceremonies, which are not easily to be forgotten, and which, with the same benevolent design, are repeated from time to time during his advancement to higher degrees, in various forms and under different circumstances. "The true Mason," says Bro. Pike, " must be, and must have a right to be, content with himself; and he can be so only when he lives not for himself alone, but for others who need his assistance and have a claim upon his sympathy." And the same eloquent writer lays down this rule for a Mason's almsgiving: " Give, looking for nothing again, without consideration of future advantages; give to children, to old men, to the unthankful, and the dying, and to those you shall never see again; for else your alms or courtesy is not charity, but traffic and merchandise. And omit not to relieve the needs of your enemy and him who does you injury." (See *Exclusiveness of Masonry.*)

Alnwick Manuscript. This manuscript, which is now in the possession of the Newcastle College of the "Societas Rosicruciana in Anglia," is written on twelve quarto pages as a preface to the minute-book of the "Company and Fellowship of Freemasons of a Lodge held at Alnwick," where it appears under the heading of "The Masons' Constitutions." The date of the document is September 29, 1701, "being the general head meeting day." It was first published in 1871 in Hughan's *Masonic Sketches and Reprints* (Amer. ed.), and again in 1872 by the same author in his *Old Charges of the British Freemasons*. In this latter work, Bro. Hughan says of the records of this old Lodge that, "ranging from 1703 to 1757 they mostly refer to indentures, fines, and initiations, the Lodge from first to last remaining true to its operative origin. The members were required annually to 'appear at the Parish Church of Alnwicke with their aprons on and common squares as aforesaid on St. John's Day in Christmas, when a sermon was provided and preached by some clergyman at their appointment.' A. D. 1708." The MS. has since been reproduced in facsimile by the Newcastle College of Rosicrucians in 1895.

Al-om-Jah. In the Egyptian mysteries, this is said to have been the name given to the aspirant in the highest degree as the secret name of the Supreme Being. In its component parts we may recognize the אל, Al or El of the Hebrews, the Aum or triliteral name of the Indian mysteries, and the יה Jah of the Syrians.

Aloyau, Société de l'. The word *Aloyau* is the French name for *a sirloin of beef* and hence the title of this society in English would be *The Society of the Sirloin*. It was a Masonic association, which existed in France before the revolution of 1789, until its members were dispersed at that time. They professed to be the possessors of many valuable documents relating to the Knights Templar and, besides, to be (*Acta Latomorum*, i., 292) their successors. (See *Temple, Order of the*.)

Alpha and Omega. The first and last letters of the Greek language, referred to in the Royal Master and some of the higher degrees. They are explained by this passage in Revelations, ch. xxii., v. 13.: "I am Alpha and Omega, the beginning and the end, the first and the last." Alpha and Omega is, therefore, one of the appellations of God, equivalent to the beginning and end of all things, and so referred to in Isaiah xliv. 6, "I am the first and I am the last."

Alphabet, Angels'. In the old rituals of the Fourth or Secret Master's Degree of the Scottish and some other Rites, we find this passage: "The seventy-two names, like the name of the Divinity, are to be taken to the Kabbalistic Tree and the Angels' Alphabet." The Kabbalistic Tree is a name given by the Kabbalists to the arrangement of the *ten Sephiroth* (which see). The Angels' Alphabet is called by the Hebrews כתב המלכים, *chetab hamalachim*, or the writing of the angels. Gaffarel says (*Curios. Inouis.*, ch. xiii., 2) that the stars, according to the opinion of the Hebrew writers, are ranged in the heavens in the form of letters, and that it is possible to read there whatsoever of importance is to happen throughout the universe. And the great English Hermetic philosopher, Robert Fludd, says, in his *Apology for the Brethren of the Rosy Cross*, that there are characters in the heavens formed from the disposition of the stars, just as geometric lines and ordinary letters are formed from points; and he adds, that those to whom God has granted the hidden knowledge of reading these characters will also know not only whatever is to happen, but all the secrets of philosophy. The letters thus arranged in the form of stars are called the Angels' Alphabet. They have the power and articulation but not the form of the Hebrew letters, and the Kabbalists say that in them Moses wrote the tables of the law. The astrologers, and after them the alchemists, made much use of this alphabet; and its introduction into any of the high degree rituals is an evidence of the influence exerted on these degrees by the Hermetic philosophy. Agrippa in his *Occult Philosophy*, and Kircher in his *Œdipus Egyptiacus*, and some other writers, have given copies of this alphabet. It may also be found in Johnson's *Typographia*. But it is in the mystical books of the Kabbalists that we must look for full instructions on this subject.

Alphabet, Hebrew. Nearly all of the significant words in the Masonic rituals are of Hebrew origin, and in writing them in the rituals the Hebrew letters are frequently used. For convenience of reference, that alphabet is here given. The Hebrews, like other ancient nations, had no figures, and therefore made use of the letters of their alphabet instead of numbers, each letter having a particular numerical value. They are, therefore, affixed in the following table:

Aleph	א	A	1
Beth	ב	B	2
Gimel	ג	G	3
Daleth	ד	D	4
He	ה	H	5
Vau	ו	V or O	6
Zain	ז	Z	7
Cheth	ח	CH	8
Teth	ט	T	9
Yod	י	I or Y	10
Caph	כ	C or K	20
Lamed	ל	L	30
Mem	מ	M	40
Nun	נ	N	50
Samech	ס	S	60
Ain	ע	Guttural	70
Pe	פ	P	80
Tsaddi	צ	Tz	90
Koph	ק	Q or K	100
Resh	ר	R	200
Shin	ש	SH	300
Tau	ת	T	400
Final Caph	ך	C or K	500
Final Mem	ם	M	600
Final Nun	ן	N	700
Final Pe	ף	P	800
Final Tsaddi	ץ	TZ	900

Alphabet, Masonic. See *Cipher Writing*.

Alphabet, Number of Letters in. In the Sandwich Island alphabet there are 12 letters; the Burmese, 19; Italian, 20; Bengalese, 21; Hebrew, Syrian, Chaldee, Phœnician, and Samaritan, 22 each; Latin, 23; Greek, 24; French, 25; German, Dutch, and English, 26 each; Spanish and Sclavonic, 27 each; Persian and Coptic, 32 each; Georgian, 35; Armenian, 38; Russian, 41; Muscovite, 43; Sanskrit and Japanese, 50 each; Ethiopic and Tartarian, 202 each.

Alphabet, Samaritan. It is believed by scholars that, previous to the captivity, the alphabet now called the Samaritan was employed by the Jews in transcribing the copies of the law, and that it was not until their return from Babylon that they adopted, instead of their ancient characters, the Chaldee or square letters, now called the Hebrew, in which the sacred text, as restored by Ezra, was written. Hence, in the more recent rituals of the Scottish Rite, especially those used in the United States, the Samaritan character is beginning to be partially used. For convenience of reference, it is therefore here inserted. The letters are the same in number as the Hebrew, with the same power and the same names; the only difference is in form.

Aleph		Lamed	
Beth		Mem	
Gimel		Nun	
Daleth		Samech	
He		Ayin	
Vau		Pe	
Zain		Tsade	
Cheth		Koph	
Teth		Resch	
Yod		Shin	
Kaph		Tau	

Alpina. In 1836, and some years afterward, General Assemblies of the Masons of Switzerland were convened at Zurich, Berne, and Basle, which resulted in the union of the two Masonic authorities of that confederation, under the name of the Grand Lodge Alpina. The new Grand Lodge was organized at Zurich, by fourteen Lodges, on the 24th of July, 1844.

In 1910 it had 34 Lodges under its jurisdiction with a membership of 3,842.

Altar. The most important article of furniture in a Lodge room is undoubtedly the altar. It is worth while, then, to investigate its character and its relation to the altars of other religious institutions. The definition of an altar is very simple. It is a structure elevated above the ground, and appropriated to some service connected with worship, such as the offering of oblations, sacrifices, or prayers.

Altars, among the ancients, were generally made of turf or stone. When permanently erected and not on any sudden emergency, they were generally built in regular courses of Masonry, and usually in a cubical form. Altars were erected long before temples. Thus, Noah is said to have erected one as soon as he came forth from the ark. Herodotus gives the Egyptians the credit of being the first among the heathen nations who invented altars.

Among the ancients, both Jews and Gentiles, altars were of two kinds—for incense and for sacrifice. The latter were always erected in the open air, outside and in front of the Temple. Altars of incense only were permitted within the Temple walls. Animals were slain, and offered on the altars of burnt-offerings. On the altars of incense, bloodless sacrifices were presented and incense was burnt to the Deity.

The Masonic altar, which, like everything else in Masonry, is symbolic, appears to combine the character and uses of both of these altars. It is an altar of sacrifice, for on it the candidate is directed to lay his passions and vices as an oblation to the Deity, while he offers up the thoughts of a pure heart as a fitting incense to the Grand Architect of the Universe. The altar is, therefore, the most holy place in a Lodge.

Among the ancients, the altar was always invested with peculiar sanctity. Altars were places of refuge, and the supplicants who fled to them were considered as having placed themselves under the protection of the Deity to whom the altar was consecrated, and to do violence even to slaves and criminals at the altar, or to drag them from it, was regarded as an act of violence to the Deity himself, and was hence a sacrilegious crime.

The marriage covenant among the ancients was always solemnized at the altar, and men were accustomed to make all their solemn contracts and treaties by taking oaths at altars. An oath taken or a vow made at the altar was considered as more solemn and binding than one assumed under other circumstances. Hence, Hannibal's father brought him to the Carthaginian altar when he was about to make him swear eternal enmity to the Roman power.

In all the religions of antiquity, it was the usage of the priests and the people to pass around the altar in the course of the sun, that is to say, from the east, by the way of the south, to the west, singing pæans or hymns of praise as a part of their worship.

From all this we see that the altar in Masonry is not merely a convenient article of furniture, intended, like a table, to hold a Bible. It is a sacred utensil of religion, intended, like the altars of the ancient temples, for religious uses, and thus identifying Masonry, by its necessary existence in our Lodges, as a religious institution. Its presence should also lead the contemplative Mason to view the ceremonies in which it is employed with solemn reverence, as being part of a really religious worship.

The situation of the altar in the French and Scottish Rites is in front of the Worshipful Master, and, therefore, in the East. In the York Rite, the altar is placed in the center of the room, or more properly a little to the East of the center.

The form of a Masonic altar should be a cube, about three feet high, and of corresponding proportions as to length and width, having, in imitation of the Jewish altar, four horns, one at each corner. The Holy Bible with the Square and Compass should be spread open

upon it, while around it are to be placed three lights. These lights are to be in the East, West, and South, and should be arranged as in the annexed diagram. The stars show the position of the light in the East, West, and South. The black dot represents the position North of the altar where there is no light, because in Masonry the North is the place of darkness.

Altenburg, Congress of. Altenberg is a small place in the Grand Dukedom of Weimar, about two miles from the city of Jena. Here in the month of June, 1764, the notorious Johnson, or Leucht, who called himself the Grand Master of the Knights Templar and the head of the Rite of Strict Observance, assembled a Masonic congress for the purpose of establishing this Rite and its system of Templar Masonry. But he was denounced and expelled by the Baron de Hund, who, having proved Johnson to be an impostor and charlatan, was himself proclaimed Grand Master of the German Masons by the congress. (See *Johnson* and *Hund;* also *Strict Observance, Rite of.*)

Altenburg, Lodge at. One of the oldest Lodges in Germany is the Lodge of " Archimedes of the Three Tracing Boards " (*Archimedes zu den drei Reissbreutern*) in Altenburg. It was instituted January 31, 1742, by a deputation from Leipsic. In 1775 it joined the Grand Lodge of Berlin, but in 1788 attached itself to the Eclectic Union at Frankfort-on-the-Main, which body it left in 1801, and established a directory of its own, and installed a Lodge at Gera and another at Schneeberg. In the year 1803 the Lodge published a *Book of Constitutions* in a folio of 244 pages, a work which is now rare, and which Lenning says is one of the most valuable contributions to Masonic literature. Three Masonic journals were also produced by the Altenburg school of historians and students, one of which —the *Bruderblätter*—continued to appear until 1854. In 1804 the Lodge struck a medal upon the occasion of erecting a new hall. In 1842 it celebrated its centennial anniversary.

Amal-sagghi. (Great labor.) The name of the 5th step of the mystic ladder of Kadosh, A. A. Scottish Rite.

Amaranth. A plant well known to the ancients, the Greek name of which signifies " never withering." It is the *Celosia cristata* of the botanists. The dry nature of the flowers causes them to retain their freshness for a very long time, and Pliny says, although incorrectly, that if thrown into water they will bloom anew. Hence it is a symbol of immortality, and was used by the ancients in their funeral rites. It is often placed on coffins at the present day with a like symbolic meaning, and is hence one of the decorations of a Sorrow Lodge.

Amaranth, Order of the. Instituted by Queen Christina of Sweden in 1653, and numbering 31, composed of 15 knights, 15 ladies, and the Queen as the Grandmistress. The insignia consisted of two letters A interlaced, one being inverted, within a laurel crown, and bearing the motto, *Dolce nella memoria.* The annual festival of this equestrian Order was held at the Epiphany. A society of a similar name, androgynous in its nature, was instituted in 1883, under the supervision of Robert Macoy, of New York, to supplement the Order of the Eastern Star, having a social and charitable purpose, the ritual of which, as well as its constitutional government, has met with much commendation.

Amar-jah. Hebrew אמריה, *God spake;* a significant word in the high degrees of the Ancient and Accepted Scottish Rite.

Amen. Sometimes used as a response to a Masonic prayer, though in England the formula is " so mote it be." The word Amen signifies in Hebrew *verily, truly, certainly.* "Its proper place," says Gesenius, " is where one person confirms the words of another, and adds his wish for success to the other's vows." It is evident, then, that it is the brethren of the Lodge, and not the Master or Chaplain, who should pronounce the word. Yet the custom in the United States is for the Master or Chaplain to say "Amen " and the brethren respond, " So mote it be." It is a response to the prayer. The Talmudists have many superstitious notions in respect to this word. Thus, in one treatise (*Uber Musar*), it is said that whosoever pronounces it with fixed attention and devotion, to him the gates of Paradise will be opened; and, again, whosoever enunciates the word rapidly, his days shall pass rapidly away, and whosoever dwells upon it, pronouncing it distinctly and slowly, his life shall be prolonged.

Amendment. All amendments to the by-laws of a Lodge must be submitted to the Grand or Provincial or District Lodge for its approval.

An amendment to a motion pending before a Lodge takes precedence of the original motion, and the question must be put upon the amendment first. If the amendment be lost, then the question will be on the motion; if the amendment be adopted, then the question will be on the original motion as so amended;

and if then this question be lost, the whole motion falls to the ground.

The principal Parliamentary rules in relation to amendments which are applicable to the business of a Masonic Lodge are the following:

1. An amendment must be made in one of three ways: by adding or inserting certain words, by striking out certain words, or by striking out certain words and inserting others.

2. Every amendment is susceptible of an amendment of itself, but there can be no amendment of the amendment of an amendment; such a piling of questions one upon another would tend to embarrass rather than to facilitate business. " The object which is proposed to be effected by such a proceeding must be sought by rejecting the amendment to the amendment, and then submitting the proposition in the form of an amendment of the first amendment in the form desired." Cushing (*Elem. Law and Pract. Leg. Ass.*, § 1306) illustrates this as follows: " If a proposition consists of AB, and it is proposed to amend by inserting CD, it may be moved to amend the amendment by inserting EF; but it cannot be moved to amend this amendment, as, for example, by inserting G. The only mode by which this can be reached is to reject the amendment in the form in which it is presented, namely, to insert EF, and to move it in the form in which it is desired to be amended, namely, to insert EFG."

3. An amendment once rejected cannot be again proposed.

4. An amendment to strike out certain words having prevailed, a subsequent motion to restore them is out of order.

5. An amendment may be proposed which will entirely change the character and substance of the original motion. The inconsistency or incompatibility of a proposed amendment with the proposition to be amended, though an argument, perhaps, from its rejection by the Lodge, is no reason for its suppression by the presiding officer.

6. An amendment, before it has been proposed to the body for discussion, may be withdrawn by the mover; but after it has once been in possession of the Lodge, it can only be withdrawn by leave of the Lodge. In the Congress of the United States, leave must be obtained by unanimous consent; but the usage in Masonic bodies is to require only a majority vote.

7. An amendment having been withdrawn by the mover, may be again proposed by another member.

8. Several amendments may be proposed to a motion or several amendments to an amendment, and the question will be put on them in the order of their presentation. But as an amendment takes precedence of a motion, so an amendment to an amendment takes precedence of the original amendment.

9. An amendment does not require a seconder, although an original motion always does.

There are many other rules relative to amendments which prevail in Parliamentary bodies, but these appear to be the only ones which regulate this subject in Masonic assemblies.

Amenti. See *Book of the Dead.*

American Mysteries. Among the many evidences of a former state of civilization among the Aborigines of America which seem to prove their origin from the races that inhabit the Eastern hemisphere, not the least remarkable is the existence of Fraternities bound by mystic ties, and claiming, like the Freemasons, to possess an esoteric knowledge, which they carefully conceal from all but the initiated. De Witt Clinton relates, on the authority of a respectable native minister, who had received the signs, the existence of such a society among the Iroquois. The number of the members was limited to fifteen, of whom six were to be of the Seneca tribe, five of the Oneidas, two of the Cayugas, and two of the St. Regis. They claim that their institution has existed from the era of the creation. The times of their meeting they keep secret, and throw much mystery over all their proceedings.

Brinton tells us in his interesting and instructive work on *The Myths of the New World* (p. 285), that among the red race of America " the priests formed societies of different grades of illumination, only to be entered by those willing to undergo trying ordeals, whose secrets were not to be revealed under the severest penalties. The Algonkins had three such grades—the *waubeno*, the *meda*, and the *jossakeed*, the last being the highest. To this no white man was ever admitted. All tribes appear to have been controlled by these secret societies. Alexander von Humboldt mentions one, called that of the Botuto, or Holy Trumpet, among the Indians of the Orinoco, whose members must vow celibacy, and submit to severe scourgings and fasts. The Collahuayas of Peru were a guild of itinerant quacks and magicians, who never remained permanently in one spot."

American Rite. It has been proposed, and I think with propriety, to give this name to the series of degrees conferred in the United States. The York Rite, which is the name by which they are usually designated, is certainly a misnomer, for the York Rite properly consists of only the degrees of Entered Apprentice, Fellow-Craft, and Master Mason, including in the last degree the Holy Royal Arch. This was the Masonry that existed in England at the time of the revival of the Grand Lodge in 1717. The abstraction of the Royal Arch from the Master's Degree, and its location as a separate degree, produced that modification of the York Rite which now exists in England, and which should properly be called the Modern York Rite, to distinguish it from the Ancient York Rite, which consisted of only three degrees. But in the United States still greater additions have been made to the Rite, through the labors of Webb and other lecturers, and the influence insensibly exerted on the Order by the introduction of the Ancient and Accepted Scottish Rite into this country. The American modification of the York Rite, or the American Rite, consists of nine degrees, viz.:

1. Entered Apprentice. 2. Fellow-Craft. 3. Master Mason.	Given in Symbolic Lodges, and under the control of Grand Lodges.
4. Mark Master. 5. Past Master. 6. Most Excellent Master. 7. Holy Royal Arch.	Given in Chapters, and under the control of Grand Chapters.
8. Royal Master. 9. Select Master.	Given in Councils, and under the control of Grand Councils.

A tenth degree, called Super-Excellent Master, is conferred in some Councils as an honorary rather than as a regular degree; but even as such it is repudiated by many Grand Councils. To these, perhaps, should be added three more degrees, namely, Knight of the Red Cross, Knight Templar, and Knight of Malta, which are given in Commanderies, and are under the control of Grand Commanderies, or, as they are sometimes called, Grand Encampments. But the degrees of the Commandery, which are also known as the degrees of Chivalry, can hardly be called a part of the American Rite. The possession of the Eighth and Ninth Degrees is not considered a necessary qualification for receiving them. The true American Rite consists only of the nine degrees above enumerated.

There is, or may be, a Grand Lodge, Grand Chapter, Grand Council, and Grand Commandery in each State, whose jurisdiction is distinct and sovereign within its own territory. There is no General Grand Lodge, or Grand Lodge of the United States, though several efforts have been made to form one (see *General Grand Lodge*); there is a General Grand Chapter, but all Grand Chapters are not subject to it, and a Grand Encampment to which all Grand Commanderies of the States are subject.

American (Military) Union Lodge. In 1776 six Master Masons, four Fellow-Crafts, and one Entered Apprentice, all but one, officers in the Connecticut Line of the Continental army in camp at Roxbury, Mass., petitioned Richard Gridley, Deputy Grand Master of St. John's Grand Lodge, for a warrant forming them into a regular Lodge. On the 15th of February, a warrant was issued to Joel Clark, appointing and constituting him First Master of American Union Lodge, " erected at Roxbury, or wherever your body shall remove on the Continent of America, provided it is where no Grand Master is appointed." The Lodge was duly constituted and almost immediately moved to New York, and met on April 23, 1776, by permission of Dr. Peter Middleton, Grand Master of Masons in the Province of New York. It was agreed at this meeting to petition him to confirm the Massachusetts warrant as, under its terms, they were without authority to meet in New York. Dr. Middleton would not confirm the warrant of Ameri-

can Union Lodge, but in April, 1776, caused a new warrant to be issued to the same brethren, under the name of Military Union Lodge, No. 1, without recalling the former warrant. They thus presented an anomaly of a Lodge holding warrants from and yielding obedience to two Grand Bodies in different jurisdictions. The spirit of the brethren, though, is shown in their adherence to the name American Union in their minutes, and the only direct acknowledgment of the new name is in a minute providing that the Lodge furniture purchased by American Union " be considered only as lent to the Military Union Lodge."

This Lodge followed the Connecticut Line of the Continental army throughout the War of Independence. It was Gen. Samuel Holden Parsons of American Union who returned to the British army Lodge Unity, No. 18, their warrant, which had come into possession of the American army at the taking of Stony Point in 1779. American Union participated in a convention at Morristown, N. J., January 31, 1780, when it was proposed to nominate Gen. Washington as " Grand Master over the thirteen United States of America," and it was on the suggestion of Rev. Israel Evans of American Union that the " Temple of Virtue," for the use of the army and the army Lodges, was erected at New Windsor (Newburgh), N. Y., during the winter of 1782-83. The Lodge followed the army to the Northwest Territory after the War of Independence, and participated in the formation of the Grand Lodge of Ohio. Shortly afterward the Lodge withdrew from the Grand Lodge of Ohio and did not appear on the roll thereafter, but pursued an independent existence for some years. The present American Union Lodge at Marietta, Ohio, No. 1 on the roll of the Grand Lodge of Ohio, was organized by members of the old Lodge. The first minute-book, from the original constitution to April 23, 1783, is in the library of the Grand Lodge of New York. During the war many prominent patriots were members, and several times Washington was recorded as a visitor.

[C. A. B.]

Ameth. Properly, *Emeth*, which see.

Amethyst. Hebrew אחלמה, *achlemah*. The ninth stone in the breastplate of the high priest. The amethyst is a stone in hardness next to the diamond, and of a deep red and blue color resembling the breast of a dove.

Amicists, Order of. A secret association of students, once very extensively existing among the universities of Northern Germany. Thory (*Acta Latomorum*, i., 292) says that this association was first established in the College of Clermont, at Paris. An account of it was published at Halle, in 1799, by F. C. Laukhard, under the title of *Der Mosellaner—oder Amicisten—Orden nach seiner Entstehung, innern Verfassung und Verbreitung auf den deutschen Universitäten*, &c. The Order was finally suppressed by the imperial government.

Amis Réunis, Loge des. The Lodge of United Friends, founded at Paris in 1771, was distinguished for the talents of many of its members, among whom was Savalette de Langes, and played for many years an important part in the affairs of French Masonry. In its bosom was originated, in 1775, the Rite of Philalethes. In 1784 it convoked the first Congress of Paris, which was held in 1785, for the laudable purpose of endeavoring to disentangle Freemasonry from the almost inextricable confusion into which it had fallen by the invention of so many rites and new degrees. The Lodge was in possession of a valuable library for the use of its members, and had an excellent cabinet of the physical and natural sciences. Upon the death of Savalette, who was the soul of the Lodge, it fell into decay, and its books, manuscripts, and cabinet were scattered. (Clavel, p. 171.) All of its library that was valuable was transferred to the archives of the Mother Lodge of the Philosophic Scottish Rite. Barruel gives a brilliant picture of the concerts, balls, and suppers given by this Lodge in its halcyon days, to which " les Crésus de la Maçonnerie " congregated, while a few superior members were engaged, as he says, in hatching political and revolutionary schemes, but really in plans for the elevation of Masonry as a philosophic institution. (Barruel, *Mémoires pour servir à l'Histoire du Jacobinisme,* iv., 343.)

Ammon. See *Amun.*

Ammonitish War. A war to which allusion is made in the Fellow-Craft's Degree. The Ammonites were the descendants of the younger son of Lot, and dwelt east of the river Jordan, but originally formed no part of the land of Canaan, the Israelites having been directed not to molest them for the sake of their great progenitor, the nephew of Abraham. But in the time of Jephthah, their king having charged the Israelites with taking away a part of his territory, the Ammonites crossed the river Jordan and made war upon the Israelites. Jephthah defeated them with great slaughter, and took an immense amount of spoil. It was on account of this spoil—in which they had no share—that the Ephraimites rebelled against Jephthah, and gave him battle. (See *Ephraimites.*)

Amor Honor et Justitia. A motto of the Grand Lodge of England used prior to the union of 1813, which is to be found graven on the " Masonic Token " of 1794, commemorative of the election of the Prince of Wales as M. W. Grand Master, November 24, 1790.

Amphibalus. See *Saint Amphibalus.*

Ample Form. When the Grand Master is present at the opening or closing of the Grand Lodge, it is said to be opened or closed " in ample form." Any ceremony performed by the Grand Master is said to be done " in ample form"; when performed by the Deputy, it is said to be "in due form"; and by any other temporarily presiding officer, it is "in form." (See *Form.*)

Amru. The name given to the Phœnician carpenter, who is represented in some legends as one of the Assassins, Fanor and Metusael being the other two.

Amshaspands. The name given in the Per-

sian Avesta to the six good genii or powerful angels who continuously wait round the throne of Ormudz, or Ormazd. Also the name of the six summer months and the six productive working properties of nature.

Amulet. See *Talisman.*

Amun. The Supreme God among the Egyptians. He was a concealed god, and is styled " the Celestial Lord who sheds light on hidden things." From him all things emanated, though he created nothing. He corresponded with the Jove of the Greeks, and, consequently, with the Jehovah of the Jews. His symbol was a ram, which animal was sacred to him. On the monuments he is represented with a human face and limbs free, having two tall straight feathers on his head, issuing from a red cap; in front of the plumes a disk is sometimes seen. His body is colored a deep blue. He is sometimes, however, represented with the head of a ram, and the Greek and Roman writers in general agree in describing him as being ram-headed. There is some confusion on this point. Kenrick says that Nouf was, in the majority of instances, the ram-headed god of the Egyptians; but he admits that Amun may have been sometimes so represented.

Anachronism. Ritual makers, especially when they have been ignorant and uneducated, have often committed anachronisms by the introduction into Masonic ceremonies of matters entirely out of time. Thus, the use of a bell to indicate the hour of the night, practised in the Third Degree; the placing of a celestial and a terrestrial globe on the summit of the pillars of the porch, in the Second Degree; and quotations from the New Testament and references to the teachings of Christ, in the Mark Degree, are all anachronisms. But, although it were to be wished that these disturbances of the order of time had been avoided, the fault is not really of much importance. The object of the ritualist was simply to convey an idea, and this he has done in the way which he supposed would be most readily comprehended by those for whom the ritual was made. The idea itself is old, although the mode of conveying it may be new. Thus, the bell is used to indicate a specific point of time, the globes to symbolize the universality of Masonry, and passages from the New Testament to inculcate the practise of duties whose obligations are older than Christianity.

Anagram. The manufacture of anagrams out of proper names or other words has always been a favorite exercise, sometimes to pay a compliment — as when Dr. Burney made *Honor est a Nilo* out of Horatio Nelson—and sometimes for purposes of secrecy, as when Roger Bacon concealed under an anagram one of the ingredients in his recipe for gunpowder, that the world might not too easily become acquainted with the composition of so dangerous a material. The same method was adopted by the adherents of the house of Stuart when they manufactured their system of high degrees as a political engine, and thus, under an anagrammatic form, they made many words to designate their friends or, principally, their enemies of the opposite party. Most of these words it has now become impossible to restore to their original form, but several are readily decipherable. Thus, among the Assassins of the Third Degree, who symbolized, with them, the foes of the monarchy, we recognize *Romvel* as *Cromwell*, and *Hoben* as *Bohun*, Earl of Essex. It is only thus that we can ever hope to trace the origin of such words in the high degrees as Tercy, Stolkin, Morphey, etc. To look for them in any Hebrew root would be a fruitless task. The derivation of many of them, on account of the obscurity of the persons to whom they refer, is, perhaps, forever lost; but of others the research for their meaning may be more successful.

Ananiah. The name of a learned Egyptian, who is said to have introduced the Order of Mizraim from Egypt into Italy. Dr. Oliver (*Landm.*, ii., 75) states the tradition, but doubts its authenticity. It is in all probability apocryphal. (See *Mizraim, Rite of.*)

Anchor and Ark. The anchor, as a symbol of hope, does not appear to have belonged to the ancient and classic system of symbolism. The Goddess *Spes*, or Hope, was among the ancients represented in the form of an erect woman, holding the skirts of her garments in her left hand, and in her right a flower-shaped cup. As an emblem of hope, the anchor is peculiarly a Christian, and thence a Masonic, symbol. It is first found inscribed on the tombs in the catacombs of Rome, and the idea of using it is probably derived from the language of St. Paul (Heb. vi. 19), "which

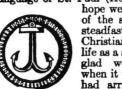

hope we have as an anchor of the soul both sure and steadfast." The primitive Christians "looked upon life as a stormy voyage, and glad were the voyagers when it was done, and they had arrived safe in port. Of this the anchor was a symbol, and when their brethren carved it over the tomb, it was to them an expression of confidence that he who slept beneath had reached the haven of eternal rest." (Kip, *Catacombs of Rome*, p. 112.) The strict identity between this and the Masonic idea of the symbol will be at once observed.

"The anchor," says Mrs. Jameson (*Sac. and Legend*, Art. I., 34), "is the Christian symbol of immovable firmness, hope, and patience; and we find it very frequently in the catacombs, and on the ancient Christian gems." It is the peculiar attribute of St. Clement, and is often inscribed on churches dedicated to him.

But there is a necessary connection between an anchor and a ship, and hence, the latter image has also been adopted as a symbol of the voyage of life; but, unlike the anchor, it was not confined to Christians, but was with the heathens also a favorite emblem of the close of life. Kip thinks the idea may have

been derived from them by the Christian Fathers, who gave it a more elevated meaning. The ship is in Masonry substituted by the ark. Mrs. Jameson says (*ut supra*) that "the Ark of Noah floating safe amid the deluge, in which all things else were overwhelmed, was an obvious symbol of the Church of Christ. . . . The bark of St. Peter tossed in the storm, and by the Redeemer guided safe to land, was also considered as symbolical."

These symbolical views have been introduced into Masonry, with, however, the more extended application which the universal character of the Masonic religious faith required. Hence, in the Third Degree, whose teachings all relate to life and death, "the ark and anchor are emblems of a well-grounded hope and a well-spent life. They are emblematical of that Divine ark which safely wafts us over this tempestuous sea of troubles, and that anchor which shall safely moor us in a peaceful harbor where the wicked cease from troubling and the weary shall find rest." Such is the language of the lecture of the Third Degree, and it gives all the information that is required on the esoteric meaning of these symbols. The history I have added of their probable origin will no doubt be interesting to the Masonic student.

Anchor, Knight of the. See *Knight of the Anchor*.

Anchor, Order of Knights and Ladies of the. A system of androgynous Masonry which arose in France in the year 1745. It was a schism which sprang out of the Order of Felicity, from which it differed only in being somewhat more refined. Its existence was not more durable than that of its predecessor. (Clavel, *Hist. pitt. de la F. M.*, p. 111.) (See *Felicity, Order of.*)

Ancient and Accepted Rite. See *Scottish Rite*.

Ancient Craft Masonry. This is the name given to the three symbolic degrees of Entered Apprentice, Fellow-Craft, and Master Mason. The degree of Royal Arch is not generally included under this appellation; although, when considered (as it really is) a complement of the Third Degree, it must of course constitute a part of Ancient Craft Masonry. In the articles of union between the two Grand Lodges of England, adopted in 1813, it is declared that "pure Antient Masonry consists of three degrees and no more, viz.: those of the Entered Apprentice, the Fellow Craft, and the Master Mason, including the Supreme Order of the Holy Royal Arch."

Ancient Free and Accepted Masons. The title most generally assumed by the English and American Grand Lodges. (See *Titles of Grand Lodges*.)

Ancient or Antient or Atholl Masons. In 1751 some Irish Masons in London established a body which they called the "Grand Lodge of England according to the Old Institutions," and they styled themselves "Ancients" and the members of the regular Grand Lodge, established in 1717, "Moderns." Thus Dermott, in his *Ahiman Rezon*, divides the Masons of England into two classes, as follows:

" The Ancients, under the name of Free and Accepted Masons, according to the old Institutions; the Moderns, under the name of Freemasons of England. And though a similarity of names, yet they differ exceedingly in makings, ceremonies, knowledge, Masonic language, and installations; so much, that they always have been, and still continue to be, *two distinct societies*, totally independent of each other." (7th ed., p. xxx.)

The " Ancients " maintained that they alone preserved the ancient tenets and practises of Masonry, and that the regular Lodges had altered the Landmarks and made innovations, as they undoubtedly had done about the year 1730, when Prichard's *Masonry Dissected* appeared.

For a long time it was supposed that the " Ancients " were a schismatic body of seceders from the Premier Grand Lodge of England, but Bro. Henry Sadler, in his *Masonic Facts and Fictions*, has proved that this view is erroneous, and that they were really Irish Masons who settled in London.

In the year 1756, Laurence Dermott, then Grand Secretary, and subsequently the Deputy Grand Master of the Grand Lodge of the Ancients, published a *Book of Constitutions* for the use of the Ancient Masons, under the title of *Ahiman Rezon*, which work went through several editions, and became the code of Masonic law for all who adhered, either in England or America, to the Grand Lodge of the Ancients, while the Grand Lodge of the Moderns, or the regular Grand Lodge of England, and its adherents, were governed by the regulations contained in Anderson's *Constitutions*, the first edition of which had been published in 1723.

The dissensions between the two Grand Lodges of England lasted until the year 1813, when, as will be hereafter seen, the two bodies became consolidated under the name and title of the United Grand Lodge of Ancient Freemasons of England. Four years afterward a similar and final reconciliation took place in America, by the union of the two Grand Lodges in South Carolina. At this day all distinction between the Ancients and Moderns has ceased, and it lives only in the memory of the Masonic student.

What were the precise differences in the rituals of the Ancients and the Moderns, it is now perhaps impossible to discover, as from their esoteric nature they were only orally communicated; but some shrewd and near approximations to their real nature may be drawn by inference from the casual expressions which have fallen from the advocates of each in the course of their long and generally bitter controversies.

It has already been said that the regular Grand Lodge is stated to have made certain changes in the modes of recognition, in consequence of the publication of Samuel Prichard's spurious revelation. These changes were, as we traditionally learn, a simple transposition of certain words, by which that which had originally been *the first became the second*, and that which had been *the second became the first*. Hence Dr. Dalcho, the compiler of the original *Ahiman Rezon* of South Carolina, who was himself made in an Ancient Lodge, but was acquainted with both systems, says (Edit. 1822, p. 193), " *The real difference in point of importance was no greater than it would be to dispute whether the glove should be placed first upon the right or on the left.*" A similar testimony as to the character of these changes is furnished by an address to the Duke of Atholl, the Grand Master of the Grand Lodge of Ancients, in which it is said: " I would beg leave to ask, whether two persons standing in the Guildhall of London, the one facing the statues of Gog and Magog, and the other with his back turned on them, could, with any degree of propriety, quarrel about their stations; as Gog must be on the right of one, and Magog on the right of the other. Such then, and far more insignificant, is the disputatious temper of the seceding brethren, that on no better grounds than the above they choose to usurp a power and to aid in open and direct violation of the regulations they had solemnly engaged to maintain, and by every artifice possible to be devised endeavored to increase their numbers." It was undoubtedly to the relative situation of the pillars of the porch, and the appropriation of their names in the ritual, that these innuendoes referred. As we have them now, they were made by the change effected by the Grand Lodge of Moderns, which transposed the original order in which they existed before the change, and in which order they are still preserved by the continental Lodges of Europe.

It is then admitted that the Moderns did make innovations in the ritual; and although Preston asserts that the changes were made by the regular Grand Lodge to distinguish its members from those made by the Ancient Lodges, it is evident, from the language of the address just quoted, that the innovations were the cause and not the effect of the schism, and the inferential evidence is that the changes were made in consequence of, and as a safeguard against, spurious publications, and were intended, as has already been stated, to distinguish impostors from true Masons, and not schismatic or irregular brethren from those who were orthodox and regular.

But outside of and beyond this transposition of words, there was another difference existing between the Ancients and the Moderns. Dalcho, who was acquainted with both systems, says that the Ancient Masons were in possession of marks of recognition known only to themselves. His language on this subject is positive. " The Ancient York Masons," he says, " were certainly in possession of the original, universal marks, as they were known and given in the Lodges they had left, and which had descended through the Lodge of York, and that of England, down to their day. Besides these, we find they had *peculiar marks of their own*, which were unknown to the body from which they had separated, and were unknown to the rest of the Masonic world. We have, then, the evidence that they had *two sets of marks;* viz.: those which they had brought with them from the original body, and those which they had, we must suppose, themselves devised." (P. 192.)

Dermott, in his *Ahiman Rezon,* confirms this statement of Dalcho, if, indeed, it needs confirmation. He says that "a Modern Mason may with safety communicate all his secrets to an Ancient Mason, but that an Ancient Mason cannot, with like safety, communicate all his secrets to a Modern Mason without further ceremony." And he assigns as a reason for this, that "as a science comprehends an art (though an art cannot comprehend a science), even so Ancient Masonry contains everything valuable among the Moderns, as well as many other things that cannot be revealed without additional ceremonies."

Now, what were these "other things" known by the Ancients, and not known by the Moderns? What were these distinctive marks, which precluded the latter from visiting the Lodges of the former? Written history is of course silent as to these esoteric matters. But tradition, confirmed by, and at the same time explaining, the hints and casual intimations of contemporary writers, leads us to the almost irresistible inference that they were to be found in the different constructions of the Third, or Master's Degree, and the introduction into it of the Royal Arch element; for, as Dr. Oliver (*Hist. Eng. R. A.,* p. 21) says, "the division of the third degree and the fabrication of the English Royal Arch appear, on their own showing, to have been the work of the Ancients." And hence the Grand Secretary of the regular Grand Lodge, or that of the Moderns, replying to the application of an Ancient Mason from Ireland for relief, says: "Our society (*i. e.,* the Moderns) is neither Arch, Royal Arch, nor Ancient, so that you have no right to partake of our charity."

This, then, is the solution of the difficulty. The Ancients, besides preserving the regular order of the words in the First and Second Degrees, which the Moderns had transposed (a transposition which has been retained in the Lodges of Britain and America, but which has never been observed by the continental Lodges of Europe, who continue the usage of the Ancients), also finished the otherwise imperfect Third Degree with its natural complement, the Royal Arch, a complement with which the Moderns were unacquainted, or which they, if they knew it once, had lost.

The following is a list of t e Grand Masters of the Grand Lodge of Ancients from its organization to its dissolution: 1753, Robert Turner; 1754–55, Edward Vaughan; 1756–59, Earl of Blessington; 1760–65, Earl of Kelly; 1766–70, The Hon. Thomas Matthew; 1771–74, third Duke of Atholl; 1775–81, fourth Duke of Atholl; 1782–90, Earl of Antrim; 1791–1813, fourth Duke of Atholl; 1813, Duke of Kent, under whom the reconciliation of the two Grand Lodges was accomplished.

The Grand Lodge of Ancient Masons was, shortly after its organization, recognized by the Grand Lodges of Scotland and Ireland, and, through the ability and energy of its officers, but especially Laurence Dermott, at one time its Grand Secretary, and afterward its Deputy Grand Master, and the author of its *Ahiman Rezon,* or *Book of Constitutions,* it extended its influence and authority into foreign countries and into the British Colonies of America, where it became exceedingly popular, and where it organized several Provincial Grand Lodges, as, for instance, in Massachusetts, New York, Pennsylvania, Virginia, and South Carolina, where the Lodges working under this authority were generally known as "Ancient York Lodges."

In consequence of this, dissensions existed, not only in the mother country, but also in America, for many years, between the Lodges which derived their warrants from the Grand Lodge of Ancients and those which derived theirs from the regular or so-called Grand Lodge of Moderns. But the Duke of Kent having been elected, in 1813, the Grand Master of the Ancients, while his brother, the Duke of Sussex, was Grand Master of the Moderns, a permanent reconciliation was effected between the rival bodies, and by mutual compromises the present "United Grand Lodge of Ancient Freemasons of England" was established.

Similar unions were consummated in America, the last being that of the two Grand Lodges of South Carolina, in 1817, and the distinction between the Ancients and the Moderns was forever abolished, or remains only as a melancholy page in the history of Masonic controversies. From their connection with the Dukes of Atholl, the "Ancient" Masons are sometimes known as "Atholl" Masons.   [E. L. H.]

Ancient Reformed Rite. A Rite differing very slightly from the French Rite, or *Rite Moderne,* of which, indeed, it is said to be only a modification. It is practised by the Grand Lodge of Holland and the Grand Orient of Belgium. It was established in 1783 as one of the results of the Congress of Wilhelmsbad.

Ancient of Days. A title applied, in the visions of Daniel, to Jehovah, to signify that his days are beyond reckoning. Used by Webb in the Most Excellent Master's song.

> "Fulfilled is the promise
> By the ANCIENT OF DAYS,
> To bring forth the cape-stone
> With shouting and praise."

Ancients. See *Ancient Masons.*

Ancient, The. The Third Degree of the German Union of Twenty-two.

Ancient York Masons. One of the names assumed by the Lodges of *Ancient Masons,* which see.

Anderson, James. The Rev. James Anderson, D.D., is well known to all Masons as the compiler of the celebrated *Book of Constitutions.* The date and place of his birth have not yet been discovered with certainty, but the date was probably 1680, and the place, Aberdeen in Scotland, where he was educated and where he probably took the degrees of M.A. and D.D. At some unascertained period he migrated to London, and our first precise knowledge of him, derived from a document in the State Records, is that on February 15, 1709–10. he, as a Presbyterian minister, took over the lease of a chapel in Swallow Street, Piccadilly, from a congregation of French Protestants which desired to dispose of it because of their decreasing prosperity. During the following decade he published several sermons, and is said to have lost a considerable sum of money dabbling in the South Sea scheme.

Where and when his connection with Freemasonry commenced has not yet been discovered, but he must have been a fairly prominent member of the Craft, because on September 29, 1721, he was ordered by the Grand Lodge, which had been established in London in 1717, to "digest the old Gothic Constitutions in a new and better method." On the 27th of December following, his work was finished, and the Grand Lodge appointed a committee of fourteen learned brethren to examine and report upon it. Their report was made on the 25th of March, 1722; and, after a few amendments, Anderson's work was formally approved, and ordered to be printed for the benefit of the Lodges, which was done in 1723. This is now the well-known *Book of Constitutions*, which contains the history of Masonry (or, more correctly, architecture), the *Ancient Charges*, and the *General Regulations*, as the same were in use in many old Lodges. In 1738 a second edition was published. Both editions have become exceedingly rare, and copies of them bring fancy prices among the collectors of old Masonic books. Its intrinsic value is derived only from the fact that it contains the first printed copy of the *Old Charges* and also the *General Regulations*. The history of Masonry which precedes these, and constitutes the body of the work, is fanciful, unreliable, and pretentious to a degree that often leads to absurdity. The Craft is greatly indebted to Anderson for his labors in reorganizing the Institution, but doubtless it would have been better if he had contented himself with giving the records of the Grand Lodge from 1717 to 1738, which are contained in his second edition, and with preserving for us the *Charges* and *Regulations*, which, without his industry, might have been lost. No Masonic writer would now venture to quote Anderson as authority for the history of the Order anterior to the eighteenth century. It must also be added that in the republication of the *Old Charges* in the edition of 1738, he made several important alterations and interpolations, which justly gave some offense to the Grand Lodge, and which render the second edition of no authority in this respect.

In the year 1723, when his first edition of the *Constitutions* appeared, he was Master of Lodge 17, and he was appointed Grand Warden, and also became Chaplain to the Earl of Buchan; in 1732 he published a voluminous work entitled *Royal Genealogies, or the Genealogical Tables of Emperors, Kings and Princes, from Adam to these times;* in 1733 he issued a theological pamphlet on *Unity in Trinity, and Trinity in Unity;* in 1734 he removed with a part of his congregation from his chapel in Swallow Street to one in Lisle Street, Leicester Fields, in consequence of some difference with his people, the nature of which is unknown; in 1735 he represented to Grand Lodge that a new edition of the *Book of Constitutions* was become necessary, and he was ordered to lay his materials before the present and former Grand Officers; in 1738 the new *Book of Constitutions* was approved of by Grand Lodge and ordered to be printed.

Anderson died on May 28, 1739, and was buried in Bunhill Fields with a Masonic funeral, which is thus reported in *The Daily Post* of June 2d: "Last night was interr'd the corpse of Dr. Anderson, a Dissenting Teacher, in a very remarkable deep Grave. His Pall was supported by five Dissenting Teachers, and the Rev. Dr. Desaguliers: It was followed by about a Dozen of Free-Masons, who encircled the Grave; and after Dr. Earle had harangued on the Uncertainty of Life, &c., without one word of the Deceased, the Brethren, in a most solemn dismal Posture, lifted up their Hands, sigh'd, and struck their aprons three times in Honour to the Deceased."

Soon after his death another of his works, entitled *News from Elysium or Dialogues of the Dead*, was issued, and in 1742 there appeared the first volume of a *Genealogical History of the House of Yvery*, also from his pen.

[E. L. H.]

Anderson Manuscript. In the first edition of the *Constitutions of the Freemasons*, published by Dr. Anderson in 1723, the author quotes on pp. 32, 33 from "a certain record of Freemasons, written in the reign of King Edward IV." Preston also cites it in his *Illustrations*, (p. 182, ed. 1788), but states that it is said to have been in the possession of Elias Ashmole, but was unfortunately destroyed, with other papers on the subject of Masonry, at the Revolution. Anderson makes no reference to Ashmole as the owner of the MS., nor to the fact of its destruction. If the statement of Preston was confirmed by other evidence, its title would properly be the "Ashmole MS."; but as it was first mentioned by Anderson, Bro. Hughan has very properly called it the "Anderson Manuscript." It contains the Prince Edwin legend.

André, Christopher Karl. An active Mason, who resided at Brünn, in Moravia, where, in 1798, he was the Director of the Evangelical Academy. He was very zealously employed, about the end of the last century, in connection with other distinguished Masons, in the propagation of the Order in Germany. He was the editor and author of a valuable periodical work, which was published in 5 numbers, 8vo, from 1793 to 1796, at Gotha and Halle under the title of *Der Freimaurer oder compendiöse Bibliothek* *alles Wissenswürdigen über geheime Gesell-schaften* ("The Freemason, or a Compendious Library of everything worthy of notice in relation to Secret Societies"). Besides valuable extracts from contemporary Masonic writers, it contains several essays and treatises by the editor.

Andreä, John Valentine. This distinguished philosopher and amiable moralist, who has been claimed by many writers as the founder of the Rosicrucian Order, was born on the 17th of August, 1586, at the small town of Herrenberg, in Württemberg, where his father exercised clerical functions of a respectable rank. After receiving an excellent education in his native province, he traveled extensively through the principal countries of Europe, and on his return home received the appointment, in 1614, of deacon in the town of Vaihingen. Four years after he was promoted to the office of superintendent at Kalw. In 1639 he was appointed court chaplain and a spiritual privy councilor, and subsequently Protestant prelate of Adelberg, and almoner of the Duke of Württemberg. He died on the 27th of June, 1654, at the age of sixty-eight years.

Andreä was a man of extensive acquirements and of a most feeling heart. By his great abilities he was enabled to elevate himself beyond the narrow limits of the prejudiced age in which he lived, and his literary labors were exerted for the reformation of manners, and for the supply of the moral wants of the times. His writings, although numerous, were not voluminous, but rather brief essays full of feeling, judgment, and chaste imagination, in which great moral, political, and religious sentiments were clothed in such a language of sweetness, and yet told with such boldness of spirit, that, as Herder says, he appears, in his contentious and anathematizing century, like a rose springing up among thorns. Thus, in his *Menippus*, one of the earliest of his works, he has, with great skill and freedom, attacked the errors of the Church and of his contemporaries. His *Herculis Christiani Luctus*, xxiv., is supposed by some persons to have given indirectly, if not immediately, hints to John Bunyan for his *Pilgrim's Progress*.

One of the most important of his works, however, or at least one that has attracted most attention, is his *Fama Fraternitatis*, published in 1615. This and the *Chemische Hochzeit Christiani Rosencreuz*, or "Chemical Nuptials, by Christian Rosencreuz," which is also attributed to him, are the first works in which the Order of the Rosicrucians is mentioned. Arnold, in his *Ketzergeschichte* or "History of Heresy," contends, from these works, that Andreä was the founder of the Rosicrucian Order; others claim a previous existence for it, and suppose that he was simply an annalist of the Order; while a third party deny that any such Order was existing at the time, or afterward, but that the whole was a mere mythical rhapsody, invented by Andreä as a convenient vehicle in which to convey his ideas of reform.

But the whole of this subject is more fully discussed under the head of *Rosicrucianism*, which see.

Andrew, Apprentice and Fellow-Craft of St. (Fr., *Apprenti et Compagnon de St. André;* Ger., *Andreas lehrling und Geselle.*) The Fourth Degree of the Swedish Rite, which is almost precisely the same as the *Elu Secret* of the French Rite.

Andrew, Cross of St. See *Cross, St. Andrew's.*

Andrew, Favorite of St. (Fr., *Favori de St. André.*) Usually called "Knight of the Purple Collar." The Ninth Degree of the Swedish Rite.

Andrew, Grand Scottish Knight of St. See *Knight of St. Andrew.*

Androgynous Degrees. (From ἀνήρ, a man, and γυνή, a woman.) Those degrees of Masonry which are conferred on both men and women. Besides the degrees of the Adoptive Rite, which are practised in France, there are several of these degrees which are, as "side degrees," conferred in America. Such are the "Mason's Wife," conferred on the wives, daughters, sisters, and mothers of Master Masons, and the "Knight and Heroine of Jericho," conferred on the wives and daughters of Royal Arch Masons. A few years ago, Rob. Morris invented, and very generally promulgated through the Western States of this country, a series of androgynous degrees, which he called "The Star of the East." There is another androgynous degree, sometimes conferred on the wives of Royal Arch Masons, known as the "Good Samaritan."

In some parts of the United States these degrees are very popular, while in other places they are never practised, and are strongly condemned as improper innovations. The fact is, that by their friends as well as by their enemies, these so-called degrees have been greatly misrepresented. When females are told that in receiving these degrees they are admitted into the Masonic Order, and are obtaining Masonic information under the name of "Ladies' Masonry," they are simply deceived. Every woman connected by ties of consanguinity to a Master Mason is peculiarly entitled to Masonic assistance and protection. If she is told this, and also told that by these androgynous degrees she is to be put in possession of the means of making her claims known by a sort of what may be called oral testimony, but that she is by their possession no nearer to the portals of Masonry than she was before, if she is honestly told this, then there is no harm, but the possibility of some good, in these forms if carefully bestowed and prudently preserved. But all attempts to make Masonry of them, and especially that anomalous thing called *Co-Masonry*, are wrong, imprudent, and calculated to produce opposition among the well-informed and cautious members of the Fraternity.

Androgynous Masonry. That so-called Masonry which is dedicated to the cultivation of the androgynous degrees. The Adoptive Rite of France is Androgynous Masonry.

Angel. Angels were originally in the Jewish theogony considered simply as messengers of God, as the name *Malachim* imports, and the word is thus continually used in the early Scriptures of the Old Testament. It was only after the captivity that the Jews brought from Babylon their mystical ideas of angels as instruments of creative ministration, such as the angel of fire, of water, of earth, or of air. These doctrines they learned from the Chaldean sages, who had probably derived them from Zoroaster and the Zendavesta. In time these doctrines were borrowed by the Gnostics, and through them they have been introduced into some of the high degrees; such, for instance, as the Knight of the Sun, in whose ritual the angels of the four elements play an important part.

Angelic Brothers. (Ger., *Engelsbrüder*.) Sometimes called, after their founder, *Gichtelites* or *Gichtelianer*. A mystical sect of religious fanatics founded by one Gichtel, about the close of the seventeenth century, in the United Netherlands. After the death of their founder in 1710, they gradually became extinct, or were continued only in secret union with the Rosicrucians.

Angels' Alphabet. See *Alphabet, Angels'*.

Angerona. The name of a pagan deity worshiped among the Romans. Pliny calls her the goddess of silence, and calmness of mind. Hence her statue has sometimes been introduced among the ornaments of Masonic edifices. She is represented with her finger pressed upon her lips. See *Harpocrates*, for what is further to be said upon this symbol.

Angle. The inclination of two lines meeting in a point. Angles are of three kinds—acute, obtuse, and right angles. The right angle, or the angle of 90 degrees, is the only one recognized in Masonry, because it is the form of the trying square, one of the most important working tools of the profession, and the symbol of morality.

Angular Triad. A name given by Oliver to the three presiding officers of a Royal Arch Chapter.

Animal Worship. The worship of animals is a species of idolatry that was especially practised by the ancient Egyptians. Temples were erected by this people in their honor, in which they were fed and cared for during life; to kill one of them was a crime punishable with death; and after death, they were embalmed, and interred in the catacombs. This worship was derived first from the earlier adoration of the stars, to certain constellations of which the names of animals had been given; next, from an Egyptian tradition that the gods being pursued by Typhon, had concealed themselves under the forms of animals; and lastly, from the doctrine of the metempsychosis, according to which there was a continual circulation of the souls of men and animals. But behind the open and popular exercise of this degrading worship the priests concealed a symbolism full of philosophical conceptions. Mr. Gliddon says in his *Otia Egyptiaca* (p. 94) that "animal worship among the Egyptians was the natural and unavoidable consequence of the misconception, by the vulgar, of those emblematical figures invented by the priests to record their own philosophical conception of absurd ideas. As the pictures and effigies suspended in early Christian churches, to commemorate a person or an event, became in time objects of worship to the vulgar, so, in Egypt, the esoteric or spiritual meaning of the emblems was lost in the gross materialism of the beholder. This esoteric and allegorical meaning was, however, preserved by the priests, and communicated in the mysteries alone to the initiated, while the uninstructed retained only the grosser conception."

Anima Mundi. (*Soul of the World*.) A doctrine of the early philosophers, who conceived that an immaterial force resided in nature and was the source of all physical and sentient life, yet not intelligential.

"Annales Chronologiques (Literaires et Historiques de la Maçonnerie de la Pays-Bas, à dater de 1 Janvier, 1814," i. e., *Chronological, Literary, and Historical Annals of the Masonry of the Netherlands from the year 1814*). This work, edited by Bros. Melton and De Margny, was published at Brussels, in five volumes, during the years 1823–26. It consists of an immense collection of French, Dutch, Italian, and English Masonic documents translated into French. Kloss extols it highly as a work which no Masonic library should be without. Its publication was unfortunately discontinued in 1826 by the Belgian revolution.

Annales Originis Magni Galliarum Orientis, etc. This history of the Grand Orient of France is, in regard to its subject, the most valuable of the works of C. A. Thory. It comprises a full account of the rise, progress, changes, and revolutions of French Freemasonry, with numerous curious and inedited documents, notices of a great number of rites, a fragment on Adoptive Masonry, and other articles of an interesting nature. It was published at Paris, in 1812, in one vol. of 471 pp., 8vo. (See *Kloss*, No. 4,088.)

Anniversary. See *Festivals*.

Anno Depositionis. *In the Year of the Deposit;* abbreviated A∴ Dep∴. The date used by Royal and Select Masters, which is found by adding 1000 to the Vulgar Era; thus, 1911 + 1000 = 2911.

Anno Egyptiaco. *In the Egyptian year.* The date used by the Hermetic Fraternity, and found by adding 5044 to the Vulgar Era prior to each July 20th, being the number of years since the consolidation of the Egyptian monarchy under Menes.

Anno Hebraico. *In the Hebrew Year;* abbreviated A∴ H∴. The same as *Anno Mundi;* which see.

Anno Inventionis. *In the Year of the Discovery;* abbreviated A∴ I∴ or A∴ Inv∴. The date used by Royal Arch Masons. Found by adding 530 to the Vulgar Era; thus, 1911 + 530 = 2441.

Anno Lucis. *In the Year of Light;* abbreviated A∴ L∴. The date used in ancient Craft

Masonry; found by adding 4000 to the Vulgar Era; thus, 1911 + 4000 = 5911.

Anno Mundi. *In the Year of the World.* The date used in the Ancient and Accepted Rite; found by adding 3760 to the Vulgar Era until September. After September, add one year more; this is because the year used is the Hebrew one, which begins in September. Thus, July, 1911 + 3760 = 5671, and October, 1911 + 3760 + 1 = 5672.

Anno Ordinis. *In the Year of the Order;* abbreviated A∴O∴. The date used by Knights Templars; found by subtracting 1118 from the Vulgar Era; thus, 1911 − 1118 = 793.

Annuaire. Some French Lodges publish annually a record of their most important proceedings for the past year, and a list of their members. This publication is called an *Annuaire,* or Annual.

Annual Communication. All the Grand Lodges of the United States, except those of Massachusetts, Maryland, the District of Columbia, and Pennsylvania, hold only one annual meeting; thus reviving the ancient custom of a yearly Grand Assembly. The Grand Lodge of Massachusetts, like that of England, holds Quarterly Communications. At these annual communications it is usual to pay the representatives of the subordinate Lodges a per diem allowance, which varies in different Grand Lodges from one to three dollars, and also their mileage or traveling expenses.

Annual Proceedings. Every Grand Lodge in the United States publishes a full account of its proceedings at its Annual Communication, to which is also almost always added a list of the subordinate Lodges and their members. Some of these Annual Proceedings extend to a considerable size, and they are all valuable as giving an accurate and official account of the condition of Masonry in each State for the past year. They also frequently contain valuable reports of committees on questions of Masonic law. The reports of the Committees of Foreign Correspondence are especially valuable in these pamphlets. (See *Committee on Foreign Correspondence.*)

Annuities. In England, one of the modes of distributing the charities of a Lodge is to grant annuities to aged members or to the widows and orphans of those who are deceased. In 1842 the "Royal Masonic Annuity for Males" was established, which has since become the "Royal Masonic Benevolent Institution for Aged Freemasons and Their Widows," and grants annuities to both males and females, having also an asylum at Croydon in Surrey, England, into which the annuitants are received in the order of their seniority on the list. (See *Asylum for Aged Freemasons.*)
[E. L. H.]

Anointing. The act of consecrating any person or thing by the pouring on of oil. The ceremony of anointing was emblematical of a particular sanctification to a holy and sacred use. As such it was practised by both the Egyptians and the Jews, and many represen-

tations are to be seen among the former of the performance of this holy Rite. Wilkinson informs us (*Anc. Egypt.,* iv., 280) that with the Egyptians the investiture to any sacred office was confirmed by this external sign; and that priests and kings at the time of their consecration were, after they had been attired in their full robes, anointed by the pouring of oil upon the head. The Jewish Scriptures mention several instances in which unction was administered, as in the consecration of Aaron as high priest, and of Saul and David, of Solomon and Joash, as kings. The process of anointing Aaron is fully described in Exodus (xxix. 7). After he had been clothed in all his robes, with the miter and crown upon his head, it is said, "then shalt thou take the anointing oil and pour it upon his head, and anoint him."

The ceremony is still used in some of the high degrees of Masonry, and is always recognized as a symbol of sanctification, or the designation of the person so anointed to a sacred use, or to the performance of a particular function. Hence, it forms an important part of the ceremony of installation of a high priest in the order of High Priesthood as practised in America.

As to the form in which the anointing oil was poured, Buxtorf (*Lex. Talm.,* p. 267) quotes the Rabbinical tradition that in the anointment of kings the oil was poured on the head in the form of a crown, that is, in a circle around the head; while in the anointment of the priests it was poured in the form of the Greek letter X, that is, on the top of the head, in the shape of a St. Andrew's cross.

Anonymous Society. A society formerly existing in Germany, which consisted of 72 members, namely, 24 Apprentices, 24 Fellow-Crafts, and 24 Masters. It distributed much charity, but its real object was the cultivation of the occult sciences. Its members pretended that its Grand Master was one Tajo, and that he resided in Spain. (*Acta Latomorum,* i., 294.)

Ansyreeh. A sect found in the mountains of Lebanon, of Northern Syria. Like the Druses, toward whom, however, they entertain a violent hostility, and the Assassins, they have a secret mode of recognition and a secret religion, which does not appear to be well understood by them. "However," says Rev. Mr. Lyde, who visited them in 1852, "there is one in which they all seem agreed, and which acts as a kind of Freemasonry in binding together the scattered members of their body, namely, secret prayers which are taught to every male child of a certain age, and are repeated at stated times, in stated places, and accompanied with religious rites." The Ansyreeh arose about the same time with the Assassins, and, like them, their religion appears to be an ill-digested mixture of Judaism, Christianity, and Mohammedanism. To the Masonic scholars these secret sects of Syria present an interesting study, because of their supposed connection with the Templars during the Crusades, the entire results of which are yet to be investigated.

Antediluvian Masonry. Among the traditions of Masonry, which, taken literally, become incredible, but which, considered allegorically, may contain a profound meaning, not the least remarkable are those which relate to the existence of a Masonic system before the Flood. Thus, Anderson (*Const.*, 1st ed., p. 3) says: "Without regarding uncertain accounts, we may safely conclude the Old World, that lasted 1656 years, could not be ignorant of Masonry." Dr. Oliver has devoted the twenty-eighth lecture in his *Historical Landmarks* to an inquiry into "the nature and design of Freemasonry before the Flood"; but he admits that any evidence of the existence at that time of such an Institution must be based on the identity of Freemasonry and morality. "We may safely assume," he says, "that whatever had for its object and end an inducement to the practice of that morality which is founded on the love of God, may be identified with primitive Freemasonry."

The truth is, that antediluvian Masonry is alluded to only in what is called the "ineffable degrees"; and that its only important tradition is that of Enoch, who is traditionally supposed to be its founder, or, at least, its great heirophant. (See *Enoch.*)

Anthem. The anthem was originally a piece of church music sung by alternate voices. The word afterward, however, came to be used as a designation of that kind of sacred music which consisted of certain passages taken out of the Scriptures, and adapted to particular solemnities. In the permanent poetry and music of Masonry the anthem is very rarely used. The spirit of Masonic poetry is lyrical, and therefore the ode is almost altogether used (except on some special occasions) in the solemnities and ceremonials of the Order. There are really no Masonic anthems.

Antient and Primitive Rite of Masonry, otherwise of Memphis. This rite claims a derivation from Egypt, and an organization from the High Grades which had entered Egypt before the arrival of the French Army, and it has been asserted that Napoleon and Kleber were invested with a ring at the hands of an Egyptian sage at the Pyramid of Cheops. However that may be, in 1814 the Disciples of Memphis were constituted as a Grand Lodge at Montauban in France by G. M. Marconis and others, being an incorporation of the various rites worked in the previous century and especially of the Primitive Rite of Philadelphes of Narbonne (*q. v.*). In the political troubles that followed in France the Lodge of the Disciples of Memphis was put to sleep on March 7, 1816, and remained somnolent until July 7, 1838, when J. E. Marconis was elected Grand Hierophant and arranged the documents, which the Rite then possessed, into 90 degrees. The first Assembly of the Supreme Power was held on September 25, 1838, and proclaimed on October 5th following. The father of the new Grand Hierophant seems to have been living and to have

sanctioned the proceedings. Lodges were established in Paris and Brussels until the government of France forbade the meetings in 1841; however, in 1848 work was resumed and the Rite spread to Roumania, Egypt, America, and elsewhere.

In 1862 J. E. Marconis united the Rite with the Grand Orient of France, retaining apparently the rank of Grand Hierophant; and in 1865 a Concordat was executed between the two bodies by which the relative value of their different degrees was settled.

In 1872 a Sovereign Sanctuary of the Rite was established in England by some American members with Bro. John Yarker as Grand Master General, and has since continued at work.

An official journal entitled *The Kneph* was at one time issued by the authority of the Sovereign Sanctuary, from which we learn that the Antient and Primitive Rite of Masonry is "universal and open to every Master Mason who is in good standing under some constitutional Grand Lodge, and teaches the Fatherhood of God and the Brotherhood of Man." The degrees of the Rite are 95 in number, starting with the three Craft degrees, and divided into three series, and appear to have been rearranged and renamed at various times. [E. L. H.]

Anti-Masonic Books. There is no country of the civilized world where Freemasonry has existed, in which opposition to it has not, from time to time, exhibited itself; although it has always been overcome by the purity and innocence of the Institution. The Roman Catholic religion has always been anti-Masonic, and hence edicts have constantly been promulgated by popes and sovereigns in Roman Catholic countries against the Order. The most important of these edicts is the bull of Pope Clement XII., which was issued on the 24th of April, 1738, the authority of which bull is still in existence, and forbids any pious Catholic from uniting with a Masonic Lodge, under the severest penalties of ecclesiastical excommunication.

In the United States, where there are neither popes to issue bulls nor kings to promulgate edicts, the opposition to Freemasonry had to take the form of a political party. Such a party was organized in this country in the year 1826, soon after the disappearance of one William Morgan. The object of this party was professedly to put down the Masonic Institution as subversive of good government, but really for the political aggrandizement of its leaders, who used the opposition to Freemasonry merely as a stepping-stone to their own advancement to office. But the public virtue of the masses of the American people repudiated a party which was based on such corrupt and mercenary views, and its ephemeral existence was followed by a total annihilation.

A society which has been deemed of so much importance as to be the victim of so many persecutions, must needs have had its enemies in the press. It was too good an Institution not to be abused. Accordingly, Freemasonry had no sooner taken its commanding position as one of the teachers of the world, than a host of adversaries sprang up to malign its character and to misrepresent its objects. Hence, in the catalogue of a Masonic library, the anti-Masonic books will form no small part of the collection.

Anti-Masonic works may very properly be divided into two classes. 1. Those written simply for the purposes of abuse, in which the character and objects of the Institution are misrepresented. 2. Those written for the avowed purpose of revealing its ritual and esoteric doctrines. The former of these classes is always instigated by malignity, the latter by mean cupidity. The former class alone comes strictly within the category of "anti-Masonic books," although the two classes are often confounded; the attack on the principles of Masonry being sometimes accompanied with a pretended revelation of its mysteries, and, on the other hand, the *pseudo*-revelations are not unfrequently enriched by the most liberal abuse of the Institution.

The earliest authentic work which contains anything in opposition to Freemasonry is *The Natural History of Staffordshire, by Robert Plot*, which was printed at Oxford in the year 1686. It is only in one particular part of the work that Dr. Plot makes any invidious remarks against the Institution; and we should freely forgive him for what he has said against it, when we know that his recognition of the existence, in the seventeenth century, of a society which was already of so much importance that he was compelled to acknowledge that he had "found persons of the most eminent quality that did not disdain to be of this fellowship," gives the most ample refutation of those writers who assert that no traces of the Masonic Institution are to be found before the beginning of the eighteenth century. A triumphant reply to the attack of Dr. Plot is to be found in the third volume of Oliver's *Golden Remains of the Early Masonic Writers.*

A still more virulent attack on the Order was made in 1730, by Samuel Prichard, which he entitled *Masonry dissected, being an universal and genuine description of all its branches from the original to the present time.* Toward the end of the year a reply was issued entitled *A Defence of Masonry, occasioned by a pamphlet called Masonry Dissected.* It was published anonymously, but it has recently been established that its author was Martin Clare A.M., F.R.S., a schoolmaster of London, who was a prominent Freemason from 1734 to 1749. (*Ars Quatuor Coronatorum*, iv., 33–41.) No copy of this Defence is known to exist, but it was reproduced in the *Free Masons' Pocket Companion* for 1738, and in the second edition of the *Book of Constitutions*, which was published in the same year.   [E. L. H.]

It is a learned production, well worth peru-

sal for the information that it gives in reference to the sacred rites of the ancients, independent of its polemic character. About this time the English press was inundated by pretended revelations of the Masonic mysteries, published under the queerest titles, such as *Jachin and Boaz; or, An authentic key to the door of Freemasonry, both Ancient and Modern*, published in 1762; *Hiram, or the Grand Master Key to both Ancient and Modern Freemasonry*, which appeared in 1764; *The Three Distinct Knocks*, published in 1760, and a host of others of a similar character, which were, however, rather intended, by ministering to a morbid and unlawful curiosity, to put money into the purses of their compilers, than to gratify any vindictive feelings against the Institution.

Some, however, of these works were amiable neither in their inception nor in their execution, and appear to have been dictated by a spirit that may be characterized as being anything else except Christian. Thus, in the year 1768, a sermon was preached, we may suppose, but certainly published, at London, with the following ominous title: *Masonry the Way to Hell; a Sermon wherein is clearly proved, both from Reason and Scripture, that all who profess the Mysteries are in a State of Damnation.* This sermon appears to have been a favorite with the ascetics, for in less than two years it was translated into French and German. But, on the other hand, it gave offense to the liberal-minded, and many replies to it were written and published, among which was one entitled *Masonry the Turnpike-Road to Happiness in this Life, and Eternal Happiness Hereafter*, which also found its translation into German.

In 1797 appeared the notorious work of John Robison, entitled *Proofs of a Conspiracy against all the Religions and Governments of Europe, carried on in the secret meetings of Freemasons, Illuminati, and Reading Societies.* Robison was a gentleman and a scholar of some repute, a professor of natural philosophy, and Secretary of the Royal Society of Edinburgh. Hence, although his theory is based on false premises and his reasoning fallacious and illogical, his language is more decorous and his sentiments less malignant than generally characterize the writers of anti-Masonic books. A contemporary critic in the *Monthly Review* (vol. xxv., p. 315) thus correctly estimates the value of his work: "On the present occasion," says the reviewer, "we acknowledge that we have felt something like regret that a lecturer in natural philosophy, of whom his country is so justly proud, should produce any work of literature by which his high character for knowledge and for judgment is liable to be at all depreciated." Robison's book owes its preservation at this day from the destruction of time only to the permanency and importance of the Institution which it sought to destroy, Masonry, which it vilified, has alone saved it from the tomb of the Capulets.

This work closed the labors of the anti-

Masonic press in England. No work abusive of the Institution of any importance has appeared in that country since the attack of Robison. The Manuals of Richard Carlile and the Theologico-astronomical sermons of the Rev. Robert Taylor are the productions of men who do not profess to be the enemies of the Order, but who have sought, by their peculiar views, to give to Freemasonry an origin, a design, and an interpretation different from that which is received as the general sense of the Fraternity. The works of these writers, although erroneous, are not inimical.

The French press was prolific in the production of anti-Masonic publications. Commencing with *La Grande Lumière*, which was published at Paris, in 1734, soon after the modern introduction of Masonry into France, but brief intervals elapsed without the appearance of some work adverse to the Masonic Institution. But the most important of these was certainly the ponderous effort of the Abbé Barruel, published in four volumes, in 1797, under the title of *Mémoires pour servir à l'histoire du Jacobinisme*. The French Revolution was at the time an accomplished fact. The Bourbons had passed away, and Barruel, as a priest and a royalist, was indignant at the change, and, in the bitterness of his rage, he charged the whole inception and success of the political movement to the machinations of the Freemasons, whose Lodges, he asserted, were only Jacobinical clubs. The general scope of his argument was the same as that which was pursued by Professor Robison; but while both were false in their facts and fallacious in their reasoning, the Scotchman was calm and dispassionate, while the Frenchman was vehement and abusive. No work, perhaps, was ever printed which contains so many deliberate misstatements as disgrace the pages of Barruel. Unfortunately, the work was, soon after its appearance, translated into English. It is still to be found on the shelves of Masonic students and curious work collectors, as a singular specimen of the extent of folly and falsehood to which one may be led by the influences of bitter party prejudices.

The anti-Masonic writings of Italy and Spain have, with the exception of a few translations from French and English authors, consisted only of bulls issued by popes and edicts pronounced by the Inquisition. The anti-Masons of those countries had it all their own way, and, scarcely descending to argument or even to abuse, contented themselves with practical persecution.

In Germany, the attacks on Freemasonry were less frequent than in England or France. Still there were some, and among them may be mentioned one whose very title would leave no room to doubt of its anti-Masonic character. It is entitled *Beweiss dass die Freimaurer-Gesellschaft in allen Staaten, u. s. w.,* that is, " Proofs that the Society of Freemasons is in every country not only useless, but. if not restricted, dangerous, and ought to be

interdicted." This work was published at Dantzic, in 1764, and was intended as a defense of the decree of the Council of Dantzic against the Order. The Germans, however, have given no such ponderous works in behalf of anti-Masonry as the capacious volumes of Barruel and Robison. The attacks on the Order in that country have principally been by pamphleteers.

In the United States anti-Masonic writings were scarcely known until they sprung out of the Morgan excitement in 1826. The disappearance and alleged abduction of this individual gave birth to a rancorous opposition to Masonry, and the country was soon flooded with anti-Masonic works. Most of these were, however, merely pamphlets, which had only an ephemeral existence and have long since been consigned to the service of the trunk-makers or suffered a literary metempsychosis in the paper-mill. Two only are worthy, from their size (their only qualification), for a place in a Masonic catalogue. The first of these is entitled *Letters on Masonry and Anti-Masonry, addressed to the Hon. John Quincy Adams. By William L. Stone.* This work, which was published at New York in 1832, is a large octavo of 556 pages.

The work of Mr. Stone, it must be acknowledged, is not abusive. If his arguments are illogical, they are at least conducted without malignity. If his statements are false, his language is decorous. He was himself a Mason, and he has been compelled, by the force of truth, to make many admissions which are favorable to the Order. The book was evidently written for a political purpose, and to advance the interests of the anti-Masonic party. It presents, therefore, nothing but partisan views, and those, too, almost entirely of a local character, having reference only to the conduct of the Institution as exhibited in what is called " the Morgan affair." Masonry, according to Mr. Stone, should be suppressed because a few of its members are supposed to have violated the laws in a village of the State of New York. As well might the vices of the Christians of Corinth have suggested to a contemporary of St. Paul the propriety of suppressing Christianity.

The next anti-Masonic work of any prominence published in this country is also in the epistolary style, and is entitled *Letters on the Masonic Institution. By John Quincy Adams.* It is an octavo of 284 pages, and was published at Boston in 1847. Mr. Adams, whose eminent public services have made his life a part of the history of his country, has very properly been described as " a man of strong points and weak ones, of vast reading and wonderful memory, of great credulity and strong prejudice." In the latter years of his life, he became notorious for his virulent opposition to Freemasonry. Deceived and excited by the misrepresentations of the anti-Masons, he united himself with that party, and threw all his vast energies and abilities into the political contests then waging. The result was this series of letters, abusive of the Masonic Institution, which he directed to leading politicians of the country, and which were published in the public journals from 1831 to 1833. These letters, which are utterly unworthy of the genius, learning, and eloquence of the author, display a most egregious ignorance of the whole design and character of the Masonic Institution. The " oath " and " the murder of Morgan " are the two bugbears which seem continually to float before the excited vision of the writer, and on these alone he dwells from the first to the last page.

Except the letters of Stone and Adams, there is hardly another anti-Masonic book published in America that can go beyond the literary dignity of a respectably sized pamphlet. A compilation of anti-Masonic documents was published at Boston, in 1830, by James C. Odiorne, who has thus in part preserved for future reference the best of a bad class of writings. In 1831, Henry Gassett, of Boston, a most virulent anti-Mason, distributed, at his own expense, a great number of anti-Masonic books, which had been published during the Morgan excitement, to the principal libraries of the United States, on whose shelves they are probably now lying covered with dust; and, that the memory of his good deed might not altogether be lost, he published a catalogue of these donations in 1852, to which he has prefixed an attack on Masonry.

Anti-Masonic Party. A party organized in the United States of America soon after the commencement of the Morgan excitement, professedly, to put down the Masonic Institution as subversive of good government, but really for the political aggrandizement of its leaders, who used the opposition to Freemasonry merely as a stepping-stone to their own advancement to office. The party held several conventions; endeavored, sometimes successfully, but oftener unsuccessfully, to enlist prominent statesmen in its ranks, and finally, in 1831, nominated William Wirt and Amos Ellmaker as its candidates for the Presidency and the Vice-Presidency of the United States. Each of these gentlemen received but seven votes, being the whole electoral vote of Vermont, which was the only State that voted for them. So signal a defeat was the death-blow of the party, that in the year 1833 it quietly withdrew from public notice, and now is happily no longer in existence. William L. Stone, the historian of anti-Masonry, has with commendable impartiality expressed his opinion of the character of this party, when he says that " the fact is not to be disguised—contradicted it cannot be—that anti-Masonry had become thoroughly political, and its spirit was vindictive towards the Freemasons without distinction as to guilt or innocence." (*Letters*, xxxviii., p. 418.) Notwithstanding the opposition that from time to time has been exhibited to Freemasonry in every country, America is the only one where it assumed the form of a political party. This, however, may very justly be attributed to the peculiar nature of its popular institutions. There, the ballot-box is considered the most potent engine for the government of rulers as well as people, and is, therefore, resorted to in cases in which, in more despotic governments, the powers of the Church and State would be exercised. Hence, the anti-Masonic convention held at Philadelphia, in 1830, did not hesitate to make the following declaration as the cardinal principle of the party. " The object of anti-Masonry, in nominating and electing candidates for the Presidency and Vice-Presidency, is to deprive Masonry of the support which it derives from the power and patronage of the executive branch of the United States Government. To effect this object, will require that candidates besides possessing the talents and virtues requisite for such exalted stations, be known as men decidedly opposed to secret societies." This issue having been thus boldly made was accepted by the people; and as principles like these were fundamentally opposed to all the ideas of liberty, personal and political, into which the citizens of the country had been indoctrinated, the battle was made, and the anti-Masonic party was not only defeated for the time, but forever annihilated.

Anti-Masonry. *Opposition to Freemasonry.* There is no country in which Masonry has ever existed in which this opposition has not from time to time exhibited itself; although, in general, it has been overcome by the purity and innocence of the Institution. The earliest opposition by a government, of which we have any record, is that of 1425, in the third year of the reign of Henry VI., of England, when the Masons were forbidden to confederate in Chapters and Congregations. This law was, however, never executed. Since that period, Freemasonry has met with no permanent opposition in England. The Roman Catholic religion has always been anti-Masonic, and hence edicts have always existed in the Roman Catholic countries against the Order. But the anti-Masonry which has had a practical effect in inducing the Church or the State to interfere with the Institution, and endeavor to suppress it, will come more properly under the head of *Persecutions*, to which the reader is referred.

Antin, Duke d'. Elected perpetual Grand Master of the Masons of France, on the 24th of June, 1738. He held the office until 1743, when he died, and was succeeded by the Count of Clermont. Clavel (*Hist. Pittoresq.*, p. 141) relates an instance of the fidelity and intrepidity with which, on one occasion, he guarded the avenues of the Lodge from the official intrusion of a commissary of police accompanied by a band of soldiers.

Antipodeans. (*Les Antipodiens.*) The name of the Sixtieth Degree of the seventh series of the collection of the Metropolitan Chapter of France. (*Acta Latomorum*, i., 294.)

Antiquity, Lodge of. The oldest Lodge in England, and one of the four which concurred in February, 1717, in the meeting at the Apple-Tree Tavern, London, in the formation of the Grand Lodge of England. At that time, the Lodge of Antiquity met at the Goose and Gridiron, in St. Paul's Church-yard. This Lodge and three others met on St. John Baptist's Day (June 24), 1717, at the Goose and Gridiron Tavern, and by a majority of hands elected Mr. Anthony Sayer Grand Master, he being the oldest Master present. Capt. Joseph Elliot, and Mr. Jacob Lamball, carpenter, he elected Grand Wardens. This and the other three Lodges did not derive their warrants from the Grand Lodge, but " acted by immemorial Constitution."

Antiquity Manuscript. This celebrated MS. is now, and has long been, in the possession of the Lodge of Antiquity, at London. It is stated in the subscription to have been written, in 1686, by " Robert Padgett, Clearke to the Worshipful Society of the Freemasons of the city of London." The whole manuscript was first published by W. J. Hughan in his *Old Charges of British Freemasons* (p. 64), but a part had been previously inserted by Preston in his *Illustrations* (b. ii., sect. vi.). And here we have evidence of a criminal inaccuracy of the Masonic writers of the last century, who never hesitated to alter or interpolate passages in old documents whenever it was required to confirm a preconceived theory. Thus, Preston had intimated that there was before 1717 an Installation ceremony for newly elected Masters of Lodges (which is not true), and inserts what he calls " the ancient Charges that were used on this occasion," taken from the MS. of the Lodge of Antiquity. To confirm the statement, that they were used for this purpose, he cites the conclusion of the MS. in the following words: " These be all the charges and covenants that ought to be read at the *installment of Master*, or making of a Freemason or Freemasons." The words in italics are not to be found in the original MS., but were inserted by Preston. Bro. E. Jackson Barron had an exact transcript made of this MS., which he carefully collated, and which was published by Bro. Hughan. Bro. Barron gives the following description of the document:

" The MS. copy of the Charges of Freemasons is on a roll of parchment nine feet long by eleven inches wide, the roll being formed of four pieces of parchment glued together; and some few years ago it was partially mounted (but not very skilfully) on a backing of parchment for its better preservation.

" The Rolls are headed by an engraving of the Royal Arms, after the fashion usual in deeds of the period; the date of the engraving in this case being fixed by the initials at the top, I. 2. R.

" Under this engraving are emblazoned in separate shields the Arms of the city of London, which are two well known to require description, and the Arms of the Masons Company of London, *Sable on a chevron between three castles argent, a pair of compasses of the first surrounded by appropriate mantling.*

" The writing is a good specimen of the ordinary law writing of the times, interspersed with words in text. There is a margin of about an inch on the left side, which is marked by a continuous double red ink line throughout, and there are similar double lines down both edges of the parchment. The letter U is used throughout the MS. for V, with but two or three exceptions." (Hughan's *Old Charges*, 1872, p. 14.)

Antiquity of Freemasonry. Years ago in writing an article on this subject under the impressions made upon me by the fascinating theories of Dr. Oliver, though I never completely accepted his views, I was led to place the organization of Freemasonry, as it now exists, at the building of Solomon's Temple. Many years of subsequent research have led me greatly to modify the views I had previously held. Although I do not rank myself among those modern iconoclasts who refuse credence to every document whose authenticity, if admitted, would give to the Order a birth anterior to the beginning of the last century, I confess that I cannot find any incontrovertible evidence that would trace Masonry, as now organized, beyond the Building Corporations of the Middle Ages. In this point of view I speak of it only as an architectural brotherhood, distinguished by signs, by words, and by brotherly ties which have not been essentially changed, and by symbols and legends which have only been developed and extended, while the association has undergone a transformation from an operative art to a speculative science.

But then these Building Corporations did not spring up in all their peculiar organization —different, as it was, from that of other guilds—like Autochthones, from the soil. They, too, must have had an origin and an archetype, from which they derived their peculiar character. And I am induced, for that purpose, to look to the Roman Colleges of Artificers, which were spread over Europe by the invading forces of the empire. But these have been traced to Numa, who gave to them that mixed practical and religious character which they are known to have possessed, and in which they were imitated by the medieval architects.

We must, therefore, look at Freemasonry in two distinct points of view: First, as it is—a society of Speculative Architects engaged in the construction of spiritual temples, and in this respect a development from the Operative Architects of the tenth and succeeding centuries, who were themselves offshoots from the Traveling Freemasons of Como, who traced their origin to the Roman Colleges of Builders. In this direction, I think, the line of descent is plain, without any demand upon our credulity for assent to its credibility.

But Freemasonry must be looked at also from another standpoint. Not only does it present the appearance of a speculative science, based on an operative art, but it also very significantly exhibits itself as the *symbolic expression of a religious idea*. In other and plainer words, we see in it the important lesson of eternal life, taught by a legend which, whether true or false, is used in Masonry as a symbol and an allegory.

But whence came this legend? Was it invented in 1717 at the revival of Freemasonry in England? We have evidence of the strongest circumstantial character, derived from the Sloane Manuscript No. 3,329, recently exhumed from the shelves of the British Museum, that this very legend was known to the Masons of the seventeenth century at least.

Then, did the Operative Masons of the Middle Ages have a legend also? The evidence is that they did. The Compagnons de la Tour, who were the offshoots of the old Masters' Guilds, had a legend. We know what the legend was, and we know that its character was similar to, although not in all the details precisely the same as, the Masonic legend. It was, however, connected with the Temple of Solomon.

Again: Did the builders of the Middle Ages invent their legend, or did they obtain it from some old tradition? The question is interesting, but its solution either way would scarcely affect the Antiquity of Freemasonry. It is not the form of the legend, but its spirit and symbolic design, with which we have to do.

This legend of the Third Degree as we now have it, and as we have had it for a certain period of two hundred and fifty years, is intended, by a symbolic representation, to teach the resurrection from death, and the Divine dogma of eternal life. All Masons know its character, and it is neither expedient nor necessary to dilate upon it.

But can we find such a legend elsewhere? Certainly we can. Not indeed the same legend; not the same personage as its hero; not the same details; but a legend with the same spirit and design; a legend funereal in character, celebrating death and resurrection, solemnized in lamentation and terminating in joy. Thus, in the Egyptian Mysteries of Osiris, the image of a dead man was borne in an *argha*, ark or coffin, by a procession of initiates; and this enclosure in the coffin or interment of the body was called the aphanism, or disappearance, and the lamentation for him formed the first part of the Mysteries. On the third day after the interment, the priests and initiates carried the coffin, in which was also a golden vessel, down to the river Nile. Into the vessel they poured water from the river; and then with a cry of Ευρήκαμεν ἀγαλλώμεθα, "We have found him, let us rejoice," they declared that the dead Osiris, who had descended into Hades, had returned from thence, and was restored again to life; and the rejoicings which ensued constituted the second part of the Mysteries. The analogy between this and the legend of Freemasonry must be at once apparent. Now, just such a legend, everywhere differing in particulars, but everywhere coinciding in general character, is to be found in all the old religions—in sun worship, in tree worship, in animal worship. It was often perverted, it is true,

from the original design. Sometimes it was applied to the death of winter and the birth of spring, sometimes to the setting and the subsequent rising of the sun, but always indicating a *loss* and a *recovery*.

Especially do we find this legend, and in a purer form, in the Ancient Mysteries. At Samothrace, at Eleusis, at Byblos—in all places where these ancient religions and mystical rites were celebrated—we find the same teachings of eternal life inculcated by the representation of an imaginary death and apotheosis. And it is this legend, and this legend alone, that connects Speculative Freemasonry with the Ancient Mysteries of Greece, of Syria, and of Egypt.

The theory, then, that I advance on the subject of the Antiquity of Freemasonry is this: I maintain that, in its present peculiar organization, it is the successor, with certainty, of the Building Corporations of the Middle Ages, and through them, with less certainty but with great probability, of the Roman Colleges of Artificers. Its connection with the Temple of Solomon, as its birthplace, may have been accidental—a mere arbitrary selection by its inventors—and bears, therefore, only an allegorical meaning; or it may be historical, and to be explained by the frequent communications that at one time took place between the Jews and the Greeks and the Romans. This is a point still open for discussion. On it I express no fixed opinion. The historical materials upon which to base an opinion are as yet too scanty. But I am inclined, I confess, to view the Temple of Jerusalem and the Masonic traditions connected with it as a part of the great allegory of Masonry.

But in the other aspect in which Freemasonry presents itself to our view, and to which I have already adverted, the question of its antiquity is more easily settled. As a brotherhood, composed of symbolic Masters and Fellows and Apprentices, derived from an association of Operative Masters, Fellows, and Apprentices—those building spiritual temples as these built material ones—its age may not exceed five or six hundred years; but as a secret association, containing within itself the symbolic expression of a religious idea, it connects itself with all the Ancient Mysteries, which, with similar secrecy, gave the same symbolic expression to the same religious idea. These Mysteries were not the cradles of Freemasonry: they were only its analogues. But I have no doubt that all the Mysteries had one common source, perhaps, as it has been suggested, some ancient body of priests; and I have no more doubt that Freemasonry has derived its legend, its symbolic mode of instruction, and the lesson for which that instruction was intended, either directly or indirectly from the same source. In this view the Mysteries become interesting to the Mason as a study, and in this view only. And so, when I speak of the Antiquity of Masonry, I must say, if I would respect the axioms of historical science, that its *body* came out of the Middle Ages, but that its *spirit* is to be traced to a far remoter period.

Anton, Dr. Carl Gottlob von. A German Masonic writer of considerable reputation, who died at Gorlitz on the 17th of November, 1818. He is the author of two historical works on Templarism, both of which are much esteemed. 1. *Versuch einer Geschichte des Tempelherren ordens* (i. e., An Essay on the Order of Knights Templars), Leipzig, 1779. 2. *Untersuchung über das Geheimniss und die Gebräuche der Tempelherren* (i. e., An Inquiry into the Mystery and Usages of the Knights Templars), Dessau, 1782. He also published at Gorlitz, in 1805, and again in 1819, A brief essay on the Culdees (*Ueber die Culdeer*).

Anton Hieronymus. In the examination of a German "steinmetz," or STONEMASON, this is said to have been the name of the first Mason. It is unquestionably a corruption of *Adon Hiram*.

Anubis or **Anepu.** Egyptian deity, son of Osiris and Nephthys. The Greek Hermes. Having the head of a jackal, with pointed ears and snout, which the Greeks frequently changed to those of a dog. At times represented as wearing a double crown. His duty was to accompany the souls of the deceased to Hades (Amenthes), and assist Horus in weighing their actions under the inspection of Osiris.

Ape and Lion, Knight of the. See *Knight of the Ape and Lion.*

Apex, Rite of. See *Sät B'hai, Order of.*

Aphanism. In the Ancient Mysteries, there was always a legend of the death or disappearance of some hero god, and the subsequent discovery of the body and its resurrection. The concealment of this body by those who had slain it was called the aphanism, from the Greek, αφανιζω, *to conceal.* As these Mysteries may be considered as a type of Masonry, as some suppose, and as, according to others, both the Mysteries and Masonry are derived from one common and ancient type, the aphanism, or concealing of the body, is of course to be found in the Third Degree. Indeed, the purest kind of Masonic aphanism is the loss or concealment of the WORD. (See *Mysteries*, and *Euresis.*)

Apis. The sacred bull, held in high reverence by the Egyptians as possessing Divine powers, especially the gift of prophecy. As it was deemed essential the animal should be peculiarly marked by nature, much difficulty was experienced in procuring it. The bull was required to be black, with a white triangle on its forehead, a white crescent on its side, and a knotted growth, like a scarabæus, under the tongue. Such an animal being found, it was fed for four months in a building facing the East. At new moon it was embarked on a special vessel, prepared with exquisite care, and with solemn ceremony conveyed to Heliopolis, where for forty days it was fed by priests and women. In its sanctified condition it was taken to Memphis and housed in a temple with two chapels and a court wherein to exercise. The omen was good or evil in accordance with which chapel it entered from the court. At the age of 25 years it was led to its death, amid great mourning and lamentations. The bull or apis was an important religious factor in the Isian worship, and was continued as a creature of reverence during the Roman domination of Egypt.

Apocalypse, Masonry of the. The adoption of St. John the Evangelist as one of the patrons of our Lodges, has given rise, among the writers on Freemasonry, to a variety of theories as to the original cause of his being thus connected with the Institution. Several traditions have been handed down from remote periods, which claim him as a brother, among which the Masonic student will be familiar with that which represents him as having assumed the government of the Craft, as Grand Master, after the demise of John the Baptist. I confess that I am not willing to place implicit confidence in the correctness of this legend, and I candidly subscribe to the prudence of Dalcho's remark, that " it is unwise to assert more than we can prove, and to argue against probability." There must have been, however, in some way, a connection more or less direct between the Evangelist and the institution of Freemasonry, or he would not from the earliest times have been so universally claimed as one of its patrons. If it was simply a Christian feeling—a religious veneration—which gave rise to this general homage, I see no reason why St. Matthew, St. Mark, or St. Luke might not as readily and appropriately have been selected as one of the " lines parallel." But the fact is that there is something, both in the life and in the writings of St. John the Evangelist, which closely connects him with our mystic Institution. He may not have been a Freemason in the sense in which we now use the term; but it will be sufficient, if it can be shown that he was familiar with other mystical institutions, which are themselves generally admitted to have been more or less intimately connected with Freemasonry by deriving their existence from a common origin.

Such a society was the Essenian Fraternity —a mystical association of speculative philosophers among the Jews, whose organization very closely resembled that of the Freemasons, and who are even supposed by some to have derived their tenets and their discipline from the builders of the Temple. As Oliver observes, their institution " may be termed Freemasonry, retaining the same form but practised under another name." Now there is little doubt that St. John was an Essene. Calmet positively asserts it; and the writings and life of St. John seem to furnish sufficient internal evidence that he was originally of that brotherhood.

But it seems to me that St. John was more particularly selected as a patron of Freemasonry in consequence of the mysterious and emblematic nature of the Apocalypse, which evidently assimilated the mode of teaching adopted by the Evangelist to that practised by the Fraternity. If anyone who has investigated the ceremonies performed in the Ancient Mysteries, the Spurious Freemasonry, as it has been called, of the Pagans, will compare them with the mystical machinery used in the Book of Revelations, he will find himself irresistibly led to the conclusion that St. John the Evangelist was intimately acquainted with the whole process of initiation into these mystic associations, and that he has selected its imagery for the ground-work of his prophetic book. Mr. Faber, in his *Origin of Pagan Idolatry* (vol. ii., b. vi., ch. 6), has, with great ability and clearness, shown that St. John in the Apocalypse applies the ritual of the ancient initiations to a spiritual and prophetic purpose.

" The whole machinery of the Apocalypse," says Mr. Faber, " from beginning to end, seems to me very plainly to have been borrowed from the machinery of the Ancient Mysteries; and this, if we consider the nature of the subject, was done with the very strictest attention to poetical decorum.

" St. John himself is made to personate *an aspirant* about to be initiated; and, accordingly, the images presented to his mind's eye closely resemble the pageants of the Mysteries both *in nature* and *in order of succession.*

" The prophet first beholds *a door opened* in the magnificent temple of heaven; and into this he is invited to enter by the voice of one who plays *the hierophant.* Here he witnesses the unsealing of a *sacred book,* and forthwith he is appalled by a troop of *ghastly apparitions,* which flit in horrid succession before his eyes. Among these are preëminently conspicuous *a vast serpent,* the well-known symbol of the great father; and two portentous *wild beasts,* which severally come up out of the sea and out of the earth. Such hideous figures correspond with the canine phantoms of the Orgies, which seem to rise out of the ground, and with the polymorphic images of the hero god who was universally deemed the offspring of the sea.

" Passing these terrific monsters in safety, the prophet, constantly attended by his *angel hierophant,* who acts the part of an interpreter, is conducted into the presence of a *female,* who is described as closely resembling the great mother of pagan theology. Like Isis emerging from the sea and exhibiting herself to the aspirant Apuleius, this female divinity, upborne upon the marine wild beast, appears to float upon the surface of many waters. She is said to be *an open and systematical harlot,* just as the great mother was the declared female principle of fecundity; and as she was always propitiated by literal fornication reduced to a religious system, and as the initiated were made to drink a prepared liquor out of a sacred goblet, so this harlot is represented as intoxicating the kings of the earth with the *golden cup* of her prostitution. On her forehead the very name of MYSTERY is inscribed; and the label teaches us that, in point of character, she is *the great universal mother* of idolatry.

" The nature of this mystery *the officiating hierophant* undertakes to explain; and an im-portant prophecy is most curiously and artfully veiled under the very language and imagery of the Orgies. To the sea-born great father was ascribed a threefold state—*he lived, he died, and he revived;* and these changes of condition were duly exhibited in the Mysteries. To the sea-born wild beast is similarly ascribed a threefold state—*he lives, he dies, he revives.* While dead, he lies floating on the mighty ocean, just like Horus or Osiris, or Siva or Vishnu. When he revives again, like those kindred deities, he emerges from the waves; and, whether dead or alive, he bears seven heads and ten horns, corresponding in number with the seven ark-preserved Rishis and the ten aboriginal patriarchs. Nor is this all: as the worshipers of the great father bore his special mark or stigma, and were distinguished by his name, so the worshipers of the maritime beast equally bear his mark and are equally decorated by his appellation.

" At length, however, *the first or doleful part* of these sacred Mysteries draws to a close, and *the last or joyful part* is rapidly approaching. After the prophet has beheld the enemies of God plunged into a dreadful lake or inundation of liquid fire, which corresponds with the infernal lake or deluge of the Orgies, he is introduced into a *splendidly-illuminated region,* expressly adorned with the characteristics of that Paradise which was the ultimate scope of the ancient aspirants; while *without* the holy gate of admission are the whole multitude of the profane, *dogs, and sorcerors, and whoremongers, and murderers, and idolators, and whosoever loveth and maketh a lie.*"

Such was the imagery of the Apocalypse. The close resemblance to the machinery of the Mysteries, and the intimate connection between their system and that of Freemasonry, very naturally induced our ancient brethren to claim the patronage of an apostle so preëminently mystical in his writings, and whose last and crowning work bore so much of the appearance, in an outward form, of a ritual of initiation.

Apocalypse, Order of the. An Order instituted about the end of the seventeenth century, by one Gabrino, who called himself the Prince of the Septenary Number or Monarch of the Holy Trinity. He enrolled a great number of artisans in his ranks who went about their ordinary occupations with swords at their sides. According to Thory, some of the provincial Lodges of France made a degree out of Gabrino's system. The arms of the Order were a naked sword and a blazing star. (*Acta Latomorum,* i., 294.) Reghellini (iii., 72) thinks that this Order was the precursor of the degrees afterward introduced by the Masons who practised the Templar system.

Apocalyptic Degrees. Those degrees which are founded on the Revelation of St. John, or whose symbols and machinery of initiation are derived from that work, are called Apocalyptic degrees. Of this nature are several of the high degrees: such, for instance, as the Seventeenth, or Knight of the East and West of the Scottish Rite.

Aporrheta. Greek, ἀπόρρητα. The holy things in the Ancient Mysteries which were known only to the initiates, and were not to be disclosed to the profane, were called the *aporrheta.* What are the aporrheta of Freemasonry? what are the arcana of which there can be no disclosure? is a question that for some years past has given rise to much discussion among the disciples of the Institution. If the sphere and number of these aporrheta be very considerably extended, it is evident that much valuable investigation by public discussion of the science of Masonry will be prohibited. On the other hand, if the aporrheta are restricted to only a few points, much of the beauty, the permanency, and the efficacy of Freemasonry which are dependent on its organization as a secret and mystical association will be lost. We move between Scylla and Charybdis, and it is difficult for a Masonic writer to know how to steer so as, in avoiding too frank an exposition of the principles of the Order, not to fall by too much reticence, into obscurity. The European Masons are far more liberal in their views of the obligation of secrecy than the English or the American. There are few things, indeed, which a French or German Masonic writer will refuse to discuss with the utmost frankness. It is now beginning to be very generally admitted, and English and American writers are acting on the admission, that the only real aporrheta of Freemasonry are the modes of recognition, and the peculiar and distinctive ceremonies of the Order; and to these last it is claimed that reference may be publicly made for the purpose of scientific investigation, provided that the reference be so made as to be obscure to the profane, and intelligible only to the initiated.

Appeal, Right of. The right of appeal is an inherent right belonging to every Mason, and the Grand Lodge is the appellate body to whom the appeal is to be made.

Appeals are of two kinds: 1st, from the decision of the Master; 2d, from the decision of the Lodge. Each of these will require a distinct consideration.

1. *Appeals from the Decision of the Master.* It is now a settled doctrine in Masonic law that there can be no appeal from the decision of a Master of a Lodge to the Lodge itself. But an appeal always lies from such decision to the Grand Lodge, which is bound to entertain the appeal and to inquire into the correctness of the decision. Some writers have endeavored to restrain the despotic authority of the Master to decisions in matters strictly relating to the work of the Lodge, while they contend that on all questions of business an appeal may be taken from his decision to the Lodge. But it would be unsafe, and often impracticable, to draw this distinction, and accordingly the highest Masonic authorities have rejected the theory, and denied the power in a Lodge to entertain an appeal from any decision of the presiding officer.

The wisdom of this law must be apparent to anyone who examines the nature of the organization of the Masonic Institution. The Master is responsible to the Grand Lodge for the good conduct of his Lodge. To him and to him alone the supreme Masonic authority looks for the preservation of order, and the observance of the *Constitutions* and the *Landmarks* of the Order in the body over which he presides. It is manifest, then, that it would be highly unjust to throw around a presiding officer so heavy a responsibility, if it were in the power of the Lodge to overrule his decisions or to control his authority.

2. *Appeals from the Decisions of the Lodge.* Appeals may be made to the Grand Lodge from the decisions of a Lodge, on any subject except the admission of members, or the election of candidates; but these appeals are more frequently made in reference to conviction and punishment after trial.

When a Mason, in consequence of charges preferred against him, has been tried, convicted, and sentenced by his Lodge, he has an inalienable right to appeal to the Grand Lodge from such conviction and sentence.

His appeal may be either general or specific. That is, he may appeal on the ground, generally, that the whole of the proceedings have been irregular or illegal, or he may appeal specifically against some particular portion of the trial; or lastly, admitting the correctness of the verdict, and acknowledging the truth of the charges, he may appeal from the sentence, as being too severe or disproportionate to the offense.

Appendant Orders. In the Templar system of the United States, the degrees of Knight of the Red Cross and Knight of Malta are called Appendant Orders because they are conferred as appendages to that of Knight Templar, which is the principal degree of the Commandery.

Apple-Tree Tavern. The place where the four Lodges of London met in 1717, and organized the Grand Lodge of England. It was situated in Charles Street, Covent Garden.

Apprenti. French for *Apprentice.*

Apprentice. See *Apprentice, Entered.*

Apprentice Architect. (*Apprenti Architecte.*) A degree in the collection of Fustier.

Apprentice Architect, Perfect. (*Apprenti Architecte, Parfait.*) A degree in the collection of Le Page.

Apprentice Architect, Prussian. (*Apprenti Architecte, Prussien.*) A degree in the collection of Le Page.

Apprentice Cohen. (*Apprenti Coën.*) A degree in the collection of the Archives of the Mother Lodge of the Philosophic Rite.

Apprentice, Egyptian. (*Apprenti, Egyptien.*) The First Degree of the Egyptian Rite of Cagliostro.

Apprentice, Entered. The First Degree of Freemasonry, in all the rites, is that of Entered Apprentice. In French, it is called *apprenti;* in Spanish, *aprendiz;* in Italian, *apprendente;* and in German, *lehrling:* in all of which the radical meaning of the word is *a learner.* Like the lesser Mysteries of the ancient initiations, it is in Masonry a preliminary degree, intended to prepare the candidate for the higher and fuller instructions of the succeeding degrees. It is, therefore, although supplying no valuable historical information, replete, in its lecture, with instructions on the internal structure of the Order. Until late in the seventeenth century, Apprentices do not seem to have been considered as forming any part of the confraternity of Free and Accepted Masons; for although they are incidentally mentioned in the *Old Constitutions* of the fifteenth, sixteenth, and seventeenth centuries, these records refer only to Masters and Fellows as constituting the Craft, and this distinction seems to have been one rather of position than of degree. The Sloane Manuscript, No. 3,329, which Findel supposes to have been written at the end of the seventeenth century, describes a just and perfect Lodge as consisting of "two Interprintices, two Fellow Craftes, and two Masters," which shows that by that time the Apprentices had been elevated to a recognized rank in the Fraternity. In the Manuscript signed "Mark Kipling," which Hughan entitles " The York MS., No. 4," the date of which is 1693, there is a still further recognition in what is there called " the Apprentice Charge," one item of which is, that " he shall keepe councell in all things spoken in Lodge or chamber by any Masons, Fellows, or Freemasons." This indicates that they were admitted to a closer communion with the members of the Craft. But notwithstanding these recognitions, all the manuscripts up to 1704 show that only " Masters and Fellows " were summoned to the assembly. During all this time, when Masonry was in fact an operative art, there was but one degree in the modern sense of the word. Early in the eighteenth century, if not earlier, Apprentices must have been admitted to the possession of this degree; for after what is called the revival of 1717, Entered Apprentices constituted the bulk of the Craft, and they only were initiated in the Lodges, the degrees of Fellow-Craft and Master Mason being conferred by the Grand Lodge. This is not left to conjecture. The thirteenth of the General Regulations, approved in 1721, says that " Apprentices must be admitted Masters and Fellow Crafts only in the Grand Lodge, unless by a dispensation." But this having been found very inconvenient, on the 22d of November, 1725, the Grand Lodge repealed the article, and decreed that the Master of a Lodge, with his Wardens and a competent number of the Lodge assembled in due form, can make Masters and Fellows at discretion.

The mass of the Fraternity being at that time composed of Apprentices, they exercised a great deal of influence in the legislation of the Order; for although they could not represent their Lodge in the Quarterly Communications of the Grand Lodge—a duty which could only be discharged by a Master or Fellow—yet they were always permitted to be present at the grand feast, and no General Regulation could be altered or repealed without their consent; and, of course, in all the business of their particular Lodges, they took the most prominent part, for there were but few Masters or Fellows in a Lodge, in consequence of the difficulty and inconvenience of obtaining the degree, which could only be done at a Quarterly Communication of the Grand Lodge.

But as soon as the subordinate Lodges were invested with the power of conferring all the degrees, the Masters began rapidly to increase in numbers and in corresponding influence. And now, the bulk of the Fraternity consisting of Master Masons, the legislation of the Order is done exclusively by them, and the Entered Apprentices and Fellow-Crafts have sunk into comparative obscurity, their degrees being considered only as preparatory to the greater initiation of the Master's Degree.

Apprentice, Hermetic. (*Apprenti Hermétique.*) The Thirteenth Degree, ninth series, of the collection of the Metropolitan Chapter of France.

Apprentice, Kabbalistic. (*Apprenti Cabalistique.*) A degree in the collection of the Archives of the Mother Lodge of the Philosophic Rite.

Apprentice Mason. (*Apprenti Maçon.*) The Entered Apprentice of French Masonry.

Apprentice Masoness. (*Apprentie Maçonne.*) The First Degree of the French Rite of Adoption. The word *Masoness* is a neologism, but it is in accordance with the genius of our language, and it is difficult to know how else to translate into English the French word Maçonne, which means a woman who has received the degrees of the Rite of Adoption, unless by the use of the awkward phrase, Female Mason. To express this idea, we might introduce as a technicality the word *Masoness.*

Apprentice Masoness, Egyptian. (*Apprentie Maçonne Egyptienne.*) The First Degree of Cagliostro's Egyptian Rite of Adoption.

Apprentice, Mystic. (*Apprenti Mystique.*) A degree in the collection of M. Pyron.

Apprentice of Paracelsus. (*Apprenti de Paracelse.*) A degree in the collection of M. Peuvret. There existed a series of these Paracelsian degrees—Apprentice, Fellow-Craft, and Master. They were all most probably forms of Hermetic Masonry.

Apprentice of the Egyptian Secrets. (*Apprenti des secrets Egyptiens.*) The First Degree of the Order of African Architects.

Apprentice Philosopher, by the Number 3. (*Apprenti Philosophe par le Nombre 3.*) A degree in the collection of M. Peuvret.

Apprentice Philosopher, Hermetic. (*Apprenti Philosophe Hermétique.*) A degree in the collection of M. Peuvret.

Apprentice Philosopher to the Number 9. (*Apprenti Philosophe au Nombre 9.*) A degree in the collection of M. Peuvret.

Apprentice Pillar. See *Prentice Pillar.*

Apprentice, Scottish. (*Apprenti Ecossais.*) This degree and that of Trinitarian Scottish Apprentice (*Apprenti Ecossais Trinitaire*) are contained in the collection of Pyron.

Apprentice   Theosophist. (*Apprenti Théosophe.*) The First Degree of the Rite of Swedenborg.

Apron. There is no one of the symbols of Speculative Masonry more important in its teachings, or more interesting in its history, than the lambskin, or white leather apron. Commencing its lessons at an early period in the Mason's progress, it is impressed upon his memory as the first gift which he receives, the first symbol which is explained to him, and the first tangible evidence which he possesses of his admission into the Fraternity. Whatever may be his future advancement in the " royal art," into whatsoever deeper arcana his devotion to the mystic Institution or his thirst for knowledge may subsequently lead him, with the lambskin apron—his first investiture—he never parts. Changing, perhaps, its form and its decorations, and conveying, at each step, some new but still beautiful allusion, its substance is still there, and it continues to claim the honored title by which it was first made known to him, on the night of his initiation, as " the badge of a Mason."

If in less important portions of our ritual there are abundant allusions to the manners and customs of the ancient world, it is not to be supposed that the Masonic Rite of *investiture* —the ceremony of clothing the newly initiated candidate with this distinctive badge of his profession—is without its archetype in the times and practises long passed away. It would, indeed, be strange, while all else in Masonry is covered with the veil of antiquity, that the apron alone, its most significant symbol, should be indebted for its existence to the invention of a modern mind.

On the contrary, we shall find the most satisfactory evidence that the use of the apron, or some equivalent mode of investiture, as a mystic symbol, was common to all the nations of the earth from the earliest periods.

Among the Israelites the girdle formed a part of the investiture of the priesthood. In the mysteries of Mithras, in Persia, the candidate was invested with a white apron. In the initiations practised in Hindostan, the ceremony of investiture was preserved, but a sash, called the sacred zennar, was substituted for the apron. The Jewish sect of the Essenes clothed their novices with a white robe. The celebrated traveler Kæmpfer informs us that the Japanese, who practise certain rites of initiation, invest their candidates with a white apron, bound round the loins with a zone or girdle. In the Scandinavian Rites, the military genius of the people caused them to substitute a white shield, but its presentation was accompanied by an emblematic instruction not unlike that which is connected with the Mason's apron.

" The apron," says Dr. Oliver (*S. and S.*, Lect. X., p. 196), " appears to have been, in ancient times, an honorary badge of distinction. In the Jewish economy, none but the superior orders of the priesthood were permitted to adorn themselves with ornamented Girdles, which were made of blue, purple, and crimson, decorated with gold, upon a ground of fine white linen; while the inferior priests wore only plain white. The Indian, the Persian, the Jewish, the Ethiopian, and the Egyptian aprons, though equally superb, all bore a character distinct from each other. Some were plain white, others striped with blue, purple, and crimson; some were of wrought gold, others adorned and decorated with superb tassels and fringes. In a word, though the *principal honour* of the Apron may consist in its reference to innocence of conduct and purity of heart, yet it certainly appears, through all ages, to have been a most exalted badge of distinction. In primitive times it was rather an ecclesiastical than a civil decoration, although in some cases the Apron was elevated to great superiority as a national trophy. The Royal Standard of Persia was originally *an apron* in form and dimensions. At this day it is connected with ecclesiastical honours; for the chief dignitaries of the Christian church, wherever a legitimate establishment, with the necessary degrees of rank and subordination is formed, are invested with Aprons as a peculiar badge of distinction; which is a collateral proof of the fact that Masonry was originally incorporated with the various systems of divine worship used by every people in the ancient world. Masonry retains the symbol or shadow; it cannot have renounced the reality or substance."

In the Masonic apron two things are essential to the due preservation of its symbolic character—its color and its material.

1. *As to its color.* The color of a Mason's apron should be pure unspotted white. This color has, in all ages and countries, been esteemed an emblem of innocence and purity. It was with this reference that a portion of the vestments of the Jewish priesthood was directed to be white. In the Ancient Mysteries the candidate was always clothed in white. " The priests of the Romans," says Festus, " were accustomed to wear white garments when they sacrificed." In the Scandinavian Rites it has been seen that the shield presented to the candidate was white. The Druids changed the color of the garment presented to their initiates with each degree; white, however, was the color appropriated to the last, or degree of perfection. And it was, according to their ritual, intended to teach the aspirant that none were admitted to that honor but such as were cleansed from all impurities both of body and mind. In the early ages of the Christian church a white garment was always placed upon the catechumen who had been newly baptized, to denote that he had been cleansed from his former sins, and was thenceforth to lead a life of purity. Hence it was presented to him with this solemn charge: " Receive the white and undefiled garment, and produce it unspotted before the tribunal of our Lord Jesus Christ, that you may obtain eternal life." From all these instances we learn that white apparel was anciently used as an emblem of purity,

and for this reason the color has been preserved in the apron of the Freemason.

2. *As to its material.* A Mason's apron must be made of lambskin. No other substance, such as linen, silk, or satin, could be substituted without entirely destroying the emblematic character of the apron, for the material of the Mason's apron constitutes one of the most important symbols of his profession. The lamb has always been considered as an appropriate emblem of innocence. And hence we are taught, in the ritual of the First Degree, that, " by the lambskin, the Mason is reminded of that purity of life and rectitude of conduct which is so essentially necessary to his gaining admission into the Celestial Lodge above, where the Supreme Architect of the Universe forever presides."

The true apron of a Mason must, then, be of unspotted lambskin, from 14 to 16 inches wide, from 12 to 14 deep, with a fall about 3 or 4 inches deep, square at the bottom, and without device or ornament of any kind. The usage of the Craft in the United States of America has, for a few years past, allowed a narrow edging of blue ribbon in the symbolic degrees, to denote the universal friendship which constitutes the bond of the society, and of which virtue blue is the Masonic emblem. But this undoubtedly is an innovation, for the ancient apron was without any edging or ornament. In the Royal Arch Degree the lambskin is, of course, continued to be used, but, according to the same modern custom, there is an edging of red, to denote the zeal and fervency which should distinguish the possessors of that degree. All extraneous ornaments and devices are in bad taste, and detract from the symbolic character of the investiture. But the silk or satin aprons, bespangled and painted and embroidered, which have been gradually creeping into our Lodges, have no sort of connection with Ancient Craft Masonry. They are an innovation of our French brethren, who are never pleased with simplicity, and have, by their love of tinsel in their various newly invented ceremonies, effaced many of the most beautiful and impressive symbols of our Institution. A Mason who understands and appreciates the true symbolic meaning of his apron, would no more tolerate a painted or embroidered satin one than an artist would a gilded statue. By him, the lambskin, and the lambskin alone, would be considered as the badge " more ancient than the Golden Fleece, or Roman Eagle, and more honorable than the Star and Garter."

The Grand Lodge of England is precise in its regulations for the decorations of the apron which are thus laid down in its *Constitution:*

"*Entered Apprentices.*—A plain white lambskin, from fourteen to sixteen inches wide, twelve to fourteen inches deep, square at bottom, and without ornament; white strings.

"*Fellow Craft.*—A plain white lambskin, similar to that of the Entered Apprentices, with the addition only of two sky-blue rosettes at the bottom.

"*Master Masons.*—The same, with sky-blue lining and edging, not more than two inches deep, and an additional rosette on the fall or flap, and silver tassels. No other colour or ornament shall be allowed except to officers and past officers of Lodges who may have the emblems of their offices in silver or white in the centre of the apron; and except as to the members of the Prince of Wales' Lodge, No. 259, who are allowed to wear the internal half of the edging of garter-blue three-fourths of an inch wide.

"*Grand Stewards, present and past.*—Aprons of the same dimensions lined with crimson, edging of the same colour three and a half inches, and silver tassels. Provincial and District Grand Stewards, present and past, the same, except that the edging is only two inches wide. The collars of the Grand Steward's Lodge to be crimson ribbon, four inches broad.

"*Grand Officers of the United Grand Lodge, present and past.*—Aprons of the same dimensions, lined with garter-blue, edging three and a half inches, ornamented with gold, and blue strings; and they may have the emblems of their offices, in gold or blue, in the centre.

"*Provincial Grand Officers, present and past.*—Aprons of the same dimensions, lined with garter-blue, and ornamented with gold and with blue strings: they must have the emblems of their offices in gold or blue in the centre within a double circle, in the margin of which must be inserted the name of the Province. The garter-blue edging to the aprons must not exceed two inches in width.

"The apron of the Deputy Grand Master to have the emblem of his office in gold embroidery in the centre, and the pomegranate and lotus alternately embroidered in gold on the edging.

"The apron of the Grand Master is ornamented with the blazing sun embroidered in gold in the centre; on the edging the pomegranate and lotus with the seven-eared wheat at each corner, and also on the fall; all in gold embroidery; the fringe of gold bullion.

"The apron of the pro Grand Master the same.

"The Masters and Past Masters of Lodges to wear, in the place of the three rosettes on the Master Mason's apron, perpendicular lines upon horizontal lines, thereby forming three several sets of two right angles; the length of the horizontal lines to be two inches and a half each, and of the perpendicular lines one inch; these emblems to be of silver or of ribbon, half an inch broad, and of the same colour as the lining and edging of the apron. If Grand Officers, similar emblems of garter-blue or gold."

In the United States, although there is evidence in some old aprons, still existing, that rosettes were formerly worn, there are now no distinctive decorations for the aprons of the different symbolic degrees. The only mark of distinction is in the mode of wearing; and this differs in the different jurisdictions, some wearing the Master's apron turned up at the corner, and others the Fellow-Craft's. The authority of Cross, in his plate of the Royal Master's Degree in the older editions of his *Hieroglyphic Chart*, conclusively shows that he taught the former method, although the latter is now the more common usage.

As we advance to the higher degrees, we find the apron varying in its decorations and in the color of its border, which are, however, always symbolical of some idea taught in the degree.

Apron, Washington's. We here introduce a faithful representation of the emblems, wrought in needlework upon white satin by Madame Lafayette, for a Masonic apron, which the Marquis conveyed from Paris to

General Washington at Mount Vernon. It was a cherished memorial, which after Washington's death was formally presented to the "Washington Benevolent Society," at Philadelphia.

Arabici. An Arabian sect of the second century, who believed that the soul died with the body, to be again revived with it at the general resurrection.

Aranyaka. An appendage to the Veda of the Indians supplementary to the Brahmanas, but giving more prominence to the mystical sense of the rites of worship.

Araunah. See *Ornan*.

Arbitration. In the *Old Charges*, Masons are advised, in all cases of dispute or controversy, to submit to the arbitration of the Masters and Fellows, rather than to go to law.

Arbroath, Abbey of (England). Erected during the twelfth century. Rev. Charles Cordinet, in his description of the ruins of North Britain, has given an account of a seal of the Abbey Arbroath marked "Initiation." The seal was ancient before the abbey had an existence, and contains a perfectly distinct characteristic of the Scottish Rite.

Arcade de la Pelleterie. The name of derision given to the Orient of Clermont in France, that is to say, to the Old Grand Lodge, before the union in 1799.

Arcani Disciplina. The mode of initiation into the primitive Christian church. (See *Discipline of the Secret*.)

Arch, Antiquity of the. Writers on architecture have, until within a few years, been accustomed to suppose that the invention of the arch and keystone was not anterior to the era of Augustus. But the researches of modern antiquaries have traced the existence of the arch as far back as 460 years before the building of King Solomon's Temple, and thus rescued Masonic traditions from the charge of anachronism. (See *Keystone*.)

Arch, Catenarian. See *Catenarian Arch*.

Arch of Enoch. The Thirteenth Degree of the Ancient and Accepted Scottish Rite is sometimes so called. (See *Knight of the Ninth Arch*.)

Arch of Heaven. Job (xxvi. 11) compares heaven to an arch supported by pillars. "The pillars of heaven tremble and are astonished at his reproof." Dr. Cutbush, on this passage, remarks, "The arch in this instance is allegorical, not only of the arch of heaven, but of the higher degree of Masonry, commonly called the Holy Royal Arch. The pillars which support the arch are emblematical of Wisdom and Strength; the former denoting the wisdom of the Supreme Architect, and the latter the stability of the Universe."—*Am. Ed. Brewster's Encyc*.

Arch of Solomon, Royal. The Thirteenth Degree of the Ancient and Accepted Rite is sometimes so called, by which it is distinguished from the Royal Arch Degree of the English and American systems.

Arch of Steel. The grand honors are conferred, in the French Rite, by two ranks of brethren elevating and crossing their drawn swords. They call it *voute d'acier*.

Arch of Zerubbabel, Royal. The Seventh Degree of the American Rite is sometimes so called to distinguish it from the Royal Arch of the Ancient and Accepted Scottish Rite, which is called the Royal Arch of Solomon.

Arch, Royal. See *Royal Arch Degree*.

Archeology. The science which is engaged in the study of those minor branches of antiquities which do not enter into the course of general history, such as national architecture, genealogies, manners, customs, heraldic subjects, and others of a similar nature. The archeology of Freemasonry has been made, within a recent period, a very interesting study, and is much indebted for its successful pursuit to the labors of Kloss and Findel in Germany, and to Thory and Ragon in France, and to Oliver, Lyon, Hughan, Gould, Sadler, Dr. Chetwode Crawley and others, in England. The scholars of this science have especially directed their attention to the collection of old records, and the inquiry into the condition and organization of Masonic and other secret associations during the Middle Ages. In America, the late William S. Rockwell was a diligent student of Masonic archeology, and several others in this country have labored assiduously in the same inviting field.

Archetype. The principal type, figure, pattern, or example whereby and whereon a thing is formed. In the science of symbolism, the archetype is the thing adopted as a symbol, whence the symbolic idea is derived. Thus, we say the Temple is the archetype of the Lodge, because the former is the symbol whence all the Temple symbolism of the latter is derived.

Archimagus. The chief officer of the Mithraic Mysteries in Persia. He was the representative of Ormudz, or Ormazd, the type of the good, the true, and the beautiful, who overcame Ahriman, the spirit of evil, of the base, and of darkness.

Architect. In laying the corner-stones of Masonic edifices, and in dedicating them after they are finished, the architect of the building, although he may be a profane, is required to take a part in the ceremonies. In the former case, the square, level, and plumb are delivered to him with a charge by the Grand Master; and in the latter case they are returned by him to that officer.

Architect, African. See *African Architects*.

Architect, Engineer and. An officer in the French Rite, whose duty it is to take charge of the furniture of the Lodge. In the Scottish Rite such officer in the Consistory has charge of the general arrangement of all preparatory matters for the working or ceremonial of the degrees.

Architect by 3, 5, and 7, Grand. (*Grande Architecte par 3, 5, et 7.*) A degree in the manuscript of Peuvret's collection.

Architect, Grand. (*Architecte, Grande.*) 1. The Sixth Degree of the Rite of Martinism. 2. The Fourth Degree of the Rite of Elect Cohens. 3. The Twenty-third Degree of the Rite of Mizraim. 4. The Twenty-fourth Degree of the third series in the collection of the Metropolitan Chapter of France.

Architect, Grand Master. See *Grand Master Architect*.

Architect, Little. (*Architecte, Petit.*) 1. The Twenty-third Degree of the third series of the collection of the Metropolitan Chapter of France. 2. The Twenty-second Degree of the Rite of Mizraim.

Architect of Solomon. (*Architecte de Salomon.*) A degree in the manuscript collection of M. Peuvret.

Architect, Perfect. (*Architecte, Parfait.*) The Twenty-fifth, Twenty-sixth, and Twenty-seventh Degrees of the Rite of Mizraim are Apprentice, Fellow-Craft, and Master Perfect Architect.

Architect, Perfect and Sublime Grand. (*Architecte, Parfait et Sublime Grande.*) A degree in the collection of the Loge de Saint-Louis des Amis Réunis at Calais.

Architectonicus. A Greek word, adopted in Latin, signifying " belonging to architecture." Thus, Vitruvius writes, " rationes architectonicæ," the rules of architecture. But as *Architecton* signifies a Master Builder, the Grand Lodge of Scotland, in some Latin inscriptions, has used the word *architectonicus*, to denote *Masonic* or *relating to Freemasonry*. In the inscription on the corner-

6

stone of the Royal Exchange of Edinburgh, we find "fratres architectonici" used for *Freemasons;* and in the Grand Lodge diploma, a Lodge is called "societas architectonica"; but the usage of the word in this sense has not been generally adopted.

Architecture. The art of constructing dwellings, as a shelter from the heat of summer and the cold of winter, must have been resorted to from the very first moment in which man became subjected to the power of the elements. Architecture is, therefore, not only one of the most important, but one of the most ancient of sciences. Rude and imperfect must, however, have been the first efforts of the human race, resulting in the erection of huts clumsy in their appearance, and ages must have elapsed ere wisdom of design combined strength of material with beauty of execution.

As Geometry is the science on which Masonry is founded, Architecture is the art from which it borrows the language of its symbolic instruction. In the earlier ages of the Order every Mason was either an operative mechanic or a superintending architect. And something more than a superficial knowledge of the principles of architecture is absolutely essential to the Mason who would either understand the former history of the Institution or appreciate its present objects.

There are five orders of architecture: the Doric, the Ionic, the Corinthian, the Tuscan, and the Composite. The first three are the original orders, and were invented in Greece; the last two are of later formation, and owe their existence to Italy. Each of these orders, as well as the other terms of architecture, so far as they are connected with Freemasonry, will be found under its appropriate head throughout this work.

The *Books of Constitutions*, commenced by Anderson and continued by Entick and Noorthouck, contain, under the title of a *History of Freemasonry*, in reality a history of the progress of architecture from the earliest ages. In the older manuscript *Constitutions* the science of geometry, as well as architecture, is made identical with Masonry; so that he who would rightly understand the true history of Freemasonry must ever bear in mind the distinction between Geometry, Architecture, and Masonry, which is constantly lost sight of in these old records.

Architecture, Piece of. (*Morçeau d'architecture.*) The name given in French Lodges to the minutes.

Archives. This word means, properly, a place of deposit for records; but it means also the records themselves. Hence the archives of a Lodge are its records and other documents. The legend in the Second Degree, that the pillars of the Temple were made hollow to contain the archives of Masonry, is simply a myth, and a very modern one.

Archives, Grand Guardian of the. An officer in the Grand Council of Rites of Ireland who performs the duties of Secretary General.

Archives, Grand Keeper of the. An officer in some of the bodies of the high degrees whose duties are indicated by the name. In the Grand Orient of France he is called *Grand Garde des timbres et Sceaux*, as he combines the duties of a keeper of the archives and a keeper of the seals.

Archiviste. An officer in French Lodges who has charge of the archives. The Germans call him *Archivar*.

Ardarel. A word in the high degrees, used as the name of the angel of fire. It is a distorted form of *Adariel*, the splendor of God.

Arelim. A word used in some of the rituals of the high degrees. It is found in Isaiah (xxxiii. 7), where it is translated, in the A. V., "valiant ones," and by Lowth, "mighty men." It is a doubtful word, and is probably formed from *ariel*, the lion of God. D'Herbelot says that Mohammed called his uncle Hamseh, on account of his valor, the lion of God. In the Kabbala, Arelim is the angelic name of the third sephirah.

Areopagus. The third apartment in a Council of Kadosh is so called. It represents a tribunal, and the name is derived from the celebrated court of Athens.

Argonauts, Order of. A German androgynous Masonic society founded in 1775, by brethren of the Rite of Strict Observance. Much of the myth of the Argonauts was introduced into the forms and ceremonies, and many of the symbols taken from this source, such as meeting upon the deck of a vessel, the chief officer being called Grand Admiral, and the nomenclature of parts of the vessel being used. The motto was *Es Lebe die Freude*, or Joy forever.

Ariel. In the demonology of the Kabbala, the spirit of air; the guardian angel of innocence and purity: hence the Masonic synonym. A name applied to Jerusalem; a water spirit.

Arithmetic. That science which is engaged in considering the properties and powers of numbers, and which, from its manifest necessity in all the operations of weighing, numbering, and measuring, must have had its origin in the remotest ages of the world.

In the lecture of the degree of Grand Master Architect, the application of this science to Freemasonry is made to consist in its reminding the Mason that he is continually to *add* to his knowledge, never to *subtract* anything from the character of his neighbor, to *multiply* his benevolence to his fellow-creatures, and to *divide* his means with a suffering brother.

Arizona, Grand Lodge of, was established in 1882, and in 1910 had 19 Lodges and 1,410 brethren under its jurisdiction.

Ark. In the ritual of the American Royal Arch Degree three arks are referred to: 1. The Ark of Safety, or of Noah; 2. The Ark of the Covenant, or of Moses; 3. The Substitute Ark, or the Ark of Zerubbabel. In what is technically called "the passing of the veils," each of these arks has its commemorative illustration, and in the order in which they have been named. The first was constructed by Shem, Ham, and Japheth, the sons of Noah; the second by Moses, Aholiab, and Bezaleel; and the third was discovered by Joshua, Haggai, and Zerubbabel.

Ark and Anchor. See *Anchor and Ark*.

Ark and Dove. An illustrative degree, preparatory to the Royal Arch, and usually conferred, when conferred at all, immediately before the solemn ceremony of exaltation. The name of Noachite, sometimes given to it, is incorrect, as this belongs to a degree in the Ancient Scottish Rite. It is very probable that the degree, which now, however, has lost much of its significance, was derived from a much older one called the *Royal Ark Mariners*, to which the reader is referred. The legend and symbolism of the ark and dove formed an important part of the spurious Freemasonry of the ancients.

Ark Mariners. See *Royal Ark Mariners*.

Ark, Noah's, or the Ark of Safety, constructed by Shem, Ham, and Japheth, under the superintendence of Noah, and in it, as a chosen tabernacle of refuge, the patriarch's family took refuge. It has been called by many commentators a tabernacle of Jehovah; and Dr. Jarvis, speaking of the word צהר, ZoHaR, which has been translated *window*, says that, in all other passages of Scripture where this word occurs, it signifies the meridian light, the brightest effulgence of day, and therefore it could not have been an aperture, but a source of light itself. He supposes it therefore to have been the Divine Shekinah, or Glory of Jehovah, which afterward dwelt between the cherubim over the Ark of the Covenant in the tabernacle and the Temple. (*Church of the Redeemed*, i., 20.)

Ark of the Covenant. The Ark of the Covenant or of the Testimony was a chest originally constructed by Moses at God's command (Exod. xxv. 10), in which were kept the two tables of stone, on which were engraved the Ten Commandments. It contained, likewise, a golden pot filled with manna, Aaron's rod, and the tables of the covenant. It was at first deposited in the most sacred place of the tabernacle and afterward placed by Solomon in the Sanctum Sanctorum of the Temple, and was lost upon the destruction of that building by the Chaldeans. The later history of this ark is buried in obscurity. It is supposed that, upon the destruction of the first Temple by the Chaldeans, it was carried to Babylon among the other sacred utensils which became the spoil of the conquerors. But of its subsequent fate all traces have been lost. It is, however, certain that it was not brought back to Jerusalem by Zerubbabel. The Talmudists say that there were five things which were the glory of the first Temple that were wanting in the second; namely, the Ark of the Covenant, the Shekinah or Divine Presence, the Urim and Thummim, the holy fire upon the altar, and the spirit of prophecy. The Rev. Salem Towne, it is true, has endeavored to prove, by a very ingenious argument, that the original Ark of the Covenant was concealed by

Josiah, or by others, at some time previous to the destruction of Jerusalem, and that it was afterward, at the building of the second Temple, discovered and brought to light. But such a theory is entirely at variance with all the legends of the degree of Select Master and of Royal Arch Masonry. To admit it would lead to endless confusion and contradictions in the traditions of the Order. It is, besides, in conflict with the opinions of the Rabbinical writers and every Hebrew scholar. Josephus and the Rabbis allege that in the second Temple the Holy of Holies was empty, or contained only the Stone of Foundation which marked the place which the ark should have occupied.

The ark was made of shittim wood, overlaid, within and without, with pure gold. It was about three feet nine inches long, two feet three inches wide, and of the same extent in depth. It had on the side two rings of gold, through which were placed staves of shittim wood, by which, when necessary, it was borne by the Levites. Its covering was of pure gold, over which was placed two figures called cherubim, with expanded wings. The covering of the ark was called *kaphiret*, from *kaphar*, " to forgive sin," and hence its English name of " mercy-seat," as being the place where the intercession for sin was made.

The researches of archeologists in the last few years have thrown much light on the Egyptian mysteries. Among the ceremonies of that ancient people was one called the Procession of Shrines, which is mentioned in the Rosetta stone, and depicted on the Temple walls. One of these shrines was an ark, which was carried in procession by the priests, who supported it on their shoulders by staves passing through metal rings. It was thus brought into the Temple and deposited on a stand or altar, that the ceremonies prescribed in the ritual might be performed before it. The contents of these arks were various, but always of a mystical character. Sometimes the ark would contain symbols of Life and Stability; sometimes the sacred beetle, the symbol of the Sun; and there was always a representation of two figures of the goddess Theme or Truth and Justice, which overshadowed the ark with their wings. These coincidences of the Egyptian and Hebrew arks must have been more than accidental.

Ark, Substitute. The chest or coffer which constitutes a part of the furniture, and is used in the ceremonies of a Chapter of Royal Arch Masons, and in a Council of Select Masters according to the American system, is called by Masons the Substitute Ark, to distinguish it from the other ark, that which was constructed in the wilderness under the direction of Moses, and which is known as the Ark of the Covenant. This the Substitute Ark was made to represent under circumstances that are recorded in the Masonic traditions, and especially in those of the Select Degree.

The ark used in Royal Arch and Cryptic Masonry in this country is generally of this form:

Prideaux, on the authority of Lightfoot, contends that, as an ark was indispensable to the Israelitish worship, there was in the second Temple an ark which had been expressly made for the purpose of supplying the place of the first or original ark, and which, without possessing any of its prerogatives or honors, was of precisely the same shape and dimensions, and was deposited in the same place. The Masonic legend, whether authentic or not, is simple and connected. It teaches that there was an ark in the second Temple, but that it was neither the Ark of the Covenant, which had been in the Holy of Holies of the first Temple, nor one that had been constructed as a substitute for it after the building of the second Temple. It was that ark which was presented to us in the Select Master's Degree, and which being an exact copy of the Mosaical ark, and intended to replace it in case of its loss, which is best known to Freemasons as the *Substitute Ark*.

Lightfoot gives these Talmudic legends, in his *Prospect of the Temple*, in the following language: " It is fancied by the Jews, that Solomon, when he built the Temple, foreseeing that the Temple should be destroyed, caused very obscure and intricate vaults under ground to be made, wherein to hide the ark when any such danger came; that howsoever it went with the Temple, yet the ark, which was the very life of the Temple, might be saved. And they understand that passage in 2 Chron. xxxv. 3, 'Josiah said unto the Levites, Put the holy ark into the house which Solomon, the son of David, did build,' etc., as if Josiah, having heard by the reading of Moses' manuscript, and by Huldah's prophecy of the danger that hung over Jerusalem, commanded to convey the ark into this vault, that it might be secured; and with it, say they, they laid up Aaron's rod, the pot of manna, and the anointing oil. For while the ark stood in its place upon the stone mentioned—they hold that Aaron's rod and the pot of manna stood before it; but, now, were all conveyed into obscurity—and the stone upon which the ark stood lay over the mouth of the vault. But Rabbi Solomon, which useth not, ordinarily, to forsake such traditions, hath given a more serious gloss upon the place; namely, that whereas Manasseh and Amon had removed the ark out of its habitation, and set up images and abominations there of their own— Joshua speaketh to the priests to restore it to its place again. What became of the ark, at the burning of the temple by Nebuchadnezzar, we read not; it is most likely it went to the fire also. However it sped, it was not in the second Temple; and is one of the five choice things that the Jews reckon wanting there. Yet they had an ark there also of their own making, as they had a breastplate of judgment; which, though they both wanted the glory of the former, which was giving of oracles, yet did they stand current as to the other matters of their worship, as the former breastplate and ark had done."

The idea of the concealment of an ark and its accompanying treasures always prevailed in the Jewish church. The account given by the Talmudists is undoubtedly mythical; but there must, as certainly, have been some foundation for the myth, for every myth has a substratum of truth. The Masonic tradition differs from the Rabbinical, but is in every way more reconcilable with truth, or at least with probability. The ark constructed by Moses, Aholiab, and Bezaleel was burned at the destruction of the first Temple; but there was an exact representation of it in the second.

Arkansas. The modern school of historians, Masonic and profane, write history from original sources when possible, but in this case that method is no longer possible, as all the records of the Grand Lodge of this State were burned in 1864 and again in 1876 when all records gathered since 1864 were destroyed —depriving us of all early records.

From what had been previously written several accounts have appeared, and from these this article is compiled.

Passing over the tradition that the Spaniards had introduced Freemasonry into Arkansas about the time of the Revolution, we find the first Lodge was established at Post Arkansas, under authority of a dispensation granted by the Grand Master of Kentucky, November 29, 1819, and a charter was granted August 29, 1820, but was surrendered August 28, 1822. For several years Masonic matters were dormant.

The Grand Master of Tennessee granted a dispensation for Washington Lodge in Fayetteville, December 24, 1835, and for some reason it was renewed November 12, 1836, and received a charter October 3, 1837. The Grand Lodge of Tennessee granted a dispensation to Clarksville Lodge at Clarksville, October 5, 1838, and a charter October 12, 1839. These dates are taken from Drummond and you will observe he says the Grand Master issued the dispensation to Washington Lodge, but that the Grand Lodge issued the dispensation to Clarksville Lodge. As we have noticed a similar statement from a Past Grand Secretary of Arkansas, they do not conform to the usual plan of the Grand Master issuing the dispensation and the Grand Lodge issuing the charter. However, this custom was quite general.

The next attempt to form a Lodge at Post Arkansas was under the Grand Lodge of Louisiana, which granted a charter January 6, 1837, and a charter seems to have been granted to a Lodge at Little Rock on the same date, and when the capital was moved to Little Rock, Morning Star Lodge at Post Arkansas surrendered its charter.

The Grand Master of Alabama granted a dispensation to Mt. Horeb Lodge at Washington in 1838.

Washington Lodge, No. 82, under a charter from the Grand Lodge of Tennessee; Western Star Lodge, No. 43, at Little Rock, under a charter of the Grand Lodge of Louisiana; Morning Star Lodge, No. 42, at Post Arkansas, under a charter from the Grand Lodge of Louisiana; Mt. Horeb Lodge, U. D., under dispensation from the Grand Lodge of Alabama, met at Little Rock, November 21, 1838, and formed the Grand Lodge of Arkansas. The combined membership is put at 100. These Lodges took new charters and Washington Lodge became No. 1, Western Star No. 2, Morning Star No. 3, and Mt. Horeb No. 4. The first two are in existence, but the last two are defunct.

The Grand Chapter of Royal Arch Masons was organized April 28, 1851, by three Chapters, located at Fayetteville, Little Rock, and El Dorado, which had previously received charters from the General Grand Chapter of the United States.

The Grand Council of Royal and Select Masters was established in the year 1860.

The Grand Commandery of the Order of the Temple was organized on March 23, 1872.

A Lodge, Council, Chapter, Council of Kadosh, and Consistory of the Scottish Rite are established at Little Rock.

Arkite Worship. The almost universal prevalence among the nations of antiquity of some tradition of a long past deluge, gave rise to certain mythological doctrines and religious ceremonies, to which has been given the name of arkite worship, which was very extensively diffused. The evidence of this is to be found in the sacred feeling which was entertained for the sacredness of high mountains, derived, it is supposed, from recollections of an Ararat, and from the presence in all the Mysteries of a basket, chest, or coffer, whose mystical character bore apparently a reference to the ark of Noah. On the subject of this arkite worship, Bryant, Faber, Higgins, Banier, and many other writers, have made learned investigations, which may be consulted with advantage by the Masonic archeologist.

Ark Mariner, Royal, Jewel of. The jewel of this degree prefigures the teachings, which are unique, and draws their symbols from the sea, rain, ark, dove, olive-branch, and *Rainbow*. This last symbol, as El's sign, "*overshadows*" the ark, which really is the sign of Ishtar. The ark is said to have contained all the elements of Elohim's creative power, and in " about nine months and three days there came forth the pent-up energies of Maiya"; her symbol is the dove with the mystic olive, which are sacred to her. The whole underlying thought is that of creation. *See illustration on opposite page.*

Armenbüchse. The poor-box; the name given by German Masons to the box in which collections of money are made at a Table-Lodge for the relief of poor brethren and their families.

Armes. A corrupted form of *Hermes*, found in the Lansdowne and some other old manuscripts.

Armiger. 1. A bearer of arms. The title given by heralds to the esquire who waited on a knight. 2. The Sixth Degree of the Order of African Architects.

Armory. An apartment attached to the asylum of a commandery of Knights Templars, in which the swords and other parts of the costume of the knights are deposited for safe-keeping.

Armor. In English statutes, armor is used for the whole apparatus of war; offensive and defensive arms. In the Order of the Temple pieces of armor are used to a limited extent. In the chivalric degrees of the Scottish Rite, in order to carry out the symbolism as well as to render effect to its dramas, armor pieces and articles for use of knights become necessary, with mantling, crest, mottoes, etc. Some are herein enumerated:

AILLETTES—Square shields for the shoulders.

ANLACE—Short dagger worn at the girdle.

BALDRIC—Belt diagonally crossing the body.

BATTLE-AX—Weapon with ax-blade and spear-head.

BEAVER—Front of helmet, which is raised to admit food and drink.

BEAKER—The drinking-cup with mouth-lip.

BELT—For body. Badge of knightly rank.

BRASSART—Armor to protect the arm from elbow to shoulder.

BUCKLER—A long shield for protecting the body.

CORSELET—Breastplate.

CREST—Ornament on helmet designating rank.

CUIRASS—Backplate.

FASCES—Armor for the thighs, hung from the corselet.

GADLING—Sharp metallic knuckles on gauntlet.

GAUNTLET—Mailed gloves.

GORGET—Armor for the neck.

HALBERD—Long-pole ax.

HAUBERK—Shirt of mail, of rings or scales.

HELMET or CASQUE—Armor for the head.

JAMBEUX—Armor for the legs.

JUPON—Sleeveless jacket, to the hips.

LANCE—Long spear with metallic head and pennon.

MACE—Heavy, short staff of metal, ending with spiked ball.

MANTLE—Outer cloak.

MORION—Head armor without vizor.

PENNON—A pennant, or short streamer, bifurcated.

PLUME—The designation of knighthood.

SALLET—Light helmet for foot-soldiers.

SPEAR—Sword, spur, shield.

VIZOR—Front of helmet (slashed), moving on pivots.

Arms of Masonry. Stow says that the Masons were incorporated as a company in the twelfth year of Henry IV., 1412. Their arms were granted to them, in 1472, by William Hawkesloe, Clarenceux King-at-Arms, and are *azure* on a chevron between three castles *argent;* a pair of compasses somewhat extended, of the first. Crest, a castle of the second. They were adopted, subsequently, by the Grand Lodge of England. The Atholl Grand Lodge objected to this as an unlawful assumption by the Modern Grand Lodge of Speculative Freemasons of the arms of the Operative Masons. They accordingly adopted another coat, which Dermott blazons as follows: Quarterly per squares, counterchanged *vert.* In the first quarter, *azure*, a lion rampant, *or*. In the second quarter, *or*, an ox *passant sable*. In the third quarter, *or*, a man with hands erect proper, robed crimson and ermine. In the fourth quarter, *azure*, an eagle displayed *or*. Crest, the holy ark of the covenant proper, supported by cherubim. Motto, *Kodes la Adonai*, that is, *Holiness to the Lord*.

These arms are derived from the "tetrarchical" (as Sir Thos. Browne calls them), or general banners of the four principal tribes; for it is said that the twelve tribes, during their passage through the wilderness, were encamped in a hollow square, three on each side, as follows: Judah, Zebulun, and Issachar, in the East, under the general banner of Judah; Dan, Asher, and Naphtali, in the North, under the banner of Dan; Ephraim, Manasseh, and Benjamin, in the West, under the banner of Ephraim; and Reuben, Simeon, and Gad, in the South, under Reuben. See *Banners*.

Aroba. Pledge, covenant, agreement. (Latin, *Arrhabo*, a token or pledge. Hebrew, *Arab*, which is the root of *Arubbah*, surety, hostage.) This important word, in the Fourteenth Degree of the Scottish Rite, is used when the initiate partakes of the "Ancient Aroba," the pledge or covenant of friendship, by eating and drinking with his new companions. The word is of greater import than that implied in mere hospitality. The word "aroba" appears nowhere in English works, and seems to have been omitted by Masonic writers. The root "arab" is one of the oldest in the Hebrew language, and means to interweave or to mingle, to exchange, to become surety for anyone, and to pledge even the life of one person for another, or the strongest pledge that can be given. Judah pleads with Israel to let Benjamin go with him to be presented in Egypt to Joseph, as the latter had requested. He says: "Send the lad with me; I will be surety for him" (Gen. xliii. 9); and before Joseph he makes the same remark in Gen. xliv. 32. Job, in chap. xvii. 3, appealing to God, says: "Put me in a surety with thee; who is he that will strike hands with me?" (See also 1 Sam. xvii. 18.) In its pure form, the word "arubbah" occurs only once in the Old Testament (Prov. xvii. 18): "A man void of understanding striketh hands, and becometh surety in the presence of his friend." In Latin, Plautus makes use of the following phrase: "*Hunc arrhabonem amoris a me accipe.*"

Arras, Primordial Chapter of. Arras is a town in France in the department of Pas de Calais, where, in the year 1747, Charles Edward Stuart, the Pretender, is said to have established a Sovereign Primordial and Metropolitan Chapter of Rosicrucian Freemasons. A portion of the charter of this body is given by Ragon in his *Orthodoxie Maçonique.* In 1853, the Count de Hamel, prefect of the department, discovered an authentic copy, in parchment, of this document bearing the date of April 15, 1747, which he deposited in the departmental archives. This document is as follows:

"We, Charles Edward, king of England, France, Scotland, and Ireland, and as such Substitute Grand Master of the Chapter of H., known by the title of Knight of the Eagle and Pelican, and since our sorrows and misfortunes by that of Rose Croix, wishing to testify our gratitude to the Masons of Artois, and.the officers of the city of Arras, for the numerous marks of kindness which they in conjunction with the officers of the garrison of Arras have lavished upon us, and their attachment to our person, shown during a residence of six months in that city,

"We have in favor of them created and erected, and do create and erect by the present bull, in the aforesaid city of Arras, a Sovereign Primordial Chapter of Rose Croix, under the distinctive title of Scottish Jacobite, (*Écosse Jacobite,*) to be ruled and governed by the Knights Lagneau and Robespierre; Avocats Hazard, and his two sons, physicians; J. B. Lucet, our upholsterer, and Jérôme Cellier, our clock-maker, giving to them and to their successors the power not only to make knights, but even to create a Chapter in whatever town they may think fit, provided that two Chapters shall not be created in the same town however populous it may be.

"And that credit may be given to our present bull, we have signed it with our hand and caused to be affixed thereunto the secret seal, and countersigned by the secretary of our cabinet, Thursday, 15th of the second month of the year of the incarnation, 1747.

          "CHARLES EDWARD STUART.
"Countersigned,   BERKLEY."

This Chapter created a few others, and in 1780 established one in Paris, under the distinctive title of Chapter of Arras, in the valley of Paris. It united itself to the Grand Orient of France on the 27th of December, 1801. It was declared First Suffragan of the Scottish Jacobite Chapter, with the right to constitute others. The Chapter established at Arras, by the Pretender, was named the "Eagle and Pelican," and Oliver (*Orig. of R. A.*, p. 22) from this seeks to find, perhaps justifiably, a connection between it and the R. S. Y. C. S. of the Royal Order of Scotland. [The story of the establishment of this Chapter by the Pretender is doubted by some writers and it certainly lacks confirmation; even his joining the Craft at all is disputed by several who have carefully studied the subject.—E. L. H.]

Arrest of Charter. To arrest the charter of a Lodge is a technical phrase by which is meant to suspend the work of a Lodge, to prevent it from holding its usual communications, and to forbid it to transact any business or to do any work. A Grand Master cannot revoke the warrant of a Lodge; but if, in his opinion, the good of Masonry or any other sufficient cause requires it, he may suspend the operation of the warrant until the next communication of the Grand Lodge, which body is alone competent to revise or approve of his action.

Ars Quatuor Coronatorum is the name under which the Transactions of the Lodge Quatuor Coronati, No. 2076, London, the premier literary Lodge of the world, are published in annual volumes, commencing with 1888.

Arthusius, Gotthardus. A learned native of Dantzic, Rector of the Gymnasium at Frankfort-on-the-Main, who wrote many works on Rosicrucianism, under the assumed name of Irenæus Agnostus. (See *Agnostus.*)

Artisan, Chief. An officer in the Council of Knights of Constantinople.

Art, Royal. See *Royal Art.*

Arts. In the Masonic phrase, "arts, parts, and points of the Mysteries of Masonry"; *arts* means the knowledge, or things made known, *parts* the degrees into which Masonry is divided, and *points* the rules and usages. (See *Parts,* and also *Points.*)

Arts, Liberal. See *Liberal Arts and Sciences.*

Arundel, Thomas Howard, Earl of. Tradition places Arundel as the Grand Master of English Freemasons from 1633 to 1635. This is in accordance with Anderson and Preston.

Aryan. One of the three historical divisions of religion—the other two being the Turanian and the Shemitic. It produced Brahmanism, Buddhism, and the Code of Zoroaster.

Asarota. A variegated pavement used for flooring in temples and ancient edifices.

Ascension Day. Also called Holy Thursday. A festival of the Christian church held in commemoration of the ascension of our Lord forty days after Easter. It is celebrated as a feast day by Chapters of Rose Croix.

Ases. The twelve gods and as many goddesses in the Scandinavian mythology.

Ashe, D.D., Rev. Jonathan. A literary plagiarist who resided in Bristol, England. In 1814 he published *The Masonic Manual; or, Lectures on Freemasonry*. Ashe does not, it is true, pretend to originality, but abstains from giving credit to Hutchinson, from whom he has taken at least two-thirds of his book. A second edition appeared in 1825, and in 1843 an edition was published by Spencer, with valuable notes by Dr. Oliver.

Asher, Dr. Carl Wilhelm. The first translator into German of the Halliwell or "Regius" MS., which he published at Hamburg, in 1842, under the title of *Aelteste Urkunde der Freimaurerei in England*. This work contains both the original English document and the German translation.

Ashlar. "Freestone as it comes out of the quarry."—*Bailey*. In Speculative Masonry we adopt the ashlar in two different states, as symbols in the Apprentice's Degree. The Rough Ashlar, or stone in its rude and unpolished condition, is emblematic of man in his natural state—ignorant, uncultivated, and vicious. But when education has exerted its wholesome influence in expanding his intellect, restraining his passions, and purifying his life, he then is represented by the Perfect Ashlar, which, under the skilful hands of the workmen, has been smoothed, and squared, and fitted for its place in the building. In the older lectures of the eighteenth century the Perfect Ashlar is not mentioned, but its place was supplied by the Broached Thurnel.

Ashmole, Elias. A celebrated antiquary, and the author of, among other works, the well-known *History of the Order of the Garter*, and founder of the Ashmolean Museum at Oxford. He was born at Litchfield, in England, on the 23d of May, 1617, and died at London on the 18th of May, 1692. He was made a Freemason on the 16th of October, 1646, and gives the following account of his reception in his *Diary*, p. 303.

"1646. Oct: 16. 4 H 30' p. m., I was made a Freemason at Warrington, in Lancashire, with Colonel Henry Mainwaring, of Karincham, in Cheshire. The names of those that were then of the Lodge, Mr. Richard Penket Warden, Mr. James Collier, Mr. Rich: Sankey, Henry Littler, John Ellam, Rich: Ellam and Hugh Brewer."

In another place he speaks of his attendance at a meeting (*Diary*, p. 362), and thirty-six years afterward makes the following entry:

"1682. March 10. About 5 H p. m., I received a summons to appear at a Lodge to be held the next day at Masons' Hall, London.

"11. Accordingly, I went, and about Noone were admitted into the Fellowship of Freemasons, Sir William Wilson, knight, Capt. Richard Borthwick, Mr. William Woodman, Mr. William Wise.

"I was the senior fellow among them, (it being thirty-five years since I was admitted;) there was present besides myself the Fellowes afternamed: Mr. Thomas Wise, Master of the Masons' company this present year; Mr. Thomas Shorthofe, Mr. Thomas Shadbolt, —— Waindsford, Esq., Mr. Nicholas Young, Mr. John Shorthofe, Mr. William Hamon, Mr. John Thompson, and Mr. William Stanton. We all dyned at the halfe Moone Taverne in Cheapeside, at a noble dinner prepared at the charge of the new Accepted Masons."*

It is to be regretted that the intention expressed by Ashmole to write a history of Freemasonry was never carried into effect. His laborious research as evinced in his exhaustive work on the *Order of the Garter*, would lead us to have expected from his antiquarian pen a record of the origin and early progress of our Institution more valuable than any that we now possess. The following remarks on this subject, contained in a letter from Dr. Knipe, of Christ Church, Oxford, to the publisher of Ashmole's *Life*, while it enables us to form some estimate of the loss that Masonic literature has suffered, supplies interesting particulars which are worthy of preservation.

"As to the ancient society of Freemasons, concerning whom you are desirous of knowing what may be known with certainty, I shall only tell you, that if our worthy Brother, E. Ashmole, Esq., had executed his intended design, our Fraternity had been as much obliged to him as the Brethren of the most noble Order of the Garter. I would not have you surprised at this expression, or think it all too assuming. The sovereigns of that Order have not disdained our fellowship, and there have been times when emperors were also Freemasons. What from Mr. E. Ashmole's collection I could gather was, that the report of our society's taking rise from a bull granted by the Pope, in the reign of Henry III., to some Italian architects to travel over all Europe, to erect chapels, was ill-founded. Such a bull there was, and those architects were Masons; but this bull, in the opinion of the learned Mr. Ashmole, was confirmative only, and did not by any means create our Fraternity, or even establish them in this kingdom. But as to the time and manner of that establishment, something I shall relate from the same collections. St. Alban the Proto-Martyr of England, established Masonry here; and from his time it flourished more or less, according as the world went, down to the days of King Athelstan, who, for the sake of his brother Edwin, granted the Masons a charter under our Norman princes. They frequently received extraordinary marks of royal favor. There is no doubt to be made, that the skill of Masons, which was always transcendent, even in the most barbarous times,—their wonderful kindness and attachment to each other, how different soever in condition, and their inviolable fidelity in keeping religiously their secret,—must expose them in ignorant, troublesome, and suspicious times

---

* These entries have been reproduced in facsimile in Vol. XI of *Ars Quatuor Coronatorum* (1898).

to a vast variety of adventures, according to the different fate of parties and other alterations in government. By the way, I shall note that the Masons were always loyal, which exposed them to great severities when power wore the trappings of justice, and those who committed treason punished true men as traitors. Thus, in the third year of the reign of Henry VI., an act of Parliament was passed to abolish the society of Masons, and to hinder, under grievous penalties, the holding Chapters, Lodges, or other regular assemblies. Yet this act was afterwards repealed, and even before that, King Henry VI., and several of the principal lords of his court, became fellows of the Craft.''

Asia. In the French Rite of Adoption, the East end of the Lodge is called *Asia*.

Asia, Initiated Knights and Brothers of. This Order was introduced in Berlin, or, as some say, in Vienna, in the year 1780, by a schism of several members of the German Rose Croix. They adopted a mixture of Christian, Jewish, and Mohammedan ceremonies, to indicate, as Ragon supposes, their entire religious tolerance. Their object was the study of the natural sciences and the search for the universal panacea to prolong life. Thory charges them with this; but may it not have been, as with the Alchemists, merely a symbol of immortality? They forbade all inquiries into the art of transmutation of metals. The Grand Synédrion, properly the Grand Sanhedrim, which consisted of seventy-two members and was the head of the Order, had its seat at Vienna. The Order was founded on the three symbolic degrees, and attached to them nine others, as follows: 4. Seekers; 5. Sufferers; 6. Initiated Knights and Brothers of Asia in Europe; 7. Masters and Sages; 8. Royal Priests, or True Brothers of Rose Croix; 9. Melchizedek. The Order no longer exists. Many details of it will be found in Luchet's *Essai sur les Illumines*.

Asia, Perfect Initiates of. A rite of very little importance, consisting of seven degrees, and said to have been invented at Lyons. A very voluminous manuscript, translated from the German, was sold at Paris, in 1821, to M. Bailleul, and came into the possession of Ragon, who reduced its size, and, with the assistance of Des Etangs, modified it. I have no knowledge that it was ever worked.

Ask, Seek, Knock. In referring to the passage of Matthew vii. 7, "Ask, and it shall be given you; seek, and ye shall find; knock, and it shall be opened unto you," Dr. Clarke says: "These three words—*ask, seek, knock*—include the ideas of *want, loss*, and *earnestness*." The application made to the passage theologically is equally appropriate to it in a Masonic Lodge. You *ask* for *acceptance*, you *seek* for *light*, you *knock* for *initiation*, which includes the other two.

Aspirant. One who eagerly seeks to know or to attain something. Thus, Warburton speaks of "the aspirant to the Mysteries." It is applied also to one about to be initiated into Masonry. There seems, however, to be

a shade of difference in meaning between the words *candidate* and *aspirant*. The candidate is one who asks for admission; so called from the Lat. *candidatus* "clothed in white," because candidates for office at Rome wore a white dress. The aspirant is one already elected and in process of initiation, and coming from *aspiro*, to seek eagerly, refers to the earnestness with which he prosecutes his search for light and truth.

Assassins. The Ishmaelites, or Assassins, constituted a sect or confraternity, which was founded by Hassan Sabah, about the year 1090, in Persia. The name is derived, it is supposed, from their immoderate use of the plant haschish, or henbane, which produced a delirious frenzy. The title given to the chief of the Order was *Sheikh-el-Jebel*, which has been translated the "Old Man of the Mountain," but which Higgins has shown (*Anacal.*, i., 700) to mean literally "The Sage of the Kabbala or Traditions." Von Hammer has written a *History of the Assassins*, but his opposition to secret societies has led him to speak with so much prejudice that, although his historical statements are interesting, his philosophical deductions have to be taken with many grains of allowance. Godfrey Higgins has probably erred on the other side, and by a too ready adherence to a preconceived theory has, in his *Anacalypsis*, confounded them with the Templars, whom he considers as the precursors of the Freemasons. In this, as in most things, the middle course appears to be the most truthful.

The Assassins were a secret society, that is to say, they had a secret esoteric doctrine, which was imparted only to the initiated. Hammer says that they had a graduated series of initiations, the names of which he gives as Apprentices, Fellows, and Masters; they had, too, an oath of passive obedience, and resembled, he asserts, in many respects, the secret societies that subsequently existed in Europe. They were governed by a Grand Master and Priors, and had regulations and a special religious code, in all of which Von Hammer finds a close resemblance to the Templars, the Hospitalers, and the Teutonic Knights. Between the Assassins and the Templars history records that there were several amicable transactions not at all consistent with the religious vows of the latter and the supposed religious faith of the former, and striking coincidences of feeling, of which Higgins has not been slow to avail himself in his attempt to prove the close connection, if not absolute identity, of the two Orders. It is most probable, as Sir John Malcolm contends, that they were a race of Sofis, the teachers of the secret doctrine of Mohammed. Von Hammer admits that they produced a great number of treatises on mathematics and jurisprudence; and, forgetting for a time his bigotry and his prejudice, he attributes to Hassan, their founder, a profound knowledge of philosophy and mathematical and metaphysical sciences, and an enlightened spirit, under whose influence the civilization of

Persia attained a high degree; so that during his reign of forty-six years the Persian literature attained a point of excellence beyond that of Alexandria under the Ptolemies, and of France under Francis I. The old belief that they were a confederacy of murderers—whence we have taken our English word *assassins*—must now be abandoned as a figment of the credulity of past centuries, and we must be content to look upon them as a secret society. of philosophers, whose political relations, however, merged them into a dynasty. If we interpret Freemasonry as a generic term, signifying a philosophic sect which teaches truth by a mystical initiation and secret symbols, then Higgins was not very far in error in calling them the Freemasons of the East.

Assassins of the Third Degree. There is in Freemasonry a legend of certain unworthy Craftsmen who entered into a conspiracy to extort from a distinguished brother a secret of which he was the possessor. The legend is altogether symbolic, and when its symbolism is truly comprehended, becomes surpassingly beautiful. By those who look at it as having the pretension of an historical fact, it is sometimes treated with indifference, and sometimes considered an absurdity. But it is not thus that the legends and symbols of Masonry must be read, if we would learn their true spirit. To behold the goddess in all her glorious beauty, the veil that conceals her statue must be withdrawn. Masonic writers who have sought to interpret the symbolism of the legend of the conspiracy of the three assassins, have not agreed always in the interpretation, although they have finally arrived at the same result, namely, that it has a spiritual signification. Those who trace Speculative Masonry to the ancient solar worship, of whom Ragon may be considered as the exponent, find in this legend a symbol of the conspiracy of the three winter months to destroy the life-giving heat of the sun. Those who, like the disciples of the Rite of Strict Observance, trace Masonry to a Templar origin, explain the legend as referring to the conspiracy of the three renegade knights who falsely accused the Order, and thus aided King Philip and Pope Clement to abolish Templarism, and to slay its Grand Master. Hutchinson and Oliver, who labored to give a Christian interpretation to all the symbols of Masonry, referred the legend to the crucifixion of the Messiah, the type of which is, of course, the slaying of Abel by his brother Cain. Others, of whom the Chevalier Ramsay was the leader, sought to give it a political significance; and, making Charles I. the type of the Builder, symbolized Cromwell and his adherents as the conspirators. The Masonic scholars whose aim has been to identify the modern system of Freemasonry with the Ancient Mysteries, and especially with the Egyptian, which they supposed to be the germ of all the others, interpret the conspirators as the symbol of the Evil Principle, or Typhon, slaying the Good Principle, or Osiris; or, when they refer to the Zoroastic Mysteries of Persia,

as Ahriman contending against Ormuzd. And lastly, in the Philosophic degrees, the myth is interpreted as signifying the war of Falsehood, Ignorance, and Superstition against Truth. Of the supposed names of the three Assassins, there is hardly any end of variations, for they materially differ in all the principal rites. Thus, we have Jubela, Jubelo, and Jubelum in the York and American Rites. In the Adonhiramite system we have Romvel, Gravelot, and Abiram. In the Scottish Rite we find the names given in the old rituals as Jubelum Akirop, sometimes Abiram, Jubelo Romvel, and Jubela Gravelot. Schterke and Oterfüt are in some of the German rituals, while other Scottish rituals have Abiram, Romvel, and Hobhen. In all these names there is manifest corruption, and the patience of many Masonic scholars has been well-nigh exhausted in seeking for some plausible and satisfactory derivation.

Assembly. The meetings of the Craft during the operative period in the Middle Ages, were called "assemblies," which appear to have been tantamount to the modern *Lodges*, and they are constantly spoken of in the *Old Constitutions*. The word assembly was also often used in these documents to indicate a larger meeting of the whole Craft, which was equivalent to the modern Grand Lodge, and which was held annually. The York MS., No. 1, about the year 1600, says " that Edwin procured of ye King his father a charter and commission to hold every yeare an assembly wheresoever they would within ye realm of England," and this statement, whether true or false, is repeated in all the old records. Preston says, speaking of that medieval period, that "a sufficient number of Masons met together within a certain district, with the consent of the sheriff or chief magistrate of the place, were empowered at this time to make Masons," etc. To this assembly, every Mason was bound, when summoned, to appear. Thus, in the Harleian MS., *circa* 1660, it is ordained that "every Master and Fellow come to the Assembly, if it be within five miles about him, if he have any warning." The term "General Assembly," to indicate the annual meeting, is said to have been first used at the meeting, held on December 27, 1663, as quoted by Preston. In the *Old Constitutions* printed in 1722 by Roberts, and which claims to be taken from a MS. of the eighteenth century, the term used is "Yearly Assembly." Anderson speaks of an *Old Constitution* which used the word "General;" but his quotations are not always verbally accurate.

Assistance. See *Aid and Assistance*.

Associates of the Temple. During the Middle Ages, many persons of rank, who were desirous of participating in the spiritual advantages supposed to be enjoyed by the Templars in consequence of the good works done by the Fraternity, but who were unwilling to submit to the discipline of the brethren, made valuable donations to the Order, and were, in consequence, admitted into a sort of spiritual connection with it. These persons were termed "Associates of the Temple." The custom was most probably confined to England, and many "of these Associates" had monuments and effigies erected to them in the Temple Church at London.

Association. Although an association is properly the union of men into a society for a common purpose, the word is scarcely ever applied to the Order of Freemasonry. Yet its employment, although unusual, would not be incorrect, for Freemasonry is an association of men for a common purpose. Washington uses the term when he calls Freemasonry "an *association* whose principles lead to purity of morals, and are beneficial of action." (*Letter to G. L. of So. Ca.*)

Assyrian Architecture. The discovery in 1882 of the remains of a town, close to, and north of, Nineveh, built by Sargon, about 721 B.C., in size about a mile square, with its angles facing the cardinal points, and the enclosure containing the finest specimens of their architecture, revived much interest in archeologists. The chief place of regard is the royal palace, which was like unto a city of itself, everything being on a colossal scale. The walls of the town were 45 feet thick. The inclined approach to the palace was flanked by strangely formed bulls from 15 to 19 feet high. There were terraces, courts, and passage-ways to an innermost square of 150 feet, surrounded by state apartments and temples. The Hall of Judgment was prominent, as also the astronomical observatory. All entrances to great buildings were ornamented by colossal animals and porcelain decorations and inscriptions.

Astræa. The Grand Lodge established in Russia, on the 30th of August, 1815, assumed the title of the Grand Lodge of Astræa. It held its Grand East at St. Petersburg, and continued in existence until 1822, when the Czar issued a Ukase, dated August 1, 1822, closing all Lodges in Russia and forbidding them to reopen at any future time.

Astrology. A science demanding the respect of the scholar, notwithstanding its designation as a "black art," and, in a reflective sense, an occult science; a system of divination foretelling results by the relative positions of the planets and other heavenly bodies toward the earth. Men of eminence have adhered to the doctrines of astrology as a science. It is a study well considered in, and forming an important part of, the ceremonies of the "Philosophus," or fourth grade of the First Order of the Society of Rosicrucians. Astrology has been deemed the twin science of astronomy, grasping knowledge from the heavenly bodies, and granting a proper understanding of many of the startling forces in nature. It is claimed that the constellations of the zodiac govern the earthly animals, and that every star has its peculiar nature, property, and function, the seal and character of which it impresses through its rays upon plants, minerals, and animal life. This science was known to the ancients as the "divine art." (See *Magic*.)

Astronomy. The science which instructs us in the laws that govern the heavenly bodies. Its origin is lost in the mists of antiquity; for the earliest inhabitants of the earth must have been attracted by the splendor of the glorious firmament above them, and would have sought in the motions of its luminaries for the readiest and most certain method of measuring time. With astronomy the system of Freemasonry is intimately connected. From that science many of our most significant emblems are borrowed. The Lodge itself is a representation of the world; it is adorned with the images of the sun and moon, whose regularity and precision furnish a lesson of wisdom and prudence; its pillars of strength and establishment have been compared to the two columns which the ancients placed at the equinoctial points as supporters of the arch of heaven; the blazing star, which was among the Egyptians a symbol of Anubis, or the dog-star, whose rising foretold the overflowing of the Nile, shines in the East; while the clouded canopy is decorated with the beautiful Pleiades. The connection between our Order and astronomy is still more manifest in the spurious Freemasonry of antiquity, where, the pure principles of our system being lost, the symbolic instruction of the heavenly bodies gave place to the corrupt Sabean worship of the sun, and moon, and stars—a worship whose influences are seen in all the mysteries of Paganism.

Asylum. During the session of a Commandery of Knights Templars, a part of the room is called the *asylum;* the word has hence been adopted, by the figure synecdoche, to signify the place of meeting of a Commandery.

Asylum for Aged Freemasons. The Asylum for Aged and Decayed Freemasons is a magnificent edifice at Croydon in Surrey, England. The charity was established by Dr. Crucefix, after sixteen years of herculean toil, such as few men but himself could have sustained. He did not live to see it in full operation, but breathed his last at the very time when the cope-stone was placed on the building. (See *Annuities*.)

Atelier. The French thus call the place where the Lodge meets, or the Lodge room. The word signifies a workshop or place where several workmen are assembled under the same master. The word is applied in French Masonry not only to the place of meeting of a Lodge, but also to that of a Chapter, Council, or any other Masonic body. Bazot says (*Man. Maçon,* 65) that *atelier* is more particularly applied to the Table-Lodge, or Lodge when at banquet, but that the word is also used to designate any reunion of the Lodge.

Atheist. One who does not believe in the existence of God. Such a state of mind can only arise from the ignorance of stupidity or a corruption of principle, since the whole universe is filled with the moral and physical proofs of a Creator. He who does not look to a superior and superintending power as his maker and his judge, is without that coercive principle of salutary fear which should prompt him to do good and to eschew evil, and his oath can, of necessity, be no stronger than his word. Masons, looking to the dangerous tendency of such a tenet, have wisely discouraged it, by declaring that no atheist can be admitted to participate in their Fraternity; and the better to carry this law into effect, every candidate, before passing through any of the ceremonies of initiation, is required, publicly and solemnly, to declare his trust in God.

Athelstan. The grandson of the great Alfred ascended the throne of England in 924, and died in 940. The *Old Constitutions* describe him as a great patron of Masonry. Thus, one of them, the Roberts MS., printed in 1722, and claiming to be five hundred years old, says: "He began to build many Abbeys, Monasteries, and other religious houses, as also castles and divers Fortresses for defence of his realm. He loved *Masons* more than his father; he greatly study'd *Geometry*, and sent into many lands for men expert in the science. He gave them a very large charter to hold a yearly assembly, and power to correct offenders in the said science; and the king himself caused a General Assembly of all *Masons* in his realm, at *York*, and there made many *Masons*, and gave them a deep charge for observation of all such articles as belonged unto *Masonry*, and delivered them the said Charter to keep."

Atholl Masons. The "Ancient" Masons are sometimes called "Atholl" Masons, because they were presided over by the Third Duke of Atholl as their Grand Master from 1771 to 1774, and by the Fourth Duke from 1775 to 1781, and also from 1791 to 1813. (See *Ancient Masons*.)

Atossa. The daughter of King Cyrus of Persia, Queen of Cambyses, and afterward of Darius Hystaspes, to whom she bore Xerxes. Referred to in the degree of Prince of Jerusalem, the Sixteenth of the Scottish Rite.

Attendance. See *Absence*.

Attouchement. The name given by the French Masons to what the English call the *grip*.

Attributes. The collar and jewel appropriate to an officer are called his attributes. The working tools and implements of Masonry are also called its attributes. The word in these senses is much more used by French than by English Masons.

Atwood, Henry C. At one time of considerable notoriety in the Masonic history of New York. He was born in Connecticut about the beginning of the present century, and removed to the city of New York about 1825, in which year he organized a Lodge for the purpose of introducing the system taught by Jeremy L. Cross, of whom Atwood was a pupil. This system met with great opposition from some of the most distinguished Masons of the State, who favored the ancient ritual, which had existed before the system of Webb had been invented, from whom Cross received his lectures. Atwood, by great smart-ness and untiring energy, succeeded in making the system which he taught eventually popular. He took great interest in Masonry, and being intellectually clever, although not learned, he collected a great number of admirers, while the tenacity with which he maintained his opinions, however unpopular they might be, secured for him as many enemies. He was greatly instrumental in establishing, in 1837, the schismatic body known as the St. John's Grand Lodge, and was its Grand Master at the time of its union, in 1850, with the legitimate Grand Lodge of New York. Atwood edited a small Masonic periodical called *The Sentinel*, which was remarkable for the virulent and unmasonic tone of its articles. He was also the author of a *Masonic Monitor* of some pretensions. He died in 1860.

Atys. The Mysteries of Atys in Phrygia, and those of Cybele his mistress, like their worship, much resembled those of Adonis and Bacchus, Osiris and Isis. Their Asiatic origin is universally admitted, and was with great plausibility claimed by Phrygia, which contested the palm of antiquity with Egypt. They, more than any other people, mingled allegory with their religious worship, and were great inventors of fables; and their sacred traditions as to Cybele and Atys, whom all admit to be Phrygian gods, were very various. In all, as we learn from Julius Firmicus, they represented by allegory the phenomena of nature, and the succession of physical facts under the veil of a marvelous history.

Their feasts occurred at the equinoxes, commencing with lamentation, mourning, groans, and pitiful cries for the death of Atys, and ending with rejoicings at his restoration to life.

" Audi, Vide, Tace." (*Hear, see, and be silent*.) A motto frequently found on Masonic medals, and often appropriately used in Masonic documents. It was adopted as its motto by the United Grand Lodge of England at the union between the "Ancients" and the "Moderns" in 1813.

Auditor. An officer in the Supreme Council of the Ancient and Accepted Scottish Rite for the Southern Jurisdiction of the United States. His duty is, with the Committee on Finance, to examine and report on the accounts of the Inspector and other officers. This duty of auditing the accounts of the Secretary and Treasurer is generally entrusted, in Masonic bodies, to a special committee appointed for the purpose. In the Grand Lodge of England, the accounts are audited annually by a professional auditor, who must be a Master Mason.

Auditors. The first class of the secret system adopted by the Christians in their early days. The second class were *Catechumens*, and the third were *The Faithful*.

Aufseher. The German name for the Warden of a Lodge. The Senior Warden is called Erste Aufseher, and the Junior Warden, Zweite Aufseher. The word literally means an overseer. Its Masonic application is technical.

Auger. An implement used as a symbol in the Ark Mariners Degree.

Augustine, St. See *Saint Augustine.*

Augustus William, Prince of Prussia. Born in 1722, died in 1758. Brother of Frederick the Great, and father of King Frederick William II. A member of Lodge "Drei Weltkugeln," Berlin.

Aum. A mystic syllable among the Hindus, signifying the Supreme God of Gods, which the Brahmans, from its awful and sacred meaning, hesitate to pronounce aloud, and in doing so place one of their hands before the mouth so as to deaden the sound. This triliteral name of God, which is as sacred among the Hindus as the Tetragrammatam is among the Jews, is composed of three Sanskrit letters, sounding AUM. The first letter, A, stands for the Creator; the second, U, for the Preserver; and the third, M, for the Destroyer, or Brahma, Vishnu, and Siva. Benfey, in his *Sanskrit-English Dictionary,* defines the word as "a particle of reminiscence"; and this may explain the Brahmanical saying, that a Brahman beginning or ending the reading of a part of the Veda or Sacred Books, must always pronounce, *to himself,* the syllable AUM; for unless that syllable precede, his learning will slip away from him, and unless it follow, nothing will be long retained. An old passage in the Parana says, "All the rites ordained in the Vedas, the sacrifices to fire, and all sacred purifications, shall pass away, but the word AUM shall never pass away, for it is the symbol of the Lord of all things." The word has been indifferently spelled, O'M, AOM, and AUM; but the last is evidently the most proper, as the second letter is OO = U in the Sanskrit alphabet.

Aumont. Said to have been the successor of Molay as Grand Master, and hence called the Restorer of the Order of the Templars. There is a tradition, altogether fabulous, however, which states that he, with seven other Templars, fled, after the dissolution of the Order, into Scotland, disguised as Operative Masons, and there secretly and under another name founded a new Order; and to preserve as much as possible the ancient name of Templars, as well as to retain the remembrance of the clothing of Masons, in which disguise they had fled, they chose the name of Freemasons, and thus founded Freemasonry. The society thus formed, instead of conquering or rebuilding the Temple of Jerusalem, was to erect symbolical temples. This is one of the forms of the Templar theory of the origin of Freemasonry.

Aurora. In Hebrew the light is called *Aur,* and in its dual capacity *Aurim.* Hence *Urim,* lights—as, *Thme,* Thummim, perfections. *Ra* is the sun, the symbolic god of the Egyptians, and *Ouro,* royalty. Hence we have Aur, Ouro, Ra, which is the double symbolic capacity of "Light." Referring to the Urim and Thummim, *Re* is physical and intellectual light, while *Thme* is the divinity of truth and justice.

Aurora is the color of the baldric worn by the brethren in the Sixteenth Degree of the Scottish Rite, which in the legend is said to have been presented by King Darius to the captive Zerubbabel on presentation of his liberty, and that of all his people, who had been slaves in Babylon for seventy years.

Auserwählten. German for *Elu* or *Elect.*

Austin. See *Saint Augustine.*

Australasia. The first Masonic Lodge in this region was held in 1803 at Sydney, but was suppressed by the Governor, and it was not until the year 1820 that the parent Lodge of Australasia was warranted to meet at Sydney by the Grand Lodge of Ireland; it is now No. 1 on the New South Wales register and named the "Australian Social Mother Lodge." After that many Lodges were warranted under the three *Constitutions* of England, Scotland and Ireland, out of which in course of time no less than six independent Grand Lodges have been formed, viz., South Australia (founded in 1884), New South Wales (1888), Victoria (1889), Tasmania (1890), New Zealand (1890), and Western Australia (1900). [E. L. H.]

Austria. Freemasonry was introduced into Austria in 1742, by the establishment at Vienna of the Lodge of the Three Cannons. But it was broken up by the government in the following year, and thirty of its members were imprisoned for having met in contempt of the authorities. Maria Theresa was an enemy of the Institution, and prohibited it in 1764. Lodges, however, continued to meet secretly in Vienna and Prague. In 1780, Joseph II. ascended the throne, and under his liberal administration Freemasonry, if not actually encouraged, was at least tolerated, and many new Lodges were established in Austria, Hungary, Bohemia, and Transylvania, under the authority of the Grand Lodge of Germany, in Berlin. Delegates from these Lodges met at Vienna in 1784, and organized the Grand Lodge of Austria, electing the Count of Dietrichstein, Grand Master. The attempt of the Grand Lodge at Berlin to make this a Provincial Grand Lodge was successful for only a short time, and in 1785 the Grand Lodge of Austria again proclaimed its independence.

During the reign of Joseph II., Austrian Masonry was prosperous. Notwithstanding the efforts of its enemies, the monarch could never be persuaded to prohibit it. But in 1785 he was induced to issue instructions by which the number of the Lodges was reduced, so that not more than three were permitted to exist in each city; and he ordered that a list of the members and a note of the times of meeting of each Lodge should be annually delivered to the magistrates.

Joseph died in 1790, and Leopold II. expressed himself as not unfriendly to the Fraternity, but his successor in 1792, Francis II., yielded to the machinations of the anti-Masons, and dissolved the Lodges. In 1801, he issued a decree which forbade the employment of anyone in the public service who was attached to any secret society. Masonry is in operation in Austria, as it is in most non-Masonic countries, but not in any public form as in other countries. The Catholics do not so persistently persecute it as they once did through royal sanction.

Authentic. Formerly, in the science of Diplomatics, ancient manuscripts were termed authentic when they were originals, and in opposition to copies. But in modern times the acceptation of the word has been enlarged, and it is now applied to instruments which, although they may be copies, bear the evidence of having been executed by proper authority. So of the old records of Masonry, the originals of many have been lost, or at least have not yet been found. Yet the copies, if they can be traced to unsuspected sources within the body of the Craft and show the internal marks of historical accuracy, are to be reckoned as authentic. But if their origin is altogether unknown, and their statements or style conflict with the known character of the Order at their assumed date, their authenticity is to be doubted or denied.

Authenticity of the Scriptures. A belief in the authenticity of the Scriptures of the Old and New Testament as a religious qualification of initiation does not constitute one of the laws of Masonry, for such a regulation would destroy the universality of the Institution, and under its action none but Christians could become eligible for admission. But in 1856 the Grand Lodge of Ohio declared "that a distinct avowal of a belief in the Divine authority of the Holy Scriptures should be required of every one who is admitted to the privileges of Masonry, and that a denial of the same is an offence against the Institution, calling for exemplary discipline." It is hardly necessary to say that the enunciation of this principle met with the almost universal condemnation of the Grand Lodges and Masonic jurists of this country. The Grand Lodge of Ohio subsequently repealed the regulation. In 1857, the Grand Lodge of Texas adopted a similar resolution; but the general sense of the Fraternity has rejected all religious tests except a belief in God.

Autopsy. (Greek, *aὐτοψία, a seeing with one's own eyes.*) The complete communication of the secrets in the Ancient Mysteries, when the aspirant was admitted into the sacellum, or most sacred place, and was invested by the hierophant with all the aporrheta, or sacred things, which constituted the perfect knowledge of the initiate. A similar ceremony in Freemasonry is called the Rite of Intrusting. (See *Mysteries.*)

Auxiliary Degrees. According to Oliver (*Landm.*, ii., 345), the Supreme Council of France, in addition to the thirty-three regular degrees of the Rite, confers six others, which he calls "Auxiliary Degrees." They are, 1. Elu de Perignan. 2. Petit Architecte. 3. Grand Architecte, or Compagnon Écossais. 4. Maître Écossais. 5. Knight of the East. 6. Knight Rose Croix.

Avenue. Forming avenue is a ceremony sometimes practised in the lower degrees, but more generally in the higher ones, on certain occasions of paying honors to superior officers. The brethren form in two ranks facing each other. If the degree is one in which swords are used, these are drawn and elevated, being crossed each with the opposite sword. The swords thus crossed constitute what is called "the arch of steel." The person to whom honor is to be paid passes between the opposite ranks and under the arch of steel.

Avignon, Illuminati of. (*Illuminés d'Avignon.*) A rite instituted by Pernetti at Avignon, in France, in 1770, and transferred in the year 1778 to Montpellier, under the name of the *Academy of True Masons.* The Academy of Avignon consisted of only four degrees, the three of symbolic or St. John's Masonry, and a fourth called the *True Mason*, which was made up of instructions, Hermetical and Swedenborgian. (See *Pernetti.*)

Avouchment. See *Vouching.*

Award. In law, the judgment pronounced by one or more arbitrators, at the request of two parties who are at variance. "If any complaint be brought," say the *Charges* published by Anderson, "the brother found guilty shall stand to the award and determination of the Lodge." (*Constitutions*, ed. 1723, p. 54.)

Ayes and Noes. It is not according to Masonic usage to call for the ayes and noes on any question pending before a Lodge. By a show of hands is the old and usual custom.

Aynon. Aynon, Agnon, Ajuon, and Dyon are all used in the old manuscript *Constitutions* for one whom they call the son of the King of Tyre, but it is evidently meant for Hiram Abif. Each of these words is most probably a corruption of the Hebrew *Adon* or *Lord*, so that the reference would clearly be to Adon Hiram or Adoniram, with whom Hiram was often confounded; a confusion to be found in later times in the Adonhiramite Rite.

Azariah. The old French rituals have *Azarias.* A name in the high degrees signifying *Helped of God.*

Azazel. "Scapegoat," the "demon of dry places." Translated by others to be the fallen angel mentioned in the Book of Enoch, and identical with Sammael, the Angel of Death. Symmachus says, "the goat that departs"; Josephus, "the averter of ills," "caper emissarius."

Two he-goats, in all respects alike and equal, were brought forward for the day of atonement. The urn was shaken and two lots cast; one was "For the Name," and the other "For Azazel." A scarlet tongue-shaped piece of wood was twisted on the head of the goat to be sent away, and he was placed before the gate and delivered to his conductor. The high priest, placing his two hands on the goat, made confession for the people, and pronounced THE NAME clearly, which the people hearing, they knelt and worshiped, and fell on their faces and said, "*Blessed be the Name. The Honor of His kingdom forever and ever.*"

The goat was then led forth to the mountain-side and rolled down to death.

Azrael. (Heb., help of God.) In the Jewish and the Mohammedan mythology, the name of the angel who watches over the dying and separates the soul from the body. Prior to the intercession of Mohammed, Azrael inflicted the death-penalty visibly, by striking down before the eyes of the living those whose time for death was come. (See Henry W. Longfellow's exquisite poem *Azrael.*)

Aztec Writings. The key to the Aztec writings, it is alleged, has been discovered by Rev. Father Damago Soto, of Concordia, Vera Cruz.

Azure. The clear, blue color of the sky. Cerulean. The appropriate color of the symbolic degrees sometimes termed Blue Degrees.

B

B. (ב, *Beth.*) A labial consonant standing second in most alphabets, and in the Hebrew or Phœnician signifies *house*, probably from its form of a tent or house, thus:

and finally the Hebrew ב, having the numerical value *two.* When united with the leading letter of the alphabet, אב, it signifies *Ab*, Father, Master, or the one in authority, as applied to Hiram the Architect. This is the root of *Baal.* The Hebrew name of the Deity connected with this letter is בחור, Bakhur.

Baal. Hebrew, בעל. He was the chief divinity among the Phœnicians, the Canaanites, and the Babylonians. The word signifies in Hebrew *lord* or *master.* It was among the Orientalists a comprehensive term, denoting divinity of any kind without reference to class or to sex. The Sabaists understood Baal as the sun, and Baalim, in the plural, were the sun, moon, and stars, "the host of heaven." Whenever the Israelites made one of their almost periodical deflections to idolatry, Baal seems to have been the favorite idol to whose worship they addicted themselves. Hence he became the especial object of denunciation with the prophets. Thus, in 1 Kings (xviii.), we see Elijah showing, by practical demonstration, the difference between Baal and Jehovah. The idolaters, at his instigation, called on Baal, as their sun-god, to light the sacrificial fire, from morning until noon, because at noon he had acquired his greatest intensity. And after noon, no fire having been kindled on the altar, they began to cry aloud, and to cut themselves in token of mortification, because as the sun descended there was no hope of his help. But Elijah, depending on Jehovah, made his sacrifice toward sunset, to show the greatest contrast between Baal and the true God. And when the people saw the fire come down and consume the offering, they acknowledged the weakness of their idol, and falling on their faces cried out, *Jehovah hu hahelohim*—"Jehovah, he is the God." And Hosea afterward promises the people that they shall abandon their idolatry, and that he would take away from them the *Shemoth hahbaalim*, the names of the Baalim, so that they should be no more remembered by their names, and the people should in that day "know Jehovah."

Hence we see that there was an evident antagonism in the orthodox Hebrew mind between Jehovah and Baal. The latter was, however, worshiped by the Jews, whenever they became heterodox, and by all the Oriental or Shemitic nations as a supreme divinity, representing the sun in some of his modifications as the ruler of the day. In Tyre, Baal was the sun, and Ashtaroth, the moon. *Baalpeor*, the lord of priapism, was the sun represented as the generative principle of nature, and identical with the phallus of other religions. *Baal-gad* was the lord of the multitude (of stars), that is, the sun as the chief of the heavenly host. In brief, Baal seems to have been wherever his cultus was established, a development or form of the old sun worship.

Babel. In Hebrew, בבל; which the writer of Genesis connects with בלל, *balal*, "to confound," in reference to the confusion of tongues; but the true derivation is probably from BAB-EL, the "gate of El" or the "gate of God," because perhaps a temple was the first building raised by the primitive nomads. It is the name of that celebrated tower attempted to be built on the plains of Shinar, A.M. 1775, about one hundred and forty years after the deluge, which tower, Scripture informs us, was destroyed by a special interposition of the Almighty. The Noachite Masons date the commencement of their Order from this destruction, and much traditionary information on this subject is preserved in the degree of "Patriarch Noachite." At Babel, Oliver says that what has been called Spurious Freemasonry took its origin. That is to say, the people there abandoned the worship of the true God, and by their dispersion lost all knowledge of his existence, and of the principles of truth upon which Masonry is founded. Hence it is that the rituals speak of the lofty tower of Babel as the place *where language was confounded and Masonry lost.*

This is the theory first advanced by Anderson in his *Constitutions*, and subsequently developed more extensively by Dr. Oliver in all his works, but especially in his *Landmarks.* As history, the doctrine is of no value, for it wants the element of authenticity. But in a symbolic point of view it is highly suggestive. If the tower of Babel represents the profane world of ignorance and darkness, and the threshing-floor of Ornan the Jebusite is the symbol of Freemasonry, because the Solomonic Temple, of which it was the site, is the prototype of the spiritual temple which Masons are erecting, then we can readily understand how Masonry and the true use of language is lost in one and recovered in the other, and how the progress of the candidate in his initiation may properly be compared to the progress of truth from the confusion and ignorance of the Babel builders to the perfection and illumination of the temple builders, which temple builders all Freemasons are. And so, when in the ritual the neophyte, being asked "whence he comes and whither is he travelling," replies, "from the lofty tower of Babel, where language was confounded and Masonry lost, to the threshing-floor of Ornan the Jebusite, where language was restored and Masonry found," the questions and answers become intelligible from this symbolic point of view. (See *Ornan.*)

Babylon. The ancient capital of Chaldea, situated on both sides of the Euphrates, and once the most magnificent city of the ancient world. It was here that, upon the destruction of Solomon's Temple by Nebuchadnezzar in the year of the world 3394, the Jews of the tribes of Judah and Benjamin, who were the inhabitants of Jerusalem, were conveyed and detained in captivity for seventy-two years, until Cyrus, King of Persia, issued a decree for restoring them, and permitting them to rebuild their temple, under the superintendence of Zerubbabel, the Prince of the Captivity, and with the assistance of Joshua the High Priest and Haggai the Scribe.

Babylon the Great, as the prophet Daniel calls it, was situated four hundred and seventy-five miles in a nearly due east direction from Jerusalem. It stood in the midst of a large and fertile plain on each side of the river Euphrates, which ran through it from north to south. It was surrounded with walls which were eighty-seven feet thick, three hundred and fifty in height, and sixty miles in compass. These were all built of large bricks cemented together with bitumen. Exterior to the walls was a wide and deep trench lined with the same material. Twenty-five gates on each side, made of solid brass, gave admission to the city. From each of these gates proceeded a wide street fifteen miles in length, and the whole was separated by means of other smaller divisions, and contained six hundred and seventy-six squares, each of which was two miles

and a quarter in circumference. Two hundred and fifty towers placed upon the walls afforded the means of additional strength and protection. Within this immense circuit were to be found palaces and temples and other edifices of the utmost magnificence, which have caused the wealth, the luxury, and splendor of Babylon to become the favorite theme of the historians of antiquity, and which compelled the prophet Isaiah, even while denouncing its downfall, to speak of it as "the glory of kingdoms, the beauty of the Chaldees' excellency."

Babylon, which, at the time of the destruction of the Temple of Jerusalem, constituted a part of the Chaldean empire, was subsequently taken, B.C. 538, after a siege of two years, by Cyrus, King of Persia.

Babylon, Red Cross of. Another name for the degree of *Babylonish Pass*, which see.

Babylonish Captivity. See *Captivity.*

Babylonish Pass. A degree given in Scotland by the authority of the Grand Royal Arch Chapter. It is also called the Red Cross of Babylon, and is almost identical with the Companion of the Red Cross conferred in Commanderies of Knights Templar in America as a preparatory degree.

Back. Freemasonry, borrowing its symbols from every source, has not neglected to make a selection of certain parts of the human body. From the back an important lesson is derived, which is fittingly developed in the Third Degree. Hence, in reference to this symbolism, Oliver says: "It is a duty incumbent on every Mason to support a brother's character in his absence equally as though he were present; not to revile him *behind his back*, nor suffer it to be done by others, without using every necessary attempt to prevent it." And Hutchinson, referring to the same symbolic ceremony, says: "The most material part of that brotherly love which should subsist among us Masons is that of speaking well of each other to the world; more especially it is expected of every member of this Fraternity that he should not traduce his brother. Calumny and slander are detestable crimes against society. Nothing can be viler than to traduce a man *behind his back;* it is like the villainy of an assassin who has not virtue enough to give his adversary the means of self-defence, but, lurking in darkness, stabs him whilst he is unarmed and unsuspicious of an enemy." (*Spirit of Masonry*, p. 205.) (See *Points of Fellowship.*)

Bacon, Francis. Baron of Verulam, commonly called Lord Bacon. Nicolai thinks that a great impulse was exercised upon the early history of Freemasonry by the *New Atlantis* of Lord Bacon. In this learned romance Bacon supposes that a vessel lands on an unknown island, called Bensalem, over which a certain King Solomon reigned in days of yore. This king had a large establishment, which was called the House of Solomon, or the college of the workmen of six days, namely, the days of the creation. He afterward describes the immense apparatus which was there employed in physical researches. There were, says he, deep grottoes and towers for the successful observation of certain phenomena of nature; artificial mineral waters; large buildings, in which meteors, the wind, thunder, and rain were imitated; extensive botanic gardens; entire fields, in which all kinds of animals were collected, for the study of their instincts and habits; houses filled with all the wonders of nature and art; a great number of learned men, each of whom, in his own country, had the direction of these things; they made journeys and observations; they wrote, they collected, they determined results, and deliberated together as to what was proper to be published and what concealed.

This romance became at once very popular, and everybody's attention was attracted by the allegory of the House of Solomon. But it also contributed to spread Bacon's views on experimental knowledge, and led afterward to the institution of the Royal Society, to which Nicolai attributes a common object with that of the Society of Freemasons, established, he says, about the same time, the difference being only that one was esoteric and the other exoteric in its instructions. But the more immediate effect of the romance of Bacon was the institution of the Society of Astrologers, of which Elias Ashmole was a leading member. Of this society Nicolai, in his work on the *Origin and History of Rosicrucianism and Freemasonry*, says:

"Its object was to build the House of Solomon, of the *New Atlantis*, in the literal sense, but the establishment was to remain as secret as the island of Bensalem—that is to say, they were to be engaged in the study of nature—but the instruction of its principles was to remain in the society in an esoteric form. These philosophers presented their idea in a strictly allegorical method. First, there were the ancient columns of Hermes, by which Iamblichus pretended that he had enlightened all the doubts of Porphyry. You then mounted, by several steps, to a chequered floor, divided into four regions, to denote the four superior sciences; after which came the types of the six days' work, which expressed the object of the society, and which were the same as those found on an engraved stone in my possession. The sense of all which was this: God created the world, and preserves it by fixed principles, full of wisdom; he who seeks to know these principles—that is to say, the interior of nature—approximates to God, and he who thus approximates to God obtains from his grace the power of commanding nature."

This society, he adds, met at Masons' Hall in Basinghall Street, because many of its members were also members of the Masons' Company, into which they all afterward entered and assumed the name of *Free and Accepted Masons*, and thus he traces the origin of the Order to the *New Atlantis* and the House of Solomon of Lord Bacon. It is only a theory, but it seems to throw some light on that long process of incubation which terminated at last, in 1717, in the production of the Grand Lodge of England. The connection of Ashmole with the Masons is a singular one, and has led to some controversy. The views of Nicolai, if not altogether correct, may suggest the possibility of an explanation. Certain it is that the eminent astrologers of England, as we learn from Ashmole's *Diary*, were on terms of intimacy with the Masons in the seventeenth century, and that many Fellows of the Royal Society were also prominent members of the early Grand Lodge of England which was established in 1717.

Bacon, Roger. An English monk who made wonderful discoveries in many sciences. He was born in Ilchester in 1214, educated at Oxford and Paris, and entered the Franciscan Order in his twenty-fifth year. He explored the secrets of nature, and made many discoveries, the application of which was looked upon as magic. He denounced the ignorance and immorality of the clergy, resulting in accusations, through revenge, and final imprisonment. He was noted as a Rosicrucian. Died in 1292.

Baculus. The staff of office borne by the Grand Master of the Templars. In ecclesiology, *baculus* is the name given to the pastoral staff carried by a bishop or an abbot as the ensign of his dignity and authority. In pure Latinity, *baculus* means a long stick or staff, which was commonly carried by travelers, by shepherds, or by infirm and aged persons, and afterward, from affectation, by the Greek philosophers. In early times, this staff, made a little longer, was carried by kings and persons in authority, as a mark of distinction, and was thus the origin of the royal scepter. The Christian church, borrowing many of its usages from antiquity, and alluding also, it is said, to the sacerdotal power which Christ conferred when he sent the apostles to preach, commanding them to take with them staves, adopted the pastoral staff, to be borne by a bishop, as symbolical of his power to inflict pastoral correction; and Durandus says, "By the pastoral staff is likewise understood the authority of doctrine. For by it the infirm are supported, the wavering are confirmed, those going astray are drawn to repentance." Catalin also says that "the baculus, or episcopal staff, is an ensign not only of honor, but also of dignity, power, and pastoral jurisdiction."

Honorius, a writer of the twelfth century, in his treatise *De Gemma Animæ*, gives to this pastoral staff the names both of *baculus* and *virga*. Thus he says, "Bishops bear the staff (*baculum*), that by their teaching they may strengthen the weak in their faith; and they carry the rod (*virgam*), that by their power they may correct the unruly." And this is strikingly similar to the language used by St. Bernard in the *Rule* which he drew up for the government of the Templars. In Art. lxviii., he says, "The Master ought to hold the staff and the rod (*baculum et virgam*) in his hand, that is to say, the staff (*baculum*), that he may support the infirmities of the weak, and the

rod (*virgam*), that he may with the zeal of rectitude strike down the vices of delinquents."

The transmission of episcopal ensigns from bishops to the heads of ecclesiastical associations was not difficult in the Middle Ages; and hence it afterward became one of the insignia of abbots, and the heads of confraternities connected with the Church, as a token of the possession of powers of ecclesiastical jurisdiction.

Now, as the Papal bull, *Omne datum Optimum*, invested the Grand Master of the Templars with almost episcopal jurisdiction over the priests of his Order, he bore the *baculus*, or pastoral staff, as a mark of that jurisdiction, and thus it became a part of the Grand Master's insignia of office.

The *baculus* of the bishop, the abbot, and the confraternities was not precisely the same in form. The earliest episcopal staff terminated in a globular knob, or a tau cross. This was, however, soon replaced by the simple-curved termination, which resembles and. is called a crook, in allusion to that used by shepherds to draw back and recall the sheep of their flock which have gone astray, thus symbolizing the expression of Christ, "I am the good Shepherd, and know my sheep, and am known of mine."

The *baculus* of the abbot does not differ in form from that of a bishop, but as the bishop carries the curved part of his staff pointing forward, to show the extent of his episcopal jurisdiction, so the abbot carries his pointing backward, to signify that his authority is limited to his monastery.

The *baculi*, or staves of the confraternities, were surmounted by small tabernacles, with images or emblems, on a sort of carved cap, having reference to the particular guild or confraternity by whom they were borne.

The *baculus* of the Knights Templars, which was borne by the Grand Master as the ensign of his office, in allusion to his *quasi*-episcopal jurisdiction, is described and delineated in Münter, Burnes, Addison, and all the other authorities, as a staff, on the top of which is an octagonal figure, surmounted with a cross patée. The cross, of course, refers to the Christian character of the Order, and the octagon alludes, it is said, to the eight beatitudes of our Savior in his Sermon on the Mount.

The pastoral staff is variously designated, by ecclesiastical writers, as *virga, ferula, cambutta, crocia*, and *pedum*. From *crocia*, whose root is the Latin *crux*, and the Italian *croce*, a cross, we get the English *crozier*.

Pedum, another name of the *baculus*, signifies, in pure Latinity, a shepherd's crook, and thus strictly carries out the symbolic idea of a pastoral charge. Hence, looking to the pastoral jurisdiction of the Grand Master of the Templars, his staff of office is described under the title of "*pedum magistrale seu patriarchale*," that is, a "magisterial or patriarchal staff," in the *Statuta Commilitonum Ordinis Templi*, or the "Statutes of the Fellow-soldiers of the Order of the Temple," as a part of the investiture of the Grand Master, in the following words:

7

"*Pedum magistrale seu patriarchale, aureum, in cacumine cujus crux Ordinis super orbem exaltatur*"; that is, "A magisterial or patriarchal staff of gold, on the top of which is a cross of the Order, surmounting an orb or globe." (*Stat.*, xxviii., art. 358.) But of all these names, *baculus* is the one more commonly used by writers to designate the Templar pastoral staff.

In the year 1859 this staff of office was first adopted at Chicago by the Templars of the United States, during the Grand Mastership of Sir William B. Hubbard. But, unfortunately, at that time it received the name of *abacus*, a misnomer, which has continued to the present day, on the authority of a literary blunder of Sir Walter Scott, so that it has fallen to the lot of American Masons to perpetuate, in the use of this word, an error of the great novelist, resulting from his too careless writing, at which he would himself have been the first to smile, had his attention been called to it.

Abacus, in mathematics, denotes an instrument or table used for calculation, and in architecture an ornamental part of a column; but it nowhere, in English or Latin, or any known language, signifies any kind of a staff.

Sir Walter Scott, who undoubtedly was thinking of *baculus*, in the hurry of the moment and a not improbable confusion of words and thoughts, wrote *abacus*, when, in his novel of *Ivanhoe*, he describes the Grand Master, Lucas Beaumanoir, as bearing in his hand "that singular *abacus*, or staff of office," committed a very gross, but not very uncommon, literary blunder, of a kind that is quite familiar to those who are conversant with the results of rapid composition, where the writer often thinks of one word and writes another.

Baden. In 1778 the Lodge "Karl of Unity " was established in Mannheim, which at that time belonged to Bavaria. In 1785 an electoral decree was issued prohibiting all secret meetings in the Bavarian Palatinate and the Lodge was closed. In 1803 Mannheim was transferred to the Grand Duchy of Baden, and in 1805 the Lodge was reopened, and in the following year accepted a warrant from the Grand Orient of France and took the name of "Karl of Concord." Then it converted itself into the Grand Orient of Baden and was acknowledged as such by the Grand Orient of France in 1807.

Lodges were established at Bruchsal, Heidelberg, and Mannheim, and the Grand Orient of Baden ruled over them until 1813, when all secret societies were again prohibited, and it was not until 1846 that Masonic activity recommenced in Baden, when the Lodge "Karl of Concord " was awakened.

There is no longer a Grand Orient of Baden, but the Lodges in the Duchy, of which several have been established, are under the Grand National Mother-Lodge "Zu den drei Weltkugeln " (Of the three Globes) in Berlin.

[E. L. H.]

Badge. A mark, sign, token, or thing, says Webster, by which a person is distinguished in a particular place or employment, and designating his relation to a person or to a particular occupation. It is in heraldry the same thing as a cognizance: thus, the followers and retainers of the house of Percy wore a silver crescent as a badge of their connection with that family; the white lion borne on the left arm was the badge of the house of Howard, Earl of Surrey; the red rose that of the house of Lancaster; and the white rose, of York. So the apron, formed of white lambskin, is worn by the Freemason as a badge of his profession and a token of his connection with the Fraternity. (See *Apron*.)

Badge of a Mason. The lambskin apron is so called. (See *Apron*.)

Badge, Royal Arch. The Royal Arch badge is the *triple tau*, which see.

Bafomet. See *Baphomet*.

Bag. In the early days of the Grand Lodge of England the Secretary used to carry a Bag in processions; thus in the procession round the tables at the Grand Feast of 1724 we find "Secretary Cowper with the Bag" (*Constitutions*, ed. 1738, p. 117); and in 1729 Lord Kingston, the Grand Master, provided at his own cost "a fine Velvet Bag for the Secretary," besides his badge of "Two golden Pens a-cross on his Breast" (*ibid*., p. 124); and in the Procession of March from St. James' Square to Merchant Taylor's Hall on January 29, 1730, there came "The Secretary alone with his Badge and Bag, clothed, in a Chariot." (*Ibid*., p. 125.)

This practise continued throughout the Eighteenth century, for at the dedication of Freemasons' Hall in London in 1776 we find in the procession "Grand Secretary with the bag." (*Constitutions*, 1784, p. 318.) But at the union of the two rival Grand Lodges in 1813 the custom was changed, for in the order of procession at public ceremonies laid down in the *Constitutions* of 1815, we find "Grand Secretary with book of constitutions on a cushion" and "Grand Registrar with his bag"; and the Grand Registrar of England still carries on ceremonial occasions a bag with the arms of the Grand Lodge embroidered on it. [E. L. H.]

Bagulkal. A significant word in the high degrees. Lenning says it is a corruption of the Hebrew *Begoal-kol*, "all is revealed." Pike says, *Bagulkol*, with a similar reference to a revelation. Rockwell gives in his MS., *Bekalkel*, without any meaning. The old rituals interpret it as signifying "the faithful guardian of the sacred ark," a derivation clearly fanciful.

Bahrdt, Karl Friederich. A German Doctor of Theology, who was born, in 1741, at Bischofswerda, and died in 1792. He is described by one of his biographers as being "notorious alike for his bold infidelity and for his evil life." We know not why Thory and Lenning have given his name a place in their vocabularies, as his literary labors bore no relation to Freemasonry, except inasmuch as that he was a Mason, and that in 1787, with several other Masons, he founded at Halle a secret society called the "German Union,"

or the "Two and Twenty," in reference to the original number of its members. The object of this society was said to be the enlightenment of mankind. It was dissolved in 1790, by the imprisonment of its founder for having written a libel against the Prussian Minister Woellner. It is incorrect to call this system of degree a Masonic Rite. (See *German Union*.)

Baldachin. In architecture, a canopy supported by pillars over an insulated altar. In Masonry, it has been applied by some writers to the canopy over the Master's chair. The German Masons give this name to the *covering of the Lodge*, and reckon it therefore among the symbols.

Balder or **Baldur.** The ancient Scandinavian or older German divinity. The hero of one of the most beautiful and interesting of the myths of the Edda; the second son of Odin and Frigga, and the husband of the maiden Nanna. In brief, the myth recites that Balder dreamed that his life was threatened, which being told to the gods, a council was held by them to secure his safety. The mother proceeded to demand and receive from every inanimate thing, iron and all metals, fire and water, stones, earth, plants, beasts, birds, reptiles, poisons, and diseases, that they would not injure Balder. Balder then became the subject of sport with the gods, who wrestled, cast darts, and in innumerable ways playfully tested his invulnerability. This finally displeased the mischievous, cunning Loki, the Spirit of Evil, who, in the form of an old woman, sought out the mother, Frigga, and ascertained from her that there had been excepted or omitted from the oath the little shrub Mistletoe. In haste Loki carried some of this shrub to the assembly of the gods, and gave to the blind Hoder, the god of war, selected slips, and directing his aim, Balder fell pierced to the heart.

Sorrow among the gods was unutterable, and Frigga inquired who, to win her favor, would journey to Hades and obtain from the goddess Hel the release of Balder. The heroic Helmod or Hermoder, son of Odin, offered to undertake the journey. Hel consented to permit the return if all things animate and inanimate should weep for Balder.

All living beings and all things wept, save the witch or giantess Thock (the stepdaughter of Loki), who refused to sympathize in the general mourning. Balder was therefore obliged to linger in the kingdom of Hel until the end of the world.

Baldrick. A portion of military dress, being a scarf passing from the shoulder over the breast to the hip. In the dress regulations of the Grand Encampment of Knights Templar of the United States, adopted in 1862, it is called a "scarf," and is thus described: "Five inches wide in the whole, of white bordered with black, one inch on either side, a strip of navy lace one-fourth of an inch wide at the inner edge of the black. On the front centre of the scarf, a metal star of nine points, in allusion to the nine founders of the Temple Order, inclosing the Passion Cross, surrounded by the Latin motto, *In hoc signo vinces;* the star to be three and three-quarter inches in diameter. The scarf to be worn from the right shoulder to the left hip, with the ends extending six inches below the point of intersection."

Baldwyn II. The successor of Godfrey of Bouillon as King of Jerusalem. In his reign the Order of Knights Templar was instituted, to whom he granted a place of habitation within the sacred enclosure of the Temple on Mount Moriah. He bestowed on the Order other marks of favor, and, as its patron; his name has been retained in grateful remembrance, and often adopted as a name of Commanderies of Masonic Templars.

Baldwyn Encampment. There is at Bristol in England a famous Preceptory of Knights Templar, called the "Baldwyn," which claims to have existed from time immemorial, and of which no one has yet been able to discover the origin. This, together with the Chapter of Knights Rosæ Crucis, is the continuation of the old Baldwyn Encampment, the name being derived from the Crusader, King of Jerusalem.

The earliest record preserved by this Preceptory is an authentic and important document dated December 20, 1780, and headed:

"In the name of the Grand Architect of the Universe.

"The Supreme Grand and Royal Encampment of the Order of Knights Templars of St. John of Jerusalem, Knights Hospitallers and Knights of Malta, &c., &c.," and commencing "Whereas by Charter of Compact our Encampment is constituted the Supreme Grand and Royal Encampment of this Noble Order with full Power when Assembled to issue, publish and make known to all our loving Knights Companions whatever may contribute to their knowledge not inconsistent with its general Laws. Also to constitute and appoint any Officer or Officers to make and ordain such laws as from time to time may appear necessary to promote the Honor of our Noble Order in general and the more perfect government of our Supreme degree in particular. We therefore the MOST EMINENT GRAND MASTER The Grand Master of the Order, the Grand Master Assistant General, and two Grand Standard Bearers and Knights Companions for that purpose in full Encampment Assembled do make known."

Then follow twenty Statutes or Regulations for the government of the Order, and the document ends with "Done at our Castle in Bristol 20th day of December 1780."

It is not clear who were the parties to this "Compact," but it is thought probable that it was the result of an agreement between the Bristol Encampment and another ancient body at Bath (the Camp of Antiquity) to establish a supreme direction of the Order. However that may be, it is clear that the Bristol Encampment was erected into a Supreme Grand Encampment in 1780.

The earliest reference to the Knights Templar as yet discovered occurs in a Bristol newspaper of January 25, 1772, so it may fairly be assumed that the Baldwyn Preceptory had been in existence before the date of the Charter of Compact.

In 1791 the well-known Brother Thomas Dunckerley, who was Provincial Grand Master and Grand Superintendent of the Royal Arch Masons at Bristol, was requested by the Knights Templar of that city to be their Grand Master. He at once introduced great activity into the Order throughout England, and established the Grand Conclave in London —the forerunner of the Great Priory.

The "seven degrees" of the Camp of Baldwyn at that time probably consisted of the three of the Craft and that of the Royal Arch (which were necessary qualifications of all candidates as set forth in the Charter of Compact), (5) Knights Templar of St. John of Jerusalem, Palestine, Rhodes and Malta, (6) Knights Rose Croix of Heredom, (7) Grand Elected Knights Kadosh.

About the year 1813 the three degrees of "Nine Elect," "Kilwinning," and "East, Sword and Eagle" were adopted by the Encampment. The "Kadosh" having afterward discontinued, the five "Royal Orders of Masonic Knighthood," of which the Encampment consisted, were: (1) Nine Elect, (2) Kilwinning, (3) East, Sword and Eagle, (4) Knight Templar, (5) Rose Croix.

For many years the Grand Conclave in London was in abeyance, but when H.R.H. the Duke of Sussex, who had been Grand Master since 1813, died in 1843, it was revived, and attempts were made to induce the Camp of Baldwyn to submit to its authority, but without avail, and in 1857 Baldwyn reasserted its position as a Supreme Grand and Royal Encampment, and shortly afterward issued charters to six subordinate Encampments. The chief cause of difference with the London Grand Conclave was the question of giving up the old custom of working the Rose Croix Degree within the Camp. At last, in 1862, the Baldwyn was enrolled by virtue of a Charter of Compact "under the Banner of the Grand Conclave of Masonic Knights Templar of England and Wales." It was arranged that the Baldwyn Preceptory (as it was then called) should take precedence (with five others "of time immemorial") of the other Preceptories; that it should be constituted a Provincial Grand Commandery or Priory of itself; and should be entitled to confer the degree of Knights of Malta.

In 1881 a "Treaty of Union" was made with the Supreme Council of the 33°, whereby the Baldwyn Rose Croix Chapter retained its "time immemorial" position and was placed at the head of the list of Chapters. It also became a "District" under the Supreme Council of the 33° and is therefore placed under an "Inspector General" of its own.

(The preceding article is contributed by Bro. Cecil Powell, joint-author of "Freemasonry in Bristol," published in 1910.)

Balkis. The name given by the Orientalists to the Queen of Sheba, who visited King

Solomon, and of whom they relate a number of fables. (See *Sheba, Queen of*.)

Ballot. In the election of candidates, Lodges have recourse to a ballot of white and black balls. Unanimity of choice, in this case, was originally required; one black ball only being enough to reject a candidate, because as the Old Regulations say, " The members of a particular Lodge are the best judges of it; and because, if a turbulent member should be imposed on them, it might spoil their harmony or hinder the freedom of their communication, or even break up and disperse the Lodge, which ought to be avoided by all true and faithful." (*Constitutions*, 1738, p. 155.)

"But it was found inconvenient to insist upon unanimity in several cases: and therefore the Grand Masters have allowed the Lodges to admit a member, if not above three Ballots are against him; though some Lodges desire no such allowance." (*Ibid*.)

And this is still the rule under the English Constitution. (Rule 190.)

In balloting for a candidate for initiation, every member is expected to vote. No one can be excused from sharing the responsibility of admission or rejection, except by the unanimous consent of the Lodge. Where a member has himself no personal or acquired knowledge of the qualifications of the candidate, he is bound to give faith to the recommendation of his brethren of the reporting committee, who, he is to presume, would not make a favorable report on the petition of an unworthy applicant.

The most correct usage in balloting for candidates is as follows:

The committee of investigation having reported favorably, the Master of the Lodge directs the Senior Deacon to prepare the ballot-box. The mode in which this is accomplished is as follows: The Senior Deacon takes the ballot-box, and, opening it, places all the white and black balls indiscriminately in one compartment, leaving the other entirely empty. He then proceeds with the box to the Junior and Senior Wardens, who satisfy themselves by an inspection that no ball has been left in the compartment in which the votes are to be deposited. The box in this and the other instance to be referred to hereafter, is presented to the inferior officer first, and then to his superior, that the examination and decision of the former may be substantiated and confirmed by the higher authority of the latter. Let it, indeed, be remembered, that in all such cases the usage of Masonic *circumambulation* is to be observed, and that, therefore, we must first pass the Junior's station before we can get to that of the Senior Warden.

These officers having thus satisfied themselves that the box is in a proper condition for the reception of the ballots, it is then placed upon the altar by the Senior Deacon, who retires to his seat. The Master then directs the Secretary to call the roll, which is done by commencing with the Worshipful Master, and proceeding through all the officers down to the youngest member. As a matter of con-

venience, the Secretary generally votes the last of those in the room, and then, if the Tiler is a member of the Lodge, he is called in, while the Junior Deacon tiles for him, and the name of the applicant having been told him, he is directed to deposit his ballot, which he does and then retires.

As the name of each officer and member is called, he approaches the altar, and having made the proper Masonic salutation to the Chair, he deposits his ballot and retires to his seat. The roll should be called slowly, so that at no time should there be more than one person present at the box, for the great object of the ballot being secrecy, no brother should be permitted so near the member voting as to distinguish the color of the ball he deposits.

The box is placed on the altar, and the ballot is deposited with the solemnity of a Masonic salutation, that the voters may be duly impressed with the sacred and responsible nature of the duty they are called on to discharge. The system of voting thus described, is, therefore, far better on this account than that sometimes adopted in Lodges, of handing round the box for the members to deposit their ballots from their seats.

The Master having inquired of the Wardens if all have voted, then orders the Senior Deacon to "take charge of the ballot-box." That officer accordingly repairs to the altar, and taking possession of the box, carries it, as before, to the Junior Warden, who examines the ballot, and reports, if all the balls are white, that "the box is clear in the South," or, if there is one or more black balls, that "the box is foul in the South." The Deacon then carries it to the Senior Warden, and afterward to the Master, who, of course, make the same report, according to the circumstance, with the necessary verbal variations of "West" and "East."

If the box is *clear*—that is, if all the ballots are white—the Master then announces that the applicant has been duly elected, and the Secretary makes a record of the fact. But if the box is *foul*, the Master inspects the number of black balls; if he finds only one, he so states the fact to the Lodge, and orders the Senior Deacon again to prepare the ballot-box. Here the same ceremonies are passed through that have already been described. The balls are removed into one compartment, the box is submitted to the inspection of the Wardens, it is placed upon the altar, the roll is called, the members advance and deposit their votes, the box is scrutinized, and the result declared by the Wardens and Master. If again one black ball be found, or if two or more appeared on the first ballot, the Master announces that the petition of the applicant has been rejected, and directs the usual record to be made by the Secretary and the notification to be given to the Grand Lodge.

Balloting for membership or affiliation is subject to the same rules. In both cases "previous notice, one month before," must be given to the Lodge, "due inquiry into the reputation and capacity of the candidate" must be made, and "the unanimous consent of all the members then present" must be obtained. Nor can this unanimity be dispensed with in one case any more than it can in the other. It is the inherent privilege of every Lodge to judge of the qualifications of its own members, "nor is this inherent privilege subject to a dispensation."

Ballot-Box. The box in which the ballots or little balls used in voting for a candidate are deposited. It should be divided into two compartments, one of which is to contain both black and white balls, from which each member selects one, and the other, which is closed with an aperture, to receive the ball that is to be deposited. Various methods have been devised by which secrecy may be secured, so that a voter may select and deposit the ball he desires without the possibility of its being seen whether it is black or white. That now most in use in this country is to have the aperture so covered by a part of the box as to prevent the hand from being seen when the ball is deposited.

Ballot, Reconsideration of the. See *Reconsideration of the Ballot.*

Ballot, Secrecy of the. The secrecy of the ballot is as essential to its perfection as its unanimity or its independence. If the vote were to be given *viva voce*, it is impossible that the improper influences of fear or interest should not sometimes be exerted, and timid members be thus induced to vote contrary to the dictates of their reason and conscience. Hence, to secure this secrecy and protect the purity of choice, it has been wisely established as a usage, not only that the vote shall in these cases be taken by a ballot, but that there shall be no subsequent discussion of the subject. Not only has no member a right to inquire how his fellows have voted, but it is wholly out of order for him to explain his own vote. And the reason of this is evident. If one member has a right to rise in his place and announce that he deposited a white ball, then every other member has the same right; and in a Lodge of twenty members, where an application has been rejected by one black ball, if nineteen members state that they did not deposit it, the inference is clear that the twentieth Brother has done so, and thus the secrecy of the ballot is at once destroyed. The rejection having been announced from the Chair, the Lodge should at once proceed to other business, and it is the sacred duty of the presiding officer peremptorily and at once to check any rising discussion on the subject. Nothing must be done to impair the inviolable secrecy of the ballot.

Ballot, Unanimity of the. Unanimity in the choice of candidates is considered so essential to the welfare of the Fraternity, that the Old Regulations have expressly provided for its preservation in the following words:

"But no man can be entered a Brother in any particular Lodge, or admitted to be a member thereof, without the unanimous consent of all the members of that Lodge then present when the candidate is proposed, and their consent is formally asked by the Master; and they are to signify their consent or dissent in their own prudent way, either virtually or in form, but with unanimity; nor is this inherent privilege subject to a dispensation; because the members of a particular Lodge are the best judges of it; and if a fractious member should be imposed on them, it might spoil their harmony, or hinder their freedom; or even break and disperse the Lodge, which ought to be avoided by all good and true brethren." (*Constitutions*, 1723, p. 59.)

The rule of unanimity here referred to is, however, applicable only to the United States of America, in all of whose Grand Lodges it is strictly enforced. Anderson tells us, in the second edition of the *Constitutions*, under the head of New Regulations (p. 155), that "it was found inconvenient to insist upon unanimity in several cases; and, therefore, the Grand Masters have allowed the Lodges to admit a member if not above three ballots are against him; though some Lodges desire no such allowance." And accordingly, the present Constitution of the Grand Lodge of England, says: "No person can be made a Mason in or admitted a member of a Lodge, if, on the ballot, three black balls appear against him; but the by-laws of a Lodge may enact that one or two black balls shall exclude a candidate; and by-laws may also enact that a prescribed period shall elapse before any rejected candidate can be again proposed in that Lodge." (Rule 190.) The Grand Lodge of Ireland prescribes unanimity, unless there is a by-law of the subordinate Lodge to the contrary. (Law 127.) The Constitution of Scotland provides that "Three black balls shall exclude a candidate. Lodges in the Colonies and in Foreign parts may enact that two black balls shall exclude." (Rule 181.) In the continental Lodges, the modern English regulation prevails. It is only in the Lodges of the United States that the ancient rule of unanimity is strictly enforced.

Unanimity in the ballot is necessary to secure the harmony of the Lodge, which may be as seriously impaired by the admission of a candidate contrary to the wishes of one member as of three or more; for every man has his friends and his influence. Besides, it is unjust to any member, however humble he may be, to introduce among his associates one whose presence might be unpleasant to him, and whose admission would probably compel him to withdraw from the meetings, or even altogether from the Lodge. Neither would any advantage really accrue to a Lodge by such a forced admission; for while receiving a new and untried member into its fold, it would be losing an old one. For these reasons, in this country, in every one of its jurisdictions, the unanimity of the ballot is expressly insisted on; and it is evident, from what has been here said, that any less stringent regulation is a violation of the ancient law and usage.

Balsamo, Joseph. See *Cagliostro.*

Baltimore Convention. A Masonic Congress which met in the city of Baltimore on the 8th of May, 1843, in consequence of a recommendation made by a preceding convention which had met in Washington, D. C., in March, 1842. It consisted of delegates from the States of New Hampshire, Rhode Island, New York, Maryland, District of Columbia, North Carolina, South Carolina, Georgia, Alabama, Florida, Tennessee, Ohio, Missouri, and Louisiana. Its professed objects were to produce uniformity of Masonic work and to recommend such measures as should tend to the elevation of the Order. It continued in session for nine days, during which time it was principally occupied in an attempt to perfect the ritual, and in drawing up articles for the permanent organization of a Triennial Masonic Convention of the United States, to consist of delegates from all the Grand Lodges. In both of these efforts it failed, although several distinguished Masons took part in its proceedings; the body was too small (consisting, as it did, of only twenty-three members) to exercise any decided popular influence on the Fraternity. Its plan of a Triennial Convention met with very general opposition, and its proposed ritual, familiarly known as the "Baltimore work," has almost become a myth. Its only practical result was the preparation and publication of Moore's *Trestle Board*, a Monitor which has, however, been adopted only by a limited number of American Lodges. The "Baltimore work" did not materially differ from that originally established by Webb. Moore's *Trestle Board* professes to be an exposition of its monitorial part; a statement which, however, is denied by Dr. Dove, who was the President of the Convention, and the controversy on this point at the time between these two eminent Masons was conducted with too much bitterness.

Baluster. A small column or pilaster, corruptly called a *bannister;* in French, *balustre.* Borrowing the architectural idea, the Scottish Rite Masons apply the word *baluster* to any official circular or other document issuing from a Supreme Council.

Balzac, Louis Charles. A French architect of some celebrity, and member of the Institute of Egypt. He founded the Lodge of the Great Sphinx at Paris. He was also a poet of no inconsiderable merit, and was the author of many Masonic canticles in the French language, among them the well-known hymn entitled *Taisons nous, plus de bruit,* the music of which was composed by M. Riguel. He died March 31, 1820, at which time he was inspector of the public works in the prefecture of the Seine.

Band. The neck ribbon bearing the jewel of the office in Lodge, Chapter, or Grand Lodge of various countries, and of the symbolic color pertaining to the body in which it is worn.

Banner-Bearer. The name of an officer known in the higher degrees in the French Rite. One who has in trust the banner; similar in station to the Standard-Bearer of a Grand Lodge, or of a Supreme Body of the Scottish Rite.

Banneret. A small banner. An officer known in the Order of the Knights Templar, who, with the Marshal, had charge of warlike undertakings. A title of an order known as Knight Banneret, instituted by Edward I. The banneret of the most ancient order of knighthood called Knight Bachelor was

(Fig. 1.)   (Fig. 2.)   (Fig. 3.)

shaped like Fig. 1. The Knights Banneret, next in age, had a pennon like Fig. 2. That of the Barons like Fig. 3.

Banners, Royal Arch. Much difficulty has been experienced by ritualists in reference to the true colors and proper arrangements of the banners used in an American Chapter of Royal Arch Masons. It is admitted that they are four in number, and that their colors are blue, purple, scarlet, and white; and it is known too, that the devices on these banners are a lion, an ox, a man, and an eagle; but the doubt is constantly arising as to the relation between these devices and these colors, and as to which of the former is to be appropriated to each of the latter. The question, it is true, is one of mere ritualism, but it is important that the ritual should be always uniform, and hence the object of the present article is to attempt the solution of this question.

The banners used in a Royal Arch Chapter are derived from those which are supposed to have been borne by the twelve tribes of Israel during their encampment in the wilderness, to which reference is made in the second chapter of the Book of Numbers, and the second verse: "Every man of the children of Israel shall pitch by his own standard." But as to what were the devices on the banners, or what were their various colors, the Bible is absolutely silent. To the inventive genius of the Talmudists are we indebted for all that we know or profess to know on this subject. These mystical philosophers have given to us with wonderful precision the various devices which they have borrowed from the death-bed prophecy of Jacob, and have sought, probably in their own fertile imaginations, for the appropriate colors.

The English Royal Arch Masons, whose system differs very much from that of their American Companions, display in their Chapters the twelve banners of the tribes in accordance with the Talmudic devices and colors. These have been very elaborately described by Dr. Oliver in his *Historical Landmarks* (ii., 583–97), and beautifully exemplified by Companion Harris in his *Royal Arch Tracing Boards.*

But our American Royal Arch Masons, as we have seen, use only four banners, being those attributed by the Talmudists to the four principal tribes—Judah, Ephraim, Reuben, and Dan. The devices on these banners are respectively a lion, an ox, a man, and an eagle. As to this there is no question, all authorities, such as they are, agreeing on this point. But, as has been before said, there is some diversity of opinion as to the colors of each, and necessarily as to the officers by whom they should be borne.

Some of the Targumists, or Jewish biblical commentators, say that the color of the banner of each tribe was analogous to that of the stone which represented that tribe in the breastplate of the High Priest. If this were correct, then the colors of the banners of the four leading tribes would be red and green, namely, red for Judah, Ephraim, and Reuben, and green for Dan; these being the colors of the precious stones sardonyx, ligure, carbuncle, and chrysolite, by which these tribes were represented in the High Priest's breastplate. Such an arrangement would not, of course, at all suit the symbolism of the American Royal Arch banners.

Equally unsatisfactory is the disposition of the colors derived from the arms of Speculative Masonry, as first displayed by Dermott in his *Ahiman Rezon*, which is familiar to all American Masons, from the copy published by Cross, in his *Hieroglyphic Chart*. In this piece of blazonry, the two fields occupied by Judah and Dan are *azure*, or blue, and those of Ephraim and Reuben are *or*, or golden yellow; an appropriation of colors altogether uncongenial with Royal Arch symbolism.

We must, then, depend on the Talmudic writers solely for the disposition and arrangement of the colors and devices of these banners. From their works we learn that the color of the banner of Judah was white; that of Ephraim, scarlet; that of Reuben, purple; and that of Dan, blue; and that the devices of the same tribes were respectively the lion, the ox, the man, and the eagle.

Hence, under this arrangement—and it is the only one upon which we can depend—the four banners in a Chapter of Royal Arch Masons, working in the American Rite, must be distributed as follows among the banner-bearing officers:

1st. An eagle, on a blue banner. This represents the tribe of Dan, and is borne by the Grand Master of the first veil.

2d. A man, on a purple banner. This represents the tribe of Reuben, and is borne by the Grand Master of the second veil.

3d. An ox, on a scarlet banner. This represents the tribe of Ephraim, and is borne by the Grand Master of the third veil.

4th. A lion, on a white banner. This represents the tribe of Judah, and is borne by the Royal Arch Captain.

Banquet. See *Table-Lodge.*

Baphomet. The imaginary idol, or, rather, symbol, which the Knights Templars were accused of employing in their mystic rights. The forty-second of the charges preferred against them by Pope Clement is in these words: *Item quod ipsi per singulas provincias habeant idola: videlicet capita quorum aliqua habebant tres facies, et alia unum: et aliqua cranium humanum habebant.* Also, that in all of the provinces they have idols,

namely, heads, of which some had three faces, some one, and some had a human skull. Von Hammer, a bitter enemy of the Templars, in his book entitled *The Mystery of Baphomet Revealed*, revived this old accusation, and attached to the Baphomet an impious signification. He derived the name from the Greek words, βαφή, baptism, and μῆτις, wisdom, and thence supposed that it represented the admission of the initiated into the secret mysteries of the Order. From this gratuitous assumption he deduces his theory, set forth even in the very title of his work, that the Templars were convicted, by their own monuments, of being guilty as Gnostics and Ophites, of apostasy, idolatry, and impurity. Of this statement he offers no other historical testimony than the Articles of Accusation, themselves devoid of proof, but through which the Templars were made the victims of the jealousy of the Pope and the avarice of the King of France.

Others again have thought that they could find in *Baphomet* a corruption of *Mahomet*, and hence they have asserted that the Templars had been perverted from their religious faith by the Saracens, with whom they had so much intercourse, sometimes as foes and sometimes as friends. Nicolai, who wrote an *Essay on the Accusations brought against the Templars*, published at Berlin, in 1782, supposes, but doubtingly, that the figure of the Baphomet, *figura Baffometi*, which was depicted on a bust representing the Creator, was nothing else but the Pythagorean pentagon, the symbol of health and prosperity, borrowed by the Templars from the Gnostics, who in turn had obtained it from the School of Pythagoras.

King, in his learned work on the Gnostics, thinks that the Baphomet may have been a symbol of the Manicheans, with whose wide-spreading heresy in the Middle Ages he does not doubt that a large portion of the inquiring spirits of the Temple had been intoxicated.

Amid these conflicting views, all merely speculative, it will not be uncharitable or unreasonable to suggest that the Baphomet, or skull of the ancient Templars, was, like the *relic* of their modern Masonic representatives, simply an impressive symbol teaching the lesson of mortality, and that the latter has really been derived from the former.

Baptism, Masonic. The term "Masonic Baptism" has been recently applied in this country by some authorities to that ceremony which is used in certain of the high degrees, and which, more properly, should be called "Lustration." It has been objected that the use of the term is calculated to give needless offense to scrupulous persons who might suppose it to be an imitation of a Christian sacrament. But, in fact, the Masonic baptism has no allusion whatsoever, either in form or design, to the sacrament of the Church. It is simply a lustration or purification by water, a ceremony which was common to all the ancient initiations. (See *Lustration.*)

Bard. A title of great dignity and importance among the ancient Britons, which was conferred only upon men of distinguished rank in society, and who filled a sacred office. It was the third or lowest of the three degrees into which Druidism was divided. (See *Druidical Mysteries*.)

There is an officer of the Grand Lodge of Scotland called the "Grand Bard."

Bastard. The question of the ineligibility of bastards to be made Freemasons was first brought to the attention of the Craft by Brother Chalmers I. Paton, who, in several articles in *The London Freemason*, in 1869, contended that they were excluded from initiation by the Ancient Regulations. Subsequently, in his compilation entitled *Freemasonry and its Jurisprudence*, published in 1872, he cites several of the *Old Constitutions* as explicitly declaring that the men made Masons shall be "no bastards." This is a most nnwarrantable interpolation not to be justified in any writer on jurisprudence; for on a careful examination of all the old manuscript copies which have been published, no such words are to be found in any one of them. As an instance of this literary disingenuousness (to use no harsher term), I quote the following from his work (p. 60): "The charge in this second edition [of Anderson's *Constitutions*] is in the following unmistakable words: 'The men made Masons must be freeborn, no bastard, (or no bondmen,) of mature age and of good report, hale and sound, not deformed or dismembered at the time of their making.'"

Now, with a copy of this second edition lying open before me, I find the passage thus printed: "The men made Masons must be freeborn, (or no bondmen,) of mature age and of good report, hale and sound, not deformed or dismembered at the time of their making." The words "no bastard" are Paton's interpolation.

Again, Paton quotes from Preston the Ancient Charges at makings, in these words: "That he that be made be able in all degrees; that is, freeborn, of a good kindred, true, and no bondsman or bastard, and that he have his right limbs as a man ought to have."

But on referring to Preston (edition of 1775, and all subsequent editions) we find the passage to be correctly thus: "That he that be made be able in all degrees; that is, freeborn, of a good kindred, true, and no bondsman, and that he have his limbs as a man ought to have."

Positive law authorities should not be thus cited, not merely carelessly, but with designed inaccuracy to support a theory.

But although there is no regulation in the *Old Constitutions* which *explicitly* prohibits the initiation of bastards, it may be implied from their language that such prohibition did exist. Thus, in all the old manuscripts, we find such expressions as these: he that shall be made a Mason "must be freeborn and *of good kindred*" (Sloane MS., No. 3323), or "come of good kindred" (Edinburgh Kilwinning MS.), or, as the Roberts Print more definitely has it, "of honest parentage."

It is not, I therefore think, to be doubted that formerly bastards were considered as ineligible for initiation, on the same principle that they were, as a degraded class, excluded from the priesthood in the Jewish and the primitive Christian church. But the more liberal spirit of modern times has long since made the law obsolete, because it is contrary to the principles of justice to punish a misfortune as if it was a crime.

Barbati Fratres. Bearded Brothers—at an earlier date known as the Conversi—craftsmen known among the Conventual Builders, admitted to the Abbey Corbey in the year 851, whose social grade was more elevated than the ordinary workmen, and were freeborn. The Conversi were filiates in the Abbeys, used a *quasi*-monastic dress, could leave their profession whenever they chose and could return to civil life. Converts who abstained from secular pursuits as sinful and professed conversion to the higher life of the Abbé, without becoming monks. Scholæ or guilds of such Operatives lodged within the convents. We are told by Bro. Geo. F. Fort (in his *Critical Inquiry Concerning the Mediæval Conventual Builders*, 1884) that the scholæ of dextrous Barbati Fratres incurred the anger of their coreligionists, by their haughty deportment, sumptuous garb, liberty of movement, and refusal to have their long, flowing beards shaven—hence their name—thus tending to the more fascinating attractions of civil life as time carried them forward through the centuries to the middle of the thirteenth, when William Abbott, of Premontré, attempted to enforce the rule of shaving the beard. "These worthy ancestors of our modern craft deliberately refused," and said, "if the execution of this order were pressed against them, 'they would fire every cloister and cathedral in the country.'" The decretal was withdrawn.

Barefeet. See *Discalceation*.

Barruel, Abbé. Augustin Barruel, generally known as the Abbé Barruel, who was born, October 2, 1741, at Villeneuve de Berg, in France, and who died October 5, 1820, was an implacable enemy of Freemasonry. He was a prolific writer, but owes his reputation principally to the work entitled *Mémoires pour servir a l'Histoire du Jacobinisme*, 4 vols., 8vo, published in London in 1797. In this work he charges the Freemasons with revolutionary principles in politics and with infidelity in religion. He seeks to trace the origin of the Institution first to those ancient heretics, the Manicheans, and through them to the Templars, against whom he revives the old accusations of Philip the Fair and Clement V. His theory of the Templar origin of Masonry is thus expressed (ii., 382): "Your whole school and all your Lodges are derived from the Templars. After the extinction of their Order, a certain number of guilty knights, having escaped the proscription, united for the preservation of their horrid mysteries. To their impious code they added the vow of vengeance against the kings and priests who destroyed their Order, and against all religion which anathematized their dogmas. They made adepts, who should transmit from generation to generation the same mysteries of iniquity, the same oaths, and the same hatred of the God of the Christians, and of kings, and of priests. These mysteries have descended to you, and you continue to perpetuate their impiety, their vows, and their oaths. Such is your origin. The lapse of time and the change óf manners have varied a part of your symbols and your frightful systems; but the essence of them remains, the vows, the oaths, the hatred, and the conspiracies are the same." It is not astonishing that Lawrie (*History of Freemasonry*, p. 50) should have said of the writer of such statements, that "that charity and forbearance which distinguish the Christian character are never exemplified in the work of Barruel; and the hypocrisy of his pretensions is often betrayed by the fury of his zeal. The tattered veil behind which he attempts to cloak his inclinations often discloses to the reader the motives of the man and the wishes of his party." Although the attractions of his style and the boldness of his declamation gave Barruel at one time a prominent place among anti-Masonic writers, his work is now seldom read and never cited in Masonic controversies, for the progress of truth has assigned their just value to its extravagant assertions.

Bartolozzi, Francesco (1728–1813). A famous engraver who lived for some time in London and engraved the frontispiece of the 1784 edition of the *Book of Constitutions*. He was initiated in the Lodge of the Nine Muses in London on February 13, 1777. [E. L. H.]

Basilica. Literally and originally a royal palace. A Roman Pagan basilica was a rectangular hall whose length was two or three times its breadth, divided by two or more lines of columns, bearing entablatures, into a broad central nave and side aisles. It was generally roofed with wood, sometimes vaulted. At one end was the entrance. From the center of the opposite end opened a semicircular recess as broad as the nave, called in Latin the "Tribuna" and in Greek the "Apsis." The uses of the basilica were various and of a public character, courts of justice being held in them. Only a few ruins remain, but sufficient to establish the form and general arrangement.

The significance of the basilica to Freemasons is that it was the form adopted for early Christian churches, and for its influence on the building guilds.

For the beginning of Christian architecture, which is practically the beginning of Operative Masonry, we must seek very near the beginning of the Christian religion. For three centuries the only places in Pagan Rome where Christians could meet with safety were in the catacombs. When Constantine adopted Christianity in 324, the Christians were no longer forced to worship in the catacombs. They were permitted to worship in the basilica and chose days for special worship of the Saints on or near days of Pagan celebrations or feast days, so as not to attract the attention or draw the contempt of the Romans not

Christians. Examples of this have come down to us, as, Christmas, St. John the Baptist Day, St. John the Evangelist Day, etc.

The Christian basilicas spread over the Roman Empire, but in Rome applied specially to the seven principal churches founded by Constantine, and it was their plan that gave Christian churches this name. The first builders were the Roman Artificers, and after the fall of the Western Empire, we find a decadent branch at Como (see *Como*) that developed into the Comacine Masters, who evolved, aided by Byzantine workmen and influence, Lombard architecture.

Basket. The basket or fan was among the Egyptians a symbol of the purification of souls. The idea seems to have been adopted by other nations, and hence, "initiations in the Ancient Mysteries," says Mr. Rolle (*Culte de Bacch.*, i., 30), "being the commencement of a better life and the perfection of it, could not take place till the soul was purified. The fan had been accepted as the symbol of that purification because the mysteries purged the soul of sin, as the fan cleanses the grain." John the Baptist conveys the same idea of purification when he says of the Messiah, "His fan is in his hand, and he will thoroughly purge his floor." The sacred basket in the Ancient Mysteries was called the λίκνον, and the one who carried it was termed the λικνόφορος, or basket-bearer. Indeed, the sacred basket, containing the first fruits and offerings, was as essential in all solemn processions of the mysteries of Bacchus and other divinities as the Bible is in the Masonic procession. As lustration was the symbol of purification by water, so the mystical fan or winnowing-basket was, according to Sainte Croix (*Myst. du Pag.*, t. ii., p. 81), the symbol in the Bacchic rites of a purification by air.

Basle, Congress of. A Masonic Congress was held September 24, 1848, at Basle, in Switzerland, consisting of one hundred and six members, representing eleven Lodges under the patronage of the Swiss Grand Lodge Alpina. The Congress was principally engaged upon the discussion of the question, "What can and what ought Freemasonry to contribute towards the welfare of mankind locally, nationally, and internationally?" The conclusion to which the Congress appeared to arrive upon this question was briefly this: "Locally, Freemasonry ought to strive to make every brother a good citizen, a good father, and a good neighbor; whilst it ought to teach him to perform every duty of life faithfully. Nationally, a Freemason ought to strive to promote and to maintain the welfare and the honor of his native land, to love and to honor it himself, and, if necessary, to place his life and fortune at its disposal; Internationally, a Freemason is bound to go still further: he must consider himself as a member of that one great family, —the whole human race,—who are all children of one and the same Father, and that it is in this sense, and with this spirit, that the Freemason ought to work if he would appear worthily before the throne of Eternal Truth and Justice." The Congress appears to have accomplished no practical result.

Baton. The truncheon or staff of a Grand Marshal, and always carried by him in processions as the ensign of his office. It is a wooden rod about eighteen inches long. In the military usage of England, the baton of the Earl Marshal was originally of wood, but in the reign of Richard II. it was made of gold, and delivered to him at his creation, a custom which is still continued. In the patent or commission granted by that monarch to the Duke of Surrey the baton is minutely described as "baculum aureum circa utramque finem de nigro annulatum," *a golden wand, having black rings around each end*—a description that will very well suit for a Masonic baton.

Bats, Parliament of. The Parliament which assembled in England in the year 1426, during the minority of Henry VI., to settle the disputes between the Duke of Gloucester, the Regent, and the Bishop of Winchester, the guardian of the young king's person, and which was so called because the members, being forbidden by the Duke of Gloucester to wear swords, armed themselves with clubs or bats. It has been stated by Preston (*Illustrations*) that it was in this Parliament that the Act forbidding Masons to meet in Chapters or Congregations was passed; but this is erroneous, for that act was passed in 1425 by the Parliament at Westminster, while the Parliament of Bats met at Leicester in 1426.   [E. L. H.]
(See *Laborers, Statutes of.*)

Battery. A given number of blows by the gavels of the officers, or by the hands of the Brethren, as a mark of approbation, admiration, or reverence, and at times accompanied by the acclamation.

Bavaria. Freemasonry was introduced into Bavaria, from France, in 1737. The meetings of the Lodges were suspended in 1784 by the reigning duke, Charles Theodore, and the Act of suspension was renewed in 1799 and 1804 by Maximilian Joseph, the King of Bavaria. The Order was subsequently revived in 1812 and in 1817. The Grand Lodge of Bayreuth was constituted in 1811 under the appellation of the "Grand Lodge zur Sonne." In 1868 a Masonic conference took place of the Lodges under its jurisdiction, and a constitution was adopted, which guarantees to every confederated Lodge perfect freedom of ritual and government, provided the Grand Lodge finds these to be Masonic.

Bay-Tree. An evergreen plant, and a symbol in Freemasonry of the immortal nature of Truth. By the bay-tree thus referred to in the ritual of the Companion of the Red Cross, is meant the laurel, which, as an evergreen, was among the ancients a symbol of immortality. It is, therefore, properly compared with truth, which Josephus makes Zerubbabel say is "immortal and eternal."

Bazot, Étienne François. A French Masonic writer, born at Nievre, March 31, 1782. He published at Paris, in 1810, a *Vocabulaire des Francs-Maçons*, which was translated into

Italian, and in 1811 a *Manuel du Franc-Maçon*, which is one of the most judicious works of the kind published in France. He was also the author of *Morale de la Franc-Maçonnerie*, and the *Tuileur Expert des 33 degrés*, which is a complement to his *Manuel*. Bazot was distinguished for other literary writings on subjects of general literature, such as two volumes of *Tales and Poems, A Eulogy on the Abbé de l'Epée*, and as the editor of the *Biographie Nouvelle des Contemporaires*, in 20 volumes.

B. D. S. P. H. G. F. In the French rituals of the Knights of the East and West, these letters are the initials of Beauté, Divinité, Sagesse, Puissance, Honneur, Gloire, Force, which correspond to the letters of the English rituals, B. D. W. P. H. G. S., which are the initials of equivalent words.

Beadle. An officer in a Council of Knights of the Holy Sepulcher, corresponding to the Junior Deacon of a symbolic Lodge. The beadle, *bedellus* (DuCange), is one, says Junius, who proclaims and executes the will of superior powers.

Beaton, Mrs. One of those fortunate females who are said to have obtained possession of the Masons' secrets. The following account of her is given in *A General History of the County of Norfolk*, published in 1829 (vol. 2, p. 1304). Mrs. Beaton, who was a resident of Norfolk, England, was commonly called the Freemason, from the circumstance of her having contrived to conceal herself, one evening, in the wainscoting of a Lodge-room, where she learned the secret—at the knowledge of which thousands of her sex have in vain attempted to arrive. She was, in many respects, a very singular character, of which one proof adduced is that the secret of the Freemasons died with her. She died at St. John Maddermarket, Norwich, July, 1802, aged eighty-five.

Beaucenifer. From *Beauseant*, and *fero*, to carry. The officer among the old Knights Templar whose duty it was to carry the Beauseant in battle. The office is still retained in some of the high degrees which are founded on Templarism.

Beauchaine. The Chevalier Beauchaine was one of the most fanatical of the irremovable Masters of the Ancient Grand Lodge of France. He had established his Lodge at the "Golden Sun," an inn in the Rue St. Victor, Paris, where he slept, and for six francs conferred all the degrees of Freemasonry. On August 17, 1747, he organized the *Order of Fendeurs*, or *Woodcutters*, at Paris.

Beauseant. The vexillum belli, or war-banner of the ancient Templars, which is also used by the modern Masonic Order. The upper half of the banner was black, and the lower half white: black, to typify terror to foes, and white, fairness to friends. It bore the pious inscription, *Non nobis, Domine non nobis, sed nomini*

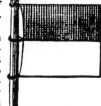

tuo da gloriam. It is frequently, says Barrington (*Intro. to Her.*, p. 121), introduced among the decorations in the Temple Church, and on one of the paintings on the wall, Henry I. is represented with this banner in his hand. As to the derivation of the word, there is some doubt among writers. *Bauseant* or *Bausant* was, in old French, a piebald or party-colored horse; and the word *Bawseant* is used in the Scottish dialect with a similar reference to two colors. Thus, Burns says:

"His honest, sonsie, baws'nt face,"

where Dr. Currie, in his *Glossary of Burns,* explains *bawsent* as meaning "having a white stripe down the face." It is also supposed by some that the word *bauseant* may be only a form, in the older language, of the modern French word *bienséant,* which signifies something decorous or handsome; but the former derivation is preferable, in which beauseant would signify simply a party-colored banner. With regard to the double signification of the white and black banner, the Orientalists have a legend of Alexander the Great, which may be appropriately quoted on the present occasion, as given by Weil in his *Biblical Legends* (p. 70).

Alexander was the lord of light and darkness: when he went out with his army the light was before him, and behind him was the darkness, so that he was secure against all ambuscades; and by means of a miraculous white and black standard he had also the power to transform the clearest day into midnight and darkness, or black night into noonday, just as he unfurled the one or the other. Thus he was unconquerable, since he rendered his troops invisible at his pleasure, and came down suddenly upon his foes. Might there not have been some connection between the mythical white and black standard of Alexander and the Beauseant of the Templars? We know that the latter were familiar with Oriental symbolism.

Beauseant was also the war-cry of the Ancient Templars.

Beauty. Said to be symbolically one of the three supports of a Lodge. It is represented by the Corinthian column, because the Corinthian is the most beautiful of the ancient orders of Architecture; and by the Junior Warden, because he symbolizes the meridian sun—the most beautiful object in the heavens. Hiram Abif is also said to be represented by the Column of Beauty, because the Temple was indebted to his skill for its splendid decorations. The idea of Beauty as one of the supports of the Lodge is found in the earliest rituals of the eighteenth century, as well as the symbolism which refers it to the Corinthian column and the Junior Warden. Preston first introduced the reference to the Corinthian column and to Hiram Abif. Beauty, תּאראה, *tiphiret,* was the sixth of the Kabbalistic Sephiroth, and, with Justice and Mercy, formed the second Sephirotic triad; and from the Kabbalists the Masons most probably derived the symbol. (See *Supports of the Lodge.*)

Beauty and Bands. The names of the two rods spoken of by the prophet Zechariah as symbolic of his pastoral office. This expression was in use in portions of the old Masonic ritual in England; but in the system of Dr. Hemming, which was adopted at the union of the two Grand Lodges in 1813, this symbol, with all reference to it, was expunged, and, as Dr. Oliver says (*Sym. Dic.*), "it is nearly forgotten, except by a few old Masons, who may perhaps recollect the illustration as an incidental subject of remark among the Fraternity of that period."

Becker. See *Johnson.*

Becker, Rudolph Zacharias. A very zealous Mason of Gotha, who published, in 1786, an historical essay on the Bavarian Illuminati, under the title of *Grundsatze Verfassung und Schicksale des Illuminatens Order in Baiern.* He was a very popular writer on educational subjects; his *Instructive Tales of Joy and Sorrow* was so highly esteemed, that a half million copies were printed in German and other languages. He died in 1802.

Bédarride, The Brothers. The Brothers Marc, Michel, and Joseph Bédarride were Masonic charlatans, notorious for their propagation of the Rite of Mizraim, having established in 1813, at Paris, under the partly real and partly pretended authority of Lechangeur, the inventor of the Rite, a Supreme Puissance for France, and organized a large number of Lodges. Of these three brothers, who were Israelites, Michel, who assumed the most prominent position in the numerous controversies which arose in French Masonry on account of their Rite, died February 16, 1856. Marc died ten years before, in April, 1846. Of Joseph, who was never very prominent, we have no record as to the time of his death. (See *Mizraim, Rite of.*)

Beehive. The bee was among the Egyptians the symbol of an obedient people, because, says Horapollo, of all insects, the bee alone had a king. Hence, looking at the regulated labor of these insects when congregated in their hive, it is not surprising that a beehive should have been deemed an appropriate emblem of systematized industry. Freemasonry has therefore adopted the beehive as a symbol of industry, a virtue taught in the ritual, which says that a Master Mason "works that he may receive wages, the better to support himself and family, and contribute to the relief of a worthy, distressed brother, his widow and orphans"; and in the Old Charges, which tell us that "all Masons shall work honestly on working days, that they may live creditably on holidays." There seems, however, to be a more recondite meaning connected with this symbol. The ark has already been shown to have been an emblem common to Freemasonry and the Ancient Mysteries, as a symbol of regeneration—of the second birth from death to life. Now, in the Mysteries, a hive was the type of the ark. "Hence," says Faber (*Orig. of Pag. Idol.*, vol. ii., 133), "both the diluvian priestesses and the regenerated souls were called bees; hence, bees were feigned to be produced from the carcass of a cow, which also symbolized the ark; and hence, as the great father was esteemed an infernal god, honey was much used both in funeral rites and in the Mysteries."[*]

Behavior. The subject of a Mason's behavior is one that occupies much attention in both the ritualistic and the monitorial instructions of the Order. In "the Charges of a Freemason," extracted from the ancient records, and first published in the *Constitutions* of 1723, the sixth article is exclusively appropriated to the subject of "Behavior." It is divided into six sections, as follows: 1. Behavior in the Lodge while constituted. 2. Behavior after the Lodge is over and the Brethren not gone. 3. Behavior when Brethren meet without strangers, but not in a Lodge formed. 4. Behavior in presence of strangers not Masons. 5. Behavior at home and in your neighborhood. 6. Behavior toward a strange brother. The whole article constitutes a code of moral ethics remarkable for the purity of the principles it inculcates, and is well worthy of the close attention of every Mason. It is a complete refutation of the slanders of anti-Masonic revilers. As these charges are to be found in all the editions of the *Book of Constitutions*, and in many recent Masonic works, they are readily accessible to everyone who desires to read them.

Behold Your Master. When, in the installation services, the formula is used, "Brethren, behold your master," the expression is not simply exclamatory, but is intended, as the original use of the word *behold* implies, to invite the members of the Lodge to fix their attention upon the new relations which have sprung up between them and him who has just been elevated to the Oriental Chair, and to impress upon their minds the duties which they owe to him and which he owes to them. In like manner, when the formula is continued, "Master, behold your brethren," the Master's attention is impressively directed to the same change of relations and duties. These are not mere idle words, but convey an important lesson, and should never be omitted in the ceremony of installation.

Bel. בל, *Bel*, is the contracted form of בעל, *Baal*, and was worshiped by the Babylonians as their chief deity. The Greeks and Romans so considered and translated the word by Zeus and Jupiter. It has, with *Jah* and *On*, been introduced into the Royal Arch system as a representative of the Tetragrammaton, which it and the accompanying words have sometimes ignorantly been made to displace. At the session of the General Grand Chapter of the United States, in 1871, this error was corrected; and while the Tetragrammaton was declared to be the true omnific word, the other three were permitted to be retained as merely explanatory.

Belenus. Belenus, the Baal of the Scripture, was identified with Mithras and with

Apollo, the god of the sun. A forest in the neighborhood of Lausanne is still known as Sauvebelin, or the forest of Belenus, and traces of this name are to be found in many parts of England. The custom of kindling fires about midnight on the eve of the festival of St. John the Baptist, at the moment of the summer solstice, which was considered by the ancients a season of rejoicing and of divination, is a vestige of Druidism in honor of this deity. It is a significant coincidence that the numerical value of the letters of the word Belenus, like those of Abraxas and Mithras, all representatives of the sun, amounts to 365, the exact number of the days in a solar year. (See *Abraxas*.)

Belgium. Soon after the separation of Belgium from the Netherlands, an independent Masonic jurisdiction was demanded by the former. Accordingly, in May, 1833, the Grand Orient of Belgium was established, which has under its jurisdiction twenty-one Lodges. There is also a Supreme Council of the Ancient and Accepted Scottish Rite, which was constituted in the year 1817.

Belief, Religious. The fundamental law of Masonry contained in the first of the Old Charges collected in 1723, and inserted in the *Book of Constitutions* published in that year, sets forth the true doctrine as to what the Institution demands of a Mason in reference to his religious belief in the following words: "A Mason is obliged, by his tenure, to obey the moral law; and if he rightly understands the art, he will never be a stupid atheist nor an irreligious libertine. But though in ancient times Masons were charged in every country to be of the religion of that country or nation, whatever it was, yet it is now thought more expedient only to oblige them to that religion in which all men agree, leaving their particular opinions to themselves." Anderson, in his second edition, altered this article, calling a Mason a true Noachida, and saying that Masons "all agree in the three great articles of Noah," which is incorrect, since the Precepts of Noah were seven. (See *Religion of Masonry*.)

Bells. The use of a bell in the ceremonies of the Third Degree, to denote the hour, is, manifestly, an anachronism, for bells were not invented until the fifth century. But Freemasons are not the only people who have imagined the existence of bells at the building of the Temple. Henry Stephen tells us (*Apologie pour Herodote*, ch. 39) of a monk who boasted that when he was at Jerusalem he obtained a vial which contained some of the sounds of King Solomon's bells. The blunders of a ritualist and the pious fraud of a relic-monger have equal claims to authenticity. The Masonic anachronism is, however, not worth consideration, because it is simply intended for a notation of time—a method of expressing intelligibly the hour at which a supposed event occurred.

Benac. A significant word in Symbolic Masonry, obsolete in many of the modern systems, whose derivation is uncertain. (See *Macbenac*.)

---

[*] Bee, Evans, *Animal Symbolism in Ecclesiastical Architecture.*

Benai. See *Bonaim.*

Benakar. The name of a cavern to which certain assassins fled for concealment.

Bendekar. A significant word in the high degrees. One of the Princes or Intendants of Solomon, in whose quarry some of the traitors spoken of in the Third Degree were found. He is mentioned in the catalogue of Solomon's princes, given in 1 Kings iv. 9. The Hebrew word is בן־דקר, *the son of him who divides or pierces.* In some old rituals we find a corrupt form, *Bendaca.*

Benedict XIV. A Roman pontiff whose family name was Prosper Lambertini. He was born at Bologna in 1675, succeeded Clement XII. as Pope in 1740, and died in 1758. He was distinguished for his learning and was a great encourager of the Arts and Sciences. He was, however, an implacable enemy of secret societies, and issued on the 18th of May, 1751, his celebrated bull, renewing and perpetuating that of his predecessor which excommunicated the Freemasons. (See *Bull.*)

Benediction. The solemn invocation of a blessing in the ceremony of closing a Lodge is called the benediction. The usual formula is as follows:

"May the blessing of Heaven rest upon us, and all regular Masons; may brotherly love prevail, and every moral and social virtue cement us." The response is, "So mote it be. Amen"; which should always be audibly pronounced by all the Brethren.

Beneficiary. One who receives the support or charitable donations of a Lodge. Those who are entitled to these benefits are affiliated Masons, their wives or widows, their widowed mothers, and their minor sons and unmarried daughters. Unaffiliated Masons cannot become the beneficiaries of a Lodge, but affiliated Masons cannot be deprived of its benefits on account of non-payment of dues. Indeed, as this non-payment often arises from poverty, it thus furnishes a stronger claim for fraternal charity.

Benefit Society, Masonic. In 1798, a society was established in London, under the patronage of the Prince of Wales, the Earl of Moira, and all the other acting officers of the Grand Lodge, whose object was "the relief of sick, aged, and imprisoned brethren, and for the protection of their widows, children, and orphans." The payment of one guinea per annum entitled every member, when sick or destitute, or his widow and orphans in case of his death, to a fixed contribution. After a few years, however, the Society came to an end, as it was considered improper to turn Freemasonry into a Benefit Club.

Benefit funds of this kind have been generally unknown to the Masons of America, although some Lodges have established a fund for the purpose. The Lodge of Strict Observance in the City of New York, and others in Troy, Ballston, Schenectady, etc., some years ago, adopted benefit funds. In 1844, several members of the Lodges in Louisville, Kentucky, organized a society under the title of the "Friendly Sons of St. John." It was constructed after the model of the English society already mentioned. No member was received after forty-five years of age, or who was not a contributing member of a Lodge; the per diem allowance to sick members was seventy-five cents; fifty dollars were appropriated to pay the funeral expenses of a deceased member, and twenty-five for those of a member's wife; on the death of a member a gratuity was given to his family; ten per cent of all fees and dues was appropriated to an orphan fund; and it was contemplated, if the funds would justify, to pension the widows of deceased members, if their circumstances required it.

But the establishment in Lodges of such benefit funds is in opposition to the pure system of Masonic charity, and they have, therefore, been very properly discouraged by several Grand Lodges, though several still exist in Scotland.

Benevolence. Cogan, in his work *On the Passions,* thus defines Benevolence: "When our love or desire of good goes forth to others, it is termed good-will or *benevolence.* Benevolence embraces all beings capable of enjoying any portion of good; and thus it becomes universal benevolence, which manifests itself by being pleased with the share of good every creature enjoys, in a disposition to increase it, in feeling an uneasiness at their sufferings, and in the abhorrence of cruelty under every disguise or pretext." This spirit should pervade the hearts of all Masons, who are taught to look upon mankind as formed by the Great Architect of the Universe for the mutual assistance, instruction, and support of each other.

Benevolence, Fund of. This Fund was established in 1727 by the Grand Lodge of England under the management of a Committee of seven members, to whom twelve more were added in 1730. It was originally supported by voluntary contributions from the various Lodges, and intended for the relief of distressed Brethren recommended by the contributing Lodges. The Committee was called the Committee of Charity.

The Fund is now derived partly from the fees of honor payable by Grand Officers, and the fees for dispensations, and partly from an annual payment of four shillings from each London Mason and of two shillings from each country Mason; it is administered by the Board of Benevolence, which consists of all the present and past Grand Officers, all actual Masters of Lodges and twelve Past Masters. The Fund is solely devoted to charity, and during the year 1909 a sum of £15,275 was voted and paid to petitioners.

In the United States of America there are several similar organizations known as "Boards of Relief." (See *Relief, Board of.*) [E. L. H.]

Benevolent Institutions, U. S. There are five institutions in the United States of an educational and benevolent character, deriving their existence in whole or in part from Masonic beneficence: 1. Girard College,

Philadelphia, Pennsylvania; 2. Masonic Widows' and Orphans' Home, Louisville, Kentucky; 3. Oxford Orphan Asylum, Oxford, North Carolina; 4. St. John's Masonic College, Little Rock, Arkansas; 5. Masonic Female College, Covington, Georgia.

Besides the *Stephen Girard Charity Fund*, founded over a half century ago in Philadelphia, the capital investment of which is $62,000, the annual interest being devoted "to relieve all Master Masons in good standing," there is a Charity Fund of $60,000 for the relief of the widows and orphans of deceased Master Masons, and an incorporated Masonic Home. The District of Columbia has an organized Masonic charity, entitled St. John's Mite Association. Idaho has an Orphan Fund, to which every Master Mason pays annually one dollar. Indiana has organized the Masonic Widows' and Orphans' Home Society. Maine has done likewise; and Nebraska has an Orphans' School Fund, although no building has been proposed.

Bengabee. Found in some old rituals of the high degrees for Bendekar, as the name of an Intendant of Solomon. It is *Bengeber* in the catalogue of Solomon's officers, 1 Kings iv. 13, the son of Geber, or the son of the strong man.

Bengal. In 1728 a "Deputation" was granted by Lord Kingston, Grand Master of England, to Brother George Pomfret to constitute a Lodge at Bengal in East India, that had been requested by some Brethren residing there; and in the following year a Deputation was granted to Captain Ralph Far Winter, to be Provincial Grand Master of East India at Bengal (*Constitutions*, 1738, p. 194); and in 1730 a Lodge was established at the "East India Arms, Fort William, Calcutta, Bengal," and numbered 72. There is a District Grand Lodge of Bengal with 74 subordinate Lodges, and also a District Grand Chapter with 21 subordinate Chapters.   [E. L. H.]

Benjamin. A significant word in several of the degrees which refer to the second Temple, because it was only the tribes of Judah and Benjamin that returned from the captivity to rebuild it. Hence, in the Masonry of the second Temple, Judah and Benjamin have superseded the columns of Jachin and Boaz; a change the more easily made because of the identity of the initials.

Benkhurim. Corruptly spelled *benchorim* in most of the old rituals. A significant word in the high degrees, probably signifying *one that is freeborn*, from בן־חורים, *son of the freeborn*.

Benyah, or *Beniah.* Lenning gives this form, *Benayah.* The son of Jah, a significant word in the high degrees.

Berith. Heb., ברית, *a covenant.* A significant word in several of the high degrees.

Berlin. The capital of the kingdom of Prussia, and the seat of three Grand Lodges, namely: the Grand National Mother Lodge, founded in 1744; the Grand Lodge of Germany, founded in 1770; and the Grand Lodge of Royal York of Friendship, founded in 1798. (See *Germany.*)

Bernard, David. An expelled Mason, under whose name was published, in the year 1829, a pretended exposition entitled *Light on Masonry.* It was one of the fruits of the anti-Masonic excitement of the day. It is a worthless production, intended as a libel on the Institution.

Bernard, Saint. St. Bernard, born in France, in 1091, was the founder of the Order of Cistercian Monks. He took great interest in the success of the Knights Templar, whose Order he cherished throughout his whole life. His works contain numerous letters recommending them to the favor and protection of the great. In 1128, he himself drew up the Rule of the Order, and among his writings is to be found a *Sermo exhortatorius ad Milites Templi,* or an "Exhortation to the Soldiers of the Temple," a production full of sound advice. To the influence of Bernard and his untiring offices of kindness, the Templars were greatly indebted for their rapid increase in wealth and consequence. He died in the year 1153.

Beryl. Heb., תרשיש. A precious stone, the first in the fourth row of the high priest's breastplate. Its color is bluish-green. It was ascribed to the tribe of Benjamin.

Beyerle, François Louis de. A French Masonic writer of some prominence toward the close of the eighteenth century. He was a leading member of the Rite of Strict Observance, in which his adopted name was *Eques à Flore.* He wrote a criticism on the Masonic Congress of Wilhelmsbad, which was published under the title of *Oratio de Conventu generali Latomorum apud aquas Wilhelminas, prope Hanauviam.* He also wrote an *Essai sur la Franc-Maçonnerie, ou du but essentiel et fondamental de la Franc-Maçonnerie;* translated the second volume of Frederic Nicolai's essay on the crimes imputed to the Templars, and was the author of several other Masonic works of less importance. He was a member of the French Constitutional Convention of 1792. He wrote also some political essays on finances, and was a contributor on the same subject to the *Encyclopédie Méthodique.*

Bezaleel. One of the builders of the Ark of the Covenant. (See *Aholiab.*)

Bible. The Bible is properly called a greater light of Masonry, for from the center of the Lodge it pours forth upon the East, the West, and the South its refulgent rays of Divine truth. The Bible is used among Masons as a symbol of the will of God, however it may be expressed. And, therefore, whatever to any people expresses that will may be used as a substitute for the Bible in a Masonic Lodge. Thus, in a Lodge consisting entirely of Jews, the Old Testament alone may be placed upon the altar, and Turkish Masons make use of the Koran. Whether it be the Gospels to the Christian, the Pentateuch to the Israelite, the Koran to the Mussulman, or the Vedas to the Brahman, it everywhere Masonically conveys the same idea—that of the symbolism of the Divine Will revealed to man.

The history of the Masonic symbolism of the Bible is interesting. It is referred to in the manuscripts before the revival as the book upon which the covenant was taken, but it was never referred to as a great light. In the old ritual, of which a copy from the Royal Library of Berlin is given by Krause (*Drei alt. Kunsturk*, i. 32), there is no mention of the Bible as one of the lights. Preston made it a part of the furniture of the Lodge; but in rituals of about 1760 it is described as one of the three great lights. In the American system, the Bible is both a piece of furniture and a great light.

Bible–Bearer. In Masonic processions the oldest Master Mason present is generally selected to carry the open Bible, Square, and Compasses on a cushion before the Chaplain. This brother is called the Bible-Bearer. The "Grand Bible-Bearer" is an officer of the Grand Lodge of Scotland.

Bibliography. In French, we have a *Bibliographie des Ouvrages, Opuscules Encycliques ou écrits les plus remarquables, publiés sur l'histoire de la Franc-Maçonnerie depuis, 1723, jusques en 1814.* It is by Thory, and is contained in the first volume of his *Acta Latomorum.* Though not full, it is useful, especially in respect to French works, and it is to be regretted that it stops at a period anterior to the Augustan age of Masonic literature. In German, we have the work of Dr. Georg Kloss, entitled *Bibliographie der Freimaurerei,* published at Frankfort in 1844. At the time of its publication it was an almost exhaustive work, and contains the titles of about six thousand volumes. See also *Bibliography* in this work (vol. ii.).

Bielfeld, Jacob Frederick. Baron Bielfeld was born March 31, 1717, and died April 5, 1770. He was envoy from the court of Prussia to The Hague, and a familiar associate of Frederick the Great in the youthful days of that Prince before he ascended the throne. He was one of the founders of the Lodge of the Three Globes in Berlin, which afterward became a Grand Lodge. Through his influence Frederick was induced to become a Mason. In Bielfeld's *Freundschaftlicher Briefe,* or "Familiar Letters," are to be found an account of the initiation of the Prince, and other curious details concerning Freemasonry.

Birkhead, Matthew. A Mason who owes his reputation to the fact that he was the author of 'the universally known Entered Apprentice's song, beginning:

> "Come let us prepare,
> We Brothers that are
> Assembled on merry occasions;
> Let's drink, laugh, and sing;
> Our wine has a spring.
> Here's a health to an Accepted Mason."

This song first appeared in Read's *Weekly Journal* for December 1, 1722, and then was published in the *Book of Constitutions* in 1723, after the death of its author, which occurred on December 30, 1722.

Birkhead was a singer and actor at Drury Lane Theater in London, and was Master of Lodge V when Dr. Anderson was preparing his *Constitutions.* His funeral is thus described in Read's *Weekly Journal* for January 12, 1723: "Mr. Birkhead was last Saturday night carried from his Lodgings in Which-street to be interr'd at St. Clements Danes; the Pall was supported by six Free-Masons belonging to Drury-Lane Play-house; the other Members of that particular Lodge of which he was a Warden, with a vast number of other Accepted-Masons, followed two and two; both the Pall-bearers and others were in their white-aprons." (See *Tune, Freemasons.*) [E. L. H.]

Black. Black, in the Masonic ritual, is constantly the symbol of grief. This is perfectly consistent with its use in the world, where black has from remote antiquity been adopted as the garment of mourning.

In Masonry this color is confined to but a few degrees, but everywhere has the single meaning of sorrow. Thus in the French Rite, during the ceremony of raising a candidate to the Master's Degree, the Lodge is clothed in black strewed with tears, as a token of grief for the loss of a distinguished member of the Fraternity, whose tragic history is commemorated in that degree. This usage is not, however, observed in the York Rite. The black of the Elected Knights of Nine, the Illustrious Elect of Fifteen, and the Sublime Knights Elected, in the Scottish Rite, has a similar import.

In the degree of Noachite, black appears to have been adopted as a symbol of grief, tempered with humility, which is the virtue principally dilated on in the degree.

The garments of the Knights Templar were originally white, but after the death of their martyred Grand Master, James de Molay, the modern Knights assumed a black dress as a token of grief for his loss. The same reason led to the adoption of black as the appropriate color in the Scottish Rite of the Knights of Kadosh and the Sublime Princes of the Royal Secret. The modern American modification of the Templar costume destroys all reference to this historical fact.

One exception to this symbolism of black is to be found in the degree of Select Master, where the vestments are of black bordered with red, the combination of the two colors showing that the degree is properly placed between the Royal Arch and Templar degrees, while the black is a symbol of silence and secrecy, the distinguishing virtues of a Select Master.

Blackball. The ball used in a Masonic ballot by those who do not wish the candidate to be admitted. Hence, when an applicant is rejected, he is said to be "blackballed." The use of black balls may be traced as far back as the ancient Romans. Thus, Ovid says (*Met.*, xv. 41), that in trials it was the custom of the ancients to condemn the prisoner by black pebbles or to acquit him by white ones.

> "Mos erat antiquus, niveis atrisque lapillis,
> His damnare reos, illis absolvere culpæ."

Blackboard. In German Lodges the *Schwarze Tafel,* or Blackboard, is that on which the names of applicants for admission are inscribed, so that every visitor may make the necessary inquiries whether they are or are not worthy of acceptance.

Black Brothers, Order of the. Lenning says that the *Schwarze Brüder* was one of the College Societies of the German Universities. The members of the Order, however, denied this, and claimed an origin as early as 1675. Thory (*Act. Lat.*, i., 313) says that it was largely spread through Germany, having its seat for a long time at Giessen and at Marburg, and in 1783 being removed to Frankfort on the Oder. The same writer asserts that at first the members observed the dogmas and ritual of the Kadosh, but that afterward the Order, becoming a political society, gave rise to the Black Legion, which in 1813 was commanded by M. Lutzow.

Blayney, Lord. Grand Master of the English Grand Lodge of the "Moderns," 1764-6.

Blazing Star. The Blazing Star, which is not, however, to be confounded with the Five-Pointed Star, is one of the most important symbols of Freemasonry, and makes its appearance in several of the degrees. "It is," says Hutchinson, "the first and most exalted object that demands our attention in the Lodge." It undoubtedly derives this importance, first, from the repeated use that is made of it as a Masonic emblem; and secondly, from its great antiquity as a symbol derived from other and older systems.

Extensive as has been the application of this symbol in the Masonic ritual, it is not surprising that there has been a great difference of opinion in relation to its true signification. But this difference of opinion has been almost entirely confined to its use in the First Degree. In the higher degrees, where there has been less opportunity of innovation, the uniformity of meaning attached to the star has been carefully preserved.

In the Twenty-eighth Degree of the Ancient and Accepted Scottish Rite, the explanation given of the Blazing Star, is, that it is symbolic of a true Mason, who, by perfecting himself in the way of truth, that is to say, by advancing in knowledge, becomes like a blazing star, shining with brilliancy in the midst of darkness. The star is, therefore, in this degree, a symbol of truth.

In the Fourth Degree of the same Rite, the star is again said to be a symbol of the light of Divine Providence pointing out the way of truth.

In the Ninth Degree, this symbol is called "the star of direction"; and while it primitively alludes to an especial guidance given for a particular purpose expressed in the degree, it still retains, in a remoter sense, its usual signification as an emblem of Divine Providence guiding and directing the pilgrim in his journey through life.

When, however, we descend to Ancient Craft Masonry, we shall find a considerable diversity in the application of this symbol.

In the earliest rituals, immediately after the revival of 1717, the Blazing Star is not mentioned, but it was not long before it was introduced. In the ritual of 1735 it is detailed as a part of the furniture of a Lodge, with the explanation that the "Mosaic Pavement is the Ground Floor of the Lodge, the Blazing Star, the Centre, and the Indented Tarsel, the Border round about it!" In a primitive Tracing Board of the Entered Apprentice, copied by Oliver, in his *Historical Landmarks* (i., 133), without other date than that it was "published early in the last century," the Blazing Star occupies a prominent position in the center of the Tracing Board. Oliver says that it represented BEAUTY, and was called "the glory in the centre."

In the lectures subsequently prepared by Dunckerley, and adopted by the Grand Lodge, the Blazing Star was said to represent "the star which led the wise men to Bethlehem, proclaiming to mankind the nativity of the Son of God, and here conducting our spiritual progress to the Author of our redemption."

In the Prestonian lecture, the Blazing Star, with the Mosaic Pavement and the Tesselated Border, are called the Ornaments of the Lodge, and the Blazing Star is thus explained:

"The Blazing Star, or glory in the centre, reminds us of that awful period when the Almighty delivered the two tables of stone, containing the ten commandments, to His faithful servant Moses on Mount Sinai, when the rays of His divine glory shone so bright that none could behold it without fear and trembling. It also reminds us of the omnipresence of the Almighty. overshadowing us with His divine love, and dispensing His blessings amongst us; and by its being placed in the centre, it further reminds us, that wherever we may be assembled together, God is in the midst of us, seeing our actions, and observing the secret intents and movements of our hearts."

In the lectures taught by Webb, and very generally adopted in this country, the Blazing Star is said to be "commemorative of the star which appeared to guide the wise men of the East to the place of our Saviour's nativity," and it is subsequently explained as hieroglyphically representing Divine Providence. But the commemorative allusion to the Star of Bethlehem seeming to some to be objectionable, from its peculiar application to the Christian religion, at the revision of the lectures made in 1843 by the Baltimore Convention, this explanation was omitted, and the allusion to Divine Providence alone retained.

In Hutchinson's system, the Blazing Star is considered a symbol of Prudence. "It is placed," says he, "in the centre, ever to be present to the eye of the Mason, that his heart may be attentive to her dictates and steadfast in her laws;—for Prudence is the rule of all Virtues; Prudence is the path which leads to every degree of propriety; Prudence is the channel where self-approbation flows for ever; she leads us forth to worthy actions, and, as a Blazing Star, enlighteneth us through the dreary and darksome paths of this life." (*Sp. of Mas.*, ed. 1775, Lect. V., p. 111.) Hutchinson also adopted Dunckerley's allusion to the Star of Bethlehem, but only as a secondary symbolism.

In another series of lectures formerly in use in America, but which I believe is now abandoned, the Blazing Star is said to be "emblematical of that Prudence which ought to appear conspicuous in the conduct of every Mason; and is more especially commemorative of the star which appeared in the east to guide the wise men to Bethlehem, and proclaim the birth and the presence of the Son of God."

The Masons on the Continent of Europe, speaking of the symbol, say: "It is no matter whether the figure of which the Blazing Star forms the centre be a square, triangle, or circle, it still represents the sacred name of God, as an universal spirit who enlivens our hearts, who purifies our reason, who increases our knowledge, and who makes us wiser and better men."

And lastly, in the lectures revised by Dr. Hemming and adopted by the Grand Lodge of England at the union in 1813, and now constituting the authorized lectures of that jurisdiction, we find the following definition: "The Blazing Star, or glory in the centre, refers us to the sun, which enlightens the earth with its refulgent rays, dispensing its blessings to mankind at large, and giving light and life to all things here below."

Hence we find that at different times the Blazing Star has been declared to be a symbol of Divine Providence, of the Star of Bethlehem, of Prudence, of Beauty, and of the Sun. Before we can attempt to decide upon these various opinions, and adopt the true signification, it is necessary to extend our investigations into the antiquity of the emblem, and inquire what was the meaning given to it by the nations who first established it as a symbol.

Sabaism, or the worship of the stars, was one of the earliest deviations from the true system of religion. One of its causes was the universally established doctrine among the idolatrous nations of antiquity, that each star was animated by the soul of a hero god, who had once dwelt incarnate upon earth. Hence, in the hieroglyphical system, the star denoted a god. To this signification, allusion is made by the prophet Amos, when he says to the Israelites, while reproaching them for their idolatrous habits: "But ye have borne the tabernacle of your Moloch and Chiun your images, the star of your god, which ye made to yourselves." (Amos v. 26.)

This idolatry was early learned by the Israelites from their Egyptian taskmasters; and so unwilling were they to abandon it, that Moses found it necessary strictly to forbid the worship of anything "that is in heaven above"; notwithstanding which we find the Jews repeatedly committing the sin which had been so expressly forbidden. Saturn was the star to whose worship they were more particularly addicted under the names of Moloch and Chiun, already mentioned in the passage quoted from Amos. The planet Saturn was worshiped under the names of Moloch, Malcom or Milcom by the Ammonites, the Canaanites, the Phœnicians, and the Carthaginians, and under that of Chiun by the Israelites in the desert. Saturn was worshiped among the Egyptians under the name of *Raiphan*, or, as it is called in the Septuagint, *Remphan*. St. Stephen, quoting the passage of Amos, says, "ye took up the tabernacle of Moloch and the star of your god Remphan." (Acts vii. 43.)

Hale, in his *Analysis of Chronology*, says, in alluding to this passage: "There is no direct evidence that the Israelites worshipped the dog-star in the wilderness, except this passage; but the indirect is very strong, drawn from the general prohibition of the worship of the sun, moon, and stars, to which they must have been prone. And this was peculiarly an Egyptian idolatry, where the dog-star was worshiped, as notifying by his heliacal rising, or emersion from the sun's rays, the regular commencement of the periodical inundation of the Nile. And the Israelite sculptures at the cemetery of Kibroth-Hattaavah, or graves of lust, in the neighborhood of Sinai, remarkably abound in hieroglyphics of the dog-star, represented as a human figure with a dog's head. That they afterwards sacrificed to the dog-star, there is express evidence in Josiah's description of idolatry, where the Syriac Mazaloth (improperly termed planets) denotes the dog-star; in Arabic, Mazaroth."

Fellows, in his *Exposition of the Mysteries* (p. 7), says that this dog-star, the Anubis of the Egyptians, is the Blazing Star of Masonry, and supposing that the latter is a symbol of Prudence, which indeed it was in some of the ancient lectures, he goes on to remark: "What connection can possibly exist between a *star* and *prudence*, except allegorically in reference to the caution that was indicated to the Egyptians by the first appearance of *this star,* which warned them of approaching danger." But it will hereafter be seen that he has totally misapprehended the true signification of the Masonic symbol. The work of Fellows, it may be remarked, is an unsystematic compilation of undigested learning; but the student who is searching for truth must carefully eschew all his deductions as to the genius and spirit of Freemasonry.

Notwithstanding a few discrepancies that may have occurred in the Masonic lectures, as arranged at various periods and by different authorities, the concurrent testimony of the ancient religions, and the hieroglyphic language, prove that the star was a symbol of God. It was so used by the prophets of old in their metaphorical style, and it has so been generally adopted by Masonic instructors. The application of the Blazing Star as an emblem of the Savior, has been made by those writers who give a Christian explanation of our emblems, and to the Christian Mason such an application will not be objectionable. But

8

those who desire to refrain from anything that may tend to impair the tolerance of our system, will be disposed to embrace a more universal explanation, which may be received alike by all the disciples of the Order, whatever may be their peculiar religious views. Such persons will rather accept the expression of Dr. Oliver, who, though much disposed to give a Christian character to our Institution, says "the great Architect of the Universe is therefore symbolized in Freemasonry by the Blazing Star, as the herald of our salvation." (*Symb. Glory*, p. 292.)

Before concluding, a few words may be said as to the form of the Masonic symbol. It is not an heraldic star or *estoile*, for that always consists of six points, while the Masonic star is made with five points. This, perhaps, was with some involuntary allusion to the five Points of Fellowship. But the error has been committed in all our modern Tracing Boards of making the star with straight points, which form, of course, does not represent a blazing star. Guillim (*Disp. of Herald*) says: "All stars should be made with waved points, because our eyes tremble at beholding them."

In the early Tracing Board already referred to, the star with five straight points is superimposed upon another of five waving points. But the latter are now abandoned, and we have in the representations of the present day the incongruous symbol of a blazing star with five straight points. In the center of the star there was always placed the letter **G**, which, like the Hebrew *yod*, was a recognized symbol of God, and thus the symbolic reference of the Blazing Star to Divine Providence is greatly strengthened.

Blazing Star, Order of the. The Baron Tschoudy was the author of a work entitled *The Blazing Star*. (See *Tschoudy*.) On the principles inculcated in this work, he established, says Thory (*Acta Latomorum*, i., 94), at Paris, in 1766, an order called "The Order of the Blazing Star," which consisted of degrees of chivalry ascending to the Crusades, after the Templar system of Ramsay. It never, however, assumed the prominent position of an active rite.

Blesington, Earl of. Grand Master of Ireland, 1738–9; also of the English Grand Lodge of the "Ancients," 1756–63.

Blessing. See *Benediction*.

Blind. A blind man cannot be initiated into Masonry under the operation of the old regulation, which requires physical perfection in a candidate.

Blindness. Physical blindness in Masonry, as in the language of the Scriptures, is symbolic of the deprivation of moral and intellectual light. It is equivalent to the darkness of the Ancient Mysteries in which the neophytes were enshrouded for periods varying from a few hours to many days. The Masonic candidate, therefore, represents one immersed in intellectual darkness, groping in the search for that Divine light and truth which are the objects of a Mason's labor. (See *Darkness*.)

Blow. The three blows given to the Builder, according to the legend of the Third Degree, have been differently interpreted as symbols in the different systems of Masonry, but always with some reference to adverse or malignant influences exercised on humanity, of whom Hiram is considered as the type. Thus, in the symbolic degrees of Ancient Craft Masonry, the three blows are said to be typical of the trials and temptations to which man is subjected in youth and manhood, and to death, whose victim he becomes in old age. Hence the three Assassins are the three stages of human life. In the high degrees, such as the Kadoshes, which are founded on the Templar system of Ramsay, the reference is naturally made to the destruction of the Order, which was effected by the combined influences of Tyranny, Superstition, and Ignorance, which are therefore symbolized by the three blows; while the three Assassins are also said sometimes to be represented by Squire de Floreau, Naffodei, and the Prior of Montfaucon, the three perjurers who swore away the lives of De Molay and his Knights. In the astronomical theory of Freemasonry, which makes it a modern modification of the ancient sun-worship, a theory advanced by Ragon, the three blows are symbolic of the destructive influences of the three winter months, by which Hiram, or the Sun, is shorn of his vivifying power. Des Etangs has generalized the Templar theory, and, supposing Hiram to be the symbol of eternal reason, interprets the blows as the attacks of those vices which deprave and finally destroy humanity. However interpreted for a special theory, Hiram the Builder always represents, in the science of Masonic symbolism, the principle of good; and then the three blows are the contending principles of evil.

Blue. This is emphatically the color of Masonry. It is the appropriate tincture of the Ancient Craft degrees. It is to the Mason a symbol of universal friendship and benevolence, because, as it is the color of the vault of heaven, which embraces and covers the whole globe, we are thus reminded that in the breast of every brother these virtues should be equally as extensive. It is therefore the only color, except white, which should be used in a Master's Lodge. Decorations of any other color would be highly inappropriate.

Among the religious institutions of the Jews, blue was an important color. The robe of the high priest's ephod, the ribbon for his breastplate, and for the plate of the miter, were to be blue. The people were directed to wear a ribbon of this color above the fringe of their garments; and it was the color of one of the veils of the tabernacle, where, Josephus says, it represented the element of air. The Hebrew word used on these occasions to designate the color blue is תכלת, *tekelet;* and this word seems to have a singular reference to the symbolic character of the color, for it is derived from a root signifying *perfection;* now it is well known that, among the ancients, initiation into the mysteries and perfection were synonymous terms; and hence the appropriate color of the greatest of all the systems of initiation may well be designated by a word which also signifies perfection.

This color also held a prominent position in the symbolism of the Gentile nations of antiquity. Among the Druids, blue was the symbol of *truth*, and the candidate, in the initiation into the sacred rites of Druidism, was invested with a robe composed of the three colors, white, blue, and green.

The Egyptians esteemed blue as a sacred color, and the body of Amun, the principal god of their theogony, was painted light blue, to imitate, as Wilkinson remarks, "his peculiarly exalted and heavenly nature."

The ancient Babylonians clothed their idols in blue, as we learn from the prophet Jeremiah. The Chinese, in their mystical philosophy, represented blue as the symbol of the Deity, because, being, as they say, compounded of black and red, this color is a fit representation of the obscure and brilliant, the male and female, or active and passive principles.

The Hindus assert that their god, Vishnu, was represented of a celestial blue, thus indicating that wisdom emanating from God was to be symbolized by this color.

Among the medieval Christians blue was sometimes considered as an emblem of immortality, as red was of the Divine love. Portal says that blue was the symbol of perfection, hope, and constancy. "The color of the celebrated dome, azure," says Weale, in his treatise on *Symbolic Colors*, "was in divine language the symbol of eternal truth; in consecrated language, of immortality; and in profane language, of fidelity."

Besides the three degrees of Ancient Craft Masonry, of which blue is the appropriate color, this tincture is also to be found in several other degrees, especially of the Scottish Rite, where it bears various symbolic significations; all, however, more or less related to its original character as representing universal friendship and benevolence.

In the degree of Grand Pontiff, the Nineteenth of the Scottish Rite, it is the predominating color, and is there said to be symbolic of the mildness, fidelity, and gentleness which ought to be the characteristics of every true and faithful brother.

In the degree of Grand Master of all Symbolic Lodges, the blue and yellow, which are its appropriate colors, are said to refer to the appearance of Jehovah to Moses on Mount Sinai in clouds of azure and gold, and hence in this degree the color is rather an historical than a moral symbol.

The blue color of the tunic and apron, which constitutes a part of the investiture of a Prince of the Tabernacle, or Twenty-fourth Degree in the Scottish Rite, alludes to the whole symbolic character of the degree, whose teachings refer to our removal from this tabernacle of clay to "that house not made with hands, eternal in the heavens." The blue in this degree is, therefore, a symbol of heaven, the seat of our celestial tabernacle.

Blue Blanket. The Lodge of Journeymen, in the city of Edinburgh, is in possession of a blue blanket, which is used as a banner in Masonic processions. The history of it is thus given in the *London Magazine:*

"A number of Scotch mechanics followed Allan, Lord Steward of Scotland, to the holy wars in Palestine, and took with them a banner, on which were inscribed the following words from the 51st Psalm, viz.: 'In bona voluntate tua edificentur muri Hierosolymæ.' Fighting under the banner, these valiant Scotchmen were present at the capture of Jerusalem, and other towns in the Holy Land; and, on their return to their own country, they deposited the banner, which they styled 'The Banner of the Holy Ghost,' at the altar of St. Eloi, the patron saint of the Edinburgh Tradesmen, in the church of St. Giles. It was occasionally unfurled, or worn as a mantle by the representatives of the trades in the courtly and religious pageants that in former times were of frequent occurrence in the Scottish capital. In 1482, James III., in consequence of the assistance which he had received from the Craftsmen of Edinburgh, in delivering him from the castle in which he was kept a prisoner, and paying a debt of 6,000 Marks which he had contracted in making preparations for the marriage of his son, the Duke of Rothsay, to Cecil, daughter of Edward IV., of England, conferred on the good town several valuable privileges, and renewed to the Craftsmen their favorite banner of 'The Blue Blanket.' James's queen, Margaret of Denmark, to show her gratitude and respect to the Crafts, painted on the banner, with her own hands, a St. Andrew's cross, a crown, a thistle, and a hammer, with the following inscription: 'Fear God and honor the king; grant him a long life and a prosperous reign, and we shall ever pray to be faithful for the defence of his sacred majesty's royal person till death.' The king decreed that in all time coming, this flag should be the standard of the Crafts within burgh, and that it should be unfurled in defence of their own rights, and in protection of their sovereign. The privilege of displaying it at the Masonic procession was granted to the journeymen, in consequence of their original connection with the Masons of Mary's Chapel, one of the fourteen incorporated trades of the city.

"'The Blue Blanket' was long in a very tattered condition; but some years ago it was repaired by lining it with blue silk, so that it can be exposed without subjecting it to much injury."

An interesting little book was published with this title in 1722 and later editions describing the Operative Companies of Edinburgh.

Blue Degrees. The first three degrees of Freemasonry are so called from the blue color which is peculiar to them.

Blue Lodge. A Symbolic Lodge, in which the first three degrees of Masonry are conferred, is so called from the color of its decorations.

Blue Masonry. The degrees of Entered Apprentice, Fellow-Craft, and Master Mason are called Blue Masonry.

Blue Master. In some of the high degrees, these words are used to designate a Master Mason.

Board of General Purposes. An organization attached to the Grand Lodge of England, consisting of the Grand Master, Pro Grand Master, Deputy Grand Master, the Grand Wardens of the year, the Grand Treasurer, the Grand Registrar, the Deputy Grand Registrar, a President, Past Presidents, the President of the Board of Benevolence, the Grand Director of Ceremonies, and twenty-four other members. The President and six of the twenty-four members are annually nominated by the Grand Master, and the remaining eighteen are elected by the Grand Lodge from the Masters and Past Masters of the Lodges. This board has authority to hear and determine all subjects of Masonic complaints, or irregularity respecting Lodges or individual Masons, when regularly brought before it, and generally to take cognizance of all matters relating to the Craft.

Board of Relief. See *Relief, Board of.*

Boaz. The name of the left hand (or *north*) pillar that stood at the porch of King Solomon's Temple. It is derived from the Hebrew ב, *b*, "in," and עז, *oaz*, "strength," and signifies "in strength." (See *Pillars of the Porch.*)

Bochim. (בכים, weepings.) A password in the Order of Ishmael. An angel spoke to Hagar as she wept at the well when in the wilderness with her son Ishmael. The angel is looked upon as a spiritual being, possibly the Great Angel of the Covenant, the Michael who appeared to Moses in the burning bush, or the Joshua, the captain of the hosts of Jehovah.

Bode, Johann Joachim Christoph. Born in Brunswick, 16th of January, 1730. One of the most distinguished Masons of his time. In his youth he was a professional musician, but in 1757 he established himself at Hamburg as a bookseller, and was initiated into the Masonic Order. He obtained much reputation by the translation of Sterne's *Sentimental Journey* and *Tristram Shandy*, of Goldsmith's *Vicar of Wakefield;* Smollett's *Humphrey Clinker;* and of Fielding's *Tom Jones,* from the English; and of Montaigne's works from the French. To Masonic literature he made many valuable contributions; among others, he translated from the French Bonneville's celebrated work entitled *Les Jésuites chassés de la Maçonnerie et leur poignard brisé par les Maçons,* which contains a comparison of Scottish Masonry with the Templarism of the fourteenth century. Bode was at one time a zealous promoter of the Rite of Strict Observance, but afterward became one of its most active opponents. In 1790 he joined the Order of the Illuminati, obtaining the highest degree in its second class, and at the Congress of Wilhelmsbad he advocated the opinions of Weishaupt. No man of

his day was better versed than he in the history of Freemasonry, or possessed a more valuable and extensive library; no one was more diligent in increasing his stock of Masonic knowledge, or more anxious to avail himself of the rarest sources of learning. Hence, he has always held an exalted position among the Masonic scholars of Germany. The theory which he had conceived on the origin of Freemasonry—a theory, however, which the investigations of subsequent historians have proved to be untenable—was, that the Order was invented by the Jesuits, in the seventeenth century, as an instrument for the reestablishment of the Roman Church in England, covering it for their own purposes under the mantle of Templarism. Bode died at Weimar on the 13th of December, 1793.

Boeber, Johann. A Royal Councilor of State and Director of the School of Cadets at St. Petersburg during the reign of Alexander I. In 1805 he induced the emperor to revoke the edicts made by Paul I. and himself against the Freemasons. His representations of the true character of the Institution induced the emperor to seek and obtain initiation. Boeber may be considered as the reviver of Masonry in the Russian dominions, and was Grand Master of the Grand Lodge from 1811 to 1814.

Boehmen, Jacob. The most celebrated of the Mystics of the sixteenth and seventeenth centuries, born near Gorlitz, in 1575, and died in 1624. His system attracted, and continued to attract long after his death, many disciples in Germany. Among these, in time, were several Freemasons, who sought to incorporate the mystical dogmas of their founder with the teachings of Freemasonry, so as to make the Lodges merely schools of theosophy. Indeed, the Theosophic Rites of Freemasonry, which prevailed to a great extent about the middle of the last century in Germany and France, were indebted for most of their ideas to the mysticism of Jacob Boehmen.

Bohemann, Karl Adolf Anderson. Born in 1770, at Jönköping in the south of Sweden. H was a very zealous member of the Order of Asiatic Brethren, and was an active promulgator of the high degrees. Invited to Sweden, in 1802, by the Duke of Sudermania, who was an ardent inquirer into Masonic science, he was appointed Court Secretary. He attempted to introduce his system of high degrees into the kingdom, but having been detected in the effort to intermingle revolutionary schemes with his high degrees, he was first imprisoned and then banished from the country, his society being interdicted. He returned to Germany, but is not heard of after 1815, when he published at Pyrmont a justification of himself. Findel (*Hist.*, p. 560) calls him an impostor, but he seems rather to have been a Masonic fanatic, who was ignorant of or had forgotten the wide difference between Freemasonry and political intrigue.

Bohemia. A Lodge named "The Three Stars" is said to have been established at Prague in 1726, and other Lodges were subsequently constituted in Bohemia, but in consequence of the French Revolution they were closed in 1793 by the Austrian Government.

Bohmann, F. Otto. A merchant in Stockholm (1695–1767), who left a legacy of 100,000 Thalers to the Asylum for the Orphans of Freemasons that was founded in Stockholm in 1753. A medal wa struck in his honor in 1768. (Marvin's *Masonic Medals*, p. 172.)   [E. L. H.]

Bombay. The earliest Lodge in Bombay was established in 1758, followed by another in 1798, and by others until in 1861 a District Grand Lodge of Bombay was established by the Grand Lodge of England, which has 33 Lodges under it. There is also a District Grand Chapter with 13 subordinate Chapters; and 9 Lodges owing allegiance to the Grand Lodge of Scotland.   [E. L. H.]

Bonaim. The word is really an incorrect transliteration of the Hebrew word for builders, which should be "Bonim"; the construct form of which ("Bonai") is used in 1 Kings v. 18 to designate a portion of the workmen on the Temple: "And Solomon's builders and Hiram's builders did hew them." Oliver, in his *Dictionary* and in his *Landmarks* (i., 402), gives a mythical account of them as Fellow-Crafts, divided into Lodges by King Solomon, but, by a grammatical blunder, he calls them *Benai*, substituting the Hebrew construct for the absolute case, and changing the participial *o* into *e*. The *Bonaim* seem to be distinguished, by the author of the Book of Kings, from the *Gibalim*, and the translators of the authorized version have called the former *builders* and the latter *stone-squarers*. It is probable that the Bonaim were an order of workmen inferior to the Gibalim. Anderson, in both of his editions of the *Book of Constitutions*, blunders grammatically, like Oliver, and calls them *Bonai*, saying that they were "setters, layers, or builders, or light Fellow Crafts, in number 80,000." This idea seems to have been perpetuated in the modern rituals. From this construct plural form "Bonai" some one has formed the slightly incorrect form "Bonaim."   [E. L. H.]

Bondman. In the fourth article of the Halliwell or Regius MS., which is the earliest Masonic document known, it is said that the Master shall take good care that he make no bondman an apprentice, or, as it is in the original language:

> "The fourthe artycul thys moste be,
> That the Mayster hymn wel be-se,
> That he no bondemon prentys make."

The regulation is repeated in all the subsequent regulations, and is still in force. (See *Freeborn*.)

Bone. This word, which is now corruptly pronounced in one syllable, is the Hebrew word *boneh*, בונה, "builder," from the verb *banah*, בנה, "to build." It was peculiarly applied, as an epithet, to Hiram Abif, who superintended the construction of the Temple as its chief builder. Master Masons will recognize it as the terminal portion of a significant word.

Its true pronunciation would be, in English letters, *bonay;* but the corruption into one syllable as *bone* has become too universal ever to be corrected.

Bone Box. In the early lectures of the last century, now obsolete, we find the following catechism:

"*Q*. Have you any key to the secrets of a Mason?

"*A*. Yes.

"*Q*. Where do you keep it?

"*A*. In a bone box, that neither opens nor shuts but with ivory keys."

The bone box is the mouth, the ivory keys the teeth. And the key to the secrets is afterward said to be the tongue. These questions were simply used as tests, and were subsequently varied. In a later lecture it is called the "bone-bone box."

Bonneville, Chevalier de. On the 24th of November, 1754, he founded the Chapter of the high degrees known as the Chapter of Clermont. All the authorities assert this except Rebold (*Hist. de trois G. L.*, p. 46), who says that he was not its founder but only the propagator of its degrees.

Bonneville, Nicolas de. A bookseller and man of letters, born at Evreux, in France, March 13, 1760. He was the author of a work, published in 1788, entitled *Les Jésuites chassés de la Maçonnerie et leur poignard brisé par les Maçons*, divided into two parts, of the first of which the subtitle was *La Maçonnerie écossaise comparée avec les trois professions et le Secret des Templiers du 14e Siecle;* and of the second, *Mêmeté des quatre voeux de la Compagnie de S. Ignace, et des quatre grades de la Maç nnerie de S. Je n*. He also translated into French, Thomas Paine's *Essay on the Origin of Freemasonry;* a work, by the way, which was hardly worth the trouble of translation. De B nneville had an exalted idea of the difficulties attendant upon writing a history of Freemasonry, for he says that, to compose such a work, supported by dates and authentic facts, it would require a period equal to ten times the age of man; a statement which, although exaggerated, undoubtedly contains an element of truth. His Masonic theory was that the Jesuits had introduced into the symbolic degrees the history of the life and death of the Templars, and the doctrine of vengeance for the political and religious crime of their destruction; and that they had imposed upon four of the higher degrees the four vows of their congregation. De Bonneville was imprisoned as a Girondist in 1793. He was the author of a *History of Modern Europe*, in 3 vols., published in 1792. He died in 1828.

Book of Charges. There seems, if we may judge from the references in the old records of Masonry, to have formerly existed a book under this title, containing the Charges of the Craft; equivalent, probably, to the *Book of Constitutions*. Thus, the Matthew Cooke MS. f the first half of the fifteenth century (l. 534) speaks of "othere chargys mo that ben wryten in the Boke of Chargys."

Book of Constitutions. The *Book of Constitutions* is that work in which is contained the rules and regulations adopted for the government of the Fraternity of Freemasons. Undoubtedly, a society so orderly and systematic must always have been governed by a prescribed code of laws; but, in the lapse of ages, the precise regulations which were adopted for the direction of the Craft in ancient times have been lost. The earliest record that we have of any such *Constitutions* is in a manuscript, first quoted, in 1723, by Anderson (*Constitutions*, 1723, pp. 32, 33), which he said was written in the reign of Edward IV. Preston (p. 182, ed. 1788) quotes the same record, and adds, that "it is said to have been in the possession of the famous Elias Ashmole, and unfortunately destroyed," a statement which had not been previously made by Anderson. To Anderson, therefore, we must look in our estimation of the authenticity of this document; and that we cannot too much rely upon his accuracy as a transcriber is apparent, not only from the internal evidence of style, but also from the fact that he made important alterations in his copy of it in his edition of 1738. Such as it is, however, it contains the following particulars:

"Though the ancient records of the Brotherhood in England were many of them destroyed or lost in the wars of the Saxons and Danes, yet King Athelstan (the grandson of King Alfrede the Great, a mighty Architect), the first anointed king of England, and who translated the Holy Bible into the Saxon tongue (A.D. 930), when he had brought the land into Rest and Peace, built many great works, and encourag'd many Masons from France, who were appointed Overseers thereof, and brought with them the Charges and Regulations of the Lodges preserv'd since the Roman times, who also prevail'd with the King to improve the Constitution of the English Lodges according to the foreign Model, and to increase the Wages of Working Masons.

"The said king's youngest son, Prince Edwin, being taught Masonry, and taking upon him the Charges of a Master Mason, for the love he had to the said Craft and the honourable Principles whereon it is grounded, purchased a free charter of King Athelstan his Father, for the Masons having a Correction among themselves (as it was anciently express'd), or a Freedom and Power to regulate themselves, to amend what might happen amiss, and to hold a yearly Communication and General Assembly.

"Accordingly, Prince Edwin summoned all the Masons in the Realm to meet him in a Congregation at York, who came and composed a General Lodge, of which he was Grand Master; and having brought with them all the Writings and Records extant, some in Greek, some in Latin, some in French, and other languages, from the Contents thereof that Assembly did frame the Constitution and Charges of an English Lodge, and made a law to preserve and observe the same in all time

coming, and ordain'd good Pay for Working Masons, &c."

Other records have from time to time been discovered, most of them recently, which prove beyond all doubt that the Fraternity of Freemasons was, at least in the fourteenth, fifteenth, sixteenth, and seventeenth centuries, in possession of manuscript *Constitutions* containing the rules and regulations of the Craft.

In the year 1717, Freemasonry, which had somewhat fallen into decay in the south of England, was revived by the organization of the Grand Lodge at London; and, in the next year, the Grand Master having desired, says Anderson, "any brethren to bring to the Grand Lodge any old writings and records concerning Masons and Masonry, in order to show the usages of ancient times, several old copies of the Gothic Constitutions were produced and collated." (*Constitutions*, 1738, p. 110.)

But these *Constitutions* having been found to be very erroneous and defective, probably from carelessness or ignorance in their frequent transcription, in September, 1721, the Duke of Montagu, who was then Grand Master, ordered Bro. James Anderson to digest them "in a new and better method." (*Ibid.*, p. 113.)

Anderson having accordingly accomplished the important task that had been assigned him, in December of the same year a committee, consisting of fourteen learned Brethren, was appointed to examine the book; and, in the March communication of the subsequent year, having reported their approbation of it, it was, after some amendments, adopted by the Grand Lodge, and published, in 1723, under the title of *The Constitutions of the Freemasons, containing the History, Charges, Regulations, etc., of that Most Ancient and Right Worshipful Fraternity. For the use of the Lodges.*

A second edition was published in 1738, under the superintendence of a committee of Grand Officers. (*Ibid.*, p. 133.) But this edition contained so many alterations, interpolations, and omissions of the Charges and Regulations as they appeared in the first, as to show the most reprehensible inaccuracy in its composition, and to render it utterly worthless except as a literary curiosity. It does not seem to have been very popular, for the printers, to complete their sales, were compelled to commit a fraud, and to present what they pretended to be a new edition in 1746, but which was really only the edition of 1738, with a new title-page neatly pasted in, the old one being canceled.

In 1754, Bro. Jonathan Scott presented a memorial to the Grand Lodge, "showing the necessity of a new edition of the *Book of Constitutions.*" It was then ordered that the book "should be revised, and necessary alterations and additions made consistent with the laws and rules of Masonry"; all of which would seem to show the dissatisfaction of the Fraternity with the errors of the second edition. Accordingly, a third edition was published in

1756, under the editorship of the Rev. John Entick. The fourth edition, prepared by a committee, was published in 1767. In 1769, G. Kearsly, of London, published an unauthorized edition of the 1767 issue, with an appendix to 1769; this was also published by Thomas Wilkinson in Dublin in the same year, with several curious plates; both issues are now very scarce. And an authorized supplement appeared in 1776.

In 1784, John Noorthouck published by authority the fifth edition. This was well printed in quarto, with numerous notes, and is considered the most valuable edition; it is the last to contain the Historical Introduction.

After the union of the two rival Grand Lodges of England (see *Ancient Masons*) in 1813, the sixth edition was issued in 1815, edited by Bro. William Williams, Prov. Grand Master for Dorsetshire; the seventh appeared in 1819, being the last in quarto; and the eighth in 1827; these were called the "Second Part," and contained only the Ancient Charges and the General Regulations. The ninth edition of 1841 contained no reference to the First or Historical Part, and may be regarded as the first of the present issue in octavo with the plates of jewels at the end.

Numerous editions have since been issued. In the early days of the Grand Lodge of England in all processions the *Book of Constitutions* was carried on a cushion by the Master of the Senior Lodge (*Constitutions*, 1738, pp. 117, 126), but this was altered at the time of the union and it is provided in the *Constitutions* of 1815 and in the subsequent issues that the *Book of Constitutions* on a cushion shall be carried by the Grand Secretary. [E. L. H.]

Book of Constitutions Guarded by the Tiler's Sword. An emblem painted on the Master's carpet, and intended to admonish the Mason that he should be guarded in all his words and actions, preserving unsullied the Masonic virtues of silence and circumspection. Such is Webb's definition of the emblem (*Freemasons' Monitor*, ed. 1818, p. 69), which is a very modern one, and I am inclined to think was introduced by that lecturer. The interpretation of Webb is a very unsatisfactory one. The *Book of Constitutions* is rather the symbol of constituted law than of silence and circumspection, and when guarded by the Tiler's sword it would seem properly to symbolize regard for and obedience to law, a prominent Masonic duty.

Book of Gold. In the Ancient and Accepted Scottish Rite, the book in which the transactions, statutes, decrees, balusters, and protocols of the Supreme Council or a Grand Consistory are contained.

Book of the Law. The Holy Bible, which is always open in a Lodge as a symbol that its light should be diffused among the Brethren. The passages at which it is opened differ in the different degrees. (See *Scriptures, Reading of the.*)

Masonically, the *Book of the Law* is that sacred book which is believed by the Mason of any particular religion to contain the revealed will of God; although, technically, among the Jews the Torah, or *Book of the Law*, means only the Pentateuch or five books of Moses. Thus, to the Christian Mason the *Book of the Law* is the Old and New Testaments; to the Jew, the Old Testament; to the Mussulman, the Koran; to the Brahman, the Vedas; and to the Parsee, the Zendavesta.

The *Book of the Law* is an important symbol in the Royal Arch Degree, concerning which there was a tradition among the Jews that the *Book of the Law* was lost during the captivity, and that it was among the treasures discovered during the building of the second Temple. The same opinion was entertained by the early Christian fathers, such, for instance, as Irenæus, Tertullian, and Clemens Alexandrinus; "for," says Prideaux, "they (the Christian fathers) hold that all the Scriptures were lost and destroyed in the Babylonish captivity, and that Ezra restored them all again by Divine revelation." The truth of the tradition is very generally denied by Biblical scholars, who attribute its origin to the fact that Ezra collected together the copies of the law, expurgated them of the errors which had crept into them during the captivity, and arranged a new and correct edition. But the truth or falsity of the legend does not affect the Masonic symbolism. The *Book of the Law* is the will of God, which, lost to us in our darkness, must be recovered as precedent to our learning what is TRUTH. As captives to error, truth is lost to us; when freedom is restored, the first reward will be its discovery.

Book of Mormon. This sacred book of the Mormons was first published in 1830 by Joseph Smith, who claimed to have translated it from gold plates which he had found under Divine guidance secreted in a stone box. The number of Mormons is estimated at about 150,000 in the United States, and 50,000 in other countries. The seat of their church is at Salt Lake, Utah.

Book of the Dead. By some translated the *Book of the Master*, containing the ancient Egyptian philosophy as to death and the resurrection. A portion of these sacred writings was invariably buried with the dead. The Book in facsimile has been published by Dr. Lepsius, and translated by Dr. Birch. The myth of the "Judgment of Amenti" forms a part of the *Book of the Dead*, and shadows forth the verities and judgments of the unseen world.

The Amenti was the Place of Judgment of the Dead, situated in the West, where Osiris was presumed to be buried. There were forty-two assessors of the amount of sin committed, who sat in judgment, and before whom the adjudged passed in succession.

There seems to be a tie which binds Freemasonry to the noblest of the cults and mysteries of antiquity. The most striking exponent of the doctrines and language of the Egyptian Mysteries of Osiris is this *Book of the Dead*, or Ritual of the Underworld, or Egyptian Bible of 165 chapters, the Egyptian title of which was *The Manifestation to Light*, *or the Book Revealing Light to the Soul.* Great dependence was had, as to the immediate attainment of celestial happiness, upon the human knowledge of this wonderful Book, especially of the principal chapters. On a sarcophagus of the eleventh dynasty (chronology of Prof. Lepsius, say B.C. 2420) is this inscription: "He who knows this book is one who, in the day of the resurrection of the underworld, arises and enters in; but if he does not know this chapter, he does not enter in so soon as he arises." The conclusion of the first chapter says: "If a man knows this book thoroughly, and has it inscribed upon his sarcophagus, he will be manifested in the day in all the forms that he may desire, and entering into his abode will not be turned back" (Tiele's *Hist. Egyptian Rel.*, p. 25.)

The Egyptian belief was that portions of the Book were written by the finger of Thoth, back in the mist of time, B.C. 3000. The one hundred and twenty-fifth chapter describes the last judgment. The oldest preserved papyrus is of the eighteenth dynasty (B.C. 1591, Lep.). The most perfect copy of this Book is in the Turin Museum, where it covers one side of the walls, in four pieces, 300 feet in length.

The following extract is from the first chapter:

"Says Thot to Osiris, King of Eternity, I am the great God in the divine boat; I fight for thee; I am one of the divine chiefs who are the TRUE LIVING WORD of Osiris. I am Thot, who makes to be real the word of Horus against his enemies. The word of Osiris against his enemies made truth in Thot, and the order is executed by Thot. I am with Horus on the day of celebrating the festival of Osiris, the good Being, whose Word is truth; I make offerings to Ra (the Sun); I am a simple priest in the underworld, anointing in Abydos, *elevating to higher degrees of initiation;* I am prophet in Abydos on the day of opening or upheaving the earth. I behold the mysteries of the door of the underworld; I direct the ceremonies of Mendes; I am the assistant in the exercise of their functions; I AM GRAND MASTER OF THE CRAFTSMEN WHO SET UP THE SACRED ARCH FOR A SUPPORT." (See *Truth.*)

Book of the Fraternity of Stonemasons. Some years ago, a manuscript was discovered in the archives of the city of Cologne bearing the title of *Brüderschaftsbuch der Steinmetzen,* with records going back to the year 1396. Steinbrenner (*Orig. and Early Hist. of Masonry,* p. 104) says: "It fully confirms the conclusions to be derived from the German Constitutions, and those of the English and Scotch Masons, and conclusively proves the inauthenticity of the celebrated Charter of Cologne."

Books, Anti-Masonic. See *Anti-Masonic Books.*

Border, Tesselated. See *Tesselated Border.*

Bosonien, The (*or* Bossonius). The Fourth Degree of the African Architects, also called the "Christian Philosopher." (Thory, *A. L.*, i., 297.)

Boswell, John (of Auchinleck). A Scottish laird of the family of the biographer of Dr. Johnson. His appearance in the Lodge of Edinburgh at a meeting held at Holyrood in June, 1600, affords the earliest authentic instance of a person being a member of the Masonic Fraternity who was not an architect or builder by profession. He signed his name and made his mark as did the Operatives.

Bourn. A limit or boundary; a word familiar to the Mason in the Monitorial Instructions of the Fellow-Craft's Degree, where he is directed to remember that we are traveling upon the level of time to that undiscovered country from whose bourn no traveler returns; and to the reader of Shakespeare, from whom the expression is borrowed, in the beautiful soliloquy of Hamlet:

"Who would fardels bear,
To grunt and sweat under a weary life;
But that the dread of something after death—
The undiscovered country, from whose bourn
No traveller returns—puzzles the will."
                                        Act III., Scene 1.

Box of Fraternal Assistance. A box of convenient shape and size under the charge of the Hospitaler or Almoner, in the Modern French and A. A. Scottish Rites, wherein is collected the obligatory contributions of the duly assembled Brethren at every convocation, which collections can only be used for secret charitable purposes, first among the members, but if not there required, among worthy profane; the Master and the Hospitaler being the only ones cognizant of the name of the beneficiary, together with the brother who suggests an individual in need of the assistance.

Box-Master. In the Lodges of Scotland the Treasurer was formerly sometimes so called. Thus, in the minutes of the Lodge of Journeymen Masons of Edinburgh, it was resolved, on December 27, 1726, that the Warden be instructed "to uplift and receive for the use of the society all such sum or sums of money which are due and indebted to them or their former Box-masters or his predecessors in office."

Boys' School. The Royal Masonic Institution for Boys is a charity of the Masons of England. It was founded in the year 1798, for clothing and educating the sons of indigent and deceased Brethren, according to the situation in life they are most probably destined to occupy, and inculcating such religious instruction as may be conformable to the tenets of their parents, and ultimately apprenticing them to suitable trades. It is still existing in a flourishing condition. Similar schools have been established by the Masons of France and Germany.

Brahmanism. The religious system practised by the Hindus. It presents a profound and spiritual philosophy, strangely blended with the basest superstitions. The Veda is the Brahmanical *Book of the Law,* although the older hymns springing out of the primitive Aryan religion have a date far anterior to that of comparatively modern Brahmanism. The "Laws of Menu" are really the text-book of Brahmanism; yet in the Vedic hymns we find the expression of that religious thought that has been adopted by the Brahmans and the rest of the modern Hindus. The learned Brahmans have an esoteric faith, in which they recognize and adore one God, without form or quality, eternal, unchangeable, and occupying all space; but confining this hidden doctrine to their interior schools, they teach, for the multitude, an open or esoteric worship, in which the incomprehensible attributes of the supreme and purely spiritual God are invested with sensible and even human forms. In the Vedic hymns all the powers of nature are personified, and become the objects of worship, thus leading to an apparent polytheism. But, as Mr. J. F. Clarke (*Ten Great Religions*, p. 90) remarks, "behind this incipient polytheism lurks the original monotheism; for each of these gods, in turn, becomes the Supreme Being." And Max Müller says (*Chips*, i., 2) that "it would be easy to find in the numerous hymns of the Veda passages in which almost every important deity is represented as supreme and absolute." This most ancient religion—believed in by one-seventh of the world's population, that fountain from which has flowed so much of the stream of modern religious thought, abounding in mystical ceremonies and ritual prescriptions, worshiping, as the Lord of all, "the source of golden light," having its ineffable name, its solemn methods of initiation, and its symbolic rites—is well worth the serious study of the Masonic scholar, because in it he will find much that will be suggestive to him in the investigations of the dogmas of his Order.

Brant, Joseph. A Mohawk Indian, who was initiated in London in 1776. During the War of American Independence he was in command of some Indian troops on the British side, by whom Captain McKinsty, of the United States Army, had been captured. The Indians had tied their prisoner to a tree and were preparing to torture him, when he made the mystic appeal of a Mason in the hour of danger. Brant interposed and rescued his American brother from his impending fate, took him to Quebec, and placed him in the hands of some English Masons, who returned him, uninjured, to the American outposts. (Hawkins's *Concise Cyclopædia of F. M.*)

Clavel has illustrated the occurrence on p. 283 of his *Histoire Pittoresque de la F. M.*
[E. L. H.]

Brazen Laver. See *Laver.*
Brazen Pillars. See *Pillars of the Porch.*
Brazen Serpent. See *Serpent and Cross.*
Brazen Serpent, Knight of the. See *Knight of the Brazen Serpent.*
Brazil. The first organized Masonic authority at Brazil, the Grande Oriente do Brazil, was established in Rio de Janeiro, in the year 1821, by the division into three of a Lodge at Rio de Janeiro, which is said to have been established under a French warrant in 1815.

The Emperor, Dom Pedro I., was soon after initiated in one of these Lodges, and immediately proclaimed Grand Master; but finding that the Lodges of that period were nothing but political clubs, he ordered them to be closed in the following year, 1822. After his abdication in 1831, Masonic meetings again took place, and a new authority, under the title of "Grande Oriente Brazileiro," was established.

Some of the old members of the "Grande Oriente do Brazil" met in November of the same year and reorganized that body; so that two supreme authorities of the French Rite existed in Brazil.

In 1832, the Visconde de Jequitinhonha, having received the necessary powers from the Supreme Council of Belgium, established a Supreme Council of the Ancient and Accepted Rite; making thus a third contending body, to which were soon added a fourth and fifth, by the illegal organizations of the Supreme Councils of their own, by the contending Grand Orientes. In 1835, disturbances broke out in the legitimate Supreme Council, some of its Lodges having proclaimed the Grand Master of the Grand Orient of Brazil their Grand Commander, and thus formed another Supreme Council. In 1842, new seeds of dissension were planted by the combination of this revolutionary faction with the Grande Oriente Brazileiro, which body then abandoned the French Rite, and the two formed a new Council, which proclaimed itself the only legitimate authority of the Scottish Rite in Brazil. But it would be useless as well as painful to continue the record of these dissensions, which, like a black cloud, darkened for years the Masonic sky of Brazil.

Things are now in a better condition, and Freemasonry in Brazil is united under the one head of the Grand Orient.

Bread, Consecrated. Consecrated bread and wine, that is to say, bread and wine used not simply for food, but made sacred by the purpose of symbolizing a bond of brotherhood, and the eating and drinking of which are sometimes called the "Communion of the Brethren," is found in some of the higher degrees, such as the Order of High Priesthood in the American Rite, and the Rose Croix of the French and Scottish Rites.

It was in ancient times a custom religiously observed, that those who sacrificed to the gods should unite in partaking of a part of the food that had been offered. And in the Jewish church it was strictly commanded that the sacrificers should "eat before the Lord," and unite in a feast of joy on the occasion of their offerings. By this common partaking of that which had been consecrated to a sacred purpose, those who partook of the feast seemed to give an evidence and attestation of the sincerity with which they made the offering; while the feast itself was, as it were, the renewal of the covenant of friendship between the parties.

Breadth of the Lodge. See *Form of the Lodge.*

Breast. In one of the Old Lectures, quoted by Dr. Oliver, it is said: "A Mason's breast should be a safe and sacred repository for all your just and lawful secrets. A brother's secrets, delivered to me as such, I would keep as my own; as to betray that trust might be doing him the greatest injury he could sustain in this mortal life; nay, it would be like the villany of an assassin who lurks in darkness to stab his adversary when unarmed and least prepared to meet an enemy."

It is true, that the secrets of a Mason, confided as such, should be as inviolate in the breast of him who has received them as they were in his own before they were confided. But it would be wrong to conclude that in this a Mason is placed in a position different from that which is occupied by every honorable man. No man of honor is permitted to reveal a secret which he has received under the pledge of secrecy. But it is as false as it is absurd, to assert that either the man of honor or the Mason is bound by any such obligation to protect the criminal from the vindication of the law. It must be left to every man to determine by his own conscience whether he is at liberty to betray a knowledge of facts with which he could not have become acquainted except under some such pledge. No court of law would attempt to extort a communication of facts made known by a penitent to his confessor or a client to his lawyer; for such a communication would make the person communicating it infamous. In this case, Masonry supplies no other rule than that which is found in the acknowledged codes of Moral Ethics.

Breastplate. Called in Hebrew חשן, *chosen,* or חשן משפט, *chosen mishpet,* the *breastplate of judgment,* because through it the high priest received divine responses, and uttered his decisions on all matters relating to the good of the commonwealth. It was a piece of embroidered cloth of gold, purple, scarlet, and fine white, twined linen. It was a span, or about nine inches square, when doubled, and made thus strong to hold the precious stones that were set in it. It had a gold ring at each corner, to the uppermost of which were attached golden chains, by which it was fastened to the shoulder-pieces of the ephod; while from the two lowermost went two ribbons of blue, by which it was attached to the girdle of the ephod, and thus held secure in its place. In the breastplate were set twelve precious jewels, on each of which was engraved the name of one of the twelve tribes. The stones were arranged in four rows, three stones in each row. As to the order of arrangement and the names of the stones, there has been some difference among the authorities. The authorized version of the Bible gives them in this order: Sardius, topaz, carbuncle, emerald, sapphire, diamond, ligure, agate, amethyst, beryl, onyx, jasper. This is the pattern generally followed in the construction of Masonic breastplates, but modern researches into the true meaning of the Hebrew names of the stones have shown its inaccuracy. Espe-

cially must the diamond be rejected, as no engraver could have cut a name on this impenetrable gem, to say nothing of the pecuniary value of a diamond of a size to match the rest of the stones. Josephus (*Ant.,* III., vii.) gives the stones in the following order: Sardonyx, topaz, emerald; carbuncle, jasper, sapphire; ligure, amethyst, agate; chrysolite, onyx, beryl. Kalisch, in his *Commentary on Exodus,* gives a still different order: Cornelian (or sardius), topaz, smaragdus; carbuncle, sapphire, emerald; ligure, agate, amethyst; chrysolite, onyx, jasper. But perhaps the Vulgate translation is to be preferred as an authority, because it was made in the fifth century, at a time when the old Hebrew names of the precious stones were better understood than now. The order given in that version is shown in the following diagram:

EMERALD.	TOPAZ.	SARDIUS.
JASPER.	SAPPHIRE.	CARBUNCLE.
AMETHYST.	AGATE.	LIGURE.
BERYL.	ONYX.	CHRYSOLITE.

A description of each of these stones, with its symbolic signification, will be found under the appropriate head.

On the stones were engraved the names of the twelve tribes, one on each stone. The order in which they were placed, according to the Jewish Targums, was as follows, having a reference to the respective ages of the twelve sons of Jacob:

LEVI.	SIMEON.	REUBEN.
ZEBULUN.	ISSACHAR.	JUDAH.
GAD.	NAPHTALI.	DAN.
BENJAMIN.	JOSEPH.	ASHER.

The differences made by different writers in the order of the names of the stones arise only from their respective translations of the Hebrew words. These original names are detailed in Exodus (xxviii.), and admit of no doubt, whatever doubt there may be as to the gems which they were intended to represent. These Hebrew names are given on opposite page.

The breastplate which was used in the first Temple does not appear to have been returned after the Captivity, for it is not mentioned in the list of articles sent back by Cyrus. The stones, on account of their great beauty and value, were most probably removed from their original arrangement and reset in various ornaments by their captors. A new one was made for the services of the second Temple, which, according to Josephus, when worn by the High Priest, shot forth brilliant rays of fire that manifested the immediate presence of Jehovah. But he adds that two hundred years before his time this miraculous power had become extinct in consequence of the impiety of the nation. It was subsequently

ברקת	פטרה	אדם
*	*	*
BABEKET.	PITDAH.	ODEM.
יהלם	ספיר	נפך
*	*	*
YAHALOM.	SAPHIR.	NOPECH.
אחלמה	שבו	לשם
*	*	*
AOHLAMAH.	SHEBO.	LESHEM.
ישפה	שהם	תרשיש
*	*	*
YASHPAH.	SHOHAM.	TABSHISH.

carried to Rome together with the other spoils of the Temple. Of the subsequent fate of these treasures, and among them the breastplate, there are two accounts: one, that they were conveyed to Carthage by Genseric after his sack of Rome, and that the ship containing them was lost on the voyage; the other, and, as King thinks (*Ant. Gems*, p. 137), the more probable one, that they had been transferred long before that time to Byzantium, and deposited by Justinian in the treasury of St. Sophia.

The breastplate is worn in American Chapters of the Royal Arch by the High Priest as an essential part of his official vestments. The symbolic reference of it, as given by Webb, is that it is to teach him always to bear in mind his responsibility to the laws and ordinances of the Institution, and that the honor and interests of his Chapter should be always near his heart. This does not materially differ from the ancient symbolism, for one of the names given to the Jewish breastplate was the "memorial," because it was designed to remind the High Priest how dear the tribes whose names it bore should be to his heart.

The breastplate does not appear to have been original with or peculiar to the Jewish ritual. The idea was, most probably, derived from the Egyptians. Diodorus Siculus says (l. i., c. 75) that among them the chief judge bore about his neck a chain of gold, from which hung a figure or image ((ζώδιον), composed of precious stones, which was called TRUTH, and the legal proceedings only commenced when the chief judge had assumed this image. Ælian

(lib. 34) confirms this account by saying that the image was engraved on sapphire, and hung about the neck of the chief judge with a golden chain. Peter du Val says that he saw a mummy at Cairo, round the neck of which was a chain, to which a golden plate was suspended, on which the image of a bird was engraved. (See *Urim and Thummim*.)

Breast, The Faithful. One of the three precious jewels of a Fellow-Craft. It symbolically teaches the initiate that the lessons which he has received from the instructive tongue of the Master are not to be listened to and lost, but carefully treasured in his heart, and that the precepts of the Order constitute a covenant which he is faithfully to observe.

Breast to Breast. See *Points of Fellowship*.

Brethren. This word, being the plural of Brother in the solemn style, is more generally used in Masonic language, instead of the common plural, *Brothers*. Thus Masons always speak of "The Brethren of the Lodge," and not of "The Brothers of the Lodge."

Brethren of the Bridge. See *Bridge Builders of the Middle Ages*.

Brethren of the Mystic Tie. The term by which Masons distinguish themselves as the members of a confraternity or brotherhood united by a mystical bond. (See *Mystic Tie*.)

Brewster, Sir David. See *Lawrie, Alexander*.

Bridge. A most significant symbol in the Fifteenth and Sixteenth Degrees of the Scottish Rite, at which an important event transpires. The characteristic letters which appear on the Bridge, L. o. P., refer to that liberty of thought which is ever thereafter to be the inheritance of those who have been symbolically captive for seven weeks of years. It is the new era of the freedom of expression, the liberation of the former captive thought. Liberty, but not License. (See *Lakak Deror Pessah;* also *Liber;* also *Liberty of Passage*.) It is also a symbol in the Royal Order.

Bridge Builders of the Middle Ages. Before speaking of the *Pontifices*, or the "Fraternity of Bridge Builders," whose history is closely connected with that of the Freemasons of the Middle Ages, it will be as well to say something of the word which they assumed as the title of their brotherhood.

The Latin word *pontifex*, with its equivalent English *pontiff*, literally signifies "the builder of a bridge," from *pons*, " a bridge," and *facere* "to make." But this sense, which it must have originally possessed, it seems very speedily to have lost, and we, as well as the Romans, only recognize *pontifex or pontiff* as significant of a sacerdotal character.

Of all the colleges of priests in ancient Rome, the most illustrious was that of the Pontiffs. The College of Pontiffs was established by Numa, and originally consisted of five, but was afterward increased to sixteen. The whole religious system of the Romans, the management of all the sacred rites, and the government of the priesthood, was under the control and direction of the College of Pontiffs, of which the *Pontifex Maximus*, or High Priest, was the presiding officer and the organ through which its decrees were communicated to the people. Hence, when the Papal Church established its seat at the city of Rome, its Bishop assumed the designation of *Pontifex Maximus* as one of his titles, and Pontiff and Pope are now considered equivalent terms.

The question naturally arises as to what connection there was between religious rites and the building of bridges, and why a Roman priest bore the name which literally denoted a bridge builder. Etymologists have in vain sought to solve the problem, and, after all their speculation, fail to satisfy us. One of the most tenable theories is that of Schmitz, who thinks the *Pontifices* were so called because they superintended the sacrifices on a bridge, alluding to the Argean sacrifices on the Sublician bridge. But Varro gives a more probable explanation when he tells us that the Sublician bridge was built by the *Pontifices;* and that it was deemed, from its historic association, of so sacred a character, that no repairs could be made on it without a previous sacrifice, which was to be conducted by the Chief Pontiff in person. The true etymology is, however, undoubtedly lost; yet it may be interesting, as well as suggestive, to know that in old Rome there was, even in a mere title, supposing that it was nothing more, some sort of connection between the art or practise of bridge building and the mysterious sacerdotal rites established by Numa, a connection which was subsequently again developed in the Masonic association which is the subject of the present article. Whatever may have been this connection in Pagan Rome, we find, after the establishment of Christianity and in the Middle Ages, a secret Fraternity organized, as a branch of the Traveling Freemasons of that period, whose members were exclusively devoted to the building of bridges, and who were known as *Pontifices*, or "Bridge Builders," and styled by the French *les Frères Pontifes*, or *Pontifical Brethren*, and by the Germans *Brückenbrüder*, or "Brethren of the Bridge." It is of this Fraternity that, because of their association in history with the early corporations of Freemasons, it is proposed to give a brief sketch.

In the eleventh and twelfth centuries, the methods of intercommunication between different countries were neither safe nor convenient. Travelers could not avail themselves of the comforts of either macadamized roads or railways. Stage-coaches were unknown. He who was compelled by the calls of business to leave his home, trudged as a pedestrian wearily on foot, or as an equestrian, if his means permitted that mode of journeying; made his solitary ride through badly constructed roads, where he frequently became the victim of robbers, who took his life as well as his purse, or submitted to the scarcely less heavy exactions of some lawless Baron, who claimed it as his high prerogative to levy a tax on every wayfarer who passed through his domains. Inns

were infrequent, incommodious, and expensive, and the weary traveler could hardly have appreciated Shenstone's declaration, that

"Whoe'er has travelled life's dull round,
    Where'er his stages may have been,
May sigh to think he still has found
    His warmest welcome at an inn."

But one of the greatest embarrassments to which the traveler in this olden time was exposed occurred when there was a necessity to cross a stream of water. The noble bridges of the ancient Greeks and Romans had been destroyed by time or war, and the intellectual debasement of the dark ages had prevented their renewal. Hence, when refinement and learning began to awaken from that long sleep which followed the invasion of the Goths and Vandals and the decline and fall of the Roman Empire, the bridgeless rivers could only be crossed by swimming through the rapid current, or by fording the shallow places.

The earliest improvement toward a removal of these difficulties consisted in the adoption of rafts or boats, and guilds or corporations of raftsmen and boatmen, under the names of *Linuncularii*, *Lintrarii*, and *Utricularii*, were formed to transport travelers and merchandise across rivers. But the times were lawless, and these watermen oftener plundered than assisted their patrons. Benevolent persons, therefore, saw the necessity of erecting hostelries on the banks of the rivers at frequented places, and of constructing bridges for the transportation of travelers and their goods.

All the architectural labors of the period were, as is well known, entrusted to the guilds or corporations of builders who, under the designation of " Traveling Freemasons," passed from country to country, and, patronized by the Church, erected those magnificent cathedrals, monasteries, and other public edifices, many of which have long since crumbled to dust, but a few of which still remain to attest the wondrous ability of these Operative Brethren. Alone skilled in the science of architecture, from them only could be derived workmen capable of constructing safe and enduring bridges.

Accordingly, a portion of these "Freemasons," withdrawing from the general body, united, under the patronage of the Church, into a distinct corporation of *Frères Pontifes*, or *Bridge Builders*. The name which they received in Germany was that of *Brückenbrüder*, or *Brethren of the Bridge*.

A legend of the Church attributes their foundation to Saint Benezet, who accordingly became the patron of the Order, as Saint John was of the Freemasons proper. Saint Benezet was a shepherd of Avilar, in France, who was born in the year 1165. "He kept his mother's sheep in the country," says Butler, the historian of the saints, "being devoted to the practices of piety beyond his age; when moved by charity to save the lives of many poor persons, who were frequently drowned in crossing the Rhone, and, being inspired by God, he undertook to build a bridge over that rapid river at Avignon. He obtained the approbation of the Bishop, proved his mission by miracles, and began the work in 1177, which he directed during seven years. He died when the difficulty of the undertaking was over, in 1184. His body was buried upon the bridge itself, which was not completely finished till four years after his decease, the structure whereof was attended with miracles from the first laying of the foundations till it was completed, in 1188."

Divesting this account, which Butler has drawn from the *Acta Sanctorum* of the Bollandists, of the miraculous, the improbable, and the legendary, the naked fact remains that Benezet was engaged, as the principal conductor of the work, in the construction of the magnificent bridge at Avignon, with its eighteen arches. As this is the most ancient of the bridges of Europe built after the commencement of the restoration of learning, it is most probable that he was, as he is claimed to have been, the founder of that Masonic corporation of builders who, under the name of *Brethren of the Bridge*, assisted him in the undertaking, and who, on the completion of their task, were engaged in other parts of France, of Italy, and of Germany, in similar labors.

After the death of Saint Benezet, he was succeeded by Johannes Benedictus, to whom, as "Prior of the Bridge," and to his *brethren*, a charter was granted in 1187, by which they obtained a chapel and cemetery, with a chaplain.

In 1185, one year after the death of Saint Benezet, the Brethren of the Bridge commenced the construction of the Bridge of Saint Esprit, over the Rhone at Lyons. The completion of this work greatly extended the reputation of the Bridge Builders, and in 1189 they received a charter from Pope Clement III. The city of Avignon continued to be their headquarters, but they gradually entered into Italy, Spain, Germany, Sweden, and Denmark. The Swedish chronicles mention one Benedict, between the years 1178 and 1191, who was a Bishop and bridge builder at Skara, in that kingdom. Could he have been the successor, already mentioned, of Benezet, who had removed from Avignon to Sweden? As late as 1590 we find the Order existing at Lucca, in Italy, where, in 1562, John de Medicis exercised the functions of its chief under the title of *Magister*, or *Master*. How the Order became finally extinct is not known; but after its dissolution much of the property which it had accumulated passed into the hands of the Knights Hospitalers or Knights of Malta.

The guild or corporation of Bridge Builders, like the corporation of Traveling Freemasons, from which it was an offshoot, was a religious institution, but admitted laymen into the society. In other words, the workmen, or the great body of the guild, were of course secular, but the patrons were dignitaries of the Church.

When by the multiplication of bridges the necessity of their employment became less urgent, and when the numbers of the workmen were greatly increased, the patronage of the Church was withdrawn, and the association was dissolved, or soon after fell into decay; its members, probably, for the most part, reuniting with the corporations of Masons from whom they had originally been derived. Nothing has remained in modern Masonry to preserve the memory of the former connection of the Order with the bridge builders of the Middle Ages, except the ceremony of opening a bridge, which is to be found in the rituals of the last century; but even this has now become almost obsolete.

Lenning, who has appropriated a brief article in his *Encyclopädie der Freimaurerei* to the *Brückenbrüder*, or *Brethren of the Bridge*, incorrectly calls them an Order of Knights. They took, he says, vows of celibacy and poverty, and also to protect travelers, to attend upon the sick, and to build bridges, roads, and hospitals. Several of the inventors of high degrees have, he thinks, sought to revive the Order in some of the degrees which they have established, and especially in the Knights of the Sword, which appears in the Ancient and Accepted Rite as the Fifteenth Degree, or Knights of the East; but I can find no resemblance except that in the Knights of the Sword there is in the ritual a reference to a river and a bridge. I am more inclined to believe that the Nineteenth Degree of the same Rite, or Grand Pontiff, was once connected with the Order we have been considering; and that, while the primitive ritual has been lost or changed so as to leave no vestige of a relationship between the two, the name which is still retained may have been derived from the *Frères Pontifes* of the twelfth century.

This, however, is mere conjecture, without any means of proof. All that we do positively know is, that the bridge builders of the Middle Ages were a Masonic association, and as such are entitled to a place in all Masonic histories.

Brief. The diploma or certificate in some of the high degrees is so called.

Bright. A Mason is said to be "bright" who is well acquainted with the ritual, the forms of opening and closing, and the ceremonies of initiation. This expression does not, however, in its technical sense, appear to include the superior knowledge of the history and science of the Institution, and many bright Masons are, therefore, not necessarily learned Masons; and, on the contrary, some learned Masons are not well versed in the exact phraseology of the ritual. The one knowledge depends on a retentive memory, the other is derived from deep research. It is scarcely necessary to say which of the two kinds of knowledge is the more valuable. The Mason whose acquaintance with the Institution is confined to what he learns from its esoteric ritual will have but a limited idea of its science and philosophy. And yet a knowledge of the ritual as the foundation of higher knowledge is essential.

Brithering. The Scotch term for Masonic initiation.

British Columbia. The first Lodge established in this Province was Victoria, No. 783, by the Grand Lodge of England, March 19, 1859, and the first chartered by the Grand Lodge of Scotland was Vancouver Lodge in 1862.

In 1871 the Grand Lodge of England had three Lodges in the Province, and the Grand Lodge of Scotland six Lodges. A convention was held on the 21st day of October, 1871, and the Grand Lodge of British Columbia duly organized. Eight out of the nine Lodges in the Province were represented. The Provincial Grand Master of Scotland and the District Grand Master of England both took an active interest in the formation of the new Grand Body, and M. W. Bro. Israel Wood Powell, M.D., was unanimously elected Grand Master.   [Will H. Whyte.]

Broached Thurnel. In the lectures of the early part of the eighteenth century the Immovable Jewels of the Lodge are said to be "the Tarsel Board, Rough Ashlar, and Broached Thurnel"; and in describing their uses it is taught that "the Rough Ashlar is for the Fellow Crafts to try their jewels on, and the Broached Thurnel for the Entered Apprentices to learn to work upon." Much difficulty has been met with in discovering what the Broached Thurnel really was. Dr. Oliver, most probably deceived by the use to which it was assigned, says (*Dict. Symb. Mas.*) that it was subsequently called the Rough Ashlar. This is evidently incorrect, because a distinction is made in the original lecture between it and the Rough Ashlar, the former being for the Apprentices and the latter for the Fellow-Crafts. Krause (*Kunsturkunden*, i., 73) has translated it by *Drehbank*, which means a turning-lathe, an implement not used by Operative Masons. Now what is the real meaning of the word? If we inspect an old tracing board of the Apprentice's Degree of the date when the Broached Thurnel was in use, we shall find depicted on it three symbols, two of which will at once be recognized as the Tarsel, or Trestle Board, and the Rough Ashlar, just as we have them at the present day; while the third symbol will be that depicted in the margin, namely, a cubical stone with a pyramidal apex. This is the Broached Thurnel. It is the symbol which is still to be found, with precisely the same form, in all French tracing boards, under the name of the *pierre cubique*, or cubical stone, and which has been replaced in English and American tracing boards and rituals by the Perfect Ashlar. For the derivation of the words, we must go to old and now almost obsolete terms of architecture. On inspection, it will at once be seen that the Broached Thurnel has the form of a little square turret with a spire springing from it. Now, broach, or broche, says Parker (*Gloss. of Terms in Architect.*, p. 97), is "an old English term for a spire, still in use in some parts of the country, as in Leicestershire, where it is said to denote a spire springing

from the tower without any intervening parapet. *Thurnel* is from the old French *tournelle*, a turret or little tower. The Broached Thurnel, then, was the Spired Turret. It was a model on which apprentices might learn the principles of their art, because it presented to them, in its various outlines, the forms of the square and the triangle, the cube and the pyramid."

[But in *Ars Quatuor Coronatorum* (xii., 205), Bro. G. W. Speth quotes from the Imperial Dictionary:

"*Broach*, in Scotland, a term among masons, signifying to rough hew. *Broached Work*, in Scotland, a term among masons, signifying work or stones that are rough-hewn, and thus distinguished from Ashlar or polished work. *Broaching-Thurmal, Thurmer, Turner*, names given to the chisels by which broached work is executed."

And he suggests that the Broached Thurnel was really a chisel for the Entered Apprentices to learn to work *with*.

The new English Dictionary explains "Broached" as a term used "of stone; chiselled with a broach," or narrow-pointed chisel used by masons; but this still leaves it uncertain what a "Thurnel" is.—E. L. H.]

Broken Column. Among the Hebrews, columns, or pillars, were used metaphorically to signify princes or nobles, as if they were the pillars of a state. Thus, in Psalm xi. 3, the passage, reading in our translation, "If the foundations be destroyed, what can the righteous do?" is, in the original, "when the columns are overthrown," i. e., when the firm supporters of what is right and good have perished. So the passage in Isaiah xix. 10 should read: "her (Egypt's) columns are broken down," that is, the nobles of her state. In Freemasonry, the broken column is, as Master Masons well know, the emblem of the fall of one of the chief supporters of the Craft. The use of the column or pillar as a monument erected over a tomb was a very ancient custom, and was a very significant symbol of the character and spirit of the person interred. It is accredited to Jeremy L. Cross that he first introduced the Broken Column into the ritual, but this may not be true. (See *Monument*.)

Brother. The term which Freemasons apply to each other. Freemasons are Brethren, not only by common participation of the human nature, but as professing the same faith; as being jointly engaged in the same labors, and as being united by a mutual covenant or tie, whence they are also emphatically called "Brethren of the Mystic Tie." (See *Companion*.)

Brotherhood. When our Savior designated his disciples as his brethren, he implied that there was a close bond of union existing between them, which idea was subsequently carried out by St. Peter in his direction to "love the brotherhood." Hence the early Christians designated themselves as a *brotherhood*, a relationship unknown to the Gentile religions; and the ecclesiastical and other confraternities of the Middle Ages assumed the same title to designate any association of men engaged in the same common object, governed by the same rules, and united by an identical interest. The association or Fraternity of Freemasons is, in this sense, called a brotherhood.

Brotherly Kiss. See *Kiss, Fraternal*.

Brotherly Love. At a very early period in the course of his initiation, a candidate for the mysteries of Freemasonry is informed that the great principles of the Order are BROTHERLY LOVE, RELIEF, and TRUTH. These virtues are illustrated, and their practise recommended to the aspirant, at every step of his progress; and the instruction, though continually varied in its mode, is so constantly repeated, as infallibly to impress upon his mind their absolute necessity in the constitution of a good Mason.

BROTHERLY LOVE might very well be supposed to be an ingredient in the organization of a society so peculiarly constituted as that of Freemasonry. But the Brotherly Love which we inculcate is not a mere abstraction, nor is its character left to any general and careless understanding of the candidate, who might be disposed to give much or little of it to his brethren, according to the peculiar constitution of his own mind, or the extent of his own generous or selfish feelings. It is, on the contrary, closely defined; its object plainly denoted; and the very mode and manner of its practise detailed in words, and illustrated by symbols, so as to give neither cause for error nor apology for indifference.

Every Mason is acquainted with the Five Points of Fellowship—he knows their symbolic meaning—he can never forget the interesting incidents that accompanied their explanation; and while he has this knowledge, and retains this remembrance, he can be at no loss to understand what are his duties, and what must be his conduct, in relation to the principle of Brotherly Love. (See *Points of Fellowship*.)

Brothers of the Bridge. See *Bridge Builders of the Middle Ages*.

Brothers of the Rosy Cross. See *Rosicrucianism*.

Brown, Dr. John. See *Latin Lodge*.

Browne, John. In 1798 John Browne published, in London, a work entitled *The Master Key through all the Degrees of a Free-Mason's Lodge, to which is added, Eulogiums and Illustrations upon Freemasonry*. In 1802, he published a second edition under the title of *Browne's Masonic Master Key through the three degrees, by way of polyglot. Under the sanction of the Craft in general, containing the exact mode of working, initiation, passing and raising to the sublime degree of a Master. Also, the several duties of the Master, officers, and brethren while in the Lodge, with every requisite to render the accomplished Mason an explanation of all the hieroglyphics. The whole interspersed with illustrations on Theology, Astronomy, Architecture, Arts, Sciences, &c., many of which are by the editor*. Browne had been, he

says, the Past Master of six Lodges, and wrote his work not as an offensive exposition, but as a means of giving Masons a knowledge of the ritual. It is considered to be a very complete representation of the Prestonian lectures, and as such was incorporated by Krause in his *drei ältesten Kunsturkunden*. The work is printed in a very complicated cipher, the key to which, and without which the book is wholly unintelligible, was, by way of caution, delivered only personally and to none but those who had reached the Third Degree. The explanation of this "mystical key," as Browne calls it, is as follows: The word *Browne* supplies the vowels, thus, $\dfrac{\text{b r o w n e}}{\text{a e i o u y}}$, and these six vowels in turn represent six letters, thus, $\dfrac{\text{a e i o u y}}{\text{k c o l n u}}$. Initial capitals are of no value, and supernumerary letters are often inserted. The words are kept separate, but the letters of one word are often divided between two or three. Much therefore is left to the shrewdness of the decipherer. The initial sentence of the work may be adduced as a specimen. *Ubs Rplrbsrt wbss oslm ronwprn Pongth Mrlwdgr*, which is thus deciphered: *Please to assist me in opening the Lodge*. The work is now exceedingly rare.

Bru. See *Vielle Bru, Rite of*.

Bruce, Robert. The introduction of Freemasonry into Scotland has been attributed by some writers to Robert, King of Scotland, commonly called Robert Bruce, who is said to have established in 1314 the Order of Herodom, for the reception of those Knights Templars who had taken refuge in his dominions from the persecutions of the Pope and the King of France. Thory (*Act. Lat.*, i., 6) copies the following from a manuscript in the library of the Mother Lodge of the Philosophical Rite:

"Robert Bruce, King of Scotland, under the name of Robert the First, created, on the 24th June, 1314, after the battle of Bannockburn, the Order of St. Andrew of the Thistle, to which has been since united that of Herodom (H-D-M) for the sake of the Scotch Masons, who composed a part of the thirty thousand men with whom he had conquered an army of a hundred thousand Englishmen. He reserved, in perpetuity, to himself and his successors, the title of Grand Master. He founded the Royal Grand Lodge of the Order of H-D-M at Kilwinning, and died, full of glory and honours, the 9th of July, 1329."

Dr. Oliver (*Landm.*, ii., 13), referring to the abolition of the Templar Order in England, when the Knights were compelled to enter the Preceptories of the Knights of St. John, as dependents, says:

"In Scotland, Edward, who had overrun the country at the time, endeavoured to pursue the same course; but, on summoning the Knights to appear, only two, Walter de Clifton, the Grand Preceptor, and another, came forward. On their examination, they confessed that all the rest had fled; and as Bruce was advancing with his army to meet Edward, nothing further was done. The Templars, being debarred from taking refuge either in England or Ireland, had no alternative but to join Bruce, and give their active support to his cause. Thus, after the battle of Bannockburn, in 1314, Bruce granted a charter of lands to Walter de Clifton, as Grand Master of the Templars, for the assistance which they rendered on that occasion. Hence the Royal Order of H-R-D-M was frequently practised under the name of Templary."

Lawrie, or the author of Lawrie's *History of Freemasonry*, who is excellent authority for Scottish Masonry, does not appear, however, to give any credit to the narrative. Whatever Bruce may have done for the higher degrees, there is no doubt that Ancient Craft Masonry was introduced into Scotland at an earlier period. But it cannot be denied that Bruce was one of the patrons and encouragers of Scottish Freemasonry.

Brün, Abraham Van. A wealthy Mason of Hamburg, who died at an advanced age in 1748. For many years he had been the soul of the "Société des anciens Rose-Croix" in Germany, which soon after his death was dissolved. (Thory, *Act. Lat.*, ii., 295.)

Brunswick, Congress of. It was convoked, in 1775, by Ferdinand, Duke of Brunswick. Its object was to effect a fusion of the various Rites; but it terminated its labors, after a session of six weeks, without success.

Buchanan MS. This parchment roll—one of the "Old Charges"—is so named because it was presented to the Grand Lodge of England in 1880 by Mr. George Buchanan, of Whitby, by whom it was found amongst the papers of a partner of his father's. It is considered to be of the latter part of the seventeenth century—say from 1660 to 1680.

It was first published at length in Gould's *History of Freemasonry* (vol. i., p. 93), being adopted as an example of the ordinary class of text, and since has been reproduced in facsimile by the Quatuor Coronati Lodge of London in vol. iv., of their Masonic reprints.

[E. L. H.]

Buddhism. The religion of the disciples of Buddha. It prevails over a great extent of Asia, and is estimated to be equally popular with any other form of faith among mankind. Its founder, Buddha—a word which seems to be an appellative, as it signifies the enlightened—lived about five hundred years before the Christian era, and established his religion as a reformation of Brahmanism.

The moral code of Buddhism is very perfect, surpassing that of any other heathen religion. But its theology is not so free from objection. Max Müller admits that there is not a single passage in the Buddhist canon of scripture which presupposes the belief in a personal God or a Creator, and hence he concludes that the teaching of Buddha was pure atheism. Yet Upham (*Hist. and Doct. of Bud.*, p. 2) thinks that, even if this be capable of proof, it also recognizes "the operation of Faith (called *Damata*), whereby much of the necessary process of conservation or government is infused into the system."

The doctrine of Nirvana, according to Burnouf, taught that absolute nothing or annihilation was the highest aim of virtue, and hence the belief in immortality was repudiated. Such, too, has been the general opinion of Oriental scholars; but Müller (*Science of Religion*, p. 141) adduces evidence, from the teachings of Buddha, to show that Nirvana may mean the extinction of many things—of selfishness, desire, and sin—without going so far as the extinction of subjective consciousness.

The sacred scripture of Buddhism is the Tripitaka, literally, the Three Baskets. The first, or the Vinaya, comprises all that relates to morality; the second, or the Sitras, contains the discourses of Buddha; and the third, or Abhidharma, includes all works on metaphysics and dogmatic philosophy. The first and second Baskets also receive the general name of Dharma, or the Law. The principal seat of Buddhism is the island of Ceylon, but it has extended into China, Japan, and many other countries of Asia. (See *Aranyaka, Aithakatha, Mahabharata, Pitaka, Puranas, Ramayana, Shaster, Sruti, Upanishad, Upadevas, Vedas*, and *Vedanga*.)

Buenos Ayres. A Lodge was chartered in this city, and named the Southern Star, by the Grand Lodge of Pennsylvania in 1825. Others followed, but in 1846 in consequence of the unsettled state of affairs their labors were suspended. A revival occurred in 1852, when a Lodge named "L'Ami des Naufragés" was established in Buenos Ayres by the Grand Orient of France; and in 1853 the Grand Lodge of England erected a Lodge named "Excelsior" (followed in 1859 by the "Teutonia," which worked in German and was erased in 1872), and in 1864 by the "Star of the South." In 1856 there was an irregular body working in the Ancient and Accepted Rite, which claimed the prerogatives of a Grand Lodge, but it was never recognized, and soon ceased to exist. On September 13, 1858, a Supreme Council and Grand Orient was established by the Supreme Council of Uruguay. In 1861 a treaty was concluded between the Grand Lodge of England and the Grand Orient of the Argentine Republic, which empowered the former to establish Lodges in La Plata and to constitute a District Grand Lodge therein, which has 13 Lodges under its rule, while 108 acknowledge the authority of the "Supreme Council and Grand Orient of the Argentine Republic in Buenos Ayres," which was formed in 1895 by combination of the Grand Orient and Supreme Council.

[E. L. H.]

Buh. A monstrous corruption, in the American Royal Arch, of the word Bel. Up to a recent period, it was combined with another corruption, *Lun*, in the mutilated form of *Buh-Lun*, under which disguise the words *Bel* and *On* were presented to the neophyte.

Buhle, Johann Gottlieb. Professor of Philosophy in the University of Göttingen, who, not being himself a Mason, published, in 1804, a work entitled *Ueber den Ursprung und die vornehmsten Schicksale des Ordens der Rosenkreuzer und Freimaurer*, that is, "On the Origin and the Principal Events of the Orders of Rosicrucianism and Freemasonry." This work, illogical in its arguments, false in many of its statements, and confused in its arrangement, was attacked by Frederick Nicolai in a critical review of it in 1806, and is spoken of very slightingly even by De Quincey, himself no very warm admirer of the Masonic Institution, who published, in 1824, in the *London Magazine* (vol. ix.), a loose translation of it, "abstracted, re-arranged, and improved," under the title of *Historicocritical Inquiry into the Origin of the Rosicrucians and the Freemasons*. Buhle's theory was that Freemasonry was invented in the year 1629, by John Valentine Andreä. Buhle was born at Brunswick in 1753, became Professor of Philosophy at Göttingen in 1787, and, having afterward taught in his native city, died there in 1821.

Builder. The chief architect of the Temple of Solomon is often called "the Builder." But the word is also applied generally to the Craft; for every speculative Mason is as much a builder as was his operative predecessor. An American writer (F. S. Wood) thus alludes to this symbolic idea: "Masons are called moral builders. In their rituals, they declare that a more noble and glorious purpose than squaring stones and hewing timbers is theirs,—fitting immortal nature for that spiritual building not made with hands, eternal in the heavens." And he adds, "The builder builds for a century; Masons for eternity." In this sense, "the Builder" is the noblest title that can be bestowed upon a Mason.

Builder, Smitten. See *Smitten Builder.*

Builders, Corporations of. See *Stone-Masons of the Middle Ages.*

Bul. Oliver says that this is one of the names of God among the ancients. (*Landmarks*, ii., 551.) It is also said to be an Assyrian word signifying "Lord" or "Powerful."

Bul. The primitive designation of the month *Marchesvan.* (See *Zif.*)

Bull, Papal. An edict or proclamation issued from the Apostolic Chancery, with the seal and signature of the Pope, written in Gothic letters and upon coarse parchment. It derives its name from the leaden seal which is attached to it by a cord of hemp or silk, and which in medieval Latin is called *bulla*. Several of these bulls have from time to time been fulminated against Freemasonry and other secret societies, subjecting them to the heaviest ecclesiastical punishments, even to the greater excommunication. According to these bulls, a Freemason is *ipso facto* excommunicated by continuing his membership in the society, and is thus deprived of all spiritual privileges while living, and the rites of burial when dead.

The several important Bulls which have been issued by the Popes of Rome intended to affect the Fraternity of Freemasons are as fol-

lows: the Bull *In Eminenti* of Clement XII., dated 24th of April, 1738. This Bull was confirmed and renewed by that beginning *Providas*, of Benedict XIV., 18th of May, 1751; then followed the edict of Pius VII., 13th of September, 1821; the apostolic edict *Quo Graviora* of Leo XII., 13th of March, 1825; that of Pius VIII., 21st of May, 1829; that of Gregory XVI., 15th of August, 1832; Pius IX. in 1846 and 1865; and finally that of Leo XIII., who ascended to the papacy in 1878, and issued his Bull, or encyclical letter, *Humanum Genus*, on April 20, 1884.

Whatever may have been the severity of the Bulls issued by the predecessors of Leo XIII., he with great clearness ratifies and confirms them all in the following language: "Therefore, whatsoever the popes our predecessors have decreed to hinder the designs and attempts of the sect of Freemasons; whatsoever they have ordained to deter or recall persons from societies of this kind, each and all do we ratify and confirm by our Apostolic authority." At the same time acknowledging that this "society of men are most widely spread and firmly established."

This letter of the Roman hierarchy thus commences: "The human race, after its most miserable defection, through the wiles of the devil, from its Creator, God, the giver of celestial gifts, has divided into two different and opposite factions, of which one fights ever for truth and virtue, the other for their opposites. One is the kingdom of God on earth . . . the other is the kingdom of Satan."

That, "by accepting any that present themselves, no matter of what religion, they (the Masons) gain their purpose of urging that great error of the present day, viz., that questions of religion ought to be left undetermined, and that there should be no distinction made between varieties. And this policy aims at the destruction of all religions, especially at that of the Catholic religion, which, since it is the only true one, cannot be reduced to equality with the rest without the greatest injury."

"But, in truth, the sect grants great license to its initiates, allowing them to defend either position, that there is a God, or that there is no God."

Thus might we quote continuous passages, which need only to be stated to proclaim their falsity, and yet there are those who hold to the doctrine of the infallibility of the Pope.

Bulletin. The name given by the Grand Orient of France to the monthly publication which contains the official record of its proceedings. A similar work is issued by the Supreme Council of the Ancient and Accepted Rite for the Southern Jurisdiction of the United States of America, and by several other Supreme Councils and Grand Orients.

Bunyan, John. The well-known author of the *Pilgrim's Progress*. He lived in the seventeenth century, and was the most celebrated allegorical writer of England. His work entitled *Solomon's Temple Spiritualized* will supply the student of Masonic symbolism with many valuable suggestions.

9

Burdens, Bearers of. A class of workmen at the Temple mentioned in 2 Chron. ii. 18, and referred to by Dr. Anderson (*Const.*, 1738, p. 11) as the *Ish Sabbal*, which see.

Buri or **Bure.** The first god of Norse mythology. In accordance with the quaint cosmogony of the ancient religion of Germany or that of Scandinavia, it was believed that before the world came into existence there was a great void, on the north side of which was a cold and dark region, and on the south side one warm and luminous. In Niflheim was a well, or the "seething caldron," out of which flowed twelve streams into the great void and formed a huge giant. In Iceland the first great giant was called Ymir, by the Germans Tuisto (Tacitus, *Germania*, ch. 2), whose three grandchildren were regarded as the founders of three of the German races.

Cotemporary with Ymir, and from the great frost-blocks of primeval chaos, was produced a man called Buri, who was wise, strong, and beautiful. His son married the daughter of another giant, and their issue were the three sons Odin, Wili, and We, who ruled as gods in heaven and earth.

By some it is earnestly believed that upon these myths and legends many symbols of Masonry were founded.

Burial. The right to be buried with the ceremonies of the Order is one that, under certain restrictions, belongs to every Master Mason.

None of the ancient *Constitutions* contain any law upon this subject, nor can the exact time be now determined when funeral processions and a burial service were first admitted as regulations of the Order.

The first official notice, however, that we have of funeral processions is in November, 1754. A regulation was then adopted which prohibited any Mason from attending a funeral or other procession clothed in any of the jewels or clothing of the Craft, except by dispensation of the Grand Master or his deputy. (*Constitutions*, 1756, p. 303.)

There are no further regulations on this subject in any of the editions of the *Book of Constitutions* previous to the modern code which is now in force in the Grand Lodge of England. But Preston gives us the rules on this subject, which have now been adopted by general consent as the law of the Order, in the following words:

"No Mason can be interred with the formalities of the Order unless it be by his own special request communicated to the Master of the Lodge of which he died a member, foreigners and sojourners excepted; nor unless he has been advanced to the third degree of Masonry, from which restriction there can be no exception. Fellow Crafts or Apprentices are not entitled to the funeral obsequies." (*Illustrations*, 1792, p. 118.)

The only restrictions prescribed by Preston are, it will be perceived, that the deceased must have been a Master Mason, that he had himself made the request, and that he was affiliated, which is implied by the expression that he must have made the request for burial of the Master of the Lodge *of which he was a member.*

The regulation of 1754, which requires a dispensation from the Grand Master for a funeral procession, is not considered of force in the United States of America, where, accordingly, Masons have generally been permitted to bury their dead without the necessity of such dispensation.

Burning Bush. In the third chapter of Exodus it is recorded that, while Moses was keeping the flock of Jethro on Mount Horeb, "the angel of the Lord appeared unto him in a flame of fire out of the midst of a bush," and there communicated to him for the first time his Ineffable Name. This occurrence is commemorated in the "Burning Bush" of the Royal Arch Degree. In all the systems of antiquity, fire is adopted as a symbol of Deity; and the "Burning Bush," or the bush filled with fire which did not consume, whence came forth the Tetragrammaton, the symbol of Divine Light and Truth, is considered, in the higher degrees of Masonry, like the "Orient" in the lower, as the great source of true Masonic light; wherefore Supreme Councils of the Thirty-third Degree date their balustres, or official documents, "near the B∴ B∴," or "Burning Bush," to intimate that they are, in their own rite, the exclusive source of all Masonic instruction.

Burnes, Sir James. A distinguished Mason, and formerly Provincial Grand Master of Western India under the Grand Lodge of Scotland (1836–46). In 1846 he was appointed Grand Master of Scottish Freemasons in India. He returned home in 1849, and died in 1862. after serving for thirty years in the Indian Medical Service. He was the author of an interesting work entitled a *Sketch of the History of the Knights Templars. By James Burnes, LL.D., F.R.S., Knight of the Royal Hanoverian Guelphic Order;* published at London, in 1840, in 74 + 60 pages in small quarto.

Burns, Robert. The celebrated Scottish poet, of whose poetry William Pitt has said, "that he could think of none since Shakespeare's that had so much the appearance of sweetly coming from nature," was born at Kirk Alloway, near the town of Ayr, on the 25th of January, 1759, and died on the 22d of July, 1796. He was initiated into Freemasonry in St. David's Lodge, Tarbolton, on July 4, 1781, and was at one time the Master of a Lodge at Mauchline, where he presided with great credit to himself, as appears from the following remarks of the philosophic Dugald Stewart. "In the course of the same season, I was led by curiosity to attend for an hour or two a Masonic Lodge in Mauchline, where Burns presided. He had occasion to make some short, unpremeditated compliments to different individuals from whom he had no reason to expect a visit, and everything he said was happily conceived and forcibly as well as fluently expressed." The slanderous charge that he acquired the habits of dissipation, to which he was unfortunately addicted, at the festive meetings of the Masonic Lodges, has been triumphantly refuted by a writer in the *London Freemasons' Magazine* (vol. v., p. 291), and by the positive declarations of his brother Gilbert, who asserts that these habits were the result of his introduction, several years after his attendance on the Lodges, to the hospitable literary society of the Scottish metropolis.

Burns consecrated some portion of his wonderful poetic talent to the service of the Masonic Order, to which he appears always to have been greatly attached. Among his Masonic poetic effusions every Mason is familiar with that noble farewell to his Brethren of Tarbolton Lodge, commencing,

> " Adieu! a heart-warm, fond adieu!
> Dear brothers of the mystic tie! "

On the 25th of January, 1820, a monument was erected to his memory, by public subscription, at his birthplace; the corner-stone of which was laid with appropriate Masonic honors by the Deputy Grand Master of the Ancient Mother Lodge Kilwinning, assisted by all the Masonic Lodges in Ayrshire.

Business. Everything that is done in a Masonic Lodge, relating to the initiation of candidates into the several degrees, is called its *work* or *labor;* all other transactions such as are common to other associations come under the head of *business,* and they are governed with some peculiar differences by rules of order, as in other societies. (See *Order, Rules of.*)

Byblos. An ancient city of Phœnicia, celebrated for the mystical worship of Adonis, who was slain by a wild boar. It was situated on a river of the same name, whose waters, becoming red at a certain season of the year by the admixture of the clay which is at its source, were said by the celebrants of the mysteries of Adonis to be tinged with the blood of that god. This city, so distinguished for the celebration of these mysteries, was the Gebal of the Hebrews, the birthplace of the Giblemites, or stone-squarers, who wrought at the building of King Solomon's Temple; and thus those who have advanced the theory that Freemasonry is the successor of the Ancient Mysteries, think that they find in this identity of Byblos and Gebal another point of connection between these Institutions.

By-Laws. Every subordinate Lodge is permitted to make its own by-laws, provided they do not conflict with the regulations of the Grand Lodge, nor with the ancient usages of the Fraternity. But of this, the Grand Lodge is the only judge, and therefore the original by-laws of every Lodge, as well as all subsequent alterations of them, must be submitted to the Grand Lodge for approval and confirmation before they can become valid, having under the English Constitution previously been approved by the Provincial or District Grand Master.

C

C. The third letter of the English alphabet, which was not known in the Hebrew, Phœnician, or early Aryan languages.

Caaba or **Kaaba.** (Arabic, Ka'abah, cubic building.) The square building or temple in Mecca. More especially the small cubical oratory within, held in adoration by the Mohammedans, as containing the black stone said to have been given by an angel to Abraham. (See *Allah.*)

The inner as well as the outer structure receives its name from Ka'ab, cube.

Cabala. Now more correctly and generally written *Kabbala,* which see.

Cabiric Mysteries. The Cabiri were gods whose worship was first established in the island of Samothrace, where the Cabiric Mysteries were practised. The gods called the Cabiri were originally two, and afterward four, in number, and are supposed by Bryant (*Anal. Ant. Myth.,* iii., 342) to have referred to Noah and his three sons, the Cabiric Mysteries being a modification of the arkite worship. In these mysteries there was a ceremony called the "Cabiric Death," in which was represented amid the groans and tears and subsequent rejoicings of the initiates, the death and restoration to life of Cadmillus, the youngest of the Cabiri. The legend recorded that he was slain by his three brethren, who afterward fled with his virile parts in a mystic basket. His body was crowned with flowers, and was buried at the foot of Mount Olympus. Clement of Alexandria speaks of the legend as *the sacred mystery of a brother slain by his brethren,* "frater trucidatus à fratribus."

There is much perplexity connected with the subject of these mysteries, but it is generally supposed that they were instituted in honor of Atys, the son of Cybele or Demeter, of whom Cadmillus was but another name. According to Macrobius, Atys was one of the appellations of the sun, and we know that the mysteries were celebrated at the vernal equinox. They lasted three days, during which they represented in the person of Atys, or Cadmillus, the enigmatical death of the sun in winter, and his regeneration in the spring. In all probability, in the initiation, the candidate passed through a drama, the subject of which was the violent death of Atys. The "Cabiric Death" was, in fact, a type of the Hiramic, and the legend, so far as it can be understood from the faint allusions of ancient authors, was very analogous in spirit and design to that of the Third Degree of Freemasonry.

Many persons annually resorted to Samothrace to be initiated into the celebrated mysteries, among whom are mentioned Cadmus, Orpheus, Hercules, and Ulysses. Jamblichus says, in his *Life of Pythagoras*, that from those of Lemnos that sage derived much of his wisdom. The mysteries of the Cabiri were much respected among the common people, and great care was taken in their concealment. The priests made use of a language peculiar to the Rites.

The mysteries were in existence at Samothrace as late as the eighteenth year of the Christian era, at which time the Emperor Germanicus embarked for that island, to be initiated, but was prevented from accomplishing his purpose by adverse winds.

Cable Tow. The word "tow" signifies, properly, a line wherewith to draw. Richardson (*Dict.*) defines it as " that which tuggeth, or with which we tug or draw." A cable tow is a rope or line for drawing or leading. The word is purely Masonic, and in some of the writers of the early part of the last century we find the expression "cable rope." Prichard so uses it in 1730. The German word for a cable or rope is *kabeltau*, and thence our *cable tow* is probably derived.

In its first inception, the cable tow seems to have been used only as a physical means of controlling the candidate, and such an interpretation is still given in the Entered Apprentice's Degree. But in the Second and Third degrees a more modern symbolism has been introduced, and the cable tow is in these grades supposed to symbolize the covenant by which all Masons are tied, thus reminding us of the passage in Hosea (xi. 4), "I drew them with cords of a man, with bands of love."

Cable Tow's Length. Gädicke says that, "according to the ancient laws of Freemasonry, every brother must attend his Lodge if he is within the length of his cable tow." The old writers define the length of a cable tow, which they sometimes called "a cable's length," to be three miles for an Entered Apprentice. But the expression is really symbolic, and, as it was defined by the Baltimore Convention in 1842, means the scope of a man's reasonable ability.

Cabul. A district containing twenty cities which Solomon gave to Hiram, King of Tyre, for his assistance in the construction of the Temple. Clark (*Comm.*) thinks it likely that they were not given to Hiram so that they should be annexed to his Tyrian dominions, but rather to be held as security for the money which he had advanced. This, however, is merely conjectural. The district containing them is placed by Josephus in the northwest part of Galilee, adjacent to Tyre. Hiram does not appear to have been satisfied with the gift; why, is uncertain. Kitto thinks because they were not situated on the coast. A Masonic legend says because they were ruined and dilapidated villages, and in token of his dis-

satisfaction, Hiram called the district *Cabul*. The meaning of this word is not known. Josephus, probably by conjecture from the context, says it means "unpleasing." Hiller (*Onomast.*) and, after him, Bates (*Dict.*) suppose that כבול is derived from the particle כ, *as*, and כל, *nothing*. The Talmudic derivation from CBL, *tied with fetters*, is Talmudically childish. The dissatisfaction of Hiram and its results constitute the subject of the legend of the degree of Intimate Secretary in the Scottish Rite.

Cadet-Gassicourt, Charles Louis. The author of the celebrated work entitled *Le Tombeau de Jacques Molay*, which was published at Paris, in 1796, and in which he attempted, like Barruel and Robison, to show that Freemasonry was the source and instigator of all the political revolutions which at that time were convulsing Europe. Cadet-Gassicourt was himself the victim of political persecution, and, erroneously attributing his sufferings to the influences of the Masonic Lodges in France, became incensed against the Order, and this gave birth to his libelous book. But subsequent reflection led him to change his views, and he became an ardent admirer of the Institution which he had formerly maligned. He sought initiation into Freemasonry, and in 1805 was elected as Master of the Lodge l'Abeille in Paris. He was born at Paris, January 23, 1769, and died in the same city November 21, 1821.

Cadmillus. The youngest of the Cabiri, and as he is slain in the Cabiric Mysteries, he becomes the analogue of the Builder in the legend of Freemasonry.

Caduceus. The *Caduceus* was the magic wand of the god Hermes. It was an olive staff twined with fillets, which were gradually converted to wings and serpents. Hermes, or Mercury, was the messenger of Jove. Among his numerous attributes, one of the most important was that of conducting disembodied spirits to the other world, and, on necessary occasions, of bringing them back. He was the guide of souls, and the restorer of the dead to life. Thus, Horace, in addressing him, says:

> "Unspotted spirits you consign
> To blissful seats and joys divine,
> And powerful with your golden wand
> The light unburied crowd command."

Virgil also alludes to this attribute of the magic wand when he is describing the flight of Mercury on his way to bear Jove's warning message to Æneas:

> "His wand he takes; with this pale ghost he calls
> From Pluto's realms, or sends to Tartarus'
> shore."

And Statius, imitating this passage, makes the same allusion in his *Thebaid* (i., 314), thus translated by Lewis:

> "He grasps the wand which draws from hollow
> graves,
> Or drives the trembling shades to Stygian
> waves;
> With magic power seals the watchful eye
> In slumbers soft or causes sleep to fly."

The history of this *Caduceus*, or magic wand, will lead us to its symbolism. Mercury, who had invented the lyre, making it out of the shell of the tortoise, exchanged it with Apollo for the latter's magical wand. This wand was simply an olive branch around which were placed two fillets of ribbon. Afterward, when Mercury was in Arcadia, he encountered two serpents engaged in deadly combat. These he separated with his wand; hence the olive wand became the symbol of peace, and the two fillets were replaced by the two serpents, thus giving to the *Caduceus* its well-known form of a staff, around which two serpents are entwined.

Such is the legend; but we may readily see that in the olive, as the symbol of immortality, borne as the attribute of Mercury, the giver of life to the dead, we have a more ancient and profounder symbolism. The serpents, symbols also of immortality, are appropriately united with the olive wand. The legend also accounts for a later and secondary symbolism —that of peace.

The *Caduceus* then—the original meaning of which word is *a herald's staff*—as the attribute of a life-restoring God, is in its primary meaning the symbol of immortality; so in Freemasonry the rod of the Senior Deacon, or the Master of Ceremonies, is but an analogue of the Hermean Caduceus. This officer, as leading the aspirant through the forms of initiation into his new birth or Masonic regeneration, and teaching him in the solemn ceremonies of the Third Degree the lesson of eternal life, may well use the magic wand as a representation of it, which was the attribute of that ancient deity who brought the dead into life.

Cæmentarius. Latin. A builder of walls, a mason, from *cœmentum*, a rough, unhewn stone as it comes from the quarry. In medieval Latin, the word is used to designate an Operative Mason. Du Cange cites *Magister Cœmentariorum* as used to designate him who presided over the building of edifices, that is, the Master of the works. It has been adopted by some modern writers as a translation of the word *Freemason*. Its employment for that purpose is perhaps more correct than that of the more usual word *latomus*, which owes its use to the authority of Thory.

Cagliostro. Of all the Masonic charlatans who flourished in the eighteenth century the Count Cagliostro was most prominent, whether we consider the ingenuity of his schemes of deception, the extensive field of his operations through almost every country of Europe, or the distinguished character and station of many of those whose credulity made them his victims. The history of Masonry in that century would not be complete without a reference to this prince of Masonic impostors. To write the history of Masonry in the eighteenth century and to leave out Cagliostro, would be like enacting the play of Hamlet and leaving out the part of the Prince of Denmark. And yet Carlyle has had occasion to complain of the paucity of materials for such a work. Indeed, of one so notorious as Cagliostro comparatively little is to be found in print. The only works upon which he who would write his life must depend are a *Life* of him published in London, 1787; *Memoirs*, in Paris, 1786; and *Memoirs Authentiques*, Strasburg, 1786; a *Life*, in Germany, published at Berlin, 1787; another in Italian, published at Rome in 1791; and a few fugitive pieces, consisting chiefly of manifestoes of himself and his disciples.

Joseph Balsamo, subsequently known as Count Cagliostro, was the son of Peter Balsamo and Felicia Braconieri, both of mean extraction, and was born on the 8th of June, 1743, in the city of Palermo. Upon the death of his father, he was taken under the protection of his maternal uncles, who caused him to be instructed in the elements of religion and learning, by both of which he profited so little that he eloped several times from the Seminary of St. Roch, near Palermo, where he had been placed for his instruction. At the age of thirteen he was carried to the Convent of the Good Brotherhood at Castiglione. There, having assumed the habit of a novice, he was placed under the tuition of the apothecary, from whom he learned the principles of chemistry and medicine. His brief residence at the convent was marked by violations of many of its rules; and finally, abandoning it altogether, he returned to Palermo. There he continued his vicious courses, and was frequently seized and imprisoned for infractions of the law. At length, having cheated a goldsmith, named Marano, of a large amount of gold, he was compelled to flee from his native country.

He then repaired to Messina, where he became acquainted with one Altotas, who pretended to be a great chemist. Together they proceeded to Alexandria in Egypt, where, by means of certain chemical, or perhaps rather by financial, operations, they succeeded in collecting a considerable amount of money. In 1776 Cagliostro appeared in London. During this visit, Cagliostro became connected with the Order of Freemasonry. In the month of April he received the degrees in Esperance Lodge, No. 289, which then met at the King's Head Tavern. Cagliostro did not join the Order with disinterested motives, or at least he determined in a very short period after his initiation to use the Institution as an instrument for the advancement of his personal interests. Here he is said to have invented, in 1777, that grand scheme of imposture under the name of "Egyptian Masonry," by the propagation of which he subsequently became so famous as the great Masonic charlatan of his age.

London did not fail to furnish him with a fertile field for his impositions, and the English Masons seemed noway reluctant to become his dupes; but, being ambitious for the extension of his Rite, and anxious for the greater income which it promised, he again passed over to the Continent, where he justly anticipated abundant success in its propagation. This Egyptian Masonry constituted the great pursuit of the rest of his life, and was the instrument which he used for many years to make dupes of thousands of credulous persons.

During Cagliostro's residence in England, on his last visit, he was attacked by the editor Morand, in the *Courier de l'Europe*, in a series of abusive articles, to which Cagliostro replied in a letter to the English people. But, although he had a few Egyptian Lodges in London under his government, he appears, perhaps from Morand's revelations of his character and life, to have lost his popularity, and he left England permanently in May, 1787.

He went to Savoy, Sardinia, and other places in the south of Europe, and at last, in May, 1789, by an act of rash temerity, proceeded to Rome, where he organized an Egyptian Lodge under the very shadow of the Vatican. But this was more than the Church, which had been excommunicating Freemasons for fifty years, was willing to endure. On the 27th of December of that year, on the festival of St. John the Evangelist, to whom he had dedicated his Lodges, the Holy Inquisition arrested him, and locked him up in the castle of San Angelo. There, after such a trial as the Inquisition is wont to give to the accused—in which his wife is said to have been the principal witness against him—he was convicted of having formed "societies and conventicles of Freemasonry." His manuscript entitled *Maçonnerie Egyptienne* was ordered to be burned by the public executioner, and he himself was condemned to death; a sentence which the Pope subsequently commuted for that of perpetual imprisonment. Cagliostro appealed to the French Constituent Assembly, but of course in vain. Thenceforth no more is seen of him. For four years this adventurer, who had filled during his life so large a space in the world's history—the associate of princes, prelates, and philosophers; the inventor of a spurious Rite, which had, however, its thousands of disciples—languished within the gloomy walls of the prison of St. Leo, in the Duchy of Urbino, and at length, in the year 1795, in a fit of apoplexy, bade the world adieu.

Cahier. French. A number of sheets of parchment or paper fastened together at one end. The word is used by French Masons to designate a small book printed, or in manuscript, containing the ritual of a degree. The word has been borrowed from French history, where it denotes the reports and proceedings of certain assemblies, such as the clergy, the States-General, etc.

Cairns. Celtic, carns. Heaps of stones of a conical form erected by the Druids. Some suppose them to have been sepulchral monuments, others altars. They were undoubtedly of a religious character, since sacrificial fires were lighted upon them, and processions were made around them. These processions were analogous to the circumambulations in Masonry, and were conducted, like them, with reference to the apparent course of the sun. Thus, Toland, in his *Letters on the Celtic Re-*

ligion (Let. II., xvii.), says of these mystical processions, that the people of the Scottish islands "never come to the ancient sacrificing and fire-hallowing Carns but they walk three times round them from east to west, according to the course of the sun. This sanctified tour, or round by the south, is called *Deaseal*, as the unhallowed contrary one by the north, *Tuapholl*"; and he says that *Deaseal* is derived from "*Deas*, the *right* (understanding hand), and *soil*, one of the ancient names of the sun, the right hand in this round being ever next the heap." In all this the Mason will be reminded of the Masonic ceremony of circumambulation around the altar and the rules which govern it.

Calatrava, Military Order of. Instituted 1158, during the reign of Sancho III., King of Castile, who conquered and gave the Castle of Calatrava, an important fortress of the Moors of Andalusia, to the Knights Templars, who subsequently relinquished their possession of it to the king. The king, being disappointed in the ability of the Templars to retain it, then offered the defense of the place to Don Raymond of Navarre, Abbot of St. Mary of Hitero, a Cistercian convent, who accepted it. Don Raymond being successful, the king gave the place to him and his companions, and instituted the Order of Calatrava. A Grand Master was appointed and approved of by the Pope, Alexander III., 1164, which was confirmed by Innocent III. in 1198. The knights had been granted the power of electing their own Grand Master; but on the death of Don Garcias Lopez de Pardella, 1489, Ferdinand and Isabella annexed the Grand Mastership to the Crown of Castile, which was sanctioned by Pope Innocent VIII.

Calcott, Wellins. A distinguished Masonic writer of the eighteenth century, and the author of a work published in 1769, under the title of *A Candid Disquisition of the Principles and Practices of the Most Ancient and Honourable Society of Free and Accepted Masons; together with some Strictures on the Origin, Nature, and Design of that Institution,* in which he has traced Masonry from its origin, explained its symbols and hieroglyphics, its social virtues and advantages, suggested the propriety of building halls for the peculiar and exclusive practise of Masonry, and reprehended its slanderers with great but judicious severity. This was the first extended effort to illustrate philosophically the science of Masonry, and was followed, a few years after, by Hutchinson's admirable work; so that Oliver justly says that "Calcott opened the mine of Masonry, and Hutchinson worked it."

Calendar. Freemasons, in affixing dates to their official documents, never make use of the Common Epoch or Vulgar Era, but have one peculiar to themselves, which, however, varies in the different rites. Era and epoch are, in this sense, synonymous.

Masons of the York, American, and French Rites, that is to say, the Masons of England,

Scotland, Ireland, France, Germany, and America date from the creation of the world, calling it "Anno Lucis," which they abbreviate A∴ L∴, signifying *in the Year of Light.* Thus with them the year 1872 is A∴ L∴ 5872. This they do, not because they believe Freemasonry to be coeval with the creation, but with a symbolic reference to the light of Masonry.

In the Scottish Rite, the epoch also begins from the date of the creation, but Masons of that Rite, using the Jewish chronology, would call the year 1872 A∴ M∴ or Anno Mundi (in the Year of the World) 5632. They sometimes use the initials A∴ H∴, signifying Anno Hebraico, or, *in the Hebrew year.* They have also adopted the Hebrew months, and the year, therefore, begins with them in the middle of September. (See *Months, Hebrew.*)

Masons of the York and American Rites begin the year on the 1st of January, but in the French Rite it commences on the 1st of March, and instead of the months receiving their usual names, they are designated numerically, as first, second, third, etc. Thus, the 1st of January, 1872, would be styled, in a French Masonic document, the "1st day of the 11th Masonic month, Anno Lucis, 5872." The French sometimes, instead of the initials A∴ L∴, use *L'an de la V∴ L∴,* or *Vraie Lumiere,* that is, Year of True Light.

Royal Arch Masons commence their epoch with the year in which Zerubbabel began to build the second Temple, which was 530 years before Christ. Their style for the year 1872 is, therefore, A∴ Inv∴, that is, *Anno Inventionis,* or, in the Year of the Discovery, 2402.

Royal and Select Masters very often make use of the common Masonic date, *Anno Lucis,* but properly they should date from the year in which Solomon's Temple was completed; and their style would then be, *Anno Depositionis,* or, in the Year of the Deposite, and they would date the year 1872 as 2872.

Knights Templars use the epoch of the organization of their Order in 1118. Their style for the year 1872 is A∴ O∴, *Anno Ordinis,* or, in the Year of the Order, 754.

We subjoin, for the convenience of reference, the rules for discovering these different dates.

1. *To find the Ancient Craft date.* Add 4000 to the Vulgar Era. Thus 1872 and 4000 are 5872.

2. *To find the date of the Scottish Rite.* Add 3760 to the Vulgar Era. Thus 1872 and 3760 are 5632. After September add one year more.

3. *To find the date of Royal Arch Masonry.* Add 530 to the Vulgar Era. Thus 530 and 1872 are 2402.

4. *To find the Royal and Select Masters' date.* Add 1000 to the Vulgar Era. Thus 1000 and 1872 are 2872.

5. *To find the Knights Templars' date.* Subtract 1118 from the Vulgar Era. Thus 1118 from 1872 is 754.

The following will show, in one view, the date of the year 1872 in all the branches of the Order:

Year of the Lord, A.D. 1872—Vulgar Era.

Year of Light, A∴ L∴ 5872—Ancient Craft Masonry.

Year of the World, A∴ M∴ 5632—Scottish Rite.

Year of the Discovery, A∴ I∴ 2402—Royal Arch Masonry.

Year of the Deposite, A∴ Dep∴ 2872—Royal and Select Masters.

Year of the Order, A∴ O∴ 754—Knights Templars.

California. The Grand Lodge of California was organized on the 19th of April, 1850, in the city of Sacramento, by the delegates of three legally constituted Lodges working, at the time, under charters from the Grand Lodges of the District of Columbia, Connecticut, and Missouri. Its present seat is at San Francisco, and there are 308 Lodges under its jurisdiction. The Grand Chapter and Grand Commandery were organized in 1854.

Calling Off. A technical term in Masonry, which signifies the temporary suspension of labor in a Lodge without passing through the formal ceremony of closing. The full form of the expression is to *call from labor to refreshment,* and it took its rise from the former custom of dividing the time spent in the Lodge between the work of Masonry and the moderate enjoyment of the banquet. The banquet formed in the last century an indispensable part of the arrangements of a Lodge meeting. "At a certain hour of the evening," says Brother Oliver, "with certain ceremonies, the Lodge was called from labor to refreshment, when the brethren enjoyed themselves with decent merriment." That custom no longer exists; and although in England almost always, and in this country occasionally, the labors of the Lodge are concluded with a banquet; yet the Lodge is formally closed before the Brethren proceed to the table of refreshment. Calling off in American Lodges is now only used, in a certain ceremony of the Third Degree, when it is desired to have another meeting at a short interval, and the Master desires to avoid the tediousness of closing and opening the Lodge. Thus, if the business of the Lodge at its regular meeting has so accumulated that it cannot be transacted in one evening, it has become the custom to call off until a subsequent evening, when the Lodge, instead of being opened with the usual ceremony, is simply "called on," and the latter meeting is considered as only a continuation of the former. This custom is very generally adopted in Grand Lodges at their Annual Communications, which are opened at the beginning of the session, called off from day to day, and finally closed at its end. I do not know that any objection has ever been advanced against this usage in Grand Lodges, because it seems necessary as a substitute for the adjournment, which is resorted to in other legislative bodies, but which is not admitted in Masonry. But much discussion has taken place in reference to the practise of calling off in Lodges, some authorities sustaining and others condemning it. Thus, twenty years ago, the Committee of Correspondence of the Grand Lodge of Mississippi proposed this question: "In case of excess of business, cannot the unfinished be laid over until the next or another day, and must the Lodge be closed in form, and opened the next, or the day designated for the transaction of that business?" To this question some authorities, and among others Brother C. W. Moore (*Mag.*, vol. xii., No. 10), reply in the negative, while other equally good jurists differ from them in opinion.

The difficulty seems to be in this, that if the regular meeting of the Lodge is closed in form, the subsequent meeting becomes a special one, and many things which could be done at a regular communication cease to be admissible. The recommendation, therefore, of Brother Moore, that the Lodge should be closed, and, if the business be unfinished, that the Master shall call a special meeting to complete it, does not meet the difficulty, because it is a well-settled principle of Masonic law that a special meeting cannot interfere with the business of a preceding regular one.

As, then, the mode of briefly closing by adjournment is contrary to Masonic law and usage, and cannot, therefore, be resorted to, as there is no other way except by calling off to continue the character of a regular meeting, and as, during the period that the Lodge is called off, it is under the government of the Junior Warden, and Masonic discipline is thus continued, I am clearly of opinion that calling off from day to day for the purpose of continuing work or business is, as a matter of convenience, admissible. The practise may indeed be abused. But there is a well-known legal maxim which says, *Ex abusu non arguitur in usum.* "No argument can be drawn from the abuse of a thing against its use." Thus, a Lodge cannot be called off except for continuance of work and business, nor to an indefinite day, for there must be a good reason for the exercise of the practise, and the Brethren present must be notified before dispersing of the time of reassembling; nor can a Lodge at one regular meeting be called off until the next, for no regular meeting of a Lodge is permitted to run into another, but each must be closed before its successor can be opened.

Calling On. When a Lodge that is called off at a subsequent time resumes work or business, it is said to be "called on." The full expression is "called on from refreshment to labor."

Calumny. See *Back*.

Calvary. Mount Calvary is a small hill or eminence, situated due west from Mount Moriah, on which the Temple of Solomon was built. It was originally a hillock of notable eminence, but has, in more modern times, been greatly reduced by the excavations made in it for the construction of the Church of the Holy Sepulcher. There are several coincidences which identify Mount Calvary with the small hill where the "newly-made grave," referred to in the Third Degree, was discovered

by the weary brother. Thus, Mount Calvary was a small hill; it was situated in a *westward direction* from the Temple, and *near Mount Moriah;* and it was on the direct road from Jerusalem to Joppa, and is the very spot where a *weary brother,* traveling on that road, would find it convenient to *sit down to rest and refresh himself;* it was *outside* the gate of the Temple; it has at least *one cleft in the rock,* or cave, which was the place which subsequently became the sepulcher of our Lord. Hence Mount Calvary has always retained an important place in the legendary history of Freemasonry, and there are many traditions connected with it that are highly interesting in their import.

One of these traditions is, that it was the burial-place of Adam, in order, says the old legend, that where he lay, who effected the ruin of mankind, there also might the Savior of the world suffer, die, and be buried. Sir R. Torkington, who published a pilgrimage to Jerusalem in 1517, says that "under the Mount of Calvary is another chapel of our Blessed Lady and St. John the Evangelist, that was called Golgotha; and there, right under the mortise of the cross, was found the head of our forefather, Adam." Golgotha, it will be remembered, means, in Hebrew, "the place of a skull"; and there may be some connection between this tradition and the name of Golgotha, by which, the Evangelists inform us, in the time of Christ Mount Calvary was known. Calvary, or Calvaria, has the same signification in Latin.

Another tradition states that it was in the bowels of Mount Calvary that Enoch erected his nine-arched vault, and deposited on the foundation-stone of Masonry that Ineffable Name, whose investigation, as a symbol of Divine truth, is the great object of Speculative Masonry.

A third tradition details the subsequent discovery of Enoch's deposit, by King Solomon, whilst making excavations in Mount Calvary during the building of the Temple.

On this hallowed spot was Christ the Redeemer slain and buried. It was there that, rising on the third day from his sepulcher, he gave, by that act, the demonstrative evidence of the resurrection of the body and the immortality of the soul.

And it is this spot that has been selected, in the legendary history of Freemasonry, to teach the same sublime truth, the development of which by a symbol evidently forms the design of the Third or Master's Degree.

Camp. A portion of the paraphernalia decorated with tents, flags, and pennons of a Consistory of Sublime Princes of the Royal Secret, or Thirty-second Degree of the Ancient and Accepted Scottish Rite. It constitutes the tracing board, and is worn on the apron of the degree. It is highly symbolic, and represents an imaginary Masonic camp. Its symbolism is altogether esoteric.

Campe, Joachim Heinrich. A Doctor of Theology, and Director of Schools in Dessau and Hamburg, who was born in 1746 and died October 22, 1818. He was the author of many works on philosophy and education, and was a learned and zealous Mason, as is shown in his correspondence with Lessing.

Canada. Upon the advent of Confederation, July 1, 1867, local control in each Province for the government of the Masonic Fraternity of the Dominion took a strong hold as a predominant idea, and prevailed. Each Province has now a Grand Lodge, and in order of their organization are as follows: Canada, having jurisdiction only in Ontario, 1855; Nova Scotia, 1866; New Brunswick, 1867; Quebec, 1869; British Columbia, 1871; Manitoba, 1875; Prince Edward Island, 1875; Alberta, 1905; Saskatchewan, 1906. The first marks of the Ancient Craftsman have been found in Nova Scotia. A mineralogical survey in 1827 found on the shore of Goat Island in the Annapolis Basin, partly covered with sand, a slab of rock $2\frac{1}{2} \times 2$ feet, bearing on it those well-known Masonic emblems, "the Square and Compasses," and the date 1606. Who were the Craftsmen and how the stone came there, must be left to conjecture. [Will H. Whyte, P. G. M. ∴ K. T. of Canada.]

Cancellarius. An office of high rank and responsibility among the Knights Templar of the Middle Ages, performing the duties of, or similar to, the Chancellor.

Candidate. An applicant for admission into Masonry is called a candidate. The Latin *candidatus* means clothed in white, *candidis vestibus indutus*. In ancient Rome, he who sought office from the people wore a white shining robe of a peculiar construction, flowing open in front, so as to exhibit the wounds he had received in his breast. From the color of his robe or *toga candida*, he was called *candidatus*, whence the word *candidate*. The derivation will serve to remind the Mason of the purity of conduct and character which should distinguish all those who are candidates for admission into the Order. The qualifications of a candidate in Masonry are somewhat peculiar. He must be free-born (under the English Constitution it is enough that he is a freeman), under no bondage, of at least twenty-one years of age, in the possession of sound senses, free from any physical defect or dismemberment, and of irreproachable manners, or, as it is technically termed, "under the tongue of good report." No Atheist, eunuch, or woman can be admitted. The requisites as to age, sex, and soundness of body have reference to the operative character of the Institution. We can only expect able workmen in able-bodied men. The mental and religious qualifications refer to the duties and obligations which a Freemason contracts. An idiot could not understand them, and an Atheist would not respect them. Even those who possess all these necessary qualifications can be admitted only under certain regulations which differ under different Masonic *Constitutions*.

Candidates, Advancement of. See *Advancement, Hurried.*

Candlestick, Golden. The golden candlestick of seven branches, which is a part of the furniture of a Royal Arch Chapter, is derived from "the holy candlestick" which Moses was instructed to construct of beaten gold for the use of the tabernacle. Smith (*Dict. of the Bible*) thus abbreviates Lightfoot's explanation of the description given in Exodus: "The foot of it was gold, from which went up a shaft straight, which was the middle light. Near the foot was a golden dish wrought almondwise; and a little above that a golden knop, and above that a golden flower. Then two branches one on each side bowed,—and coming up as high as the middle shaft. On each of them were three golden cups placed almondwise, in sharp, scallop-shell fashion; above which was a golden knop, a golden flower, and the socket. Above the branches on the middle shaft was a golden boss, above which rose two shafts more; above the coming out of these was another boss and two more shafts, and then on the shaft upwards were three golden scallop-cups, a knop, and a flower; so that the heads of the branches stood an equal height." In the tabernacle, the candlestick was placed opposite the table of shewbread, which it was intended to illumine, in an oblique position, so that the lamps looked to the east and south. What became of the candlestick between the time of Moses and that of Solomon is unknown; but it does not appear to have been present in the first Temple, which was lighted by ten golden candlesticks similarly embossed, which were connected by golden chains and formed a sort of railing before the veil.

These ten candlesticks became the spoil of the Chaldean conqueror at the time of the destruction of the Temple, and could not have been among the articles afterward restored by Cyrus; for in the second Temple, built by Zerubbabel, we find only a single candlestick of seven branches, like that of the tabernacle. Its form has been perpetuated on the Arch of Titus, on which it was sculptured with other articles taken by that monarch, and carried to Rome as *spolia opima*, after he had destroyed the Herodian Temple. This is the candlestick which is represented as a decoration in a Royal Arch Chapter.

In Jewish symbolism, the seven branches were supposed by some to refer to the seven planets, and by others to the seventh day or Sabbath. The primitive Christians made it allusive to Christ as the "light of the world," and in this sense it is a favorite symbol in early Christian art. In Masonry it seems to have no symbolic meaning, unless it be the general one of light; but is used in a Royal Arch Chapter simply to indicate that the room is a representation of the tabernacle erected near the ruins of the first Temple, for the purpose of temporary worship during the building of the second, and in which tabernacle this candlestick is supposed to have been present.

Canopy. Oliver says that in the Masonic processions of the Continent the Grand Master walks under a gorgeous canopy of blue, purple, and crimson silk, with gold fringes and tassels, borne upon staves, painted purple and ornamented with gold, by eight of the oldest Master Masons present; and the Masters of private Lodges walk under canopies of light blue silk with silver tassels and fringes, borne by four members of their own respective companies. The canopies are in the form of an oblong square, and are in length six feet, in breadth and height three feet, having a semicircular covering. The framework should be of cedar, and the silken covering ought to hang down two feet on each side. This is, properly speaking, a *Baldachin.* (See Baldachin.)

Canopy, Celestial. Ritualists seem divided in the use of the terms "Clouded Canopy " and "Celestial Canopy " in the First Degree. (For the former, see *Canopy, Clouded,* and *Covering of the Lodge.*) It would seem that the unclouded grandeur of the heavens should not be without advocates.

Sir John Lubbock gives the following description of the heavens filled with stars in connection with the latest discoveries: "Like the sand of the sea, the stars of heaven are used as a symbol of numbers. We now know that our earth is but a fraction of one part of, at least 75,000,000 worlds. But this is not all. In addition to the luminous heavenly bodies, we cannot doubt there are countless others invisible to us from their great distance, smaller size, or feebler light; indeed, we know that there are many dark bodies which now emit no light, or comparatively little. Thus the floor of heaven is not only 'thick inlaid with patines of bright gold,' but studded also with extinct stars, once probably as brilliant as our own sun."

Canopy, Clouded. The *clouded canopy,* or starry-decked heaven, is a symbol of the First Degree, and is of such important significance that Lenning calls it a "fundamental symbol of Freemasonry." In the lectures of the York Rite, the *clouded canopy* is described as the covering of the Lodge, teaching us, as Krause says, "that the primitive Lodge is confined within no shut up building, but that it is universal, and reaches to heaven, and especially teaching that in every clime under heaven Freemasonry has its seat." And Gädicke says, "Every Freemason knows that by the clouded canopy we mean the heavens, and that it teaches how widely extended is our sphere of usefulness. There is no portion of the inhabited world in which our labor cannot be carried forward, as there is no portion of the globe without its clouded canopy." Hence, then, the German interpretation of the symbol is that it denotes the universality of Freemasonry, an interpretation that does not precisely accord with the English and American systems, in which the doctrine of universality is symbolized by the form and extent of the Lodge. The clouded canopy as the covering of the Lodge seems rather to teach the doctrine of aspiration for a higher sphere; it is thus defined in this work under the head of *Covering of the Lodge,* which see.

Canzler, Carl Christian. A librarian of Dresden, born September 30, 1733, died October 16, 1786. He was an earnest, learned Freemason, who published in a literary journal, conducted by himself and A. G. Meissner at Leipsic, in 1783–85, under the title of *Für ältere Litteratur und neuere Lectüre,* many interesting articles on the subject of Freemasonry.

Cape-Stone, or, as it would more correctly be called, the cope-stone (but the former word has been consecrated to us by universal Masonic usage), is the topmost stone of a building. To bring it forth, therefore, and to place it in its destined position, is significative that the building is completed, which event is celebrated, even by the Operative Masons of the present day, with great signs of rejoicing. Flags are hoisted on the top of every edifice by the builders engaged in its construction, as soon as they have reached the topmost post, and thus finished their labors. This is the "celebration of the cape-stone"—the celebration of the completion of the building—when tools are laid aside, and rest and refreshment succeed, for a time, labor. This is the event in the history of the Temple which is commemorated in the degree of Most Excellent Master, the sixth in the American Rite. *The day set apart for the celebration of the cape-stone of the Temple* is the day devoted to rejoicing and thanksgiving for the completion of that glorious structure. Hence there seems to be an impropriety in the ordinary use of the Mark Master's keystone in the ritual of the Most Excellent Master. That keystone was deposited in silence and secrecy; while the cape-stone, as the legend and ceremonies tell us, was placed in its position in the presence of all the Craft.

Capitular Degrees. The degrees conferred under the charter of an American Royal Arch Chapter, which are Mark Master, Past Master, Most Excellent Master, and Royal Arch Mason. The capitular degrees are almost altogether founded on and composed of a series of events in Masonic history. Each of them has attached to it some tradition or legend which it is the design of the degree to illustrate, and the memory of which is preserved in its ceremonies and instructions. Most of these legends are of symbolic signification. But this is their interior sense. In their outward and ostensible meaning, they appear before us simply as legends. To retain these legends in the memory of Masons appears to have been the primary design in the establishment of the higher degrees; and as the information intended to be communicated in these degrees is of an historical character, there can of course be but little room for symbols or for symbolic instruction; the profuse use of which would rather tend to an injury than to a benefit, by complicating the purposes of the ritual and confusing the mind of the aspirant. These remarks refer exclusively to the Mark and Most Excellent Master's Degree of the American Rite, but are not so applicable to the Royal Arch, which is eminently symbolic. The legends of the second Temple, and the lost word, the peculiar legends of that degree, are among the most prominent symbols of the Masonic system.

Capitular Masonry. The Masonry conferred in a Royal Arch Chapter of the York and American Rites. There are Chapters in the Ancient and Accepted, Scottish, and in the French and other Rites; but the Masonry therein conferred is not called capitular.

Capitular Statistics. See *Statistics of Capitular Masonry.*

Capripede Ratier et Lucifuge. A burlesque dining degree, mentioned in the collection of Fustier. (Thory, *Acta Latomorum,* i., 298.)

Captain-General. The third officer in a Commandery of Knights Templar. He presides over the Commandery in the absence of his superiors, and is one of its representatives in the Grand Commandery. His duties are to see that the council chamber and asylum are duly prepared for the business of the meetings, and to communicate all orders issued by the Grand Council. His station is on the left of the Grand Commander, and his jewel is a level surmounted by a cock. (See *Cock.*)

Captain of the Guard. The sixth officer in a Council of Royal and Select Masters. In the latter degree he is said to represent Azariah, the son of Nathan, who had command of the officers of the king's household. (1 Kings iv. 5.) His duties correspond in some measure with those of a Senior Deacon in the primary degrees. His post is, therefore, on the right of the throne, and his jewel is a trowel and battle-ax within a triangle.

Captain of the Host. The fourth officer in a Royal Arch Chapter. He represents the general or leader of the Jewish troops who returned from Babylon, and who was called "*Sar el hatzaba,*" and was equivalent to a modern general. The word Host in the title means *army.* He sits on the right of the Council in front, and wears a white robe and cap or helmet, with a red sash, and is armed with a sword. His jewel is a triangular plate, on which an armed soldier is engraved.

Captivity. The Jews reckoned their national captivities as four:—the Babylonian, Medean, Grecian, and Roman. The present article will refer only to the first, when there was a forcible deportation of the inhabitants of Jerusalem by Nebuzaradan, the general of King Nebuchadnezzar, and their detention at Babylon until the reign of Cyrus, which alone is connected with the history of Masonry, and is commemorated in the Royal Arch Degree.

Between that portion of the ritual of the Royal Arch which refers to the destruction of the first Temple, and that subsequent part which symbolizes the building of the second, there is an interregnum (if we may be allowed the term) in the ceremonial of the degree, which must be considered as a long interval in history, the filling up of which, like the interval between the acts of a play, must be left to the imagination of the spectator. This interval represents the time passed in the captivity of the Jews at Babylon. That captivity lasted for seventy years—from the reign of Nebuchadnezzar until that of Cyrus —although but fifty-two of these years are commemorated in the Royal Arch Degree. This event took place in the year 588 B.C. It was not, however, the beginning of the "seventy years' captivity," which had been foretold by the prophet Jeremiah, which commenced eighteen years before. The captives were conducted to Babylon. What was the exact number removed we have no means of ascertaining. We are led to believe, from certain passages of Scripture, that the deportation was not complete. Calmet says that Nebuchadnezzar carried away only the principal inhabitants, the warriors and artisans of every kind, and that he left the husbandmen, the laborers, and, in general, the poorer classes, that constituted the great body of the people. Among the prisoners of distinction, Josephus mentions the high priest, Seraiah, and Zephaniah, the priest that was next to him, with the three rulers that guarded the Temple, the eunuch who was over the armed men, seven friends of Zedekiah, his scribe, and sixty other rulers. Zedekiah, the king, had attempted to escape previous to the termination of the siege, but being pursued, was captured and carried to Riblah, the headquarters of Nebuchadnezzar, where, having first been compelled to behold the slaughter of his children, his eyes were then put out, and he was conducted in chains to Babylon.

A Masonic tradition informs us that the captive Jews were bound by their conquerors with triangular chains, and that this was done by the Chaldeans as an additional insult, because the Jewish Masons were known to esteem the triangle as an emblem of the sacred name of God, and must have considered its appropriation to the form of their fetters as a desecration of the Tetragrammaton.

Notwithstanding the ignominious mode of their conveyance from Jerusalem and the vindictiveness displayed by their conqueror in the destruction of their city and Temple, they do not appear, on their arrival at Babylon, to have been subjected to any of the extreme rigors of slavery. They were distributed into various parts of the empire, some remaining in the city, while others were sent into the provinces. The latter probably devoted themselves to agricultural pursuits, while the former were engaged in commerce or in the labors of architecture. Smith says that the captives were treated not as slaves but as colonists. They were permitted to retain their personal property, and even to purchase lands and erect houses. Their civil and religious government was not utterly destroyed, for they kept up a regular succession of kings and high priests, one of each of whom returned with them, as will be seen hereafter, on their restoration. Some of the principal captives were advanced to offices of dignity and power in the royal palace, and were permitted to share in the councils of state. Their prophets, Daniel and Ezekiel, with their associates, preserved among their countrymen the pure doctrines of their religion. Although they had neither place nor time of national gathering, nor temple, and therefore offered no sacrifices, yet they observed the Mosaic laws with respect to the rite of circumcision. They preserved their tables of genealogy and the true succession to the throne of David. The rightful heir being called the Head of the Captivity,* Jehoiachin, who was the first king of Judea carried captive to Babylon, was succeeded by his son Shealtiel, and he by his son Zerubbabel, who was the Head of the Captivity, or nominal prince of Judea at the close of the captivity. The due succession of the high-priesthood was also preserved, for Jehosadek, who was the high priest carried by Nebuchadnezzar to Babylon, where he died during the captivity, was succeeded by his eldest son, Joshua. The Jewish captivity terminated in the first year of the reign of Cyrus, B.C. 536. Cyrus, from his conversations with Daniel and the other Jewish captives of learning and piety, as well as from his perusal of their sacred books, more especially the prophecies of Isaiah, had become imbued with a knowledge of true religion, and hence had even publicly announced to his subjects his belief in the God "which the nation of the Israelites worshipped." He was consequently impressed with an earnest desire to fulfil the prophetic declarations of which he was the subject, and to rebuild the Temple of Jerusalem. Cyrus therefore issued a decree by which the Jews were permitted to return to their country. According to Milman, 42,360 besides servants availed themselves of this permission, and returned to Jerusalem under Zerubbabel their prince and Joshua their high priest, and thus ended the first or Babylonian captivity, the only one which has any connection with the legends of Freemasonry as commemorated in the Royal Arch Degree.

Capuchin. One of the monks of the Order of St. Francis. They went barefooted, were long-bearded, and wore a gown or cloak of dark color made like a woman's garment with a hood.

Carausius. A Roman emperor, who assumed the purple A.D. 287. Of him Preston gives the following account, which may or may not be deemed apocryphal, according to the taste and inclination of the reader: "By assuming the character of a Mason, he acquired the love and esteem of the most enlightened part of his subjects. He possessed real merit, encouraged learning and learned men, and improved the country in the civil arts. In order to establish an empire in Britain, he brought into his dominions the best workmen and artificers from all parts; all of whom, under his auspices, enjoyed peace and tranquillity. Among the first class of his favorites he enrolled the Masons: for their

tenets he professed the highest veneration, and appointed Albanus, his steward, the principal superintendent of their assemblies. Under his patronage, Lodges and conventions of the Fraternity were formed, and the rites of Masonry regularly practised. To enable the Masons to hold a general council, to establish their own government and correct errors among themselves, he granted to them a charter, and commanded Albanus to preside over them in person as Grand Master." (*Illustrations*, ed. 1812, p. 142.) Anderson also gives the legend of Carausius in the second edition of his *Constitutions*, and adds that "this is asserted by all the old copies of the Constitutions, and the old English Masons firmly believed it." (*Constitutions*, 1738, p. 57.) But the fact is that Anderson himself does not mention the tradition in his first edition, published in 1723, nor is any reference to Carausius to be found in any of the old manuscripts now extant. The legend is, it is true, inserted in Krause's Manuscript; but this document is of very little authority, having been, most probably, a production of the early part of the eighteenth century, and of a contemporary of Anderson, written perhaps between 1723 and 1738, which would account for the omission of it in the first edition of the *Book of Constitutions*, and its insertion in the second. The reader may hence determine for himself what authenticity is to be given to the Carausian legend.

Carbuncle. In Hebrew, ברקת, *baraketh*, the third stone in the first row of the high priest's breastplate, according to the authorized version, but the first stone in the second row, according to the Septuagint. Braun, a writer on the sacerdotal vestments of the Hebrews (Amsterdam, 1680), supposes that the *baraketh* was a *smaragdus* or emerald, which view is sustained by Kalisch, and is in accordance with the Septuagint translation. The Talmudists derive *baraketh* from a word signifying "to shine with the brightness of fire," which would seem to indicate some stone of a coruscant color, and would apply to the bright green of the emerald as well as to the bright red of the carbuncle. The stone, whatever it was, was referred to the tribe of Judah. The carbuncle in Christian iconography signifies blood and suffering, and is symbolical of the Lord's passion. Five carbuncles placed on a cross symbolize the five wounds of Christ.

Cardinal Points. The north, west, east, and south are so called from the Latin *cardo*, a hinge, because they are the principal points of the compass on which all the others hinge or hang. Each of them has a symbolic signification in Masonry, which will be found under their respective heads. Dr. Brinton, in an interesting *Treatise on the Symbolism and Mythology of the Red Race of America*, has a chapter on the sacred number four; the only one, he says, that has any prominence in the religions of the red race, and which he traces to the four cardinal points. The reason, he declares, is to be "found in the *adoration of*

---

* So says the Talmud, but Smith (*Dict. of the Bible*) affirms that the assertion is unsupported by proof. The Masonic legends conform to the Talmudic statement.

the cardinal points "; and he attributes to this cause the prevalence of the cross as a symbol among the aborigines of America, the existence of which so surprised the Catholic missionaries that they "were in doubt whether to ascribe the fact to the pious labors of St. Thomas or the sacrilegious subtlety of Satan." The arms of the cross referred to the cardinal points, and represented the four winds, the bringers of rain. The theory is an interesting one, and the author supports it with many ingenious illustrations. In the symbolism of Freemasonry each of the cardinal points has a mystical meaning. The East represents Wisdom; the West, Strength; the South, Beauty; and the North, Darkness.

Cardinal Virtues. The preeminent or principal virtues on which all the others hinge or depend. They are temperance, fortitude, prudence, and justice. They are referred to in the ritual of the First Degree, and will be found in this work under their respective heads. Oliver says (*Revelations of a Square*, ch. i.) that in the eighteenth century the Masons delineated the symbols of the four cardinal virtues by an acute angle variously disposed. Thus, suppose you face the east, the angle symbolizing temperance will point to the south, >. It was called a Guttural. Fortitude was denoted by a saltire, or St. Andrew's Cross, ✕. This was the Pectoral. The symbol of prudence was an acute angle pointing toward the southeast, >, and was denominated a Manual; and justice had its angle toward the north, <, and was called a Pedestal or Pedal. The possession of cardinal virtues is no special distinction of Freemasons, for other societies have had them. They are in evidence in the Christian church. The fifteen cardinal virtues, in mosaic, in the dome of Ascension of St. Mark's at Venice is a famous example. [E. E. C.]

Carlile, Richard. A printer and bookseller of London, who in 1819 was fined and imprisoned for the publication of Paine's *Age of Reason*, and Palmer's *Light of Nature*. He also wrote and published several pretended expositions of Masonry, which, after his death, were collected, in 1845, in one volume, under the title of a *Manual of Freemasonry, in three parts*. Carlile was a professed Atheist, and, although a fanatical reformer of what he supposed to be the errors of the age, was a man of some ability. His Masonic works are interspersed with considerable learning, and are not as abusive of the Order as expositions generally are. He was born in 1790, and died in 1843, in London. For ten years before his death his religious opinions had been greatly modified.

Carmelites. Monks of an order established on Mount Carmel, in Syria, during the twelfth century. They wore a brown scapular passing over the shoulder and diagonally across the back and body, thus crossing the gown from right to left.

Carpenters, Order of. An organized body in Holland and Belgium, with central point of assembly at Antwerp. Their gatherings were at night in some neighboring forest.

Carpet. The chart or tracing board on which the emblems of a degree are depicted for the instruction of a candidate. "Carpets" were originally drawn on the floor with chalk or charcoal, and at the close of the Lodge obliterated. To avoid this trouble, they were subsequently painted on cloth, which was laid on the floor; hence they were called carpets. Carpets, or charts, as they are at the present time commonly designated, are now generally suspended from the wall, or from a framework in the Lodge. (See *Steps on Master's Carpet*.)

Carthusians. A religious order founded by Bruno in 1080, and named from Chartreux, in France, the place of their institution. They were noted for their austerity.

Cartulary. An officer who has charge of the register or other books of record.

Casmaran. The angel of air. Referred to in the degree of Scottish Knight of St. Andrew. The etymology is uncertain.

Cassia. A corruption of acacia, which undoubtedly arose from the common habit, among illiterate people, of sinking the sound of the letter A in the pronunciation of any word of which it constitutes the initial syllable, as *pothecary* for *apothecary*, and *prentice* for *apprentice*. The word *prentice*, by the way, is almost altogether used in the old records of Masonry, which were, for the most part, the productions of uneducated men. Unfortunately, however, the corruption of *acacia* into *cassia* has not always been confined to the illiterate; but the long employment of the corrupted form has at length introduced it, in some instances, among a few of our writers. Even Dr. Oliver has sometimes used the objectionable corruption, notwithstanding he has written so much upon the symbolism of the acacia.

There is a plant which was called by the ancients *cassia*, but it is entirely different from the acacia. The acacia was a sacred plant; the cassia an ignoble plant, having no sacred character. The former is in Masonry profoundly symbolic; the latter has no symbolism whatever. The cassia is only three times mentioned in Scripture, but always as an aromatic plant forming a portion of some perfume. There is, indeed, strong reason for believing that the cassia was only a coarse kind of cinnamon, and that it did not grow in Palestine, but was imported from the East. Cassia, therefore, has no rightful place in Masonic language, and its use should be avoided as a vulgar corruption.

Castellan. In Germany, the Superintendent or Steward of a Lodge building, in which he resides. He is either a serving brother or an actual member of the Lodge, and has the care of the building and its contents.

Casting Voice or **Vote.** The twelfth of the thirty-nine General Regulations prescribes that "All matters are to be determined in the Grand Lodge by a majority of votes, each member having one vote and the Grand Master having two votes." (*Constitutions*, 1723,

p. 61.) From this law has arisen the universal usage of giving to the Master of the Lodge a casting vote in addition to his own when there is a tie. The custom is so universal, and has been so long practised, that, although I can find no specific law on the subject, the right may be considered as established by prescription. It may be remarked that the Masonic usage is probably derived from the custom of the London Livery Companies or Guilds, where the casting vote has always been given by the presiding officers in all cases of equality, a rule that has been recognized by Act of Parliament.

Catacomb. A grotto for burial; a sepulchral vault. A subterranean place for the burial of the dead, consisting of galleries or passages with recesses excavated at their sides for tombs. Later applied in the plural to all the subterranean cemeteries lying around Rome which, after having been long covered up and forgotten, were fortuitously discovered in 1578. They are found elsewhere, as, at Naples, at Syracuse, in Egypt, at Paris, etc. (See *Oxford Dictionary* for full definitions.)

The term is chiefly applied to those lying about Rome, the principal ones lying along the Appian Way. The following engraving shows a small portion of the Northern section of the Catacomb of St. Calixtus.

THE NORTHERN SECTION OF THE CATACOMB
OF CALIXTUS

There seems to have been no plan for these excavations, for they shoot off in the most unexpected directions, forming such a labyrinth of connected passages that persons often have been lost for several days at a time, giving the monk attendants much trouble. They are several miles in extent. Those about Rome are under the care of various monks of the church, and are a source of considerable revenue from tourists.

They are now entered by narrow passages and some (St. Calixtus) descend to considerable depth. Along the passages are small chambers at the sides for tombs, one above another, each of which generally closed by a slab of stone on which was placed the letters D. M. (Deo Maximo) or X. P., the Greek letters for Christ. Tombs of saints bore inscriptions of identification.

The passages are generally three or four feet wide and were at intervals along their course enlarged into chambers, usually square or rectangular, that were used for worship. One

in St. Calixtus was an irregular semicircle and about 32 feet in diameter. In these chambers is usually found a stone bench or chair for the bishop or teacher. They were ventilated and partially lighted by shafts that extended to the surface of the ground. Some frescoes were found on the walls.

Many catacombs were destroyed and traces of them lost when the Goths, Lombards, and others besieged Rome at various times.

The foregoing would not justify a place in a work of this character, were it not for the influence it sheds on the beginning of Christian architecture, as for three centuries Pagan Rome would not permit Christians to meet above ground.

The Twenty-sixth Degree in the Ancient and Accepted Rite refers to catacombs.

[E. E. C.]

Catafalque. A temporary structure of wood, appropriately decorated with funereal symbols and representing a tomb or cenotaph. It forms a part of the decorations of a Sorrow Lodge, and is also used in the ceremonies of the Third Degree in Lodges of the French Rite.

Catch Questions. Questions not included in the Catechism, but adopted from an early period to try the pretensions of a stranger, such as this used by American Masons: "Where does the Master hang his hat?" and by the French, "Comment êtes vous entré dans le Temple de Salomon?" Such as these are of course unsanctioned by authority. But Dr. Oliver, in an essay on this subject preliminary to the fourth volume of his *Golden Remains*, gives a long list of these "additional tests," which had been reduced to a kind of system, and were practised by the English Masons of the eighteenth century. Among them were such as these: "What is the punishment of a cowan?" "What does this stone smell of?" "If a brother were lost, where would you look for him?" "How blows a Mason's wind?" and many others of the same kind. Of these tests or catch questions, Dr. Oliver says "that they were something like the conundrums of the present day—difficult of comprehension; admitting only of one answer, which appeared to have no direct correspondence with the question, and applicable only in consonance with the mysterious terms and symbols of the Institution." Catch questions in this country, at least, seem to be getting out of use, and some of the most learned Masons at the present day would find it difficult to answer them.

Catechism. From the earliest times the oral instructions of Masonry have been communicated in a catechetical form. Each degree has its peculiar catechism, the knowledge of which constitutes what is called a "bright Mason." The catechism, indeed, should be known to every Mason, for every aspirant should be thoroughly instructed in that of the degree to which he has attained before he is permitted to make further progress. The rule, however, is not rigidly observed; and many Masons, unfortunately, are very ignorant of all but the rudimentary parts of their catechism, which they derive only from hearing portions of it communicated at the opening and closing of the Lodge.

Catechumen. One who had attained the Second Degree of the Essenian or early Christian Mysteries and assumed the name of Constans. There were three degrees in the ceremonies, which, to a limited extent, resembled the Pagan services. Of the three classes, the first were Auditors, the second Catechumens, and the third the Faithful. The Auditors were novices, prepared by ceremonies and instruction to receive the dogmas of Christianity. A portion of these dogmas was made known to the Catechumens, who, after particular purifications, received baptism, or the initiation of the *theogenesis* (Divine regeneration); but in the grand mysteries of that religion—the incarnation, nativity, passion, and resurrection of Christ—none was initiated but the Faithful. The Mysteries were divided into two parts—the first, styled the Mass of the Catechumens; the second, the Mass of the Faithful.

Many beautiful ceremonies and much instruction touching these matters will be found in that most enticing degree called Prince of Mercy, and known as the Twenty-sixth in the Scottish Rite services.

Catenarian Arch. If a rope be suspended loosely by its two ends, the curve into which it falls is called a catenarian curve, and this inverted forms the catenarian arch, which is said to be the strongest of all arches. As the form of a symbolic Lodge is an oblong square, that of a Royal Arch Chapter, according to the English ritual, is a catenarian arch.

Catharine II. Catharine the Great, Empress of Russia, in 1762, prohibited by an edict all Masonic meetings in her dominions. But subsequently better sentiments prevailed, and having learned the true character of the Institution, she not only revoked her order of prohibition, but invited the Masons to reestablish their Lodges and to constitute new ones, and went so far in 1763 as to proclaim herself the Protectress of the Order and "Tutrice" of the Lodge of Clio, at Moscow. (Thory, *Acta Latomorum*, i., 82.) During the remainder of her reign Freemasonry was in a flourishing condition in Russia, and many of the nobles organized Lodges in their palaces. But in 1794 her feelings changed and she became suspicious that the Lodges of Moscow were intriguing against the Court and the Ministers; this idea, coupled with the horrors of the French Revolution and other crimes said to be due to secret societies, caused her to cease to protect the Order, and without any express prohibition emanating from her, the Lodges ceased to work. (*Ibid.*, i., 195.) She died November 6, 1796, and in 1797 her successor, Paul I., forbade all secret societies in Russia.

Caution. It was formerly the custom to bestow upon an Entered Apprentice, on his initiation, a new name, which was "caution." The custom is now very generally discontinued, although the principle which it inculcated should never be forgotten.

The *Old Charges* of 1723 impress upon a Mason the necessity, when in the presence of strangers not Masons, to be "cautious in your words and carriage, that the most penetrating stranger shall not be able to discover or find out what is not proper to be intimated"; as these *Charges* were particularly directed to Apprentices, who then constituted the great body of the Fraternity, it is evident that the "new name" gave rise to the *Charge*, or, more likely, that the *Charge* gave rise to the "new name."

Cavern. In the Pagan mysteries of antiquity the initiations were often performed in caverns, of which a few, like the cave of Elephanta in India, still remain to indicate by their form and extent the character of the rites that were then performed. The cavern of Elephanta, which was the most gorgeous temple in the world, is one hundred and thirty feet square, and eighteen feet high. It is supported by four massive pillars, and its walls are covered with statues and carved symbolic decorations. The sacellum, or sacred place, which contained the phallic symbol, was in the western extremity, and accessible only to the initiated. The caverns of Salsette greatly exceeded in magnitude that of Elephanta, being three hundred in number, all adorned with symbolic figures, among which the phallic emblems were predominant, which were placed in the most secret caverns, accessible only by private entrances. In every cavern was a basin to contain the consecrated water of ablution, on the surface of which floated the sacred lotus flower. All these caverns were places of initiation into the Hindu mysteries, and every arrangement was made for the performance of the most impressive ceremonies.

Faber (*Mys. Cab.*, ii., 257) says that "wherever the Cabiric Mysteries were practised, they were always in some manner or other connected with caverns"; and he mentions, among other instances, the cave Zirinthus, within whose dark recesses the most mysterious Rites of the Samothracian Cabiri were performed.

Maurice (*Ind. Ant.*, iii., 536), speaking of the subterranean passages of the Temple of Isis, in the island of Phile in the river Nile, says "it was in these gloomy caverns that the grand and mystic arcana of the goddess were unfolded to the adoring aspirant, while the solemn hymns of initiation resounded through the long extent of these stony recesses."

Many of the ancient oracles, as, for instance, that of Trophonius in Bœotia, were delivered in caves. Hence, the cave—subterranean, dark, and silent—was mingled in the ancient mind with the idea of mystery.

In the ceremonies of Masonry, we find the cavern or vault in what is called the Cryptic Masonry of the American Rite, and also in the high degrees of the French and Scottish Rites, in which it is a symbol of the darkness of ignorance and crime impenetrable to the light of truth.

In reference to the practical purposes of the cavern, as recorded in the legend of these degrees, it may be mentioned that caverns, which abounded in Palestine in consequence of the geological structure of the country, are spoken of by Josephus as places of refuge for banditti; and Mr. Phillott says, in Smith's *Dictionary*, that it was the caves which lie beneath and around so many of the Jewish cities that formed the last hiding-places of the Jewish leaders in the war with the Romans.

Cedars of Lebanon. In Scriptural symbology, the cedar-tree, says Wemyss (*Symb. Lang. Scrip.*), was the symbol of eternity, because its substance never decays nor rots. Hence, the Ark of the Covenant was made of cedar; and those are said to utter things worthy of cedar who write that which no time ought to obliterate.

The Cedars of Lebanon are frequently referred to in the legends of Masonry, especially in the higher degrees; not, however, on account of any symbolical signification, but rather because of the use made of them by Solomon and Zerubbabel in the construction of their respective Temples. Mr. Phillott (Smith's *Bible Dict.*) thus describes the grove so celebrated in Scriptural and Masonic history:

"The grove of trees known as the Cedars of Lebanon consists of about four hundred trees, standing quite alone in a depression of the mountain with no trees near, about six thousand four hundred feet above the sea, and three thousand below the summit. About eleven or twelve are very large and old, twenty-five large, fifty of middle size, and more than three hundred younger and smaller ones. The older trees have each several trunks and spread themselves widely round, but most of the others are of cone-like form, and do not send out wide lateral branches. In 1550, there were twenty-eight old trees, in 1739, Pococke counted fifteen, but the number of trunks makes the operation of counting uncertain. They are regarded with much reverence by the native inhabitants as living records of Solomon's power, and the Maronite patriarch was formerly accustomed to celebrate there the festival of the Transfiguration at an altar of rough stones."

Celebration. The Third Degree of Fessler's Rite. (See *Fessler, Rite of.*)

Celestial Alphabet. See *Alphabet, Angels'*.

Celtic Mysteries. See *Druidical Mysteries*.

Celts. The early inhabitants of Italy, Gaul, Spain, and Britain. They are supposed to have left Asia during one of the Aryan emigrations, and, having traveled in a westerly direction, to have spread over these countries of Europe. The Celtic Mysteries or the Sacred Rites which they instituted are known as *Druidical Mysteries*, which see.

Cement. The cement which in Operative Masonry is used to unite the various parts of a building into one strong and durable mass, is borrowed by Speculative Masonry as a symbol to denote that brotherly love which binds the Masons of all countries in one common brotherhood. As this brotherhood is recognized as being perfected among Master Masons only, the symbol is very appropriately referred to the Third Degree.

Cemeteries, Masonic. The desire to select some suitable spot wherein to deposit the remains of our departed kindred and friends seems almost innate in the human breast. The stranger's field was bought with the accursed bribe of betrayal and treason, and there is an abhorrence to depositing our loved ones in places whose archetype was so desecrated by its purchase-money. The church-yard, to the man of sentiment, is as sacred as the church itself. The cemetery bears a hallowed character, and we adorn its graves with vernal flowers or with evergreens, to show that the dead, though away from our presence visibly, still live and bloom in our memories. The oldest of all the histories that time has saved to us contains an affecting story of this reverence of the living for the dead, when it tells us how Abraham, when Sarah, his beloved wife, had died in a strange land, reluctant to bury her among strangers, purchased from the sons of Heth the cave of Machpelah for a burial-place for his people.

It is not, then, surprising that Masons, actuated by this spirit, should have been desirous to consecrate certain spots as resting-places for themselves and for the strange Brethren who should die among them. A writer in the *London Freemason's Magazine* for 1858 complained that there was not in England a Masonic cemetery, nor portion of an established cemetery especially dedicated to the interment of the Brethren of the Craft. This neglect cannot be charged against the Masons of America, for there is scarcely a city or town of considerable size in which the Masons have not purchased and appropriated a suitable spot as a cemetery to be exclusively devoted to the use of the Fraternity. These cemeteries are often, and should always be, dedicated with impressive ceremonies; and it is to be regretted that our rituals have provided no sanctioned form of service for these occasions.

Censer. A small vessel of metal fitted to receive burning coals from the altar, and on which the incense for burning was sprinkled by the priest in the Temple. Among the furniture of a Royal Arch Chapter is to be found the censer, which is placed upon the altar of incense within the sanctuary, as a symbol of the pure thoughts and grateful feelings which, in so holy a place, should be offered up as a fitting sacrifice to the great I AM. In a similar symbolic sense, the censer, under the name of the "*pot of incense*," is found among the emblems of the Third Degree. (See *Pot of Incense.*) The censer also constitutes a part of the Lodge furniture in many of the high degrees.

Censor. Gädicke says he is not an officer, but is now and then introduced into some of the Lodges of Germany. He is commonly found where the Lodge has its own private house, in which, on certain days, mixed assemblies are held of Freemasons and their families and friends. Of those assemblies the Censor has the superintendence.

Censure. In Masonic law, the mildest form of punishment that can be inflicted, and may be defined to be a formal expression of disapprobation, without other result than the effect produced upon the feelings of him who is censured. It is adopted by a resolution of the Lodge on a motion made at a regular communication; it requires only a bare majority of votes, for its passage does not affect the Masonic standing of the person censured, and may be revoked at any subsequent regular communication.

Centaine, Order of. A mystical society of the last century which admitted females. It was organized at Bordeaux, in 1735. (Thory, *Acta Latomorum*, i., 298.)

Centennial. That which happens every hundred years. Masonic bodies that have lasted for that period very generally celebrate the occasion by a commemorative festival. On the 4th of November, 1852, almost all of the Lodges of the United States celebrated the centennial anniversary of the initiation of George Washington as a Freemason.

Centralists. A society which existed in Europe from 1770 to 1780. It made use of Masonic forms at its meetings simply to conceal its secrets. Lenning calls it an alchemical association, but says that it had religious and political tendencies. Gädicke thinks that its object was to propagate Jesuitism.

Central Point. See *Point within a Circle.*

Center, Opening on the. In the English ritual, a Master Mason's Lodge is said to be opened on the center, because the Brethren present, being all Master Masons, are equally near and equally distant from that imaginary central point which among Masons constitutes perfection. Neither of the preliminary degrees can assert the same conditions, because the Lodge of an Entered Apprentice may contain all the three classes, and that of a Fellow-Craft may include some Master Masons; and therefore the doctrine of perfect equality is not carried out in either. An attempt was made, but without success, in the *Trestle Board*, published under the sanction of the Baltimore Masonic Convention, to introduce the custom into the American Lodges.

Cephas. A word which in the Syriac signifies a rock or stone, and is the name which was bestowed by Christ upon Simon, when he said to him, "Thou art a rock," which the Greeks rendered by Πέτρος, and the Latins by *Petrus*, both words meaning "a rock." It is used in the degree of Royal Master, and there alludes to the *Stone of Foundation*, which see.

Ceremonies. The outer garments which cover and adorn Freemasonry as clothing does the human body. Although ceremonies give neither life nor truth to doctrines or principles, yet they have an admirable influence, since by their use certain things are made to acquire a sacred character which they would not otherwise have had; and hence, Lord Coke has most wisely said that "prudent antiquity did, for more solemnity and better memory and observation of that which is to be done, express substances under ceremonies."

Ceremonies, Master of. See *Master of Ceremonies.*

Ceres. Among the Romans, the goddess of agriculture; but among the more poetic Greeks she was worshiped under the name of Demeter, as the symbol of the prolific earth. To her is attributed the institution of the Eleusinian Mysteries in Greece, the most popular of all the ancient initiations.

Ceridwen. The Isis of the Druids.

Cerneau, Joseph. A French jeweler, born at Villeblerin, in 1763, who in the beginning of the nineteenth century removed to the City of New York, where in 1807 he established a spurious body under the title of "Sovereign Grand Consistory of the United States of America, its Territories and Dependencies." This Masonic charlatan, who claimed the right to organize bodies of the Ancient and Accepted Scottish Rite, was expelled and his pretensions denounced, in 1813, by the legal Supreme Council sitting at Charleston, South Carolina. Cerneau and his adherents gave much trouble in the Scottish Rite for many years, and the bodies which he had formed were not entirely dissolved until long after the establishment of a legal Supreme Council for the Northern Jurisdiction.

Certificate. A diploma issued by a Grand Lodge or by a subordinate Lodge under its authority, testifying that the holder thereof is a true and trusty Brother, and recommending him to the hospitality of the Fraternity abroad. The character of this instrument has sometimes been much misunderstood. It is by no means intended to act as a *voucher* for the bearer, nor can it be allowed to supersede the necessity of a *strict examination.* A stranger, however, having been tried and proved by a more unerring standard, his certificate then properly comes in as an auxiliary testimonial, and will be permitted to afford good evidence of his correct standing in his Lodge at home; for no body of Masons, true to the principles of their Order, would grant such an instrument to an unworthy Brother, or to one who, they feared, might make an improper use of it. But though the presence of a Grand Lodge certificate be in general required as collateral evidence of worthiness to visit, or receive aid, its accidental absence, which may arise in various ways, as from fire, captivity, or shipwreck, should not debar a strange Brother from the rights guaranteed to him by our Institution, provided he can offer other evidence of his good character. The Grand Lodge of New York has, upon this subject, taken the proper stand in the following regulation: "That no Mason be admitted to any subordinate Lodge under the jurisdiction of this Grand Lodge, or receive the charities of any Lodge, unless he

10

shall, on such application, exhibit a Grand Lodge certificate, duly attested by the proper authorities, *except he is known to the Lodge to be a worthy brother.*"

The certificate system has been warmly discussed by the Grand Lodges of the United States, and considerable opposition to it has been made by some of them on the ground that it is an innovation. If it is an innovation, it certainly is not one of the present day, as we may learn from the Regulations made in General Assembly of the Masons of England, on St. John the Evangelist's day, 1663, during the Grand Mastership of the Earl of St. Albans, one of which reads as follows:

"That no person hereafter who shall be accepted a Freemason shall be admitted into any Lodge or Assembly, until he has brought a certificate of the time and place of his acceptation from the Lodge that accepted him, unto the Master of that limit or division where such Lodge is kept." (*Constitutions*, 1738, p. 101.)

Chaillou de Joinville. He played an important part in the Freemasonry of France about the middle of the last century, especially during the schisms which at that time existed in the Grand Lodge. In 1761, he was an active member of the Council of Emperors of the East and West, or Rite of Perfection, which had been established in 1758. Under the title of "Substitute General of the Order, Ven. Master of the First Lodge in France, called St. Anthony's, Chief of the Eminent Degrees, Commander, and Sublime Prince of the Royal Secret, etc., etc., etc.," he signed the Patent of Stephen Morin, authorizing him to extend the Royal Order in America, which was the first step that subsequently led to the establishment of the Ancient and Accepted Rite in the United States. In 1762, the Prince of Clermont, Grand Master of the Grand Lodge of France, removed the dancing-master Lacorne, whom he had previously appointed his Substitute General, and who had become distasteful to the respectable members of the Grand Lodge, and put Chaillou de Joinville in his place. This action created a schism in the Grand Lodge, during which De Joinville appears to have acted with considerable energy, but eventually he became almost as notorious as his predecessor, by issuing irregular charters and deputations. On the death of the Prince of Clermont, in 1771, the Lacornists regained much of their influence, and De Joinville appears quietly to have passed away from the field of French Masonry and Masonic intrigues.

Chain, Mystic. To form the mystic chain is for the Brethren to make a circle, holding each other by the hands, as in surrounding a grave, etc. Each Brother crosses his arms in front of his body, so as to give his right hand to his left-hand neighbor, and his left hand to his right-hand neighbor. The French call it *chaine d'union.* It is a symbol of the close connection of all Masons in one common brotherhood.

Chain of Flowers. In French Masonry,

when a Lodge celebrates the day of its foundation, or the semicentennial membership of one of the Brethren, or at the initiation of a *louveteau* (*q. v.*) the room is decorated with wreaths of flowers called "chaine de fleurs."

Chain of Union. See *Chain, Mystic.*

Chain, Triangular. One of the legends of Freemasonry tells us that when the Jewish Masons were carried as captives from Jerusalem to Babylon by Nebuchadnezzar they were bound by triangular chains, which was intended as an additional insult, because to them the triangle, or delta, was a symbol of the Deity, to be used only on sacred occasions. The legend is of course apocryphal, and is worth nothing except as a legendary symbol.

Chair. A technical term signifying the office of Master of a Lodge. Thus "he is eligible to the chair" is equivalent to "he is eligible to the office of Master." The word is applied in the same sense to the presiding officer in other Masonic bodies.

Chairman. The presiding officer of a meeting or committee. In all committees of a Lodge, the Worshipful Master, if he chooses to attend, is *ex-officio* chairman; as is the Grand Master of any meeting of the Craft when he is present.

Chair, Master in the. The German Masons call the Worshipful Master "der Meister im Stuhl," or the Master in the Chair.

Chair, Oriental. The seat or office of the Master of a Lodge is thus called—sometimes, more fully, the "Oriental Chair of King Solomon."

Chair, Passing the. The ceremony of inducting the Master-elect of a Lodge into his office is called "passing the chair." He who has once presided over a Lodge as its Master is said to have "passed the chair," hence the title "Past Master."

Chaldea. A large tract of country, lying in a nearly northwest and southeast direction for a distance of four hundred miles along the course of the rivers Euphrates and Tigris, with an average width of one hundred miles. The kingdom of Chaldea, of which Babylon was the chief city, is celebrated in Masonic history as the place where the Jewish captives were conducted after the destruction of Jerusalem. At that time Nebuchadnezzar was the king. His successors, during the captivity, were Evilmerodach, Neriglissar, Labosordacus, and Belshazzar. In the seventeenth year of his reign, the city of Babylon was taken and the Chaldean kingdom subverted by Cyrus, King of Persia, who terminated the captivity of the Jews, and restored them to their native country.

Chaldean Cylinder. The cylinder so recently discovered by Mr. Rassam in the course of his excavations in Babylonia, which has greatly attracted the attention of the London Society of Biblical Archeology, is one of the most remarkable yet made known, by reason of the light it throws upon the ancient chronology of the Chaldean Empire. It dates from the time of Nabonides, and records, among various things, that this sovereign, digging under the foundations of the Temple of the Sun-god at Sippara, forty-five years after the death of King Nebuchadnezzar, came upon a cylinder of Naramsin, the son of Nargon, which no one had seen for "3200 years." This gives as the date of the ancient sovereign named 3750 B.C. This, and the fact pointed out by Prof. Oppert, that there was in those early days already "lively intercourse between Chaldea and Egypt," will have to be taken into account by future Bible critics. This destroys the conception of Abraham, the founder of the Jews, as a wanderer or nomad, and establishes the existence of two highly civilized, as well as cultured, empires in Egypt and Chaldea more than 5,500 years ago; that the highroad between them lay direct through Southern Palestine, and that Abraham was a native of the one great empire and an honored visitor in the other. Thus has been opened up a new field for investigation in the matter of Akkad and Akkadian civilization.

Chaldeans or **Chaldees.** The ancient— Diodorus Siculus says the "most ancient "— inhabitants of Babylonia. There was among them, as among the Egyptians, a true priestly caste, which was both exclusive and hereditary; for although not every Chaldean was a priest, yet no man could be a priest among them unless he were a Chaldean. "At Babylon," says Dr. Smith (*Anc. Hist. of the East*, p. 398), "they were in all respects the ruling order in the body politic, uniting in themselves the characters of the English sacerdotal and military classes. They filled all the highest offices of state under the king, who himself belonged to the order." The Chaldean priests were famous for their astronomical science, the study of which was particularly favored by the clear atmosphere and the cloudless skies of their country, and to which they were probably urged by their national worship of the sun and the heavenly hosts. Diodorus Siculus says that they passed their whole lives in meditating questions of philosophy, and acquired a great reputation for their astrology. They were addicted especially to the art of divination, and framed predictions of the future. They sought to avert evil and to insure good by purifications, sacrifices, and enchantments. They were versed in the arts of prophesying and explaining dreams and prodigies. All this learning among the Chaldeans was a family tradition; the son inheriting the profession and the knowledge of the priesthood from his father, and transmitting it to his descendants. The Chaldeans were settled throughout the whole country, but there were some special cities, such as Borsippa, Ur, Sippera, and Babylon, where they had regular colleges. The reputation of the Chaldeans for prophetic and magical knowledge was so great, that astrologers, and conjurers in general, were styled Babylonians and Chaldeans, just as the wandering fortune-tellers of modern times are called Egyptians or gipsies, and *Ars Chaldæorum* was the name given to all occult sciences.

Chalice. A cup used in religious rites. It forms a part of the furniture of a Commandery of Knights Templar, and of some of the higher degrees of the French and Scottish Rites. It should be made either of silver or of gilt metal. The stem of the chalice should be about four inches high and the diameter from three to six.

Chalk, Charcoal, and Clay. By these three substances are beautifully symbolized the three qualifications for the servitude of an Entered Apprentice—freedom, fervency, and zeal. Chalk is the freest of all substances, because the slightest touch leaves a trace behind. Charcoal, the most fervent, because to it, when ignited, the most obdurate metals yield; and clay, the most zealous, because it is constantly employed in man's service, and is as constantly reminding us that from it we all came, and to it we must all return. In the earlier lectures of the last century, the symbols, with the same interpretation, were given as "Chalk, Charcoal, and Earthen Pan."

Chamber, Middle. See *Middle Chamber.*

Chamber of Reflection. In the French and Scottish Rites, a small room adjoining the Lodge, in which, preparatory to initiation, the candidate is enclosed for the purpose of indulging in those serious meditations which its somber appearance and the gloomy emblems with which it is furnished are calculated to produce. It is also used in some of the high degrees for a similar purpose. Its employment is very appropriate, for, as Gädicke well observes, "It is only in solitude that we can deeply reflect upon our present or future undertakings, and blackness, darkness, or solitariness, is ever a symbol of death. A man who has undertaken a thing after mature reflection seldom turns back."

Chancellor. An officer in a Council of Companions of the Red Cross, corresponding in some respects to the Senior Warden of a Symbolic Lodge.

Chancellor, Grand. An officer in the Supreme Councils and Grand Consistories of the Ancient and Accepted Scottish Rite, whose duties are somewhat similar to those of a Corresponding Secretary.

Chaos. A confused and shapeless mass, such as is supposed to have existed before God reduced creation into order. It is a Masonic symbol of the ignorance and intellectual darkness from which man is rescued by the light and truth of Masonry. Hence, *ordo ab chao*, or, "order out of chaos," is one of the mottoes of the Institution.

Chaos Disentangled. One of the names formerly given to the Twenty-eighth Degree of the Ancient and Accepted Scottish Rite, or Knight of the Sun. It is likewise found in the collection of M. Pyron. Discreet and Wise Chaos are the Forty-ninth and Fiftieth degrees of the Rite of Mizraim.

Chapeau. The cocked hat worn in this country by Knights Templar. The regulations of the Grand Encampment of the United States, in 1862, prescribe that it shall be "the military chapeau, trimmed with black binding, one white and two black plumes, and appropriate cross on the left side."

Chapel. The closets and anterooms so necessary and convenient to a Lodge for various purposes are dignified by German Masons with the title of "Capellen," or chapels.

Chapel, Mary's (or the Lodge of Edinburgh). The oldest Lodge in Edinburgh, Scotland, whose minutes extend as far back as the year 1599. This long stood as the oldest minute, but in 1912 one was found of Aitchison's-Haven Lodge dated 1598. (See *Aitchison's-Haven.*) They show that John Boswell, Esq., of Auchinleck, was present in the Lodge in the year 1600, and that the Hon. Robert Moray, Quartermaster-General of the Army of Scotland, was created a Master Mason in 1641 at Newcastle by some members of the Lodge of Edinburgh who were present there with the Scotch Army. These facts show that at that early period persons who were not Operative Masons by profession were admitted into the Order. The Lodge of Edinburgh (Mary's Chapel) is No. 1 on the roll of the Grand Lodge of Scotland; the date of its formation is unknown, and at one time it stood first on the roll, but in 1807 the Mother Kilwinning Lodge was placed before it as No. 0. It met at one time in a chapel dedicated to the Virgin Mary; hence comes the second part of its name. Its history was published in 1873 by D. M. Lyon. [E. L. H.]

Chapiter. The uppermost part of a column, pillar, or pilaster, serving as the head or crowning, and placed immediately over the shaft and under the entablature. The pillars which stood in front of the porch of King Solomon's Temple were adorned with chapiters of a peculiar construction, which are largely referred to, and their symbolism explained, in the Fellow-Craft's Degree. (See *Pillars of the Porch.*)

Chaplain. The office of Chaplain of a Lodge is one which is not recognized in the ritual of the United States of America, although often conferred by courtesy. The Master of a Lodge in general performs the duties of a Chaplain.

Chaplain, Grand. An office of very modern date in a Grand Lodge. It was first instituted on the 1st of May, 1775, on the occasion of the laying of the foundation of Freemasons' Hall in London. It is stated in the English *Constitutions* of 1784 (p. 314) that the office "which had been discontinued for several years, was this day revived," but there is no record of any appointment to it before the date given. This office is now universally recognized by the Grand Lodges of America. His duties are confined to offering up prayer at the communications of the Grand Lodge, and conducting its devotional exercises on public occasions.

Chapter. In early times the meetings of Masons were called not only Lodges, but Chapters and Congregations. Thus, the statute enacted in the third year of the reign of Henry VI., of England, A.D. 1425, declares that "Masons shall not confederate in Chapiters and Congregations." The word is now exclusively appropriated to designate the bodies in which degrees higher than the symbolic are conferred. Thus there are Chapters of Royal Arch Masons in the York and American Rites and Chapters of Rose Croix Masons in the Ancient and Accepted.

Chapter, General Grand. See *General Grand Chapter.*

Chapter, Grand. See *Grand Chapter.*

Chapter Mason. A colloquialism denoting a Royal Arch Mason.

Chapter Masonry. A colloquialism intended to denote the degrees conferred in a Royal Arch Chapter.

Chapter of R. Arch Masons, An Old. There is in Boston, Mass., a Chapter of Royal Arch Masons which was holden in St. Andrew's Lodge and formed about the year 1769. (See *Royal Arch Masons, Massachusetts;* also, *Pennsylvania.*)

Chapter, Rose Croix. See *Rose Croix, Prince of.*

Chapter, Royal Arch. A convocation of Royal Arch Masons is called a Chapter. In Great Britain, Royal Arch Masonry is connected with and practically under the same government as the Grand Lodge; but in America the jurisdictions are separate. In America a Chapter of Royal Arch Masons is empowered to give the preparatory degrees of Mark, Past, and Most Excellent Master; although, of course, the Chapter, when meeting in either of these degrees, is called a Lodge. In some Chapters the degrees of Royal and Select Master are also given as preparatory degrees; but in most of the States, the control of these is conferred upon separate bodies, called "Councils of Royal and Select Masters."

The presiding officers of a Chapter are the High Priest, King, and Scribe, who are, respectively, representatives of Joshua, Zerubbabel, Haggai, and son of Josedech. In the English Chapters, these officers are generally styled either by the founders' names, as above, or as First, Second, and Third Principals. In the Chapters of Ireland the order of the officers is King, High Priest, and Chief Scribe. Chapters of Royal Arch Masons in America are primarily under the jurisdiction of State Grand Chapters, as Lodges are under Grand Lodges; and secondly, under the General Grand Chapter of the United States, whose meetings are held triennially, and which exercises a general supervision over this branch of the Order throughout the Union. (See *Royal Arch Degree.*)

Chapters, Irish. See *Irish Chapters.*

Characteristic Name. See *Order Name.*

Characteristics. The prefix to signatures of brethren of the A. A. Scottish Rite is as follows: To that of the Sovereign Grand Commander, the triple cross crosslet, as in (1), in red ink. To that of an Inspector-General other than a Commander (2), in red ink. To that of a Brother of the Royal Secret, Thirty-second Degree (3), in red ink. In the Northern Jurisdiction of the U. S., a Rose Croix Knight will suffix a triangle surmounted by a cross in red ink, as in (4). In all cases, it is usual to place the degree rank in a triangle after the name.

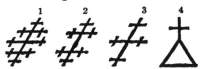

Charcoal. See *Chalk, Charcoal, and Clay.*

Charge. So called from the "Old Charges," because, like them, it contains an epitome of duty. It is the admonition which is given by the presiding officer, at the close of the ceremony of initiation, to the candidate, and which the latter receives standing, as a token of respect. There is a charge for each degree, which is to be found in all the monitors and manuals from Preston onward.

Charges, Old. The Masons' *Constitutions* are old records, containing a history, very often somewhat apocryphal, of the origin and progress of Masonry, and regulations for the government of the Craft. These regulations are called *Charges*, and are generally the same in substance, although they differ in number, in the different documents. These *charges* are divided into "Articles" and "Points"; although it would be difficult to say in what the one section differs in character from the other, as each details the rules which should govern a Mason in his conduct toward his "lord," or employer, and to his brother workmen. The oldest of these *charges* is to be found in the York *Constitutions* (if they are authentic), and consists of Fifteen Articles and Fifteen Points. It was required by the *Constitutions* of the time of Edward III., "that, for the future, at the making or admission of a brother, the constitutions and charges should be read." This regulation is still preserved in form, in modern Lodges, by the reading of *the charge* by the Master to a candidate at the close of the ceremony of his reception into a degree. (For a list of the *Old Charges,* see *Manuscripts, Old.*)

Charges of 1722. The Fraternity had long been in possession of many records, containing the ancient regulations of the Order; when, in 1722, the Duke of Montague being Grand Master of England, the Grand Lodge finding fault with their antiquated arrangement, it was directed that they should be collected, and after being properly digested, be annexed to the *Book of Constitutions,* then in course of publication under the superintendence of Dr. James Anderson. This was accordingly done, and the document now well known under the title of *The Old Charges of the Free and Accepted Masons,* constitutes, by universal consent, a part of the fundamental law of our Order. The *charges* are divided into six general heads of duty, as follows: 1. Concerning God and religion. 2. Of the civil magistrate, supreme and subordinate. 3. Of Lodges. 4. Of Masters, Wardens, Fellows, and Apprentices. 5. Of the management of the Craft in working. 6. Of behavior under different circumstances and in various conditions. These *charges* contain succinct directions for the proper discharge of a Mason's duties, in whatever position he may be placed, and are as modern researches have shown, a collation of the *charges* contained in the *Old Records* and from them have been abridged, or by them suggested, all those well-known directions found in our monitors, which Masters are accustomed to read to candidates on their reception. (See *Records, Old.*)

Charity. "Though I speak with the tongues of men and of angels, and have not charity, I am become as sounding brass, or a tinkling cymbal. And though I have the gift of prophecy, and understand all mysteries and all knowledge; and though I have all faith, so that I could remove mountains, and have not charity, I am nothing." (1 Corinth. xiii. 1, 2.) Such was the language of an eminent apostle of the Christian church, and such is the sentiment that constitutes the cementing bond of Freemasonry. The apostle, in comparing it with faith and hope, calls it the greatest of the three, and hence in Masonry it is made the topmost round of its mystic ladder. We must not fall into the too common error that charity is only that sentiment of commiseration which leads us to assist the poor with pecuniary donations. Its Masonic, as well as its Christian application is more noble and more extensive. The word used by the apostle is, in the original, ἀγάπη, or *love,* a word denoting that kindly state of mind which renders a person full of good-will and affectionate regard toward others. John Wesley expressed his regret that the Greek had not been correctly translated as *love* instead of *charity,* so that the apostolic triad of virtues would have been, not "faith, hope, and charity," but "faith, hope, and love." Then would we have understood the comparison made by St. Paul, when he said, "Though I bestow all my goods to feed the *poor,* and though I give my body to be burned, and have not *love,* it profiteth me nothing." Guided by this sentiment, the true Mason will "suffer long and be kind." He will be slow to anger and easy to forgive. He will stay his falling brother by gentle admonition, and warn him with kindness of approaching danger. He will not open his ear to his slanderers, and will close his lips against all reproach. His faults and his follies will be locked in his breast, and the prayer for mercy will ascend to Jehovah for his brother's sins. Nor will these sentiments of benevolence be confined to those who are bound to him by ties of kindred or worldly friendship alone; but, extending them throughout the globe, he will love and cherish all who sit beneath the broad canopy of our universal Lodge. For it is the boast of our Institution, that a Mason, destitute and worthy, may find in every clime a brother, and in every land a home.

Charity, Committee on. See *Committee of Charity.*

Charity Fund. Many Lodges and Grand Lodges have a fund especially appropriated to charitable purposes, which is not used for the disbursement of the current expenses, but which is appropriated to the relief of indigent brethren, their widows, and orphans. The charity fund of the Grand Lodge of Pennsylvania, which was bequeathed to it by Stephen Girard, and which is the largest in America, considerably exceeds fifty thousand dollars.

Charlatan. A charlatan is a babbling mountebank, who imposes on the populace by large pretensions and high-sounding words. A charlatan in Masonry is one who seeks by a display of pompous ceremonial, and often by claims to supernatural powers, to pervert the Institution of Masonry to the acquisition of gain, or the gratification of a paltry ambition. Every man, says a distinguished writer, is a charlatan who extorts money by charging for sixpenny trash the amount that should only be paid for works of science, and that, too, under the plea of conveying knowledge that cannot otherwise be obtained. (*Lond. Freem. Mag.*, 1844, p. 505.) The eighteenth century presented many examples of these Masonic charlatans, of whom by far the greatest was Cagliostro; nor has the nineteenth century been entirely without them.

Charlemagne. The great Charles, King of France, who ascended the throne in the year 768, is claimed by some Masonic writers as a patron of Masonry. This is perhaps because architecture flourished in France during his reign, and because he encouraged the arts by inviting the architects and traveling Freemasons, who were then principally confined to Italy, to visit France and engage in the construction of important edifices. The claim has been made that at his castle at Aix-la-Chapelle he set apart a room or rooms in which the seven liberal arts and sciences were taught. This comprised a liberal education for that period.   [E. E. C.]

Charles Martel. He was the founder of the Carlovingian dynasty, and governed France with supreme power from 720 to 741, under the title of Duke of the Franks, the nominal kings being only his puppets. He is claimed by the authors of the *Old Records* as one of the patrons of Masonry. Thus, the Lansdowne MS. says: "There was one of the Royall Line of France called *Charles Marshall*, and he was a man that loved well the said Craft and took upon him the Rules and Manners, and after that BY THE GRACE OF GOD he was elect to be the *King* of France, and when he was in his Estate he helped to make those Masons that were now, and sett them on Work and gave them Charges and Manners and good pay as he had learned of other Masons, and confirmed them a Charter from yeare to yeare to hold their Assembly when they would, and cherished them right well, and thus came this Noble Craft into France and England."

Rebold (*Hist. Gen.*) has accepted this legend as authentic, and says: "In 740, Charles Martel, who reigned in France under the title of Mayor of the Palace, at the request of the Anglo-Saxon kings, sent many workmen and Masters into England."

Charles I. and II. For their supposed connection with the origin of Freemasonry, see *Stuart Masonry*.

Charles XIII. The Duke of Südermanland was distinguished for his attachment to Masonry. In 1809 he ascended the throne of Sweden under the title of Charles XIII. Having established the Masonic Order of Knighthood of that name, he abdicated in favor of Charles John Bernadotte, but always remained an active and zealous member of the Order. There is no king on record so distinguished for his attachment to Freemasonry as Charles XIII., of Sweden, and to him the Swedish Masons are in a great measure indebted for the high position that the Order has maintained during the present century in that country.

Charles XIII., Order of. An order of knighthood instituted in 1811 by Charles XIII., King of Sweden, which was to be conferred only on the principal dignitaries of the Masonic Institution in his dominions. In the manifesto establishing the Order, the king says: "To give to this society (the Masonic) a proof of our gracious sentiments towards it, we will and ordain that its first dignitaries to the number which we may determine, shall in future be decorated with the most intimate proof of our confidence, and which shall be for them a distinctive mark of the highest dignity." The number of Knights are twenty-seven, all Masons, and the King of Sweden is the perpetual Grand Master. The color of the ribbon is red, and the jewel a maltese cross pendant from an imperial crown.

Charleston. A city in the United States of America, and the metropolis of the State of South Carolina. It was there that the first Supreme Council of the Ancient and Accepted Scottish Rite was established in 1801, whence all other Supreme Councils have emanated, directly or indirectly. Hence, it has assumed the title of "Mother Council of the world." Its seat was removed in 1870 to the city of Washington. (See *Scottish Rite*.)

Charms, Magical. See *Talisman*.

Chart. 1. A map on which is delineated the emblems of a degree, to be used for the instruction of candidates, formerly called a *carpet*, which see. 2. The title given by Jeremy L. Cross to his *Hieroglyphic Monitor*, which acquired on its first appearance in the Lodges of America a popularity that it has not yet entirely lost. Hence the word chart is still sometimes used colloquially and improperly to designate any other Masonic manual of monitorial instruction.

Charter. Often used for *Warrant of Constitution*, which see.

Chartered Lodge. A Lodge working under the authority of a Charter or Warrant of Constitution issued by a Grand Lodge as distinguished from a Lodge working under a dispensation issued by a Grand Master. Chartered Lodges only are entitled to representation in the Grand Lodge. They alone can make by-laws, elect members, or have their officers installed. They are the constituent bodies of a jurisdiction, and by their representatives compose the Grand Lodge.

Charter Member. A Mason whose name is attached to the petition upon which a Charter or Warrant of Constitution has been granted to a Lodge, Chapter, or other subordinate body.

Charter of Cologne. See *Cologne, Charter of.*

Charter of Transmission. See *Transmission, Charter of.*

Chasidim. In Hebrew, חסידים, meaning *saints*. The name of a sect which existed in the time of the Maccabees, and which was organized for the purpose of opposing innovations upon the Jewish faith. Their essential principles were to observe all the ritual laws of purification, to meet frequently for devotion, to submit to acts of self-denial and mortification, to have all things in common, and sometimes to withdraw from society and to devote themselves to contemplation. Lawrie, who seeks to connect them with the Masonic Institution as a continuation of the Masons of the Solomonic era, describes them under the name of "Kasideans" as "a religious Fraternity, or an order of the KNIGHTS OF THE TEMPLE OF JERUSALEM, who bound themselves to adorn the porches of that magnificent structure, and to preserve it from injury and decay. This association was composed of the greatest men of Israel, who were distinguished for their charitable and peaceful dispositions, and always signalized themselves by their ardent zeal for the purity and preservation of the Temple." (*History of Freemasonry*, p. 38.)

Chastanier, Benedict. A French surgeon, who in the year 1767 introduced into England a modification of the Rite of Pernetty, in nine degrees, and established a Lodge in London under the name of the "Illuminated Theosophists"; which, however, according to Lenning, soon abandoned the Masonic forms, and was converted into a mere theosophic sect, intended to propagate the religious system of Swedenborg. Mr. White, in his *Life of Emanuel Swedenborg* (Lond., 1868, p. 683), gives an account of "The Theosophical Society, instituted for the purpose of promoting the Heavenly Doctrines of the New Jerusalem by translating, printing, and publishing the theological writings of Emanuel Swedenborg." This society was formed in 1784, and met on Sundays and Thursdays at chambers in New Court, Middle Temple, for the discussion of Swedenborg's writings. Among the twenty-five persons mentioned by White as having either joined the society or sympathized with its object, we find the name of "Benedict Chastanier, French Surgeon, 62 Tottenham Court." The nine degrees of Chastanier's Rite of Illuminated Theosophists are as follows: 1, 2, and 3, Symbolic degrees; 4, 5, 6, Theosophic Apprentice, Fellow-Craft, and Master; 7, Sublime Scottish Mason, or Celestial Jerusalem; 8, Blue Brother; and 9, Red Brother.

Chastity. In the Regius or Halliwell MS.

of the *Constitutions* of Masonry, written not later than the latter part of the fourteenth century, the seventh point is in these words:

> "Thou schal not by thy maystres wyf ly,
> Ny by thy felows yn no manner wyse,
> Lest the Craft wolde the despyse;
> Ny by thy felows concubyne,
> No more thou woldest he dede by thyne."

Again, in the *Constitutions* known as the Matthew Cooke MS., the date of which is about the latter part of the fifteenth century, the same regulation is enforced in these words: "The 7th Point. That he covet not the wyfe ne the daughter of his masters, nother of his fellows but if [unless] hit be in maryage." So all through the *Old Constitutions* and *Charges*, we find this admonition to respect the chastity of our brethren's wives and daughters; an admonition which, it is scarcely necessary to say, is continued to this day.

Chasuble. The outer dress which is worn by the priest at the altar service, and is an imitation of the old Roman toga. It is a circular cloth, which falls down over the body so as completely to cover it, with an aperture in the center for the head to pass through. It is used in the ceremonies of the Rose Croix Degree.

Checkered Floor. See *Mosaic Pavement.*

Chef-d'œuvre. It was a custom among many of the guilds, and especially among the *Compagnons du Devoir*, who sprang up in the sixteenth century in France, on the decay of Freemasonry in that kingdom, and as one of its results, to require every Apprentice, before he could be admitted to the freedom of the guild, to present a piece of finished work as a proof of his skill in the art in which he had been instructed. The piece of work was called his *chef-d'œuvre*, or masterpiece.

Chereau, Antoine Guillaume. A painter in Paris, who published, in 1806, two hermetico-philosophical brochures entitled *Explication de la Pierre Cubique*, and *Explication de la Croix Philosophique;* or Explanations of the Cubical Stone and of the Philosophical Cross. These works are brief, but give much interesting information on the ritualism and symbolism of the high degrees. They have been republished by Tessier in his *Manuel Général*, without, however, any acknowledgment to the original author.

Cherubim. The second order of the angelic hierarchy, the first being the seraphim. The two cherubim that overtopped the mercy-seat or covering of the ark, in the holy of holies, were placed there by Moses, in obedience to the orders of God: "And thou shalt make two cherubims of gold, of beaten work shalt thou make them, in the two ends of the mercy-seat. And the cherubims, shall stretch forth their wings on high, covering the mercy-seat with their wings, and their faces shall look one to another; towards the mercy-seat shall the faces of the cherubims be." (Exod. xxv. 18, 20.) It was between these cherubim that the Shekinah or Divine presence rested, and from which issued the Bathkol or voice of God. Of the form of these cherubim, we are ignorant. Josephus says, that they resembled no known creature, but that Moses made them in the form in which he saw them about the throne of God; others, deriving their ideas from what is said of them by Ezekiel, Isaiah, and St. John, describe them as having the face and breast of a man, the wings of an eagle, the belly of a lion, and the legs and feet of an ox, which three animals, with man, are the symbols of strength and wisdom. But all agree in this, that they had wings, and that these wings were extended. The cherubim were purely symbolic. But although there is great diversity of opinion as to their exact signification, yet there is a very general agreement that they allude to and symbolize the protecting and overshadowing power of the Deity. Reference is made to the *extended wings of the cherubim* in the degree of Royal Master.

* Much light has been thrown upon the plastic form of these symbols during the past few years, not only as to the Cherubim of the Ark of the Covenant spoken of in Exodus, Samuel, Kings, and Chronicles, but those of Chaldeo-Assyrian art which beautified the gates of the palace of Sennacherib at Nineveh, and other structures.

The Kirubi of the Assyrian type, in the shape of bulls with extended wings, in nowise meet the description given above. The figures which can be found in various places upon Egyptian monuments, placed face to face on either side of the Naos of the gods, and stretching out their arms, furnished with great wings, as though to envelop them (Wilkinson, *Manners and Customs of Ancient Egyptians*, 1878, vol. iii.), more fully meet the idea—in fact, it is convincing, when we remember the period, and note that all else about the sacred furnishings of the Tabernacle, or Ohel-mo'ed, are exclusively Egyptian in form, as well as the sacerdotal costumes. (See *L'Égypte et Moïse*, by Abbé Ancessi, Paris, 1875.) Furthermore, this was most natural, since the period was immediately after the exodus. The Kerubim of the Ark were remodeled by Solomon after designs furnished by his father, David. (1 Chron. xxviii. 18.)

THE ISMIAN CAR.

At this epoch, says François Lenormant, Professor of Archeology at the National Library of France, in his *Beginnings of History*, 1882, the Egyptian influence was no longer supreme in its sway over the Hebrews; that the Assyro-Babylonian influence balanced it; that the new Kerubim, then executed, may

(* From this point the article is from the pen of C. T. McClenachan.)

have been different from the ancient ones as described in Exodus; in fact, Kirubi after the Assyrian type, which formed a Merkâbâh (a chariot, 1 Chron. xxviii. 18), upon which Yahveh was seated. In the Egyptian monuments the gods are often represented between the forward-stretching wings of sparrow-hawks or

THE ARK OF PHILE.

vultures, placed face to face, and birds of this kind often enfold with their wings the divine Naos.

The adornment of the Tabernacle, as mentioned in Exodus, excluded every figure susceptible of an idolatrous character, which is far from being the case in what we know of the Temple of Solomon. In the matter of plastic images, none was admitted save only the Kerubim, which were not only placed upon the Ark, but whose representations are woven into the hangings of the Mishkân and the veil which separates the Holy Place from the Holy of Holies. It is therefore most probable that the Kerubim of Exodus were great eagles or birds—Kurubi—while under the remodeling by Solomon these were changed to Kirubi with human faces.

The prophet Ezekiel describes four hayyôth or Kerubim, two and two, back to back, and going "each one straight forward" toward the four quarters. The Kerubim of the Merkâbâh of Ezekiel have four wings—two lifted up and two covering their back—and four human faces set in pairs, to the right and to the left, one of a man, one of a bull, one of a lion, and one of an eagle—the faces of creatures which combine all the emblems of strength depicted by the Chaldeo-Assyrian bull. Ezekiel (Yehezqel) thus describes the Kerubim with several faces which, alternately with the palm-trees, decorated the frieze around the interior of the temple at Jerusalem: "Each Kerub had two faces, a man's face turned one way toward the palm-tree, and a lion's face turned the other way toward the other palm-tree; and it was in this wise all around the house."

The following information, furnished by Prof. Lenormant, on the subject of Cherubim, is important: "Deductions were formerly made from the Aryan theory to support primitive tradition as to origin and form, but these have been overthrown, and the Semitic interpretation made manifest through finding the name of the Kerubim in the cuneiform inscriptions; that in place of referring the Hebrew word *kerub* to the Aryan root *grabh*, 'to seize,' the word is more properly of Semitic origin, from the root *kârab*, signifying 'bull,' or a creature strong and powerful (כרובא). Referring to the prophet Ezekiel i. 10 and x. 14, the two parallel passages use the word *kerûb* interchangeably with *shor*, 'bull,' the 'face of a bull' and 'face of a cherub,' which are synonymous expressions. Since we have come to know those colossal images of winged bulls with human faces, crowned with the lofty cidaris, decorated with several pairs of horns, which flanked the gateways of the Assyrian palaces, a number of scholars, intimately acquainted with antique sculpture, have been zealous in associating them with the Kerubim of the Bible. . . . The winged bull with a human head figures in a bas-relief in the palace of Khorsabad as a favoring and protecting genius, which watches over the safe navigation of the transports that carry the wood of Lebanon by sea. The bulls whose images are placed at the gateways of the palaces and temples, as described in the above ideographic group, are the guardian genii, who are looked upon as living beings. As the result of a veritable magical operation, the supernatural creature is supposed to reside within these bodies of stone.'

In a bilingual document, Akkadian with an Assyrian version, we read invocations to the two bulls who flanked the gate of the infernal abode, which were no longer simulacra of stone, but living beings, like the bulls at the gates of the celestial palaces of the gods. The following is one of the unique expressions made in the ears of the bull which stands to the right of the bronze enclosure:

"Great Bull, most great Bull, stamping before the holy gates, he opens the interior; director of Abundance, who supports the god Nirba, he who gives their glory to the cultivated fields, my pure hands sacrifice toward thee."

Similar expressions were then made in the bull's left ear.

These genii, in the form of winged bulls with human countenances, were stationed as guardians at the portals of the edifices of Babylonia and Assyria, and were given the name of Kirubi; thus, *Kirubu damqu lippaqid*, "May the propitious Kirub guard." Numerous authorities may be given to show that the Chaldeo-Assyrians' Kirub, from the tenth to the fifth century before our era, whose name is identical with the Hebrew Kerub, was the winged bull with a human head. The Israelites, during the times of the Kings and the Prophets, pictured to themselves the Kerubim under this form.[*]

Chesed. A word which is most generally corrupted into Hesed. It is the Hebrew חסד, and signifies *mercy*. Hence, it very appropriately refers to that act of kindness and compassion which is commemorated in the degree of Select Master of the American system. It

---

[*] "The figures of the Cherubim are said to have defeated Dante's power of constructive imagination."

is the fourth of the Kabbalistic Sephiroth, and is combined in a triad with *Beauty* and *Justice.*

Chevalier. Employed by the French Masons as the equivalent of *Knight* in the name of any degree in which the latter word is used by English Masons, as *Chevalier du Soleil* for Knight of the Sun, or *Chevalier de l'Orient* for Knight of the East. The German word is *Ritter.*

Chibbelum. A significant word used in the rituals of the last century, which define it to mean "a worthy Mason." It is a corruption of *Giblim.*

Chicago, Congress of. A convention of distinguished Masons of the United States, held at the city of Chicago in September, 1859, during the session of the Grand Encampment and General Grand Chapter, for the purpose of establishing a General Grand Lodge, or a Permanent Masonic Congress. Its results were not of a successful character; and the death of its moving spirit, Cyril Pearl, which occurred soon after, put an end to all future attempts to carry into effect any of its preliminary proceedings.

Chief of the Tabernacle. The Twenty-third Degree in the Ancient and Accepted Scottish Rite. It commemorates the institution of the order of the priesthood in Aaron and his sons Eleazar and Ithamar. Its principal officers are three, a Sovereign Sacrificer and two High Priests, now called by the Supreme Councils of America the Most Excellent High Priest and Excellent Priests, and the members of the "Hierarchy" or "Court," as the Lodge is now styled, are called Levites. The apron is white, lined with deep scarlet and bordered with red, blue, and purple ribbon. A golden chandelier of seven branches is painted or embroidered on the center of the apron. The jewel, which is a thurible, is worn from a broad yellow, purple, blue, and scarlet sash from the left shoulder to the right hip.

Chief of the Twelve Tribes. (*Chef des douze Tribus.*) The Eleventh Degree of the Chapter of Emperors of the East and West. It is also called Illustrious Elect.

Chiefs of Masonry. A title formerly given in the Ancient and Accepted Scottish Rite to Princes of Jerusalem. It seems now to be more appropriate to Inspectors-General of the Thirty-third Degree.

Chili. Freemasonry was introduced into Chili, in 1841, by the Grand Orient of France. Lodges were subsequently organized in 1850 and 1851 by the Grand Lodges of Massachusetts and California. On the 24th of May, 1862, a Grand Lodge was formed.

China. Masonry was introduced into China by the Grand Lodge of England in the Eighteenth century. There are two District Grand Lodges under the Grand Lodge of England: 1. That of Hong Kong and South China with 7 Lodges. 2. That of Northern China with 11 Lodges. There are also Chapters and an Encampment of Knights Templars, under the English authority.

A secret society, akin to Masonry and indigenous to China, is the "Most Ancient Order of Suastica," or the Brotherhood of the Mystic Cross, said to have been founded 1027 B.C. by Fohi, and introduced into China 975 B.C. It contains three degrees: Apprentice Brothers, Tao Sze (or Doctors of Reason), and Grand Master. The Apprentice wears the *Jaina Cross*, worked on a blue silk ribbon; the Tao Sze wears a cross of silver; and the Grand Master one in gold. The meetings are called "Tents."

Chinese Classics and Symbolism. Mr. Giles, well versed in matters pertaining to Chinese literature, customs, and archeology, is the authority for stating that in the written language of the Chinese many curious expressions were in use seven hundred years before the Christian era, or only about two hundred years after the death of King Solomon, bearing close proximity to those used prominently in Masonry. The following quotation from the works of Mencius, the great disciple of Confucius, is given in illustration: "A Master Mason, in teaching his apprentices, makes use of the compasses and the square. Ye who are engaged in the pursuit of wisdom must also make use of the compasses and the square." These two words, "compasses" and "square," in the Chinese language represent "order, regularity, and propriety." Mr. Giles points out that in the oldest of the Chinese classics, "which embraces a period from the twenty-fourth to the seventh century before Christ, there are distinct allusions to this particular symbolism."

Chinese Secret Societies. In China, as in all other countries, secret societies have existed, such as the Tien-tee-whee, or Association of Heaven and Earth, and the Tien-lee, or Society of Celestial Reason. But the attempt to trace any analogy between them and Freemasonry is a mistaken one. These societies have in general been of a political character, with revolutionary tendencies, and as such, have been prohibited by the government, sometimes under the penalty of the death or banishment of their members. Their similarity to Masonry consists only in these points: that they have forms of initiation, an esoteric instruction, and secret modes of recognition. Beyond these all further resemblance fails.

Chisel. In the American Rite the chisel is one of the working tools of a Mark Master, and symbolizes the effects of education on the human mind. For as the artist, by the aid of this instrument, gives form and regularity to the shapeless mass of stone, so education, by cultivating the ideas and by polishing the rude thoughts, transforms the ignorant savage into the civilized being.

In the English ritual, the chisel is one of the working tools of the Entered Apprentice. With the same reference to the advantages of education. Preston (B. II., Sect. vi.) thus elaborates its symbolism as one of the implements of Masonry: "The chisel demonstrates the advantages of discipline and education. The mind, like the diamond in its original state, is unpolished; but as the effects of the chisel on the external coat soon present to view the latent beauties of the diamond, so education discovers the latent virtues of the mind and draws them forth to range the large field of matter and space, in order to display the summit of human knowledge, our duty to God and to man." (*Illustrations*, ed. 1812, p. 86, footnote.) But the idea is not original with Preston. It is found in Hutchinson, who, however, does not claim it as his own. It formed, most probably, a portion of the lectures of the period. In the French system, the chisel is placed on the tracing board of the ·Fellow-Craft as an implement with which to work upon and polish the Rough Ashlar. It has, therefore, there the same symbolic significa-tion.

Chivalry. The origin of chivalry is involved in very great obscurity. Almost every author who has written on this subject has adopted an hypothesis of his own. Some derive the institution from the equestrian order of ancient Rome, while others trace it to the tribes who, under the name of Northmen, about the ninth century, invaded the southern parts of Europe. Warburton ascribes the origin of chivalry to the Arabians; Pinkerton, Mallet, and Percy, to the Scandinavians. Clavel derives it from the secret societies of the Persians, which were the remains of the mysteries of Mithras. In Christendom, it gave rise to the orders of knighthood, some of which have been incorporated into the Masonic system. (See *Knighthood*.)

Christ, Order of. After the overthrow of the Order of Knights Templars throughout Europe, Dennis I., King of Portugal, in 1317 solicited of Pope John XXII. permission to re·establish the Order of the Temple in his dominions under the name of the Order of Christ, and to restore to it the possessions which had been wrested from the Templars. The Pope consented, approved the statutes which had been submitted to him, and, in 1319, confirmed the institution, reserving to himself and to his successors the right of creating knights, which has given rise to the pontifical branch of the Order which exists at Rome. The knights follow the rule of St. Benedict, and conform in all points to the statutes of the Order of the Temple. The Grand Mastership is vested in the King of Portugal, and the Order having been secularized in 1789, the members were divided into the three classes of six Grand Crosses, four hundred and fifty Commanders, and an unlimited number of knights. It was designated the Most Noble Order, and none but those *nobly descended*, of unsullied character, could be admitted. That the grandfather had been a mechanic was an impediment to the exaltation even of knights of the third class. The Grand Crosses and Commanders had generally valuable grants and great privileges; the latter were also enjoyed by the knights, with pensions with reversion to their wives.

Christianization of Freemasonry. The interpretation of the symbols of Freemasonry from a Christian point of view is a theory adopted by some of the most distinguished Masonic writers of England and this country, but one which I think does not belong to the ancient system. Hutchinson, and after him Oliver—profoundly philosophical as are the Masonic speculations of both—have, I am constrained to believe, fallen into a great error in calling the Master Mason's Degree a Christian institution. It is true that it embraces within its scheme the great truths of Christianity upon the subject of the immortality of the soul and the resurrection of the body; but this was to be presumed, because Freemasonry is truth, and all truth must be identical. But the origin of each is different; their histories are dissimilar. The principles of Freemasonry preceded the advent of Christianity. Its symbols and its legends are derived from the Solomonic Temple and from the people even anterior to that. Its religion comes from the ancient priesthood; its faith was that primitive one of Noah and his immediate descendants. If Masonry were simply a Christian institution, the Jew and the Moslem, the Brahman and the Buddhist, could not conscientiously partake of its illumination. But its universality is its boast. In its language citizens of every nation may converse; at its altar men of all religions may kneel; to its creed disciples of every faith may subscribe.

Yet it cannot be denied that since the advent of Christianity a Christian element has been almost imperceptibly infused into the Masonic system, at least among Christian Masons. This has been a necessity; for it is the tendency of every predominant religion to pervade with its influence all that surrounds it or is about it, whether religious, political, or social. This arises from a need of the human heart. To the man deeply imbued with the spirit of his religion, there is an almost unconscious desire to accommodate and adapt all the business and the amusements of life—the labors and the employments of his everyday existence—to the indwelling faith of his soul.

The Christian Mason, therefore, while acknowledging and appreciating the great doctrines taught in Masonry, and also while grateful that these doctrines were preserved in the bosom of his ancient Order at a time when they were unknown to the multitudes of the surrounding nations, is still anxious to give to them a Christian character; to invest them, in some measure, with the peculiarities of his own creed, and to bring the interpretation of their symbolism more nearly home to his own religious sentiments.

The feeling is an instinctive one, belonging to the noblest aspirations of our human nature; and hence we find Christian Masonic writers indulging in it to an almost unwarrantable excess, and, by the extent of their sectarian interpretations, materially affecting the cosmopolitan character of the Institution.

This tendency to Christianization has, in some instances, been so universal, and has prevailed for so long a period, that certain symbols and myths have been, in this way, so deeply and thoroughly imbued with the Christian element as to leave those who have not penetrated into the cause of this peculiarity, in doubt whether they should attribute to the symbol an ancient or a modern and Christian origin.

Chromatic Calendar. "The Five Points." In the great Temple, usually known as the Ocean Banner Monastery, at Honam, a suburb of Canton, China, we find four colossal idols occupying a large porch, each image being painted a different color. Ch'i-kwoh, who rules the north and grants propitious winds, is dark; Kwang-muh is red, and to him it is given to rule the south and control the fire, air, and water; To-man' rules the west, and grants or withholds rain, his color being white; while Chang-tsang, whose color is green, rules the winds and keeps them within their proper bounds, his supreme control being exercised over the east. The old custom of associating colors with the four quarters of the globe has probably led to the habit of describing the winds from these respective points as possessed of the same colors. The fifth, the earth, the central remaining point, still is conjectural. Thus, we also find in China a set of deities known as the five rulers; their colors, elements, and points may be thus represented:

1. Black. Water. North. Back.
2. Red. Fire. South. Breast.
3. Green. Wood. East. Mouth.
4. White. Metal. West. Knee.
5. Yellow. Earth. Middle. Foot.

These again are in turn associated with the planets, and the study of Chinese and Babylonian planet-colors is full of curious points of similarity.

BLACK, typifying the north, has two direct opponents in symbolic colors, and these are red and white. The first as implying ignorance arising from evil passions, the second indicating ignorance of mind. Red-black is called in Hebrew חם, *Heum*, from which comes Heume, *an enclosing* wall. Black from white, in Hebrew, is שהר, *sehher*, signifying *the dawn* of light to the mind of the Masonic profane. *The hand to back*, as the words of wisdom are about to be spoken.

In the Egyptian, the black Osiris appears at the commencement of the Funereal Ritual, representing the state of the soul which passes into the world of light. Anubis, one of the sons of Osiris, who weighs the soul in the scales of Amenti, and is the god of the dead, is black. The Conductor, or Master of Ceremonies, Thoth Psychopompe, has the head of the black Ibis. (See *Truth*.)

RED. In Hebrew, the fire of love, which burns in the south, is ארה, *are*, to burn. On Egyptian monuments, and in their temples, the flesh of men is painted red, and that of women, yellow. The same difference exists between the gods and goddesses, except where specially otherwise defined. Man's name in Hebrew signifies red, and as the image of fire is love, it is the universal tie of beings from *breast to breast*.

GREEN. ירק, *Irq*, viridis, verdure. רקיע, the firmament, also the winds. Green designates the beginning, the creation, the birth, as the world was called into being in the *wisdom of God by his word of mouth*, and Light was to appear in the *East*. Phtha was the Egyptian Creator of the world; he was at times represented with his flesh painted green, and holding a scepter of four colors, red, blue, green, and yellow: fire, air, water, and earth. The god Lunus, the Moon, in Hebrew ירה, *irhe*, is formed of one of the roots of green, signifying to found or set in order. Green is the symbol of Victory as well as Hope, in the symbolic colors. (See *Green*.)

WHITE. הור, *Heur*, to be white; הורים, *Heurim*, to be noble and pure. The Egyptian spirits of the dead were clothed in white, like the priests. Phtha, the creator and regenerator, was frequently robed in a white vestment, symbol of the egg from which he was born, enveloped in the white or albumen. The head of Osiris was draped in a white tunic. While the Chinese metaphorically represented Metal by this color, the Egyptians and Hebrews made it the symbol of Earth. Its reference to the West would imply the first point whereat the profane *bent the knee in supplication to the Deity*.

YELLOW. צהב, *Tseb*, gold color, designates a radiation of light, signifying to shine, to be resplendent. Man, or the male principle, symbolized by ardent fire, was represented by red, and the female principle, identified with the idea of light or flame, represented by yellow or light-colored earth, over which the *swift-footed messenger bears the tidings* of a Mason's distress and the return of obligatory succor. This light of the fire, the female of Divine beauty, the Egyptian Venus, was called Athor, signifying *dwelling of Horus*, and was thus represented.

Church, Freemasons of the. An Architectural College was organized in London, in the year 1842, under the name of "Freemasons of the Church for the Recovery, Maintenance, and Furtherance of the True Principles and Practice of Architecture." The founders announced their objects to be "the rediscovery of the ancient principles of architecture; the sanction of good principles of building, and the condemnation of bad ones; the exercise of scientific and experienced judgment in the choice and use of the most proper materials; the infusion, maintenance, and advancement of science throughout architecture; and eventually, by developing the powers of the College upon a just and beneficial footing, to reform the whole practice of architecture, to raise it from its present vituperated condition, and to bring around it the same unquestioned honor which is at present enjoyed by almost every other profession." (*The Builder*, vol. i., p. 23.)

One of their own members has said that "the title was not intended to express any conformity with the general body of Freemasons, but rather as indicative of the professed views of the College, namely, the recovery, maintenance, and furtherance of the free principles and practice of architecture." And that, in addition, they made it an object of their exertions to preserve or effect the restoration of architectural remains of antiquity threatened unnecessarily with demolition or endangered by decay. But it is evident, from the close connection of modern Freemasonry with the building guilds of the Middle Ages, that any investigations into the condition of medieval architecture must throw light on Masonic history.

Cipher Writing. Cryptography, or the art of writing in cipher, so as to conceal the meaning of what is written from all except those who possess the key, may be traced to remote antiquity. De la Guilletiere (*Lacedæmon*) attributes its origin to the Spartans, and Polybius says that more than two thousand years ago Æneas Tacitus had collected more than twenty different kinds of cipher which were then in use. Kings and generals communicated their messages to officers in distant provinces, by means of a preconcerted cipher; and the system has always been employed wherever there was a desire or a necessity to conceal from all but those who were entitled to the knowledge the meaning of a written document.

The Druids, who were not permitted by the rules of their Order to commit any part of their ritual to ordinary writing, preserved the memory of it by the use of the letters of the Greek alphabet. The Kabbalists concealed many words by writing them backward: a method which is still pursued by the French Masons. The old alchemists also made use of cipher writing, in order to conceal those processes the knowledge of which was intended only for the adepts. Thus Roger Bacon, who discovered the composition of gunpowder, is said to have concealed the names of the ingredients under a cipher made by a transposition of the letters.

Cornelius Agrippa tells us, in his *Occult Philosophy*, that the ancients accounted it unlawful to write the mysteries of God with those characters with which profane and vulgar things were written; and he cites Porphyry as saying that the ancients desired to conceal God, and divine virtues, by sensible figures which were visible, yet signified invisible things, and therefore delivered their great mysteries in sacred letters, and explained them by symbolical representations. Porphyry here, undoubtedly, referred to the invention and use of hieroglyphics by the Egyptian priests; but these hieroglyphic characters were in fact nothing else but a form of cipher intended to conceal their instructions from the uninitiated profane.

Peter Aponas, an astrological writer of the thirteenth century, gives us some of the old ciphers which were used by the Kabbalists, and among others one alphabet called "the passing of the river," which is referred to in some of the high degrees of Masonry.

But we obtain from Agrippa one alphabet in cipher which is of interest to Masons, and which he says was once in great esteem among the Kabbalists, but which has now, he adds, become so common as to be placed among profane things. He describes this cipher as follows (*Philos. Occult.*, lib. iii., cap. 3): The twenty-seven characters (including the finals) of the Hebrew alphabet were divided into three classes of nine in each, and these were distributed into nine squares, made by the intersection of two horizontal and two vertical lines, forming the following figure:

8	2	1
6	5	4
9	8	7

In each of these compartments three letters were placed; as, for instance, in the first compartment, the first, tenth, and nineteenth letters of the alphabet; in the second compartment, the second, eleventh, and twentieth, and so on. The three letters in each compartment were distinguished from each other by dots or accents. Thus, the first compartment, or ∟, represented the first letter, or א; the same compartment with a dot, thus, ∟·, represented the tenth letter, or י; or with two dots, thus, ∟··, it represented the nineteenth letter, or ק; and so with the other compartments; the ninth or last representing the ninth, eighteenth, and twenty-seventh letters, ט, צ, or ץ, accordingly as it was figured ⅂, ⅂· or ⅂··, without a dot in the center or with one or two.

About the middle of the last century, the French Masons adopted a cipher similar to this in principle, but varied in the details, among which was the addition of four compartments, made by the oblique intersection of two lines in the form of a St. Andrew's Cross. This cipher was never officially adopted by the Masons of any other country, but was at one time assumed by the American Royal Arch; although it is now becoming obsolete there. It is, however, still recognized in all the "Tuilleurs" of the French Rite. It has become so common as to be placed, as Agrippa said of the original scheme, "among profane things." Its use would certainly no longer subserve any purpose of concealment. Rockwell openly printed it in his *Ahiman Rezon of Georgia;* and it is often used by those who are not initiated, as a means of amusement.

There is, therefore, really no recognized cipher in use in Ancient Craft Masonry. Browne and Finch, who printed rituals intended only for the use of Masons, and not as expositions, invented ciphers for their own use, and supplied their initiated readers with the key. Without a key, their works are unintelligible, except by the art of the decipherer.

Although not used in symbolic Masonry, the cipher is common in the high degrees, of which there is scarcely one which has not its peculiar cipher. But for the purposes of concealment, the cipher is no longer of any practical use. The art of deciphering has been brought to so great a state of perfection that there is no cipher so complicated as to bid defiance for many hours to the penetrating skill of the experienced decipherer. Hence, the cipher has gone out of use in Masonry as it has among diplomatists, who are compelled to communicate with their respective countries by methods more secret than any that can be supplied by a dispatch written in cipher. Edgar A. Poe has justly said, in his story of *The Gold Bug,* that "it may well be doubted whether human ingenuity can construct an enigma of the kind, which human ingenuity may not, by proper application, resolve."

Cipriani, Jean Baptiste. (1727–85.) A famous Florentine artist, who came to England in 1755, and cooperated with Bartolozzi in the production of the frontispiece of the 1784 Edition of the *Book of Constitutions.*

Circle. The circle being a figure which returns into itself, and having therefore neither beginning nor end, has been adopted in the symbology of all countries and times as a symbol sometimes of the universe and sometimes of eternity. With this idea in the Zoroastrian mysteries of Persia, and frequently in the Celtic mysteries of Druidism, the temple of initiation was circular. In the obsolete lectures of the old English system, it was said that "the circle has ever been considered symbolical of the Deity; for as a circle appears to have neither beginning nor end, it may be justly considered a type of God, without either beginning of days or ending of years. It also reminds us of a future state, where we hope to enjoy everlasting happiness and joy." But whatever refers especially to the Masonic symbolism of the circle will be more appropriately contained in the article on the *Point within a Circle.*

Circles (Kränzchen). There are in Germany many small Masonic clubs, or Circles, which are formed in subordination to some Lodge which exercises a supervision over them and is responsible for their good behavior to the Grand Lodge, by whose permission they have been established. The members devote themselves to Masonic work, organize lectures, etc., and acquire a Masonic library. (*Ars Quatuor Coronatorum*, ix., 66.) [E. L. H.]

Circuit. Fort, in his *Early History and Antiquities of Freemasonry*, says: "Northern kings, immediately upon acceding to the throne, made a 'gait' or procession about their realms. According to the Scandinavian laws, when real property was sold, granted, or conveyed, the transfer of possession was incomplete until a circuit was made around the estate by the buyer and vendor, in which tour all the inhabitants of the nearest hamlet united. . . ."

"During the installation ceremonies of the Master of a Masonic Lodge, a procession of all the Craftsmen march around the room before the Master, to whom an appropriate salute is tendered. This Circuit is designed to signify that the new incumbent reduces the Lodge to his possession in this symbolic manner." (P. 320.)

Circular Temples. These were used in the initiations of the religion of Zoroaster. Like the square temples of Masonry, and the other mysteries, they were symbolic of the world; and the symbol was completed by making the circumference of the circle a representation of the zodiac. In the mysteries of Druidism also, the temples were sometimes circular.

Circumambulation, Rite of. Circumambulation is the name given by sacred archeologists to that religious rite in the ancient initiations which consisted in a formal procession around the altar, or other holy and consecrated object. The same Rite exists in Freemasonry.

In ancient Greece, when the priests were engaged in the rite of sacrifice, they and the people always walked three times round the altar while singing a sacred hymn. In making this procession, great care was taken to move in imitation of the course of the sun. For this purpose, they commenced at the east, and passing on by the way of the south to the west and thence by the north, they arrived at the east again.* By this means, as it will be observed, the right hand was always placed to the altar.†

This ceremony the Greeks called moving, ἐκ δεξίας εἰς δεξίαν, *from the right to the right*, which was the direction of the motion, and the Romans applied to it the term *dextrovorsum*, or *dextrorsum*, which signifies the same thing. Thus, Plautus (*Curcul.*, I., i., 70) makes Palinurus, a character in his comedy of *Curculio*, say: "If you would do reverence to the gods, you must turn to the right hand." *Si deos salutas dextroversum censeo.* Gronovius,

---

* The *strophe* of the ancient hymn was sung in going from the east to the west; the *antistrophe* in returning to the east, and the *epode* while standing still.

† "After this," says Potter, "they stood about the altar, and the priest, turning towards the right hand, went round it and sprinkled it with meal and holy water." (*Antiquities of Greece*, B. II., ch. iv., p. 206.)

---

in commenting on this passage of Plautus, says: "In worshiping and praying to the gods, they were accustomed to *turn to the right hand*."

A hymn of Callimachus has been preserved, which is said to have been chanted by the priests of Apollo at Delos, while performing this ceremony of circumambulation, the substance of which is "we imitate the example of the sun, and follow his benevolent course."

Among the Romans, the ceremony of circumambulation was always used in the rites of sacrifice, of expiation or purification. Thus, Virgil (*Æn.*, vi., 229) describes Corynæus as purifying his companions at the funeral of Misenus, by passing three times around them while aspersing them with the lustral waters; and to do so conveniently, it was necessary that he should have moved with his right hand toward them.

> *Idem ter socios pura circumtulit unda,*
> *Spargens rore levi et ramo felicis olivæ.*

That is:

> "Thrice with pure water compass'd he the crew,
> Sprinkling, with olive branch, the gentle dew."

In fact, so common was it to unite the ceremony of circumambulation with that of expiation or purification, or, in other words, to make a circuitous procession in performing the latter rite, that the term *lustrare*, whose primitive meaning is "to purify," came at last to be synonymous with *circumire*, to walk round anything, and hence a purification and a circumambulation were often expressed by the same word.

Among the Hindus, the same Rite of Circumambulation has always been practised. As an instance, we may cite the ceremonies which are to be performed by a Brahman, upon first rising from bed in the morning, an accurate account of which has been given by Mr. Colebrooke in the sixth volume of the *Asiatic Researches*. The priest having first adored the sun, while directing his face to the east, then walks toward the west by the way of the south, saying, at the same time, "I follow the course of the sun," which he thus explains: "As the sun in his course moves round the world by way of the south, so do I follow that luminary, to obtain the benefit arising from a journey round the earth by the way of the south."

Lastly, we may refer to the preservation of this Rite among the Druids, whose "mystical dance" around the *cairn*, or sacred stones, was nothing more nor less than the Rite of Circumambulation. On these occasions, the priest always made three circuits from east to west, by the right hand, around the altar or *cairn*, accompanied by all the worshipers. And so sacred was the rite once considered, that we learn from Toland (*Celt. Rel. and Learn.*, II., xvii.) that in the Scottish Isles, once a principal seat of the Druidical religion, the people "never come to the ancient sacrificing and fire-hallowing *cairns*, but they walk three times around them, from east to west, according to the course of the sun." This sanctified tour, or round by the south, he observes, is called *Deaseal*, as the contrary, or unhallowed one by the north, is called *Tuapholl*. And, he further remarks, that this word *Deaseal* was derived "from *Deas*, the *right* (understanding *hand*) and *soil*, one of the ancient names of the sun; the right hand in this round being ever next the heap."

This Rite of Circumambulation undoubtedly refers to the doctrine of sun-worship, because the circumambulation was always made around the sacred place, just as the sun was supposed to move around the earth; and although the dogma of sun-worship does not of course exist in Freemasonry, we find an allusion to it in the Rite of Circumambulation, which it preserves, as well as in the position of the officers of a Lodge and in the symbol of a point within a circle.

Circumspection. A necessary watchfulness is recommended to every man, but in a Mason it becomes a positive duty, and the neglect of it constitutes a heinous crime. On this subject, the *Old Charges* of 1722 (vi., 4) are explicit. "You shall be cautious in your words and carriage, that the most penetrating stranger shall not be able to discover or find out what is not proper to be imitated; and sometimes you shall divert a discourse and manage it prudently for the Honour of the Worshipful Fraternity." (*Constitutions*, 1723, p. 55.)

City of David. A section in the southern part of Jerusalem, embracing Mount Zion, where a fortress of the Jebusites stood, which David reduced, and where he built a new palace and city, to which he gave his own name.

City of the Great King. Jerusalem, so called in Psalm xlviii. 2, and by the Savior in Matt. v. 35.

Civilization and Freemasonry. Those who investigate in the proper spirit the history of Speculative Masonry will be strongly impressed with the peculiar relations that exist between the history of Masonry and that of civilization. They will find these facts to be patent: that Freemasonry has ever been the result of civilization; that in the most ancient times the spirit of Masonry and the spirit of civilization have always gone together; that the progress of both has been with equal strides; that where there has been no appearance of civilization there has been no trace of Masonry; and, finally, that wherever Masonry has existed in any of its forms, there it has been surrounded and sustained by civilization, which social condition it in turn elevated and purified.

Speculative Masonry, therefore, seems to have been a necessary result of civilization. It is, even in its primitive and most simple forms, to be found among no barbarous or savage people. Such a state of society has never been capable of introducing or maintaining its abstract principles of Divine truth.

But while Speculative Masonry is the result of civilization, existing only in its bosom and never found among barbarous or savage races,

it has, by a reactionary law of sociology, proved the means of extending and elevating the civilization to which it originally owed its birth. Civilization has always been progressive. That of Pelasgic Greece was far behind that which distinguished the Hellenic period of the same country. The civilization of the ancient world was inferior to that of the modern, and every century shows an advancement in the moral, intellectual, and social condition of mankind. But in this progress from imperfection to perfection the influence of those speculative systems that are identical with Freemasonry has always been seen and felt. Let us, for an example, look at the ancient heathen world and its impure religions. While the people of Paganism bowed, in their ignorance, to a many-headed god, or, rather, worshiped at the shrines of many gods, whose mythological history and character must have exercised a pernicious effect on the moral purity of their worshipers, Speculative Philosophy, in the form of the "Ancient Mysteries," was exercising its influence upon a large class of neophytes and disciples, by giving this true symbolic interpretation of the old religious myths. In the adyta of their temples in Greece and Rome and Egypt, in the sacred caves of India, and in the consecrated groves of Scandinavia and Gaul and Britain, these ancient sages were secretly divesting the Pagan faith of its polytheism and of its anthropomorphic deities, and were establishing a pure monotheism in its place, and illustrating, by a peculiar symbolism, the great dogmas—since taught in Freemasonry—of the unity of God and the immortality of the soul. And in modern times, when the religious thought of mankind, under a better dispensation, has not required this purification, Masonry still, in other ways, exerts its influence in elevating the tone of civilization; for through its working the social feelings have been strengthened, the amenities and charities of life been refined and extended, and, as we have had recent reason to know and see, the very bitterness of strife and the blood-guiltiness of war have been softened and oftentimes obliterated.

We then arrive at these conclusions, namely, that Speculative Masonry is a result of civilization, for it exists in no savage or barbarous state of society, but has always appeared with the advent in any country of a condition of civilization, "grown with its growth and strengthened with its strength"; and, in return, has proved, by a reactionary influence, a potent instrument in extending, elevating, and refining the civilization which gave it birth, by advancing its moral, intellectual, and religious character.

Clandestine. The ordinary meaning of this word is secret, hidden. The French word *clandestin*, from which it is derived, is defined by Boiste to be something "fait en cachette et contre les lois," done in a hiding-place and against the laws, which better suits the Masonic signification, which is *illegal*, *not authorized*. *Irregular* is often used for small departures from custom.

Clandestine Lodge. A body of Masons uniting in a Lodge without the consent of a Grand Lodge, or, although originally legally constituted, continuing to work after its charter has been revoked, is styled a "Clandestine Lodge." Neither Anderson nor Entick employ the word. It was first used in the *Book of Constitutions* in a note by Noorthouck, on page 239 of his edition. (*Constitutions*, 1784.) Irregular Lodge would be the better term.

Clandestine Mason. One made in or affiliated with a clandestine Lodge. With clandestine Lodges or Masons, regular Masons are forbidden to associate or converse on Masonic subjects.

Clare, Martin. A London schoolmaster and a celebrated Mason of England in the last century. He was a man of some distinction in literary circles, for he was a Fellow of the Royal Society. He was a Grand Steward in 1734, Junior Grand Warden in 1735, and in 1741, Deputy Grand Master. He was distinguished for zeal and intelligence in Masonry, and it has been pretty well established that he was the author of *A Defence of Masonry*, which was issued in 1730 in answer to Prichard's *Masonry Dissected*, and which was reproduced in the 1738 Edition of the *Constitutions*. (*Ars Quatuor Coronatorum*, vol. iv., 33–41.) He translated into English a work which had been published the preceding year, in Dublin, under the title of *Relation Apologique et Historique de la Société des Franc-Maçons*. In 1735, he delivered an address before the Grand Lodge, which was translated into French and German. He died in 1751. [E. L. H.]

Clarence, H. R. H. the Duke of, afterward King William IV., was initiated in Lodge 86, Plymouth, on March 9, 1796.

Classification of Masons. Oliver says, in his *Dictionary of Symbolical Masonry* (*s. v. Classes*), that ancient Masonic tradition informs us that the Speculative and Operative Masons who were assembled at the building of the Temple were arranged in nine classes, under their respective Grand Masters; viz., 30,000 Entered Apprentices, under their Grand Master Adoniram; 80,000 Fellow-Crafts, under Hiram Abif; 2,000 Mark Men, under Stolkyn; 1,000 Master Masons, under Mohabin; 600 Mark Masters, under Ghiblim; 24 Architects, under Joabert; 12 Grand Architects, under Adoniram; 45 Excellent Masons, under Hiram Abif; 9 Super-Excellent Masons, under Tito Zadok; besides the Ish Sabbal or laborers. The tradition is, however, rather apocryphal.

Clavel, F. T. Begue. An abbé. A French Masonic writer, who published, in 1842, a *Histoire Pittoresque de la Franc-Maçonnerie et des Sociétés Secrètes Anciennes et Modernes.* This work contains a great amount of interesting and valuable information, notwithstanding many historical inaccuracies, especially in reference to the Ancient Accepted Scottish Rite, of which the author was an adversary. For the publication of the work without authority he was suspended by the Grand Orient for two months, and condemned to pay a fine. Clavel appealed to the intelligence of the Fraternity against this sentence. In 1844, he commenced the publication of a Masonic Journal called the *Grand Orient*, the title of which he subsequently changed to the *Orient*. As he had not obtained the consent of the Grand Orient, he was again brought before that body, and the sentence of perpetual exclusion from the Grand Orient pronounced against him. Rebold says that it was the act of a faction, and obtained by unfair means. It was not sustained by the judgment of the Craft in France, with whom Clavel gained reputation and popularity. Notwithstanding the Masonic literary labors of Clavel, an account of the time of his birth, or of his death, appears to be obscure. His desire seemed to be to establish as history, by publication, those views which he personally entertained and formed; gathered from sources of doubtful character, he desired they should not be questioned in the future, *semel pro semper.*

Clay. See *Chalk, Charcoal, and Clay.*

Clay Ground. In the clay ground between Succoth and Zeredatha, Hiram Abif cast all the sacred vessels of the Temple, as well as the pillars of the porch. This spot was about thirty-five miles in a northeast direction from Jerusalem; and it is supposed that Hiram selected it for his foundry, because the clay which abounded there was, by its great tenacity, peculiarly fitted for making molds. The Masonic tradition on this subject is sustained by the authority of Scripture. (See 1 Kings vii. 46, and 2 Chron. iv. 17.) Morris, in his *Freemasonry in the Holy Land*, gives the following interesting facts in reference to this locality. "A singular fact came to light under the investigations of my assistant at Jerusalem. He discovered that the jewellers of that city, at the present day, use a particular species of *brown, arenaceous clay* in making moulds for casting small pieces in brass, etc. Inquiring whence this clay comes, they reply, 'From *Seikoot*, about two days' journey north-east of Jerusalem.' Here, then, is a satisfactory reply to the question, Where was the 'clay ground' of Hiram's foundries? It is the best matrix-clay existing within reach of Hiram Abif, and it is found only in 'the clay ground between Succoth and Zeredatha'; and considerable as was the distance, and extremely inconvenient as was the locality, so important did that master-workman deem it, to secure a sharp and perfect mould for his castings, that, as the Biblical record informs us, he established his furnaces there."

Clean Hands. Clean hands are a symbol of purity. The psalmist says "that he only shall ascend into the hill of the Lord, or shall stand in his holy place, who hath clean hands and a pure heart." Hence, the washing of the hands is an outward sign of an internal purification; and the psalmist says in another place, "I will wash my hands in innocence. And I will encompass thine altar, Jehovah." In the Ancient Mysteries the washing of the hands was always an introductory ceremony to the initiation; and, of course, it was used symbolically to indicate the necessity of purity from crime as a qualification of those who sought admission into the sacred rites; and hence, on a temple in the Island of Crete, this inscription was placed: "Cleanse your feet, wash your hands, and then enter." Indeed, the washing of hands, as symbolic of purity, was among the ancients a peculiarly religious rite. No one dared to pray to the gods until he had cleansed his hands. Thus, Homer makes Hector say:

"Χερσὶ δ' ἀνίπτοισιν Διὶ λείβειν αἴθοπα οἶνον
"Ἄζομαι."   (*Iliad*, vi., 266.)

"I dread with unwashed hands to bring
My incensed wine to Jove an offering."

In a similar spirit of religion, Æneas, when leaving burning Troy, refuses to enter the Temple of Ceres until his hands, polluted by recent strife, had been washed in the living stream.

"Me bello e tanto digressum et corde recenti,
Attrectare nefas, donec me flumine vivo
Abluero."   (*Æn.*, ii., 718.)

"In me, now fresh from war and recent strife,
'T is impious the sacred things to touch,
Till in the living stream myself I bathe."

The same practise prevailed among the Jews, and a striking instance of the symbolism is exhibited in that well-known action of Pilate, who, when the Jews clamored for Jesus that they might crucify him, appeared before the people, and, having taken water, washed his hands, saying at the same time, "I am innocent of the blood of this just man, see ye to it."

The white gloves worn by Masons as a part of their clothing, alluded to this symbolizing of clean hands; and what in some of the high degrees has been called "Masonic Baptism" is nothing else but the symbolizing, by a ceremony, this doctrine of clean hands as the sign of a pure heart.

Cleave. The word to cleave is twice used in Masonry, and each time in an opposite sense. First, in the sense of adhering, where the sentence in which it is employed is in the Past Master's Degree, and is taken from the 137th Psalm: "Let my tongue cleave to the roof of my mouth"; second, in the Master's Degree, where, in the expression "The flesh cleaves from the bone," it has the intransitive meaning of to separate, and is equivalent to "the flesh parts, or separates, itself from the bone." In this latter use the word is obsolete, and used only technically as a Masonic term.

Cleche. A cross charged with another of the same figure, but whose color is that of the field.

Clefts of the Rocks. The whole of Palestine is very mountainous, and these mountains abound in deep clefts or caves, which were anciently places of refuge to the inhabitants in time of war, and were often used as lurking places for robbers. It is, therefore, strictly in accordance with geographical truth that the statement, in relation to the concealment of certain persons in the clefts of the rocks, is made in the Third Degree. (See the latter part of the article *Caverns*.)

Clement XII. A Pope who assumed the pontificate on the 12th of August, 1730, and died on the 6th of February, 1740. On the 24th of April, 1738, he published his celebrated bull of excommunication, entitled *In Eminenti Apostolatus Specula*, in which we find these words: "For which reason the temporal and spiritual communities are enjoined, in the name of holy obedience, neither to enter the society of Freemasons, to disseminate its principles, to defend it, nor to admit nor conceal it within their houses or palaces, or elsewhere, under pain of excommunication *ipso facto*, for all acting in contradiction to this, and from which the pope only can absolve the dying." Clement was a bitter persecutor of the Masonic Order, and hence he caused his Secretary of State, the Cardinal Firrao, to issue on the 14th of January, 1739, a still more stringent edict for the Papal States, in which death and confiscation of property, without hope of mercy, was the penalty, or, as the original has it, "sotto Pena della morte, e confiscazione de beni da incorressi, irremissibilmente senz a speranza di grazia."

Clerks of Strict Observance. Known also as the Spiritual Branch of the Templars, or Clerici Ordinis Templarii. This was a schism from the Order or Rite of Strict Observance, and was founded by Starck in 1767. The members of this Rite established it as a rival of the latter system. They claimed a preeminence not only over the Rite of Strict Observance, but also over all the Lodges of ordinary Masonry, and asserted that they alone possessed the true secrets of the Order, and knew the place where the treasures of the Templars were deposited. (For a further history of this Rite, see *Starck*.) The Rite consisted of seven degrees, viz.: 1, 2, and 3. Symbolic Masonry. 4. Junior Scottish Mason, or Jungschotte. 5. Scottish Master, or Knight of St. Andrew. 6. Provincial Capitular of the Red Cross. 7. Magus, or Knight of Purity and Light. Clavel (*Histoire Pittoresque*, p. 186) gives different names to some of the degrees. This last was subdivided into five sections, as follows: I. Knight Novice of the third year. II. Knight Novice of the fifth year. III. Knight Novice of the seventh year. IV. Levite, and V. Priest. Ragon errs in calling this the Rite of Lax Observance.

Clermont, Chapter of. On the 24th of November, 1754, the Chevalier de Bonneville established in Paris a Chapter of the high degrees under this name, which was derived from the Jesuitical Chapter of Clermont. This society was composed of many distinguished persons of the court and city, who, disgusted with the dissensions of the Parisian Lodges, determined to separate from them. They adopted the Templar system, which had been created at Lyons, in 1743, and their Rite consisted at first of but six degrees, viz.: 1, 2, 3. St. John's Masonry. 4. Knight of the

11

Eagle. 5. Illustrious Knight or Templar. 6. Sublime Illustrious Knight. But soon after the number of these degrees was greatly extended. The Baron de Hund received the high degrees in this Chapter, and derived from them the idea of the Rite of Strict Observance, which he subsequently established in Germany.

Clermont, College of. A college of Jesuits in Paris, where James II., after his flight from England, in 1688, resided until his removal to St. Germains. During his residence there, he is said to have sought the establishment of a system of Freemasonry, the object of which should be the restoration of the House of Stuart to the throne of England. Relics of this attempted system are still to be found in many of the high degrees, and the Chapter of Clermont, subsequently organized in Paris, appears to have had some reference to it.

Clermont, Count of. Louis of Bourbon, prince of the blood and Count of Clermont, was elected by sixteen of the Paris Lodges perpetual Grand Master, for the purpose of correcting the numerous abuses which had crept into French Masonry. He did not, however, fulfil the expectations of the French Masons; for the next year he abandoned the supervision of the Lodges, and new disorders arose. He still, however, retained the Grand Mastership, and died in 1771, being succeeded by his nephew, the Duke of Chartres.

Clinton, De Witt. A distinguished statesman, who was born at Little Britain, New York, March 2, 1769, and died on the 11th of February, 1828. He entered the Masonic Order in 1793, and the next year was elected Master of his Lodge. In 1806, he was elevated to the position of Grand Master of the Grand Lodge of New York, and in 1814, to that of Grand Master of the Grand Encampment. In 1816, he was elected General Grand High Priest of the General Grand Chapter of the United States. In 1813, he became unwittingly complicated with the Spurious Consistory, established by Joseph Cerneau in the city of New York, but he took no active part in its proceedings, and soon withdrew from all connection with it. When the anti-Masonic excitement arose in this country in 1826, in consequence of the affair of William Morgan, whom the Masons were accused of having put to death, Mr. Clinton was Governor of the State of New York, and took all the necessary measures for the arrest of the supposed criminals. But, although he offered a liberal reward for their detection, he was charged by the anti-Masons with official neglect and indifference, charges which were undoubtedly false and malicious. Spenser, the special attorney of the State, employed for the prosecution of the offenders, went so far as to resign his office, and to assign, as a reason for his resignation, the want of sympathy and support on the part of the Executive. But all of the accusations and insinuations are properly to be attributed to political excitement, anti-Masonry having been adopted soon after its origin by the politicians as an engine for their advancement to office. Clinton was an honorable man and a true patriot. He was also an ardent and devoted Mason.

Closing. The duty of closing the Lodge is as imperative, and the ceremony as solemn, as that of opening; nor should it ever be omitted through negligence, nor hurried over with haste, but everything should be performed with order and precision, so that no brother shall go away dissatisfied. From the very nature of our Constitution, a Lodge cannot properly be adjourned. It must be closed either in due form, or the brethren called off to refreshment. But an adjournment on motion, as in other societies, is unknown to the Order. The Master can alone dismiss the brethren, and that dismission must take place after a settled usage. In Grand Lodges which meet for several days successively, the session is generally continued from day to day, by calling to refreshment at the termination of each day's sitting.

Clothed. A Mason is said to be properly clothed when he wears white leather gloves, a white apron, and the jewel of his Masonic rank. The gloves are now often, but improperly, dispensed with, except on public occasions. "No Mason is permitted to enter a Lodge or join in its labors unless he is properly clothed." Lenning, speaking of Continental Masonry, under the article *Kleidung* in his *Lexicon*, says that the clothing of a Freemason consists of apron, gloves, sword, and hat. In the York and American Rites, the sword and hat are used only in the degrees of chivalry. In the catechisms of the early eighteenth century the Master of a Lodge was described as clothed in a yellow jacket and a blue pair of breeches, in allusion to the brass top and steel legs of a pair of compasses. After the middle of the century, he was said to be "clothed in the old colors, viz., purple, crimson, and blue"; and the reason assigned for it was "because they are royal, and such as the ancient kings and princes used to wear." The actual dress of a Master Mason was, however, a full suit of black, with white neck-cloth, apron, gloves, and stockings; the buckles being of silver, and the jewels being suspended from a white ribbon by way of collar. (For the clothing and decorations of the different degrees, see *Regalia*.)

Clothing the Lodge. In the "General Regulations," approved by the Grand Lodge of England in 1721, it is provided in article seven that "Every *new* Brother at his making is decently to *cloath* the *Lodge*, that is, all the Brethren present; and to deposit something for the relief of indigent and decayed Brethren." By "clothing the Lodge" was meant furnishing the Brethren with gloves and aprons. The regulation no longer exists. It is strange that Oliver should have quoted as the authority for this usage a subsequent regulation of 1767. In Scotland this was practised in several Lodges to a comparatively recent date.

Clouded Canopy. See *Canopy, Clouded.*

Cloud, Pillar of. See *Pillars of Cloud and Fire*.

Cloudy. A word sometimes improperly used by the Wardens of a Lodge when reporting an unfavorable result of the ballot. The proper word is *foul*.

Clubs. The eighteenth century was distinguished in England by the existence of numerous local and ephemeral associations under the name of *clubs*, where men of different classes of society met for amusement and recreation. Each profession and trade had its club, and "whatever might be a man's character or disposition," says Oliver, "he would find in London a club that would square with his ideas." Addison, in his paper on the origin of clubs (*Spectator*, No. 9), remarks: "Man is said to be a social animal, and as an instance of it we may observe that we take all occasions and pretences of forming ourselves into those little nocturnal assemblies which are commonly known by the name of clubs. When a set of men find themselves agree in any particular, though never so trivial, they establish themselves into a kind of fraternity and meet once or twice a week, upon the account of such a fantastic resemblance." Hard drinking was characteristic of those times, and excesses too often marked the meetings of these societies. It was at this time that the Institution of Freemasonry underwent its revival commonly known as the revival of 1717, and it is not strange that its social character was somewhat affected by the customs of the day. The Lodges therefore assumed at that time too much of a convivial character, derived from the customs of the existing clubs and coteries; but the moral and religious principles upon which the Institution was founded prevented any undue indulgence; and although the members were permitted the enjoyment of decent refreshment, there was a standing law which provided against all excess.

Coat of the Tiler. In olden times it was deemed proper that the Tiler of a Lodge, like the beadle of a parish—whose functions were in some respects similar—should be distinguished by a tawdry dress. In a schedule of the regalia, records, etc., of the Grand Lodge of all England, taken at York in 1779, to be found in Hughan's *Masonic Sketches and Reprints* (p. 33), we find the following item: "a blue cloth coat with a red collar for the Tyler."

Cochleus. A very corrupt word in the Fourth Degree of the Scottish Rite; there said to signify *in the form of a screw*, and to be the name of the winding staircase which led to the middle chamber. The true Latin word is *cochlea*. But the matter is so historically absurd that the word ought to be and is rejected in the modern rituals.

Cock. The ancients made the cock a symbol of courage, and consecrated him to Mars, Pallas, and Bellona, deities of war. Some have supposed that it is in reference to this quality that the cock is used in the jewel of the Captain-General of an Encampment of Knights Templar.

Reghellini, however, gives a different ex- planation of this symbol. He says that the cock was the emblem of the sun and of life, and that as the ancient Christians allegorically deplored the death of the solar orb in Christ, the cock recalled its life and resurrection. The cock, we know, was a symbol among the early Christians, and is repeatedly to be found on the tombs in the catacombs of Rome. Hence it seems probable that we should give a Christian interpretation to the jewel of a Knights Templar as symbolic of the resurrection.

Cockade. Some few of the German Lodges have a custom of permitting their members to wear a blue cockade in the hat as a symbol of equality and freedom—a symbolism which, as Lenning says, it is difficult to understand, and the decoration is inappropriate as a part of the clothing of a Mason. Yet it is probable that it was a conception of this kind that induced Cagliostro to prescribe the cockade as a part of the investiture of a female candidate in the initiation of his Lodges. Clavel says the Venerable or Master of a French Lodge wears a black cockade.

Cockle-Shell. The cockle-shell was worn by pilgrims in their hats as a token of their profession; now used in the ceremonies of Templarism.

Cœtus. Latin. An assembly. It is incorrectly used in some old Latin Masonic diplomas for a Lodge. It is used by Laurence Dermott in a diploma dated September 10, 1764, where he signs himself "Sec. M. Cœtus," or Secretary of the Grand Lodge.

Coffin. In the Ancient Mysteries the aspirant could not claim a participation in the highest secrets until he had been placed in the Pastos, bed or coffin. The placing him in the coffin was called the symbolical death of the mysteries, and his deliverance was termed a raising from the dead. "The mind," says an ancient writer, quoted by Stobæus, "is affected in *death* just as it is in the *initiation* into the mysteries. And word answers to word, as well as thing to thing; for τελευτᾶν is *to die*, and τελεῖσθαι, *to be initiated*." The coffin in Masonry is found on tracing boards of the early part of the last century, and has always constituted a part of the symbolism of the Third Degree, where the reference is precisely the same as that of the Pastos in the Ancient Mysteries.

Cohen. כהן. A Hebrew word signifying a priest. The French Masonic writers, indulging in a Gallic custom of misspelling all names derived from other languages, universally spell it *coën*.

Cohens, Elected. See *Paschalis, Martinez*.

Cole, Benjamin. He published at London, in 1728, and again in 1731, the *Old Constitutions*, engraved on thirty copper plates, under the title of *A Book of the Ancient Constitutions of the Free and Accepted Masons*. In 1751, Cole printed a third edition with the title of *The Ancient Constitutions and Charges of Freemasons, with a true representation of their noble Art in several Lectures or Speeches*.

Subsequent editions were published up to 1794. Bro. Richard Spencer, the well-known Masonic bibliographer, says that Cole engraved his plates from a MS. which he calls the *Constitutions of 1726*, or from a similar MS. by the same scribe. Bro. Hughan published in 1869 in his *Constitutions of the Freemasons*, in a limited edition of seventy copies, a lithograph facsimile of the 1729 Edition of Cole, and in 1897 a facsimile of the 1731 Edition, which was limited to 200 copies, was published by Mr. Richard Jackson of Leeds, with an introduction by Bro. Hughan.

Cole, Samuel. He was at one time the Grand Secretary of the Grand Lodge of Maryland, and the author of a work entitled *The Freemason's Library, or General Ahiman Rezon*, the first edition of which appeared in 1817, and the second in 1826. It is something more than a mere monitor or manual of the degrees, and greatly excels in literary pretensions the contemporary works of Webb and Cross.

Cole's Manuscript. The MS. from which Cole is supposed to have made his engraved *Constitutions*, now known as the Spencer MS. It was in the possession of Bro. Richard Spencer, who published it in 1871, under the title of *A Book of the Ancient Constitutions of the Free and Accepted Masons. Anno Dom., 1726.* The subtitle is *The Beginning and First Foundation of the Most Worthy Craft of Masonry, with the charges thereunto belonging.* In 1875 it was bought by Mr. E. T. Carson of Cincinnati, U. S. A.

Collar. An ornament worn around the neck by the officers of Lodges, to which is suspended a jewel indicative of the wearer's rank. The color of the collar varies in the different grades of Masonry. That of a symbolic Lodge is blue; of a Past Master, purple; of a Royal Arch Mason, scarlet; of a Secret Master, white bordered with black; of a Perfect Master, green, etc. These colors are not arbitrary, but are each accompanied with a symbolic signification.

In the United States, the collar worn by Grand Officers in the Grand Lodge is, properly, purple edged with gold. In the Grand Lodge of England, the Grand Officers wear chains of gold or metal gilt instead of collars, but on other occasions, collars of ribbon, garter blue, four inches broad, embroidered or plain.

The use of the collar in Masonry, as an official decoration, is of very old date. It is a regulation that its form should be triangular; that is, that it should terminate on the breast in a point. The symbolical reference is evident. The Masonic collar is derived from the practises of heraldry; collars are worn not only by municipal officers and officers of State, but also by knights of the different orders as a part of their investiture.

College. The regular Convocation of the subordinate bodies of the Society of Rosicrucians is called an Assemblage of the College, at which their mysteries are celebrated by initiation and advancement, at the conclusion of which the Mystic Circle is broken.

Colleges, Irish. These were established in Paris between 1730 and 1740, and were rapidly being promulgated over France, when they were superseded by the Scottish Chapters.

Colleges, Masonic. There was at one time a great disposition exhibited by the Fraternity of the United States to establish colleges, to be placed under the supervision of Grand Lodges. The first one ever endowed in this country was that at Lexington, in Missouri, established by the Grand Lodge of that State, in October, 1841, which for some time pursued a prosperous career. Other Grand Lodges, such as those of Kentucky, Mississippi, Arkansas, North Carolina, Florida, and a few others, subsequently either actually organized or took the preliminary steps for organizing Masonic colleges in their respective jurisdictions. But experience has shown that there is an incongruity between the official labors of a Grand Lodge as the Masonic head of the Order, and the superintendence and support of a college. Hence, these institutions have been very generally discontinued, and the care of providing for the education of indigent children of the Craft has been wisely committed to the subordinate Lodges.

The late Thomas Brown, the distinguished Grand Master of Florida, thus expressed the following correct views on this subject:

"We question if the endowment of colleges and large seminaries of learning, under the auspices and patronage of Masonic bodies, be the wisest plan for the accomplishment of the great design, or is in accordance with the character and principles of the Fraternity. Such institutions savor more of pageantry than utility; and as large funds, amassed for such purposes, must of necessity be placed under the control and management of comparatively few, it will have a corrupting influence, promote discord, and bring reproach upon the Craft. The principles of Masonry do not sympathize with speculations in stock and exchange brokerage. Such, we fear, will be the evils attendant on such institutions, to say nothing of the questionable right and policy of drawing funds from the subordinate Lodges, which could be appropriated by their proper officers more judiciously, economically, and faithfully to the accomplishment of the same great and desirable object in the true Masonic spirit of charity, which is the bond of peace."

Collegia Artificum. Colleges of Artificers. (See *Roman Colleges of Artificers*.)

Collegium. In Roman jurisprudence, a collegium, or college, expressed the idea of several persons united together in any office or for any common purpose. It required not less than three to constitute a college, according to the law maxim, "Tres faciunt collegium" (Three make a college), and hence, perhaps, the Masonic rule that not fewer than three Master Masons can form a Lodge.

Collocatio. The Greek custom of exposing the corpse on a bier over night, near the threshold, that all might be convinced of the normal death.

Cologne, Cathedral of. The city of Cologne, on the banks of the Rhine, is memorable in the history of Freemasonry for the connection of its celebrated Cathedral with the labors of the Steinmetzen of Germany, whence it became the seat of one of the most important Lodges of that period. It has been asserted that Albertus Magnus designed the plan, and that he there also altered the Constitution of the Fraternity, and gave it a new code of laws. It is at least clear that in this Cathedral the symbolic principles of Gothic architecture, the distinguishing style of the Traveling Freemasons, were carried out in deeper significance than in any other building of the time. Whether the document known as the *Charter of Cologne* be authentic or not, and it is fairly well established that it is not, the fact that it is claimed to have emanated from the Lodge of that place, gives to the Cathedral an importance in the views of the Masonic student.

The Cathedral of Cologne is one of the most beautiful religious edifices in the world, and the vastest construction of Gothic architecture. The primitive Cathedral, which was consecrated in 873, was burned in 1248. The present one was commenced in 1249, and the work upon it continued until 1509. But during that long period the labors were often interrupted by the sanguinary contests which raged between the city and its archbishops, so that only the choir and the chapels which surrounded it were finished. In the eighteenth century it suffered much from the ignorance of its own canons, who subjected it to unworthy mutilations, and during the French Revolution it was used as a military depot. In 1820, this edifice, ravaged by men and mutilated by time, began to excite serious anxieties for the solidity of its finished portions. The *débris* of the venerable pile were even about to be overthrown, when archeologic zeal and religious devotion came to the rescue. Societies were formed for its restoration by the aid of permanent subscriptions, which were liberally supplied; and it was resolved to finish the gigantic structure according to the original plans which had been conceived by Gerhard de Saint Trond, the ancient master of the works. The works were renewed under the direction of M. Zwiner. The building is now completed; Mr. Seddon says (*Ramb. on the Rhine*, p. 16), "It is without question, one of the most stupendous structures ever conceived."

There is a story, that may be only a tradition, that there was a book written by Albertus Magnus called *Liber Constructionum Alberti*, which contained the secrets of the Operative Masons, and particularly giving directions of how to lay the foundations of cathedrals.

Even though these builders had a special treatise on laying the foundations of cathedrals, they had not made provision for inventions which came later. It has been shown that lately the foundations of the Cathedral were being loosened by the constant shaking from the railway trains that now run near, so that they became unsafe and seriously threatened the destruction of this wonderful masterpiece of Gothic architecture. The German Government came to the relief and saved the structure.   [E. E. C.]

Cologne, Charter of. This is an interesting Masonic document, originally written in Latin, and purporting to have been issued in 1535. Its history, as given by those who first offered it to the public, and who claim that it is authentic, is as follows: From the year 1519 to 1601, there existed in the city of Amsterdam, in Holland, a Lodge whose name was Het Vredendall, or The Valley of Peace. In the latter year, circumstances caused the Lodge to be closed, but in 1637 it was revived, by four of its surviving members, under the name of Frederick's Vredendall, or Frederick's Valley of Peace. In this Lodge, at the time of its restoration, there was found a chest, bound with brass and secured by three locks and three seals, which, according to a protocol published on the 29th of January, 1637, contained the following documents:

1. The original warrant of constitution of the Lodge Het Vredendall, written in the English language. 2. A roll of all the members of the Lodge from 1519 to 1601. 3. The original charter given to the Brotherhood at the city of Cologne, and which is now known among Masonic historians as the Charter of Cologne.

It is not known how long these documents remained in possession of the Lodge at Amsterdam. But they were subsequently remitted to the charge of Bro. James Van Vasner, Lord of Opdem, whose signature is appended to the last attestation of The Hague register, under the date of the 2d of February, 1638. After his death, they remained among the papers of his family until 1790, when M. Walpenaer, one of his descendants, presented them to Bro. Van Boetzelaer, who was then the Grand Master of the Lodges of Holland. Subsequently they fell into the hands of some person whose name is unknown, but who, in 1816, delivered them to Prince Frederick.

There is a story that the Prince received these documents accompanied by a letter, written in a female hand, and signed "C., child of V. J." In this letter the writer states that she had found the documents among the papers of her father, who had received them from Mr. Van Boetzelaer. It is suspected that the authoress of the letter was the daughter of Bro. Van Jeylinger, who was the successor of Van Boetzelaer as Grand Master of Holland.

There is another version of the history which states that these documents had long been in the possession of the family of Wassenaer Van Opdem, by a member of which they were presented to Van Boetzelaer, who subsequently gave them to Van Jeylinger, with strict injunctions to preserve them until the restitution of the Orange regency. The originals are now, or were very lately, deposited in the archives of a Lodge at Namur, on the Meuse; but copies of the charter were given to the Fraternity under the following circumstances:

In the year 1819, Prince Frederick of Nassau, who was then the Grand Master of the National Grand Lodge of Holland, contemplating a reformation in Masonry, addressed a circular on this subject to all the Lodges under his jurisdiction, for the purpose of enlisting them in behalf of his project, and accompanied this circular with copies of the charter, which he had caused to be taken in facsimile, and also of the register of the Amsterdam Lodge, Valley of Peace, to which I have already referred as contained in the brass-mounted chest. A transcript of the charter in the original Latin, with all its errors, was published, in 1818, in the *Annales Maçonniques*. The document was also presented to the public in a German version, in 1819, by Dr. Fred. Heldmann; but his translation has been proved, by Lenning and others, to be exceedingly incorrect. In 1821, Dr. Krause published it in his celebrated work entitled *The Three Oldest Masonic Documents*. It has been frequently published since in a German translation, in whole or in part, but is accessible to the English reader only in Burnes' *Sketch of the History of the Knights Templars* (London, 1840); in the English translation of Findel's *History of Freemasonry*, and in the *American Quarterly Review of Freemasonry*, where it was published with copious notes by the author of the present work. P. J. Schouten, a Dutch writer on the history of Freemasonry, who had undoubtedly seen the original document, describes it as being written on parchment in Masonic cipher, in the Latin language, the characters uninjured by time, and the subscription of the names not in cipher, but in the ordinary cursive character. The Latin is that of the Middle Ages, and is distinguished by many incorrectly spelled words, and frequent grammatical solecisms. Thus, we find "bagistri" for "magistri," "trigesimo" for "tricesimo," "ad nostris ordinem" for "ad nostrum ordinem," etc.

Of the authenticity of this document, it is but fair to say that there are well-founded doubts among many Masonic writers. The learned antiquaries of the University of Leyden have testified that the paper on which the register of the Lodge at The Hague is written, is of the same kind that was used in Holland at the commencement of the seventeenth century, which purports to be its date, and that the characters in which it is composed are of the same period. This register, it will be remembered, refers to the Charter of Cologne as existing at that time; so that if the learned men of Leyden have not been deceived, the fraud—supposing that there is one in the charter—must be more than two centuries old.

Dr. Burnes professes to have no faith in the document, and the editors of the *Hermes* at once declare it to be surreptitious. But the condemnation of Burnes is too sweeping in its character, as it includes with the charter all other German documents on Freemasonry; and the opinion of the editors of the *Hermes* must be taken with some grains of allowance, as they were at the time engaged in a controversy with the Grand Master of Holland, and in the defense of the high degrees, whose claims to antiquity this charter would materially impair. Dr. Oliver, on the other hand, quotes it unreservedly, in his *Landmarks*, as an historical document worthy of credit; and Reghellini treats it as authentic. In Germany, the Masonic authorities of the highest reputation, such as Heldermann, Morsdorf, Kloss, and many others, have repudiated it as a spurious production, most probably of the beginning of the present century. Kloss objects to the document, that customs are referred to in it that were not known in the rituals of initiation until 1731; that the higher degrees were nowhere known until 1725; that none of the eighteen copied documents have been found; that the declaimer against Templar Masonry was unnecessary in 1535, as no Templar degrees existed until 1741; that some of the Latin expressions are not such as were likely to have been used; and a few other objections of a similar character. Bobrik, who published, in 1840, the *Text, Translation, and Examination of the Cologne Document*, also advances some strong critical arguments against its authenticity. On the whole, the arguments to disprove the genuineness of the charter appear to be very convincing, and are strong enough to throw at least great doubt upon it as being anything else but a modern forgery. [See Gould's *History of Freemasonry* (i., 496), where the question of the authenticity of the document is examined, and it is classed among Apocryphal Manuscripts.—E. L. H.]

Cologne, Congress of. A Congress which is said to have been convened in 1525, by the most distinguished Masons of the time, in the city of Cologne, as the representatives of nineteen Grand Lodges, who are said to have issued the celebrated manifesto, in defense of the character and aims of the Institution, known as the Charter of Cologne. Whether this Congress was ever held is a moot point among Masonic writers, most of them contending that it never was, and that it is simply an invention of the early part of the present century. (See *Cologne, Charter of.*)

Colonial Lodges. Lodges in the colonies of Great Britain are under the immediate supervision and jurisdiction of District Grand Lodges, to which title the reader is referred.

Colorado. Freemasonry was introduced into the territory of Colorado in 1860, in which year the Grand Lodge of Kansas chartered Golden City Lodge at Golden City. In 1861 two other Lodges, Rocky Mountain at Gold Hill and Summit Lodge at Parkville, were chartered by the Grand Lodge of Nebraska. On August 2, 1861, representatives from these three Lodges met in convention at Golden City, and organized the Grand Lodge of Colorado, the Grand East of which was placed at Denver. J. M. Chivington was elected first Grand Master. Chapters of Royal Arch Masons and a Commandery of Knights Templar were subsequently introduced.

Colored Fraternities. The secret societies of negroes claiming to be Masonic are quite extensive, embracing Grand Lodges in practically every State. (See *Negro Masonry*.)

Colors, Symbolism of. Wemyss, in his *Clavis Symbolica*, says: "Color, which is outwardly seen on the habit of the body, is symbolically used to denote the true state of the person or subject to which it is applied, according to its nature." This definition may appropriately be borrowed on the present occasion, and applied to the system of Masonic colors. The color of a vestment or of a decoration is never arbitrarily adopted in Freemasonry. Every color is selected with a view to its power in the symbolic alphabet, and it teaches the initiate some instructive moral lesson, or refers to some important historical fact in the system.

Frederic Portal, a French archeologist, has written a valuable treatise on the symbolism of colors, under the title of *Des Couleurs Symboliques dans l'antiquite, le moyen âge et les temps modernes*, which is well worth the attention of Masonic students. The Masonic colors are seven in number, namely: 1, blue; 2, purple; 3, red; 4, white; 5, black; 6, green; 7, yellow; 8, violet. (See those respective titles.)

Columbia, District of. The Grand Lodge of the District of Columbia was organized December 11, 1810, by Lodges having warrants from Maryland and Virginia, and Valentine Reintzel was elected Grand Master. It has 27 Lodges under it. The Grand Chapter formed, originally, a component part of the Grand Chapter of Maryland and the District of Columbia; but the connection was dissevered in 1867, and an independent Grand Chapter formed, which has now five Chapters under its jurisdiction. There is neither a Grand Commandery nor Grand Council in the Territory, but several Commanderies subordinate to the Grand Encampment of the United States and a Council of Royal and Select Masters chartered by the Grand Council of Massachusetts. The Scottish Rite has also been successfully cultivated, and there are in operation a Lodge of Perfection and a Chapter of Rose Croix.

Column. A round pillar made to support as well as to adorn a building, whose construction varies in the different orders of architecture. In Masonry, columns have a symbolic signification as the supports of a Lodge, and are known as the Columns of Wisdom, Strength, and Beauty. The broken column is also a symbol in Masonry. (See the titles *Supports of the Lodge* and *Broken Column*.)

Comacine Masters. It has long been a theory of some writers, secular and Masonic, that there was a direct succession of the operative gilds from the Roman Colleges to those who merged into Speculative Masonry in 1717, and as investigation proceeded, the proofs became stronger and stronger until now it can no longer reasonably be doubted. At first it was not attempted to prove the succession, it was only inferred, but recently more careful investigators have come to view, whose results go far in establishing the direct succession from Roman Colleges to Speculative Masonry.

The principal purpose of this article is to put a link in the chain of operative gilds and establish a continuous connection from the oldest gild formation (Roman Colleges, which see) through the Lombard period and Renaissance to the formation of Speculative Masonry by the English gilds.

Before beginning the description of the Comacine Masters, which, from the controversial character of the subject, must of necessity be kindred to a discussion resting heavily on citations and quoted authorities who have worked in this special field, it will be necessary to draw a fair picture of the Roman possessions and civilization at this period.

When Rome had passed the zenith of her power and had begun to decline from internal and external causes, it is but natural to suppose that her neighboring enemies noticed this, and as they had long looked upon Italy with avaricious eyes, felt the time had arrived for them to attain what they had most desired. The year 476 A.D., when the last of the nominal Cæsars ceased to rule in the West, is usually taken by historians as marking the fall of the Roman Empire. However true that may be, the falling began when Constantine established the seat of his empire at Constantinople, in 327, and drew much strength from Rome, thereby making it easier for the Vandals and Goths to renew their attacks. For five centuries horde after horde of barbarians flung themselves against the Roman frontiers, each striking deeper than the last, and being repelled with greater and greater difficulty, the Empire sinking beneath internal decay more than from her external enemies.

When the Western Empire ceased in the fifth century and Europe was plunged into what has been called "The Dark Ages" and all progress in letters and the arts of peace is supposed to have ceased, it is refreshing to quote what John Fiske said in *Old and New Ways of Treating History*, when speaking of that period: "In truth the dull ages which no Homer has sung or Tacitus described, have sometimes been critical ages for human progress. . . . This restriction of the views to literary ages has had much to do with the popular misconception of the 1,000 years that elapsed between the reign of Theodoric the Great and the Discovery of America. For many reasons that period might be called the Middle Ages; but the popular mind is apt to lump these ten centuries together, as if they were all alike, and apply to them the misleading epithet 'Dark Ages.' A portion of the darkness is in the minds of those who use the epithet."

I, also, wish to take exception to their position and conclusions, for in the success of my exceptions lies the potency and possibility of my subject, the Comacine Masters, who lived and built at this period, having descended from branches of the Roman Colleges of Artificers who had come to Como as colonists or had fled to this free republic for safety during barbaric invasions, creating and developing what is called Lombard architecture, and forming a powerful gild which later not only influenced, but had a connection with the gilds of France and Germany at the Renaissance, thereby establishing a direct line of descent of Roman Colleges to the operative gilds that grew into Speculative Masonry.

It can be understood how a tribe or a small section of people may, from various causes, recede in letters, science and civilization, but how the world could do so is difficult to comprehend, yet the historians and literature attempted to confirm this in describing the "gloom when the sun of progress was in a total or partial eclipse from the fifth to the twelfth centuries," or, between the period of ancient Classic Art of Rome and that early rise of Art in the twelfth century, which led to the Renaissance. Leder Scott says that "this hiatus is supposed to be a time when Art was utterly dead and buried, its corpse in Byzantine dress lying embalmed in its tomb at Ravenna. But all death is nothing but the germ of new life. Art was not a corpse; it was only a seed laid in Italian soil to germinate and it bore several plants before the great reflowering period of the Renaissance."

Those who produced these several plants which it bore before the great Cathedral Building period that followed the Renaissance, will furnish the subject of this article, and trust it will be as interesting and important to the Masonic student as it is new in the literature of Masonry.

Most things will, I trust, become more and more clear as we follow up the traces of the Comacine Gild from the chrysalis state, in which Roman Art hibernated during the dark winter of the usually called Dark Ages, as Scott says "through the grub state of the Lombard period to the glorious winged flight of the full Gothic of the Renaissance."

Many historians, Masonic and profane, who wrote as long as a generation ago, are inclined to give the impression that there was but little or nothing that transpired during the so-called Dark Ages which was essential to the world's progress at the time, or worthy of contemplation at present. Had their views of the importance of historical matter prevailed, we would now know very little of what transpired from the Fall of the Western part of the Roman Empire to the Renaissance. We know that many cities in Italy were rebuilt after they had been sacked and partly destroyed by the Goths and Huns. Many cathedrals were built during this period, some of which work lasts till to-day, and is worthy workmanship. The historical architects have approached this period from another angle and the results of their efforts now make this article possible and open up a new and important field for Masonic students.

Toward the end of the fifth century a new wave of barbaric invasions swept over the West. North and East Gaul—all not previously held by the Visigoths—fell into the hands of the Franks (486). Theodoric and the Ostrogoths wrested Italy from Odoacer and established the Ostrogothic Kingdom in Italy, with its capital at Ravenna. This kingdom was established and governed on exceptionally enlightened lines. Theodoric, often called The Great, was the most broad-minded and advanced of all the German conquerors. He was a man of culture, yet some have said that he could not read. He had been educated from his eighth to his eighteenth year at Constantinople. His rule was, therefore, more like the revival of Roman ideas than a barbarous conquest. Accordingly we need not be surprised to find him decorating his capital city, Ravenna, during the period of his occupation, (493–526) with a series of monuments which, although strongly tinctured with Byzantine influence, yet constitute, perhaps, the finest examples we possess of the early Christian style. Theodoric was an Aryan and opposed to the Bishop of Rome. This fact and his education at Constantinople are sufficient to explain the strong Byzantine elements so noticeable even in those monuments at Ravenna, which antedate the Byzantine conquest. Charles A. Cummings in his *History of Architecture in Italy* says: "One of the earliest acts of Theodoric after his accession to the throne was the appointment of an architect to have charge of all the public buildings—including the aqueducts and the city walls—of Ravenna and Rome, putting at his disposal for this purpose, yearly, twelve hundred pounds of gold, two hundred and fifty thousand bricks, and the income of the Lucrine Haven. A remarkable letter from Theodoric to this official on his appointment is preserved by Cassiodorus, who was the minister of the Empire. 'These excellent buildings,' he says, 'are my delight. They are the noble image of the power of the Empire, and bear witness to its grandeur and glory. The palace of the sovereign is shown to ambassadors as a monument worthy of their admiration, and seems to declare to them his greatness. It is then a great pleasure for an enlightened prince to inhabit a palace where all the perfections of art are united, and to find there relaxation from the burden of public affairs. . . . I give you notice that your intelligence and talents have determined me to confide to your hands the care of my palace. It is my wish that you preserve in its original splendor all which is ancient, and that whatever you add to it may be conformable to it in style. It is not a work of small importance which I place in your hands, since it will be your duty to fulfill by your art the lively desire which I feel to illustrate my reign by many new edifices; so that whether the matter in hand be the rebuilding of a city, the construction of new castles, or the building of a Pretorium, it will be for you to translate my projects into accomplished realities. And this is a service highly honorable and worthy of any man's ambition:—to leave to future ages the monuments which shall be the admiration of new generations of men. It will be your duty to direct the mason, the sculptor, the painter, the worker in stone, in bronze, in plaster, in mosaic. What they know not, you will teach them. The difficulties which they find in their work, you will solve for them. But behold what various knowledge you must possess, thus to instruct artificers of so many sorts. But if you can direct their work to a good and satisfactory end, their success will be your eulogy, and will form the most abundant and flattering reward you could desire.' "

From this it may be seen that an architect of those days was a complete Master of the art of building. He was required to be able to construct a building from foundation to roof and also to be able to decorate it with sculpture and painting, mosaics and bronzes. This broad education prevailed in all the schools or Lodges up to 1335, when the painters seceded, which was followed by other branches separating themselves into distinct gilds.

It is a well-known fact that when the barbarians were sacking and carrying away the riches of many Italian cities and particularly of Rome, people fled to more secure places for the better protection of their lives and property. Of the various places to which they fled only one interests us in this article. Como was a free republic and many fled there for the protection it afforded. Rome had previously colonized many thousands in Como before the Christian Era. (See *Como*.)

The first we hear of the Comacines was that they were living on an island called Isola Comacina in Lake Como, that most beautiful of lakes. They were so well fortified that it was years before the island was captured and then only by treachery. Their fortifications and buildings were similar to those built by the Colleges of Artificers at Rome, which gave rise to the belief that they were the direct descendants from these Roman builders, who had built for the Roman Empire for several centuries.

In offering the form of building as best evidence of the descent of the Comacines from the Roman Colleges, it is appreciated how recorded literature, which is usually the word and opinions of one person, can be biased, changed and often wrong. But all who have studied a people in their social, political or religious aspects, know how permanent these things are and how subject to slow changes. Their forms of dress, songs, folk-lore and language undergo changes but slowly, climate, unsuccessful wars and amalgamation proving the most disastrous. But probably none of these change so slowly as forms of building, unless the latter be subjected to a marked change of climate from migration. Architecture is one of the noblest and most useful of arts and one of the first to attract the attention of barbarous people when evoluting into a higher civilization, and is at all times an accurate measure of a people's standing in civilization.

A law we learn from biology in the morphology of animals is that nature never makes a new organ when she can modify an old one so as to perform the required functions. New styles of architecture do not spring from human intellect as "creations." Cattaneo says: "Monuments left by a people are truer than documents, which often prove fallacious and mislead and prove no profit for those who blindly follow them. The story of a people or a nation, if not known by writings, might be guessed through its monuments and works of art."

The Lombards, who had come from northern Germany and settled in northern Italy in 568, at once began to develop along many lines which made Lombardy known all over Europe—the result of which influence Europe feels to-day. They developed along lines which in our every-day parlance may be called business. They were not primarily architects or builders and they employed the Comacines for this kind of work and it was the Comacines who developed what is known to-day as Lombard architecture, covering a period that we may roughly put as from the seventh century to the Renaissance.

The first to draw attention to the name Magistri Comacini was the erudite Muratori, that searcher out of ancient manuscripts, who unearthed from the archives an edict, dated November 22, 643, signed by Rotharis, in which are included two clauses treating of the Magistri Comacini and their colleagues. The two clauses, Nos. 143 and 144, out of the 388 inscribed in cribbed Latin, says Leder Scott, are, when anglicized, to the following intent:

"Art. 143. Of the Magister Comacinus. If the Comacine Master with his colleagues shall have contracted to restore or build a house of any person whatsoever, the contract for payment being made, and it chances that someone shall die by the fall of the said house, or any material or stone from it, the owner of said house shall not be cited by the Master Comacinus or his brethren to compensate them for homicide or injury; because having for their own gain contracted for the payment of the building, they just sustain the risk and injuries thereof.

"Art. 144. Of the engaging and hiring of Magistri. If any person has engaged or hired one or more of the Comacine Masters to design a work, or to daily assist his workmen in building a palace or a house, and it shall happen by reason of the house some Comacine shall be killed, the owner of the house is not considered responsible; but if a pole or stone shall injure some extraneous person, the Master builder shall not bear the blame, but the person who hired him shall make compensation."

Charles A. Cummings says: "The code of Luitprand, eighty years later, contains further provisions regulating the practice of Comacini, which had now become much more numerous and important. Fixed rates of payment were established for their services, varying according to the kind of building on which they were engaged; definite prices being allowed for walls of various thicknesses, for arches and vaults, for chimneys, plastering and joiners' work. The difficulty which these early builders found in the construction of vaults is indicated by the allowance of a charge per superficial foot, from fifteen to eighteen times as great as in the case of a wall. The price of provisions and wine furnished to the workmen is also determined and is counted as part of their pay."

Scott maintains that "these laws prove that in the seventh century the Magistri Comacini were a compact and powerful gild, capable of asserting their rights, and that the gild was properly organized, having degrees of different ranks; that the higher orders were entitled Magistri, and could 'design' or 'undertake' a work; i. e., act as architects; and that the colligantes or colleagues worked under, or with, them. In fact, a powerful organization altogether—so powerful and so solid that it spoke of a very ancient foundation. Was it a surviving branch of a Roman Collegium? Or a decadent group of Byzantine artists stranded in Italy?"

Professor Merzario says: "In this darkness which extended all over Italy, only one small lamp remained alight, making a bright spark in the vast Italian metropolis. It was from the Magistri Comacini. Their respective names are unknown, their individual work unspecialized, but the breath of their spirit might be felt all through those centuries and their names collectively is legion. We may safely say that of all the works of art between A.D. 800 and 1000, the greater and better part are due to that brotherhood—always faithful and often secret—of the Magistri Comacini. The authority and judgment of learned men justify the assertion."

Quaternal de Quincy, in his *Dictionary of Architecture*, under the heading Comacines, remarks that "to these men who were both designers and executors, architects, sculptors and mosaicists, may be attributed the Renaissance of art and its propagation in the southern countries, where it marched with Christianity. Certain it is that we owe to them that the heritage of antique ages was not entirely lost, and it is only by their tradition and imitation that the art of building was kept alive, producing works which we still admire and which become surprising when we think of the utter ignorance of all science in those Dark Ages."

Hope, in his well-balanced style, draws quite a picture of the gilds at this period which, upon the whole, is fairly accurate. He says: "When Rome, the Eternal City, was first abandoned for Milan, Ravenna and other cities in the more fertile North, which became seats of new courts and the capitals of new kingdoms, we find in northern Italy a rude and barbarous nation—The Lombards—in the space of two short centuries, producing in trade, in legislation, in finance, in industry of every description, new developments so great, that from them, and from the regions to which they attach their names, has issued the whole of that ingenious and complex system of bills of exchange, banks, insurance, double-entry bookkeeping, commercial and marine laws and public loans, since adopted all over Europe—all over Europe retaining, in their peculiar appellations the trace and landmarks of their origin—and all over Europe affording to capital and commerce an ease of captivity and a security unknown before.

"To keep pace with this progress, kings, lesser lords and the municipalities that by degrees arose, were induced, at one time from motives of public policy, at others, of private advantage, to encourage artificers of different professions. Thus of their own accord, they granted licenses to form associations possessed of the exclusive privilege of exercising their peculiar trades, and making them an object of profit; of requiring that youths anxious to be associated with their body, and ultimately to be endowed with the mastery of the profession, should submit to a fixed and often severe course of study, under the name of apprenticeship, for their master's profit, and in addition should frequently be compelled to pay a considerable premium; and of preventing any individual not thus admitted into their body, from establishing a competition against them. These associations were called Corporations or Gilds.

"These bodies in order to enjoy exclusive exercise of their profession, and that its profits should be secure to them, not only by law, but by the inability of others to violate it, by degrees made their business, or craft, as they called it, a profound mystery from the world at large, and only suffered their own apprentices to be initiated in its higher branches and improvements, most gradually; and in every place where a variety of paths of industry and art were struck out, these crafts, these corporations, these masterships and these mysteries became so universally prevalent, that not only the arts of a wholly mechanical nature, but even those of the most exalted and intellectual nature—those which in ancient times had been considered the exclusive privilege of freemen and citizens, and those dignified with the name liberal—were submitted to all those narrow rules of corporations and connected with all the servile offices of apprenticeship." While Hope and writers of his time recognized that some well-organized body of workers had dominated the building trades at the Lombard period of history, they never attempted to trace their genealogy. Later historical critics of architecture have given some attention to origin and succession of these building crafts. One of the latest Italian students, Rivoiri, has devoted a separate chapter to the Comacine Masters. As his extensive work on *Lombard Architecture, Its Origin, Development and Derivatives* may be accessible to but few, I shall give a generous quotation from him for the importance of his sound conclusions: "The origin of the Comacine Masters in the diocese of Como is explained quite naturally, according to De Dartein, Merzario, and others, by the custom, which has always existed among the craftsmen and workmen of that region, of leaving their native places in order to betake themselves in gangs wherever building works are about to be or have been begun, urged thereto by their barren mountain soil, pecuniary gain, their innate ability and enterprising character. Another explanation is to be found in the presence on the shores of the lakes of Como, Lugano and the Maggiore, of numerous stones, marble and timber yards which furnished building material for the cities of the plains. These yards gave scope for the practice of the crafts of carver, carpenter, builder, etc.; and these, in their turn, by constant practice and continuous progress, ultimately developed architects and sculptors.

" And here we may naturally feel surprise at the appearance, amid the darkness of the early centuries of the Middle Ages, of a corporation of craftsmen who, though of Roman origin, none the less enjoyed Lombard citizenship and the rights belonging to it; while the Roman or Italian subjects of Lombard rule were, if not slaves, nothing better than 'aldi,' that is to say, midway between freedmen and serfs, manumitted on the condition of performing the manual tasks assigned them by the manumittor. A corporation, too, which had a legal monopoly of public and private building work within the territories occupied by the Lombards, as the code of Rotharis proves, and can claim the honor of filling up the gap which for so long was believed, especially by non-Italian writers, to exist between the incorporated artisans of the Roman epoch, supposed to have vanished with the fall of the Empire, and the gilds of craftsmen which sprang up so luxuriantly in the XIIIth and XIVth centuries. Such surprise, however, may easily be allayed if we consider that in reality the fraternity of craftsmen, in Italy at least, by no means came to an end with the Barbarian invasions, and particularly that of the Lombards, who actually preserved those Roman institutions which best fulfilled their aim of keeping the conquered people in subjection. Accordingly, they would have maintained the corporation of artisans in order to make the exaction of tribute easier, and at the same time to be able to keep a hold over the individuals composing them.

" Hence we have good grounds for inferring that the corporation of 'Comacini,' who apparently were neither more nor less than the successors of the Master Masons who in the days of the Empire had directed the operations of the *collegia* specially devoted to building, survived the barbarian invasions which were so disastrous to Italy in the centuries preceding the accession of Rotharis to the Lombard throne. This view is confirmed by the undoubted fact that from this time onwards the 'Comacini' formed a very important gild, as is shown by the need which he felt of making regulations for it in his laws.

This gild cannot have sprung into existence full grown, and, as it were, by magic, just when the Code of Rotharis made its appearance in 643. It must have already been in existence and have attained some degree of importance well before Alboin's descent on Italy (568). Troya, in fact, remarks that when the Lombards of the time of Autharis (583–590) and of Agilulf and Theodelinda (590–625) wanted to erect buildings, they must have made use of it; and that everything leads one to think that before the promulgation of the Code of Rotharis, some of the members (*i.e.* those of the highest capacity and reputation) had already been enfranchised by 'impans' or express grace of the King. However that may be, the mention of the associations of Comacini in the reign of Rotharis and Luitprand is one of the earliest in the Barbarian world, and earlier than that of any gild of architects or builders belonging to the Middle Ages. . . . Whatever may have been the organization of the Comacine or Lombard gilds, and however these may have been affected by outward events, *they did not cease to exist in consequence of the fall of the Lombard kingdom.* With the first breath of municipal freedom, and with the rise of the new brotherhoods of artisans, they, too, perhaps, may have reformed themselves like the latter, who were nothing but the continuation of the 'collegium' of Roman times preserving its existence through the barbarian ages, and transformed little by little into the mediæval corporation. The members may have found themselves constrained to enter into a more perfect unity of thought and sentiment, to bind themselves into a more compact body, and thus put themselves in a condition to maintain their ancient supremacy in carrying out the most important building works in Italy. But we cannot say anything more. And even putting aside all tradition, the monuments themselves are there to confirm what we have said.

" Finally, toward the end of the XIth century, the Comacine brotherhoods began to relax their bonds of union, to make room gradually for personality, and for artistic and scientific individuality, till at length they vanish at the close of the XVth century, with the disappearance of the Lombardic style which they had created, and the rise of the architecture of the Renaissance." Leder Scott has reasonably inferred: " 1. That the architects of the same gild worked at Rome and in Ravenna in the early centuries after Christ. 2. That though the architects were Roman, the decorations up to the fourth century were chiefly Byzantine, or had imbibed that style, as their paintings show. 3. That in the time when Rome lay in a heap of ruins under the barbarians, the Collegium, or a Collegium, I know not which, fled to independent Como, and there, in after centuries they were employed by the Lombards, and ended in again becoming a powerful gild."

There was the greatest similarity in form

of the cathedrals of this period and when changes were introduced they became general, thereby creating a unity of purpose and an interchange of ideas, which spoke the existence of some kind of gild or fraternity with a perfected organization. That the Comacines received ideas which somewhat influenced their building art is probably true, particularly their decorations. On the latter question Müller in his *Archæology der Kunst* says: "From Constantinople as a center of mechanical skill, a knowledge of art radiated to distant countries, and corporations of builders of Grecian birth were permitted to exercise a judicial government among themselves, according to the laws of the country to which they owed allegiance."

This was the age when more symbolism was made use of than at any other period, the reason being that the Christian religion having so lately supplanted Paganism, and as most converts could not read, the Bible was spread over the front of the cathedrals in the form of sculptured saints, animals and symbolic figures. Hope says: "Pictures can always be read by all people and when symbolic uses are made and once explained will be ever after understood."

The Eastern branch of the Church at Constantinople prohibited imagery and other forms of adornment of their churches, and like disputants, when one denies, the other affirms, the Western branch of Rome espoused the carving of images and beautiful sculpture. This caused the Eastern sculptors to come to Italy, where they were welcomed by the Roman branch of the Church. That policy of the Roman branch was carried throughout the cathedral building period that followed in Europe for several centuries and to this day is a dominant element with them, for they still believe that to properly spread their religion, noble architecture, fine sculpturing and painting, and inspiring music are prime requisites. We Speculative Masons should give full credit to the Roman Catholic Church for employing and fostering our Operative Brethren through many centuries and making possible Speculative Freemasonry of to-day, even though the Church is now our avowed enemy.

Combining some arguments that have been reasonably put forward for the maintenance of this theory, and adding others, it may be pointed out that the identical form of Lodges in different cities is a strong argument that the same ruling body governed them all. An argument equally strong is the ubiquity of the members. We find the same men employed in one Lodge after another, as work required. Not only were these changes or migrations from one cathedral to another accomplished in Italy, but we have many examples of Masters and special workmen going into France, Germany and other countries. Unfortunately, no documents exist of the early Lombard times, but the archives of the Opera, which in most cities have been faithfully kept since the

thirteenth century, would, if thoroughly examined, prove to be valuable stores from which to draw a history of the Masonic Gild. They have only begun to examine carefully these records, and when completed we may reasonably expect to learn much concerning this period. Leder Scott has examined several and gives continuous lists of Masters of the School or Lodge in different cities. In Sienese School, a list of sixty-seven Masters in continuous succession from 1259 to 1423; at Florence Lodge, seventy-eight Masters from 1258 to 1418; at Milan Lodge, seventy-nine Masters from 1387 to 1647. She (for Leder Scott was a woman, whose real name was Mrs. Lucy Baxter) gives headings of laws for these Lodges, and it may be interesting to glance over the headings of statutes of these Masonic Gilds, which will throw light on all the organizations. The Sienese Gild is a typical one and will serve our purpose. There are forty-one chapters, but the headings of only twelve will be selected:

C.1. One who curses God or the Saints. A fine of 25 lira.

C.2. One who opposes the Signora of city. A fine of 25 lira.

C.5. How to treat underlings (sottoposti or apprentices).

C.11. That no one take work from another Master.

C.13. How the feast of the Four Holy Martyrs is to be kept. Feast of the Dead, November. Two half-pound candles and offering; grand fête of the Gild in June.

C.16. The camerlingo shall hand all receipts to Grand Master.

C.19. One who is sworn to another Gild cannot be either Grand Master or camerlingo.

C.22. How members are to be buried.

C.23. How to insure against risks.

C.24. No argument or business discussion to be held in public streets.

C.30. That no Master shall undertake a second work till the first has been paid.

C.34. On those who lie against others.

These statutes are very fair and well composed and must certainly have been made from long experience in the Gild.

The genealogy of the styles of architecture has baffled many. Leder Scott believes this to be the line of descent: First, the Comacines continued Roman traditions, as the Romans continued Etruscan ones; next, they orientalized their style by their connection with the East through Aquileia, and the influx of the Greek exiles into the Gild. Later came a different influence through the Saracens into the South, and the Italian-Gothic was born. In the old times (sixth to the tenth centuries) before the painters and sculptors, and after them the metal workers, split off and formed companies of their own, every kind of decoration was practised by the Masters, as the letter of Theodoric plainly shows. A church was not complete unless it was adorned in its whole height and breadth with sculpture on the outside, mosaics or paintings on the inside, and in its completeness formed the peoples' Bible and dogma of religious belief, and this from the very early times of Constantine and his Byzantine mosaicists, and of Queen Theolinda and her fresco-painters, up to the revival of mosaics by the Cosmati and the fresco-painting in the Tuscan schools, but never were these arts entirely lost.

For the first, we have the identity of form and ornamentation in their works and the similarity of nomenclature and organization between the Roman Collegio and the Lombard Gild of Magistri. Besides this, the well-known fact that the free republic of Como was used as a refuge by Romans who fled from barbaric invasions makes a strong argument. For the second, we may plead again the same identity of form and organization and a like similarity of ornamentation and nomenclature. Just as King Luitprand's architects were called Magistri, and the Grand Master the Gadtaldo, so we have the great architectural Gilds in Venice, in the thirteenth, fourteenth and fifteenth centuries, using the very same titles and having the very same laws.

Again the hereditary descent is marked by the patron saints of the Lombard and Tuscan Lodges, being the Four Martyr Brethren from a Roman Collegio. (See *Four Crowned Martyrs*.)

All these and other indications are surely as strong as documental proof, and are practically the summary of the conclusions of Leder Scott and are not overdrawn, being amply borne out by facts already known. Older writers recognized the presence of a compact gild in the work, but did not connect them with the builders of the Renaissance. More recent writers, such as Rivoira, Porter, and others declare the connection. This connection is probably without the field of historical architects, whose work is the study of the product of the workmen, and not the workmen themselves, while our interest is centered on the workmen and their relations to those who follow them in connected sequence, and not on the product of their work, further than to show and prove relationships of the building crafts.

There are many most interesting and important things pertaining to the Comacines that must be omitted in a cyclopedic article. Their rich, varied and curious symbolism, which even Ruskin failed to understand, would furnish matter for a fair-sized volume.

While it is recognized that history should always be written from as nearly original sources as is possible, it has not been realized in this instance, as I have had to rely solely on those who have made their investigations at first-hand, and while some liberties have been taken, no violence has been done to their conclusions.

The reader will find a rich field in the following bibliography:

The Cathedral Builders, The Story of a Great Masonic Guild, by Leder Scott.

The Comacines, Their Predecessors and their Successors, by W. Ravencroft.

Lombard Architecture, Its Origin, Development and Derivatives, by G. T. Rivoira.

A History of Architecture in Italy, from the Time of Constantine to the Dawn of the Renaissance, by Charles A. Cummings.

Medieval Architecture, by A. K. Porter.

Architecture in Italy from the Sixth to the Eleventh Century, Historical and Critical Researches, by Raffaele Cattaneo.

Historical Essay on Architecture, by Thomas Hope.

These are English works or have been translated into English. From them an extensive bibliography embracing other languages will be found. [E. E. C.]

Combination of Masons. The combination of the Freemasons in the fourteenth and fifteenth centuries to demand a higher rate of wages, which eventually gave rise to the enactment of the Statutes of Laborers, is thus described by a writer in the *Gentleman's Magazine* (January, 1740, p. 17): "King Edward III. took so great an affection to Windsor, the place of his birth, that he instituted the Order of the Garter there, and rebuilt and enlarged the castle, with the church and chapel of St. George. This was a great work and required a great many hands; and for the carrying of it on writs were directed to the sheriffs of several counties to send thither, under the penalty of £100 each, such a number of masons by a day appointed. London sent forty, so did Devon, Somerset, and several other counties; but several dying of the plague, and others deserting the service, new writs were issued to send up supplies. Yorkshire sent sixty, and other counties proportionably, and orders were given that no one should entertain any of these runaway masons, under pain of forfeiture of all their goods. Hereupon, the Masons entered into a combination not to work, unless at higher wages. They agreed upon tokens, etc., to know one another by, and to assist one another against being impressed, and not to work unless *free* and on their own terms. Hence they called themselves Freemasons; and this combination continued during the carrying on of these buildings for several years. The wars between the two Houses coming on in the next reign, the discontented herded together in the same manner, and the gentry also underhand supporting the malcontents, occasioned several Acts of Parliament against the combination of Masons and other persons under that denomination, the titles of which Acts are still to be seen in the printed statutes of those reigns." Ashmole, in his *History of the Order of the Garter* (p. 80), confirms the fact of the impressment of workmen by King Edward; and the combination that followed seems but a natural consequence of this oppressive act; but the assertion that the origin of Freemasonry as an organized institution of builders is to be traced to such a combination, is not supported by the facts of history, and, indeed, the writer himself admits that the Masons denied its truth.

Commander. 1. The presiding officer in a Commandery of Knights Templar. His style is "Eminent," and the jewel of his office is a cross, from which issue rays of light. In England and Canada he is now styled "Preceptor." 2. The Superintendent of a Commandery, as a house or residence of the Ancient Knights of Malta, was so called.

Commander, Grand. See *Grand Commander.*

Commander-in-Chief. The presiding officer in a Consistory of Sublime Princes of the Royal Secret in the Ancient and Accepted Scottish Rite. His style is "Illustrious." In a Grand Consistory the presiding officer is a Grand Commander-in-Chief, and he is styled "Very Illustrious."

Commandery. 1. In the United States all regular assemblies of Knights Templar are called Commanderies, and must consist of the following officers: Eminent Commander, Generalissimo, Captain-General, Prelate, Senior Warden, Junior Warden, Treasurer, Recorder, Warder, Standard-Bearer, Sword-Bearer, and Sentinel. These Commanderies derive their warrants of Constitution from a Grand Commandery, or, if there is no such body in the State in which they are organized, from the Grand Encampment of the United States. They confer the degrees of Companion of the Red Cross, Knight Templar, and Knight of Malta.

In a Commandery of Knights Templars, the throne is situated in the East. Above it are suspended three banners: the center one bearing a cross, surmounted by a glory; the left one having inscribed on it the emblems of the Order, and the right one, a paschal lamb. The Eminent Commander is seated on the throne; the Generalissimo, Prelate, and Past Commanders on his right; the Captain-General on his left; the Treasurer and Recorder, as in a Symbolic Lodge; the Senior Warden at the southwest angle of the triangle, and upon the right of the first division; the Junior Warden at the northwest angle of the triangle, and on the left of the third division; the Standard-Bearer in the West, between the Sword-Bearer on his right, and the Warder on his left; and in front of him is a stall for the initiate. The Knights are arranged in equal numbers on each side, and in front of the throne. In England and Canada a body of Knights Templars is called a "Preceptory."

2. The houses or residences of the Knights of Malta were called Commanderies, and the aggregation of them in a nation was called a Priory or Grand Priory.

Commandery, Grand. When three or more Commanderies are instituted in a State, they may unite and form a Grand Commandery under the regulations prescribed by the Grand Encampment of the United States. They have the superintendence of all Commanderies of Knights Templars that are holden in their respective jurisdictions.

A Grand Commandery meets at least an-

nually, and its officers consist of a Grand Commander, Deputy Grand Commander, Grand Generalissimo, Grand Captain-General, Grand Prelate, Grand Senior and Junior Warden, Grand Treasurer, Grand Recorder, Grand Warder, Grand Standard-Bearer, and Grand Sword-Bearer.

Committee. To facilitate the transaction of business, a Lodge or Grand Lodge often refers a subject to a particular committee for investigation and report. By the usages of Masonry, committees of this character are always appointed by the presiding officer; and the Master of a Lodge, when present at the meeting of a committee, may act, if he thinks proper, as its chairman; for the Master presides over any assemblage of the Craft in his jurisdiction.

Committee, General. By the Constitution of the Grand Lodge of England, all matters of business to be brought under the consideration of the Grand Lodge must previously be presented to a General Committee, consisting of the President of the Board of Benevolence, the Present and Past Grand Officers, and the Master of every regular Lodge, who meet on the fourteenth day immediately preceding each quarterly communication. No such regulation exists in any of the Grand Lodges of America.

Committee of Charity. In most Lodges there is a standing Committee of Charity, appointed at the beginning of the year, to which, in general, applications for relief are referred by the Lodge. In cases where the Lodge does not itself take immediate action, the committee is also invested with the power to grant relief to a limited amount during the recess of the Lodge.

Committee of Finance. In many Lodges the Master, Wardens, Treasurer, and Secretary constitute a Committee of Finance, to which is referred the general supervision of the finances of the Lodge.

Committee on Foreign Correspondence. In none of the Grand Lodges of this country, forty years ago, was such a committee as that on foreign correspondence ever appointed. A few of them had corresponding secretaries, to whom were entrusted the duty of attending to the correspondence of the body: a duty which was very generally neglected. A report on the proceedings of other bodies was altogether unknown. Grand Lodges met and transacted the local business of their own jurisdictions without any reference to what was passing abroad.

But within the last twenty or thirty years, improvements in this respect began to show themselves. Intelligent Masons saw that it would no longer do to isolate themselves from the Fraternity in other countries, and that, if any moral or intellectual advancement was to be expected, it must be derived from the intercommunication and collision of ideas; and the first step toward this advancement was the appointment in every Grand Lodge of a committee, whose duty it should be to collate the proceedings of other jurisdictions, and to eliminate from them the most important items. These committees were, however, very slow in assuming the functions which devolved upon them, and in coming up to the full measure of their duties. At first their reports were little more than "reports of progress." No light was derived from their collation, and the bodies which had appointed them were no wiser after their reports had been read than they were before.

As a specimen of the first condition and subsequent improvement of these committees on foreign correspondence, let us take at random the transactions of any Grand Lodge old enough to have a history and intelligent enough to have made any progress; and, for this purpose, the proceedings of the Grand Lodge of Ohio, two volumes of which lie conveniently at hand, will do as well as any other. The Grand Lodge of Ohio was organized in January, 1808. From that time to 1829, its proceedings contain no reference to a committee on correspondence; and except, I think, a single allusion to the Washington Convention, made in the report of a special committee, the Masons of Ohio seem to have had no cognizance, or at least to have shown no recognition, of any Masonry which might be outside of their own jurisdiction.

But in the year 1830, for the first time, a committee was appointed to report on the foreign correspondence of the Grand Lodge. This committee bore the title of the "Committee on Communications from Foreign Grand Lodges," etc., and made during the session a report of *eight lines* in length, which contained just the amount of information that could be condensed in that brief space, and no more. In 1831, the report was *fifteen lines* long; in 1832, *ten lines;* in 1833, *twelve lines;* and so on for several years, the reports being sometimes a little longer and sometimes a little shorter; but the length being always measured by lines, and not by pages, until, in 1837, there was a marked falling off, the report consisting only of *one line and a half.* Of this report, which certainly cannot be accused of verbosity, the following is an exact copy: "Nothing has been presented for the consideration of your committee requiring the action of the Grand Lodge."

In 1842, the labors of the committee began to increase, and their report fills *a page* of the proceedings. Things now rapidly improved. In 1843, the report was *three pages* long; in 1845, *four pages;* in 1846, *seven;* in 1848, nearly *thirteen;* in 1853, *fourteen;* in 1856, *thirty;* and in 1857, *forty-six.* Thenceforward there is no more fault to be found. The reports of the future committees were of full growth, and we do not again hear such an unmeaning phrase as "nothing requiring the action of the Grand Lodge."

The history of these reports in other Grand Lodges is the same as that in Ohio. Beginning with a few lines, which announced the absence of all matters worthy of consideration, they have grown up to the full stature of elaborate essays, extending to one hundred and some-times to one hundred and fifty pages, in which the most important and interesting subjects of Masonic history, philosophy, and jurisprudence are discussed, generally with much ability.

At this day the reports of the committees on foreign correspondence in all the Grand Lodges of this country constitute an important portion of the literature of the Institution. The chairmen of these committees—for the other members fill, for the most part, only the post of "sleeping partners"—are generally men of education and talent, who, by the very occupation in which they are employed, of reading the published proceedings of all the Grand Lodges in correspondence with their own, have become thoroughly conversant with the contemporary history of the Order, while a great many of them have extended their studies in its previous history.

The "reportorial corps," as these hard-laboring brethren are beginning to call themselves, exercise, of course, a not trifling influence in the Order. These committees annually submit to their respective Grand Lodges a mass of interesting information, which is read with great avidity by their brethren. Gradually—for at first it was not their custom—they have added to the bare narration of facts their comments on Masonic law and their criticisms on the decisions made in other jurisdictions. These comments and criticisms have very naturally their weight, sometimes beyond their actual worth; and it will not therefore be improper to take a glance at what ought to be the character of a report on foreign correspondence.

In the first place, then, a reporter of foreign correspondence should be, in the most literal sense of Shakespeare's words, "a brief chronicler of the times." His report should contain a succinct account of everything of importance that is passing in the Masonic world, so far as his materials supply him with the information. But, remembering that he is writing for the instruction of hundreds, perhaps thousands, many of whom cannot spare much time, and many others who have no inclination to spare it, he should eschew the sin of tediousness, never forgetting that "brevity is the soul of wit." He should omit all details that have no special interest; should husband his space for important items, and be exceedingly parsimonious in the use of unnecessary expletives, whose only use is to add to the length of a line. In a word, he should remember that he is not an orator but an historian. A rigid adherence to these principles would save the expense of many printed pages to his Grand Lodge, and the waste of much time to his readers. These reports will form the germ of future Masonic history. The collected mass will be an immense one, and it should not be unnecessarily enlarged by the admission of trivial items.

In the next place, although I admit that these "brethren of the reportorial corps" have peculiar advantages in reading the opinions of their contemporaries on subjects of

Masonic jurisprudence, they would be mistaken in supposing that these advantages must necessarily make them Masonic lawyers. *Ex quovis ligno non fit Mercurius.* It is not every man that will make a lawyer. A peculiar turn of mind and a habit of close reasoning, as well as a thorough acquaintance with the law itself, are required to fit one for the investigation of questions of jurisprudence. Reporters, therefore, should assume the task of adjudicating points of law with much diffidence. They should not pretend to make a decision *ex cathedra*, but only to express an opinion; and that opinion they should attempt to sustain by arguments that may convince their readers. Dogmatism is entirely out of place in a Masonic report on foreign correspondence.

But if tediousness and dogmatism are displeasing, how much more offensive must be rudeness and personality. Courtesy is a Masonic as well as a knightly virtue, and the reporter who takes advantage of his official position to speak rudely of his brethren, or makes his report the vehicle of scurrility and abuse, most strangely forgets the duty and respect which he owes to the Grand Lodge which he represents and the Fraternity to which he addresses himself.

And, lastly, a few words as to style. These reports, I have already said, constitute an important feature of Masonic literature. It should be, then, the object and aim of everyone to give to them a tone and character which shall reflect honor on the society whence they emanate, and enhance the reputation of their authors. The style cannot always be scholarly, but it should always be chaste; it may sometimes want eloquence, but it should never be marked by vulgarity. Coarseness of language and slang phrases are manifestly out of place in a paper which treats of subjects such as naturally belong to a Masonic document. Wit and humor we would not, of course, exclude. The Horatian maxim bids us sometimes to unbend, and old Menander thought it would not do always to appear wise. Even the solemn Johnson could sometimes perpetrate a joke, and Sidney Smith has enlivened his lectures on moral philosophy with numerous witticisms. There are those who delight in the stateliness of Coleridge; but for ourselves we do not object to the levity of Lamb, though we would not care to descend to the vulgarity of Rabelais.

To sum up the whole matter in a few words, these reports on foreign correspondence should be succinct, and, if you please, elaborate chronicles of all passing events in the Masonic world; they should express the opinions of their authors on points of Masonic law, not as judicial *dicta*, but simply as *opinions*, not to be dogmatically enforced, but to be sustained and supported by the best arguments that the writers can produce; they should not be made the vehicles of personal abuse or vituperation; and, lastly, they should be clothed in language worthy of the literature of the Order.

Committee, Private. The well-known regulation which forbids private committees in the Lodge, that is, select conversations between two or more members, in which the other members are not permitted to join, is derived from the *Old Charges:* "You are not to hold private committees or separate conversation, without leave from the Master, nor to talk of anything impertinent or unseemly, nor to interrupt the Master or Wardens, or any brother speaking to the Master." (*Constitutions*, 1723, p. 53.)

Committee, Report of. See *Report of a Committee.*

Common Gavel. See *Gavel.*

Communication. The meeting of a Lodge is so called. There is a peculiar significance in this term. "To communicate," which, in the Old English form, was "to common," originally meant to share in common with others. The great sacrament of the Christian church, which denotes a participation in the mysteries of the religion and a fellowship in the church, is called a "communion," which is fundamentally the same as a "communication," for he who partakes of the communion is said "to communicate." Hence, the meetings of Masonic Lodges are called *communications*, to signify that it is not simply the ordinary meeting of a society for the transaction of business, but that such meeting is the fellowship of men engaged in a common pursuit, and governed by a common principle, and that there is therein a communication or participation of those feelings and sentiments that constitute a true brotherhood.

The communications of Lodges are regular or stated and special or emergent. Regular communications are held under the provision of the by-laws, but special communications are called by order of the Master. It is a regulation that no special communication can alter, amend, or rescind the proceedings of a regular communication.

Communication, Grand. The meeting of a Grand Lodge.

Communication of Degrees. When the peculiar mysteries of a degree are bestowed upon a candidate by mere verbal description of the bestower, without his being made to pass through the constituted ceremonies, the degree is technically said to be *communicated*. This mode is, however, entirely confined in America to the Ancient and Accepted Scottish Rite. The degrees may in that Rite be thus conferred in any place where secrecy is secured; but the prerogative of communicating is restricted to the presiding officers of bodies of the Rite, who may communicate certain of the degrees upon candidates who have been previously duly elected, and to Inspectors and Deputy Inspectors-General of the Thirty-third Degree, who may communicate all the degrees of the Rite, except the last, to any persons whom they may deem qualified to receive them.

Communication, Quarterly. Anciently Grand Lodges, which were then called General Assemblies of the Craft, were held annually.

But it is said that the Grand Master Inigo Jones instituted quarterly communications at the beginning of the seventeenth century (*Constitutions*, 1738, p. 99), which were continued by his successors, the Earl of Pembroke and Sir Christopher Wren, until the infirmities of the latter compelled him to neglect them. On the revival in 1717, provision was made for their resumption; and in the twelfth of the thirty-nine Regulations of 1721 it was declared that the Grand Lodge must have a quarterly communication about Michaelmas, Christmas, and Lady-Day. (*Constitutions*, 1723, p. 61.) These quarterly communications are still retained by the Grand Lodge of England, and in America by the Grand Lodge of Massachusetts, but all other American Grand Lodges have adopted the old system of annual communications.

Communion of the Brethren. See *Bread, Consecrated.*

Como. Capital of the Province of Como in northern Italy, situated at S. end of W. branch of Lake of Como, about thirty miles from Milan, and to-day is an industrial city.

Its interest to Masons is on account of it being the center from which radiated the Comacine Masters, who descended from the Roman Colleges of Artificers and who built for the Lombards and others during their reign and carried their Art and influence into the Cathedral building of the Renaissance. (See *Comacine Masters.*)

The archeologists have determined the form of the older city of Roman times to have been rectangular, enclosed by walls. Towers were constructed on walls in the twelfth century. Portions of the walls are now to be seen in the garden of Liceo Volta. Baths common in all Roman cities have been discovered. Fortifications erected previous to 1127 were largely constructed with Roman inscribed sepulchral urns and other remains, in which most all Roman cities were unusually rich.

It is usual to record that Como was the birthplace of the elder and younger Pliny. The younger Pliny had a villa here called Comedia and was much interested in building the city,

PARAPET OF THE OLD CHURCH OF ST. ABBONDIO. MILAN, NINTH CENTURY.

having founded baths, a library, and aided in charity for the support of orphan children.

Of the many letters of the younger Pliny that remain, one is to his builder, Mustio, a Comacine architect, commissioning him to restore the temple of the Eleusinian Ceres, in which, after explaining the form of design he wished it to take, he concludes: ". . . at least, unless you think of something better, you, whose Art can always overcome difficulties of position."

There was an early church of SS. Peter and Paul in the fifth century that stood outside of the town, and the site is now occupied by the Romanesque church of St. Abbondio, founded 1013, and consecrated 1095. There are found many interesting intrecci remains of early carvings of the Comacine or Solomon's Knob. (See cut.)

On a site of an earlier church stands the present Cathedral of Como, which is built entirely of marble. It was begun in 1396, but was altered in 1487–1526 into Renaissance. Authors disagree as to whether the church was restored or rebuilt. The façade, 1457–86, follows in its lines the old Lombard form but the dividing pilasters are lavishly enriched, being perpendicular niches with a statue in each.

Scott says that "During the years from 1468 to 1492, the books of the Lodge, preserved in the archives, abound in names of *Magistri* from the neighborhood of Como, both architects and sculptors, and among them was Tommaso Rodari, who entered the Lodge in 1490, with a letter of recommendation from the Duke, advising that he be specially trained in the Art of Sculpture. He and four others were sent to Rome to remain ten years, and perfect themselves in sculpture, to study the antique, and to return to the *laborerium* as fully qualified masters." Rodari returned and sculptured a most beautiful North door of the Cathedral in rich ornate Renaissance style, although the lions are still under the columns, thus preserving a Comacine symbol so universally common in earlier times of pure Lombard style.

The history of Como as a city with her various fortunes and defeats during the invasions of barbarians and her long conflicts with her old enemy, Milan, may be found elsewhere. What interests us is the early colonization by Rome and her subsequent relations to Architecture at the Renaissance.

Soon after 89 B.C. Rome sent 3,000 colonists to Como, and Artificers were certainly among them, and in 59 B.C. Cæsar sent 5,000 more, and the place received the name Novum Comum and received Latin rights. (See *Comacine Masters.*)

Compagnon. In French Masonry, a Fellow-Craft is so called, and the *grade du Compagnon* is the degree of Fellow-Craft.

Compagnonage. This is the name which is given in France to certain mystical associations formed between workmen of the same or an analogous handicraft, whose object is to afford mutual assistance to the members. It was at one time considered among handicraftsmen as the Second Degree of the novitiate, before arriving at the *maîtrise*, or mastership, the first being, of course, that of apprentice; and workmen were admitted into it only after five years of apprenticeship, and on the production of a skilfully constructed piece of work, which was called their *chef-d'œuvre*.

Tradition gives to Compagnonage a Hebraic origin, which to some extent assimilates it to the traditional history of Freemasonry as springing out of the Solomonic Temple. It is, however, certain that it arose, in the twelfth century, out of a part of the corporation of workmen. These, who prosecuted the labors of their Craft from province to province, could not shut their eyes to the narrow policy of the gilds or corporations, which the masters were constantly seeking to make more exclusive. Thence they perceived the necessity of forming for themselves associations or confraternities, whose protection should accompany them in all their laborious wanderings, and secure to them employment and fraternal intercourse when arriving in strange towns.

The *Compagnons de la Tour*, which is the title assumed by those who are the members of the brotherhoods of Compagnonage, have legends, which have been traditionally transmitted from age to age, by which, like the Freemasons, they trace the origin of their association to the Temple of King Solomon. These legends are three in number, for the different societies of Compagnonage recognize three different founders, and hence made three different associations, which are:

1. The Children of Solomon.
2. The Children of Maître Jacques.
3. The Children of Père Soubise.

These three societies or classes of the Compagnons are irreconcilable enemies and reproach each other with the imaginary contests of their supposed founders.

The Children of Solomon pretend that King Solomon gave them their *devoir*, or gild, as a reward for their labors at the Temple, and that he had there united them into a brotherhood.

The Children of Maître Jacques say that their founder, who was the son of a celebrated architect named Jacquain, or Jacques, was one of the chief Masters of Solomon, and a colleague of Hiram. He was born in a small city of Gaul named Carte, and now St. Romille, but which we should in vain look for on the maps.

From the age of fifteen he was employed in stone-cutting. He traveled in Greece, where he learned sculpture and architecture; afterward went to Egypt, and thence to Jerusalem, where he constructed two pillars with so much skill that he was immediately received as a Master of the Craft. Maître Jacques and his colleague Père Soubise, after the labors of the Temple were completed, resolved to go together to Gaul, swearing that they would never separate; but the union did not last very long in consequence of the jealousy excited in Père Soubise by the ascendency of Maître Jacques over their disciples. They parted, and the former landed at Bordeaux, and the latter at Marseilles.

One day, Maître Jacques, being far away from his disciples, was attacked by ten of those of Père Soubise. To save himself, he fled into a marsh, where he sustained himself from sinking by holding on to the reeds, and was eventually rescued by his disciples. He then retired to St. Baume, but being soon after betrayed by a disciple, named, according to some, Jeron, and according to others, Jamais, he was assassinated by five blows of a dagger, in the forty-seventh year of his age, four years and nine days after his departure from Jerusalem. On his robe was subsequently found a reed which he wore in memory of his having been saved in the marsh, and thenceforth his disciples adopted the reed as the emblem of their Order.

Père Soubise is not generally accused of having taken any part in the assassination. The tears which he shed over the tomb of his colleague removed in part the suspicions which had at first rested on him. The traitor who committed the crime, subsequently, in a moment of deep contrition, cast himself into a well, which the disciples of Maître Jacques filled up with stones. The relics of the martyr were long preserved in a sacred chest, and, when his disciples afterward separated into different crafts, his hat was given to the hatters, his tunic to the stone-cutters, his sandals to the locksmiths, his mantle to the joiners, his girdle to the carpenters, and his staff to the cartwrights.

According to another tradition, Maître Jacques was no other than Jacques de Molay, the last Grand Master of the Templars, who had collected under his banner some of the Children of Solomon that had separated from the parent society, and who, about 1268, conferred upon them a new *devoir* or gild. Père Soubise is said, in the same legend, to have been a Benedictine monk, who gave to the carpenters some special statutes. This second legend is generally recognized as more truthful than the first. From this it follows that the division of the society of Compagnonage into three classes dates from the thirteenth century, and that the Children of Maître Jacques and of Père Soubise are more modern than the Children of Solomon, from whom they were a dismemberment.

The organization of these associations of Compagnonage reminds one very strongly of the somewhat similar organization of the Stonemasons of Germany and of other countries in the Middle Ages. To one of these classes every handicraftsman in France was expected to attach himself. There was an initiation, and a system of degrees which were four in number: the Accepted Companion, the Finished Companion, the Initiated Companion, and, lastly, the Affiliated Companion. There were also signs and words as modes of recognition, and decorations, which varied in the different devoirs; but to all, the square and compasses was a common symbol.

As soon as a Craftsman had passed through his apprenticeship, he joined one of these gilds, and commenced his journey over France, which was called the *tour de France*, in the course of which he visited the principal cities, towns, and villages, stopping for a time wherever he could secure employment. In almost every town there was a house of call, presided over always by a woman, who was affectionately called "la Mère," or the Mother, and the same name was given to the house itself. There the Compagnons held their meetings and annually elected their officers, and traveling workmen repaired there to obtain food and lodging, and the necessary information which might lead to employment.

When two Companions met on the road, one of them addressed the other with the *topage*, or challenge, being a formula of words, the conventional reply to which would indicate that the other was a member of the same devoir. If such was the case, friendly greetings ensued. But if the reply was not satisfactory, and it appeared that they belonged to different associations, a war of words, and even of blows, was the result. Such was formerly the custom, but through the evangelic labors of Agricol Perdiquier, a journeyman joiner of Avignon, who traveled through France inculcating lessons of brotherly love, a better spirit now exists.

In each locality the association has a chief, who is annually elected by ballot at the General Assembly of the Craft. He is called the First Compagnon of Dignity. He presides over the meetings, which ordinarily take place on the first Sunday of every month, and represents the society in its intercourse with other bodies, with the Masters, or with the municipal authorities.

Compagnonage has been exposed, at various periods, to the persecutions of the Church and the State, as well as to the opposition of the Corporations of Masters, to which, of course, its designs were antagonistic, because it opposed their monopoly. Unlike them, and particularly the Corporation of Freemasons, it was not under the protection of the Church. The practise of its mystical receptions was condemned by the Faculty of Theology at Paris, in 1655, as impious. But a hundred years before, in 1541, a decree of Francis I. had interdicted the *Compagnons de la Tour* from binding themselves by an oath, from wearing swords or canes, from assembling in a greater number than five outside of their Masters' houses, or from having banquets on any occasion. During the sixteenth, seventeenth, and eighteenth centuries, the parliaments were continually interposing their power against the associations of Compagnonage, as well as against other fraternities. The effects of these persecutions, although embarrassing, were not absolutely disastrous. In spite of them, Compagnonage was never entirely dissolved, although a few of the trades abandoned their devoirs; some of which, however —such as that of the shoemakers—were subsequently renewed. And at this day the gilds of the workmen still exist in France having lost, it is true, much of their original code of religious dogmas and symbols, and, although not recognized by the law, always tolerated by the municipal authorities and undisturbed by the police. To the Masonic scholar, the history of these devoirs or gilds is peculiarly interesting. In nearly all of them the Temple of Solomon prevails as a predominant symbol, while the square and compass, their favorite and constant device, would seem, in some way, to identify them with Freemasonry so far as respects the probability of a common origin.

Compagnons de la Tour. The title assumed by the workmen in France who belong to the different gilds of Compagnonage, which see.

Companion. A title bestowed by Royal Arch Masons upon each other, and equivalent to the word brother in Symbolic Lodges. It refers, most probably, to the companionship in exile and captivity of the ancient Jews, from the destruction of the Temple by Nebuchadnezzar to its restoration by Zerubbabel, under the auspices of Cyrus. In using this title in a higher degree, the Masons who adopted it seem to have intimated that there was a shade of difference between its meaning and that of brother. The latter refers to the universal fatherhood of God and the universal brotherhood of man; but the former represents a companionship or common pursuit of one object—the common endurance of suffering or the common enjoyment of happiness. *Companion* represents a closer tie than *brother*. The one is a natural relation shared by all men; the other a connection, the result of choice and confined to a few. All men are our brethren, not all our companions.

Companions, The Twelve. George F. Fort says that the "twelve Companions of Master Hiram correspond unquestionably to the twelve zodiacal signs, or the twelve months of the year. The ground-work of this tradition is a fragment of ancient natural religion, common to both Oriental and European nations; or, more properly, was derived from identical sources. The treacherous Craftsmen of Hiram the Good are the three winter months which slew him. He is the sun surviving during the eleven consecutive months, but subjected to the irresistible power of three ruffians, the winter months; in the twelfth and last month, that luminary, Hiram, the good, the beauteous, the bright, the sun god, is extinguished." (*The Early History and Antiquities of Freemasonry*, p. 408.)

Compasses. As in Operative Masonry, the compasses are used for the admeasurement of the architect's plans, and to enable him to give those just proportions which will ensure beauty as well as stability to his work; so, in Speculative Masonry, is this important implement symbolic of that even tenor of deportment, that true standard of rectitude which alone can bestow happiness here and felicity hereafter. Hence are the compasses the most prominent emblem of virtue, the true and only measure of a Mason's life and conduct. As the *Bible* gives us *light* on our duties to God, and the *square* illustrates our duties to our neighborhood and brother, so the *compasses* give that additional *light* which is to instruct us in the duty we owe to ourselves —the great, imperative duty of circumscribing our passions, and keeping our desires within due bounds. "It is ordained," says the philosophic Burke, "in the eternal constitution of things, that men of intemperate passions cannot be free; their passions forge their fetters." Those brethren who delight to trace our emblems to an astronomical origin, find in the compasses a symbol of the sun, the circular pivot representing the body of the luminary, and the diverging legs his rays.

In the earliest rituals of the last century, the compasses are described as a part of the furniture of the Lodge, and are said to belong to the Master. Some change will be found in this respect in the ritual of the present day. (See *Square and Compasses.*)

Composite. One of the five orders of architecture introduced by the Romans, and compounded of the other four, whence it derives its name. Although it combines strength with beauty, yet, as it is a comparatively modern invention, it is held in little esteem among Freemasons.

Concealment of the Body. See *Aphanism.*

Conclave. Commanderies of Knights Templars in England and Canada were called Conclaves, and the Grand Encampment, the Grand Conclave, but the terms now in use are "Preceptory" and "Great Priory" respectively. The word is also applied to the meetings in some other of the high degrees. The word is derived from the Latin *con,* "with," and *clavis,* "a key," to denote the idea of being locked up in seclusion, and in this sense was first applied to the apartment in which the cardinals are literally locked up when met to elect a Pope.

Concordists. A secret order established in Prussia, by M. Lang, on the wreck of the Tugendverein, which latter body was instituted in 1790 as a successor of the Illuminati, and suppressed in 1812 by the Prussian Government, on account of its supposed political tendencies.

Confederacies. A title given to the yearly meetings of the Masons in the time of Henry VI., of England, and used in the celebrated statute passed in the third year of his reign, which begins thus: "Whereas, by the yearly congregations and confederacies made by the Masons in their General Chapiters assembled, etc." (See *Laborers, Statutes of.*)

Conference Lodges. Assemblies of the members of a Lodge sometimes held in Germany. Their object is the discussion of the financial and other private matters of the Lodge. Lodges of this kind held in France are said to be "en famille." There is no such arrangement in English or American Masonry.

Conferring Degrees. When a candidate is initiated into any degree of Masonry in due form, the degree is said to have been conferred,

in contradistinction to the looser mode of imparting its secrets by *communication.*

Confusion of Tongues. The Tower of Babel is referred to in the ritual of the Third Degree as the place where *language was confounded and Masonry lost.* Hence, in Masonic symbolism, as Masonry professes to possess a universal language, the confusion of tongues at Babel is a symbol of that intellectual darkness from which the aspirant is seeking to emerge on his passage to that intellectual light which is imparted by the Order. (See *Threshing-Floor.*)

Congregations. In the *Old Records* and *Constitutions* of Masonry the yearly meetings of the Craft are so called. Thus, in the Halliwell or Regius MS. it is said, "Every Master that is a Mason must be at the General Congregation." (Line 107.) What are now called "Communications of a Grand Lodge" were then called "Congregations of the Craft." (See *Assembly.*)

Congresses, Masonic. At various times in the history of Freemasonry conferences have been held, in which, as in the General Councils of the Church, the interests of the Institution have been made the subject of consideration. These conferences have received the name of Masonic Congresses. Whenever a respectable number of Masons invested with deliberative powers, assemble as the representatives of different countries and jurisdictions, to take into consideration matters relating to the Order, such a meeting will be properly called a Congress. Of these Congresses some have been productive of little or no effect, while others have undoubtedly left their mark; nor can it be doubted, that if a General or Ecumenical Congress, consisting of representatives of all the Masonic powers of the world, were to meet, with an eye single to the great object of Masonic reform, and were to be guided by a liberal and conciliatory spirit of compromise, such a Congress might at the present day be of incalculable advantage.

The most important Congresses that have met since the year 926 are those of York, Strasburg, Ratisbon, Spire, Cologne, Basle, Jena, Altenberg, Brunswick, Lyons, Wolfenbuttel, Wilhelmsbad, Paris, Washington, Baltimore, Lexington, and Chicago. (See them under their respective titles.)

Connecticut. The first Lodge organized in Connecticut was Hiram Lodge, at New Haven, which was warranted by the Grand Lodge of the "Moderns" on November 12, 1750; it remained on the English register until the formation of the Grand Lodge of Connecticut in 1789, when it became No. 1 on the roll of that Grand Lodge. Other Lodges were instituted, some by authority from Massachusetts, others from that derived from New York. A convention of delegates from twelve Lodges assembled at New Haven, July 8, 1789, and organized the Grand Lodge of Connecticut, Pierpont Edwards being elected Grand Master.

In 1796, there were three Royal Arch Chapters in Connecticut. In 1797, these Chapters had entered into an association, probably with the idea of establishing a Grand Chapter. On January 24, 1798, a convention of delegates from Massachusetts, Rhode Island, Connecticut, and New York was held at Hartford, when a conference was had on the subject of the two conventions, the delegates from Connecticut uniting with those from the other States in forming the "Grand Royal Arch Chapter of the Northern States of America." By the Constitution then adopted, the "Deputy Grand Chapter" of Connecticut was established. The title was changed in the subsequent year for that of "Grand Chapter." Webb gives the precise date of the organization of the Grand Chapter as May 17, 1798. (See *Royal Arch Grand Bodies in America*.)

The Grand Council of Royal and Select Masters was organized in 1819.

The Grand Encampment of Knights Templar was organized September 13, 1827, but is now known as the Grand Commandery.

Consecration. The appropriating or dedicating, with certain ceremonies, anything to sacred purposes or offices by separating it from common use. Hobbes, in his *Leviathan* (p. iv., c. 44), gives the best definition of this ceremony. "To consecrate is, in Scripture, to offer, give, or dedicate, in pious and decent language and gesture, a man, or any other thing, to God, by separating it from common use." Masonic Lodges, like ancient temples and modern churches, have always been consecrated. The rite of consecration is performed by the Grand Master, when the Lodge is said to be consecrated in *ample form;* by the Deputy Grand Master, when it is said to be consecrated in *due form;* or by the proxy of the Grand Master, when it is said to be consecrated in *form.* The Grand Master, accompanied by his officers, proceeds to the hall of the new Lodge, where, after the performance of those ceremonies which are described in all manuals and monitors, he solemnly consecrates the Lodge with the elements of corn, wine, and oil, after which the Lodge is dedicated and constituted, and the officers installed.

Consecration, Elements of. Those things, the use of which in the ceremony as constituent and elementary parts of it, are necessary to the perfecting and legalizing of the act of consecration. In Freemasonry, these elements are *corn, wine,* and *oil,* which see.

Conservators of Masonry. About the year 1859, a Mason of some distinction in America professed to have discovered, by his researches, what he called "the true Preston-Webb Work," and attempted to introduce it into various jurisdictions, sometimes in opposition to the wishes of the Grand Lodge and leading Masons of the State. To aid in the propagation of this ritual, he communicated it to several persons, who were bound to use all efforts—to some, indeed, of questionable propriety—to secure its adoption by their respective Grand Lodges. These Masons were called by him "Conservators," and the order or society which they constituted was called

the "Conservators' Association." This association, and the efforts of its chief to extend his ritual, met with the very general disapproval of the Masons of the United States, and in some jurisdictions led to considerable disturbance and bad feeling.

Conservators, Grand. See *Grand Conservators.*

Consistory. The meetings of members of the Thirty-second Degree, or Sublime Princes of the Royal Secret in the Ancient and Accepted Scottish Rite, are called Consistories. The elective officers are, according to the ritual of the Southern Jurisdiction of the United States, a Commander-in-Chief, Seneschal, Preceptor, Chancellor, Minister of State, Almoner, Registrar, and Treasurer. In the Northern Jurisdiction it is slightly different, the second and third officers being called Lieutenant-Commanders. A Consistory confers the Thirty-first and Thirty-second degrees of the Rite.

Consistory, Grand. See *Grand Consistory.*

Constable, Grand. The fourth officer in a Grand Consistory. It is the title which was formerly given to the leader of the land forces of the Knights Templars.

Constantine. See *Red Cross of Rome and Constantine.*

Constituted, Legally. The phrase, a legally constituted Lodge, is often used Masonically to designate any Lodge working under proper authority, which necessarily includes Lodges working under dispensation; although, strictly, a Lodge cannot be legally constituted until it has received its warrant or charter from the Grand Lodge. But so far as respects the regularity of their work, Lodges under dispensation and warranted Lodges have the same standing.

Constitution of a Lodge. Any number of Master Masons, not less than seven, being desirous of forming a new Lodge, having previously obtained a dispensation from the Grand Master, must apply by petition to the Grand Lodge of the State in which they reside, praying for a Charter, or Warrant of Constitution, to enable them to assemble as a regular Lodge. Their petition being favorably received, a warrant is immediately granted, and the Grand Master appoints a day for its consecration and for the installation of its officers. The Lodge having been consecrated, the Grand Master, or person acting as such, declares the brethren "to be constituted and formed into a regular Lodge of Free and Accepted Masons," after which the officers of the Lodge are installed. In this declaration of the Master, accompanied with the appropriate ceremonies, consists the *constitution* of the Lodge. Until a Lodge is thus *legally constituted,* it forms no component of the constituency of the Grand Lodge, can neither elect officers nor members, and exists only as a *Lodge under dispensation* at the will of the Grand Master.

Constitutions of 1762. This is the name of one of that series of Constitutions, or Regulations, which have always been deemed of importance in the history of the Ancient and Accepted Scottish Rite; although the *Constitutions of 1762* have really nothing to do with that Rite, having been adopted long before its establishment. In the year 1758, there was founded at Paris a Masonic body which assumed the title of the Chapter, or Council, of Emperors of the East and West, and which organized a Rite known as the Rite of Perfection, consisting of twenty-five degrees, and in the same year the Rite was carried to Berlin by the Marquis de Bernez. In the following year, a Council of Princes of the Royal Secret, the highest degree conferred in the Rite, was established at Bordeaux. On September 21, 1762, nine Commissioners met and drew up *Constitutions* for the government of the Rite of Perfection, which have been since known as the *Constitutions of 1762*. Of the place where the Commissioners met, there is some doubt. Of the two copies, hereafter to be noticed, which are in the archives of the Southern Supreme Council, that of Delahogue refers to the Orients of Paris and Berlin, while that of Aveilhé says that they were made at the Grand Orient of Bordeaux. Thory also (*Act. Lat.*, i., 79) names Bordeaux as the place of their enactment, and so does Ragon (*Orthod. Maç.*, 133); although he doubts their authenticity, and says that there is no trace of any such document at Bordeaux, nor any recollection there of the Consistory which is said to have drawn up the *Constitutions*. To this it may be answered, that in the Archives of the Mother Supreme Council at Charleston there are two manuscript copies of these *Constitutions*—one written by Jean Baptiste Marie Delahogue in 1798, which is authenticated by Count de Grasse, under the seal of the Grand Council of the Princes of the Royal Secret, then sitting at Charleston; and another, written by Jean Baptiste Aveilhé in 1797. This copy is authenticated by Long, Delahogue, De Grasse, and others. Both documents are written in French, and are almost substantially the same. The translated title of Delahogue's copy is as follows:

"Constitutions and Regulations drawn up by nine Commissioners appointed by the Grand Council of the Sovereign Princes of the Royal Secret at the Grand Orients of Paris and Berlin, by virtue of the deliberation of the fifth day of the third week of the seventh month of the Hebrew Era, 5662, and of the Christian Era, 1762. To be ratified and observed by the Grand Councils of the Sublime Knights and Princes of Masonry as well as by the particular Councils and Grand Inspectors regularly constituted in the two Hemispheres." The title of Aveilhé's manuscript differs in this, that it says the *Constitutions* were enacted "at the Grand Orient of Bordeaux," and that they were "transmitted to our Brother Stephen Morin, Grand Inspector of all the Lodges in the New World." Probably this is a correct record, and the *Constitutions* were prepared at Bordeaux.

The *Constitutions of 1762* consist of thirty-

five articles, and are principally occupied in providing for the government of the Rite established by the Council of Emperors of the East and West and of the bodies under it.

The Constitutions of 1762 were published at Paris, in 1832, in the *Recueil des Actes du Supreme Conseil de France*. They were also published, in 1859, in America; but the best printed exemplar of them is that published in French and English in the *Book of Grand Constitutions*, edited by Bro. Albert Pike, which is illustrated with copious and valuable annotations by the editor, who was the Sovereign Grand Commander of the Southern Supreme Council.

Constitutions of 1786. These are regarded by the members of the Ancient and Accepted Scottish Rite as the fundamental law of their Rite. They are said to have been established by Frederick II., of Prussia, in the last year of his life; a statement, however, that has been denied by some writers (see Findel's *History of Freemasonry* under "Declaration of the Grande Lodge of the Three Globes at Berlin"; also Gould's *History of Freemasonry* under "The Ancient and Accepted Scottish Rite"), and the controversies as to their authenticity have made them a subject of interest to all Masonic scholars. Bro. Albert Pike, the Grand Commander of the Supreme Council for the Southern Jurisdiction of the United States, published them, in 1872, in Latin, French, and English; and his exhaustive annotations are valuable because he has devoted to the investigation of their origin and their authenticity more elaborate care than any other writer.

Of these *Constitutions*, there are two exemplars, one in French and one in Latin, between which there are, however, some material differences. For a long time the French exemplar only was known in this country. It is supposed by Bro. Pike that it was brought to Charleston by Count de Grasse, and that under its provisions he organized the Supreme Council in that place. They were accepted by the Southern Supreme Council, and are still regarded by the Northern Council as the only authentic *Constitutions*. But there is abundant internal evidence of the incompleteness and incorrectness of the French *Constitutions*, of whose authenticity there is no proof, nor is it likely that they were made at Berlin and approved by Frederick, as they profess.

The Latin *Constitutions* were probably not known in France until after the Revolution. In 1834, they were accepted as authentic by the Supreme Council of France, and published there in the same year. A copy of this was published in America, in 1859, by Bro. Pike. These Latin *Constitutions* of 1786 have been recently accepted by the Supreme Council of the Southern Jurisdiction in preference to the French version. Most of the other Supreme Councils—those, namely, of England and Wales, of Italy, and of South America—have adopted them as the law of the Rite, repudiating the French version as of no authority.

The definite and well-authorized conclusions to which Bro. Pike has arrived on the subject of these *Constitutions* have been expressed by that eminent Mason in the following language:

"We think we may safely say, that the charge that the *Grand Constitutions* were forged at Charleston is completely disproved, and that it will be contemptible hereafter to repeat it. No set of speculating Jews constituted the Supreme Council established there; and those who care for the reputations of Colonel Mitchell, and Doctors Dalcho, Auld, and Moultrie, may well afford to despise the scurrilous libels of the Ragons, Clavels, and Folgers.

"And, secondly, that it is not by any means *proven* or *certain* that the *Constitutions* were *not* really made at Berlin, as they purport to have been, and approved by Frederick. We think that the preponderance of the evidence, internal and external, is on the side of their authenticity, apart from the positive evidence of the certificate of 1832.

"And, thirdly, that the Supreme Council at Charleston had a perfect right to adopt them as the law of the new Order; no matter where, when, or by whom they were made, as Anderson's *Constitutions* were adopted in Symbolic Masonry; that they are and always have been the law of the Rite, because they *were* so adopted; and because no man has ever lawfully received the degrees of the Rite without swearing to maintain them as its supreme law; for as to the articles themselves, there is no substantial difference between the French and Latin copies.

"And, fourthly, that there is not one particle of *proof* of any sort, circumstantial or historical, or by argument from improbability, that they are not genuine and authentic. In law, documents of great age, found in the possession of those interested under them, to whom they rightfully belong, and with whom they might naturally be expected to be found, are admitted in evidence without proof, to establish title or facts. They prove themselves, and to be avoided must be disproved by evidence. *There is no evidence against the genuineness of these Grand Constitutions.*"

Constitutions, Old. See *Records, Old.*

Consummatum est. Latin. *It is finished.* A phrase used in some of the higher degrees of the Ancient and Accepted Scottish Rite. It is borrowed from the expression used by our Lord when he said, on the cross, "It is finished," meaning that the work which had been given him to do had been executed. It is, therefore, appropriately used in the closing ceremonies to indicate that the sublime work of the degrees is finished, so that all may retire in peace.

Contemplative. To contemplate is, literally, to watch and inspect the Temple. The augur among the Romans, having taken his stand on the Capitoline Hill, marked out with his wand the space in the heavens he intended to consult. This space he called the *templum.* Having divided his templum into two parts

from top to bottom, he watched to see what would occur. The watching of the templum was called *contemplating;* and hence those who devoted themselves to meditation upon sacred subjects assumed this title. Thus, among the Jews, the Essenes and the Therapeutists, and, among the Greeks, the school of Pythagoras, were contemplative sects. Among the Freemasons, the word speculative is used as equivalent to contemplative. (See *Speculative Masonry.*)

Continental Lodges. This expression is used throughout this work, as it constantly is by English writers, to designate the Lodges on the Continent of Europe which retain many usages which have either been abandoned by, or never were observed in, the Lodges of England, Ireland, and Scotland, as well as the United States of America. The words *Continental Masonry* are employed in the same sense.

Contumacy. In civil law, it is the refusal or neglect of a party accused to appear and answer to a charge preferred against him in a court of justice. In Masonic jurisprudence, it is disobedience of or rebellion against superior authority, as when a Mason refuses to obey the edict of his Lodge, or a Lodge refuses to obey that of the Grand Master or the Grand Lodge. The punishment, in the former case, is generally suspension or expulsion; in the latter, arrest of charter or forfeiture of warrant.

Convention. In a State or Territory where there is no Grand Lodge, but three or more Lodges holding their Warrants of Constitution from Grand Lodges outside of the Territory, these Lodges may meet together by their representatives—who should properly be the first three officers of each Lodge—and take the necessary steps for the organization of a Grand Lodge in that State or Territory. This preparatory meeting is called a Convention. A President and Secretary are chosen, and a Grand Lodge is formed by the election of a Grand Master and other proper officers, when the old warrants are returned to the Grand Lodges, and new ones taken out from the newly formed Grand Lodge. Not less than three Lodges are required to constitute a Convention. The first Convention of this kind ever held was that of the four old Lodges of London, which met at the Apple-Tree Tavern, in 1716, and in the following year formed the Grand Lodge of England.

Convention Night. A title sometimes given in the minutes of English Lodges to a Lodge of emergency. Thus, in the minutes of Constitution Lodge, No. 390 (London), we read: "This being a Convention Night to consider the state of the Lodge," etc. (Sadler's *History and Records of the Lodge of Emulation,* p. 64.)

Conventions or Congresses of Masons in chronological order:

926. York, under Prince Edwin of England.

1275. Strasburg, under Edwin Von Steinbach.

1459. Ratisbon, under Jost Dolsinger.

1464. Ratisbon, under Grand Lodge of Strasburg.

1469. Spire, under Grand Lodge of Strasburg.

1535. Cologne, by Hermann, Bishop of Cologne.

1563. Basle, by Grand Lodge of Strasburg.

1717. London, by the Four Old Lodges. Organization of Grand Lodge.

1730. Dublin, by the Dublin Lodges.

1736. Edinburgh. Organization and institution of Grand Lodge.

1756. The Hague, by the Royal Union Lodge.

1762. Paris and Berlin, by nine commissioners nominated by the Sov. G. Council of P. of Masonry.

1763. Jena, by the Lodge of Strict Observance.

1764. Jena, by Johnson or Becker, denounced by Baron Hund.

1765. Altenberg, a continuation wherein Hund was elected G. M. of Rite of Strict Observance.

1772. Kohl, by Ferdinand of Brunswick and Baron Hund, without success.

1775. Brunswick, by Ferdinand, Duke of Brunswick.

1778. Lyons, by Lodge of Chevaliers Bienfaisants.

1778. Wolfenbüttel, by Duke of Brunswick.

1782. Wilhelmsbad, an impotent session for purification.

1784. Paris, a medley of Lovers of Truth and United Friends.

1786. Berlin, alleged to have been convened by Frederick II of Prussia.

1822. Washington, a mutual assemblage of American Lodges.

1843. Baltimore, a mutual assemblage of American Lodges.

1847. Baltimore, a mutual assemblage of American Lodges.

1853. Lexington, Ky., a mutual assemblage of American Lodges.

1855. Paris, by Grand Orient of France.

1859. Chicago. A volunteer assemblage.

1875. Lausanne. A convention of the Supreme Councils of the Scottish Rite of the World, which subsequently led to an eternal bond of unity both offensive and defensive.

Conversation. Conversation among the brethren during Lodge hours is forbidden by the *Charges of 1722* in these words: "You are not to hold private committees or separate conversation without leave from the Master." (*Constitutions*, 1723, p. 53.)

Convocation. The meetings of Chapters of Royal Arch Masons are so called from the Latin *convocatio*, a calling together. It seems very properly to refer to the convoking of the dispersed Masons at Jerusalem to rebuild the second Temple, of which every Chapter is a representation.

Convocation, Grand. The meeting of a Grand Chapter is so styled.

Cooke's Manuscript. The old document commonly known among Masonic scholars as *Matthew Cooke's Manuscript*, because it was first given to the public by that distinguished Brother, was published by him, in 1861, from the original in the British Museum, which institution purchased it, on the 14th of October, 1859, from Mrs. Caroline Baker. It was also published in facsimile by the Quatuor Coronati Lodge, No. 2076, London, in 1890. Its principal value is derived from the fact, as Bro. Cooke remarks, that until its appearance "there was no prose work of such undoubted antiquity known to be in existence on the subject."

Bro. Cooke gives the following account of the MS. in his preface to its republication:

"By permission of the Trustees of the British Museum, the following little work has been allowed to be copied and published in its entire form. The original is to be found among the additional manuscripts in that national collection, and is numbered 23,198.

"Judging from the character of the handwriting and the form of contractions employed by the scribe, it was most probably written in the latter portion of the fifteenth century, and may be considered a very clear specimen of the penmanship of that period.

"By whom or for whom it was originally penned there is no means of ascertaining; but from the style, it may be conjectured to have belonged to some Master of the Craft, and to have been used in assemblies of Masons as a text-book of the traditional history and laws of the Fraternity."

Cope-Stone. See *Cape-Stone*.

Cord, Hindu Sacred. See *Zennaar*.

Cord, Silver. See *Silver Cord*.

Cord, Threefold. See *Threefold Cord*.

Cordon. The Masonic decoration, which in English is called the collar, is styled by the French Masons the *cordon*.

Corinthian Order. This is the lightest and most ornamental of the pure orders, and possesses the highest degree of richness and detail that architecture attained under the Greeks. Its capital is its great distinction, and is richly adorned with leaves of acanthus, olive, etc., and other ornaments. The column of Beauty which supports the Lodge is of the Corinthian order, and its appropriate situation and symbolic officer are in the South.

Corner, Northeast. See *Northeast Corner*.

Corner-Stone, Symbolism of the. The corner-stone is the stone which lies at the corner of two walls and forms the corner of the foundation of an edifice. In Masonic buildings it is now always placed in the Northeast; but this rule was not always formerly observed. As the foundation on which the entire structure is supposed to rest it is considered by Operative Masons as the most important stone in the edifice. It is laid with impressive ceremonies; the assistance of Speculative Masons is often, and ought always to be, invited to give dignity to the occasion; and for this purpose Freemasonry has provided an especial ritual which is to govern the proper performance of that duty.

Among the ancients the corner-stone of important edifices was laid with impressive ceremonies. These are well described by Tacitus in the history of the rebuilding of the Capitol. After detailing the preliminary ceremonies, which consisted of a procession of vestals, who with chaplets of flowers encompassed the ground and consecrated it by libations of living water, he adds that, after solemn prayer, Helvidius Priscus, to whom the care of rebuilding the Capitol had been committed, "laid his hand upon the fillets that adorned the foundation stone, and also the cords by which it was to be drawn to its place. In that instant the magistrates, the priests, the senators, the Roman knights, and a number of citizens, all acting with one effort and general demonstrations of joy, laid hold of the ropes and dragged the ponderous load to its destined spot. They then threw in ingots of gold and silver, and other metals which had never been melted in the furnace, but still retained, untouched by human art, their first formation in the bowels of the earth." (*Histories*, iv., 53.)

The symbolism of the corner-stone when duly laid with Masonic rites is full of significance, which refers to its form, to its situation, to its permanence, and to its consecration.

As to its form, it must be perfectly square on its surfaces, and in its solid contents a cube. Now the square is a symbol of morality, and the cube, of truth. In its situation it lies between the north, the place of darkness, and the east, the place of light; and hence this position symbolizes the Masonic progress from darkness to light, and from ignorance to knowledge. The permanence and durability of the corner-stone, which lasts long after the building in whose foundation it was placed has fallen into decay, is intended to remind the Mason that, when this earthly house of his tabernacle shall have passed away, he has within him a sure foundation of eternal life—a corner-stone of immortality—an emanation from that Divine Spirit which pervades all nature, and which, therefore, must survive the tomb, and rise, triumphant and eternal, above the decaying dust of death and the grave.

The stone, when deposited in its appropriate place, is carefully examined with the necessary implements of Operative Masonry—the square, the level, and the plumb, themselves all symbolic in meaning—and is then declared to be "well formed, true, and trusty." Thus the Mason is taught that his virtues are to be tested by temptation and trial, by suffering and adversity, before they can be pronounced by the Master Builder of souls to be materials worthy of the spiritual building of eternal life, fitted, "as living stones, for that house not made with hands, eternal in the heavens."

And lastly, in the ceremony of depositing the corner-stone, the elements of Masonic consecration are produced, and the stone is solemnly set apart by pouring corn, wine, and oil upon its surface, emblematic of the Nourishment, Refreshment, and Joy which are to be the rewards of a faithful performance of duty.

The corner-stone does not appear to have been adopted by any of the heathen nations, but to have been as the *eben pinah*, peculiar to the Jews, from whom it descended to the Christians. In the Old Testament, it seems always to have denoted a prince or high personage, and hence the Evangelists constantly use it in reference to Christ, who is called the "chief corner-stone." In Masonic symbolism, it signifies a true Mason, and therefore it is the first character which the Apprentice is made to represent after his initiation has been completed.

Corn of Nourishment. One of the three elements of Masonic consecration. (See *Corn, Wine, and Oil.*)

Corn, Wine, and Oil. Corn, wine, and oil are the Masonic elements of consecration. The adoption of these symbols is supported by the highest antiquity. Corn, wine, and oil were the most important productions of Eastern countries; they constituted the wealth of the people, and were esteemed as the supports of life and the means of refreshment. David enumerates them among the greatest blessings that we enjoy, and speaks of them as "*wine* that maketh glad the heart of man, and *oil* to make his face to shine, and *bread* which strengtheneth man's heart." (Ps. civ. 15.) In devoting anything to religious purposes, the anointing with oil was considered as a necessary part of the ceremony, a rite which has descended to Christian nations. The tabernacle in the wilderness, and all its holy vessels, were, by God's express command, anointed with oil; Aaron and his two sons were set apart for the priesthood with the same ceremony; and the prophets and kings of Israel were consecrated to their offices by the same rite. Hence, Freemasons' Lodges, which are but temples to the Most High, are consecrated to the sacred purposes for which they were built by strewing corn, wine, and oil upon the "*Lodge*," the emblem of the Holy Ark. Thus does this mystic ceremony instruct us to be nourished with the hidden manna of righteousness, to be refreshed with the Word of the Lord, and to rejoice with *joy* unspeakable in the riches of divine grace. "Wherefore, my brethren," says the venerable Harris (*Disc.*, iv., 81), "wherefore do you carry *corn, wine,* and *oil* in your processions, but to remind you that in the pilgrimage of human life you are to impart a portion of your *bread* to feed the hungry, to send a cup of your *wine* to cheer the sorrowful, and to pour the healing *oil* of your consolation into the wounds which sickness hath made in the bodies, or affliction rent in the hearts, of your fellow-travellers?"

In processions, the corn alone is carried in a golden pitcher, the wine and oil are placed in silver vessels, and this is to remind us that the first, as a necessity and the "staff of life," is of more importance and more worthy of honor than the others, which are but comforts.

Cornucopia. The horn of plenty. The old Pagan myth tells us that Zeus was nourished during his infancy in Crete by the daughters of Melissus, with the milk of the goat Amalthea. Zeus, when he came to the empire of the world, in gratitude placed Amalthea in the heavens as a constellation, and gave one of her horns to his nurses, with the assurance that it should furnish them with a never-failing supply of whatever they might desire. Hence it is a symbol of abundance, and as such has been adopted as the jewel of the Stewards of a Lodge, to remind them that it is their duty to see that the tables are properly furnished at refreshment, and that every brother is suitably provided for. Among the deities whose images are to be found in the ancient Temples at Elora, in Hindustan, is the goddess *Ana Purna*, whose name is compounded of *Ana*, signifying corn, and *Purna*, meaning plenty. She holds a corn measure in her hand, and the whole therefore very clearly has the same allusion as the Masonic *Horn of plenty*.

Coronet, Ducal. (Italian, *Coronetta*.) An inferior crown worn by noblemen; that of a

British duke is adorned with strawberry leaves; that of a marquis has leaves with pearls interposed; that of an earl has the pearls above the leaves; that of a viscount is surrounded with pearls only; that of a baron has only four pearls. The ducal coronet is a prominent symbol in the Thirty-third Degree of the A. A. Scottish Rite.

Correspondence. See *Committee on Foreign Correspondence*.

Corresponding Grand Secretary. An officer of a Grand Lodge to whom was formerly entrusted, in some Grand Lodges, the Foreign Correspondence of the body. The office is now disused, being retained only in the Grand Lodge of Massachusetts.

Corybantes, Mysteries of. Rites instituted in Phrygia in honor of Atys, the lover of Cybele. The goddess was supposed first to bewail the death of her lover, and afterward to rejoice for his restoration to life. The ceremonies were a scenical representation of this alternate lamentation and rejoicing, and of the sufferings of Atys, who was placed in an ark or coffin during the mournful part of the orgies. If the description of these rites, given by Sainte-Croix from various ancient authorities, be correct, they were but a modification of the Eleusinian mysteries.

Cosmist. A religious faith of late recognition, having for its motto, "Deeds, not Creeds," and for its principle the service of humanity is the supreme duty. The design of Cosmism is to join all men and women into one family, in which the principle of equality, together with that of brotherly love (that is, love of the human race), is the predominant one, and the moral and material welfare of all the sole aim and purpose.

The Cosmists are enjoined to act as follows: To give one another encouragement and aid, both material and moral; to cultivate all their faculties; to contemplate all mankind as brethren; to be courteous and forbearing to each and all; to practise charity without publicity or ostentation.

Freemasonry is an intensely theistical institution; but its principles could scarcely be better expressed than those above enumerated as the foundation of the Cosmistic faith; more especially in the motto, "Deeds, not Creeds."

There is an observable difference between Cosmists and Secularists, Collectivists and Positivists.

Cosmopolite. The Third Degree of the Second Temple of the Rite of African Architects (*q. v.*).

Council. In several of the high degrees of Masonry the meetings are styled Councils; as, a Council of Royal and Select Masters, or Princes of Jerusalem, or Companions of the Red Cross.

Council Chamber. A part of the room in which the ceremonies of the Companions of the Red Cross are performed.

Council, Grand. See *Grand Council*.

Council of Allied Masonic Degrees. An organization formed in England in 1880 to embosom, protect, and promulgate all side degrees of a Masonic or other secret character, and those otherwise unclaimed that may appear as waifs. The central organization is termed the "Grand Council of Allied Masonic Degrees."

Council of Companions of the Red Cross. A body in which the First Degree of the Templar system in this country is conferred. It is held under the Charter of a Commandery of Knights Templar, which, when meeting as a council, is composed of the following officers: A Sovereign Master, Chancellor, Master of the Palace, Prelate, Master of Despatches, Master of Cavalry, Master of Infantry, Standard-Bearer, Sword-Bearer, Warder, and Sentinel.

Council of Royal and Select Masters. The united body in which the Royal and Select degrees are conferred. In some jurisdictions this Council confers also the degree of Super-Excellent Master.

Council of Royal Masters. The body in which the degree of Royal Master, the eighth in the American Rite, is conferred. It receives its Charter from a Grand Council of Royal and Select Masters, and has the following officers: Thrice Illustrious Grand Master, Illustrious Hiram of Tyre, Principal Conductor of the Works, Master of the Exchequer, Master of Finances, Captain of the Guards, Conductor of the Council, and Steward.

Council of Select Masters. The body in which the degree of Select Masters, the ninth in the American Rite, is conferred. It receives its Charter from a Grand Council of Royal and Select Masters. Its officers are: Thrice Illustrious Grand Master, Illustrious Hiram of Tyre, Principal Conductor of the Works, Treasurer, Recorder, Captain of the Guards, Conductor of the Council, and Steward.

Council of the Trinity. An independent Masonic jurisdiction, in which are conferred the degrees of Knight of the Christian Mark, and Guard of the Conclave, Knight of the Holy Sepulcher, and the Holy and Thrice Illustrious Order of the Cross. They are conferred after the Encampment degrees. They are Christian degrees, and refer to the crucifixion.

Council, Supreme. See *Supreme Council.*

Courtesy. Politeness of manners, as the result of kindness of disposition, was one of the peculiar characteristics of the knights of old. "No other human laws enforced," says M. de St. Palaye, "as chivalry did, sweetness and modesty of temper, and that politeness which the word *courtesy* was meant perfectly to express." We find, therefore, in the ritual of Templarism, the phrase "a true and courteous knight"; and Knights Templars are in the habit of closing their letters to each other with the expression, *Yours in all knightly courtesy.* Courtesy is also a Masonic virtue, because it is the product of a feeling of kindness; but it is not so specifically spoken of in the symbolic degrees, where *brotherly love* assumes its place, as it is in the orders of knighthood.

Coustos, John. The sufferings inflicted, in 1743, by the Inquisition at Lisbon, on John Coustos, a Freemason, and the Master of a Lodge in that city; and the fortitude with which he endured the severest tortures, rather than betray his trusts and reveal the secrets that had been confided to him, constitute an interesting episode in the history of Freemasonry. Coustos, after returning to England, published, in 1746, a book, detailing his sufferings, from which the reader is presented with the following abridged narrative.

John Coustos was born at Berne, in Switzerland, but emigrated, in 1716, with his father to England, where he became a naturalized subject. In 1743 he removed to Lisbon, in Portugal, and began the practise of his profession, which was that of a lapidary, or dealer in precious stones.

In consequence of the bull or edict of Pope Clement XII. denouncing the Masonic institution, the Lodges at Lisbon were not held at public houses, as was the custom in England and other Protestant countries, but privately, at the residences of the members. Of one of these Lodges, Coustos, who was a zealous Mason, was elected the Master. A female, who was cognizant of the existence of the Lodge over which Coustos presided, revealed the circumstance to her confessor, declaring that, in her opinion, the members were "monsters in nature, who perpetrated the most shocking crimes." In consequence of this information, it was resolved, by the Inquisition, that Coustos should be arrested and subjected to the tender mercies of the "Holy Office." He was accordingly seized, a few nights afterward, in a coffee-house—the public pretense of the arrest being that he was privy to the stealing of a diamond, of which they had

falsely accused another jeweler, the friend and Warden of Coustos, whom also they had a short time previously arrested.

Coustos was then carried to the prison of the Inquisition, and after having been searched and deprived of all his money, papers, and other things that he had about him, he was led to a lonely dungeon, in which he was immured, being expressly forbidden to speak aloud or knock against the walls, but if he required anything, to beat with a padlock that hung on the outward door, and which he could reach by thrusting his arm through the iron grate. "It was there," says he, "that, struck with the horrors of a place of which I had heard and read such baleful descriptions, I plunged at once into the blackest melancholy; especially when I reflected on the dire consequences with which my confinement might very possibly be attended."

On the next day he was led, bareheaded, before the President and four Inquisitors, who, after having made him reply on oath to several questions respecting his name, his parentage, his place of birth, his religion, and the time he had resided in Lisbon, exhorted him to make a full confession of all the crimes he had ever committed in the whole course of his life; but, as he refused to make any such confession, declaring that, from his infancy, he had been taught to confess not to man but to God, he was again remanded to his dungeon.

Three days after, he was again brought before the Inquisitors, and the examination was renewed. This was the first occasion on which the subject of Freemasonry was introduced, and there Coustos for the first time learned that he had been arrested and imprisoned solely on account of his connection with the forbidden Institution.

The result of this conference was that Coustos was conveyed to a deeper dungeon, and kept there in close confinement for several weeks, during which period he was taken three times before the Inquisitors. In the first of these examinations they again introduced the subject of Freemasonry, and declared that if the Institution was as virtuous as their prisoner contended that it was, there was no occasion for concealing so industriously the secrets of it. Coustos did not reply to this objection to the Inquisitorial satisfaction, and he was remanded back to his dungeon, where a few days after he fell sick.

After his recovery, he was again taken before the Inquisitors, who asked him several new questions with regard to the tenets of Freemasonry—among others, whether he, since his abode in Lisbon, had received any Portuguese into the society? He replied that he had not.

When he was next brought before them, "they insisted," he says, "upon my letting them into the secrets of Freemasonry; threatening me, in case I did not comply." But Coustos firmly and fearlessly refused to violate his obligations.

After several other interviews, in which the effort was unavailingly made to extort from him a renunciation of Masonry, he was subjected to the torture, of which he gives the following account:

"I was instantly conveyed to the torture-room, built in form of a square tower, where no light appeared but what two candles gave; and to prevent the dreadful cries and shocking groans of the unhappy victims from reaching the ears of the other prisoners, the doors are lined with a sort of quilt.

"The reader will naturally suppose that I must be seized with horror, when, at my entering this infernal place, I saw myself, on a sudden, surrounded by six wretches, who, after preparing the tortures, stripped me naked, (all to linen drawers,) when, laying me on my back, they began to lay hold of every part of my body. First, they put round my neck an iron collar, which was fastened to the scaffold; they then fixed a ring to each foot; and this being done, they stretched my limbs with all their might. They next wound two ropes round each arm, and two round each thigh, which ropes passed under the scaffold, through holes made for that purpose, and were all drawn tight at the same time, by four men, upon a signal made for this purpose.

"The reader will believe that my pains must be intolerable, when I solemnly declare that these ropes, which were of the size of one's little finger, pierced through my flesh quite to the bone, making the blood gush out at eight different places that were thus bound. As I persisted in refusing to discover any more than what has been seen in the interrogatories above, the ropes were thus drawn together four different times. At my side stood a physician and a surgeon, who often felt my temples, to judge of the danger I might be in—by which means my tortures were suspended, at intervals, that I might have an opportunity of recovering myself a little.

"Whilst I was thus suffering, they were so barbarously unjust as to declare, that, were I to die under the torture, I should be guilty, by my obstinacy, of self-murder. In fine, the last time the ropes were drawn tight, I grew so exceedingly weak, occasioned by the blood's circulation being stopped, and the pains I endured, that I fainted quite away; insomuch that I was carried back to my dungeon, without perceiving it.

"These barbarians, finding that the tortures above described could not extort any further discovery from me; but that, the more they made me suffer, the more fervently I addressed my supplications, for patience, to heaven; they were so inhuman, six weeks after, as to expose me to another kind of torture, more grievous, if possible, than the former. They made me stretch my arms in such a manner that the palms of my hands were turned outward; when, by the help of a rope that fastened them together at the wrist, and which they turned by an engine, they drew them gently nearer to one another behind, in such a manner that the back of each hand touched, and stood exactly parallel one to another; whereby both my shoulders were dislocated,

and a considerable quantity of blood issued from my mouth. This torture was repeated thrice; after which I was again taken to my dungeon, and put into the hands of physicians and surgeons, who, in setting my bones, put me to exquisite pain.

"Two months after, being a little recovered, I was again conveyed to the torture-room, and there made to undergo another kind of punishment twice. The reader may judge of its horror, from the following description thereof. "The torturers turned twice around my body a thick iron chain, which, crossing upon my stomach, terminated afterwards at my wrists. They next set my back against a thick board, at each extremity whereof was a pulley, through which there ran a rope, that catched the ends of the chains at my wrists. The tormentors then stretched these ropes, by means of a roller, pressed or bruised my stomach, in proportion as the means were drawn tighter. They tortured me on this occasion to such a degree, that my wrists and shoulders were put out of joint.

"The surgeons, however, set them presently after; but the barbarians not yet having satiated their cruelty, made me undergo this torture a second time, which I did with fresh pains, though with equal constancy and resolution. I was then remanded back to my dungeon, attended by the surgeons, who dressed by bruises; and here I continued until their *auto-da-fé*, or gaol delivery."

On that occasion, he was sentenced to work at the galleys for four years. Soon, however, after he had commenced the degrading occupation of a galley slave, the injuries which he had received during his inquisitorial tortures having so much impaired his health, that he was unable to undergo the toils to which he had been condemned, he was sent to the infirmary, where he remained until October, 1744, when he was released upon the demand of the British minister, as a subject to the King of England. He was, however, ordered to leave the country. This, it may be supposed, he gladly did, and repaired to London, where he published the account of his sufferings in a book entitled *The Sufferings of John Coustos for Freemasonry, and for refusing to turn Roman Catholic, in the Inquisition at Lisbon, etc., etc.* London, 1746; 8vo, 400 pages. (Reprinted at Birmingham, 1790.) Such a narrative is well worthy of being read. John Coustos has not, by his literary researches, added anything to the learning or science of our Order; yet, by his fortitude and fidelity under the severest sufferings, inflicted to extort from him a knowledge he was bound to conceal, he has shown that Freemasonry makes no idle boast in declaring that its secrets "are locked up in the depository of faithful breasts."

Couvreur. The title of an officer in a French Lodge, equivalent to the English Tiler.

Couvrir le Temple. A French expression for the English one to close the Lodge. But it has also another signification. "To cover the Temple to a brother," means, in French Masonic language, to exclude him from the Lodge.

Covenant of Masonry. As a covenant is defined to be a contract or agreement between two or more parties on certain terms, there can be no doubt that when a man is made a Mason he enters into a covenant with the Institution. On his part he promises to fulfil certain promises, and to discharge certain duties, for which, on the other part, the Fraternity bind themselves by an equivalent covenant of friendship, protection, and support. This covenant must of course be repeated and modified with every extension of the terms of agreement on both sides. The covenant of an Entered Apprentice is different from that of a Fellow-Craft, and the covenant of the latter from that of a Master Mason. As we advance in Masonry our obligations increase, but the covenant of each degree is not the less permanent or binding because that of a succeeding one has been superadded. The second covenant does not impair the sanctity of the first.

This covenant of Masonry is symbolized and sanctioned by the most important and essential of all the ceremonies of the Institution. It is the very foundation-stone which supports the whole edifice, and, unless it be properly laid, no superstructure can with any safety be erected. It is indeed the covenant that makes the Mason.

A matter so important as this, in establishing the relationship of a Mason with the Craft—this baptism, so to speak, by which a member is inaugurated into the Institution—must of course be attended with the most solemn and binding ceremonies. Such has been the case in all countries. Covenants have always been solemnized with certain solemn forms and religious observances which gave them a sacred sanction in the minds of the contracting parties. The Hebrews, especially, invested their covenants with the most imposing ceremonies.

The first mention of a covenant in form that is met with in Scripture is that recorded in the fifteenth chapter of Genesis, where, to confirm it, Abraham, in obedience to the Divine command, took a heifer, a she-goat, and a ram, "and divided them in the midst, and laid each piece one against another." (v. 10.) This dividing a victim into two parts, that the covenanting parties might pass between them, was a custom not confined to the Hebrews, but borrowed from them by all the heathen nations.

In the Book of Jeremiah it is again alluded to, and the penalty for the violation of the covenant is also expressed.

"And I will give the men that have transgressed my covenant, which have not performed the words of the covenant which they had made before me, when *they cut the calf in twain*, and passed between the parts thereof,

"The princes of Judah, and the princes of Jerusalem, the eunuchs, and the priests, and all the people of the land, which passed between the parts of the calf;

"I will even give them into the hand of their enemies, and into the hand of them that seek their life: and their dead bodies shall be for meat *unto the fowls of the heaven, and to the beasts of the earth.*" (Jeremiah xxxiv. 18, 19, 20.)

These ceremonies, thus briefly alluded to in the passages which have been quoted, were performed in full, as follows. The attentive Masonic student will not fail to observe the analogies to those of his own Order.

The parties entering into a covenant first selected a proper animal, such as a calf or a kid among the Jews, a sheep among the Greeks, or a pig among the Romans. The throat was then cut across, with a single blow, so as to completely divide the windpipe and arteries, without touching the bone. This was the first ceremony of the covenant. The second was to tear open the breast, to take from thence the heart and vitals, and if on inspection the least imperfection was discovered, the body was considered unclean, and thrown aside for another. The third ceremony was to divide the body in twain, and to place the two parts to the north and south, so that the parties to the covenant might pass between them, coming from the east and going to the west. The carcass was then left as a prey to the wild beasts of the field and the vultures of the air, and thus the covenant was ratified.

Covering of the Lodge. As the lectures tell us that our ancient brethren met on the highest hills and lowest vales, from this it is inferred that, as the meetings were thus in the open air, the only covering must have been the overarching vault of heaven. Hence, in the symbolism of Masonry the *covering of the Lodge* is said to be "a clouded canopy or starry-decked heaven." The terrestrial Lodge of labor is thus intimately connected with the celestial Lodge of eternal refreshment. The symbolism is still further extended to remind us that the whole world is a Mason's Lodge, and heaven its sheltering cover.

Cowan. This is a purely Masonic term, and signifies in its technical meaning an *intruder*, whence it is always coupled with the word *eavesdropper*. It is not found in any of the old manuscripts of the English Masons anterior to the eighteenth century, unless we suppose that *lowen*, met with in many of them, is a clerical error of the copyists. It occurs in the Schaw manuscript, a Scotch record which bears the date of 1598, in the following passage: "That no Master or Fellow of Craft receive any *cowans* to work in his society or company, nor send none of his servants to work with *cowans*." In the second edition of Anderson's *Constitutions*, published in 1738, we find the word in use among the English Masons, thus: "But Free and Accepted Masons shall not allow *cowans* to work with them; nor shall they be employed by *cowans* without an urgent necessity; and even in that case they must not teach *cowans*, but must have a separate communication." (P. 146.) There can be but little doubt that the word, as a Masonic term, comes to us from Scotland, and it is therefore in the Scotch language that we must look for its signification.

Now, Jamieson, in his Scottish *Dictionary*, gives us the following meanings of the word:

"Cowan, s. 1. A term of contempt; applied to one who does the work of a Mason, but has not been regularly bred.

"2. Also used to denote one who builds dry walls, otherwise denominated a *dry-diker*.

"3. One unacquainted with the secrets of Freemasonry."

And he gives the following examples as his authorities:

"'A boat-carpenter, joiner, *cowan* (or builder of stone without mortar), get 1s. at the *minimum* and good maintenance.' P. Morven, *Argyles. Statistic. Acct.*, X., 267. N.

"'*Cowans*. Masons who build dry-stone dikes or walls.' P. Halkirk, *Carthn. Statistic. Acct.*, XIX., 24. N."

In the *Rob Roy* of Scott, the word is used by Allan Inverach, who says:

"She does not value a Cawmil mair as a *cowan*."

The word has therefore, I think, come to the English Fraternity directly from the Operative Masons of Scotland, among whom it was used to denote a pretender, in the exact sense of the first meaning of Jamieson.

There is no word that has given Masonic scholars more trouble than this in tracing its derivation. By some it has been considered to come from the Greek κύων, *kuŏn*, a dog; and referred to the fact that in the early ages of the Church, when the mysteries of the new religion were communicated only to initiates under the veil of secrecy, infidels were called "dogs," a term probably suggested by such passages as Matthew vii. 6, "Give not that which is holy unto the dogs"; or, Philip. iii. 2, "Beware of dogs, beware of evil workers, beware of the concision." This derivation has been adopted by Oliver, and many other writers. Jamieson's derivations are from the old Swedish *kujon*, *kuzhjohn*, a silly fellow, and the French *coion*, *coyon*, a coward, a base fellow. No matter how we get the word, it seems always to convey an idea of contempt. The attempt to derive it from the *chouans* of the French Revolution is manifestly absurd, for it has been shown that the word was in use long before the French Revolution was even meditated. [Dr. Murray in the *New English Dictionary* says that the derivation of the word is unknown.—E. L. H.]

Craft. It is from the Saxon *craft*, which indirectly signifies skill or dexterity in any art. In reference to this skill, therefore, the ordinary acceptation is a trade or mechanical art, and collectively, the persons practising it. Hence, "the Craft," in Speculative Masonry, signifies the whole body of Freemasons, wherever dispersed.

Craft Masonry, Ancient. See *Ancient Craft Masonry*.

Craft Statistics. See *Statistics of Craft Masonry*.

Crafted. A word sometimes colloquially used, instead of the Lodge term "passed," to designate the advancement of a candidate to the Second Degree.

Craftsman. A Mason. The word originally meant anyone skilful in his art, and is so used by our early writers. Thus Chaucer, in his *Knights' Tale*, v. 1897, says:

"For in the land there was no craftesman,
That geometry or arsmetrike can,
Nor pourtrayor, nor carver of images,
That Theseus ne gave him meat and wages.
The theatre to make and to devise."

Crata Repoa. See *Egyptian Priests, Initiations of the*.

Create. In chivalry, when anyone received the order of knighthood, he was said to be *created a knight*. The word "dub" had also the same meaning. The word *created* is used in Commanderies of Knights Templar to denote the elevation of a candidate to that degree. (See *Dub*.)

Creation. Preston (*Illust.*, B. I., Sect. 3) says: "From the commencement of the world, we may trace the foundation of Masonry. Ever since symmetry began, and harmony displayed her charms, our Order has had a being." Language like this has been deemed extravagant, and justly, too, if the words are to be taken in their literal sense. The idea that the Order of Masonry is coeval with the creation is so absurd that the pretension cannot need refutation. But the fact is, that Anderson, Preston, and other writers who have indulged in such statements, did not mean by the word *Masonry* anything like an organized Order or Institution bearing any resemblance to the Freemasonry of the present day. They simply meant to indicate that the great moral principles on which Freemasonry is founded, and by which it professes to be guided, have always formed a part of the Divine government, and been presented to man from his first creation for his acceptance. The words quoted from Preston are unwise, because they are liable to misconstruction. But the symbolic idea which they intended to convey, namely, that Masonry is truth, and that truth is coexistent with man's creation, is correct, and cannot be disputed.

Creed, A Mason's. Although Freemasonry is not a dogmatic theology, and is tolerant in the admission of men of every religious faith, it would be wrong to suppose that it is without a creed. On the contrary, it has a creed, the assent to which it rigidly enforces, and the denial of which is absolutely incompatible with membership in the Order. This creed consists of two articles: First, a belief in God, the Creator of all things, who is therefore recognized as the Great Architect of the Universe; and secondly, a belief in the eternal life, to which this present life is but a preparatory and probationary state. To the first of these articles assent is explicitly required as soon as the threshold of the Lodge is crossed. The second is expressively taught by legends and symbols, and must be implicitly assented to by every Mason, especially by those who have received the Third Degree, which is altogether founded on the doctrine of the resurrection to a second life.

At the revival of Masonry in 1717, the Grand Lodge of England set forth the law, as to the religious creed to be required of a Mason, in the following words, to be found in the *Charges* approved by that body.

"In ancient times, Masons were charged in every country to be of the religion of that country or nation, whatever it was; yet it is now thought more expedient only to oblige them to that religion in which all men agree, leaving their particular opinions to themselves." (*Constitutions*, 1723, p. 50.)

This is now considered universally as the recognized law on the subject.

Cresset. An open lamp formerly having a cross-piece filled with combustible material, such as naphtha, and recognized as the symbol of Light and Truth.

Creuzer, Georg Friederich. George Frederick Creuzer, who was born in Germany in 1771, and was a professor at the University of Heidelberg, devoted himself to the study of the ancient religions, and, with profound learning, established a peculiar system on the subject. His theory was, that the religion and mythology of the ancient Greeks were borrowed from a far more ancient people—a body of priests coming from the East—who received them as a revelation. The myths and traditions of this ancient people were adopted by Hesiod, Homer, and the later poets, although not without some misunderstanding of them; and they were finally preserved in the Mysteries, and became subjects of investigation for the philosophers. This theory Creuzer has developed in his most important work, entitled *Symbolik und Archäologie der alten Völker, besonders der Griechen*, which was published at Leipsic in 1819–21. There is no translation of this work into English; but Guigniaut published at Paris, in 1829, a paraphrastic translation of it, under the title of *Religions de l'Antiquité considerées principalement dans leur Formes Symboliques et Mythologiques*. Creuzer's views throw much light on the symbolic history of Freemasonry. He died in 1858.

Crimes, Masonic. In Masonry, every offense is a crime, because, in every violation of a Masonic law there is not only sometimes an infringement of the rights of an individual, but always, superinduced upon this, a breach and violation of public rights and duties, which affect the whole community of the Order considered as a community.

The first class of crimes which are laid down in the *Constitutions*, as rendering their perpetrators liable to Masonic jurisdiction, are offenses against the moral law. "Every Mason," say the *Old Charges of 1722*, "is obliged by his tenure to obey the moral law." The same charge continues the precept by asserting, that if he rightly understands the art, he will never be a stupid atheist, nor an irreligious libertine. Atheism, therefore, which is a rejection of a supreme, superintending Creator, and irreligious libertinism, which, in the language of that day, signified a denial of all moral responsibility, are offenses against the moral law, because they deny its validity and contemn its sanctions; and hence they are to be classed as Masonic crimes.

Again: the moral law inculcates love of God, love of our neighbor, and duty to ourselves. Each of these embraces other incidental duties which are obligatory on every Mason, and the violation of any one of which constitutes a Masonic crime.

The love of God implies that we should abstain from all profanity and irreverent use of his name. Universal benevolence is the necessary result of love of our neighbor. Cruelty to one's inferiors and dependents, uncharitableness to the poor and needy, and a general misanthropical neglect of our duty as men to our fellow-beings, exhibiting itself in extreme selfishness and indifference to the comfort or happiness of all others, are offenses against the moral law, and therefore Masonic crimes. Next to violations of the moral law, in the category of Masonic crimes, are to be considered the transgressions of the municipal law, or the law of the land. Obedience to constituted authority is one of the first duties which is impressed upon the mind of the candidate; and hence he who transgresses the laws of the government under which he lives violates the teachings of the Order, and is guilty of a Masonic crime. But the Order will take no cognizance of ecclesiastical or political offenses. And this arises from the very nature of the society, which eschews all controversies about national religion or state policy. Hence apostasy, heresy, and schisms, although considered in some governments as heinous offenses, and subject to severe punishment, are not viewed as Masonic crimes. Lastly, violations of the Landmarks and Regulations of the Order are Masonic crimes. Thus, disclosure of any of the secrets which a Mason has promised to conceal; disobedience and want of respect to Masonic superiors; the bringing of "private piques or quarrels" into the Lodge; want of courtesy and kindness to the brethren; speaking calumniously of a Mason behind his back, or in any other way attempting to injure him, as by striking him except in self-defense, or violating his domestic honor, is each a crime in Masonry. Indeed, whatever is a violation of fidelity to solemn engagements, a neglect of prescribed duties, or a transgression of the cardinal principles of friendship, morality, and brotherly love, is a Masonic crime.

Crimson. (Crimoysin, O. Eng.) A deep-red color tinged with blue, emblematical of fervency and zeal; belonging to several degrees of the Scottish Rite as well as to the Holy Royal Arch.

Cromlech. A large stone resting on two or more stones, like a table. Cromlechs are found in Brittany, Denmark, Germany, and some other parts of Europe, and are supposed to have been used in the Celtic *Mysteries*.

Cromwell. The Abbé Larudan published at Amsterdam, in 1746, a book entitled *Les Francs-Maçons Ecrasés*, of which Kloss says (*Bibliog. der Freimaurerei*, No. 1874) that it is the armory from which all the abuse of Freemasonry by its enemies has been derived. Larudan was the first to advance in this book the theory that Oliver Cromwell was the founder of Freemasonry. He says that Cromwell established the Order for the furtherance of his political designs; adopting with this view, as its governing principles, the doctrines of liberty and equality, and bestowed upon its members the title of Freemasons, because his object was to engage them in the building of a new edifice, that is to say, to reform the human race by the extermination of kings and all regal powers. He selected for this purpose the design of rebuilding the Temple of Solomon. This Temple, erected by Divine command, had been the sanctuary of religion. After years of glory and magnificence, it had been destroyed by a formidable army. The people who there worshiped had been conveyed to Babylon, whence, after enduring a rigorous captivity, they had been permitted to return to Jerusalem and rebuild the Temple. This history of the Solomonic Temple Cromwell adopted, says Larudan, as an allegory on which to found his new Order. The Temple in its original magnificence was man in his primeval state of purity; its destruction and the captivity of its worshipers typified pride and ambition, which have abolished equality and introduced dependence among men; and the Chaldean destroyers of the glorious edifice are the kings who have trodden on an oppressed people.

It was, continues the Abbé, in the year 1648 that Cromwell, at an entertainment given by him to some of his friends, proposed to them, in guarded terms, the establishment of a new society, which should secure a true worship of God, and the deliverance of man from oppression and tyranny. The proposition was received with unanimous favor; and a few days after, at a house in King Street, and at six o'clock in the evening (for the Abbé is particular as to time and place), the Order of Freemasonry was organized, its degrees established, its ceremonies and ritual prescribed, and several of the adherents of the future Protector initiated. The Institution was used by Cromwell for the advancement of his projects, for the union of the contending parties in England, for the extirpation of the monarchy, and his own subsequent elevation to supreme power. It extended from England into other countries, but was always careful to preserve the same doctrines of equality and liberty among men, and opposition to all monarchical government. Such is the theory of the Abbé Larudan, who, although a bitter enemy of Masonry, writes with seeming fairness and mildness. But it is hardly necessary to say that this theory of the origin of Freemasonry finds no support either in the legends of the Institution, or in the authentic history that is connected with its rise and progress.

Crosier. The staff surmounted by a cross carried before a bishop on occasions of solemn

ceremony. They are generally gilt, and made light; frequently of tin, and hollow. The pastoral staff has a circular head.

Cross. We can find no symbolism of the cross in the primitive degrees of Ancient Craft Masonry. It does not appear among the symbols of the Apprentice, the Fellow-Craft, the Master, or the Royal Arch. This is undoubtedly to be attributed to the fact that the cross was considered, by those who invented those degrees, only in reference to its character as a Christian sign. The subsequent archeological investigations that have given to the cross a more universal place in iconography were unknown to the rituals. It is true, that it is referred to, under the name of the *rode* or *rood*, in the manuscript of the fourteenth century, published by Halliwell; this was, however, one of the Constitutions of the Operative Freemasons, who were fond of the symbol, and were indebted for it to their ecclesiastical origin, and to their connection with the Gnostics, among whom the cross was a much used symbol. But on the revival in 1717, when the ritual was remodified, and differed very greatly from that meager one in practise among the medieval Masons, all allusion to the cross was left out, because the revivalists laid down the principle that the religion of Speculative Masonry was not sectarian but universal. And although this principle was in some points, as in the "lines parallel," neglected, the reticence as to the Christian sign of salvation has continued to the present day; so that the cross cannot be considered as a symbol in the primary and original degrees of Masonry.

But in the high degrees, the cross has been introduced as an important symbol. In some of them—those which are to be traced to the Temple system of Ramsay—it is to be viewed with reference to its Christian origin and meaning. Thus, in the original Rose Croix and Kadosh—no matter what may be the modern interpretation given to it—it was simply a representation of the cross of Christ. In others of a philosophical character, such as the Ineffable degrees, the symbolism of the cross was in all probability borrowed from the usages of antiquity, for from the earliest times and in almost all countries the cross has been a sacred symbol. It is depicted on the oldest monuments of Egypt, Assyria, Persia, and Hindustan. It was, says Faber (*Cabir.*, ii., 390), a symbol throughout the Pagan world long previous to its becoming an object of veneration to Christians. In ancient symbology it was a symbol of eternal life. M. de Mortillet, who, in 1866, published a work entitled *Le Signe de la Croix avant le Christianisme*, found in the very earliest epochs three principal symbols of universal occurrence: viz., the *circle*, the *pyramid*, and the *cross*. Leslie (*Man's Origin and Destiny*, p. 312), quoting from him in reference to the ancient worship of the cross, says: "It seems to have been a worship of such a peculiar nature as to exclude the worship of idols." This sacredness of the crucial symbol may be one reason why its form was often adopted, especially by the Celts, in the construction of their temples.

Of the Druidical veneration of the cross, Higgins quotes from the treatise of Schedius (*De Moribus Germanorum*, xxiv.) the following remarkable paragraph:

"The Druids seek studiously for an oaktree, large and handsome, growing up with two principal arms in the form of a cross, beside the main, upright stem. If the two horizontal arms are not sufficiently adapted to the figure, they fasten a cross beam to it. This tree they consecrate in this manner. Upon the right branch they cut in the bark, in fair characters, the word HESUS; upon the middle or upright stem, the word TARAMIS; upon the left branch, BELENUS; over this, above the going off of the arms, they cut the name of God, THAU. Under all the same repeated, THAU. This tree, so inscribed, they make their *kebla* in the grove, cathedral, or summer church, towards which they direct their faces in the offices of religion."

Mr. Brinton, in his interesting work entitled *Symbolism; The Myths of the New World*, has the following remarks:

"The symbol that beyond all others has fascinated the human mind, THE CROSS, finds here its source and meaning. Scholars have pointed out its sacredness in many natural religions, and have reverently accepted it as a mystery, or offered scores of conflicting, and often debasing, interpretations. *It is but another symbol of the four cardinal points, the four winds of heaven.* This will luminously appear by a study of its use and meaning in America." (P. 95.) And Mr. Brinton gives many instances of the religious use of the cross by several of the aboriginal tribes of this continent, where the allusion, it must be confessed, seems evidently to be to the four cardinal points, or the four winds, or four spirits of the earth. If this be so, and if it is probable that a similar reference was adopted by the Celtic and other ancient peoples, then we would have in the cruciform temple as much a symbolism of the world, of which the four cardinal points constitute the boundaries, as we have in the square, the cubical, and the circular.

18

Cross, Double. See *Cross, Patriarchal.*

Cross, Jerusalem. A Greek cross between four crosslets. It was adopted by Baldwyn as the arms of the kingdom of Jerusalem, and has since been deemed a symbol of the Holy Land. It is also the jewel of the Knights of the Holy Sepulcher. Symbolically, the four small crosses typify the four wounds of the Savior in the hands and  feet, and the large central cross shows forth his death for that world to which the four extremities point.

Cross, Maltese. A cross of eight points, worn by the Knights of Malta. It is heraldically described as "a cross pattée, but the extremity of each pattée notched at a deep angle." The eight points are said to refer symbolically to the eight beatitudes.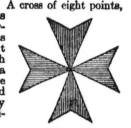

Cross of Constantine. See *Labarum.*

Cross of Salem. Called also the Pontifical Cross, because it is borne before the Pope. It is a cross, the upright piece being crossed by three lines, the upper and lower shorter than the middle one. It is the insignia of the Grand Master and Past Grand Masters of the Grand Encampment of Knights Templar of the United States, and also of the Sovereign Grand Commander of the Supreme  Council of the Ancient and Accepted Scottish Rite.

Cross, Passion. The cross on which Jesus suffered crucifixion. It is the most common form of the cross. When *rayonnant*, or having rays issuing from the point of intersection of the limbs, it is the insignia of the Commander of a Commandery of Knights Templar, according to the American system.

Cross, Patriarchal. A cross, the upright piece being twice crossed, the upper arms shorter than the lower. It is so called because it is borne before a Patriarch in the Roman Church. It is the insignia of the officers of the Grand Encampment of Knights Templars of the United States, and of all possessors of the Thirty-third Degree in the Ancient and Accepted Scottish Rite.

Cross, St. Andrew's. A saltier or cross whose decussation is in the form of the letter X. Said to be the form of 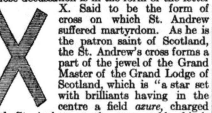 cross on which St. Andrew suffered martyrdom. As he is the patron saint of Scotland, the St. Andrew's cross forms a part of the jewel of the Grand Master of the Grand Lodge of Scotland, which is "a star set with brilliants having in the centre a field *azure*, charged with St. Andrew on the cross, gold; this is pendant from the upper band of the collar, while from the lower band is pendant the jewel proper, the Compasses extended, with the Square and Segment of a Circle of 90°; the points of the Compasses resting on the Segment, and in the centre, the Sun between the Square and Compasses." The St. Andrew's cross is also the jewel of the Twenty-ninth Degree of the Ancient and Accepted Scottish Rite, or Grand Scottish Knight of St. Andrew.

Cross, Tau. The cross on which St. Anthony is said to have suffered martyrdom. It is in the form of the letter T. (See *Tau.*)

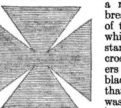

Cross, Templar. André Favin, a French heraldic writer, says that the original badge of the Knights Templar was a Patriarchal Cross, and Clarke, in his *History of Knighthood*, states the same fact; this but is an error. At first, the Templars wore a white mantle without any cross. But in 1146 Pope Eugenius III. prescribed for them a red cross on the breast, as a symbol of the martyrdom to which they were constantly exposed. The cross of the Hospitallers was white on a black mantle, and that of the Templars was different in color but of the same form, namely, a cross pattée. In this it differed from the true Maltese Cross, worn by the Knights of Malta, which was a cross pattée, the limbs deeply notched so as to make a cross of eight points. Sir Walter Scott, with his not unusual heraldic inaccuracy, and Higgins, who is not often inaccurate, but only fanciful at times, both describe the Templar cross as having eight points, thus confounding it with the cross of Malta. In the statutes of the Order of the Temple, the cross prescribed is that depicted in the Charter of Transmission, and is a cross pattée.

Cross, Teutonic. The cross formerly worn by the Teutonic Knights. It is described in heraldry as "a cross potent, *sable*, (black,) charged with another cross double potent *or*, (gold,) and surcharged with an escutcheon *argent* (silver,) bearing a double-headed eagle

(sable)." It has been adopted as the jewel of the Kadosh of the Ancient and Accepted Scottish Rite in the United States, but the original jewel of the degree was a Latin or Passion Cross.

Cross, Thrice Illustrious Order of the. A degree formerly conferred in this country on Knights Templar, but now extinct. Its meetings were called Councils, and under the authority of a body which styled itself the Ancient Council of the Trinity. The degree is no longer conferred.

Cross, Triple. See *Cross of Salem.*

Cross-Bearing Men. (*Viri Crucigeri.*) A name sometimes assumed by the Rosicrucians. Thus, in the *Miracula Naturæ* (Anno 1619), there is a letter addressed to the Fraternity of the Rosy Cross, which begins: "Philosophi Fratres, Viri Crucigeri"—*Brother Philosophers, Cross-Bearing Men.*

Cross, Jeremy L. A teacher of the Masonic ritual, who, during his lifetime, was extensively known, and for some time very popular. He was born June 27, 1783, at Haverhill, New Hampshire, and died at the same place in 1861. Cross was admitted into the Masonic Order in 1808, and soon afterward became a pupil of Thomas Smith Webb, whose modifications of the Preston lectures and of the higher degrees were generally accepted by the Masons of the United States. Cross, having acquired a competent knowledge of Webb's system, began to travel and disseminate it throughout the country. In 1819 he published *The True Masonic Chart or Hieroglyphic Monitor*, in which he borrowed liberally from the previous work of Webb. In fact, the *Chart* of Cross is, in nearly all its parts, a mere transcript of the *Monitor* of Webb, the first edition of which was published in 1797. Webb, it is true, took the same liberty with Preston, from whose *Illustrations of Masonry* he borrowed largely. The engraving of the emblems constituted, however, an entirely new and original feature in the *Hieroglyphic Chart*, and, as furnishing aids to the memory, rendered the book of Cross at once very popular; so much so, indeed, that for a long time it almost altogether superseded that of Webb. In 1820 Cross published *The Templars' Chart*, which, as a monitor of the degrees of chivalry, met with equal success. Both of these works have passed through numerous editions.

Cross received the appointment of Grand Lecturer from many Grand Lodges, and traveled for many years very extensively through the United States, teaching his system of lectures to Lodges, Chapters, Councils, and Encampments.

He possessed little or no scholarly attainments, and his contributions to the literature of Masonry are confined to the two compilations already cited. In his latter years he became involved in an effort to establish a Supreme Council of the Ancient and Accepted

Rite. But he soon withdrew his name, and retired to the place of his nativity, where he died at the advanced age of seventy-eight.

Although Cross was not a man of any very original genius, yet a recent writer has announced the fact that the symbol of the monument in the Third Degree, the broken column, unknown to the system of either Preston or Webb, was invented by him. (See *Monument*.)

Crosses. In referring to the philosophic triads and national crosses, there will be found in a work entitled *The Celtic Druids*, by Godfrey Higgins, the following: "Few causes have been more powerful in producing mistakes in ancient history than the idea, hastily formed by all ages, that every monument of antiquity marked with a cross, or with any of those symbols which they conceived to be monograms of Christ the Saviour, was of Christian origin. The cross is as common in India as in Egypt or Europe." The Rev. Mr. Maurice remarks (*Indian Antiquities*): "Let not the piety of the Catholic Christian be offended at the assertion that the cross was one of the most usual symbols of Egypt and India. The emblem of universal nature is equally honored in the Gentile and Christian world. In the Cave of Elephanta, in India, over the head of the principal figure may be seen the cross, with other symbols." Upon the breast of one of the Egyptian mummies in the museum of the London University is a cross upon a Calvary or mount. People in those countries marked their sacred water-jars, dedicated to Canopus, with a Tau cross, and sometimes even that now known as the Teutonic cross. The fertility of the country about the river Nile, in Egypt, was designated, in distance on its banks from the river proper, by the Nilometer, in the form of a cross. The erudite Dr. G. L. Ditson says: "The Rabbins say that when Aaron was made High Priest he was marked in the forehead by Moses with a cross in the shape of that now known as St. Andrew's." Proselytes, when admitted into the religious mysteries of Eleusis, were marked with a cross.

Crossing the River. The Kabbalists have an alphabet so called, in allusion to the crossing of the river Euphrates by the Jews on their return from Babylon to Jerusalem to rebuild the Temple. It has been adopted in some of the high degrees which refer to that incident. Cornelius Agrippa gives a copy of the alphabet in his *Occult Philosophy*.

Cross-Legged Knights. In the Middle Ages it was the custom to bury the body of a Knights Templar with one leg crossed over the other; and on many monuments in the churches of Europe, the effigies of these knights are to be found, often in England, of a diminutive size, with the legs placed in this position. The cross-legged posture was not confined to the Templars, but was appropriated to all persons who had assumed the cross and taken a vow to fight in defense of the Christian religion. The posture, of course, alluded to the position of the Lord while on the cross.

Cross-Legged Masons. A name given to the Knights Templar, who, in the sixteenth century, united themselves with the Masonic Lodge at Sterling, in Scotland. The allusion is evidently to the funeral posture of the Templars, so that a "cross-legged Mason" must have been at the time synonymous with a Masonic Knights Templar.

Crotona. One of the most prominent cities of the Greek colonists in Southern Italy, where, in the sixth century, Pythagoras established his celebrated school. As the early Masonic writers were fond of citing Pythagoras as a brother of their Craft, Crotona became connected with the history of Masonry, and was often spoken of as one of the most renowned seats of the Institution. Thus, in the Leland MS., whose authenticity is now, however, doubted, it is said that Pythagoras "framed a grate Lodge at Groton, and maked many Maconnes," in which sentence *Groton*, it must be remarked, is an evident corruption of *Crotona*.

Crow. An iron implement used to raise heavy stones. It is one of the working-tools of a Royal Arch Mason, and symbolically teaches him to raise his thoughts above the corrupting influence of worldly-mindedness.

Crown. A portion of Masonic regalia worn by officers who represent a king, more especially King Solomon. In Ancient Craft Masonry, however, the crown is dispensed with, the hat having taken its place.

Crown, Knight of the. See *Knight of the Crown*.

Crown, Princesses of the. (*Princesses de la Couronne*.) A species of androgynous Masonry established in Saxony in 1770. (Thory, *Acta Latomorum*, i., 303.) It existed for only a brief period.

Crowned Martyrs. See *Four Crowned Martyrs*.

Crowning of Masonry. *Le couronnement de la Maçonnerie.* The Sixty-first Degree, 7th series, of the collection of the Metropolitan Chapter of France. (Thory, *Acta Latomorum*, i., 303.)

Crowns. As the result of considerable classification, Bro. Robert Macoy presents nine principal crowns recognized in heraldry and symbolism: 1st. The Triumphal crown, of which there were three kinds—a laurel wreath, worn by a General while in the act of triumph; a golden crown, in imitation of laurel leaves; and the presentation golden crown to a conquering General. 2d. The Blockade crown of wild flowers and grass, presented by the army to the Commander breaking and relieving a siege. 3d. The Civic crown of oak leaves, presented to a soldier who saved the life of his comrade. 4th. The Olive crown, conferred upon the soldiery or commander who consummated a triumph. 5th. The Mural crown, which rewarded the soldier who first scaled the wall of a besieged city. 6th. The Naval crown, presented to the Admiral who won a naval victory. 7th. The Vallary crown, or circlet of gold, bestowed on that soldier who first surmounted the stockade and forced an entrance into the enemy's camp. 8th. The Ovation crown, or chaplet of myrtle, awarded to a General who had destroyed a despised enemy and thus obtained the honor of an ovation. 9th. The Eastern or Radiated crown, a golden circle set with projecting rays.

The crown of Darius, used in Red Cross knighthood and in the Sixteenth Degree, Scottish Rite, was one of seven points, the central front projection being more prominent than the other six in size and height.

Crucefix, Robert T. An English Mason, distinguished for his services to the Craft. Robert Thomas Crucefix, M.D., LL.D., was born in Holborn, Eng., in the year 1797, and received his education at Merchant Tailors' School. After leaving school, he became the pupil of Mr. Chamberlayne, a general and celebrated practitioner of his day, at Clerkenwell; he afterward became a student at St. Bartholomew's Hospital and was a pupil of the celebrated Abernethy. On receiving his diploma as a member of the Royal College of Surgeons, in 1810, he went out to India, where he remained but a short time; upon his return he settled in London, and he continued to reside there till the year 1845, when he removed to Milton-on-Thames, where he spent the rest of his life till within a few weeks before his decease, when he removed, for the benefit of his declining health, to Bath, where he expired February 25, 1850. Dr. Crucefix was initiated into Masonry in 1829, and during the greater part of his life discharged the duties of important offices in the Grand Lodge of England, of which he was a Grand Deacon, and in several subordinate Lodges, Chapters, and Encampments. He was an earnest promoter of all the Masonic charities of England, of one of which, the "Asylum for Aged and Decrepit Freemasons," he was the founder. In 1834, he established the *Freemasons' Quarterly Review*, and continued to edit it for six years, during which period he contributed many valuable articles to its pages.

In 1840, through the machinations of his enemies (for he was too great a man not to have had some), he incurred the displeasure of the ruling powers; and on charges which, undoubtedly, were not sustained by sufficient evidence, he was suspended by the Grand Lodge for six months, and retired from active Masonic life. But he never lost the respect of the Craft, nor the affection of the leading Masons who were his contemporaries. On his restoration, he again began to labor in behalf of the Institution, and spent his last days in advancing its interests. To his character, his long-tried friend, the venerable Oliver, pays this tribute: "Dr. Crucefix did not pretend to infallibility, and, like all other public men, he might be sometimes wrong; but his errors were not from the heart, and always leaned to the side of virtue and beneficence. He toiled incessantly for the benefit of his brethren, and was anxious that all inestimable blessings should be conveyed by Masonry on mankind. In sickness or in health he was ever found at his post, and his sympathy was the most active in behalf of the destitute brother, the widow, and the orphan. His perseverance never flagged for a moment; and he acted as though he had made up his mind to live and die in obedience to the calls of duty."

Crucifix. A cross with the image of the Savior suspended on it. A part of the furniture of a Commandery of Knights Templar and of a Chapter of Princes of Rose Croix.

Crusades. There was between Freemasonry and the Crusades a much more intimate relation than has generally been supposed. In the first place, the communications frequently established by the Crusaders, and especially the Knights Templar, with the Saracens, led to the acquisition, by the former, of many of the dogmas of the secret societies of the East, such as the Essenes, the Assassins, and the Druses. These were brought by the knights to Europe, and subsequently, on the establishment by Ramsay and his contemporaries and immediate successors of Templar Masonry, were incorporated into the high degrees, and still exhibit their influence. Indeed, it is scarcely to be doubted that many of these degrees were invented with a special reference to the events which occurred in Syria and Palestine. Thus, for instance, the Scottish degree of Knights of the East and West must have originally alluded, as its name imports, to the legend which teaches a division of the Masons after the Temple was finished, when the Craft dispersed—a part remaining in Palestine, as the Assideans, whom Lawrie, citing Scaliger, calls the "Knights of the Temple of Jerusalem," and another part passing over into Europe, whence they returned on the breaking out of the Crusades. This, of course, is but a legend, yet the influence is felt in the invention of the higher rituals.

But the influence of the Crusades on the Freemasons and the architecture of the Middle Ages is of a more historical character. In 1836, Mr. Westmacott, in a course of lectures on art before the Royal Academy, remarked that the two principal causes which materially tended to assist the restoration of literature and the arts in Europe were Freemasonry and the Crusades. The adventurers, he said, who returned from the Holy Land brought back some ideas of various improvements, particularly in architecture, and, along with these, a strong desire to erect castellated, ecclesiastical, and palatial edifices, to display the taste they had acquired; and in less than a century from the first Crusade above six hundred buildings of the above description had been erected in Southern and Western Europe. This taste was spread into almost all countries by the establishment of the Fraternity of Freemasons, who, it appears, had, under some peculiar form of brotherhood, existed for an immemorial period in Syria and other parts of the East, from whence some bands of them migrated to Europe, and after a time a great efflux of these ingenious men — Italian, German, French, Spanish, etc.—had spread themselves in communities through all civilized Europe; and in all countries where they settled we find the same style of architecture from that period, but differing in some points of treatment, as suited the climate.

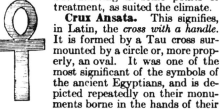

Crux Ansata. This signifies, in Latin, the *cross with a handle*. It is formed by a Tau cross surmounted by a circle or, more properly, an oval. It was one of the most significant of the symbols of the ancient Egyptians, and is depicted repeatedly on their monuments borne in the hands of their deities, and especially Phtha. Among them it was the symbol of life, and with that meaning it has been introduced into some of the higher degrees of Masonry. The Crux Ansata, surrounded by a serpent in a circle, is the symbol of immortality, because the cross was the symbol of life, and the serpent of eternity.

Crypt. From the Greek, κρύπτω (to hide). A concealed place, or subterranean vault. The caves, or cells underground, in which the primitive Christians celebrated their secret worship, were called cryptæ; and the vaults beneath our modern churches receive the name of crypts. The existence of crypts or vaults under the Temple of Solomon is testified to by the earliest as well as the most recent topographers of Jerusalem. Their connection with the legendary history of Masonry is more fully noticed under the head of *Vault Secret*.

Cryptic Degrees. The degrees of Royal and Select Master. Some modern ritualists have added to the list the degree of Superexcellent Master; but this, although now often conferred in a Cryptic Council, is not really a Cryptic degree, since its legend has no connection with the crypt or secret vault.

Cryptic Masonry. That division of the Masonic system which is directed to the investigation and cultivation of the Cryptic degrees. It is, literally, the Masonry of the secret vault.

Cteis. Greek, κτείς. The female personification of the productive principle. It generally accompanied the phallus, as the Indian yoni did the lingam; and as a symbol of the prolific powers of nature, was extensively venerated by the nations of antiquity. (See *Phallic Worship*.)

Cubical Stone. This symbol is called by the French Masons, *pierre cubique*, and by the German, *cubik stein*. It is the Perfect Ashlar of the English and American systems. (See *Ashlar*.)

Cubit. A measure of length, originally denoting the distance from the elbow to the extremity of the middle finger, or the fourth part of a well-proportioned man's stature. The Hebrew cubit, according to Bishop Cumberland, was twenty-one inches; but only eighteen according to other authorities. There were two kinds of cubits, the sacred and profane—the former equal to thirty-six, and the latter to eighteen inches. It is by the common cubit that the dimensions of the various parts of the Temple are to be computed.

Culdees. When St. Augustine came over, in the beginning of the sixth century, to Britain, for the purpose of converting the natives to Christianity, he found the country already occupied by a body of priests and their disciples, who were distinguished for the pure and simple apostolic religion which they professed. These were the *Culdees*, a name said by some to be derived from *Cultores Dei*, or worshipers of God; but by others, with perhaps more plausibility, from the Gaelic, *Cuildich*, which means a secluded corner, and evidently alludes to their recluse mode of life. The Culdees are said to have come over into Britain with the Roman legions; and thus it has been conjectured that these primitive Christians were in some way connected with the Roman Colleges of Architects, branches of which body, it is well known, everywhere accompanied the legionary armies of the empire. The chief seat of the Culdees was in the island of Iona, where St. Columba, coming out of Ireland, with twelve brethren, in the year 563, established their principal monastery. At Avernethy, the capital of the kingdom of the Picts, they founded another in the year 600, and subsequently other principal seats at Dunkeld, St. Andrew's, Brechin, Dunblane, Dumferline, Kirkaldy, Melrose, and many other places in Scotland. A writer in the London *Freemasons' Quarterly Review* (1842, p. 36) says they were little solicitous to raise architectural structures, but sought chiefly to civilize and socialize mankind by imparting to them the knowledge of those pure principles which they taught in their Lodges. Lenning and Gädicke, however, both state that the Culdees had organized within themselves, and as a part of their social system, Corporations of Builders; and that they exercised the architectural art in the construction of many sacred edifices in Scotland, Ireland, and Wales, and even in other countries of Northern Europe. Gädicke also claims that the *York Constitutions* of the tenth century were derived from them. But neither of these German lexicographers has furnished us with authorities upon which these statements are founded. It is, however, undeniable, that Masonic writers have always claimed that there was a connection—it might be only a mythical one—between these apostolic Christians and the early Masonry of Ireland and Scotland. The Culdees were opposed and persecuted by the adherents of St. Augustine, and were eventually extinguished in Scotland. But their complete suppression did not take place until about the fourteenth century.

Cumulation of Rites. The practise by a Lodge of two or more Rites, as the American or York and the Ancient Accepted Scottish, or the Scottish and French Modern Rites. This cumulation of Rites has been practised to a considerable extent in France, and in Louisiana in the United States.

Cunning. Used by old English writers in the sense of *skilful*. Thus, in 1 Kings vii. 14, it is said of the architect who was sent by the King of Tyre to assist King Solomon in the construction of his Temple, that he was "*cunning* to work all works in brass."

Cup of Bitterness. (*Calice d'Amertume*.) A ceremony in the First Degree of the French Rite. It is a symbol of the misfortunes and sorrows that assail us in the voyage of life, and which we are taught to support with calmness and resignation.

Curetes. Priests of ancient Crete, whose mysteries were celebrated in honor of the Mother of the Gods, and bore, therefore, some resemblance to the Eleusinian Rites. The neophyte was initiated in a cave, where he remained closely confined for thrice nine days. Porphyry tells us that Pythagoras repaired to Crete to receive initiation into their rites.

Curiosity. It is a very general opinion among Masons that a candidate should not be actuated by curiosity in seeking admission into the Order. But, in fact, there is no regulation nor landmark on the subject. An idle curiosity is, it is true, the characteristic of a weak mind. But to be influenced by a laudable curiosity to penetrate the mysteries of an Institution venerable for its antiquity and its universality, is to be controlled by a motive which is not reprehensible. There are, indeed, in legends of the high degrees, some instances where curiosity is condemned; but the curiosity, in these instances, led to an intrusion into forbidden places, and is very different from the curiosity or desire for knowledge which leads a profane to seek fairly and openly an acquaintance with mysteries which he has already learned to respect.

Curious. Latin, *curiosus*, from *cura*, care. An archaic expression for careful. Thus in Masonic language, which abounds in archaisms, an evidence, indeed, of its antiquity, Hiram Abif is described as a "curious and cunning workman," that is to say, "careful and skilful."

Customs, Ancient. See *Usages*.

Cynocephalus. The figure of a man with the head of a dog. A very general and important hieroglyphic among the ancient Egyptians. It was with them a symbol of the sun and moon; and in their mysteries they taught that it had indicated to Isis the place where the body of Osiris lay concealed. The possessor of the high degrees of Masonry will be familiar with the symbol of a dog, which is used in those degrees because that animal is said to have pointed out on a certain occasion an important secret. Hence the figure of a dog is sometimes found engraved among the symbols on old Masonic diplomas.

Cyrus. Cyrus, King of Persia, was a great conqueror, and after having reduced nearly all Asia, he crossed the Euphrates, and laid siege to Babylon, which he took by diverting the course of the river which ran through it. The Jews, who had been carried away by Nebuchadnezzar on the destruction of the Temple, were then remaining as captives in Babylon. These Cyrus released A.M. 3466, or B.C. 538, and sent back to Jerusalem to rebuild the house of God, under the care of Joshua, Zerubbabel, and Haggai. Hence,

from this connection of Cyrus with the history of Masonry, he plays an important part in the rituals of many of the high degrees.

But from late discoveries of inscriptions pertaining to Cyrus, as mentioned in the excellent little London work called *Fresh Light from the Ancient Monuments* (pp. 166–186), A. H. Sayce, M.A., it would appear that this king was a polytheist, and that he was not a king of Persia, although he acquired that country after his conquest of Astyages, B.C. 559 between the sixth and ninth years of Nabonidos. Cyrus was king of Elam. The empire he founded was not a Persian one; Darius, the son of Hystaspes, at a subsequent period, was the real founder of that kingdom. Prof. Sayce continues: "It was only as the predecessor of Darius, and for the sake of intelligibility to the readers of a later day, that Cyrus could be called a king of Persia." (Ezra i. 2.) The original words of his proclamation, "King of Elam," have been changed into the more familiar and intelligible "King of Persia." Elsewhere in the Bible (Isa. xxi. 1–10), when the invasion of Babylon is described, there is no mention of Persia, only of Elam and Media, the ancestral dominions of Cyrus. This is in strict accordance with the revelations of the Monuments, and testifies to the accuracy of the Old Testament records.

Cyrus never besieged Babylon, a city fifteen miles square. It opened its gates to his general without battle, B.C. 538. The description by Herodotus belongs to the reign of Darius. Mr. Bosanquet asserts that the Darius of the Book of Daniel is Darius the son of Hystaspes.

Cyrus had learned that a disaffected conquered people imported into a kingdom was a constant menace and danger, and he returned the Jewish exiles to Jerusalem to rebuild their city and be a fortress and check upon Egypt. The nations which had been brought from East and West were restored to their lands along with their gods. So it was with the captives of Judah. His dominions extended from the Hellespont almost to India.

Cyrus was a worshiper of Merodach, originally the Sun-god, who is mentioned and intended by the name Bel, and Nebo, his prophet. (Isa. xlvi. 1.) His first act after acquiring Babylonia was to restore the Babylonian gods to their shrines, from which they had been removed by Nabonidos, and further asks for their intercession. The theory that Cyrus believed in but one supreme god—Ormudz—must be abandoned. God consecrated Cyrus to be His instrument in restoring His chosen people to their land, not because the King of Elam was a Monotheist, but because the period of prophecy, "ten weeks of years," was drawing to a close.

These statements are made upon the authority of the three inscriptions among the clay documents lately discovered in Babylonia by Mr. Rassam, and translated by Sir Henry Rawlinson and Mr. Pinches. The first of these is a cylinder, inscribed by order of Cyrus; the second a tablet, which describes the conquest of Babylonia by Cyrus; while the third is an account given by Nabonidos of his restoration of the temple of the Moon-god at Haran, and of the temples of the Sun-god and of Anunit at Sepharvaim.

Cyrus ascended the throne B.C. 559, and was slain in battle against the Massagetæ, B.C. 529. He was followed by Cambyses (son) until B.C. 521, when he was succeeded by Smerdis, a Magian usurper, who reigned seven months. Darius I., son of Hystaspes, a nobleman, conspired with six others and murdered Smerdis, when, by device, Darius obtained the throne over his companions, B.C. 521. The celebrated siege of Babylon lasted two years; the city finally succumbed to the strategy of General Zopyrus, 516. Darius reigned 36 years, died B.C. 485. (C. T. McClenachan, *Zendavesta.*)

D

D. The fourth letter of the Phœnician, the Hebrew, the Greek, the Roman, and of nearly all alphabets. In Hebrew it is ד, Daleth, signifying the *door of life*, a representation of which was probably its original hieroglyph, thus:

1 shows the approximation to the Hebrew Daleth; 2, the Greek Delta, resembling the opening of a tent. The numerical value of ד is four; as a Roman numeral it stands for 500. The Divine name in Hebrew connected with this letter is רגול, Daghul, Insignis.

Da Costa, Hippolyto Joseph. A native of Colonia-do-Sacramento, on the river La Plata. He was made a Freemason in Philadelphia in the United States and afterward settled in Lisbon. He was subsequently persecuted by the Inquisition, and was rescued only in time to save his life by the aid of English brethren who got him under the protection of the English flag. He then passed over into England, where he lived for several years, becoming a zealous Mason and devoting himself to Masonic literature. In 1811, he published in London a *Narrative of his persecution in Lisbon, by the Inquisition, for the pretended crime of Freemasonry*, in 2 vols., 8vo. He wrote also a *History of the Dionysian Artificers*, in which he attempts to connect Freemasonry with the Dionysian and other mysteries of the ancients. He begins with the Eleusinian mysteries, assuming that Dionysus, Bacchus, Adonis, Thammuz, and Apollo were all various names for the sun, whose apparent movements are represented by the death and resurrection referred to in the ceremonies. But as the sun is typified as being dead or hidden for three months under the horizon, he thinks that these mysteries must have originated in a cold climate as far north as latitude 66°, or among a people living near the polar circle. He therefore attributes the invention of these mysteries to the ancient Scythians or Massagetæ, of whom he confesses that we know nothing. He afterward gives the history of the Dionysiac or Orphic mysteries of Eleusis, and draws a successful parallel between the initiation into these and the Masonic initiation. His disquisitions are marked by much learning, although his reasoning may not always carry conviction.

Dactyli. Priests of Cybele, in Phrygia, of whom there were five, which number could not be exceeded, and alluded to the salutation and blessing by the five fingers of the hand.

Daduchos. A torch-bearer. The title given to an officer in the Eleusinian mysteries, who bore a torch in commemoration of the torch lit by Ceres at the fire of Mt. Etna, and carried by her through the world in her search for her daughter.

Dædalus. A famous artist and mechanician, whose genealogy is traced in the Greek myths as having sprung from the old Athenian race of kings, the Erechtheidæ. He is said to have executed the Cretan labyrinth, the reservoir near Megaris in Sicily, the Temple of Apollo at Capua, and the celebrated altar sculptured with lions on the Libyan coast. He is said to be the inventor of a number of the "Working Tools" used in the various degrees of Masonry, the plumb-line and the ax, most of the tools used in carpentry, and of glue. Of him is told the fable of his flying safely over the Ægean by means of wings made by himself. His nephew, Perdix, is the reputed inventor of the third Great Light in Masonry, the Compasses, which are dedicated to the Craft. Through envy Dædalus is said to have hurled his nephew, Perdix, from the Temple Athene.

Dagger. In the high degrees a symbol of Masonic vengeance, or the punishment of crime. (See *Vengeance.*)

Dagrain, Louis. A writer in the *Amsterdam Journal* of November 3, 1735, of an article on the subject of Freemasonry, which caused an edict from the States General forbidding Masonic gatherings throughout the country. (Thory, *Acta Lat.*, ii., 306.)

Dagran, Louis. President of a General Assembly of thirty Lodges, held on St. John's Day, 1756, at The Hague, for the formation of the Grand Lodge of Holland. It was at this December meeting that Baron Van Aerssen Beyeren Van Hogerheide was appointed Grand Master. (Thory, *Acta Lat.*, i., 72.)

Dais. From the French *dais*, a canopy. The raised floor at the head of a banqueting room, designed for guests of distinction; so called because it used to be decorated with a canopy. In Masonic language, the dais is the elevated portion of the eastern part of the Lodge room, which is occupied by Past Masters and the dignitaries of the Order. This should be elevated three steps above the floor. The station of the Junior Warden is raised one, and that of the Senior two.

Dakota. The first Lodge organized in Dakota was St. John's Lodge, at Yankton, which received from the Grand Lodge of Iowa, December 5, 1862, a dispensation, and afterward a Charter, dated June 3, 1863; Incense Lodge, at Vermillion, received a dispensation, January 14, 1869, and a Charter, June 2, 1869; Elk Point Lodge, at Elk Point, received a dispensation, March 23, 1870, and a Charter, June 8, 1871; Minnehaha Lodge, at Sioux Falls received a dispensation, July 13, 1873, and a Charter, June 3, 1874; Silver Star Lodge, at Canton, received a dispensation, February 6, 1875, and a Charter, June 2, 1875; and Mount Zion Lodge, at Springfield, received a dispensation, February 16, 1875, and a Charter, June 2, 1875. All of the above warrants were granted by authority of the Grand Lodge of Iowa. A dispensation was issued by the Grand Master of Minnesota, November 22, 1872, for Shiloh Lodge, at Fargo, and a Charter was issued January 14, 1874. He also issued a dispensation to Bismarck Lodge in 1874, and again in 1875, and on January 12, 1876, the Lodge received a Charter.

June 21, 1875, a convention was held of the representatives of St. John's, Incense, Elk Point, Minnehaha, and Silver Star Lodges. Those of Mt. Zion Lodge, U. D., were present but did not participate in the proceedings, the Lodge not having a Charter. A constitution was adopted and they elected their Grand Officers.

July 21, 1875, the convention met again and the Grand Officers were installed in public, by Illustrious Brother Theodore S. Parvin, P. G. Master and Grand Secretary of the Grand Lodge of Iowa.

This Grand Lodge continued until the session of June 11–13, 1889, when by Act of Congress, approved February 22, 1889, the division of the Territory of Dakota into North and South Dakota was likely to be accomplished within a few months. The report of a committee on division of the Grand Lodge was adopted, and certain Lodges located in North Dakota were permitted to organize a Grand Lodge of North Dakota.

A Grand Chapter of Dakota was constituted in 1885, which was divided in 1890 into the Grand Chapters of North and South Dakota. On May 14, 1884, a Grand Commandery of Knights Templar was organized, with five Commanderies,

Dalcho, Frederick, M.D. One of the founders of the Supreme Council of the Ancient and Accepted Scottish Rite for the Southern Jurisdiction of the United States. He was born in the city of London in the year 1770, of Prussian parents. His father had been a distinguished officer under Frederick the Great, and, having been severely wounded, was permitted to retire to England for his health. He was a very earnest Mason, and transmitted his sentiments to his son. At his death, this son was sent for by an uncle, who had a few years before emigrated to Baltimore. Here he obtained a good classical education, after which he devoted himself successfully to the study of medicine, including a more extensive course of botany than is common in medical schools.

Having received his degree of Doctor of Medicine, he took a commission in the medical department of the American army. With his division of the army he came to South Carolina, and was stationed at Fort Johnson, in Charleston harbor. Here some difficulty arose between Dr. Dalcho and his brother officers, in consequence of which he resigned his place in the army in 1799. He then removed to Charleston, where he formed a partnership in the practise of physic with Isaac Auld, and he became a member of the Medical Society, and a trustee of the Botanic Garden, established through its influence.

On the 12th of June, 1818, Dr. Dalcho was admitted to the priesthood of the Protestant Episcopal Church. On the 23d of February, he was elected assistant minister of St. Michael's Church, in Charleston. He died on the 24th of November, 1836, in the sixty-seventh year of his age, and the seventeenth of his ministry in St. Michael's Church.

The principal published work of Dr. Dalcho is, *An Historical Account of the Protestant Episcopal Church in South Carolina.* He also published a work entitled *The Evidence from Prophecy for the Truth of Christianity and the Divinity of Christ;* besides several sermons and essays, some of which were the result of considerable labor and research. He was also the projector, and for a long time the principal conductor, of the *Gospel Messenger,* then the leading organ of the Episcopal Church in South Carolina.

The Masonic career of Dr. Dalcho closely connects him with the history of York Masonry in South Carolina, and with that of the Ancient and Accepted Scottish Rite throughout the United States.

He was initiated in a York or Atholl Lodge at the time when the jurisdiction of South Carolina was divided by the existence and the dissensions of two Grand Lodges, the one deriving its authority from the Grand Lodge of Free and Accepted Masons of England, and the other from the rival Atholl Grand Lodge.

His constant desire appears, however, to have been to unite these discordant elements, and to uproot the evil spirit of Masonic rivalry and contention which at that time prevailed— a wish which was happily gratified, at length, by the union of the two Grand Lodges of South Carolina in 1817, a consummation to which he himself greatly contributed.

In 1801 Dr. Dalcho received the Thirty-third and ultimate degree, or Sovereign Grand Inspector of the Ancient and Accepted Scottish Rite; and May 31, 1801, he became instrumental in the establishment at Charleston of the Supreme Council for the Southern Jurisdiction of the United States, of which body he was appointed Grand Secretary, and afterward Grand Commander; which latter position he occupied until 1823, when he resigned.

September 23, 1801, he delivered an oration before the Sublime Grand Lodge in Charleston. This and another delivered March 21, 1803, before the same body, accompanied by a learned historical appendix, were published in the latter year under the general name of *Dalcho's Orations*. The work was soon after republished in Dublin by the Grand Council of Heredom, or Prince Masons of that city; and McCosh says that there were other editions issued in Europe, which, however, I have never seen. The oration of 1803 and the appendix furnish the best information that up to that day, and for many years afterward, was accessible to the Craft in relation to the history of the Ancient and Accepted Scottish Rite in this country.

In 1807, at the request of the Grand Lodge of York Masons of South Carolina, he published an *Ahiman Rezon*, which was adopted as the code for the government of the Lodges under the jurisdiction of that body. This work, as was to be expected from the character of the Grand Lodge which it represented, was based on the previous book of Laurence Dermott.

In 1808 he was elected Corresponding Grand Secretary of the Grand Lodge of Ancient York Masons, and from that time directed the influences of his high position to the reconciliation of the Masonic difficulties in South Carolina.

In 1817 the Grand Lodge of Free and Accepted Masons and that of Ancient York Masons of South Carolina became united under the name of "the Grand Lodge of Ancient Freemasons of South Carolina." Dr. Dalcho took a very active part in this reunion, and at the first annual communication he was elected Grand Chaplain. The duties of this office he faithfully performed, and for many years delivered a public address or sermon on the Festival of St. John the Evangelist.

In 1822 he prepared a second edition of the *Ahiman Rezon*, which was published the following year, enriched with many notes. Some of these notes he would have hardly written, with the enlarged experience of the present day; but on the whole the second edition was an improvement on the first. Although retaining the peculiar title which had been introduced by Dermott, it ceased in a great measure to follow the principles of the "Ancient Masons."

In 1823 Dalcho became involved in an unpleasant controversy with some of his Masonic associates, in consequence of difficulties and dissensions which at that time existed in the Scottish Rite; and his feelings were so wounded by the unmasonic spirit which seemed to actuate his antagonists and former friends, that he resigned the office of Grand Chaplain, and retired for the remainder of his life from all participation in the active duties of Masonry.

Dalmatic. A robe worn by deacons in some Christian churches. Originally made of linen, as shown by early Christian paintings on the walls of the catacombs at Rome, but now generally made of heavy woolen or silk material, as the planeta worn by the priest. This article of dress has become quite common in many of the degrees of various Rites.

Damascus. An ancient and important city of Syria, situated on the road between Babylon and Jerusalem, and said in Masonic tradition to have been one of the resting-places of the Masons who, under the proclamation of Cyrus, returned from the former to the latter city to rebuild the Temple. An attempt was made in 1868 to introduce Freemasonry into Damascus, and a petition, signed by fifteen applicants, for a charter for a Lodge was sent to the Grand Lodge of England; but the petition was rejected on the ground that all the petitioners were members of Grand Lodges under other Grand Lodge jurisdictions.

Dambool. The vast rock temple of the Buddhists in Ceylon, containing a profusion of carvings, figures of Buddha of extraordinary magnitude. Monuments of this deity are, in the common Singhalese term, called Dagoba, but the more general name is Stupa or Tope. (See *Topes*.)

Dame. In the *York Roll No. 4* and some of the other old manuscripts, we find the direction to the Apprentice that he shall not so act as to bring harm or shame, during his apprenticeship, "either to his Master or Dame." It is absurd to suppose that this gives any color to the theory that in the ancient Masonic gilds women were admitted. The word was used in the same sense as it still is in the public schools of England, where the old lady who keeps the house at which the pupils board and lodge, is called "the dame." The Compagnons de la Tour in France called her "la mère," or the mother. It must, however, be acknowledged, that women, under the title of *sisters*, were admitted as members, and given the freedom of the company, in the old Livery Companies of London—a custom which Herbert (*Hist. Liv. Comp.*, i., 83) thinks was borrowed, on the reconstitution of the companies by Edward III., from the religious gilds. (See this subject discussed under the title *Sisters of the Gild*.)

Dames of Mt. Tabor. An androgynous Masonic society, established about the year 1818, under the auspices of the Grand Orient of France. Its design was to give charitable relief to destitute females.

Dames of the Order of St. John. Religious ladies who, from its first institution, had been admitted into the Fraternity of Knights Hospitalers of St. John of Jerusalem. The rules for their reception were similar to those for the Knights, and the proofs of noble descent which were required of them were sometimes more rigid. They had many conventual establishments in France, Italy, and Spain.

Damoisel. A name given in the times of chivalry to a page or candidate for knighthood.

Dan. One of the twelve tribes of Israel, whose blue banner, charged with an eagle, is borne by the Grand Master of the First Veil in a Royal Arch Chapter.

Danger. In all the old *Constitutions* and *Charges*, Masons are taught to exercise brotherly love, and to deal honestly and truly with each other, whence results the duty incumbent upon every Mason to warn his Brother of approaching danger. That this duty may never be neglected, it is impressed upon every Master Mason by a significant ceremony.

Daniel. The countersign with "Darius" for Monday in the Thirty-second Degree, Scottish Rite. A Hebrew prophet, contemporary of Ezekiel, about 600 B.C. Carried captive to Babylon in the fourth year of Jehoiakim, but selected for instruction in all the learning of the Chaldeans by order of the Court. His skill in the interpretation of dreams was famed. He became Governor of Babylon under Nebuchadnezzar, and the first ruler of the whole Medo-Persian Empire, inferior only to Darius, the king. Under Cyrus he had been Grand Master of the Palace and Interpreter of Visions, as narrated in the Fifteenth Degree, Scottish Rite. He did not return with his countrymen to Judea when granted their liberty. It is a dispute as to when he died, or where, but the majority favor Sushan, in Persia, when he was 90 years of age. At the present day a tomb is shown in this ancient city bearing his name; in fact, it is the only standing structure there. Daniel was noted and famed for his piety, and as well for his worldly possessions.

Dannebrog. The banner of Denmark containing a red cross. It is founded upon the tradition, which reminds us of that of Constantine, that Waldemar II., of Denmark, in 1219 saw in the heavens a fiery cross, which betokened his victory over the Esthonians.

Dantzic. In the year 1768, on the 3d of October, the burgomaster and magistrates of the city of Dantzic commenced a persecution against Freemasonry, which Institution they charged with seeking to undermine the foundations of Christianity, and to establish in its place the religion of nature. Hence, they issued a decree forbidding every citizen, inhabitant, and even stranger sojourning in the city, from any attempt to reestablish the society of Freemasons, which was thenceforth to be regarded "as forever abolished," under penalties of fine and imprisonment.

Dao. The Zend name for light, from *Daer*, to shine.

Daraklel. A responsive word in the Twenty-third Degree of the Scottish Rite. דרכיאל. Latin, *Directio Dei.*

Darius. The successor of Cyrus on the throne of Persia, Babylon, and Medea. He pursued the friendly policy of his predecessor in reference to the Jews, and confirmed the decrees of that monarch by a new edict. In the second year of his reign, Haggai and Zechariah, encouraged by this edict, induced their countrymen to resume the work of restoring the Temple, which was finished four years afterward. Darius is referred to in the degrees of Princes of Jerusalem, the Sixteenth of the Ancient and Accepted Scottish Rite, and the Companion of the Red Cross in the American Rite.

Darkness. Darkness has, in all the systems of initiation, been deemed a symbol of ignorance, and so opposed to light, which is the symbol of knowledge. Hence the rule, that the eye should not see until the heart has conceived the true nature of those beauties which constitute the mysteries of the Order. In the Ancient Mysteries, the aspirant was always shrouded in darkness, as a preparatory step to the reception of the full light of knowledge. The time of this confinement in darkness and solitude varied in the different mysteries. Among the Druids of Britain the period was nine days and nights; in the Grecian Mysteries it was three times nine days; while among the Persians, according to Porphyry, it was extended to the almost incredible period of fifty days of darkness, solitude, and fasting.

Because, according to all the cosmogonies, darkness existed before light was created, darkness was originally worshiped as the firstborn, as the progenitor of day and the state of existence before creation. The apostrophe of Young to Night embodies the feelings which gave origin to this debasing worship of darkness:

"O majestic night!
Nature's great ancestor! day's elder born!
And fated to survive the transient sun!
By mortals and immortals seen with awe!"

Freemasonry has restored darkness to its proper place as a state of preparation; the symbol of that antemundane chaos from whence light issued at the Divine command; of the state of nonentity before birth, and of ignorance before the reception of knowledge. Hence, in the Ancient Mysteries, the release of the aspirant from solitude and darkness was called the act of regeneration, and he was said to be born again, or to be raised from the dead. And in Masonry, the darkness which envelops the mind of the uninitiated being removed by the bright effulgence of Masonic light, Masons are appropriately called "the sons of light."

In Dr. Oliver's *Signs and Symbols* there is a lecture "On the Mysterious Darkness of the Third Degree." This refers to the ceremony of enveloping the room in darkness when that degree is conferred—a ceremony once always observed, but now, in this country at least, frequently but improperly omitted. The darkness here is a symbol of death, the lesson taught in the degree, while the subsequent renewal of light refers to that other and subsequent lesson of eternal life.

Darmstadt, Grand Lodge of. The Grand Lodge of Darmstadt, in Germany, under the distinctive appellation of the Grand Lodge zur Eintracht (of Concord), was established on the 22d of March, 1846, by three Lodges, in consequence of a dissension between them and the Eclectic Union. The latter body had declared that the religion of Freemasonry was universal, and that Jews could be admitted into the Order. Against this liberal declaration a Lodge at Frankfort had protested, and had been erased from the roll for contumacy. Two other Lodges, at Mainz and at Darmstadt, espoused its cause, and united with it in forming a new Grand Lodge for southern Germany, founded on the dogma "that Christian principles formed the basis on which they worked." It was, in fact, a dispute between tolerance and intolerance. Nevertheless, the body was taken under the patronage of the Grand Duke of Hesse, and was recognized by most of the Grand Lodges of Germany. It has eight Lodges under its jurisdiction.

Dassigny, Fifield, M.D. A Mason of Dublin, Ireland, who published, in 1744, at Dublin, *A Serious and Impartial Enquiry into the Cause of the present Decay of Freemasonry in the Kingdom of Ireland.* It contained an abstract of the history of Freemasonry, and an allusion to the Royal Arch Degree, on account of which it has been cited by Dermott in his *Ahiman Rezon.* The work is important on account of its reference to Royal Arch Masonry, but is very scarce, only three copies of it being known to exist, of which one belongs to the Grand Lodge of Iowa, and one to the West Yorkshire Masonic Library, of which a facsimile was published in 1893, while a third copy was discovered in 1896. The writer's name is spelled D'Assigny or Dassigny, but is given in the latter form on the title-page of the *Serious Enquiry.* Dr. W. J. Chetwode Crawley has investigated the history of the D'Assigny family. (*Comentaria Hibernica. Fasc. II.*)   [E. L. H.]

Dates, Masonic. See *Calendar.*

Dathan. A Reubenite who, with Korah and Abiram, revolted against Moses and unlawfully sought the priesthood. In the first chapter of the Book of Numbers, where the whole account is given, it is said that as a punishment the earth opened and swallowed them up. The incident is referred to in the Order of High Priesthood, an honorary degree of the American Rite, which is conferred upon the installed High Priests of Royal Arch Chapters.

Daughter, Mason's. See *Mason's Wife and Daughter.*

Daughter of a Mason. The daughter of a Mason is entitled to certain peculiar privileges and claims upon the Fraternity arising from her relationship to a member of the Craft. There has been some difference of opinion as to the time and manner in which the privileges cease. Masonic jurists, however, very generally incline to the opinion that they are terminated by marriage. If a Mason's daughter marries a profane, she absolves her connection with the Fraternity. If she marries a Mason, she exchanges her relation of a Mason's daughter for that of a Mason's wife.

David. David has no place in Masonic history, except that which arises from the fact that he was the father of King Solomon, and his predecessor on the throne of Israel. To him, however, were the Jews indebted for the design of a Temple in Jerusalem, the building of which was a favorite object with him. For this purpose he purchased Mt. Moriah, which had been the threshing-floor of Ornan the Jebusite; but David had been engaged in so many wars, that it did not seem good to the Lord that he should be permitted to construct so sacred an edifice. This duty, therefore, he left to his son, whom, before dying, he furnished with plans and with means to accomplish the task. Though David is a favorite subject among the Kabbalists and the Mussulmans, who relate many curious traditions concerning him, he is not alluded to in the legends or symbolism of Masonry, except incidentally as the father of Solomon.

David, Shield of. See *Shield of David.*

Dazard, Michel François. Born at Chateaudun, in France, May 2, 1781. He was a devoted student of Masonry, and much occupied in the investigation of the high degrees of all the Rites. He was an opponent of the Supreme Council, against which body he wrote, in 1812, a brochure of forty-eight pages entitled *Extrait des colonnes gravées du Père de Famille, vallée d'Angers.* Kloss calls it an important and exhaustive polemic document. It attempts to expose, supported by documents, what the author and his party called the illegal pretensions of the Supreme Council, and the arrogance of its claim to exclusive jurisdiction in France. Dazard was the author of several other interesting discourses on Masonic subjects.

Deacon. In every Symbolic Lodge, there are two officers who are called the Senior and Junior Deacons. In America the former is appointed by the Master and the latter by the Senior Warden; in England both are appointed by the Master. It is to the Deacons that the introduction of visitors should be properly entrusted. Their duties comprehend, also, a general surveillance over the security of the Lodge, and they are the proxies of the officers by whom they are appointed. Hence their jewel, in allusion to the necessity of circumspection and justice is a square and compasses. In the center, the Senior Deacon wears a sun, and the Junior Deacon a moon, which serve to distinguish their respective ranks. In the English system, the jewel of the Deacons is a dove, in allusion to the dove sent forth by Noah. In the Rite of Mizraim the Deacons are called acolytes.

The office of Deacons in Masonry appears to have been derived from the usages of the primitive church. In the Greek church, the

Deacons were always the πυλωροί, pylori or doorkeepers, and in the *Apostolical Constitutions* the Deacon was ordered to stand at the men's door, and the Subdeacon at the women's, to see that none came in or went out during the oblation.

In the earliest rituals of the last century, there is no mention of Deacons, and the duties of those officers were discharged partly by the Junior Warden and partly by the Senior and Junior Entered Apprentices, and they were not generally adopted in England until the Union of 1813.

Deacon's Rod. See *Rod, Deacon's*.

Deaf and Dumb. Deaf mutes, as imperfect men, come under the provisions of the *Old Constitutions*, and are disqualified for initiation. Some years ago, however, a Lodge in Paris, captivated by the éclat of the proceeding, and unmindful of the ancient landmark, initiated a deaf mute, who was an intelligent professor in the Deaf and Dumb Asylum. All the instructions were given through the medium of the language of the deaf mutes. It scarcely need be said that this cannot be recognized as a precedent.

Death. The Scandinavians, in their Edda, describing the residence of Death in Hell, where she was cast by her father, Loke, say that she there possesses large apartments, strongly built, and fenced with gates of iron. Her hall is Grief; her table, Famine; Hunger, her knife; Delay, her servant; Faintness, her porch; Sickness and Pain, her bed; and her tent, Cursing and Howling. But the Masonic idea of death, like the Christian's, is accompanied with no gloom, because it is represented only as a sleep, from whence we awaken into another life. Among the ancients, sleep and death were fabled as twins. Old Gorgias, when dying, said, "Sleep is about to deliver me up to his brother"; but the death sleep of the heathen was a sleep from which there was no awaking. The popular belief was annihilation, and the poets and philosophers fostered the people's ignorance, by describing death as the total and irremediable extinction of life. Thus Seneca says—and he was too philosophic not to have known better—"that after death there comes nothing"; while Virgil, who doubtless had been initiated into the Mysteries of Eleusis, nevertheless calls death "an iron sleep, an eternal night": yet the Ancient Mysteries were based upon the dogma of eternal life, and their initiations were intended to represent a resurrection. Masonry, deriving its system of symbolic teachings from these ancient religious associations, presents death to its neophytes as the gate or entrance to eternal existence. To teach the doctrine of immortality is the great object of the Third Degree. In its ceremonies we learn that life here is the time of labor, and that, working at the construction of a spiritual temple, we are worshiping the Great Architect, for whom we build that temple. But we learn also that, when that life is ended, it closes only to open upon a newer and higher one, where, in a second temple and a purer Lodge, the Mason will find eternal truth. Death, therefore, in Masonic philosophy, is the symbol of initiation completed, perfected, and consummated.

Death of the Mysteries. Each of the ancient religious Mysteries, those quasi-Masonic associations of the heathen world, was accompanied by a legend—which was always of a funereal character—representing the death, by violence, of the deity to whom it was dedicated, and his subsequent resurrection or restoration to life. Hence, the first part of the ceremonies of initiation was solemn and lugubrious in character, while the latter part was cheerful and joyous. These ceremonies and this legend were altogether symbolical, and the great truths of the unity of God and the immortality of the soul were by them intended to be dramatically explained.

This representation of death, which finds its analogue in the Third Degree of Masonry, has been technically called the Death of the Mysteries. It is sometimes more precisely defined, in reference to any special one of the Mysteries, as "the Cabiric death" or "the Bacchic death," as indicating the death represented in the Mysteries of the Cabiri or of Dionysus.

Debate. Debates in a Masonic Lodge must be conducted according to the fraternal principles of the Institution. In the language of Dr. Oliver, "the strictest courtesy should be observed during a debate, in a Mason's Lodge, on questions which elicit a difference of opinion; and any gross violation of decorum and good order is sure to be met by an admonition from the chair." It must be always remembered that the object of a Masonic discussion is to elicit truth, and not simply to secure victory.

When, in a debate, a brother desires to speak, he rises and addresses the chair. The presiding officer calls him by his name, and thus recognizes his right to the floor. While he is speaking, he is not to be interrupted by any other member, except on a point of order. If called to order by any member, the speaker is immediately to take his seat until the point is stated, when the Master will make his decision without debate. The speaker will then rise and resume his discourse, if not ruled out by the Master. During the time that he is speaking, no motion is permissible. Every member is permitted to speak once on the subject under discussion; nor can he speak a second time, except by permission of the Master, unless there is a more liberal provision in the by-laws of the Lodge. There are to this rule two exceptions, namely, when a member rises to explain, and when the mover of the resolution closes the debate by a second speech to which he is entitled by parliamentary law.

Decalogue. The ten commandments of the Masonic law, as delivered from Mt. Sinai and recorded in the twentieth chapter of Exodus, are so called. They are not obligatory upon a Mason as a Mason, because the Institution is tolerant and cosmopolite, and cannot require its members to give their adhesion to any religious dogmas or precepts, excepting those which express a belief in the existence of God, and the immortality of the soul. No partial law prescribed for a particular religion can be properly selected for the government of an Institution whose great characteristic is its universality. (See *Moral Law*.)

Decanus. An officer in the Knights Templar system of Baron Hund, who, in the absence of the Grand Master and his Prior, possessed the right to preside in the Chapter.

Decius. The *nom de plume* of C. L. Reinhold, a distinguished Masonic writer. (See *Reinhold*.)

Declaration of Candidates. Every candidate for initiation is required to make, "upon honor," the following declaration before an appropriate officer or committee. That, unbiased by the improper solicitation of friends and uninfluenced by mercenary motives, he freely and voluntarily offers himself as a candidate for the Mysteries of Masonry; that he is prompted to solicit the privileges of Masonry by a favorable opinion conceived of the Institution and a desire of knowledge; and that he will cheerfully conform to all the ancient usages and established customs of the Fraternity. This form is very old. It is to be found in precisely the same words in the earliest edition of Preston. It is required by the English Constitution, that the candidate should subscribe his name to this declaration. But in America the declaration is made orally, and usually before the Senior Deacon.

Declaration of the Master. Every Master of a Lodge, after his election and before his installation, is required to give, in the presence of the brethren, his assent to the following fifteen charges and regulations:

1. Do you promise to be a good man and true, and strictly to obey the moral law? 2. Do you promise to be a peaceable citizen, and cheerfully to conform to the laws of the country in which you reside? 3. Do you promise not to be concerned in plots and conspiracies against the government of the country in which you live, but patiently to submit to the decisions of the law and the constituted authorities? 4. Do you promise to pay proper respect to the civil magistrates, to work diligently, live creditably, and act honorably by all men? 5. Do you promise to hold in veneration the original rulers and patrons of the Order of Freemasonry. and their regular successors, supreme and subordinate, according to their stations; and to submit to the awards and resolutions of your brethren in Lodge convened, in every case consistent with the constitutions of the Order? 6. Do you promise, as much as in you lies, to avoid private piques and quarrels, and to guard against intemperance and excess? 7. Do you promise to be cautious in your behavior, courteous to your brethren, and faithful to your Lodge? 8. Do you promise to respect genuine and true brethren, and to discountenance impostors and all dissenters from the Ancient Landmarks and Constitutions of Masonry? 9. Do you

promise, according to the best of your abilities, to promote the general good of society, to cultivate the social virtues, and to propagate the knowledge of the mystic art, according to our statutes? 10. Do you promise to pay homage to the Grand Master for the time being, and to his officers when duly installed; and strictly to conform to every edict of the Grand Lodge or General Assembly of Masons that is not subversive of the principles and groundwork of Masonry? 11. Do you admit that it is not in the power of any man, or body of men, to make innovations in the body of Masonry? 12. Do you promise a regular attendance on the committees and communications of the Grand Lodge, on receiving proper notice, and to pay attention to all the duties of Masonry, on convenient occasions? 13. Do you admit that no new Lodge can be formed without permission of the Grand Lodge; and that no countenance ought to be given to any irregular Lodge, or to any person clandestinely initiated therein, as being contrary to the ancient charges of the Order? 14. Do you admit that no person can be regularly made a Freemason in, or admitted a member of, any regular Lodge, without previous notice, and due inquiry into his character? 15. Do you agree that no visitors shall be received into your Lodge without due examination, and producing proper vouchers of their having been initiated in a regular Lodge?

Declaring Off. "When a brother ceases to visit and pay his monthly subscription, he thereby declares himself off the Lodge." (*Symbolical Dictionary*.) In England, the brother "resigns." Various designations rule in the United States, the chief one being "dropped from the roll." In some States the brother is punished by "suspension." If, however, in certain States, he is *clear of the books*, upon application he can receive a certificate to that effect, and be dropped from the roll. In England he gets a "clearance certificate." In Scotland a "demit" is issued by the Daughter Lodge and countersigned by the Grand Secretary.

Decorations. A Lodge room ought, besides its necessary furniture, to be ornamented with decorations which, while they adorn and beautify it, will not be unsuitable to its sacred character. On this subject, Dr. Oliver, in his *Book of the Lodge* (ch. v., p. 70), makes the following judicious remarks: "The expert Mason will be convinced that the walls of a Lodge room ought neither to be absolutely naked nor too much decorated. A chaste disposal of symbolical ornaments in the right places, and according to propriety, relieves the dulness and vacuity of a blank space, and, though but sparingly used, will produce a striking impression, and contribute to the general beauty and solemnity of the scene."

Dedication of a Lodge. Among the ancients every temple, altar, statue, or sacred place was dedicated to some divinity. The Romans, during the Republic, confided this duty to their consuls, pretors, censors, or other chief magistrates, and afterward to the emperors. According to the Papirian law, the dedication must have been authorized by a decree of the senate and the people, and the consent of the college of augurs. The ceremony consisted in surrounding the temple or object of dedication with garlands of flowers, whilst the vestal virgins poured on the exterior of the temple the lustral water. The dedication was completed by a formula of words uttered by the Pontiff, and the immolation of a victim, whose entrails were placed upon an altar of turf. The dedication of a temple was always a festival for the people, and was annually commemorated. While the Pagans dedicated their temples to different deities—sometimes to the joint worship of several—the monotheistic Jews dedicated their religious edifices to the one supreme Jehovah. Thus, David dedicated with solemn ceremonies the altar which he erected on the threshing-floor of Ornan the Jebusite, after the cessation of the plague which had afflicted his people; and Calmet conjectures that he composed the thirtieth Psalm on this occasion. The Jews extended this ceremony of dedication even to their private houses, and Clarke tells us, in reference to a passage on this subject in the Book of Deuteronomy, that "it was a custom in Israel to dedicate a new house to God with prayer, praise, and thanksgiving; and this was done in order to secure the divine presence and blessing, for no pious or sensible man could imagine he could dwell safely in a house that was not under the immediate protection of God."

According to the learned Selden, there was a distinction among the Jews between consecration and dedication, for sacred things were both consecrated and dedicated, while profane things, such as private dwelling-houses, were only dedicated. Dedication was, therefore, a less sacred ceremony than consecration. This distinction has also been preserved among Christians, many of whom, and, in the early ages, all, consecrated their churches to the worship of God, but dedicated them to, or placed them under, the especial patronage of some particular saint. A similar practise prevails in the Masonic Institution; and therefore, while we consecrate our Lodges "to the honor of God's glory," we dedicate them to the patrons of our Order.

Tradition informs us that Masonic Lodges were originally dedicated to King Solomon, because he was our first Most Excellent Grand Master. In the sixteenth century St. John the Baptist seems to have been considered as the peculiar patron of Freemasonry; but subsequently this honor was divided between the two Saints John, the Baptist and the Evangelist; and modern Lodges, in this country at least, are universally *erected* or *consecrated* to God, and dedicated to the Holy Saints John. In the Hemming lectures, adopted in 1813, at the time of the union of the two Grand Lodges of England, the dedication was changed from the Saints John to King Solomon, and this usage now prevails very generally in England [where Lodges are dedicated to "God and His

Service, also to the memory of the Royal Solomon, under whose auspices many of our Masonic mysteries had their origin."—[E. L. H.]; but the ancient dedication to the Saints John has never been abandoned by the American Lodges.

The formula in Webb which dedicates the Lodge "to the memory of the Holy Saint John," was, undoubtedly, an inadvertence on the part of that lecturer, since in all his oral teachings he adhered to the more general system, and described a Lodge in his esoteric work as being "dedicated to the Holy Saints John." This is now the universal practise, and the language used by Webb becomes contradictory and absurd when compared with the fact that the festivals of both saints are equally celebrated by the Order, and that the 27th of December is not less a day of observance in the Order than the 24th of June.

In one of the old lectures of the last century, this dedication to the two Saints John is thus explained:

"*Q*. Our Lodges being finished, furnished, and decorated with ornaments, furniture, and jewels, to whom were they consecrated?

"*A*. To God.

"*Q*. Thank you, brother; and can you tell me to whom they were first dedicated?

"*A*. To Noah, who was saved in the ark.

"*Q*. And by what name were the Masons then known?

"*A*. They were called Noachidæ, Sages, or Wise Men.

"*Q*. To whom were the Lodges dedicated during the Mosaic dispensation?

"*A*. To Moses, the chosen of God, and Solomon, the son of David, king of Israel, who was an eminent patron of the Craft.

"*Q*. And under what name were the Masons known during that period?

"*A*. Under the name of Dionysiacs, Geometricians, or Masters in Israel.

"*Q*. But as Solomon was a Jew, and died long before the promulgation of Christianity, to whom were they dedicated under the Christian dispensation?

"*A*. From Solomon the patronage of Masonry passed to St. John the Baptist.

"*Q*. And under what name were they known after the promulgation of Christianity?

"*A*. Under the name of Essenes, Architects, or Freemasons.

"*Q*. Why were the Lodges dedicated to St. John the Baptist?

"*A*. Because he was the forerunner of our Saviour, and, by preaching repentance and humiliation, drew the first parallel of the Gospel.

"*Q*. Had St. John the Baptist any equal?

"*A*. He had; St. John the Evangelist.

"*Q*. Why is he said to be equal to the Baptist?

"*A*. Because he finished by his learning what the other began by his zeal, and thus drew a second line parallel to the former; ever since which time Freemasons' Lodges, in all Christian countries, have been dedicated to the one or the other, or both, of these worthy and worshipful men.''

There is another old lecture, adopted into the Prestonian system, which still further developed these reasons for the Johannite dedication, but with slight variations in some of the details.

"From the building of the first Temple at Jerusalem to the Babylonish captivity, Freemasons' Lodges were dedicated to King Solomon; from thence to the coming of the Messiah, they were dedicated to Zerubbabel, the builder of the second Temple; and from that time to the final destruction of the Temple by Titus, in the reign of Vespasian, they were dedicated to St. John the Baptist; but owing to the many massacres and disorders which attended that memorable event, Freemasonry sunk very much into decay; many Lodges were entirely broken up, and but few could meet in sufficient numbers to constitute their legality; and at a general meeting of the Craft, held in the city of Benjamin, it was observed that the principal reason for the decline of Masonry was the want of a Grand Master to patronize it. They therefore deputed seven of their most eminent members to wait upon St. John the Evangelist, who was at that time Bishop of Ephesus, requesting him to take the office of Grand Master. He returned for answer, that though well stricken in years (being upwards of ninety), yet having been initiated into Masonry in the early part of his life, he would take upon himself that office. He thereby completed by his learning what the other St. John effected by his zeal, and thus drew what Freemasons term a 'line parallel'; ever since which time Freemasons' Lodges, in all Christian countries, have been dedicated both to St. John the Baptist and St. John the Evangelist.''

So runs the tradition, but, as it lacks every claim to authenticity, a more philosophical reason may be assigned for this dedication to the two Saints John.

One of the earliest deviations from the pure religion of the Noachidæ was distinguished by the introduction of sun worship. The sun, in the Egyptian mysteries, was symbolized by Osiris, the principal object of their rites, whose name, according to Plutarch and Macrobius, signified the prince and leader, the soul of the universe and the governor of the stars. Macrobius (*Saturn.*, l. i., c. 18) says that the Egyptians worshiped the sun as the only divinity; and they represented him under different forms, according to the different phases, of his infancy at the winter solstice in December, his adolescence at the vernal equinox in March, his manhood at the summer solstice in June, and his old age at the autumnal equinox in September.

Among the Phœnicians, the sun was adored under the name of Adonis, and in Persia, under that of Mithras. In the Grecian mysteries, the orb of day was represented by one of the officers who superintended the ceremony of initiation; and in the Druidical rites his worship was introduced as the visible representa-

tive of the invisible, creative, and preservative principle of nature. In short, wherever the spurious Freemasonry existed, the adoration of, or, at least, a high respect for, the solar orb constituted a part of its system.

In Freemasonry, the sun is still retained as an important symbol. This fact must be familiar to every Freemason of any intelligence. It occupies, indeed, its appropriate position, simply as a symbol, but, nevertheless, it constitutes an essential part of the system. "As an emblem of God's power," says Hutchinson (*Sp. of Mas.*, *Lect. IV*., p. 86), "his goodness, omnipresence, and eternity, the Lodge is adorned with the image of the sun, which he ordained to arise from the east and open the day; thereby calling forth the people of the earth to their worship and exercise in the walks of virtue."

"The government of a Mason's Lodge," says Oliver (*Signs and Sym.*, p. 204), "is vested in three superior officers, who are seated in the East, West, and South, to represent the rising, setting, and meridian sun."

The sun, obedient to the all-seeing eye, is an emblem in the ritual of the Third Degree, and the sun displayed within an extended compass constitutes the jewel of the Past Master in the American system, and that of the Grand Master in the English.

But it is a needless task to cite authorities or multiply instances to prove how intimately the sun, as a symbol, is connected with the whole system of Freemasonry.

It is then evident that the sun, either as an object of worship, or of symbolization, has always formed an important part of what has been called the two systems of Freemasonry, the Spurious and the Pure.

To the ancient sun worshipers, the movements of the heavenly bodies must have been something more than mere astronomical phenomena; they were the actions of the deities whom they adored, and hence were invested with the solemnity of a religious character. But, above all, the particular periods when the sun reached his greatest northern and southern declination, at the winter and summer solstices, by entering the zodiacal signs of Cancer and Capricorn, marked as they would be by the most evident effects on the seasons, and on the length of the days and nights, could not have passed unobserved, but, on the contrary, must have occupied an important place in their ritual. Now these important days fall respectively on the 21st of June and the 21st of December. Hence, these solstitial periods were among the principal festivals observed by the Pagan nations. Du Pauw (*Diss. on Egyp. and Chinese*, ii., 159) remarks of the Egyptians, that "they had a fixed festival at each new moon; one at the summer, and one at the winter solstice, as well as the vernal and autumnal equinoxes."

The Druids always observed the festivals of midsummer and midwinter in June and December. The former for a long time was celebrated by the Christian descendants of the Druids. "The eve of St. John the Baptist," says Chambers (*Inf. for the People*, No. 89), "variously called midsummer eve, was formerly a time of high observance amongst the English, as it still is in Catholic countries. Bonfires were everywhere lighted, round which the people danced with joyful demonstrations, occasionally leaping through the flame." Higgins (*Celt. Druids*, p. 165) thus alludes to the celebration of the festival of midwinter in the ancient world:

"The festival of the 25th of December was celebrated, by the Druids in Britain and Ireland, with great fires lighted on the tops of the hills. . . . On the 25th of December, at the first moment of the day, throughout all the ancient world, the birthday of the god *Sol* was celebrated. This was the moment when, after the supposed winter solstice and the lowest point of his degradation below our hemisphere, he began to increase and gradually to ascend. At this moment, in all the ancient religions, his birthday was kept; from India to the Ultima Thule, these ceremonies partook of the same character: everywhere the god was feigned to be born, and his festival was celebrated with great rejoicings."

Our ancestors finding that the Church, according to its usage of purifying Pagan festivals by Christian application, had appropriated two days near those solstitial periods to the memory of two eminent saints, incorporated these festivals by the lapse of a few days into the Masonic calendar, and adopted these worthies as patrons of our Order. To this change, the earlier Christian Masons were the more persuaded by the peculiar character of these saints. St. John the Baptist, by announcing the approach of Christ, and by the mystic ablution to which he subjected his proselytes, and which was afterward adopted in the ceremony of initiation into Christianity, might well be considered as the Grand Hierophant of the Church; while the mysterious and emblematic nature of the Apocalypse assimilated the mode of instruction adopted by St. John the Evangelist to that practised by the Fraternity.

We are thus led to the conclusion that the connection of the Saints John with the Masonic Institution is rather of a symbolic than of an historical character. In dedicating our Lodges to them, we do not so much declare our belief that they were eminent members of the Order, as demonstrate our reverence for the great Architect of the Universe in the symbol of His most splendid creation, the great light of day.

In conclusion it may be observed that the ceremony of dedication is merely the enunciation of a form of words, and this having been done, the Lodge is thus, by the consecration and dedication, set apart as something sacred to the cultivation of the principles of Masonry, under that peculiar system which acknowledges the two Saints John as its patrons.

Royal Arch Chapters are dedicated to Zerubbabel, Prince or Governor of Judah, and Commanderies of Knights Templar to St. John the Almoner. Mark Lodges should be dedicated to Hiram the Builder; Past Masters' to the Saints John, and Most Excellent Masters' to King Solomon.

Dedication of the Temple. There are five dedications of the Temple of Jerusalem which are recorded in Jewish history: 1. The dedication of the Solomonic Temple; B.C. 1004. 2. The dedication in the time of Hezekiah, when it was purified from the abominations of Ahaz, B.C. 726. 3. The dedication of Zerubbabel's Temple, B.C. 513. 4. The dedication of the Temple when it was purified after Judas Maccabæus had driven out the Syrians, B.C. 164. 5. The dedication of Herod's Temple, B.C. 22. The fourth of these is still celebrated by the Jews in their "Feast of the Dedication." The first only is connected with the Masonic ritual, and is commemorated in the Most Excellent Master's Degree of the American Rite as the "Celebration of the Cape-Stone." This dedication was made by King Solomon in the year of the world 3000, and lasted eight days, commencing in the month of Tisri, 15th day, during the Feast of Tabernacles. The dedication of the Temple is called, in the English system of Lectures, "the third grand offering which consecrates the floor of a Mason's Lodge." The same Lectures contain a tradition that on that occasion King Solomon assembled the nine Deputy Grand Masters in the holy place, from which all natural light had been carefully excluded, and which only received the artificial light which emanated from the east, west, and south, and there made the necessary arrangements. The legend must be considered as a myth; but the inimitable prayer and invocation which were offered up by King Solomon on the occasion are recorded in the eighth chapter of the 1st Book of Kings, which contains the Scriptural account of the dedication.

Defamation. See *Back*.

Definition of Freemasonry. "The definitions of Freemasonry," says Oliver, in his *Historical Landmarks of Freemasonry*, "have been numerous; but they all unite in declaring it to be a system of morality, by the practice of which its members may advance their spiritual interest, and mount by the theological ladder from the Lodge on earth to the Lodge in heaven. It is a mistake, however, to suppose that Freemasonry is a system of religion. It is but the handmaiden to religion, although it largely and effectually illustrates one great branch of it, which is practice." The definition in the English Lectures is most often quoted, which says that "Freemasonry is a peculiar system of morality veiled in allegory and illustrated by symbols."

But a more comprehensive and exact definition is, that it is *a science which is engaged in the search after Divine Truth, and which employs symbolism as its method of instruction.*

Deformity. The *old Constitutions* declare that the candidate for Masonry must be a "perfect youth, having no maim or defect in his body." The Masonic law of physical qualifications is derived from the Mosaic, which excluded from the priesthood a man having any blemishes or deformities. The regulation in Masonry constitutes one of the landmarks, and is illustrative of the symbolism of the Institution. The earliest of the *old Constitutions*, that of the Halliwell or Regius MS., has this language on the subject:

> "To the Craft it were great shame
> To make a halt man and a lame,
> For an imperfect man of such blood
> Should do the Craft but little good."
> (Lines 153–6.)

This question has been fully discussed in Dr. Mackey's *Text Book of Masonic Jurisprudence*, pp. 96–113.

Degrees. The word *degree*, in its primitive meaning, signifies a *step*. The *degrees* of Freemasonry are, then, the steps by which the candidate ascends from a lower to a higher condition of knowledge. It is now the opinion of the best scholars, that the division of the Masonic system into degrees was the work of the revivalists of the beginning of the eighteenth century; that before that period there was but one degree, or rather one common platform of ritualism; and that the division into Masters, Fellows, and Apprentices was simply a division of ranks, there being but one initiation for all. In 1717 the whole body of the Fraternity consisted only of Entered Apprentices, who were recognized by the thirty-nine Regulations, compiled in 1720, as among the law-givers of the Craft, no change in those Regulations being allowed unless first submitted "even to the youngest Apprentice." In the *old Charges*, collected by Anderson and approved in 1722, the degree of Fellow-Craft is introduced as being a necessary qualification for Grand Master, although the word *degree* is not used. "No brother can be a . . . Grand Master unless he has been a Fellow Craft before his election." And in the *Manner of constituting a New Lodge* of the same date, the Master and Wardens are taken from "among the Fellow Crafts," which Dermott explains by saying that "they were called Fellow Crafts because the Masons of old times never gave any man the title of Master Mason until he had first passed the chair." In the thirteenth of the Regulations of 1720, approved in 1721, the orders or degrees of Master and Fellow-Craft are recognized in the following words: "Apprentices must be admitted Masters and Fellow Crafts only in the Grand Lodge." Between that period and 1738, the system of degrees had been perfected; for Anderson, who, in that year, published the second edition of the *Book of Constitutions*, changed the phraseology of the *old Charges* to suit the altered condition of things, and said, "a Prentice, when of age and expert, may become an Enter'd Prentice or a Free-Mason of the lowest degree, and upon his due improvements a Fellow-Craft and a Master-Mason." (*Old Charge* IV., *Constitutions*, 1738, p. 145.) No such words are found in the Charges as printed in 1723; and if at that time the distinction of the three degrees had been as well defined as in 1738, Anderson would not have

14

failed to insert the same language in his first edition. That he did not, leads to the fair presumption that the ranks of Fellow-Craft and Master were not then absolutely recognized as distinctive degrees. The earliest ritual extant, which is contained in the *Grand Mystery*, published in 1725, makes no reference to any degrees, but gives only what we may suppose was the common initiation in use about that time. The division of the Masonic system into three degrees must have grown up between 1717 and 1730, but in so gradual and imperceptible a manner that we are unable to fix the precise date of the introduction of each degree. In 1717 there was evidently but one degree, or rather one form of initiation, and one catechism. Perhaps about 1721 the three degrees were introduced, but the second and third were not perfected for many years. Even as late as 1735 the Entered Apprentice's Degree contained the most prominent form of initiation, and he who was an Apprentice was, for all practical purposes, a Freemason. It was not until repeated improvements, by the adoption of new ceremonies and new regulations, that the degree of Master Mason took the place which it now occupies; having been confined at first to those who had passed the chair.

Degrees, Ancient Craft. See *Ancient Craft Masonry*.

Degrees, Androgynous. Degrees that are conferred on females as well as males. (See *Androgynous Degrees*.)

Degrees, Apocalyptic. See *Apocalyptic Degrees*.

Degrees, High. See *High Degrees*.

Degrees, Honorary. See *Honorary Degrees*.

Degrees, Ineffable. See *Ineffable Degrees*.

Degrees of Chivalry. The religious and military orders of knighthood which existed in the Middle Ages, such as the Knights Templar and Knights of Malta, which were incorporated into the Masonic system and conferred as Masonic degrees, have been called Degrees of Chivalry. They are Christian in character, and seek to perpetuate in a symbolic form the idea on which the original Orders were founded. The Companion of the Red Cross, although conferred, in this country, in a Commandery of Knights Templar, and as preliminary to that degree, is not properly a degree of chivalry.

Degrees of Knowledge. Fessler was desirous of abolishing all the high degrees, but being unable to obtain the consent of the Royal York Grand Lodge, he composed out of them a new system of five degrees which he called Degrees of Knowledge, *Erkenntnis-Stufen*, to each of which was annexed a form of initiation. "The Degrees of Knowledge," says Findel (*Hist.*, 496), "consisted of a regular detailed course of instruction in each system of the Lodges, whether extinct or in full activity, and were to end with a complete critical remodelling of the history of Freemasonry, and of the Fraternity of Freemasons from the most ancient period down to our own day." (See *Fessler, Rite of*.)

Degrees, Philosophical. See *Philosophic Degrees*.

Degrees, Symbolic. See *Symbolic Degrees*.

Deiseil. The counterpart of *Tuathal*. Mackenzie, in the *Royal Masonic Cyclopædia*, says "Deiseil is used by the Druids as a term for the circumambulation of the sacred cairns. Derived from *deas*, south, and *tul*, a course; that is, in a southward direction following the course of the sun. The opposite is *Tuathal*, in a northward direction, as is observed at the present day in approaching the grave with a corpse."

Deism. In an abstract sense, Deism, or Theism, is the belief in God, but the word is generally used to designate those who, believing in God, reject a belief in the Scriptures as a revelation. The sect of Deists—which, in the seventeenth and eighteenth centuries, enrolled among its followers many great intellects, such as Toland, Collins, Lord Herbert of Cherbury, Hume, Gibbon, and Voltaire—is said by Findel (*Hist.*, p. 126) to have "necessarily exercised an important influence on the Fraternity of Masons"; and, he adds, that "we cannot doubt that it contributed essentially to its final transformation from an operative to a universal speculative society." The refutation of this remarkable assertion is best found in the first of the Charges adopted at the revival in 1717, and which was published in the *Constitutions* of 1723: "A Mason is obliged, by his tenure, to obey the moral law; and if he rightly understands the art, he will never be a stupid atheist nor an irreligious libertine," where the words *irreligious libertine* refer to the Freethinkers or Deists of that period. It is evident, then, that the Deists could have had no influence at that time in molding the Masonic organization. There is still better evidence to be found in the old records of Freemasonry during several preceding centuries, when the Operative was its dominant character, and when the dogmas of Christianity were fully recognized, which must necessarily have been the case, since Freemasonry during that period was under the patronage of the Church. There is, in fact, no evidence to sustain Findel's theory, that in the transition stage from the Operative to the Speculative, when such men as the deeply religious Ashmole were among its members, the Deists could have infused any of their principles into its organization or exercised any influence in changing its character.

Freemasonry, at that time sectarian, demanded almost a Christian belief—at all events, a Christian allegiance—from its disciples. It is now more tolerant, and Deism presents no disqualification for initiation. An atheist would be rejected, but none would now be refused admission on religious grounds who subscribed to the dogmas of a belief in God and a resurrection to eternal life.

Deity. See *Great Architect of the Universe.*

Delalande, Charles Florent Jacques. A French litterateur of this century, who was the author of many didactic and poetic articles on Masonry inserted in the *Miroir de la Vérité*, the *Annales Maçonniques*, and other collections. He was also the author of the *Defense et Apologie de la Franche-Maçonnerie, ou Réfutation des Accusations dirigées contre elle à différentes Époques et par divers Autems*, a prize essay before a Lodge in Leghorn, published in 1814. He founded the archives of the Lodge of the Philosophic Rite at Douay, France.

Delalande, Joseph Jérôme François. One of the most distinguished French astronomers of the eighteenth century. He was born in 1732 and died in 1807. He was one of the founders of the Grand Orient of France, and published, in 1774, an able memoir upon the *History of Freemasonry*, which was subsequently incorporated in the twentieth volume of the *Encyclopédie Méthodique*.

Delaunay, François H. Stanislaus. A French litterateur and historian, and author of many works on Masonry, the principal of which is the *Tuileur des trente trois degrés de l'Ecossisme du Rite Ancien et Accepté*. This is a work of great erudition, and of curious research in reference to the etymology of the words of the Rite. These etymologies, however, are not always correct; and, indeed, some of them are quite absurd, betraying a want of the proper appreciation of the construction of Hebrew, from which language all of the words are derived.

Delaware. The Grand Lodge of Delaware was organized on the 7th of June, 1806. Its seat is at Wilmington. The Grand Chapter was instituted in 1818, but having suspended labor for many years, a new organization was established by the General Grand High Priest of the United States in 1869.

Delegates. Past Masters, or others, sent by a Lodge to represent it in the Grand Lodge, in place of the Master and Wardens, if these are absent, are in some of the American jurisdictions called delegates. The word is a modern one, and without good authority. Those who represent a Lodge in the Grand Lodge, whether the Master and Wardens or their proxies, are properly *representatives*.

Delta. A triangle. The name of a piece of furniture in a Commandery of Knights Templar, which, being of a triangular form, derives its name from the Greek letter Δ, delta. It is also the title given, in the French and Scottish Rites, to the luminous triangle which encloses the Ineffable name. (See *Triangle*.)

Demeter. The Greek name of *Ceres*, which see.

Demit. A Mason is said *to demit* from his Lodge when he withdraws his membership; and a *demit* is a document granted by the Lodge which certifies that that demission has been accepted by the Lodge, and that the demitting brother is clear of the books and in good standing as a Mason. *To demit*, which is the act of the member, is, then, to resign; and to grant *a demit*, which is the act of the Lodge, is to grant a certificate that the resignation has been accepted. It is derived from the French reflective verb *se démettre*, which, according to the dictionary of the Academy, means "to withdraw from an office, to resign an employment." Thus it gives as an example, "Il s'est démis de sa charge en faveur d'un tel," *he resigned (demitted) his office in favor of such a one.*

The application for a demit is a matter of form, and there is no power in the Lodge to refuse it, if the applicant has paid all his dues and is free of all charges. It is true that a regulation of 1722 says that no number of brethren shall withdraw or separate themselves from the Lodge in which they were made, without a dispensation; yet it is not plain how the law can be enforced, for Masonry being a voluntary association, there is no power in any Lodge to insist on any brother continuing a connection with it which he desires to sever. (See, on this subject, Dr. Mackey's *Text Book of Masonic Jurisprudence*, book iii., chap. iii., sect. vi.)

The usual object in applying for a demit is to enable the brother to join some other Lodge, into which he cannot be admitted without some evidence that he was in good standing in his former Lodge. This is in accordance with an old law found in the Regulations of 1663 in the following words: "No person hereafter who shall be accepted a Freemason, shall be admitted into any Lodge or Assembly until he has brought a certificate of the time and place of his acceptation from the Lodge that accepted him, unto the Master of that limit or division where such Lodge is kept." (See the corrupt word *Dimit*.)

Denderah. A ruined town of Upper Egypt, of great interest in consequence of its astronomical allusions on the ceiling of the main portico supported on twenty-four columns, which is covered with figures and hieroglyphics. This is in the principal temple, which is 220 by 50 feet. The numerous mythological figures are arranged in zodiacal fashion. Recent archeological travelers doubt the reference to astronomy, in consequence of the absence of the Crab. The temple dates from the period of Cleopatra and the earlier Roman emperors, and is one of the finest and best preserved structures of the kind in Egypt. The chief deity was Athor, the goddess of night, corresponding with the Greek Aphrodite. (See *Zodiac*.)

Denmark. The first Masonic Lodge in Denmark was opened in Copenhagen, by Baron G. O. Münnich, on the 11th of November, 1743, under a charter, as he claimed, from the Lodge of the Three Globes in Berlin. In the next year a new Lodge named Zerubbabel was formed by members who separated from the former Lodge. Both of these bodies, however, appear to have been imperfect in their constitution. This imperfection was subsequently rectified. The first Lodge, having changed its name to St. Martin, received in 1749 a warrant from Lord Byron, who was then Grand Master of England. Lord Cranstoun had previously, in October, 1745, granted a warrant to the second Lodge. In 1749 Lord Byron, Grand Master of England, granted a patent to Count Danneskiold Laurvig as Provincial Grand Master of Denmark and Norway. A Lodge had been established at Copenhagen, by the Grand Lodge of Scotland, under the name of "Le petit Nombre"; and in 1753 its Master was elevated by that body to the rank of a Provincial Grand Master. In 1792 Prince Charles became the sole head of the Danish Lodges, and the Grand Lodge of Denmark may be considered to have been then established. He died in 1836, and the Crown Prince, afterward Christian VIII., became the Protector of the Danish Lodges, and his son and successor, Frederick VII., became Grand Master of the Grand Lodge of Denmark on ascending the throne in 1848. He remodeled Danish Masonry on the Swedish system. Now King Frederick VIII. is Protector of the Craft, with the Crown Prince as Grand Master, and there are three St. Andrew's, ten St. John's, and fifteen "Instruction" Lodges under his rule.   [E. L. H.]

Deposite. The deposite of the substitute ark is celebrated in the degree of Select Master, and is supposed to have taken place in the last year of the building of Solomon's Temple, or 1000 B.C. This is therefore adopted as the date in Cryptic Masonry.

In the legendary history of Freemasonry as preserved in the Cryptic degrees, two *deposites* are spoken of; the deposite of the substitute Ark, and the deposite of the Word, both being referred to the same year and being different parts of one transaction. They have, therefore, sometimes been confounded. The deposite of the Ark was made by the three Grand Masters; that of the Word by Hiram Abif alone.

Deposite, Year of. See *Anno Depositionis*.

Depth of the Lodge. This is said to be from the surface to the center, and is the expression of an idea connected with the symbolism of the form of the Lodge as indicating the universality of Masonry. The oldest definition was that the depth extended "to the centre of the earth," which, says Dr. Oliver, is the greatest extent that can be imagined. (See *Form of the Lodge*.)

Deputation. The authority granted by the Grand Master to a brother to act as Provincial Grand Master was formerly called a *deputation*. Thus, in Anderson's *Constitutions* (2d edition, 1738, p. 191), it is said, "Lovel, Grand Master, granted a deputation to Sir Edward Matthews to be Provincial Grand Master of Shropshire." It was also used in the sense in which dispensation is now employed to denote the Grand Master's authority for opening a Lodge. In German Masonry, a *deputation* is a committee of one Lodge appointed to visit and confer with some other Lodge.

Depute Grand Master. Depute is a Scotticism used in the "Laws and Regulations of the Grand Lodge of Scotland" to designate the officer known in England and America as *Deputy Grand Master*.

Deputy. In French Masonry, the officers who represent a Lodge in the Grand Orient are called its deputies. The word is also used in another sense. When two Lodges are affiliated, that is, have adopted a compact of union, each appoints a deputy to represent it at the meetings of the other. He is also called *garant d'amitié*, and is entitled to a seat in the East.

Deputy Grand Chapter. In the Constitution adopted in January, 1798, by the "Grand Royal Arch Chapter of the Northern States of America," which afterward became the "General Grand Chapter," it was provided that Grand Bodies of the system should be established in the different States, which should be known as "Deputy Grand Royal Arch Chapters." But in the succeeding year, on the adoption of a new Constitution, the title was changed to "State Grand Chapters." Massachusetts, Rhode Island, and New York are the only States in which Deputy Grand Chapters were organized.

Deputy Grand Master. The assistant and, in his absence, the representative of the Grand Master. The office originated in the year 1720, when it was agreed that the Grand Master might appoint both his Grand Wardens and a Deputy Grand Master. (*Constitutions*, 1738, p. 111.) The object evidently was to relieve a nobleman, who was Grand Master, from troublesome details of office. The Constitutions give a Deputy Grand Master no other prerogatives than those which he claims in the Grand Master's right. He presides over the Craft in the absence of the Grand Master, and, on the death of that officer, succeeds to his position until a new election. In England, and in a few States of America, he is appointed by the Grand Master; but the general usage in America is to elect him.

Deputy Lodge. In Germany, a *Deputations-Loge*, or Deputy Lodge, was formed by certain members of a Lodge who lived at a remote distance from it, and who met under the name and by the authority of the mother Lodge, through whom alone it was known to the Grand Lodge, or the other Lodges. Such bodies are not known in England or America, and are not now so common in Germany as formerly.

Deputy Master. In England, when a Prince of the Blood Royal is Master of a private Lodge, his functions are performed by an officer appointed by him, and called a Deputy Master, who exercises all the prerogatives and enjoys all the privileges of a regular Master. In Germany, the Master of every Lodge is assisted by a Deputy Master, who is either appointed by the Master, or elected by the members, and who exercises the powers of the Master in the absence of that officer.

Dermott, Laurence. He was at first the Grand Secretary, and afterward the Deputy Grand Master, of that body of Masons who in 1751 formed the Grand Lodge of the "Ancients" (*q. v.*), stigmatizing the regular Masons as "Moderns." In 1756, Dermott published the Book of Constitutions of his Grand Lodge, under the title of *Ahiman Rezon; or a help to all that are or would be Free and Accepted Masons, containing the quintessence of all that has been published on the subject of Freemasonry*. This work passed through several editions, the last of which was edited, in 1813, by Thomas Harper, the Deputy Grand Master of the Ancient Masons, under the title of *The Constitutions of Freemasonry, or Ahiman Rezon*.

Dermott was undoubtedly the moving and sustaining spirit of the great schism which, from the middle of the eighteenth to the beginning of the nineteenth century, divided the Masons of England; and his character has not been spared by the adherents of the constitutional Grand Lodge. Lawrie (*Hist.*, p. 117) says of him: "The unfairness with which he has stated the proceedings of the moderns, the bitterness with which he treats them, and the quackery and vainglory with which he displays his own pretensions to superior knowledge, deserve to be reprobated by every class of Masons who are anxious for the purity of their Order and the preservation of that charity and mildness which ought to characterize all their proceedings." There is perhaps much truth in this estimate of Dermott's character. As a polemic, he was sarcastic, bitter, uncompromising, and not altogether sincere or veracious. But in intellectual attainments he was inferior to none of his adversaries, and in a philosophical appreciation of the character of the Masonic institution he was in advance of the spirit of his age. It has often been asserted that he invented the Royal Arch Degree by dismembering the Third Degree, but that this is entirely unfounded is proved by the fact that he was exalted to the Royal Arch Degree in 1746, while the degree was being conferred in London before 1744. (See *Royal Arch Degree*.) [He died in 1791.—E. L. H.]

Derwentwater. Charles Radcliffe, titular Earl of Derwentwater, which title he assumed on the death of the unmarried son of his brother, James Radcliffe, Earl of Derwentwater, who was executed for rebellion in 1716, in London, was the first Grand Master of the Grand Lodge of France, to which office he was elected on the organization of the Grand Lodge in 1725. Charles Radcliffe was arrested with his brother, Lord Derwentwater, in 1715, for having taken part in the rebellion of that year to restore the house of Stuart to the throne. Both were convicted of treason, and the Earl suffered death, but his brother Charles made his escape to France, and thence to Rome, where he received a trifling pension from the Pretender. After a residence of some years, he went to Paris, where, with the Chevalier Maskelyne, Mr. Heguetty, and some other Englishmen, he established a

Lodge in the Rue des Boucheries, which was followed by the organization of several others, and Radcliffe, who had taken the title of Earl of Derwentwater on the death of his youthful nephew, the son of the last Earl, was elected Grand Master. Leaving France for a time, in 1736 he was succeeded in the Grand Mastership by Lord Harnouester. [Such is the statement usually made, but R. F. Gould, in his *Concise History of Freemasonry*, suggests that "Harnouester" is a corruption of "Darwentwater" and that the two persons are identical, the Earl of Derwentwater being really elected G. M. in 1736.—E. L. H.] Radcliffe made many visits to England after that time in unsuccessful pursuit of a pardon. Finally, on the attempt of the young Pretender to excite a rebellion in 1745, he sailed from France to join him, and the vessel in which he had embarked having been captured by an English cruiser, he was carried to London and decapitated December 8, 1746.

Desaguliers, John Theophilus. Of those who were engaged in the revival of Freemasonry in the beginning of the eighteenth century, none performed a more important part than he to whom may be well applied the epithet of the Father of Modern Speculative Masonry, and to whom, perhaps, more than any other person, is the present Grand Lodge of England indebted for its existence. A sketch of his life, drawn from the scanty materials to be found in Masonic records, and in the brief notices of a few of his contemporaries, cannot fail to be interesting to the student of Masonic history.

The Rev. John Theophilus Desaguliers, LL.D., F.R.S., was born on the 12th of March, 1683, at Rochelle, in France. He was the son of a French Protestant clergyman; and, his father having removed to England as a refugee on the revocation of the Edict of Nantes, he was educated at Christ Church, Oxford, where he took lessons of the celebrated Keill in experimental philosophy. In 1712 he received the degree of Master of Arts, and in the same year succeeded Dr. Keill as a lecturer on experimental philosophy at Hert Hall (now Hertford College). In the year 1713 he removed to Westminster, where he continued his course of lectures, being the first one, it is said, who ever lectured upon physical science in the metropolis. At this time he attracted the notice and secured the friendship of Sir Isaac Newton. His reputation as a philosopher obtained for him a fellowship in the Royal Society. He was also about this time admitted to clerical orders, and appointed by the Duke of Chandos his chaplain, who also presented him to the living of Whitchurch. In 1718 he received from the University of Oxford the degree of Doctor of Civil Law, and was presented by the Earl of Sunderland to a living in Norfolk, which he afterward exchanged for one in Essex. He maintained, however, his residence in London, where he continued to deliver his lectures until his death in 1744.

His contributions to science consist of a *Treatise on the Construction of Chimneys*, translated from the French, and published in 1716; *Lectures of Experimental Philosophy*, of which a second edition was issued in 1719; *A Course of Experimental Philosophy*, in two volumes, 4to, published in 1734; and in 1735 he edited an edition of Gregory's *Elements of Catoptrics and Dioptrics*. He also translated from the Latin Gravesandes' *Mathematical Elements of Natural Philosophy*.

In the clerical profession he seems not to have been an ardent worker, and his theological labors were confined to the publication of a single sermon on repentance. He was in fact more distinguished as a scientist than as a clergyman, and Priestly calls him "an indefatigable experimental philosopher."

It is, however, as a Mason that Dr. Desaguliers will most attract our attention. But nothing is known as to his connection with Freemasonry until 1719, when, he was elevated to the throne of the Grand Lodge, succeeding George Payne, and being thus the third Grand Master after the revival. He paid much attention to the interests of the Fraternity, and so elevated the character of the Order, that the records of the Grand Lodge show that during his administration several of the older brethren who had hitherto neglected the Craft resumed their visits to the Lodges, and many noblemen were initiated into the Institution.

Dr. Desaguliers was peculiarly zealous in the investigation and collection of the old records of the society, and to him we are principally indebted for the preservation of the "Charges of a Freemason" and the preparation of the "General Regulations," which are found in the first edition of the *Constitutions;* which, although attributed to Dr. Anderson, were undoubtedly compiled under the supervision of Desaguliers. Anderson, we suppose, did the work, while Desaguliers furnished much of the material and the thought. One of the first controversial works in favor of Freemasonry, namely, *A Detection of Dr. Plots' Account of the Freemasons*, was also attributed to his pen; but he is said to have repudiated the credit of its authorship, of which indeed the paper furnishes no internal evidence. In 1721 he delivered before the Grand Lodge what the records call "an eloquent oration about Masons and Masonry." It does not appear that it was ever published, at least no copy of it is extant, although Kloss puts the title at the head of his *Catalogue of Masonic Orations*. It is, indeed, the first Masonic address of which we have any notice, and would be highly interesting, because it would give us, in all probability, as Kloss remarks, the views of the Masons of that day in reference to the design of the Institution.

After his retirement from the office of Grand Master, in 1720, Desaguliers was three times appointed Deputy Grand Master: in 1723, by the Duke of Wharton; in June of the same year, by the Earl of Dalkeith; in 1725, by Lord Paisley; and during this period of service he did many things for the benefit of the Craft; among others, initiating that scheme of charity which was subsequently developed in what is now known in the Grand Lodge of England as the Fund of Benevolence.

After this, Dr. Desaguliers passed over to the Continent, and resided for a few years in Holland. In 1731 he was at The Hague, and presided as Worshipful Master of a Lodge organized under a special dispensation for the purpose of initiating and passing the Duke of Lorraine, who was subsequently Grand Duke of Tuscany, and then Emperor of Germany. The Duke was, during the same year, made a Master Mason in England.

On his return to England, Desaguliers was considered, from his position in Masonry, as the most fitting person to confer the degrees on the Prince of Wales, who was accordingly entered, passed, and raised in an occasional Lodge, held on two occasions at Kew, over which Dr. Desaguliers presided as Master.

Dr. Desaguliers was very attentive to his Masonic duties, and punctual in his attendance on the communications of the Grand Lodge. His last recorded appearance by name is on the 8th of February, 1742, but a few years before his death.

Of Desaguliers' Masonic and personal character, Dr. Oliver gives, from tradition, the following description:

"There were many traits in his character that redound to his immortal praise. He was a grave man in private life, almost approaching to austerity; but he could relax in the private recesses of a Tyled Lodge, and in company with brothers and fellows, where the ties of social intercourse are not particularly stringent. He considered the proceedings of the Lodge as strictly confidential; and being persuaded that his brothers by initiation actually occupied the same position as brothers by blood, he was undisguisedly free and familiar in the mutual interchange of unrestrained courtesy. In the Lodge he was jocose and free-hearted, sang his song, and had no objection to his share of the bottle, although one of the most learned and distinguished men of his day." (*Revelations of a Square*, p. 10.)

In 1713, Desaguliers had married a daughter of William Pudsey, Esq., by whom he had two sons—Alexander, who was a clergyman, and Thomas, who went into the army, and became a colonel of artillery and an equerry to George III.

The latter days of Dr. Desaguliers are said to have been clouded with sorrow and poverty. De Feller, in the *Biographie Universelle*, says that he became insane, dressing sometimes as a harlequin, and sometimes as a clown, and that in one of these fits of insanity he died. And Cawthorn, in a poem entitled *The Vanity of Human Enjoyments*, intimates, in the following lines, that Desaguliers was in very necessitous circumstances at the time of his death:

"How poor, neglected Desaguliers fell!
How he who taught two gracious kings to view
All Boyle ennobled and all Bacon knew,
Died in a cell, without a friend to save,
Without a guinea, and without a grave."

But the accounts of the French biographer and the English poet are most probably both apocryphal, or, at least, much exaggerated; for Nichols, who knew him personally, and has given a fine portrait of him in the ninth volume of his *Literary Anecdotes*, says that he died on the 29th of February, 1744, at the Bedford Coffee House, and was buried in the Savoy.

To few Masons of the present day, except to those who have made Freemasonry a subject of especial study, is the name of Desaguliers very familiar. But it is well they should know that to him, perhaps, more than to any other man, are we indebted for the present existence of Freemasonry as a living institution, for it was his learning and social position that gave a standing to the Institution, which brought to its support noblemen and men of influence, so that the insignificant assemblage of four London Lodges at the Apple-Tree Tavern has expanded into an association which now overshadows the entire civilized world. And the moving spirit of all this was John Theophilus Desaguliers.

Desert. The outer court of a tent in the Order of Ishmael, or of Esau and Reconciliation.

Des Etangs, Nicholas Charles. A Masonic reformer, who was born at Allichamps, in France, on the 7th of September, 1766, and died at Paris on the 6th of May, 1847. He was initiated, in 1797, into Masonry in the Lodge l'Heureuse Rencontre. He subsequently removed to Paris, where, in 1822, he became the Master of the Lodge of Trinosophs, which position he held for nine years. Thinking that the ceremonies of the Masonic system in France did not respond to the dignity of the Institution, but were gradually being diverted from its original design, he determined to commence a reform in the recognized dogmas, legends, and symbols, which he proposed to present in new forms more in accord with the manners of the present age. There was, therefore, very little of conservation in the system of Des Etangs. It was, however, adopted for a time by many of the Parisian Lodges, and Des Etangs was loaded with honors. His Rite embraced five degrees, viz., 1, 2, 3, the Symbolic degrees; 4, the Rose Croix rectified; 5, the Grand Elect Knight Kadosh. He gave to his system the title of "Masonry Restored to its True Principles," and fully developed it in his work entitled *Veritable Lien des Peuples*, which was first published in 1823. Des Etangs also published in 1825 a very able reply to the calumnies of the Abbé Barruel, under the title of *La Franc-Maçonnerie justifée de toute les calomnies repandues contre elles*. In the system of Des Etangs, the Builder of the Temple is supposed to symbolize the Good Genius of Humanity destroyed by Ignorance, Falsehood, and Ambition; and hence the Third Degree is supposed to typify the battle between liberty and despotism. In the same spirit, the justness of destroying impious kings is considered the true dogma of the Rose Croix. In fact, the tumults of the French Revolution, in which Des Etangs took no inconsiderable share, had infected his spirit with a political temperament, which unfortunately appears too prominently in many portions of his Masonic system. Notwithstanding that he incorporated two of the high degrees into his Rite, Des Etangs considered the three Symbolic degrees as the only legitimate Masonry, and says that all other degrees have been instituted by various associations and among different peoples on occasions when it was desired to revenge a death, to reestablish a prince, or to give success to a sect.

Design of Freemasonry. It is neither charity nor almsgiving, nor the cultivation of the social sentiment; for both of these are merely incidental to its organization; but it is the search after truth, and that truth is the unity of God and the immortality of the soul. The various degrees or grades of initiation represent the various stages through which the human mind passes, and the many difficulties which men, individually or collectively, must encounter in their progress from ignorance to the acquisition of this truth.

Destruction of the Temple. The Temple of King Solomon was destroyed by Nebuchadnezzar, King of the Chaldees, during the reign of Zedekiah, A.M. 3416, B.C. 588, and just four hundred and sixteen years after its dedication. Although the city was destroyed and the Temple burnt, the Masonic legends state that the deep foundations of the latter were not affected. Nebuchadnezzar caused the city of Jerusalem to be leveled to the ground, the royal palace to be burned, the Temple to be pillaged as well as destroyed, and the inhabitants to be carried captive to Babylon. These events are symbolically detailed in the Royal Arch, and, in allusion to them, the passage of the Book of Chronicles which records them is appropriately read during the ceremonies of this part of the degree.

Detached Degrees. Side or honorary degrees outside of the regular succession of degrees of a Rite, and which, being conferred without the authority of a supreme controlling body, are said to be to the *side of* or *detached from* the regular *régime*. The word detached is peculiar to the Ancient and Accepted Scottish Rite. Thus, in the circular of the Southern Supreme Council, October 10, 1802, is the following: "Besides those degrees which are in regular succession, most of the Inspectors are in possession of a number of *detached degrees*, given in different parts of the world, and which they generally communicate, free of expense, to those brethren who are high enough to understand them."

Deuchar Charters. Warrants, some of which are still in existence in Scotland, and which are used to authorize the working of the Knights Templar Degree by certain Encampments in that country. They were designated "Deuchar Charters," on account of Alexander Deuchar, an engraver and heraldic writer, having been the chief promoter of the Grand Conclave and its first Grand Master. To his exertions, also, the Supreme Grand Royal Arch Chapter of Scotland may be said to have owed its origin. He appears to have become acquainted with Knights Templarism early in the present century through brethren who had been dubbed under a warrant emanating from Dublin, which was held by Fratres serving in the Shropshire Militia. This corps was quartered in Edinburgh in 1798; and in all probability it was through the instrumentality of its members that the first Grand Assembly of Knights Templar was first set up in Edinburgh. Subsequently, this gave place to the Grand Assembly of High Knights Templar in Edinburgh, working under a charter, No. 31, of the Early Grand Encampment of Ireland, of which in 1807 Deuchar was Grand Master. The Deuchar Charters authorized Encampments to install "Knights Templar and Knights of St. John of Jerusalem"—one condition on which these warrants were held being "that no communion or intercourse shall be maintained with any Chapter or Encampment, or body assuming that name, holding meetings of Knights Templar under a Master Mason's Charter." In 1837 the most of these warrants were forfeited, and the Encampments erased from the roll of the Grand Conclave, on account of not making the required returns.

Deus Meumque Jus. *God and my right.* The motto of the Thirty-third Degree of the Ancient and Accepted Scottish Rite, and hence adopted as that also of the Supreme Council of the Rite. It is a Latin translation of the motto of the royal arms of England, which is "Dieu et mon droit," and concerning which we have the following tradition. Richard Cœur de Leon, besieging Gisors, in Normandy, in 1198, gave, as a parole, "Dieu et mon droit," because Philip Augustus, King of France, had, without *right*, taken that city, which then belonged to England. Richard, having been victorious with that righteous parole, hence adopted it as his motto; and it was afterward marshaled in the arms of England.

Development. The ancients often wrote their books on parchment, which were made up into a roll, hence called a *volume*, from *volvere*, "to roll up." Thus, he who read the book commenced by unrolling it, a custom still practised by the Jews in reading their Sacred Law, and it was not until the whole volume was unrolled and read that he became the master of its contents. Now, in the Latin language, to unfold or to unroll was *devolvere*, whence we get our English word *to develop*. The figurative signification thus elicited from etymology may be well applied to the idea of the development of Masonry. The system of Speculative Masonry is a volume closely folded from unlawful eyes, and he who would understand its true intent and meaning must follow the old proverb, and "commence at the beginning." There is no royal road of arriving at this knowledge. It can be attained only by laborious research. The student must begin as an Apprentice, by studying the rudiments that are unfolded on its first page. Then as a Fellow-Craft still more of the precious writing is unrolled, and he acquires new ideas. As a Master he continues the operation, and possesses himself of additional material for thought. But it is not until the entire volume lies unrolled before him, in the highest degree, and the whole speculative system of its philosophy is lying outspread before him, that he can pretend to claim a thorough comprehension of its plan. It is then only that he has solved the problem, and can exclaim, "the end has crowned the work." The Mason who looks only on the ornamental covering of the roll knows nothing of its contents. Masonry is a scheme of development; and he who has learned nothing of its design, and who is daily adding nothing to his stock of Masonic ideas, is simply one who is not unrolling the parchment. It is a custom of the Jews on their Sabbath, in the synagogue, that a member should pay for the privilege of unrolling the Sacred Law. So, too, the Mason, who would uphold the law of his Institution, must pay for the privilege, not in base coin, but in labor and research, studying its principles, searching out its design, and imbibing all of its symbolism; and the payment thus made will purchase a rich jewel.

Device. A term in heraldry signifying any emblem used to represent a family, person, nation, or society, and to distinguish such from any other. The device is usually accompanied with a suitable motto applied in a figurative sense, and its essence consists in a metaphorical similitude between the thing representing and that represented. Thus, the device of a lion represents the courage of the person bearing it. The oak is the device of strength; the palm, of victory; the sword, of honor; and the eagle, of sovereign power. The several sections of the Masonic sodality are distinguished by appropriate devices.

1. *Ancient Craft Masonry.* Besides the arms of Speculative Masonry, which are described in this work under the appropriate head, the most common device is a *square and compass.*

2. *Royal Arch Masonry.* The device is a *triple tau within a triangle.*

3. *Knight Templarism.* The ancient device, which was borne on the seals and banners of the primitive Order, was two knights riding on one horse, in allusion to the vow of poverty taken by the founders. The modern device of Masonic Templarism is a *cross pattée.*

4. *Scottish Rite Masonry.* The device is a *double-headed eagle crowned, holding in his claws a sword.*

5. *Royal and Select Masters.* The device is a *trowel suspended within a triangle,* in which the allusion is to the tetragrammaton

symbolized by the triangle or delta, and the workmen at the first Temple symbolized by the trowel.

6. *Rose Croix Masonry.* The device is a *cross charged with a rose; at its foot an eagle and a pelican.*

7. *Knight of the Sun.* This old degree of philosophical Masonry has for its device *rays of light issuing from a triangle inscribed within a circle of darkness,* which "teaches us," says Oliver, "that when man was enlightened by the Deity with reason, he became enabled to penetrate the darkness and obscurity which ignorance and superstition have spread abroad to allure men to their destruction."

Each of these devices is accompanied by a motto which properly forms a part of it. These mottoes will be found under the head of *Motto.*

The Italian heralds have paid peculiar attention to the subject of devices, and have established certain laws for their construction, which are generally recognized in other countries. These laws are, 1. That there be nothing extravagant or monstrous in the figures. 2. That figures be never joined together which have no relation or affinity with one another. 3. That the human body should never be used. 4. That the figures should be few in number, and 5. That the motto should refer to the device, and express with it a common idea. According to P. Bouhours, the figure or emblem was called the body, and the motto the soul of the device.

Devoir. The gilds or separate communities in the system of French compagnonage are called devoirs. (See *Compagnonage.*)

Devoir of a Knight. The original meaning of devoir is duty; and hence, in the language of chivalry, a knight's devoir comprehended the performance of all those duties to which he was obligated by the laws of knighthood and the vows taken at his creation. These were the defense of widows and orphans, the maintenance of justice, and the protection of the poor and weak against the oppressions of the strong and great. Thus, in one of Beaumont and Fletcher's plays, the knight says to the lady:

"Madame, if any service or *devoir*
Of a poor errant knight may right your wrongs,
Command it; I am prest to give you succor,
For to that holy end I bear my armor."
Knight of the Burning Pestle. Act II., Scene 1.

The devoir of a Knights Templar was originally to protect pilgrims on their visit to the Holy Land, and to defend the holy places. The devoir of a modern Knights Templar is to defend innocent virgins, destitute widows, helpless orphans, and the Christian religion.

Devotions. The prayers in a Commandery of Knights Templar are technically called the devotions of the knights.

Dialectics. That branch of logic which teaches the rules and modes of reasoning. *Dialecticke* and *dialecticus* are used as corruptions of the Latin *dialectica* in some of the old manuscript Constitutions, instead of logic, in the enumeration of the seven liberal arts and sciences.

Diamond. A precious stone; in Hebrew, םהלי. It was the third stone in the second row of the high priest's breastplate, according to the enumeration of Aben Ezra, and corresponded to the tribe of Zebulun. But it is doubtful whether the diamond was known in the time of Moses; and if it was, its great value and its insusceptibility to the impression of a graving-tool would have rendered it totally unfit as a stone in the breastplate. The Vulgate more properly gives the jasper.

Dieseal. A term used by the Druids to designate the circumambulation around the sacred cairns, and is derived from two words signifying "on the right of the sun," because the circumambulation was always in imitation of the course of the sun, with the right hand next to the cairn or altar. (See *Circumambulation* and *Deiseil*.)

Dieu et mon Droit. See *Deus Meumque Jus*.

Dieu le Veut. *God wills it.* The war-cry of the old Crusaders, and hence adopted as a motto in the degrees of Templarism.

Dignitaries. The Master, the Wardens, the Orator, and the Secretary in a French Lodge are called dignitaries. The corresponding officers in the Grand Orient are called Grand Dignitaries. In English and American Masonic language the term is usually restricted to high officers of the Grand Lodge.

Dimit. A modern, American, and wholly indefensible corruption of the technical word *Demit*. As the use of this corrupt form is beginning to be very prevalent among American Masonic writers, it is proper that we should inquire which is the correct word, *Demit* or *Dimit*.

For almost a century and a half the Masonic world has been content, in its technical language, to use the word *demit*. But within a few years, a few admirers of neologisms—men who are always ready to believe that what is old cannot be good, and that new fashions are always the best—have sought to make a change in the well-established word, and, by altering the *e* in the first syllable into an *i*, they make another word *dimit*, which they assert is the right one. It is simply a question of orthography, and must be settled first by reference to usage, and then to etymology, to discover which of the words sustains, by its derivation, the true meaning which is intended to be conveyed.

It is proper, however, to premise that although in the seventeenth century Sir Thomas Browne used the word *demit* as a verb, meaning "to depress," and Bishop Hall used *dimit* as signifying *to send away*, yet both words are omitted by all the early lexicographers. Neither of them is to be found in Phillips, in 1706, nor in Blunt, in 1707, nor in Bailey, in 1732. Johnson and Sheridan, of a still later date, have inserted in their dictionaries *demit*, but not *dimit*; but Walker, Richardson, and Webster give both words, but only as verbs. The verb *to demit* or *to dimit* may be found, but

never the noun *a demit* or *a dimit*. As a noun substantive, this word, however it may be spelled, is unknown to the general language, and is strictly a technical expression peculiar to Freemasonry.

As a Masonic technicality we must then discuss it. And, first, as to its meaning.

Dr. Oliver, who omits *dimit* in his *Dictionary of Symbolical Masonry*, defines *demit* thus: "A Mason is said to demit from the Order when he withdraws from all connection with it." It will be seen that he speaks of it here only as a verb, and makes no reference to its use as a noun.

Macoy, in his *Cyclopœdia*, omits *demit*, but defines *dimit* thus: "From the Latin *dimitto*, to permit to go. The act of withdrawing from membership." To say nothing of the incorrectness of this definition, to which reference will hereafter be made, there is in it a violation of the principles of language which is worthy of note. No rule is better settled than that which makes the verb and the noun derived from it have the same relative signification. Thus, "to discharge" means "to dismiss"; "a discharge" means "a dismission"; "to approve" means "to express liking"; "an approval" means "an expression of liking"; "to remit" means "to relax"; "a remission" means "a relaxation," and so with a thousand other instances. Now, according to this rule, if "to demit" means "to permit to go," then "a dimit" should mean "a permission to go." The withdrawal is something subsequent and consequent, but it may never take place. According to Macoy's definition of the verb, the granting of "a dimit" does not necessarily lead to the conclusion that the Mason who received it has left the Lodge. He has only been permitted to do so. This is contrary to the universally accepted definition of the word. Accordingly, when he comes to define the word as a noun, he gives it the true meaning, which, however, does not agree with his previous definition as a verb.

In instituting the inquiry which of these two words is the true one, we must first look to the general usage of Masonic writers; for, after all, the rule of Horace holds good, that in the use of words we must be governed by custom or usage,

——"whose arbitrary sway
Words and the forms of language must obey."

If we shall find that the universal usage of Masonic writers until a very recent date has been to employ the form *demit*, then we are bound to believe that it is the correct form, notwithstanding a few writers have very recently sought to intrude the form *dimit* upon us.

Now, how stands the case? The first time that we find the word *demit* used is in the second edition of Anderson's *Constitutions*, Anno 1738, p. 153. There it is said that on the 25th of November, 1723, "it was agreed that if a Master of a particular Lodge is deposed, or *demits*, the Senior Warden shall forthwith fill the Master's Chair."

The word continued in use as a technical word in the Masonry of England for many years. In the editions of the *Constitutions* published in 1756, p. 311, the passage just quoted is again recited, and the word *demit* is again employed in the fourth edition of the *Constitutions* published in 1767, p. 345.

In the second edition of Dermott's *Ahiman Rezon*, published in 1764 (I have not the first), p. 52, and in the third edition, published in 1778, p. 58, the word *demit* is employed. Oliver, it will be seen, uses it in his *Dictionary*, published in 1853. But the word seems to have become obsolete in England, and *to resign* is now constantly used by English Masonic writers in the place of *to demit*.

In America, however, the word has been and continues to be in universal use, and has always been spelled, until very recently, *demit*.

Thus we find it used by Taunehill, *Manual*, 1845, p. 59; Morris, *Code of Masonic Law*, 1856, p. 289; by Hubbard, in 1851; by Chase, *Digest*, 1859, p. 104; by Mitchell, *Masonic History*, vol. ii., pp. 556, 592, and by all the Grand Lodges whose proceedings I have examined up to the year 1860, and probably beyond that date.

On the contrary, the word *dimit* is of very recent origin, and has been used only within a few years. Usage, therefore, both English and American, is clearly in favor of *demit*, and *dimit* must be considered as an interloper, and ought to be consigned to the tomb of the Capulets.

And now we are to inquire whether this usage is sustained by the principles of etymology. First, let us obtain a correct definition of the word.

To demit, in Masonic language, means simply to resign. The Mason who demits from his Lodge resigns from it. The word is used in the exact sense, for instance, in the Constitution of the Grand Lodge of Wisconsin, where it is said: "No brother shall be allowed *to demit* from any Lodge unless for the purpose of uniting with some other." That is to say: "No brother shall be allowed *to resign* from any Lodge."

Now what are the respective meanings of *demit* and *dimit* in ordinary language?

There the words are found to be entirely different in signification.

To demit is derived first from the Latin *demittere* through the French *demettre*. In Latin the prefixed particle *de* has the weight of *down;* added to the verb *mittere*, to send, it signifies to let down from an elevated position to a lower. Thus, Cæsar used it in this very sense, when, in describing the storming of Avaricum, (*Bel. Gal.*, vii., 28), he says that the Roman soldiers did not let themselves down, that is, descend from the top of the wall to the level ground. The French, looking to this reference to a descent from a higher to a lower position, made their verb *se demettre*, used in a reflective sense, signify to give up a post, office, or occupation, that is to say, to resign it. And thence the English use of the word is

reducible, which makes *to demit* signify *to resign*. We have another word in our language also derived from *demettre*, and in which the same idea of resignation is apparent. It is the word *demise*, which was originally used only to express a royal death. The old maxim was that "the king never dies." So, instead of saying "the death of the king," they said "the demise of the king," thereby meaning his resignation of the crown to his successor. The word is now applied more generally, and we speak of the demise of Mr. Pitt, or any other person.

To dimit is derived from the Latin *dimittere*. The prefixed particle *di* or *dis* has the effect of *off from*, and hence *dimittere* means to send away. Thus, Terence uses it to express the meaning of dismissing or sending away an army.

Both words are now obsolete in the English language. They were formerly used, but in the different senses already indicated.

Thus, Hollinshed employs *demit* to signify a surrender, yielding up, or resignation of a franchise.

Bishop Hall uses *dimit* to signify a sending away of a servant by his master.

Demit, as a noun, is not known in good English; the correlative nouns of the verbs *to demit* and *to dimit* are *demission* and *dimission*. "A demit" is altogether a Masonic technicality, and is, moreover, an Americanism of very recent usage.

It is then evident that *to demit* is the proper word, and that to use *to dimit* is to speak and write incorrectly. When a Mason "demits from a Lodge," we mean that he "resigns from a Lodge," because *to demit* means *to resign*. But what does anyone mean when he says that a Mason "dimits from a Lodge"? *To dimit* means, as we have seen, *to send away*, therefore "he dimits from the Lodge" is equivalent to saying "he sends away from the Lodge," which of course is not only bad English, but sheer nonsense. If *dimit* is to be used at all, as it is an active, transitive verb, it must be used only in that form, and we must either say that "a Lodge dimits a Mason," or that "a Mason is dimitted by his Lodge."

I think that I have discovered the way in which this blunder first arose. Robert Morris, in his *Code of Masonic Law*, p. 289, has the following passage:

"A 'demit,' technically considered, is *the act of withdrawing*, and applies to the Lodge and not to the individual. A Mason cannot *demit*, in the strict sense, but the Lodge may demit (dismiss) him."

It is astonishing how the author of this passage could have crowded into so brief a space so many violations of grammar, law, and common sense. First, *to demit* means *to withdraw*, and then this withdrawal is made the act of the Lodge and not of the individual, as if the Lodge withdrew the member instead of the member withdrawing himself. And immediately afterward, seeing the absurdity of this doctrine, and to make the demission the act of the Lodge, he changes the signification of the word, and makes *to demit* mean *to dismiss*. Certainly it is impossible to discuss the law of Masonic demission when such contrary meanings are given to the word in one and the same paragraph.

But certain wiseacres, belonging probably to that class who believe that there is always improvement in change, seizing upon this latter definition of Morris, that *to demit* meant *to dismiss*, and seeing that this was a meaning which the word never had, and, from its derivation from *demittere*, never could have, changed the word from *demit* to *dimit*, which really does have the meaning of sending away or dismissing. But as the Masonic act of *demission* does not mean a dismissal from the Lodge, because that would be an expulsion, but simply a resignation, the word *dimit* cannot properly be applied to the act.

A Mason demits from the Lodge; he resigns. He takes out his demit (a strictly technical expression and altogether confined to this country); he asks for and receives an acceptance of his resignation.

Diocesan. The Fifth Degree of Bahrdt's German Union.

Dionysian Architects. The priests of Bacchus, or, as the Greeks called him, Dionysus, having devoted themselves to architectural pursuits, established about 1000 years before the Christian era a society or fraternity of builders in Asia Minor, which is styled by the ancient writers the Fraternity of Dionysian Architects, and to this society was exclusively confined the privilege of erecting temples and other public buildings.

The members of the Fraternity of Dionysian Architects were linked together by the secret ties of the Dionysian mysteries, into which they had all been initiated. Thus constituted, the Fraternity was distinguished by many peculiarities that strikingly assimilate it to our Order. In the exercise of charity, the "more opulent were sacredly bound to provide for the exigencies of the poorer brethren." For the facilities of labor and government, they were divided into communities called συνοικίαι, each of which was governed by a Master and Wardens. They held a general assembly or grand festival once a year, which was solemnized with great pomp and splendor. They employed in their ceremonial observances many of the implements which are still to be found among Freemasons, and used, like them, a universal language, by which one brother could distinguish another in the dark as well as in the light, and which served to unite the members scattered over India, Persia, and Syria, into one common brotherhood. The existence of this order in Tyre, at the time of the building of the Temple, is universally admitted; and Hiram, the widow's son, to whom Solomon entrusted the superintendence of the workmen, as an inhabitant of Tyre, and as a skilful architect and cunning and curious workman, was, very probably, one of its members. Hence, we may legitimately suppose that the Dionysians were sent by Hiram, King of Tyre, to assist King Solomon in the construction of the house he was about to dedicate to Jehovah, and that they communicated to their Jewish fellow-laborers a knowledge of the advantages of their Fraternity, and invited them to a participation in its mysteries and privileges. In this union, however, the apocryphal legend of the Dionysians would naturally give way to the true legend of the Masons, which was unhappily furnished by a melancholy incident that occurred at the time. The latter part of this statement is, it is admitted, a mere speculation, but one that has met the approval of Lawrie, Oliver, and our best writers; and although this connection between the Dionysian Architects and the builders of King Solomon may not be supported by documentary evidence, the traditionary theory is at least plausible, and offers nothing which is either absurd or impossible. If accepted, it supplies the necessary link which connects the Pagan with the Jewish mysteries.

The history of this association subsequent to the Solomonic era has been detailed by Masonic writers, who have derived their information sometimes from conjectural and sometimes from historical authority. About 300 years B.C., they were incorporated by the kings of Pergamos at Teos, which was assigned to them as a settlement, and where they continued for centuries as an exclusive society engaged in the erection of works of art and the celebration of their mysteries. Notwithstanding the edict of the Emperor Theodosius which abolished all mystical associations, they are said to have continued their existence down to the time of the Crusades, and during the constant communication which was kept up between the two continents passed over from Asia to Europe, where they became known as the "Traveling Freemasons" of the Middle Ages, into whose future history they thus became merged.

Dionysian Mysteries. These mysteries were celebrated throughout Greece and Asia Minor, but principally at Athens, where the years were numbered by them. They were instituted in honor of Bacchus, or, as the Greeks called him, Dionysus, and were introduced into Greece from Egypt. In these mysteries, the murder of Dionysus by the Titans was commemorated, in which legend he is evidently identified with the Egyptian Osiris, who was slain by his brother Typhon. The aspirant, in the ceremonies through which he passed, represented the murder of the god and his restoration to life, which, says the Baron de Sacy (*Notes on Sainte-Croix*, ii., 86), were the subject of allegorical explanations altogether analogous to those which were given to the rape of Proserpine and the murder of Osiris.

The commencement of the mysteries was signalized by the consecration of an egg, in allusion to the mundane egg from which all things were supposed to have sprung. The candidate having been first purified by water, and crowned with a myrtle branch, was introduced into the vestibule, and there clothed in the sacred habiliments. He was then delivered to the conductor, who, after the mystic warning, ἑκάς, ἑκάς, ἔστε, βέβηλοι, "Depart hence, all ye profane!" exhorted the candidate to exert all his fortitude and courage in the dangers and trials through which he was about to pass. He was then led through a series of dark caverns, a part of the ceremonies which Stobæus calls "a rude and fearful march through night and darkness." During this passage he was terrified by the howling of wild beasts, and other fearful noises; artificial thunder reverberated through the subterranean apartments, and transient flashes of lightning revealed monstrous apparitions to his sight. In this state of darkness and terror he was kept for three days and nights, after which he commenced the aphanism or mystical death of Bacchus. He was now placed on the pastos or couch, that is, he was confined in a solitary cell, where he could reflect seriously on the nature of the undertaking in which he was engaged. During this time, he was alarmed with the sudden crash of waters, which was intended to represent the deluge. Typhon, searching for Osiris, or Dionysus, for they are here identical, discovered the ark in which he had been secreted, and, tearing it violently asunder, scattered the limbs of his victim upon the waters. The aspirant now heard the lamentations which were instituted for the death of the god. Then commenced the search of Rhea for the remains of Dionysus. The apartments were filled with shrieks and groans; the initiated mingled with their howlings of despair the frantic dances of the Corybantes; everything was a scene of distraction, until, at a signal from the hierophant, the whole drama changed—the mourning was turned to joy; the mangled body was found; and the aspirant was released from his confinement, amid the shouts of Εὑρήκαμεν, Ευγχαίρωμεν, "We have found it; let us rejoice together." The candidate was now made to descend into the infernal regions, where he beheld the torments of the wicked and the rewards of the virtuous. It was now that he received the lecture explanatory of the Rites, and was invested with the tokens which served the initiated as a means of recognition. He then underwent a lustration, after which he was introduced into the holy place, where he received the name of epopt, and was fully instructed in the doctrine of the mysteries, which consisted in a belief in the existence of one God and a future state of rewards and punishments. These doctrines were inculcated by a variety of significant symbols. After the performance of these ceremonies, the aspirant was dismissed, and the Rites concluded with the pronunciation of the mystic words, *Konx Ompax.* Sainte-Croix (*Myst. du Pag.*, ii., 90), says that the murder of Dionysus by the Titans was only an allegory of the physical revolutions of the world; but these were in part, in the ancient initiations, significant of the changes of life and death and resurrection.

Dionysus. The Greek name of Bacchus. (See *Dionysian Mysteries.*)

Diploma. Literally means something

folded. From the Greek, διπλόω. The word is applied in Masonry to the certificates granted by Lodges, Chapters, and Commanderies to their members, which should always be written on parchment. The more usual word, however, is *Certificate*, which see. In the Scottish Rite they are called Patents.

Director of Ceremonies, Grand. An officer in the Grand Lodge of England, who has the arrangement and direction of all processions and ceremonies of the Grand Lodge and the care of the regalia, clothing, insignia, and jewels belonging to the Grand Lodge. His jewel is two rods in saltire, tied by a ribbon.

Directory. In German Lodges, the Master and other officers constitute a council of management, under the name of *Directorium* or *Directory*.

Directory, Roman Helvetic. The name assumed in 1739 by the Supreme Masonic authority at Lausanne, in Switzerland. (See *Switzerland.*)

Discalceation, Rite of. The ceremony of taking off the shoes, as a token of respect, whenever we are on or about to approach holy ground. It is referred to in Exodus iii. 5, where the angel of the Lord, at the burning bush, exclaims to Moses: "Draw not nigh hither; put off thy shoes from off thy feet, for the place whereon thou standest is holy ground." It is again mentioned in Joshua v. 15, in the following words: "And the captain of the Lord's host said unto Joshua, Loose thy shoe from off thy foot; for the place whereon thou standest is holy." And lastly, it is alluded to in the injunction given in Ecclesiastes v. 1: "Keep thy foot when thou goest to the house of God."

The Rite, in fact, always was, and still is, used among the Jews and other Oriental nations when entering their temples and other sacred edifices. It does not seem to have been derived from the command given to Moses; but rather to have existed as a religious custom from time immemorial, and to have been borrowed, as Mede supposes, by the Gentiles, through tradition, from the patriarchs.

The direction of Pythagoras to his disciples was in these words: Ἀνυπόδητος θύε καὶ προσκύνει—that is, "Offer sacrifice and worship with thy shoes off."

Justin Martyr says that those who came to worship in the sanctuaries and temples of the Gentiles were commanded by their priests to put off their shoes.

Drusius, in his *Notes on the Book of Joshua*, says that among most of the Eastern nations it was a pious duty to tread the pavement of the temple with unshod feet.

Maimonides, the great expounder of the Jewish law, asserts (*Beth Habbechirah*, c. vii.) that "it was not lawful for a man to come into the mountain of God's house with his shoes on his feet, or with his staff, or in his working garments, or with dust on his feet."

Rabbi Solomon, commenting on the command in Leviticus xix. 30, "Ye shall reverence my sanctuary," makes the same remark in relation to this custom. On this subject, Oliver (*Hist. Landm.*, ii., 471) observes: "Now the act of going with naked feet was always considered a token of humility and reverence, and the priests, in the temple worship, always officiated with feet uncovered, although it was frequently injurious to their health."

Mede quotes Zago Zaba, an Ethiopian bishop, who was ambassador from David, King of Abyssinia, to John III., of Portugal, as saying: "We are not permitted to enter the church except barefooted."

The Mohammedans, when about to perform their devotions, always leave their slippers at the door of the mosque. The Druids practised the same custom whenever they celebrated their sacred rites; and the ancient Peruvians are said always to have left their shoes at the porch when they entered the magnificent temple consecrated to the worship of the sun.

Adam Clarke (*Comm. on Exod.*) thinks that the custom of worshiping the Deity barefooted, was so general among all nations of antiquity, that he assigns it as one of his thirteen proofs that the whole human race have been derived from one family.

Finally, Bishop Patrick, speaking of the origin of this Rite, says, in his *Commentaries:* "Moses did not give the first beginning to this Rite, but it was derived from the patriarchs before him, and transmitted to future times from that ancient, general tradition; for we find no command in the law of Moses for the priests performing the service of the temple without shoes, but it is certain they did so from immemorial custom; and so do the Mohammedans and other nations at this day."

Disciplina Arcani. See *Discipline of the Secret.*

Discipline. This word is used by Masons, in its ecclesiastical sense, to signify the execution of the laws by which a Lodge is governed and the infliction of the penalties enjoined against offenders who are its members, or, not being members, live within its jurisdiction. *To discipline a Mason* is to subject him to punishment. (See *Jurisdiction* and *Punishments.*)

Discipline of the Secret. There existed in the earlier ages of the Christian church a mystic and secret worship, from which a portion of the congregation was peremptorily excluded, and whose privacy was guarded, with the utmost care, from the obtrusive eyes of all who had not been duly initiated into the sacred rites that qualified them to be present.

This custom of communicating only to a portion of the Christian community the more abstruse doctrines and more sacred ceremonies of the church, is known among ecclesiastical writers by the name of "DISCIPLINA ARCANI," or "The Discipline of the Secret."

Converts were permitted to attain a knowledge of all the doctrines, and participate in the sacraments of the church, only after a long and experimental probation. The young Christian, like the disciple of Pythagoras, was made to pass through a searching ordeal of time and patience, by which his capacity, his fidelity,

and his other qualifications were strictly tested. For this purpose, different ranks were instituted in the congregation. The lowest of these were the *Catechumens.* These were occupied in a study of the elementary principles of the Christian religion. Their connection with the church was not consummated by baptism, to which rite they were not admitted, even as spectators, it being the symbol of a higher degree; but their initiation was accompanied with solemn ceremonies, consisting of prayer, signing with the cross, and the imposition of hands by the priest. The next degree was that of the *Competentes,* or seekers.

When a Catechumen had exhibited satisfactory evidences of his proficiency in religious knowledge, he petitioned the Bishop for the Sacrament of baptism. His name was then registered in the books of the church. After this registration, the candidate underwent the various ceremonies appropriate to the degree upon which he was about to enter. He was examined by the bishop as to his attainments in Christianity, and, if approved, was exorcised for twenty days, during which time he was subjected to rigorous fasts, and, having made confession, the necessary penance was prescribed. He was then, for the first time, instructed in the words of the Apostles' creed, a symbol of which the Catechumens were entirely ignorant.

Another ceremony peculiar to the Competentes was that of going about with their faces veiled. St. Augustine explains the ceremony by saying that the Competentes went veiled in public as an image of the slavery of Adam after his expulsion from Paradise, and that, after baptism, the veils were taken away as an emblem of the liberty of the spiritual life which was obtained by the sacrament of regeneration. Some other significant ceremonies, but of a less important character, were used, and the Competent, having passed through them all, was at length admitted to the highest degree.

The *Fideles,* or *Faithful,* constituted the Third Degree or order. Baptism was the ceremony by which the Competentes, after an examination into their proficiency, were admitted into this degree. "They were thereby," says Bingham, "made complete and perfect Christians, and were, upon that account, dignified with several titles of honor and marks of distinction above the Catechumens." They were called *Illuminati,* or Illuminated, because they had been enlightened as to those secrets which were concealed from the inferior orders. They were also called *Initiati,* or Initiated, because they were admitted to a knowledge of the sacred mysteries; and so commonly was this name in use, that, when Chrysostom and the other ancient writers spoke of their concealed doctrines, they did so in ambiguous terms, so as not to be understood by the Catechumens, excusing themselves for their brief allusions, by saying, "the Initiated know what we mean." And so complete was the understanding of the ancient Fathers of a hidden mystery, and an initiation into them, that

St. Ambrose has written a book, the title of which is, *Concerning those who are Initiated into the Mysteries.* They were also called the Perfect, to intimate that they had attained to a perfect knowledge of all the doctrines and sacraments of the church.

There were certain prayers, which none but the Faithful were permitted to hear. Among these was the Lord's prayer, which, for this reason, was commonly called *Oratio Fidelium,* or, "The Prayer of the Faithful." They were also admitted to hear discourses upon the most profound mysteries of the church, to which the Catechumens were strictly forbidden to listen. St. Ambrose, in the book written by him to the Initiated, says that sermons on the subject of morality were daily preached to the Catechumens; but to the Initiated they gave an explanation of the Sacraments, which, to have spoken of to the unbaptized, would have rather been like a betrayal of mysteries than instruction. And St. Augustine, in one of his sermons to the Faithful, says: "Having now dismissed the Catechumens, you alone have we retained to hear us, because, in addition to those things which belong to all Christians in common, we are now about to speak in an especial manner of the Heavenly Mysteries, which none can hear except those who, by the gift of the Lord, are able to comprehend them."

The mysteries of the church were divided, like the Ancient Mysteries, into the lesser and the greater. The former was called "Missa Catechumenorum," or the Mass of the Catechumens, and the latter, "Missa Fidelium," or the Mass of the Faithful. The public service of the church consisted of the reading of the Scripture, and the delivery of a sermon, which was entirely of a moral character. These being concluded, the lesser mysteries, or Mass of the Catechumens, commenced. The deacon proclaimed in a loud voice, "*Ne quis audientium, ne quis infidelium,*" that is, "Let none who are simply hearers, and let no infidels be present." All then who had not acknowledged their faith in Christ by placing themselves among the Catechumens, and all Jews and Pagans, were caused to retire, that the Mass of the Catechumens might begin. And now, for better security, a deacon was placed at the men's door and a subdeacon at the women's, for the deacons were the door-keepers, and, in fact, received that name in the Greek church. The Mass of the Catechumens—which consisted almost entirely of prayers, with the Episcopal benediction—was then performed.

This part of the service having been concluded, the Catechumens were dismissed by the deacons, with the expression, "Catechumens, depart in peace." The Competentes, however, or those who had the Second or intermediate degree, remained until the prayers for those who were possessed of evil spirits, and the supplications for themselves, were pronounced. After this, they too were dismissed, and none now remaining in the church but the Faithful, the Missa Fidelium, or greater mysteries, commenced.

The formula of dismission used by the dea-con on this occasion was: "Holy things for the holy, let the dogs depart," *Sancta sanctis, foris canes.*

The Faithful then all repeated the creed, which served as an evidence that no intruder or uninitiated person was present; because the creed was not revealed to the Catechumens, but served as a password to prove that its possessor was an initiate. After prayers had been offered up—which, however, differed from the supplications in the former part of the service, by the introduction of open allusions to the most abstruse doctrines of the church, which were never named in the presence of the Catechumens—the oblations were made, and the Eucharistical Sacrifice, or Lord's Supper, was celebrated. Prayers and invocations followed, and at length the service was concluded, and the assembly was dismissed by the benediction, "Depart in peace."

Bingham records the following rites as having been concealed from the Catechumens, and entrusted, as the sacred mysteries, only to the Faithful: the manner of receiving baptism; the ceremony of confirmation; the ordination of priests; the mode of celebrating the Eucharist; the liturgy, or Divine service; and the doctrine of the Trinity, the creed, and the Lord's prayer, which last, however, were begun to be explained to the Competentes.

Such was the celebrated Discipline of the Secret in the early Christian church. That its origin, so far as the outward form was concerned, is to be found in the Mysteries of Paganism, there can be no doubt, as has been thus expressed by the learned Mosheim: "Religion having thus, in both its branches, the speculative as well as the practical, assumed a twofold character,—the one public or common, the other private or mysterious,—it was not long before a distinction of a similar kind took place also in the Christian discipline and form of divine worship; for, observing that in Egypt, as well as in other countries, the heathen worshippers, in addition to their public religious ceremonies,—to which everyone was admitted without distinction,—had certain secret and most sacred rites, to which they gave the name of 'mysteries,' and at the celebration of which none but persons of the most approved faith and discretion were permitted to be present, the Alexandrian Christians first, and after them others, were beguiled into a notion that they could not do better than make the Christian discipline accommodate itself to this model."

Discovery of the Body. See *Euresis.*

Discovery, Year of the. "Anno Inventionis," or "in the Year of the Discovery," is the style assumed by the Royal Arch Masons, in commemoration of an event which took place soon after the commencement of the rebuilding of the Temple by Zerubbabel.

Dispensation. A permission to do that which, without such permission, is forbidden by the Constitutions and usages of the Order. Du Cange (*Glossarium*) defines a dispensation to be a prudent relaxation of a general law. *Provida juris communis relaxatio.* While showing how much the ancient ecclesiastical authorities were opposed to the granting of dispensations, since they preferred to pardon the offense after the law had been violated, rather than to give a previous license for its violation, he adds, "but however much the Roman Pontiffs and pious Bishops felt of reverence for the ancient Regulations, they were often compelled to depart in some measure from them, for the utility of the church; and this milder measure of acting the jurists called a dispensation."

This power to dispense with the provisions of law in particular cases appears to be inherent in the Grand Master; because, although frequently referred to in the old Regulations, it always is as if it were a power already in existence, and never by way of a new grant. There is no record of any Masonic statute or constitutional provision conferring this prerogative in distinct words. The instances, however, in which this prerogative may be exercised are clearly enumerated in various places of the Old Constitutions, so that there can be no difficulty in understanding to what extent the prerogative extends.

The power of granting dispensations is confided to the Grand Master, or his representative, but should not be exercised except on extraordinary occasions, or for excellent reasons. The dispensing power is confined to only four circumstances: 1. A Lodge cannot be opened and held unless a Warrant of Constitution be first granted by the Grand Lodge; but the Grand Master may issue his dispensation, empowering a constitutional number of brethren to open and hold a Lodge until the next communication of the Grand Lodge. At this communication, the dispensation of the Grand Master is either revoked or confirmed. A Lodge under dispensation is not permitted to be represented, nor to vote in the Grand Lodge. 2. Not more than five candidates can be made at the same communication of a Lodge; but the Grand Master, on the showing of sufficient cause, may extend to a Lodge the privilege of making as many more as he may think proper. 3. No Brother can, at the same time, belong to two Lodges within three miles of each other. But the Grand Master may dispense with this regulation also. 4. Every Lodge must elect and install its officers on the constitutional night, which, in most Masonic jurisdictions, precedes the anniversary of St. John the Evangelist. Should it, however, neglect this duty, or should any officer die, or be expelled, or removed permanently, no subsequent election or installation can take place, except under dispensation of the Grand Master.

Dispensation, Lodges under. See *Lodge*.

Dispensations of Religion. An attempt has been made to symbolize the Pagan, the Jewish, and the Christian dispensations by a certain ceremony of the Master's Degree which dramatically teaches the resurrection of the body and the immortality of the soul. The reference made in this ceremony to portions of the First, Second, and Third degrees is used to demonstrate the difference of the three dispensations in the reception of these two dogmas. It is said that the unsuccessful effort in the Entered Apprentice's Degree refers to the heathen dispensation, where neither the resurrection of the body nor the immortality of the soul was recognized; that the second unsuccessful effort in the Fellow-Craft's Degree refers to the Jewish dispensation, where, though the resurrection of the body was unknown, the immortality of the soul was dimly hinted; and that the final and successful effort in the Master's Degree symbolizes the Christian dispensation, in which, through the teachings of the Lion of the tribe of Judah, both the resurrection of the body and the immortality of the soul were clearly brought to light. This symbolism, which was the invention of a peripatetic lecturer in the South about fifty years ago, is so forced and fanciful in its character, that it did not long survive the local and temporary teachings of its inventor, and is only preserved here as an instance of how symbols, like metaphors, may sometimes run mad.

But there is another symbolism of the three degrees, as illustrating three dispensations, which is much older, having originated among the lecture-makers of the eighteenth century, which for a long time formed a portion of the authorized ritual, and is still repeated with approbation by some distinguished writers. In this the three degrees are said to be symbols in the progressive knowledge which they impart of the Patriarchal, the Mosaic, and the Christian dispensations.

The First, or Entered Apprentice's Degree, in which but little Masonic light is communicated, and which, indeed, is only preparatory and introductory to the two succeeding degrees, is said to symbolize the first, or Patriarchal dispensation, the earliest revelation, where the knowledge of God was necessarily imperfect, His worship only a few simple rites of devotion, and the religious dogmas merely a general system of morality. The Second, or Fellow-Craft's Degree, is symbolic of the second or Mosaic dispensation, in which, while there were still many imperfections, there was also a great increase of religious knowledge, and a nearer approximation to Divine truth, with a promise in the future of a better theodicy. But the Third, or Master Mason's Degree, which, in its original conception, before it was dismembered by the innovations of the Royal Arch, was perfect and complete in its consummation of all Masonic light, symbolizes the last, or Christian dispensation, where the great and consoling doctrine of the resurrection to eternal life is the crowning lesson taught by its Divine founder. This subject is very fully treated by the Rev. James Watson, in an address delivered at Lancaster, Eng., in 1795, and contained in Jones's *Masonic Miscellanies*, p. 245; better, I think, by him than even by Hutchinson.

Beautiful as this symbolism may be, and appropriately fitting in all its parts to the laws of symbolic science, it is evident that its origin cannot be traced farther back than to the period when Masonry was first divided into three distinctive degrees; nor could it have been invented later than the time when Masonry was deemed, if not an exclusively Christian organization, at least to be founded on and fitly illustrated by Christian dogmas. At present, this symbolism, though preserved in the speculations of such Christian writers as Hutchinson and Oliver, and those who are attached to their peculiar school, finds no place in the modern cosmopolitan rituals. It may belong, as an explanation, to the history of Masonry, but can scarcely make a part of its symbolism.

Dispersion of Mankind. The dispersion of mankind at the tower of Babel and on the plain of Shinar, which is recorded in the Book of Genesis, has given rise to a Masonic tradition of the following purport. The knowledge of the great truths of God and immortality were known to Noah, and by him communicated to his immediate descendants, the Noachidæ or Noachites, by whom the true worship continued to be cultivated for some time after the subsidence of the deluge; but when the human race were dispersed, a portion lost sight of the Divine truths which had been communicated to them from their common ancestor, and fell into the most grievous theological errors, corrupting the purity of the worship and the orthodoxy of the religious faith which they had primarily received.

These truths were preserved in their integrity by but a very few in the patriarchal line, while still fewer were enabled to retain only dim and glimmering portions of the true light.

The first class was confined to the direct descendants of Noah, and the second was to be found among the priests and philosophers, and, perhaps, still later, among the poets of the heathen nations, and among those whom they initiated into the secrets of these truths.

The system of doctrine of the former class has been called by Masonic writers the "Pure or Primitive Freemasonry" of antiquity, and that of the latter class the "Spurious Freemasonry" of the same period. These terms were first used by Dr. Oliver, and are intended to refer—the word *pure* to the doctrines taught by the descendants of Noah in the Jewish line, and the word *spurious* to those taught by his descendants in the heathen or Gentile line.

Disputes. The spirit of all the *Ancient Charges* and *Constitutions* is, that disputes among Masons should be settled by an appeal to the brethren, to whose award the disputants were required to submit. Thus, in an Old Record of the fifteenth century, it is provided, among other charges, that "yf any discorde schall be bitwene hym and his felows, he schall abey hym mekely and be stylle at the byddyng of his Master or of the Wardeyne of his Master, in his Master's absens, to the holy day folowyng, and that he accorde then at the dispocition of his felows." A similar regulation is to be found in all the other old *Charges* and *Constitutions*, and is continued in opera-

tion at this day by the Charges approved in 1722, which express the same idea in more modern language.

Distinctive Title. In the rituals, all Lodges are called Lodges of St. John, but every Lodge has also another name by which it is distinguished. This is called its distinctive title. This usage is preserved in the diplomas of the continental Masons, especially the French, where the specific name of the Lodge is always given as well as the general title of St. John, which it has in common with all other Lodges. Thus, a diploma issued by a French Lodge whose name on the Register of the Grand Orient would perhaps be La Vérité, will purport to have been issued by the Lodge of St. John, under the distinctive title of La Vérité, "Par la Loge de St. Jean sub la title distinctive de la Vérité." The expression is never used in English or American diplomas.

Distress, Sign of. See *Sign of Distress.*

District Deputy Grand Master. An officer appointed to inspect old Lodges, consecrate new ones, install their officers, and exercise a general supervision over the Fraternity in the districts where, from the extent of the jurisdiction, the Grand Master or his Deputy cannot conveniently attend in person. He is considered as a Grand Officer, and as the representative of the Grand Lodge in the district in which he resides. In England, officers of this description are called Provincial Grand Masters.

District Grand Lodges. In the Constitution of the Grand Lodge of England, Grand Lodges in colonies and foreign parts are called District Grand Lodges, to distinguish them from Provincial Grand Lodges in England.

Diu. (The "Shining Light of Heaven.") An Indian word applied to the Supreme God, of the same signification as the Greek words Zeus and Theos, and the Latin Deus, Jupiter (Jovis); in Sanskrit, Dewas; in Lettish, Dews, in Gothic, Thius; and in North German, Tyr.

Divining-Rod or **Pedum.** The Moderator, or Royal Master, was imaged with the *ureus* on his forehead, the *pedum* and the *whip* between his knees. The Divining-Rod was a symbol of moderation. הק, *Heq,* signifies a law, a statute, or custom; הקק, *Heqq,* a legislator, a scepter, a king, moderator, and a pedum. Hence, a staff. It is represented by a crook surmounted on a pole. The rod of the Rose Croix Knight is dissimilar; it is straight, white, like a wand, and yet may be used as a helping or leaning staff.

Documents, Three Oldest. See *Krause.*

Dodd's Constitutions. This is a printed pamphlet of twenty pages, in quarto, the title being *The beginning and the first foundation of the Most Worthy Craft of Masonry; with the Charges thereunto belonging. By a deceased Brother, for the benefit of his widow. London: printed for Mrs. Dodd at the Peacock without Temple Bar.* 1739. Price, sixpence.

Probably this pamphlet was printed from the Spencer MS.; it is very rare, but the Grand Lodges of England and Iowa each have a copy, and so had Mr. Carson of Cincinnati, who reprinted 125 copies of it in 1886; it has also been reproduced in facsimile by the Quatuor Coronati Lodge in Volume IV. of their Masonic Reprints.   [E. L. H.]

Dog. A symbol in the higher degrees. (See *Cynocephalus*.)

Dolmen. A name given in France to the Celtic stone tables termed in England "cromlechs."

Domatic. At one time, especially in Scotland, Operative Masons were styled "Domatic," while the Speculative ones were known as "Geomatic"; but the origin and derivation of the terms are unknown.   [E. L. H.]

Domine Deus Meus. (*Adonai elohai.*) Found in the Third Degree of the Scottish Rite.

Dominicans, Order of. Founded at Toulouse, in 1215, by Dominic (Domingo) de Guzman, who was born at Calahorra, in Old Castile, 1170. He became an itinerant to convert the heretical Albigenses, and established the Order for that purpose and the cure of souls. The Order was confirmed by Innocent III. and Honorius III., in 1216. Dress, white garment, with black cloak and pointed cap. Dominic died at Bologna, 1221, and was canonized by Gregory IX. in 1233.

Dominican Republic. Masonry, in the Dominican Republic, has for its center the National Grand Orient, which possesses the supreme authority and which practises the Ancient and Accepted Scottish Rite. The Grand Orient is divided into a National Grand Lodge, under which are fifteen Symbolic Lodges; a sovereign Grand Chapter General, under which are all Chapters; and a Supreme Council, which controls the higher degrees of the Rite.

San Domingo was the headquarters of Morin (*q. v.*) in 1763, when he was establishing the Scottish Rite in America.

Donats. A class of men who were attached to the Order of St. John of Jerusalem, or Knights of Malta. They did not take the vows of the Order, but were employed in the different offices of the convent and hospital. In token of their connection with the Order, they wore what was called the demi-cross. (See *Knights of Malta*.)

Door. Every well-constructed Lodge room should be provided with two doors—one on the left hand of the Senior Warden, communicating with the preparation room, the other on his right hand, communicating with the Tiler's apartment. The former of these is called the *inner door*, and is under the charge of the Senior Deacon; the latter is called the *outer door*, and is under the charge of the Junior Deacon. In a well-furnished Lodge, each of these doors is provided with two knockers, one on the inside and the other on the outside; and the outside door has sometimes a small aperture in the center to facilitate communications between the Junior

Deacon and the Tiler. This, however, is a modern innovation, and its propriety and expediency are very doubtful. No communication ought legally to be held between the inside and the outside of the Lodge except through the door, which should be opened only after regular alarm duly reported, and on the order of the Worshipful Master.

Doric Order. The oldest and most original of the three Grecian orders. It is remarkable for robust solidity in the column, for massive grandeur in the entablature, and for harmonious simplicity in its construction. The distinguishing characteristic of this order is the want of a base. The flutings are few, large, and very little concave. The capital has no astragal, but only one or more fillets, which separate the flutings from the torus. The column of strength which supports the Lodge is of the Doric order, and its appropriate situation and symbolic officer are in the West. (See *Orders of Architecture*.)

Dormant Lodge. A Lodge whose Charter has not been revoked, but which has ceased to meet and work for a long time, is said to be dormant. It can be restored to activity only by the authority of the Grand Master or the Grand Lodge on the petition of some of its members, one of whom, at least, ought to be a Past Master.

Dormer. In the Lectures, according to the present English system, the ornaments of a Master Mason's Lodge are said to be the porch, dormer, and square pavement. The dormer is the window which is supposed to give light to the Holy of Holies. In the *Glossary of Architecture*, a dormer is defined to be a window pierced through a sloping roof, and placed in a small gable which rises on the side of the roof. This symbol is not preserved in the American system.

Dotage. The regulations of Masonry forbid the initiation of an old man in his dotage; and very properly, because the imbecility of his mind would prevent his comprehension of the truths presented to him.

Double Cube. A cubical figure, whose length is equal to twice its breadth and height. Solomon's Temple is said to have been of this figure, and hence it has sometimes been adopted as the symbol of a Masonic Lodge. Dr. Oliver (*Dict. Symb. Mas.*) thus describes the symbolism of the double cube: "The heathen deities were many of them represented by a cubical stone. Pausanius informs us that a cube was the symbol of Mercury, because, like the cube, he represented Truth. In Arabia, a black stone in the form of a double cube was reputed to be possessed of many occult virtues. Apollo was sometimes worshiped under the symbol of a square stone; and it is recorded that when a fatal pestilence raged at Delphi, the oracle was consulted as to the means proper to be adopted for the purpose of arresting its progress, and it commanded that the cube should be doubled. This was understood by the priests to refer to the altar, which was of a cubical form. They obeyed the injunction,

15

increasing the altitude of the altar to its pre-scribed dimensions, like the pedestal in a Masons' Lodge, and the pestilence ceased."

Double - Headed Eagle. See *Eagle, Double-Headed.*

Dove. In ancient symbolism, the dove represented purity and innocence; in ecclesiology, it is a symbol of the Holy Spirit. In Masonry, the dove is only viewed in reference to its use by Noah as a messenger. Hence, in the Grand Lodge of England, doves are the jewels of the Deacons, because these officers are the messengers of the Masters and Wardens. They are not so used in America. In an honorary or side degree formerly conferred in America, and called the "Ark and Dove," that bird is a prominent symbol.

Dove, Knights and Ladies of the. An extinct secret society, of a Masonic model, but androgynous, instituted at Versailles, in 1784.

Dowland Manuscript. First published by James Dowland, in the *Gentleman's Magazine*, May, 1815, Vol. LXXXV., p. 489. "Written on a long roll of parchment, in a very clear hand, apparently early in the seventeenth century, and very probably is copied from a manuscript of earlier date." Bro. William J. Hughan says: "Brother Woodford, Mr. Sims, and other eminent authorities, consider the *original of the copy*, from which the manuscript for the *Gentleman's Magazine* was written, to be a scroll of at least a century earlier than the date ascribed to Mr. Dowland's MS., that is, about 1550." The original MS. from which Dowland made his copy has not yet been traced. Hughan's *Old Charges* (ed. 1872) contains a reprint of the Dowland MS.

Draeseke, Johan Heinrich Dernhardt. A celebrated pulpit orator of great eloquence, who presided over the Lodge "*Oelzweig*," in Bremen, for three years, and whose contributions to Masonic literature were collected and published in 1865, by A. W. Müller, under the title of *Bishop Dräseke as a Mason.* Of this work Findel says that it "contains a string of costly pearls full of Masonic eloquence."

Drake, Francis, M.D. Francis Drake, M.D., F.R.S., a celebrated antiquary and historian, was initiated in the city of York in 1725, and, as Hughan says, "soon made his name felt in Masonry." His promotion was rapid; for in the same year he was chosen Junior Grand Warden of the Grand Lodge of York, and in 1726 delivered an address, which was published with the following title: *A Speech delivered to the Worshipful and Ancient Society of Free and Accepted Masons, at a Grand Lodge held at Merchants' Hall, in the city of York, on St. John's Day, December the 27th, 1726. The Right Worshipful Charles Bathurst, Esq., Grand Master. By the Junior Grand Warden. Olim meminisse Juvabit. York.* The address was published in York without any date, but probably in 1727, and reprinted in London in 1729 and 1734. It has often been reproduced since and can be found in Hughan's *Masonic Sketches and Reprints.* In

this work Drake makes the important statement that the first Grand Lodge in England was held at York; and that while it recognizes the Grand Master of the Grand Lodge in London as Grand Master of England, it claims that its own Grand Master is Grand Master of *all England.* The speech is also important for containing a very early reference to the three degrees of Entered Apprentice, Fellow-Craft. and Master Mason.

Dramatic Literature of Masonry. Freemasonry has frequently supplied play-writers with a topic for the exercise of their genius. Kloss (*Bibliog.*, p. 300) gives the titles of no less than forty-one plays of which Freemasonry has been the subject. The earliest Masonic play is noticed by Thory (*Fond. G. O.*, p. 360), as having been performed at Paris, in 1739, under the title of *Les Frimaçons.* Editions of it were subsequently published at London, Brunswick, and Strasburg. In 1741, we have *Das Geheimniss der Freimaurer* at Frankfort and Leipsic. France and Germany made many other contributions to the Masonic drama. Even Denmark supplied one in 1745, and Italy in 1785. The English dramatists give us only a pantomime, *Harlequin Freemason*, which was brought out at Covent Garden in 1781, and *Solomon's Temple*, an oratorio. Templarism has not been neglected by the dramatists. Kalchberg, in 1788, wrote *Die Tempelherren*, a dramatic poem in five acts. *Odon de Saint-Amand, Grand Maître des Templiers*, a melodrama in three acts, was performed at Paris in 1806. *Jacques Molai*, a melodrama, was published at Paris in 1807, and *La Mort de Jacques Molai*, a tragedy, in 1812. Some of the plays on Freemasonry were intended to do honor to the Order, and many to throw ridicule upon it.

Dresden, Congress of. A General Congress of the Lodges of Saxony was held in Dresden, where the representatives of twelve Lodges were present. In this Congress it was determined to recognize only the Masonry of St. John, and to construct a National Grand Lodge. Accordingly, on September 28, 1811, the National Grand Lodge of Saxony was established in the city of Dresden, which was soon joined by all the Saxon Lodges, with the exception of one in Leipsic. Although it recognizes only the Symbolic degrees, it permits great freedom in the selection of a ritual; and, accordingly, some of its Lodges work in the Rite of Fessler, and others in the Rite of Berlin.

Dress of a Mason. See *Clothed.*

Drop Cloth. A part of the furniture used in America in the ceremony of initiation into the Third Degree. It should be made of very strong material, with a looped rope at each corner and one in the middle of each side, by which it may be securely held.

Drops, Three. The mystic number of drops of blood from the White Giant, that in the Persian mysteries restored sight to the captives in the cell of horrors when applied by the conqueror Rustam. In India, a girdle of three triple threads was deemed holy; so were three drops of water in Brittany, and the same number of drops of blood in Mexico.

Druidical Mysteries. The Druids were a sacred order of priests who existed in Britain and Gaul, but whose mystical rites were practised in most perfection in the former country, where the isle of Anglesea was considered as their principal seat. Higgins thinks that they were also found in Germany, but against this opinion we have the positive statement of Cæsar.

The meanings given to the word have been very numerous, and most of them wholly untenable. The Romans, seeing that they worshiped in groves of oak, because that tree was peculiarly sacred among them, derived their name from the Greek word, Δρôς, *drus;* thus absurdly seeking the etymology of a word of an older language in one comparatively modern. Their derivation would have been more reasonable had they known that in Sanskrit *druma* is an oak, from *dru,* wood. It has also been traced to the Hebrew with equal incorrectness, for the Druids were not of the Semitic race. Its derivation is rather to be sought in the Celtic language. The Gaelic word *Druiah* signifies a holy or wise man; in a bad sense, a magician; and this we may readily trace to the Aryan *druh,* applied to the spirit of night or darkness, whence we have the Zend *dru,* a magician. Druidism was a mystical profession, and in the olden time mystery and magic were always confounded. Vallencey (*Coll. Reb. Hib.,* iii., 503) says: "Welsh, *Drud,* a Druid, *i. e.* the absolver or remitter of sins; so the Irish *Drui,* a Druid, most certainly is from the Persic *duru,* a good and holy man"; and Ousely (*Coll. Orient.,* iv., 302) adds to this the Arabic *dari,* which means a wise man. Bosworth (*A. S. Dict.*) gives *dry,* pronounced *dru,* as the Anglo-Saxon for "a magician, sorcerer, druid." Probably with the old Celts the Druids occupied the same place as the *Magi* did with the old Persians.

Druidism was divided into three orders or degrees, which were, beginning with the lowest, the *Bards,* the *Prophets,* and the *Druids.* Higgins thinks that the prophets were the lowest order, but he admits that it is not generally allowed. The constitution of the Order was in many respects like that of the Freemasons. In every country there was an Arch-Druid in whom all authority was placed. In Britain it is said that there were under him three arch-flamens or priests, and twenty-five flamens. There was an annual assembly for the administration of justice and the making of laws, and, besides, four quarterly meetings, which took place on the days when the sun reached his equinoctial and solstitial points. The latter two would very nearly correspond at this time with the festivals of St. John the Baptist and St. John the Evangelist. It was not lawful to commit their ceremonies or doctrines to writing, and Cæsar says (*Bell. Gall.,* vi., 14) that they used the Greek letters, which was, of course, as a cipher; but Higgins (p. 90) says that one of the Irish

Ogum alphabets, which Toland calls *secret writing,* "was the original, sacred, and secret character of the Druids."

The places of worship, which were also places of initiation, were of various forms: circular, because a circle was an emblem of the universe; or oval, in allusion to the mundane egg, from which, according to the Egyptians, our first parents issued; or serpentine, because a serpent was a symbol of Hu, the druidical Noah; or winged, to represent the motion of the Divine Spirit; or cruciform, because a cross was the emblem of regeneration. Their only covering was the *clouded canopy,* because they deemed it absurd to confine the Omnipotent beneath a roof; and they were constructed of embankments of earth, and of unhewn stones, *unpolluted with a metal tool.* Nor was anyone permitted to enter their sacred retreats, unless *he bore a chain.*

The ceremony of initiation into the Druidical Mysteries required much preliminary mental preparation and physical purification. The aspirant was clothed with the three sacred colors, white, blue, and green; white as the symbol of Light, blue of Truth, and green of Hope. When the rites of initiation were passed, the tri-colored robe was changed for one of green; in the Second Degree, the candidate was clothed in blue; and having surmounted all the dangers of the Third, and arrived at the summit of perfection, he received the red tiara and flowing mantle of purest white. The ceremonies were numerous, the physical proofs painful, and the mental trials appalling. They commenced in the First Degree, with placing the aspirant in the pastos, bed or coffin, where his symbolical death was represented, and they terminated in the Third, by his regeneration or restoration to life from the womb of the giantess Ceridwin, and the committal of the body of the *newly born* to the waves in a small boat, symbolical of the ark. The result was, generally, that he succeeded in reaching the safe landing-place, but if his arm was weak, or his heart failed, death was the almost inevitable consequence. If he refused the trial through timidity, he was contemptuously rejected, and declared forever ineligible to participate in the sacred rites. But if he undertook it and succeeded, he was joyously invested with all the privileges of Druidism.

The doctrines of the Druids were the same as those entertained by Pythagoras. They taught the existence of one Supreme Being; a future state of rewards and punishments; the immortality of the soul, and a metempsychosis; and the object of their mystic rites was to communicate these doctrines in symbolic language, an object and a method common alike to Druidism, to the Ancient Mysteries and to Modern Freemasonry.

Druses. A sect of mystic religionists who inhabit Mounts Lebanon and Anti-Lebanon, in Syria. They settled there about the tenth century, and are said to be a mixture of Cuthites or Kurds, Mardi Arabs, and possibly of

Crusaders; all of whom were added, by subsequent immigrations, to the original stock to constitute the present or modern race of Druses. Their religion is a heretical compound of Judaism, Christianity, and Mohammedism; the last of which, greatly modified, predominates in their faith. They have a regular order of priesthood, the office being filled by persons consecrated for the purpose, comprising principally the emirs and sheiks, who form a secret organization divided into several degrees, keep the sacred books, and hold secret religious assemblies. Their sacred books are written in antiquated Arabic. The Druses are divided into three classes or degrees, according to religious distinctions. To enable one Druse to recognize another, a system of passwords is adopted, without an interchange of which no communication is made that may give an idea of their religious tenets. (Tien's *Druse Religion Unveiled.*)

Dr. Clarke tells us in his *Travels* that "one class of the Druses are to the rest what the initiated are to the profane, and are called Okkals, which means spiritualists; and they consider themselves superior to their countrymen. They have various degrees of initiation."

Colonel Churchill, in his *Ten Years' Residence on Mount Lebanon*, tells us that among this singular people there is an order having many similar customs to the Freemasons. It requires a twelvemonth's probation previous to the admission of a member. Both sexes are admissible. In the second year the novice assumes the distinguishing mark of the white turban, and afterward, by degrees, is allowed to participate in the whole of the mysteries. Simplicity of attire, self-denial, temperance, and irreproachable moral conduct are essential to admission to the order.

All of these facts have led to the theory that the Druses are an offshoot from the early Freemasons, and that their connection with the latter is derived from the Crusaders, who, according to the same theory, are supposed to have acquired their Freemasonry during their residence in Palestine. Some writers go so far as to say that the degree of Prince of Lebanon, the Twenty-second in the Ancient and Accepted Scottish Rite, refers to the ancestors of these mystical mountaineers in Syria.

Duad. The number two in the Pythagorean system of numbers.

Dualism. In the old mythologies, there was a doctrine which supposed the world to have been always governed by two antagonistic principles, distinguished as the good and the evil principle. This doctrine pervaded all the Oriental religions.

Thus in the system of Zoroaster we have Ahriman and Ormuzd, and in the Hebrew cosmogony we find the Creator and the Serpent. There has been a remarkable development of this system in the three degrees of Symbolic Masonry, which everywhere exhibit in their organization, their symbolism, and their design, the pervading influences of this principle of dualism. Thus, in the First De-

gree, there is Darkness overcome by Light; in the Second, Ignorance dispersed by Knowledge, and in the Third, Death conquered by Eternal Life.

Dub. In the ancient ceremonies of chivalry, a knight was made by giving him three strokes on the neck with the flat end of the sword, and he was then said to be "dubbed a knight." Dubbing is from the Saxon, *dubban*, to strike with a blow. Sir Thomas Smith (*Eng. Commonwealth*), who wrote in the sixteenth century, says: "And when any man is made a knight, he, kneeling down, is strooken of the prince, with his sword naked, upon the back or shoulder, the prince saying, *Sus* or *sois chevalier au nom de Dieu*, and (in times past) they added St. George, and at his arising the prince sayeth, *Avancey*. This is the manner of *dubbing* of knights at this present; and that terme *dubbing* was the old terme in this point, and not *creation*."

Due East and West. A Lodge is said to be situated due East and West for reasons which have varied at different periods in the ritual and lectures. (See *Orientation*.)

Due Examination. That sort of examination which is correct and prescribed by law. It is one of the three modes of proving a strange brother; the other two being *strict trial* and *lawful information*. (See *Vouching*.)

Due Form. When the Grand Lodge is opened, or any other Masonic ceremony performed, by the Deputy Grand Master in the absence of the Grand Master, it is said to be done in *due form*. Subordinate Lodges are always said to be opened and closed in *due form*. It is derived from the French word *du*, and that from *devoir*, "to owe,"—that which is owing or ought to be done. Due form is the form in which an act ought to be done to be done rightly. French: *En due forme*. (See *Ample Form*.)

Due Guard. A mode of recognition which derives its name from its object, which is to *duly guard* the person using it in reference to his obligations, and the penalty for their violation. The Due Guard is an Americanism, and of comparatively recent origin, being unknown to the English and continental systems. In some of the old rituals of the date of 1757, the expression is used, but only as referring to what is now called the Sign.

Dueling. Dueling has always been considered a Masonic crime, and most of the Grand Lodges have enacted statutes by which Masons who engage in duels with each other are subject to expulsion. The *Monde Maçonnique* (May, 1858) gives the following correct view on this subject: "A Freemason who allows himself to be involved in a duel, and who possesses not sufficient discretion to be able to make reparation without cowardice, and without having recourse to this barbarous extremity, destroys by that impious act the contract which binds him to his brethren. His sword or his pistol, though it may seem to spare his adversary, still commits a murder, for it destroys his brothers—from that time fraternity no longer exists for him."

Dues. The payment of annual dues by a member to his Lodge is a comparatively modern custom, and one that certainly did not exist before the revival of 1717. As previous to that period, according to Preston, Lodges received no warrants, but a sufficient number of brethren meeting together were competent to practise the Rites of Masonry, and as soon as the special business which called them together had been accomplished, they separated, there could have been no permanent organization of Speculative Masons, and no necessity for contributions to constitute a Lodge fund. Dues must therefore have been unknown except in the Lodges of Operative Masons, which, as we find, especially in Scotland, had a permanent existence. There is, accordingly, no regulation in any of the old Constitutions for the payment of dues. It is not a general Masonic duty, in which the Mason is affected to the whole of the Craft, but an arrangement between himself and his Lodge, with which the Grand Lodge ought not to interfere. As the payment of dues is not a duty owing to the Craft in general, so the non-payment of them is not an offense against the Craft, but simply against his Lodge, the only punishment for which should be striking from the roll or discharge from membership. It is now the almost universal opinion of Masonic jurists that suspension or expulsion from the Order is a punishment that should never be inflicted for non-payment of dues.

Dumbness. Although the faculty of speech is not one of the five human senses, it is important as the medium of communicating instruction, admonition, or reproof, and the person who does not possess it is unfitted to perform the most important duties of life. Hence dumbness disqualifies a candidate for Masonic initiation.

Dummy. A word used in the Grand Chapter of Minnesota to signify what is more usually called a *substitute* in the Royal Arch Degree.

Dunckerley, Thomas. No one, among the Masons of England, occupied a more distinguished position or played a more important part in the labors of the Craft during the latter part of the eighteenth century than Thomas Dunckerley, whose private life was as romantic as his Masonic was honorable.

Thomas Dunckerley was born in the city of London on the 23d of October, 1724. He was the reputed son of Mr. —— and Mrs. Mary Dunckerley, but really owed his birth to a personage of a much higher rank in life, being the natural son of the Prince of Wales, afterward George II., to whom he bore, as his portrait shows, a striking resemblance. It was not until after his mother's death that he became acquainted with the true history of his birth; so that for more than half of his life this son of a king occupied a very humble position on the stage of the world, and was sometimes even embarrassed with the pressure of poverty and distress.

At the age of ten he entered the navy, and continued in the service for twenty-six years, acquiring, by his intelligence and uniformly good conduct, the esteem and commendation of all his commanders. But having no personal or family interest, he never attained to any higher rank than that of a gunner. During all this time, except at brief intervals, he was absent from England on foreign service.

He returned to his native country in January, 1760, to find that his mother had died a few days before, and that on her death-bed she had made a solemn declaration, accompanied by such details as left no possible doubt of its truth, that Thomas was the illegitimate son of King George II., born while he was Prince of Wales. The fact of the birth had, however, never been communicated by the mother to the prince, and George II. died without knowing that he had such a son living.

Dunckerley, in the account of the affair which he left among his posthumous papers, says: "This information gave me great surprise and much uneasiness; and as I was obliged to return immediately to my duty on board the *Vanguard*, I made it known to no person at that time but Captain Swanton. He said that those who did not know me would look on it to be nothing more than a gossip's story. We were then bound a second time to Quebec, and Captain Swanton did promise me that on our return to England he would endeavour to get me introduced to the king, and that he would give me a character; but when we came back to England the king was dead."

Dunckerley had hoped that his case would have been laid before his royal father, and that the result would have been an appointment equal to his birth. But the frustration of these hopes by the death of the king seems to have discouraged him, and no efforts appear for some time to have been made by him or his friends to communicate the facts to George III., who had succeeded to the throne.

In 1761 he again left England as a gunner in Lord Anson's fleet, and did not return until 1764, at which time, finding himself embarrassed with a heavy debt, incurred in the expenses of his family (for he had married in early life, in the year 1744), knowing no person who could authenticate the story of his birth, and seeing no probability of gaining access to the ear of the king, he sailed in a merchant vessel for the Mediterranean. He had previously been granted superannuation in the navy in consequence of his long services, and received a small pension, the principal part of which he left for the support of his family during his absence.

But the romantic story of his birth began to be publicly known and talked about, and in 1766 attracted the attention of several persons of distinction, who endeavored, but without success, to excite the interest of the Princess Dowager of Wales in his behalf.

In 1767, however, the declaration of his mother was laid before the king, who was George III., the grandson of his father. It made an impression on him, and inquiry into his previous character and conduct having proved satisfactory, on May 7, 1767, the king ordered Dunckerley to receive a pension of £100, which was subsequently increased to £800, together with a suite of apartments in Hampton Court Palace. He also assumed, and was permitted to bear, the royal arms, with the distinguishing badge of the bend sinister, and adopted as his motto the appropriate words "*Fato non merito.*" In his familiar correspondence, and in his book-plates, he used the name of "Fitz-George."

In 1770 he became a student of law, and in 1774 was called to the bar; but his fondness for an active life prevented him from ever making much progress in the legal profession.

Dunckerley died at Portsmouth in the year 1795, at the ripe age of seventy-one; but his last years were embittered by the misconduct of his son, whose extravagance and dissolute conduct necessarily afflicted the mind while it straitened the means of the unhappy parent. Every effort to reclaim him proved utterly ineffectual; and on the death of his father, no provision being left for his support, he became a vagrant, living for the most part on Masonic charity. At last he became a bricklayer's laborer, and was often seen ascending a ladder with a hod on his shoulders. His misfortunes and his misconduct at length found an end, and the grandson of a king of England died a pauper in a cellar at St. Giles.

Dunckerley was initiated into Masonry on January 10, 1754, in a Lodge, No. 31, which then met at the Three Tuns, Portsmouth; in 1760 he obtained a warrant for a Lodge to be held on board the *Vanguard*, in which ship he was then serving; in the following year the *Vanguard* sailed for the West Indies, and Dunckerley was appointed to the *Prince*, for which ship a Lodge was warranted in 1762; this warrant Dunckerley appears to have retained when he left the service, and in 1766 the Lodge was meeting at Somerset House, where Dunckerley was then living. In 1768 the Vanguard Lodge was revived in London, with Dunckerley as its first Master, and it exists to the present day under the name of the "London Lodge," No. 108.

In 1767 he joined the present "Lodge of Friendship"; in 1785 he established a Lodge at Hampton Court, now No. 255. In 1767 he was appointed Provincial Grand Master of Hampshire, and in 1776 Provincial Grand Master for Essex, and at various dates he was placed in charge of the provinces of Bristol, Dorsetshire, Gloucestershire, Somersetshire,

and Herefordshire. In Royal Arch Masonry Dunckerley displayed equal activity as in Craft Masonry; he was exalted at Portsmouth in 1754 and in 1766 joined the London Chapter, which in the following year became a Grand Chapter.

He was especially active in promoting Arch Masonry all over the country and was in charge of Essex, Hants, Wilts, Dorset, Devon, Somersetshire, Gloucestershire, Kent, Suffolk, Sussex and Durham.

He was also a most zealous Knight Templar, being in 1791 the first Grand Master of the Order when the Grand Conclave was formed in London.

He was also a Mark Mason. A Charge, or Oration, is still extant, which was delivered by him at Plymouth in April, 1757, entitled "The Light and Truth of Masonry Explained." He was also the author of "A Song for the Knights Templars," and of an "Ode for an Exaltation of Royal Arch Masons." These will be found in *Thomas Dunckerley—his Life, Labours and Letters*, by H. Sadler (1891).

It is often asserted that Dunckerley revised the Craft Lectures and reconstructed the Royal Arch Degree, but there is no proof forthcoming of these statements. [E. L. H.]

Dupaty, Louis Emanuel Charles Mercier. The author of many Masonic songs and other fugitive pieces inserted in the *Annales Maçonniques*. He wrote in 1810, with Révéroui de Saint-Cyr, a comic opera entitled "Cagliostro ou les Illuminés." In 1818, he published a Masonic tale entitled "l'Harmonie." He was a poet and dramatic writer of some reputation. He was born in the Gironde in 1775, elected to the French Academy in 1835, and died in 1851.

Duty. The duty of a Mason as an honest man is plain and easy. It requires of him honesty in contracts, sincerity in affirming, simplicity in bargaining, and faithfulness in performing. To sleep little, and to study much; to say little, and to hear and think much; to learn, that he may be able to do; and then to do earnestly and vigorously whatever the good of his fellows, his country, and mankind requires, are the duties of every Mason.

Dyaus. Sanskrit for sky; bright, exalted. The Deity, the sun, the celestial canopy, the firmament.

"Dye na Sore," or "*Die Wanderer aus dem Sanskrit Ubersetzt.*" A Masonic romance, by Von Meyern, which appeared at Vienna in 1789, and contains a complete account of Masonic festivities.

E

E. (Heb., ה.) The fifth letter in the English and in the Græco-Roman alphabets. In form the Hebrew ה is quite similar to *Cheth*, ח, which has a numerical value of eight, while that of *He* is five. The signification is *window*, and in the Egyptian hieroglyphs is represented by a hand extending the thumb and two fingers. It also represents the fifth name of God, הדור (Hadur), *Formosus, Majestuosus*.

Eagle. The eagle, as a symbol, is of great antiquity. In Egypt, Greece, and Persia, this bird was sacred to the sun. Among the Pagans it was an emblem of Jupiter, and with the Druids it was a symbol of their supreme god. In the Scriptures, a distinguished reference is in many instances made to the eagle; especially do we find Moses (Exod. xix. 4) representing Jehovah as saying, in allusion to the belief that this bird assists its feeble young in their flight by bearing them upon its own pinions, "Ye have seen what I did unto the Egyptians, and how I bare you on eagles' wings, and brought you unto myself." Not less elevated was the symbolism of the eagle among the Pagans. Thus, Cicero, speaking of the myth of Ganymede carried up to Jove on an eagle's back, says that it teaches us that the truly wise, irradiated by the shining light of virtue, become more and more like God, until by wisdom they are borne aloft and soar to Him. The heralds explain the eagle as signifying the same thing among birds as the lion does among quadrupeds. It is, they say, the most swift, strong, laborious, generous, and bold of all birds, and for this reason it has been made, both by ancients and moderns, the symbol of majesty. In the jewel of the Rose Croix Degree is found an eagle displayed at the foot of the cross; and it is there very appropriately selected as a symbol of Christ, in His Divine character, bearing the children of His adoption on his wings, teaching them with unequaled love and tenderness to poise their unfledged wings and soar from the dull corruptions of earth to a higher and holier sphere. And for this reason the eagle in the jewel of that degree is very significantly represented as having the wings displayed as if in the very act of flight.

Eagle and Pelican, Knight of the. See *Knight of the Eagle and Pelican*.

Eagle, Double-Headed. The *eagle displayed*, that is, with extended wings, as if in the act of flying, has always, from the majestic character of the bird, been deemed an emblem of imperial power. Marius, the consul, first consecrated the eagle, about eight years B.C., to be the sole Roman standard at the head of every legion, and hence it became the standard of the Roman Empire ever afterward. As the single-headed eagle was thus adopted as the symbol of imperial power, the double-headed eagle naturally became the representative of a double empire; and on the division of the Roman dominions into the eastern and western empire, which were after-ward consolidated by the Carlovingian race into what was ever after called the Holy Roman Empire, the double-headed eagle was assumed as the emblem of this double empire; one head looking, as it were, to the West, or Rome, and the other to the East, or Byzantium. Hence the escutcheons of many persons now living, the descendants of the princes and counts of the Holy Roman Empire, are placed upon the breast of a double-headed eagle. Upon the dissolution of that empire, the emperors of Germany, who claimed their empire to be the representative of ancient Rome, assumed the double-headed eagle as their symbol, and placed it in their arms, which were blazoned thus: *Or*, an eagle displayed *sable*, having two heads, each enclosed within an amulet, *or* beaked and armed *gules*, holding in his right claw a sword and scepter *or*, and in his left the imperial mound. Russia also bears the double-headed eagle, having added, says Brewer, that of Poland to her own, and thus denoting a double empire. It

is, however, probable that the double-headed eagle of Russia is to be traced to some assumed representation of the Holy Roman Empire based upon the claim of Russia to Byzantium; for Constantine, the Byzantine emperor, is said to have been the first who assumed this device to intimate the division of the empire into East and West.

The statement of Millington (*Heraldry in History, Poetry, and Romance*, p. 290) is doubtful that "the double-headed eagle of the Austrian and Russian empires was first assumed during the Second Crusade and typified the great alliance formed by the Christian sovereigns of Greece and Germany against the enemy of their common faith, and it is retained by Russia and Austria as representations of those empires." The theory is more probable as well as more generally accepted which connects the symbol with the eastern and western empires of Rome. It is, however, agreed by all that while the single-headed eagle denotes imperial dignity, the extension and multiplication of that dignity is symbolized by the two heads.

The double-headed eagle was probably first introduced as a symbol into Masonry in the year 1758. In that year the body calling itself the Council of Emperors of the East and West was established in Paris. The double-headed eagle was likely to have been assumed by this Council in reference to the double jurisdiction which it claimed, and which is represented so distinctly in its title. Its ritual, which consisted of twenty-five degrees, all of which are now contained in the Ancient and Accepted Scottish Rite, was subsequently established in the city of Berlin, and adopted by the Grand Lodge of the Three Globes.

The jewel of the Thirty-third Degree, or Sovereign Grand Inspector-General of the Ancient and Accepted Scottish Rite, is a double-headed eagle (which was originally black, but is now generally of silver), a golden crown resting on both heads, wings displayed, beak and claws of gold, his talons grasping a wavy sword, the emblem of cherubic fire, the hilt held by one talon, the blade by the other. The banner of the Order is also a double-headed eagle crowned.

Eagle, Knight of the. See *Knight of the Eagle*.

Eagle, Knight of the American. See *Knight of the American Eagle*.

Eagle, Knight of the Black. See *Knight of the Black Eagle*.

Eagle, Knight of the Golden. See *Knight of the Golden Eagle*.

Eagle, Knight of the Prussian. See *Knight of the Prussian Eagle*.

Eagle, Knight of the Red. See *Knight of the Red Eagle*.

Eagle, Knight of the White and Black. See *Knight of the White and Black Eagle*.

Eagles, Knight of the Two Crowned. See *Knight of the Two Crowned Eagles*.

Ear of Corn. This was, among all the ancients, an emblem of plenty. Ceres, who was universally worshiped as the goddess of abundance, and even called by the Greeks *Demeter*, a manifest corruption of *Gemeter*, or *mother earth*, was symbolically represented with a garland on her head composed of ears of corn, a lighted torch in one hand, and a cluster of poppies and ears of corn in the other. And in the Hebrew, the most significant of all languages, the two words, which signify an ear of corn, are both derived from roots which give the idea of abundance. For *shibboleth*, which is applicable both to an ear of corn and a flood of water, has its root in *shabal*, to increase or to flow abundantly; and the other name of corn, *dagan*, is derived from the verb *dagah*, signifying to multiply, or to be increased.

Ear of corn, which is a technical expression in the Second Degree, has been sometimes ignorantly displaced by a *sheaf of wheat*. This is done in America, under the mistaken supposition that *corn* refers only to *Indian maize*, which was unknown to the ancients. But *corn* is a generic word, and includes wheat and every other kind of grain. This is its legitimate English meaning, and hence an *ear of corn*, which is an old expression, and the right one, would denote a stalk, but not a sheaf of wheat. (See *Shibboleth*.)

Ear, The Listening. The listening ear is one of the three precious jewels of a Fellow-Craft Mason. In the Hebrew language, the verb שמע, *shemong*, signifies not only to hear, but also to understand and to obey. Hence, when Jesus said, after a parable, "he that hath ears to hear, let him hear," he meant to denote that he who hears the recital of allegories should endeavor to discover their hidden meaning, and be obedient to their teaching. This is the true meaning of the symbol of the listening ear, which admonishes the Fellow-Craft not only that he should receive lessons of instruction from his teacher, but that he should treasure them in his breast, so as to ponder over their meaning and carry out their design.

Earthen Pan. In the lectures of the early part of the eighteenth century used as a symbol of zeal, together with chalk and charcoal, which represented freedom and fervency. In the modern lectures clay has been substituted for it. *Pan* once signified *hard earth*, a meaning which is now obsolete, though from it we derive the name of a cooking utensil.

East. The East has always been considered peculiarly sacred. This was, without exception, the case in all the Ancient Mysteries. In the Egyptian rites, especially, and those of Adonis, which were among the earliest, and from which the others derived their existence, the sun was the object of adoration, and his revolutions through the various seasons were fictitiously represented. The spot, therefore, where this luminary made his appearance at the commencement of day, and where his worshipers were wont anxiously to look for the first darting of his prolific rays, was esteemed as the figurative birthplace of their god, and honored with an appropriate degree of reverence. And even among those nations where sun-worship gave place to more enlightened doctrines, the respect for the place of sun-rising continued to exist. The camp of Judah was placed by Moses in the East as a mark of distinction; the tabernacle in the wilderness was placed due East and West; and the practise was continued in the erection of Christian churches. Hence, too, the primitive Christians always turned toward the East in their public prayers, which custom St. Augustine (*Serm. Dom. in Monte*, c. 5), accounts for "because the East is the most honorable part of the world, being the region of light whence the glorious sun arises." And hence all Masonic Lodges, like their great prototype the Temple of Jerusalem, are built, or supposed to be built, due East and West; and as the North is esteemed a place of darkness, the East, on the contrary, is considered a place of light.

In the primitive Christian church, according to St. Ambrose, in the ceremonies accompanying the baptism of a catechumen, "he turned towards the West, the image of darkness, to abjure the world, and towards the East, the emblem of light, to denote his alliance with

Jesus Christ." And so, too, in the oldest lectures of the last century, the Mason is said to travel from the West to the East, that is, from darkness to light. In the Prestonian system, the question is asked, "What induces you to leave the West to travel to the East?" And the answer is: "In search of a Master, and from him to gain instruction." The same idea, if not precisely the same language, is preserved in the modern and existing rituals.

The East, being the place where the Master sits, is considered the most honorable part of the Lodge, and is distinguished from the rest of the room by a dais, or raised platform, which is occupied only by those who have passed the Chair.

Bazot (*Manuel*, p. 154) says: "The veneration which Masons have for the East, confirms the theory that it is from the East that the Masonic cult proceeded, and that this bears a relation to the primitive religion whose first degeneration was sun-worship."

East and West, Knight of the. See *Knight of the East and West.*

East, Grand. The place where a Grand Lodge holds its communications, and whence are issued its edicts, is often called its Grand East. Thus, the Grand East of Boston would, according to this usage, be placed at the head of documents emanating from the Grand Lodge of Massachusetts. Grand Orient has sometimes been used instead of Grand East, but improperly. Orient might be admissible as signifying East, but Grand Orient having been adopted as the name of certain Grand Bodies, such as the Grand Orient of France, which is tantamount to the Grand Lodge of France, the use of the term might lead to confusion. Thus, the Orient of Paris is the seat of the Grand Orient of France. The expression Grand East, however, is almost exclusively confined to America, and even there is not in universal use.

East Indies. See *India.*

East, Knight of the. See *Knight of the East.*

Easter. Easter Sunday, being the day celebrated by the Christian church in commemoration of the resurrection of the Lord Jesus, is appropriately kept as a feast-day by Rose Croix Masons.

Easter Monday. On this day, in every third year, Councils of Kadosh in the Ancient and Accepted Scottish Rite hold their elections.

Eastern Star, Order of the. An American Adoptive Rite, called the "Order of the Eastern Star," invented by Bro. Robert Morris, and somewhat popular in America. It consists of five degrees, viz., 1, Jephtha's Daughter, or the Daughter's Degree; 2, Ruth, or the Widow's Degree; 3, Esther, or the Wife's Degree; 4, Martha, or the Sister's Degree; 5, Electa, or the Benevolent. It is entirely different from European or French Adoptive Masonry. Recently, this Order has undergone a thorough organization, and been extended into other countries, especially into South America and Great Britain.

East Port. An error of ignorance in the Lansdowne Manuscript, where the expression "the city of East Port" occurs as a corruption of "the cities of the East."

Eavesdropper. A listener. The punishment which was directed in the old lectures, at the revival of Masonry in 1717, to be inflicted on a detected cowan was: "To be placed under the eaves of the house in rainy weather, till the water runs in at his shoulders and out at his heels." The French inflict a similar punishment. "On le met sous une gouttière, une pompe, ou une fontaine, jusqu'à ce qu'il soit mouillé depuis la tête jusqu'aux pieds." Hence a listener is called an eavesdropper. The word is not, as has by some been supposed, a peculiar Masonic term, but is common to the language. Skinner gives it in his *Etymologicon*, and calls it "vox sane elegantissima"; and Blackstone (*Comm.*,iv.,13) thus defines it: "Eavesdroppers, or such as listen under walls, or windows, or the eaves of a house, to hearken after discourse, and thereupon to frame slanderous and mischievous tales, are a common nuisance and presentable at the court leet; or are indictable at the sessions, and punishable by fine and finding sureties for their good behavior."

Ebal. According to Mackenzie (*Royal Masonic Cyclopœdia s.v.*) the following was introduced into the lectures of Masonry in the last century: "Moses commanded Israel that as soon as they had passed the Jordan, they should go to Shechem, and divide into two bodies, each composed of six tribes: one placed on, that is, adjacent to, Mount Ebal; the other on, or adjacent to, Mount Gerizim. The six tribes on or at Gerizim were to pronounce blessings on those who should faithfully observe the law; and the six on Mount Ebal were to pronounce curses against those who should violate it. This Joshua executed. (Deut. xxvii; Joshua viii. 30–35.) Moses enjoined them to erect an altar of unhewn stones on Mount Ebal, and to plaster them over, that the law might be written on the altar. Shechem is the modern Nablous."

Eben Bohan. The stone which Bohan set up as a witness-stone, and which afterward served as a boundary-mark on the frontier between Judah and Benjamin. (Joshua xv. 6; xviii. 17.)

Eben-Ezer. (Heb., אבן־העזר, stone of help.) A stone set up by Samuel between Mizpeh and Shen in testimony of the Divine assistance obtained against the Philistines. (1 Sam. vii. 12.)

Eblis. The Arabian name of the prince of the apostate angels, exiled to the infernal regions for refusing to worship Adam at the command of the Supreme, Eblis claiming that he had been formed of ethereal fire, while Adam was created from clay. The Mohammedans assert that at the birth of their prophet the throne of Eblis was precipitated to the bottom of hell. The Azazel of the Hebrews.

Ebony Box. A symbol in the high degrees of the human heart, which is intended to teach reserve and taciturnity, which should be inviolably maintained in regard to the incommunicable secrets of the Order. When it is said that the ebony box contained the plans of the Temple of Solomon, the symbolic teaching is, that in the human heart are deposited the secret designs and motives of our conduct by which we propose to erect the spiritual temple of our lives.

Ecbatana. An ancient city of great interest to those who study the history of the rebuilding of the Temple. Its several names were Agbatana, Hagmatana, and Achmeta. Tradition attributes the founding of the city to Solomon, Herodotus to Deioces, 728 B.C., the Book of Judith to Arphaxad. It was the ancient capital of Media. Vast quantities of rubbish now indicate where the palace and citadel stood. The Temple of the Sun crowned a conical hill enclosed by seven concentric walls. According to Celsus, there was thus exhibited a scale composed of seven steps or stages, with an eighth at the upper extremity. The first stage was composed of lead, and indicated Saturn; the second, of tin, denoted Venus; the third, of copper, denoted Jupiter; the fourth, of iron, denoted Mars; the fifth, of divers metals, denoted Mercury; the sixth, of silver, denoted the Moon; the seventh, of gold, denoted the Sun; then the highest, Heaven. As they rose in gradation toward the pinnacle, all the gorgeous battlements represented at once—in Sabean fashion—the seven planetary spheres. The principal buildings were the Citadel, a stronghold of enormous dimensions, where also the archives were kept, in which Darius found the edict of Cyrus the Great concerning the rebuilding of the Holy Temple in Jerusalem.

Eclectic Masonry. From the Greek, ἐκλεκτικὸς, eklektikos, which means selecting. Those philosophers who, in ancient times, selected from the various systems of philosophy such doctrines as appeared most conformable to truth were called "eclectic philosophers." So the confederation of Masons in Germany, which consisted of Lodges that selected the degrees which they thought most comformable to ancient Freemasonry, was called the eclectic union, and the Masonry which it adopted received the name of Eclectic Masonry. (See Eclectic Union.)

Eclectic Rite. The Rite practised by the Eclectic Union, which see.

Eclectic Union. The fundamental idea of a union of the German Lodges for the purpose of purifying the Masonic system of the corruptions which had been introduced by the numerous degrees founded on alchemy, theosophy, and other occult sciences which at that time flooded the continent of Europe, originated, in 1779, with the Baron Von Ditfurth, who had been a prominent member of the Rite of Strict Observance; although Lenning attributes the earlier thought of a circular letter to Von Knigge. But the first practical step toward this purification was taken in 1783 by the Provincial Grand Lodges of Frankfort-on-the-Main and of Wetzlar. These two bodies addressed an encyclical letter to the Lodges of Germany, in which they invited them to enter into an alliance for the purpose of "re-establishing the Royal Art of Freemasonry." The principal points on which this union or alliance was to be founded were, 1. That the three symbolic degrees only were to be acknowledged by the united Lodges. 2. That each Lodge was permitted to practise for itself such high degrees as it might select for itself, but that the recognition of these was not to be made compulsory on the other Lodges. 3. That all the united Lodges were to be equal, none being dependent on any other. These propositions were accepted by several Lodges, and thence resulted the Eklectischer Bund, or Eclectic Union of Germany. at the head of which is the "Mother Grand Lodge of the Eclectic Union" at Frankfort-on-the-Main which has 21 Lodges and 3,166 brethren under its jurisdiction. The system of Masonry practised by this union is called the Eclectic system, and the Rite recognized by it is the Eclectic Rite, which consists of only the three degrees of Apprentice, Fellow-Craft, and Master Mason.

Ecossais. This is a French word, which is most generally to be translated as Scottish Master. There are numerous degrees under the same or a similar name; all of them, however, concurring in one particular, namely, that of detailing the method adopted for the preservation of the true Word. The American Mason will understand the character of the system of Ecossaism, as it may be called, when he is told that the Select Master of his own Rite is really an Ecossais Degree. It is found, too, in many other Rites. Thus, in the French Rite, it is the Fifth Degree. In the Ancient and Accepted Scottish Rite, the Thirteenth Degree or Knights of the Ninth Arch is properly an Ecossais Degree. The Ancient York Rite is without an Ecossais Degree, but its principles are set forth in the instructions of the Royal Arch.

Some idea of the extent to which these degrees have been multiplied may be formed from the fact that Oliver has a list of eighty of them; Ragon enumerates eighty-three; and the Baron Tschoudy, rejecting twenty-seven which he does not consider legitimate, retains a far greater number to whose purity he does not object.

In the Ecossais system there is a legend, a part of which has been adopted in all the Ecossais degrees, and which has in fact been incorporated into the mythical history of Masonry. It is to the effect that the builder of the Temple engraved the word upon a triangle of pure metal, and, fearing that it might be lost, he always bore it about his person, suspended from his neck, with the engraved side next to his breast. In a time of great peril to himself, he cast it into an old dry well, which was in the southeast corner of the Temple, where it was afterward found by three Masters. They were passing near the well at the hour of meridian, and were attracted by its brilliant appearance; whereupon one of them, descending with the assistance of his comrades, obtained it, and carried it to King Solomon. But the more modern form of the legend dispenses with the circumstance of the dry well, and says that the builder deposited it in the place which had been purposely prepared for it, and where centuries afterward it was found. And this amended form of the legend is more in accord with the recognized symbolism of the loss and the recovery of the Word.

Ecossais. 1. The Fourth Degree of Ramsay's Rite, and the original whence all the degrees of Ecossaism have sprung. 2. The Fifth Degree of the French Rite. 3. The Ecossais degrees constitute the fourth class of the Rite of Mizraim—from the Fourteenth to the Twenty-first Degree. In the subsequent articles only the principal Ecossais degrees will be mentioned.

Ecossais Architect, Perfect. (*Ecossais Architecte Parfait.*) A degree in the collection of M. Pyron.

Ecossais d'Angers or **Ecossais d'Alcidony.** Two degrees mentioned in a work entitled *Philosophical Considerations on Freemasonry.*

Ecossais, English. (*Ecoss. Angiais.*) A degree in the Mother Lodge of the Philosophic Rite.

Ecossais, Faithful. (*Ecossais Fidèle.*) (See *Vielle Bru.*)

Ecossais, French. The Thirty-fifth Degree of the collection of the Metropolitan Chapter of France.

Ecossais, Grand. The Fourteenth Degree of the Scottish Rite is so called in some of the French rituals.

Ecossais, Grand Architect. (*Grand Architect Ecossais.*) The Forty-fifth Degree of the Metropolitan Chapter of France.

Ecossais, Grand Master. Formerly the Sixth Degree of the Capitular system, practised in Holland.

Ecossais, Knight. A synonym of the Ninth Degree of Illuminism. It is more commonly called Illuminatus Dirigens.

Ecossais, Master. The Fifth Degree of the Rite of Zinnendorf. It was also formerly among the high degrees of the German Chapter and those of the Rite of the Clerks of Strict Observance. It is said to have been composed by Baron Hund.

Ecossais Novice. A synonym of the Eighth Degree of Illuminism. It is more commonly called Illuminatus Major.

Ecossais of Clermont. The Thirteenth Degree of the Metropolitan Chapter of France.

Ecossais of England. A degree in the collection of M. Le Rouge.

Ecossais of Franville. The Thirty-first Degree of the Metropolitan Chapter of France.

Ecossais of Hiram. A degree in the Mother Lodge of the Philosophic Scotch Rite.

Ecossais of Messina. A degree in the nomenclature of M. Fustier.

Ecossais of Montpellier. The Thirty-sixth Degree of the Metropolitan Chapter of France.

Ecossais of Naples. The Forty-second Degree of the collection of the Metropolitan Chapter of France.

Ecossais of Perfection. The Thirty-ninth Degree of the collection of the Metropolitan Chapter of France.

Ecossais of Prussia. A degree in the archives of the Mother Lodge of the Philosophic Scottish Rite.

Ecossais of St. Andrew. A not unusual form of Ecossaism, and found in several Rites. 1. The Second Degree of the Clerks of Strict Observance; 2. The Twenty-first Degree of the Rite of Mizraim; 3. The Twenty-ninth Degree of the Ancient and Accepted Scottish Rite is also an Ecossais of St. Andrew; 4. The Sixty-third Degree of the collection of the Metropolitan Chapter of France is an Ecossais of St. Andrew of Scotland; 5. The Seventy-fifth Degree of the same collection is called Ecossais of St. Andrew of the Thistle.

Ecossais of St. George. A degree in the collection of Le Page.

Ecossais of the Forty. (*Ecossais des Quarante.*) The Thirty-fourth Degree of the collection of the Metropolitan Chapter of France.

Ecossais of the Lodge of Prince Edward. A degree in the collection of Pyron. This was probably a Stuart degree, and referred to Prince Charles Edward, the young Pretender.

Ecossais of the Sacred Vault of James VI. 1. The Thirty-third Degree of the collection of the Metropolitan Chapter of France, said to have been composed by the Baron Tschoudy. 2. The Twentieth Degree of the Rite of Mizraim. 3. In the French rituals, this name has been given to the Fourteenth Degree of the Scottish Rite. Chemin Dupontès says that the degree was a homage paid to the kings of Scotland. Nothing, however, of this can be found in its present ritual; but it is very probable that the degree, in its first conception, and in some ritual that no longer exists, was an offspring of the house of Stuart, of which James VI. was the first English king.

Ecossais of the Three J. J. J. 1. The Thirty-second Degree of the collection of the Metropolitan Chapter of France. 2. The Nineteenth Degree of the Rite of Mizraim. The three J. J. J. are the initials of Jourdain, Jaho, Jachin.

Ecossais of Toulouse. A degree in the archives of the Mother Lodge of the Philosophic Scottish Rite.

Ecossais of the Triple Triangle. The Thirty-seventh Degree of the collection of the Metropolitan Chapter of France.

Ecossais, Parisian. So Thory has it; but Ragon, and all the other nomenclators, give it as Écossais Panissière. The Seventeenth Degree of the Rite of Mizraim.

Ecossais, Perfect. A degree in the archives of the Mother Lodge of the Philosophic Scottish Rite.

Ecossism. A name given by French Masonic writers to the thirty-three degrees of the Ancient and Accepted Scottish Rite. This, in English, would be equivalent to *Scottish Masonry*, which see.

Ecuador. Masonry was introduced into the Republic of Ecuador, in the year 1857, by the Grand Orient of Peru, which organized a Symbolic Lodge and Chapter of the Eighth Degree in Guayaquil; but in consequence of the opposition of the priests, these bodies did not flourish, and at the end of two years their members surrendered their warrants and ceased to pursue their Masonic labors. But, since then the Craft has revived and there are in Ecuador two Lodges under the Grand Lodge of Peru.

Edda. An Icelandic word, literally translated *great-grandmother*, as referred to in Scandinavian poetry. There are in reality two books of this name which were deemed inspired by the ancient Germans, Norwegians, and Swedes, and there grew out so many myths from these canonical writings, that great difficulty is now experienced as to what were apocryphal. The myths springing from the old German theology are full of beauty; they pervade Freemasonry extensively and so intimately that they are believed by many of the best students to be the origin of a large number of its legends and symbols.

The older of the two, called *The Edda of Sämund the Learned*, was written in a language existing in Denmark, Sweden, and Norway as early as the eighth century. Sämund Sigfusson, an Icelandic priest born in 1056, collected thirty-nine of these poems during the earlier portion of the twelfth century. The most remarkable of these poems is the *Oracle of the Prophetess*, containing the cosmogony, under the Scandinavian belief, from the creation to the destruction of the world. A well-preserved copy was found in Iceland in 1643.

The younger *Edda* is a collection of the myths of the gods, and of explanations or meters of Pagan poetry, and is intended for instruction of young scalds or poets. The first copy was found complete in 1628. The prologue is a curious compendium of Jewish, Greek, Christian, Roman, and Icelandic legend. Its authorship is ascribed to Snorro Sturleson, born in 1178; hence called *Edda of Snorro*.

Edict of Cyrus. Five hundred and thirty-six years before the Christian era, Cyrus issued his edict permitting the Jews to return from the captivity at Babylon to Jerusalem, and to rebuild the House of the Lord. At the same time he restored to them all the sacred vessels and precious ornaments of the first Temple, which had been carried away by Nebuchadnezzar, and which were still in existence. This is commemorated in the Royal Arch Degree of the York and American Rites. It is also referred to in the Fifteenth Degree, or Knight of the East of the Scottish Rite.

Edicts. The decrees of a Grand Master or of a Grand Lodge are called Edicts, and obedience to them is obligatory on all the Craft.

Edinburgh. The capital of Scotland. [The Lodge of Edinburgh (Mary's Chapel) is No. 1 on the "Roll of Lodges holding under the Grand Lodge of Scotland," and is described therein as instituted "Before 1598." Nothing more precise is known as to the date of its foundation, but it possesses minutes commencing in July, 1599. It met at one time in a chapel dedicated to the Virgin Mary, and from this is derived the second part of its name. Its history has been written by D. M. Lyon (1873).—E. L. H.] (See *Scotland*.)

Edinburgh, Congress of. It was convoked, in 1736, by William St. Clair of Roslin, Patron of the Masons of Scotland (whose mother Lodge was Canongate Kilwinning), with the view of abdicating his dignity as hereditary Grand Patron, with all the privileges granted to the family of St. Clair of Roslin by the Operative Masons of Scotland early in the seventeenth century (see *St. Clair Charters*), and afterward to organize Masonry upon a new basis. The members of thirty-three Lodges uniting for this purpose, constituted the new Grand Lodge of Scotland, and elected St. Clair Grand Master on November 30, 1736. (See *St. Clair*.)

Edinburgh - Kilwinning Manuscript. One of the "Old Charges," probably written about 1665. It is in the custody of the "Mother Lodge Kilwinning, No. 0," which heads the Roll of Scotch Lodges. It has been reproduced in Hughan's *Masonic Sketches and Reprints*, and in D. M. Lyon's *History of the Lodge of Edinburgh*. [E. L. H.]

Edward the Confessor, King. Said to have been a patron of Masonry in England in 1041.

Edward, Kings. The four kings, numerically known as the First, Second, Third, and Fourth, appear as favorers, abettors, and protectors of the Institution of Freemasonry.

Edward, Prince. Son of George III., and Duke of Kent, was initiated in 1790, at Geneva, in the Lodge *De l'Union des Cœurs;* was Grand Master of the Ancients, and resigned to the Duke of Sussex on the memorable occasion of the Union in England, 1813.

Edward III. Manuscript. A manuscript quoted by Anderson in his second edition (p. 71), and also by Preston, as an old record referring to "the glorious reign of King Edward III." The whole of the record is not cited, but the passages that are given are evidently the same as those contained in what is now known as the Cooke MS., the archaic phraseology having been modernized and interpolations inserted by Anderson, as was, unfortunately, his habit in dealing with those old documents. Compare, for instance, the following passages:

From the Cooke MS. "When the master and the felawes be forwarned ben y come to such congregacions if nede be the Schereffe of the countre or the mayer of the Cyte or alderman of the towne in wyche the congregacions is holde schall be felaw and sociat to the master of the congregacion in helpe of hym a yest rebelles and upberyng (upbearing) the rygt of the reme." (Ll. 901-912.)

Edward III. MS., as quoted by Anderson. "That when the Master and Wardens preside in a Lodge, the sheriff if need be, or the mayor or the alderman (if a brother) where the Chapter is held, shall be sociate to the Master, in help of him against rebels and for upholding the rights of the realm."

The identity of the two documents is apparent. Either the Edward III. MS. was copied from the Cooke, or both were derived from a common original.

Edwin. The son of Edward, Saxon king of England, who died in 924, and was succeeded by his eldest son, Athelstan. The Masonic tradition is that Athelstan appointed his brother Edwin the Patron of Masonry in England, and gave him what the Old Records call a free Charter to hold an Annual Communication or General Assembly, under the authority of which he summoned the Masons of England to meet him in a Congregation at York, where they met in 926 and formed the Grand Lodge of England. The Old Records say that these Masons brought with them many old writings and records of the Craft, some in Greek, some in Latin, some in French, and other languages, and from these framed the document now known as the York Constitutions, whose authenticity has been in recent years so much a subject of controversy among Masonic writers. Prince Edwin died two years before his brother, and a report was spread of his being put wrongfully to death by him; "but this," says Preston, "is so improbable in itself, so inconsistent with the character of Athelstan, and, indeed, so slenderly attested, as to be undeserving a place in history." William of Malmesbury, the old chronicler, relates the story, but confesses that it had no better foundation than some old ballads. But now come the later Masonic antiquaries, who assert that Edwin himself is only a myth, and that, in spite of the authority of a few historical writers, Athelstan had no son or brother of the name of Edwin. Woodford (*Old Charges of the Brit. Freemasons,* p. xiv.) thinks that the Masonic tradition points to Edwin, King of Northumbria, whose rendezvous was once at Auldby, near York, and who in 627 aided in the building of a stone church at York, after his baptism there, with Roman workmen. "Tradition," he says, "sometimes gets confused after the lapse of time; but I believe the tradition is in itself true which links Masonry to the church building at York by the Operative Brotherhood, under Edwin, in 627, and to a gild Charter under Athelstan, in 927."

The legend of Prince Edwin, of course, requires some modification, but we should not be too hasty in rejecting altogether a tradition which has been so long and so universally accepted by the Fraternity, and to which Anderson, Preston, Krause, Oliver, and a host of other writers, have subscribed their assent. The subject will be fully discussed under the head of *York Legend,* which see.

Edwin Charges. The charges said to have been given by Prince Edwin, and contained in the Antiquity MS., are sometimes so called. (See *Antiquity Manuscript.*)

Egg, Mundane. It was a belief of almost all the ancient nations, that the world was hatched from an egg made by the Creator, over which the Spirit of God was represented as hovering in the same manner as a bird broods or flutters over her eggs. Faber (*Pag. Idol.,* i., 4), who traced everything to the Arkite worship, says that this egg, which was a symbol of the resurrection, was no other than the ark; and as Dionysus was fabled in the Orphic hymns to be born from an egg, he and Noah were the same person; wherefore the birth of Dionysus or Brahma, or any other hero god from an egg, was nothing more than the egress of Noah from the ark. Be this as it may, the egg has been always deemed a symbol of the resurrection, and hence the Christian use of Easter eggs on the great feast of the resurrection of our Lord. As this is the most universally diffused of all symbols, it is strange that it has found no place in the symbolism of Freemasonry, which deals so much with the doctrine of the resurrection, of which the egg was everywhere the recognized symbol. It was, however, used by the ancient architects, and from them was adopted by the Operative Masons of the Middle Ages, one of whose favorite ornaments was the ovolo, or egg-molding.

Eglinton Manuscript. An Old Record dated December 28, 1599. It is so named from its having been discovered some years ago in the charter chest at Eglinton Castle. It is a Scottish manuscript, and is valuable for its details of early Masonry in Scotland. In it, Edinburgh is termed "the first and principal Lodge," and Kilwinning is called "the heid and secund Ludge of Scotland in all tyme cuming." An exact copy of it was taken by Bro. D. Murray Lyon, and published in his *History of the Lodge of Edinburgh.* (P. 12.) It has also been printed in Hughan's *Masonic Sketches and Reprints.*

Egyptian Hieroglyphs. The extent of parallelism between the innumerable hieroglyphs on the tombs and monuments of India and Egypt and the symbols and emblems of Freemasonry, taken together with their esoteric interpretation, has caused very many well-thinking Masons to believe in an Indian or Egyptian origin of our speculative institution of the present day: So close and numerous are these symbols and their meaning that it becomes difficult for the mind to free itself from a fixed conclusion; and some of the best students feel confident in their judgment to this end, more especially when tracing the Leader, "Moses, learned in all the wisdom of the Egyptians," from **MSS or MES,** that country to Palestine with the twelve tribes of Israel and their successors building that Holy House in Jerusalem, which has become the chief Masonic symbol. Some have abominated this theory on the ground of alleged polytheism existing among the Egyptians; but this existed only at a later day in the life of the nation, as it also existed among the corrupted Jews in its worst form, for which see 2 Kings ch. 17–21.

Bro. Thomas Pryer presents this evidence of a monotheistic belief, of pristine purity, among the early Egyptians, ages prior to Abraham's day. We give the hieroglyphs and their interpretation:

May

thy soul

attain (come)

to

KHNUM (Spirit of God, one of the forms of AMON, the Creator),

The Creator (the idea denoted by a man building the walls of a city)

of all

mankind (literally men and women.)

May thy soul attain to KHNUM, *the Creator of all mankind.*

How prophetical were the Books of Hermes, "O Egypt, Egypt! a time shall come, when, in lieu of a pure religion, and of a pure belief, thou wilt possess naught but ridiculous fables, incredible to posterity; and nothing will remain to thee, but *words engraven on stone,* the only monuments that will attest thy piety."

Egyptian Masonry.   See *Cagliostro.*

Egyptian Months.   Named Thoth, Paophi, Athyr, Choiak, Tybi, Mechir, Phamenoth, Pharmuthi, Pashons, Payni, Epiphi, and Mesore. The above twelve months, commencing with March 1st, were composed of thirty days each, and the five supplementary days were dedicated to Hesiri (Osiris), Hor (Horus), Set (Typhon), His (Isis), and Nebti (Nephthys). The sacred year commenced July 20th; the Alexandrian year, August 29th, B.C. 25.

Egyptian Mysteries.   Egypt has always been considered as the birthplace of the mysteries. It was there that the ceremonies of initiation were first established. It was there that truth was first veiled in allegory, and the dogmas of religion were first imparted under symbolic forms. From Egypt—"the land of the winged globe"—the land of science and philosophy, "peerless for stately tombs and magnificent temples—the land whose civilization was old and mature before other nations, since called to empire, had a name"—this system of symbols was disseminated through Greece and Rome and other countries of Europe and Asia, giving origin, through many intermediate steps, to that mysterious association which is now represented by the Institution of Freemasonry.

To Egypt, therefore, Masons have always looked with peculiar interest as the cradle of that mysterious science of symbolism whose peculiar modes of teaching they alone, of all modern institutions, have preserved to the present day.

The initiation into the Egyptian mysteries was, of all the systems practised by the ancients, the most severe and impressive. The Greeks at Eleusis imitated it to some extent, but they never reached the magnitude of its forms nor the austerity of its discipline. The system had been organized for ages, and the priests, who alone were the hierophants—the explainers of the mysteries, or, as we should call them in Masonic language, the Masters of the Lodges—were educated almost from childhood for the business in which they were engaged. That "learning of the Egyptians," in which Moses is said to have been so skilled, was all imparted in these mysteries. It was confined to the priests and to the initiates; and the trials of initiation through which the latter had to pass were so difficult to be endured, that none but those who were stimulated by the most ardent thirst for knowledge dared to undertake them or succeeded in submitting to them.

The priesthood of Egypt constituted a sacred caste, in whom the sacerdotal functions were hereditary. They exercised also an important part in the government of the state, and the kings of Egypt were but the first subjects of its priests. They had originally organized, and continued to control, the ceremonies of initiation. Their doctrines were of two kinds—exoteric or public, which were communicated to the multitude, and esoteric or secret, which were revealed only to a chosen few; and to obtain them it was necessary to pass through an initiation which was characterized by the severest trials of courage and fortitude.

The principal seat of the mysteries was at Memphis, in the neighborhood of the great Pyramid. They were of two kinds, the greater and the less; the former being the mysteries of Osiris and Serapis, the latter those of Isis. The mysteries of Osiris were celebrated at the autumnal equinox, those of Serapis at the summer solstice, and those of Isis at the vernal equinox.

The candidate was required to exhibit proofs of a blameless life. For some days previous to the commencement of the ceremonies of initiation, he abstained from all unchaste acts, confined himself to an exceedingly light diet, from which animal food was rigorously excluded, and purified himself by repeated ablutions.

Apuleius (*Met.*, lib. xi.), who had been initiated in all of them, thus alludes, with cautious reticence, to those of Isis: "The priest, all the profane being removed to a distance, taking hold of me by the hand, brought me into the inner recesses of the sanctuary itself, clothed in a new linen garment. Perhaps, curious reader, you may be eager to know what was then said and done. I would tell you were it lawful for me to tell you; you should know it if it were lawful for you to hear. But both the ears that heard those things and the tongue that told them would reap the evil results of their rashness. Still, however, kept in suspense, as you probably are, with religious longing, I will not torment you with long-protracted anxiety. Hear, therefore, but believe what is the truth. *I approached the confines of death*, and, having trod on the threshold of Proserpine, I returned therefrom, being borne through all the elements. At midnight I saw the sun shining with its brilliant light; and I approached the presence of the gods beneath and the gods above, and stood near and worshiped them. Behold, I have related to you things of which, though heard by you, you must necessarily remain ignorant."

The first degree, as we may term it, of Egyptian initiation was that into the mysteries of Isis. What was its peculiar import, we are unable to say. Isis, says Knight, was, among the later Egyptians, the personification of universal nature. To Apuleius she says: "I am nature—the parent of all things, the sovereign of the elements, the primary progeny of time." Plutarch tells us that on the front of the temple of Isis was placed this inscription: "I, Isis, am all that has been, that is, or shall be, and no mortal hath ever unveiled me." Thus we may conjecture that the Isiac mysteries were descriptive of the alternate decaying and renovating powers of nature. Higgins (*Anacal.*, ii., 102), it is true, says that during the mysteries of Isis were celebrated the misfortunes and tragical death of Osiris in a sort of drama; and Apuleius asserts that the initiation into her mysteries is celebrated as bearing a close resemblance to a voluntary death, with a precarious chance of recovery. But Higgins gives no authority for his statement, and that of Apuleius cannot be constrained into any reference to the enforced death of Osiris. It is, therefore, probable that the ceremonies of this initiation were simply preparatory to that of the Osirian, and taught, by instructions in the physical laws of nature, the necessity of moral purification, a theory which is not incompatible with all the mystical allusions of Apuleius when he describes his own initiation.

The *Mysteries of Serapis* constituted the second degree of the Egyptian initiation. Of these rites we have but a scanty knowledge. Herodotus is entirely silent concerning them, and Apuleius, calling them "the nocturnal orgies of Serapis, a god of the first rank," only intimates that they followed those of Isis, and were preparatory to the last and greatest initiation. Serapis is said to have been only Osiris while in Hades; and hence the Serapian initiation might have represented the death of Osiris, but leaving the lesson of resurrection for a subsequent initiation. But this is merely a conjecture.

In the mysteries of Osiris, which were the consummation of the Egyptian system, the lesson of death and resurrection was symbolically taught; and the legend of the murder of Osiris, the search for the body, its discovery and restoration to life is scenically represented. This legend of initiation was as follows: Osiris, a wise king of Egypt, left the care of his kingdom to his wife Isis, and traveled for three years to communicate to other nations the arts of civilization. During his absence, his brother Typhon formed a secret conspiracy to destroy him and to usurp his throne. On his return, Osiris was invited by Typhon to an entertainment in the month of November, at which all the conspirators were present. Typhon produced a chest inlaid with gold, and promised to give it to any person present whose body would most exactly fit it. Osiris was tempted to try the experiment; but he had no sooner laid down in the chest, than the lid was closed and nailed down, and the chest thrown into the river Nile. The chest containing the body of Osiris was, after being for a long time tossed about by the waves, finally cast up at Byblos in Phœnicia, and left at the foot of a tamarisk tree. Isis, overwhelmed with grief for the loss of her husband, set out on a journey, and traversed the earth in search of the body. After many adventures, she at length discovered the spot whence it had been thrown up by the waves and returned with it in triumph to Egypt. It was then proclaimed, with the most extravagant demonstrations of joy, that Osiris was risen from the dead and had become a god. Such, with slight variations of details by different writers, are the general outlines of the Osiric legend which was represented in the drama of initiation. Its resemblance to the Hiramic legend of the Masonic system will be readily seen, and its symbolism will be easily understood. Osiris and Typhon are the representatives of the two antagonistic principles—good and evil, light and darkness, life and death.

There is also an astronomical interpretation of the legend which makes Osiris the sun and Typhon the season of winter, which suspends the fecundating and fertilizing powers of the sun or destroys its life, to be restored only by the return of invigorating spring.

The sufferings and death of Osiris were the great mystery of the Egyptian religion. His being the abstract idea of the Divine goodness, his manifestation upon earth, his death, his resurrection, and his subsequent office as judge of the dead in a future state, look, says Wilkinson, like the early revelation of a future manifestation of the Deity converted into a mythological fable.

Into these mysteries Herodotus, Plutarch, and Pythagoras were initiated, and the former two have given brief accounts of them. But their own knowledge must have been extremely limited, for, as Clement of Alexandria (*Strom.*, v., 7) tells us, the more important secrets were not revealed even to all the priests, but to a select number of them only.

Egyptian Priests, Initiations of the. In the year 1770, there was published at Berlin a work entitled *Crata Repoa; oder Einweihungen der Egyptischen Priester*, i. e., Crata Repoa; or, Initiations of the Egyptian Priests. This book was subsequently republished in 1778, and translated into French under the revision of Ragon, and published at Paris in 1821, by Bailleul. It professed to give the whole formula of the initiation into the mysteries practised by the ancient Egyptian priests. Lenning cites the work, and gives an outline of the system as if he thought it an authentic relation; but Gädicke more prudently says of it that he doubts that there are more mysteries described in the book than were ever practised by the ancient Egyptian priests. The French writers have generally accepted it as genuine. Forty years before, the Abbé Terrasson had written a somewhat similar work, in which he pretended to describe the initiation of a Prince of Egypt. Kloss, in his *Bibliography*, has placed this latter work under the head of "Romances of the Order"; and a similar place should doubtless be assigned to the *Crata Repoa*. The curious may, however, be gratified by a brief detail of the system.

According to the *Crata Repoa*, the priest of Egypt conferred their initiation at Thebes. The mysteries were divided into the following seven degrees: 1. Pastophoros. 2. Neocoros. 3. Melanophoros. 4. Kistophoros. 5. Balahate. 6. Astronomos. 7. Propheta. The first degree was devoted to instructions in the physical sciences; the second, to geometry and architecture. In the third degree, the candidate was instructed in the symbolical death of Osiris, and was made acquainted with the hieroglyphical language. In the fourth he was presented with the book of the laws of Egypt, and became a judge. The instructions of the fifth degree were dedicated to chemistry, and of the sixth to astronomy and the mathematical sciences. In the seventh and last degree the candidate received a detailed explanation of all the mysteries, his head was shaved, and he was presented with a cross, which he was constantly to carry, a white mantle, and a square head dress. To each degree was attached a word and sign. Anyone who should carefully read the *Crata Repoa* would be convinced that, so far from being founded on any ancient system of initiation, it was simply a modern invention made up out of the high degrees of continental Masonry. It is indeed surprising that Lenning and Ragon should have treated it as if it had the least claims to antiquity.

[It has been suggested that *Crata Repoa* may be an anagram for *Arcta Opera* or "close finished works."—E. L. H.]

Eheyeh asher Eheyeh. The pronunciation of אהיה אשר אהיה, which means, *I am that I am*, and is one of the pentateuchal names of God. It is related in the third chapter of Exodus, that when God appeared to Moses in the burning bush, and directed him to go to Pharaoh and to the children of Israel in Egypt, Moses required that, as preliminary to his mission, he should be instructed in the name of God, so that, when he was asked by the Israelites, he might be able to prove his mission by announcing what that name was; and God said to him, אהיה (Eheyeh), *I am that I am;* and he directed him to say, "*I am* hath sent you." *Eheyeh asher eheyeh* is, therefore, the name of God, in which Moses was instructed at the burning bush.

Maimonides thinks that when the Lord ordered Moses to tell the people that אהיה (Eheyeh) sent him, he did not mean that he should only mention his name; for if they were already acquainted with it, he told them nothing new, and if they were not, it was not likely that they would be satisfied by saying such a name sent me, for the proof would still be wanting that this was really the name of God; therefore, he not only told them the name, but also *taught* them its signification. In those times, Sabaism being the predominant religion, almost all men were idolaters, and occupied themselves in the contemplation of the heavens and the sun and the stars, without any idea of a personal God in the world. Now, the Lord, to deliver his people from such an error, said to Moses, "Go and tell them I AM THAT I AM hath sent me unto you," which name אהיה (Eheyeh), signifying Being, is derived from היה (heyeh), the verb of existence, and which, being repeated so that the second is the predicate of the first, contains the mystery. This is as if he had said, "Explain to them that *I am what I am:* that is, that my Being is within myself, independent of every other, different from all other beings, who *are* so alone by virtue of my distributing it to them, and might not have *been*, nor could actually *be* such without it." So that אהיה denotes the Divine Being Himself, by which he taught Moses not only the name, but the infallible demonstration of the Fountain of Existence, as the name itself denotes. The Kabbalists say that Eheyeh is the *crown* or highest of the Sephiroth, and that it is the name that was hidden in the most secret place of the tabernacle.

The Talmudists had many fanciful exercitations on this word אהיה, and, among others, said that it is equivalent to יהיה, and the four letters of which it is formed possess peculiar properties. א is in Hebrew numerically equivalent to 1, and י to 10, which is equal to 11; a result also obtained by taking the second and third letters of the holy name, or ה and ו, which are 5 and 6, amounting to 11. But the 5 and 6 invariably produce the same number in their multiplication, for 5 times 5 are 25, and 6 times 6 are 36, and this invariable product of ה and ו was said to denote the unchangeableness of the First Cause. Again, *I am*, אהיה, commences with א or 1, the beginning of numbers, and *Jehovah*, יהוה, with י or 10, the end of numbers, which signified that God was the beginning and end of all things. The phrase *Eheyeh asher eheyeh* is of importance in the study of the legend of the Royal Arch system. Some years ago, that learned Mason, William S. Rockwell, while preparing his *Ahiman Rezon* for the State of Georgia, undertook, but beyond that jurisdiction unsuccessfully, to introduce it as a password to the veils.

Eight. Among the Pythagoreans the number *eight* was esteemed as the first cube, being formed by the continued multiplication of $2 \times 2 \times 2$, and signified friendship, prudence, counsel, and justice; and, as the cube or reduplication of the first even number, it was made to refer to the primitive law of nature, which supposes all men to be equal. Christian numerical symbologists have called it the symbol of the resurrection, because Jesus rose on the 8th day, i. e. the day after the 7th, and because the name of Jesus in Greek numerals, corresponding to its Greek letters, is 10, 8, 200, 70, 400, 200, which, being added up, is 888. Hence, too, they call it the Dominical Number. As 8 persons were saved in the ark, those who, like Faber, have adopted the theory that the Arkite Rites pervaded all the religions of antiquity, find an important symbolism in this number, and as Noah was the type of the resurrection, they again find in it a reference to that doctrine. It can, however, be scarcely reckoned among the numerical symbols of Masonry.

Eighty-One. A sacred number in the high degrees, because it is the square of *nine*, which is again the square of *three*. The Pythagoreans, however, who considered the *nine* as a fatal number, especially dreaded eighty-one, because it was produced by the multiplication of nine by itself.

El, אל. One of the Hebrew names of God, signifying the *Mighty One*. It is the root of many of the other names of Deity, and also, therefore, of many of the sacred words in the high degrees. Bryant (*Anc. Myth.*, i., 16) says it was the true name of God, but transferred by the Sabians to the sun, whence the Greeks borrowed their *helios*.

Elai beni almanah (Hebrew, בני אלמנה אלי, *Huc venite filii viduæ*). Third Degree A. A. Scottish Rite.

Elai beni emeth (Heb., אלי בני אמת, *Huc venite filii veritatis*). Sometimes applied to the Twenty-sixth Degree of the A. A. Scottish Rite.

Elchanan, אלחנן. *God has graciously given.* In the authorized version, it is improperly translated *Elhanan.* Jerome says that it meant David, because in 2 Sam. xxi. 19 it is said that Elchanan slew Goliath. A significant word in the high degrees, which has undergone much corruption and various changes of form. In the old rituals it is Eleham. Lenning gives Elchanam, and incorrectly translates, *mercy of God;* Delaunay calls it Eliham, and translates it, *God of the people*, in which Pike concurs.

Elders. This word is used in some of the old Constitutions to designate those Masons who, from their rank and age, were deputed to obligate Apprentices when admitted into the Craft. Thus in the *Constitutions of Masonrie*, preserved in the archives of the York

Lodge, No. 236 (*York Roll No. 2*), with the date of 1704, we find this expression, *Tum unus ex Senioribus Teneat librum*, etc., which in another manuscript, dated 1693, preserved in the same archives (*York Roll No. 4*), is thus translated: "Then one of the *elders* takeing the Booke, and that hee or shee that is to bee made Mason shall lay their hands thereon, and the charge shall be given." These old MSS. have been published by W. J. Hughan in *Ancient Masonic Rolls of Constitutions, &c.*, 1894.

Elect. See *Elu.*

Elect Brother. The Seventh Degree of the Rite of Zinnendorf and of the National Grand Lodge of Berlin.

Elect Cohens, Order of. See *Paschalis, Martinez.*

Elect Commander. (*Elu Commandeur.*) A degree mentioned in Fustier's nomenclature of degrees.

Elect, Depositary. A degree mentioned in Pyron's collection.

Elect, Grand. (*Grand Elu.*) The Fourteenth Degree of the Chapter of the Emperors of the East and West. The same as the Grand Elect, Perfect and Sublime Mason or the Scottish Rite.

Elect, Grand Prince of the Three. A degree mentioned in Pyron's collection.

Elect, Irish. (*Elu Irlandais.*) The first of the high grades of the Chapters of that name.

Elect Lady, Sublime. (*Dame, Elu Sublime.*) An androgynous degree contained in the collection of Pyron.

Elect, Little English. (*Petit Elu Anglais.*) The Little English Elect was a degree of the Ancient Chapter of Clermont. The degree is now extinct.

Elect Master. (*Maître Elu.*) 1. The Thirteenth Degree of the collection of the Metropolitan Chapter of France. 2. The Fifth Degree of the Rite of Zinnendorf.

Elect of Fifteen. (*Elu des Quinze.*) The Tenth Degree in the Ancient and Accepted Scottish Rite. The place of meeting is called a Chapter; the emblematic color is black, strewed with tears; and the principal officers are a Thrice Illustrious Master and two Inspectors. The history of this degree develops the continuation and conclusion of the punishment inflicted on three traitors who, just before the conclusion of the Temple, had committed a crime of the most atrocious character. The degree is now more commonly called *Illustrious Elu of the Fifteen.* The same degree is found in the Chapter of Emperors of the East and West, and in the Rite of Mizraim.

Elect of London. (*Elus des Londres.*) The Seventieth Degree of the collection of the Metropolitan Chapter of France.

Elect of Nine. (*Elu des Neuf.*) The Ninth Degree of the Ancient and Accepted Rite. In the old rituals there were two officers who represented Solomon and Stolkin. But in the revised ritual of the Southern Jurisdiction, the principal officers are a Master and

16

two Inspectors. The meetings are called Chapters. The degree details the mode in which certain traitors, who, just before the completion of the Temple, had been engaged in an execrable deed of villany, received their punishment. The symbolic colors are red, white, and black; the white emblematic of the purity of the knights; the red, of the crime which was committed; and the black, of grief. This is the first of the *Elu* degrees, and the one on which the whole *Elu* system has been founded.

Elect of Nine and Fifteen. (*Auserwählte der Neun und der Fünfzehn.*) The first and second points of the Fourth Degree of the old system of the Royal York Lodge of Berlin.

Elect of Perignan. (*Elu de Perignan.*) A degree illustrative of the punishment inflicted upon certain criminals whose exploits constitute a portion of the legend of Symbolic Masonry. The substance of this degree is to be found in the Elect of Nine and Elect of Fifteen in the Scottish Rite, with both of which it is closely connected. It is the Sixth Degree of the Adonhiramite Rite. (See *Perignan.*)

Elect of the New Jerusalem. Formerly the Eighth and last of the high degrees of the Grand Chapter of Berlin.

Elect of the Twelve Tribes. (*Elu des douze Tribus.*) The Seventeenth Degree of the collection of the Metropolitan Chapter of France.

Elect of Truth, Rite of. (*Rite des Elus de la Vérité.*) This Rite was instituted in 1776, by the Lodge of Perfect Union, at Rennes, in France. A few Lodges in the interior of France adopted this *régime;* but, notwithstanding its philosophical character, it never became popular, and finally, about the end of the eighteenth century, fell into disuse. It consisted of twelve degrees divided into two classes, as follows:

1st Class. *Knights Adepts.* 1. Apprentice; 2. Fellow-Craft; 3. Master; 4. Perfect Master. 2d Class. *Elects of Truth.* 5. Elect of Nine; 6. Elect of Fifteen; 7. Master Elect; 8. Architect; 9. Second Architect; 10. Grand Architect; 11. Knight of the East; 12. Prince of Rose Croix.

Elect of Twelve. See *Knight Elect of Twelve.*

Elect, Perfect. (*Parfait Elu.*) The Twelfth Degree of the Metropolitan Chapter of France, and also of the Rite of Mizraim.

Elect, Perfect and Sublime Mason. See *Perfection, Lodge of.*

Elect Philosopher. A degree under this name is found in the instructions of the philosophic Scottish Rite, and in the collection of Viany.

Elect Secret, Severe Inspector. (*Elu Secret, Sévère Inspecteur.*) The Fourteenth Degree of the collection of the Metropolitan Chapter of France.

Elect, Sovereign. (*Elu Souverain.*) The Fifty-ninth Degree of the Rite of Mizraim.

Elect, Sublime. (*Elu Sublime.*) The Fifteenth Degree of the collection of the Metropolitan Chapter of France.

Elect, Supreme. (*Elu Suprême.*) The Seventy-fourth Degree of the collection of the Metropolitan Chapter of France. It is also a degree in the collection of M. Pyron, and, under the name of Tabernacle of Perfect Elect, is contained in the archives of the Mother Lodge of the Philosophic Rite.

Elect, Symbolical. Fifth Degree of the Reformed Rite of Baron Von Tschoudy.

Electa. Fifth Degree in the American Adoptive system of the *Eastern Star.* [So named from the lady, whose real name is unknown, to whom the 2d Epistle of St. John is addressed, and who, according to tradition, "joyfully rendered up home, husband, children, good name and life, that she might testify to her Christian love by a martyr's death."—E. L. H.]

Election of Officers. The election of the officers of a Lodge is generally held on the meeting which precedes the festival of St. John the Evangelist, and sometimes on that festival itself. Should a Lodge fail to make the election at that time, no election can be subsequently held except by dispensation; and it is now very generally admitted, that should any one of the officers die or remove from the jurisdiction during the period for which he was elected, no election can take place to supply the vacancy, but the office must be filled temporarily until the next election. If it be the Master, the Senior Warden succeeds to the office. For the full exposition of the law on this subject, see *Vacancies in Office.*

Elective Officers. In America, all the offices of a Symbolic Lodge except the Deacons, Stewards, and sometimes the Tiler, are elected by the members of the Lodge. In England, the rule is different. There the Master, Treasurer, and Tiler only are elected; the other officers are appointed by the Master.

Eleham. See *Elchanan.*

Elements. It was the doctrine of the old philosophies, sustained by the authority of Aristotle, that there were four principles of matter—fire, air, earth, and water—which they called elements. Modern science has shown the fallacy of the theory. But it was also taught by the Kabbalists, and afterward by the Rosicrucians, who, according to the Abbé de Villars (*Le Comte de Gabalis*), peopled them with supernatural beings called, in the fire, Salamanders; in the air, Sylphs; in the earth, Gnomes; and in the water, Undines. From the Rosicrucians and the Kabbalists, the doctrine passed over into some of the high degrees of Masonry, and is especially referred to in the Ecossais or Scottish Knight of St. Andrew, originally invented by the Chevalier Ramsay. In this degree we find the four angels of the four elements described as Andarel, the angel of fire; Casmaran, of air; Talliad, of water; and Furlac, of earth; and the signs refer to the same elements.

Elements, Test of the. A ceremonial in the First and Twenty-fourth degrees of the A. A. Scottish Rite.

Elephanta. The cavern of Elephanta, situated on the island of Gharipour, in the Gulf of Bombay, is the most ancient temple in the world, and was the principal place for the celebration of the mysteries of India. It is one hundred and thirty-five feet square and eighteen feet high, supported by four massive pillars, and its walls covered on all sides with statues and carved decorations. Its adytum at the western extremity, which was accessible only to the initiated, was dedicated to the Phallic worship. On each side were cells and passages for the purpose of initiation, and a sacred orifice for the mystical representation of the doctrine of regeneration. (See Maurice's *Indian Antiquities,* for a full description of this ancient scene of initiation.)

Eleusinian Mysteries. Of all the mysteries of the ancient religions, those celebrated at the village of Eleusis, near the city of Athens, were the most splendid and the most popular. To them men came, says Cicero, from the remotest regions to be initiated. They were also the most ancient, if we may believe St. Epiphanius, who traces them to the reign of Inachus, more than eighteen hundred years before the Christian era. They were dedicated to the goddess Demeter, the Ceres of the Romans, who was worshiped by the Greeks as the symbol of the prolific earth; and in them were scenically represented the loss and the recovery of Persephone, and the doctrines of the unity of God and the immortality of the soul were esoterically taught. The learned Faber believed that there was an intimate connection between the Arkite worship and the mysteries of Eleusis; but Faber's theory was that the Arkite Rites, which he traced to almost all the nations of antiquity, symbolized, in the escape of Noah and the renovation of the earth, the doctrines of the resurrection and the immortal life. Plutarch (*De Is. et Os.*) says that the travels of Isis in search of Osiris were not different from those of Demeter in search of Persephone; and this view has been adopted by St. Croix (*Myst. du Pag.*) and by Creuzer (*Symb.*); and hence we may well suppose that the recovery of the former at Byblos, and of the latter in Hades, were both intended to symbolize the restoration of the soul after death to eternal life. The learned have generally admitted that when Virgil, in the sixth book of his *Æneid,* depicted the descent of Æneas into hell, he intended to give a representation of the Eleusinian mysteries.

The mysteries were divided into two classes, the lesser and the greater. The lesser mysteries were celebrated on the banks of the Ilissus, whose waters supplied the means of purification of the aspirants. The greater mysteries were celebrated in the temple at Eleusis. An interval of six months occurred between them, the former taking place in March and the latter in September; which has led some writers to suppose that there was some mystical reference to the vernal and autumnal equinoxes. But, considering the character of Demeter as the goddess of Agriculture, it might be imagined, although this is a mere conjecture, that the reference was to seed-time and harvest. A year, however, was required to elapse before the initiate into the lesser mysteries was granted admission into the greater.

In conducting the mysteries, there were four officers, namely: 1. The Hierophant, or explainer of the sacred things. As the pontifex maximus in Rome, so he was the chief priest of Attica; he presided over the ceremonies and explained the nature of the mysteries to the initiated. 2. The Dadouchus, or torch-bearer, who appears to have acted as the immediate assistant of the Hierophant. 3. The Hieroceryx, or sacred herald, who had the general care of the temple, guarded it from the profanation of the uninitiated, and took charge of the aspirant during the trials of initiation. 4. The Epibomus, or altar-server, who conducted the sacrifices.

The ceremonies of initiation into the lesser mysteries were altogether purificatory, and intended to prepare the neophyte for his reception into the more sublime rites of the greater mysteries. This, an ancient poet, quoted by Plutarch, illustrates by saying that sleep is the lesser mysteries of the death. The candidate who desired to pass through this initiation entered the modest temple, erected for that purpose on the borders of the Ilissus, and there submitted to the required ablutions, typical of moral purification. The Dadouchus then placed his feet upon the skins of the victims which had been immolated to Jupiter. Hesychius says that only the left foot was placed on the skins. In this position he was asked if he had eaten bread, and if he was pure; and his replies being satisfactory, he passed through other symbolic ceremonies, the mystical signification of which was given to him, an oath of secrecy having been previously administered. The initiate into the lesser mysteries was called a *mystes,* a title which, being derived from a Greek word meaning to shut the eyes, signified that he was yet blind as to the greater truths thereafter to be revealed.

The greater mysteries lasted for nine days, and were celebrated partly on the Thriasian plain, which surrounded the temple, and partly in the temple of Eleusis itself. Of this temple, one of the most magnificent and the largest in Greece, not a vestige is now left. Its antiquity was very great, having been in existence, according to Aristides the rhetorician, when the Dorians marched against Athens. It was burned by the retreating Persians under Xerxes, but immediately rebuilt, and finally destroyed with the city by Alaric, "the Scourge of God," and all that is now left of Eleusis and its spacious temple is the mere site occupied by the insignificant Greek village of Lepsina, an evident corruption of the ancient name.

The public processions on the plain and on the sacred way from Athens to Eleusis were made in honor of Demeter and Persephone, and made mystical allusions to events in the life of both, and of the infant Iacchus. These processions were made in the daytime, but the initiation was nocturnal, and was reserved for the nights of the sixth and seventh days.

The herald opened the ceremonies of initiation into the greater mysteries by the proclamation, ἐκάς, ἐκάς, ἔστε βέβηλοι, "Retire, O ye profane." Thus were the sacred precincts tiled. The aspirant was clothed with the skin of a calf. An oath of secrecy was administered, and he was then asked, "Have you eaten bread?" The reply to which was, "I have fasted; I have drunk the sacred mixture; I have taken it out of the chest; I have spun; I have placed it in the basket, and from the basket laid it in the chest." By this reply, the aspirant showed that he had been duly prepared by initiation into the lesser mysteries; for Clement of Alexandria says that this formula was a shibboleth, or password, by which the mystæ, or initiates, into the lesser mysteries were known as such, and admitted to the epopteia or greater initiation. The gesture of spinning wool, in imitation of what Demeter did in the time of her affliction, seemed also to be used as a sign of recognition.

The aspirant was now clothed in the sacred tunic, and awaited in the vestibule the opening of the doors of the sanctuary.

What subsequently took place must be left in great part to conjecture, although modern writers have availed themselves of all the allusions that are to be found in the ancients. The temple consisted of three parts: the *megaron*, or sanctuary, corresponding to the holy place of the Temple of Solomon; the *anactoron*, or holy of holies, and a subterranean apartment beneath the temple. Each of these was probably occupied at a different portion of the initiation. The representation of the infernal regions, and the punishment of the uninitiated impious was appropriated to the subterranean apartment, and was, as Sylvestre de Sacy says (*Notes to St. Croix*, i., 360), an episode of the drama which represented the adventures of Isis, Osiris, and Typhon, or of Demeter, Persephone, and Pluto. This drama, the same author thinks, represented the carrying away of Persephone, the travels of Demeter in search of her lost daughter, her descent into hell; the union of Pluto with Persephone, and was terminated by the return of Demeter into the upper world and the light of day. The representation of this drama commenced immediately after the profane had been sent from the temple. And it is easy to understand how the groans and wailings with which the temple at one time resounded might symbolize the sufferings and the death of man, and the subsequent rejoicings at the return of the goddess might be typical of the joy for the restoration of the soul to eternal life. Others have conjectured that the drama of the mysteries represented, in the deportation of Persephone to Hades by Pluto, the departure, as

it were, of the sun, or the deprivation of its vivific power during the winter months, and her reappearance on earth, the restoration of the prolific sun in summer. Others again tell us that the last act of the mysteries represented the restoration to life of the murdered Zagreus, or Dionysus, by Demeter. Diodorus says that the members of the body of Zagreus lacerated by the Titans was represented in the ceremonies of mysteries, as well as in the Orphic hymns; but he prudently adds that he was not allowed to reveal the details to the uninitiated. Whatever was the precise method of symbolism, it is evident that the true interpretation was the restoration from death to eternal life, and that the funereal part of the initiation referred to a loss, and the exultation afterward to a recovery. Hence it was folly to deny the coincidence that exists between this Eleusinian drama and that enacted in the Third Degree of Masonry. It is not claimed that the one was the uninterrupted successor of the other, but there must have been a common ideal source for the origin of both. The lesson, the dogma, the symbol, and the method of instruction are the same. Having now, as Pindar says, "descended beneath the hollow earth, and beheld those mysteries," the initiate ceased to be a *mystes*, or blind man, and was thenceforth called an *epopt*, a word signifying *he who beholds*.

The Eleusinian mysteries, which, by their splendor, surpassed all contemporary institutions of the kind, were deemed of so much importance as to be taken under the special protection of the state, and to the council of five hundred were entrusted the observance of the ordinances which regulated them. By a law of Solon, the magistrates met every year at the close of the festival, to pass sentence upon any who had violated or transgressed any of the rules which governed the administration of the sacred rites. Any attempt to disclose the esoteric ceremonies of initiation was punished with death. Plutarch tells us, in his *Life of Alcibiades*, that that votary of pleasure was indicted for sacrilege, because he had imitated the mysteries, and shown them to his companions in the same dress as that worn by the Hierophant; and we get from Livy (xxxi. 14), the following relation:

Two Acarnanian youths, who had not been initiated, accidentally entered the temple of Demeter during the celebration of the mysteries. They were soon detected by their absurd questions, and being carried to the managers of the temple, although it was evident that their intrusion was accidental, they were put to death for so horrible a crime. It is not, therefore, surprising that, in the account of them, we should find such uncertain and even conflicting assertions of the ancient writers, who hesitated to discuss publicly so forbidden a subject.

The qualifications for initiation were maturity of age and purity of life. Such was the theory, although in practise these qualifications were not always rigidly regarded. But the early doctrine was that none but the pure, morally and ceremonially, could be admitted to initiation. At first, too, the right of admission was restricted to natives of Greece; but even in the time of Herodotus this law was dispensed with, and the citizens of all countries were considered eligible. So in time these mysteries were extended beyond the limits of Greece, and in the days of the empire they were introduced into Rome, where they became exceedingly popular.

The scenic representations, the participation in secret signs and words of recognition, the instruction in a peculiar dogma, and the establishment of a hidden bond of fraternity, gave attraction to these mysteries, which lasted until the very fall of the Roman Empire, and exerted a powerful influence on the mystical associations of the Middle Ages. The bond of union which connects them with the modern initiations of Freemasonry is evident in the common thought which pervades and identifies both; though it is difficult, and perhaps impossible, to trace all the connecting links of the historic chain. We see the beginning and we see the end of one pervading idea, but the central point is hidden from us to await some future discoverer.

Eleven. In the Prestonian lectures, eleven was a mystical number, and was the final series of steps in the winding stairs of the Fellow-Craft, which were said to consist of 3, 5, 7, 9, and 11. The eleven was referred to the eleven apostles after the defection of Judas, and to the eleven sons of Jacob after Joseph went into Egypt. But when the lectures were revived by Hemming, the eleven was struck out. In Templar Masonry, however, eleven is still significant as being the constitutional number required to open a Commandery; and here it is evidently allusive of the eleven true disciples.

Eligibility for Initiation. See *Qualifications of Candidates.*

Elihoreph. One of Solomon's secretaries. (See *Ahiah.*)

Elizabeth of England. Anderson (*Constitutions*, 1738, p. 80) states that the following circumstance is recorded of this sovereign: Hearing that the Masons were in possession of secrets which they would not reveal, and being jealous of all secret assemblies, she sent an armed force to York, with intent to break up their annual Grand Lodge. This design, however, was happily frustrated by the interposition of Sir Thomas Sackville, who took care to initiate some of the chief officers whom she had sent on this duty. They joined in communication with the Masons, and made so favorable a report to the queen on their return that she countermanded her orders, and never afterward attempted to disturb the meetings of the Fraternity. [What authority, if any, Anderson had for the story is unknown.]

Elizabeth of Portugal. In May, 1792, this queen, having conceived a suspicion of the Lodges in Madeira, gave an order to the gov-

ernor to arrest all the Freemasons in the island, and deliver them over to the Inquisition. The rigorous execution of this order occasioned an emigration of many families, ten of whom repaired to New York, and were liberally assisted by the Masons of that city.

Elohim. אלהים. A name applied in Hebrew to any deity, but sometimes also to the true God. According to Lanci, it means *the most beneficent.* It is not, however, much used in Masonry.

It is an expression used throughout the first chapter of Genesis, as applied to God in the *exercise of His creative power*, and signifies the "Divine Omnipotence, the Source of all power, the Power of all powers," which was in *activity* in the Creation. After which the expression used for Deity is Jehovah, which implies the *Providence* of God, and which could not have been active until the world had been created by Elohim.

Eloquence of Masonry. Lawyers boast of the eloquence of the bar, and point to the arguments of counsel in well-known cases; the clergy have the eloquence of the pulpit exhibited in sermons, many of which have a world-wide reputation; and statesmen vaunt of the eloquence of Congress—some of the speeches, however, being indebted, it is said, for their power and beauty, to the talent of the stenographic reporter rather than to the member who is supposed to be the author.

Freemasonry, too, has its eloquence, which is sometimes, although not always, of a very high order. This eloquence is to be found in the addresses, orations, and discourses which have usually been delivered on the great festivals of the Order, at consecrations of Lodges, dedications of halls, and the laying of foundation-stones. These addresses constitute, in fact, the principal part of the early literature of Freemasonry. (See *Addresses, Masonic.*)

Elu. The Fourth Degree of the French Rite. (See *Elus.*)

Elul. אלל. The sixth month of the ecclesiastical and the twelfth of the civil year of the Jews. The twelfth also, therefore, of the Masonic calendar used in the Ancient and Accepted Scottish Rite. It begins on the new moon of August or September, and consists of twenty-nine days.

Elus. The French word *elu* means *elected;* and the degrees, whose object is to detail the detection and punishment of the actors in the crime traditionally related in the Third Degree, are called Elus, or the degrees of the Elected, because they referred to those of the Craft who were chosen or elected to make the discovery, and to inflict the punishment. They form a particular system of Masonry, and are to be found in every Rite, if not in all in name, at least in principle. In the York and American Rites, the Elu is incorporated in the Master's Degree; in the French Rite it constitutes an independent degree; and in the Scottish Rite it consists of three degrees, the Ninth, Tenth, and Eleventh. Ragon counts the five preceding degrees among the Elus, but they more properly belong to the Order of Masters.

The symbolism of these Elu degrees has been greatly mistaken and perverted by anti-Masonic writers, who have thus attributed to Masonry a spirit of vengeance which is not its characteristic. They must be looked upon as conveying only a symbolic meaning. Those higher degrees, in which the object of the election is changed and connected with Templarism, are more properly called *Kadoshes*. Thory says that all the Elus are derived from the degree of Kadosh, which preceded them. The reverse, we think, is the truth. The Elu system sprang naturally from the Master's Degree, and was only applied to Templarism when De Molay was substituted for Hiram the Builder.

Emanation. Literally, "a flowing forth." The doctrine of emanations was a theory predominant in many of the Oriental religions, such, especially, as Brahmanism and Parseeism, and subsequently adopted by the Kabbalists and the Gnostics, and taught by Philo and Plato. It assumed that all things emanated, flowed forth (which is the literal meaning of the word), or were developed and descended by degrees from the Supreme Being. Thus, in the ancient religion of India, the *anima mundi*, or soul of the word, the mysterious source of all life, was identified with Brahma, the Supreme God. The doctrine of Gnosticism was that all beings emanated from the Deity; that there was a progressive degeneration of these beings from the highest to the lowest emanation, and a final redemption and return of all to the purity of the Creator. Philo taught that the Supreme Being was the Primitive Light or the Archetype of Light, whose rays illuminate, as from a common source, all souls. The theory of emanations is interesting to the Mason, because of the reference in many of the higher degrees to the doctrines of Philo, the Gnostics, and the Kabbalists.

Emanuel. A sacred word in some of the high degrees, being one of the names applied in Scripture to the Lord Jesus Christ. It is a Greek form from the Hebrew, Immanuel, עמנואל, and signifies "God is with us."

Embassy. The embassy of Zerubbabel and four other Jewish chiefs to the court of Darius, to obtain the protection of that monarch from the encroachments of the Samaritans, who interrupted the labors in the reconstruction of the Temple, constitutes the legend of the Sixteenth Degree of the Ancient and Accepted Scottish Rite, and also of the Red Cross Degree of the American Rite, which is surely borrowed from the former. The history of this embassy is found in the eleventh book of the *Antiquities* of Josephus, whence the Masonic ritualists have undoubtedly taken it. The only authority of Josephus is the apocryphal record of Esdras, and the authenticity of the whole transaction is doubted or denied by modern historians.

Emblem. The emblem is an occult representation of something unknown or concealed by a sign or thing that is known. Thus, a square is in Freemasonry an emblem of morality; a plumb line, of rectitude of conduct; and a level, of equality of human conditions. *Emblem* is very generally used as synonymous with *symbol*, although the two words do not express exactly the same meaning. An emblem is properly a representation of an idea by a visible object, as in the examples quoted above; but a symbol is more extensive in its application, includes every representation of an idea by an image, whether that image is presented immediately to the senses as a visible and tangible substance, or only brought before the mind by words. Hence an action or event as described, a myth or legend, may be a symbol; and hence, too, it follows that while all emblems are symbols, all symbols are not emblems. (See *Symbol*.)

Emerald. In Hebrew, נפך, *caphak*. It was the first stone in the first row of the high priest's breastplate, and was referred to Levi. Adam Clarke says it is the same stone as the smaragdus, and is of a bright green color. Josephus, the Septuagint, and the Jerusalem Targum understood by the Hebrew word the carbuncle, which is red. The modern emerald, as everybody knows, is green.

Emergency. The general law of Masonry requires a month to elapse between the time of receiving a petition for initiation and that of balloting for the candidate, and also that there shall be an interval of one month between the reception of each of the degrees of Craft Masonry. Cases sometimes occur when a Lodge desires this probationary period to be dispensed with, so that the candidate's petition may be received and balloted for at the same communication, or so that the degrees may be conferred at much shorter intervals. As some reason must be assigned for the application to the Grand Master for the dispensation, such reason is generally stated to be that the candidate is about to go on a long journey, or some other equally valid. Cases of this kind are called, in the technical language of Masonry, *cases of emergency*. It is evident that the emergency is made for the sake of the candidate, and not for that of the Lodge or of Masonry. The too frequent occurrence of applications for dispensations in cases of emergency have been a fruitful source of evil, as thereby unworthy persons, escaping the ordeal of an investigation into character, have been introduced into the Order; and even where the candidates have been worthy, the rapid passing through the degrees prevents a due impression from being made on the mind, and the candidate fails to justly appreciate the beauties and merits of the Masonic system. Hence, these cases of emergency have been very unpopular with the most distinguished members of the Fraternity. In the olden time the Master and Wardens of the Lodge were vested with the prerogative of deciding what was a case of emergency; but modern law and usage (in America, at least) make the Grand Master the sole judge of what constitutes a case of emergency. [Under the English Constitution the emergency must be real in the opinion of the Master of the Lodge concerned. (Rule 185.)]

Emergent Lodge. A Lodge held at an emergent meeting.

Emergent Meeting. The meeting of a Lodge called to elect a candidate, and confer the degrees in a case of emergency, or for any other sudden and unexpected cause, has been called an emergent meeting. The term is not very common, but it has been used by W. S. Mitchell and a few other writers.

Emeritus. Latin; plural, *emeriti.* The Romans applied this word—which comes from the verb *emerere,* to gain by service—to a soldier who had served out his time; hence, in the Supreme Councils of the Ancient and Accepted Scottish Rite of this country, an active member, who resigns his seat by reason of age, infirmity, or for other cause deemed good by the Council, may be elected an Emeritus member, and will possess the privilege of proposing measures and being heard in debate, but not of voting.

Emeth. Hebrew, אמת. One of the words in the high degrees. It signifies *integrity, fidelity, firmness,* and constancy in keeping a promise, and especially TRUTH, as opposed to falsehood. In the Scottish Rite, the Sublime Knights Elect of Twelve of the Eleventh Degree are called "Princes Emeth," which mean simply men of exalted character who are devoted to truth.

Eminent. The title given to the Commander or presiding officer of a Commandery of Knights Templar, and to all officers below the Grand Commander in a Grand Commandery. The Grand Commander is styled "Right Eminent," and the Grand Master of the Grand Encampment of the United States, "Most Eminent." The word is from the Latin *eminens,* "standing above," and literally signifies "exalted in rank." Hence, it is a title given to the cardinals in the Roman Church.

Emounah. (*Fidelity, Truth.*) The name of the Fourth Step of the mystic ladder of the Kadosh of the A. A. Scottish Rite.

Emperor of Lebanon. (*Empereur du Liban.*) This degree, says Thory (*Act. Lat.*, i., 311), which was a part of the collection of M. Le Rouge, was composed in the isle of Bourbon, in 1778, by the Marquis de Beurnonville, who was then National Grand Master of all the Lodges of India.

Emperors of the East and West. In 1758 there was established in Paris a Chapter called the "Council of Emperors of the East and West." The members assumed the titles of "Sovereign Prince Masons," "Substitutes General of the Royal Art," "Grand Superintendents and Officers of the Grand and Sovereign Lodge of St. John of Jerusalem." Their ritual, which was based on the Templar system, consisted of twenty-five degrees, as follows: 1 to 19, the same as the Scottish Rite; 20, Grand Patriarch Noachite; 21, Key of Masonry; 22, Prince of Lebanon; 23, Knight of the Sun; 24, Kadosh; 25, Prince of the Royal Secret. It granted warrants for Lodges of the high degrees, appointed Grand Inspectors and Deputies, and established several subordinate bodies in the interior of France,

among which was a "Council of Princes of the Royal Secret," at Bordeaux. In 1763, one Pincemaille, the Master of the Lodge *La Candeur,* at Metz, began to publish an exposition of these degrees in the serial numbers of a work entitled *Conversations Allegoriques sur la Franche-Maçonnerie.* In 1764, the Grand Lodge of France offered him 300 livres to suppress the book. Pincemaille accepted the bribe, but continued the publication, which lasted until 1766.

In 1758, the year of their establishment in France, the degrees of this Rite of Heredom, or of Perfection, as it was called, were carried by the Marquis de Bernez to Berlin, and adopted by the Grand Lodge of the Three Globes.

Between the years 1760 and 1765, there was much dissension in the Rite. A new Council, called the Knights of the East, was established at Paris, in 1760, as the rival of the Emperors of the East and West. The controversies of these two bodies were carried into the Grand Lodge, which, in 1766, was compelled, for the sake of peace, to issue a decree in opposition to the high degrees, excluding the malcontents, and forbidding the symbolical Lodges to recognize the authority of these Chapters. But the excluded Masons continued to work clandestinely and to grant warrants. From that time until its dissolution, the history of the Council of the Emperors of the East and West is but a history of continuous disputes with the Grand Lodge of France. At length, in 1781, it was completely absorbed in the Grand Orient, and has no longer an existence.

The assertion of Thory (*Act. Lat.*), and of Ragon (*Orthod. Mac.*), that the Council of the Emperors of the East and West was the origin of the Ancient and Accepted Rite, although it has been denied, does not seem destitute of truth. It is very certain, if the documentary evidence is authentic, that the Constitutions of 1672 were framed by this Council; and it is equally certain that under these Constitutions a patent was granted to Stephen Morin, through whom the Ancient and Accepted Scottish Rite was established in America.

Emunah. אמונה. Sometimes spelled *Amunah,* but not in accordance with the Masoretic points. A significant word in the high degrees signifying fidelity, especially in fulfilling one's promises.

Encampment. All regular assemblies of Knights Templar were formerly called Encampments. They are now styled Commanderies in America, and Grand Encampments of the States are called Grand Commanderies. In England they are now called "Preceptories." (See *Commandery* and *Commandery, Grand.*)

Encampment, General Grand. The title, before the adoption of the Constitution of 1856, of the Grand Encampment of the United States.

Encampment, Grand. The Grand Encampment of the United States was instituted on the 22d of June, 1816, in the city of New York. It consists of a Grand Master, Deputy Grand Master, and other Grand Officers who are similar to those of a Grand Commandery, with Past Grand Officers and the representatives of the various Grand Commanderies, and of the subordinate Commanderies deriving their warrants immediately from it. It exercises jurisdiction over all the Templars of the United States, and meets triennially. The term Encampment is borrowed from military usage, and is very properly applied to the temporary congregation at stated periods of the army of Templars, who may be said to be, for the time being, in camp.

Encyclical. Circular; sent to many places or persons. Encyclical letters, containing information, advice, or admonition, are sometimes issued by Grand Lodges or Grand Masters to the Lodges and Masons of a jurisdiction. The word is not in very common use; but in 1848 the Grand Lodge of South Carolina issued "an encyclical letter of advice, of admonition, and of direction," to the subordinate Lodges under her jurisdiction; and a similar letter was issued in 1865 by the Grand Master of Iowa.

En famille. French, meaning *as a family*. In French Lodges, during the reading of the minutes, and sometimes when the Lodge is engaged in the discussion of delicate matters affecting only itself, the Lodge is said to meet "en famille," at which time visitors are not admitted.

England. The following is a brief *résumé* of the history of Freemasonry in England as it has hitherto been written, and is now generally received by the Fraternity. It is but right, however, to say, that recent researches have thrown doubts on the authenticity of many of the statements—that the legend of Prince Edwin has been doubted; the establishment of a Grand Lodge at York in the beginning of the eighteenth century denied; and the existence of anything but Operative Masonry before 1717 controverted. These questions are still in dispute; but the labors of Masonic antiquaries, through which many old records and ancient constitutions are being continually exhumed from the British Museum and from Lodge libraries, will eventually enable us to settle upon the truth.

According to Anderson and Preston, the first charter granted in England to the Masons, as a body, was bestowed by King Athelstan, in 926, upon the application of his brother, Prince Edwin. "Accordingly," says Anderson, quoting from the "Old Constitutions" (*Constitutions*, 1738, p. 64), "Prince Edwin summon'd all the Free and Accepted Masons in the Realm, to meet him in a Congregation at York, who came and form'd the Grand Lodge under him as their Grand Master, A.D. 926.

"They brought with them many old Writings and Records of the Craft, some in Greek, some in Latin, some in French, and other Languages; and from the Contents thereof, they fram'd the Constitutions of the English Lodges, and made a Law for Themselves, to preserve and observe the same in all Time coming, &c, &c, &c."

From this assembly at York, the rise of Masonry in England is generally dated; from the statutes there enacted are derived the English Masonic Constitutions; and from the place of meeting, the ritual of the English Lodges is designated as the "Ancient York Rite."

For a long time the York Assembly exercised the Masonic jurisdiction over all England; but in 1567 the Masons of the southern part of the island elected Sir Thomas Gresham, the celebrated merchant, their Grand Master, according to Anderson. (*Constitutions*, 1738, p. 81.) He was succeeded by the Earl of Effingham, the Earl of Huntingdon, and by the illustrious architect, Inigo Jones.

In the beginning of the eighteenth century, Masonry in the south of England had fallen into decay. The disturbances of the revolution, which placed William III. on the throne, and the subsequent warmth of political feelings which agitated the two parties of the state, had given this peaceful society a wound fatal to its success. But in 1716 "the few Lodges at London finding themselves neglected by Sir Christopher Wren, thought fit to cement under a Grand Master as the Center of Union and Harmony," and so four of the London Lodges "met at the Apple-Tree Tavern; and having put into the chair the oldest Master Mason, (now the Master of a Lodge,) they constituted themselves a Grand Lodge, *pro tempore*, in due form, and forthwith revived the quarterly communication of the officers of Lodges, (called the Grand Lodge,) resolved to hold the annual assembly and feast, and then to choose a Grand Master from among themselves, till they should have the honor of a noble brother at their head." (Anderson, *Constitutions*, 1738, p. 109.)

Accordingly, on St. John the Baptist's Day, 1717, the annual assembly and feast were held, and Mr. Anthony Sayer duly proposed and elected Grand Master. The Grand Lodge adopted, among its regulations, the following: "That the privilege of assembling as Masons, which had hitherto been unlimited, should be vested in certain Lodges or assemblies of Masons convened in certain places; and that every Lodge to be hereafter convened, except the four old Lodges at this time existing, should be legally authorized to act by a warrant from the Grand Master for the time being, granted to certain individuals by petition, with the consent and approbation of the Grand Lodge in communication; and that, without such warrant no Lodge should be hereafter deemed regular or constitutional."

In compliment, however, to the four old Lodges, the privileges which they had always possessed under the old organization were particularly reserved to them; and it was enacted that "no law, rule, or regulation, to be hereafter made or passed in Grand Lodge, should deprive them of such privilege, or encroach on any landmark which was at that time established as the standard of Masonic government." (Preston, *Illustrations*, ed. 1792, pp. 248, 249.)

The Grand Lodges of York and of London kept up a friendly intercourse, and mutual interchange of recognition, until the latter body, in 1725, granted a warrant of constitution to some Masons who had seceded from the former. This unmasonic act was severely reprobated by the York Grand Lodge, and produced the first interruption to the harmony that had long subsisted between them. It was, however, followed some years after by another unjustifiable act of interference. In 1735, the Earl of Crawford, Grand Master of England, constituted two Lodges within the jurisdiction of the Grand Lodge of York, and granted, without its consent, deputations for Lancashire, Durham, and Northumberland. "This circumstance," says Preston (*Illust.*, ed. 1792, p. 279), "the Grand Lodge at York highly resented, and ever afterward viewed the proceedings of the brethren in the south with a jealous eye. All friendly intercourse ceased, and the York Masons, from that moment, considered their interests distinct from the Masons under the Grand Lodge in London."

Three years after, in 1738, several brethren, dissatisfied with the conduct of the Grand Lodge of England, seceded from it, and held unauthorized meetings for the purpose of initiation. Taking advantage of the breach between the Grand Lodges of York and London, they assumed the character of York Masons. On the Grand Lodge's determination to put strictly in execution the laws against such seceders, they still further separated from its jurisdiction, and assumed the appellation of "*Ancient York Masons.*" They announced that the ancient landmarks were alone preserved by them; and, declaring that the regular Lodges had adopted new plans, and sanctioned innovations, they branded them with the name of "*Modern Masons.*" In 1739, they established a new Grand Lodge in London, under the name of the "Grand Lodge of Ancient York Masons," and, persevering in the measures they had adopted, held communications and appointed annual feasts. They were soon afterward recognized by the Masons of Scotland and Ireland, and were encouraged and fostered by many of the nobility. The two Grand Lodges continued to exist, and to act in opposition to each other, extending their schisms into other countries, especially into America, until the year 1813, when, under the Grand Mastership of the Duke of Sussex, they were united under the title of the United Grand Lodge of England.

Such is the history of Freemasonry in England as uninterruptedly believed by all Masons and Masonic writers for nearly a century and a half. Recent researches have thrown great doubts on its entire accuracy. Until the year 1717, the details are either traditional, or supported only by manuscripts whose authenticity has not yet been satisfactorily proved. Much of the history is uncertain; some of it, especially as referring to York, is deemed apocryphal by Hughan and other laborious writers, and Bro. Henry Sadler in his *Masonic Facts and Fictions* has proved that the "Ancients"

were not really a schismatic body of seceders from the Premier Grand Lodge of England, but were Irish Masons settled in London, who, in 1751, established a body which they called the "Grand Lodge of England according to the Old Institutions," maintaining that they alone preserved the ancient tenets and practises of Masonry. (See *Ancient Masons.*) [E. L. H.]

England, Grand Lodges in. During one period of the eighteenth century there existed four Grand Lodges in England: 1. "The G. Lodge of England," located at London; 2. "The G. Lodge of all England," located at York; 3. "The G. Lodge of England according to the Old Institutions"; and, 4. "The G. Lodge of England south of the river Trent," which last two had their G. East at London.

The first Grand Lodge was formed in 1717. The second G. Lodge bears date 1725, and emanated from that immemorial Masonic Lodge that gave such reverence to the city of York. The third was established in 1751 by some Irish Masons settled in London. (See *Ancient Masons.*) And the fourth, whose existence lasted from 1779 to 1789, was instituted by the York Grand Lodge in compliance with the request of members of the Lodge of Antiquity, of London; but its existence was ephemeral, in consequence of the removal of the disturbing cause with the regular G. Lodge. Recently evidence has been found pointing to the existence in London from 1770 to 1775 of a fifth Grand Lodge, formed by Scotch Masons, with some four or five Lodges under its control. (*Ars Quatuor Coronatorum*, xviii., pp. 69–90.) [E. L. H.]

All subordinate Lodges existing at present, which had their being prior to the union, in December, 1813, were subjects of either the first or the third of the above designated four G. Lodges, and known respectively as the "Moderns" or the "Ancients," these titles, however, having no recognized force as to the relative antiquity of either.

England, The First Record of Grand Lodge of. Bro. R. F. Gould (*Hist. of F. M.*, ii., 373) furnishes the valuable information that the minutes of Grand Lodge commence 24th June, 1723, and those bearing such date are signed by "John Theophilus Desaguliers, Deputy Grand Master." They are entered in a *different handwriting*, under date of 25th November, 1723, 19th February, 1724, 28th "Aprill 1724," and are *not* signed at foot. On 24th June, 1724, the Earl of Dalkeith presided in Grand Lodge, and the following signatures are appended to the recorded minutes:

"Dalkeith, G. M., 1724."
"J. T. Desaguliers, G. M."
"Fra Sorrell, Senr., G. W."
"John Senex, Junr."

The minutes of 21st November, 1724, 17th March, 20th May, 24th June, and 27th November, 1725, are unsigned. But to those of 27th December, 1725, are appended the signatures of

"Richmond & Lenox, G. M., 1725,"
"M. ffolkes, D. G. M.,"
and two G. Wardens.

Signatures are again wanting to the proceedings of 28th February and 12th December, 1726, but reappear under date of 27th "ffebry 1726" [27], viz.:

"Paisley, G. Mr., 1726,"

and the next three succeeding officers.

The minutes of the following 10th May (1727) were signed by "Inchiquin, G. M., 1727," and the three officers next in rank.

The *earliest* minutes were not signed on confirmation at the next meeting but were verified by the *four* Grand Officers, or such of them as took part in the proceedings recorded. In consequence of the reelection of Dr. Desaguliers as Dep. G. M. the minutes say that "the late Grand Master went away from the Hall without any ceremony." [E. L. H.]

Englet. A corruption of *Euclid*, found in the Old Constitutions known as the Matthew Cooke MS., "wherefore yᵉ forsayde maister *Englet* ordeynet thei were passing of conying schold be passing honoured." (Ll. 674–7.) Perhaps the copyist mistook a badly made old English **u** for an **n**, and the original had *Euglet*, which would be a nearer approximation to Euclid.

Engrave. In French Lodges, *buriner*, to engrave, is used instead of *ecrire*, to write. The "engraved tablets" are the "written records."

Enlightened. This word, equivalent to the Latin *illuminatus*, is frequently used to designate a Freemason as one who has been rescued from darkness, and received intellectual light. Webster's definition shows its appositeness: "Illuminated; instructed; informed; furnished with clear views." Many old Latin diplomas commence with the heading, "Omnibus illuminatis," i. e., "to all the enlightened."

Enlightenment, Shock of. See *Shock of Enlightenment*.

Enoch. Though the Scriptures furnish but a meager account of Enoch, the traditions of Freemasonry closely connect him, by numerous circumstances, with the early history of the Institution. All, indeed, that we learn from the Book of Genesis on the subject of his life is, that he was the seventh of the patriarchs; the son of Jared, and the great-grand-father of Noah; that he was born in the year of the world 622; that his life was one of eminent virtue, so much so, that he is described as "walking with God"; and that in the year 987 his earthly pilgrimage was terminated (as the commentators generally suppose), not by death, but by a bodily translation to heaven.

In the very commencement of our inquiries, we shall find circumstances in the life of this great patriarch that shadow forth, as it were, something of that mysticism with which the traditions of Masonry have connected him. His name, in the Hebrew language, הנך, *Henoch*, signifies *to initiate and to instruct*, and seems intended to express the fact that he was, as Oliver remarks, the first to give a decisive character to the rite of initiation and to add to the practise of Divine worship the study and application of human science. In confirmation of this view, a writer in the *Freemasons' Quarterly Review* says, on this subject, that "it seems probable that Enoch introduced the speculative principles into the Masonic creed, and that he originated its exclusive character," which theory must be taken, if it is accepted at all, with very considerable modifications.

The years of his life may also be supposed to contain a mystic meaning, for they amounted to three hundred and sixty-five, being exactly equal to a solar revolution. In all the ancient rites this number has occupied a prominent place, because it was the representative of the annual course of that luminary which, as the great fructifier of the earth, was the peculiar object of divine worship.

Of the early history of Enoch, we know nothing. It is, however, probable that, like the other descendants of the pious Seth, he passed his pastoral life in the neighborhood of Mount Moriah. From the other patriarchs he differed only in this, that, enlightened by the Divine knowledge which had been imparted to him, he instructed his contemporaries in the practise of those rites, and in the study of those sciences, with which he had himself become acquainted.

The Oriental writers abound in traditionary evidence of the learning of the venerable patriarch. One tradition states that he received from God the gift of wisdom and knowledge, and that God sent him thirty volumes from heaven, filled with all the secrets of the most mysterious sciences. The Babylonians supposed him to have been intimately acquainted with the nature of the stars; and they attribute to him the invention of astrology. The Rabbis maintain that he was taught by God and Adam how to sacrifice, and how to worship the Deity aright. The Kabbalistic book of Raziel says that he received the Divine mysteries from Adam, through the direct line of the preceding patriarchs.

The Greek Christians supposed him to have been identical with the first Egyptian Hermes, who dwelt at Sais. They say he was the first to give instruction on the celestial bodies; that he foretold the deluge that was to overwhelm his descendants; and that he built the Pyramids, engraving thereon figures of artificial instruments and the elements of the sciences, fearing lest the memory of man should perish in that general destruction. Eupolemus, a Grecian writer, makes him the same as Atlas, and attributes to him, as the Pagans did to that deity, the invention of astronomy.

Mr. Wait, in his *Oriental Antiquities*, quotes a passage from Bar Hebræus, a Jewish writer, which asserts that Enoch was the first who invented books and writing; that he taught men the art of building cities; that he discovered the knowledge of the Zodiac and the course of the planets; and that he inculcated the worship of God by fasting, prayer, alms, votive offerings, and tithes. Bar Hebræus adds, that he also appointed festivals for sacrifices to the sun at the periods when that luminary entered each of the zodiacal signs; but this statement, which would make him the author of idolatry, is entirely inconsistent with all that we know of his character, from both history and tradition, and arose, as Oliver supposes, most probably from a blending of the characters of Enos and Enoch.

In the study of the sciences, in teaching them to his children and his contemporaries, and in instituting the rites of initiation, Enoch is supposed to have passed the years of his peaceful, his pious, and his useful life, until the crimes of mankind had increased to such a height that, in the expressive words of Holy Writ, "every imagination of the thoughts of man's heart was only evil continually." It was then, according to a Masonic tradition, that Enoch, disgusted with the wickedness that surrounded him, and appalled at the thought of its inevitable consequences, fled to the solitude and secrecy of Mount Moriah, and devoted himself to prayer and pious contemplation. It was on that spot—then first consecrated by this patriarchal hermitage, and afterward to be made still more holy by the sacrifices of Abraham, of David, and of Solomon—that we are informed that the Shekinah, or sacred presence, appeared to him, and gave him those instructions which were to preserve the wisdom of the antediluvians to their posterity when the world, with the exception of but one family, should have been destroyed by the forthcoming flood. The circumstances which occurred at that time are recorded in a tradition which forms what has been called the great Masonic "Legend of Enoch," and which runs to this effect:

Enoch, being inspired by the Most High, and in commemoration of a wonderful vision, built a temple under ground, and dedicated it to God. His son, Methuselah, constructed the building; although he was not acquainted with his father's motives for the erection. This temple consisted of nine brick vaults, situated perpendicularly beneath each other, and communicating by apertures left in the arch of each vault.

Enoch then caused a triangular plate of gold to be made, each side of which was a cubit long; he enriched it with the most precious stones, and encrusted the plate upon a stone of agate of the same form. On the plate he engraved, in ineffable characters, the true name of Deity, and, placing it on a cubical pedestal of white marble, he deposited the whole within the deepest arch.

When this subterranean building was completed, he made a door of stone, and attaching to it a ring of iron, by which it might be occasionally raised, he placed it over the opening of the uppermost arch, and so covered it over that the aperture could not be discovered. Enoch himself was permitted to enter it but once a year; and on the death of Enoch, Methuselah, and Lamech, and the destruction of the world by the deluge, all knowledge of this temple, and of the sacred treasure which it contained, was lost until, in after times, it was accidentally discovered by another worthy of Freemasonry, who, like Enoch,

was engaged in the erection of a temple on the same spot.

The legend goes on to inform us that after Enoch had completed the subterranean temple, fearing that the principles of those arts and sciences which he had cultivated with so much assiduity would be lost in that general destruction of which he had received a prophetic vision, he erected two pillars—the one of marble, to withstand the influence of fire, and the other of brass, to resist the action of water. On the pillar of brass he engraved the history of the creation, the principles of the arts and sciences, and the doctrines of Speculative Freemasonry as they were practised in his times; and on the one of marble he inscribed characters in hieroglyphics, importing that near the spot where they stood a precious treasure was deposited in a subterranean vault.

Josephus gives an account of these pillars in the first book of his *Antiquities*. He ascribes them to the children of Seth, which is by no means a contradiction of the Masonic tradition, since Enoch was one of these children. "That their inventions," says the historian, "might not be lost before they were sufficiently known, upon Adam's prediction that the world was to be destroyed at one time by the force of fire and at another time by the violence and quantity of water, they made two pillars—the one of brick, the other of stone; they inscribed their discoveries on them both, that in case the pillar of brick should be destroyed by the flood, the pillar of stone might remain and exhibit those discoveries to mankind, and also inform them that there was another pillar of brick erected by them. Now this remains in the land of Siriad to this day."

Enoch, having completed these labors, called his descendants around him on Mount Moriah, and having warned them in the most solemn manner of the consequences of their wickedness, exhorted them to forsake their idolatries and return once more to the worship of the true God. Masonic tradition informs us that he then delivered up the government of the Craft to his grandson, Lamech, and disappeared from earth.

Enoch, Brother. (*Frère Enoch.*) Evidently the *nom de plume* of a French writer and the inventor of a Masonic rite. He published at Liege, in 1773, two works: 1. *Le Vrai Franc-Maçon*, in 276 pages; 2. *Lettres Maçonniques pour servir de Supplement au Vrai Franc-Maçon.* The design of the former of these works was to give an account of the origin and object of Freemasonry, a description of all the degrees, and an answer to the objections urged against the Institution. The historical theories of Frère Enoch were exceedingly fanciful and wholly untenable. Thus, he asserts that in the year 814, Louis the Fair of France, being flattered by the fidelity and devotion of the Operative Masons, organized them into a society of four degrees, granting the Masters the privilege of wearing swords in the Lodge—a custom still continued in French Lodges—and, having been received into the Order himself, accepted the Grand Mastership on the festival of St. John the Evangelist in the year 814. Other equally extravagant opinions make his book rather a source of amusement than of instruction. His definition of Freemasonry is, however, good. He says that it is "a holy and religious society of men who are friends, which has for its *foundation*, discretion; for its *object*, the service of God, fidelity to the sovereign, and love of our neighbor; and for its *doctrine*, the erection of an allegorical building dedicated to the virtues, which it teaches with certain signs of recognition."

Enoch, Legend of. This legend is detailed in a preceding article. It never formed any part of the old system of Masonry, and was first introduced from Talmudic and Rabbinical sources into the high degrees, where, however, it is really to be viewed rather as symbolical than as historical. Enoch himself is but the symbol of initiation, and his legend is intended symbolically to express the doctrine that the true Word or Divine truth was preserved in the ancient initiations.

Enoch, Rite of. A Rite attempted to be established at Liege, in France, about the year 1773. It consisted of four degrees, viz., 1. *Manouvre*, or Apprentice, whose object was friendship and benevolence. 2. *Ouvrier*, or Fellow-Craft, whose object was fidelity to the Sovereign. 3. *Maître*, or Master, whose object was submission to the Supreme Being. 4. *Architecte*, whose object was the perfection of all the virtues. The Rite never made much progress.

Enochian Alphabet. One of the most important alphabets, or ciphers, known to historic Masons is the *Enochian*, in consequence of the revelations made in that char-

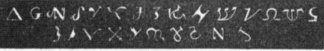

acter. Tradition says the Christian princes were accompanied in their journey to Palestine by Freemasons, who fought by their side, and who, when at the Holy City, discovered important MSS., on which some of the historic degrees were founded; that some of these MSS. were in Syriac and others in Enochian characters; and that on their return, when at Venice, it was ascertained that the characters were identical with those in the Syriac column, spoken of by Josephus, and with the oldest copies in which the Book of Enoch was written, and are of great antiquity. The brethren in the A. A. Scottish Rite are largely instructed as to matters pertaining hereto in the Thirteenth and Fourteenth degrees.

We present an exact copy of the alphabet, as may be found by comparison with that in the Bodleian Library.

The name He No C H, in Hebrew, signifies "*taught*," or, more properly, "*dedicated*." In the *Koran* Enoch is called "Edris," from *dar-*

asa, to study, which word, more liberally translated, means, "to read or to study with attention." (See *Enoch*.)

En Soph. סוֹף אֵין. In the Kabbalistic doctrines, the Divine Word, or Supreme Creator, is called the En Soph, or rather the Or En Soph, the Infinite Intellectual Light. The theory is, that all things emanated from this Primeval Light. (See *Kabbala*.)

Entered. When a candidate receives the First Degree of Masonry he is said *to be entered*. It is used in the sense of *admitted*, or *introduced*; a common as well as a Masonic employment of the word, as when we say, "the youth *entered* college"; or, "the soldier *entered* the service."

Entered Apprentice. See *Apprentice, Entered*.

Entick, John. An English clergyman, born about 1703, who took much interest in Freemasonry about the middle of the eighteenth century. He revised the third edition of Anderson's *Constitutions*, by order of the Grand Lodge, which was published in 1756. The next issue of the *Book of Constitutions* (1767) also has his name on the title-page as successor to Dr. Anderson, and is often attributed to him, but it is described as "A new edition . . . by a Committee appointed by the Grand Lodge," and it does not appear that he had anything to do with its preparation. (*Ars Quatuor Coronatorum*, xxi., p. 80.) Entick was also the author of many Masonic sermons, a few of which were published. Oliver speaks of him as a man of grave and sober habits, a good Master of his Lodge, a fair disciplinarian, and popular with the Craft. But Entick did not confine his literary labors to Masonry. He was the author of a *History of the War which ended in 1763*, in 5 vols., 8vo; and a *History of London*, in 4 vols., 8vo. As an orthoepist he had considerable reputation and published a *Latin and English Dictionary*, and an *English Spelling Dictionary*. He died in 1773.   [E. L. H.]

Entombment. An impressive ceremony in the degree of Perfect Master of the Scottish Rite.

Entrance, Points of. See *Points of Entrance, Perfect*.

Entrance, Shock of. See *Shock of Entrance*.

Entrusting. That portion of the ceremony of initiation which consists in communicating to the candidate the modes of recognition.

Envy. This meanest of vices has always been discouraged in Masonry. The fifth of the Old Charges says: "None shall discover envy at the prosperity of a brother." (*Constitutions*, 1723, p. 53.)

Eons. In the doctrine of Gnosticism, Divine spirits occupying the intermediate state which was supposed to exist between the Supreme Being and the Jehovah of the Jewish theology, whom the Gnostics called only a secondary deity. These spiritual beings were indeed no more than abstractions, such as *Wisdom, Faith, Prudence*, etc. They derived their name from the Greek αἰων, *an age*, in reference to the long duration of their existence. Valentinius said there were but thirty of them; but Basilides reckons them as three hundred and sixty-five, which certainly has an allusion to the days of the solar year. In some of the philosophical degrees, references are made to the Eons, whose introduction into them is doubtless to be attributed to the connection of Gnosticism with certain of the high degrees.

Eons, Rite of the. Ragon (*Tuilleur Gen.*, p. 186) describes this Rite as one full of beautiful and learned instruction, but scarcely known, and practised only in Asia, being founded on the religious dogmas of Zoroaster. The existence of it as a genuine Rite is doubtful, for Ragon's information is very meager.

Eostre. Easter, a name given to the paschal festival in the spring of the year.

Ephod. The sacred vestment worn by the high priest of the Jews over the tunic and outer garment. It was without sleeves, and divided below the arm-pits into two parts or halves, one falling before and the other behind, and both reaching to the middle of the thighs. They were joined above on the shoulders by buckles and two large precious stones, on which were inscribed the names of the twelve tribes, six on each. The ephod was a distinctive mark of the priesthood. It was of two kinds, one of plain linen for the priests, and another, richer and embroidered, for the high priest, which was composed of blue, purple, crimson, and fine linen. The robe worn by the high priest in a Royal Arch Chapter is intended to be a representation, but hardly can be called an imitation, of the ephod.

Ephraimites. The descendants of Ephraim. They inhabited the center of Judea between the Mediterranean and the river Jordan. The character given to them in the ritual of the Fellow-Craft's Degree, of being "a stiff-necked and rebellious people," coincides with history, which describes them as haughty, tenacious to a fault of their rights, and ever ready to resist the pretensions of the other tribes, and more especially that of Judah, of which they were peculiarly jealous. The circumstance in their history which has been appropriated for a symbolic purpose in the ceremonies of the Second Degree of Masonry, may be briefly related thus. The Ammonites, who were the descendants of the younger son of Lot, and inhabited a tract of country east of the river Jordan, had been always engaged in hostility against the Israelites. On the occasion referred to, they had commenced a war upon the pretext that the Israelites had deprived them of a portion of their territory. Jephthah, having been called by the Israelites to the head of their army, defeated the Ammonites, but had not called upon the Ephraimites to assist in the victory. Hence, that high-spirited people were incensed, and more especially as they had had no share in the rich spoils obtained by Jephthah from the Ammonites. They accordingly gave him battle, but were defeated with great slaughter by the Gileadites, or countrymen of Jephthah, with

whom alone he resisted their attack. As the land of Gilead, the residence of Jephthah, was on the west side of the Jordan, and as the Ephraimites lived on the east side, in making their invasion it was necessary that they should cross the river, and after their defeat, in attempting to effect a retreat to their own country, they were compelled to recross the river. But Jephthah, aware of this, had placed forces at the different fords of the river, who intercepted the Ephraimites, and detected their nationality by a peculiar defect in their pronunciation. For although the Ephraimites did not speak a dialect different from that of the other tribes, they had a different pronunciation of some words, and an inability to pronounce the letter *ע* or SH, which they pronounced as if it were *ס* or S. Thus, when called upon to say SHIBBOLETH, they pronounced it SIBBOLETH, "which trifling defect," says the ritual, "proved them to be enemies." The test to a Hebrew was a palpable one, for the two words have an entirely different signification; *shibboleth* meaning an *ear of corn*, and *sibboleth*, *a burden*. The biblical relation will be found in the twelfth chapter of the Book of Judges.

Epoch. In chronology, a certain point of time marked by some memorable event at which the calculation of years begins. Different peoples have different epochs or epochas. Thus, the epoch of Christians is the birth of Christ; that of Jews, the creation of the world; and that of Mohammedans, the flight of their prophet from Mecca. See *Calendar.*

Epopt. This was the name given to one who had passed through the Great Mysteries, and been permitted to behold what was concealed from the *mystæ*, who had only been initiated into the Lesser. It signifies an eye-witness, and is derived from the Greek, ἐφοράω, *to look over, to behold.* The epopts repeated the oath of secrecy which had been administered to them on their initiation into the Lesser Mysteries, and were then conducted into the lighted interior of the sanctuary and permitted to behold what the Greeks emphatically termed "the sight," αὐτοψία. The epopts alone were admitted to the sanctuary, for the mystæ were confined to the vestibule of the temple. The epopts were, in fact, the Master Masons of the Mysteries, while the mystæ were the Apprentices and Fellow-Crafts; these words being used, of course, only in a comparative sense.

Equality. Among the ancient iconologists, equality was symbolized by a female figure holding in one hand a pair of scales equipoised and in the other a nest of swallows. The moderns have substituted a level for the scales. And this is the Masonic idea. In Masonry, the level is the symbol of that equality which, as Higgins (*Anac.*, i., 790), says, is the very essence of Freemasonry. "All, let their rank in life be what it may, when in the Lodge are brothers—brethren with the Father at their head. No person can read the Evangelists and not see that this is correctly Gospel Christianity."

Equerry. An officer in some courts who has the charge of horses. For some unknown reason the title has been introduced into some of the high degrees.

Eques. A Latin word signifying *knight*. Every member of the Rite of Strict Observance, on attaining to the seventh or highest degree, received a "characteristic name," which was formed in Latin by the addition of a noun in the ablative case, governed by the preposition *a* or *ab*, to the word *Eques*, as "Eques à Serpente," or *Knight of the Serpent*, "Eques ab Aquila," or *Knight of the Eagle*, etc., and by this name he was ever afterward known in the Order. Thus Bode, one of the founders of the Rite, was recognized as "Eques à Lilio Convallium," or *Knight of the Lily of the Valleys*, and the Baron Hund, another founder, as "Eques ab Ense," or *Knight of the Sword*. A similar custom prevailed among the Illuminati and in the Royal Order of Scotland. *Eques* signified among the Romans a *knight*, but in the Middle Ages the knight was called *miles*; although the Latin word *miles* denoted only a soldier, yet, by the usage of chivalry, it received the nobler signification. Indeed, Muratori says, on the authority of an old inscription, that *Eques* was inferior in dignity to *Miles*. (See *Miles*.)

Eques Professus. *Professed Knight.* The seventh and last degree of the Rite of Strict Observance. Added, it is said, to the original series by Von Hund.

Equilateral Triangle. (See *Triangle*.)

Equity. The equipoised balance is an ancient symbol of equity. On the medals, this virtue is represented by a female holding in the right hand a balance, and in the left a measuring wand, to indicate that she gives to each one his just measure. In the Ancient and Accepted Rite, the Thirty-first Degree, or Grand Inspector Inquisitor Commander, is illustrative of the virtue of equity; and hence the balance is a prominent symbol of that degree, as it is also of the Sixteenth Degree, or Princes of Jerusalem, because according to the old rituals, they were chiefs in Masonry, and administered justice to the inferior degrees.

Equivocation. The words of the covenant of Masonry require that it should be made without *evasion*, *equivocation*, or *mental reservation*. This is exactly in accordance with the law of ethics in relation to promises made. And it properly applies in this case, because the covenant, as it is called, is simply a promise, or series of promises, made by the candidate to the Fraternity—to the brotherhood into whose association he is about to be admitted. In making a promise, an *evasion* is the eluding or avoiding the terms of the promise; and this is done, or attempted to be done, by *equivocation*, which is by giving to the words used a secret signification, different from that which they were intended to convey by him who imposed the promise, so as to mislead, or by a *mental reservation*, which is a concealment or withholding in the mind of the promiser of certain conditions under which he makes it, which conditions are not known to the one to whom the promise is made. All of this is in direct violation of the law of veracity. The doctrine of the Jesuits is very different. Suarez, one of their most distinguished casuists, lays it down as good law, that if any one makes a promise or contract, he may secretly understand that he does not sincerely promise, or that he promises without any intention of fulfilling the promise. This is not the rule of Masonry, which requires that the words of the covenant be taken in the patent sense which they were intended by the ordinary use of language to convey. It adheres to the true rule of ethics, which is, as Paley says, that a promise is binding in the sense in which the promiser supposed the promisee to receive it.

Eranoi. Among the ancient Greeks there were friendly societies, whose object was, like the modern Masonic Lodges, to relieve the distresses of their necessitous members. They were permanently organized, and had a common fund by the voluntary contributions of the members. If a member was reduced to poverty, or was in temporary distress for money, he applied to the *eranos*, and, if worthy, received the necessary assistance, which was, however, advanced rather as a loan than a gift, and the amount was to be returned when the recipient was in better circumstances. In the days of the Roman Empire these friendly societies were frequent among the Greek cities, and were looked on with suspicion by the emperors, as tending to political combinations. Smith says (*Dict. Gr. and Rom. Ant.* s. v. *Evani*) that the Anglo-Saxon gilds, or fraternities for mutual aid, resembled the eranoi of the Greeks. In their spirit, these Grecian confraternities partook more of the Masonic character, as charitable associations, than of the modern friendly societies, where relief is based on a system of mutual insurance; for the assistance was given only to cases of actual need, and did not depend on any calculation of natural contingencies.

Erica. The Egyptians selected the *erica* as a sacred plant. The origin of the consecration of this plant will be peculiarly interesting to the Masonic student. There was a legend in the mysteries of Osiris, which related that Isis, when in search of the body of her murdered husband, discovered it interred at the brow of a hill near which an erica grew; and hence, after the recovery of the body and the resurrection of the god, when she established the mysteries to commemorate her loss and her recovery, she adopted the erica as a sacred plant, in memory of its having pointed out the spot where the *mangled remains* of Osiris were concealed.

Ragon (*Cours des Initiations*, p. 151), thus alludes to this mystical event: "Isis found the body of Osiris in the neighborhood of Biblos, and near a tall plant called the *erica*. Oppressed with grief, she seated herself on the margin of a fountain, whose waters issued from a rock. This rock is the *small hill* mentioned in the ritual; the erica has been replaced by the acacia, and the grief of Isis has been changed for that of the Fellow-Crafts."

The lexicographers define ἀρείκη as "the heath or heather"; but it is really, as Plutarch asserts, the tamarisk tree; and Schwenk (*Die Mythologie der Semiten*, p. 248) says that Phylœ, so renowned among the ancients as one of the burial-places of Osiris, and among the moderns for its wealth of architectural remains, contains monuments in which the grave of Osiris is overshadowed by the *tamarisk*.

Erlking. A name found in one of the sacred sagas of the Scandinavian mythology, entitled *Sir Olaf and the Erlking's Daughter*, and applied to the mischievous goblin haunting the black forest of Thuringia.

Ernest and Falk. *Ernst und Falk. Gespräche für Freimaurer*, i. e., "Ernest and Falk. Conversations for Freemasons," is the title of a German work written by Gotthold Ephraim Lessing, and first published in 1778. Ernest is an inquirer, and Falk a Freemason, who gives to his interlocutor a very philosophical idea of the character, aims, and objects of the Institution. The work has been faithfully translated by Bro. Kenneth R. H. Mackenzie, F.S.A., in the London *Freemasons' Quarterly Magazine*, in 1854, and continued and finished, so far as the author had completed it, in the London *Freemason* in 1872. Findel says of this work, that it "is one of the best things that has ever been written upon Freemasonry." (*Hist. of F. M.*, p. 373.)

Erwin von Steinbach. A distinguished German, who was born, as his name imports, at Steinbach, near Bühl, about the middle of the thirteenth century. He was the master of the works at the Cathedral of Strasburg, the tower of which he commenced in 1275. He finished the tower and doorway before his death, which was in 1318. He was at the head of the German Fraternity of Stonemasons, who were the precursors of the modern Freemasons. (See *Strasburg*.)

Esoteric Masonry. That secret portion of Masonry which is known only to the initiates as distinguished from *exoteric Masonry*, or *monitorial*, which is accessible to all who choose to read the manuals and published works of the Order. The words are from the Greek, ἐσωτερικὸς, *internal*, and ἐξωτερικὸς, *external*, and were first used by Pythagoras, whose philosophy was divided into the exoteric, or that taught to all, and the esoteric, or that taught to a select few; and thus his disciples were divided into two classes, according to the degree of initiation to which they had attained, as being either fully admitted into the society, and invested with all the knowledge that the Master could communicate, or as merely postulants, enjoying only the public instructions of the school, and awaiting the gradual reception of further knowledge. This double mode of instruction was borrowed by Pythagoras from the Egyptian priests, whose theology was of two kinds—the one exoteric, and addressed to the people in general; the other esoteric, and confined to a select num-

ber of the priests and to those wno possessed, or were to possess, the regal power. And the mystical nature of this concealed doctrine was expressed in their symbolic language by the images of sphinxes placed at the entrance of their temples. Two centuries later, Aristotle adopted the system of Pythagoras, and, in the Lyceum at Athens, delivered in the morning to his select disciples his subtle and concealed doctrines concerning God, Nature, and Life, and in the evening lectured on more elementary subjects to a promiscuous audience. These different lectures he called his Morning and his Evening Walk.

Espérance. Under the name of "Chevaliers et Dames de l'Espérance" was founded in France, and subsequently an androgynous order in Germany. It is said to have been instituted by Louis XV., at the request of the Marquis de Chatelet, and was active about 1750. The Lodge "Irene," at Hamburg, was founded in 1757.

Essenes. Lawrie, in his *History of Freemasonry*, in replying to the objection, that if the Fraternity of Freemasons had flourished during the reign of Solomon, it would have existed in Judea in after ages, attempts to meet the argument by showing that there did exist, after the building of the Temple, an association of men resembling Freemasons in the nature, ceremonies, and object of their institution (p. 33.) The association to which he here alludes is that of the Essenes, whom he subsequently describes as an ancient Fraternity originating from an association of architects who were connected with the building of Solomon's Temple.

Lawrie evidently seeks to connect historically the Essenes with the Freemasons, and to impress his readers with the identity of the two Institutions. I am not prepared to go so far; but there is such a similarity between the two, and such remarkable coincidences in many of their usages, as to render this Jewish sect an interesting study to every Freemason, to whom therefore some account of the usages and doctrines of this holy brotherhood will not, perhaps, be unacceptable.

At the time of the advent of Jesus Christ, there were three religious sects in Judea—the Pharisees, the Sadducees, and the Essenes; and to one of these sects every Jew was compelled to unite himself. The Savior has been supposed by many writers to have been an Essene, because, while repeatedly denouncing the errors of the two other sects, he has nowhere uttered a word of censure against the Essenes; and because, also, many of the precepts of the New Testament are to be found among the laws of this sect.

In ancient authors, such as Josephus, Philo, Porphyry, Eusebius, and Pliny, who have had occasion to refer to the subject, the notices of this singular sect have been so brief and unsatisfactory, that modern writers have found great difficulty in properly understanding the true character of Essenism. And yet our antiquaries, never weary of the task of investigation, have at length, within a recent period, succeeded in eliciting, from the collation of all that has been previously written on the subject, very correct details of the doctrines and practises of the Essenes. Of these writers none have been more successful than the laborious German critics Frankel and Rappaport. Their investigations have been ably and thoroughly condensed by Dr. Christian D. Ginsburg, whose essay on *The Essenes, their History and Doctrines* (Lond., 1864), has supplied the most material facts contained in the present article.

It is impossible to ascertain the precise date of the development of Essenism as a distinct organization. The old writers are so exaggerated in their statements, that they are worth nothing as historical authorities. Philo says, for instance, that Moses himself instituted the order, and Josephus that it existed ever since the ancient time of the Fathers; while Pliny asserts, with mythical liberality, that it has continued for thousands of ages. Dr. Ginsburg thinks that Essenism was a gradual development of the prevalent religious notions out of Judaism, a theory which Dr. Döllinger repudiates. But Rappaport, who was a learned Jew, thoroughly conversant with the Talmud and other Hebrew writings, and who is hence called by Ginsburg "the corypheus of Jewish critics," asserts that the Essenes were not a distinct sect, in the strict sense of the word, but simply an order of Judaism, and that there never was a rupture between them and the rest of the Jewish community. This theory is sustained by Frankel, a learned German, who maintains that the Essenes were simply an intensification of the Pharisaic sect, and that they were the same as the Chasidim, whom Lawrie calls the Kassideans, and of whom he speaks as the guardians of King Solomon's Temple. If this view be the correct one, and there is no good reason to doubt it, then there will be another feature of resemblance and coincidence between the Freemasons and the Essenes; for, as the latter was not a religious sect, but merely a development of Judaism, an order of Jews entertaining no heterodox opinions, but simply carrying out the religious dogmas of their faith with an unusual strictness of observance, so are the Freemasons not a religious sect, but simply a development of the religious idea of the age. The difference, however, between Freemasonry and Essenism lies in the spirit of universal tolerance prominent in the one and absent in the other. Freemasonry is Christian as to its membership in general, but recognizing and tolerating in its bosom all other religions: Essenism, on the contrary, was exclusively and intensely Jewish in its membership, its usages, and its doctrines.

The Essenes are first mentioned by Josephus as existing in the days of Jonathan the Maccabæan, one hundred and sixty-six years before Christ. The Jewish historian repeatedly speaks of them at subsequent periods; and there is no doubt that they constituted one of the three sects which divided the Jewish religious world at the advent of our Savior, and

of this sect he is supposed, as has been already said, to have been a member.

On this subject, Ginsburg says: "Jesus, who in all things conformed to the Jewish law, and who was holy, harmless, undefiled, and separate from sinners, would, therefore, naturally associate himself with that order of Judaism which was most congenial to his holy nature. Moreover, the fact that Christ, with the exception of once, was not heard of in public till his thirtieth year, implying that he lived in seclusion with this Fraternity, and that, though he frequently rebuked the Scribes, Pharisees, and Sadducees, he never denounced the Essenes, strongly confirms this decision." But he admits that Christ neither adopted nor preached their extreme doctrines of asceticism.

After the establishment of Christianity, the Essenes fade out of notice, and it has been supposed that they were among the earliest converts to the new faith. Indeed, De Quincey rather paradoxically asserts that they were a disguised portion of the early Christians.

The etymology of the word has not been settled. Yet, among the contending opinions, the preferable one seems to be that it is derived from the Hebrew CHASID,—*holy, pious,*—which connects the Essenes with the *Chasidim,* a sect which preceded them, and of whom Lawrie says (quoting from Scaliger), that they were "an order of the Knights of the Temple of Jerusalem, who bound themselves to adorn the porches of that magnificent structure, and to preserve it from injury and decay." (*Hist. of F. M.,* p. 38.)

The Essenes were so strict in the observance of the Mosaic laws of purity, that they were compelled for the purpose of avoiding contamination, to withdraw altogether from the rest of the Jewish nation and to form a separate community, which thus became a brotherhood. The same scruples which led them to withdraw from their less strict Jewish brethren induced most of them to abstain from marriage, and hence the unavoidable depletion of their membership by death could only be repaired by the initiation of converts. They had a common treasury, in which was deposited whatever anyone of them possessed, and from this the wants of the whole community were supplied by stewards appointed by the brotherhood, so that they had everything in common. Hence there was no distinction among them of rich and poor, or masters and servants; but the only gradation of rank which they recognised was derived from the degrees or orders into which the members were divided, and which depended on holiness alone. They lived peaceably with all men, reprobated slavery and war, and would not even manufacture any warlike instruments. They were governed by a president, who was elected by the whole community; and members who had violated their rules were, after due trial, excommunicated or expelled.

As they held no communication outside of

their own fraternity, they had to raise their own supplies, and some were engaged in tilling, some in tending flocks, others in making clothing, and others in preparing food. They got up before sunrise, and, after singing a hymn of praise for the return of light, which they did with their faces turned to the east, each one repaired to his appropriate task. At the fifth hour, or eleven in the forenoon, the morning labor terminated. The brethren then again assembled, and after a lustration in cold water, they put on white garments and proceeded to the refectory, where they partook of the common meal, which was always of the most frugal character. A mysterious silence was observed during this meal, which, to some extent, had the character of a sacrament. The feast being ended, and the priest having returned thanks, the brethren withdrew and put off their white garments, resumed their working-clothes and their several employments until evening, when they again assembled as before, to partake of a common meal.

They observed the Sabbath with more than Judaic strictness, regarding even the removal of a vessel as a desecration of the holy day. On that day, each took his seat in the synagogue in becoming attire; and, as they had no ordained ministers, any one that liked read out of the Scriptures, and another, experienced in spiritual matters, expounded the passages that had been read. The distinctive ordinances of the brotherhood and the mysteries connected with the Tetragrammaton and the angelic worlds were the prominent topics of Sabbatical instruction. In particular, did they pay attention to the mysteries connected with the Tetragrammaton, or the Shem hamphorash, the *expository name*, and the other names of God which play so important a part in the mystical theosophy of the Jewish Kabbalists, a great deal of which has descended to the Freemasonry of our own days.

Josephus describes them as being distinguished for their brotherly love, and for their charity in helping the needy, and showing mercy. He says that they are just dispensers of their anger, curbers of their passions, representatives of fidelity, ministers of peace, and every word with them is of more force than an oath. They avoid taking an oath, and regard it as worse than perjury; for they say that he who is not believed without calling on God to witness, is already condemned of perjury. He also states that they studied with great assiduity the writings of the ancients on distempers and their remedies, alluding, as it is supposed, to the magical works imputed by the Talmudists to Solomon.

It has already been observed that, in consequence of the celibacy of the Essenes, it was found necessary to recruit their ranks by the introduction of converts, who were admitted by a solemn form of initiation. The candidate, or aspirant, was required to pass through a novitiate of two stages, which extended over three years, before he was admitted to a full participation in the privileges of the Order. Upon entering the first

stage, which lasted for twelve months, the novice cast all his possessions into the common treasury. He then received a copy of the regulations of the brotherhood, and was presented with a *spade*, and *apron*, and a *white robe*. The spade was employed to bury excrement, the apron was used at the daily lustrations, and the white robe was worn as a symbol of purity. During all this period the aspirant was considered as being outside the order, and, although required to observe some of the ascetic rules of the society, he was not admitted to the common meal. At the end of the probationary year, the aspirant, if approved, was advanced to the second stage, which lasted two years, and was then called an *approacher*. During this period he was permitted to unite with the brethren in their lustrations, but was not admitted to the common meal, nor to hold any office. Should this second stage of probation be passed with approval, the *approacher* became an *associate*, and was admitted into full membership, and at length allowed to partake of the common meal.

There was a third rank or degree called the *disciple* or *companion*, in which there was a still closer union. Upon admission to this highest grade, the candidate was bound by a solemn oath to love God, to be just to all men, to practise charity, maintain truth, and to conceal the secrets of the society and the mysteries connected with the Tetragrammaton and the other names of God.

These three sections or degrees, of Aspirant, Associate, and Companion, were subdivided into four orders or ranks, distinguished from each other by different degrees of holiness; and so marked were these distinctions, that if one belonging to a higher degree of purity touched one of a lower order, he immediately became impure, and could only regain his purity by a series of lustrations.

The earnestness and determination of these Essenes, says Ginsburg, to advance to the highest state of holiness, were seen in their self-denying and godly life; and it may fairly be questioned whether any religious system has ever produced such a community of saints. Their absolute confidence in God and resignation to the dealings of Providence; their uniformly holy and unselfish life; their unbounded love of virtue and utter contempt for worldly fame, riches, and pleasures; their industry, temperance, modesty, and simplicity of life; their contentment of mind and cheerfulness of temper; their love of order, and abhorrence of even the semblance of falsehood; their benevolence and philanthropy; their love for the brethren, and their following peace with all men; their hatred of slavery and war; their tender regard for children, and reverence and anxious care for the aged; their attendance on the sick, and readiness to relieve the distressed; their humility and magnanimity; their firmness of character and power to subdue their passions; their heroic endurance under the most agonizing sufferings for righteousness' sake; and their cheer-

17

fully looking forward to death, as releasing their immortal souls from the bonds of the body, to be forever in a state of bliss with their Creator,—have hardly found a parallel in the history of mankind.

Lawrie, in his *History of Freemasonry*, gives, on the authority of Pictet, of Basnage, and of Philo, the following condensed recapitulation of what has been said in the preceding pages of the usages of the Essenes:

"When a candidate was proposed for admission, the strictest scrutiny was made into his character. If his life had hitherto been exemplary, and if he appeared capable of curbing his passions, and regulating his conduct, according to the virtuous, though austere maxims of their order, he was presented, at the expiration of his novitiate, with a white garment, as an emblem of the regularity of his conduct, and the purity of his heart. A solemn oath was then administered to him, that he would never divulge the mysteries of the Order; that he would make no innovations on the doctrines of the society; and that he would continue in that honorable course of piety and virtue which he had begun to pursue. Like Freemasons, they instructed the young member in the knowledge which they derived from their ancestors. They admitted no women into their order. They had particular signs for recognizing each other, which have a strong resemblance to those of Freemasons. They had colleges or places of retirement, where they resorted to practise their rites and settle the affairs of the society; and, after the performance of these duties, they assembled in a large hall, where an entertainment was provided for them by the president, or master of the college, who alloted a certain quantity of provisions to every individual. They abolished all distinctions of rank; and if preference was ever given, it was given to piety, liberality, and virtue. Treasurers were appointed in every town, to supply the wants of indigent strangers." (pp. 34, 35.)

Lawrie thinks that this remarkable coincidence between the chief features of the Masonic and Essenian fraternities can be accounted for only by referring them to the same origin; and, to sustain this view, he attempts to trace them to the Kasideans, or Assideans, more properly the Chasidim, "an association of architects who were connected with the building of Solomon's Temple." But, aside from the consideration that there is no evidence that the Chasidim were a body of architects—for they were really a sect of Jewish puritans, who held the Temple in especial honor—we cannot conclude, from a mere coincidence of doctrines and usages, that the origin of the Essenes and the Freemasons is identical. Such a course of reasoning would place the Pythagoreans in the same category: a theory that has been rejected by the best modern critics.

The truth appears to be that the Essenes, the School of Pythagoras, and the Freemasons, derive their similarity from that spirit of brotherhood which has prevailed in all ages of the civilized world, the inherent principles of which, as the results of any fraternity,—all the members of which are engaged in the same pursuit and assenting to the same religious creed,—are brotherly love, charity, and that secrecy which gives them their exclusiveness. And hence, between all fraternities, ancient and modern, these "remarkable coincidences" will be found.

Esther. The Third Degree of the American Adoptive Rite of the Eastern Star. It is also called "the wife's degree," and in its ceremonies comprises the ·history of Esther the wife and queen of Ahasuerus, King of Persia, as related in the Book of Esther.

Eternal Life. The doctrine of eternal life is taught in the Master's Degree, as it was in the Ancient Mysteries of all nations. (See *Immortality of the Soul*.)

Eternity. The ancient symbol of eternity was a serpent in the form of a circle, the tail being placed in the mouth. The simple circle, the figure which has neither beginning nor end, but returns continually into itself, was also a symbol of eternity.

Ethanim or **Tishri.** The seventh sacred month, or the first month of the Hebrew civil year, commencing with the new moon in September.

Ethics of Freemasonry. There is a Greek word, ἔθος (*ethos*), which signifies *custom*, from which Aristotle derives another word ἠθος, (*ethos*),¹ which means *ethics*; because, as he says, from the custom of doing good acts arises the habit of moral virtue. Ethics, then, is the science of morals teaching the theory and practise of all that is good in relation to God and to man, to the state and the individual; it is, in short, to use the emphatic expression of a German writer, "the science of the good." Ethics being thus engaged in the inculcation of moral duties, there must be a standard of these duties, an authoritative ground-principle on which they depend, a doctrine that requires their performance, making certain acts just those that *ought* to be done, and which, therefore, are duties, and that forbid the performance of others which are, therefore, offenses. Ethics, then, as a science, is divisible into several species, varying in name and character, according to the foundation on which it is built.

Thus we have the *Ethics of Theology*, which is founded on that science which teaches the nature and attributes of God; and, as this forms a part of all religious systems, every religion, whether it be Christianity or Judaism, Brahmanism or Buddhism, or any other form of recognized worship, has within its bosom a science of theological ethics which teaches, according to the lights of that religion, the duties which are incumbent on man from his relations to a Supreme Being. And then we have the *Ethics of Christianity*, which being founded on the Scriptures, recognized by Christians as the revealed will of God, is nothing other than theological ethics applied to and limited by Christianity.

Then, again, we have the *Ethics of Philoso-*

phy, which is altogether speculative, and derived from and founded on man's speculations concerning God and himself. There might be a sect of philosophers who denied the existence of a Superintending Providence; but it would still have a science of ethics referring to the relations of man to man, although that system would be without strength, because it would have no Divine sanction for its enforcement.

And, lastly, we have the *Ethics of Freemasonry,* whose character combines those of the three others. The first and second systems in the series above enumerated are founded on religious dogmas; the third on philosophical speculations. Now, as Freemasonry claims to be a religion, in so far as it is founded on a recognition of the relations of man and God, and a philosophy in so far as it is engaged in speculations on the nature of man, as an immortal, social, and responsible being, the ethics of Freemasonry will be both religious and philosophical.

The symbolism of Masonry, which is its peculiar mode of instruction, inculcates all the duties which we owe to God as being his children, and to men as being their brethren. "There is," says Dr. Oliver, "scarcely a point of duty or morality which man has been presumed to owe to God, his neighbor, or himself, under the Patriarchal, the Mosaic, or the Christian dispensation, which, in the construction of our symbolical system, has been left untouched." Hence, he says, that these symbols all unite to form "a code of moral and theological philosophy"; the term of which expression would have been better if he had called it a "code of philosophical and theological ethics."

At a very early period of his initiation, the Mason is instructed that he owes a threefold duty,—to God, his neighbor, and himself,—and the inculcation of these duties constitutes the ethics of Freemasonry.

Now, the Tetragrammaton, the letter G, and many other symbols of a like character, impressively inculcate the lesson that there is a God in whom "we live, and move, and have our being," and of whom the apostle, quoting from the Greek poet, tells us that "we are his offspring." To him, then, as the Universal Father, does the ethics of Freemasonry teach us that we owe the duty of loving and obedient children.

And, then, the vast extent of the Lodge, making the whole world the common home of all Masons, and the temple, in which we all labor for the building up of our bodies as a spiritual house, are significant symbols, which teach us that we are not only the children of the Father, but fellow-workers, laboring together in the same task and owing a common servitude to God as the Grand Architect of the universe—the Algabil or Master Builder of the world and all that is therein; and thus these symbols of a joint labor, for a joint purpose, tell us that there is a brotherhood of man: to that brotherhood does the ethics of Freemasonry teach us that we owe the duty of fraternal kindness in all its manifold phases.

And so we find that the ethics of Freemasonry is really founded on the two great ideas of the universal fatherhood of God and the universal brotherhood of man.

Ethiopia. A tract of country to the south of Egypt, and watered by the upper Nile. The reference to Ethiopia, in the Master's Degree of the American Rite, as a place of attempted escape for certain criminals, is not to be found in the English or French rituals, and I am inclined to think that this addition to the Hiramic legend is an American interpolation. The selection of Ethiopia, by the ritualist, as a place of refuge, seems to be rather inappropriate when we consider what must have been the character of that country in the age of Solomon.

Etymology. For the etymology of the word Mason, see *Mason, Derivation of the Word.*

Euclid. In the year of the world 3650, which was 646 years after the building of King Solomon's Temple, Euclid, the celebrated geometrician, was born. His name has been always associated with the history of Freemasonry, and in the reign of Ptolemy Soter, the Order is said to have greatly flourished in Egypt, under his auspices. The well known forty-seventh problem of his first book, although not discovered by him, but long before by Pythagoras, has been adopted as a symbol in the Third Degree.

Euclid, Legend of. All the old manuscript Constitutions contain the well known "legend of Euclid," whose name is presented to us as the "Worthy Clerk Euclid" in every conceivable variety of corrupted form. The legend as given in the Dowland MS. (*q. v.*) is in the following words:

"Moreover, when Abraham and Sara his wife went into Egypt, there he taught the Seaven Scyences to the Egiptians; and he had a worthy Scoller that height Ewclyde, and he learned right well, and was a master of all the vij Sciences liberall. And in his dayes it befell that the lord and the estates of the realme had soe many sonns that they had gotten, some by their wifes and some by other ladyes of the realm; for that land is a hott land and a plentious of generacion. And they had not competent livelode to find with their children; wherefore they made much care. And then the King of the land made a great Counsell and a parliament, to witt, how they might find their children honestly as gentlemen; And they could find no manner of good way. And then they did crye through all the realme, if their were any man that could informe them, that he should come to them, and he should be soe rewarded for his travail, that he should hold him pleased.

"After that this cry was made, then came this worthy clarke Ewclyde, and said to the King and to all his great lords: 'If yee will, take me your children to governe, and to teach them one of the Seaven Scyences, wherewith they may live honestly as gentlemen should, under a condicion, that yee will grant me and them a commission that I may have power to rule them after the manner that the science ought to be ruled.' And that the King and all his counsell granted to him anone, and sealed their commission. And then this worthy Doctor tooke to him these lords' sonns, and taught them the scyence of Geometrie in practice, for to work in stones all manner of worthy worke that belongeth to buildinge churches, temples, castells, towres, and mannors, and all other manner of buildings; and he gave them a charge on this manner:"

Here follow the usual "charges" of a Freemason as given in all the old Constitutions; and then the legend concludes with these words:

"And thus was the science grounded there; and that worthy Mr. Ewclyde gave it the name of Geometrie. And now it is called through all this land Masonrye." (Hughan's *Old Charges*, ed. 1872, p. 26.)

This legend, considered historically, is certainly very absurd, and the anachronism which makes Euclid the contemporary of Abraham adds, if possible, to the absurdity. But interpreted as all Masonic legends should be interpreted, as merely intended to convey a Masonic truth in symbolic language, it loses its absurdity, and becomes invested with an importance that we should not otherwise attach to it.

Euclid is here very appropriately used as a type of geometry, that science of which he was so eminent a teacher; and the myth or legend then symbolizes the fact that there was in Egypt a close connection between that science and the great moral and religious system which was among the Egyptians, as well as other ancient nations, what Freemasonry is at the present day—a secret institution, established for the inculcation of the same principles, and inculcating them in the same symbolic manner. So interpreted, this legend corresponds to all the developments of Egyptian history, which teach us how close a connection existed in that country between the religious and scientific systems. Thus Kenrick (*Anc. Eg.*, i., 383) tells us that "when we read of foreigners [in Egypt] being obliged to submit to painful and tedious ceremonies of initiation, it was not that they might learn the secret meaning of the rites of Osiris or Isis, but that they might partake of the knowledge of astronomy, physic, geometry, and theology."

The legend of Euclid belongs to that class of narrations which, in another work, Dr. Mackey calls "The Mythical Symbols of Freemasonry."

Eulogy. Masonry delights to do honor to the memory of departed brethren by the delivery of eulogies of their worth and merit, which are either delivered at the time of their burial, or at some future period. The eulogy forms the most important part of the ceremonies of a Sorrow Lodge. But the language of the eulogist should be restrained within certain limits; while the veil of charity should be thrown over the frailties of the deceased, the praise of his virtues should not be expressed with exaggerated adulation.

Eumolpus. A king of Eleusis, who founded, about the year 1374 B. C., the Mysteries of Eleusis. His descendants, the Eumoipidæ, presided for twelve hundred years over these Mysteries as Hierophants.

Eunuch. It is usual, in the most correct rituals of the third degree, especially to name *eunuchs* as being incapable of initiation. In none of the old Constitutions and Charges is this class of persons alluded to by name, although of course they are comprehended in the general prohibition against making persons who have any blemish or maim. However, in the Charges which were published by Dr. Anderson, in his second edition (*Constitutions*, 1738, p. 144), they are included in the list of prohibited candidates. It is probable from this that at that time it was usual to name them in the point of OB. referred to; and this presumption derives strength from the fact that Dermott, in copying his Charges from those of Anderson's second edition, added a note complaining of the "moderns" for having disregarded this ancient law, in at least one instance. (*Ahiman Rezon*, ed. 1778.) The question is, however, not worth discussion, except as a matter of ritual history, since the legal principle is already determined that eunuchs cannot be initiated because they are not perfect men, "having no maim or defect in their bodies."

Euphrates. One of the largest and most celebrated rivers of Asia. Rising in the mountains of Armenia and flowing into the Persian gulf, it necessarily lies between Jerusalem and Babylon. In the ritual of the higher degrees it is referred to as the stream over which the Knights of the East won a passage by their arms in returning from Babylon to Jerusalem.

Euresis. From the Greek, εὕρεσις, a *discovery*. That part of the initiation in the Ancient Mysteries which represented the finding of the body of the god or hero whose death and resurrection was the subject of the initiation. The euresis has been adopted in Freemasonry, and forms an essential portion of the ritual of the Third Degree.

Europe. An appellation at times given to the west end of the Lodge.

Eva. The acclamation used in the French Rite of Adoption.

Evangelicon. The gospel belonging to the so-called "Ordre du Temple" at Paris, and professedly a relic of the real Templars. Some believe in its antiquity; but others, from external and internal evidence, fix its date subsequent to the fifteenth century. It is apparently a garbled version of St. John's Gospel. It is sometimes confounded with the "*Leviticon*"; but, though bound up in the same printed volume, it is entirely distinct.

Evangelist. (See *St. John the Evangelist*.)

Evates. The second degree in the Druidical system. Of the three degrees the first was the Bards, the second Evates or Prophets, and the third Druids or Sanctified Authorities.

Eveillés, Secte des. (Sect of the Enlightened.) According to Thory (*Acta Lat.*, i., 312), a society presumed to be a branch of Weishaupt's *Illumines* that existed in Italy.

Evergeten, Bund der. (From the Greek εὐεργέτης, a benefactor.) A secret order after the manner of the *Illuminati*. It was founded in Silesia about 1792, by a certain Zerboni of Glogau, Lieut. von Leipzinger, the merchant Contessa, Herr von Reibnitz, and five others; that Fessler worked in it; that it used Masonic forms. Some of the members were imprisoned at Breslau in 1796, and about 1801 the society became defunct. (Kenning's *Cyclopædia of F. M. s.v.*)

Evergreen. An evergreen plant is a symbol of the immortality of the soul. The ancients, therefore, as well as the moderns, planted evergreens at the heads of graves. Freemasons wear evergreens at the funerals of their brethren, and cast them into the grave. The acacia is the plant which should be used on these occasions, but where it cannot be obtained, some other evergreen plant, especially the cedar, is used as a substitute. (See *Acacia*.)

Evora, Knights of. There is a very ancient city in Portugal of 1200 population. Quintus Sertorius took it 80 B.C. The Roman antiquities are unrivaled. The aqueduct erected by Sertorius has at one end a marvelous architectural tower rising high above the city, perfect in its condition as when built, 70 B.C. In 1147, King Alfonso I., of Portugal, instituted the Order of the New Militia in consequence of the prowess exhibited by the troops in the siege of Lisbon against the Moors. When they conquered Evora in 1166, the king by decree changed their name to Knights of Evora.

Exalted. A candidate is said to be exalted, when he receives the Degree of Holy Royal Arch, the seventh in American Masonry. Exalted means *elevated* or *lifted up*, and is applicable both to a peculiar ceremony of the degree, and to the fact that this degree, in the Rite in which it is practised, constitutes the summit of ancient Masonry.

The rising of the sun of spring from his wintry sleep into the glory of the vernal equinox was called by the old sun-worshipers his "exaltation"; and the Fathers of the Church afterward applied the same term to the resurrection of Christ. St. Athanasius says that by the expression, "God hath exalted him," St. Paul meant the resurrection. Exaltation, therefore, technically means a rising from a lower to a higher sphere, and in Royal Arch Masonry may be supposed to refer to the being lifted up out of the first temple of this life into the second temple of the future life. The candidate is *raised* in the Master's Degree, he is *exalted* in the Royal Arch. In both the symbolic idea is the same.

Examination of Candidates. It is an almost universal rule of the modern Constitutions of Masonry, that an examination upon the subjects which had been taught in the preceding degree shall be required of every brother who is desirous of receiving a higher degree; and it is directed that this examination shall take place in an open Lodge of the degree upon which the examination is made, that all the members present may have an opportunity of judging from actual inspection of the proficiency and fitness of the candidate for the advancement to which he aspires. The necessity of an adequate comprehension of the mysteries of one degree, before any attempt is made to acquire a higher one, seems to have been duly appreciated from the earliest times; and hence the 13th Article of the Regius MS. requires that if a Master has an Apprentice he shall teach him fully, that he may know his Craft ably wherever he may go. (vv., 239–244.) But there is no evidence that the system of examining candidates as to their proficiency, before their advancement, is other than a modern improvement, and first adopted not very early in the present century.

Examination of the Ballot-Box. This is sometimes done during the ballot for a candidate, by presenting the box first to the Junior Warden, then to the Senior, and lastly to the Master, each of whom proclaims the result as "clear" or "foul." This order is adopted so that the declaration of the inferior officer, as to the state of the ballots, may be confirmed and substantiated by his superior.

Examination of Visitors. The due examination of strangers who claim the right to visit, should be entrusted only to the most skilful and prudent brethren of the Lodge. And the examining committee should never forget, that no man applying for admission is to be considered as a Mason, however strong may be his recommendations, until by undeniable evidence he has proved himself to be such.

All the necessary forms and antecedent cautions should be observed. Inquiries should be made as to the time and place of initiation, as a preliminary step the Tiler's OB, of course, never being omitted. Then remember the good old rule of "commencing at the beginning." Let everything proceed in regular course, not varying in the slightest degree from the order in which it is to be supposed that the information sought was originally received. Whatever be the suspicions of imposture, let no expression of those suspicions be made until the final decree for rejection is uttered. And let that decree be uttered in general terms, such as, "I am not satisfied," or "I do not recognize you," and not in more specific language, such as, "You did not answer this inquiry," or "You are ignorant on that point." The candidate for examination is only entitled to know that he has not complied generally with the requisitions of his examiner. To descend to particulars is always improper and often dangerous. Above all, never ask what the lawyers call "leading questions," which include in themselves the answers, nor in any manner aid the memory or prompt the forgetfulness of the party examined, by the slightest hints. If he has it in him it will come out without assistance, and if he has it not, he is clearly entitled to no aid. The Mason who is so unmindful of his obligations as to have forgotten the instructions he has received, must pay the penalty of his carelessness, and be deprived of his contemplated visit to that society whose secret modes of recognition he has so little valued as not to have treasured them in his memory.

Lastly, never should an unjustifiable delicacy weaken the rigor of these rules. Remember, that for the wisest and most evident reasons, the merciful maxim of the law, which says that it is better that ninety-nine guilty men should escape than that one innocent man should be punished, is with us reversed, and that in Masonry *it is better that ninety and nine true men should be turned away from the door of a Lodge than that one cowan should be admitted.*

Excalibar. King Arthur's famous sword, which he unfixed from a miraculous stone after the unavailing efforts of 200 of his most puissant barons. Hence, Arthur was proclaimed king. When dying, Arthur commanded a servant to throw the sword into a neighboring lake, but the servant twice eluded this command. When he finally complied, a hand and arm arose from the water, seized the sword by the hilt, waved it thrice, then sinking into the lake, was seen no more?

Excavations. Excavations beneath Jerusalem have for some years past been in progress, under the direction of the English society, which controls the "Palestine Exploration Fund," and many important discoveries, especially interesting to Masons, have been made.

Excellent. A title conferred on the Grand Captain of the Host, and Grand Principal Sojourner of a Grand Chapter, and on the King and Scribe of a subordinate Chapter of Royal Arch Masons in America.

Excellent Masons. Dr. Oliver (*Hist. Landm.*, i., 420–8) gives a tradition that at the building of Solomon's Temple there were nine Lodges of Excellent Masons, having nine in each, which were distributed as follows: Six Lodges, or fifty-four Excellent Masons in the quarries; three Lodges, or twenty-seven Excellent Masons in the forest of Lebanon; eight Lodges, or seventy-two Excellent Masons engaged in preparing the materials; and nine Lodges, or eighty-one Excellent Masons subsequently employed in building the Temple. Of this tradition there is not the slightest support in authentic history, and it must have been invented altogether for a symbolic purpose, in reference perhaps to the mystical numbers which it details.

Excellent Master. A degree which, with Super-Excellent Master, was at one time given as preparatory to the Royal Arch. They now form part of what is known as Cryptic Masonry.

Excellent, Most. (See *Most Excellent.*)

Excellent, Right. (See *Right Excellent.*)

Excellent, Super. (See *Super-Excellent Masons.*)

Exclusion. In England the Grand Lodge alone can expel from the rights and privileges of Masonry. But a subordinate Lodge may *exclude* a member after giving him due notice of the charge preferred against him, and of the time appointed for its consideration. The name of any one so excluded, and the cause of his exclusion must be sent to the Grand Secretary and to the Provincial or District Grand Secretary if the Lodge be in a Province or District. No Mason excluded is eligible to any other Lodge until the Lodge to which he applies has been made acquainted with his exclusion, and the cause, so that the brethren may exercise their discretion as to his admission. (*Constitutions*, Rules 210 and 212.) In America, the word used as synonymous with *exclusion* is *striking from the roll*, except that the latter punishment is only inflicted for non-payment of Lodge dues.

Exclusiveness of Masonry. The exclusiveness of Masonic benevolence is a charge that has frequently been made against the Order; and it is said that the charity of which it boasts is always conferred on its own members in preference to strangers. It cannot be denied that Masons, simply as Masons, have ever been more constant and more profuse in their charities to their own brethren than to the rest of the world; that in apportioning the alms which God has given them to bestow, they have first looked for the poor in their own home before they sought those who were abroad; and that their hearts have felt more deeply for the destitution of a Brother than a stranger.

The principle that governs the Institution of Freemasonry, in the distribution of its charities, and the exercise of all the friendly affections, is that which was laid down by St. Paul for the government of the infant church at Galatia: "As we have therefore opportunity, let us do good unto all men, especially unto them who are of the household of faith." (Galatians vi. 10.)

This sentiment of preference for those of one's own faith, thus sanctioned by apostolic authority, is the dictate of human nature, and the words of Scripture find their echo in every heart. "Blood," says the Spanish proverb, "is thicker than water," and the claims of kindred, of friends and comrades to our affections, must not be weighed in the same scale with those of the stranger, who has no stronger tie to bind him to our sympathies, than that of a common origin from the founder of our race. All associations of men act on this principle. It is acknowledged in the church, which follows with strict obedience the injunction of the apostle; and in the relief it affords to the distressed, in the comforts and consolations which it imparts to the afflicted, and in the rights and privileges which it bestows upon its own members, distinguishes between those who have no community with it of religious belief, and those who, by worshiping at the same altar, have established the higher claim of being of the household of faith.

It is recognized by all other societies, which, however they may, from time to time, and under the pressure of peculiar circumstances, extend temporary aid to accidental cases of distress, carefully preserve their own peculiar funds for the relief of those who, by their election as members, by their subscription to a written constitution, and by the regular payment of arrears, have assumed the relationship which St. Paul defines as being of the household of faith.

It is recognized by governments, which, however liberally they may frame their laws, so that every burden may bear equally on all, and each may enjoy the same civil and religious rights, never fail, in the privileges which they bestow, to discriminate between the alien and foreigner, whose visit is but temporary or whose allegiance is elsewhere, and their own citizens. This principle of preference is universally diffused, and it is well that it is so. It is well that those who are nearer should be dearer; and that a similitude of blood, an identity of interest, or a community of purpose, should give additional strength to the ordinary ties that bind man to man. Man, in the weakness of his nature, requires this security. By his own unaided efforts, he cannot accomplish the objects of his life nor supply the necessary wants of his existence. In this state of utter helplessness, God has wisely and mercifully provided a remedy by implanting in the human breast a love of union and an ardent desire for society. Guided by this instinct of preservation, man eagerly seeks the communion of man, and the weakness of the individual is compensated by the strength of association. It is to this consciousness of mutual dependence, that nations are indebted for their existence, and governments for their durability. And under the impulse of the same instinct of society, brotherhoods and associations are formed, whose members, concentrating their efforts for the attainment of one common object, bind themselves by voluntary ties of love and friendship, more powerful than those which arise from the ordinary sentiments and feelings of human nature.

Excuse. Many Lodges in the last century and in the beginning of this inflicted pecuniary fines for non-attendance at Lodge meetings, and of course excuses were then required to avoid the penalty. But this has now grown out of use. Masonry being considered a voluntary institution, fines for absence are not inflicted, and excuses are therefore not now required. The infliction of a fine would, it is supposed, detract from the solemnity of the obligation which makes attendance a duty. The old *Constitutions*, however, required excuses for non-attendance, although no penalty was prescribed for a violation of the rule. Thus, in the Matthew Cooke MS. (fifteenth century), it is said, "that every master of this art should be warned to come to his congregation that they come duly, but if (*unless*) they may be *excused* by some manner of cause." (lines 740–4.) And in the Regius MS. it is written:

"That every mayster, that is a Mason,
Must ben at the generale congregacyon,
So that he hyt resonebly y-tolde
Where that the semble shall be holde;
And to that semble he must nede gon,
But he have a resenabul skwsacyon."
                              vv. 107–112.

Executive Powers of a Grand Lodge. (See *Grand Lodge.*)

Exegetical and Philanthropical Society. According to Thory (*Acta Lat.*, i., 312), founded at Stockholm in 1787. It united Magnetism to Swedenborgianism; it was at first secret, but when it became known it was killed by ridicule.

Exemplification of the Work. This term is of frequent use in American Masonry. When a lecturer or teacher performs the ceremonies of a degree for instruction, using generally one of the Masons present as a substitute for the candidate, he is said "to exemplify the work." It is done for instruction, or to enable the members of the Grand or subordinate Lodge to determine on the character of the ritual that is taught by the exemplifier.

Exoteric. Public, not secret. (See *Esoteric.*)

Exodus. The date of the Exodus has been determined by the excavations recently made at Tel el-Maskhûta. This is the name of large mounds near Tel el-Kebêr, excavated by M. Naville for the Egyptian Exploration Fund, wherein he found inscriptions showing that they represent the ancient city of Pithom, or Succoth, the "treasure-cities" (Ex. i. 11), and that Ramses II. was the founder. This was the Pharaoh of the oppression. The walls of the treasure-chambers were about six hundred and fifty feet square and twenty-two feet thick. From Pithom, or Succoth, where the Israelites were at work, they started on their Exodus toward Etham (Khetam), then to Pihachiroth (Ex. xiv. 2), and so on north and east. The Exodus took place under Meneptah II., who ascended the throne B.C. 1325, and reigned but a short period. It was along the isthmus that the Egyptian army perished pursuing the retreating Israelites as they crossed between Lake Serbonis and the waters of the Mediterranean, amidst the "sea of papyrus reeds," the *yâm sûph*, that has often proved disastrous to single or congregated travelers. (See S. Birch, LL.D., in *Ancient History from the Monuments*, Brugsch-Bey's lecture, 17th September, 1874; but more particularly the late discoveries above referred to, in *Fresh Lights*, etc., by A. H. Sayce.

Expert. In Lodges of the French Rite, there are two officers called First and Second Experts, whose duty it is to assist the Master of Ceremonies in the initiation of a candidate. In Lodges of Perfection of the Scottish Rite, there are similar officers who are known as the Senior and Junior Expert.

Expert, Perfect. Conferred in three grades, and cited in Fustier's collection. (Thory, *Acta Lat.* i., 312.)

Expert, Sublime English. Mentioned in Fustier's collection. (Thory, *Acta Lat.*, i., 312.)

Expositions. Very early after the revival of Masonry, in the beginning of the eighteenth century, pretended expositions of the ritual of Masonry began to be published. The following catalogue comprises the most notorious of these pseudo-revelations. The leading titles only are given.

1. *A Mason's Examination*, which appeared in *The Flying Post* for April 11–13, 1723. (Gould's *Hist. of F. M.*, iii., 487.)

2. *The Grand Mystery of Freemasons Discovered.* London, 1724. (Gould's *Hist. of F. M.*, iii., 475.)

3. *The Secret History of the Freemasonry.* London, 1724.

4. *Masonry Dissected*, by Samuel Prichard. London, 1730. There were several subsequent editions, and a French translation in 1737, and a German one in 1736.

5. *The Secrets of Masonry made known to all men*, by S. P. [Samuel Prichard.] London, 1737.

6. *The Mystery of Masonry.* London, 1737.

7. *Masonry further dissected.* London, 1738.

8. *Le Secret des Franc-Maçons*, par M. l'Abbé Perau. Geneva, 1742.

9. *Catéchisme des Franc-Maçons*, par Leonard Gabanon (Louis Travenol). Paris, 1745. He published several editions, varying the titles.

10. *L'Ordre de Franc-Maçons trahi et le Secret des Mopses revélé.* Amsterdam, 1745. Many subsequent editions, and a German and a Dutch translation.

11. *Le Maçon démarqué.* 1751.

12. *A Master Key to Freemasonry.* 1760.

13. *The Three Distinct Knocks.* 1760.

14. *Jachin and Boaz.* 1762.

15. *Hiram; or, The Grand Master Key.* London, 1764.

16. *Shibboleth, or Every Man a Freemason.* 1765.

17. *Solomon in all his Glory.* 1766.

18. *Mahhabone, or the Grand Lodge Door Open'd.* 1766.

19. *Tubal Kain.* 1767.

20. *The Freemason Stripped Naked*, by Charles Warren. London, 1769.

21. *Receuil precieux de la Maçonnerie Adonhiramite*, par Louis Guillemain de St. Victor. Paris, 1781. This work was not written with an unfriendly purpose, and many editions of it were published.

22. *The Master Key*, by I. Browne. London, 1794. Scarcely an exposition, since the cipher in which it is printed renders it a sealed book to all who do not possess the key.

23. *A Masonic Treatise, with an Elucidation on the Religious and Moral Beauties of Freemasonry*, etc., by W. Finch. London, 1801.

24. *Manual of Freemasonry*, by Richard Carlisle. London, 1825.

25. *Illustrations of Masonry*, by William Morgan. The first edition is without date or place, but it was probably printed at Batavia, N. Y., in 1828.

26. *Light on Masonry*, by David Bernard. Utica, N. Y., 1829.

27. *A Ritual of Freemasonry*, by Avery Allyn. New York, 1852.

There have been several other American expositions, but the compilers have only been servile copyists of Morgan, Bernard, and Allyn. It has been, and continues to be, simply the pouring out of one vial into another.

The expositions which abound in the French, German, and other continental languages, are not attacks upon Freemasonry, but are written often under authority, for the use of the Fraternity. The usages of continental Masonry permit a freedom of publication that would scarcely be tolerated by the English or American Fraternity.   [E. L. H.]

Expulsion. Expulsion is, of all Masonic penalties, the highest that can be inflicted on a member of the Order, and hence it has been often called a Masonic death. It deprives the expelled of all the rights and privileges that he ever enjoyed, not only as a member of the particular Lodge from which he has been ejected, but also of those which were inherent in him as a member of the Fraternity at large. He is at once as completely divested of his Masonic character as though he had never been admitted, so far as regards his rights, while his duties and obligations remain as firm as ever, it being impossible for any human power to cancel them. He can no longer demand the aid of his brethren, nor require from them the performance of any of the duties to which he was formerly entitled, nor visit any Lodge, nor unite in any of the public or private ceremonies of the Order. He is considered as being without the pale, and it would be criminal in any brother, aware of his expulsion, to hold communication with him on Masonic subjects.

The only proper tribunal to impose this heavy punishment is a Grand Lodge. A subordinate Lodge tries its delinquent member, and if guilty declares him expelled. But the sentence is of no force until the Grand Lodge, under whose jurisdiction it is working, has confirmed it. And it is optional with the Grand Lodge to do so, or, as is frequently done, to reverse the decision and reinstate the brother. Some of the Lodges in this country claim the right to expel independently of the action of the Grand Lodge, but the claim is not valid. The very fact that an expulsion is a penalty, affecting the general relations of the punished brother with the whole Fraternity, proves that its exercise never could with propriety be entrusted to a body so circumscribed in its authority as a subordinate Lodge. Besides, the general practise of the Fraternity is against it. The English Constitutions vest the power to expel exclusively in the Grand Lodge. A Private Lodge has only the power to exclude an offending member from its own meetings.

All Masons, whether members of Lodges or not, are subject to the infliction of this punishment when found to merit it. Resignation or withdrawal from the Order does not cancel a Mason's obligations, nor exempt him from that wholesome control which the Order exercises over the moral conduct of its members. The fact that a Mason, not a member of any particular Lodge, who has been guilty of immoral or unmasonic conduct, can be tried and punished by any Lodge within whose jurisdiction he may be residing, is a point on which there is no doubt.

Immoral conduct, such as would subject a candidate for admission to rejection, should be the only offense visited with expulsion. As the punishment is general, affecting the relation of the one expelled with the whole Fraternity, it should not be lightly imposed for the violation of any Masonic act not general in its character. The commission of a grossly immoral act is a violation of the contract entered into between each Mason and his Order. If sanctioned by silence or impunity, it would bring discredit on the Institution, and tend to impair its usefulness. A Mason who is a bad man is to the Fraternity what a mortified limb is to the body, and should be treated with the same mode of cure,—he should be cut off, lest his example spread, and disease be propagated through the constitution.

Expulsion from one of what is called the higher degrees of Masonry, such as a Chapter or an Encampment, does not affect the relations of the expelled party to Blue Masonry. A Chapter of Royal Arch Masons is not and cannot be recognized as a Masonic body by a Lodge of Master Masons by any of the modes of recognition known to Masonry. The acts, therefore, of a Chapter cannot be recognized by a Master Mason's Lodge any more than the acts of a literary or charitable society wholly unconnected with the Order. Besides, by the present organization of Freemasonry, Grand Lodges are the supreme Masonic tribunals. If, therefore, expulsion from a Chapter of Royal Arch Masons involved expulsion from a Blue Lodge, the right of the Grand Lodge to hear and determine causes, and to regulate the internal concerns of the Institution, would be interfered with by another body beyond its control. But the converse of this proposition does not hold good. Expulsion from a Blue Lodge involves expulsion from all the higher degrees; because, as they are composed of Blue Masons, the members could not of right sit and hold communications on Masonic subjects with one who was an expelled Mason.

Extended Wings of the Cherubim. An expression used in the ceremonies of Royal Master, the Tenth Degree of the American Rite, and intended to teach symbolically that he who comes to ask and to seek Divine Truth symbolized by the True Word, should begin by placing himself under the protection of that Divine Power who alone is Truth, and from whom alone Truth can be obtained. Of him the cherubim with extended wings in the Holy of Holies were a type.

Extent of the Lodge. The extent of a Mason's Lodge is said to be in height from the earth to the highest heavens; in depth, from the surface to the center; in length, from east to west; and in breadth, from north to south. The expression is a symbolic one, and is intended to teach the extensive boundaries of Masonry and the coterminal extension of Masonic charity. (See *Form of the Lodge.*)

Exterior. The name of the First Degree of the "Rite d'Orient," according to the nomenclature of M. Fustier. (Thory, *Acta Lat.,* i., 312.)

External Qualifications. The external qualifications of candidates for initiation are those which refer to their outward fitness, based upon moral and religious character, the frame of body, the constitution of the mind, and social position. Hence they are divided into *Moral, Religious, Physical, Mental,* and *Political,* for which see *Qualifications of Candidates.* The expression in the ritual, that "it is the internal and not the external qualifications that recommend a man to be made a Mason," it is evident, from the context, refers entirely to "worldly wealth and honors," which, of course, are not to be taken "into consideration in inquiring into the qualifications of a candidate."

Extinct Lodge. A Lodge is said to be extinct which has ceased to exist and work, which is no longer on the registry of the Grand Lodge, and whose Charter had been revoked for misuse or forfeited for nonuse.

Extra Communication. The same as *Special Communication.* (See *Communication.*)

Extraneous. Not regularly made; clandestine. The word is now obsolete in this signification, but was so used by the Grand Lodge of England in a motion adopted March 31, 1735, and reported by Anderson in his 1738 edition of the *Constitutions,* p. 182. "No extraneous brothers, that is, not regularly made, but clandestinely, . . . shall be ever qualified to partake of the Mason's general charity."

Extrusion. Used in the Constitution of the Royal Order of Scotland for expulsion. "If a brother shall be convicted of crime by any Court of Justice, such brother shall be permanently extruded." (Sect. 29.) Not in use elsewhere as a Masonic term.

Eye. (See *All-Seeing Eye.*)

Ezekiel, Temple of. (See *Temple of Ezekiel.*)

Ezel. In Hebrew, אֶבֶן הָאָזֶל, *eben hahezel,* the stone of the departure, viz., a mile-stone. An old testimonial stone in the neighborhood of Saul's residence, the scene of the parting of David and Jonathan, and the mark beyond which the falling of Jonathan's arrow indicated danger. (1 Sam. xx. 19.) Hence, a word adopted in the honorary degree called the "Mason's wife and daughter."

Ezra. There are two persons named Ezra who are recorded in Scripture. 1. Ezra, a leading priest among the first colonists who came up to Jerusalem with Zerubbabel, and who is mentioned by Nehemiah (xii. i); and, 2, Ezra, the celebrated Jewish scribe and restorer of the law, who visited Jerusalem forty-two years after the second Temple had been completed. Calmet, however, says that this second Ezra had visited Jerusalem previously in company with Zerubbabel. Some explanation of this kind is necessary to reconcile an otherwise apparent inconsistency in the English system of the Royal Arch, which makes two of its officers represent Ezra and Nehemiah under the title of scribes, while at the same time it makes the time of the ritual refer to the laying of the foundation of the second Temple, and yet places in the scene, as a prominent actor, the later Ezra, who did not go up to Jerusalem until more than forty years after the completion of the building. It is more probable that the Ezra who is said in the ritual to have wrought with Joshua, Haggai, and Zerubbabel, was intended by the original framer of the ritual to refer to the first Ezra, who is recorded by Nehemiah as having been present; and that the change was made in the reference, without due consideration, by some succeeding ritualist, whose mistake has been carelessly perpetuated by those who followed him. Dr. Oliver (*Hist. Landmarks,*

ii., 428) attempts to reconcile the difficulty, and to remove the anachronism, by saying that Esdras was the scribe under Joshua, Haggai, and Zerubbabel, and that he was succeeded in this important office by Ezra and Nehemiah. But the English ritual makes no allusion to this change of succession; and if it did, it would not enable us to understand how Ezra and Nehemiah could be present as scribes when the foundations of the second Temple were laid, and the important secrets of the Royal Arch degree were brought to light, unless the Ezra meant is the one who came to Jerusalem with Nehemiah. There is a confusion in all this which should be rectified.

F

F. The sixth letter in the English and Latin alphabets, and the same as the Greek digamma or the ϕ or ph, and the *vau* of the Hebrew, which has a numerical value of six.

F∴. In French Masonic documents the abbreviation of *Frère*, or *Brother*. FF∴. is the abbreviation of *Frères*, or *Brethren.*

Fabre-Palaprat, Bernard Raymond. The restorer, or, to speak more correctly, the organizer of the Order of the Temple at Paris, of which he was elected Grand Master in 1804. He died at Pau, in the lower Pyrenees, February 18, 1838. (See *Temple, Order of the.*)

Faculty of Abrac. In the so-called Leland Manuscript, it is said that Masons "conceal the way of wynninge the facultye of Abrac." That is, that they conceal the method of acquiring the powers bestowed by a knowledge of the magical talisman that is called Abracadabra. (See *Abracadabra* and *Leland Manuscript.*)

Faith. In the theological ladder, the explanation of which forms a part of the ritual of the First Degree of Masonry, *faith*, is said to typify the lowest round. Faith, here, is synonymous with *confidence* or *trust*, and hence we find merely a repetition of the lesson which had been previously taught that the first, the essential qualification of a candidate for initiation, is that he should *trust in God.*

In the lecture of the same degree, it is said that "Faith may be lost in sight; Hope ends in fruition; but Charity extends beyond the grave, through the boundless realms of eternity." And this is said, because as faith is "the evidence of things not seen," when we see we no longer believe by faith but through demonstration; and as hope lives only in the expectation of possession, it ceases to exist when the object once hoped for is at length enjoyed, but charity, exercised on earth in acts of mutual kindness and forbearance, is still found in the world to come, in the sub-

limer form of mercy from God to his erring creatures.

Faithful Breast. (See *Breast, the Faithful.*)

Falk, De, Rabbi. A native Israelite of Fürth, who attracted some attention in London at the close of the eighteenth century in consequence of his presumed extraordinary powers, acquired through the secrets of the Kabbala, as a Thaumaturgist. It was alleged that he could and did transmute metals, and thereby acquired large sums with which he was liberal to the poor. A merry incident is perhaps familiar to the reader. An invitation was extended by the Baal Shem (the sacerdotal pronouncer of the Holy Name) to the Doctor to call as a visitor for a friendly and philosophical discussion. This was assented to, when the Doctor was asked to fix a time. He did so by taking from his pocket a small taper and, handing it to his new friend, saying: "Light this, sir, when you get home, and I shall be with you as soon as it goes out." This the gentleman did next morning, expecting an early call, but the taper appeared to have a charmed life, and it was deposited in a special closet, where it continued to burn for three weeks, and until in the evening, when Doctor drove up to the door and alighted, much to the surprise of the host, who, with wonderment, had watched the bright-burning taper. As soon as his visitor was announced, the light and candlestick disappeared. The Doctor was asked if the candlestick would be returned, when he replied, "It is already in the kitchen"; and so it was found. A further incident is mentioned of his leaving upon his death a sealed box to his particular friend, Aaron Goldsmid, stating that to open it portended evil. Aaron could not withstand his curiosity, and one day opened it, and ere the night came Aaron was picked up dead.

Fall of Water. (See *Waterfall.*)

Family Lodge. A Lodge held especially for the transaction of private and local business of so delicate a nature that it is found necessary to exclude, during the session, the presence of all except members. In France a Lodge when so meeting is said to be en famille, and the meeting is called a tenue de famille or family session; in Germany such Lodges are called, sometimes, Familien-Logen, but more generally Conferenz-Logen. (See Conference Lodges.)

Fanaticism. The English interpretation of the name of the second assassin of the G. Master, or mankind. The frenzy that overbalances the mind. The Gravelot or Romvel of philosophical Masonry.

Fanor. The name given to the Syrian Mason, who is represented in some legends as one of the assassins. Amru and Metusael being the other two.

Fasces. The bundle of rods borne before the Roman magistrates as an ensign of their authority. In French Masonry, faisceau, or fasces, is used to denote a number of speeches or records tied up in a roll and deposited in the archives.

Favorite of Solomon. The Seventh Degree, 3d division, of the system of the Chapter of the High Degrees of Stockholm. (Thory, Acta Lat., i, 313.)

Favorite Brother of St. Andrew. The Ninth Degree of the Swedish Rite.

Favorite Brother of St. John. The Eighth Degree of the Swedish Rite.

Feast. The convocation of the Craft together at an annual feast, for the laudable purpose of promoting social feelings, and cementing the bonds of brotherly love by the interchange of courtesies, is a time-honored custom, which is unfortunately growing into disuse. The "Assembly and Feast" are words constantly conjoined in the Book of Constitutions. At this meeting, no business of any kind, except the installation of officers, was transacted, and the day was passed in innocent festivity. The election of officers always took place at a previous meeting, in obedience to a regulation adopted by the Grand Lodge of England, in 1720, as follows: "It was agreed, in order to avoid disputes on the annual feast-day, that the new Grand Master for the future shall be named and proposed to the Grand Lodge some time before the feast." (Constitutions, 1738, p. 111.)

Feasts of the Order. The festivals of St. John the Baptist and St. John the Evangelist, June 24th and December 27th, are so called.

Feeling. One of the five human senses, and esteemed by Masons above all the others. For as Anthony Brewer, an old dramatist, says:

"Though one hear, and see, and smell, and taste, If he wants touch, he is counted but a block."

Fees of Honor. In the Grand Lodge of England every Grand Officer, on his election or reelection, is required to pay a sum of money, varying from two to twenty guineas. The sums thus paid for honors bestowed are technically called "fees of honor." A similar custom prevails in the Grand Lodges of Ireland and Scotland; but the usage is unknown in America.

Feix-Feax. A word signifying School of Thought, which is found in the First Degree of the French Adoptive Rite.

Felicity, Order of. An androgynous secret society, founded in 1743, at Paris, by M. Chambonnet. It was among the first of the pseudo-Masonic associations, or coteries, invented by French Masons to gratify the curiosity and to secure the support of women. It had a ritual and a vocabulary which were nautical in their character, and there was a rather too free indulgence in the latitude of gallantry. It consisted of four degrees, Cabin Boy, Master, Commodore, and Vice Admiral. The chief of the order was called Admiral, and this position was of course occupied by M. Chambonnet, the inventer of the system. (Clavel, Historie Pittoresque, p. 111.)

Feld Loge. What is designated in England and America as a Military or Traveling Lodge is called in Germany a Feld Loge. Sometimes, "ein ambulante Loge."

Fellow. The Saxon word for fellow is felaw. Spelman derives it from two words, fe and loy, which signifies bound in mutual trust; a plausible derivation, and not unsuited to the meaning of the word. But Hicks gives a better etymology when he derives it from the Anglo-Saxon folgian, "to follow," and thus a fellow would be a follower, a companion, an associate. In the Middle Ages, the Operative Masons were divided into Masters and Fellows. Thus in the Harleian MS., No. 2054, it is said: "Now I will reherse other charges in singular for Maisters & ffellowes." Those who were of greater skill held a higher position and were designated as Masters, while the masses of the fraternity, the commonalty, as we might say, were called Fellows. In the Matthew Cooke MS. this principle is very plainly laid down. There it is written that Euclid "ordained that they who were passing of cunning should be passing honored, and commanded to call the cunninger Master . . . . and commanded that they that were less of wit should not be called servant nor subject, but Fellow, for nobility of their gentle blood." (Lines 675–688.) From this custom has originated the modern title of Fellow-Craft, given to the Second Degree of Speculative Masonry; although not long after the revival of 1717 the Fellows ceased to constitute the main body of the Fraternity, the Masters having taken and still holding that position.

Fellow-Craft. The Second Degree of Freemasonry in all the Rites is that of the Fellow-Craft. In French it is called Compagnon; in Spanish, Compañero; in Italian, Compagno; and in German, Gesell; in all of which the radical meaning of the word is a fellow workman, thus showing the origin of the title from an operative institution. Like the Degree of Apprentice, it is only preparatory in the higher initiation of the Master; and yet it differs essentially from it in its symbolism. For, as the First Degree was typical of youth, the Second is supposed to represent the stage of manhood, and hence the acquisition of science is made its prominent characteristic. While the former is directed in all its symbols and allegorical ceremonies to the purification of the heart, the latter is intended by its lessons to cultivate the reasoning faculties and improve the intellectual powers. Before the eighteenth century, the great body of the Fraternity consisted of Fellow-Crafts, who are designated in all the old manuscripts as "Fellows." After the revival in 1717, the Fellow-Crafts, who then first began to be called by that name, lost their prominent position, and the great body of the brotherhood was, for a long time, made up altogether of Apprentices, while the government of the Institution was committed to the Masters and Fellows, both of whom were made only in the Grand Lodge until 1725, when the regulation was repealed, and subordinate Lodges were permitted to confer these two degrees.

Fellow-Craft Perfect Architect. (*Compagnon Parfait Architect.*) The Twenty-sixth Degree of the Rite of Mizraim. There are several other degrees which, like this, are so called, not because they have any relation to the original Second Degree of Symbolic Masonry, but to indicate that they constitute the second in any particular series of degrees which are preparatory to the culmination of that series. Thus, in the Rite of Mizraim, we have the Master Perfect Architect, which is the Twenty-seventh Degree, while the Twenty-fifth and Twenty-sixth are Apprentice and Fellow-Craft Perfect Architect. So we have in other rites and systems the Fellow-Craft Cohen, Hermetic, and Kabbalistic Fellow-Craft, where Master Cohen and Hermetic and Kabbalistic Master are the topmost degrees of the different series. Fellow-Craft in all these, and many other instances like them, means only the second preparation toward perfection.

Fellowship, Five Points of. (See *Points of Fellowship, Five.*)

Female Masonry. (See *Adoptive Masonry.*)

Female Masons. The landmarks of Speculative Masonry peremptorily exclude females from any active participation in its mysteries. But there are a few instances in which the otherwise unalterable rule of female exclusion has been made to yield to the peculiar exigencies of the occasion; and some cases are well authenticated where this "Salique law" has been violated from necessity, and females have been permitted to receive at least the First Degree. Such, however, have been only the exceptions which have given confirmation to the rule. (See *Aldworth, Beaton,* and *Xaintrailles.*)

Fendeurs. *L'Ordre des Fendeurs,* i. e. the Order of Woodcutters, was a secret society, established at Paris, in 1743, by the Chevalier Beauchaine. The Lodge represented a forest, and was generally held in a garden. It was androgynous, and had secret signs and words, and an allegorical language borrowed from the profession of woodcutting. The Abbé Barruel (tom. ii., p. 350, ed. 1797)

thought that the Order originated in the forests among the actual woodcutters, and that many intelligent inhabitants of the city having united with them, the operative business of felling trees was abandoned, and Philosophic Lodges were established—a course of conversion from Operative to Speculative precisely like that, he says, which occurred in Masonry, and this conversion was owing to the number of Fendeurs who were also Freemasons.

A complete ritual of the Fendeurs is given in *Ars Quatuor Coronatorum*, vol. XXII, pp. 37–52.]

Ferdinand IV. This King of the two Sicilies, on the 12th of September, 1775, issued an edict forbidding the meeting of Masons in Lodges in his dominions, under penalty of death. In 1777, at the solicitation of his queen, Caroline, this edict was repealed, and Masonry was once more tolerated; but in 1781 the decree was renewed.

Ferdinand VI. In 1751, Ferdinand VI., King of Spain, at the solicitation of Joseph Ferrubia, Visitor of the Holy Inquisition, enforced in his dominions the bull of excommunication of Pope Benedict XIV., and forbade the congregation of Masons under the highest penalties of law. In the *Journal of Freemasonry,* Vienna, 1784 (pp. 176–224), will be found a translation from Spanish into German of Ferrubia's "Act of Accusation," which gave rise to this persecution.

Ferdinand VII. The King of Spain who bore this title was one of the greatest bigots of his time. He had no sooner ascended the throne in 1814, than he reestablished the Inquisition, which had been abolished by his predecessor, proscribed the exercise of Freemasonry, and ordered the closing of all the Lodges, under the heaviest penalties. In September following, twenty-five persons, among whom were several distinguished noblemen, were arrested as "suspected of Freemasonry." On March 30, 1818, a still more rigorous edict was issued, by which those convicted of being Freemasons were subjected to the most severe punishments, such as banishment to India and confiscation of goods, or sometimes death by a cruel form of execution. But the subsequent resolution of 1820 and the abolition of the Inquisition removed these blots from the Spanish records.

Fervency. From the middle of the last century, ardent devotion to duty, fervor or fervency, was taught as a Masonic virtue in the lectures of the First Degree, and symbolized by charcoal, because, as later rituals say, all metals were dissolved by the fervor of ignited charcoal. Subsequently, in the higher degrees, fervency and zeal were symbolized by the color scarlet, which is the appropriate tincture of Royal Arch Masonry.

Fessler, Ignaz Aurelius. A distinguished German writer and Masonic reformer, who was born at Czurendorf, in Hungary, in 1756. He was the son of very poor parents. His mother, who was a bigoted Catholic, had devoted him to a monastic life, and having been educated at the Jesuit school of Raab, he took holy orders in 1772, and was removed to the Capuchin monastery in Vienna. In consequence, however, of his exposure to the Emperor Joseph II. of monastic abuses, he incurred the persecutions of his superiors. But the emperor, having taken him under his protection, nominated him, in 1783, as ex-professor of the Oriental languages in the University of Lemberg. But the monks having threatened him with legal proceedings, he fled to Breslau in 1788, where he subsequently was appointed the tutor of the son of the Prince of Corolath. Here he established a secret Order, called by him the "Evergreen," which bore a resemblance to Freemasonry in its organization, and was intended to effect moral reforms, which at the time he thought Masonry incapable of producing. The Order, however, never really had an active existence, and the attempt of Fessler failed by the dissolution, in 1793, of the society. In 1791 he adopted the Lutheran faith, and, having married, settled in Berlin, where until 1806 he was employed as a superintendent of schools. He wrote during this period several historical works, which gave him a high reputation as an author. But the victorious progress of the French army in Prussia caused him to lose his official position. Having been divorced from his wife in 1802, he again married, and, retiring in 1803 from Berlin, betook himself to the quietude of a country life. Becoming now greatly embarrassed in pecuniary matters, he received adequate relief from several of the German Lodges, for which he expressed the most lively gratitude. In 1808 he accepted the position of a professor in the University of St. Petersburg, which, however, he was soon compelled to relinquish in consequence of the intrigues of the clergy, who were displeased with his liberal views. Subsequently he was appointed superintendent of the Evangelical community, over nine Russian departments, and Ecclesiastical President of the consistory at Saratow, with a large salary. In 1827, on the invitation of the Emperor Alexander, he removed permanently to St. Petersburg, where, in 1833, he received the appointment of Ecclesiastical Counsellor, and died there December 15, 1839, at the advanced age of eighty-three years.

Fessler was initiated into Masonry at Lemberg, in 1783, and immediately devoted himself to the study of its science and history. In June, 1796, he affiliated with the Lodge Royal York, zur Freundschaft, in Berlin, and having been made one of its Sublime Council, was invested with the charge of revising and remodeling the entire ritual of the Lodge, which was based on the high degrees of the French system. To the accomplishment of this laborious task, Fessler at once, and for a long time afterward, devoted his great intellect and his indefatigable energies. In a very short period he succeeded in a reformation of the symbolic degrees, and finding the brethren unwilling to reject the high degrees, which were four in number, then practised by the Lodge, he remodeled them, retaining a con-

siderable part of the French ritual, but incorporated with it a portion of the Swedish system. The work thus accomplished met with general approbation. In his next task of forming a new Constitution he was not so successful, although at length he induced the Royal York Lodge to assume the character and rank of a Grand Lodge, which it did in 1798, with seven subordinate Lodges under its obedience. Again Fessler commenced the work of a revision of the ritual. He had always been opposed to the high degree system. He proposed, therefore, the abolition of everything above the Degree of Master. In this, however, he was warmly opposed, and was compelled to abandon his project of reducing German Masonry to the simplicity of the English system. Yet he was enabled to accomplish something, and had the satisfaction, in 1800, of metamorphosing the Elu, the Ecossais, and the Rose Croix, of the old ritual of the Royal York Lodge into the "degrees of knowledge," which constitute the Rite known as the Rite of Fessler.

In 1798, Fessler had been elected Deputy Grand Master when there were but three Lodges under the Grand Lodge. In 1801, by his persevering activity, the number had been increased to sixteen. Still, notwithstanding his meritorious exertions in behalf of Masonry, he met with that ingratitude, from those whom he sought to serve, which appears to be the fate of almost all Masonic reformers. In 1802, wearied with the opposition of his antagonists, he renounced all the offices that he had filled, and resigned from the Grand Lodge. Thenceforth he devoted himself in a more retired way to the pursuits of Masonry.

Before Fessler resigned, he had conceived and carried out the scheme of establishing a great union of scientific Masons, who should devote themselves to the investigation of the history of Masonry. Of this society Mossdorf, Fischer, and many other distinguished Masons, were members. (See *Scientific Masonic Association*.)

Fessler's contributions to the literature of Freemasonry were numerous and valuable. His chief work was, *An Attempt to Furnish a Critical History of Freemasonry and the Masonic Fraternity from the earliest times to the year 1802*. This work was never printed, but only sold in four folio manuscript volumes, at the price of £30, to persons who pledged themselves eventually to return it. It was a mistake to circumscribe the results of his researches within so narrow a field. But he published many other works. His productions were mostly historical and judicial, and made a great impression on the German Masonic mind. His collected works were published in Berlin, from 1801 to 1807, but, unfortunately, they have never been translated into English. The object of all he wrote was to elevate Freemasonry to the highest sphere of intellectual character.

Fessler, Rite of. This Rite, which was prepared by Fessler at the request of the

Grand Lodge Royal York of Berlin, consisted of nine degrees, as follows:

1. *Entered Apprentice.*
2. *Fellow-Craft.*
3. *Master Mason.*

These differ but slightly from the same degrees in all the Rites, and are followed by six other degrees, which he called the *higher knowledge*, namely:

4. *The Holy of Holies.*—This degree is occupied in a critical exposition of the various hypotheses which have been proposed as to the origin of Freemasonry; as, whether it sprang from the Templars, from the Cathedral of Strasburg, from the Rose Croix of the seventeenth century, from Oliver Cromwell, from the Cathedral of St. Paul's at London, from that of the Palace of Kensington, or from the Jesuits.

5. *Justification.*—Critical examination of the origin of certain of the high degrees, such as the Écossais and the Chapter of Clermont.

6. *Celebration.*—Critical examination of the four following systems: Rose Croix, Strict Observance, African Architects, and Initiated Brothers of Asia.

7. *True Light.*—Critical examination of the Swedish System, the System of Zinnendorf, the Royal Arch of England, of the succession of the Mysteries, and of all systems and their ramifications.

8. *The Country.*—Examination of the origin of the Mysteries of the Divine Kingdom, introduced by Jesus of Nazareth; of the exoteric doctrines communicated by him immediately to his disciples, and of those which sprang up after his death, up to the time of the Gnostics.

9. *Perfection.*—A complete critical history of all Mysteries comprehended in actual Freemasonry.

Both Clavel and Ragon say that the rituals of these degrees were drawn up from the rituals of the Golden Rose Croix, of the Rite of Strict Observance, of the Illuminated Chapter of Sweden, and the Ancient Chapter of Clermont. Fessler's Rite was, perhaps, the most abstrusely learned and philosophical of all the Masonic systems; but it did not have a long existence, as it was abandoned by the Grand Lodge, which had at first accepted it, for the purpose of adopting the Ancient York Rite under the Constitutions of England.

Festivals. In all religions there have been certain days consecrated to festive enjoyment, and hence called festivals. Sir Isaac Newton (on Daniel, p. 204) says: "The heathen were delighted with the festivals of their gods, and unwilling to part with these delights; and, therefore, Gregory Thaumaturgus, who died in 265, and was Bishop of Neocæsarea, to facilitate their conversion, instituted annual festivals to the saints and martyrs. Hence it came to pass that, for exploding the festivals of the heathens, the principal festivals of the Christians succeeded in their room; as the keeping of Christmas with joy, and feasting, and playing, and sports, in the room of the *Bacchinalia* and *Saturnalia;* the celebrating of May day with flowers, in the room of the *Floralia;* and the keeping of festivals to the Virgin Mary, John the Baptist, and divers of the apostles, in the room of the solemnities at the entrance of the sun into the signs of the Zodiac, in the old Julian Calendar." The Masons, borrowing from and imitating the usage of the Church, have also always had their festivals or days of festivity and celebration. The chief festivals of the Operative or Stonemasons of the Middle Ages were those of St. John the Baptist on the 24th of June, and the Four Crowned Martyrs on the 8th of November. The latter was, however, discarded by the Speculative Masons; and the festivals now most generally celebrated by the Fraternity are those of St. John the Baptist, June 24th, and St. John the Evangelist, December 27th. These are the days kept in this country. Such, too, was formerly the case in England; but the annual festival of the Grand Lodge of England now falls on the Wednesday following St. George's day, April 23d, that saint being the patron of England. For a similar reason, St. Andrew's day, November 30th, is kept by the Grand Lodge of Scotland. In Ireland the festival kept is that of St. John on December 27th.

Feuillans. An androgynous system, found in Fustier's collection, and governed by the statutes of St. Bernard.

Fidelity. (See *Fides.*)

Fidelity of Baden Durlach, Order of. Instituted in 1716 by Charles Margrave of Baden Durlach. The members of the Order were knighted, selections being made only from the nobles of ancient family. The reigning princes were hereditary Grand Masters.

Fides. In the Lecture of the First Degree, it is said that "our ancient brethren worshipped deity under the name of Fides or Fidelity, which was sometimes represented by two right hands joined, and sometimes by two human figures holding each other by the right hands." The deity here referred to was the goddess Fides, to whom Numa first erected temples, and whose priests were covered by a white veil as a symbol of the purity which should characterize Fidelity. No victims were slain on her altars, and no offerings made to her except flowers, wine, and incense. Her statues were represented clothed in a white mantle, with a key in her hand and a dog at her feet. The virtue of Fidelity is, however, frequently symbolized in ancient medals by a heart in the open hand, but more usually by two right hands clasped. Horace calls her "incorrupta fides," and makes her the sister of Justice; while Cicero says that that which is religion toward God and piety toward our parents is fidelity toward our fellow-men. There was among the Romans another deity called Fidius, who presided over oaths and contracts, a very usual form of imprecation being "Me Dius Fidius adjuvet," that is, so help me the god Fidius. Noël (*Dict. Fab.*) says that there was an ancient marble at Rome consecrated to the god Fidius, on which was depicted two figures clasping each other's hands as the representatives of Honor and Truth, without which there can be no fidelity nor truth among men. Masonry, borrowing its ideals from the ancient poets, also makes the right hand the symbol of Fidelity.

Fiducial Sign. That is, the sign of confiding trust, called also the sign of Truth and Hope. One of the signs of the English Royal Arch system, which is thus explained by Dr. Oliver (*Dict. Symb. Mas.*): "The fiducial sign shows us if we prostrate ourselves with our face to the earth, we thus throw ourselves on the mercy of our Creator and Judge, looking forward with humble confidence to his holy promises, by which alone we hope to pass through the Ark of our redemption into the mansion of eternal bliss and glory to the presence of Him who is the great I AM, the Alpha and Omega, the Beginning and the Ending, the First and the Last."

Field Lodge, or Army Lodge. A lodge duly instituted under proper authority from a grand body of competent jurisdiction, and authorized to exercise during its peripatetic existence all the powers and privileges that it might possess if permanently located. Charters of this nature, as the name implies, are intended for the tented field, and have been of the greatest service to humanity in its trying hours, when the worst of passions are appealed to.

Fifteen. A sacred number symbolic of the name of God, because the letters of the holy name יה, JAH, are equal, in the Hebrew mode of numeration by the letters of the alphabet, to fifteen; for י is equal to ten, and ה is equal to five. Hence, from veneration for this sacred name, the Hebrews do not, in ordinary computations, when they wish to express the number fifteen, make use of these two letters, but of two others, which are equivalent to nine and six.

Finances. According to universal usage in Masonry, the Treasurer of the Lodge or other body is the banker or depositary of the finances of the Lodge. They are first received by the Secretary, who receipts for them, and immediately pays them over to the Treasurer. The Treasurer distributes them under the orders of the Master and the consent of the Lodge. This consent can only be known officially to him by the statement of the Secretary, and hence all orders drawn on the Treasurer for the disbursement of money should be countersigned by the Secretary.

Finch, William. A Masonic charlatan, who flourished at the end of the last and the beginning of the present century. Finch was a tailor in Canterbury, who, having been expelled for some misconduct by the Grand Lodge, commenced a system of practical Masonry on his own account, and opened a Lodge in his house, where he undertook to initiate candidates and to give instructions in Masonry. He published a great number of pamphlets, many of them in a cipher of his own, which he pretended were for the instruction of the Fraternity. Among the books published by him are: *A Masonic Treatise, with an Eluci-*

dation on the Religious and Moral Beauties of Freemasonry, etc.; printed at Canterbury in 1802. *The Lectures, Laws, and Ceremonies of the Holy Arch Degree of Freemasonry, etc.;* Lambeth, 1812. *The Origin of Freemasons, etc.;* London, 1816. Finch found many dupes, and made a great deal of money. But having on one occasion been sued by an engraver named Smith, for money due for printing his plates, Finch pleaded an offset of money due by Smith for initiation and instruction in Masonry. Smith brought the Grand Secretary and other distinguished Masons into court, who testified that Finch was an impostor. In consequence of this exposure, Finch lost credit with the community, and, sinking into obscurity, died sometime after, in abject poverty.

As it is impossible to read Finch's *Treatises* without a knowledge of the cipher employed by him, the following key will be found useful. We owe it to the researches of Bro. H. C. Levander (*Freem. Mag. and Rev.*, 1859, p. 490). In the first part of the book the cipher used is formed by reversing the alphabet, writing z for a, y for b, etc. The cipher used on the title-page differs somewhat from this, as will be seen from the following tables:

FOR THE TITLE-PAGE.

Cipher. a, b, c, d, e, f, g, h, i, j, k, l, m, n, o, p, q, r, s, t, u, v, w, x, y, z.
Key. b, d, f, h, j, l, n, p, r, t, v, x, z, y, w, u, s, q, o, m, k, i, g, e, c, a.

FOR THE FIRST PART.

Cipher. a, b, c, d, e, f, g, h, i, j, k, l, m, n, o, p, q, r, s, t, u, v, w, x, z.
Key. z, y, x, w, v, u, t, s, r, q, p, o, n, m, l, k, j, i, h, g, f, e, d, c, b, a.

In the second part of the work, a totally different system is employed. The words may be deciphered by taking the last letter, then the first, then the last but one, then the second, and so on. Two or three words are also often run into one; for example, *ereetemhdrdoh*, is *he ordered them.* The nine digits represent certain words of frequent recurrence, a repetition of the same digit denoting the plural; thus, 1 stands for Lodge; 11, for Lodges; 3, Fellow-Craft; 33, Fellow-Crafts, etc.

Findel, J. G. A Masonic writer of more than ordinary note, who was admitted in the lodge "Eleusis zur Verschwiegenheit," at Baireuth, in 1856. He was editor of the *Bauhütte*, an interesting journal, at Leipsic, in 1858, and added materially to Masonic literature in founding the *Verein Deutscher Freimaurer*, about 1860, and publishing, in 1874, *Geist und Form der Freimaurerei.*

His best known and most important work is his *Geschichte der Freimaurerei* (or General History of Freemasonry) published in 1861, which has been translated into English, French, and other languages, and was the first attempt at a critical history of the Craft. He died in 1905.

Fines. Fines for non-attendance or neglect of duty are not now usually imposed in

Masonic bodies, because each member is bound to the discharge of these duties by a motive more powerful than any that could be furnished by a pecuniary penalty. The imposition of such a penalty would be a tacit acknowledgment of the inadequacy of that motive, and would hence detract from its solemnity and its binding nature. It cannot, however, be denied that the records of old Lodges show that it was formerly a common custom to impose fines for a violation of the rules.

Fire. The French, in their Table Lodges, called the drinking a toast, *feu,* or *fire.*

Fire Philosophers. (See *Theosophists.*)

Fire, Pillar of. (See *Pillars of Cloud and Fire.*)

Fire, Purification by. (See *Purification.*)

Fire-Worship. Of all the ancient religions, fire-worship was one of the earliest, next to Sabaism; and even of this it seems only to have been a development, as with the Sabaists the sun was deemed the Universal Fire. "Darius," says Quintus Curtius, "invoked the sun as Mithras, the sacred and eternal fire." It was the faith of the ancient Magi and the old Persians, still retained by their modern descendants the Parsees. But with them it was not an idolatry. The fire was venerated only as a visible symbol of the Supreme Deity, of the creative energy, from whom all things come, and to whom all things ascend. The flame darting upward to meet its divine original, the mundane fire seeking an ascension to and an absorption into the celestial fire, or God himself, constituted what has been called "the flame-secret" of the fire-worshipers. This religion was not only very ancient, but also very universal. From India it passed over into Egypt, and thence extended to the Hebrews and to the Greeks, and has shown its power and prevalence even in modern thought. On the banks of the Nile, the people did not, indeed, fall down like the old Persians and worship fire, but they venerated the fire-secret and its symbolic teaching. Hence the Pyramids (*pyr* is Greek for fire), the representation of ascending flame; and Jennings Hargrave shrewdly says that what has been supposed to be a tomb, in the center of the Great Pyramid, was in reality a depository of the sacred, ever-burning fire. Monoliths were everywhere in antiquity erected to fire or to the sun, as the type of fire. Among the Hebrews, the sacred idea of fire, as something connected with the Divine Being, was very prominent. God appeared to Moses in a flame of fire; he descended on Mount Sinai in the midst of flames; at the Temple the fire descended from heaven to consume the burnt-offering. Everywhere in Scripture, fire is a symbol of the holiness of God. The lights on the altar are the symbols of the Christian God. The purifying power of fire is naturally deduced from this symbol of the holiness of the element. And in the high degrees of Masonry, as in the ancient institutions, there is a purification by fire, coming down to us insensibly

and unconsciously from the old Magian cultus. In the Medieval ages there was a sect of "fire-philosophers"—*philosophi per ignem*—who were a branch or offshoot of Rosicrucianism, with which Freemasonry has so much in common. These fire-philosophers kept up the veneration for fire, and cultivated the "fire-secret," not as an idolatrous belief, but modified by their hermetic notions. They were also called "theosophists," and through them, or in reference to them, we find the theosophic degrees of Masonry, which sprang up in the eighteenth century. As fire and light are identical, so the fire, which was to the Zoroastrians the symbol of the Divine Being, is to the Mason, under the equivalent idea of light, the symbol of Divine Truth, or of the Grand Architect.

Firrao, Joseph. *A cardinal priest* who, in 1738, published the edict of Pope Clement XII. against Freemasonry.

Fish. The Greek word for *fish* is ΙΧΘΥΣ. Now these five letters are the initials of the five words Ιησους Χριστος Θεου Υιος Σωτηρ, that is, *Jesus Christ the Son of God, the Savior.* Hence the early Christians adopted the *fish* as a Christian symbol; and it is to be found on many of their tombs, and was often worn as an ornament. Clement of Alexandria, in writing of the ornaments that a Christian may constantly wear, mentions the fish as a proper device for a ring, as serving to remind the Christian of the origin of his spiritual life, the fish referring to the waters of baptism. The *Vesica Piscis,* which is an oval figure, pointed at both ends, and representing the air bladder of a fish, was adopted, and is still often used as the form of the seal of religious houses and confraternities. Margoliouth (*Vest. of Gen. Freem.,* 45) says: "In former days, the Grand Master of our Order used to wear a silver fish on his person; but it is to be regretted that, amongst the many innovations which have been of late introduced into the society to conciliate the prejudices of some who cannot consistently be members of it, this beautiful emblem has disappeared."

Five. Among the Pythagoreans *five* was a mystical number, because it was formed by the union of the first even number and the first odd, rejecting unity; and hence it symbolized the mixed conditions of order and disorder, happiness and misfortune, life and death. The same union of the odd and even, or male and female, numbers made it the symbol of marriage. Among the Greeks it was a symbol of the world, because, says Diodorus, it represented ether and the four elements. It was a sacred round number among the Hebrews. In Egypt, India, and other Oriental nations, says Gesenius, the five minor planets and the five elements and elementary powers were accounted sacred. It was the pentas of the Gnostics and the Hermetic Philosophers; it was the symbol of their quintessence, the fifth or highest essence of power in a natural body. In Masonry, five is a sacred number, inferior only in importance to three and seven. It is especially significant in the Fellow-Craft's

Degree, where five are required to hold a Lodge, and where, in the winding stairs, the five steps are referred to the orders of architecture and the human senses. In the Third Degree, we find the reference to the five points of fellowship and their symbol, the five-pointer star. Geometry, too, which is deemed synonymous with Masonry, is called the fifth science; and, in fact, throughout nearly all the degrees of Masonry, we find abundant allusions to five as a sacred and mystical number.

Five-Pointed Star. The five-pointed star, which is not to be confounded with the blazing star, is not found among the old symbols of Masonry; indeed, some writers have denied that it is a Masonic emblem at all. It is undoubtedly of recent origin, and was probably introduced by Jeremy Cross, who placed it among the plates in the emblems of the Third Degree prefixed to his *Hieroglyphic Chart.* It is not mentioned in the ritual or the lecture of the Third Degree, but the Masons of this country have, by tacit consent, referred to it as a symbol of the Five Points of Fellowship. The outlines of the five-pointed star are the same as those of the pentalpha of Pythagoras, which was the symbol of health. M. Jomard, in his *Description de l'Egypte* (tom. viii., p. 423), says that the star engraved on the Egyptian monuments, where it is a very common hieroglyphic, has constantly five points, never more nor less.

Five Points of Fellowship. (See *Points of Fellowship, Five.*)

Five Senses. The five senses of Hearing, Seeing, Feeling, Tasting, and Smelling are introduced into the lecture of the Fellow-Craft as a part of the instructions of that Degree. See each word in its appropriate place. In the earlier lectures of the eighteenth century, the five senses were explained in the First Degree as referring to the *five* who make a Lodge. Their subsequent reference to the winding stairs, and their introduction into the second degree, were modern improvements. As these senses are the avenues by which the mind receives its perceptions of things exterior to it, and thus becomes the storehouse of ideas, they are most appropriately referred to that degree of Masonry whose professed object is the pursuit and acquisition of knowledge.

Fixed Lights. In the old lectures of the last century, the *fixed lights* were the three windows always supposed to exist in the East, South, and West. Their uses were, according to the ritual, "to light the men to, at, and from their work." In the modern lectures they have been omitted, and their place as symbols supplied by the *lesser lights.*

Flaming Sword. A sword whose blade is of a spiral or twisted form is called by the heralds a flaming sword, from its resemblance to the ascending curvature of a flame of fire. Until very recently, this was the form of the Tiler's sword. Carelessness or ignorance has now in many Lodges substituted for it a common sword of any form. The flaming sword of the Tiler refers to the flaming sword which guarded the entrance to Paradise, as described

in Genesis (iii., 24): "So he drove out the man; and he placed at the east of the garden of Eden cherubims and a *flaming sword* which turned every way, to keep the way of the tree of life"; or, as Raphall has translated it, "the *flaming sword* which revolveth, to guard the way to the tree of life." In former times, when symbols and ceremonies were more respected than they are now; when collars were worn, and not ribbons in the buttonhole; and when the standing column of the Senior Warden, and the recumbent one of the Junior during labor, to be reversed during refreshment, were deemed necessary for the complete furniture of the Lodge, the cavalry sword was unknown as a Masonic implement, and the Tiler always bore a flaming sword. It were better if we could get back to the old customs.

Floats. Pieces of timber, made fast together with rafters, for conveying burdens down a river with the stream. The use of these floats in the building of the Temple is thus described in the letter of King Hiram to Solomon: "And we will cut wood out of Lebanon, as much as thou shalt need; and we will bring it to thee in flotes by sea to Joppa; and thou shalt carry it up to Jerusalem." (2 Chron. ii., 16.)

Floor. The floor of a properly constructed Lodge room should be covered with alternate squares of black and white, to represent the Mosaic pavement which was the ground floor of King Solomon's Temple.

Floor-Cloth. A framework of board or canvas, on which the emblems of any particular degree are inscribed, for the assistance of the Master in giving a lecture. It is so called because formerly it was the custom to inscribe these designs on the floor of the Lodge room in chalk, which were wiped out when the Lodge was closed. It is the same as the "Carpet," or "Tracing Board."

Flooring. The same as *floor-cloth*, which see.

Florian, Squin de. The first accuser of Grand Master Jacques de Molay and the Knights Templar. He was subsequently assassinated.

Florida. Freemasonry was first introduced into Florida, in 1806, by the organization, in the city of St. Augustine, of St. Fernando Lodge by the Grand Lodge of Georgia. In the year 1811, it was suppressed by a mandate of the Spanish government. In 1820, the Grand Lodge of South Carolina granted a Charter to Floridian Virtue Lodge, No. 28, but, in consequence of the hostility of the political and religious authorities, it did not long exist. In 1824, the Grand Lodge of South Carolina granted another Charter for Esperanza Lodge at St. Augustine, which body, however, became extinct after a year by the removal of most of its members to Havana. In 1826, the Grand Lodges of Tennessee and Georgia granted warrants for the establishment respectively of Jackson Lodge at Tallahassee,

18

Washington Lodge at Quincy, and Harmony Lodge at Mariana. On the 5th of July, 1830, delegates from these three Lodges met at Tallahassee, and organized the Grand Lodge of Florida, which has 166 subordinate Lodges under its rule.

Fludd, Robert. Robert Fludd, or, as he called himself in his Latin writings, Robertus de Fluctibus, was in the seventeenth century a prominent member of the Rosicrucian Fraternity. He was born in England in 1574, and having taken the degrees of Bachelor and Master of Arts at St. John's College, Oxford, he commenced the study of physic, and in due time took the degree of Doctor of Medicine. He died in 1637. In 1616, he commenced the publication of his works and became a voluminous writer, whose subject and style were equally dark and mysterious. The most important of his publications are: *Apologia Compendaria, Fraternitatem de Rosea Cruce, suspicionis et infamiæ maculis aspersum abluens,* (Leyden, 1616), i. e., *A Brief Apology, clearing the Fraternity of the Rosy Cross from the stigma of suspicion and infamy with which they have been aspersed;* and *Tractatus Apologeticus integritatem Societatis de Rosea Cruce defendens contra Libanium et alios* (Leyden, 1617), or, *An Apologetic Tract defending the purity of the Society of the Rosy Cross from the attacks of Libanius and others.* And last, and wildest of all, was his extravagant work on magic, the kabbala, alchemy, and Rosicrucianism, entitled *Summum bonum, quod est verum magiæ, cabacel, alchymiæ, fratrum Rosæ Crucis verorum veræ subjectum.* Rosicrucianism was perhaps indebted more to Fludd than to any other person for its introduction from Germany into England, and it may have had its influence in molding the form of Speculative Freemasonry; but we are not prepared to go as far as a distinguished writer in the London *Freemasons' Magazine* (April, 1858, p. 677), who says that "Fludd must be considered as the immediate father of Freemasonry as Andreä was its remote father." Nicolai more rationally remarks that Fludd, like Andreä, exerted a considerable and beneficial influence on the manners of his age. His explanation of the Rose Croix is worth quoting. He says that it symbolically signifies the cross dyed with the blood of the Savior; a Christian idea which was in advance of the original Rosicrucians.

Folkes, Martin. From his acquaintance with Sir Christopher Wren, and his intimacy with Dr. Desaguliers, Martin Folkes was induced to take an active part in the reorganization of Freemasonry in the beginning of the last century, and his literary attainments and prominent position in the scientific world enabled him to exercise a favorable influence on the character of the Institution. He was descended from a good family, being the eldest son of Martin Folkes, Esq., Counsellor at Law, and Dorothy, the daughter of the Sir William Howell, Knt., of the county of Norfolk. He was born in Queen Street, Leicester Inn Fields, Westminster, October 29, 1690. In 1707 he was entered at Clare Hall, Cambridge, and in 1713 elected a Fellow of the Royal Society, of which, in 1723, he was appointed Vice-President. In 1727, on the death of Sir Isaac Newton, he became a candidate for the Presidency, in which he was defeated by Sir Hans Sloane, who, however, renewed his appointment as Vice-President, and in 1741, on the resignation of Sloane as President, he was elected his successor. In 1742 he was elected a member of the Royal Academy of Sciences of Paris, and in 1746 received the degree of Doctor of Laws from the Universities of Oxford and Cambridge.

In 1750, he was elected President of the Society of Antiquaries. To this and to the Royal Society he contributed many essays, and published a work entitled, *A Table of English Silver Coins,* which is still much esteemed as a numismatic authority. On September 26, 1751, he was struck with paralysis, from which he never completely recovered. On November 30, 1753, he resigned the Presidency of the Royal Society, but retained that of the Society of Antiquaries until his death. In 1733, he visited Italy, and remained there until 1735, during which time he appears to have ingratiated himself with the Masons of that country, for in 1742 they struck a medal in his honor, a copy of which is to be found in Thory's *History of the Foundation of the Grand Orient of France.* On one side is a pyramid, a sphinx, some Masonic ciphers, and the two pillars, and on the obverse a likeness of Folkes.

Of the Masonic life of Folkes we have but few records. In 1725, he was appointed Deputy Grand Master of the Grand Lodge of England, and is recorded as having paid great attention to the duties of his office. Anderson says that he presided over the Grand Lodge in May of that year, and "prompted a most agreeable communication." (*Constitutions,* 1738, p. 119.) But he held no office afterward; yet he is spoken of as having taken great interest in the Institution. Of his literary contributions to Masonry nothing remains.

The *Pocket Companion* cites an address by him, in 1725, before the Grand Lodge, probably at that very communication to which Anderson has alluded, but it is unfortunately no longer extant. He died June 28, 1754, and was buried in the Chancel of Hillington Church near Lynn, Norfolk. He left a wife and two daughters, an only son having died before him.

Nichols, who knew him personally, says (*Lit. Anecd.,* ii., 591) of him: "His knowledge was very extensive, his judgment exact and accurate, and the precision of his ideas appeared from the perspicuity and conciseness of his expression in his discourses and writings on abstruse and difficult topics. . . . He had turned his thoughts to the study of antiquity and the polite arts with a philosophical spirit, which he had contracted by the cultivation of the mathematical sciences from his earliest youth." His valuable library of more than five thousand volumes was sold for £3,090 at auction after his decease.

Fool. A fool, as one not in possession of sound reason, a natural or idiot, is intellectually unfit for initiation into the mysteries of Freemasonry, because he is incapable of comprehending the principles of the Institution, and is without any moral responsibility for a violation or neglect of its duties.

Footstone. The corner-stone. "To level the footstone": to lay the corner-stone. Thus, Oliver = "Solomon was enabled to level the footstone of the Temple in the fourth year of his reign."

Foot to Foot. The old lectures of the last century descanted on the symbolism of foot to foot as teaching us "that indolence should not permit the foot to halt or wrath to turn our steps out of the way; but forgetting injuries and selfish feelings, and remembering that man was born for the aid of his fellow-creatures, not for his own enjoyments only, but to do that which is good, we should be swift to extend our mercy and benevolence to all, but more particularly to a brother Mason." The present lecture on the same subject gives the same lesson more briefly and more emphatically, when it says, "we should never halt nor grow weary in the service of a brother Mason."

Fords of the Jordan. The slaughter of the Ephraimites at the *passages* or *fords of the river Jordan*, which is described in the twelfth chapter of the Book of Judges, is referred to in the ritual of the Fellow-Craft's Degree. Morris, in his *Freemasonry in the Holy Land* (p. 316), says: "The exact locality of these fords (or 'passages,' as the Bible terms them), cannot now be designated, but most likely they were those nearly due east of *Seikoot* and opposite Mizpah. At these fords, in summer time, the water is not more than three or four feet deep, the bottom being composed of a hard limestone rock. If, as some think, the fords, thirty miles higher up, are those referred to, the same description will apply. At either place, the Jordan is about eighty feet wide, its banks encumbered by a dense growth of tamarisks, cane, willows, thorn-bushes, and other low vegetation of the shrubby and thorny sorts, which make it difficult even to approach the margin of the stream. The Arabs cross the river at the present day, at stages of low water, at a number of fords, from the one near the point where the Jordan leaves the Sea of Galilee down to the Pilgrims' Ford, six miles above the Dead Sea."

Foreign Country. The lecture of the Third Degree begins by declaring that the recipient was induced to seek that sublime degree "that he might perfect himself in Masonry, so as to travel into *foreign countries*, and work and receive wages as a Master Mason."

Thousand have often heard this ritualistic expression at the opening and closing of a Master's Lodge, without dreaming for a moment of its hidden and spiritual meaning, or, if they think of any meaning at all, they content themselves by interpreting it as referring to the actual travels of the Masons, after the completion of the Temple, into the surrounding countries in search of employment, whose wages were to be the gold and silver which they could earn by the exercise of their skill in the operative art.

But the true symbolic meaning of the *foreign country* into which the Master Mason travels in search of wages is far different.

The symbolism of this life terminates with the Master's Degree. The completion of that degree is the lesson of death and the resurrection to a future life, where the TRUE WORD, or Divine Truth, not given in this, is to be received as the reward of a life worthily spent in its search. Heaven, the future life, the higher state of existence after death, is the *foreign country* in which the Master Mason is to enter, and there he is to receive his wages in the reception of that TRUTH which can be imparted only in that better land.

Foresters' Degrees. This title has been given to certain secret associations which derive their symbols and ceremonies from trades practised in forests, such as the Carbonari, or Charcoal-burners; the Fendeurs, or Wood-cutters; the Sawyers, etc. They are all imitative of Freemasonry.

Forest of Lebanon. (See *Lebanon*.)

Forfeiture of Charter. A Lodge may forfeit its charter for misconduct, and when forfeited, the warrant or charter is revoked by the Grand Lodge.

Form. In Masonry, an official act is said to be done, according to the rank of the person who does it, either in *ample form*, in *due form*, or simply in *form*. Thus, when the Grand Lodge is opened by the Grand Master in person, it is said to be opened in *ample form;* when by the Deputy Grand Master, it is said to be in *due form;* when by any other qualified officer, it is said to be in *form*. The legality of the act is the same whether it be done in form or in ample form; and the epithet refers only to the dignity of the officer by whom the act is performed.

Form of the Lodge. The terms "Ample" and "Due" Form appear to have been introduced by Anderson in the 1738 ed. of the *Constitutions* (p. 110). The form of a Mason's Lodge is said to be an oblong square, having its greatest length from east to west, and its greatest breadth from north to south. This oblong form of the Lodge has, I think, a symbolic allusion that has not been adverted to by any other writer.

If, on a map of the world, we draw lines which shall circumscribe just that portion which was known and inhabited at the time of the building of Solomon's Temple, these lines, running a short distance north and south of the Mediterranean Sea, and extending from Spain to Asia Minor, will form an *oblong square*, whose greatest length will be from east to west, and whose greatest breadth will be from north to south, as is shown in the annexed diagram.

There is a peculiar fitness in this theory, which is really only making the Masonic Lodge a symbol of the world. It must be remembered that, at the era of the Temple, the earth was supposed to have the form of a parallelogram, or "oblong square." Such a figure inscribed upon a map of the world, and including only that part of it which was known in the days of Solomon, would present just such a square, embracing the Mediterranean Sea and the countries lying immediately on its northern, southern, and eastern borders. Beyond, far in the north, would be Cimmerian deserts as a place of darkness, while the pillars of Hercules in the west, on each side of the Straits of Gades—now Gibraltar—might appropriately be referred to the

two pillars that stood at the porch of the Temple. Thus the world itself would be the true Mason's Lodge, in which he was to live and labor. Again: the solid contents of the earth below, "from the surface to the centre," and the profound expanse above, "from the earth to the highest heavens," would give to this parallelogram the outlines of a double cube, and meet thereby that definition which says that "the form of the Lodge ought to be a double cube, as an expressive emblem of the powers of light and darkness in the creation."

Formula. A prescribed mode or form of doing or saying anything. The word is derived from the technical language of the Roman law, where, after the old legal actions had been abolished, suits were practised according to certain prescribed forms called *formulæ.*

Formulas in Freemasonry are very frequent. They are either oral or monitorial. Oral formulas are those that are employed in various parts of the ritual, such as the opening and closing of a Lodge, the investiture of a candidate, etc. From the fact of their oral transmission they are frequently corrupted or altered, which is one of the most prolific sources of non-conformity so often complained of by Masonic teachers. Monitorial formulas are those that are committed to writing, and are to be found in the various monitors and manuals. They are such as relate to public installations, to laying foundation-stones, to dedications of halls, to funerals, etc. Their monitorial character ought to preserve them from change; but uniformity is not even here always attained, owing to the whims of the compilers of manuals or of monitors, who have often unnecessarily changed the form of words from the original standard.

Fort Hiram. An earthwork erected on October 3, 1814, at Fox Point, Rhode Island, by the Grand Lodge, with the members of the subordinate Lodges, about two hundred and thirty in number. The object was to build a fortification for the defense of the harbor of Providence, and the G. Lodge, of which Thomas Smith Webb was Grand Master, through its Deputy, Sen. G. Warden, and W. Bro. Carlisle, were authorized to work on the defenses. They formed a procession, marched in the early morning to the Point, and by sunset had completed their labors, consisting of a breastwork four hundred and thirty feet in length, ten wide, and five high. They then marched and countermarched upon the parapet from one extremity to the other, when the G. Master gave the work the appellation of Fort Hiram, which was approved and sanctioned by the Governor.

Fort Masonic. A redoubt of the fortifications on what was known as the Heights of Brooklyn, located between, what is now, Bond and Nevins Streets, Brooklyn, the south point of the quadrangle resting on State Street and extending north nearly to Schermerhorn Street; built by members of the fourteen Lodges located in New York City, who, agreeable to a resolution of the Grand Lodge, of which De Witt Clinton was Grand Master, adopted August 22, 1814, assembled at sunrise on the morning of Thursday, September 1st, and, accompanied by the officers of the Grand Lodge, proceeded to Brooklyn where they were joined by the members of Fortitude and Newton Union Lodges, marched to the Height and performed one day's work on the fortifications; the redoubt was not completed, however, until September 17th, when another day's labor was performed.   [W. J. A.]

Fortitude. One of the four cardinal virtues, whose excellencies are dilated on in the First Degree. It not only instructs the worthy Mason to bear the ills of life with becoming resignation, "taking up arms against a sea of trouble," but, by its intimate connection with a portion of our ceremonies, it teaches him to let no dangers shake, no pains dissolve the inviolable fidelity he owes to the trusts reposed in him. Or, in the words of the old Prestonian lecture, it is "a fence or security against any attack that might be made upon him by force or otherwise, to extort from him any of our Royal Secrets."

Spence, in his *Polymetis* (p. 139), when describing the moral virtues, says of Fortitude: " She may be easily known by her erect air and military dress, the spear she rests on with one hand, and the sword which she holds in the other. She has a globe under her feet; I suppose to show that the Romans, by means of this virtue, were to subdue the whole world."

Forty. The multiple of two perfect numbers—four and ten. This was deemed a sacred number, as commemorating many events of religious signification, some of which are as follows: The alleged period of probation of our first parents in Eden; the continuous deluge of forty days and nights, and the same number of days in which the waters remained upon the face of the earth; the Lenten season of forty days' fast observed by Christians with reference to the fast of Jesus in the Wilderness, and by the Hebrews to the earlier desert fast for a similar period; of the forty years spent in the Desert by Moses and Elijah and the Israelites, which succeeded the concealment of Moses the same number of years in the land of Midian. Moses was forty days and nights on the Mount. The days for embalming the dead were forty. The forty years of the reign of Saul, of David, and of Solomon; the forty days of grace allotted to Nineveh for repentance; the forty days' fast before Christmas in the Greek Church; as well as its being the number of days of mourning in Assyria, Phenicia, and Egypt, to commemorate the death and burial of their Sun God; and as well the period in the festivals of the resurrection of Adonis and Osiris; the period of forty days thus being a bond by which the whole world, ancient and modern, Pagan, Jewish, and Christian, is united in religious sympathy. Hence, it was determined as the period of mourning by the Supreme Council of the A. A. Scottish Rite of the Northern Jurisdiction U. S.

Forty-Seventh Problem. The forty-seventh problem of Euclid's first book, which has been adopted as a symbol in the Master's Degree, is thus enunciated: "In any right-angled triangle, the square which is described upon the side subtending the right angle is equal to the squares described upon the sides which contain the right angle." Thus, in a triangle whose perpendicular is 3 feet, the square of which is 9, and whose base is 4 feet, the square of which is 16, the hypothenuse, or subtending side, will be 5 feet, the square of which will be 25, which is the sum of 9 and 16. This interesting problem, on account of its great utility in making calculations and drawing plans for buildings, is sometimes called the "Carpenter's Theorem."

For the demonstration of this problem the world is indebted to Pythagoras, who, it is said, was so elated after making the discovery, that he made an offering of a hecatomb, or a sacrifice of a hundred oxen, to the gods. The devotion to learning which this religious act indicated in the mind of the ancient philosopher has induced Masons to adopt the problem as a memento, instructing them to be lovers of the arts and sciences.

The triangle, whose base is 4 parts, whose perpendicular is 3, and whose hypothenuse is 5, and which would exactly serve for a demonstration of this problem, was, according to Plutarch, a symbol frequently employed by the Egyptian priests, and hence it is called by M. Jomard, in his *Exposition du Système Métrique des Anciens Egyptiens*, the Egyptian triangle. It was, with the Egyptians, the symbol of universal nature, the base representing Osiris, or the male principle; the perpendicular, Isis, or the female principle; and the hypothenuse, Horus, their son, or the

produce of the two principles. They added that 3 was the first perfect odd number, that 4 was the square of 2, the first even number, and that 5 was the result of 3 and 2.

But the Egyptians made a still more important use of this triangle. It was the standard of all their measures of extent, and was applied by them to the building of the pyramids. The researches of M. Jomard, on the Egyptian system of measures, published in the magnificent work of the French savants on Egypt, has placed us completely in possession of the uses made by the Egyptians of this forty-seventh problem of Euclid, and of the triangle which formed the diagram by which it was demonstrated.

If we inscribe within a circle a triangle, whose perpendicular shall be 300 parts, whose base shall be 400 parts, and whose hypothenuse shall be 500 parts, which, of course, bear the same proportion to each other as 3, 4, and 5; then if we let a perpendicular fall from the angle of the perpendicular and base to the hypothenuse, and extend it through the hypothenuse to the circumference of the circle, this chord or line will be equal to 480 parts, and the two segments of the hypothenuse, on each side of it, will be found equal, respectively, to 180 and 320. From the point where this chord intersects the hypothenuse let another line fall perpendicularly to the shortest side of the triangle, and this line will be equal to 144 parts, while the shorter segment, formed by its junction with the perpendicular side of the triangle, will be equal to 108 parts. Hence, we may derive the following measures from the diagram: 500, 480, 400, 320, 180, 144, and 108, and all these without the slightest fraction. Supposing, then, the 500 to be cubits, we have the measure of the base of the great pyramid of Memphis. In the 400 cubits of the base of the triangle we have the exact length of the Egyptian stadium. The 320 gives us the exact number of Egyptian cubits contained in the Hebrew and Babylonian stadium. The stadium of Ptolemy is represented by the 480 cubits, or length of the line falling from the right angle to the circumference of the circle, through the hypothenuse. The number 180, which expresses the smaller segment of the hypothenuse being doubled, will give 360 cubits, which will be the stadium of Cleomedes. By doubling the 144, the result will be 288 cubits, or the length of the stadium of Archimedes; and by doubling the 108, we produce 216 cubits, or the precise value of the lesser Egyptian stadium. In this manner, we obtain from this triangle all the measures of length that were in use among the Egyptians; and since this triangle, whose sides are equal to 3, 4, and 5, was the very one that most naturally would be used in demonstrating the forty-seventh problem of Euclid; and since by these three sides the Egyptians symbolized Osiris, Isis, and Horus, or the two producers and the product, the very principle, expressed in symbolic language, which constitutes the terms of the problem as enunciated by Pythagoras, that the sum of the squares of the two sides will produce the square of the third, we have no reason to doubt that the forty-seventh problem was well known to the Egyptian priests, and by them communicated to Pythagoras.

Dr. Lardner, in his edition of Euclid, says: "Whether we consider the forty-seventh proposition with reference to the peculiar and beautiful relation established in it, or to its innumerable uses in every department of mathematical science, or to its fertility in the consequences derivable from it, it must certainly be esteemed the most celebrated and important in the whole of the elements, if not in the whole range, of mathematical science. It is by the influence of this proposition, and that which establishes the similitude of equiangular triangles (in the sixth book), that geometry has been brought under the dominion of algebra; and it is upon the same principles that the whole science of trigonometry is founded.

"The XXXIId and XLVIIth propositions are said to have been discovered by Pythagoras, and extraordinary accounts are given of his exultation upon his first perception of their truth. It is, however, supposed by some that Pythagoras acquired a knowledge of them in Egypt, and was the first to make them known in Greece."

Forty-Two. The number of judges required to sit by the body of the Egyptian dead pending the examination, and without which the deceased had no portion in Amenti. (See *Truth.*)

Forty-Two-Lettered Name. (See *Twelve-Lettered Name.*)

Foul. The ballot-box is said to be "foul" when, in the ballot for the initiation or advancement of a candidate, one or more black balls are found in it.

Foundation-Stone. This term has been repeatedly used by Dr. Oliver, and after him by some other writers, to designate the chief or corner-stone of the Temple or any other building. Thus, Oliver says, "the Masonic days proper for laying the foundation-stone of a Mason's Lodge are from the 15th of April to the 15th of May"; evidently meaning the corner-stone. The usage is an incorrect one. The *foundation-stone*, more properly the *stone of foundations*, is very different from the *corner-stone*.

Foundation, Stone of. (See *Stone of Foundation.*)

Fountain. In some of the high degrees a fountain constitutes a part of the furniture of the initiation. In the science of symbology, the fountain, as representing a stream of continually flowing water, is a symbol of refreshment to the weary; and so it might be applied in the degrees in which it is found, although there is no explicit interpretation of it in the ritual, where it seems to have been introduced rather as an exponent of the dampness and darkness of the place which was a refuge for criminals and a spot fit for crime. Brother Pike refers to the fountain as "tra-

dition, a slender stream flowing from the Past into the Present, which, even in the thickest darkness of barbarism, keeps alive some memory of the Old Truth in the human heart." But this beautiful idea is not found in the symbolism as interpreted in the old rituals.

Four. Four is the *tetrad* or *quarternary* of the Pythagoreans, and it is a sacred number in the high degrees. The Pythagoreans called it a perfect number, and hence it has been adopted as a sacred number in the Degree of Perfect Master. In many nations of antiquity the name of God consists of four letters, as the ADAD, of the Syrians, the AMUM of the Egyptians, the ΘΕΟΣ of the Greeks, the DEUS of the Romans, and preeminently the Tetragrammaton or four-lettered name of the Jews. But in Symbolic Masonry this number has no special significance.

Four Crowned Martyrs. The legend of "The Four Crowned Martyrs" should be interesting to Masonic scholars, because it is one of the few instances, perhaps the only one, in which the church has been willing to do honor to those old workers in stone, whose services it readily secured in the Medieval ages, but with whom, as with their successors the modern Freemasons, it has always appeared to be in a greater or less degree of antagonism. Besides, these humble but true-hearted confessors of the faith of Christianity were adopted by the Stonemasons of Germany as the patron saints of Operative Masonry, just as the two Saints John have been since selected as the patrons of the Speculative branch of the Institution.

The late Dr. Christian Ehrmann, of Strasburg, who for thirty years had devoted his attention to this and to kindred subjects of Masonic archeology, has supplied us with the most interesting details of the life and death of the Four Crowned Martyrs.

The Roman Church has consecrated the 8th of November to the commemoration of these martyrs, and yearly, on that day, offers up the prayer: "Grant, we beseech thee, O Almighty God, that as we have been informed of the constancy of the glorious martyrs in the profession of Thy faith, so we may experience their kindness in recommending us to Thy mercy." The *Roman Breviary* of 1474 is more explicit, and mentions them particularly by name.

It is, therefore, somewhat remarkable, that, although thus careful in their commemoration, the missals of the church give us no information of the deeds of these holy men. It is only from the breviaries that we can learn anything of the act on which the commemoration in the calendar was founded. Of these breviaries, Ehrmann has given full citations from two: the *Breviary of Rome*, published in 1474, and the *Breviary of Spire*, published in 1478. These, with some few extracts from other books on the subject, have been made accessible to us by George Kloss, in his interesting work entitled, *Freimaurerei in ihrer wahren Bedeutung*, or Freemasonry in its true significance.

The *Breviarium Romanum* is much more

complete in its details than the *Breviarium Spirense;* and yet the latter contains a few incidents that are not related in the former. Both agree in applying to the Four Crowned Martyrs the title of *"quadratarii."* Now *quadratarius,* in the Latin of the lower age, signified a Stone-squarer or a Mason. This will remind us of the passage in the Book of Kings, thus translated in the authorized version: "And Solomon's builders and Hiram's builders did hew them, and the *stone-squarers.*" It is evident from the use of this word *"quadratarii"* in the ecclesiastical legends, as well as from the incidents of the martyrdom itself, that the four martyrs were not simply sculptors, but stone-cutters and builders of temples: in other words, Operative Masons. Nor can we deny the probability of the supposition, that they were members of one of those colleges of architects, which afterward gave birth to the gilds of the Middle Ages, the corporations of builders, and through these to the modern Lodges of Freemasons. Supposing the legend to be true, or even admitting that it is only symbolical, we must acknowledge that there has been good reason why the Operative Masons should have selected these martyrs as the patron saints of their profession.

And now let us apply ourselves to the legend. Taking the *Roman Breviary* as the groundwork, and only interpolating it at the proper points with the additional incidents related in the *Breviary of Spire,* we have the following result as the story of the Four Crowned Martyrs.

In the last quarter of the third century Diocletian was emperor of the Roman Empire. In his reign commenced that series of persecutions of the Christian church, which threatened at one time to annihilate the new religion, and gave to the period among Christain writers the name of the Era of Martyrs. Thousands of Christians, who refused to violate their consciences by sacrificing to the heathen gods, became the victims of the bigotry and intolerance, the hatred and the cruelty, of the Pagan priests and the Platonic philosophers; and the scourge, the cross, or the watery grave daily testified to the constancy and firmness of the disciples of the prophet of Nazareth.

Diocletian had gone to the province of Pannonia, that he might by his own presence superintend the bringing of metals and stones from the neighboring mines of Noricum, wherewith to construct a temple consecrated to the sun-god, Apollo. Among the six hundred and twenty-two artisans whom he had collected together for this purpose were four—by name Claudius, Castorius, Symphorianus, and Nichostratus—said to have been distinguished for their skill as Stonemasons. They had abandoned the old heathen faith and were in secret Christians, doing all their work as Masons in the name of the Lord Jesus Christ.

The *Breviary of Spires* relates here an additional occurrence, which is not contained in the *Breviary of Rome,* and which, as giving a miraculous aspect to the legend, must have made it doubly acceptable to the pious Christians of the fifteenth century, upon whose religious credulity one could safely draw without danger of a protest.

It seems that, in company with our four blessed martyrs, there worked one Simplicius, who was also a Mason, but a heathen. While he was employed in labor near them, he wondered to see how much they surpassed in skill and cunning all the other artisans. They succeeded in all that they attempted, while he was unfortunate, and always breaking his working tools. At last he approached Claudius, and said to him:

"Strengthen, I beseech thee, my tools, that they may no longer break."

Claudius took them in his hands, and said:

"In the name of the Lord Jesus Christ be these tools henceforth strong and faithful to their work."

From this time, Simplicius did his work well, and succeeded in all that he attempted to do. Amazed at the change, Simplicius was continually asking his fellow-workmen how it was that the tools had been so strengthened that now they never broke. At length Claudius replied:

"God, who is our Creator, and the Lord of all things, has made his creatures strong."

Then Simplicius inquired:

"Was not this done by the God Zeus?"

To this Claudius replied:

"Repent, O my brother, of what thou hast said, for thou hast blasphemed God, our Creator, whom alone we worship; that which our own hands have made we do not recognise as a God."

With these and such sentences they converted Simplicius to the Christian faith, who, being baptized by Cyrillus, bishop of Antioch, soon afterward suffered martyrdom for his refusal to sacrifice to the Pagan gods.

But to return from this episode to the legend of the Four Martyrs: It happened that one day Diocletian issued an order, that out of a piece of marble should be constructed a noble statue of Apollo sitting in his chariot. And now all the workmen and the philosophers began to consult on the subject, and each one had arrived at a different opinion.

And when at length they had found a huge block of stone, which had been brought from the Island of Thasos, it proved that the marble was not fit for the statue which Diocletian had commanded; and now began a great war of words between the masters of the work and the philosophers. But one day the whole of the artisans, six hundred and twenty-two in number, with five philosophers, came together, that they might examine the defects and the veins of the stone, and there arose a still more wonderful contest between the workmen and the philosophers.

Then began the philosophers to rail against Claudius, Symphorianus, Nichostratus, and Simplicius, and said:

"Why do ye not hearken to the commands

of our devout emperor, Diocletian, and obey his will."

And Claudius answered and said:

"Because we cannot offend our Creator and commit a sin, whereof we should be found guilty in his sight."

Then said the philosophers:

"From this it appears that you are Christians."

And Claudius replied:

"Truly we are Christians."

Hereupon the philosophers chose other Masons, and caused them to make a statue of Esculapius out of the stone which had been rejected, which, after thirty-one days, they finished and presented to the philosophers. These then informed the emperor that the statue of Esculapius was finished, when he ordered it to be brought before him for inspection. But as soon as he saw it he was greatly astonished, and said:

"This is a proof of the skill of these men, who receive my approval as sculptors."

It is very apparent that this, like all other legends of the church, is insufficient in its details, and that it leaves many links in the chain of the narrative to be supplied by the fancy or the judgment of the readers. It is equally evident from what has already been said, in connection with what is subsequently told, that the writer of the legend desired to make the impression that it was through the influence of Claudius and the other Christian Masons that the rest of the workmen were persuaded that the Thasian stone was defective and unfit for the use of a sculptor; that this was done by them because they were unwilling to engage in the construction of the statue of a Pagan god; that this was the cause of the controversy between the workmen and the philosophers; that the latter denied the defectiveness of the stone; and, lastly, that they sought to prove its fitness by causing other Masons, who were not Christians, to make out of it a statue of Esculapius. These explanations are necessary to an understanding of the legend, which proceeds as follows:

As soon as Diocletian had expressed his admiration of the statue of Esculapius, the philosopher said:

"Most mighty Cæsar, know that these men whom your majesty has praised for their skill in Masonry, namely, Claudius, Symphorianus, Nichostratus, and Castorius, are Christians, and by magic spells or incantations make men obedient to their will."

Then said Diocletian:

"If they have violated the laws, and if your accusations be true, let them suffer the punishment of sacrilege."

But Diocletian, in consideration of their skill, sent for the Tribune Lampadius, and said to him:

"If they refuse to offer sacrifice to the sun-god Apollo, then let them be scourged with scorpions. But if they are willing to do so, then treat them with kindness."

For five days sat Lampadius in the same place, before the temple of the sun-god, and called on them by the proclamation of the herald, and showed them many dreadful things, and all sorts of instruments for the punishment of martyrs, and then he said to them:

"Hearken to me and avoid the doom of martyrs, and be obedient to the mighty prince, and offer a sacrifice to the sun-god, for no longer can I speak to you in gentle words."

But Claudius replied for himself and for his companions with great boldness:

"This let the Emperor Diocletian know: that we truly are Christians, and never can depart from the worship of our God."

Thereupon the Tribune Lampadius, becoming enraged, caused them to be stripped and to be scourged with scorpions, while a herald, by proclamation, announced that this was done because they had disobeyed the commands of the emperor. In the same hour Lampadius, being seized by an evil spirit, died on his seat of judgment.

As soon as the wife and the domestics of Lampadius heard of his death, they ran with great outcries to the palace. Diocletian, when he had learned what had happened, ordered four leaden coffins to be made, and that—Claudius and his three companions being placed therein alive—they should be thrown into the river Danube. This order Nicetius, the assistant of Lampadius, caused to be obeyed, and thus the faithful Masons suffered the penalty and gained the crown of martyrdom.

There are some legend books which give the names of the Four Crowned Martyrs as Severus, Severianus, Carpophorus, and Victorinus, and others again which speak of five confessors who, a few years afterward, suffered martyrdom for refusing to sacrifice to the Pagan gods, and whose names being at the time unknown, Pope Melchiades caused them to be distinguished in the church calendar as the Four Crowned Martyrs: an error, says Jacob de Voragine, which, although subsequently discovered, was never corrected. But the true legend of the Four Crowned Martyrs is that which has been given above from the best authority, the *Roman Breviary* of 1474.

"On the other side of the Esquiline," says Mrs. Jameson (in her *Sacred and Legendary Art*, vol. ii., p. 624), "and on the road leading from the Coliseum to the Lateran, surmounting a heap of sand and ruins, we come to the church of the 'Quattro Coronati,' the Four Crowned Brothers. On this spot, some time in the fourth century, were found the bodies of four men who had suffered decapitation, whose names being then unknown, they were merely distinguished as CORONATI, *crowned*—that is, with the crown of martyrdom."

There is great obscurity and confusion in the history of these.

Their church, Mrs. Jameson goes on to say, is held in particular respect by the builders and stone-cutters of Rome. She has found allusion to these martyr Masons not only in

Roman art, but in the old sculpture and stained glass of Germany. Their effigies, she tells us, are easily distinguished by the fact, that they stand in a row, bearing palms, with crowns upon their heads and various Masonic implements at their feet—such as the rule, the square, the mallet, and the chisel.

They suffered death on the 8th of November, 287, and hence in the Roman Catholic missal that day is dedicated to their commemoration. From their profession as Stonemasons and from the pious firmness with which they refused, at the cost of their lives, to consecrate their skill in their art to the construction of Pagan temples, they have been adopted by the Stonemasons of Germany as the *Patron Saints of Operative Masonry.* Thus the oldest regulation of the Stonemasons of Strasburg, which has the date of the year 1459, commences with the following invocation: "In the name of the Father, and of the Son, and of the Holy Ghost, and of our gracious Mother Mary, and also of her Blessed Servants, the Four Crowned Martyrs of everlasting memory."

Such allusions are common in the German Masonic documents of the Middle Ages. It is true, however, that the English Masons ceased at a later period to refer in their Constitutions to those martyrs, although they undoubtedly borrowed many of their usages from Germany. Yet the Regius Manuscript of the Constitutions of Masonry, the oldest of the English Records, which is supposed to have been written about the year 1390, under the title of "*Ars Quatuor Coronatorum*," gives a rather copious detail of the legend, which is here inserted with only those slight alterations of its antiquated phraseology which are necessary to render it intelligible to modern readers, although in doing so the rhyme of the original is somewhat destroyed:

"Pray we now to God Almighty,
And to His Mother, Mary bright,
That we may keep these articles here
And these points well altogether,
As did those holy martyrs four
That in this Craft were of great honour.
They were as good Mason as on earth shall go,
Gravers and image makers they were also,
For they were workmen of the best,
The emperor had them in great liking;
He willed of them an image to make,
That might be worshiped for his sake;
Such idols he had in his day
To turn the people from Christ's law,
But they were steadfast in Christ's law
And to their Craft, without denial;
They loved well God and all his lore,
And were in his service evermore.
True men they were, in that day,
And lived well in God's law;
They thought no idols for to make,
For no good that they might take;
To believe on that idol for their god,
They would not do so, though he were mad,
For they would not forsake their true faith,
And believe on his false law.
The emperor caused to take them at once
And put them in a deep prison.
The sorer he punished them in that place,
The more joy was to them of Christ's grace.

Then when he saw no other one,
To death he let them then go.
Who so will of their life more know,
By the book he may it show,
In the legends of the saints,
The names of the four crowned ones.
Their feast will be, without denial,
After All Hallows, the eighth day."
               (vv. 497–534.)

The devotion of these saints, which led to the introduction of their legend into an ancient Constitution of Masonry, shows how much they were reverenced by the Craft. In fact, the Four Crowned Martyrs were to the Stone-cutters of Germany and to the earlier Operative Masons of England what St. John the Baptist and St. John the Evangelist became to their successors, the Speculative Freemasons of the eighteenth century. [From them the famous literary Lodge—the Quatuor Coronati, of London, England—has been so named.]

Fourfold Cord. In the ritual of the Past Master's Degree in America we find the following expression: "A twofold cord is strong, a threefold cord is stronger, but a fourfold cord is not easily broken." The expression is taken from a Hebrew proverb which is to be found in the Book of Ecclesiastes (iv. 12): "And if one prevail against him, two shall withstand him; and a threefold cord is not quickly broken." The form of the Hebrew proverb has been necessarily changed to suit the symbolism of the degree.

Four New Years. According to the Talmud there were four New Years. The first of Nisan was the new year for kings and festivals; the reign of a king was calculated from this date. The first of Elul was a new year for the tithing of cattle. The first of Tishri was a new year for civil years, for years of release, jubilees, and planting. The first of Shebat was a new year for the tithing of trees.

"Four Old Lodges." Of the four old Lodges which constituted the Grand Lodge of England, on St. John the Baptist's day, 1717, the "*Lodge of Antiquity*," No. 2, London, was the first. The Lodge meets by "Time Immemorial Constitution," having no warrant, and, until the "Union," was first on the roll; a decision, however, by ballot, lost it its numerical priority. As Lodges were known by the house in which they met, Antiquity Lodge was designated "*The West India and American.*"

"*The Royal Somerset House and Inverness*," No. 4, London, is the junior of the four Lodges which constituted the Grand Lodge. At that time it met at the "*Rummer and Grapes*" Tavern, Westminster, and subsequently at the "*Horn*," which latter gave the Lodge a name for many years. This Lodge now represents three united Lodges, the names of two of which are to be found in its present designation.

Of the four "*original*" Lodges, two only have been on the roll from 1740 as of "Time Immemorial Constitution." The original "No. 2" ceased working about 1736 and was erased in 1740, and "No. 3" accepted a "New Constitution" (now No. 12), and is known as "Fortitude and Cumberland." .

The four original Lodges, after the issue of the "Regulations" of 1723, simply enjoyed the advantage of being ahead of all the Warrant Lodges, the privilege of assembling by "Time Immemorial Constitution," and the honor of having established the first Grand Lodge in the universe. (See *Freemasonry, Early British*.)

Fourteen. It is only necessary to remind the well-informed Mason of the fourteen days of burial mentioned in the legend of the Third Degree. Now, this period of fourteen was not in the opinion of Masonic symbologists, an arbitrary selection, but was intended to refer to or symbolize the fourteen days of lunary darkness, or decreasing light, which intervene between the full moon and its continued decrease until the end of the lunar month. In the Egyptian mysteries, the body of Osiris is said to have been cut into *fourteen* pieces by Typhon, and thrown into the Nile. Plutarch, speaking of this in his treatise *On Isis and Osiris*, thus explains the symbolism of the number fourteen, which comprises the Masonic idea: "The body of Osiris was cut," says Plutarch, "into fourteen pieces; that is, into as many parts as there are days between the full moon and the new. This circumstance has reference to the gradual diminution of the lunary light during the *fourteen* days that follow the full moon. The moon, at the end of fourteen days, enters Taurus, and becomes united to the sun, from whom she collects fire upon her disk during the fourteen days which follow. She is then found every month in conjunction with him in the superior parts of the signs. The equinoctial year finishes at the moment when the sun and moon are found united with Orion, or the star of Orus, a constellation placed under Taurus, which unites itself to the Neomenia of spring. The moon renews herself in Taurus, and a few days afterward is seen, in the form of a crescent, in the following sign, that is, Gemini, the home of Mercury. Then Orion, united to the sun in the attitude of a formidable warrior, precipitates Scorpio, his rival, into the shades of night; for he sets every time Orion appears above the horizon. The day becomes lengthened, and the germs of evil are by degrees destroyed. It is thus that the poet Nonnus pictures to us Typhon conquered at the end of winter, when the sun arrives in Taurus, and when Orion mounts into the heavens with him."

France. The early history of Masonry in France is, from the want of authentic documents, in a state of much uncertainty. Kloss, in his *Geschichte der Freimaurerei in Frankreich* (vol. i., p. 14) says, in reference to the introduction of Freemasonry into that kingdom, that the earliest date of any certainty is 1725. Yet he copies the statement of the *Sçeau Rompu*—a work published in 1745—that the earliest recognized date of its introduction is 1718; and the Abbé Robin says that

nothing of it is to be found farther back than 1720.

Lalande, the great astronomer, was the author of the article on Freemasonry in the *Encyclopédié Méthodique*, and his account has been generally recognized as authentic by succeeding writers. According to him, Lord Derwentwater, the Chevalier Maskeleyne, Mr. Heguetty, and some other Englishmen (the names being corrupted, of course, according to French usage), founded, in 1725, the first Lodge in Paris. It was held at the house of an English confectioner named Hure, in the Rue de Boucheries. In ten years the number of Lodges in Paris had increased to six, and there were several also in the provincial towns.

As the first Paris Lodge had been opened by Lord Derwentwater, he was regarded as the Grand Master of the French Masons, without any formal recognition on the part of the brethern, at least until 1736, when the six Lodges of Paris formally elected Lord Harnouester as Provincial Grand Master*; in 1738, he was succeeded by the Duke d'Antin; and on the death of the Duke, in 1743, the Count de Clermont was elected to supply his place.

Organized Freemasonry in France dates its existence from this latter year. In 1735, the Lodges of Paris had petitioned the Grand Lodge of England for the establishment of a Provincial Grand Lodge, which, on political grounds, had been refused. In 1743, however, it was granted, and the Provincial Grand Lodge of France was constituted under the name of the "Grand Loge Anglaise de France." The Grand Master, the Count de Clermont, was, however, an inefficient officer; anarchy and confusion once more invaded the Fraternity; the authority of the Grand Lodge was prostrated; and the establishment of Mother Lodges in the provinces, with the original intention of superintending the proceedings of the distant provincial Lodges, instead of restoring harmony, as was vainly expected, widened still more the breach. For, assuming the rank and exercising the functions of Grand Lodges, they ceased all correspondence with the metropolitan body, and became in fact its rivals.

Under these circumstances, the Grand Lodge declared itself independent of England in 1755, and assumed the title of the "*Grande Loge de France.*" It recognized only the three degrees of Apprentice, Fellow-Craft, and Master Mason, and was composed of the Grand Officers to be elected out of the body of the Fraternity, and of the Masters for life of the Parisian Lodges; thus formally excluding the provincial Lodges from any participation in the government of the Craft.

But the proceedings of this body were not less stormy than those of its predecessor. The Count de Clermont appointed, in suc-

*Bro. R. F. Gould, in his *Concise History of Freemasonry* (p. 355), considers that the name "*Harnouester*" is probably a corruption of "*Derwentwater*."

cession, two deputies, both of whom had been displeasing to the Fraternity. The last, Lacorne, was a man of such low origin and rude manners, that the Grand Lodge refused to meet him as their presiding officer. Irritated at this pointed disrespect, he sought in the taverns of Paris those Masters who had made a traffic of initiations, but who, heretofore, had submitted to the control, and been checked by the authority of, the Grand Lodge. From among them he selected officers devoted to his service, and undertook a complete reorganization of the Grand Lodge.

The retired members, however, protested against these illegal proceedings; and in the subsequent year, the Grand Master consented to revoke the authority he had bestowed upon Lacorne, and appointed as his deputy, M. Chaillou de Jonville. The respectable members now returned to their seats in the Grand Lodge; and in the triennial election which took place in June, 1765, the officers who had been elected during the Deputy Grand Mastership of Lacorne were all removed. The displaced officers protested, and published a defamatory memoir on the subject, and were in consequence expelled from Masonry by the Grand Lodge. Ill feeling on both sides was thus engendered, and carried to such a height, that, at one of the communications of the Grand Lodge, the expelled brethren, attempting to force their way in, were resisted with violence. The next day the lieutenant of police issued an edict, forbidding the future meetings of the Grand Lodge.

The expelled party, however, still continued their meetings. The Count de Clermont died in 1771; and the excluded brethren having invited the Duke of Chartres (afterward Duke of Orleans) to the Grand Mastership, he accepted the appointment. They now offered to unite with the Grand Lodge, on condition that the latter would revoke the decree of expulsion. The proposal was accepted, and the Grand Lodge went once more into operation.

Another union took place, which has since considerably influenced the character of French Masonry. During the troubles of the preceding years, Masonic bodies were instituted in various parts of the kingdom, which professed to confer degrees of a higher nature than those belonging to Craft Masonry, and which have since been known by the name of the High Degrees. These Chapters assumed a right to organize and control Symbolic or Blue Lodges, and this assumption has been a fertile source of controversy between them and the Grand Lodge. By the latter body they had never been recognized, but the Lodges under their direction had often been declared irregular, and their members expelled. They now, however, demanded a recognition, and proposed, if their request was complied with, to bestow the government of the "hautes grades" upon the same person who was at the head of the Grand Lodge. The compromise was made, the recognition was decreed, and the Duke of Chartres was elected Grand Mas-

ter of all the Councils, Chapters, and Scotch Lodges of France.

But peace was not yet restored. The party who had been expelled, moved by a spirit of revenge for the disgrace formerly inflicted on them, succeeded in obtaining the appointment of a committee which was empowered to preparé the new Constitution. All the Lodges of Paris and the provinces were requested to appoint deputies, who were to form a convention to take the new Constitution into consideration. This convention, or, as they called it, National Assembly, met at Paris in December, 1771. The Duke of Luxemburg presided, and on the twenty-fourth of that month the Ancient Grand Lodge of France was declared extinct, and in its place another substituted with the title of *Grand Orient de France*.

Notwithstanding the declaration of extinction by the National Assembly, the Grand Lodge continued to meet and to exercise its functions. Thus the Fraternity of France continued to be harassed, by the bitter contentions of these rival bodies, until the commencement of the revolution compelled both the Grand Orient and the Grand Lodge to suspend their labors.

On the restoration of civil order, both bodies resumed their operations, but the Grand Lodge had been weakened by the death of many of the perpetual Masters, who had originally been attached to it; and a better spirit arising, the Grand Lodge was, by a solemn and mutual declaration, united to the Grand Orient on the 28th of June, 1799.

Dissensions, however, continued to arise between the Grand Orient and the different Chapters of the high degrees. Several of those bodies had at various periods given in their adhesion to the Grand Orient, and again violated the compact of peace. Finally, the Grand Orient, perceiving that the pretensions of the Scottish Rite Masons would be a perpetual source of disorder, decreed on the 16th of September, 1805, that the Supreme Council of the Thirty-third Degree should thenceforth become an independent body, with the power to confer warrants of constitution for all the degrees superior to the Eighteenth, or Rose Croix; while the Chapters of that and the inferior degrees were placed under the exclusive control of the Grand Orient.

But the concordat was not faithfully observed by either party, and dissensions continued to exist with intermittent and unsuccessful attempts at reconciliation, which was, however, at last effected in some sort in 1841. The Masonic obedience of France is now divided between the two bodies, and the Grand Orient and the Supreme Council now both exist as independent powers in French Masonry. The constant tendency of the former to interfere in the administration of other countries would furnish an unpleasant history for the succeeding thirty years, at last terminated by the refusal of all the Grand Lodges in the United States, and some in Europe, to hold further Masonic communication with it; a breach which every good Mason must desire to see eventually healed. One of the most extraordinary acts of the Grand Orient of France has been the abolition in 1871 of the office of Grand Master, the duties being performed by the President of the Council of the Order.

Discussion and an attempted avoidance of a threatening Masonic calamity by a large number of the Fraternity of France did not avail to prevent the General Assembly of the Grand Orient of France from completing its overthrow and that of its subordinates by the almost unanimous adoption of the now famous amendment of Art. I. of the Constitution of Masonry, on September 14, 1877.

The following is the text of the amendment and of the original second paragraph which was expunged:

Original paragraph: "Freemasonry has for its principles the existence of God, the immortality of the soul, and the solidarity of mankind."

Substituted amendment: "Whereas, Freemasonry is not a religion, and has therefore no doctrine or dogma to affirm in its Constitution, the Assembly adopting the Väeu IX., has decided and decreed that the second paragraph of Article I. of the Constitution shall be erased, and that for the words of the said article the following shall be substituted: I. Being an institution essentially philanthropic, philosophic, and progressive, Freemasonry has for its object, search after truth, study of universal morality, sciences and arts, and the practice of benevolence. It has for its principles, absolute liberty of conscience and human solidarity, it excludes no person on account of his belief and its motto is Liberty, Equality, and Fraternity."

The adoption of the above was after a full and deliberate consideration by its constituents, who for more than a year were in the throes of deep deliberation and judgment.

[The Grand Lodge of England appointed a committee to consider this action of the Grand Orient in thus expunging the existence of T. G. A. O. T. U. from its tenets, and they reported that such alteration is "opposed to the traditions, practice and feelings of all true and genuine Masons from the earliest to the present time"; and it was resolved that foreign brethren could only be received as visitors if they had been initiated in a Lodge professing belief in T. G. A. O. T. U., and would themselves acknowledge such belief to be an essential landmark of the Order. Similar action was taken by other Grand Lodges, and wherever the English language is spoken the Grant Orient of France is no longer regarded as a Masonic body. E. L. H]

Francis II., Emperor of Germany, was a bitter enemy of Freemasonry. In 1789, he ordered all the Lodges in his dominions to be closed, and directed all civil and military functionaries to take an oath never to unite with any secret society, under pain of exemplary punishment and destitution of office. In 1794, he proposed to the diet of Ratisbon the suppression of the Freemasons, the Illumi-

nati, and all other secret societies. The diet, controlled by the influence of Prussia, Brunswick, and Hanover, refused to accede to the proposition, replying to the emperor that he might interdict the Lodges in his own states. but that others claimed Germanic liberty. In 1801, he renewed his opposition to secret societies, and especially to the Masonic Lodges, and all civil, military, and ecclesiastical functionaries were restrained from taking any part in them under the penalty of forfeiting their offices.

Francken, Henry A. The first Deputy Inspector General appointed by Stephen Morin, under his commission from the Emperors of the East and West. Francken received his degrees and his appointment at Kingston, Jamaica. The date is not known, but it must have been between 1762 and 1767. Francken soon afterward repaired to the United States, where he gave the appointment of a Deputy to Moses M. Hayes, at Boston, and organized a council of Princes of Jerusalem at Albany. He may be considered as the first propagator of the high degrees in the United States.

Franc-Macon, Franc-Maçonnerie. The French names of *Freemason* and of *Freemasonry*. The construction of these words is not conformable to the genius or the idiom of the French language, which would more properly employ the terms "Maçon libre," and "Maçonnerie libre"; and hence Laurens, in his *Essais historiques et critiques sur la Franç Maçonnerie*, adduces their incorporation into the language as an evidence that the Institution in France was derived directly from England, the words being a literal and unidiomatic translation of the English titles. But he blunders in supposing that *Franc-Mason* and *Franc-Masonry* are any part of the English language.

Frankfort-on-the-Main. A Provincial Grand Lodge was established in this city, in 1766, by the Grand Lodge of England. In the dissensions which soon after prevailed among the Masons of Germany, the Provincial Grand Lodge of Frankfort, not finding itself supported by its mother Grand Lodge, declared itself independent in 1783. Since 1823, it has worked under the title of the "Grosse Mutterloge des Eklektischen Freimaurer-Bandes zu Frankfurt A. M."

It has now 21 Lodges and 9 "Circles" under its jurisdiction.

Franklin, Benjamin. This sage and patriot was born in the city of Boston, Massachusetts, on the 6th of January, 1706. He was most probably initiated in 1731 in the St. John's Lodge at Philadelphia (Gould's *Hist. of F. M.*, iii. 429.) In 1734 he was elected Grand Master of the Provincial Grand Lodge of Pennsylvania; and in November of the same year Franklin applied to Henry Price, who had received from England authority to establish Masonry in this country, for a confirmation of those powers conferred by the first deputation or warrant. It is probable that the request was granted, although no record of the fact can be found. In 1734, Franklin edited an edition of Anderson's *Constitutions*, which was probably the first Masonic work published in America.

In 1743 Thomas Oxnard was appointed Provincial Grand Master of all North America, and he appointed Franklin Provincial Grand Master of Pennsylvania.

While Franklin was in France as the Ambassador from this country, he appears to have taken much interest in Masonry. He affiliated with the celebrated Lodge of the Nine Sisters, of which Lalande, Count de Gebelin, and other celebrities of French literature, were members. He took a prominent part in the initiation of Voltaire, and on his death acted as Senior Warden of the Lodge of Sorrow held in his memory. The Lodge of the Nine Sisters held Franklin in such esteem that it struck a medal in his honor, of which a copy, supposed to be the only one now in existence, belongs to the Provincial Grand Lodge of Mecklenburg. [E. L. H.]

Franks, Order of Regenerated. A political brotherhood that was instituted in France in 1815, flourished for a while, and imitated in its ceremonies the Masonic fraternity.

Frater. Latin, Brother. A term borrowed from the monks by the Military Orders of the Middle Ages, and applied by the members to each other. It is constantly employed in England by the Masonic Knights Templars, and is beginning to be adopted, although not very generally, in the United States. When speaking of two or more, it is an error of ignorance, sometimes committed, to call them *fraters*. The correct plural is *fratres*.

Fraternally. The usual mode of subscription to letters written by one Mason to another is, "I remain, fraternally, yours."

Fraternity. The word was originally used to designate those associations formed in the Roman Catholic Church for the pursuit of special religious and ecclesiastical purposes, such as the nursing of the sick, the support of the poor, the practise of particular devotions, etc. They do not date earlier than the thirteenth century. The name was subsequently applied to secular associations, such as the Freemasons. The word is only a Latin form of the Anglo-Saxon *Brotherhood*.

In the earliest lectures of the last century we find the word *fraternity* alluded to in the following formula:

"*Q.* How many particular points pertain to a Freemason?

"*A.* Three: Fraternity, Fidelity, and Taciturnity.

"*Q.* What do they represent?

"*A.* Brotherly Love, Relief, and Truth among all Right Masons."

Fraternize. To recognize as a brother; to associate with Masonically.

Frederick of Nassau. Prince Frederick, son of the King of the Netherlands, and for many years the Grand Master of the National Grand Lodge of that kingdom. He was ambitious of becoming a Masonic reformer, and in addition to his connection with the Charter of Cologne, an account of which has been given under that head, he attempted, in 1819, to introduce a new Rite. He denounced the high degrees as being contrary to the true intent of Masonry; and in a circular to all the Lodges under the obedience of the National Grand Lodge, he proposed a new system, to consist of five degrees, namely, the three symbolic, and two more as complements or illustrations of the third, which he called *Elect Master* and *Supreme Elect Master*. Some few Lodges adopted this new system, but most of them rejected it. The Grand Chapter, whose existence it had attacked, denounced it. The Lodges practising it in Belgium were dissolved in 1830, but a few of them probably still remain in Holland. The full rituals of the two supplementary degrees are printed in the second volume of *Hermes*, and an attentive perusal of them does not give an exalted idea of the inventive genius of the Prince.

Frederick the Great. Frederick II., King of Prussia, surnamed the Great, was born on the 24th of January, 1712, and died on the 17th of August, 1786, at the age of seventy-four years and a few months. He was initiated as a Mason, at Brunswick, on the night of the 14th of August, 1738, not quite two years before he ascended the throne.

In English, we have two accounts of this initiation,—one by Campbell, in his work on *Frederick the Great and his Times*, and the other by Carlyle in his *History of Frederick the Second*. Both are substantially the same, because both are merely translations of the original account given by Bielfeld in his *Freundschaftliche Briefe*, or *Familiar Letters*. The Baron von Bielfeld was, at the time, an intimate companion of the Prince, and was present at the initiation.

Bielfeld tells us that in a conversation which took place on the 6th of August at Loo (but Carlyle corrects him as to time and place, and says it probably occurred at Minden, on the 17th of July), the Institution of Freemasonry had been enthusiastically lauded by the Count of Lippe Buckeburg. The Crown Prince soon after privately expressed to the Count his wish to join the society. Of course, this wish was to be gratified. The necessary furniture and asistance for conferring the degrees were obtained from the Lodge at Hamburg. Biefeld gives an amusing account of the embarrassments which were encountered in passing the chest containing the Masonic implements through the customhouse without detection. Campbell, quoting from Bielfeld, says:

"The whole of the 14th (August) was spent in preparations for the Lodge, and at twelve at night the Prince Royal arrived, accompanied by Count Wartensleben, a captain in the king's regiment at Potsdam. The Prince introduced him to us as a candidate whom he very warmly recommended, and begged that he might be admitted immediately after himself. At the same time, he desired that he might be treated like any private individual, and that none of the usual ceremonies might be altered on his account. Accordingly, he was admitted in the customary form, and I could not sufficiently admire his fearlessness, his composure, and his address. After the double reception, a Lodge was held. All was over by four in the morning, and the Prince returned to the ducal palace, apparently as well pleased with us as we were charmed with him.'

Of the truth of this account there never has been any doubt. Frederick the Great was certainly a Mason. But Carlyle, in his usual sarcastic vein, adds: "The Crown Prince prosecuted his Masonry at Reinsberg or elsewhere, occasionally, for a year or two, but was never ardent in it, and very soon after his accession left off altogether. . . . A Royal Lodge was established at Berlin, of which the new king consented to be patron; but he never once entered the palace, and only his portrait (a welcomely good one, still to be found there) presided over the mysteries of that establishment."

Now how much of truth with the sarcasm, and how much of sarcasm without the truth, there is in this remark of Carlyle, is just what the Masonic world is bound to discover. Until further light is thrown upon the subject by documentary evidence from the Prussian Lodges, the question can not be definitely answered. But what is the now known further Masonic history of Frederick?

Bielfeld tells us that the zeal of the Prince for the Fraternity induced him to invite the Baron Von Oberg and himself to Reinsberg, where, in 1739, they founded a Lodge, into which Keyserling, Jordan, Moolendorf, Queis, and Fredersdorf (Frederick's valet) were admitted.

Bielfeld is again our authority for stating that on the 20th of June, 1740, King Frederick—for he had then ascended the throne—held a Lodge at Charlottenburg, and, as Master in the chair, initiated Prince William of Prussia, his brother, the Margrave Charles of Brandenburg, and Frederick William, Duke of Holstein. The Duke of Holstein was seven years afterward elected Adjutant Grand Master of the Grand Lodge of the Three Globes at Berlin.

We hear no more of Frederick's Masonry in the printed records until the 16th of July, 1774, when he granted his protection to the National Grand Lodge of Germany, and officially approved of the treaty with the Grand Lodge of England, by which the National Grand Lodge was established. In the year 1777, the Mother Lodge, "Royal York of Friendship," at Berlin, celebrated, by a festival, the king's birthday, on which occasion Frederick wrote the following letter, which, as it is the only printed declaration of his opinion of Freemasonry that is now extant, is well worth copying:

"I cannot but be sensible of the new homage of the Lodge 'Royal York of Friendship' on the occasion of the anniversary of my birth, bearing, as it does, the evidence of its zeal and attachment for my person. Its orator has

well expressed the sentiments which animate all its labors; and a society which employs itself only in sowing the seed and bringing forth the fruit of every kind of virtue in my deminions may always be assured of my protection. It is the glorious task of every good sovereign, and I will never cease to fulfil it. And so I pray God to take you and your Lodge under his holy and deserved protection. Potsdam, this 14th of February, 1777.—Frederick." *

Frederick Henry Louis, Prince of Prussia, was received into Masonry at Berlin by Frederick the Great, his brother, in 1740.

Frederick William III. King of Prussia, and, although not a Freemason, a generous patron of the Order. On December 29, 1797, he wrote to the Lodge Royal York of Friendship, at Berlin, these words: "I have never been initiated, as every one knows, but I am far from conceiving the slightest distrust of the intentions of the members of the Lodge. I believe that its design is noble, and founded on the cultivation of virtue; that its methods are legitimate, and that every political tendency is banished from its operations. Hence, I shall take pleasure in manifesting on all occasions my good-will and my affection to the Lodge Royal York of Friendship, as well as to every other Lodge in my dominions." In a similar tone of kindness toward Masonry, he wrote three months afterward to Fessler. And when he issued, October 20, 1798, an edict forbidding secret societies, he made a special exemption in favor of the Masonic Lodges. To the time of his death, he was always the avowed friend of the Order.

Free. The word "free," in connection with "Mason," originally signified that the person so called was free of the company or gild of incorporated Masons. For those Operative Masons who were not thus made free of the gild, were not permitted to work with those who were. A similar regulation still exists in many parts of Europe, although it is not known to this country. The term appears to have been first thus used in the tenth century, when the traveling Freemasons were incorporated by the Roman Pontiff. (See *Traveling Freemasons.*)

In reference to the other sense of *free* as meaning *not bound, not in captivity*, it is a rule of Masonry that no one can be initiated who is at the time restrained of his liberty.

The Grand Lodge of England extends this doctrine, that Masons should be free in all their thoughts and actions, so far, that it will not permit the initiation of a candidate who is

---

*Frederick did not in his latter days take the active interest in Masonry that had distinguished his early life before coming to the throne. It cannot be established that he ever attended a meeting after he became king, though many such efforts have been attempted. Some over-zealous persons have claimed that he established the A. and A.S.R. of the Thirty-third Degree, but the Grand Lodge of the Three Globes at Berlin, as well as many European historians, have often shown this to have been impossible.   [E. E. C.]

only temporarily in a place of confinement. In the year 1783, the Master of the Royal Military Lodge at Woolwich (No. 371) being confined, most probably for debt, in the King's Bench prison, at London, the Lodge, which was itinerant in its character and allowed to move from place to place with its regiment, adjourned, with its warrant of Constitution, to the Master in prison, where several Masons were made. The Grand Lodge, being informed of the circumstances, immediately summoned the Master and Wardens of the Lodge "to answer for their conduct in making Masons in the King's Bench prison," and, at the same time, adopted a resolution, affirming that "it is inconsistent with the principles of Masonry for any Freemasons' Lodge to be held, for the purposes of making, passing, or raising Masons, in any prison or place of confinement." (*Constitutions*, 1784, p. 349.)

Free and Accepted. The title "Free and Accepted" first occurs in the Roberts Print of 1722, which is headed *The Old Constitutions belonging to the Ancient and Honourable Society of Free and Accepted Masons*, and was adopted by Dr. Anderson in the second edition of the *Book of Constitutions*, published in 1738, the title of which is *The New Book of Constitutions of the Antient and Honourable Fraternity of Free and Accepted Masons*. In the first edition of 1723 the title was, *The Constitutions of the Freemasons*. The newer title continued to be used by the Grand Lodge of England, in which it was followed by those of Scotland and Ireland; and a majority of the Grand Lodges in this country have adopted the same style, and call themselves Grand Lodges of Free and Accepted Masons. (See *Accepted*.) The old lectures formerly used in England give the following account of the origin of the term:

"The Masons who were selected to build the Temple of Solomon were declared FREE and were exempted, together with their descendants, from imposts, duties, and taxes. They had also the privilege to bear arms. At the destruction of the Temple by Nebuchadnezzar, the posterity of these Masons were carried into captivity with the ancient Jews. But the good-will of Cyrus gave them permission to erect a second Temple, having set them at liberty for that purpose. It is from this epoch that we bear the name of Free and Accepted Masons."

Free Born. In all the old Constitutions, free birth is required as a requisite to the reception of Apprentices. Thus the Lansdowne MS. says, "That the prentice be able of birth, that is, free born." So it is in the Edinburgh Kilwinning, the York, the Antiquity, and in every other manuscript that has been so far discovered. And hence, the modern Constitutions framed in 1721 continue the regulation. After the abolition of slavery in the West Indies by the British Parliament, the Grand Lodge of England on September 1, 1847, changed the word "free-born" into "freeman," but the ancient landmark never has been removed in America.

The non-admission of a slave seems to have been founded upon the best of reasons; because, as Freemasonry involves a solemn contract, no one can legally bind himself to its performance who is not a free agent and the master of his own actions. That the restriction is extended to those who were originally in a servile condition, but who may have since acquired their liberty, seems to depend on the principle that birth in a servile condition is accompanied by a degradation of mind and abasement of spirit which no subsequent disenthralment can so completely efface as to render the party qualified to perform his duties, as a Mason, with that "freedom, fervency, and zeal" which are said to have distinguished our ancient brethren. "Children," says Oliver, "cannot inherit a free and noble spirit except they be born of a free woman."

The same usage existed in the spurious Freemasonry or the mysteries of the ancient world. There, no slave, or man born in slavery, could be initiated; because the prerequisites imperatively demanded that the candidate should not only be a man of irreproachable manners, but also a free-born denizen of the country in which the mysteries were celebrated.

Some Masonic writers have thought that in this regulation, in relation to free birth, some allusion is intended, both in the mysteries and in Freemasonry, to the relative conditions and characters of Isaac and Ishmael. The former—the accepted one, to whom the promise was given—was the son of a free woman, and the latter, who was cast forth to have "his hand against every man and every man's hand against him," was the child of a slave. Wherefore, we read that Sarah demanded of Abraham, "Cast out this bondwoman and her son; for the son of the bondwoman shall not be heir with my son." Dr. Oliver, in speaking of the grand festival with which Abraham celebrated the weaning of Isaac, says that he "had not paid the same compliment at the weaning of Ishmael, because he was the son of a bondwoman, and consequently could not be admitted to participate in the Freemasonry of his father, which could only be conferred on free men born of free women." The ancient Greeks were of the same opinion; for they used the word δουλοπρεπεια, or "slave manners," to designate any very great impropriety of manners.

Freedom. This is defined to be a state of exemption from, the control or power of another. The doctrine that Masons should enjoy unrestrained liberty, and be free in all their thoughts and actions, is carried so far in Masonry, that the Grand Lodge of England will not permit the initiation of a candidate who is only temporarily deprived of his liberty, or even in a place of confinement. (See *Free*.)

It is evident that the word freedom is used in Masonry in a symbolical or metaphysical sense differing from its ordinary signification. While, in the application of the words *free born* and *freeman*, we use them in their usual legal acceptation, we combine *freedom* with *fervency* and *zeal* as embodying a symbolic idea. Gädicke, under the word *Freiheit*, in his *Freimaurer-Lexicon*, thus defines the word:

"A word that is often heard among us, but which is restricted to the same limitation as the freedom of social life. We have in our assemblies no freedom to act each one as he pleases. But we are, or should be, free from the dominion of passion, pride, prejudice, and all the other follies of human nature. We are free from the false delusion that we need not be obedient to the laws." Thus he makes it equivalent to *integrity;* a sense that I think it bears in the next article.

Freedom, Fervency, and Zeal. The earliest lectures in the eighteenth century designated freedom, fervency, and zeal as the qualities which should distinguish the servitude of Apprentices, and the same symbolism is found in the ritual of the present day. The word *freedom* is not here to be taken in its modern sense of *liberty*, but rather in its primitive Anglo-Saxon meaning of *frankness, generosity, a generous willingness to work or perform one's duty.* So Chaucer uses it in the Prologue to the *Canterbury Tales* (l. 43):

"A knight there was, and that a worthy man,
That fro the time that he first began
To riden out, he loved chivalrie,
Trouthe and Honour, *Freedom* and Courtesy."

(See *Fervency* and *Zeal.*)

Freeman. The Grand Lodge of England, on September 1, 1847, erased from their list of the qualifications of candidates the word "free-born," and substituted for it "free-man." Their rule now reads, "every candidate must be a freeman." This has been generally considered an unauthorized violation of a landmark.

Freemason. One who has been initiated into the mysteries of the Fraternity of Freemasonry. Freemasons are so called to distinguish them from the Operative or Stone-Masons, who constituted an inferior class of workmen, and out of whom they sprang. (See *Stone-Masons* and *Traveling Freemasons.*) The meaning of the epithet *free*, as applied to *Mason*, is given under the word *Free.* In the old lectures of the last century a Freemason was described as being "a freeman, born of a freewoman, brother to a king, fellow to a prince, or companion to a beggar, if a Mason," and by this was meant to indicate the universality of the brotherhood.

The word "Freemason" was until recently divided into two words, sometimes with and sometimes without a hyphen; and we find in all the old books and manuscripts "Free Mason" or "Free-Mason." But this usage has been abandoned by all good writers, and "Freemason" is now always spelled as one word. The old Constitutions constantly used the word *Mason.* Yet the word was employed at a very early period in the parish registers of England, and by some writers. Thus, in the register of the parish of Astbury we find these items:

"1685. Smallwood, Jos., fils Jos. Henshaw, Freemason, bapt. 3° die Nov.

"1697. Jos. fil Jos. Henshaw, Freemason, buried 7 April."

But the most singular passage is one found in Cawdray's *Treasurie of Similies*, published in 1609, and which he copied from Bishop Coverdale's translation of Werdmuller's *A Spiritual and most Precious Perle*, which was published in 1550. It is as follows: "As the Free-Mason heweth the hard stones . . . . even so God the Heavenly Free-Mason buildeth a Christian church." But, in fact, the word was used at a much earlier period, and occurs, Steinbrenner says (*Orig. and Early Hist. of Mas.*, p. 110), for the first time in a statute passed in 1350, in the twenty-fifth year of Edward I., where the wages of a master Freemason are fixed at 4 pence, and of other masons at 3 pence. The original French text of the statute is "Mestre de franche-peer." "Here," says Steinbrenner, "the word Freemason evidently signifies a free-stone mason—one who works in free-stone, (Fr. *franche-peer*, i. e., franche-pierre,) as distinguished from the *rough* mason, who merely built walls of rough, unhewn stone." This latter sort of workmen was that class called by the Scotch Masons *cowans*, whom the Freemasons were forbidden to work with, whence we get the modern use of that word. Ten years after, in 1360, we have a statute of Edward III., in which it is ordained that "every mason shall finish his work, be it of free-stone or of rough-stone," where the French text of the statute is "de franche-pere ou de grosse-pere." Thus it seems evident that the word *free-mason* was originally used in contradistinction to *rough-mason.* The old Constitutions sometimes call these latter masons *rough-layers.*

[Dr. Murray's *New English Dictionary* has the following (*s.v.* Freemason):

"The precise import with which the adj. was originally used in this designation has been much disputed. Three views have been propounded. (1) The suggestion that *free mason* stands for *free-stone mason* would appear unworthy of attention, but for the curious fact that the earliest known instances of any similar appellation are *mestre mason de franche peer*, 'master mason of free stone' (Act 25, Edw. III., st. II., c. 3, A. D. 1350), and *sculptores lapidum liberorum*, 'carvers of free stones,' alleged to occur in a document of 1217 (tr. Findel's *Hist. Mas.*, 51, citing Wyatt Papworth): the coincidence, however, seems to be merely accidental. (2) The view most generally held is that *free masons* were those who were 'free' of the masons' guild. Against this explanation many forcible objections have been brought by Mr. G. W. Speth, who suggests (3) that the itinerant masons were called 'free' because they claimed exemption from the control of the local guilds of the towns in which they temporarily settled. (4) Perhaps the best hypothesis is that the term refers to the mediæval practice of emancipating skilled artisans, in order that they might be able to travel and render their services wherever any great building was in process of construction."

And then the following meanings are given: "1. A member of a certain class of skilled workers in stone, in the 14th and following centuries often mentioned in contradistinction to 'rough masons,' 'ligiers,' etc. They travelled from place to place, finding employment wherever important buildings were being erected, and had a system of secret signs and passwords by which a craftsman who had been admitted on giving evidence of competent skill could be recognized. In later use (16–18th c.) the term seems often to be used merely as a more complimentary synonym of 'mason,' implying that the workman so designated belonged to a superior grade."

The earliest instance quoted of the word in this sense is in a list of the London City Companies of 1376.

"2. A member of the fraternity called more fully, *Free and Accepted Masons*.

"Early in the 17th c., the societies of freemasons (in sense 1) began to admit honorary members, not connected with the building trades, but supposed to be eminent for architectural or antiquarian learning. These were called *accepted masons*, though the term *free masons* was often loosely applied to them; and they were admitted to a knowledge of the secret signs, and instructed in the legendary history of the craft, which had already begun to be developed. The distinction of being an 'accepted mason' became a fashionable object of ambition, and before the end of the 17th c. the object of the societies of freemasons seems to have been chiefly social and convivial. In 1717, under the guidance of the physicist J. T. Desaguliers, four of these societies or 'lodges' in London united to form a 'grand lodge,' with a new constitution and ritual, and a system of secret signs: the object of the society as reconstituted being mutual help and the promotion of brotherly feeling among its members."

The earliest instance quoted of the word in this sense is in Ashmole's diary under date 1646. (See *Ashmole*.)   [E. L. H.]

Gould in his concise *History* says: "Two curious coincidences have been connected with the above year (1375). The first, that the earliest copy of the manuscript constitutions (Regius MS.) refers to the customs of that period; the second, that the formation of a wonderful society, occasioned by a combination of masons undertaking not to work without an advance of wages, when summoned from several counties by writs of Edward III., to rebuild and enlarge Windsor Castle, under the direction of William of Wykeham, has been placed at the same date. It is said also that these masons agreed on certain signs and tokens by which they might know one another, and render mutual assistance against impressment; and further agreed not to work unless *free* and on their own terms. Hence they called themselves *Free-Masons*."
        [E. E. C.]

Freemasonry, Early British. Bro. Robert Freke Gould, in his *History of F. M.* (i., p, 381), writes: "The minutes of Scottish

19

Lodges from the sixteenth century, and evidences of British Masonic life dating farther back by some two hundred years (than the second decade of the last century) were actually left unheeded by our premier historiographer, although many of such authentic and invaluable documents lay ready to hand, only awaiting examination, amongst the muniments in the old Lodge chests. . . . By the collection and comparatively recent publication of many of the interesting records above alluded to, so much evidence has been accumulated respecting the early history, progress, and character of the craft as to be almost embarrassing, and the proposition may be safely advanced, that the Grand Lodges of Great Britain are the direct descendants, by continuity and absorption, of the ancient Freemasonry which immediately preceded their institution, which will be demonstrated without requiring the exercise of either dogmatism or credulity.

"The oldest Lodges in Scotland possess registers of members and meetings, as well as particulars of their laws and customs, ranging backward nearly three hundred years. (These) will form an important link in the chain which connects what is popularly known as the Lodges of Modern Freemasonry, with their operative and speculative ancestors."

There are no Lodge records in England of the seventeenth century, and records of only one between 1700 and 1717.

The original *St. Clair Charters* (*q. v.*) in the custody of the Grand Lodge of Scotland, dated, respectively, 1601-2 and 1628, are referred to by Gould. Then are considered the Schaw Statutes, No. 1, of A.D. 1598 (see *Schaw Manuscript*), the Schaw Statutes, No. 2, of A.D. 1599, and their relevancy to "*Mother Kilwinning*" Lodge, *Ayrshire, No. 0*, with an important certificate from William Schaw, which proves that the document of 1599 was intended exclusively for the Masons under the jurisdiction of the Kilwinning Lodge. The subject of the "*Lodge of Edinburgh*," *No. 1*, and its career from its earliest records, dating back to 1599, down to the year 1736, when the Grand Lodge of Scotland was inaugurated, as most fully described in Lyon's history of this ancient Lodge, passes under review; then appears, as Bro. Gould says, one of the adornments of that history in the facsimile of the record of that Lodge, showing that the earliest minute of the presence of a *speculative* freeman Mason in a Lodge, and taking part in its deliberations, is dated June 8, 1600. (*Hist. of F. M.*, i., 406.) It is to be noted that "the admission of General Alexander Hamilton, on May 20, 1640, and of the Right Hon. Sir Patrick Hume, Bart., on December 27, 1667, are specially recorded as constituting these intrants '*Felow and Mr off the forsed craft*,' and '*Fellow of craft (and Master) of this lodg*,' respectively." (*Ibid.*, p. 408.) It is assumed that *Master* simply meant a compliment; certainly, there was nothing corresponding with the ceremony of a Master Mason's Degree at that time. Many of the operatives did not view the introduction

of the *speculative* element with favor, and
at one time they were arrayed in hostile
camps; but eventually those who supported
the "Gentlemen" or "Geomatic Masons"
won the day, the "Domatics" having to succumb. In the Lodge of Aberdeen, the
majority in A.D. 1670 were actually non-
operative or *speculative* members.

On March 2, 1653, appears the important
fact of the election of a *"joining member."*
Again, Lyon declares that the reference to
"frie mesones," in the minute of December
27, 1636, is the earliest instance yet discovered
of "Free-Mason" being applied to designate members of the Mason craft, and considers that it is used as an abbreviation of
the term "Freemen Masons." But while
concurring therein, as did Bro. Hughan,
Gould thinks *the word freemason* may be
traced back to 1581, when the "Melrose"
version of the "Old Charges" was originally
written.

"Canongate Kilwinning" Lodge, No. 2,
was commissioned or warranted by the Lodge
of Kilwinning, No. 0, granting powers to
several of their own members resident in
the Canongate, Edinburgh, and dated December 20, 1677. This, Bro. Gould says, was
a direct invasion of jurisdiction, for it was
not simply a charter to enable their members to meet as Masons in Edinburgh, but
also to act as independently as "Mother Kilwinning" herself, with a separate existence,
which was the actual result that ensued.
(*Ibid.*, p. 410.)

"Scoon and Perth" Lodge, No. 3, is much
older than No. 2, although fourth on the
roll, though the authorities state that it
existed *"before* 1658," and the Grand Lodge
acknowledges this date at the present time,
placing Nos. 0 and 1, however, as *"before*
1598," and No. 57 (Haddington) at 1599,
there being also many bearing seventeenth
century designations. (*Ibid.*, p. 411.)

The Lodge of *"Glasgow St. John,"* No. 3,
bis, is next mentioned as "an old Lodge,
undoubtedly, though its documents do not
date back as far as some of its admirers have
declared." (*Ibid.*, p. 413.) The Rev. A. T.
Grant is quoted as saying that every line is
inconsistent with the charter phraseology of
the period to which it has been *assigned.* But
Mr. W. P. Buchan states that the first notice
in the minutes of the "Glasgow Incorporation
of Masons" bears date September 22, 1620,
viz., "Entry of Apprentices to the Lodge
of Glasgow, the last day of Dec., 1613 years,
compeared John Stewart, &c." It was
placed on the roll of the Grand Lodge of
Scotland in 1850 as No. 3, *bis;* it was exclusively *operative.*

"Glasgow Kilwinning" Lodge, No. 4, dates
from 1735.

*"Canongate and Leith, Leith and Canongate"
Lodge, No. 5,* is authoritatively acknowledged
as dating from 1688.

Lodge of "Old Kilwinning St. John," Inverness, No. 6, was granted a Charter of
Confirmation on November 30, 1737, its exist-

ence being admitted from the year 1678, but
a cloud rests upon the latter record.

"Hamilton Kilwinning" Lodge, No. 7, is
considered to date from the year 1695.

Thus Bro. Gould, in his remarkable *History,* continues quoting old Charters, Laws,
Statutes, etc., back even to the sixteenth century, in a most interesting manner, dissenting largely from the early history of Bro.
George H. Fort, and as well from the *Antiquities of Freemasonry,* by Bro. Findel. (See
"Four Old Lodges.")

Freemasonry, History of. See: *The History of Freemasonry,* by Albert Gallatin Mackey
and William R. Singleton, published in seven
volumes by The Masonic History Company,
New York. *The History of Freemasonry,* by
Robert Freke Gould, published in six volumes,
London. *The History of Freemasonry,* by J.
G. Findel, published in eight volumes, Leipzig; second edition, London, 1869.

See also: *The Antiquity of Freemasonry;
Origin of Freemasonry; Operative Freemasonry
and Speculative Freemasonry.*

Freemasons of the Church. An architectural college was organized in London,
in the year 1842, under the name of "Freemasons of the Church for the Recovery,
Maintenance, and Furtherance of the True
Principles and Practice of Architecture."
The founders of the association announced
their objects to be "the rediscovery of the
ancient principles of architecture; the sanction of good principles of building, and the
condemnation of bad ones; the exercise of
scientific and experienced judgment in the
choice and use of the proper materials; the
infusion, maintenance, and advancement of
science throughout architecture; and eventually, by developing the powers of the college
upon a just and beneficial footing, to reform
the whole practice of architecture, to raise
it from its present vituperated condition,
and to bring around it the same unquestioned honor which is at present enjoyed
by almost every other profession." One of
their members has said that the title assumed
was not intended to express any conformity
with the general body of Freemasons, but
rather as indicative of the profound views of
the college, namely, the recovery, maintenance, and furtherance of the free principles and
practise of architecture; and that, in addition,
they made it an object of their exertions to
preserve or effect the restoration of architectural remains of antiquity, threatened unnecessarily with demolition or endangered by decay.
But it is evident, from the close connection of
modern Freemasonry with the building gilds
of the Middle Ages, that any investigation
into the condition of Medieval architecture
must throw light on Masonic history.

Free-Will and Accord. There is one
peculiar feature in the Masonic Institution
that must commend it to the respect of every
generous mind. In other associations it is
considered meritorious in a member to exert
his influence in obtaining applications for
admission; but it is wholly uncongenial with

the spirit of our Order to persuade anyone to become a Mason. Whosoever seeks a knowledge of our mystic rites, must first be prepared for the ordeal in his heart; he must not only be endowed with the necessary moral qualifications which would fit him for admission into our ranks, but he must come, too, uninfluenced by friends and unbiased by unworthy motives. This is a settled landmark of the Order; and, therefore, nothing can be more painful to a true Mason than to see this landmark violated by young and heedless brethren. For it cannot be denied that it is sometimes violated; and this habit of violation is one of those unhappy influences sometimes almost insensibly exerted upon Masonry by the existence of the many secret societies to which the present age has given birth, and which resemble Masonry in nothing except in having some sort of a secret ceremony of initiation. These societies are introducing into some parts of America such phraseology as a "card" for a "demit," or "worthy" for "worshipful," or "brothers" for "brethren." And there are some men who, coming among us imbued with the principles and accustomed to the usages of these modern societies, in which the persevering solicitation of candidates is considered as a legitimate and even laudable practise, bring with them these preconceived notions, and consider it their duty to exert all their influence in persuading their friends to become members of the Craft. Men who thus misunderstand the true policy of our Institution should be instructed by their older and more experienced brethren that it is wholly in opposition to all our laws and principles to ask any man to become a Mason, or to exercise any kind of influence upon the minds of others, except that of a truly Masonic life and a practical exemplification of its tenets, by which they may be induced to ask admission into our Lodges. We must not seek — we are to be sought.

And if this were not an ancient law, embedded in the very cement that upholds our system, policy alone would dictate an adherence to the voluntary usage. We need not now fear that our Institution will suffer from a deficiency of members. Our greater dread should be that, in its rapid extension, less care may be given to the selection of candidates than the interests and welfare of the Order demand. There can, therefore, be no excuse for the practise of persuading candidates, and every hope of safety in avoiding such a practise. It should always be borne in mind that the candidate who comes to us not of his own "free-will and accord," but induced by the persuasions of his friends —no matter how worthy he otherwise may be —violates, by so coming, the requirements of our Institution on the very threshold of its temple, and, in ninety-nine cases out of a hundred, fails to become imbued with that zealous attachment to the Order which is absolutely essential to the formation of a true Masonic character.

Freimaurer. German for *Freemason.* *Mauer* means "a wall," and *mauern*, "to build a wall." Hence, literally, *freimaurer* is a "builder of walls" who is free of his gild, from the fact that the building of walls was the first occupation of masons.

Freimaurerei. German for *Freemasonry.*

French, Benjamin Brown. A distinguished Mason of the United States, who was born at Chester, in New Hampshire, September 4, 1800, and died at the city of Washington, where he had long resided, on August 12, 1870. He was initiated into Masonry in 1825, and during his whole life took an active interest in the affairs of the Fraternity. He served for many years as General Grand Secretary of the General Grand Chapter, and Grand Recorder of the Grand Encampment of the United States. In 1846, soon after his arrival in Washington, he was elected Grand Master of the Grand Lodge of the District, a position which he repeatedly occupied. In 1859, he was elected Grand Master of the Templars of the United States, a distinguished position which he held for six years, having been reelected in 1862. His administration, during a period of much excitement in the country, was marked by great firmness, mingled with a spirit of conciliation. He was also a prominent member of the Ancient and Accepted Scottish Rite, and at the time of his death was the Lieutenant Grand Commander of the Supreme Council for the Southern Jurisdiction of the United States.

Bro. French was possessed of much intellectual ability, and contributed no small share of his studies to the literature of Masonry. His writings, which have not yet been collected, were numerous, and consisted of Masonic odes, many of them marked with the true poetic spirit, eloquent addresses on various public occasions, learned dissertations on Masonic law, and didactic essays, which were published at the time in various periodicals. His decisions on Templar law have always been esteemed of great value.

French Rite. (*Rite Français ou Moderne.*) The French or Modern Rite is one of the three principal Rites of Freemasonry. It consists of seven degrees, three symbolic and four higher, viz.: 1. Apprentice; 2. Fellow-Craft; 3. Master; 4. Elect; 5. Scotch Master; 6. Knight of the East; 7. Rose Croix. This Rite is practised in France, in Brazil, and in Louisiana. It was founded, in 1786, by the Grand Orient of France, who, unwilling to destroy entirely the high degrees which were then practised by the different Rites, and yet anxious to reduce them to a smaller number and to greater simplicity, extracted these degrees out of the Rite of Perfection, making some few slight modifications. Most of the authors who have treated of this Rite have given to its symbolism an entirely astronomical meaning. Among these writers, we may refer to Ragon, in his *Cours Philosophique*, as probably the most scientific.

Ragon, in his *Tuileur Général* (p. 51), says that the four degrees of the French Rite, which were elaborated to take the place of the thirty degrees of the Scottish Rite, have for their basis the four physical proofs to which the recipiendary submits in the First Degree. And that the symbolism further represents the sun in his annual progress through the four seasons. Thus, the Elect Degree represents the element of *Earth* and the season of *Spring;* the Scottish Master represents *Air* and the *Summer;* the Knight of the East represents *Water* and *Autumn;* and the Rose Croix represents *Fire;* but he does not claim that it is consecrated to *Winter,* although that would be the natural conclusion.

The original Rose Croix was an eminently Christian degree, which, being found inconvenient, was in 1860 substituted by the Philosophic Rose Croix, which now forms the summit of the French Rite.

Frères Pontifes. See *Bridge Builders of the Middle Ages.*

Frey or **Freia.** Grimme, in his *Deutsche Mythologie* (pp. 191, 279), traces the name Freia through the ancient Teutonic dialects and explains it to signify *plenty* and *beauty.* Also, see Thorpe, *Northern Mythology,* (vol. i., pp. 197, 198). The column or pillar set apart to the goddess Frey in the temple of Upsala became the pillar of beauty or plenteousness. Bro. Fort says, in his *Antiquities* (ch. 27), the three divinities in the Norse temple at Upsala, in Denmark, Odin, Thor, and Frey, were typical supports of the universe—Wisdom, Strength, and Beauty—or the three of the ten columns in the Hebrew sephiroth, in the Jewish philosophy, designated as *Sapientia, Pulchritudo,* and *Fundamentum;* which, like the three columns existing in a Lodge of Freemasons, symbolize the moralistic pillars of the world, represented by the Lodge itself. An additional significant fact confronts us at this point: the column of Beauty or Plenty, originally emblematic of Frey, is situated in the south of the Lodge. A Masonic symbol—sheaf of grain—always suspended above that station, denotes plenteousness. Freia may also be comparatively described as the Scandinavian Isis.

Friendly Societies. Societies first established toward the end of the last century, in England, for the relief of mechanics, laborers, and other persons who derived their support from their daily toil. By the weekly payment of a stipulated sum, the members secured support and assistance from the society when sick, and payment of the expenses of burial when they died. These societies gave origin to the Odd Fellows and other similar associations, but they have no relation whatever to Freemasonry.

Friend of St. John. The Sixth Degree of the system practised by the Grand Lodge of Sweden. It is comprehended in the degree of Knight of the East and West.

Friend of Truth. The Fifth Degree of the Rite of African Architects.

Friendship. Leslie, in 1741, delivered the first descant on Friendship, as peculiarly a Masonic virtue. He was followed by Hutchinson, Preston, and other writers, and now in the modern lectures it is adopted as one of the precious jewels of a Master Mason. Of universal friendship, blue is said to be the symbolic color. "In regular gradation," says Munkhouse (*Disc.,* i., 17), "and by an easy descent, brotherly love extends itself to lesser distinct societies or to particular individuals, and thus becomes friendship either of convenience or of personal affection." Cicero says, "Amicitia nisi inter bonos non potest," Friendship can exist only among the good.

Fund of Benevolence. A fund established in 1727 by the Grand Lodge of England, and solely devoted to charity. The regulations for its management are as follows: Its distribution and application is directed by the Constitutions to be monthly, for which purpose a Board of Benevolence is holden on the last Wednesday of every month except December, when it is on the third Wednesday. This Lodge consists of all the present and past Grand Officers, all actual Masters of Lodges, and twelve Past Masters. The brother presiding is bound strictly to enforce all the regulations of the Craft respecting the distribution of the fund, and must be satisfied, before any petition is read, that all the required formalities have been complied with. To every petition must be added a recommendation, signed in open Lodge by the Master, Wardens, and a majority of the members then present, to which the petitioner does or did belong, or from some other contributing Lodge, certifying that they have known him to have been in reputable, or at least tolerable, circumstances, and that he has been not less than five years a subscribing member to a regular Lodge.

Fund, Grand Masters'. A fund over which the G. Master of the United G. Lodge of England exercises exclusive control. It originated with a sum of £2,730 subscribed by the Craft in 1870, when the Earl of Zetland retired from the Grand Mastership, and is known as "The Zetland Fund."

Funds of the Lodge. The funds of the Lodge are placed in the keeping of the Treasurer, to whom all moneys received by the Secretary must be immediately paid. Hence each of these officers is a check on the other. And hence, too, the "Thirtynine Regulations" of 1721 say that the Grand Treasurer should be "a brother of good worldly substance" (*Constitutions,* 1723, p. 62), lest impecuniosity should tempt him to make use of the Lodge funds.

Funeral Rites. See *Burial.*

Furlac. A word in the high degrees, whose etymology is uncertain, but probably Arabic. It is said to signify the angel of the earth.

Furniture of a Lodge. The Bible, square, and compasses are technically said to constitute the furniture of a Lodge. They are respectfully dedicated to God, the Master of the Lodge, and the Craft. Our English brethren differ from us in their explanation of the furniture. Oliver gives their illustration, from the English lectures, as follows:

"The Bible is said to derive from God to man in general; because the Almighty has been pleased to reveal more of His divine will by that holy book than by any other means. The Compasses being the chief implement used in the construction of all architectural plans and designs, are assigned to the Grand Master in particular as emblems of his dignity, he being the chief head and ruler of the Craft. The square is given to the whole Masonic body, because we are all obligated within it, and are consequently bound to act thereon." (*Landmarks*, i., 169.) But the lecture of the early part of the last century made the furniture consist of the Mosaic Pavement, Blazing Star, and the Indented Tarsel, while the Bible, square, and compass were considered as additional furniture.

Fustier. An officer of the Grand Orient of France in the beginning of this century. In 1810, he published, and presented to the Grand Orient, a *Geographical Chart of the Lodges in France and its Dependencies*. He was the author of several memoirs, dissertations, etc., on Masonic subjects, and of a manuscript entitled *Nomenclature Alphabetique des Grades*. Oliver (*Landmarks*, ii., 95) says that he promulgated a new system of sixty-four degrees. But he seems to have mistaken Fustier's catalogue of degrees invented by others for a system established by himself. No record can be found elsewhere of such a system. Lenning says (*Encyc. der Freimaurerei*) that Fustier was a dealer in Masonic decorations and in the transcript of rituals, of which he had made a collection of more than four hundred, which he sold at established prices.

Future Life. Lorenzo de Medici said that all those are dead, even for the present life, who do not believe in a future state. The belief in that future life, it is the object of Freemasonry, as it was of the ancient initiations, to teach.

Fylfot. An ancient symbol well known among Heralds. It is sometimes known as the *crux dissimulata*, found in the catacombs of Rome, and forms one of the symbols of the degree of Prince of Mercy, Scottish Rite System. It is a form of the "Swastika." (See *Jaina Cross*.)

G

G. (Hebrew, ג. Chaldaic, or hieroglyphic.) The seventh letter of the English and Roman alphabets. In the Greek and many other alphabets it is the third in place; in the Russian, Wallachian, and some others it is the fourth; in the Arabic the fifth, and in the Ethiopian the twentieth.

In Hebrew it is called "Gimel," is of the numerical value of 3, and its signification is *camel*. It is associated with the third sacred name of God in Hebrew, גרול (Ghadol), *magnus*. In Masonry it is given as the initial of God. The Masonic use of the letter tends to the belief of a modern form in the ceremony of the Fellow-Craft Degree. (See *G.O.D.*)

G. As in all Roman Catholic and in many Protestant churches the cross, engraved or sculptured in some prominent position, will be found as the expressive symbol of Christianity, so in every Masonic Lodge a letter G may be seen in the east, either painted on the wall or sculptured in wood or metal, and suspended over the Master's chair. This is, in fact, if not the most prominent, certainly the most familiar, of all the symbols of Freemasonry. It is the one to which the poet Burns alluded in those well-known and often-quoted lines, in which he speaks of

"——that hieroglyphic bright,
Which none but Craftsmen ever saw";

that is to say, ever saw understandingly—ever saw, knowing at the same time what it meant.

There is an uncertainty as to the exact time when this symbol was first introduced into Speculative Masonry. It was not derived, in its present form, from the Operative Masons of the Middle Ages, who bestowed upon Freemasonry so much of its symbolism, for it is not found among the architectural decorations of the old cathedrals. Dr. Oliver says it was "in the old lectures"; but this is an uncertain expression. From Prichard's *Masonry Dissected*, which was published in 1730, it would seem that the symbol was not in use at that date. But it may have been omitted. If *Tubal Cain*, which was published in 1767, is, as it purported to be, identical with Prichard's work, the question is settled; for it contains the lecture on the letter G, to which reference will directly be made.

It is, however, certain that the symbol was well known and recognized in 1766, and some few years before. The book entitled *Solomon in all his Glory*, the first edition of which appeared in that year, and which is a translation of "*Le Maçon démasque*," contains the reference to and the explanation of the symbol. The work contains abundant internal evidence that it is a translation, and hence the symbol may, like some others of the system subsequent to 1717, have been first introduced on the Continent, and then returned in the translation, all of which would indicate a date some years anterior to 1776 for the time of its adoption.

In the ritual contained in *Tubal Cain* (p. 18), or, if that be only a reprint, in *Masonry Dissected*, that is to say, in 1768 or in 1730, there is a test which is called "The Repeating the Letter G," and which Dr. Oliver gives in his *Landmarks* (i., 454) as a part of the "old lectures." It is doggerel verse, and in the form of a catechism between an examiner and a respondent, a form greatly affected in these old lectures, and is as follows:

"Resp.—In the Midst of Solomon's Temple
　　　　　there stands a G,
　　　A letter for all to read and see;
　　　But few there be that understand
　　　What means the letter G.

"Ex.—My friend, if you pretend to be
　　　Of this Fraternity,
　　　You can forthwith and rightly tell
　　　What means that letter G.

"Resp.—By sciences are brought about,
　　　Bodies of various kinds,
　　　Which do appear to perfect sight;
　　　But none but males shall know my
　　　　　mind.

"Ex.—the Right shall.

"Resp.—If Worshipful.

"Ex.—Both Right and Worshipful I am;
　　　To hail you I have command,
　　　That you forthwith let me know,
　　　As I you may understand.

"Resp.—By letters four and science five,
　　　This G aright doth stand,
　　　In a due art and proportion;
　　　You have your answer, Friend."

And now as to the signification of the symbol. We may say, in the first place, that the explanation is by no means, and never has been, esoteric. As the symbol itself has always been exposed to public view, forming, as it does, a prominent part of the furniture of a Lodge, to be seen by everyone, so our Masonic authors, from the earliest times, have not hesitated to write, openly and in the plainest language, of its signification. The fact is, that the secret instruction in reference to this symbol relates not to the knowledge of the symbol itself, but to the mode in which, and the object for which, that knowledge has been obtained.

Hutchinson, who wrote as early as 1776, says, in his *Spirit of Masonry* (Lect. viii.), "It is now incumbent on me to demonstrate to you the great signification of the letter G, wherewith Lodges and the medals of Masons are ornamented.

"To apply its signification to the name of God only is depriving it of part of its Masonic import; although I have already shown that the symbols used in Lodges are expressive of the Divinity's being the great object of Masonry, as Architect of the world.

"This significant letter denotes Geometry, which, to artificers, is the science by which all their labours are calculated and formed; and to Masons, contains the determination, definition, and proof of the order, beauty, and wonderful wisdom of the power of God in His creation."

Again, Dr. Frederick Dalcho, a distinguished Mason of South Carolina, in one of his *Orations*, delivered and published in 1801, uses the following language:

"The *letter* G, which ornaments the Master's Lodge, is not only expressive of the name of the Grand Architect of the universe, but also denotes the science of Geometry, so necessary to artists. But the adoption of it by Masons implies no more than their respect for those inventions which demonstrate to the world the power, the wisdom, and beneficence of the Almighty Builder in the works of the creation." (P. 27.)

Lastly, Dr. Oliver has said, in his *Golden Remains of the Early Masonic Writers*, that "the term G. A. O. T. U. is used among Masons for this great and glorious Being, designated by the letter G, that it may be applied by every brother to the object of his adoration."

More quotations are unnecessary to show that from the earliest times, since the adoption of the letter as a symbol, its explanation has not been deemed an esoteric or secret part of the ritual. No Masonic writer has hesitated openly to give an explanation of its meaning. The mode in which, and the purpose for which, that explanation was obtained are the only hidden things about the symbol.

It is to be regretted that the letter G, as a symbol, was ever admitted into the Masonic system. The use of it, as an initial, would necessarily confine it to the English language and to modern times. It wants, therefore, as a symbol, the necessary characteristics of both universality and antiquity. The Greek letter *gamma* is said to have been venerated by the Pythagoreans because it was the initial of γεωμέτρια, or *Geometry*. But this veneration could not have been shared by other nations whose alphabet had no *gamma*, and where the word for *geometry* was entirely different.

There can be no doubt that the letter G is a very modern symbol, not belonging to any old system anterior to the origin of the English language. It is, in fact, a corruption of the old Hebrew Kabbalistic symbol, the letter *yod*, י, by which the sacred name of God—in fact, the most sacred name, the Tetragrammaton—is expressed. This letter, *yod*, is the initial letter of the word יהוה,

or Jehovah, and is constantly to be met with among Hebrew writers, as the abbreviation or symbol of that most holy name, which, indeed, was never written at length. Now, as G is in like manner the initial of God, the English equivalent of the Hebrew Jehovah, the letter has been adopted as a symbol intended to supply to modern Lodges the place of the Hebrew symbol. First adopted by the English ritual makers, it has, without remark, been transferred to the Masonry of the Continent, and it is to be found as a symbol in all the systems of Germany, France, Spain, Italy, Portugal, and every other country where Masonry has been introduced; although in Germany only can it serve, as it does in England, for an intelligent symbol.

The letter G, then, has in Masonry the same force and signification that the letter *yod* had among the Kabbalists. It is only a symbol of the Hebrew letter, and, as that is a symbol of God, the letter G is only a symbol of a symbol. As for its reference to geometry, Kloss, the German Masonic historian, says that the old Operative Masons referred the entire science of geometry to the art of building, which gave to the modern English Masons occasion to embrace the whole system of Freemasonry under the head of Geometry, and hence the symbol of that science, as well as of God, was adopted for the purpose of giving elevation to the Fellow-Craft's Degree.

Indeed, the symbol, made sacred by its reference to the Grand Geometrician of the universe, was well worthy to be applied to that science which has, from the remotest times, been deemed synonymous with Masonry.

Gabaon. A significant word in the high degrees. Oliver says (*Landm.*, i., 335), "in philosophical Masonry, heaven, or, more correctly speaking, *the third heaven*, is denominated Mount Gabaon, which is feigned to be accessible only by the seven degrees that compose the winding staircase. These are the degrees terminating in the Royal Arch." *Gabaon* is defined to signify "a high place." It is the Septuagint and Vulgate form of גבעון, *Gibeon*, which was the city in which the tabernacle was stationed during the reigns of David and Solomon. The word means *a city built on a hill*, and is referred to in 2 Chron. i. 3. "So Solomon, and all the congregation with him, went to the high place that was at Gibeon; for there was the tabernacle of the congregation of God."

In a ritual of the middle of the last century, it is said that Gabanon is the name of a Master Mason. This word is a striking evidence of the changes which Hebrew words have undergone in their transmission to Masonic rituals, and of the almost impossibility of tracing them to their proper root. It would seem difficult to find a connection between *Gabanon* and any known Hebrew word. But if we refer to Guillemain's *Ritual of Adonhiramite Masonry*, we will find the following passage:

"*Q*. How is a Master called?
"*A*. Gabaon, which is the name of the place where the Israelites deposited the ark in the time of trouble.
"*Q*. What does this signify?
"*A*. That the heart of a Mason ought to be pure enough to be a temple suitable for God." (P. 95.)

There is abundant internal evidence that these two rituals came from a common source, and that *Gabaon* is a French distortion, as *Gabanon* is an English one, of some unknown word—connected, however, with the Ark of the Covenant as the place where that article was deposited.

Now, we learn from the Jewish records that the Philistines, who had captured the ark, deposited it "in the house of Abinadab that was in Gibeah"; and that David, subsequently recapturing it, carried it to Jerusalem, but left the tabernacle at Gibeon. The ritualist did not remember that the tabernacle at Gibeon was without the ark, but supposed that it was still in that sacred shrine. Hence, *Gabaon* or *Gabanon* must have been corrupted from either *Gibeah* or *Gibeon*, because the ark was considered to be at some time in both places. But Gibeon had already been corrupted by the Septuagint and the Vulgate versions into *Gabaon*; and this undoubtedly is the word from which *Gabanon* is derived, through either the Septuagint or the Vulgate, or perhaps from Josephus, who calls it *Gabao*.

Gabaonne. In French Masonic language, the widow of a Master Mason. Derived from *Gabaon*.

Gabor. Heb., גבר, *strong*. A significant word in the high degrees.

Gabriel. Heb., גבריאל, *a man of God*. The name of one of the archangels, referred to in some of the high degrees. He interpreted to Daniel the vision of the ram and the he-goat, and made the prophecy of the "seventy weeks" (Dan. viii. and ix.); he announced the future appearance of the Messiah (Dan. ix. 21, 27). In the New Testament he foretold to Zacharias the birth of John the Baptist (Luke i. 19), and to Mary the birth of Christ (Luke i. 26). Among the Rabbis Gabriel is entrusted with the care of the souls of the dead, and is represented as having taught Joseph the seventy languages spoken at Babel. In addition, he was the only angel who could speak Chaldee and Syriac. The *Talmud* speaks of him as the Prince of Fire, the Spirit presiding over thunder. The Mohammedans term him the Spirit of Truth, and believe that he dictated the *Koran* to Mohammed.

Gaedicke, Johann Christian. A bookseller of Berlin, born on the 14th of December, 1763, and initiated into Masonry in 1804. He took much interest in the Order, and was the author of several works, the most valuable and best known of which is the *Freimaurer-Lexicon*, or *Freemasons' Lexicon*, published in 1818; which, although far inferior to that of Lenning, which appeared four years afterward, is, as a pioneer work, very creditable to its author. The *Lexicon* was translated into

English and published in the London *Free-masons' Magazine*.

Gage. See *Twenty-four-Inch Gage*.

Galahad. Also spelled *Galaad*. Most probably a corruption of *Gilead*. Said in the old rituals to have been the keeper of the Seals in the Scottish degree of Knights of the Ninth, Arch or Sacred Vault of James VI.

G∴A∴O∴T∴U∴ An abbreviation of *Great Architect of the Universe*, which see.

Gangler. The title given to the candidate in the Scandinavian mysteries, signifying *wanderer*. The application is also made to the sun.

Garinus. Said in the old ritual of the degree of Knights of the East and West to have been the Patriarch of Jerusalem, between whose hands the first Knights of that Order took, in 1182, their vows. It is a corruption, by the French ritualists, of Garimond or Garimund, Patriarch of Jerusalem, before whom the Hospitalers took their three vows of obedience, chastity, and poverty.

Gassicourt, Cadet de. An apothecary of Paris, who, in the year 1796, published a work entitled *Le Tombeau de Jacques Molai, ou histoire secrète et abregée des initiés anciens et modernes*. In this book, which embraced all the errors of Barruel and Robison, he made the same charges of atheism and conspiracy against the Fraternity, and loaded the Chevalier Ramsay with the most vehement indignation as a libertine and traitor. But De Gassicourt subsequently acknowledged his folly in writing against a society of which he really knew nothing. In fact, in 1805, he solicited admission into the Order, and was initiated in the Lodge "l'Abeille," at Paris, where, in the various offices of Orator and Master, which he filled, he taught and recommended that Institution which he had once abused; and even on a public occasion pronounced the eulogy of that Ramsay whom he had formerly anathematized.

Gaston, John. Grand Duke of Tuscany; in 1737 he inaugurated a persecution against the Freemasons in his dominions.

Gates of the Temple. In the system of Freemasonry, the Temple of Solomon is represented as having a gate on the east, west, and south sides, but none on the north. In reference to the historical Temple of Jerusalem, such a representation is wholly incorrect. In the walls of the building itself there were no places of entrance except the door of the porch, which gave admission to the house. But in the surrounding courts there were gates at every point of the compass. The Masonic idea of the Temple is, however, entirely symbolic. The Temple is to the Speculative Mason only a symbol, not an historical building, and the gates are imaginary and symbolic also. They are, in the first place, symbols of the progress of the sun in his daily course, rising in the east, culminating to the meridian in the south, and setting in the west. They are also, in the allegory of life, which it is the object of the Third Degree to illustrate, symbols of the three stages of youth, manhood, and old age, or, more properly, of birth, life, and death.

Gaudini, Theobald de. Known as the monk Gaudini. Elected Grand Master of Templars, 1291; died 1301.

Gauntlets. Gloves formerly made of steel and worn by knights as a protection to their hands in battle. They have been adopted in the United States, as a part of the costume of a Knights Templar, under a regulation of the Grand Encampment, which directs them to be "of buff leather, the flap to extend four inches upwards from the wrist, and to have the appropriate cross embroidered in gold, on the proper colored velvet, two inches in length."

Gavel. The common gavel is one of the working tools of an Entered Apprentice. It is made use of by the Operative Mason to break off the corners of the rough ashlar, and thus fit it the better for the builder's use, and is therefore adopted as a symbol in Speculative Masonry, to admonish us of the duty of divesting our minds and consciences of all the vices and impurities of life, thereby fitting our bodies as living stones for that spiritual building not made with hands, eternal in the heavens.

It borrows its name from its shape, being that of the *gable* or *gavel* end of a house; and this word again comes from the German *gipfel*, a summit, top, or peak—the idea of a pointed extremity being common to all.

The true form of the gavel is that of the stone-mason's hammer. It is to be made with a cutting edge, as in the annexed engraving, that it may be used "to break off the corners of rough stones," an operation which could never be effected by the common hammer or mallet. The gavel thus shaped will give, when looked at in front, the exact representation of the *gavel* or *gable* end of a house, whence, as has been already said, the name is derived.

The gavel of the Master is also called a "Hiram," because, like that architect, it governs the Craft and keeps order in the Lodge, as he did in the Temple.

Gebal. A city of Phœnicia, on the Mediterranean, and under Mount Lebanon. It was the Byblos of the Greeks, where the worship of Adonis, the Syrian Thammuz, was celebrated. The inhabitants, who were Giblites or, in Masonic language, Giblemites, are said to have been distinguished for the art of stone-carving, and are called in the 1st Book of Kings "stone-squarers." (See *Giblim*.)

Gedaliah. The second officer in a Council of Superexcellent Masters represents Gedaliah the son of Pashur. An historical error has crept into the ritual of this degree in reference to the Gedaliah who is represented in it. I have sought to elucidate the question in my work on *Cryptic Masonry* in the following manner:

There are five persons of the name of Gedaliah who are mentioned in Scripture, but only two of them were contemporary with the destruction of the Temple.

Gedaliah the son of Pashur is mentioned by the prophet Jeremiah (xxxviii. 1) as a prince of the court of Zedekiah. He was present at its destruction, and is known to have been one of the advisers of the king. It was through his counsels, and those of his colleagues, that Zedekiah was persuaded to deliver up the prophet Jeremiah to death, from which he was rescued only by the intercession of a eunuch of the palace.

The other Gedaliah was the son of Ahikam. He seems to have been greatly in favor with Nebuchadnezzar, for after the destruction of Jerusalem, and the deportation of Zedekiah, he was appointed by the Chaldean monarch as his satrap or governor over Judea. He took up his residence at Mizpah, where he was shortly afterward murdered by Ishmael, one of the descendants of the house of David.

The question now arises, which of these two is the one referred to in the ceremonies of a Council of Superexcellent Masters? I think there can be no doubt that the founders of the degree intended the second officer of the Council to represent the former, and not the latter Gedaliah—the son of Pashur, and not Gedaliah the son of Ahikam; the prince of Judah, and not the governor of Judea.

We are forced to this conclusion by various reasons. The Gedaliah represented in the degree must have been a resident of Jerusalem during the siege, and at the very time of the assault, which immediately preceded the destruction of the Temple and the city. Now, we know that Gedaliah the son of Pashur was with Hezekiah as one of his advisers. On the other hand, it is most unlikely that Gedaliah the son of Ahikam could have been a resident of Jerusalem, for it is not at all probable that Nebuchadnezzar would have selected such a one for the important and confidential office of a satrap or governor. We should rather suppose that Gedaliah the son of Ahikam had been carried away to Babylon after one of the former sieges; that he had there, like Daniel, gained by his good conduct the esteem and respect of the Chaldean monarch; that he had come back to Judea with the army; and that, on the taking of the city, he had been appointed governor by Nebuchadnezzar. Such being the facts, it is evident that he could not have been in the council of King Zedekiah, advising and directing his attempted escape.

The modern revivers of the degree of Superexcellent Master have, therefore, been wrong in supposing that Gedaliah the son of Ahikam, and afterward governor of Judea, was the person represented by the second officer of the Council. He was Gedaliah the son of Pashur, a wicked man, one of Zedekiah's princes, and was most probably put to death by Nebuchadnezzar, with the other princes and nobles whom he captured in the plains of Jericho.

Gemara. See *Talmud*.

General Assembly. See *Assembly*.

General Grand Chapter. Until the year 1797, the Royal Arch Degree and the degrees subsidiary to it were conferred in America, either in irresponsible bodies calling themselves Chapters, but obedient to no superior authority, or in Lodges working under a Grand Lodge Warrant. On the 24th of October, 1797, a convention of committees from three Chapters, namely, St. Andrew's Chapter of Boston, Temple Chapter of Albany, and Newburyport Chapter, was held at Boston, which recommended to the several Chapters within the States of New Hampshire, Massachusetts, Rhode Island, Connecticut, Vermont, and New York to hold a convention at Hartford on the fourth Wednesday of January ensuing, to form a Grand Chapter for the said States.

Accordingly, on the 24th of January, 1798, delegates from St. Andrew's Chapter of Boston, Mass.; King Cyrus Chapter of Newburyport, Mass.; Providence Chapter of Providence, R. I.; Solomon Chapter of Derby, Conn.; Franklin Chapter of Norwich, Conn.; Franklin Chapter of New Haven, Conn.; and Hudson Chapter of Hudson, N. Y.; to which were the next day added Temple Chapter of Albany, N. Y., and Horeb Chapter of Whitestown, N. Y., assembled at Hartford in Convention, and, having adopted a Constitution, organized a governing body which they styled "The Grand Royal Arch Chapter of the Northern States of America." This body assumed in its Constitution jurisdiction over only the States of New England and New York, and provided that Deputy Grand Chapters, subject to its obedience, should be organized in those States. Ephraim Kirby, of Litchfield, Conn., was elected Grand High Priest; and it was ordered that the first meeting of the Grand Chapter should be held at Middletown, Conn., on the third Wednesday of September next ensuing.

On that day the Grand Chapter met, but the Grand Secretary and Grand Chaplain were the only Grand Officers present. The Grand King was represented by a proxy. The Grand Chapter, however, proceeded to an election of Grand Officers, and the old officers were elected. The body then adjourned to meet in January, 1799, at Providence, R. I.

On the 9th of January, 1799, the Grand Chapter met at Providence, the Deputy Grand Chapters of Massachusetts, Rhode Island, and New York being represented. At this meeting, the Constitution was very considerably modified, and the Grand Chapter assumed the title of "The General Grand Chapter of Royal Arch Masons for the six Northern States enumerated in the preamble." The meetings were directed to be held septennially; and the Deputy Grand Chapters were in future to be called "State Grand Chapters." No attempt was, however, made in words to extend the jurisdiction of the General Grand Chapter beyond the States already named.

On the 9th of January, 1806, a meeting of the General Grand Royal Arch Chapter was held at Middletown, representatives being present from the States of Rhode Island, Connecticut, Vermont, and New York. The Constitution was again revised. The title was for the first time assumed of "The General Grand Chapter of Royal Arch Masons for the United States of America," and jurisdiction was extended over the whole country. This year may, therefore, be considered as the true date of the establishment of the General Grand Chapter.

In 1826 the septennial meetings were abolished, and the General Grand Chapter has ever since met triennially.

The General Grand Chapter consists of the present and past Grand High Priests, Deputy Grand High Priests, Grand Kings and Scribes of the State Grand Chapters, and the Past General Grand Officers.

The officers are a General Grand High Priest, Deputy General Grand High Priest, General Grand King, General Grand Scribe, General Grand Treasurer, General Grand Secretary, General Grand Chaplain, General Grand Captain of the Host, and General Grand Royal Arch Captain.

It originally possessed large prerogatives, extending even to the suspension of Grand Chapters; but by its present Constitution it has "no power of discipline, admonition, censure, or instruction over the Grand Chapters, nor any legislative powers whatever not specially granted" by its Constitution. It may, indeed, be considered as scarcely more than a great Masonic Congress meeting triennially for consultation. But even with these restricted powers, it is capable of doing much good.

General Grand High Priest. The presiding officer of the General Grand Chapter of the United States of America. He is elected every third year by the General Grand Chapter. The title was first assumed in 1799, although the General Grand Chapter did not at that time extend its jurisdiction beyond six of the Northern States.

General Grand Lodge. Ever since the Grand Lodges of this country began, at the commencement of the Revolutionary War, to abandon their dependence on the Grand Lodges of England and Scotland—that is to say, as soon as they emerged from the subordinate position of Provincial Grand Lodges, and were compelled to assume a sovereign and independent character—attempts have, from time to time, been made by members of the Craft to destroy this sovereignty of the State Grand Lodges, and to institute in its place a superintending power, to be constituted either as a Grand Master of North America or as a General Grand Lodge of the United States. Led, perhaps, by the analogy of the united Colonies under one federal head, or, in the very commencement of the Revolutionary struggle, controlled by long habits of dependence on the mother Grand Lodges of Europe, the contest had no sooner begun, and a disseverance of political relations between England and America taken place, than the attempt was made to institute the office of Grand Master of the United States, the object being—of

which there can hardly be a doubt—to invest Washington with the distinguished dignity.

The effort emanated, it appears, with the military Lodges in the army. For a full account of it we are indebted to the industrious researches of Bro. E. G. Storer, who published the entire Minutes of the "American Union Lodge," attached to the Connecticut line, in his work on *The Early Records of Freemasonry in the State of Connecticut.*

On the 27th of December, 1779, the Lodge met to celebrate the day at Morristown, in New Jersey, which, it will be remembered, was then the winter-quarters of the army. At that communication—at which, it may be remarked, by the way, "Bro. Washington" is recorded among the visitors—a petition was read, representing the present state of Freemasonry to the several Deputy Grand Masters in the United States of America, desiring them to adopt some measures for appointing a Grand Master over said States.

The petition purports to emanate from "Ancient Free and Accepted Masons in the several lines of the army"; and on its being read, it was resolved that a committee be appointed from the different Lodges in the army, and from the staff, to meet in convention at Morristown on the 7th of February next. Accordingly, on the 7th of February, 1780, a convention, called in the records "a committee," met at Morristown. This convention adopted an address to the "Grand Masters of the several Lodges in the respective United States." The recommendations of this address were that the said Grand Masters should adopt and pursue the most necessary measures for establishing one Grand Lodge in America, to preside over and govern all other Lodges of whatsoever degree or denomination, licensed or to be licensed, upon the continent; that they should nominate, as Grand Master of said Lodge, a brother whose merit and capacity may be adequate to a station so important and elevated; and that his name should be transmitted "to our Grand Mother Lodge in Europe" for approbation and confirmation.

This convention contained delegates from the States of Massachusetts, Connecticut, New York, New Jersey, Pennsylvania, Delaware, and Maryland. Between the time of its conception, on the 27th of December, 1779, and that of its meeting on the 7th of February, 1780, that is to say in January, 1780, the Grand Lodge of Pennsylvania had held an emergent meeting, and in some measure anticipated the proposed action of the convention by electing General Washington *Grand Master of the United States.*

From the contemporaneous character of these events, it would seem probable that there was some concert of action between the Grand Lodge of Pennsylvania and the Masons of Morristown. Perhaps, the initiative having been taken by the latter in December, the former determined to give its influence, in January, to the final recommendations which were to be made in the following February.

All this, however, although plausible, is but conjecture. Nothing appears to have resulted from the action of either body. The only further reference which I find to the subject, in subsequent Masonic documents, is the declaration of a convention held in 1783, to organize the Grand Lodge of Maryland, where it is remarked that "another Grand Lodge was requisite before an election could be had of a Grand Master for the United States."

But the attempt to form a General Grand Lodge, although, on this occasion, unsuccessful, was soon to be renewed. In 1790, the proposition was again made by the Grand Lodge of Georgia, and here, true to the Roman axiom, *Tempora mutantur et nos mutamur in illis*, the Grand Lodge of Pennsylvania became the opponent of the measure, and declared it to be impracticable.

Again, in 1799, the Grand Lodge of South Carolina renewed the proposition, and recommended a convention to be held at the city of Washington for the purpose of establishing a "Superintending Grand Lodge of America." The reasons assigned by the Grand Lodge of South Carolina for making this proposition are set forth in the circular which it issued on the subject to its sister Grand Lodges. They are "to draw closer the bonds of union between the different Lodges of the United States, and to induce them to join in some systematic plan whereby the drooping spirit of the Ancient Craft may be revived and become more generally useful and beneficial, and whereby Ancient Masonry, so excellent and beautiful in its primitive institution, may be placed upon such a respectable and firm basis in this western world as to bid defiance to the shafts of malice or the feeble attempts of any foreign disclaimers to bring it into disrepute." The allusion here is to the Abbé Barruel, who had just published his abusive and anti-Masonic *History of Jacobinism*.

Several Grand Lodges acceded to the proposition for holding a convention, although they believed the scheme of a "Superintending Grand Lodge" inexpedient and impracticable; but they were willing to send delegates for the purpose of producing uniformity in the Masonic system. The convention, however, did not assemble.

The proposition was again made in 1803, by the Grand Lodge of North Carolina, and with a like want of success.

In 1806, the subject of a General Grand Lodge was again presented to the consideration of the Grand Lodges of the Union, and propositions were made for conventions to be held in Philadelphia in 1807, and in Washington city in 1808, neither of which was convened. The *Proceedings* of the various Grand Lodges in the years 1806, 1807, and 1808 contain allusions to this subject, most of them in favor of a convention to introduce uniformity, but unfavorable to the permanent establishment of a General Grand Lodge. North Carolina, however, in 1807, expressed the opinion that "a National Grand Lodge should possess controlling and corrective powers over all Grand Lodges under its jurisdiction."

An unsuccessful attempt was again made to hold a convention at Washington in January, 1811, "for the purpose of forming a Superintending Grand Lodge of America."

After the failure of this effort, the Grand Lodge of North Carolina, which seems to have been earnest in its endeavors to accomplish its favorite object, again proposed a convention, to be convoked at Washington in 1812. But the effort, like all which had preceded it, proved abortive. No convention was held.

The effort seems now, after all these discouraging attempts, to have been laid upon the shelf for nearly ten years. At length, however, the effort for a convention which had so often failed was destined to meet with partial success, and one rather extemporaneous in its character was held in Washington on the 8th of March, 1822. Over this convention, which the Grand Lodge of Maryland rather equivocally describes as "composed of members of Congress and strangers," the renowned orator and statesman Henry Clay presided. A strong appeal, most probably from the facile pen of its eloquent president, was made to the Grand Lodges of the country to concur in the establishment of a General Grand Lodge. But the appeal fell upon unwilling ears, and the Grand Lodges continued firm in their opposition to the organization of such a superintending body.

The subject was again brought to the attention of the Fraternity by the Grand Lodge of Maryland, which body, at its communication in May, 1845, invited its sister Grand Lodges to meet in convention at Baltimore on the 23d of September, 1847, for the purpose of reporting a Constitution of a General Grand Lodge.

This convention met at the appointed time and place, but only seven Grand Lodges were represented by twice that number of delegates. A Constitution was formed for a "Supreme Grand Lodge of the United States," which was submitted for approval or rejection to the Grand Lodges of the Union. The opinion expressed of that Constitution by the Grand Lodge of Ohio, "that it embraced, in several of its sections, indefinite and unmeaning powers, to which it was impossible to give a definite construction, and that it gave a jurisdiction to the body which that Grand Lodge would in no event consent to," seems to have been very generally concurred in by the other Grand bodies, and the "Supreme Grand Lodge of the United States" never went into operation. The formation of its Constitution was its first, its last, and its only act.

The next action that we find on this much discussed subject was by the Grand Lodge of New York, which body recommended, in 1848, that each of the Grand Lodges should frame the outlines of a General Grand Constitution such as would be acceptable to it, and send it with a delegate to a convention to be holden at Boston in 1850, at the time of meeting of the General Grand Chapter and General

Grand Encampment. The committee of the Grand Lodge of New York, who made this recommendation, also presented the outlines of a General Grand Constitution.

This instrument defines the jurisdiction of the proposed General Grand Lodge as intended to be "over all controversies and disputes between the different Grand Lodges which may become parties to the compact, when such controversies are referred for decision; and the decisions in all cases to be final when concurred in by a majority of the Grand Lodges present"; but it disclaims all appeals from State Grand Lodges or their subordinates in matters relating to their own internal affairs. It is evident that the friends of the measure had abated much of their pretensions since the year 1779, when they wanted a Grand Lodge of America, "to preside over and govern all other Lodges of whatsoever degree or denomination, licensed or to be licensed, on the continent."

The Grand Lodge of Rhode Island also submitted the draft of a General Grand Constitution, more extensive in its details than that presented by New York, but substantially the same in principle. The Grand Lodge of the District of Columbia also concurred in the proposition. The convention did not, however, meet; for the idea of a Supreme Grand Lodge was still an unpopular one with the Craft. In January, 1850, Texas expressed the general sentiment of the Fraternity when it said: "The formation of a General Grand Lodge will not accomplish the desired end. The same feeling and spirit that now lead to difficulties between the different Grand Lodges would produce insubordination and disobedience of the edicts of a General Grand Lodge."

But another attempt was to be made by its friends to carry this favorite measure, and a convention of delegates was held at Lexington, Ky., in September, 1853, during the session of the General Grand Chapter and Encampment at that city. This convention did little more than invite the meeting of a fuller convention, whose delegates should be clothed with more plenary powers, to assemble at Washington in January, 1855.

The proposed convention met at Washington, and submitted a series of nine propositions styled "Articles of Confederation." The gist of these articles is to be found in the initial one, and is in these words: "All matters of difficulty which may hereafter arise in any Grand Lodge, or between two or more Grand Lodges of the United States, which cannot by their own action be satisfactorily adjusted or disposed of, shall, if the importance of the case or the common welfare of the Fraternity demand it, be submitted, with accompanying evidence and documents, to the several Grand Lodges in their individual capacities; and the concurrent decision thereon of two-thirds of the whole number, officially communicated, shall be held authoritative, binding, and final on all parties concerned."

The provisions of these articles were to be considered as ratified, and were to take effect as soon as they were approved by twenty Grand Lodges of the United States. It is needless to say that this approbation was never received, and the proposed confederation failed to assume a permanent form.

It will be perceived that the whole question of a General Grand Lodge is here, at once and in full, abandoned. The proposition was simply for a confederated league, with scarcely a shadow of power to enforce its decisions, with no penal jurisdiction whatsoever, and with no other authority than that which, from time to time, might be delegated to it by the voluntary consent of the parties entering into the confederation. If the plan had been adopted, the body would, in all probability, have died in a few years of sheer debility. There was no principle of vitality to keep it together.

But the friends of a General Grand Lodge did not abandon the hope of effecting their object, and in 1857 the Grand Lodge of Maine issued a circular, urging the formation of a General Grand Lodge at a convention to be held at Chicago in September, 1859, during the session of the General Grand Chapter and General Grand Encampment at that city. This call was generally and courteously responded to; the convention was held, but it resulted in a failure. Other attempts have been made by its friends to carry this measure, but with no results.

Generalissimo. The second officer in a Commandery of Knights Templar, and one of its representatives in the Grand Commandery. His duty is to receive and communicate all orders, signs, and petitions; to assist the Eminent Commander, and, in his absence, to preside over the Commandery. His station is on the right of the Eminent Commander, and his jewel is a square, surmounted by a paschal lamb.

The use of the title in Templarism is of very recent origin, and peculiar to America. No such officer was known in the old Order. It is, besides, inappropriate to a subordinate officer, being derived from the French *generalissime*, and that from the Italian *generalissimo*, both signifying a supreme commander. It has the same meaning in English.

Gentleman Mason. In some of the old lectures of the last century this title is used as equivalent to Speculative Freemason. Thus they had the following catechism:

"*Q.* What do you learn by being a Gentleman Mason?

"*A.* Secrecy, Morality, and Good-Fellowship.

"*Q.* What do you learn by being an Operative Mason?

"*A.* Hew, Square, Mould stone, lay a Level, and raise a Perpendicular."

Hence we see that Gentleman Mason was in contrast with Operative Mason.

Genuflection. Bending the knees has, in all ages of the world, been considered as an act of reverence and humility, and hence Pliny, the Roman naturalist, observes, that "a certain degree of religious reverence is attributed to the knees of a man." Solomon placed himself in this position when he prayed at the consecration of the Temple; and Masons use the same posture in some portions of their ceremonies, as a token of solemn reverence. In Ancient Craft Masonry, during prayer, it is the custom for the members to stand, but in the higher degrees, kneeling, and generally on one knee, is the more usual form.

Geomatic. See *Domatic.*

Geometrical Master Mason. A term in use in England during the last century. By the primitive regulations of the Grand Chapter, an applicant for the Royal Arch Degree was required to produce a certificate that he was "a Geometrical Master Mason," and had passed the chair. The word Geometrical was here synonymous with Speculative.

Geometric Points. In the language of French Masonry, this name is given to the four cardinal points of the compass, because they must agree with the four sides of a regular Temple or Lodge. They are a symbol of regularity and perfection.

Geometry. In the modern rituals, geometry is said to be the basis on which the superstructure of Masonry is erected; and in the *Old Constitutions* of the Medieval Freemasons of England the most prominent place of all the sciences is given to geometry, which is made synonymous with Masonry. Thus, in the Regius MS., which dates not later than the latter part of the fourteenth century, the Constitutions of Masonry are called "the Constitutions of the art of geometry according to Euclid," the words geometry and Masonry being used indifferently throughout the document; and in the Harleian No. 2054 MS. it is said, "thus the craft Geometry was governed there, and that worthy Master (Euclid) gave it the name of Geometry, and it is called Masonrie in this land long after." In another part of the same MS. it is thus defined: "The fifth science is called Geometry, and it teaches a man to mete and measure of the earth and other things, which science is Masonrie."

The Egyptians were undoubtedly one of the first nations who cultivated geometry as a science. "It was not less useful and necessary to them," as Goguet observes (*Orig. des Lois.*, I., iv., 4), "in the affairs of life, than agreeable to their speculatively philosophical genius." From Egypt, which was the parent both of the sciences and the mysteries of the Pagan world, it passed over into other countries; and geometry and Operative Masonry have ever been found together, the latter carrying into execution those designs which were first traced according to the principles of the former.

Speculative Masonry is, in like manner, intimately connected with geometry. In deference to our operative ancestors, and, in fact, as a necessary result of our close connection with them, Speculative Freemasonry derives its most important symbols from this parent science. Hence it is not strange that Euclid, the most famous of geometricians, should be spoken of in all the *Old Records* as a founder of Masonry in Egypt, and that a special legend should have been invented in honor of his memory.

Georgia. Freemasonry was introduced at a very early period into the province of Georgia. Roger Lacey is said to have been the first Provincial Grand Master, and to him the warrant for Solomon's Lodge, at Savannah, was directed in 1735. Rockwell (*Ahim. Rez.*, p. 323) denies this, and thinks that there was an earlier Lodge organized by Lacey, perhaps in 1730. The original warrant of Solomon's Lodge has, however, been destroyed, and we have no authentic evidence on the subject; although it is very generally conceded that the introduction of organized Masonry into Georgia does not date later than the year 1735. There is no evidence, except tradition, of the existence of an earlier Lodge. In 1786, the Independent Grand Lodge of Georgia was formed, Samuel Elbert, the last Provincial Grand Master resigning his position to William Stephens, who was elected the first Grand Master.

Gerbier, Doctor. An energetic Mason, and, as mentioned in *The Royal Masonic Cyclopædia*, one of their removable Masters of the ancient Grand Lodge of France. He is said to have fabricated the title of the Metropolitan Chapter of France, which it was pretended had emanated from Edinburgh, in 1721.

German Union of Two and Twenty. A secret society founded in Germany, in 1786, by Dr. Bahrdt, whose only connection with Freemasonry was that Bahrdt and the twenty-one others who founded it were Masons, and that they invited to their cooperation the most distinguished Masons of Germany. The founder professed that the object of the association was to diffuse intellectual light, to annihilate superstition, and to perfect the human race. Its instruction was divided into six degrees, as follows: 1. The Adolescent; 2. The Man; 3. The Old Man; 4. The Mesopolite; 5. The Diocesan; 6. The Superior. The first three degrees were considered a preparatory school for the last three, out of which the rules of the society were chosen. It lasted only four years, and was dissolved by the imprisonment of its founder for a political libel, most of its members joining the Illuminati. The publication of a work in 1789 entitled *Mehr Noten als Text*, etc., i. e., *More Notes than Text*, or *The German Union of XXII.*, which divulged its secret organization, tended to hasten its dissolution. (See *Bahrdt*.)

Germany. Of all countries Germany plays the most important part in the history of ancient Masonry, since it was there that the gilds of Operative Stone-Masons first assumed that definite organization which subsequently led to the establishment of Speculative Freemasonry. But it was not until a later date that the latter institution obtained a footing on German soil. Findel (*Hist.*, p. 238) says that as early as 1730 temporary Lodges, occupied only in the communication of Masonic knowledge and in the study of the ritual, were formed at different points. But the first regular Lodge was established at Hamburg, in 1733, under a warrant of Lord Strathmore, Grand Master of England; which did not, however, come into active operation until four years later. Its progress was at first slow; and nowhere is Freemasonry now more popular or more deserving of popularity. Its scholars have brought to the study of its antiquities and its philosophy all the laborious research that distinguishes the Teutonic mind, and the most learned works on these subjects have emanated from the German press. The detailed history of its progress would involve the necessity of no ordinary volume.

Ghemoul Binah Thebounah. (Prudence in the midst of vicissitude.) The name of the seventh step of the mystical Kadosh ladder of the A. A. Scottish Rite.

Ghiblim. The form in which Dr. Anderson spells *Giblim*. In the *Book of Constitutions* (ed. 1738, page 70) it is stated that in 1350 "John de Spoulee, call'd *Master of the Ghiblim*," rebuilt St. George's chapel.

Gibalim. A Masonic corruption of *Giblim*, the Giblites, or men of Gebal. (See *Giblim*.)

Gibeah. A Hebrew word signifying a "hill," and giving name to several towns and places in ancient Palestine. The only one requiring special mention is "Gibeah of Benjamin," a small city about four miles north of Jerusalem. It was the residence, if not the birthplace, of King Saul.

In the French Rite it symbolically refers to the Master, who must be pure in heart, that the High and Holy One may dwell therein. The word is also used in the Swedish Rite.

Giblim. Heb., גבלים. A significant word in Masonry. It is the plural of the Gentile noun Gibli (the *g* pronounced hard), and means, according to the idiom of the Hebrew, *Giblites*, or inhabitants of the city of Gebal. The Giblim, or Giblites, are mentioned in Scripture as assisting Solomon's and Hiram's builders to prepare the trees and the stones for building the Temple, and from this passage it is evident that they were clever artificers. The passage is in 1 Kings v. 18, and, in our common version, is as follows: "And Solomon's builders and Hiram's builders did hew them, and the stone-squarers; so they prepared timber and stones to build the house," where the word translated in the authorized version by *stone-squarers* is, in the original, *Giblim*. It is so also in that translation known as the *Bishop's Bible*. The Geneva version has *masons*. The French version of Martin has *tailleurs de pierres*, following the English; but Luther, in his German version, retains the original word *Giblim*.

It is probable that the English translation followed the Jewish Targum, which has a word of similar import in this passage. The error has, however, assumed importance in the Masonic ritual, where *Giblim* is supposed to be synonymous with a Mason. And Sir Wm. Drummond confirms this by saying in his *Origines* (vol. iii., b. v., ch. iv., p. 129) that

"the Gibalim were Master Masons who put the finishing hand to King Solomon's Temple." (See *Gebal*.)

Gilds. The word gild, guild, or geld, from the Saxon *gildan*, to pay, originally meant a tax or tribute, and hence those fraternities which, in the early ages, contributed sums to a common stock, were called Gilds. Cowell, the old English jurist, defines a Gild to be "a fraternity or commonalty of men gathered together into one combination, supporting their common charge by mutual contribution."

Societies of this kind, but not under the same name, were known to the ancient Greeks and Romans, and their artificers and traders were formed into distinct companies which occupied particular streets named after them. But according to Dr. Lujo Brentano, who published, in 1870, an essay on *The History and Development of Gilds*, England is the birthplace of the Medieval Gilds, from whom he says that the modern Freemasons emerged. They existed, however, in every country of Europe, and we identify them in the Compagnons de la Tour of France, and the Bau-corporationen of Germany. The difference, however, was that while they were patronized by the municipal authorities in England, they were discouraged by both the Church and State on the Continent.

The Gilds in England were of three kinds, Religious Gilds, Merchant Gilds, and Craft Gilds, specimens of all of which still exist, although greatly modified in their laws and usages. The Religious or Ecclesiastical Gilds are principally found in Roman Catholic countries, where, under the patronage of the Church, they often accomplish much good by the direction of their benevolence to particular purposes. Merchant Gilds are exemplified in the twelve great Livery Companies of London. And the modern Trades Unions are nothing else but Craft Gilds under another name. But the most interesting point in the history of the Craft Gilds is the fact that from them arose the Brotherhoods of the Freemasons.

Brentano gives the following almost exhaustive account of the organization and customs of the Craft Gilds:

"The Craft Gilds themselves first sprang up amongst the free craftsmen, when they were excluded from the fraternities which had taken the place of the family unions, and later among the bondmen, when they ceased to belong to the *familia* of their lord. Like those Frith Gilds, the object of the early Craft Gilds was to create relations as if among brothers; and above all things, to grant to their members that assistance which the member of a family might expect from that family. As men's wants had become different, this assistance no longer concerned the protection of life, limbs, and property, for this was provided for by the Frith Gilds, now recognized as the legitimate authority; but the principal object of the Craft Gilds was to secure their members in the independent, unimpaired, and regular earning of their daily bread by means of their craft.

"The very soul of the Craft Gild was its meetings, which brought all the Gild brothers together every week or quarter. These meetings were always held with certain ceremonies, for the sake of greater solemnity. The box, having several locks like that of the Trade Unions, and containing the charters of the Gild, the statutes, the money, and other valuable articles, was opened on such occasions, and all present had to uncover their heads. These meetings possessed all the rights which they themselves had not chosen to delegate. They elected the presidents (originally called Aldermen, afterwards Masters and Wardens) and other officials, except in those cases already mentioned, in which the Master was appointed by the king, the bishop, or the authorities of the town. As a rule, the Gilds were free to choose their Masters, either from their own members, or from men of higher rank, though they were sometimes limited in their choice to the former.

"The Wardens summoned and presided at the meetings, with their consent enacted ordinances for the regulation of the trade, saw these ordinances properly executed, and watched over the maintenance of the customs of the Craft. They had the right to examine all manufactures, and a right of search for all unlawful tools and products. They formed, with the assistance of a quorum of Gild brothers, the highest authority in all the concerns of the Gild. No Gild member could be arraigned about trade matters before any other judge. We have still numerous documentary proofs of the severity and justice with which the Wardens exercised their judicial duties. Whenever they held a court, it was under special forms and solemnities; thus, for instance, in 1275 the chief Warden of the masons building Strasburg cathedral held a court sitting under a canopy.

"Besides being brotherhoods for the care of the temporal welfare of their members, the Craft Gilds were, like the rest of the Gilds, at the same time religious fraternities. In the account of the origin of the Company of Grocers, it is mentioned that at the very first meeting they fixed a stipend for the priest, who had to conduct their religious services and pray for their dead. In this respect the Craft Gilds of all countries are alike; and in reading their statutes, one might fancy sometimes that the old craftsmen cared only for the wellbeing of their souls. All had particular saints for patrons, after whom the society was frequently called; and, where it was possible, they chose one who had some relation to their trade. They founded masses, altars, and painted windows in cathedrals; and even at the present day their coats of arms and their gifts range proudly by the side of those of kings and barons. Sometimes individual Craft Gilds appear to have stood in special relation to a particular church, by virtue of which they had to perform special services, and received in return a special share in all the prayers of the clergy of that church. In later times, the Craft Gilds frequently went in solemn procession to their churches. We find innumerable ordinances also as to the support of the sick and poor; and to afford a settled asylum for distress, the London Companies early built dwellings near their halls. The chief care, however, of the Gildmen was always directed to the welfare of the souls of the dead. Every year a requiem was sung for all departed Gild brothers, when they were all mentioned by name; and on the death of any member, special services were held for his soul, and distribution of alms was made to the poor, who, in return, had to offer up prayers for the dead, as is still the custom in Roman Catholic countries."

In a *History of the English Guilds*, edited by Toulmin Smith from old documents in the Record Office at London, and published by the Early English Text Society, we find many facts confirmatory of those given by Brentano, as to the organization of these Gilds.

The testimony of these old records shows that a religious element pervaded the Gilds, and exercised a very powerful influence over them. Women were admitted to all of them, which Herbert (*Liv. Comp.*, i., 83) thinks was borrowed from the Ecclesiastical Gilds of Southern Europe; and the brethren and sisters were on terms of complete equality. There were fees on entrance, yearly and special payments, and fines for wax for lights to burn at the altar or in funeral rites. The Gilds had set days of meeting, known as "moming speeches," or "days of spekyngges totiedare for here comune profyte," and a grand festival on the patron saint's day, when the members assembled for worship, almsgiving, feasting, and for nourishing of brotherly love. Mystery plays were often performed. They had a treasure-chest, the opening of which was a sign that business had begun. While it remained open all stood with uncovered heads, when cursing and swearing and all loose conduct were severely punished. The Gild property consisted of land, cattle, money, etc. The expenditure was on the sick poor and aged, in making good losses by robbery, etc. Loans were advanced, pilgrims assisted, and, in one city, "any good girl of the Gild" was to have a dowry on marriage, if her father could not provide it. Poor travelers were lodged and fed. Roads were kept in repair, and churches were sustained and beautified. They wore a particular costume, which was enforced by their statutes, whence come the liveries of the London Companies of the present day and the "clothing" of the Freemasons.

An investigation of the usages of these Medieval Gilds, and a comparison of their regulations with the old Masonic Constitutions, will furnish a fertile source of interest to the Masonic archeologist, and will throw much light on the early history of Freemasonry. (See Gilds in Eleventh Edition of the *Britannica Cyclopedia*.)

Gilead. See *Galahad*.

Gilgul, Doctrine of. We learn from Bro. Kenneth R. H. Mackenzie's *Royal Masonic Cyclopædia* that "Certain of the learned Jews have believed, for many centuries, in the doctrine of Gilgul, according to which the bodies of Jews deposited in foreign tombs contain within them a principle of soul which cannot rest until, by a process called by them 'the whirling of the soul,' the immortal particle reaches once more the sacred soil of the Promised Land. This whirling of souls was supposed to be accomplished by a process somewhat similar to that of the *metempsychosis* of the Hindus, the psychical spark being conveyed through bird, beast, or fish, and, sometimes, the most minute insect. The famous Rabbi Akiba (followed by the Rabbis Judah and Meir) declared that none could come to the resurrection save those of the Jews who were buried in the Holy Land, or whose remains were, in the process of ages, gradually brought thither. In Picart's wonderful and laborious work there are many references to this doctrine. The learned may consult further authorities on this curious subject in the *Kabbala Denudata* of Heinrich Khunrath, 1677."

Gilkes, Peter William. Born in London in 1765, and died in 1833. He was celebrated for his perfect knowledge of the ritual of Ancient Craft Masonry according to the English ritual, which he successfully taught for many years. His reputation in England as a Masonic teacher was very great.

Girdle. In ancient symbology the girdle was always considered as typical of chastity and purity. In the Brahmanical initiations, the candidate was presented with the Zennar, or sacred cord, as a part of the sacred garments; and Gibbon says that "at the age of puberty the faithful Persian was invested with a mysterious girdle; fifteen genuflections were required after he put on the sacred girdle." The old Templars assumed the obligations of poverty, obedience, and chastity; and a girdle was given them, at their initiation, as a symbol of the last of the three vows. As a symbol of purity, the girdle is still used in many chivalric initiations, and may be properly considered as the analogue of the Masonic apron.

Glaire, Peter Maurice. A distinguished Mason, who was born in Switzerland in 1743, and died in 1819. In 1764, he went to Poland, and became the intimate friend of King Stanislaus Poniatowski, who confided to him many important diplomatic missions. During his residence in Poland, Glaire greatly patronized the Freemasons of that kingdom, and established there a Rite of seven degrees. He returned to Switzerland in 1788, where he continued to exercise an interest in Freemasonry, and in 1810 was elected Grand Master for three years, and in 1813 for life, of the Roman Grand Orient of Helvetia, which body adopted his Rite.

Glastonbury, Holy Thorn of. There is an ancient market town in County Somerset, Eng., with a population of 3,700, which owes its origin to a celebrated abbey, founded, according to tradition, in 60 A.D. We are further told that Joseph of Arimathea was the founder, and the "miraculous thorn" which flowered on Christmas day was believed by the common people to be the veritable staff with which Joseph aided his steps from the Holy Land. The tree was destroyed during the civil wars, but grafts flourish in neighboring gardens. Glastonbury has the honor of ranking St. Patrick (415 A.D.) and St. Dunstan among its abbots. In 1539, Henry VIII. summoned Abbot Whiting to surrender the town and all its treasures, and on his refusal condemned him to be hanged and quartered, and the monastery confiscated to the king's use, which sentence was immediately carried into execution. King Arthur is said to be buried in this place.

Gleason, Benjamin. A lecturer and teacher of the Masonic ritual, according to the system of Webb, in the Grand Lodge of Massachusetts, from 1806 to 1842. Gleason is said to have been a man of liberal education, and a graduate in 1802 of Brown University. He became soon after a pupil of Thomas Smith Webb, whose lectures he taught in Massachusetts and elsewhere. The assertion of some writers that Gleason went to England and lectured before the Grand Lodge of England, which recognized his or Webb's system as being the same as that of Preston, is highly improbable and wants confirmation.

Globe. In the Second Degree, the celestial and terrestrial globes have been adopted as symbols of the universal extension of the Order, and as suggestive of the universal claims of brotherly love. The symbol is a very ancient one, and is to be found in the religious systems of many countries. Among the Mexicans the globe was the symbol of universal power. But the Masonic symbol appears to have been derived from, or at least to have an allusion to, the Egyptian symbol of the *winged globe*. There is nothing more common among the Egyptian monuments than the symbol of a globe supported on each side by a serpent, and accompanied with wings extended wide beyond them, occupying nearly the whole of the entablature above the entrance of many of their temples. We are thus reminded of the globes on the pillars at the entrance of the Temple of Solomon. The winged globe, as the symbol of Cneph, the Creator Sun, was adopted by the Egyptians as their national device, as the Lion is that of England, or the Eagle of the United States. In the eighteenth chapter of Isaiah (v. i.), where the authorized version of King James's Bible has "Woe to the land shadowing with wings," Lowth, after Bochart, translates, "Ho! to the land of the winged cymbal," supposing the Hebrew עלצל to mean the sistrum, which was a round instrument, consisting of a broad rim of metal, having rods passing through it, and some of which, extending beyond the sides, would, says Bishop Lowth, have the appearance of wings, and be expressed by the same Hebrew word. But Rosellini translates the passage differently, and says, "Ho, land of the winged globe."

Dudley, in his *Naology* (p. 13), says that the knowledge of the spherical figure of the earth was familiar to the Egyptians in the early ages, in which some of their temples were constructed. Of the round figure described above, he says that although it be called a globe, an egg, the symbol of the world was perhaps intended; and he thinks that if the globes of the Egyptian entablatures were closely examined, they would perhaps be found of an oval shape, figurative of the creation, and not bearing any reference to the form of the world.

The interpretation of the Masonic globes, as a symbol of the universality of Masonry, would very well agree with the idea of the Egyptian symbol referring to the extent of creation. That the globes on the pillars, placed like the Egyptian symbol before the temple, were a representation of the celestial and terrestrial globes, is a very modern idea. In the passage of the Book of Kings, whence Masonry has derived its ritualistic description, it is said (1 Kings vii. 16), "And he made two chapiters of molten brass, to set upon the tops of the pillars." In the Masonic ritual it is said that "the pillars were surmounted by two pomels or globes." Now *pomel*, פומיל, is the very word employed by Rabbi Solomon in his commentary on this passage, a word which signifies a globe or spherical body. The Masonic globes were really the chapiters described in the Book of Kings. Again it is said (1 Kings vii. 22), "Upon the top of the pillars was lily work." We now know that the plant here called the lily was really the lotus, or the Egyptian water-lily. But among the Egyptians the lotus was a symbol of the universe; and hence, although the Masons in their ritual have changed the expanded flower of the lotus, which crowned the chapiter and surmounted each pillar of the porch, into a globe, they have retained the interpretation of universality. The Egyptian globe or egg and lotus or lily and the Masonic globe are all symbols of something universal, and the Masonic idea has only restricted by a natural impulse the idea to the universality of the Order and its benign influences. But it is a pity that Masonic ritualists did not preserve the Egyptian and Scriptural symbol of the lotus surrounding a ball or sphere, and omit the more modern figures of globes celestial and terrestrial.

Glory, Symbol of. The Blazing Star in the old lectures was called "the glory in the center," because it was placed in the center of the floor-cloth, and represented the glorious name of Deity. Hence, Dr. Oliver gives to one of his most interesting works, which treats of the symbolism of the Blazing Star, the title of *The Symbol of Glory*.

Gloves. In the continental Rites of Masonry, as practised in France, in Germany, and in other countries of Europe, it is an invariable custom to present the new-

20

ly initiated candidate not only, as we do, with a white leather apron, but also with two pair of white kid gloves—one a man's pair for himself, and the other a woman's—to be presented by him in turn to his wife or his betrothed, according to the custom of the German Masons, or, according to the French, to the female whom he most esteems, which, indeed, amounts, or should amount, to the same thing.

There is in this, of course, as there is in everything else which pertains to Freemasonry, a symbolism. The gloves given to the candidate for himself are intended to teach him that the acts of a Mason should be as pure and spotless as the gloves now given to him. In the German Lodges, the word used for *acts* is, of course, *handlung*, or *handlings*, "the works of his hands," which makes the symbolic idea more impressive.

Dr. Robert Plot—no friend of Masonry, but still a historian of much research—says, in his *Natural History of Staffordshire*, that the Society of Freemasons in his time (and he wrote in 1686) presented their candidates with gloves for themselves and their wives. This shows that the custom, still preserved on the Continent of Europe, once was practised in England; although there, as well as in America, it is discontinued, which is perhaps to be regretted.

But although the presentation of the gloves to the candidate is no longer practised as a ceremony in England or America, yet the use of them as a part of the proper professional clothing of a Mason in the duties of the Lodge or in processions, is still retained; and in many well-regulated Lodges the members are almost as regularly clothed in their white gloves as in their white aprons.

The symbolism of the gloves, it will be admitted, is in fact but a modification of that of the apron. They both signify the same thing, both are allusive to a purification of life. "Who shall ascend," says the Psalmist, "into the hill of the Lord? or who shall stand in his holy place? He that hath clean hands and a pure heart." The apron may be said to refer to the "pure heart"; the gloves, to the "clean hands." Both are significant of that purification which was always symbolized by the ablution which preceded the ancient initiations into the sacred mysteries. But while our American and English Masons have adhered only to the apron, and rejected the gloves as a Masonic symbol, the latter appear to be far more important in symbolic science, because the allusions to pure or clean hands are abundant in all the ancient writers.

"Hands," says Wemyss, in his *Clavis Symbolica*, "are the symbols of human actions—pure hands are pure actions; unjust hands are deeds of injustice." There are numerous references in sacred or profane writers to this symbolism. The washing of the hands has the outward sign of an internal purification. Hence, the Psalmist says, "I will wash my hands in innocence, and I will encompass thine altar, Jehovah."

In the Ancient Mysteries, the washing of the hands was always an introductory ceremony to the initiation, and, of course, it was used symbolically to indicate the necessity of purity from crime as a qualification of those who sought admission into the sacred Rites; and hence on a temple in the island of Crete this inscription was placed: "Cleanse your feet, wash your hands, and then enter."

Indeed, the washing of hands, as symbolic of purity, was among the ancients a peculiarly religious rite. No one dared to pray to the gods until he had cleansed his hands. Thus, Homer makes Hector say,

"I dread with unwashed hands to bring
My incensed wine to Jove an offering."

The same practise existed among the Jews; and a striking instance of the symbolism is exhibited in that well-known action of Pilate, who, when the Jews clamored for Jesus that they might crucify him, appeared before the people, and, having taken water, washed his hands, saying at the same time, "I am innocent of the blood of this just man. See ye to it." In the Christian church of the Middle Ages, gloves were always worn by bishops or priests when in the performance of ecclesiastical functions. They were made of linen and were white; and Durandus, a celebrated ritualist, says that "by the white gloves were denoted chastity and purity, because the hands were thus kept clean and free from all impurity."

There is no necessity to extend examples any further. There is no doubt that the use of the gloves in Masonry is a symbolic idea, borrowed from the ancient and universal language of symbolism, and was intended, like the apron, to denote the necessity of purity of life.

The builders, who associated in companies, who traversed Europe and were engaged in the construction of palaces and cathedrals, have left to us, as their descendants, their name, their technical language, and the apron, that distinctive piece of clothing by which they protected their garments from the pollutions of their laborious employment. Did they also bequeath to us their gloves? This is a question which some modern discoveries will at last enable us to solve.

M. Didron, in his *Annales Archéologiques*, presents us with an engraving copied from the painted glass of a window in the Cathedral of Chartres, in France. The painting was executed in the thirteenth century, and represents a number of Operative Masons at work. *Three* of them are adorned with laurel crowns. May not these be intended to represent the three officers of a Lodge? All of the Masons wear gloves. M. Didron remarks that in the old documents which he has examined mention is often made of gloves which are intended to be presented to Masons and stone-cutters. In a subsequent number of the *Annales*, he gives the following three examples of this fact:

In the year 1331, the Chatelan of Villaines, in Duemois, bought a considerable quantity of gloves to be given to the workmen, in order, as it is said, "to shield their hands from the stone and lime."

In October, 1383, as he learns from a document of that period, three dozen pair of gloves were bought and distributed to the Masons when they commenced the buildings at the Chartreuse of Dijon.

And, lastly, in 1486 or 1487, twenty-two pair of gloves were given to the Masons and stone-cutters who were engaged in work at the city of Amiens.

It is thus evident that the builders—the Operative Masons—of the Middle Ages wore gloves to protect their hands from the effects of their work. It is equally evident that the Speculative Masons have received from their operative predecessors the gloves as well as the apron, both of which, being used by the latter for practical uses, have been, in the spirit of symbolism, appropriated by the former to "a more noble and glorious purpose."

Gnostics. The general name of Gnostics has been employed to designate several sects that sprung up in the eastern parts of the Roman Empire about the time of the advent of Christianity; although it is supposed that their principal doctrines had been taught centuries before in many of the cities of Asia Minor. The word Gnosticism is derived from the Greek *Gnosis* or knowledge, and was a term used in the earliest days of philosophy to signify the science of Divine things, or, as Matter says, "superior or celestial knowledge." He thinks the word was first used by the Jewish philosophers of the famous school of Alexandria. The favorite opinion of scholars is that the sect of Gnostics arose among the philosophers who were the converts of Paul and the other Apostles, and who sought to mingle the notions of the Jewish Egyptian school, the speculations of the Kabbalists, and the Grecian and Asiatic doctrines with the simpler teachings of the new religion which they had embraced. They believed that the writings of the Apostles enunciated only the articles of the vulgar faith; but that there were esoteric traditions which had been transmitted from generation to generation in mysteries, to which they gave the name of Gnosticism or Gnosis. King says (*Gnostics*, p. 7) that they drew the materials out of which they constructed their system from two religions, viz., the Zend-Avesta and its modifications in the Kabbala, and the reformed Brahmanical religion, as taught by the Buddhist missionaries.

Notwithstanding the large area of country over which this system of mystical philosophy extended, and the number of different sects that adopted it, the same fundamental doctrine was everywhere held by the chiefs of Gnosticism. This was, that the visible creation was not the work of the Supreme Deity, but of the Demiurgus, a simple emanation, and several degrees removed from the Godhead. To the latter, indeed, styled by them "the unknown Father," they attributed the creation of the intellectual world, the Æons and Angels, while they made the creation of the world of matter the work of the Demiurgus.

Gnosticism abounded in symbols and legends, in talismans and amulets, many of which were adopted into the popular superstitions of the Medieval ages. It is, too, interesting to the student of Masonic antiquities because of its remote connection with that Order, some of whose symbols have been indirectly traced to a Gnostic origin. The Druses of Mount Lebanon were supposed to be a sect of Gnostics; and the constant intercourse which was maintained during the Crusades between Europe and Syria produced an effect upon the Western nations through the influence of the pilgrims and warriors.

Toward the Manicheans, the most prominent offshoot of Gnosticism, the Templars exercised a tolerant spirit very inconsistent with the professed objects of their original foundation, which led to the charge that they were affected by the dogmas of Manicheism.

The strange ceremonies observed in the initiation into various secret societies that existed in the Lower Empire are said to have been modeled on the Gnostic Rites of the Mithraic Cave.

The architects and stone-masons of the Middle Ages borrowed many of the principles of ornamentation, by which they decorated the ecclesiastical edifices which they constructed, from the abstruse symbols of the Gnostics.

So, too, we find Gnostic symbols in the Hermetic Philosophy and in the system of Rosicrucianism; and lastly, many of the symbols still used by Freemasonry—such, for instance, as the triangle within a circle, the letter G, and the pentacle of Solomon—have been traced to a Gnostic source.

Goat, Riding the. The vulgar idea that "riding the goat" constitutes a part of the ceremonies of initiation in a Masonic Lodge has its real origin in the superstition of antiquity. The old Greeks and Romans portrayed their mystical god Pan in horns and hoof and shaggy hide, and called him "goat-footed." When the demonology of the classics was adopted and modified by the early Christians, Pan gave way to Satan, who naturally inherited his attributes; so that to the common mind the Devil was represented by a he-goat, and his best known marks were the horns, the beard, and the cloven hoofs. Then came the witch stories of the Middle Ages, and the belief in the witch orgies, where, it was said, the Devil appeared *riding on a goat*. These orgies of the witches, where, amid fearfully blasphemous ceremonies, they practised initiation into their Satanic Rites, became, to the vulgar and the illiterate, the type of the Masonic Mysteries; for, as Dr. Oliver says, it was in England a common belief that the Freemasons were accustomed in their Lodges "to raise the Devil." So the "riding of the goat," which was believed to be practised by the witches, was transferred to the Freemasons; and the saying remains to this day, although the belief has very long since died out.

G. O. D. The initials of Gomer, Oz, Dabar. It is a singular coincidence, and worthy of thought, that the letters composing the English name of Deity should be the initials of the Hebrew words wisdom, strength, and beauty; the three great pillars, or metaphorical supports, of Masonry. They seem to present almost the only reason that can reconcile a Mason to the use of the initial "G" in its conspicuous suspension in the East of the Lodge in place of the Delta. The incident seems to be more than an accident.

דבר Dabar, Wisdom, D.

עז Oz, Strength, O.

גמר Gomer, Beauty, G.

Thus the initials conceal the true meaning.

God. A belief in the existence of God is an essential point of Speculative Masonry—so essential, indeed, that it is a landmark of the Order that no Atheist can be made a Mason. Nor is this left to an inference; for a specific declaration to that effect is demanded as an indispensable preparation for initiation. And hence Hutchinson says that the worship of God "was the first and corner-stone on which our originals thought it expedient to place the foundation of Masonry." The religion of Masonry is cosmopolitan, universal; but the required belief in God is not incompatible with this universality; for it is the belief of all peoples. "Be assured," says Godfrey Higgins, "that God is equally present with the pious Hindoo in the temple, the Jew in the synagogue, the Mohammedan in the mosque, and the Christian in the church." There never has been a time since the revival of Freemasonry, when this belief in God as a superintending power did not form a part of the system. The very earliest rituals that are extant, going back almost to the beginning of the eighteenth century, contain precisely the same question as to the trust in God which is found in those of the present day; and the oldest *manuscript constitutions*, dating as far back as the fifteenth century at least, all commence with, or contain, an invocation to the "Mighty Father of Heaven." There never was a time when the dogma did not form an essential part of the Masonic system.

God and His Temple, Knight of. A degree mentioned by Fustier.

Godfather. In French Lodges the member who introduces a candidate for initiation is called his "parrain," or "godfather."

Goethe, John Wolfgang von. This illustrous German poet was much attached to Freemasonry. He was initiated on the eve of the festival of St. John the Baptist, in 1780; and on the eve of the same festival, in 1830, the Masons of Weimar celebrated the semi-centennial anniversary of his admission into the Order, of which, in a letter to the musical composer, Zeeter, who had been, like himself, initiated on the same day fifty years before, he speaks with great gratification as his "Masonic jubilee." He says, "The gentlemen have treated this epoch with the greatest courtesy. I responded to it in the most friendly manner on the following day." Goethe's writings contain many favorable allusions to the Institution.

Goetia. A contradistinctive term to Theurgia, the first signifying black magic, the latter white magic. The demons of darkness were invoked and no crime or horror stayed the power. Alchemy and chemistry were the powerful arms relied on.

Golden Candlestick. The golden candlestick which was made by Moses for the service of the tabernacle, and was afterward deposited in the holy place of the temple to throw light upon the altar of incense, and the table of shewbread, was made wholly of pure gold, and had seven branches; that is, three on each side, and one in the center. These branches were at equal distances, and each one was adorned with flowers like lilies, gold knobs after the form of an apple, and similar ones resembling an almond. Upon the extremities of the branches were seven golden lamps, which were fed with pure olive-oil, and lighted every evening by the priests on duty. Its seven branches are explained in the Ineffable degrees as symbolizing the seven planets. It is also used as a decoration in Chapters of the Royal Arch, but apparently without any positive symbolic signification.

Golden Fleece. In the lecture of the First Degree, it is said of the Mason's apron, that it is "more ancient than the Golden Fleece or Roman Eagle, more honorable than the Star and Garter." The reference is here evidently not to the Argonautic expedition in search of the golden fleece, nor to the deluge, of which that event is supposed to have been a figure, as Dr. Oliver incorrectly supposes (*Symb. Dict.*), but to certain decorations of honor with which the apron is compared. The eagle was to the Romans the ensign of imperial power; the Order of the Golden Fleece was of high repute as an Order of Knighthood. It was established in Flanders, in 1429, by the Duke of Burgundy, who selected the fleece for its badge because wool was the staple production of the country. It has ever been considered, says Clark, one of the most illustrious Orders in Europe. The Order of the Garter was, and is still considered, the highest decoration that can be bestowed upon a subject by a sovereign of Great Britain. Thus, the apron is proudly compared with the noblest decorations of ancient Rome and of modern Europe. But the Masons may have been also influenced in their selection of a reference to the Golden Fleece, by the fact that in the Middle Ages it was one of the most important symbols of the Hermetic philosophers.

Golden Key, Knight of the. See *Knight of the Golden Key.*

Golden Lion of Hesse-Cassel, Order of the. Instituted by Frederick II., 14th of August, 1770, under a decree of 6th July, to recompense virtue and merit. The Grand Master is the reigning sovereign of Hesse-Cassel. Motto, "Virtute et Fidelitate."

Golden Stole of Venice. (*Cavalieri della Stola d'Oro.*) An ancient order of knighthood, conferred by the republic of Venice. The number of knights was unlimited. The decoration, worn over the left shoulder, was richly embroidered with flowers of gold, and being in width a handbreadth, fell behind and before to the knee. An ambassador, for some distinctive service, was deemed worthy. The ducal robe was of red material.

Gold Thaler, or Gold Gülden, we are informed in Kenning's *Cyclopædia of Freemasonry*, is the St. John's offering, as it was called under the strict observance in Germany, and which amounted to one ducat, or, at the least, one and two-thirds of a thaler, which was paid by every member on St. John's Day. This practise is still kept up in many German Lodges for the benefit of the poor fund.

Golgotha. Greek, Γολγοθᾶ, from the Hebrew, גלגלת, *Gulgoleth,* "a skull." The name given by the Jews to Calvary, the place of Christ's crucifixion and burial. It is a significant word in Templar Masonry. (See *Calvary.*)

Gomel. (Heb., גמל, L., *retribuens.*) Irregularly given as Gomer and Gomez. A word found in the Twenty-sixth Degree A. A. Scottish Rite, signifying *reward.*

Gonfalon. (Ital., *Gonfalone*, O. German, *Gundfano.*) An ecclesiastical war flag or banner, a standard; used in several of the

chivalric degrees of Masonry. The chief magistrates in Italian cities when bearing this ensign are known as Gonfaloniers. The banner is triune, of white silk, trimmed and mounted with gold.

Goodall. The reputed author of the exposure of Masonry, known as "Jachin and Boaz." It is said that he was at one time Master of the W. India and American Lodge, now known as the Lodge of Antiquity; but this statement has never been confirmed.

Good Samaritan. An androgynous, honorary or side degree conferred in the United States with rather impressive ceremonies. It is, of course, as a degree to be conferred on females, unconnected with Masonic history or traditions, but draws its allusions from the fate of Lot's wife, and from the parable of the Good Samaritan related in the Gospels. The passages of Scripture which refer to these events are read during the ceremony of initiation. This degree is to be conferred only on Royal Arch Masons and their wives, and in conferring it two Good Samaritans must always be present, one of whom must be a Royal Arch Mason. Much dignity and importance has been given to this degree by its possessors; and it is usual in many places for a certain number of Good Samaritans to organize themselves into regular, but of course independent, bodies to hold monthly meetings under the name of Assemblies, to elect proper officers, and receive applications for initiation. In this manner the assemblies of Good Samaritans, consisting of male and female members, bear a very near resemblance to the female Lodges, which, under the name of "Maçonnerie d'Adoption," prevail in France.

Good Shepherd. Our Savior called himself the Good Shepherd. Thus, in St. John's Gospel (x. 14, 15, 16), he says: "I am the Good Shepherd, and know my sheep, and am known of mine. As the Father knoweth me, even so know I the Father: and I lay down my life for the sheep. And other sheep I have, which are not of this fold: them also must I bring, and they shall hear my voice; and there shall be one fold, and one Shepherd." Hence, in Masonic as well as in Christian symbolism, Christ is naturally called the Good Shepherd.

Good Shepherd, Sign of the. When Jesus was relating (Luke xv.) the parable in which one having lost a sheep goes into the wilderness to search for it, he said: "And when he hath found it, he layeth it on his shoulders, rejoicing." Mr. Hettner, a German writer on Greek customs, says: "When the Greek carries home his lamb, he slings it round his neck, holding it by the feet crossed over the breast. This is to be seen with us also, but the sight is especially attractive at Athens, for it was in this manner that the ancients represented Hermes as the guardian and multiplier of flocks; so stood the statue of Hermes at Olympia, Occhalia, and Tanagra. Small marble statues of this kind have even come down to us, one of which is to be seen in the Pembroke collection at Wilton House; another, a smaller one, in the Stoa of Hadrian, at Athens. This representation, however, appears most frequently in the oldest works of Christian art, in which the laden Hermes is turned into a laden Christ, who often called himself the Good Shepherd, and expressly says in the Gospel of St. Luke, that when the shepherd finds the sheep, he lays it joyfully on his shoulder."

Now, although the idea of the Good Shepherd may have been of Pagan origin, yet derived from the parable of our Savior in St. Luke and his language in St. John, it was early adopted by the Christians as a religious emblem. The Good Shepherd bearing the sheep upon his shoulders, the two hands of the Shepherd crossed upon his breast and holding the legs of the sheep, is a very common subject in the paintings of the earliest Christian era. It is an expressive symbol of the Savior's love—of him who taught us to build the new temple of eternal life—and, consequently, as Didron says, "the heart and imagination of Christians have dwelt fondly upon this theme; it has been unceasingly repeated under every possible aspect, and may be almost said to have been worn threadbare by Christian art. From the earliest ages, Christianity completely made it her own." And hence the Christian degree of Rose Croix has very naturally appropriated the "sign of the Good Shepherd," the representation of Christ bearing his once lost but now recovered sheep upon his shoulders, as one of its most impressive symbols.

Goose and Gridiron. An alehouse with this sign, in St. Paul's Church Yard, London. In 1717, the Lodge of Antiquity met at the Goose and Gridiron, and it was there that the first quarterly communication of the Grand Lodge of England, after the revival of 1717, was held on the 24th of June, 1717. It was the headquarters of a musical society, whose arms—a lyre and a swan—were converted into Goose and Gridiron.

Gormogons. A secret society established in 1724, in England, in opposition to Freemasonry. One of its rules was that no Freemason could be admitted until he was first degraded, and had then renounced the Masonic Order. It was absurdly and intentionally pretentious in its character; claiming, in ridicule of Freemasonry, a great antiquity, and pretending that it was descended from an ancient society in China. There was much antipathy between the two associations, as will appear from the following doggerel, published in 1729, by Henry Carey:

"The Masons and the Gormogons
    Are laughing at one another,
While all mankind are laughing at them;
    Then why do they make such a pother?

"They bait their hook for simple gulls,
    And truth with bam they smother;
But when they 've taken in their culls,
    Why then 't is—Welcome, Brother!"

The Gormogons made a great splutter in their day, and published many squibs against

Freemasonry; yet that is still living, while the Gormogons were long ago extinguished. They seemed to have flourished for but a very few years.

[Bro. R. F. Gould has collected all that is known about the Gormogons in his article on the Duke of Wharton, in vol. viii. of *Ars Quatuor Coronatorum*.]

Gothic Architecture. Of all the styles of architecture, the Gothic is that which is most intimately connected with the history of Freemasonry, having been the system peculiarly practised by the Freemasons of the Middle Ages. To what country or people it owes its origin has never been satisfactorily determined; although it has generally been conjectured that it was of Arabic or Saracenic extraction, and that it was introduced into Europe by persons returning from the Crusades. The Christians who had been in the Holy Wars received there an idea of the Saracenic works, which they imitated on their return to the West, and refined on them as they proceeded in the building of churches. The Italians, Germans, French, and Flemings, with Greek refugees, united in a fraternity of architects and ranged from country to country, and erected buildings according to the Gothic style, which they had learned during their visits to the East, and whose fundamental principles they improved by the addition of other details derived from their own architectural taste and judgment. Hence Sir Christopher Wren thinks that this style of the Medieval Freemasons should be rather called the Saracenic than the Gothic. This style, which was distinguished, by its pointed arches, and especially by the perpendicularity of its lines, from the rounded arch and horizontal lines of previous styles, was altogether in the hands of those architects who were known, from the tenth to the sixteenth centuries, as Freemasons, and who kept their system of building as a secret, and thus obtained an entire monopoly of both domestic and ecclesiastical architecture. At length, when the gilds or fraternities of Freemasons, "who alone," says Mr. Hope, "held the secrets of Gothic art," were dissolved, the style itself was lost, and was succeeded by what Paley says (*Man. of Goth. Arch.*, p. 15) was "a worse than brazen era of architecture." (For further details, see *Traveling Freemasons*.)

Gothic Constitutions. A title sometimes given to the Constitutions which are supposed to have been adopted by the Freemasons at the City of York, in the tenth century, and so called in allusion to the Gothic architecture which was introduced into England by the Fraternity. A more correct and more usual designation of these laws is the *York Constitutions*, which see.

Gould, Robert Freke. This well-known historian of Freemasonry has had a very varied career. Born in 1836, and died March 26, 1915. He entered the English army at the age of eighteen, becoming a lieutenant in the same year, and serving with distinction in North China in 1860–2. On his return to England he studied law and became a barrister in 1868.

He was initiated at Ramsgate in the Royal Navy Lodge, No. 429, and was Master of the Inhabitants' Lodge at Gibraltar, also of the Meridian Lodge, No. 743, a Military Lodge attached to his regiment. Afterward he held the Chair of the Moira, Quatuor Coronati and Jerusalem Lodges. In 1880 he was appointed Senior Grand Deacon of England.

He has been a constant writer in the Masonic press since 1858; in 1879 he published *The Four Old Lodges* and *The Atholl Lodges*, and in 1899 a book on *Military Lodges*.

But his "magnum opus" is his stupendous *History of Freemasonry* in three large volumes, which occupied him from 1882 to 1887, which was followed in 1903 by *A Concise History of Freemasonry* abridged from the larger work and brought up to date.   [E. L. H.]

Gourgas, John James Joseph. A merchant of New York, who was born in France in 1777, and received a member of the Scottish Rite in 1806. His name is intimately connected with the rise and progress of the Ancient and Accepted Scottish Rite in the Northern Jurisdiction of the United States. Through his representations and his indefatigable exertions, the Mother Council at Charleston was induced to denounce the Consistory of Joseph Cerneau in the City of New York, and to establish there a Supreme Council for the Northern Jurisdiction, of which Bro. Gourgas was elected the Secretary-General. He continued to hold this office until 1832, when he was elected Sovereign Grand Commander. In 1851, on the removal of the Grand East of the Supreme Council to Boston, he resigned his office in favor of Bro. Giles Fonda Yates, but continued to take an active interest, so far as his age would permit, in the Rite until his death, which occurred at New York on February 14, 1865, at the ripe old age of eighty-eight, and being at the time probably the oldest possessor of the Thirtieth Degree in the world. Bro. Gourgas was distinguished for the purity of his life and the powers of his intellect. His Masonic library was very valuable, and especially rich in manuscripts. His correspondence with Dr. Moses Holbrook, at one time Grand Commander of the Southern Council, is in the Archives of that body, and bears testimony to his large Masonic attainments.

Grades. Degrees in Masonry are sometimes so called. It is a French word. (See *Degrees*.)

Grain of Mustard, Order of the. (Ger., *Der Orden vom Senf Korn*.) An order instituted in Germany, based on Mark iv. 30 and 32, the object being the propagation of morality.

Grammar. One of the seven liberal arts and sciences, which forms, with Logic and Rhetoric, a triad dedicated to the cultivation of language. "God," says Sanctius, "created man the participant of reason; and as he willed him to be a social being, he bestowed upon him the gift of language, in the perfecting of which there are three aids. The first is *Grammar*, which rejects from language all solecisms and barbarous expressions; the second is *Logic*, which is occupied with the truthfulness of language; and the third is *Rhetoric*, which seeks only the adornment of language."

Grand Architect. A degree in several of the Rites modeled upon the Twelfth of the Ancient and Accepted Scottish Rite. It is, 1. The Sixth Degree of the Reform of St. Martin; 2. The Fourteenth of the Rite of Elected Cohens; 3. The Twenty-third of the Rite of Mizraim; and 4. The Twenty-fourth of the Metropolitan Chapter of France.

Grand Chapter. A Grand Chapter consists of the High Priests, Kings, and Scribes for the time being, of the several Chapters under its jurisdiction, of the Past Grand and Deputy Grand High Priests, Kings, and Scribes of the said Grand Chapter. In some Grand Chapters Past High Priests are admitted to membership, but in others they are not granted this privilege, unless they shall have served as Grand and Deputy Grand High Priests, Kings, or Scribes. Grand Chapters have the sole government and superintendence of the several Royal Arch Chapters and Lodges of Most Excellent Past and Mark Masters within their several jurisdictions.

Until the year 1797, there was no organization of Grand Chapters in the United States. Chapters were held under the authority of a Master's Warrant, although the consent of a neighboring Chapter was generally deemed expedient. But in 1797, delegates from several of the Chapters in the Northern States assembled at Boston for the purpose of deliberating on the expediency of organizing a Grand Chapter for the government and regulation of the several Chapters within the said States. This convention prepared an address to the Chapters in New York and New England, disclaiming the power of any Grand Lodge to exercise authority over Royal Arch Masons, and declaring it expedient to establish a Grand Chapter. In consequence of this address, delegates from most of the States above mentioned met at Hartford in January, 1798, and organized a Grand Chapter, formed and adopted a Constitution, and elected and installed their officers. This example was quickly followed by other parts of the Union, and Grand Chapters now exist in nearly all the States. (See *General Grand Chapter*.)

The officers of a Grand Chapter are usually the same as those of a Chapter, with the distinguishing prefix of "Grand" to the titles. The jewels are also the same, but enclosed within a circle. In England and Scotland the Grand Chapter bears the title of Supreme Grand Chapter.

Grand Commander. The presiding officer of a Grand Commandery of Knights Templar.

Grand Commander of the Eastern Star. *(Grand Commandeur de l'Etoile d'Orient.)* A degree in Pyron's collection.

Grand Conclave. The title of the presiding body of Templarism in England is the "Grand Conclave of the Religious and Military Order of Masonic Knights Templar."

Grand Conservators. On July 1, 1814, the Grand Mastership of the Order in France, then held by Prince Cambacérès, was, in consequence of the political troubles attendant upon the restoration of the monarchy, declared vacant by the Grand Orient. On August 12th, the Grand Orient decreed that the functions of Grand Master should be provisionally discharged by a commission consisting of three Grand Officers, to be called Grand Conservators, and Macdonald, Duke of Tarentum, the Count de Beurnonville, and Timbrune, Count de Valénce, were appointed to that office.

Grand Consistory. The governing body over a State of the Ancient and Accepted Scottish Rite; subject, however, to the superior jurisdiction of the Supreme Council of the Thirty-third. The members of the Grand Consistory are required to be in possession of the Thirty-second Degree.

Grand Council. The title given to the first three officers of a Royal Arch Chapter. Also the name of the superintending body of Cryptic Masonry in any jurisdiction. It is composed of the first three officers of each Council in the jurisdiction. Its officers are: Most Puissant Grand Master, Thrice Illustrious Deputy Grand Master, Illustrious Grand Conductor of the Works, Grand Treasurer, Grand Recorder, Grand Chaplain, Grand Marshal, Grand Captain of the Guards, Grand Conductor of the Council, and Grand Steward.

Grand Director of the Ceremonies. An important officer in the United Grand Lodge of England; a similar office to that of Grand Master-General of Ceremonies of a Supreme Council, upon whom the order of the Grand Body largely depends, and who has charge of the service or ceremonies of whatever nature that may transpire.

Grand East. The city in which the Grand Lodge, or other governing Masonic Body, is situated, and whence its official documents emanate, is called the Grand East. Thus, a document issued by the Grand Lodge of Massachusetts would be dated from the "Grand East of Boston," or if from the Grand Lodge of Louisiana, it would be the "Grand East of New Orleans." The place where a Grand Lodge meets is therefore called a Grand East. The word is in constant use on the Continent of Europe and in America, but seldom employed in England, Scotland, or Ireland.

Grand Elect, Perfect and Sublime Mason. The Fourteenth Degree of the A. A. Scottish Rite. (See *Perfection, Lodge of*.)

Grand Encampment. See *Encampment, Grand*.

Grand High Priest. The presiding officer of a Grand Royal Arch Chapter in the American system. The powers and prerogatives of a Grand High Priest are far more circumscribed than those of a Grand Master. As the office has been constitutionally created by the Grand Chapter, and did not precede it as that of Grand Masters did the Grand Lodges, he possesses no inherent prerogatives, but those only which are derived from and delegated to him by the Constitution of the Grand Chapter and regulations formed under it for the government of Royal Arch Masonry.

Grand Inquiring Commander. The Sixty-sixth Degree of the Rite of Mizraim.

Grand Inspector, Inquisitor Commander. The Thirty-first Degree of the Ancient and Accepted Scottish Rite. It is not an historical degree, but simply a judicial power of the higher degrees. The place of meeting is called a Supreme Tribunal. The decorations are white, and the presiding officer is styled Most Perfect President. The jewel of the degree is a Teutonic cross of silver attached to white watered ribbon.

Grand Lodge. A Grand Lodge is the dogmatic and administrative authority of Ancient Craft Masonry, or the three Symbolic degrees. It is defined in the Regulations of 1721 as "consisting of and formed by the Masters and Wardens of all the regular Lodges upon record, with the Grand Master at their head, and his Deputy on his left hand, and the Grand Wardens in their proper places." (*Constitutions*, 1723, p. 61.) This definition refers to a very modern organization, for of Grand Lodges thus constituted we have no written evidence previous to the year 1717, when Freemasonry was revived in England. Previous to that time the administrative authority of the Craft was exercised by a General Assembly of the Masons of a jurisdiction which met annually. (See *Assembly*.) The true history of Grand Lodges commences, therefore, from what has been called the era of the revival.

In 1716, four old Lodges in London, determined, if possible, to revive the Institution from its depressed state, and accordingly they met in February, 1717, at the Apple-Tree Tavern (whose name has thus been rendered famous for all time); and after placing the oldest Master Mason, who was the Master of a Lodge, in the chair, they constituted themselves into a Grand Lodge, and forthwith "revived the quarterly communications of the officers of Lodges (call'd the Grand Lodge)." (*Constitutions*, 1738, p. 109.) On the following St. John the Baptist's Day, the Grand Lodge was duly organized, and Mr. Anthony Sayer was elected Grand Master, who appointed his Wardens, and commanded the Masters and Wardens of Lodges to meet the Grand Officers every quarter in communication. From that time Grand Lodges have been uninterruptedly held; receiving, however, at different periods, various modifications.

A Grand Lodge is invested with power and authority over all the Craft within its jurisdiction. It is the Supreme Court of Appeal in all Masonic cases, and to its decrees implicit obedience must be paid by every Lodge and every Mason situated within its control. The government of Grand Lodges is, therefore, completely despotic. While a Grand Lodge exists, its edicts must be respected and obeyed without examination by its subordinate Lodges.

This autocratic power of a Grand Lodge is based upon a principle of expediency, and derived from the fundamental law established at the organization of Grand Lodges in the beginning of the last century. In so large a body as the Craft, it is absolutely necessary that there should be a supreme controlling body to protect the Institution from anarchy, and none could be more conveniently selected than one which, by its representative character, is, or ought to be, composed of the united wisdom, prudence, and experience of all the subordinate Lodges under its obedience; so that the voice of the Grand Lodge is nothing else than the voice of the Craft expressed by their representatives. Hence the twelfth of the General Regulations declares that "the Grand Lodge consists of, and is formed by, the Masters and Wardens of all the particular Lodges upon record." (*Constitutions*, 1738, p. 158.)

So careful has the Institution been to preserve the dogmatic and autocratic power of the Grand Lodge, that all elected Masters are required, at the time of their installation, to make the following declaration:

"You agree to hold in veneration the original rulers and patrons of the Order of Freemasonry, and their regular successors, supreme and subordinate, according to their stations; and to submit to the awards and resolutions of your brethren in general Lodge convened, in every case, consistent with the Constitutions of the Order.

"You promise to pay homage to the Grand Master for the time being, and to his officers when duly installed, and *strictly to conform to every edict of the Grand Lodge.*"

The organization of new Grand Lodges in America has followed that adopted, in essential particulars, by the four Lodges which established the Grand Lodge of England in 1717. When it is desired to organize a Grand Lodge, three or more legally constituted Lodges, working in any State, territory, or other independent political division, where no Grand Lodge already exists, may meet in convention, adopt by-laws, elect officers, and organize a Grand Lodge. The Lodges within its jurisdiction then surrender their Warrants of constitution to the Grand Lodges from which they respectively had received them, and accept others from the newly organized Grand Lodge, which thenceforward exercises all Masonic jurisdiction over the State in which it has been organized.

A Grand Lodge thus organized consists of the Masters and Wardens of all the Lodges under its jurisdiction, and such Past Masters as may enroll themselves or be elected as members. Past Masters are not, however, members of the Grand Lodge by inherent right, but only by courtesy, and no Past Master can remain a member of the Grand Lodge unless he is attached to some subordinate Lodge in its jurisdiction.

All Grand Lodges are governed by the following officers: Grand Master, Deputy Grand Master, Senior and Junior Grand Wardens, Grand Treasurer, and Grand Secretary. These are usually termed the Grand Officers; in addition to them there are subordinate officers appointed by the Grand Master and the Grand Wardens, such as Grand Deacons, Grand Stewards, Grand Marshal, Grand Pursuivant, Grand Sword-Bearer, and Grand Tiler; but their number and titles vary in different Grand Lodges.

Grand Lodge Manuscript, No. 1. A roll of parchment, nine inches in length and five in breadth, containing the Legend of the Craft and the Old Charges. It is preserved in the Archives of the Grand Lodge of England, having been bought in 1839 for £25. It was dated by its writer 1583. It has been reproduced in Hughan's *Old Charges*, 1872; in Sadler's *Masonic Facts and Fictions*, and in facsimile by the Quatuor Coronati Lodge.

Grand Master. The presiding officer of the Symbolic degrees in a jurisdiction. He presides, of course, over the Grand Lodge, and has the right not only to be present, but also to preside in every Lodge, with the Master of the Lodge on his left hand, and to order his Grand Wardens to attend him, and act as Wardens in that particular Lodge. He has the right of visiting the Lodges and inspecting their books and mode of work as often as he pleases, or, if unable to do so, he may depute his Grand Officers to act for him. He has the power of granting dispensations for the formation of new Lodges; which dispensations are of force until revoked by himself or the Grand Lodge. He may also grant dispensations for several other purposes, for which see the article *Dispensation*. Formerly, the Grand Master appointed his Grand Officers, but this regulation has been repealed, and the Grand Officers are now all elected by the Grand Lodges. [Except in England, where the Grand Master appoints all but the Grand Treasurer.]

When the Grand Master visits a Lodge, he must be received with the greatest respect, and the Master of the Lodge should always offer him the chair, which the Grand Master may or may not accept at his pleasure.

Should the Grand Master die, or be absent from the jurisdiction during his term of office, the Deputy Grand Master assumes his powers, or, if there be no Deputy, then the Grand Wardens according to seniority.

The following is a list of the Grand Masters of the Grand Lodge of England, established in 1717 and afterward known as the "Moderns":

1717.	Anthony Sayer.
1718.	George Payne.
1719.	J. T. Desaguliers, LL.D., F.R.S.
1720.	George Payne.
1721.	John, Duke of Montague.
1722.	Philip, Duke of Wharton.
1723.	Francis, Earl of Dalkeith.
1724.	Charles, Duke of Richmond.
1725.	James, Lord Paisley.

1726.	William, Earl of Inchiquin.
1727.	Henry, Lord Coleraine.
1728.	James, Lord Kingston.
1729–30.	Thomas, Duke of Norfolk.
1731.	Thomas, Lord Lovel.
1732.	Anthony, Viscount Montague.
1733.	James, Earl of Strathmore.
1734.	John, Earl of Crawford.
1735.	Thomas, Viscount Weymouth.
1736.	John, Earl of Loudoun.
1737.	Edward, Earl of Darnley.
1738.	Henry, Marquess of Carnarvon.
1739.	Robert, Lord Raymond.
1740.	John, Earl of Kintore.
1741.	James, Earl of Morton.
1742–3.	John, Viscount Dudley and Ward.
1744.	Thomas, Earl of Strathmore.
1745–6.	James, Lord Cranstoun.
1747–51.	Wm., Lord Byron.
1752–3.	John, Lord Carysfort.
1754–6.	James, Marquess of Carnarvon.
1757–61.	Sholts, Lord Aberdour.
1762–3.	Washington, Earl Ferrers.
1764–6.	Cadwallader, Lord Blaney.
1767–71.	Henry, Duke of Beaufort.
1772–6.	Robert, Lord Petre.
1777–82.	George, Duke of Manchester.
1782–90.	H. R. H. The Duke of Cumberland.
1790– 1813.	} H. R. H. The Prince of Wales.
1813.	H. R. H. The Duke of Sussex.

The following is a list of the Grand Masters of the Atholl or "Ancients" Grand Lodge:

1753.	Robert Turner.
1754–5.	Hon. Edward Vaughan.
1756–9.	Earl of Blessington.
1760–65.	Thomas, Earl of Kelly.
1766–70.	Hon. Thos. Mathew.
1771–4.	John, 3d Duke of Atholl.
1775–81.	John, 4th Duke of Atholl.
1782.	Vacant.
1783–90.	Randal, Earl of Antrim.
1791– 1813.	} John, 4th Duke of Atholl.
1813.	H. R. H. The Duke of Kent.

The following is a list of the Grand Masters of the United Grand Lodge of England from the union of "Ancients" and "Moderns" in 1813:

1813–43.	H. R. H. The Duke of Sussex.
1844–70.	Earl of Zetland.
1870–4.	Marquess of Ripon.
1874– 1901.	} H. R. H. The Prince of Wales.
1901.	H. R. H. The Duke of Connaught.

Grand Master Architect. (*Grand Maître Architect.*) The Twelfth Degree in the Ancient and Accepted Scottish Rite. This is strictly a scientific degree, resembling in that respect the degree of Fellow-Craft. In it the principles of architecture and the connection of the liberal arts with Masonry are unfolded. Its officers are three—a Master, and two Wardens. The Chapter is decorated with white and red hangings, and furnished with the five orders of architecture, and a case of mathematical instruments. The apron is white, lined with blue; and the jewel is a gold medal, on which are engraved the orders of architecture. It is suspended by a stone-colored ribbon.

Grand Master Mason. The title given to the Grand Master in the Grand Lodge of Scotland.

Grand Master of all Symbolic Lodges. (*Vénérable Maître de toutes les Loges.*) The Twentieth Degree in the Ancient and Accepted Scottish Rite. The presiding officer is styled Venerable Grand Master, and is assisted by two Wardens in the west. The decorations of the Lodge are blue and yellow. The old ritual contains some interesting instructions respecting the first and second Temple.

Among the traditions preserved by the possessors of this degree, is one which states that after the third Temple was destroyed by Titus, the son of Vespasian, the Christian Freemasons who were then in the Holy Land, being filled with sorrow, departed from home with the determination of building a fourth, and that, dividing themselves into several bodies, they dispersed over the various parts of Europe. The greater number went to Scotland, and repaired to the town of Kilwinning, where they established a Lodge and built an abbey, and where the records of the Order were deposited. This tradition, preserved in the original rituals, is a very strong presumptive evidence that the degree owed its existence to the Templar system of Ramsay.

Grand Master of Light. One of the various names bestowed on the degree of Knight of St. Andrew.

Grand Offerings. According to the English system of lectures, three important events recorded in Scripture are designated as the three grand offerings of Masonry, because they are said to have occurred on Mount Moriah, which symbolically represents the ground floor of the Lodge. These three grand offerings are as follows: The first grand offering was when Abraham prepared to offer up his son Isaac; the second was when David built an altar to stay the pestilence with which his people were afflicted; and the third was when Solomon dedicated to Jehovah the Temple which he had completed. (See *Ground Floor of the Lodge.*)

Grand Officers. The elective officers of a superintending Masonic body, such as Grand Lodge, Grand Chapter, etc., are so called. The appointed officers are designated as subordinate officers, but this distinction is not always strictly observed.

Grand Orient. Most of the Grand Lodges established by the Latin races, such as those of France, Spain, Italy, and the South American States, are called Grand Orients. The word is thus, in one sense, synonymous with Grand Lodge; but these Grand Orients have often a more extensive obedience than Grand Lodges, frequently exercising jurisdiction over the highest degrees, from which English and American Grand Lodges refrain.

Thus, the Grand Orient of France exercises jurisdiction not only over the seven degrees of its own Rite, but also over the thirty-three of the Ancient and Accepted, and over all the other Rites which are practised in France.

Grand Orient is also used in English, and especially in American, Masonry to indicate the seat of the Grand Lodge of highest Masonic power, and is thus equivalent to *Grand East*, which see.

Grand Pontiff. (*Grand Pontife ou Sublime Ecossais.*) The Nineteenth Degree of the Ancient and Accepted Scottish Rite. The degree is occupied in an examination of the Apocalyptic mysteries of the New Jerusalem. Its officers are a Thrice Puissant and one Warden. The Thrice Puissant is seated in the east on a throne canopied with blue, and wears a white satin robe. The Warden is in the west, and holds a staff of gold. The members are clothed in white, with blue fillets embroidered with twelve stars of gold, and are called True and Faithful Brothers. The decorations of the Lodge are blue sprinkled with gold stars.

Grand Principals. The first three officers of the Grand Chapter of England are so called. They are respectively designated as Z., H., and J., meaning Zerubbabel, Haggai, and Joshua.

Grand Prior. 1. Each chief or conventual bailiff of the eight languages of the Order of Malta was called a Grand Prior. There were also other Grand Priors, under whom were several Commanderies. The Grand Priors of the Order were twenty-six in number. 2. The third officer in the Supreme Council of the Ancient and Accepted Scottish Rite for the Southern Jurisdiction of the United States. (See *Prior.*)

Grand Secretary. The recording and corresponding officer of a Grand Lodge, whose signature must be attached to every document issued from the Grand Lodge; where there is no Grand Register or Keeper of the Seals, he is the custodian of the Seal of the Grand Lodge. The Regulations of 1722 had provided for the office, but no appointment was made until 1723, when William Cowper was chosen by the Grand Lodge. The office was therefore at first an elective one, but Anderson, in his edition of 1738, says that "ever since, the new Grand Master, upon his commencement, appoints the Secretary, or continues him by returning him the books." (P. 161.) This usage is still pursued by the modern Grand Lodge of England; but in every jurisdiction of this country the office of Grand Secretary is an elective one. The jewel of the Grand Secretary is a circle enclosing two pens crossed. His badge of office was formerly a bag. (See *Bag.*)

Grand Stewards. Officers of a Grand Lodge, whose duty it is to prepare and serve at the Grand Feast. This duty was at first performed by the Grand Wardens, but in 1721 they were authorized "to take some Stewards to their assistance." (*Constitutions*, 1738, p. 112.) This was sometimes done and sometimes omitted, so that often there were no Stewards. In 1728 (*ibid.*, p. 123), the Stewards, to the number of twelve, were made permanent officers; and it was resolved that in future, at the annual election, each Steward should nominate his successor. At present, in the Grand Lodge of England, nineteen Grand Stewards are annually appointed from nineteen different Lodges. Each Lodge recommends one of its subscribing members, who is nominated by the former Steward of that Lodge, and the appointment is made by the Grand Master. The number of Grand Stewards in this country seldom exceeds two, and the appointment is made in some Grand Lodges by the Grand Master, and in others by the Junior Grand Warden. The jewel of a Grand Steward is a cornucopia within a circle, and his badge of office a white rod.

Grand Stewards' Lodge. According to the Constitutions of England, the past and present Grand Stewards constitute a Lodge, which has no number, but is registered in the Grand Lodge books at the head of all other Lodges. It is represented in the Grand Lodge by its Master, Wardens, and Past Masters, but has no power of making Masons. The institution has not been introduced into this country except in the Grand Lodge of Maryland, where the Grand Stewards' Lodge acts as a Committee of Grievances during the recess of the Grand Lodge.

Grand Tiler. An officer who performs in a Grand Lodge the same duties that a Tiler does in a subordinate Lodge. The Grand Tiler is prohibited from being a member of the Grand Lodge, because his duties outside of the door would prevent his taking part in the deliberations of the body.

Grand Treasurer. The office of Grand Treasurer was provided for by the Regulations of 1722, and in 1724, on the organization of the Committee of Charity, it was enacted that a Treasurer should be appointed. But it was not until 1727 that the office appears to have been really filled by the selection of Nathaniel Blakerby. But as he was elected Deputy Grand Master in the same year, and yet continued to perform the duties of Treasurer, it does not appear to have been considered as a distinct appointment. In 1738, he demitted the office, when Revis, the Grand Secretary, was appointed. But he declined on the ground that the offices of Secretary and Treasurer should not be held by the same person—"the one being a check on the other." (*Constitutions*, 1738, p. 184.) So that, in 1739, it was made a permanent office of the Grand Lodge by the appointment of Bro. John Jesse. It is an elective office; and it was provided, by the Old Regulations, that he should be "a brother of good worldly substance." The duties are similar to those of the Treasurer of a subordinate Lodge. The jewel is a circle enclosing two keys crossed, or in saltire. According to ancient custom, his badge of office was a white staff, but this is generally disused in this country.

Grand Wardens. The Senior and Junior Grand Wardens are the third and fourth officers of a Grand Lodge. Their duties do not differ very materially from those of the corresponding officers of a subordinate Lodge, but their powers are of course more extensive.

The Grand Wardens succeed to the government of the Craft, in order of rank, upon the death or absence from the jurisdiction of the Grand and Deputy Grand Masters. (See *Succession to the Chair.*)

It is also their prerogative to accompany the Grand Master in his visitations of the Lodges, and when there to act as his Wardens.

In the absence of the Senior Grand Warden, the Junior does not occupy the west, but retains his position in the south. Having been elected and installed to preside in the south, and to leave that station only for the east, the temporary vacancy in the west must be supplied by the appointment by the Grand Master of some other brother. (See *Wardens.*)

On the same principle, the Senior Grand Warden does not supply the place of the absent Deputy Grand Master, but retains his station in the west.

The Old Charges of 1722 required that no one could be a Grand Warden until he had been the Master of a Lodge. The rule still continues in force, either by specific regulations or by the force of usage.

By the Regulations of 1721, the Grand Master nominated the Grand Wardens, but if his nomination was not approved, the Grand Lodge proceeded to an election. By the present Constitutions of England the power of appointment is vested absolutely in the Grand Master. In this country the Grand Wardens are elected by the Grand Lodge.

Grasse Tilly, Alexandre François Auguste, Comte de. He was the son of the Comte de Grasse who commanded the French fleet that had been sent to the assistance of the Americans in their revolutionary struggle. De Grasse Tilly was born at Versailles, in France, about the year 1766. He was initiated in the Mother Scottish Lodge du Contrat Social, and subsequently, going over to America, resided for some time in the island of St. Domingo, whence he removed to the city of Charleston, in South Carolina, where, in 1796, he affiliated with the French Lodge la Candeur. In 1799, he was one of the founders of the Lodge la Reunion Française, of which he was at one time the Venerable or Master. In 1802, the Comte de Grasse was a member of the Supreme Council of the Ancient and Accepted Rite, which had been established the year before at Charleston; and in the same year he received a patent as Grand Commander for life of the French West India islands. In 1802 he returned to St. Domingo, and established a Supreme Council of the Scottish Rite at Port au Prince. In 1804 he went to Europe, and labored with great energy for the extension of the Ancient and Accepted Rite. On September 22, 1804, he founded at Paris a Supreme Council of the Ancient and Accepted Scottish Rite, of which body he was until 1806, the Grand Commander. On March 5, 1805, he organized a Supreme Council at Milan, in Italy, and on July 4, 1811, another at Madrid, in Spain. The Comte de Grasse was an officer in the French army, and was taken prisoner by the English and detained in England until 1815, when he returned to Paris. He immediately resumed his functions as Grand Commander of a body which took the unauthorized pretentious title of the Supreme Council of America. For several years Scottish Masonry in France was convulsed with dissensions, which De Grasse vainly labored to reconcile. Finally, in 1818, he resigned his post as Grand Commander, and was succeeded by the Comte Decazes. From that period he appears to have passed quietly out of the Masonic history of France, and probably died soon after.

Grave. The grave is, in the Master's Degree, the analogue of the pastos, couch or coffin, in the Ancient Mysteries, and is intended scenically to serve the same purpose. The grave is, therefore, in that degree, intended, in connection with the sprig of acacia, to teach symbolically the great Masonic doctrine of a future life.

Gravelot. The name of the second of the three conspirators in the Master's Degree, according to the Adonhiramite Rite. The others are Romvel and Abiram. The etymology of Gravelot is unknown.

Great Architect of the Universe. The title applied in the technical language of Freemasonry to the Deity. It is appropriate that a society founded on the principles of architecture, which symbolizes the terms of that science to moral purposes, and whose members profess to be the architects of a spiritual temple, should view the Divine Being, under whose holy law they are constructing that edifice, as their Master Builder or Great Architect. Sometimes, but less correctly, the title "Grand Architect of the Universe" is found.

Great Priory. The ruling body of the Order of the Temple for England, Wales and Canada is so called.

Greater Lights. See *Lights, Greater, Bible, Square and Compasses.*

Greece. , In 1867, the first steps were taken to establish a Grand Lodge in Greece by the Lodges which had been recently founded there by the Grand Orient of Italy, but owing to various causes the organization did not succeed, and until 1872 the Grecian Lodges were presided over by a Deputy Grand Master, appointed by and the representative of the Grand Orient of Italy.

On July 22, 1872, the Lodges of Greece met at Athens, and organized the Grand Lodge of Greece, electing His Imperial Highness Prince Rhodocanakis the first Grand Master.

At the same time a Supreme Council of the Ancient and Accepted Scottish Rite was organized. The seat of both bodies is at Athens.

Greece, Mysteries in. The principal Pagan mysteries celebrated in Greece were the *Eleusinian* and the *Bacchic.* (See *Eleusinian Mysteries.*)

Green. Green, as a Masonic color, is almost confined to the four degrees of Perfect Master, Knight of the East, Knight of the Red Cross, and Prince of Mercy. In the degree of Perfect Master it is a symbol of the moral resurrection of the candidate, teaching him that being dead to vice he should hope to revive in virtue.

In the degree of Knight of the Red Cross, this color is employed as a symbol of the immutable nature of truth, which, like the bay tree, will ever flourish in immortal green.

This idea of the unchanging immortality of that which is divine and true, was always connected by the ancients with the color of green. Among the Egyptians, the god Phtha, the active spirit, the creator and regenerator of the world, the goddess Pascht, the Divine preserver, and Thoth, the instructor of men in the sacred doctrines of truth, were all painted in the hieroglyphic system with green flesh.

Portal says, in his essay on *Symbolic Colors,* that "green was the symbol of victory"; and this reminds us of the motto of the Red Cross Knights, " magna est veritas et prævalebit " —*great is truth and mighty above all things;* and hence green is the symbolic color of that degree.

In the degree of Prince of Mercy, or the Twenty-sixth Degree of the Scottish Rite, green is also symbolic of truth, and is the appropriate color of the degree, because truth is there said to be the palladium of the Order.

In the degree of Knight of the East, in the Ancient and Accepted Scottish Rite, green is also the symbolic color. We may very readily suppose, from the close connection of this degree in its ritual with that of the Companion of the Red Cross, that the same symbolic explanation of the color would apply to both, and I think that such an explanation might very properly be made; but it is generally supposed by its possessors that the green of the Knights of the East alludes to the waters of the river Euphrates, and hence its symbolism is not moral but historical.

The *evergreen* of the Third Degree is to the Master Mason an emblem of immortality. Green was with the Druids a symbol of hope, and the virtue of hope with a Mason illustrates the hope of immortality. In all the Ancient Mysteries, this idea was carried out, and green symbolized the birth of the world, and the moral creation or resurrection of the initiate. If we apply this to the evergreen of the Master Mason we shall again find a resemblance, for the acacia is emblematic of a new creation of the body, and a moral and physical resurrection.

Greeting. This word means salutation, and, under the form of "Thrice Greeting," it is very common at the head of Masonic documents. In the beginning of the last century it was usual at the meeting of Masons to say, "God's good *greeting* be to this our happy meeting." Browne gives the formula as practised in 1800: "The recommendation I bring is from the right worthy and worshipful brothers and fellows of the Holy Lodge of St. John, who *greet* your worship well." This formula is obsolete, but the word *greeting* is still in use among Freemasons. In Masonic documents it is sometimes found in the form of S∴ S∴ S∴, which three letters are the initials of the Latin word *salutem* or *health*, three times repeated, and therefore equivalent to "Thrice Greeting."

Gregorians. An association established early in the eighteenth century in ridicule of and in opposition to the Freemasons. There was some feud between the two Orders, but the Gregorians at last succumbed, and long ago became extinct. They lasted, however, at least until the end of the century, for there is extant a Sermon preached before them in 1797. They must too, by that time, have changed their character, for Prince William Frederick of Gloucester was then their presiding officer; and Dr. Munkhouse, the author of that sermon, who was a very ardent Mason, speaks in high terms of the Order as an ally of Freemasonry, and distinguished for its "benign tendency and salutary effects."

Greinemann, Ludwig. A Dominican monk, who, while preaching a course of Lenten sermons at Aix-la-Chapelle in 1779, endeavored to prove that the Jews who crucified Jesus were Freemasons; that Pilate and Herod were Wardens in a Masonic Lodge; and that Judas, before he betrayed his Lord, had been initiated in the synagogue, the thirty pieces of silver which he returned being the amount of his fee for initiation. With discourses like these, Greinemann, who had threatened, if his followers would assist him, he would slay every Freemason he met with his own hand, so excited the people, that the magistrates were compelled to issue an edict forbidding the assemblies of the Freemasons. Peter Schuff, a Capuchin, also vied with Greinemann in the labor of persecution, and peace was not restored until the neighboring free imperial states threatened that, if the monks did not refrain from stirring up the mob against Freemasonry, they should be prohibited from collecting alms in their territories.

Grip. In early Masonic works this is called the "gripe." German Masons call it *der Griff*, and French ones, *l'attouchement*.

Groton. In the Leland Manuscript, a corruption of Crotona, where Pythagoras established his school.

Ground Floor of the Lodge. Mount Moriah, on which the Temple of Solomon was built, is symbolically called the *ground floor of the Lodge*, and hence it is said that "the Lodge rests on holy ground." This ground-floor of the Lodge is remarkable for three great events recorded in Scripture, which are called "the three grand offerings of Masonry." It was here that Abraham prepared, as a token of his faith, to offer up his beloved son Isaac—this was the *first grand offering;* it was here that David, when his people were afflicted with a pestilence, built an altar, and offered thereon peace-offerings and burnt-offerings to appease the wrath of God—this was the *second grand offering;* and lastly, it was here that, when

the Temple was completed, King Solomon dedicated that magnificent structure to the service of Jehovah, with the offering of pious prayers and many costly presents—and this was the *third grand offering.*

This sacred spot was once the threshing-floor of Ornan the Jebusite, and from him David purchased it for fifty shekels of silver. The Kabbalists delight to invest it with still more solemn associations, and declare that it was the spot on which Adam was created and Abel slain. (See *Holy Ground.*)

Ground Floor of King Solomon's Temple. This is said to have been a Mosaic pavement, consisting of black and white stones laid lozengewise, and surrounded by a tesselated border. The tradition of the Order is that Entered Apprentices' Lodges were held on the ground floor of King Solomon's Temple; and hence a Mosaic pavement, or a carpet representing one, is a very common decoration of Masonic Lodges. (See *Mosaic Pavement* and *Grand Offerings.*)

Grumbach, Sylvester. Mentioned in the legend of the Strict Observance, and was the reputed Grand Master of the Templars from 1330 to 1332, and was the twenty-second Grand Master.

Guard. See *Due Guard.*

Guard of the Conclave. See *Knight of the Christian Mark.*

Guards. Officers used in working the rituals of the Red Cross and Templar degrees. They do not constitute regular officers of a Council or Commandery, but are appointed *pro re natâ.*

Guerrier de Dumast. A distinguished French Mason, born at Nancy on February 26, 1796. He is the author of a poem entitled *La Maçonnerie*, in three cantos, enriched with historical, etymological, and critical notes, published in 1820. For this work he received from the Lodge Frères Artistes, of which he was the orator, a gold medal. He was the author of several other works, both Masonic and secular.

Gugomos, Baron Von. An impostor in Masonry, who, in 1775, appeared in Germany, and, being a member of the Order of Strict Observance, claimed that he had been delegated by the Unknown Superiors of the Holy See at Cyprus to establish a new Order of Knights Templars. Calling himself Dux and High Priest, he convoked a Masonic Congress at Wiesbaden, which, notwithstanding the warning of Dr. Bode, was attended by many influential members of the Fraternity. His pretensions were so absurd, that at length his imposture was detected, and he escaped secretly out of Wiesbaden. In 1786, Gugomos confessed the imposition, and, it is said, asserted that he had been employed as a tool by the Jesuits to perform this part, that Freemasonry might be injured.

Guibbs. The names given to the Assassins of the Third Degree by some of the inventors of the high degrees, are of so singular a form as to have almost irresistibly led to the conclusion that these names were bestowed by the adherents of the house of Stuart upon some of their enemies as marks of infamy. Such, for instance, is *Romvel*, the name of one of the Assassins in certain Scottish degrees, which is probably a corruption of *Cromwell*. *Jubelum Guibbs*, another name of one of these traitors, has much puzzled the Masonic etymologists. I think that I have found its origin in the name of the Rev. Adam Gib, who was an antiburgher clergyman of Edinburgh. When that city was taken possession of by the young Pretender, Charles Edward, in 1745, the clergy generally fled. But Gib removed only three miles from the city, where, collecting his loyal congregation, he hurled anathemas for five successive Sundays against the Pretender, and boldly prayed for the downfall of the rebellion. He subsequently joined the loyal army, and at Falkirk took a rebel prisoner. So active was Gib in his opposition to the cause of the house of Stuart, and so obnoxious had be become, that several attempts were made by the rebels to take his life. On Charles Edward's return to France, he erected in 1747 his "Primordial Chapter" at Arras; and in the composition of the high degrees there practised, it is very probable that he bestowed the name of his old enemy Gib on the most atrocious of the Assassins who figure in the legend of Third Degree. The letter *u* was doubtless inserted to prevent the French, in pronouncing the name, from falling into the soft sound of the G and calling the word *Jib*. The additional *b* and *s* were the natural and customary results of a French attempt to spell a foreign proper name. (See *Arras, Primordial Chapter of.*)

Guillemain de St. Victor, Louis. A distinguished French writer, who published several works on Freemasonry, the most valuable and best known of which is his *Recueil Précieux de la Maçonnerie Adonhiramite*, first issued at Paris in 1782. This work, of which several editions were published, contains the catechisms of the first four degrees of Adoniramite Masonry, and an account of several other degrees, and is enriched with many learned notes. Ragon, who speaks highly of the work, erroneously attributes its authorship to the celebrated Baron de Tschoudy.

Gustavus IV., King of Sweden. He was initiated into Masonry, at Stockholm, on the 10th of March, 1793. Ten years after, on the 9th of March, 1803, Gustavus issued an Ordonnance by which he required all the secret societies in his dominions to make known to the stadtholders of the cities where they resided, and in the provinces to his governors, not only the formula of the oath which they administered to their members, but the duties which they prescribed, and the object of their association; and also to submit at any time to a personal inspection by the officers of government. But at the end of the Ordonnance the King says: "The Freemasons, who are under our immediate protection, are alone excepted from this inspection, and from this Ordonnance in general."

Guttural Point of Entrance. From the Latin *guttur*, the throat. The throat is that avenue of the body which is most employed in the sins of intemperance, and hence it suggests to the Mason certain symbolic instructions in relation to the virtue of temperance. (See *Points of Entrance, Perfect.*)

Gymnosophist. The Eighth Degree of the Kabbalistic Rite.

Gymnosophists. (Signifying "naked sages.") A name given by the Greeks to those ancient Hindu philosophers who lived solitarily in the woods, wore little or no clothing, and addicted themselves to mystical contemplation and the practise of the most rigorous asceticism. Strabo divides them into Brahmans and Samans, the former of whom adhered to the strictest principles of caste, while the latter admitted any one into their number regarding whose character and kindred they were satisfied. They believed in the immortality of the soul and its migration into other bodies. They practised celibacy, abstained from wine, and lived on fruits. They held riches in contempt, and abstained from sensual indulgences.

Gypsies. Cornelius Van Paun, more generally known as De Paun, in his *Philosophical Researches on the Egyptians and Chinese* (Paris, 1774), advances the theory that Freemasonry originated with the Gypsies. He says: "Every person who was not guilty of some crime could obtain admission to the lesser mysteries. Those vagabonds called Egyptian priests in Greece and Italy required considerable sums for initiation; and their successors, the Gypsies, practise similar mummeries to obtain money. And thus was Freemasonry introduced into Europe." But De Paun is remarkable for the paradoxical character of his opinions. Mr. James Simpson, who has written a rather exhaustive *History of the Gypsies* (1866), finds (p. 387) "a considerable resemblance between Gypsyism, in its harmless aspect, and Freemasonry—with this difference, that the former is a general, while the latter is a special, society; that is to say, the Gypsies have the language, or some of the words and the signs peculiar to the whole race, which each individual or class will use for different purposes. The race does not necessarily, and does not in fact, have intercourse with every other member of it. In that respect they resemble any ordinary community of men." And he adds: "There are many Gypsies Freemasons; indeed, they are the very people to push their way into a Masons' Lodge; for they have secrets of their own, and are naturally anxious to pry into those of others, by which they may be benefited. I was told of a Gypsy who died, lately, the Master of a Masons' Lodge. A friend, a Mason, told me the other day of his having entered a house in Yetholm where were five Gypsies, all of whom responded to his Masonic signs." But it must be remembered that Simpson is writing of the Gypsies of Scotland, a kingdom where the race is considerably advanced above those of any other country in civilization and in social position.

H

H. (Heb. ח, *Cheth;* the hieroglyph was an altar thus, and finally the Hebrew ח.) The eighth letter in the alphabet,   and in the Hebrew has the value in number of 8, while the Heb. ה, He, which is of the same hieroglyphic formation, has the numerical valuation of 5.

H∴ A∴ B∴. An abbreviation of Hiram Abif.

Habakkuk. (Heb. הבקוק, a struggler, a favorite.) The eighth of the twelve minor prophets. No account is contained in the Book of Habakkuk, either of the events of his life or the data when he lived. He is believed by many to have flourished about 630 B.C. In the Thirty-second Degree of the A. A. Scottish Rite, his name answers to the passwords Tuesday and Xerxes.

Habin. (Heb. הבין, *intelligius.*) Name of the initiate in the Fourth Degree of the modern French Rite, sometimes given as Johaben, or Jabin.

Habramah or **Jabamiah.** (*Fanum excelsum.*) Said to be used in the Thirtieth Degree of the A. A. Scottish Rite in France; it is not used in America.

Hacquet, G. A French notary at Port-au-Prince, subsequently a member of the Grand Orient of Paris, and President of the Royal Arch Chapter at Paris in 1814.

Hadeeses. An Arabic word, signifying the traditions handed down by Mohammed and preserved by the Mohammedan doctors. They are said to amount to 5266 in number. Many of the traditions of Mohammedan Masonry are said to be borrowed from the Hadeeses, just as much of the legendary lore of European Masonry is to be found in the Jewish Talmud.

Hâfedha. The second of the four gods worshiped by the Arab tribe of Ad, before the time of Mohammed, to which Hûd, or Heber, was sent. These were Sâkia, the god of rain; Hâfedha, the preserver from danger; Râzeka, the provider of food; and Sâlema, the god of health.

Hagar. The old lectures taught the doctrine, and hence it was the theory of the Masons of the eighteenth century, that the landmark which requires all candidates for initiation to be free born is derived from the fact that the promise which was given to Isaac, the free-born son of Abraham and Sarah, was denied to Ishmael, the slave-born son of the Egyptian bondwoman Hagar. This theory is entertained by Oliver in all his writings, as a part of the old Masonic system. (See *Free Born.*)

Haggai. According to Jewish tradition, Haggai was born in Babylon during the captivity, and being a young man at the time of the liberation by Cyrus, he came to Jerusalem in company with Joshua and Zerubbabel, to aid in the rebuilding of the Temple. The work being suspended during the reigns of the two immediate successors of Cyrus, on the accession of Darius, Haggai urged the renewal of the undertaking, and for that purpose obtained the sanction of the king. Animated by the courage and patriotism of Haggai and Zechariah, the people prosecuted the work with vigor, and the second Temple was completed and dedicated in the year 516 B.C.

In the Royal Arch system of America, Haggai represents the scribe, or third officer of a Royal Arch Chapter. In the English system he represents the second officer, and is called the *prophet.*

Hague, The. A city of the Netherlands, formerly South Holland. Freemasonry was introduced there in 1731 by the Grand Lodge of England, when an occasional Lodge was opened for the initiation of Francis, Duke of Lorraine, afterward Emperor of Germany. Between that year and 1735 an English and a Dutch Lodge were regularly instituted, from which other Lodges in Holland subsequently proceeded. In 1749, the Lodge at The Hague assumed the name of "The Mother Lodge of the Royal Union," whence resulted the National Grand Lodge, which declared its independence of the Grand Lodge of England in 1770. (See *Netherlands.*)

Hah. The Hebrew definite article ה, "the." It forms the second syllable of the Substitute Word.

Hail or **Hale.** This word is used among Masons with two very different significations. 1. When addressed as an inquiry to a visiting brother it has the same import as that in which it is used under like circumstances by mariners. Thus: "Whence do you hail?" that is, "Of what Lodge are you a member?" Used in this sense, it comes from the Saxon term of salutation "HÆL," and should be spelled "hail." 2. Its second use is confined to what Masons understand by the "*tie,*" and in this sense it signifies to *conceal*, being derived from the Saxon word "HELAN," to hide, the e being pronounced in Anglo-Saxon as *a* in the word *fate.* By the rules of etymology, it should be spelled "hale," but is usually spelled "hele." The preservation of this Saxon word in the Masonic dialect, while it has ceased to exist in the vernacular, is a striking proof of the antiquity of the Order and its ceremonies in England. "In the western parts of England," says Lord King (*Crit. Hist. Ap. Creed*, p. 178), "at this very day, to *hele* over anything signifies, among the common people, to cover it; and he that covereth an house with tile or slate is called a helliar."

Hall Committee. A committee established in all Lodges and Grand Lodges which own the building in which they meet, to which is entrusted the supervision of the building. The Grand Lodge of England first appointed its Hall Committee in 1773, for the purpose of superintending the erection of the hall which had been projected.

Hall, Masonic. For a long time after the revival of Masonry in 1717, Masonic Lodges continued to meet, as they had done before that period, in taverns. Thus, the Grand Lodge of England was organized, and, to use the language of Anderson, "the quarterly communications were revived," by four Lodges, whose respective places of meeting were the Goose and Gridiron Ale-House, the Crown Ale-House, the Apple-Tree Tavern, and the Rummer and Grapes Tavern. For many years the Grand Lodge held its quarterly meetings sometimes at the Apple-Tree, but principally at the Devil Tavern, and kept the Grand Feast at the hall of one of the Livery Companies. The first Lodge in Paris was organized at a tavern kept in the Rue des Boucheries by one Hure, and the Lodges subsequently organized in France continued to meet, like those of England, in public houses. The custom was long followed in other countries of Europe. In America the practise ceased only at a comparatively recent period, and it is possible that in some obscure villages it has not yet been abandoned.

At as early a period as the beginning of the fourteenth century, the Gilds, or Livery Companies, of London, had their halls or places of meeting, and in which they stored their goods for sale. At first these were mean buildings, but gradually they rose into importance, and the Goldsmith's Hall, erected in the fifteenth century, is said to have been an edifice of large dimensions and of imposing appearance. These halls, probably, as they were very common in the eighteenth century, were suggestive to the Freemasons of similar edifices for their own Fraternity; but undoubtedly the necessity, as the Association grew into importance, of a more respectable, more convenient, and more secure locality than was afforded by temporary resort to taverns and ale-houses must have led to the erection of isolated edifices for their own special use.

The first Masonic Hall of which we have any account is the one that was erected by the Lodge at Marseilles, in France, in the year 1765. Smith describes it very fully in his *Use and Abuse of Freemasonry* (p. 165), and calls it "a very magnificent hall." In 1773, the Grand Lodge of England made preliminary arrangements for the construction of a hall, a considerable sum having been already subscribed for that purpose. On the 1st of May, 1775, the foundation-stone of the new edifice was laid in solemn form, according to a ceremonial which was then adopted, and which, with a few modifications, continues to be used at the present day on similar occasions. On the foundation-stone it was designated as *Aula Latamorum,* "The Freemasons' Hall." It was finished in less than twelve months, and was dedicated, on the 23d of May, 1776, to *Masonry, Virtue, Universal Charity* and *Benevolence;* a formula still adhered to without variation in the English and American rituals.

In the same year, the Lodge at Newcastle, stimulated by the enterprise of the London Freemasons, erected a hall; an example which was followed, two years afterward, by the Lodge of Sunderland. And after this the erection of isolated halls for Masonic purposes became common not only in England, Scotland, and Ireland, but all over the Continent, wherever the funds of a Lodge would permit of the expenditure.

In America, Lodges continued to be held in taverns up to a very recent period. It is not now considered reputable; although, as has been already remarked, the custom is, perhaps, not entirely discontinued, especially in remote country villages. It is impossible to tell at what precise period and in what locality the first Masonic Hall was erected in this country. It is true that in a Boston paper of 1773 we find (*Moore's Mag.,* xv., 162) an advertisement summoning the Masons to celebrate the festival of St. John the Evangelist at "Freemasons' Hall"; but, on examination, we learn that this was no other than a room in the Green Dragon Tavern. Other buildings, such as the Exchange Coffee-House, only partially used for Masonic purposes, were subsequently erected in Boston, and received by courtesy, but not by right, the name of "Masonic Halls"; but it was not until 1832 that the first independent hall was built in that city, which received the name of the Masonic Temple, a title which has since been very usually conferred on the halls in the larger cities. We may suppose that it was about this time, when a resuscitation of Masonic energy, which had been paralyzed by the anti-Masonic opposition, had commenced to develop itself, that the Lodges and Grand Lodges began to erect halls for their peculiar use. At present there is no dearth of these buildings for Masonic use of imposing grandeur and architectural beauty to be found scattered all over the land.

In America, as well as in Britain, the construction of Masonic Halls is governed by no specific rules, and is too often left to the judgment and taste of the architect, and hence, if that person be not an experienced Freemason, the building is often erected without due reference to the ritual requirements of the Order. But in these particulars, says Oliver, the Masons of the Continent are governed by a Ritual of Building, and he quotes, as a specimen of the Helvetian Ritual in reference to the laying of the foundation-stone of a Masonic Hall, the following directions:

"A Mason, assisted by two others, if there be a dearth of workmen, or distress, or war, or peril, or threats of danger, may begin the work of building a Lodge; but it is better to have seven known and sworn workmen. The Lodge is, as we know, due east and west; but its chief window or its chief door must look to the east. On a day allowed and a place appointed, the whole company of builders set out after high noon to lay the first stone."

Far more practical are the directions of Dr. Oliver himself for the construction of a Masonic Hall, given in his *Book of the Lodge* (ch. iii.), which is here condensed.

"A Masonic Hall should be isolated, and, if possible, surrounded with lofty walls, so as to be included in a court, and apart from any other buildings, to preclude the possibility of being overlooked by cowans or eavesdroppers. As, however, such a situation in large towns can seldom be obtained, the Lodge should be formed in an upper story; and if there be any contiguous buildings, the windows should be either in the roof, or very high from the floor. These windows ought to be all on one side—the south, if practicable—and furnished with proper ventilation, that the brethren be not incommoded, when pursuing their accustomed avocations, by the heat of the Lodge. The room, to preserve a just proportion, must, of course, be lofty. It should be furnished with a pitched roof, open within, and relieved with an ornamental framework of oak, or painted so as to represent that species of timber. It should be supported on corbels running along the cornice, on which should be engraven Masonic ornaments. The dimensions of the room, in length and breadth, will depend in a great measure on the situation of the Lodge, or the space which is assigned for its position; and this will often be extremely circumscribed in a large and populous place, where building land is scarce and dear, or the fund inadequate to any extensive operations. But in all cases a due proportion should be observed in the several members of the fabric wherever it is practicable, that no unsightly appearance may offend the eye, by disturbing that general harmony of parts which constitutes the beauty and excellence of every architectural production.

"The principal entrance to the Lodge room ought to face the east, because the east is a place of light both physical and moral; and therefore the brethren have access to the Lodge by that entrance, as a symbol of mental illumination. The approaches to the Lodge must be angular, for a straight entrance is unmasonic and cannot be tolerated. The advance from the external avenue to the east ought to consist of three lines and two angles. The first line passes through a small room or closet for the accommodation of visitors. At the extremity of this apartment there ought to be another angular passage leading to the Tiler's room adjacent to the Lodge; and from thence, by another right angle, you are admitted into the presence of the brethren with your face to the Light.

"In every convenient place the architect should contrive secret cryptæ or closets. They are of indispensable utility; but in practice are not sufficiently attended to in this country. On the Continent they are numerous, and are dignified with the name of chapels. Two of these apartments have already been mentioned—a room for visitors and the Tiler's room; added to which there ought to be a vestry, where the ornaments, furniture, jewels, and other regalia are deposited. This is called the treasury, or Tiler's conclave, because these things are under his especial charge, and a communication is usually made to this apartment from the Tiler's room. There ought to be also a chapel for preparations, hung with black, and having only one small light, placed high up, near the ceiling; a chapel for the dead furnished with a table, on which are a lamp and emblems of mortality; the Master's conclave, where the records, the warrants, the minutes, and every written document are kept. To this room the Worshipful Master retires when the Lodge is called from labor to refreshment, and at other times when his presence in the Lodge is not essential; and here he examines the visitors, for which purpose a communication is formed between his conclave and the visitor's chapel. It is furnished with blue. And here he transacts the Lodge business with his Secretary. The Ark of the Covenant is also deposited in this apartment. None of these closets should exceed twelve feet square, and may be of smaller dimensions, according to circumstances. In the middle of the hall there should be a movable trapdoor in the floor, seven feet long and three or four feet broad, opening into a small crypt, about three feet in depth, the use of which is known to none but perfect Masons, who have passed through all the symbolical degrees. All of these particulars may not be equally necessary to the construction of a Masonic Hall; but a close attendance to their general spirit and direction, or to similar regulations, should be impressed on every Lodge that undertakes the construction of a building exclusively for Masonic purposes; and such a building only is entitled to be called a Masonic Hall."

The division in the American Rite of the degrees among different bodies imposes the necessity, or at least the convenience, when erecting a Masonic Hall in this country, of appropriating some of the rooms to the uses of Ancient Craft Lodges, some to Royal Arch Chapters, some to Royal and Select Councils, and some to Commanderies of Knights Templars. It is neither proper nor convenient that a Chapter should be held in a Lodge; and it is equally expedient that the Asylum of a Commandery should be kept separate from both.

All of these rooms should be oblong in form, lofty in height, with an elevated dais or platform in the east, and two doors in the west, the one in the northwest corner leading into the preparation room, and the other communicating with the Tiler's apartment. But in other respects they differ. First, as to the color of the decorations. In a Lodge room the predominating color should be blue, in a Chapter red, and in a Council and Commandery black.

In a Lodge room the dais should be elevated on three steps, and provided with a pedestal for the Master, while on each side are seats for the Past Masters, and dignitaries who may visit the Lodge. The pedestal of the Senior Warden in the west should be elevated on two steps, and that of the Junior Warden in the south on one.

A similar arrangement, either permanent or temporary, should be provided in the Chapter room for working the intermediate degrees; but the eastern dais should be supplied with three pedestals instead of one, for the reception of the Grand Council. The tabernacle also forms an essential part of the Chapter room. This is sometimes erected in the center of the room, although the consistency of the symbolism would require that the whole room, during the working of the Royal Arch Degree, should be deemed a tabernacle, and then the veils would, with propriety, extend from the ceiling to the floor, and from one side of the room to the other. There are some other arrangements required in the construction of a Chapter room, of which it is unnecessary to speak.

Councils of Royal and Select Masters are usually held in Chapter rooms, with an entire disregard of the historical teachings of the degrees. In a properly constructed Council chamber, which, of course, would be in a distinct apartment, there should be no veils, but nine curtains of a stone color; and these, except the last, starting from one side of the room, should stop short of the other, so as to form a narrow passage between the wall and the extremities of the curtains, reaching from the door to the ninth curtain, which alone should reach across the entire extent of the room. These are used only in the Select Degree, and can be removed when the Royal Master is to be conferred. Unlike a Lodge and Chapter, in a Council there is no dais or raised platform; but three tables, of a triangular form, are placed upon the level of the floor in the east. It is, however, very seldom that the funds of a Council will permit of the indulgence in a separate room, and those bodies are content to work, although at a disadvantage, in a Chapter room.

It is impossible, with any convenience, to work a Commandery in a Lodge, or even a Chapter room. The officers and their stations are so different, that what is suitable for one is unsuitable for the other. The dais, which has but one station in a Lodge and three in a Chapter, requires four in a Commandery, the Prelate taking his proper place on the right of the Generalissimo. But there are other more important differences. The principal apartment should be capable of a division by a curtain, which should separate the Asylum proper from the rest of the room, as the mystical veil in the ancient Church shut off the prospect of the altar,

during the eucharistic sacrifice, from the view of the catechumens. There are several other rooms required in the Templar ritual which are not used by a Lodge, a Chapter, or a Council, and which makes it necessary that the apartments of a Commandery should be distinct. A banquet-room in close proximity to the Asylum is essential; and convenience requires that there should be an armory for the deposit of the arms and costume of the Knights. But it is unnecessary to speak of reflection rooms, and other places well known to those who are familiar with the ritual, and which cannot be dispensed with.

Hallelujah. (Praise the Lord.) Expression of applause in the degree of Sublime Ecossais, Heavenly Jerusalem, and others.

Halliwell Manuscript. The earliest of the old Constitutions. It is in poetic form, and was probably transcribed in 1390 from an earlier copy. The manuscript is in the King's Library of the British Museum. It was published in 1840 by James O. Halliwell, and again in 1844, under the title of *The Early History of Freemasonry in England*. The Masonic character of the poem remained unknown until its discovery by Mr. Halliwell, who was not a Mason, because it was catalogued as *A Poem of Moral Duties.*

It is now more commonly known as the "Regius MS.," because it formed part of the Royal Library commenced by Henry VII. and presented to the British Museum by George II.   [E. L. H.]

Hamaliel. The name of the angel that, in accordance with the Kabbalistical system, governs the planet Venus.

Hamburg. In 1733, the Earl of Strathmore, Grand Master of England, granted a deputation "to eleven German gentlemen, good Brothers, for constituting a Lodge at Hamburg." (Anderson, *Constitutions*, 1738, p. 194.) Of the proceedings of this Lodge we have no information. In 1740, Bro. Luettman brought from England a Warrant for the establishment of a Lodge, and a patent for himself, as Provincial Grand Master of Hamburg and Lower Saxony. In October, 1741, it assumed the name of Absalom, and in the same year the Provincial Grand Lodge of Hamburg and Saxony was opened, a body which, Findel says (p. 239), was the oldest Mother Lodge in Germany. About the year 1787, the Provincial Grand Lodge adopted the newly-invented Rite of Frederick L. Schröder, consisting of only three degrees. In 1801, it declared itself an independent Grand Lodge, and has so continued. The Grand Lodge of Hamburg practises Schröder's Rite. (See *Schröder.*) There is also in Hamburg a sort of Chapter, which was formed by Schröder, under the title of Geschichtliche Engbund, or Historical Select Union. It was intended as a substitute for Fessler's degrees of Knowledge, the members of which employ their time in studying the various systems of Masonry. The Mutter-Bund of the Confederacy of Hamburg Lodges, which make up this system, is independent of the Grand Lodge. The two authorities are entirely distinct, and bear much the same relation to each other as the Grand Lodges and Grand Chapters of the United States.

Hamilton, Hon. Robert M.A., M.D. Born 1820; died May, 1880, at Jamaica, of which island he was District Grand Master. This English gentleman was a member of the Queen's Body Guard. He was appointed District G. Master of Jamaica, November 5, 1858; District G. Supt. of Royal Arch Masons, January 10, 1859; Prov. G. M. M. M., 1877; and was a supernumerary member of the Supreme Council, 33d, of England, and Prov. G. Master of the Royal Order of Scotland.

Hand. In Freemasonry, the hand as a symbol holds a high place, because it is the principal seat of the sense of feeling so necessary to and so highly revered by Masons. The same symbol is found in the most ancient religions, and some of their analogies to Masonic symbolism are peculiar. Thus, Horapollo says that among the Egyptians the hand was the symbol of a builder, or one fond of building, because all labor proceeds from the hand. In many of the Ancient Mysteries the hand, especially the left, was deemed the symbol of equity. In Christian art a hand is the indication of a holy person or thing. In early Medieval art, the Supreme Being was always represented by a hand extended from a cloud, and generally in the act of benediction. The form of this act of benediction, as adopted by the Roman Church, which seems to have been borrowed from the symbols of the Phrygian and Eleusinian priests or hierophants, who used it in their mystical processions, presents a singular analogy, which will be interesting to Mark Master Masons, who will recognize in it a symbol of their own ritual. In the benediction

referred to, as given in the Latin Church, the thumb, index, and middle fingers are extended, and the two others bent against the palm. The church explains this position of the extended thumb and two fingers as representing the Trinity; but the older symbol of the Pagan priests, which was precisely of the same form, must have had a different meaning. A writer in the *British Magazine* (vol. i., p. 565) thinks that the hand, which was used in the Mithraic mysteries in this position, was symbolic of the Light emanating not from the sun, but from the Creator, directly as a special manifestation; and he remarks that chiromancy or divination by the hand is an art founded upon the notion that the human hand has some reference to the decrees of the supreme power peculiar to it above all other parts of the microcosmus—man. Certainly, to the Mason, the hand is most important as the symbol of that mystical intelligence by which one Mason

knows another "in the dark as well as in the light."

Hand, Left. See *Left Hand.*

Hand, Right. See *Right Hand.*

Hand to Back. See *Points of Fellowship.*

Hand to Hand. See *Points of Fellowship.*

Hands, United. Clasped hands are a symbol of fidelity and trust. A Spanish work was published at Vittoria, in 1774, where three hands are shown united in the vignette on the title.

Hanover. Freemasonry was introduced into Hanover, in the year 1744, by the organization of the Lodge "Frederick"; which did not, however, get into active operation, in consequence of the opposition of the priests, until two years after. A Provincial Grand Lodge was established in 1755, which in 1828 became an independent Grand Lodge. In 1866, in consequence of the war between Austria and Prussia, Hanover was annexed to the latter country. There being three Grand Lodges at that time in Prussia, the king deemed it inexpedient to add a fourth, and, by a cabinet order of February 17, 1867, the Grand Lodge of Hanover was dissolved. Most of the Hanoverian Lodges united with the Grand Lodge Royal York at Berlin, and a few with the Grand Lodge of the Three Globes.

Haphtziel. (Heb. הפציאל, *Voluntas Dei.*) A covered word used in the Twenty-third Degree of the A. A. Scottish Rite.

Har. The name of the second king in the Scandinavian Mysteries.

Haram, Grand. The Seventy-third Degree of the Rite of Mizraim.

Harbinger. The title of an officer in the Knights of the Holy Sepulcher, and also in the Knights of St. John the Evangelist.

Hardie, James. A Mason of New York, who published, in 1818, a work entitled *The New Freemasons' Monitor and Masonic Guide.* It evinces considerable ability, is more valuable than the *Monitors* of Webb and Cross, and deserved a greater popularity than it seems to have received.

Harleian Manuscripts. An old record of the Constitutions of Freemasonry, so called because it forms No. 2054 of the collection of manuscripts in the British Museum, which were originally collected by Robert Harley, Earl of Oxford, the celebrated prime minister of Queen Anne, and known as the "Bibliotheca Harleian," or Harleian Library. The MS. consists of four leaves, containing six and a half pages of close writing in a cramped hand, said to be that of Randle Holmes, *Chester Herald,* who died in 1699. The MS. was first published by Bro. William James Hughan, in his *Masonic Sketches and Reprints.* The Manuscript was carefully transcribed for Bro. Hughan by a faithful copyist, and its correctness was verified by Mr. Sims, of the MS. department of the British Museum. Bro. Hughan places the date of the record in the middle of the seventeenth century, and in this he is probably correct.

"The two following folios," says the Rev. Mr. Woodford, "in the volume (viz., 33 and 34) are of a very important character, inasmuch as the secrets of Freemasonry are referred to in the 'obligation' taken by Initiates, and the sums are recorded which 'William Wade give to be a Freemason,' and others who were admitted members of the Lodge. The amounts varied from five shillings to a pound, the majority being ten shillings and upwards. The fragment on folio 33 is as follows, and was written about the same time as the MS. Constitutions:

" ' There is severall words & signes of a free mason to be reveiled to yᵘ wᶜʰ as yᵘ will answʳ before God at the Great & terrible day of Judgmt yᵘ keep secret & not to revaile the same in the heares of any person or to any but to the Mʳˢ· & fellows of the said society of free masons so helpe me God, etc.' "

A facsimile of the MS. has been published by the Quatuor Coronati Lodge.

There is another MS. in the same collection marked No. 1492, the date of which is conjectured to be about 1650, or rather later. It was copied by Bro. Henry Phillips, and first published in the *Freemasons' Quarterly Review* in 1836, pp. 288–295. The copy, however, unfortunately, is not an exact one, as Mr. E. A. Bond, of the Museum, who compared a part of the transcript with the original, says that "the copyist has overlooked peculiarities in many instances." It is important in containing the "Oath of Secrecy," which is in the following words:

"I, A. B. Doe, in the presence of Almighty God, and my fellows and Brethren here present, promise and declare that I will not at any time hereafter, by any Act, or Circumstance whatsoever, directly or indirectly publish, discover, reveale, or make knowne any of the Secrets, priviledges, or Counsels of the Fraternity or fellowship of Freemasonry, which at this time, or any time hereafter shall be made known unto me; soe helpe mee God and the holy contents of this book."

A facsimile of this MS. also has been published by the Quatuor Coronati Lodge.

Harmony. It is a duty especially entrusted to the Senior Warden of a Lodge, who is figuratively supposed to preside over the Craft during the hours of labor, so to act that none shall depart from the Lodge dissatisfied or discontented, that harmony may be thus preserved, because, as the ritual expresses it, harmony is the strength and support of all well-regulated institutions.

Harmony, Universal. See *Mesmeric Masonry.*

Harnouester. Lord Harnouester is said to have been elected by the four Lodges of Paris, as the second Grand Master of France, in 1736, succeeding the Earl of Derwentwater.

Nothing is known of this nobleman in contemporary history. Burke makes no allusion to him in his *Extinct Peerages*, and probably the name has undergone one of those indecipherable mutations to which French writers are accustomed to subject all foreign names; indeed, Bro. R. F. Gould, in his *Concise History of Freemasonry* (p. 355), considers that the name may even be a corruption of "Derwentwater."   [E. L. H.]

Harodim. We owe the Masonic use of this word to Anderson, who first employed it in the *Book of Constitutions*, where he tells us that "there were employed about the Temple no less than three thousand and six hundred Princes or Master Masons to conduct the work," and in a note he says that "in 1 Kings v. 16 they are called *Harodim*, Rulers or Provosts." (*Constitutions*, 1723, p. 10.) The passage here alluded to may be translated somewhat more literally than in the authorized version, thus: "Besides from the chiefs or princes appointed by Solomon who were over the work, there were three thousand and three hundred *harodim* over the people who labored at the work." Harodim, in Hebrew הרדים, is a grammatically compounded word of the plural form, and is composed of the definite article ה, HAH, *the* or *those*, and a participle of the verb רדה, radah, *to rule over*, and means, therefore, *those who rule over*, or *overseers*. In the parallel passage of 2 Chronicles ii. 18, the word used is *Menatzchim*, which has a similar meaning. But from the use of this word Harodim in 1 Kings, and the commentary on it by Anderson, it has come to pass that Harodim is now technically used to signify "Princes in Masonry." They were really overseers of the work, and hence the Masonic use of the term is not altogether inappropriate. Whoever inspects the two parallel passages in 1 Kings v. 16 and 2 Chron. ii. 18, will notice an apparent discrepancy. In the former it is said that there were three thousand and three hundred of these overseers, and in the latter the number is increased to three thousand and six hundred. The commentators have noted but not explained the incongruity. Lee, in his *Temple of Solomon*, attempts to solve it by supposing that "possibly three hundred at a second review might be added to the number of officers for the greater care of the business." This is not satisfactory; not more so is the explanation offered by myself, many years ago, in the *Lexicon of Freemasonry*. It is much more reasonable to suspect a clerical error of some old copyist which has been perpetuated. There is room for such an inadvertence, for there is no very great difference between שלש, the Hebrew for *three*, and שש, which is *six*. The omission of the central letter would create the mistake. Masonic writers have adhered to the three thousand and six hundred, which is the enumeration in Chronicles.

[A degree bearing this name was commonly conferred by the Lodges in the county of

Durham, England, during the latter half of the eighteenth century, but what its exact nature was has now been forgotten.—E. L. H.]

Harodim, Grand Chapter of. An institution under the title of the "Grand Chapter of the Ancient and Venerable Order of Harodim" was established in London, in the year 1787, by the celebrated Masonic lecturer, William Preston. He thus defines, in his *Illustrations*, its nature and objects: (12th ed., p. 310.)

"The mysteries of this Order are peculiar to the institution itself; while the lectures of the Chapter include every branch of the Masonic system, and represent the art of Masonry in a finished and complete form.

"Different classes are established, and particular lectures restricted to each class. The lectures are divided into sections, and the sections into clauses. The sections are annually assigned by the Chief Harod to a certain number of skilful Companions in each class, who are denominated Sectionists; and they are empowered to distribute the clauses of their respective sections, with the approbation of the Chief Harod and General Director, among the private companions of the Chapter, who are denominated CLAUSEHOLDERS. Such Companions as by assiduity become possessed of all the sections in the lecture are called Lecturers; and out of these the General Director is always chosen.

"Every Clauseholder, on his appointment, is presented with a ticket, signed by the Chief Harod, specifying the clause allotted to him. This ticket entitles him to enjoy the rank and privileges of a Clauseholder in the Chapter; and no Clauseholder can transfer his ticket to another Companion, unless the consent of the Council has been obtained for that purpose, and the General Director has approved the Companion to whom it is to be transferred as qualified to hold it. In case of the death, sickness, or non-residence in London of any Lecturer, Sectionist, or Clauseholder, another Companion is appointed to fill up the vacancy for the time being, that the lectures may be always complete; and during the session a public lecture is usually delivered at stated times.

"The Grand Chapter is governed by a Grand Patron, two Vice Patrons, a chief Ruler, and two Assistants, with a Council of twelve respectable Companions, who are chosen annually at the Chapter nearest to the festival of St. John the Evangelist."

The whole system was admirably adapted to the purposes of Masonic instruction, and was intended for the propagation of the Prestonian system of lectures, but it no longer exists.

Harodim, Prince of. In the old lectures of the Ineffable degrees, it is said that Tito, the oldest of the Provosts and Judges, was the Prince of Harodim, that is, chief of the three hundred architects who were the Harodim, or additional three hundred added to the thirty-three thousand Menatzchim mentioned in Chronicles, and who thus make up the number of three thousand six hundred recorded in the 1st Book of Kings, and who in the old lecture of the degree of Provost and Judge are supposed to have been the Harodim or Rulers in Masonry. The statement is a myth; but it thus attempts to explain the discrepancy alluded to in the article *Harodim*.

Harpocrates. The Greek god of silence and secrecy. He was, however, a divinity of the Egyptian mythology; his true name being, according to Bunsen and Lepsius, Har-pi-chrati, that is, Horus the child; and he is supposed to have been the son of Osiris and Isis. He is represented as a nude figure, sitting sometimes on a lotus flower, either bareheaded or covered by an Egyptian miter, but always with his finger pressed upon his lips. Plutarch thinks that this gesture was an indication of his childlike and helpless nature; but the Greeks, and after them the Romans, supposed it to be a symbol of silence; and hence, while he is sometimes described as the god of the renewed year, whence peach blossoms were consecrated to him because of their early appearance in spring, he is more commonly represented as the god of silence and secrecy. Thus, Ovid says of him:

"Quique premit vocem digitoque silentia suadet."
He who controls the voice and persuades to silence with his finger.

In this capacity, his statue was often placed at the entrance of temples and places where the mysteries were celebrated, as an indication of the silence and secrecy that should there be observed. Hence the finger on the lips is a symbol of secrecy, and has so been adopted in Masonic symbolism.

Harris, Thaddeus Mason. The Rev. Thaddeus Mason Harris, D.D., an American Masonic writer of some reputation, was born in Charlestown, Mass., July 7, 1767, and graduated at Harvard University in 1787. He was ordained as minister of a church in Dorchester in 1793, and died at Boston, April 3, 1842. He held at different times the offices of Deputy Grand Master, Grand Chaplain, and Corresponding Grand Secretary of the Grand Lodge of Massachusetts. "His first great Masonic work," says Huntoon (*Eulogy*), "was the editing of a collation, revision, and publication of the 'Constitutions of the Ancient and Honorable Fraternity of Free and Accepted Masons,' a quarto volume, printed at Worcester, Mass., 1792; a work which he accomplished with the accustomed diligence and fidelity with which he performed every enterprise confided to his care. His various occasional addresses while Grand Chaplain of the Grand Lodge, Masonic defences, and his volume of *Masonic Discourses*, published in 1801, constitute a large and valuable portion of the Masonic classic literature of America."

Haruspices, Order of. The word Haruspex comes from a Sanskrit word "hirâ," meaning entrails; therefore implying a soothsayer or aruspice. The founder of the Etruscan order was Tages, doubtless a myth of self-creative power. This order is claimed to have been reestablished in Rome at the time of the foundation of the city. It embraced two divisions, those who formed their judgment from the movements and habits of animals as well as the flight of birds, and those who judged and foretold events by the inspection of the entrails of newly killed animals. These were the precursors of naturalists and physiologists.

Hasidim, Sovereign Prince. The Seventy-fifth and Seventy-sixth degrees of the Rite of Mizraim. It should be *Chasidim*, which see.

Hat. To uncover the head in the presence of superiors has been, among all Christian nations, held as a mark of respect and reverence. The Eastern nations uncover the feet when they enter a place of worship; the Western uncover the head. The converse of this is also true; and to keep the head covered while all around are uncovered is a token of superiority of rank or office. The king remains covered, the courtiers standing around him take off their hats.

Haupt-Hütte. Among the German Stone-Masons of the Middle Ages, the original Lodge at Strasburg was considered as the head of the Craft, under the title of the Haupt-Hütte, or Grand Lodge.

Hautes Grades. French. *High Degrees*, which see.

Hayti. Freemasonry, which had been in existence for several years in the island of Hayti, was entirely extinguished by the revolution which drove out the white inhabitants. In 1809, the Grand Lodge of England granted a charter for a Lodge at Port-au-Prince, and for one at Cayes. In 1817, it constituted two others, at Jeremias and at Jacmel. Subsequently, a Provincial Grand Lodge was established under obedience to England. January 25, 1824, this Provincial Grand Lodge declared its independence and organized the Grand Orient of Hayti, which is still in existence.

Heal. A technical Masonic term which signifies to make valid or legal. Hence one who has received a degree in an irregular manner or from incompetent authority is not recognized until he has been healed. The precise mode of healing depends on circumstances. If the Lodge which conferred the degree was clandestine, the whole ceremony of initiation would have to be repeated. If the authority which conferred the degree was only irregular, and the question was merely a technical one of legal competence, it has been supposed that it was only necessary to exact an obligation of allegiance, or in other words to renew the covenant.

Hearing. One of the five senses, and an important symbol in Masonry, because it is through it that we receive instruction when ignorant, admonition when in danger, reproof when in error, and the claim of a brother who is in distress. Without this sense, the Mason would be crippled in the performance of all his duties; and hence deafness is deemed a disqualification for initiation.

Heart. Notwithstanding that all the modern American Masonic Manuals and Masters' Carpets from the time of Jeremy L. Cross exhibit the picture of a heart among the emblems of the Third Degree, there is no such symbol in the ritual. But the theory that every man who becomes a Mason must first be prepared in his heart was advanced among the earliest lectures of the last century, and demonstrates, as Krause properly remarks, in Speculative Masonry, an internal principle which addresses itself not simply to the outward conduct, but to the inner spirit and conscience of all men who seek its instructions.

Heart of Hiram Abif. There is a legend in some of the high degrees and in continental Masonry, that the heart of Hiram Abif was deposited in an urn and placed upon a monument near the holy of holies; and in some of the tracing boards it is represented as a symbol. The myth, for such it is, was probably derived from the very common custom in the Middle Ages of persons causing their bodies to be dismembered after death for the purpose of having parts of them buried in a church, or some place which had been dear to them in life. Thus Hardynge, in his *Metrical Chronicle of England*, tells us of Richard I. that

"He queathed his corpse then to be buried
At Fount Everard, there at his father's feete;

* * * * * * * *

His herte invyncyble to Rome he sent full mete
For their great truth and stedfast great constance."

The Medieval idea has descended to modern times; for our present lectures say that the ashes of Hiram were deposited in an urn.

Hebrew Chronology. The ecclesiastical year commences 1st Nisan, March, but the civil reckoning begins 1st Tishri, September, which is New Year's Day.

The following dates are accepted by the Hebrews, as given by Dr. Zunz in *Remarks* prefacing "The 24 Books of the Holy Scriptures according to the Massoretic Text":

BEFORE COMMON ERA.

3988, Creation.
2332, Flood.
2040, Abraham born.
1575, Moses born.
1495, Exodus.
1051, David acknowledged king.
1015, First Temple commenced.
586, First Temple destroyed.
536, Cyrus's Decree.
516, Second Temple completed.
330, Alexander conquers Palestine.

The succeeding dates are in accord with the research of other authorities.

The Temple was dedicated on five occasions:

1st. B.C. 1004, 15th day of Tishri (Ethanim and Abib) (1 Kings viii. 2–62).

2d. B.C. 726, when purified from the abominations of Ahaz.

3d. B.C. 516, 3d Adar, upon completion of Zerubbabel's Temple.

4th. B.C. 164, 25th Kislev, after the victory of Judas Maccabæus over the Syrians, the service lasted eight days.

5th. B.C. 22, upon completion of Herod's Temple.

The three Temples were destroyed on the same day and month of the year. The "threefold destruction" of the Temple took place on the 9th Ab, or fifth ecclesiastical month. The destruction of the Solomonian Temple, by Nebuchadnezzar, took place B.C. 588, or four hundred and sixteen years after dedication. The taking of the city of Jerusalem by Titus is commemorated as a fast day on the 17th Tamuz.

Passover, 14th Nisan; "Little" Passover, 15th Iyar.

Pentecost, or "First Fruits," commemorating the giving of the law on Mount Sinai, 6th Sivan.

Great Day of Atonement, 10th Tishri.

Feast of Tabernacles, 15–21 Tishri.

Fast for commencement of siege of Jerusalem by Nebuchadnezzar, 10th day of Tebeth.

Feast of Purim, 14th and 15th Adar.

King Cyrus liberated the Jews, B.C. 538.

King Darius confirmed the decree, B.C. 520. (See *Cyrus*.)

Hebrew Faith. See *Talmud*.

Hécart, Gabriel Antoine Joseph. A French Masonic writer, who was born at Valenciennes in 1755, and died in 1838. He made a curious collection of degrees, and invented a system of five, namely: 1. Knight of the Prussian Eagle; 2. Knight of the Comet; 3. The Scottish Purifier; 4. Victorious Knight; 5. Scottish Trinitarian, or Grand Master Commander of the Temple. This cannot be called a Rite, because it was never accepted and practised by any Masonic authority. It is known in nomenclatures as Hécart's system. He was the author of many dissertations and didactic essays on Masonic subjects. He at one time proposed to publish his collection of degrees with a full explanation of each, but did not carry his design into execution. Many of them are cited in this work.

Height of the Lodge. From the earth to the highest heavens. A symbolic expression. (See *Form of the Lodge.*)

Heldmann, Dr. Friedrich. He was a professor of political science in the Academy of Bern, in Switzerland, and was born at Margetshochheim, in Franconia, November 24, 1770. He was one of the most profound of the German investigators into the history and philosophy of Masonry. He was initiated into the Order at Freiburg, in 1809, and, devoting himself to the study of the works of Fessler and other eminent scholars, he resolved to establish a system founded on a collation of all the rituals, and which should be more in accordance with the true design of the Institution. For this purpose, in 1816, he organized the Lodge *zur Brudertreue* at Aarau, in Switzerland, where he then resided as a professor. For the Lodge he prepared a Manual, which he proposed to publish. But the Helvetian Directory demanded that the manuscript should be given to that body for inspection and correction, which the Lodge, unwilling to submit to such a censorship, refused to do. Heldmann, being reluctant to involve the Lodge in a controversy with its superiors, withdrew from it. He subsequently published a valuable work entitled *Die drei ältesten geschichtlichen Denkmale der deutschen Freimaurerbruderschaft;* i. e., The three oldest Memorials of the German Masonic Brotherhood, which appeared at Aarau in 1819. In this work, which is chiefly founded on the learned researches of Krause, the Constitutions of the Stone-Masons of Strasburg were published for the first time.

Heler, A. A tiler or tegulator. From the Anglo-Saxon "helan." Also written "Hillyar" and "Hilliar."

Helmet. A defensive weapon wherewith the head and neck are covered. In heraldry, it is a mark of chivalry and nobility. It was, of course, a part of the armor of a knight, and therefore, whatever may be the head covering adopted by modern Knights Templars, it is in the ritual called a helmet.

Helmets, To Deposit. In Templar ritualism, to lay aside the covering of the head.

Helmets, To Recover. In Templar ritualism, to resume the covering of the head.

Help. See *Aid and Assistance*.

Hemming, Samuel, D.D. Previous to the union of the two Grand Lodges of England in 1813, the Prestonian system of lectures was practised by the Grand Lodge of Modern Masons, while the Atholl Masons recognized higher degrees, and varied somewhat in their ritual of the lower. When the union was consummated, and the United Grand Lodge of England was organized, a compromise was effected, and Dr. Hemming, who was the Senior Grand Warden, and had been distinguished for his skill as the Master of a Lodge and his acquaintance with the ritual, was appointed to frame a new system of lectures. The Prestonian system was abandoned, and the Hemming lectures adopted in its place, not without the regret of many distinguished Masons, among whom was Dr. Oliver. Among the innovations of Dr. Hemming, which are to be regretted, are the abolition of the dedication to the two Saints John, and the substitution for it of a dedication to Solomon. Some other changes that were made were certainly no improvements.

Henrietta Maria. The widow of Charles I., of England. It is asserted, by those who support the theory that the Master's Degree was invented by the adherents of the exiled house of Stuart, and that its legend refers to the death of Charles I. and the restoration of his son, that in the technical Masonic expression of the "widow's son," the allusion is to the widow of the decapitated monarch. Those who look farther for the foundation of the legend give, of course, no credence to a statement whose plausibility depends only on a coincidence.

Henry VI. King of England from 1422 to 1461. This monarch is closely connected with the history of Masonry because, in the beginning of his reign and during his minority, the celebrated "Statute of Laborers," which prohibited the congregations of the Masons, was passed by an intolerant Parliament, and because of the questions said to have been proposed to the Masons by the king, and their answers, which are contained in what is called the "Leland Manuscript," a document which, if authentic, is highly important; but of whose authenticity there are as many oppugners as there are defenders.

Heredom. In what are called the "high degrees" of the continental Rites, there is nothing more puzzling than the etymology of this word. We have the Royal Order of Heredom, given as the *ne plus ultra* of Masonry in Scotland, and in almost all the Rites the Rose Croix of Heredom, but the true meaning of the word is apparently unknown. Ragon, in his *Orthodoxie Maçonnique* (p. 91), asserts that it has a political signification, and that it was invented between the years 1740 and 1745, by the adherents of Charles Edward the Pretender, at the Court of St. Germain, which was the residence, during that period, of the unfortunate prince, and that in their letters to England, dated from *Heredom*, they mean to denote St. Germain. He supposes it to be derived from the Medieval Latin word "hœredum," signifying "a heritage," and that it alludes to the Castle of St. Germain, the only heritage left to the dethroned sovereign. But as Ragon's favorite notion was that the *hautes grades* were originally instituted for the purpose of aiding the house of Stuart in its restoration to the throne, a theory not now generally accepted, at least without modification, this etymology must be taken with some grains of allowance. The suggestion is, however, an ingenious one.

In some of the old manuscripts the word *Heroden* is found as the name of a mountain in Scotland; and we sometimes find in the French Cahiers the title of "Rose Croix de Heroden." There is not a very great difference in the French pronunciation of *Heredom* and *Heroden*, and one might be a corruption of the other. I was once inclined to this theory; but even if it were the correct one we should gain nothing, for the same difficulty would recur in tracing the root and meaning of Heroden.

The most plausible derivation is one given in 1858, by a writer in the London *Freemasons' Magazine.* He thinks it should be spelled "Heredom," and traces it to the two Greek words, ἱερὸς, *hieros*, holy, and δόμος, *domos*, house. It would thus refer to Masonry as symbolically the Holy House or Temple. In this way the title of Rose Croix of Heredom would signify the Rosy Cross of the Holy House of Masonry. This derivation is now very generally recognized as the true one. [But according to this view the word should be "Hierodom."—E. L. H.]

Hermaimes. A corruption of Hermes, found in some of the old Constitutions.

Hermandad, The. (Spanish, "Brotherhood.") An association of the principal cities of Castile and Aragon bound by a solemn league for the defense of their liberties in time of trouble. The sovereigns approved this brotherhood as agents for suppressing the increasing power of the nobles, and without cost to the government. The Hermandad was first established in Aragon in the thirteenth century, and in Castile about thirty years later, while, in 1295, thirty-five cities of Castile and Leon formed a joint confederacy, pledging themselves to take summary vengeance on every robber noble who injured a member of the association. The *Santa*, or Holy Brotherhood, finally checked so effectually the outrages of the nobles, that Isabella of Castile, in 1496, obtained the sanction of the Cortez to reorganize and extend it over the whole kingdom.

Hermes. In all the old manuscript records which contain the Legend of the Craft, mention is made of Hermes as one of the founders of Masonry. Thus, in the "Grand Lodge, No. 1, MS.," whose date is 1583—and the statement is substantially and almost verbally the same in all the others—that "The great Hermarines that was Cubys sonne, the which Cubye was Semmes sonne, that was Noes sonne. This same Hermarines was afterwards called Hernes the father of Wysdome; he found one of the two pillars of stone, and found the science written therein, and he taught it to other men."

There are two persons of the name of Hermes mentioned in sacred history. The first is the divine Hermes, called by the Romans Mercury. Among the Egyptians he was known as Thoth. Diodorus Siculus describes him as the secretary of Osiris; he is commonly supposed to have been the son of Mizraim, and Cumberland says that he was the same as Osiris. There is, however, much confusion among the mythologists concerning his attributes.

The second was Hermes Trismegistus or the Thrice Great, who was a celebrated Egyptian legislator, priest, and philosopher, who lived in the reign of Ninus, about the year of the world 2670. He is said to have written thirty-six books on theology and philosophy, and six upon medicine, all which are lost. There are many traditions of him; one of which, related by Eusebius, is that he introduced hieroglyphics into Egypt. This Hermes Trismegistus, although the reality of his existence is doubtful, was claimed by the alchemists as the founder of their art, whence it is called the Hermetic science, and whence we get in Masonry, Hermetic Rites and Hermetic degrees. It is to him that the Legend of the Craft refers; and, indeed, the York Constitutions, which are of importance, though not probably of the date of 926, assigned to them by Krause, give him that title, and say that he brought the custom of making himself understood by signs with him to Egypt. In the first ages of the Christian church, this mythical Egyptian philosopher was in fact considered as the inventor of everything known to the human intellect. It was fabled that Pythagoras and Plato had derived their knowledge from him, and that he had recorded his inventions on pillars. The Operative Masons, who wrote the old Constitutions, obtained their acquaintance with him from the *Polycronycon* of the monk Ranulf Higden, which was translated from the Latin by Trevisa, and printed by William Caxton in 1482. It is repeatedly quoted in the Cooke MS., whose probable date is the latter part of the fifteenth century, and was undoubtedly familiar to the writers of the other Constitutions.

Hermetic Art. The art or science of *Alchemy*, so termed from Hermes Trismegistus, who was looked up to by the alchemists as the founder of their art. The Hermetic philosophers say that all the sages of antiquity, such as Plato, Socrates, Aristotle, and Pythagoras, were initiated into the secrets of their science; and that the hieroglyphics of Egypt and all the fables of mythology were invented to teach the dogmas of Hermetic philosophy. (See *Alchemy*.)

Hermetic Philosophy. Pertaining or belonging to that species of philosophy which pretends to solve and explain all the phenomena of nature from the three chemical principles, salt, sulphur, and mercury. Also that study of the sciences as pursued by the Rosicrucian fraternity. A practise of the arts of alchemy and similar pursuits, involving a duplex symbolism with their peculiar distinctions.

Hermetic Rite. A Rite established by Pernetty at Avignon, in France, and more commonly called the Illuminati of Avignon. (See *Avignon, Illuminati of*.)

Herodem. See *Heredom*.

Herodem, Royal Order of. See *Royal Order of Scotland*.

Heroden. "Heroden," says a MS. of the Ancient Scottish Rite, "is a mountain situated in the northwest of Scotland, where the first or metropolitan Lodge of Europe was held." The word is not now used by Masonic writers, and was, undoubtedly, a corruption of *Heredom*.

Heroine of Jericho. An androgynous degree conferred, in America, on Royal Arch Masons, their wives, and daughters. It is intended to instruct its female recipients in the claims which they have upon the protection of their husbands' and fathers' companions, and to communicate to them an effectual method of proving those claims. An instance of friendship extended to the whole family of a benefactress by those whom she had benefited, and of the influence of a solemn contract in averting danger, is referred to in the case of Rahab, the woman of Jericho, from whom

the degree derives its name; and for this purpose the second chapter of the Book of Joshua is read to the candidate. When the degree is received by a male, he is called a Knight of Jericho, and when by a female, she is termed a Heroine. It is a side or honorary degree, and may be conferred by any Royal Arch Mason on a candidate qualified to receive it.

Herring, James. Born in London, England, January 12, 1794; died in France, October 8, 1867; buried in Greenwood Cemetery, New York, October 27, 1867. The family emigrated to America in 1805. James was initiated in Solomon's Lodge, Somerville, New Jersey, in 1816. He was Master of Clinton Lodge, New York City, in 1827, 1828, 1832, and 1834, a period when the anti-Masonic spirit was in its zenith. He, with the remaining members of Clinton Lodge, united with St. John's, No. 1, and met in union December 18, 1834. He instituted the formation of the Lodge of Strict Observance, which was constituted by Grand Lodge, December 27, 1843, R. W. Bro. Herring being the Master, with which Lodge he remained until his death. On September 3, 1828, he was appointed Assistant Grand Secretary, and on June 3, 1829, was elected Grand Secretary, which office he retained until 1846. He sided with the "Phillips" or "Herring" Grand Body at the split in Grand Lodge on June 5, 1849, and remained its Grand Secretary until 1858, when, in June, the two Grand Lodges were fused. He was a delegate to the Convention of Grand Lodges held in Washington March 7, 1842. Bro. Herring delivered the oration, on August 25, 1847, in St. John's Lodge, in commemoration of the M. W. G. Masters, Morgan Lewis and Alex. H. Robertson, and other eminent Masons, on the occasion of the First Lodge of Sorrow held in America in the English language. He was exalted in Jerusalem Chapter, No. 8, R. Arch, N. Y., January 5, 1817, dubbed a Knights Templar in Columbian Commandery, No. 1, N. Y., and was received a Sov. G. I. General, Thirty-third Degree Scottish Rite. Bro. Herring was a P. H. Priest, P. G. G. Sec. of the G. G. Chapter, U. S., P. G. Master of the G. Encampment, N. Y., and Officer of the G. G. Encampment of U. S., and P. G. Representative of the Orients of Brazil and France.

Hesed. A corruption of *Chesed*, which see.

Hesse-Cassel. Freemasonry appears to have been founded in this electorate in 1743, by a Lodge at Marburg, called "Zu den drei Löwen," which afterward took the name of "Marc Aurel zum flammenden Stern." A Lodge also appears to have existed in 1771, at Cassel, called "Zum blauen Löwen." In 1817 the Grand Mother Lodge of Hesse-Cassel was founded, which lasted until 1821, when the government closed all Lodges. In 1849 one was reopened by General von Helmschwerdt, but it was closed in 1855. It is now understood that this Lodge has been reopened.

Hexagon. A figure of six equal sides constitutes a part of the camp in the Scottish degree of Sublime Princes of the Royal Secret.

Stieglitz, in an essay on the symbols of Freemasonry, published in 1825, in the Altenburg *Zeitschrift*, says that the hexagon, formed by six triangles, whose apices converge to a point, making the following figure,

is a symbol of the universal creation, the six points crossing the central point; thus assimilating the hexagon to the older symbol of the point within a circle.

Hibbut-Hakkeber. (Beating of the sepulcher.) A Mohammedan belief as to the state of the soul after death. The form and mode of judgment is explained in *Al Koran.* The sarcophagus of an orthodox Moslem is so constructed that the deceased can sit upright when notified by his angel of the approach of the examiners, who question him as to his faith in the unity of God and the mission of Mohammed. Satisfactory answers insure peace; but if to the contrary, he is beaten on the temples with iron maces until he roars with anguish. The two angels, Monker and Nakû, then press the earth upon the body, which is gnawed and stung by ninety-nine seven-headed dragons until the day of resurrection. As the Mohammedan was an imitative religion, we naturally look for the origin of its customs and beliefs in older faiths; thus the Hibbut-Hakkeber is found in the Jewish, which taught that the angel of death would sit on a new-made grave, the soul would return to the body, which would stand up, the angel striking it thrice with a chain, half iron and half fire; at the first blow all the limbs were loosened, at the second the bones were dispersed, but gathered again by angels, and the third stroke reduces it to dust. This need not occur to those who died on the Sabbath or in the land of Israel. (See *Gilgul.*)

Hieroglyphics. From two Greek words which signify the engraving of sacred things. Hieroglyphics are properly the expressions of ideas by representations of visible objects, and the word is more peculiarly applied to that species of picture-writing which was in use among the ancient Egyptians, whose priests by this means concealed from the profane that knowledge which they communicated only to their initiates. Browne says (*Master Key*, p. 87), "The usages amongst Masons have ever corresponded with those of the ancient *Egyptians.* Their *Philosophers,* unwilling to expose their *Mysteries* to vulgar Curiosity, couched the Principles of their Learning and Philosophy under *Hieroglyphical Figures* and *Allegorical Emblems,* and expressed their notions of Government by *Signs* and *Symbols,* which they communicated to

the *Magi,* or wise *Men* only, who were solemnly obligated never to reveal them."

Hierogrammatists. The title of those priests in the Egyptian mysteries to whom were confided the keeping of the sacred records. Their duty was also to instruct the neophytes in the ritual of initiation, and to secure its accurate observance.

Hieronymites. A hermit order established in the fourteenth century, formed from the third Order of St. Francis. Followers of Thomas of Siena, who established themselves among the wild districts of the Sierra Morena, and so forming a community, obtained approval of Pope Gregory XI. in 1374.

Hierophant. From the Greek, ιεροψάντης, which signifies *one who explains the sacred things.* The Hierophant was, in the Ancient Mysteries, what the Master is in a Masonic Lodge—he who instructed the neophyte in the doctrines which it was the object of the mysteries to inculcate.

Hierophant or **Mystagog.** The Chief Priest of the Eleusinians, selected from the grade of Eumolpidens. He was selected for his imposing personal presence, and his dignity was sustained by the grandeur of his attire, his head encircled with a costly diadem. He was required to be perfect in animal structure, without blemish, and in the vigor of life, with a commanding voice. He was presumed to be surrounded by a halo of holiness. His duty was to maintain and also expound the laws. He was the introductor of the novices into the Eleusinian Temple, and passed them from the lesser into the greater mysteries, where he became the Demiurg, and impressed the initiate, while instructing him, by his manner and voice. His title of Mystagog was awarded because he alone revealed the secret or mystery.

Hierophylax. Title of the guardian of the holy vessels and vestments, as used in several Rites.

High Degrees. Not long after the introduction of Freemasonry on the Continent, in the beginning of the eighteenth century, three new degrees were invented and named, Ecossais, Novice, and Knights Templar. These gave the impulse to the invention of many other degrees, all above the Master's Degree. To these the name of *hautes grades* or *high degrees* was given. Their number is very great. Many of them now remain only in the catalogues of Masonic collectors, or are known merely by their titles; while others still exist, and constitute the body of the different Rites. The word is not properly applicable to the Royal Arch or degrees of the English and American systems, which are intimately connected with the Master's Degree, but is confined to the additions made to Ancient Craft Masonry by continental ritualists. These degrees have, from time to time, met with great opposition as innovations on Ancient Masonry, and some of the Grand Lodges have not only rejected them, but forbidden their cultivation by those who are under their obedience. But, on the other hand, they have been strenuously supported by many who have believed the Ancient Craft degrees do not afford a sufficient field for the expansion of Masonic thought. A writer in the London *Freemasons' Magazine* (1858, i., 1167) has expressed the true theory on this subject in the following language:

"It is the necessary consequence of an exclusive addiction to Craft Masonry that the intellectual and artistic development of the minds of the members must suffer, the ritual sink to formalism, and the administration fall into the hands of the lower members of the Order, by a diminution in the initiations of men of high intellectual calibre, and by the inactivity, or practical secession, of those within the Order. The suppression of the higher degrees, that is, of the higher Masonry, may be agreeable to those who are content to possess the administrative functions of the Order without genuine qualifications for their exercise, but it is a policy most fatal to the true progress of the Order. When Masonry has so fallen, to restore the higher degrees to their full activity is the measure essential for restoring the efficacy of Masonry within and without. Thus, in the last century, when Craft Masonry had spread rapidly over the whole of Europe, a reaction set in, till the heads of the Order brought the high degrees into vigor, and they continued to exercise the most powerful influence."

Highest of Hills. In the Old York Lectures was the following passage: "Before we had the convenience of such well-formed Lodges, the Brethren used to meet on the highest of hills and in the lowest of valleys. And if they were asked why they met so high, so low, and so very secret, they replied—the better to see and observe all that might ascend or descend; and in case a cowan should appear, the Tiler might give timely notice to the Worshipful Master, by which means the Lodge might be closed, the jewels put by, thereby preventing any unlawful intrusion." Commenting on this, Dr. Oliver (*Landm.*, i., 319) says: "Amongst other observances which were common to both the true and spurious Freemasonry, we find the practice of performing commemorative rites *on the highest of hills and in the lowest of valleys*. This practice was in high esteem amongst all the inhabitants of the ancient world, from a fixed persuasion that the summit of mountains made a nearer approach to the celestial deities, and the valley or holy cavern to the infernal and submarine gods than the level country; and that, therefore, the prayers of mortals were more likely to be heard in such situations." Hutchinson also says: "The highest hills and the lowest valleys were from the earliest times esteemed sacred, and it was supposed that the Spirit of God was peculiarly diffusive in those

places." The sentiment was expressed in the language of the earliest lectures of the eighteenth century, and is still retained, without change of words, in the lectures of the present day. But introduced, at first, undoubtedly with special reference to the ancient worship on "high places," and the celebration of the mysteries in the caverns of initiation, it is now retained for the purpose of giving warning and instruction as to the necessity of security and secrecy in the performance of our mystical rites, and this is the reason assigned in the modern lectures. And, indeed, the notion of thus expressing the necessity of secrecy seems to have been early adopted, while that of the sacredness of these places was beginning to be lost sight of; for in a lecture of the middle of the last century, or perhaps earlier, it was said that "the Lodge stands upon holy ground, or the highest hill or lowest vale, or in the Vale of Jehosophat, or any *other secret place*." The sacredness of the spot is, it is true, here adverted to, but there is an emphasis given to its secrecy.

This custom of meeting on the "highest hills and in the lowest valleys" seems to have prevailed at Aberdeen, Scotland, for they say: "We ordain that no Lodge be holden within a dwelling-house where there is people living in it, but in the open fields, except it be ill weather, and then let a house be chosen that no person shall heir or sie us." Also, "We ordain lykewayes that all entering prentieses be entered in our ancient outfield Lodge in the mearnes in the Parish of Negg, at the Stonnies at the poynt of the Ness."   [E. E. C.]

High Grades. Sometimes used for *High Degrees*, which see.

High Priest. The presiding officer of a Chapter of Royal Arch Masons according to the American system. His title is "Most Excellent," and he represents Joshua, or Jeshua, who was the son of Josedech, and the High Priest of the Jews when they returned from the Babylonian exile. He is seated in the east, and clothed in the apparel of the ancient High Priest of the Jews. He wears a robe of blue, purple, scarlet, and white linen, and is decorated with a breastplate and miter. On the front of the miter is inscribed the words, "HOLINESS TO THE LORD." His jewel is a miter.

High Priesthood, Order of. This order is an honorarium, to be bestowed upon the High Priest of a Royal Arch Chapter in the United States, and consequently no one is legally entitled to receive it until he has been duly elected to preside as High Priest in a regular Chapter of Royal Arch Masons. It should not be conferred when a less number than three duly qualified High Priests are present. Whenever the ceremony is performed in ample form, the assistance of at least nine High Priests, who have received it, is requisite. The General Grand Chapter of the United States has decided that although it is highly expedient that every High Priest should receive the order, yet its possession is not essentially necessary as a qualification for the discharge of his official duties.

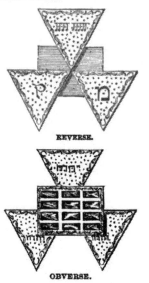

REVERSE.

OBVERSE.

The jewel of the degree consists of a plate of gold in the form of a triple triangle, a breastplate being placed over the point of union. In front, the face of each triangle is inscribed with the Tetragrammaton, יהוה; on the other side, the upper triangle has the following mystical notation, ꝏꝏ ꝏꝏꝏ; the two lower triangles have the Hebrew letters מ and ק inserted upon them. Each side of each triangle should be one inch in length, and may be ornamented at the fancy of the wearer. The breastplate may be plainly engraved or set with stones. It was adopted in 1856, on the suggestion of the author of this work, at a very general but informal meeting of Grand and Past Grand High Priests during the session of the General Grand Chapter held at Hartford, Conn. It is now in general use.

It is impossible, from the want of authentic documents, to throw much light upon the historical origin of this degree. No allusion to it can be found in any ritual works out of America, nor even here anterior to about the end of the last and beginning of this century. Webb is the first who mentions it, and gives it a place in the series of capitular degrees. The question has, however, been exhaustively examined by Bro. William Hacker, Past Grand High Priest of Indiana, who has paid much attention to the subject of American Masonic archeology. In a letter to the author in August, 1873, he sought to investigate the origin of this Order, and I gladly avail myself of the result of his inquiries.

"Thomas Smith Webb," says Bro. Hacker, "in the first edition of his *Monitor*, published in 1797, makes no mention of it. But in the second edition, published in 1802, he gives a monitorial ritual for the Order; or, as he terms it, *Observations on the Order of High Priests*.

"Now, I infer, as we find no mention of the Order in the edition of 1797, and a monitorial ritual appearing in the edition of 1802, that at some time between those dates we must look for the true origin of the Order.

"Turning then to the proceedings of the General Grand Chapter of the United States, we find that at the Communication held in the city of Providence, in the State of Rhode Island, on the 9th day of January, 1799, Benjamin Hurd, Jr., Thomas S. Webb, and James Harrison were appointed 'a committee to revise the Constitution, and report such alterations and amendments thereto as they shall find necessary to be made.'

"The next day, January 10, 1799, Webb, as chairman of the committee, submitted their report, which was adopted as reported. In Article IV. of that Constitution, we find the forms for constituting new Chapters and installing High Priests fully laid down and provided for. In those forms, after certain ceremonies had been gone through with, 'All the Companions, except High Priests and Past High Priests, are requested to withdraw, while the new High Priest is solemnly bound to the performance of his duties; and after the performance of other necessary ceremonies, not proper to be written, they are permitted to return.'

"Now, right here the question naturally arises, What were those 'other necessary ceremonies not proper to be written'? A few lines farther on we find this language laid down: 'In consequence of your cheerful acquiescence with the charges and regulations just recited, I now declare you duly installed *and anointed* High Priest of this new Chapter.' Now do not the words '*and anointed*,' as here used, fully answer the question as to what those 'other necessary ceremonies' were? It seems so to me.

"Upon this theory, then, we have Thomas Smith Webb and his associates on the committee, Benjamin Hurd, Jr., and James Harrison, as the authors of the Order. It was adopted by the General Grand Chapter on the 10th day of January, 1799, when it became a part of the constitutional requirements of Royal Arch Masonry, so far, at least, as the authority of the General Grand Chapter extended.

"Following this matter out, we find that this provision of the Constitution was retained until the Triennial Communication held in the city of Lexington, Kentucky, on the 19th day of September, 1853, when, on motion of Companion Gould, the section was repealed; thus leaving the Order of High Priesthood the exclusive property of those who were in possession of it.

"Where these Excellent Companions got

the original thought or germ out of which the Order was formed will have, perhaps, to be left to conjecture; yet even here I think we may find some data upon which to found a conclusion.

"In setting about the formation of an order suitable for the office of High Priest, what could be more natural or appropriate than to take the scriptural history of the meeting of Abraham with Melchizedek, Priest of the Most High God; the circumstances which brought that meeting about; the bringing forth the bread and wine; the blessing, etc.; and the anointing of Aaron and his sons to the Priesthood under the Mosaic dispensations. It does seem to me that these would be the most natural sources for any one to go to for facts and circumstances to work into an order of this kind.

"We can illustrate this point farther by reference to a note found in an old ritual of the 'Mediterranean Pass,' as then—and perhaps it may be so now—conferred under the Grand Priory of England and Wales, preparatory to the Order of Malta. That note read as follows:

"'In some Priories the candidate partakes of bread from the point of a sword, and wine from a chalice placed upon the blade, handed to him by the Prelate.'

"Again, in an old manuscript of the ritual of the Royal Grand Conclave of Scotland, now also lying before me, I find similar language used in the ritual of the Templars' Order. How well the thoughts contained in these extracts have been worked into the Order of High Priest, every well-informed High Priest must very well understand.

"But the question now comes up: were Webb and his associates in possession of these rituals at the time they originated the Order of High Priesthood? I think they were, and for these reasons: In these rituals to which I have referred I find these expressions used: 'That I will not shed the blood of a K. T. unlawfully;' 'the skull to be laid open, and all the brains to be exposed to the scorching rays of the sun;' with several other familiar expressions, which every Royal Arch Mason will readily recognize as appropriately wrought into Webb's Royal Arch Degree.

"From the foregoing facts, as well as others not stated, I infer that Thomas Smith Webb, with his co-advisers, Benjamin Hurd, Jr., and James Harrison, were the true authors of the Order; that it dates from the 10th day of January, 1799, at which time it was adopted by the General Grand Chapter, and became a part of the constitutional regulations and requirements of Royal Arch Masonry so far as the authority of the General Grand Chapter extended, and that it continued as such until the 19th day of September, 1853, when it was repealed, as before stated.

"A thought or two further, and I will have done. Webb, in arranging the Order, evidently intended that it should be con-

ferred as a part of the installation ceremonies of a High Priest; and whether he ever conferred it at any other time or in any other manner I have been unable to learn, as I have never met with any one who claimed to have received the Order from him. At what time and by whom it was first conferred as a separate ceremonial is equally unknown to me. All I have yet been able to find upon this point is in Cross's *Chart*, where, in the edition of 1826, and it may also be in the earlier editions, I find it arranged as a separate ceremonial, and disconnected with the ceremonies of installation.

"The earliest authentic record of the organization of a Council of High Priests I have yet found is in the proceedings of the Grand Chapter of Ohio in 1828, where it appears that a Council was duly formed, rules adopted for its government, and a full list of officers elected, with Companion John Snow as President.

"It is more than probable that the Order has always been conferred, west of the mountains, as a separate ceremonial, and never as a part of the installation ceremonies. It is well known that John Snow, who no doubt brought it with him when he came to the West, always so conferred it, and not then until the applicant had been regularly elected and installed as High Priest of his Chapter. I have also met with those who claimed to have received it from the celebrated Lorenzo Dow, of whom it is further alleged that he always required an election and installation as a prerequisite to the Order. With these facts before us, and I have no doubt of the truth of every word of them, I would ask of those who have attempted to heap such obloquy and derision upon the Order, as Dr. Mitchell and others who have followed him, to point us to any other single order or degree of Masonry that can be traced so successfully to the source from whence it came; that has in it more of the elements of sublimity and impressiveness, and that is more scripturally and Masonically appropriate for that for which it was intended, than has this much-maligned Order of High Priesthood; remembering also that it was established upon the constitutional authority of the General Grand Chapter of the United States, which is, and ever has been, the highest authority in Royal Arch Masonry in the United States. And again, among the names of those zealous companions who participated in its adoption stands that of the Honorable De Witt Clinton, for so many years the zealous and efficient General Grand High Priest. Then I say, when we take all these facts together, as they stand recorded before us, I think the question as to the origin and authenticity may be considered as fully settled."

High Priest of the Jews. The important office of the High Priesthood was instituted by Moses after the completion of the directions for erecting the tabernacle, and was restricted to Aaron and his descendants, and was so confined until the time of the Asmonean dynasty, when it passed into the family of Judas Maccabæus. The High Priest was at the head not only of ecclesiastical but of civil affairs, presiding in the Sanhedrim and judging the people. He superintended the Temple, directing the mode of worship, and preserving the building from profanation. He was inducted into his office by anointment and sacrifices, and was invested with a peculiar dress. This dress, as the Rabbis describe it, consisted of eight parts, namely, the breastplate, the ephod, with its curious girdle, the robe of the ephod, the miter, the broidered coat, and the girdle. The materials of which these were composed were gold, blue, red, purple, and fine white linen. As these garments are to a certain extent represented in the vestment of a High Priest of a Royal Arch Chapter, a brief description of them may be expedient:

The High Priest was first clothed in a pair of linen drawers. Over this was a coat or shirt of fine linen reaching to his feet, and with sleeves extending to his wrists. Over this again was a robe of blue, called the coat of ephod. It was without sleeves, but consisted of two pieces, one before and another behind, having a large opening in the top for the passage of the head, and another on each side to admit the arms. It extended only to the middle of the legs, and its skirt was adorned with little golden bells and pomegranates. Above all these vestments was placed the ephod, which has already been described as a short garment coming down only to the breast before, but somewhat longer behind, without sleeves, and artificially wrought with gold, and blue, and purple, and scarlet, in embroidery of various figures. It was looped on the shoulders with two onyx stones, on each of which was inscribed the names of six of the tribes. On the front of the ephod he wore the breastplate; at solemn ministrations a miter of fine linen of a blue color. This was wrapped in several folds, and worn about his head in the manner of a Turkish turban, except that it was without a crown, being open on top, and sitting on his head like a garland. In front of it there hung down upon his forehead a square plate of gold, called the plate of the golden crown, upon which were inscribed the words HOLINESS TO THE LORD, which were engraved in the ancient Hebrew or Samaritan characters. The vestments of a High Priest of a Royal Arch Chapter are intended to represent— though the representation is imperfect— the gorgeous apparel of the Jewish Pontiff. They are a miter, breastplate, and a robe of four colors. To these the Masonic ritualists have ascribed a symbolic signification. The miter teaches the High Priest the dignity of his office; the breastplate, his responsibility to the laws and ordinances of the Institution, and that the honor and interest of the Chapter should be always

near his heart; and the robe, the different graces and virtues which are symbolized by the various colors of which it is composed.

High Twelve. The hour of noon or twelve o'clock in the day, when the sun is high in the heavens, in contradistinction to *low twelve*, or midnight, when the sun is low down beneath the earth. The expression is always used, in Masonic language, to indicate the hour of noon, at which time, as the tradition tells us, the Craft in the Temple were called from labor to refreshment. The phrase was used in the earliest rituals of the last century. The answer in the old catechisms to the question, "What's a clock?" was always, "High Twelve."

Hindustan, Mysteries of. Of all the ethnic religions, that of Hindustan is admitted to be the oldest, for its Vedas or sacred books claim an antiquity of nearly forty centuries. However Brahmanism may have been corrupted in more modern times, in its earliest state it consisted of a series of doctrines which embraced a belief in a Supreme Being and in the immortality of the soul. All primitive religions were more or less mystical, and that of India formed no exception to the rule. Oliver, in his *History of Initiation*, has given a very succinct account of the Brahmanical mysteries, collected from the most authentic sources, such as Maurice, Colebrook, Jones, and Faber. His description refers almost exclusively to the reception and advancement of a Brahman in his sacred profession; for the initiations of India, like those of Egypt, were confined to the priesthood. All Brahmans, it is true, do not necessarily belong to the sacerdotal order, but every Brahman who has been initiated, and thus been made acquainted with the formulas of worship, may at any time become an officiating priest. The ceremonies of initiation, as they have been described by Oliver, were celebrated in spacious caverns, the principal of which were Elephanta and Salsette, both situated near Bombay. The mysteries were divided into four degrees, and the candidate was permitted to perform the probation of the first at the early age of eight years. It consisted simply in the investiture with the linen garment and Zennar or sacred cord; of sacrifices accompanied by ablutions; and of an explanatory lecture. The aspirant was now delivered into the care of a Brahman, who thenceforth became his spiritual guide, and prepared him by repeated instructions and a life of austerity for admission into the second degree. To this, if found qualified, he was admitted at the requisite age. The probationary ceremonies of this degree consisted in an incessant occupation in prayers, fastings, ablutions, and the study of astronomy. Having undergone these austerities for a sufficient period, he was led at night to the gloomy caverns of initiation, which had been duly prepared for his reception.

The interior of this cavern was brilliantly illuminated, and there sat the three chief hierophants, in the east, west, and south, representing the gods Brahma, Vishnu, and Siva, surrounded by the attendant mystagogues, dressed in appropriate vestments. After an invocation to the sun, the aspirant was called upon to promise that he would be obedient to his superiors, keep his body pure, and preserve inviolable secrecy on the subject of the mysteries. He was then sprinkled with water, an invocation of the Deity was whispered in his ear; he was divested of his shoes, and made to circumambulate the cavern three times, in imitation of the course of the sun, whose rising was personated by the hierophant representing Brahma, stationed in the east, whose meridian height by the representative of Siva in the south, and whose setting by the representative of Vishnu in the west. He was then conducted through seven ranges of dark and gloomy caverns, during which period the wailing of Mahadeva for the loss of Siva was represented by dismal howlings. The usual paraphernalia of flashes of light, of dismal sounds and horrid phantoms, was practised to intimidate or confuse the aspirant. After the performance of a variety of other ceremonies, many of which we can only conjecture, the candidate reached the extremity of the seven caverns; he was now prepared for enlightenment by requisite instruction and the administration of a solemn oath.

This part of the ceremonies being concluded, the sacred conch was blown, the folding-doors were suddenly thrown open, and the aspirant was admitted into a spacious apartment filled with dazzling light, ornamented with statues and emblematical figures, richly decorated with gems, and scented with the most fragrant perfumes. This was a representation of Paradise.

The candidate was now supposed to be regenerated, and he was invested by the chief Brahman with the white robe and tiara; a cross was marked upon his forehead, and a tau upon his breast, and he was instructed in the signs, tokens, and lectures of the Order. He was presented with the sacred belt, the magical black stone, the talismanic jewel to be worn upon his breast, and the serpent stone, which, as its name imported, was an antidote against the bite of serpents. And, lastly, he was entrusted with the sacred name, known only to the initiated. This ineffable name was AUM, which, in its triliteral form, was significant of the creative, preservative, and destroying power, that is, of Brahma, Vishnu, and Siva. It could not be pronounced, but was to be the subject of incessant silent contemplation. The symbols and the *aporrheta*, or secret things of the mysteries, were now explained.

Here ended the Second Degree. The Third took place when the candidate had grown old, and his children had all been provided for. This consisted in a total exclusion in the forest, where, as an anchorite,

he occupied himself in ablutions, prayers, and sacrifices.

In the Fourth Degree he underwent still greater austerities, the object of which was to impart to the happy sage who observed them a portion of the Divine nature, and to secure him a residence among the immortal gods.

The object of the Indian mysteries appears, says Oliver, to have been to teach the unity of God and the necessity of virtue. The happiness of our first parents, the subsequent depravity of the human race, and the universal deluge were described in a manner which showed that their knowledge must have been derived from an authentic source.

Hinnom. A deep valley south of Mt. Moriah, known as Gehenna; in which carrion was cast as food for vultures. The holy valley of judgment, Jehoshaphat, has been improperly substituted for Hinnom.

Hiram. The gavel, when wielded by the Master of the Lodge, is sometimes called the *Hiram*, because as the workmen at the Temple were controlled and directed by Hiram, the chief builder, so the Master preserves order in the Lodge by the proper use of the gavel.

Hiram or **Huram.** In Hebrew, הירם or הורם, meaning *noble-born*. The more correct pronunciation, according to the true value of the Hebrew letters, is *Khuram* or *Khurum;* but universal Masonic usage renders it now impossible, or, at least, inexpedient, to make the change. The name of the King of Tyre is spelled *Hiram* everywhere in Scripture except in 1 Chronicles xiv. 1, where it occurs as *Huram*. In 1 Chron. xiv. 1, the original Hebrew text has *Hiram*, but the Masorites in the margin direct it to be read *Huram*. In our authorized version, the name is spelled *Hiram*, which is also the form used in the Vulgate and in the Targums; the Septuagint has Χειράμ, or *Cheiram*.

Hiram Abif. There is no character in the annals of Freemasonry whose life is so dependent on tradition as the celebrated architect of King Solomon's Temple. Profane history is entirely silent in respect to his career, and the sacred records supply us with only very unimportant items. To fill up the space between his life and his death, we are necessarily compelled to resort to those oral legends which have been handed down from the ancient Masons to their successors. Yet, looking to their character, I should be unwilling to vouch for the authenticity of all; most of them were probably at first symbolical in their character; the symbol in the lapse of time having been converted into a myth, and the myth, by constant repetition, having assumed the formal appearance of a truthful narrative. Such has been the case in the history of all nations. But whatever may have been their true character, to the Mason, at least, they are interesting, and cannot be altogether void of instruction.

When King Solomon was about to build a temple to Jehovah, the difficulty of obtaining skilful workmen to superintend and to execute the architectural part of the undertaking was such, that he found it necessary to request of his friend and ally, Hiram, King of Tyre, the use of some of his most able builders; for the Tyrians and Sidonians were celebrated artists, and at that time were admitted to be the best mechanics in the world. Hiram willingly complied with his request, and despatched to his assistance an abundance of men and materials, to be employed in the construction of the Temple, and among the former, a distinguished artist, to whom was given the superintendence of all the workmen, both Jews and Tyrians, and who was in possession of all the skill and learning that were required to carry out, in the most efficient manner, all the plans and designs of the King of Israel.

Of this artist, whom Freemasons recognize sometimes as Hiram the Builder, sometimes as the Widow's Son, but more commonly as Hiram Abif, the earliest account is found in the 1st Book of Kings (vii. 13, 14), where the passage reads as follows:

"And King Solomon sent and fetched Hiram out of Tyre. He was a widow's son of the tribe of Naphtali, and his father was a man of Tyre, a worker in brass, and he was filled with wisdom and understanding, and cunning to work all works in brass. And he came to King Solomon and wrought all his work."

He is next mentioned in the 2d Book of Chronicles (ch. ii. 13, 14), in the following letter from Hiram of Tyre to King Solomon.

" And now I have sent a cunning man, endued with understanding, of Huram my father's. The son of a woman of the daughters of Dan, and his father was a man of Tyre, skilful to work in gold and in silver, in brass, in iron, in stone and in timber, in purple, in blue and in fine linen and in crimson; also to grave any manner of graving, and to find out every device which shall be put to him, with thy cunning men, and with the cunning men of my lord David, thy father."

In reading these two descriptions, everyone will be at once struck with an apparent contradiction in them in relation to the parentage of their subject. There is no doubt—for in this both passages agree—that his father was a man of Tyre; but the discrepancy is in reference to the birthplace of his mother, who in one passage is said to have been "of the tribe of Naphtali," and in the other, "of the daughters of Dan." Commentators have, however, met with no difficulty in reconciling the contradiction, and the suggestion of Bishop Patrick is now generally adopted on this subject. He supposes that she herself was of the tribe of Dan, but that her first husband was of the tribe of Naphtali, by whom she had this son; and that when she was a widow, she married a man of Tyre, who is called Hiram's father because he bred him up and was the husband of his mother.

Hiram Abif undoubtedly derived much of his knowledge in mechanical arts from that man of Tyre who had married his mother,

and we may justly conclude that he increased that knowledge by assiduous study and constant intercourse with the artisans of Tyre, who were greatly distinguished for their attainments in architecture. Tyre was one of the principal seats of the Dionysiac fraternity of artificers, a society engaged exclusively in the construction of edifices, and living under a secret organization, which was subsequently imitated by the Operative Freemasons. Of this association, it is not unreasonable to suppose that Hiram Abif was a member, and that on arriving at Jerusalem he introduced among the Jewish workmen the same exact system of discipline which he had found of so much advantage in the Dionysiac associations at home, and thus gave, under the sanction of King Solomon, a peculiar organization to the Masons who were engaged in building the Temple.

Upon the arrival of this celebrated artist at Jerusalem, which was in the year B.C. 1012, he was at once received into the intimate confidence of Solomon, and entrusted with the superintendence of all the workmen, both Tyrians and Jews, who were engaged in the construction of the building. He received the title of "Principal Conductor of the Works," an office which, previous to his arrival, had been filled by Adoniram, and, according to Masonic tradition, formed with Solomon and King Hiram of Tyre, his ancient patron, the Supreme Council of Grand Masters, in which everything was determined in relation to the construction of the edifice and the government of the workmen.

The *Book of Constitutions*, as it was edited by Entick (ed. 1756, p. 19), speaks of him in the following language: "This inspired master was, without question, the most cunning, skilful, and curious workman that ever lived; whose abilities were not confined to building only, but extended to all kinds of work, whether in gold, silver, brass or iron; whether in linen, tapestry or embroidery; whether considered as architect, statuary, founder or designer, separately or together, he equally excelled. From his designs and under his direction, all the rich and splendid furniture of the Temple and its several appendages were begun, carried on, and finished. Solomon appointed him, in his absence, to fill the Chair as Deputy Grand Master, and in his presence, Senior Grand Warden, Master of Work, and general overseer of all artists, as well those whom David had formerly procured from Tyre and Sidon, as those Hiram should now send."

This statement requires some correction. According to the most consistent systems and the general course of the traditions, there were three Grand Masters at the building of the Temple, of whom Hiram Abif was one, and hence in our Lodges he always receives the title of a Grand Master. We may, however, reconcile the assertion of Anderson, that he was sometimes a Deputy Grand Master, and sometimes a Senior Grand Warden, by supposing that the three Grand Masters were, among the Craft, possessed of equal authority, and held in equal reverence, while among themselves there was an acknowledged subordination of station and power. But in no way can the assertion be explained that he was at any time a Senior Grand Warden, which would be wholly irreconcilable with the symbolism of the Temple. In the mythical Master's Lodge, supposed to have been held in the Temple, and the only one ever held before its completion, at which the three Grand Masters alone were present, the office of Junior Warden is assigned to Hiram Abif.

According to Masonic tradition, which is in part supported by Scriptural authority, Hiram was charged with all the architectural decorations and interior embellishments of the building. He cast the various vessels and implements that were to be used in the religious service of the Temple, as well as the pillars that adorned the porch, selecting as the most convenient and appropriate place for the scene of his operations, the clay grounds which extend between Succoth and Zaredatha; and the old lectures state that the whole interior of the house, its posts and doors, its very floors and ceilings, which were made of the most expensive timber, and overlaid with plates of burnished gold, were, by his exquisite taste, enchased with magnificent designs and adorned with the most precious gems. Even the abundance of these precious jewels, in the decorations of the Temple, is attributed to the foresight and prudence of Hiram Abif; since a Masonic tradition, quoted by Dr. Oliver, informs us, that about four years before the Temple was begun, he, as the agent of the Tyrian king, purchased some curious stones from an Arabian merchant, who told him, upon inquiry, that they had been found by accident on an island in the Red Sea. By the permission of King Hiram, he investigated the truth of this report, and had the good fortune to discover many precious gems, and among the rest an abundance of the topaz. They were subsequently imported by the ships of Tyre for the service of King Solomon.

In allusion to these labors of taste and skill displayed by the widow's son, our lectures say, that while the *wisdom* of Solomon contrived the fabric, and the *strength* of King Hiram's wealth and power supported the undertaking, it was adorned by the *beauty* of Hiram Abif's curious and cunning workmanship.

In the character of the chief architect of the Temple, one of the peculiarities which most strongly attract attention was the systematic manner in which he conducted all the extensive operations which were placed under his charge. In the classification of the workmen, such arrangements were made, by his advice, as to avoid any discord or confusion; and although about two hundred thousand craftsmen and laborers were employed, so complete were his arrangements, that the general harmony was never once disturbed. In the payment of wages, such means were, at his suggestion, adopted, that every one's labor

22

was readily distinguished, and his defects ascertained, every attempt at imposition detected, and the particular amount of money due to each workman accurately determined and easily paid, so that, as Webb remarks, "the disorder and confusion that might otherwise have attended so immense an undertaking was completely prevented." It was his custom never to put off until to-morrow the work that might have been accomplished to-day, for he was as remarkable for his punctuality in the discharge of the most trifling duties, as he was for his skill in performing the most important. It was his constant habit to furnish the craftsmen every morning with a copy of the plans which he had, on the previous afternoon, designed for their labor in the course of the ensuing day. As new designs were thus furnished by him from day to day, any neglect to provide the workmen with them on each successive morning would necessarily have stopped the labors of the whole body of the workmen for that day; a circumstance that in so large a number must have produced the greatest disorder and confusion. Hence the practise of punctuality was in him a duty of the highest obligation, and one which could never for a moment have been neglected without leading to immediate observation. Such is the character of this distinguished personage, whether mythical or not, that has been transmitted by the uninterrupted stream of Masonic tradition.

The trestle-board used by him in drawing his designs is said to have been made, as the ancient tablets were, of wood, and covered with a coating of wax. On this coating he inscribed his plans with a pen or stylus of steel, which an old tradition, preserved by Oliver, says was found upon him when he was raised, and ordered by King Solomon to be deposited in the center of his monument. The same tradition informs us that the first time he used this stylus for any of the purposes of the Temple was on the morning that the foundation-stone of the building was laid, when he drew the celebrated diagram known as the forty-seventh problem of Euclid, and which gained a prize that Solomon had offered on that occasion. But this is so evidently a mere myth, invented by some myth-maker of the last century, without even the excuse of a symbolic meaning, that it has been rejected or, at least, forgotten by the Craft.

Another and more interesting legend has been preserved by Oliver, which may be received as a mythical symbol of the faithful performance of duty. It runs thus:

"It was the duty of Hiram Abif to superintend the workmen, and the reports of his officers were always examined with the most scrupulous exactness. At the opening of the day, when the sun was rising in the east, it was his constant custom, before the commencement of labor, to go into the Temple, and offer up his prayers to Jehovah for a blessing on the work; and in like manner when the sun was setting in the west. And after the labors of the day were closed, and the workmen had left the Temple, he returned his thanks to the Great Architect of the Universe for the harmonious protection of the day. Not content with this devout expression of his feelings, he always went into the Temple at the hour of high twelve, when the men were called off from labor to refreshment, to inspect the work, to draw fresh designs upon the trestle-board, if such were necessary, and to perform other scientific labors,—never forgetting to consecrate the duties by solemn prayer. These religious customs were faithfully performed for the first six years in the secret recesses of his Lodge, and for the last year in the precincts of the most holy place."

While assiduously engaged in the discharge of these arduous duties, seven years passed rapidly away, and the magnificent Temple at Jerusalem was nearly completed. The Fraternity were about to celebrate the cope-stone with the greatest demonstrations of joy; but, in the language of the venerable *Book of Constitutions*, "their joy was soon interrupted by the sudden death of their dear and worthy master, Hiram Abif." On the very day appointed for celebrating the cope-stone of the building, says one tradition, he repaired to his usual place of retirement at the meridian hour, and did not return alive. On this subject we can say no more. This is neither the time nor the place to detail the particulars of his death. It is enough to say that the circumstance filled the Craft with the most profound grief, which was deeply shared by his friend and patron, King Solomon, who, according to the *Book of Constitutions*, "after some time allowed to the Craft to vent their sorrow, ordered his obsequies to be performed with great solemnity and decency, and buried him in the Lodge near the Temple,—according to the ancient usages among Masons,—and long mourned his loss."

Hiramites. In the degree of Patriarch Noachites, the legend is, that the Masons of that degree are descended from Noah through Peleg. Distinguishing themselves, therefore, as Noachites, they call the Masons of the other degrees Hiramites, as being descended from Hiram Abif. The word is not elsewhere used.

Hiram, King of Tyre. He was the son of Abibal, and the contemporary of both David and Solomon. In the beginning of the former's reign, he sent messengers to him, and Hiram supplied the Israelitish king with "cedar-trees, and carpenters, and masons: and they built David a house." (2 Sam. v. 11.) Nearly forty years afterward, when Solomon ascended the throne and began to prepare for building the Temple, he sent to the old friend of his father for the same kind of assistance. The King of Tyre gave a favorable response, and sent workmen and materials to Jerusalem, by the aid of which Solomon was enabled to carry out his great design. Historians celebrate the friendly intercourse of these monarchs, and Josephus says that the correspondence between them in respect to the building of the Temple was, in his days, preserved in the Archives of the kingdom of Tyre. The answer of Hiram to the application of Solomon is given in the 1st Book of Kings (v. 8, 9), in the following language: "I will do all thy desire concerning timber of cedar and concerning timber of fir. My servants shall bring them down from Lebanon unto the sea; and I will convey them by sea in floats unto the place that thou shalt appoint me, and will cause them to be discharged there, and thou shalt receive them; and thou shalt accomplish my desire in giving food for my household." In return for this kindness, Solomon gave Hiram 20,000 measures, or *corim*, of wheat and the same quantity of oil, which was nearly 200,000 bushels of one and 1,500,000 gallons of the other; an almost incredible amount, but not disproportioned to the magnificent expenditure of the Temple in other respects. After Solomon had finished his work, he presented the King of Tyre with twenty towns in Galilee; but when Hiram viewed these places, he was so dissatisfied with their appearance that he called them *the land of Cabul*—which signifies barren, desolate—saying reproachfully to Solomon, "Are these, my brother, the towns which you have given me?" On this incident the Scottish Rite Masons have founded their Sixth Degree, or Intimate Secretary.

Hiram appears, like Solomon, to have been disposed to mysticism, for Dius and Menander, two Greek historians, tell us that the two kings proposed enigmas to each other for solution. Dius says that Solomon first sent some to Hiram; and that the latter king, being unable to solve them, paid a large sum of money as a forfeit, but that afterward he explained them with the assistance of one Abdemon; and that he in turn proposed some to Solomon, who, not being able to solve them, paid a much greater sum to Hiram than he had himself received on the like occasion.

The connection of the King of Tyre with King Solomon in the construction of the Temple has given him a great importance in the legendary history of Masonry. Anderson says (*Constitutions*, 1738, p. 15), "The tradition is that King Hiram had been Grand Master of all Masons; but when the Temple was finished, Hiram came to survey it before its consecration, and to commune with Solomon about wisdom and art; and finding that the Great Architect of the Universe had inspired Solomon above all mortal men, Hiram very readily yielded the pre-eminence to Solomon Jedediah, the beloved of God." He is called in the rituals one of our "Ancient Grand Masters," and when the mythical Master's Lodge was held in the Temple is supposed to have acted as the Senior Warden. It is said, too, that in the symbolic supports of Masonry he represented the pillar of strength, because "by his power and wealth he assisted the great undertaking" of constructing the Temple. He is reported, also, to have visited Jerusalem several times (a fact on which profane history is silent) for the purpose of consultation with Solomon and his great architect on the symbolism of the Word, and to have been present at the time of the death of the latter. Many other legends are related of him in the Master's Degree and those connected with it, but he is lost sight of after the completion of the first Temple, and is seldom heard of in the high degrees.

Hiram reigned over the Tyrians for thirty-four years; he permitted Solomon's ships to participate in the profitable trade of the Mediterranean, and Jewish sailors, under the instructions of Tyrian mariners, were taught how to bring from India the gold to enrich their people and beautify the temple of their king. Tradition says that Hiram gave his daughter in marriage to King Solomon.

Near Tyre there is a tomb which, to this day, has been pointed out as that of Hiram, King of Tyre, as delineated below.

Hiram the Builder. See *Hiram Abif.*

Hirschau, Wilhelm von. The Abbot Wilhelm von Hirschau, Count Palatine of Scheuren, is said to have been the founder, at the close of the eleventh century, of the German Bauhütten. Having been previously the Master of the Bauhütte, or Lodge of St. Emmerau, in Ratisbon, when he became Abbot of Hirschau, he collected together in 1080–1091 the Masons for the purpose of enlarging the convent. He incorporated the workmen, says Findel (*Hist.*, p. 54), with the monastery, as lay brethren, and greatly promoted their instruction and general improvement. Their social life was regulated by special laws; and the one most frequently inculcated by him was that brotherly concord should prevail, because only by working together and lovingly uniting all their strength would it be possible to accomplish such great works as were these undertakings for the public benefit.

Hittites. A powerful nation, whose two chief seats were at Kadesh, on the Orontes, and Carchemish, on the Euphrates, and who subjected as allies, forces from Palestine, Lydia, and the Troad. This great empire had at times contended with the Egyptian monarchs before the days of the Exodus. The Assyrians also had felt their power. They were foremost in arms and in the arts, and carried their religion to the shores of the Ægean; in fact, as shown by the explorations and discoveries of 1879, the early civilization of Greece and other European nations was as much indebted to them as it was to the Phœnicians. Egyptian inscriptions bear out the truth of these discoveries, and more firmly establish

Biblical history. Jerusalem came within the influence of this great empire. The Hittites were finally subdued by the capture of their famous capital, Carchemish, by Sargon, B.C. 717. For Biblical references, see Judges i. 26; 1 Kings x. 28, 29; 2 Kings vii. 6.

The system of writing by the Hittites was unique; their letters were hieroglyphic and their sculptures a peculiar and curious style of art, some of which may be found in the British Museum. (See *Fresh Lights*, etc., by Sayce, chap. 5.)

H∴ K∴ T∴. The abbreviation of Hiram, King of Tyre.

Hoben. The name given, in some of the high degrees, to one of the three conspirators commemorated in the Master's Degree. The derivation is uncertain. Oben, in Hebrew, means a stone; or it may be a corruption of Habbone, the Builder or Mason.

Hodin. The Blind Fate mentioned in the Scandinavian mysteries. (See *Balder.*)

Ho-Hi. A combination of the two Hebrew pronouns הו, *ho*, meaning "he," and הי, *hi*, meaning "she"; thus mystically representing the twofold sex of the Creator, and obtained by a Kabbalistic transposition or inversion of the letters of the Tetragrammaton, יהוה or IHOH. HO-HI, therefore, thus Kabbalistically obtained, denotes the male and female principle, the vis genitrix, the phallus and lingam, the point within the circle; the notion of which, in some one form or another of this double gender, pervades all the ancient systems as the representative of the creative power.

Thus, one of the names given by the mythological writers to the Supreme Jupiter was ἀρρενόθηλυς, the *man-woman.* In one of the Orphic hymns we find the following line:

Ζεὺς ἄρσην, γένετο, Ζεὺς ἄμβροτος ἔπλετο νύμφη.
Jove is a male, Jove is an immortal virgin.

And Plutarch, in his *Isis and Osiris*, says, "God, who is a male and female intelligence, being both life and light, brought forth another intelligence, the Creator of the world." All the Pagan gods and goddesses, however various their appellation, were but different expressions for the male and female principle. "In fact," says Russel, "they may all be included in the one great Hermaphrodite, the ἀρρενόθηλυς, who combines in his nature all the elements of production, and who continues to support the vast creation which originally proceeded from his will." And thus, too, may we learn something of the true meaning of the passage in Genesis (i. 27), where it is said, "So God created man *in his own image, in the image of God* created he him; *male* and *female* created he them."

The suggestion of this working of Ho-Hi out of Ih-Ho was put forward by George R. Gliddon, the great Egyptologist, who had obtained it from the writings of Lanzi, the Italian antiquary.

Holiness to the Lord. In Hebrew, קדש ליהוה, KODESH LAYEHOVAH. It was the inscription on the plate of gold that was placed in front of the high priest's miter. The letters were in the ancient Samaritan character.

Holland. See *Netherlands.*

Holy City, Knight of the. The Fifth and last of the degrees of the rectified Rite of the Benevolent Knights of the Holy City, or the Rite of Strict Observance, settled at Wilhelmsbad in 1782.

Holy Ground. A Masonic Lodge is said to be held on holy ground, according to the Prestonian lecture, because the first regularly constituted Lodge was held on that holy, consecrated ground wherein the first three grand offerings were made, which afterward met with Divine approbation. (See *Ground Floor of the Lodge.)*

Holy Lodge. The old lectures of the last century taught symbolically that there were three Lodges opened at three different periods in Masonic history; these were the Holy Lodge, the Sacred Lodge, and the Royal Lodge. The Holy Lodge was opened in the tabernacle in the wilderness, and over it presided Moses, Aholiab, and Bezaleel; the Sacred Lodge was opened on Mount Moriah during the building of the first Temple, and was presided over by Solomon, King of Israel, Hiram, King of Tyre, and Hiram the Builder; the Royal Lodge was opened among the ruins of the first Temple, at the building of the second, and was presided over by Joshua, Zerubbabel, and Haggai. Though presented as a tradition, it is really only a symbol intended to illustrate three important events in the progress of Masonic science.

Holy Name. Freemasonry teaches, in all its symbols and rituals, a reverence for the name of God, which is emphatically called the "Holy Name." In the prayer "Ahabath Olam," first introduced by Dermott, it is said, "because we trusted in thy holy, great, mighty, and terrible Name"; and in the introductory prayer of the Royal Arch, according to the American system, similar phraseology is employed: "Teach us, we pray thee, the true reverence of thy great, mighty, and terrible Name." The expression, if not the sentiment, is borrowed from the Hebrew mysteries.

Holy of Holies. Every student of Jewish antiquities knows, and every Mason who has taken the Third Degree ought to know, what was the peculiar construction, character, and uses of the Sanctum Sanctorum or Holy of Holies in King Solomon's Temple. Situated in the western end of the Temple, separated from the rest of the building by a heavy curtain, and enclosed on three sides by dead walls without any aperture or window, it contained the sacred ark of the covenant, and was secluded and set apart from all intrusion save of the high priest, who only entered it on certain solemn occasions. As it was the most sacred of the three parts of the Temple, so has it been made symbolic of a Master's Lodge, in which are performed the most sacred rites of initiation in Ancient Craft Masonry.

But as modern hierologists have found in all the Hebrew rites and ceremonies the traces of more ancient mysteries, from which they seem to have been derived, or on which they have been modified, whence we trace also to the same mysteries most of the Masonic forms which, of course, are more immediately founded on the Jewish Scriptures, so we shall find in the ancient Gentile temples the type of this same Sanctum Sanctorum or Holy of Holies, under the name of *Adyton* or *Adytum.* And what is more singular, we shall find a greater resemblance between this *Adytum* of the Pagan temples and the Lodge of Master Masons, than we will discover between the latter and the Sanctum Sanctorum of the Solomonic Temple. It will be curious and interesting to trace this resemblance, and to follow up the suggestions that it offers in reference to the antiquity of Masonic rites.

The *Adytum* was the most retired and secret part of the ancient Gentile temple, into which, as into the Holy of Holies of the Jewish Temple, the people were not permitted to enter, but which was accessible only to the priesthood. And hence the derivation of the word from the Greek *Adoein*, "not to enter," "that which it is not permitted to enter." Seclusion and mystery were always characteristic of the *Adytum*, and therefore, like the Holy of Holies, it never admitted of windows.

In the *Adytum* was to be found a *taphos* or tomb, and some relic or image or statue of the god to whom the temple was dedicated. The tomb reminds us of the characteristic feature of the Third Degree of Masonry; the image or statue of the god finds its analogue in the ark of the covenant and the overshadowing cherubim.

It being supposed that temples owed their first origin to the reverence paid by the ancients to their deceased friends, and as it was an accepted theory that the gods were once men who had been deified on account of their heroic virtues, temples were, perhaps, in the beginning only stately monuments erected in honor of the dead. Hence the interior of the temple was originally nothing more than a cell or cavity, that is to say, a grave regarded as a place of deposit for the reception of a person interred, and, therefore, in it was to be found the *soros* or coffin, and the *taphos* or tomb, or, among the Scandinavians, the *barrow* or mound grave. In time the statue or image of a god took the place of the coffin; but the reverence for the spot, as one of peculiar sanctity, remained, and this interior part of the temple became among the Greeks the *sekos* or chapel, among the Romans the *Adytum* or forbidden place, and among the Jews the *kodesh kodashim*, or Holy of Holies.

"The sanctity thus acquired," says Dudley in his *Naology* (p. 393), "by the cell of interment might readily and with propriety be assigned to any fabric capable of containing the body of the departed friend, or relic, or even the symbol of the presence or existence, of a divine personage." And thus it happened that there was in every ancient temple an *Adytum* or most holy place.

There was in the Holy of Holies of the Jewish Temple, it is true, no tomb nor coffin containing the relics of the dead. But there was an ark of the covenant which was the recipient of the rod of Aaron, and the pot of manna, which might well be considered the relics of the past life of the Jewish nation in the wilderness. There was an analogy easily understood according to the principles of the science of symbolism. There was no statue or image of a god, but there were the sacred cherubim, and, above all, the Shekinah or Divine Presence, and the *bathkol* or voice of God.

But when Masonry established its system partly on the ancient rites and partly on the Jewish ceremonies, it founded its Third Degree as the *Adytum* or holy of holies of all its mysteries, the exclusive place into which none but the most worthy—the priesthood of Masonry—the Masters in Israel—were permitted to enter; and then going back to the mortuary idea of the ancient temple, it recognized the *reverence for the dead* which constitutes the peculiar characteristic of that degree. And, therefore, in every Lodge of Master Masons there should be found, either actually or allegorically, a grave, or tomb, and coffin, because the Third Degree is the inmost sanctuary, the *kodesh kodashim*, the Holy of Holies of the Masonic temple.

Holy Place. Called also the sanctuary. It was that part of the Temple of Solomon which was situated between the Porch and the Holy of Holies. It was appropriated to the purposes of daily worship, and contained the altars and utensils used in that service. It has no symbolic meaning in Masonry; although really, as it occupied the ground floor of the Temple, it might be properly considered as represented by an Entered Apprentice's Lodge, that is to say, by the Lodge when occupied in the ceremonies of the First Degree.

Holy Sepulcher, Knight of the. See *Knight of the Holy Sepulcher.*

Hom. The tree of life and man in the Zoroastrian doctrine of the Persians.

Homaged. First employed by Entick, in his edition of the *Constitutions*, in reference to the installation of the Earl of Kintore, in 1740, as Grand Master: "Who having been homaged and duly congratulated according to the forms and solemnity of Masonry." He never repeats the word, using afterward the expression, "received the homage." Noorthouck adopts this latter expression in three or four instances, but more generally employs the word "recognized" or "selected." The expression "to do homage" to the Grand Master at his installation, although now generally disused, is a correct one—not precisely in the feudal sense of *homagium*, but in the more modern one of reverence, obedience, and loyalty.

Honorable. This was the title formerly given to the degree of Fellow-Craft.

Honorarium. When a degree of Masonry is conferred *honoris causâ*, that is, as a mark of respect, and without the payment of a fee, it is said to be conferred as an honorarium. This is seldom done in Ancient Craft Masonry; but it is not unusual in the high degrees of the Scottish Rite, which are sometimes bestowed by Inspectors on distinguished Masons as an honorarium.

Honorary Degrees. 1. The Mark Master's Degree in the American system is called the "Honorary Degree of Mark Master," because it is traditionally supposed to have been conferred in the Temple upon a portion of the Fellow-Crafts as a mark of honor and of trust. The degrees of Past Master and of High Priesthood are also styled honorary, because each is conferred as an honorarium or reward attendant upon certain offices; that of Past Master upon the elected Master of a Symbolic Lodge, and that of High Priesthood upon the elected High Priest of a Chapter of Royal Arch Masons.

2. Those degrees which are outside of the regular series, and which are more commonly known by the epithet "side degrees," are also sometimes called honorary degrees, because no fee is usually exacted for them.

Honorary Masons. A schismatic body which arose soon after the revival in the beginning of the eighteenth century, the members of which rejected the established formula of an obligation, and bound themselves to secrecy and obedience by a pledge of honor only. Like the Gregorians and the Gormogons, who arose about the same time, they soon died a natural death. A song of theirs, preserved in Carey's *Musical Century*, is almost the only record left of their existence.

Honorary Members. It is a custom in some Lodges to invest distinguished Masons with the rank and title of honorary membership. This confers upon them, as the by-laws may prescribe, sometimes all the rights of active membership and sometimes only the right of speaking, but always without the exaction of annual dues. Nor does honorary membership subject the person receiving it to the discipline of the Lodge further than to a revocation of the honor bestowed. The custom of electing honorary members is a usage of very modern date, and has not the sanction of the old Constitutions. It is common in France; less so, but not altogether unknown, in America and England. Oliver, in the title of one of his works, claimed honorary membership in more than nine Lodges. It may be considered unobjectionable as a method of paying respect to distinguished merit and Masonic services, when it is viewed only as a local regulation, and does not attempt to interfere with Masonic discipline. A Mason who is expelled forfeits, of course, with his active membership in his own Lodge, his honorary membership in other Lodges.

Honorary Thirty-Thirds. The Supreme Councils of the Ancient and Accepted Scottish Rite in this country have, within a few years past, adopted the custom of electing honorary members, who are sometimes called "Honorary Thirty-Thirds." They possess none of the rights of Inspectors-General or Active Members, except that of being present at the meetings of the Council, taking part to a limited extent in its deliberations, except when it holds an executive session.

Honors, Grand. The Grand Honors of Masonry are those peculiar acts and gestures by which the Craft have always been accustomed to express their homage, their joy, or their grief on memorable occasions. In the Symbolic degrees of the American Rite, they are of two kinds, the private and public, which are used on different occasions and for different purposes.

The private Grand Honors of Masonry are performed in a manner known only to Master Masons, since they can only be used in a Master's Lodge. They are practised by the Craft only on four occasions: when a Masonic Hall is to be consecrated, a new Lodge to be constituted, a Master Elect to be installed, or a Grand Master, or his Deputy, to be received on an official visitation to a Lodge. They are used at all these ceremonies as tokens of congratulation and homage. And as they can only be given by Master Masons, it is evident that every consecration of a hall, or constitution of a new Lodge, every installation of a Worshipful Master, and every reception of a Grand Master, must be done in the Third Degree. It is also evident, from what has been said, that the mode and manner of giving the private Grand Honors can only be personally communicated to Master Masons. They are among the *aporrheta*—the things forbidden to be divulged.

The public Grand Honors, as their name imports, do not partake of this secret character. They are given on all public occasions, in the presence of the profane as well as the initiated. They are used at the laying of corner-stones of public buildings, or in other services in which the ministrations of the Fraternity are required, and especially in funerals. They are given in the following manner: Both arms are crossed on the breast, the left uppermost, and the open palms of the hands sharply striking the shoulders; they are then raised above the head, the palms striking each other, and then made to fall smartly upon the thighs. This is repeated three times, and as there are three blows given each time, namely, on the breast, on the palms of the hands, and on the thighs, making nine concussions in all, the Grand Honors are technically said to be given " by three times three." On the occasion of funerals, each one of these honors is accompanied by the words, "*the will of God is accomplished; so mote it be,*" audibly pronounced by the brethren.

These Grand Honors of Masonry have undoubtedly a classical origin, and are but an imitation of the plaudits and acclamations practised by the ancient Greeks and Romans in their theaters, their senates, and their public games. There is abundant evidence in the writings of the ancients, that in the days of the empire, the Romans had circumscribed the mode of doing homage to their emperors and great men when they made their appearance in public, and of expressing their approbation of actors at the theater, within as explicit rules and regulations as those that govern the system of giving the Grand Honors in Freemasonry. This was not the case in the earlier ages of Rome, for Ovid, speaking of the Sabines, says that when they applauded, they did so without any rules of art:

"In medio plausu, plausus tunc arte carebat."

And Propertius speaks, at a later day, of the ignorance of the country people, who, at the theaters, destroyed the general harmony by their awkward attempts to join in the modulated applauses of the more skilful citizens.

The ancient Romans had carried their science on this subject to such an extent as to have divided these *honors* into three kinds, differing from each other in the mode in which the hands were struck against each other, and in the sound that thence resulted. Suetonius, in his life of Nero (cap. xx.), gives the names of these various kinds of applause, which he says were called *bombi, imbrices, testæ,* and Seneca, in his *Naturales Quæstiones,* gives a description of the manner in which they were executed. The "bombi," or *hums,* were produced by striking the palms of the hands together, while they were in a hollow or concave position, and doing this at frequent intervals, but with little force, so as to imitate the humming sound of a swarm of bees. The "imbrices," or *tiles,* were made by briskly striking the flattened and extended palms of the hands against each other, so as to resemble the sound of hail pattering upon the tiles of a roof. The "testæ," or *earthen vases,* were executed by striking the palm of the left hand, with the fingers of the right collected into one point. By this blow a sound was elicited which imitated that given out by an earthen vase when struck by a stick.

The Romans, and other ancient nations, having invested this system of applauding with all the accuracy of a science, used it in its various forms, not only for the purpose of testifying their approbation of actors in the theater, but also bestowed it, as a mark of respect or a token of adulation, on their emperors, and other great men, on the occasion of their making their appearance in public. Huzzas and cheers have, in this latter case, been generally adopted by the moderns, while the manual applause is only appropriated to successful public speakers and declaimers. The Freemasons, however, have altogether preserved the ancient custom of applause, guarding and regulating its use by as strict, though different rules as did the Romans; and thus showing, as another evidence of the antiquity of their Institution, that the "Grand Honors" of Freemasonry are legitimately derived from the "plausus," or applaudings, practised by the ancients on public occasions.

In the higher degrees, and in other Rites, the Grand Honors are different from those of Ancient Craft Masonry in the American Rite.

Hoodwink. A symbol of the secrecy, silence, and darkness in which the mysteries of our art should be preserved from the unhallowed gaze of the profane. It has been supposed to have a symbolic reference to the passage in St. John's Gospel (i. 5), "And the light shineth in darkness; and the darkness comprehended it not." But it is more certain that there is in the hoodwink a representation of the mystical darkness which always preceded the rites of the ancient initiations.

Hope. The second round in the theological and Masonic ladder, and symbolic of a hope in immortality. It is appropriately placed there, for, having attained the first, or *faith in God*, we are led by a belief in his wisdom and goodness to the *hope of immortality*. This is but a reasonable expectation; without it, virtue would lose its necessary stimulus and vice its salutary fear; life would be devoid of joy, and the grave but a scene of desolation. The ancients represented Hope by a nymph holding in her hand a bouquet of opening flowers, indicative of the coming fruit; but in modern and Masonic iconology it is represented by a virgin leaning on an anchor, the anchor itself being a symbol of hope.

Hope Manuscript. A manuscript copy of the old Constitutions, which is in the possession of the Lodge of Hope at Bradford, in England. The parchment roll on which this Constitution is written is six feet long and six inches wide, and is defaced and worn away at the lower edge. Its date is supposed to be about 1680. From a transcript in the possession of the late Bro. A. F. A. Woodford, whose correctness is certified to by the Master of the Lodge, Bro. Hughan first published it in his *Old Charges of the British Freemasons*.

Horn of Plenty. The jewel of the Steward of a Lodge. (See *Cornucopia*.)

Horns of the Altar. In the Jewish Temple, the altars of burnt-offering and of incense had each at the four corners four horns of shittim wood. Among the Jews, as well as all other ancient peoples, the altar was considered peculiarly holy and privileged; and hence, when a criminal, fleeing, took hold of these horns, he found an asylum and safety. As the Masonic altar is a representation of the altar of the Solomonic member, it should be constructed with these horns; and Cross has very properly so represented it in his *Hieroglyphic Chart*.

Hoschea. The word of acclamation used by the French Masons of the Scottish Rite. In some of the Cahiers it is spelled *Ozee*. It is, I think, a corruption of the word *huzza*, which is used by the English and American Masons of the same Rite.

Hospitality. This virtue has always been highly esteemed among Masons. Nothing is more usual in diplomas or certificates than to recommend the bearer "to the hospitality of all the brethren wheresoever dispersed over the globe"; a recommendation that is seldom disregarded. All of the old Constitutions detail the practise of hospitality, as one of the duties of the Craft, in language like this: "Every Mason shall receive and cherish strange fellowes when they come over the countreye."

Hospitaler. An officer in each of the bodies of the A. A. Scottish Rite, and in the Modern French Rite, whose duty it is to collect the obligatory contributions of the members, and, as the custodian, to disburse the same, under the advisement of the Master, to needy brethren, or even worthy profanes who may be in distress. The fund is entirely a secret one, and is reserved apart from all other receipts and disbursements.

Hospitaler, Knight. See *Knight Hospitaler*.

Hospitalers of Jerusalem. In the middle of the eleventh century, some merchants of Amalfi, a rich city of the kingdom of Naples, while trading in Egypt, obtained from the Calif Monstaser Billah permission to establish hospitals in the city of Jerusalem for the use of poor and sick Catholic pilgrims. A site was assigned to them close to the Holy Sepulcher, on which they erected a chapel dedicated to the Virgin, giving it the name of St. Mary ad Latinos, to distinguish it from those churches where the service was performed according to the Greek ritual. The building was completed in the year 1048; and at the same time two hospitals, one for either sex, were erected in the vicinity of the chapel for the reception of pilgrims. Subsequently each of these hospitals had a separate chapel annexed to it; that for the men being dedicated to St. John the Almoner, and that for the women to St. Mary Magdalen. Many of the pilgrims, who had experienced the kindness so liberally bestowed upon all wayfarers, abandoned all idea of returning to Europe, and formed themselves into a band of charitable assistants, and, without assuming any regular, religious profession, devoted themselves to the service of the hospital and the care of its sick inmates. The chief cities of the south of Europe subscribed liberally for the support of this institution; and the merchants of Amalfi who were its original founders acted as the stewards of their bounty, which was greatly augmented from the favorable reports of grateful pilgrims who had returned home, and the revenues of the hospital were thus much increased. The associates assumed the name of Hospitalers of Jerusalem. Afterward, taking up arms for the protection of the holy places against the Saracens, they called themselves Knights Hospitalers, a title which they subsequently changed to that of Knights of Rhodes, and finally to that of Knights of Malta.

Host, Captain of the. See *Captain of the Host*.

Houel. A Grand Officer of the G. Orient in France in 1804. G. Orator of the Grand Chapter in 1814.

Hour–Glass. An emblem used in the Third Degree, according to the Webb lectures, to remind us by the quick passage of its sands of the transitory nature of human life. As a Masonic symbol it is of comparatively modern date, but the use of the hour-glass as an emblem of the passage of time is older than our oldest rituals. Thus, in a speech before Parliament, in 1627, it is said: "We may dandle and play with the hour-glass that is in our power, but the hour will not stay for us; and an opportunity once lost cannot be regained." We are told in *Notes and Queries* (1st Ser., v. 223) that in the early part of the last century it was a custom to inter an hour-glass with the dead, as an emblem of the sand of life being run out.

Hours, Masonic. The language of Masonry, in reference to the hours of labor and refreshment, is altogether symbolical. The old lectures contained a tradition that our ancient brethren wrought six days in the week and twelve hours in the day, being called off regularly at the hour of high twelve from labor to refreshment. In the French and German systems, the Craft were said to be called from labor at low twelve, or midnight, which is therefore the supposed or fictitious time at which a French or German Lodge is closed. But in the English and American systems the Craft are supposed to be called off at high twelve, and when called on again the time for recommencing labor is said to be "one hour past high twelve": all this refers to Ancient Craft Masonry. In some of the high degrees the hours designated for labor or rest are different. So, too, in the different Rites: thus, in the system of Zinnendorf, it is said that there are in a Mason's Lodge five hours, namely, twelve struck, noon, high noon, midnight, and high midnight; which are thus explained. Twelve struck, is before the Lodge is opened and after it is closed; noon is when the Master is about to open the Lodge; high noon, when it is duly open; midnight, when the Master is about to close it; and high midnight, when it is closed and the uninitiated are permitted to draw near.

Hours of Initiation. In Masonic Lodges, as they were in the Ancient Mysteries, initiations are always at night. No Lodges ever meet in the daytime for that purpose, if it can be avoided. (See *Night*.)

How Go Squares? The question was one of the earliest of the tests which were common in the eighteenth century. In the *Grand Mystery*, published in 1724, we find it in the following form:

"*Q.* How go squares?"

"*A.* Straight."

It is noteworthy, that this phrase has an earlier date than the eighteenth century, and did not belong exclusively to the Masons. In Thomas May's comedy of *The Old Couple*, published in 1658 (Act. iv., sc. i.), will be found the following passage:

"*Sir Argent Scrape.* Ha! Mr. Frightful, welcome. How go squares? What do you think of me to make a bridegroom? Do I look young enough?" (See it in Dodsley's *Collection of Old Plays*, vol. 10.)

H∴ R∴ D∴ M∴. An abbreviation of Heredom or Herodem.

Hu. The name of the chief god among the Druids, commonly called *Hu Gadarn*, or Hu the Mighty. He is thus described by one of the Welsh bards: "The smallest of the small, Hu is the mighty in the world's judgment; yet he is the greatest and Lord over us and our God of mystery. His course is light and swift, his car is a particle of bright sunshine. He is great on land and sea, the greatest whom I shall behold, greater than the worlds. Offer not indignity to him, the Great and Beautiful." Bryant and Davies, in accordance with their arkite theory, think that he was Noah deified; but the Masonic scholar will be reminded of the Hi-hu eliminated by the Kabbalists out of the name of Jehovah.

Hughan, William James. This well-known Masonic writer was born on February 13, 1841, and died on May 20, 1911. His father was a native of Dunscore, in Scotland, who had settled at East Stonehouse in Devonshire, where W. J. H. was born. At the age of fifteen he was apprenticed to a draper at Devonport; at nineteen he entered a wholesale firm at Plymouth, going thence to Manchester and Truro, at which latter place he remained until 1883, when he retired from business and settled at Torquay, where he died.

He was initiated in 1863 in the St. Aubyn Lodge, No. 954, at Devonport; in the following year he joined the Emulation Lodge of Improvement in London, and on removing to Truro in 1864 he joined the Phenix Lodge of Honor and Prudence, No. 331, of which he was for a time Secretary, and in 1866 the Fortitude Lodge, No. 131, of which he was W. M. in 1868 and 1878.

In 1865 he was exalted in the Glasgow Chapter, No. 50, and joined Kilwinning Chapter, Ayr, No. 80, in 1868, becoming its Z. in 1873, and he was appointed Past Assistant Grand Sojourner of England in 1883; at various times he took most, if not all, of the degrees worked in England and Scotland.

In 1869 he was appointed Provincial Grand Secretary for Cornwall, which post he held for two years, and in 1874 he received the rank of Past Senior Grand Deacon of England, in recognition of his literary labors in the service of the Craft, this honor being the first of its kind to be so bestowed.

In 1876 he was given the rank of Past Senior Grand Warden of the Grand Lodge of Egypt, which was followed by many similar honors conferred upon him by various foreign Masonic bodies, including Senior Grand Warden of the Grand Lodge of Iowa.

He was devoted to Masonic study and research ever since he first saw the light of Masonry, and the Masonic periodicals of both hemispheres contain innumerable articles from his pen.

His chief published works are: *Constitutions of the Freemasons* (1869), *History of Freemasonry in York* (1871), *Unpublished Records of the Craft* (1871), *Old Charges of British Freemasons* (1872), *Memorials of the Masonic*

Union of 1813 (1874), *Numerical and Medallic Register of Lodges* (1878), *Origin of the English Rite of Freemasonry* (1884 and 1909), *Engraved List of Regular Lodges for 1734* (1889), *History of the Apollo Lodge and the R. A. York* (1889), *History of the Lion and Lamb Lodge* (1894), *Old Charges of British Freemasons* (1895), *Constitutions of the Freemasons, 1723-1896* (1899), and *The Jacobite Lodge at Rome, 1735-7* (1910).

His writings cover the whole range of Freemasonry, but he gave special attention to the *Old Charges*, in the search for which he was indefatigable.

The copyright in his books now belongs to the Lodge of Research, Leicester, England, and it is to be hoped that some of them will shortly be reissued. [E. L. H.]

Humility. The Divine Master has said, "He that humbleth himself shall be exalted" (Luke xiv. 2), and the lesson is emphatically taught by a portion of the ritual of the Royal Arch Degree. Indeed, the first step toward the acquisition of truth is a humility of mind which teaches us our own ignorance and our necessity for knowledge, so that thus we may be prepared for its reception. Dr. Oliver has greatly erred in saying (*Landmarks*, ii., 471) that bare feet are a Masonic symbol of humility. They are properly a symbol of reverence. The true Masonic symbol of humility is bodily prostration, and it is so exemplified in the Royal Arch Degree.

Hund, Baron von. Carl Gotthelf, Baron von Hund, was born in Oberlausitz, in Germany, on the 11th of September, 1722. He was a nobleman and hereditary landed proprietor in the Lausitz. He is said to have been upright in his conduct, although beset by vanity and a love of adventure. But Findel is scarcely correct in characterizing him as a man of moderate understanding, since the position which he took among his Masonic contemporaries—many of whom were of acknowledged talent—and the ability with which he defended and maintained his opinions, would indicate the possession of very respectable intelligence. In religious faith he was a Protestant. That rare work, the *Anti-Saint-Nicaise*, contains in its first volume a brief biography of von Hund, from which some details of his personal appearance and character may be obtained. He was of middling stature, but well formed; never dressed sumptuously, but always with taste and neatness; and although himself a moderate liver, was distinguished for his hospitality, and his table was always well supplied for the entertainment of friends and visitors. The record that his servants were never changed, but that those who were employed in his domestic service constantly remained with him, is a simple but conclusive testimony to the amiability of his character.

The scanty details of the life of Hund, which are supplied by Clavel in his *Histoire Pittoresque;* by Thory, in the *Acta Latomorum;* by Ragon, in his *Orthodoxie Maçonnique;* by Robison, in his *Proofs of a Conspiracy;* by

Lenning and Gädicke, in the *Encyclopädie* of each; by Oliver, in his *Historical Landmarks;* and by Findel, in his *History*, vary so much in dates and in the record of events, that he who should depend on their conflicting authority for information would be involved in almost inextricable confusion in attempting to follow any connected thread of a narrative. As Thory, however, writes as an annalist, in chronological order, it may be presumed that his dates are more to be depended on than those of the looser compilers of historical essays. He, therefore, will furnish us with at least an outline of the principal Masonic events in the life of Hund, while from other writers we may derive the material facts which the brevity of Thory does not provide. But even Thory must sometimes be abandoned, where he has evidently neglected to note a particular circumstance, and his omission must be supplied from some other source.

On the 20th of March, 1742, when still lacking some months of being twenty years of age, he was initiated into the mysteries of Freemasonry, in the Lodge of the Three Thistles at Frankfort-on-the-Main. Findel places the date of his initiation in the year 1741; but, for the reason already assigned, I prefer the authority of Thory, with whom Lenning concurs. The First and Second degrees were conferred on the same day, and in due time his initiation into the Symbolic degrees was completed.

Soon after his initiation, the Baron von Hund traveled through England and Holland, and paid a visit to Paris. Robison, who speaks of the Baron as "a gentleman of honorable character," and whose own reputation secures him from the imputation of wilful falsehood, although it could not preserve him from the effects of prejudice, says that Hund, while in Paris, became acquainted with the Earl of Kilmarnock and some other gentlemen, who were adherents of the Pretender, and received from them the new degrees, which had been invented, it is said, for political purposes by the followers of the exiled house of Stuart. Gädicke states that while there he also received the Order of the Mopses, which he afterward attempted, but without success, to introduce into Germany. This must, however, be an error; for the Order of the Mopses, an androgynous institution, which subsequently gave birth to the French Lodges of Adoption, was not established until 1776, long after the return of Hund to his native country.*

While he resided in Paris he received, says Findel, some intimations of the existence of the Order of Knights Templars in Scotland. The legend, which it is necessary to say has been deemed fabulous, is given to us by Clavel (*Hist. Pittor.*, p. 184), who tells us that, after the execution of Jacques de Molay, Pierre d'Aumont, the Provincial Grand Master of Auvergne, accompanied

---

* But the order of the Mopses was established in 1738 (see *Mopses*).—E. L. H.

by two Commanders and five Knights, escaped to Scotland, assuming during their journey, for the purpose of concealment, the costume of Operative Masons. Having landed on one of the Scottish Islands, they met several other companions, Scottish Knights, with whom they resolved to continue the existence of their Order, whose abolition had been determined by the Pope and the King of France. At a Chapter held on St. John's Day, 1313, Aumont was elected Grand Master, and the Knights, to avoid in future the persecutions to which they had been subjected, professed to be Freemasons, and adopted the symbols of that Order. In 1361, the Grand Master transported his see to the city of Aberdeen, and from that time the Order of the Temple spread, under the guise of Freemasonry, throughout the British Islands and the Continent.

The question is not now as to the truth or even the probability of this legend. It is sufficient for our present purpose to say, that the Baron von Hund accepted it as a veritable historical fact. He was admitted, at Paris, to the Order of Knights Templar, Clavel says, by the Pretender, Charles Edward, who was the Grand Master of the Order. Of this we have no other evidence than the rather doubtful authority of Clavel. Robison intimates that he was inducted by the Earl of Kilmarnock, whose signature was attached to his diploma. Gädicke says that he traveled over Brabant to the French army, and was there made a Templar by high chiefs of the Order. And this statement might be reconciled with that of Robison, for the high chiefs (*hohe Obere*) of Gädicke were possibly the followers of the Pretender, some of whom were likely to have been with the French army. The point is not, however, worth the trouble of an investigation. Two things have been well settled, namely: That in 1743 von Hund was initiated as a Knights Templar, and that at the same time he received the appointment of a Provincial Grand Master, with ample powers to propagate the Order in Germany. He returned to his native country, but does not appear to have been very active at first as a missionary of Templarism, although he continued to exhibit his strong attachment to Ancient Craft Masonry. In the year 1749 he erected, at his own expense, a Lodge on his estates at Kittlitz, near Lobau, to which he gave the name of the "Lodge of the Three Pillars." At the same time he built there a Protestant church, the corner-stone of which was laid by the brethren, with the usual Masonic ceremonies.

I am compelled to suppose, from incidents in his life which subsequently occurred, that Hund must have visited Paris a second time, and that he was there in the year 1754. On the 24th of November in that year, the Chevalier de Bonneville, supported by some of the most distinguished Masons of Paris, instituted a Chapter of the High Degrees, which received the name of the "Chapter of Clermont," and into which he introduced the Templar system, that is, the system which finds the origin of Freemasonry in Templarism. In this Chapter Baron von Hund, who was then in Paris, received the degrees of the Clermont system, and there, says Thory, he learned the doctrine upon which he subsequently founded his new Rite of Strict Observance. This doctrine was, that Freemasonry owes its existence to Knights Templarism, of which it is the natural successor; and, therefore, that every Mason is a Templar, although not entitled to all the privileges of the Order until he has attained the highest degree.

Von Hund returned to Germany possessed of powers, or a deputation granted to him in Paris by which he was authorized to disseminate the high degrees in that country. He was not slow to exhibit these documents, and soon collected around him a band of adherents. He then attempted what he termed a reform in primitive Masonry or the simple English system of the three Symbolic degrees, which alone most of the German Lodges recognized. The result was the establishment of a new system, well known as the Rite of Strict Observance.

But here we again encounter the embarrassments of conflicting authorities. The distinctive feature of the Rite of Strict Observance was, that Freemasonry is the successor of Templarism; the legend of Aumont being unhesitatingly accepted as authentic. The author of *Anti-Saint-Nicaise*, the book already referred to, asserted that between the years 1730 and 1740, there was already in Lusatia a Chapter of Templars; that he knew one, at least, who had been there initiated before the innovation of the Baron von Hund; and that the dignities of Prior, Subprior, Prefect, and Commander, which he professed to introduce into Germany for the first time, had been known there at a long antecedent period.

Ragon also asserts that the Templar system of Ramsay was known in Germany before the foundation of the Chapter of Clermont, whence von Hund derived his information and his powers; that it consisted of six degrees, to which Hund added a seventh; and that at the time of Von Hund's arrival in Germany this *régime* had Baron von Marshall as its head, to whom Hund's superiors in Paris had referred him.

This seems to be the correct version of the affair; and so the Rite of Strict Observance was not actually established, but only reformed and put into more active operation, by von Hund.

One of the peculiarities of this Rite was, that every member was called a Knight, or *Eques;* the classical Latin for a Roman knight being, by a strange inconsistency, adopted by these professed Templars, instead of the Medieval word *Miles*, which had been always appropriated to the military knights of chivalry. To this word was appended another, and the title thus formed was called the "characteristic name." Lists of these characteristic names, and of the persons whom they represented, are given in all the registers and lists of the Rite. Von Hund selected for himself the title of *Eques ab Ense*, or Knight of the Sword; and, to show the mixed military and Masonic character of his *régime*, chose for his seal a square and sword crossed, or, in heraldic language, saltierwise.

Von Hund divided Europe into nine provinces, and called himself the Grand Master of the seventh province, which embraced Lower Saxony, Prussian Poland, Livonia, and Courland. He succeeded in getting the Duke Ferdinand of Brunswick to place himself at the head of the Rite, and secured its adoption by most of the Lodges of Berlin and of other parts of Prussia. After this he retired into comparative inactivity, and left the Lodges of his Rite to take care of themselves.

But in 1763 he was aroused by the appearance of one Johnson on the Masonic stage. This man, whose real name was Leucht, was a Jew, and had formerly been the secretary of the Prince of Anhalt-Bernburg, under the assumed name of Becker. But, changing his name again to that of Johnson, he visited the city of Jena, and proclaimed himself to the Masons there as possessed of powers far more extensive than those of von Hund, which he pretended to have received from "Unknown Superiors" at Aberdeen, Scotland, the supposed seat of the Templar Order, which had been revived by Aumont. Von Hund at first admitted the claims of Johnson, and recognized him as the Grand Prior of the Order. Ragon says that this recognition was a fraud on the part of von Hund, who had really selected Johnson as his agent, to give greater strength to his Rite. I am reluctant to admit the truth of this charge, and am rather disposed to believe that the enthusiasm and credulity of von Hund had made him for a time the victim of Johnson's ostentatious pretensions. If this be so, he was soon undeceived, and, discovering the true character as well as the dangerous designs of Johnson, he proclaimed him to be an adventurer. He denied that Johnson had been sent as a delegate from Scotland, and asserted anew that he alone was the Grand Master of the Order in Germany, with the power to confer the high degrees. Johnson, accused of abstracting the papers of a Lord of Courland, in whose service he had been, and of the forgery of documents, was arrested at Magdeburg through the influence of von Hund, on the further charges of larceny and counterfeiting money, and died in 1775 in prison.

Von Hund now renewed his activity as a Mason, and assembled a Congress of the Rite at Altenberg, where he was recognized as Grand Master of the Templars, and aug-

mented his strength by numerous important initiations. His reappearance among the brethren exerted as much surprise as joy, and its good effects were speedily seen in a large increase of Chapters; and the Rite of Strict Observance soon became the predominating system in Germany.

But dissatisfaction began to appear as a consequence of the high claims of the members of the Rite to the possession of superior knowledge. The Knights looked haughtily upon the Masons who had been invested only with the primitive degrees, and these were offended at the superciliousness with which they were treated. A Mother Lodge was established at Frankfort, which recognized and worked only the three degrees. Other systems of high degrees also arose as rivals of the Rite, and von Hund's *régime* began to feel sensibly the effects of this compound antagonism.

Hitherto the Rite of Strict Observance had been cosmopolitan in its constitution, admitting the believers in all creeds to its bosom, and professing to revive only the military and chivalric character of the ancient Templars, without any reference to their religious condition. But in 1767, von Starck, the rector at Wismar, proposed to engraft upon the Rite a new branch, to be called the clerical system of Knights Templar. This was to be nominally spiritual in character; and, while announcing that it was in possession of secrets not known to the chivalric branch of the Order, demanded, as preliminary to admission, that every candidate should be a Roman Catholic, and have previously received the degrees of the Strict Observance.

Starck wrote to von Hund, proposing a fusion of the two branches; and he, "because," to borrow the language of Findel (*Hist. of F. M.*, p. 279), "himself helpless and lacking expedients, eagerly stretched out his hand to grasp the offered assistance, and entered into connection with the so-called clergy." He even, it is said, renounced Protestantism and became a Catholic, so as to qualify himself for admission.

In 1774, a Congress assembled at Kohlo, the object of which was to reconcile the difference between these two branches of the Rite. Here von Hund appears to have been divested of some portion of his dignities, for he was appointed only Provincial Superior of Upper and Lower Alsace, of Denmark and of Courland, while the Grand Mastership of the Rite was conferred on Frederick, Duke of Brunswick.

Another Congress was held in 1775, at Brunswick, where Hund again appeared. Here Findel, who seems to have no friendly disposition toward von Hund, charges him with "indulgence in his love of outward pomp and show," a charge that is not consistent with the character given him by other writers, who speak of his modesty of demeanor. The question of the *Superiores Incogniti*, or Unknown Superiors, from whom von Hund professed to derive his powers, came under consideration. His replies were not satisfactory. He denied that he was bound to give any explanations at all, and asserted that his oath precluded him from saying anything more. Confidence in him now declined, and the Rite to which he was so much attached, and of which he had been the founder and the chief supporter, began to lose its influence. The clerical branch of the Rite seceded, and formed an independent Order, and the Lodges of Strict Observance thenceforward called themselves the "United German Lodges."

With his failure at Brunswick, the functions of von Hund ceased. He retired altogether from the field of Masonic labor, and died, in the fifty-fifth year of his age, on the 8th of November, 1776, at Meiningen, in Prussia. The members of the Lodge Minerva, at Leipsic, struck a medal in commemoration of him, which contains on the obverse an urn encircled by a serpent, the symbol of immortality, and on the reverse a likeness of him, which is said to be exceedingly accurate. A copy of it may be found in the *Taschenbuche der Freimaurerei*, and in the *American Quarterly Review of Freemasonry*.

For this amiable enthusiast, as he certainly was—credulous but untiring in his devotion to Masonry; deceived but enthusiastic; generous and kind in his disposition; whose heart was better than his head—we may not entertain the profoundest veneration; but we cannot but feel an emotion of sympathy. We know not how much the antagonism and contests of years, and final defeat and failure, may have embittered his days or destroyed his energy; but we do know that he ceased the warfare of life while still there ought to have been the promise of many years of strength and vigor.

Hungary. Masonry was introduced into Hungary about the middle of the eighteenth century. In 1760, a Lodge, according to Hund's Templar system, was instituted at Presburg. Smith says (*Use and Abuse*, p. 219) that there were several Lodges there in 1783, but none working under the English Constitution. Most probably they received their Warrants from Germany. In 1870 there were seven Lodges in Hungary. On the 30th of January in that year these Lodges met in convention at Pesth, and organized the Grand Lodge of Hungary. In the next year a "Grand Orient of Hungary" was established, which, however, in 1886, amalgamated with the Grand Lodge under the title of the "Symbolic Grand Lodge of Hungary."

Hur. (Heb. הור, liberty.) A term used in the Fourth Degree of Perfect Mistress in the French Rite of Adoption.

Hutchinson, William. Of all the Masonic writers of the last century there was no one who did more to elevate the spirit and character of the Institution than William Hutchinson of Barnard Castle, in the county of Durham, England. To him are we indebted for the first philosophical explanation of the symbolism of the Order, and his *Spirit of Masonry* still remains a priceless boon to the Masonic student.

Hutchinson was born in 1732, and died April 7, 1814, at the ripe age of eighty-two years. He was by profession a solicitor; but such was his literary industry, that a very extensive practise did not preclude his devotion to more liberal studies. He published several works of fiction, which, at the time, were favorably received. His first contribution to literature was *The Hermitage, a British Story*, which was published in 1772. This was followed, in 1773, by a descriptive work, entitled *An Excursion to the Lakes of Westmoreland and Cumberland*. In 1775, he published *The Doubtful Marriage*, and in 1776 *A Week in a Cottage* and *A Romance after the Fashion of the Castle of Otranto*. In 1778, he commenced as a dramatic writer, and besides two tragedies, *Pygmalion, King of Tyre* and *The Tyrant of Onia*, which were never acted, he also wrote *The Princess of Zanfara*, which was successfully performed at several of the provincial theaters.

Hutchinson subsequently devoted himself to archeological studies, and became a prominent member of the Royal Society of Antiquaries. His labors in this direction were such as to win for him from Nichols the title of "an industrious antiquary." He published in 1776, *A View of Northumberland*, in two volumes; in 1785, 1787, and 1794, three consecutive quarto volumes of *The History and Antiquities of the County Palatinate of Durham;* and in 1794, in two quarto volumes, *A History of Cumberland*, —works which are still referred to by scholars as containing valuable information on the subjects of which they treat, and are an evidence of the learning and industry of the author.

But it is as a Masonic writer that Hutchinson has acquired the most lasting reputation, and his labors as such have made his name a household word in the Order. He was for some years the Master of Barnard Castle Lodge, where he sought to instruct the members by the composition and delivery of a series of Lectures and Charges, which were so far superior to those then in use as to attract crowds of visitors from neighboring Lodges to hear him and to profit by his instructions. Some of these were from time to time printed, and won so much admiration from the Craft that he was requested to make a selection, and publish them in a permanent form.

Accordingly, he applied, in 1774, for permission to publish, to the Grand Lodge— which then assumed to be a rigid censor of the Masonic press—and, having obtained it, he gave to the Masonic world the first edition of his now celebrated treatise entitled *The Spirit of Masonry, in Moral and Elucidatory Lectures;* but the latter part of the title was omitted in all the subsequent editions. The sanction for its publication, prefixed to the first edition, has an almost supercilious sound, when we compare the reputation of the work—which at once created a revolution in Masonic literature—with that of those who gave the sanction, and whose names are preserved only by the official titles, which were affixed to them. The sanction is in these words:

"Whereas, Brother William Hutchinson has compiled a book, entitled *The Spirit of Masonry*, and has requested our sanction for the publication thereof; we, having perused the said book and finding it will be of use to this Society, do recommend the same." This is signed by the Grand Master and his Deputy, by the Grand Wardens, and the Grand Treasurer and Secretary. But their judgment, though tamely expressed, was not amiss. A century has since shown that the book of Hutchinson has really been "of use to the Society." It opened new thoughts on the symbolism and philosophy of Masonry, which, worked out by subsequent writers, have given to Masonry the high rank it now holds, and has elevated it from a convivial association, such as it was in the beginning of the eighteenth century, to that school of religious philosophy which it now is. To the suggestions of Hutchinson, Hemming undoubtedly owed that noble definition, that "Freemasonry was a science of morality veiled in allegory, and illustrated by symbols."

The first edition of *The Spirit of Masonry* was published in 1775, the second in 1795, the third in 1802, the fourth in 1813, the fifth in 1814, and the sixth in 1815, all except the last in the lifetime of the author. Several subsequent editions have been published both in this country and in Great Britain. In 1780, it was translated into German, and published at Berlin under the title of *Der Geist der Freimaurerei, in moralischen und erläuternden Vorträgen.*

Of this great work the Craft appear to have had but one opinion. It was received on its first appearance with enthusiasm, and its popularity among Masonic scholars has never decreased. Dr. Oliver says of it: "It was the first efficient attempt to explain, in a rational and scientific manner, the true philosophy of the Order. Dr. Anderson and the writer of the Gloucester sermon indicated the mine, Calcott opened it, and Hutchinson worked it. In this book he gives to the science its proper value. After explaining his design, he enters copiously on the rites, ceremonies, and institutions of ancient nations. Then he dilates on the Lodge, with its ornaments, furniture, and jewels; the building of the Temple; geometry; and after explaining the third degree with a minuteness which is highly gratifying, he expatiates on secrecy, charity, and brotherly love; and sets at rest all the vague conjectures of cowans and unbelievers, by a description of the occupations of Masons and a masterly defence of our peculiar rites and ceremonies."

The peculiar theory of Hutchinson in reference to the symbolic design of Masonry is set forth more particularly in his ninth lecture, entitled "The Master Mason's Order." His doctrine was that the lost word was typical of the lost religious purity, which had been occasioned by the corruptions of the Jewish faith. The piety which had planted the Temple at Jerusalem had been expunged, and the reverence and adoration due to God had been buried in the filth and rubbish of the world, so that it might well be said "that the guide to heaven was lost, and the master of the works of righteousness was smitten." In the same way he extends the symbolism. "True religion," he says, "was fled. Those who sought her through the wisdom of the ancients were not able to raise her. She eluded the grasp, and their polluted hands were stretched forth in vain for her restoration. Those who sought her by the old law were frustrated, for death had stepped between, and corruption defiled the embrace."

Hence the Hutchinsonian theory is, that the Third Degree of Masonry symbolizes the new law of Christ, taking the place of the old law of Judaism, which had become dead and corrupt. With him, Hiram or Huram is only the Greek *huramen*, "I have found it," and Acacia, from the same Greek, signifies freedom from sin; and "thus the Master Mason represents a man, under the Christian doctrine, saved from the grave of iniquity and raised to the faith of salvation."

Some of Hutchinson's etymologies are unquestionably inadmissible; as, when he derives Tubal Cain from a corruption of the Greek, *tumbon choeo*, "I prepare my sepulcher," and when he translates the substitute word as meaning "I ardently wish for life." But fanciful etymologies are the besetting sin of all antiquaries. So his theory of the exclusive Christian application of the Third Degree will not be received as the dogma of the present day. But such was the universally recognized theory of all his contemporaries. Still, in his enlarged and elevated views of the symbolism and philosophy of Masonry as a great moral and religious science, he was immeasurably in advance of his age.

In his private life, Hutchinson was greatly respected for his cultivated mind and extensive literary acquirements, while the suavity of his manners and the generosity of his disposition secured the admiration of all who knew him. He had been long married to an estimable woman, whose death was followed in only two days by his own, and they were both interred in the same grave.

Hütte. A word equivalent among the Stone-Masons of Germany, in the Middle Ages, to the English word *Lodge*. Findel defines it as "a booth made of boards, erected near the edifice that was being built, where the stone-cutters kept their tools, carried on their work, assembled, and most probably occasionally ate and slept." These *hütten* accord exactly with the *Lodges* which Wren describes as having been erected by the English Masons around the edifice they were constructing.

Huzza. The acclamation in the Scottish Rite. In the old French rituals it is generally written *Hoschea.*

I

I. The ninth letter in the alphabets of Western Europe, called by the Greeks *Iota*, after its Shemitic name. The Hebrew equivalent is ׳, of the numerical value of 10, and signifies a *hand*. The oldest forms of the letter, as seen in the Phœnician and Samaritan, have a rude resemblance to a hand with three fingers, but by a gradual

simplification, the character came to be the smallest in the alphabet, and *iota*, or "jot," is a synonym for a trifle. The thumb and two fingers are much used, and are of great significance, in religious forms, as well as in Freemasonry. It is the position of the hand when the Pope blesses the congregation, and signifies the Three in One. The Hebrew letter *ain*, ע, with the numerical value of 70, possesses and gives the English sound of the letter *i*.

I. A. A. T. Reghellini (i., 29) says that the Rose Croix Masons of Germany and Italy always wear a ring of gold or silver, on which are engraved these letters, the initials of *Ignis, Aer, Aqua, Terra*, in allusion to the Egyptian mystical doctrine of the generation, destruction, and regeneration of all things by the four elements, *fire, air, water*, and *earth;* which doctrine passed over from the Egyptians to the Greeks, and was taught in the philosophy of Empedocles. But these Rose Croix Masons, probably, borrowed their doctrine from the Gnostics.

I Am that I Am. The name which the Great Architect directed Moses to use (Exod. iii. 14) that he might identify himself to the Israelites as the messenger sent to them by God. It is one of the modifications of the Tetragrammaton, and as such, in its Hebrew form of אהיה אשר אהיה, *eheyeh asher eheyeh* (the *e* pronounced like *a* in *fate*), has been adopted as a significant word in the high degrees of the York, American, and several other Rites. The original Hebrew words are actually in the future tense, and grammatically mean *I will be what I will be;* but all the versions give a present signification. Thus, the Vulgate has it, *I am who am;* the Septuagint, *I am he who exists;* and the Arabic paraphrase, *I am the Eternal who passes not away.* The expression seems intended to point out the eternity and self-existence of God, and such is the sense in which it is used in Masonry. (See *Eheyeh asher eheyeh*.)

Iatric Masonry. From ιατρική, the art of medicine. Ragon, in his *Orthodoxie Maçonnique* (p. 450), says that this system was instituted in the eighteenth century, and that its adepts were occupied in the search for the universal medicine. It must therefore have been a Hermetic Rite. Ragon knew very little of it, and mentions only one degree, called the "Oracle of Cos." The island of Cos was the birthplace of Hippocrates, the father of medicine, and to him the degree is dedicated. The Order or Rite has no longer any existence.

I-Colm-Kill. An island south of the Hebrides, once the seat of the Order of the Culdees, containing the ruins of the monastery of St. Columba, founded A.D. 565. Tradition plants the foundation of the Rite of Heredom on this island.

Iconoclasts. (Gr. *eikon*, image, and *klazo*, I break.) The name used to designate those in the Church, from the eighth century downward, who have been opposed to the use of sacred images, or, rather, to the paying of religious honor or reverence to such representations. Image-worship prevailed extensively in the sixth and seventh centuries in the Eastern Empire. The iconoclast movement commenced with the imperial edict issued, in 726, by the Emperor Leo III., surnamed the Isaurian, who allowed images only of the Redeemer. The second decree was issued in 730. This was opposed strenuously by Popes Gregory II. and III., but without avail.

Iconology. The science which teaches the doctrine of images and symbolic representations. It is a science collateral with Masonry, and is of great importance to the Masonic student, because it is engaged in the consideration of the meaning and history of the symbols which constitute so material a part of the Masonic system.

Idaho. In 1867, there were four Lodges in what was then the Territory of Idaho, three chartered by the Grand Lodge of Oregon, and one by the Grand Lodge of Washington Territory. In that year these Lodges met in convention and organized the Grand

Lodge of Idaho on December 16th. The Grand Lodge is migratory, holding its sessions on the first Monday in October, at such place as may be determined at the previous session. Royal Arch Masonry was introduced by the General Grand Chapter of the United States, which granted a charter for Idaho Chapter at Idaho City, September 18, 1868, for Cypress at Silver City, and Boise at Boise City, both September 20, 1870.

Idiot. Idiocy is one of the mental disqualifications for initiation. This does not, however, include a mere dulness of intellect and indocility of apprehension. These amount only to stupidity, and "the judgment of the heavy or stupid man," as Dr. Good has correctly remarked, "is often as sound in itself as that of the man of more capacious comprehension." The idiot is defined by Blackstone as "one that hath had no understanding from his nativity; and therefore is by law presumed never likely to attain any." A being thus mentally imperfect is incompetent to observe the obligations or to appreciate the instructions of Freemasonry. It is true that the word does not occur in any of the old Constitutions, but from their general tenor it is evident that idiots were excluded, because "cunning," or knowledge and skill, are everywhere deemed essential qualifications of a Mason. But the ritual law is explicit on the subject.

Idolatry. The worship paid to any created object. It was in some one of its forms the religion of the entire ancient world except the Jews. The forms of idolatry are generally reckoned as four in number. 1. Fetichism, the lowest form, consisting in the worship of animals, trees, rivers, mountains, and stones. 2. Sabianism or Sabaism, the worship of the sun, moon, and stars. 3. Sintooism, or the worship of deceased ancestors or the leaders of a nation. 4. Idealism, or the worship of abstractions or mental qualities. Oliver and his school have propounded the theory that among the idolatrous nations of antiquity, who were, of course, the descendants, in common with the monotheistic Jews, of Noah, there were the remains of certain legends and religious truths which they had received from their common ancestor, but which had been greatly distorted and perverted in the system which they practised. This system, taught in the Ancient Mysteries, he called "the Spurious Freemasonry" of antiquity.

Igne Natura Renovatur Integra. By fire, nature is perfectly renewed. See $I.\cdot.N.\cdot.R.\cdot.I.\cdot.$

Ignorance. The ignorant Freemason is a drone and an encumbrance in the Order. He who does not study the nature, the design, the history, and character of the Institution, but from the hour of his initiation neither gives nor receives any ideas that could not be shared by a profane, is of no more advantage to Masonry than Masonry is to him. The true Mason seeks

light that darkness may be dispelled, and knowledge that ignorance may be removed. The ignorant aspirant, no matter how loudly he may have asked for light, is still a blind groper in the dark.

Ih-ho. The Kabbalistic mode of reading Ho-hi, one of the forms of the Tetragrammaton. (See Ho-hi.)

I. H. S. A monogram, to which various meanings have been attached. Thus, these letters have been supposed to be the initials of *In hoc signo*, words which surrounded the cross seen by Constantine. But that inscription was in Greek; and besides, even in a Latin translation, the letter V, for *vinces*, would be required to complete it. The Church has generally accepted the monogram as containing the initials of *Iesus Hominum Salvator*, Jesus the Savior of Men; a sense in which it has been adopted by the Jesuits, who have taken it in this form, I. H̷. S., as the badge of their society. So, too, it is interpreted by the Masonic Templars, on whose banners it often appears. A later interpretation is advocated by the Cambridge Camden Society in a work published by them on the subject. In this work they contend that the monogram is of Greek origin, and is the first three letters of the Greek name, ΙΗΣΟΥΣ, JESUS. But the second of these interpretations is the one most generally received.

Ijar. אייר. The eighth month of the Hebrew civil year. It corresponds to a part of the months of April and May.

Illinois. The first Grand Lodge established in this State was in the year 1823; but this body yielded in a few years to the storm of anti-Masonry which swept over the country, and ceased to exist. Subsequently, Lodges were chartered by the Grand Lodges of Kentucky and other jurisdictions, and on the 30th of January, 1840, a convention of six Lodges was held in the town of Jacksonville, which organized the Grand Lodge of Illinois on April 6, 1840. The seat of the Grand Lodge is Springfield. A Grand Chapter, Grand Council, and Grand Commandery were subsequently established in 1850, 1854, and 1857 respectively.

Illiteracy. The word illiteracy, as signifying an ignorance of letters, an incapability to read and write, suggests the inquiry whether illiterate persons are qualified to be made Masons. There can be no doubt, from historic evidence, that at the period when the Institution was operative in its character, the members for the most part—that is, the great mass of the Fraternity—were unable to read or write. At a time when even kings made at the foot of documents the sign of the cross, "*pro ignorantia litterarum*," because they could not write their names, it could hardly be expected that an Operative Mason should be gifted with a greater share of education than his sovereign. But the change of the society from Operative to Speculative gave to it an intellectual elevation, and the philosophy and science of symbolism which was then introduced could hardly be understood by one who had no preliminary education. Accordingly, the provision in all Lodges, that initiation must be preceded by a written petition, would seem to indicate that no one is expected or desired to apply for initiation unless he can comply with that regulation, by writing, or at least signing, such a petition. The Grand Lodge of England does not leave this principle to be settled by implication, but in express words requires that a candidate shall know how to write, by inserting in its Constitution the provision that a candidate, "previous to his initiation, must subscribe his name at full length to a declaration." The official commentary on this, in an accompanying note, is, that "a Person who cannot write is consequently ineligible to be admitted into the Order," and this is now the very generally accepted law. The *ne varietur* in Masonic diplomas, which follows the signature in the margin, indicates that the holder is required to know how to sign his name.

Illuminated Theosophists. A modification of the system of Pernetty instituted at Paris by Benedict Chastanier, who subsequently succeeded in introducing it into London. It consisted of nine degrees, for an account of which see *Chastanier.*

Illuminati. This is a Latin word, signifying *the enlightened*, and hence often applied in Latin diplomas as an epithet of Freemasons.

Illuminati of Bavaria. A secret society, founded on May 1, 1776, by Adam Weishaupt, who was professor of canon law at the University of Ingolstadt. Its founder at first called it the Order of the Perfectibilists; but he subsequently gave it the name by which it is now universally known. Its professed object was, by the mutual assistance of its members, to attain the highest possible degree of morality and virtue, and to lay the foundation for the reformation of the world by the association of good men to oppose the progress of moral evil. To give to the Order a higher influence, Weishaupt connected it with the Masonic Institution, after whose system of degrees, of esoteric instruction, and of secret modes of recognition, it was organized. It has thus become confounded by superficial writers with Freemasonry, although it never could be considered as properly a Masonic Rite. Weishaupt, though a reformer in religion and a liberal in politics, had originally been a Jesuit; and he employed, therefore, in the construction of his association, the shrewdness and subtlety which distinguished the disciples of Loyola; and having been initiated in 1777 in a Lodge at Munich, he also borrowed for its use the mystical organization which was peculiar to Freemasonry. In this latter task he was greatly assisted by the Baron Von Knigge, a zealous and well-instructed Mason, who joined the Illuminati in 1780, and soon became a leader, dividing with

Weishaupt the control and direction of the Order.

In its internal organization the Order of Illuminati was divided into three great classes, namely, 1. The Nursery; 2. Symbolic Freemasonry; and 3. The Mysteries; each of which was subdivided into several degrees, making ten in all, as in the following table:

I. Nursery.

After a ceremony of preparation it began:

1. Novice.
2. Minerval.
3. Illuminatus Minor.

II. Symbolic Freemasonry.

The first three degrees were communicated without any exact respect to the divisions, and then the candidate proceeded:

4. Illuminatus Major, or Scottish Novice.
5. Illuminatus Dirigens, or Scottish Knight.

III. The Mysteries.

This class was subdivided into the Lesser and the Greater Mysteries.

The Lesser Mysteries were:

6. Presbyter, Priest, or Epopt.
7. Prince, or Regent.

The Greater Mysteries were:

8. Magus.
9. Rex, or King.

Anyone otherwise qualified could be received into the degree of Novice at the age of eighteen; and after a probation of not less than a year he was admitted to the Second and Third degrees, and so on to the higher degrees; though but few reached the Ninth and Tenth degrees, in which the inmost secret designs of the Order were contained, and, in fact, it is said that these last degrees were never thoroughly worked up.

The Illuminati selected for themselves Order names, which were always of a classical character. Thus, Weishaupt called himself Spartacus, Knigge was Philo, and Zwack, another leader, was known as Cato. They gave also fictitious names to countries. Ingolstadt, where the Order originated, was called Eleusis; Austria was Egypt, in reference to the Egyptian darkness of that kingdom, which excluded all Masonry from its territories; Munich was called Athens, and Vienna was Rome. The Order had also its calendar, and the months were designated by peculiar names; as, Dimeh for January, and Bemeh for February. They had also a cipher, in which the official correspondence of the members was conducted. The character ▭, now so much used by Masons to represent a Lodge, was invented and first used by the Illuminati.

The Order was at first very popular, and enrolled no less than two thousand names upon its registers, among whom were some of the most distinguished men of Germany. It extended rapidly into other countries, and its Lodges were to be found in France, Belgium, Holland, Denmark, Sweden, Poland, Hungary, and Italy.

The original design of Illuminism was undoubtedly the elevation of the human race. Knigge, who was one of its most prominent working members, and the author of several of its degrees, was a religious man, and would never have united with it had its object been, as has been charged, to abolish Christianity. But it cannot be denied, that in process of time abuses had crept into the Institution, and that by the influence of unworthy men the system became corrupted; yet the coarse accusations of such writers as Barruel and Robison are known to be exaggerated, and some of them altogether false. The *Conversations-Lexicon*, for instance, declares that the society had no influence whatever on the French Revolution, which is charged upon it by these as well as other writers.

But Illuminism came directly and professedly in conflict with the Jesuits and with the Roman Church, whose tendencies were to repress the freedom of thought. The priests became, therefore, its active enemies, and waged war so successfully against it, that on June 22, 1784, the Elector of Bavaria issued an edict for its suppression. Many of its members were fined or imprisoned, and some, among whom was Weishaupt, were compelled to flee the country. The edicts of the Elector of Bavaria were repeated in March and August, 1785, and the Order began to decline, so that by the end of the last century it had ceased to exist. Adopting Masonry only as a means for its own more successful propagation, and using it only as incidental to its own organization, it exercised while in prosperity no favorable influence on the Masonic Institution, nor any unfavorable effect on it by its dissolution.

Illuminati of Avignon. See *Avignon, Illuminati of.*

Illuminati of Stockholm. An Order but little known; mentioned by Ragon in his *Catalogue* as having been instituted for the propagation of Martinism.

Illuminism. The system or Rite practised by the German Illuminati is so called.

Illustrious. A title given in the Ancient and Accepted Scottish Rite to all those who possess the Thirty-second or Thirty-third Degree.

Illustrious Elect of the Fifteen. The title now generally given to the *Elect of Fifteen*, which see.

Imaum. The appellation given to the most honored teacher of Mohammedanism. The title of the Sultan, as the spiritual chief of all Moslems.

Imitative Societies. A title sometimes given to those secret societies which, imitating the general organization of Freemasonry, differ from it entirely in their character and object. Such, in the last century, when at

one time they abounded, were the Bucks, the Sawyers, the Gormogons, and the Gregorians; and, in the present century, the Odd Fellows, the Good Templars, and the Knights of Pythias. Most of them imitate the Masons in their external appearance, such as the wearing of aprons, collars, and jewels, and in calling their places of meeting, by a strange misnomer, Lodges. But in these points is their only resemblance to the original Institution.

Immanuel. A Hebrew word signifying "God with us," from עמנו, *immanu*, "with us," and אל, *el*, "God." It was the symbolical name given by the prophet Isaiah to the child who was announced to Ahaz and the people of Judah as the sign which God would give of their deliverance from their enemies, and afterward applied by the Apostle Matthew to the Messiah born of the Virgin. As one of the appellations of Christ, it has been adopted as a significant word in modern Templarism, where, however, the form of *Emanuel* is most usually employed.

Immaterialism. A doctrine relating to the quality of God and of the human soul, showing that He forms an absolute contrast to matter, and is the basis of the qualities of eternity, omnipotence, and unchangeableness. The immateriality of the soul includes simplicity as another of its qualities.

Immortality of the Soul. Very wisely has Max Müller said (*Chips*, i., 45) that "without a belief in personal immortality, religion is surely like an arch resting on one pillar, like a bridge ending in an abyss"; and he cites passages from the Vedas to show that to the ancient Brahmans the idea was a familiar one. Indeed, almost all the nations of the earth with whose religious faith we are acquainted recognize the dogma, although sometimes in vague and, perhaps, materialistic forms.

It was the professed teaching of the Ancient Mysteries, where, in the concluding rites of their initiation, the restoration of the hero of their legend was a symbol of the immortal life. So, too, the same doctrine is taught by a similar legendary and symbolic method in the Third Degree of Masonry.

Archdeacon Mant thus describes the differences, in the teaching of this doctrine of immortality, between what he calls, after the school of Oliver, the spurious and the true Freemasonry:

"Whereas the heathens had taught this doctrine only by the application of a fable to their purpose, the wisdom of the pious Grand Master of the Israelitish Masons took advantage of a real circumstance, which would more forcibly impress the sublime truths he intended to inculcate upon the minds of all brethren."

It will be doubted by some of our modern skeptics whether the Hiramic myth is entitled to more authenticity as an historic narrative than the Osiric or the Dionysian; but it will not be denied that, while they all taught the same dogma of immortality, the method of teaching by symbolism was in all the same.

Immovable Jewels. See *Jewels of a Lodge.*

Implements. The Operative Freemasons of the Middle Ages gave to certain of their implements—the most important of which were the square, the compasses, the stone-hammer, or gavel, and the foot-rule—a special symbolic meaning. When the Operative Institution was merged in the Speculative, the custom of thus spiritualizing, as it was called, these implements was continued; but the system of symbolic instruction has been so greatly enlarged and improved as to consti-tute, in fact, the characteristic feature of modern Freemasonry—a feature which widely distinguishes it from all other socie-ties, whether secret or open. Thus, the twenty-four-inch gage and gavel are be-stowed upon the Entered Apprentice be-cause these are the implements used in the quarries in hewing the stones and fitting them for the builder's use, an occupation which, for its simplicity, is properly suited to the un-skilled apprentice. The square, level, and plumb are employed in the still further prep-aration of these stones and in adjusting them to their proper positions. This is the labor of the craftsmen, and hence to the Fellow-Craft are they presented. But the work is not com-pleted until the stones thus adjusted have been accurately examined by the master work-man, and permanently secured in their places by cement. This is accomplished by the trowel, and hence this implement is entrusted to the Master Mason. Thus, the tools at-tached to each degree admonish the Mason, as an Apprentice, to prepare his mind for the reception of the great truths which are here-after to be unfolded to him; as a Fellow-Craft, to mark their importance and adapt them to their proper uses; and as a Master, to adorn their beauty by the practise of brotherly love and kindness, the cement that binds all Ma-sons in one common Fraternity.

There is no doubt, as Findel says (*Hist.*, p. 68), that the stone-masons were not the first who symbolized the implements of their craft. But they had reason, above all other gilds, for investing them with a far higher worth, and associating them with a spiritual mean-ing, on account of the sacred calling to which they were devoted. By the erection of churches, the Master Mason not only per-petuated his own name, but assisted in giving glory to God, in spreading the knowledge of Christianity, and in stimulating to the prac-tise of the Christian virtues. And hence the church-building Masons naturally gave a more sacred signification in their symbolism to the implements employed in such holy pur-poses. And thus it was that they transmitted to their successors, the Speculative Masons, the same sacred interpretation of their sym-bols. Modern Freemasonry has been derived from an association of church architects, and this accounts for the religious character of its symbolism. Had it been the offspring of the Templars, as Ramsay contends, its symbolism would have been undoubtedly military, some-

what like that employed by St. Paul in his epistle to the Ephesians.

Impost. The point where an arch rests on a wall or column. Husenbeth says *imposts* were "members of a secret society of Tyrian artists who were hired by King Solomon to erect the temple, in order to distinguish them from the Jews, who performed the more hum-ble labors, were honored with the epithet of *free* annexed to the name of builder or Mason, and, being talented foreigners, were freed from the usual imposts paid to the state by the sub-jects of Solomon."

Impostors. Impostors in Masonry may be either profanes who, never having been in-itiated, yet endeavor to pass themselves for regular Freemasons, or Masons who, having been expelled or suspended from the Order, seek to conceal the fact and still claim the priv-ileges of members in good standing. The false pretensions of the former class are easily de-tected, because their real ignorance must after a proper trial become apparent. The latter class, having once been invested with the proper instructions, can stand the test of an examination; and their true position must be discovered only by information derived from the Lodges which have suspended or expelled them. The Tiler's oath is intended to meet each of these cases, because it requires every strange visitor to declare that he has been lawfully initiated, and that he is in good standing. But perjury added to im-posture will easily escape this test. Hence the necessity for the utmost caution, and there-fore the Charges of 1722 say, "You are cau-tiously to examine a strange brother in such a method as prudence shall direct you, that you may not be imposed on by an ignorant false pretender, whom you are to reject with con-tempt and derision, and beware of giving him any hints of knowledge." (*Constitutions*, 1723, p. 55.) The Masonic rule is, that it is better that ninety and nine true brethren be rejected than that one impostor be admitted.

In Activity. When a Lodge is performing all its duties and functions, and is regularly represented in the Grand Lodge, it is said to be *in activity*, in contradistinction to a Lodge which has ceased to work or hold communi-cations, which is said to be *dormant*.

Inauguration. A word applied by the ancient Romans to the ceremony by which, after the *augurs* had been consulted, some thing or person was solemnly consecrated. The consecration of a Master of a Lodge to his office, which is equivalent to the ancient in-auguration of a priest or king, is in Masonic language called an *Installation*, which see.

Incense. The use of incense as a part of the Divine worship was common to all the nations of antiquity. Among the Hebrews, the Egyptians, and the Hindus it seems to have been used for no other purposes; but the Persians burnt it also before the king. The Roman Catholic Church has borrowed the usage from the ancients; and the burning of incense in certain sacred rites is also practised in Masonry, especially in the high degrees.

In Scripture, incense is continually spoken of, both in the Old and the New Testaments, as a symbol of prayer. Thus the Psalmist says (cxli. 2), "Let my prayer be set before thee as incense." It has in Masonry a similar signification; and hence the pot of incense has been adopted as a symbol in the Third Degree, typifying the pure heart from which prayers and aspirations arise, as incense does from the pot or incensorium, as an acceptable sacrifice to the Deity.

Incense, Regulations for Use of. From the Talmud we learn that the mixture of the perfume of incense was composed of balm, mycha, galbanum, frankincense, of each an equal weight, viz., 70 manehs; myrrh, cassia, spikenard, and saffron, of each an equal weight, 16 manehs; costus, 12 manehs; the rind of an odoriferous tree, 3 manehs; cinnamon, 9 manehs; soap of Carsina, 9 kabs; wine of capers, 3 seahs and 3 kabs, and if caper wine could not be had, strong white wine was substituted for it; salt of Sodom, the fourth part of a kab, and of an herb called maa-a-lay o-shon, a small quantity. Rabbi Nathan said a small quantity of the amber of Jordan. If honey was mixed with it, it was profane; and if it was deficient in any one of its ingredients, the priest was accounted worthy of death.

Rabbi Simeon, the son of Gamliel, says that the balm issues from an incision in the tree called balsamon. The soap of Carsina was to refine the omycha, that it might have a handsome appearance. The wine of capers was brought to soak the cloves or mycha therein, that it might become hard. And though the "water from the feet" was proper for the purpose, yet it was not used because it was not decent to bring it into the temple.

Inchoate Lodges. From the Latin, *inchoatus*, unfinished, incomplete. Lodges working under the dispensation of the Grand Master are said to be "inchoate" or incomplete, because they do not possess all the rights and prerogatives that belong to a Lodge working under the Warrant of constitution of a Grand Lodge. The same term is applied to Chapters which work under the dispensation of a Grand High Priest. (See *Lodges.*)

Incommunicable. The Tetragrammaton, so called because it was not common to, and could not be bestowed upon, nor shared by, any other being. It was proper to the true God alone. Thus Drusius (*Tetragrammaton, sive de Nomine Dei proprio*, p. 108) says, "Nomen quatuor literarum proprie et absolute non tribui nisi Deo vero. Unde doctores catholici dicunt *incommunicabile* [not common] esse creaturæ."

That is: "The name of four letters, which is not to be attributed, properly and absolutely, except to the true God. Whence the Catholic doctors say that it is *incommunicable*, not common to or to be shared by any creature." Oliver, in his *Symbolic Dictionary*, commits a curious blunder in supposing that the Incommunicable Name is the Name not to be communicated to or pronounced by anyone; thus incorrectly confounding the words *incommuni-*

cable and *ineffable*. Although the two epithets are applied to the same name, yet the qualities of incommunicability and ineffability are very different.

Incorporation. By an act of incorporation, the supreme legislature of a country creates a corporation or body politic, which is defined by Mr. Kyd (*Corp.*, i., 13) to be "a collection of many individuals united in one body, under a special denomination, having perpetual succession under an artificial form, and vested by the policy of the law with a capacity of acting in several respects as an individual, particularly of taking and granting property, contracting obligations, and of suing and being sued; of enjoying privileges and immunities in common, and of exercising a variety of political rights." Some Grand Lodges in America are incorporated by act of the General Assembly of their respective States; others are not, and these generally hold their property through Trustees. In 1768, an effort was made in the Grand Lodge of England to petition Parliament for incorporation, and after many discussions the question was submitted to the Lodges; a large majority of whom having agreed to the measure in 1772, a bill was introduced in Parliament by the Deputy Grand Master, but, being approved on its second reading, at the request of several of the Fraternity, who had petitioned the House against it, it was withdrawn by the mover, and thus the design of an incorporation fell to the ground. Perhaps the best system of Masonic incorporation in existence is that of the Grand Lodge of South Carolina. There the act, by which the Grand Lodge was incorporated, in 1817, delegates to that body the power of incorporating its subordinates; so that a Lodge, whenever it receives from the Grand Lodge a Warrant of constitution, acquires thereby at once all the rights of a corporate body, which it ceases to exercise whenever the said Warrant is revoked by the Grand Lodge.

Objections have been made to the incorporation of Lodges in consequence of some of the legal results which would follow. An incorporated Lodge becomes subject to the surveillance of the courts of law, from which an unincorporated Lodge is exempt. Thus, a Mason expelled by an unincorporated Lodge must look for his redress to the Grand Lodge alone. But if the Lodge be incorporated, he may apply to the courts for a restoration of his franchise as a member. Masonic discipline would thus be seriously affected. The objection to incorporation is, it seems, founded on good reasons.

Increase of Wages. (*Augmentation de gages.*) To ask for an increase of wages, is, in the technical language of French Masonry, to apply for advancement to a higher degree.

Indefeasible. Unavoidable, that which cannot be voided or taken away. The word is thus used in the second of the Charges of 1722, where, speaking of a brother who has been guilty of treason or rebellion, it is, said that he cannot for this cause be expelled from the Lodge, and that "his relation to it remains *indefeasible.*" (*Constitutions*, 1723, p. 50.) It is a law term, which is usually applied to an estate or right which cannot be defeated.

Indelibility. The indelibility of the Masonic character, as expressed in the often-repeated maxim, "once a Mason, always a Mason," is universally admitted. That is to say, no voluntary or even forced withdrawal from the Order can cancel certain obligations which have been contracted, and place the person withdrawing in precisely the same relative position toward the Institution that he had occupied before his initiation.

Indented Tarsel. In the old rituals these words were used for what is now called the tessellated border. (See *Tarsel.*)

Indented Tessel. The ornamented border which surrounds the Mosaic pavement. (See *Tessellated Border.*)

India. In 1728, Lord Kingston, Grand Master of England, granted a Deputation to George Pomfret, Esq., for Bengal, in the East Indies, but no action seems to have been taken, under that authority, until 1730, in which year a Lodge meeting at The East India Arms, Fort William, No. 72, was established at Calcutta; and this may therefore be considered as the era of the introduction of Freemasonry into India. The next was established at Madras in 1752; a third at Bombay in 1758; and a fourth at Calcutta in 1761. From that time Masonry made rapid progress in India, and in 1779 there was scarcely a town of importance in Hindustan in which there was not a Lodge. The dissensions of the Ancients and the Moderns, which commenced in England in 1751, unhappily spread to India, but all differences were reconciled in 1786, by the establishment of a Provincial Grand Lodge, of which Brigadier-General Horne was appointed Provincial Grand Master by the Duke of Cumberland. Templarism and Royal Arch Masonry were subsequently introduced, Chapters and Commanderies are now in successful operation.

Indian Calendar. The Indian or Hindu year begins in April, thus: 1st Vaisakha, 13th April; 1st Jyaishtha, 14th May; 1st Ashadha, 14th June; 1st Sravana, 16th July; 1st Bhadrapada, 16th August; 1st Asvina, 16th September; 1st Kartlika, 17th October; 1st Agrahayana or Margasirsha, 16th November; 1st Pansha, 15th December; 1st Magha, 13th January; 1st Phalguna, 12th February; 1st Caitra, 13th March. The days of the week, commencing with Sunday, are Aditya, Soma, Mangala, Budha, Guru, Sukra, and Sani. The Hindu era, until April 13, 1885, was 1937.

Indian Faith. See *Buddhism.*

Indiana. Freemasonry was introduced into the Territory now known as the State of Indiana as early as 1795, by those connected with Army Lodges on the northwest frontier, but the first Lodge organized was the Vincennes Lodge, No. 15, at Vincennes, which was constituted under a Warrant granted by the Grand Lodge of Kentucky. Five other Lodges were subsequently chartered by the same authority. On December 3, 1817, a convention assembled at Corydon, at which were present the representatives of six chartered Lodges, and two under dispensation from Kentucky, and one under dispensation from Ohio. The convention, having taken the preliminary steps, adjourned to meet at Madison on January 12, 1818, on which day the Grand Lodge was organized.

The Grand Chapter was established in 1845; the Grand Commandery on May 16, 1854, and the Grand Council of Royal and Select Masters on December 11, 1855.

Indifferents. A secret society of men and women established in Paris, in 1738, in imitation of Freemasonry. The object of the society was to protect its members from the influence of love, and hence it wore, as an appropriate device, a jewel representing an icicle.

Indische Mysterien. Indian Mysteries. In the German Cyclopædia we find the following: "The East Indians have still their mysteries, which it is very probable they received from the ancient Egyptians. (?) These mysteries are in the possession of the Brahmans, and their ancestors were the ancient Brachmen.

"It is only the sons of these priests who are eligible to initiation. Had a grown-up youth of the Brachmen sufficiently hardened his body, learned to subdue his passions, and given the requisite proofs of his abilities at school, he must submit to an especial proof of his fortitude before he was admitted into the mysteries, which proofs were given in a cavern. A second cavern in the middle of a high hill contained the statues of nature, which were neither made of gold, nor of silver, nor of earth, nor of stone, but of a very hard material resembling wood, the composition of which was unknown to any mortal.

"These statues are said to have been given by God to his Son, to serve as models by which he might form all created beings. Upon the crown of one of these statues stood the likeness of Bruma, who was the same with them as Osiris was with the Egyptians. The inner part, and the entrance also into this cavern, was quite dark, and those who wished to enter into it were obliged to seek the way with a lighted torch. A door led into the inner part, on the opening of which the water that surrounded the border of the cavern broke loose.

"If the candidate for initiation was worthy, he opened the door quite easily, and a spring of the purest water flowed gently upon him and purified him. Those, on the contrary, who were guilty of any crime, could not open the door; and if they were candid, they confessed their sins to the priest, and besought him to turn away the anger of the gods by prayer and fasting.

"In this cavern, on a certain day, the Brachmen held their annual assembly. Some of them dwelt constantly there; others came there only in the spring and harvest—conversed with each other upon the doctrines contained in their mysteries, contemplated the hieroglyphics upon the statues, and endeavored to decipher them. Those among the initiated who were in the lowest degrees, and who could not comprehend the sublime doctrines of one God, worshiped the sun and other inferior divinities. This was also the religion of the common people. The Brahmans, the present inhabitants of India, those pure descendants of the ancient Brachmen, do not admit any person into their mysteries without having first diligently inquired into his character and capabilities, and duly proved his fortitude and prudence. No one could be initiated until he had attained a certain age; and before his initiation the novice had to prepare himself by prayer, fasting, and almsgiving, and other good works, for many days.

"When the appointed day arrived he bathed himself and went to the Guru, or chief Brahman, who kept one of his own apartments ready in which to perform this ceremony. Before he was admitted he was asked if he earnestly desired to be initiated?—if it was not curiosity which induced him to do so?—if he felt himself strong enough to perform the ceremonies which would be prescribed to him for the whole of his life, without the exception of a single day?

"He was at the same time advised to defer the ceremony for a time, if he had not sufficient confidence in his strength. If the youth continued firm in his resolution, and showed a zealous disposition to enter into the paths of righteousness, the Guru addressed a charge to him upon the manner of living, to which he was about to pledge himself for the future. He threatened him with the punishment of heaven if he conducted himself wickedly; promised him, on the contrary, the most glorious rewards if he would constantly keep the path of righteousness. After this exhortation, and having received his pledge, the candidate was conducted to the prepared chamber, the door of which stood open, that all those who assembled might participate in the offering about to be made.

"Different fruits were thrown into the fire, while the High Priest, with many ceremonies, prayed that God might be present with them in that sacred place. The Guru then conducted the youth behind a curtain, both having their heads covered, and then gently pronounced into his ear a word of one or two syllables, which he was as gently to repeat into the ear of the Guru, that no other person might hear it. In this word was the prayer which the initiated was to repeat as often as he could for the whole day, yet in the greatest stillness and without ever moving the lips. Neither durst he discover this sacred word unto any person. No European has ever been able to discover this word, so sacred is this secret to them. When the newly initiated has repeated this command several times, then the chief Brahman instructs him in the ceremonies, teaches him several songs to the honor of God, and finally dismisses him with many exhortations

to pursue a virtuous course of life." (See *Pitris*.)

Induction. 1. The Master of a Lodge, when installed into office, is said to be inducted into the Oriental Chair of King Solomon. The same term is applied to the reception of a candidate into the Past Master's Degree. The word is derived from the language of the law, where the giving a clerk or parson possession of his benefice is called his induction. 2. Induction is also used to signify initiation into the degree called Thrice Illustrious Order of the Cross.

Inductor. The Senior and Junior Inductors are officers in a Council of the Thrice Illustrious Order of the Cross, corresponding to the Senior and Junior Deacons.

Industry. A virtue inculcated amongst Masons, because by it they are enabled not only to support themselves and families, but to contribute to the relief of worthy distressed brethren. "All Masons," say the Charges of 1722, "shall work honestly on working days that they may live creditably on holy days." (*Constitutions*, 1723, p. 52.) The Masonic symbol of industry is the beehive, which is used in the Third Degree.

Ineffable Degrees. From the Latin word, *ineffabilis*, that which can not or ought not to be spoken or expressed. The degrees from the Fourth to the Fourteenth inclusive, of the Ancient and Accepted Scottish Rite, which are so called because they are principally engaged in the investigation and contemplation of the Ineffable name.

Ineffable Name. It was forbidden to the Jews to pronounce the Tetragrammaton or sacred name of God; a reverential usage which is also observed in Masonry. Hence the Tetragrammaton is called the Ineffable Name. As in Masonry, so in all the secret societies of antiquity, much mystery has been attached to the Divine Name, which it was considered unlawful to pronounce, and for which some other word was substituted. Adonai was among the Hebrews the substitute for the Tetragrammaton.

Ineffable Triangle. The two triangles incrusted one upon the other, containing the Ineffable Name in Enochian characters, represented in the Eleventh of the Ineffable series. Good and evil, light and darkness, life and death, are here not wanting in symbolism, foreshadow- ing the philosophic degrees, and furnishing the true original of the two interlaced triangles adopted in modern Masonry. (See *Enochian Alphabet*.)

Ineligible. Who are and who are not ineligible for initiation into the mysteries of Freemasonry is treated of under the head of *Qualifications of Candidates*, which see.

Information, Lawful. One of the modes of recognizing a stranger as a true brother, is from the "lawful information" of a third party. No Mason can lawfully give information of another's qualifications unless he has actually tested him by the strictest trial and examination, or knows that it has been done by another. But it is not every Mason who is competent to give "lawful information." Ignorant and unskilful brethren cannot do so, because they are incapable of discovering truth or of detecting error. A "rusty Mason" should never attempt to examine a stranger, and certainly, if he does, his opinion as to the result is worth nothing. If the information given is on the ground that the party who is vouched for has been seen sitting in a Lodge, care must be taken to inquire if it was a "just and legally constituted Lodge of Master Masons." A person may forget from the lapse of time, and vouch for a stranger as a Master Mason, when the Lodge in which he saw him was only opened in the First or Second Degree. Information given by letter, or through a third party, is irregular. The person giving the information, the one receiving it, and the one of whom it is given, should all be present at the same time, for otherwise there would be no certainty of identity. The information must be positive, not founded on belief or opinion, but derived from a legitimate source. And, lastly, it must not have been received casually, but for the very purpose of being used for Masonic purposes. For one to say to another, in the course of a desultory conversation, "A. B. is a Mason," is not sufficient. He may not be speaking with due caution, under the expectation that his words will be considered of weight. He must say something to this effect: "I know this man to be a Master Mason, for such or such reasons, and you may safely recognize him as such." This alone will insure the necessary care and proper observance of prudence.

Inherent Rights of a Grand Master. This has been a subject of fertile discussion among Masonic jurists, although only a few have thought proper to deny the existence of such rights. Upon the theory which, however recently controverted, has very generally been recognized, that Grand Masters existed before Grand Lodges were organized, it must be evident that the rights of a Grand Master are of two kinds—those, namely, which he derives from the Constitution of a Grand Lodge of which he has been made the presiding officer, and those which exist in the office independent of any Constitution, because they are derived from the landmarks and ancient usages of the Craft. The rights and prerogatives which depend on and are prescribed by the Constitution may be modified or rescinded by that instrument. They differ in different jurisdictions, because one Grand Lodge may confer more or less power upon its presiding officer than another; and they differ at different times, because the Constitution of every Grand Lodge is subject, in regard to its internal regulations, to repeated alteration and amendment. These may be called the accidental rights of a Grand Master, because they are derived from the accidental provisions of a Grand Lodge, and have in them nothing essential to the integrity of the office. It is unnecessary to enumerate them, because they may be found in varied modifications in the Constitutions of all Grand Lodges. But the rights and prerogatives which Grand Masters are supposed to have possessed, not as the presiding officers of an artificial body, but as the rulers of the Craft in general, before Grand Lodges came into existence, and which are dependent, not on any prescribed rules which may be enacted to-day and repealed to-morrow, but on the long-continued usages of the Order and the concessions of the Craft from time out of mind, inhere in the office, and cannot be augmented or diminished by the action of any authority, because they are landmarks, and therefore unchangeable. These are called the *inherent rights* of a Grand Master. They comprise the right to preside over the Craft whenever assembled, to grant dispensations, and, as a part of that power, to make Masons at sight.

In Hoc Signo Vinces. On the Grand Standard of a Commandery of Knights Templar these words are inscribed over "a blood-red Passion Cross," and they constitute in part the motto of the American branch of the Order. Their meaning, "by this sign thou shalt conquer," is a substantial, but not literal, translation of the original Greek, ἐν τούτῳ νίκα. For the origin of the motto, we must go back to a well-known legend of the Church, which has, however, found more doubters than believers among the learned. Eusebius, who wrote a life of Constantine, says that while the emperor was in Gaul, in the year 312, preparing for war with his rival, Maxentius, about the middle hours of the day, as the sun began to verge toward its setting, he saw in the heavens, with his own eyes, the sun surmounted with the trophy of the cross, which was composed of light, and a legend annexed, which said *"by this conquer."* This account Eusebius affirms to be in the words of Constantine. Lactantius, who places the occurrence at a later date and on the eve of a battle with Maxentius, in which the latter was defeated, relates it not as an actual occurrence, but as a dream or vision; and this is now the generally received opinion of those who do not deem the whole legend a fabrication. On the next day Constantine had an image of this cross made into a banner, called the *labarum*, which he ever afterward used as the imperial standard. Eusebius describes it very fully. It was not a Passion Cross, such as is now used on the modern Templar standard, but the monogram of Christ. The shaft was a very long spear. On the top was a crown composed of gold and precious stones, and containing the sacred symbol, namely, the Greek letter *rho* or P, intersected by the *chi* or X, which two letters are the first and second of the name ΧΡΙΣΤΟΣ, or CHRIST. If, then, the Templars retain the motto on their banner, they should, for the sake of historical accuracy, discard the Passion Cross, and replace it with the Constantinian Chronogram, or Cross of the Labarum. But the truth is, that the ancient Templars used neither the Passion Cross, nor that of Constantine, nor yet the motto *in hoc signo vinces* on their standard. Their only banner was the black and white Beauseant, and at the bottom of it was inscribed their motto, "Non nobis Domine, non nobis, sed nomini tuo da gloriam "—*not unto us, O Lord, not unto us, but unto thee give the glory.* This was the song or shout of victory sung by the Templars when triumphant in battle.

In Memoriam. Latin. As a memorial. Words frequently placed at the heads of pages in the transactions of Grand Lodges on which are inscribed the names of brethren who have died during the past year. The fuller phrase, of which they are an abbreviated form, is "In perpetuam rei memoriam," *As a perpetual memorial of the event.* Words often inscribed on pillars erected in commemoration of some person or thing.

Inigo Jones MS. R. F. Gould (*History of F. M.*, vol. i., p. 63) informs us that this MS. was published only in the *Masonic Magazine*, July, 1881. A very curious folio MS., ornamented title and drawing by Inigo Jones, old red morocco, gilt leaves, dated 1607, was sold by Puttick & Simpson, November 12, 1879, and described as "The Ancient Constitutions of the Free and Accepted Masons." The late Bro. Woodford became its possessor, who mentions it as "a curious and valuable MS. *per se*, not only on account of its special verbiage, but because it possesses a frontispiece of Masons at work, with the words 'Inigo Jones delin.' at the bottom. It is also highly ornamented throughout, both in the capital letters and with 'finials.' It is of date 1607. . . . It is a peculiarly interesting MS. in that it differs from all known transcripts in many points, and agrees with no one copy extant." Bro. Gould remarks, "This, one of the latest 'discoveries,' is certainly to be classed amongst the most valuable of existing versions of our manuscript 'Constitutions.'" It is now the property of the Provincial Grand Lodge of Worcestershire, and has been reproduced by the Quatuor Coronati Lodge. It was probably a copy of a much earlier MS., and is considered to belong to the latter half of the seventeenth century, and never to have belonged to Inigo Jones.

Initiate. (*Initiatus.*) 1. The Fifth and last degree of the Order of the Temple; 2. The Eleventh Degree of the Rite of Philalethes; 3. The candidate in any of the degrees of Masonry is called an Initiate.

Initiate in the Egyptian Secrets. The Second Degree in the Rite of African Architects.

Initiate in the Mysteries. The Twenty-first Degree in the Metropolitan Chapter of France.

Initiate in the Profound Mysteries. The Sixty-second Degree of the collection of the Metropolitan Chapter of France.

Initiate into the Sciences, The. Bro. Kenneth Mackenzie, in the *Royal Masonic Cyclopædia*, informs us that this is the title of the Second Degree of a Masonic system founded on the doctrines and principles of Pythagoras.

Initiated Knight and Brother of Asia. The Thirty-second Degree of the Order of Initiated Brothers of Asia. (See *Asia, Initiated Knights and Brothers of*.)

Initiation. A term used by the Romans to designate admission into the mysteries of their sacred and secret rites. It is derived from the word *initia*, which signifies the first principles of a science. Thus Justin (*Lib.* xi., c. 7) says of Midas, King of Phrygia, that he was initiated into the mysteries by Orpheus. "Ab Orpheo sacrorum solemnibus initiatus." The Greeks used the term Μυσταγωγία, from μυστηριον, a mystery. From the Latin, the Masons have adopted the word to signify a reception into their Order. It is sometimes specially applied to a reception into the First Degree, but he who has been made an Entered Apprentice is more correctly said to be *Entered.* (See *Mysteries*.)

Inner Guard. An officer of a Lodge, according to the English system, whose functions correspond in some particulars with those of the Junior Deacon in the American Rite. His duties are to admit visitors, to receive candidates, and to obey the commands of the Junior Warden. This officer is unknown in the American system.

Inner Order. Name of the sixth grade of Von Hund's Templar system.

Innovations. There is a well-known maxim of the law which says *Omnis innovatio plus novitate perturbat quam utilitate prodest*, that is, every innovation occasions more harm and disarrangement by its novelty than benefit by its actual utility. This maxim is peculiarly applicable to Freemasonry, whose system is opposed to all innovations. Thus Dr. Dalcho says, in his *Ahiman Rezon* (p. 191), "Antiquity is dear to a Mason's heart; innovation is treason, and saps the venerable fabric of the Order." In accordance with this sentiment, we find the installation charges of the Master of a Lodge affirming that "it is not in the power of any man or body of men to make innovations in the body of Masonry."

By the "body of Masonry" is here meant, undoubtedly, the landmarks, which have always been declared to be unchangeable. The non-essentials, such as the local and general regulations and the lectures, are not included in this term. The former are changing every day, according as experience or caprice suggests improvement or alteration. The most important of these changes in this country has been the abolition of the Quarterly Communications of the Grand Lodge, and the substitution for them, except, perhaps, in a single State, of an Annual Communication. But, after all, this is, perhaps, only a recurrence to first usages; for, although Anderson says that in 1717 the Quarterly Communications "were revived," there is no evidence extant that before that period the Masons ever met except once a year in their "General Assembly." If so, the change in 1717 was an innovation, and not that which has almost universally prevailed in America.

The lectures, which are but the commentaries on the ritual and the interpretation of the symbolism, have been subjected, from the time of Anderson to the present day, to repeated modifications.

But notwithstanding the repugnance of Masons to innovations, a few have occurred in the Order. Thus, on the formation of the Grand Lodge of Ancients, as they called themselves in contradistinction to the regular Grand Lodge of England, which was styled the Grand Lodge of Moderns, the former body, to prevent the intrusion of the latter upon their meetings, made changes in some of the modes of recognition—changes which, although Dalcho has said that they amounted to no more than a dispute "whether the glove should be placed first upon the right hand or on the left" (*Ahim. Rez.*, p. 193), were among the causes of continuous acrimony among the two bodies, which was only healed, in 1813, by a partial sacrifice of principle on the part of the legitimate Grand Lodge, and have perpetuated differences which still exist among the English and American and the continental Freemasons.

But the most important innovation which sprang out of this unfortunate schism is that which is connected with the Royal Arch Degree. On this subject there have been two theories: One, that the Royal Arch Degree originally constituted a part of the Master's Degree, and that it was dissevered from it by the Ancients; the other, that it never had any existence until it was invented by Ramsay, and adopted by Dermott for his Ancient Grand Lodge. If the first, which is the most probable and the most generally received opinion, be true, then the regular or Modern Grand Lodge committed an innovation in continuing the disseverance at the union in 1813. If the second be the true theory, then the Grand Lodge equally perpetuated an innovation in recognizing it as legal, and declaring, as it did, that "Ancient Craft Masonry consists of three degrees, including the Holy Royal Arch." But however the innovation may have been introduced, the Royal Arch Degree has now become, so far as the York and American Rites are concerned, well settled and recognized as an integral part of the Masonic system.

About the same time there was another innovation attempted in France. The adherents of the Pretender, Charles Edward, sought to give to Masonry a political bias in favor of the exiled house of Stuarts,

and, for this purpose, altered the interpretation of the great legend of the Third Degree, so as to make it applicable to the execution or, as they called it, the martyrdom of Charles I. But this attempted innovation was not successful, and the system in which this lesson was practised has ceased to exist, although its workings are now and then seen in some of the high degrees, without, however, any manifest evil effect.

On the whole, the spirit of Freemasonry, so antagonistic to innovation, has been successfully maintained; and an investigator of the system as it prevailed in the year 1717, and as it is maintained at the present day, will not refrain from wonder at the little change which has been brought about by the long cycle of one hundred and fifty years.

I∴N∴R∴I∴ The initials of the Latin sentence which was placed upon the cross: *Jesus Nazarenus Rex Judæorum.* The Rosicrucians used them as the initials of one of their Hermetic secrets: *Igne Natura Renovatur Integra*, "By fire, nature is perfectly renewed." They also adopted them to express the names of their three elementary principles—salt, sulphur, and mercury—by making them the initials of the sentence, *Igne Nitrum Roris Invenitur.* Ragon finds in the equivalent Hebrew letters יגרי the initials of the Hebrew names of the ancient elements: *Iaminim*, water; *Nour*, fire; *Ruach*, air; and *Iebschah*, earth.

Insect Shermah. A Jewish belief that the Solomonian Temple was constructed by Divine means, that the stones were squared and polished by a specially created worm called *samis*, and that the stones by innate power came to the temple ground, and were placed in position by angelic aid. The worm has been designated "the Insect Shermah."

Insignia. See *Jewels, Official.*

Inspector. See *Sovereign Grand Inspector-General.*

Installation. The act by which an officer is put in possession of the place he is to fill. In Masonry it is, therefore, applied to the induction of one who has been elected into his office. The officers of a Lodge, before they can proceed to discharge their functions, must be installed. The officers of a new Lodge are installed by the Grand Master, or by some Past Master deputed by him to perform the ceremony. Formerly, the Master was installed by the Grand Master, the Wardens by the Grand Wardens, and the Secretary and Treasurer by the Grand Secretary and Treasurer; but now this custom is not continued. At the election of the officers of an old Lodge, the Master is installed by his predecessor or some Past Master present, and the Master elect then installs his subordinate officers. No officer after his installation can resign. At his installation, the Master receives the degree of Past Master. It is a law of Masonry that all officers hold on to their respective offices until their successors are installed. It is installation only that gives the right to exercise the franchises of an office.

The ceremony is an old one, and does not pertain exclusively to Masonry. The ancient Romans installed their priests, their kings, and their magistrates; but the ceremony was called *inauguration*, because performed generally by the augurs. The word *installation* is of comparatively modern origin, being Medieval Latin, and is compounded of *in* and *stallum*, a seat. Priests, after *ordination* or reception into the sacerdotal order, were installed into the churches or parishes to which they were appointed. The term as well as the custom is still in use.

Installation as a Masonic ceremony was early used. We find in the first edition of Anderson's *Constitutions*, a form of "Constituting a New Lodge," which was practised by the Duke of Wharton, who was Grand Master in 1723. It was probably prepared by Desaguliers, who was Deputy, or by Anderson, who was one of the Wardens, and perhaps by both. It included the ceremony of installing the new Master and Wardens. The words "Shall, in due form, *install* them" are found in this document. The usage then was for the Grand Master, or some brother for him, to install the Master, and for the Master to install his Wardens; a usage which still exists.

Installed Masters, Board of. An expression used in England to designate a committee of Masters to whom "the Master elect is presented that he may receive from his predecessor the benefit of installation." It is the same as the emergent Lodge of Past Masters assembled in this country for the same purpose.

Installing Officer. The person who performs the ceremony of installation is thus called. He should be of the same official dignity at least; although necessity has sometimes permitted a Grand Master to be installed by a Past Deputy, who in such case acts as *locum tenens* of a Grand Master. The Masonic rule is that anyone who has been installed into an office may install others into similar or inferior offices. In this it agrees with the old Rabbinical law as described by Maimonides (*Stat. de Sanhed.*, c. 4), who says: "Formerly, all Rabbis who had been installed, *hasmochachim*, could install others; but since the time of Hillel the faculty can be exercised only by those who have been invested with it by the Prince of the Grand Sanhedrim; nor then, unless there be two witnesses present, for an installation cannot be performed by less than three." So the strict Masonic rule requires the presence of three Past Masters in the complete installation of a Master and his investiture with the Past Master's Degree.

The first Master of a new Lodge can be installed only by the Grand Master, or by a Past Master especially appointed by him and acting as his proxy.

Instruction. It is the duty of the Master of the Lodge to give the necessary instruction to the candidate on his initiation. In some of the higher and in the continental Rites these instructions are imparted by an officer called the Orator; but the office is unknown in the English and American systems of Ancient Craft Masonry.

Instruction, Lodge of. See *Lodge of Instruction.*

Instrumental Masonry. Oliver by this term defines a species of Masonry which is engaged in the study of mechanical instruments. But there is no authority in any other writer for the use of the term, nor is its necessity or relevancy apparent.

Integrity. Integrity of purpose and conduct is symbolized by the *Plumb*, which see.

Intemperance. This is a vice which is wholly incompatible with the Masonic character, and the habitual indulgence in which subjects the offender to the penalty of expulsion from the Order. (See *Temperance*.)

Intendant of the Building. (*Intendant du Bâtiment.*) This degree is sometimes called "Master in Israel." It is the Eighth in the Ancient and Accepted Scottish Rite. Its emblematic color is red; and its principal officers, according to the old rituals, are a Thrice Puissant, representing Solomon; a Senior Warden, representing the illustrious Tito, one of the Harodim; and a Junior Warden, representing Adoniram the son of Abda. But in the present rituals of the two Supreme Councils of the United States the three chief officers represent Adoniram, Joabert, and Stolkin; but in the working of the degree the past officer assumes the character of Solomon. The legend of the degree is, that it was instituted to supply the place of the chief architect of the Temple.

Intention. The obligations of Masonry are required to be taken with an honest determination to observe them; and hence the Mason solemnly affirms that in assuming those responsibilities he does so without equivocation, secret evasion, or mental reservation.

Internal Preparation. See *Preparation of the Candidate.*

Internal Qualifications. Those qualifications of a candidate which refer to a condition known only to himself, and which are not patent to the world, are called internal qualifications. They are: 1st. That he comes forward of his own free-will and accord, and unbiased by the solicitations of others. 2d. That he is not influenced by mercenary motives; and, 3d, That he has a disposition to conform to the usages of the Order. The knowledge of these can only be obtained from his own statements, and hence they are included in the preliminary questions which are proposed before initiation.

Intimate Initiate. (*Intimus Initiatus.*) Latin. The Fourth Degree of the Order of the Temple.

Intimate Secretary. (*Secretaire intime.*) The Sixth Degree in the Ancient and Accepted Scottish Rite. Its emblematic color is black, strewed with tears; and its collar and the lining of the apron are red. Its officers are only three: Solomon, King of Israel; Hiram, King of Tyre; and a Captain of the Guards. Its history records an instance of unlawful curiosity, the punishment of which was only averted by the previous fidelity of the offender. The legend in this degree refers to the cities in Galilee which were presented by Solomon to Hiram, King of Tyre; and with whose character the latter was so displeased that he called them the land of Cabul.

Intolerance. The arch-enemy of Freemasonry. Toleration is one of the chief foundation-stones of the Fraternity, and Universality and Brotherly Love are ever taught. Notwithstanding, intolerance has, and ever has had, its grip upon the brotherhood, and insidiously does its silent and undermining work. Human powers are limited or circumscribed. Man by nature is weak, and is largely the creature of early education; yet no institution has such resisting power and is of such avail as Freemasonry against that great enemy of man, which has destroyed more of the human race than any other evil power. The synonym may be found in the Third and Tenth degrees, A. A. Scottish Rite.

Introductor and Introductress. Officers in a Lodge of Adoption, whose functions resemble those of a Master of Ceremonies.

Inversion of Letters. In some of the French documents of the high degrees the letters of some words were inverted—not apparently for concealment, but as a mere caprice. Hence Thory (*Fondat*, p. 128) calls them *inversions enfantines* (childish inversions). Thus they wrote Ɪosɐ ɔɹυɔıs for Rosæ crucis. But in all French Cahiers and rituals, or, as they call them, *tuilleurs*, words are inverted; that is, the letters are transposed for purposes of secrecy. Thus they would write *Nomolos* for Solomon, and *Marih* for Hiram. This was also a custom among the Kabbalists and the Alchemists to conceal secret words.

Investiture. The presentation of the apron to a candidate in the ceremony of initiation.

Invincible. The degree of Knights of the Christian Mark, formerly conferred in this country, was called the Invincible Order, and the title of the presiding officer was Invincible Knight.

Invisibles, Les. (*The Invisibles.*) A secret order of which little is known. Thory (*Acta Latomorum*, i., 319) quotes a German writer, who says: "C'est la secte la plus dangereuse; les réceptions des initiés se font la nuit, sous une voûte souterraine, et la doctrine des initians prêche l'athéisme et le suicide." We need no more upon this subject, and believe the society "sleeps the sleep that knows no waking."

Inwood, Jethro. The Rev. Jethro Inwood was curate of St. Paul's at Deptford, in England. He was born about the year 1767,

and initiated into Masonry in 1785 as a lewis, according to Oliver. He was soon after appointed Chaplain of the Provincial Grand Lodge of Kent, an office which he held for more than twenty years, during which time he delivered a great number of sermons on festival and other occasions. A volume of these sermons was published in 1799, with a portrait of the author, under the title of *Sermons, in which are explained and enforced the religious, moral, and political virtues of Freemasonry, preached upon several occasions before the Provincial Grand Officers and other Brethren in the Counties of Kent and Essex.* An edition of these sermons was published by Oliver, in 1849, in the fourth volume of his *Golden Remains*. These sermons are written, to use the author's own expression, "in a language that is plain, homely, and searching"; but, in Masonic character, surpass the generality of sermons called Masonic, simply because they have been preached before the Craft. Dr. Oliver describes him as "an assiduous Mason, who permitted no opportunity to pass unimproved of storing his mind with useful knowledge, or of imparting instruction to those who needed it."

Ionian Islands. Freemasonry appears to have been founded at Corfu, by a Lodge called "Loge de St. Napoléon," under the Grand Orient of France, in 1809, followed by a second in 1810.

Ionic Order. One of the three Grecian orders, and the one that takes the highest place in Masonic symbolism. Its distinguishing characteristic is the volute of its capital, and the shaft is cut into twenty flutes separated by fillets. It is more delicate and graceful than the Doric, and more simply majestic than the Corinthian. The judgment and skill displayed in its construction, as combining the strength of the former with the beauty of the latter, has caused it to be adopted in Masonry as the symbol of Wisdom, and being placed in the east of the Lodge it is referred to as represented by the Worshipful Master.

Iowa. Freemasonry was introduced into Iowa on November 20, 1840, by the formation of a Lodge at Burlington, under a Warrant from the Grand Lodge of Missouri. Of this Lodge, Bro. Theodore S. Parvin, since a Past Grand Master of the State, was one of the founders, and James R. Hartsock, another Past Grand Master, was the first initiate. A second Lodge was formed at Bloomington, now Muscatine, February 4, 1841; a third at Dubuque, October 20, 1842; and a fourth in Iowa City, October 10, 1842. A convention was held on January 2, 1844, and a Grand Lodge organized; Oliver Cock being elected Grand Master.

The Grand Chapter was organized June 8, 1854; the Grand Council in 1857, and the Grand Commandery, June 6, 1864. The Ancient and Accepted Scottish Rite has also been introduced into the State, and there is a Grand Consistory and several subordinate bodies.

Iram. (Heb., עירם, *aureum excelsus*.) The former ruling Prince of Idumea.

Ireland. The early history of Freemasonry in Ireland is involved in the deepest obscurity. It is vain to look in Anderson, in Preston, Smith, or any other English writer of the last century, for any account of the organization of Lodges in that kingdom anterior to the establishment of a Grand Lodge. But Dr. W. J. Chetwode Crawley, Grand Treasurer of Ireland (1911), has done much to lift the veil from the early Irish Freemasonry. A contemporary newspaper has been discovered, which gives an account of the installation of the Earl of Rosse as Grand Master of Ireland in June, 1725; and this account is so worded as to leave little room for doubt that the Grand Lodge of Ireland had already been in existence long enough to develop a complete organization of Grand Officers with at least six subordinate Lodges under its jurisdiction. (*Comentaria Hibernica, Fasc. II.*)

There is also still in existence a minute book which contains a record of a meeting of the "Grand Lodge for the Province of Munster," held on December 27, 1726, when the Hon. James O'Brien was elected Grand Master; and there is nothing to show that this was the first meeting of this body.

In 1731 Lord Kingston, who had been Grand Master of England in 1729, became Grand Master of the Grand Lodge of Munster and also of the Grand Lodge of Ireland, in connection with what appears to have been a reorganization of the latter body. No more is heard of the Grand Lodge of Munster, and from 1731 to the present date the succession of the Grand Officers of the Grand Lodge of Ireland is plain and distinct. (Gould's *Concise History of F. M.*, p. 273.)

In the year 1730, *The Constitutions of the Freemasons, Containing the History, Charges, Regulations, etc., of that most Ancient and Right Worshipful Fraternity. For the use of the Lodges*, was published at Dublin. A second edition was published in 1744, and a third, in 1751.

In 1749, the "Grand Master's Lodge" was instituted, which still exists; a singular institution, possessing several unusual privileges, among which are that its members are members of the Grand Lodge without the payment of dues, that the Lodge takes precedence of all other Lodges, and that any candidates nominated by the Grand Master are to be initiated without ballot.

In 1772, the Grand Lodge of Ireland recognized the Grand Lodge of the "Antients" and entered into an alliance with it, which was also done in the same year by the Grand Lodge of Scotland. This does not appear to have given any offense to the regular Grand Lodge of England; for when that body, in 1777, passed a vote of censure on the Lodges of Ancient Masons, it specially excepted from the censure the Lodges of Ireland and Scotland.

In 1779, an application was made to the Mother Kilwinning Lodge of Scotland, by certain brethren in Dublin, for a charter empowering them to form a Lodge to be called the "High Knights Templars," that they might confer the Templar Degree. The Kilwinning Lodge granted the petition for the three Craft degrees only, but at a later period this Lodge became, says Findel, the source of the Grand Encampment of Ireland.

The Grand Lodge holds jurisdiction over all the Blue Lodges. The Mark Degree is worked under the Grand Royal Arch Chapter. Next comes the Royal Arch, which formerly consisted of three degrees, the Excellent, Super-excellent, and Royal Arch—the first two being nothing more than passing the first two veils with each a separate obligation. But that system was abolished some years ago, and a new ritual framed something like the American, except that the king and not the high priest is made the Presiding Officer. The next degrees are the Fifteenth, Sixteenth, and Seventeenth, which are under the jurisdiction of the Templar Grand Conclave, and are given to the candidate previous to his being created a Knights Templar. Next to the Templar Degree in the Irish system comes the Eighteenth or Rose Croix, which is under the jurisdiction of the Grand Chapter of Prince Masons or Council of Rites, composed of the first three officers of all the Rose Croix Chapters, the Supreme Council having some years ago surrendered its authority over the degree. The Twenty-eighth Degree or Knight of the Sun is the next conferred, and then the Thirtieth or Kadosh in a body over which the Supreme Council has no control except to grant certificates to its members. The Supreme Council confers the Thirty-first, Thirty-second, and Thirty-third degrees, there being no Grand Consistory.

The Supreme Council of the Ancient and Accepted Scottish Rite for Ireland was established by a Patent from the Supreme Council of the United States, at Charleston, dated August 13, 1824, by which the Duke of Leinster, John Fowler, and Thomas McGill were constituted a Supreme Council for Ireland, and under that authority it continues to work.

Whence the high degrees came into Ireland is not clearly known. The Rose Croix and Kadosh degrees existed in Ireland long before the establishment of the Supreme Council. In 1808 Dr. Dalcho's *Orations* were published at Dublin, by "the Illustrious College of Knights of K. H., and the Original Chapter of Prince Masons of Ireland." It is probable that these degrees were received from Bristol, England, where are preserved the earliest English records of the Rose Croix.

Irish Chapters. These Chapters existed in Paris from the year 1730 to 1740, and were thence disseminated through France. They consisted of degrees, such as Irish Master, Perfect Irish Master, and Sublime Irish Master, which, it is said, were invented by the adherents of the house of Stuart when they sought to make Freemasonry a political means of restoring the exiled family to the throne of England. Ramsay, when he assumed his theory of the establishment of Freemasonry in

Scotland by the Templars, who had fled thither under d'Aumont, took possession of these degrees (if he did not, as some suppose, invent them himself), and changed their name, in deference to his theory, from Irish to Scottish, calling, for instance, the degree of *Maître Irlandais* or Irish Master, the *Maître, Ecossais* or Scottish Master.

Irish Colleges. The Irish Chapters are also called by some writers Irish Colleges.

Irish Degrees. See *Irish Chapters*.

Iron Tools. The lectures teach us that at the building of King Solomon's Temple there was not heard the sound of ax, hammer, or other metallic tool. But all the stones were hewn, squared, and numbered in the quarries; and the timbers felled and prepared in the forest of Lebanon, whence they were brought on floats by sea to Joppa, and thence carried by land to Jerusalem, where, on being put up, each part was found to fit with such exact nicety that the whole, when completed, seemed rather the handiwork of the Grand Architect of the Universe than of mere human hands. This can hardly be called a legend, because the same facts are substantially related in the 1st Book of Kings; but the circumstance has been appropriated in Masonry to symbolize the entire peace and harmony which should prevail among Masons when laboring on that spiritual temple of which the Solomonic Temple was the archetype.

Isaac and Ishmael. The sons of Abraham by Sarah and Hagar. They are recognized, from the conditions of their mothers, as the free born and the bondman. According to Oliver, the fact that the inheritance which was bestowed upon Isaac, the son of his freeborn wife, was refused to Ishmael, the son of a slave woman, gave rise to the Masonic theory which constitutes a landmark that none but the free born are entitled to initiation.

Ischngi. (Heb., יִשְׁעִי, *salus mea*.) One of the five Masters, according to the Masonic myth, appointed by Solomon after the death of Hiram to complete the Temple.

Ish Chotzeb. אִישׁ חֹצֵב. Literally, "men of hewing," i. e., "hewers." The phrase was first used by Anderson in the first edition of the *Constitutions* (p. 10), but is not found in the original Hebrew (1 Kings v. 18) to which he refers, where it is said that Solomon had fourscore "hewers in the mountains," *chotzeb bahar*. But *ish chotzeb* is properly constructed according to the Hebrew idiom, and is employed by Anderson to designate the hewers who, with the "Giblim," or stone-cutters, and the "Bonai," or builders, amounted to eighty thousand, all of whom he calls, in his second edition (p. 11), "bright Fellow Crafts." But he distinguishes them from the thirty thousand who cut wood on Mount Lebanon under Adoniram.

Ish Sabbal. אִישׁ סַבָּל. Men of burden. Anderson thus designates the 70,000 laborers who, in the original Hebrew, are (1 Kings v. 18) called *noshe sabal*, bearers of burdens. Anderson says "they were of the remains of the old Canaanites, and, being bondmen, are not to be reckoned among Masons." (*Constitutions*, 1738, p. 11.) But in Webb's system they constitute the Apprentices at the building of the Temple.

Ish Sodi. Corruptly, *Ish Soudy*. This expression is composed of the two Hebrew words, שׁיִא, ISH, and סוֹד, SOD. The first of these words, ISH, means *a man*, and SOD signifies primarily *a couch* on which one reclines. Hence ISH SODI would mean, first, *a man of my couch*, one who reclines with me on the same seat, an indication of great familiarity and confidence. Thence followed the secondary meaning given to SOD, of familiar intercourse, consultation, or intimacy. Job (xix. 19) applies it in this sense, when, using MATI, a word synonymous with ISH, he speaks of MATI SODI in the passage which the common version has translated thus: "all my *inward friends* abhorred me," but which the marginal interpretation has more correctly rendered, "all the men of my secret." *Ish Sodi*, therefore, in this degree, very clearly means *a man of my intimate counsel, a man of my choice*, one selected to share with me a secret task or labor. Such was the position of every Select Master to King Solomon, and in this view those are not wrong who have interpreted *Ish Sodi* as meaning a *Select Master*.

Isiac Table. Known also as the Tabula Isiaca, Mensa Isiaca, and Tabula Bembina. A monument often quoted by archeologists previous to the discovery of hieroglyphics. A flat rectangular bronze plate, inlaid with niello and silver, 56 by 36 inches in size. It consists of three compartments of figures of Egyptian deities and emblems; the central figure is Isis. It was sold by a soldier to a locksmith, bought by Cardinal Bembo in 1527, and is now in the Royal Museum in Turin.

Isis. The sister and the wife of Osiris, and worshiped by the Egyptians as the great goddess of nature. Her mysteries constituted one of the degrees of the ancient Egyptian initiation. (See *Egyptian Mysteries* and *Osiris*.)

Israfeel. In the Mohammedan faith, the name of the angel who, on the judgment morn, will sound the trumpet of resurrection.

Italy. In the year 1733, Freemasonry was introduced into Italy, by the establishment of a Lodge at Florence, by Lord George Sackville. Thory, and after him Findel, calls him Duke of Middlesex; but there was at that time no such title in the peerage of England. A medal was struck on this occasion. It is not known under what authority this Lodge was established, but most probably under that of the Grand Lodge of England. The initiation of the Grand Duke of Tuscany had a favorable influence on the prospects of the Order, and in 1735 Lodges were established at Milan, Verona, Padua, Vincenza, Venice, and Naples. In 1737, John Gaston, the last duke of the house of the Medicis, prohibited Freemasonry, but dying soon after, the Lodges continued to meet. His successor, the Grand Duke of Lorraine, declared himself the protector of the Order, and many new Lodges were established under his auspices. In 1738, Pope Clement XIV. issued his bull forbidding all congregations of Freemasons, which was followed in January, 1739, by the edict of Cardinal Firrao, which inflicted the penalty of death and confiscation of goods on all who should contravene the Papal order. Several arrests were made at Florence by the Inquisition, but, through the intercession of the Grand Duke, the persons who had been arrested were set at liberty.

For many years Freemasonry held but a precarious existence in Italy, the persecutions of the Church preventing any healthy growth. The Masons continued to meet, although generally in secret. The Masons of Rome struck a medal, in 1746, in honor of Martin Folkes; and the author of *Anti-Saint-Nicaise* says that there was a Grand Lodge at Naples in 1756, which was in correspondence with the Lodges of Germany. Naples, indeed, seems to have been for a long time the only place where the Lodges were in any kind of activity. In 1776, Queen Caroline exerted her interest in behalf of the Order. Smith, writing in 1783 (*Use and Abuse*, p. 211), says, "At present most of the Italian nobles and dignified ecclesiastics are Freemasons, who hold their meetings generally in private houses, though they have established Lodges at Naples, Leghorn, Venice, Verona, Turin, Messina, in the island of Sicily, Genoa, and Modena."

In 1805 a Supreme Council of the Ancient and Accepted Rite was established at Milan by Count de Grasse-Tilly, and Prince Eugene accepted the offices of Grand Commander of the Council and Grand Master of the Grand Orient.

When, by the defeat of Napoleon in 1814, the liberal policy of France was withdrawn from Italy, to be again substituted by the ignorance of the Bourbon dynasty and the bigotry of the Roman Church, Italian Masonry ceased any longer to have an existence nor did it revive until 1860. But the centralization of Italy, and the political movements that led to it, restored Italy to freedom and intelligence, and Freemasonry had again found, even beneath the shadow of the Vatican, a congenial soil.

A Lodge was established at Turin in 1859, and a Grand Lodge in 1861. A Grand Orient was subsequently established by Garibaldi, who adopted the system of the Scottish Rite. A Supreme Council was also formed at Naples. Internal dissensions, however, unfortunately took place. The Grand Orient was removed from Turin to Florence, when many resignations took place, and a recusant body was formed. But peace at length prevailed, and at a Constituent Assembly held at Rome on April 28, 1873, "the fundamental bases of Italian Masonic Fraternity" were adopted; and "the Grand Orient of Italy" was now in successful operation. There was also a Supreme Council of the Scottish Rite.

Itratics, Order of. A society of adepts, engaged in the search for the Universal Medicine; is now extinct. Mentioned by Fustier.

I∴V∴I∴O∴L∴. (*Inveni Verbum in Ore Leonis.*) Initial letters of significant words used in the Thirteenth Degree, A. A. Scottish Rite. They have reference to the recovery of the key of the Sacred Ark, which contains certain treasures. The Ark and its key having been lost in the forest during a battle which occurred when the Jews were journeying through the wilderness, the key was found in the mouth of a lion, who dropped it upon the ground on the approach of the Israelites. Much symbolical teaching is deduced from this historical myth.

Ivory Key. The symbolic jewel of the Fourth Degree, A. A. Scottish Rite. On the wards of the key is the Hebrew letter *zain*.

Izabud. A corruption of *Zabud*, which see.

Izads. The twenty-eight creations of the beneficent deity Ormudz, or Auramazda, in the Persian religious system.

J

J. The tenth letter in the English alphabet. It is frequently and interchangeably used with I, and written in Hebrew as Yod (י), with the numerical value of 10, and having reference to the Supreme.

Jaaborou Hammaim. (Heb., יעברודהמים, *aquæ transibunt*.) A word of covered significancy in the Fifteenth Degree of the A. A. Scottish Rite. It also has reference to the L. D. P. (See *Liber*.)

Jabescheh. (Heb., יבשה, *Earth*.) Also written Jebschah. (See *I∴N∴R∴I∴*.)

Jabulum. A corrupted word used in two of the degrees of the A. A. Scottish Rite, the Thirteenth and Seventeenth. The true word and its meaning, however, are disclosed to the initiate.

Jachin. יכין. Hence called by Dudley and some other writers, who reject the points, *ichin*. It is the name of the right-hand pillar facing eastward (i. e., on the south), that stood at the porch of King Solomon's Temple. It is derived from two Hebrew words, יה, *jah*, "God," and יכין, *iachin*, "will establish." It signifies, therefore, "God will establish," and is often called "the pillar of establishment."

Jachinai. A Gallic corruption of *Shekinah*, to be found only in the French Cahiers of the high degrees.

Jacobins. A political sect that sprang up

in the beginning of the French Revolution, and which gave origin to the Jacobin clubs, so well known as having been the places where the leaders of the Revolution concocted their plans for the abolition of the monarchy and the aristocracy. Lieber says that it is a most surprising phenomenon that "so large a body of men could be found uniting rare energy with execrable vice, political madness, and outrageous cruelty, committed always in the name of virtue." Barruel, in his *Histoire de Jacobinisme*, and Robison, in his *Proofs of a Conspiracy*, both endeavor to prove that there was a coalition of the revolutionary conspirators with the Illuminati and the Freemasons which formed the Jacobin clubs, those bodies being, as they contend, only Masonic Lodges in disguise. The falsity of these charges will be evident to anyone who reads the history of French Masonry during the Revolution, and more especially during that part of the period known as the "Reign of Terror," when the Jacobin clubs were in most vigor. The Grand Orient, in 1788, declared that a politico-Masonic work, entitled *Les Jesuites chassés de la Maçonnerie et leur Poignard brisé par les Maçons*, was the production of a perverse mind, prepared as a poison for the destruction of Masonry, and ordered it to be burned. During the Revolution, the Grand Orient suspended its labors, and the Lodges in France were dissolved; and in 1793, the Duke of Orleans, the head of the Jacobins, who was also, unfortunately, Grand Master of the French Masons, resigned the latter position, assigning as a reason that he did not believe that there should be any mystery nor any secret society in a republic. It is evident that the Freemasons, as an Order, held themselves aloof from the political contests of that period.

Jacob's Ladder. The introduction of Jacob's ladder into the symbolism of Speculative Masonry is to be traced to the vision of Jacob, which is thus substantially recorded in the twenty-eighth chapter of the Book of Genesis: When Jacob, by the command of his father Isaac, was journeying toward Padanaram, while sleeping one night with the bare earth for his couch and a stone for his pillow, he beheld the vision of a ladder, whose foot rested on the earth and whose top reached to heaven. Angels were continually ascending and descending upon it, and promised him the blessing of a numerous and happy posterity. When Jacob awoke, he was filled with pious gratitude, and consecrated the spot as the house of God.

This ladder, so remarkable in the history of the Jewish people, finds its analogue in all the ancient initiations. Whether this is to be attributed simply to a coincidence—a theory which but few scholars would be willing to accept—or to the fact that these analogues were all derived from a common fountain of symbolism, or whether, as suggested by Oliver, the origin of the symbol was lost among the practises of the Pagan rites, while the symbol itself was retained, it is, perhaps, impossible

authoritatively to determine. It is, however, certain that the ladder as a symbol of moral and intellectual progress existed almost universally in antiquity, presenting itself either as a succession of steps, of gates, of degrees, or in some other modified form. The number of the steps varied; although the favorite one appears to have been seven, in reference, apparently, to the mystical character almost everywhere given to that number.

Thus, in the Persian mysteries of Mithras, there was a ladder of seven rounds, the passage through them being symbolical of the soul's approach to perfection. These rounds were called gates, and, in allusion to them, the candidate was made to pass through seven dark and winding caverns, which process was called the ascent of the ladder of perfection. Each of these caverns was the representative of a world, or state of existence through which the soul was supposed to pass in its progress from the first world to the last, or the world of truth. Each round of the ladder was said to be of metal of increasing purity, and was dignified also with the name of its protecting planet. Some idea of the construction of this symbolic ladder may be obtained from the following table:

7 Gold,	Sun,	Truth. [Blessed.
6 Silver,	Moon,	Mansion of the
5 Iron,	Mars,	World of Births.
4 Tin,	Jupiter,	Middle World.
3 Copper,	Venus,	Heaven. [ence.
2 Quicksilver,	Mercury,	World of Preexist-
1 Lead,	Saturn,	First World.

In the mysteries of Brahma we find the same reference to the ladder of seven steps. The names of these were not different, and there was the same allusion to the symbol of the universe. The seven steps were emblematical of the seven worlds which constituted the Indian universe. The lowest was the Earth; the second, the World of Preexistence; the third, Heaven; the fourth, the Middle World, or intermediate region between the lower and upper worlds; the fifth, the World of Births, in which souls are again born; the sixth, the Mansion of the Blessed; and the seventh, or topmost round, the Sphere of Truth, and the abode of Brahma. Dr. Oliver thinks that in the Scandinavian mysteries the tree Yggrasil was the representative of the mystical ladder. But although the ascent of the tree, like the ascent of the ladder, was a change from a lower to a higher sphere—from time to eternity, and from death to life—yet the unimaginative genius of the North seems to have shorn the symbolism of many of its more salient features.

Among the Kabbalists, the ladder was represented by the ten Sephiroths, which, commencing from the bottom, were the Kingdom, Foundation, Splendor, Firmness, Beauty, Justice, Mercy, Intelligence, Wisdom, and the Crown, by which we arrive at the En Soph, or the Infinite.

In the higher Masonry we find the ladder of Kadosh, which consists of seven steps, thus commencing from the bottom: Justice, Equity, Kindness, Good Faith, Labor, Patience, and Intelligence. The arrangement of these steps, for which we are indebted to modern ritualism, does not seem to be perfect; but yet the idea of intellectual progress to perfection is carried out by making the topmost round represent Wisdom or Understanding.

The Masonic ladder which is presented in the symbolism of the First Degree ought really to consist of seven steps, which thus ascend: Temperance, Fortitude, Prudence, Justice, Faith, Hope, and Charity; but the earliest examples of it present it only with three, referring to the three theological virtues, whence it is called the theological ladder. It seems, therefore, to have been settled by general usage that the Masonic ladder has but three steps.

As a symbol of progress, Jacob's ladder was early recognized. Picus of Mirandola, who wrote in the sixteenth century, in his oration, "De Hominis Dignitate," says that Jacob's ladder is a symbol of the progressive scale of intellectual communication betwixt earth and heaven; and upon the ladder, as it were, step by step, man is permitted with the angels to ascend and descend until the mind finds blissful and complete repose in the bosom of divinity. The highest step he defines to be theology, or the study and contemplation of the Deity in his own abstract and exalted nature.

Other interpretations have, however, been given to it. The Jewish writers differ very much in their expositions of it. Thus, a writer of one of the Midrashes or Commentaries, finding that the Hebrew words for *Ladder* and *Sinai* have each the same numerical value of letters, expounds the ladder as typifying the giving of the law on that mount. Aben Ezra thought that it was a symbol of the human mind, and that the angels represented the sublime meditations of man. Maimonides supposed the ladder to symbolize nature in its operations; and, citing the authority of a Midrash which gives to it four steps, says that they represent the four elements; the two heavier, earth and water, descending by their specific gravity, and the two lighter, fire and air, ascending from the same cause. Abarbanel, assuming the Talmudic theory that Luz, where Jacob slept, was Mount Moriah, supposes that the ladder, resting on the spot which afterward became the holy of holies, was a prophetic symbol of the building of the Temple. And, lastly, Raphael interprets the ladder, and the ascent and the descent of the angels, as the prayers of man and the answering inspiration of God. Fludd, the Hermetic philosopher, in his *Philosophia Mosaica* (1638), calls the ladder the symbol of the triple world, moral, physical, and intellectual; and Nicolai says that the ladder with three steps was, among the Rosicrucian Freemasons in the seventeenth century, a symbol of the knowledge of nature. Finally, Krause says, in his *drei ältesten Kunsturkunden* (ii., 481), that a Brother Keher of Edinburgh, whom he

describes as a skilful and truthful Mason, had in 1802 assured the members of a Lodge at Altenberg that originally only one Scottish degree existed, whose object was the restoration of James II. to the throne of England, and that of that restoration Jacob's ladder had been adopted by them as a symbol. Of this fact he further said that an authentic narrative was contained in the Archives of the Grand Lodge of Scotland. Notwithstanding Lawrie's silence on the subject, Krause is inclined to believe the story, nor is it in all its parts altogether without probability. It is more than likely that the Chevalier Ramsay, who was a warm adherent of the Stuarts, transferred the symbol of the mystical ladder from the Mithraic mysteries, with which he was very familiar, into his Scottish degrees, and that thus it became a part of the symbolism of the Kadosh system. In some of the political Lodges instituted under the influence of the Stuarts to assist in the restoration of their house, the philosophical interpretation of the symbol may have been perverted to a political meaning, and to these Lodges it is to be supposed that Keher alluded; but that the Grand Lodge of Scotland had made any official recognition of the fact is not to be believed. Lawrie's silence seems to be conclusive.

In the Ancient Craft degrees of the York Rite, Jacob's ladder was not an original symbol. It is said to have been introduced by Dunckerley when he reformed the lectures. This is confirmed by the fact that it is not mentioned in any of the early rituals of the last century, nor even by Hutchinson, who had an excellent opportunity of doing so in his lecture on the *Nature of the Lodge*, where he speaks of the covering of the Lodge, but says nothing of the means of reaching it, which he would have done, had he been acquainted with the ladder as a symbol. Its first appearance is in a Tracing Board, on which the date of 1776 is inscribed, which very well agrees with the date of Dunckerley's improvements. In this Tracing Board, the ladder has but three rounds; a change from the old seven-stepped ladder of the mysteries; which, however, Preston corrected when he described it as having many rounds, but three principal ones.

As to the modern Masonic symbolism of the ladder, it is, as I have already said, a symbol of progress, such as it is in all the old initiations. Its three principal rounds, representing Faith, Hope, and Charity, present us with the means of advancing from earth to heaven, from death to life—from the mortal to immortality. Hence its foot is placed on the ground floor of the Lodge, which is typical of the world, and its top rests on the covering of the Lodge, which is symbolic of heaven.

In the Prestonian lecture, which was elaborated out of Dunckerley's system, the ladder is said to rest on the Holy Bible, and to reach to the heavens. This symbolism is thus explained:

"By the doctrines contained in the Holy

Bible we are taught to believe in the Divine dispensation of Providence, which belief strengthens our *Faith*, and enables us to ascend the first step.

"That Faith naturally creates in us a *Hope* of becoming partakers of some of the blessed promises therein recorded, which *Hope* enables us to ascend the second step.

"But the third and last being *Charity* comprehends the whole, and he who is possessed of this virtue in its ample sense, is said to have arrived at the summit of his profession, or, more metaphorically, into an ethereal mansion veiled from the mortal eye by the starry firmament."

In the modern lectures, the language is materially changed, but the idea and the symbolism are retained unaltered.

The delineation of the ladder with three steps only on the Tracing Board of 1776, which is a small one, may be attributed to notions of convenience. But the Masonic ladder should properly have seven steps, which represent the four cardinal and the three theological virtues.

Jacques de Molay. See *Molay, James de.*

Jafuhar. The second king in the Scandinavian mysteries. The synonym for Thor.

Jah. In Hebrew, יה. Maimonides calls it the "two-lettered name," and derives it from the Tetragrammaton, of which he says it is an abbreviation. Others have denied this, and assert that *Jah* is a name independent of Jehovah, but expressing the same idea of the Divine Essence. It is uniformly translated in the authorized version of the Bible by the word LORD, being thus considered as synonymous with Jehovah, except in Psalm lxviii. 4, where the original word is preserved: "Extol him that rideth upon the heavens by his name JAH," upon which the Targum comment is: "Extol him who sitteth on the throne of glory in the ninth heaven; YAH is his name." It seems, also, to have been well known to the Gentile nations as the triliteral name of God; for, although biliteral among the Hebrews, it assumed among the Greeks the triliteral form, as IAΩ. Macrobius, in his *Saturnalia*, says that this was the sacred name of the Supreme Deity; and the Clarian Oracle being asked which of the gods was Jao, replied, "The initiated are bound to conceal the mysterious secrets. Learn thou that IAΩ is the Great God Supreme who ruleth over all." (See *Jehovah*.)

Jaheb. (Heb., יהב, *concedens*.) A sacred name used in the Thirteenth Degree of the A. A. Scottish Rite.

Jaina Cross. Used by several orders, and found in the abbeys of Great Britain and on the monuments of India. Its significations are many. This cross was adopted by the Jainas, a heterodox sect of the Hindus, who dissent from Brahmanism and deny the Vedas, and whose adherents are found in every province of Upper Hindustan. They are wealthy and influential, and form an important division of the population of India. This symbol is also known as the *Fylfot* or *Swastika*. It is a religious symbol mentioned by Weaver in his *Funeral Monuments*, by Dr. H. Schliemann as having been found in the presumed ruins of Troy, by De Rossi and others in the Catacombs of Christian Rome, and there termed the *Crux dissimulata*. It has been found on almost every enduring monument on the globe, of all ages, and in both hemispheres.

Jainas. See *Jaina Cross.*

Jamblichus. It is strange that the old Masons, when inventing their legend, which gave so prominent a place to Pythagoras as "an ancient friend and brother," should have entirely forgotten his biographer, Jamblichus, whose claims to their esteem and veneration are much greater than those of the Samian sage. Jamblichus was a Neoplatonic philosopher, who was born at Chalcis, in Calo, Syria, and flourished in the fourth century. He was a pupil of Porphyry, and was deeply versed in the philosophic systems of Plato and Pythagoras, and, like the latter, had studied the mystical theology of the Egyptians and Chaldeans whose Divine origin and truth he attempts to vindicate. He maintained that man, through theurgic rites and ceremonies, might commune with the Deity; and hence he attached great importance to initiation as the means of inculcating truth. He carried his superstitious veneration for numbers and numerical formula to a far greater extent than did the school of Pythagoras; so that all the principles of his philosophy can be represented by numbers.

Thus, he taught that one, or the monad, was the principle of all unity as well as diversity; the duad, or two, was the intellect; three, the soul; four, the principle of universal harmony; eight, the source of motion; nine, perfection; and ten, the result of all the emanations of the *to en*. It will thus be seen that Jamblichus, while adopting the general theory of numbers that distinguished the Pythagorean school, differed very materially in his explanations. He wrote many philosophical works on the basis of these principles, and was the author of a *Life of Pythagoras*, and a *Treatise of the Mysteries*. Of all the ancient philosophers, his system assimilates him most—if not in its details, at least in its spirit—to the mystical and symbolic character of the Masonic philosophy.

James II. and III. of Scotland. See *Stuart Masonry.*

Jaminim or **Iaminim.** (Heb., *water.*) (See *I∴N∴R∴I∴*.)

Janitor. A door-keeper. The word *Sentinel*, which in a Royal Arch Chapter is the proper equivalent of the *Tiler* in a Lodge, is in some jurisdictions replaced by the word *Janitor*. There is no good authority for the usage.

Japan. Freemasonry was introduced in Japan by the establishment at Yokohama, in 1865, of a Lodge by the Grand Lodge of England. A Masonic hall was built at Yokohama in 1869.

Japanese Faith. See *Kojiki; also Nihongi.*

Japhet. Heb., יפת. The eldest son of Noah. It is said that the first ark—the ark of safety, the archetype of the tabernacle—was constructed by Shem, Ham, and Japhet under the superintendence of Noah. Hence these are significant words in the Royal Arch Degree.

Jasher, Book of. (Heb., Sepher hayashar, *The Book of the Upright*.) One of the lost books of the ancient Hebrews, which is quoted twice (Josh. x. 13; 2 Sam. i. 18). A Hebrew minstrelsy, recording the warlike deeds of the national heroes, and singing the praises of eminent or celebrated men. An original is said to be in the library at Samarkand.

Jasper. Heb., ישפה. A precious stone of a dullish green color, which was the last of the twelve inserted in the high priest's breastplate, according to the authorized version; but the Vulgate translation more correctly makes it the third stone of the second row. It represented the tribe of Zebulun.

Jebusite. See *Ornan*.

Jedadiah. A special name given to King Solomon at his birth. It signifies "beloved of God."

Jehoshaphat. East of Jerusalem, between Mount Zion and the Mount of Olives, lies the Valley of Jehoshaphat. In the most recent rituals this word has lost its significance, but in the older ones it played an important part. There was in reality no such valley in ancient Judea, nor is there any mention of it in Scripture, except once by the prophet Joel. The name is altogether modern. But, as the Hebrew means *the judgment of God*, and as the prophecy of Joel declared that God would there judge the heathen for their deeds against the Israelites, it came at last to be believed by the Jews, which belief is shared by the Mohammedans, that the Valley of Jehoshaphat is to be the place of the last judgment. Hence it was invested with a peculiar degree of sanctity as a holy place. The idea was borrowed by the Masons of the last century, who considered it as the symbol of holy ground. Thus, in the earliest rituals we find this language:

"Where does the Lodge stand?"

"Upon holy ground, or the highest hill or lowest vale, or in the Valley of Jehoshaphat, or any other secret place."

This reference to the Valley of Jehoshaphat as the symbol of the ground floor of the Lodge was in this country retained until a very recent period; and the expression which alludes to it in the ritual of the Second Degree has only within a few years past been abandoned. Hutchinson referred to this symbolism, when he said that the Spiritual Lodge was placed in the Valley of Jehoshaphat to imply that the principles of Masonry are derived from the knowledge of God, and are established in the judgments of the Lord.

Jehovah. JEHOVAH is, of all the significant words of Masonry, by far the most important. Reghellini very properly calls it "the basis of our dogma and of our mysteries."

24

In Hebrew it consists of four letters, יהוה, and hence is called the *Tetragrammaton*, or four-lettered name; and because it was forbidden to a Jew, as it is to a Mason, to pronounce it, it is also called the Ineffable or Unpronounceable name. For its history we must refer to the sixth chapter of Exodus (verses 2, 3). When Moses returned discouraged from his first visit to Pharaoh, and complained to the Lord that the only result of his mission had been to incense the Egyptian king, and to excite him to the exaction of greater burdens from the oppressed Israelites, God encouraged the patriarch by the promise of the great wonders which he would perform in behalf of his people, and confirmed the promise by imparting to him that sublime name by which he had not hitherto been known: "And God," says the sacred writer, "spake unto Moses, and said unto him, I am Jehovah: and I appeared unto Abraham, unto Isaac, and unto Jacob as El Shaddai, but by my name JEHOVAH was I not known unto them."

This Ineffable name is derived from the substantive verb היה, hayah, *to be;* and combining, as it does, in its formation the present, past, and future significations of the verb, it is considered as designating God in his immutable and eternal existence. This idea is carried by the Rabbis to such an extent, that Menasseh Ben Israel says that its four letters may be so arranged by permutations as to form twelve words, every one of which is a modification of the verb *to be*, and hence it is called the *nomen substantiæ vel essentiæ*, the name of his substance or existence.

The first thing that attracts our attention in the investigation of this name is the ancient regulation, still existing, by which it was made unlawful to pronounce it. This, perhaps, originally arose from a wish to conceal it from the surrounding heathen nations, so that they might not desecrate it by applying it to their idols. Whatever may have been the reason, the rule was imperative among the Jews. The Talmud, in one of its treatises, the "Sanhedrim," which treats of the question, Who of the Israelites shall have future life and who shall not? says: "Even he who *thinks* the name of God with its true letters forfeits his future life." Abraham Ben David Halevi, when discussing the names of God, says: "But the name יהוה we are not allowed to pronounce. In its original meaning it is conferred upon no other being, and therefore we abstain from giving any explanation of it." We learn from Jerome, Origen, and Eusebius that in their time the Jews wrote the name in their copies of the Bible in Samaritan instead of Hebrew letters, in order to veil it from the inspection of the profane. Capellus says that the rule that the holy name was not to be pronounced was derived from a tradition, based on a passage in Leviticus (xxiv. 16), which says that he who blasphemeth the name of Jehovah shall be put to death; and he translates this passage, "whosoever shall pronounce the name Jehovah shall suffer death," because the word *nokeb*, here translated "to blaspheme," means also "to pronounce distinctly, to call by name." Another reason for the rule is to be found in a rabbinical misinterpretation of a passage in Exodus.

In the third chapter of that book, when Moses asks of God what is His name, He replies "I AM THAT I AM; and He said, Thus shalt thou say unto the children of Israel, I AM hath sent me unto you," and he adds, "this is my name forever." Now, the Hebrew word I AM is אהיה, *Ehyeh*. But as Mendelssohn has correctly observed, there is no essential difference between אהיה, in the sixth chapter and יהוה in the third, the former being the first person singular, and the latter the third person of the same verb (the future used in the present sense of the verb *to be*); and hence what was said of the name Ehyeh was applied by the Rabbis to the name Jehovah. But of Ehyeh God had said, "this is my name *forever*." Now the word *forever* is represented in the original by לעלם, *l'olam;* but the Rabbis, says Capellus, by the change of a single letter, made *l'olam*, forever, read as if it had been written *l'alam*, which means "to be concealed," and hence the passage was translated "this is my name to be concealed," instead of "this is my name forever." And thus Josephus, in writing upon this subject, uses the following expressions: "Whereupon God declared to Moses His holy name, which had never been discovered to men before; concerning which it is not lawful for me to say any more." In obedience to this law, whenever the word Jehovah occurs to a Jew in reading, he abstains from pronouncing it, and substitutes in its place the word אדני, *Adonai*. Thus, instead of saying "holiness to Jehovah," as it is in the original, he would say "holiness to Adonai." And this same reverential reticence has been preserved by our translators in the authorized version, who, wherever Jehovah occurs, have, with a few exceptions, translated it by the word "Lord," the very passage just quoted, being rendered "holiness to the Lord."

Maimonides tells us that the knowledge of this word was confined to the *hachamin* or wise men, who communicated its true pronunciation and the mysteries connected with it only on the Sabbath day, to such of their disciples as were found worthy; but how it was to be sounded, or with what vocal sounds its four letters were to be uttered, was utterly unknown to the people. Once a year, namely, on the day of atonement, the holy name was pronounced with the sound of its letters and with the utmost veneration by the high priest in the Sanctuary. The last priest who pronounced it, says Rabbi Bechai, was Simeon the Just, and his successors used in blessing only the twelve-lettered name. After the destruction of the city and Temple by Vespasian, the pronunciation of it ceased, for it was not lawful to pronounce it anywhere except in the Temple at Jerusalem, and thus the true and genuine pronunciation of the name was entirely lost to the Jewish people. Nor is it now known how it was originally pro-

nounced. The Greeks called it JAO; the Romans, JOVA; the Samaritans always pronounced it JAHVE.

The task is difficult to make one unacquainted with the peculiarities of the Hebrew language comprehend how the pronunciation of a word whose letters are preserved can be wholly lost. It may, however, be attempted. The Hebrew alphabet consists entirely of consonants. The vowel sounds were originally supplied by the reader while reading, he being previously made acquainted with the correct pronunciation of each word; and if he did not possess this knowledge, the letters before him could not supply it, and he was, of course, unable to pronounce the word. Every Hebrew, however, knew from practise the vocal sounds with which the consonants were pronounced in the different words, in the same manner as every English reader knows the different sounds of *a* in *hat, hate, far, was*, and that *knt* is pronounced *knight*. The words "God save the republic," written in the Hebrew method, would appear thus: "Gd sv th rpblc." Now, this incommunicable name of God consists of four letters, Yod, He, Vau, and He, equivalent in English to the combination JHVH. It is evident that these four letters cannot, in our language, be pronounced, unless at least two vowels be supplied. Neither can they in Hebrew. In other words, the vowels were known to the Jew, because he heard the words continually pronounced, just as we know that *Mr.* stands for *Mister*, because we continually hear this combination so pronounced. But the name of God, of which these four letters are symbols, was never pronounced, but another word, *Adonai*, substituted for it; and hence, as the letters themselves have no vocal power, the Jew, not knowing the implied vowels, was unable to supply them, and thus the pronunciation of the word was in time entirely lost.

Hence some of the most learned of the Jewish writers even doubt whether Jehovah is the true pronunciation, and say that the recovery of the name is one of the mysteries that will be revealed only at the coming of the Messiah. They attribute the loss to the fact that the Masoretic or vowel points belonging to another word were applied to the sacred name, whereby in time a confusion occurred in its vocalization.

In the Ineffable degrees of the Scottish Rite, there is a tradition that the pronunciation varied among the patriarchs in different ages. Methuselah, Lamech, and Noah pronounced it *Juha;* Shem, Arphaxad, Selah, Heber, and Peleg pronounced it *Jeva;* Reu, Serug, Nahor, Terah, Abraham, Isaac, and Judah, called it *Jova;* by Hezrom and Ram it was pronounced *Jevo;* by Aminadab and Nasshon, *Jevah;* by Salmon, Boaz, and Obed, *Johe;* by Jesse and David, *Jehovah*. And they imply that none of these was the right pronunciation, which was only in the possession of Enoch, Jacob, and Moses, whose names are, therefore, not mentioned in this list. In all these words it must be noticed that the J is to be pronounced as Y, the *a* as in *father*, and the *e* as *a* in *fate*.

Thus, Je-ho-vah would be pronounced Yay-ho-vah.

The Jews believed that this holy name, which they held in the highest veneration, was possessed of unbounded powers. "He who pronounces it," said they, "shakes heaven and earth, and inspires the very angels with astonishment and terror. There is a sovereign authority in this name: it governs the world by its power. The other names and surnames of the Deity are ranged about it like officers and soldiers about their sovereigns and generals: from this king-name they receive their orders, and obey."

It was called the *Shem hamphorash*, the explanatory or declaratory name, because it alone, of all the Divine names, distinctly explains or declares what is the true essence of the Deity.

Among the Essenes, this sacred name, which was never uttered aloud, but always in a whisper, was one of the mysteries of their initiation, which candidates were bound by a solemn oath never to divulge.

It is reported to have been, under a modified form, a password in the Egyptian mysteries, and none, says Schiller, dare enter the temple of Serapis who did not bear on his breast or forehead the name *Jao* or *Je-ha-ho;* a name almost equivalent in sound to that of Jehovah, and probably of identical import; and no name was uttered in Egypt with more reverence.

The Rabbis asserted that it was engraved on the rod of Moses, and enabled him to perform all his miracles. Indeed, the Talmud says that it was by the utterance of this awful name, and not by a club, that he slew the Egyptian; although it fails to tell us how he got at that time his knowledge of it.

That scurrilous book of the Jews of the Middle Ages, called the *Toldoth Jeshu*, attributes all the wonderful works of Jesus Christ to the potency of this incommunicable name, which he is said to have abstracted from the Temple, and worn about him. But it would be tedious and unprofitable to relate all the superstitious myths that have been invented about this name.

And now as to the grammatical signification of this important word. Gesenius (*Thesaur.*, ii., 577) thinks—and many modern scholars agree with him—that the word is the future form of the Hiphil conjugation of the verb *to be*, pronounced *Yavah*, and therefore that it denotes "He who made to exist, called into existence," that is, the Creator. The more generally accepted definition of the name is, that it expresses the eternal and unchangeable existence of God in respect to the past, the present, and the future. The word יהוה is derived from the substantive verb היה, hayah, *to be*, and in its four letters combines those of the past, present and future of the verb. The letter י in the beginning, says Buxtorf (*de Nomine*, v.), is a characteristic of the future; the ו in the middle, of the participle or present time; and the ה at the end, of the past. Thus, out of יהוה we get היה, *he was;* הוה, *he is;* and יהיה, *he will be.* Hence, among other

titles it received that of *nomen essentiæ*, because it shows the essential nature of God's eternal existence. The other names of God define His power, wisdom, goodness, and other qualities; but this alone defines His existence.

It has been a controverted point whether this name was made known for the first time to Moses, or whether the patriarchs had been previously acquainted with it. The generally recognized opinion now is, and the records of Genesis and Exodus sustain it, that the name was known to the patriarchs, but not in its essential meaning, into which Moses was the first to be initiated. In the language of Aben Ezra, "Certainly the name was already known to the patriarchs, but only as an uncomprehended and unmeaning noun, not as a descriptive, appellative one, indicative of the attributes and qualities of the Deity." "It is manifest," says Kallisch (*Comm. on Ex.*), "that Moses, in being initiated into the holy and comprehensive name of the Deity, obtains a superiority over the patriarchs, who, although perhaps from the beginning more believing than the long-wavering Moses, lived more in the sphere of innocent, childlike obedience than of manly, spiritual enlightenment." This, too, is the Masonic doctrine. In Freemasonry the Holy Name is the representative of the Word, which is itself the symbol of the nature of God. To know the Word is to know the true nature and essence of the Grand Architect.

When the pronunciation of the name was first interdicted to the people is not certainly known. Leusden says it was a rabbinical prohibition, and was probably made at the second Temple. The statement of the Rabbi Bechai, already cited, that the word was pronounced for the last time by Simeon, before the spoliation by the Roman emperor Vespasian, would seem to indicate that it was known at the second Temple, although its utterance was forbidden, which would coincide with the Masonic tradition that it was discovered while the foundations of the second Temple were being laid. But the general opinion is, that the prohibition commenced in the time of Moses, the rabbinical writers tracing it to the law of Leviticus, already cited. This, too, is the theory of Masonry, which also preserves a tradition that the prohibition would have been removed at the first Temple, had not a well-known occurrence prevented it. But this is not to be viewed as an historic statement, but only as a medium of creating a symbol.

The Jews had four symbols by which they expressed this Ineffable name of God: the first and most common was two Yods, with a Sheva and the point Kametz underneath, thus, ; the second was three points in a radiated form like a diadem, thus, \|/, to represent, in all probability, the sovereignty of God; the third was a Yod within an equilateral triangle, which the Kabbalists explained as a ray of light, whose luster was too transcendent to be contemplated by human eyes; and the fourth was the letter ש, which is the initial letter of *Shadai*, "the Almighty," and was the symbol usually placed upon their phylacteries. Buxtorf mentions a fifth method which was by three Yods, with a Kametz underneath 'ֵי', enclosed in a circle.

In Freemasonry, the equilateral triangle, called the delta, with or without a *Yod* in the center, the Yod alone, and the letter G, are recognized as symbols of the sacred and Ineffable name.

The history of the introduction of this word into the ritualism of Freemasonry would be highly interesting, were it not so obscure. Being in almost all respects an esoteric symbol, nearly all that we know of its Masonic relations is derived from tradition; and as to written records on the subject, we are compelled, in general, to depend on mere intimations or allusions, which are not always distinct in their meaning. In Masonry, as in the Hebrew mysteries, it was under the different appellations of the Word, the True Word, or the Lost Word, the symbol of the knowledge of Divine Truth, or the true nature of God.

That this name, in its mystical use, was not unknown to the Medieval Freemasons there can be no doubt. Many of their architectural emblems show that they possessed this knowledge. Nor can there be any more doubt that through them it came to their successors, the Freemasons of the beginning of the eighteenth century. No one can read the *Defence of Masonry*, written in 1730, without being convinced that the author (probably Martin Clare, *q. v.*) was well acquainted with this name; although he is, of course, careful to make no very distinct reference to it, except in one instance. "The occasion," he says, "of the brethren searching so diligently for their Master was, it seems, to receive from him the *secret Word of Masonry*, which should be delivered down to their fraternity in after ages." (*Constitutions*, 1738, p. 225.)

It is now conceded, from indisputable evidence, that the holy name was, in the earlier years, and, indeed, up to the middle of the last century, attached to the Third Degree, and then called the Master's Word. On some early tracing boards of the Third Degree among the emblems displayed is a coffin, on which is inscribed, in capital letters, the word JEHOVAH. Hutchinson, who wrote in 1774, makes no reference whatever to the Royal Arch, although that system had, by that time, been partially established in England; but in his lectures to Master Masons and on the Third Degree refers to "the mystic word, the Tetragrammaton." (*Lecture* X., p. 180.) Oliver tells us distinctly that it was the Master's Word until Dunckerley took it out of the degree and transferred it to the Royal Arch. That it was so on the Continent, we have the unmistakable testimony of Guillemain de St. Victor, who says, in his *Adonhiramite Masonry* (p. 90), that Solomon placed a medal on the tomb of Hiram, "on which was engraved *Jehova*, the old Master's Word, and which signifies the Supreme Being."

So far, then, these facts appear to be established: that this Ineffable name was known to the Operative Freemasons of the Middle Ages; that it was derived from them by the Speculative Masons, who, in 1717, revived the Order in England; that they knew it as Master Masons; and that it continued to be the Master's Word until late in that century, when it was removed by Dunckerley into the Royal Arch.

Although there is, perhaps, no point in the esoteric system of Masonry more clearly established than that the Tetragrammaton is the true omnific word, yet innovations have been admitted, by which, in some jurisdictions in this country, that word has been changed into three others, which simply signify Divine names in other languages, but have none of the sublime symbolism that belongs to the true name of God. It is true that the General Grand Chapter of the United States adopted a regulation disapproving of the innovation of these explanatory words, and restoring the Tetragrammaton; but this declaration of what might almost be considered a truism in Masonry has been met with open opposition or reluctant obedience in some places.

The Grand Chapter of England has fallen into the same error, and abandoned the teachings of Dunckerley, the founder of the Royal Arch in that country, as some of the Grand Chapters in America did those of Webb, who was the founder of the system here. It is well, therefore, to inquire what was the omnific word when the Royal Arch system was first invented.

We have the authority of Oliver, who had the best opportunity of any man in England of knowing the facts, for saying that Dunckerley established the Royal Arch for the modern Grand Lodge; that he wisely borrowed many things from Ramsay and Dermott; and that he boldly transplanted the word Jehovah from the Master's Degree and placed it in his new system.*

Now, what was "THE WORD" of the Royal Arch, as understood by Dunckerley? We have no difficulty here, for he himself answers the question. To the first edition of the *Laws and Regulations of the Royal Arch*, published in 1782, there is prefixed an essay on Freemasonry, which is attributed to Dunckerley. In this he makes the following remarks:

"It must be observed that the expression THE WORD is not to be understood as a watchword only, after the manner of those annexed to the several degrees of the Craft; but also theologically, as a term, thereby to convey to the mind some idea of that Grand Being who is the sole author of our existence; and to carry along with it the most solemn veneration for his sacred Name and Word, as well as the most clear and perfect elucidation of his power and attributes that the human mind is capable of receiving. And this is the light in which the

---

* But more recent authorities, such as R. F. Gould (*Hist. of F. M.*) and H. Sadler (*Life of Dunckerley*), have cast great doubt on these statements (see *Dunckerley*).　　　[E. L. H.]

Name and Word hath always been considered, from the remotest ages, amongst us Christians and the Jews."

And then, after giving the well-known history from Josephus of the word, which, to remove all doubt of what it is, he says is the "Shem Hamphorash, or the Unutterable Name," he adds: "Philo, the learned Jew, tells us not only that the word was lost, but also the time when, and the reason why. But, to make an end of these unprofitable disputes among the learned, be it remembered that they all concur with the Royal Arch Masons in others much more essential: first, that the Name or Word is expressive of SELF-EXISTENCE AND ETERNITY; and, secondly, that it can be applicable only to that GREAT BEING who WAS and IS and WILL BE."

Notwithstanding this explicit and unmistakable declaration of the founder of the English Royal Arch, that the Tetragrammaton is the omnific word, the present system in England has rejected it, and substituted in its place three other words, the second of which is wholly unmeaning.

In the American system, as revised by Thomas Smith Webb, there can be no doubt that the Tetragrammaton was recognized as the omnific word. In the *Freemasons' Monitor*, prepared by him for monitorial instruction, he has inserted, among the passages of Scripture to be read during an exaltation, the following from Exodus, which is the last in order, and which anyone at all acquainted with the ritual will at once see is appropriated to the time of the *euresis* or *discovery of the Word*.

"And God spake unto Moses, and said unto him, I am the Lord; and I appeared unto Abraham, and unto Isaac, and unto Jacob by the name of God Almighty, but by my name JEHOVAH was I not known to them."

From this it will be evident that Webb recognized the word Jehovah, and not the three other words that have since been substituted for them by some Grand Chapters in America, and which it is probable were originally used by Webb as merely explanatory or declaratory of the Divine nature of the other and principal word. And this is in accordance with one of the traditions of the degree, that they were placed on the substitute ark around the real word, as a key to explain its signification.

To call anything else but this four-lettered name an omnific word—an all-creating and all-performing word—either in Masonry or in Hebrew symbolism, whence Masonry derived it, is to oppose all the doctrines of the Talmudists, the Kabbalists, and the Gnostics, and to repudiate the teachings of every Hebrew scholar from Buxtorf to Gesenius. To fight the battle against such odds is to secure defeat. It shows more of boldness than of discretion. And hence the General Grand Chapter of the United States has very wisely restored the word Jehovah to its proper place. It is only in the York and in the American Rites that this error has ever existed. In every other Rite the Tetragrammaton is recognized as the true word.

Jephthah. A Judge of Israel, and the leader of the Gileadites in their war against the Ephraimites, which terminated in the slaughter of so many of the latter at the passes of the river Jordan. (See *Ephraimites*.)

Jephthah's Daughter. The First Degree in the American Order of the Eastern Star, or Adoptive Rite. It inculcates obedience. Color, blue. (See *Eastern Star, Order of the*.)

Jericho, Heroine of. See *Heroine of Jericho*.

Jermyn, Henry. Anderson says (*Constitutions*, 1738, p. 101) that Henry Jermyn, Earl of St. Albans, was Grand Master and held a General Assembly on the 27th of December, 1663, at which six regulations (which he quotes) were made. Roberts, in his edition of the *Old Constitutions* printed in 1722, the earliest printed Masonic book that we have, refers also to this General Assembly; the date of which he, however, makes the 8th of December. Roberts gives what he calls the Additional Orders and Constitutions. The Harleian MS., in the British Museum, numbered 1942, which Hughan supposes to have the date of 1670, and which he has published in his *Old Charges of the British Freemasons* (p. 52, ed. 1872), contains also six "new articles." The articles in Roberts's and the Harleian MS. are identical, but the wording is slightly altered by Anderson after his usual fashion. Of these new articles, one of the most important is that which prescribes that the society of Freemasons shall thereafter be governed by a Master and Wardens. Bro. Hughan thinks that there is no evidence of the statement that a General Assembly was held in 1663. But it would seem that the concurring testimony of Roberts in 1722, and of Anderson in 1738, with the significant fact that the charges are found in a manuscript written seven years after, give some plausibility to the statement that a General Assembly was held at that time.

Jekson. This word is found in the French *Cahiers* of the high degrees. It is undoubtedly a corruption of *Jacquesson*, and this a mongrel word compounded of the French *Jacques* and the English *son*, and means the *son of James*, that is, James II. It refers to Charles Edward the Pretender, who was the son of that abdicated and exiled monarch. It is a significant relic of the system attempted to be introduced by the adherents of the house of Stuart, and by which they expected to enlist Masonry as an instrument to effect the restoration of the Pretender to the throne of England. For this purpose they had altered the legend of the Third Degree, making it applicable to James II., who, being the son of Henrietta Maria, the widow of Charles I., was designated as "the widow's son."

Jena, Congress of. Jena is a city of Saxe-Weimar, in Thuringia. A Masonic Congress was convoked there in 1763, by the Lodge of Strict Observance, under the presidency of Johnson, a Masonic charlatan, whose real name was Becker. In this Congress the doctrine was announced that the Freemasons were the successors of the Knights Templar, a dogma peculiarly characteristic of the Rite of Strict Observance. In the year 1764, a second Congress was convoked by Johnson or Leucht with the desire of authoritatively establishing his doctrine of the connection between Templarism and Masonry. The empirical character of Johnson was here discovered by the Baron Hund, and he was denounced, and subsequently punished at Magdeburg by the public authorities.

Jerusalem. The capital of Judea, and memorable in Masonic history as the place where was erected the Temple of Solomon. It is early mentioned in Scripture, and is supposed to be the Salem of which Melchizedek was king. At the time that the Israelites entered the Promised Land, the city was in possession of the Jebusites, from whom, after the death of Joshua, it was conquered, and afterward inhabited by the tribes of Judah and Benjamin. The Jebusites were not, however, driven out; and we learn that David purchased Mount Moriah from Ornan or Araunah the Jebusite as a site for the Temple. It is only in reference to this Temple that Jerusalem is connected with the legends of Ancient Craft Masonry. In the degrees of chivalry it is also important, because it was the city where the holy places were situated, and for the possession of which the Crusaders so long and so bravely contested. It was there, too, that the Templars and the Hospitalers were established as Orders of religious and military knighthood.

Modern Speculative Masonry was introduced into Jerusalem by the establishment of a Lodge in 1872, the warrant for which, on the application of Robert Morris and others, was granted by the Grand Lodge of Canada. Recently a Lodge has been warranted in England to meet at Chester, but to be in due course removed to Jerusalem, named "King Solomon's Temple," No. 3464.

Jerusalem, Knight of. See *Knight of Jerusalem.*

Jerusalem, New. The symbolic name of the Christian church (Rev. xxi. 2–21; iii. 12). The Apostle John (Rev. xxi.), from the summit of a high mountain, beheld, in a pictorial symbol or scenic representation, a city resplendent with celestial brightness, which seemed to descend from the heavens to the earth. It was stated to be a square of about 400 miles, or 12,000 stadia, equal to about 16,000 miles in circumference—of course, a mystical number, denoting that the city was capable of holding almost countless myriads of inhabitants. The New Jerusalem was beheld, like Jacob's ladder, extending from earth to heaven. It plays an important part in the ritual of the Nineteenth Degree, or Grand Pontiff of the Ancient and Accepted Scottish Rite, where the descent of the New Jerusalem is a symbol of the descent of the empire of Light and Truth upon the earth.

Jerusalem, Prince of. See *Prince of Jerusalem.*

Jerusalem Word. In the Grand Mystery of the Freemasons Discovered of 1724 occurs the following question and answer:

"Q. Give me the Jerusalem Word.

"A. Giblin."

The origin of this phrase may perhaps be thus traced. The theory that after the completion of the Temple a portion of the workmen traveled abroad to seek employment, while another portion remained at Jerusalem, was well known to the Fraternity at the beginning of the last century. It is amply detailed in that old manuscript known as the York MS., which is now lost, but was translated by Krause, and inserted in his *Kunsturkunden*. It may be supposed that this "Jerusalem Word" was the word which the Masons used at Jerusalem, while the "Universal Word," which is given in the next question and answer, was the word common to the Craft everywhere. The Jerusalem Word, as such, is no longer in use, but the Universal Word is still found in the First Degree.

Jesse. A large candlestick, of metal, with many sconces, hanging from the ceiling, and symbolically referring to the Branch of Jesse.

Jesuits. In the last century the Jesuits were charged with having an intimate connection with Freemasonry, and the invention of the degree of Kadosh was even attributed to those members of the Society who constituted the College of Clermont. This theory of a Jesuitical Masonry seems to have originated with the Illuminati, who were probably governed in its promulgation by a desire to depreciate the character of all other Masonic systems in comparison with their own, where no such priestly interference was permitted. Barruel scoffs at the idea of such a connection, and calls it (*Hist. de Ja.*, iv., 287) "la fable de la Franc-Maçonnerie Jésuitique." For once he is right. Like oil and water, the tolerance of Freemasonry and the intolerance of the "Society of Jesus" cannot commingle.

Yet it cannot be denied that, while the Jesuits have had no part in the construction of pure Freemasonry, there are reasons for believing that they took an interest in the invention of some degrees and systems which were intended to advance their own interests. But wherever they touched the Institution they left the trail of the serpent. They sought to convert its pure philanthropy and toleration into political intrigue and religious bigotry. Hence it is believed that they had something to do with the invention of those degrees, which were intended to aid the exiled house of Stuart in its efforts to regain the English throne, because they believed that would secure the restoration in England of the Roman Catholic religion. Almost a library of books has been written on both sides of this subject in Germany and in France.

Jetzirah, Book of. See *Jezirah.*

Jewel of an Ancient Grand Master. A Masonic tradition informs us that the jewel of an ancient Grand Master at the Temple was the square and compass with the letter G between. This was the jewel worn by Hiram Abif on the day which deprived the Craft of his invaluable services, and which was subsequently found upon him.

Jewel, Member's. In many Lodges, especially among the Germans, where it is called "Mitglieder Zeichen," a jewel is provided for every member, and presented to him on his initiation or affiliation. It is to be worn from the buttonhole, and generally contains the name of the Lodge and some Masonic device.

Jewels, Immovable. See *Jewels of a Lodge*.

Jewels, Movable. See *Jewels of a Lodge*.

Jewels of a Lodge. Every Lodge is furnished with six jewels, three of which are movable and three immovable. They are termed jewels, says Oliver, because they have a moral tendency which renders them jewels of inestimable value. The movable jewels, so called because they are not confined to any particular part of the Lodge, are the rough ashlar, the perfect ashlar, and the trestle-board. The immovable jewels are the square, the level, and the plumb. They are termed immovable, because they are appropriated to particular parts of the Lodge, where alone they should be found, namely, the square to the east, the level to the west, and the plumb to the south. In the English system the division is the reverse of this. There, the square, level, and plumb are called movable jewels, because they pass from the three officers who wear them to their successors.

Jewels, Official. Jewels are the names applied to the emblems worn by the officers of Masonic bodies as distinctive badges of their offices. For the purpose of reference, the jewels worn in Symbolic Lodges, in Chapters, Councils, and Encampments are here appended.

1. *In Symbolic Lodges.*

W∴ Master	wears	a square.
Senior Warden	"	a level.
Junior Warden	"	a plumb.
Treasurer	"	cross keys.
Secretary	"	cross pens.
Senior Deacon	"	square and compass, sun in the center.
Junior Deacon	"	square and compass, moon in the center.
Steward	"	a cornucopia.
Tiler	"	cross swords.

The jewels are of silver in a subordinate Lodge, and of gold in a Grand Lodge. In English Lodges, the jewel of the Deacon is a dove and olive branch.

2. *In Royal Arch Chapters.*

High Priest	wears a	miter.
King	"	a level surmounted by a crown.
Scribe	"	a plumb-rule surmounted by a turban.

Captain of the Host	wears	a triangular plate inscribed with a soldier.
Principal Sojourner	"	a triangular plate inscribed with a pilgrim.
Royal Arch Captain	"	a sword.
Grand Master of the Veils	"	a sword.

The other officers as in a Symbolic Lodge All the jewels are of gold, and suspended within an equilateral triangle.

3. *In Royal and Select Councils.*

T. I. Grand Master	wears	a trowel and square.
I. Hiram of Tyre	"	a trowel and level.
Principal Conductor of the Works	"	a trowel and plumb.
Treasurer	"	a trowel and cross keys.
Recorder	"	a trowel and cross pens.
Captain of the Guards	"	a trowel and sword.
Steward	"	a trowel and cross swords.
Marshal	"	a trowel and baton.

If a Conductor of the Council is used, he wears a trowel and baton, and then a scroll is added to the Marshal's baton to distinguish the two officers.

All the jewels are of silver, and are enclosed within an equilateral triangle.

4. *In Commanderies of Knights Templars.*

Em't Commander	wears	a cross surmounted by rays of light.
Generalissimo	"	a square surmounted by a paschal lamb.
Captain-General	"	a level surmounted by a cock.
Prelate	"	a triple triangle.
Senior Warden	"	a hollow square and sword of justice.
Junior Warden	"	eagle and flaming sword.
Treasurer	"	cross keys.
Recorder	"	cross pens.
Standard-Bearer	"	a plumb surmounted by a banner.
Warder	"	a square plate inscribed with a trumpet and cross swords.
Three Guards	"	a square plate inscribed with a battle-ax.

The jewels are of silver.

Jewels, Precious. In the lectures of the Second and Third degrees, allusion is made to certain moral qualities, which, as they are intended to elucidate and impress the most important moral principles of the degree, are for their great value called the Precious Jewels of a Fellow-Craft and the Precious Jewels of a Master Mason. There are three in each degree, and they are referred to by the *Alarm*. Their explanation is esoteric.

Jewish Rites and Ceremonies. A period of excitement in favor of the rites of Judaism centered upon and pervaded the people of various nations during the early portion of the fourteenth century. The ceremonies grew and took fast hold upon the minds of the Romans, and, combining with their forms, spread to Constantinople and northwest to Germany and France. The Jewish rites, traditions, and legends thus entered the mystic schools. It was during this period that the legend of Hiram first became known (Bro. G. H. Fort), and Jehovah's name, and mystic forms were transmitted from Byzantine workmen to Teutonic sodalities and German gilds. Thus, also, when the Christian enthusiasm pervaded the North, Paganism gave way, and the formal toasts at the ceremonial banquets were drunk in the name of the saints in lieu of those of the Pagan gods.

Jews, Disqualification of. The great principles of religious and political toleration which peculiarly characterize Freemasonry would legitimately make no religious faith which recognized a Supreme Being a disqualification for initiation. But, unfortunately, these principles have not always been regarded, and from an early period the German Lodges, and especially the Prussian, were reluctant to accord admission to Jews. This action has given great offense to the Grand Lodges of other countries which were more liberal in their views, and were more in accord with the Masonic spirit, and was productive of dissensions among the Masons of Germany, many of whom were opposed to this intolerant policy. But a better spirit now prevails; and very recently the Grand Lodge of the Three Globes at Berlin, the leading Masonic body of Prussia, has removed the interdict, and Judaism is there no longer a disqualification for initiation.

Jezeeds. A Mohammedan sect in Turkey and Persia, which took its name from the founder, Jezeed, a chief who slew the sons of Ali, the father-in-law of Mohammed. They were ignorant in the extreme, having faith in both the Hebrew Bible and Koran; their hymns were addressed, without distinction, to Moses, Christ, or Mohammed.

Jezirah or **Jetzirah, Book of.** יצירה ספר, i. e., Book of the Creation. A Kabbalistic work, which is claimed by the Kabbalists as their first and oldest code of doctrines, although it has no real affinity with the tenets of the Kabbala. The authorship of it is attributed to the patriarch Abraham; but the actual date of its first appearance is supposed to be about the ninth century. Steinschneider says that it opens the literature of the Secret Doctrine. Its fundamental idea is, that in the ten digits and the twenty letters of the Hebrew alphabet we are to find the origin of all things. Landauer, a German Hebraist, thinks that the author of the *Jetzirah* borrowed his doctrine of numbers from the School of Pythagoras, which is very probable. The old Masons, it is probable, derived some of their mystical ideas of sacred numbers from this work.

Joabert. This, according to the legends of the high degrees, was the name of the chief favorite of Solomon, who incurred the displeasure of Hiram of Tyre on a certain occasion, but was subsequently pardoned, and, on account of the great attachment he had shown to the person of his master, was appointed the Secretary of Solomon and Hiram in their most intimate relations. He was afterward still further promoted by Solomon, and appointed with Tito and Adoniram a Provost and Judge. He distinguished himself in his successful efforts to bring certain traitors to condign punishment, and although by his rashness he at first excited the anger of the king, he was subsequently forgiven, and eventually received the highest reward that Solomon could bestow, by being made an Elect, Perfect, and Sublime Mason. The name is evidently not Hebrew, or must at least have undergone much corruption, for in its present form it cannot be traced to a Hebrew root. Lenning says (*Encyclopädie*) that it is *Johaben*, or, more properly, *Ihaoben*, which he interprets the Son of God; but it would be difficult to find any such meaning according to the recognised rules of the Hebrew etymology.

Joachim, Order of. A secret association instituted in Germany toward the end of the last century. Its recipients swore that they believed in the Trinity, and would never waltz. None but nobles, their wives and children, were admitted. It had no connection with Masonry.

Jobel. (Heb., יובל, *jubilans*.) A name of God used in the Thirteenth Degree, A. A. Scottish Rite.

Jochebed. (Heb., יוכבר, *God-glorified*.) The wife of Amram, and mother of Miriam, Moses, and Aaron.

Johaben. (Heb., יהו־בן; Latin, *Filius Dei*.) A name of continuous use in the A. A. Scottish Rite, and also mentioned in the Fourth and Fifth degrees of the modern French Rite.

Johannite Masonry. A term introduced by Dr. Oliver to designate the system of Masonry, of which the two Sts. John are recognized as the patrons, and to whom the Lodges are dedicated, in contradistinction to the more recent system of Dr. Hemming, in which the dedication is to Moses and Solomon. Oliver was much opposed to the change, and wrote an interesting work on the subject entitled *A Mirror for the Johannite Masons*, which was published in 1848. According to his definition, the system practised in the United States is Johannite Masonry.

Johannites. A Masonico-religious sect established in Paris, in 1814, by Fabré-Paliprat, and attached to the Order of the Temple, of which he was the Grand Master. (See *Levitikon* and *Temple, Order of the*.)

John's Brothers. In the charter of Cologne, it is said that before the year 1440 the society of Freemasons was known by no other name than that of "John's Brothers," *Joannaeorum fratrum;* that they then began to be called at Valenciennes, Free and Accepted Masons; and that at that time, in some parts of Flanders, by the assistance and riches of the brotherhood, the first hospitals were erected for the relief of such as were afflicted with St. Anthony's fire. In another part of the charter it is said that the authors of the association were called "Brothers consecrated to John"—*fratres Joanni Sacros*—because "they followed the example and imitation of John the Baptist."

Johnson. Sometimes spelled Johnstone. An adventurer, and Masonic charlatan, whose real name was Leucht. He assumed Masonry as a disguise under which he could carry on his impositions. He appeared first at Jena, in the beginning of the year 1763, and proclaimed that he had been deputed by the chiefs of Templar Masonry in Scotland to introduce a reform into the German Lodges. He established a Chapter of Strict Observance (the Rite then dominating in Germany), and assumed the dignity of Grand Prior. He made war upon Rosa, the founder of the Rosaic Rite, and upon the Grand Lodge of the Three Globes, which then sustained that enthusiast. Many of the German Lodges succumbed to his pretensions, and, surrendering their Warrants, gave in their adhesion to Johnson. Von Hund himself was at first deceived by him; but in 1764, at Altenberg, having discovered that Johnson had been formerly, under the name of Becker, the secretary of the Prince of Bernberg, whose confidence he had betrayed; that during the seven years' war he had been wandering about, becoming, finally, the servant of a Mason, whose papers he had stolen, and that by means of these papers he had been passing himself as that individual, B. von Hund denounced him as an impostor. Johnson fled, but was subsequently arrested at Magdeburg, and imprisoned in the fortress of Wartzberg, where in 1773 he died suddenly.

John the Baptist. See *Saint John the Baptist.*

John the Evangelist. See *Saint John the Evangelist.*

Joinville, Chaillou de. See *Chaillou de Joinville.*

Jokshan. (Heb., יקשן, *fowler.*) The second son of Abraham and Keturah, whose sons appear to be the ancestors of the Sabeans and Dedanites, who inhabited part of Arabia Felix. (Same as *Jeksan.*)

Jones, Inigo. One of the most celebrated of English architects, and hence called the Vitruvius of England. He was born at London on July 15, 1573, and died June 21, 1652, in the seventy-ninth year of his age. He was successively the architect of three kings—James I., Charles I., and Charles II.—and during his long career superintended the erection of many of the most magnificent public and private edifices in England, among which were the Banqueting-House of Whitehall, and the old church of St. Paul's. Jones's official

position placed him, of course, in close connection with the Operative Masons. Anderson, seizing on this circumstance, says that James I. "approved of his being chosen Grand Master of England, to preside over the Lodges" (*Constitutions,* 1738, p. 98); but the Earl of Pembroke being afterward chosen Grand Master, he appointed Jones his Deputy. These statements are copied by Entick and Noorthouck in their respective editions of the *Book of Constitutions;* but it is hardly necessary to say that they need historical confirmation. Preston says:

"During his administration, several learned men were initiated into the Order, and the society considerably increased in consequence and reputation. Ingenious artists daily resorted to England, where they met with great encouragement; Lodges were instituted as seminaries of instruction in the sciences and polite arts, after the model of the Italian schools; the communications of the Fraternity were established, and the annual festivals regularly observed."

There may be exaggeration or assumption in much of this, but it cannot be denied that the office of Jones as "King's Architect," and his labors as the most extensive builder of his time, must have brought him into close intimacy with the associations of Operative Masons, which were being rapidly influenced by a speculative character. It will be remembered that six years before Jones's death, Elias Ashmole was, by his own account, made a Freemason at Warrington, and Jones the architect and builder could hardly have taken less interest in the society than Ashmole the astrologer and antiquary. We have, perhaps, a right to believe that Jones was a Freemason.

Jones, Stephen. A miscellaneous writer and Masonic author of some celebrity. He was born at London in 1764, and educated at St. Paul's school. He was, on leaving school, placed under an eminent sculptor, but, on account of some difference, was removed and apprenticed to a printer. On the expiration of his articles, he was engaged as corrector of the press, by Mr. Strahan, the king's printer. Four years afterward, he removed to the office of Mr. Thomas Wright, where he remained until 1797, when the death of his employer dissolved his immediate connection with the printing business. He then became the editor of the Whitehall *Evening Post,* and, on the decline of that paper, of the *General Evening Post,* and afterward of the *European Magazine.* His contributions to literature were very various. He supervised an edition of Reed's *Biographia Dramatica,* an abridgment of *Burke's Reflections on the French Revolution,* and also abridgments of many other popular works. But he is best known in general literature by his *Pronouncing and Explanatory Dictionary of the English Language,* published in 1798. This production, although following Walker's far superior work, was very favorably received by the public.

In Masonry, Stephen Jones occupied a very high position. He was a Past Master of the

Lodge of Antiquity, of which William Preston was a member, and of whom Jones was an intimate friend, and one of his executors. Preston had thoroughly instructed him in his system, and after the death of that distinguished Mason, he was the first to fill the appointment of Prestonian lecturer. In 1797 he published *Masonic Miscellanies in Prose and Poetry*, which went through many editions, the last being that of 1811. In a graceful dedication to Preston, he acknowledges his indebtedness to him for any insight that he may have acquired into the nature and design of Masonry. In 1816, he contributed the article "Masonry or Freemasonry" to the *Encyclopædia Londinensis*. In 1821, after the death of Preston, he published an edition of the *Illustrations*, with *Additions and Corrections*. Bro. Matthew Cooke (London *Freemasons' Magazine*, September, 1859) says of him: "In the Masonic Craft, Bro. Jones was very deeply versed. He was a man of genial sympathies, and a great promoter of social gatherings." John Britton the architect, who knew him well, says of him (*Autobiog.*, p. 302), that "he was a man of mild disposition, strict honesty, great industry, and unblemished character." In his latter days he was in embarrassed circumstances, and derived pecuniary aid from the Literary Fund. He died, on December 20, 1828, of dropsy, in King Street, Holborn, London.

Joppa. A town of Palestine and the seaport of Jerusalem, from which it is distant about forty miles in a westerly direction. It was here that the King of Tyre sent ships laden with timber and marble to be forwarded overland to Solomon for the construction of the Temple. Its shore is exceedingly rough, and much dreaded by navigators, who, on account of its exposure, and the perpendicularity of its banks, are compelled to be perpetually on their guard. The following extract from the narrative of the Baron Geramb, a Trappist, who visited the Holy Land in 1842, will be interesting to Mark Masters. "Yesterday morning at daybreak, boats put off and surrounded the vessel to take us to the town (of Joppa), *the access to which is difficult on account of the numerous rocks that present to view their bare flanks.* The walls were covered with spectators, attracted by curiosity. The boats being much lower than the bridge, *upon which one is obliged to climb,* and having no ladder, *the landing is not effected without danger.* More than once it has happened that passengers, in springing out, have broken their limbs; and we might have met with the like accident, *if several persons had not hastened to our assistance.*" (*Pilgrimage to Jerusalem and Mount Sinai,* vol. i., p. 27.) The place is now called Jaffa.

Joram. (Heb., עוֹרָם, *excelsus.*) One of three architects sent by Solomon to superintend the cutting and preparing of timber.

Jordan. A river of Judea, on the banks of which occurred the slaughter of the Ephraimites, which is alluded to in the Second Degree.

Jordan, Charles Stephen. Secret counselor of the King of Prussia, and Vice-President of the Academy of Sciences in Berlin, was born in the year 1700, and died in the year 1745. In the year 1740, he founded, with the Baron von Bielfeld, the Lodge of Three Globes at Berlin, of which he was Secretary until the time of his death.

Jordan, Fords of the. The *exact* locality of these fords (or "passages," as the Bible terms them) cannot now be designated, but most likely they were those nearly due east of Seikoot, and opposite Mizpah. At these fords, in summer time, the water is not more than three or four feet deep, the bottom being composed of a hard limestone rock. If, as some think, the fords thirty miles higher up are those referred to, the same description will apply. At either place, the Jordan is about eighty feet wide; its banks encumbered by a dense growth of tamarisks, cane, willows, thorn bushes, and other low vegetation of the shrubby and thorny sorts, which make it difficult even to approach the margin of the stream. The Arabs cross the river at the present day, at stages of low water, at a number of fords, from the one near the point where the Jordan leaves the sea of Galilee, down to the Pilgrims' Ford, six miles above the Dead Sea. (Morris, *Freemasonry in the Holy Land,* p. 316.)

Joseph II. This emperor of Germany, who succeeded his mother Maria Theresa, at one time encouraged the Masons in his dominions, and, notwithstanding the efforts of the priests to prevent it, issued a decree in 1785, written, says Lenning, by his own hand, which permitted the meetings of Lodges under certain restrictions as to number. In this decree he says:

"In return for their compliance with this ordinance, the government accords to the Freemasons welcome, protection, and liberty; leaving entirely to their own direction the control of their members and their constitutions. The government will not attempt to penetrate into their mysteries.

"Following these directions, the Order of Freemasons, in which body are comprised a great number of worthy men who are well-known to me, may become useful to the state."

But the Austrian Masons did not enjoy this tolerance long; the Emperor at length yielded to the counsels and the influence of the bigoted priesthood, and in 1789 the ordinance was rescinded, and the Lodges were forbidden to congregate under the severest penalties.

Josephus, Flavius. A Jewish author who lived in the first century, and wrote in Greek, among other works, a *History of the Jews,* to which recourse has been had in some of the high degrees, such as the Prince of Jerusalem, and Knight of the Red Cross, or Red Cross of Babylon, for details in framing their rituals.

Joshaphat, Son of Ahilud. The name of the Orator in the degree of Provost and Judge, A. A. Scottish Rite.

Joshua. The high priest who, with Zerubbabel the Prince of Judah, superintended the rebuilding of the Temple after the Babylonian captivity. He was the high priest by lineal descent from the pontifical family, for he was the son of Josadek, who was the son of Seraiah, who was the high priest when the Temple was destroyed by the Chaldeans. He was distinguished for the zeal with which he prosecuted the work of rebuilding, and opposed the interference of the Samaritans. He is represented by the High Priest in the Royal Arch Degree according to the York and American Rites.

Journey. Journeywork, or work by the day, in contradistinction to *task*, or work by the piece, and so used in all the old *Constitutions*. Thus, in the Dowland MS., there is the charge "that noe maister nor fellowe, put no lord's work to taske that was want to goe to jornaye." It was fairer to the lord and to the craftsman to work by the day than by the piece.

Journeyman. When the Lodges were altogether operative in their character, a Mason, having served his apprenticeship, began to work for himself, and he was then called a *journeyman;* but he was required, within a reasonable period (in Scotland it was two years), to obtain admission into a Lodge, when he was said to have passed a Fellow-Craft. Hence the distinction between Fellow-Crafts and journeymen was that the former were and the latter were not members of Lodges. Thus, in the minutes of St. Mary's Chapel Lodge of Edinburgh, on the 27th of December, 1689, it was declared that "No Master shall employ a person who has not been passed a Fellow Craft in two years after the expiring of his apprenticeship"; and the names of several journeymen are given who had not complied with the law. A similar regulation was repeated by the same Lodge in 1705, complaint having been made "that there are several Masteris of this house that tolerate jurnimen to work up and down this citie contrary to their oath of admission"; and such journeymen were forbidden to seek employment. The patronage of the Craft of Freemasons was bestowed only on those who had become "free of the gild."

Jova. A significant word in the high degrees. It is a corrupted form of the Tetragrammaton.

Jua. A corrupted form of the Tetragrammaton, and a significant word in the high degrees.

Jubal Cain. Erroneously used for *Tubal Cain*, which see. Jubal was the second son of Lamech by his first wife, Ada, and was the founder of the science of music; while the third son, Tubal Cain, was a famous smithwright.

Jubela-o-m. The mythical names of assassins, the true interpretation of which is only known to the initiate who is an esoteric student.

Judah. The whole of Palestine was sometimes called the land of Judah, because Judah was a distinguished tribe in obtaining possession of the country. The tribe of Judah bore a lion in its standard, and hence the Masonic allusion to the Lion of the tribe of Judah. (See also Genesis xlix. 9, "Judah is a lion's whelp.")

Judah and Benjamin. Of the twelve tribes of Israel who were, at various times, carried into captivity, only two, those of Judah and Benjamin, returned under Zerubbabel to rebuild the second Temple. Hence, in the high degrees, which are founded on events that occurred at and after the building of the second Temple, the allusions are made only to the tribes of Judah and Benjamin.

Judith. (Heb., יהודית.) Used in the French Adoptive Masonry, and in the Fifth Degree of Sovereign Illustrious Ecossais.

Jug Lodges. An opprobrious epithet bestowed, during the anti-Masonic excitement, upon certain assemblages of worthless men who pretended to confer the degrees upon candidates weak enough to confide in them. They derived their instructions from the so-called expositions of Morgan, and exacted a trifling fee for initiation, which was generally a jug of whisky, or money enough to buy one. They were found in the mountain regions of North and South Carolina and Georgia.

Junior Adept. (*Junior Adeptus.*) One of the degrees of the German Rose Croix.

Junior Entered Apprentice. According to the rituals of the early part of the last century, the Junior Entered Apprentice was placed in the North, and his duty was to keep out all cowans and eavesdroppers. There was also a Senior Entered Apprentice, and the two seem to have occupied, in some manner, the positions now occupied by the Senior and Junior Deacons. (See *Senior Entered Apprentice.*)

Junior Overseer. The lowest officer in a Mark Lodge. When Royal Arch Chapters are opened in the Mark Degree, the duties of the Junior Overseer are performed by the Grand Master of the First Veil.

Junior Warden. The third officer in a Symbolic Lodge. He presides over the Craft during the hours of refreshment, and, in the absence of the Master and Senior Warden, he performs the duty of presiding officer. Hence, if the Master and Senior Warden were to die or remove from the jurisdiction, the Junior Warden would assume the chair for the remainder of the term. The jewel of the Junior Warden is a plumb, emblematic of the rectitude of conduct which should distinguish the brethren when, during the hours of refreshment, they are beyond the precincts of the Lodge. His seat is in the South, and he represents the Pillar of Beauty. He has placed before him, and carries in procession, a column, which is the representative of the left-hand pillar which stood at the porch of the Temple. (See *Wardens.*)

The sixth officer in a Commandery of Knights Templar is also styled Junior Warden. His duties, especially in the reception of candidates, are very important. His jewel of office is an Eagle holding a Flaming Sword.

Jurisdiction of a Grand Lodge. The jurisdiction of a Grand Lodge extends over every Lodge working within its territorial limits, and over all places not already occupied by a Grand Lodge. The territorial limits of a Grand Lodge are determined in general by the political boundaries of the country in which it is placed. Thus the territorial limits of the Grand Lodge of New York are circumscribed within the settled boundaries of that State. Nor can its jurisdiction extend beyond these limits into any of the neighboring States. The Grand Lodge of New York could not, therefore, without an infringement of Masonic usage, grant a Warrant of Constitution to any Lodge located in any State where there was already a Grand Lodge. It might, however, charter a Lodge in a Territory, where there is not in existence a Grand Lodge of that Territory. Thus the Lodges of France held their allegiance to the Grand Lodge of England until the formation of a Grand Lodge of France, and the Grand Lodges of both England, Scotland, and France granted Warrants to various Lodges in America until after the Revolution, when the States began to organize Grand Lodges for themselves. For the purpose of avoiding collision and unfriendly feeling, it has become the settled usage, that when a Grand Lodge has been legally organized in a State, all the Lodges within its limits must surrender the charters which they have received from foreign bodies, and accept new ones from the newly established Grand Lodge. This is the settled and well-recognized law of American and English Masonry. But the continental Masons, and especially the Germans, have not so rigidly interpreted this law of unoccupied territory; and there have been in France, and still are in Germany, several Grand Lodges in the same kingdom exercising coordinate powers.

Jurisdiction of a Lodge. The jurisdiction of a Lodge is geographical or personal. The *geographical jurisdiction* of a Lodge is that which it exercises over the territory within which it is situated, and extends to all the Masons, affiliated and unaffiliated, who live within that territory. This jurisdiction extends to a point equally distant from the adjacent Lodge. Thus, if two Lodges are situated within twenty miles of each other, the geographical jurisdiction of each will extend ten miles from its seat in the direction of the other Lodge. But in this case both Lodges must be situated in the same State, and hold their Warrants from the same Grand Lodge;

for it is a settled point of Masonic law that no Lodge can extend its geographical jurisdiction beyond the territorial limits of its own Grand Lodge.

The *personal jurisdiction* of a Lodge is that penal jurisdiction which it exercises over its own members wherever they may be situated. No matter how far a Mason may remove from the Lodge of which he is a member, his allegiance to that Lodge is indefeasible so long as he continues a member, and it may exercise penal jurisdiction over him.

Jurisdiction of a Supreme Council. The Masonic jurisdiction of the whole territory of the United States for the Ancient and Accepted Scottish Rite was divided between the Southern and Northern Supreme Councils in accordance with a special concession made by the former body in 1813, when the latter was organized. By this concession the Northern Supreme Council has jurisdiction over the States of Maine, New Hampshire, Vermont, Massachusetts, Rhode Island, Connecticut, New York, New Jersey, Delaware, Pennsylvania, Ohio, Illinois, and Indiana; all the other States and Territories are under the jurisdiction of the Southern Supreme Council.

Justice. One of the four cardinal virtues, the practise of which is inculcated in the First Degree. The Mason who remembers how emphatically he has been charged to preserve an upright position in all his dealings with mankind, should never fail to act justly to himself, to his brethren, and to the world. This is the corner-stone on which alone he can expect "to erect a superstructure alike honorable to himself and to the Fraternity." In iconology, Justice is usually represented as a matron with bandaged eyes, holding in one hand a sword and in the other a pair of scales at equipoise. But in Masonry the true symbol of Justice, as illustrated in the First Degree, is the feet firmly planted on the ground, and the body upright.

Justification. The Fifth Degree in the Rite of Fessler.

Just Lodge. A Lodge is said to be Just, Perfect, and Regular under the following circumstances: *Just,* when it is furnished with the three Great Lights; *Perfect,* when it contains the constitutional number of members; and *Regular,* when it is working under a Charter of Warrant of Constitution emanating from the legal authority.

K

K. (Heb., כ, *Caph*, signifying hollow of the hand.) This is the eleventh letter of the English alphabet, and in Hebrew has the numerical value of 20. In the Chaldaic or hieroglyphic it is represented by a hand.

Kaaba. The name of the holy temple of Mecca, which is to the Mohammedans what the Temple of Solomon was to the Jews. It is certainly older, as Gibbon admits, than the Christian era, and is supposed, by the tradition of the Arabians, to have been erected in the nineteenth century B.C., by Abraham, who was assisted by his son Ishmael. It derives its name of Kaaba from its cubical form, it being fifteen feet long, wide, and high. It has but one aperture for light, which is a door in the east end. In the northeast corner is a black stone, religiously venerated by the Mussulmans, called "the black stone of the Kaaba," around which cluster many traditions. One of these is that it came down from Paradise, and was originally as white as milk, but that the sins of mankind turned it black; another is, that it is a ruby which was originally one of the precious stones of heaven, but that God deprived it of its brilliancy, which would have illuminated the world from one end to the other. Syed Ahmed, who, for a Mussulman, has written a very rational *History of the Holy Mecca* (London, 1870), says that the black stone is really a piece of rock from the mountains in the vicinity of Mecca; that it owes its black color to the effects of fire; and that before the erection of the temple of the Kaaba, it was no other than one of the numerous altars erected for the worship of God, and was, together with other stones, laid up in one of the corners of the temple at the time of its construction. It is, in fact, one of the relics of the ancient stone worship; yet it reminds us of the foundation-stone of the Solomonic Temple, to which building the temple of the Kaaba has other resemblances. Thus, Syed Ahmed, who, in opposition to most Christian writers, devoutly believes in its Abrahamic origin, says that (p. 6) "the temple of the Kaaba was built by Abraham in conformity with those religious practices according to which, after a lapse of time, the descendants of his second son built the Temple of Jerusalem."

Kabbala. The mystical philosophy or theosophy of the Jews is called the Kabbala. The word is derived from the Hebrew קבל, *Kabal*, signifying to receive, because it is the doctrine received from the elders. It has sometimes been used in an enlarged sense, as comprehending all the explanations, maxims, and ceremonies which have been traditionally handed down to the Jews; but in that more limited acceptation, in which it is intimately connected with the symbolic science of Freemasonry, the Kabbala may be defined to be a system of philosophy which embraces certain mystical interpretations of Scripture, and metaphysical speculations concerning the Deity, man, and spiritual beings. In these interpretations and speculations, according to the Jewish doctors, were enveloped the most profound truths of religion, which, to be comprehended by finite beings, are obliged to be revealed through the medium of symbols and allegories. Buxtorf (*Lex. Talm.*) defines the Kabbala to be a secret science, which treats in a mystical and enigmatical manner of things divine, angelical, theological, celestial, and metaphysical; the subjects being enveloped in striking symbols and secret modes of teaching. Much use is made of it in the high degrees, and entire Rites have been constructed on its principles. Hence it demands a place in any general work on Masonry.

In what estimation the Kabbala is held by Jewish scholars, we may learn from the traditions which they teach, and which Dr. Ginsburg has given in his exhaustive work (*Kabbalah*, p. 84), in the following words:

"The Kabbalah was first taught by God himself to a select company of angels, who formed a theosophic school in Paradise. After the fall, the angels most graciously communicated this heavenly doctrine to the disobedient child of earth, to furnish the protoplasts with the means of returning to their pristine nobility and felicity. From Adam it passed over to Noah, and then to Abraham, the friend of God, who emigrated with it to Egypt, where the patriarch allowed a portion of this mysterious doctrine to ooze out. It was in this way that the Egyptians obtained some knowledge of it, and the other Eastern nations could introduce it into their philosophical systems. Moses, who was learned in all the wisdom of Egypt, was first initiated into it in the land of his birth, but became most proficient in it during his wanderings in the wilderness, when he not only devoted to it the leisure hours of the whole forty years, but received lessons in it from one of the angels. By the aid of this mysterious science, the lawgiver was enabled to solve the difficulties which arose during his management of the Israelites, in spite of the pilgrimages, wars, and the frequent miseries of the nation. He covertly laid down the principles of this secret doctrine in the first four books of the Pentateuch, but withheld them from Deuteronomy. This constitutes the former the man, and the latter the woman. Moses also initiated the seventy elders into the secrets of this doctrine, and they again transmitted them from hand to hand. Of all who formed the unbroken line of tradition, David and Solomon were first initiated into the Kabbalah. No one, however, dared to write it down till Simon ben Jochai, who lived at the time of the destruction of the second Temple. Having been condemned to death by Titus, Rabbi Simon managed to escape with his son, and concealed himself in a cavern, where he remained for twelve years. Here in this subterranean abode, he occupied himself entirely with the contemplation of the sublime Kabbalah, and was constantly visited by the prophet Elias, who disclosed to him some of its secrets, which were still concealed from the theosophical Rabbi. Here, too, his disciples resorted to be initiated by their master into these divine mysteries; and here Simon ben Jochai expired with this heavenly doctrine in his mouth, whilst discoursing on it to his disciples. Scarcely had his spirit departed, when a dazzling light filled the cavern, so that no one could look at the Rabbi; whilst a burning fire appeared outside, forming as it were a sentinel at the entrance of the cave, and denying admittance to the neighbors. It was not till the light inside, and the fire outside, had disappeared, that the disciples perceived that the lamp of Israel was extinguished. As they were preparing for his obsequies, a voice was heard from heaven, saying, 'Come ye to the marriage of Simon b. Jochai; he is entering into peace, and shall rest in his chamber!' A flame preceded the coffin, which seemed enveloped by and burning like fire. And when the remains were deposited in the tomb, another voice was heard from heaven, saying, 'This is he who caused the earth to quake and the kingdoms to shake!' His son, R. Eliezer, and his secretary, R. Abba, as well as his disciples, then collated R. Simon b. Jochai's treatises, and out of these composed the celebrated work called Sohar, (סהר,) i. e., Splendor, which is the grand storehouse of Kabbalism."

The Kabbala is divided into two kinds, the Practical and the Theoretical. The Practical Kabbala is occupied in instructions for the construction of talismans and amulets, and has no connection with Masonic science. The Theoretical Kabbala is again divided into the Dogmatic and the Literal. The Dogmatic Kabbala is the summary of the rabbinical theosophy and philosophy. The Literal Kabbala is the science which teaches a mystical mode of explaining sacred things by a peculiar use of the letters of words, and a reference to their value. Each of these divisions demands a separate attention.

I. The Dogmatic Kabbala. The origin of the Kabbala has been placed by some scholars at a period posterior to the advent of Christianity, but it is evident, from the traces of it which are found in the Book of Daniel, that it arose at a much earlier day. It has been supposed to be derived originally from the system of Zoroaster, but whether its inventors were the contemporaries or the successors of that philosopher and reformer it is impossible to say. The doctrine of emanation is, says King (Gnostics, p. 10), "the soul, the essential element of the Kabbala; it is likewise the essential element of Zoroastrism." But as we advance in the study of each we will find important differences, showing that, while the idea of the Kabbalistic theosophy was borrowed from the Zendavesta,

the sacred book of the Persian sage, it was not a copy, but a development of it.

The Kabbalistic teaching of emanation is best understood by an examination of the doctrine of the Sephiroth.

The Supreme Being, say the Kabbalists, is an absolute and inscrutable unity, having nothing without him and everything within him. He is called אין סוף, EN SOPH, "The Infinite One." In this infinitude he cannot be comprehended by the intellect, nor described in words intelligible by human minds, so as to make his existence perceptible. It was necessary, therefore, that, to render himself comprehensible, the En Soph should make himself active and creative. But he could not become the direct creator; because, being infinite, he is without will, intention, thought, desire, or action, all of which are qualities of a finite being only. The En Soph, therefore, was compelled to create the world in an indirect manner, by ten emanations from the infinite light which he was and in which he dwelt. These ten emanations are the ten Sephiroth, or Splendors of the Infinite One, and the way in which they were produced was thus: At first the En Soph sent forth into space one spiritual emanation. This first Sephirah is called כתר, Kether, "the Crown," because it occupies the highest position. This first Sephirah contained within it the other nine, which sprang forth in the following order: At first a male, or active potency, proceeded from it, and this, the second Sephirah, is called חכמה, Chocmah or "Wisdom." This sent forth an opposite, female or passive potency, named בינה, Binah or "Intelligence." These three Sephiroth constitute the first triad, and out of them proceeded the other seven. From the junction of Wisdom and Intelligence came the fourth Sephirah, called חסד, Chesed or "Mercy." This was a male potency, and from it emanated the fifth Sephirah, named גבורה, Giburah or "Justice." The union of Mercy and Justice produced the sixth Sephirah, תפארת, Tiphereth or "Beauty"; and these three constitute the second triad. From the sixth Sephirah came forth the seventh Sephirah, נצח, Nitzach or "Firmness." This was a male potency, and produced the female potency named הוד, Hod or "Splendor." From these two proceeded יסוד, Isod or "Foundation"; and these three constituted the third triad of the Sephiroth. Lastly, from the Foundation came the tenth Sephirah, called מלכות, Malcuth or "Kingdom," which was at the foot of all, as the Crown was at the top.

This division of the ten Sephiroth into three triads was arranged into a form called by the Kabbalists the Kabbalistic Tree, or the Tree of Life, as shown in the diagram on opposite page.

In this diagram the vertical arrangement of the Sephiroth is called "Pillars." Thus the four Sephiroth in the center are called the "Middle Pillar"; the three on the right, the "Pillar of Mercy"; and the three on the left, the "Pillar of Justice." They allude to these two qualities of God, of which the benignity of the one modifies the rigor of the other, so that the Divine Justice is always tempered by the Divine Mercy. C. W. King, in his *Gnostics* (p. 12), refers the right-hand pillar to the Pillar Jachin, and the left-hand pillar to the Pillar Boaz, which stood at the porch of the Temple; and "these two pillars," he says, "figure largely amongst all the secret societies of modern times, and naturally so; for these

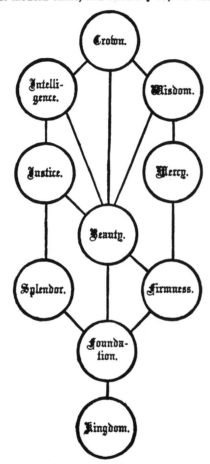

illuminati have borrowed, without understanding it, the phraseology of the Kabbalists and the Valentinians." But an inspection of the arrangement of the Sephiroth will show, if he is correct in his general reference, that he has transposed the pillars. Firmness would more naturally symbolize Boaz or Strength, as Splendor would Jachin or Establishment.

These ten Sephiroth are collectively denominated the archetypal man, the Microcosm, as the Greek philosophers called it, and each of them refers to a particular part of the body. Thus the Crown is the *head;* Wisdom, the *brain;* and Intelligence, the *heart,* which was deemed the seat of understanding. These three represent the intellectual; and the first triad is therefore called the *Intellectual World.*

Mercy is the *right arm,* and Justice the *left arm,* and Beauty is the *chest.* These three represent moral qualities; and hence the second triad is called the *Moral World.* Firmness is the *right leg,* Splendor the *left leg,* and Foundation the *privates.* These three represent power and stability; and hence the third triad is called the *Material World.* Lastly, Kingdom is the *feet,* the basis on which all stand, and represents the harmony of the whole archetypal man.

Again, each of these Sephiroth was represented by a Divine name and by an Angelic name, which may be thus tabulated:

Sephiroth.	Divine Names.	Angelic Names.
Crown,	Eheyeh,	Chajoth,
Wisdom,	Jah,	Ophanim,
Intelligence,	Jehovah,	Arelim,
Mercy,	El,	Cashmalim,
Justice,	Eloha,	Seraphim,
Beauty,	Elohim,	Shinanim,
Firmness,	Jehovah Sabaoth,	Tarshishim,
Splendor,	Elohim Sabaoth,	Beni Elohim,
Foundation,	El Chai,	Ishim,
Kingdom.	Adonai.	Cherubim.

These ten Sephiroth constitute in their totality the Atzilatic world or the world of emanations, and from it proceeded three other worlds, each having also its ten Sephiroth, namely, the Briatic world or the world of creation; the Jetziratic world or the world of formation; and the Ashiatic world or the world of action: each inhabited by a different order of beings. But to enter fully upon the nature of these worlds would carry us too far into the obscure mysticism of the Kabbala.

These ten Sephiroth, represented in their order of ascent from the lowest to the highest, from the Foundation to the Crown, forcibly remind us of the system of Mystical Ladders which pervaded all the ancient as well as the modern initiations; the Brahmanical Ladder of the Indian mysteries; the Ladder of Mithras, used in the Persian mysteries; the Scandinavian Ladder of the Gothic mysteries, and in the Masonic mysteries the Ladder of Kadosh; and lastly, the Theological Ladder of the Symbolical degrees.

II. THE LITERAL KABBALA. This division of the Kabbala, being, as has already been said, occupied in the explanation of sacred words by the value of the letters of which they are composed, has been extensively used by the inventors of the high degrees in the symbolism of their significant words. It is divided into three species: Gematria, Notaricon, and Temura.

1. *Gematria.* This word, which is evidently a rabbinical corruption of the Greek *geometria,* is defined by Buxtorf to be "a species of the Kabbala which collects the same sense of different words from their equal numerical value." The Hebrews, like other ancient nations, having no figures in their language, made use of the letters of their alphabet instead of numbers, each having a numerical value. Gematria is, therefore, a mode of con-

templating words according to the numerical value of their letters.

Any two words, the letters of which have the same numerical value, are mutually convertible, and each is supposed to contain the latent signification of the other. Thus the words in Genesis xlix. 10, "Shiloh shall come," are supposed to contain a prophecy of the Messiah, because the letters of "Shiloh shall come," יבאשילה, and of "Messiah," משיה, both have the numerical value of 358, according to the above table. By Gematria, applied to the Greek language, we find the identity of *Abraxas* and *Mithras*, the letters of each word having in the Greek alphabet the equal value of 365. This is by far the most common mode of applying the literal Kabbala.

2. *Notaricon* is derived from the Latin *notarius*, a shorthand writer or writer in cipher. The Roman Notarii were accustomed to use single letters, to signify whole words with other methods of abbreviation, by marks called "notæ." Hence, among the Kabbalists, *notaricon* is a mode of constructing one word out of the initials or finals of many, or a sentence out of the letters of a word, each letter being used as the initial of another word. Thus of the sentence in Deuteronomy xxx. 12, "Who shall go up for us to heaven?" in Hebrew מי יעלה לנו השמימה, the initial letters of each word are taken to form the word מילה, "circumcision," and the finals to form יהוה, "Jehovah"; hence it is concluded that Jehovah hath shown circumcision to be the way to heaven. Again: the six letters of the first word in Genesis, בראש.ת "in the beginning," are made use of to form the initials of six words which constitute a sentence signifying that "In the beginning God saw that Israel would accept the law," שיקבלו ישראל תורה בראשית ראה אלהים.

3. *Temura* is a rabbinical word which signifies permutation. Hence *temura* is a Kabbalistic result produced by a change or permutation of the letters of a word. Sometimes the letters are transposed to form another word, as in the modern anagram; and sometimes the letters are changed for others, according to certain fixed rules of alphabetical permutation, the 1st letter being placed for the 22d, the 2d for the 21st, the 3d for the 20th, and so on. It is in this way that Babel, בבל, is made out of Sheshach, ששך, and hence the Kabbalists say that when Jeremiah used the word Sheshach (xxv. 26), he referred to Babel.

Kabbalistic Companion. A degree found in the archives of the Mother Lodge of the Philosophical Rite of France.

Kadiri, Order of. A secret society existing in Arabia, which so much resembles Freemasonry in its object and forms, that Lieut. Burton, who succeeded in obtaining initiation into it, calls the members "Oriental Freemasons." Burton gives a very interesting account of the Order in his *Pilgrimage to El Medinah and Mecca.*

Kadosh. The name of a very important degree in many of the Masonic Rites. The word קדש is Hebrew, and signifies *holy* or *consecrated*, and is thus intended to denote the elevated character of the degree and the sublimity of the truths which distinguish it and its possessors from the other degrees. Pluche says that in the East, a person preferred to honors bore a scepter, and sometimes a plate of gold on the forehead, called a *Kadosh*, to apprise the people that the bearer of this mark or rod was a public person, who possessed the privilege of entering into hostile camps without the fear of losing his personal liberty.

The degree of Kadosh, though found in many of the Rites and in various countries, seems, in all of them, to have been more or less connected with the Knights Templar. In some of the Rites it was placed at the head of the list, and was then dignified as the *ne plus ultra* of Masonry.

It was sometimes given as a separate order or Rite within itself, and then it was divided into the three degrees of Illustrious Knight of the Temple, Knight of the Black Eagle, and Grand Elect.

Oliver enumerates five degrees of Kadosh: the Knight Kadosh; Kadosh of the Chapter of Clermont; Philosophical Kadosh; Kadosh Prince of Death; and Kadosh of the Ancient and Accepted Scottish Rite.

The French rituals speak of seven: Kadosh of the Hebrews; Kadosh of the first Christians; Kadosh of the Crusades; Kadosh of the Templars; Kadosh of Cromwell or the Puritans; Kadosh of the Jesuits; and the True Kadosh. But the correctness of this enumeration is doubtful, for it cannot be sustained by documentary evidence. In all of these Kadoshes the doctrine and the modes of recognition are substantially the same, though in most of them the ceremonies of initiation differ.

Ragon mentions a Kadosh which is said to have been established at Jerusalem in 1118; but here he undoubtedly refers to the Order of Knights Templar. He gives also in his *Tuileur Général* the nomenclature of no less than fourteen Kadosh degrees.

The doctrine of the Kadosh system is that the persecutions of the Knights Templar by Philip the Fair of France, and Pope Clement V., however cruel and sanguinary in its results, did not extinguish the Order, but it continued to exist under the forms of Freemasonry. That the ancient Templars are the modern Kadoshes, and that the builder at the Temple of Solomon is now replaced by James de Molay, the martyred Grand Master of the Templars, the assassins being represented by the King of France, the Pope, and Naffodei the informer against the Order; or, it is sometimes said, by the three informers, Squin de Florian, Naffodei, and the Prior of Montfauçon.

As to the history of the Kadosh degree, it is said to have been first invented at Lyons, in France, in 1743, where it appeared under the name of the *Petit Elu*. This degree, which is said to have been based upon the Templar doctrine heretofore referred to, was afterward developed into the Kadosh, which we find in 1758 incorporated as the *Grand Elect Kadosh* into the system of the Council of Emperors of the East and West, which was that year formed at Paris, whence it descended to the Scottish Rite Masons.

Of all the Kadoshes, two only are now important, viz.: the Philosophic Kadosh, which has been adopted by the Grand Orient of France, and the Knight Kadosh, which constitutes the Thirtieth Degree of the Ancient and Accepted Scottish Rite, this latter being the most generally diffused of the Kadoshes.

Kadosh, called also the Holy Man. (*Kadosch ou l'Homme Saint.*) The Tenth and last degree of the Rite of Martinism.

Kadosh, Grand, Elect Knight. The Sixty-fifth Degree of the Rite of Mizraim.

Kadosh, Knight. The Thirtieth Degree of the Scottish Rite. (See *Knight Kadosh.*)

Kadosh of the Jesuits. According to Thory (*Act. Lat.*, i., 320), this degree is said to have been invented by the Jesuits of the College of Clermont. The statement is not well supported. De Bonneville's Masonic Chapter of Clermont was probably, either with or without design, confounded with the Jesuitical College of Clermont. (See *Jesuits.*)

Kadosh, Philosophic. A modification of the original Kadosh, for which it has been substituted and adopted by the Grand Orient of France. The military character of the Order is abandoned, and the Philosophic Kadosh wear no swords. Their only weapon is the WORD.

Kadosh, Prince. A degree of the collection of Pyron.

Kadosh Prince of Death. The Twenty-seventh Degree of the Rite of Mizraim.

Kamea. Hebrew, קמיע, *an amulet.* More particularly applied by the Kabbalists to magic squares inscribed on paper or parchment, and tied around the neck as a safeguard against evil. (See *Magic Squares.*)

Kansas. In the year 1855 there were three Lodges in Kansas, holding warrants from the Grand Lodge of Missouri. On November 14, 1855, two of these Lodges met in convention at Leavenworth. In consequence of the absence of the third Lodge, the convention adjourned until December 27, 1855, on which day the two Lodges of Smithton and Leavenworth met, and, Wyandot Lodge being again absent, the delegates of these two Lodges organized the Grand Lodge of Kansas, and elected Richard R. Rees Grand Master.

But these proceedings were considered illegal, in consequence of the convention having been formed by two instead of three Lodges; and, accordingly, another convention of the three chartered Lodges in the Territory was held March 17, 1856, and the proceedings of the previous convention ratified by a reenactment, the same Grand Master being reelected. There are 389 Lodges under the Grand Lodge of Kansas.

The Grand Royal Arch Chapter was established January 27, 1866.

The Grand Council of Royal and Select Masters was organized December 12, 1867.

The Grand Commandery was organized December 29, 1868.

Karmatians. A Mohammedan sect that became notorious from its removal of the celebrated black stone of the Kaaba, and, after retaining it for twenty-two years, voluntarily surrendered it. Founded by Karmata at Irak in the ninth century.

Kasideans. A Latinized spelling of *Chasidim,* which see.

Katharsis. Greek, καθαρσις. The ceremony of purification in the Ancient Mysteries. Müller says (*Dorians,* i., 384) that "one of the important parts of the Pythagorean worship was the *pæan,* which was sung to the lyre in spring-time by a person sitting in the midst of a circle of listeners: this was called the *katharsis* or purification."

Keeper of the Seals. An officer called *Garde des Sceaux* in Lodges of the French Rite. It is also the title of an officer in Consistories of the Scottish Rite. The title sufficiently indicates the functions of the office.

Kellermann, Marshal. Duke de Valmy, born 1770, died 1835. Member of the Supreme Council and Grand Officer of Honor of G. O. of France; elected 1814. Served in the battles of Marengo, Austerlitz, and Waterloo.

Kelly, Christopher. A Masonic plagiarist, who stole bodily the whole of the typical part of the celebrated work of Samuel Lee entitled *Orbis Miraculum, or The Temple of Solomon pourtrayed by Scripture Light,* and published it as his own under the title of *Solomon's Temple spiritualized; setting forth the Divine Mysteries of the Temple, with an account of its Destruction.* He prefaced the book with *An Address to all Free and Accepted Masons.* The first edition was published at Dublin in 1803, and on his removal to America he published a second in 1820, at Philadelphia. Kelly was, unfortunately, a Freemason, but not an honest one.

Kenning's Masonic Cyclopædia. Edited by Rev. A. F. A. Woodford, in London, contemporaneously with the *Encyclopædia* of Dr. A. G. Mackey, in America, but published by the well-known Bro. George Kenning, 198 Fleet Street, London, to whom the work is dedicated in affectionate terms. Kenning's *Cyclopædia* is rendered unusually invaluable in consequence of the fulness of its bibliography. Kloss's well-known *Bibliographie der Freimaurer* does not become so great a necessity, having *Kenning;* yet other subjects have not been permitted to suffer in consequence of the numerous short biographic sketches. The work is an admirably arranged octavo of nearly seven hundred pages.

Kentucky. Organized Freemasonry was introduced by the Grand Lodge of Virginia, which, in the year 1788, granted a charter for Lexington Lodge, No. 25, at Lexington. This was the first Lodge instituted west of the Alleghany Mountains.

Three other Lodges were subsequently chartered by Virginia, namely, at Paris, Georgetown, and Frankford, and a dispensation granted for a fifth at Shelbyville. These five Lodges met in convention at Lexington on September 8, 1800. Having resolved that it was expedient to organize a Grand Lodge, an address was prepared to the Grand Lodge of Virginia, and the convention adjourned to October 16th. On that day it reassembled and organized the Grand Lodge of Kentucky, William Murray being elected Grand Master.

Chapters of Royal Arch Masons, independent of the Grand Lodge, were first established by Thomas Smith Webb in 1816, and the Grand Chapter was formed December 4, 1817.

The Grand Council of Royal and Select Masters was organized December 10, 1827.

The Grand Encampment (now the Grand Commandery) was organized October 5, 1847.

Scottish Masonry was introduced into Kentucky, and the Grand Consistory organized at Louisville, in August, 1852, by Bro. Albert G. Mackey, Secretary-General of the Supreme Council for the Southern Jurisdiction.

Key. "The key," says Dr. Oliver (*Landm.*, i., 180, *note*), "is one of the most important symbols of Freemasonry. It bears the appearance of a common metal instrument, confined to the performance of one simple act. But the well-instructed brother beholds in it the symbol which teaches him to keep a tongue of good report, and to abstain from the debasing vices of slander and defamation." Among the ancients the key was a symbol of silence and circumspection; and thus Sophocles alludes to it in the *Œdipus Coloneus* (1051), where he makes the chorus speak of "the golden key which had come upon the tongue of the ministering hierophant in the mysteries of Eleusis—ὦν καὶ χρυσέα κλῃς ἐπὶ γλώσσᾳ βέβακε προσπόλων εὐμολπιδᾶν." Callimachus says that the priestess of Ceres bore a key as the ensign of her mystic office. The key was in the mysteries of Isis a hieroglyphic of the opening or disclosing of the heart and conscience, in the kingdom of death, for trial and judgment.

In the old rituals of Masonry the key was an important symbol, and Dr. Oliver regrets that it has been abandoned in the modern system. In the rituals of the First Degree, in the eighteenth century, allusion is made to a key by whose help the secrets of Masonry are to be obtained, which key "is said to hang and not to lie, because it is always to hang in a brother's defence and not to lie to his prejudice." It was said, too, to hang "by the thread of life at the entrance," and was closely connected with the heart, because the tongue "ought to utter nothing but what the heart dictates." And, finally, this key is described as being "composed of no metal, but a tongue of good report." In the ritual of the Master's Degree in the Adonhiramite Rite, we find this catechism:

"*Q.* What do you conceal?

"*A.* All the secrets which have been intrusted to me.

"*Q.* Where do you conceal them?

"*A.* In the heart.

"*Q.* Have you a *key* to gain entrance there?

"*A.* Yes, Right Worshipful.

"*Q.* Where do you keep it?

"*A.* In a box of coral which opens and shuts only with ivory keys.

"*Q.* Of what metal is it composed?

"*A.* Of none. It is a tongue obedient to reason, which knows only how to speak well of those of whom it speaks in their absence as in their presence." (*Recueil Précieux*, p. 87.)

All of this shows that the key as a symbol was formerly equivalent to the modern symbol of the "instructive tongue," which, however, with almost the same interpretation, has now been transformed to the Second or Fellow-Craft's Degree. The key, however, is still preserved as a symbol of secrecy in the Royal Arch Degree; and it is also presented to us in the same sense in the ivory key of the Secret Master, or Fourth Degree of the Scottish Rite, In many of the German Lodges an ivory key is made a part of the Masonic clothing of each brother, to remind him that he should lock up or conceal the secrets of Freemasonry in his heart.

But among the ancients the key was also a symbol of power; and thus among the Greeks the title of κλειδοῦχος, or *key-bearer*, was bestowed upon one holding high office; and with the Romans, the keys are given to the bride on the day of marriage, as a token that the authority of the house was bestowed upon her; and if afterward divorced, they were taken from her, as a symbol of the deprivation of her office. Among the Hebrews the key was used in the same sense. "As the robe and the baldric," says Lowth (*Is.*, p. 2, s. 4), "were the ensigns of power and authority, so likewise was the key the mark of office, either sacred or civil." Thus in Isaiah it is said: "The key of the house of David will I lay upon his shoulders; so he shall open, and none shall shut; and he shall shut, and none shall open" (xxii. 22). Our Savior expressed a similar idea when he said to St. Peter, "I will give unto thee the keys of the kingdom of heaven." It is in reference to this interpretation of the symbol, and not that of secrecy, that the key has been adopted as the official jewel of the treasurer of a Lodge, because he has the purse, the source of power, under his command.

Key of Masonry. See *Knight of the Sun*.

Keystone. The stone placed in the center of an arch which preserves the others in their places, and secures firmness and stability to the arch. As it was formerly the custom of Operative Masons to place a peculiar mark on each stone of a building to designate the workman by whom it had been adjusted, so the Keystone was most likely to receive the most prominent mark, that of the superintendent of the structure. Such is related to have occurred to that Keystone which plays so important a part in the legend of the Royal Arch Degree.

The objection has sometimes been made, that the arch was unknown in the time of Solomon. But this objection has been completely laid at rest by the researches of antiquaries and travelers within a few years past. Wilkinson discovered arches with regular keystones in the doorways of the tombs of Thebes, the construction of which he traced to the year 1540 B.C., or 460 years before the building of the Temple of Solomon. And Dr. Clark asserts that the Cyclopean gallery of Tiryns exhibits lancet-shaped arches almost as old as the time of Abraham. In fact, at the Solomonic era, the construction of the arch must have been known to the Dionysian artificers, of whom, it is the received theory, many were present at the building of the Temple.

Khem. The Egyptian Deity, Amon, in the position metaphorically used in representations of Buddha and by the Hermetic philosophers, one hand toward Heaven and the other toward Nature.

Khepra. An Egyptian Deity, presiding over transformation, and represented with the beetle in place of a head.

Kher-heb. The Master of Ceremonies in the Egyptian system of worship.

Khesvan or **Chesvan.** (חשון.) The same Hebrew month as *Marchesvan*, which see.

Khetem el Nabiim. Mohammed, the seal of the prophets.

Khon. The title given to the dead, subject to examination as depicted in ch. 125 of the Book of the Dead in the Egyptian Ritual.

Khotbah. The Confession of Faith under the Mohammedan law.

Khurum-Abi. A variation of the name of Hiram Abi.

Ki. A word used in the old Ritual of the Eighth Degree of the A. A. Scottish Rite.

Kilwinning. As the city of York claims to be the birthplace of Masonry in England, the obscure little village of Kilwinning is entitled to the same honor with respect to the origin of the Order in the sister kingdom of Scotland. The claim to the honor, however, in each case, depends on the bare authority of a legend, the authenticity of which is now doubted by many Masonic historians. A place, which, in itself small and wholly undistinguishable in the political, the literary, or the commercial annals of its country, has become of great importance in the estimation of the Masonic antiquary from its intimate connection with the history of the Institution.

The Abbey of Kilwinning is situated in the bailiwick of Cunningham, about three miles north of the royal burgh of Irving, near the Irish Sea. The abbey was founded in the year 1140, by Hugh Morville, Constable of Scotland, and dedicated to St. Winning, being intended for a company of monks of the Tyronesian Order, who had been brought from Kelso. The edifice must have been constructed at great expense, and with much magnificence, since it is said to have occupied several acres of ground in its whole extent.

Lawrie (*Hist. of Freemasonry*, 1804) says that, by authentic documents as well as by other collateral arguments which amount almost to a demonstration, the existence of the Kilwinning Lodge has been traced back as far as the end of the fifteenth century. But we know that the body of architects who perambulated the Continent of Europe under the name of "Traveling Freemasons," flourished at a much earlier period; and we learn, also, from Lawrie himself, that several of these Masons traveled into Scotland, about the beginning of the twelfth century. Hence, we have every reason to suppose that these men were the architects who constructed the Abbey at Kilwinning, and who first established the Institution of Freemasonry in Scotland. If such be the fact, we must place the origin of the first Lodge in that kingdom at an earlier date, by three centuries, than that claimed for it by Lawrie, which would bring it much nearer, in point of time, to the great Masonic Assembly, which is traditionally said to have been convened in the year 926, by Prince Edwin, at York, in England.

There is some collateral evidence to sustain the probability of this early commencement of Masonry in Scotland. It is very generally admitted that the Royal Order of Herodem was founded by King Robert Bruce, at Kilwinning. Thory, in the *Acta Latomorum*, gives the following chronicle: "Robert Bruce, King of Scotland, under the title of Robert I., created the Order of St. Andrew of Chardon, after the battle of Bannockburn, which was fought on the 24th of June, 1314. To this Order was afterwards united that of Herodem, for the sake of the Scotch Masons, who formed a part of the thirty thousand troops with whom he had fought an army of one hundred thousand Englishmen. King Robert reserved the title of Grand Master to himself and his successors forever, and founded the Royal Grand Lodge of Herodem at Kilwinning."

Dr. Oliver says that "the Royal Order of Herodem had formerly its chief seat at Kilwinning; and there is every reason to think that it and St. John's Masonry were then governed by the same Grand Lodge."

In 1820, there was published at Paris a record which states that in 1286, James, Lord Stewart, received the Earls of Gloucester and Ulster into his Lodge at Kilwinning; which goes to prove that a Lodge was then existing and in active operation at that place.

The modern iconoclasts, however, who are leveling these old legends with unsparing hands, have here been at work. Bro. D. Murray Lyon has attacked the Bruce legend, and in the London *Freemasons' Magazine* (1868, p. 141) says: "Seeing that the fraternity of Kilwinning never at any period practised or acknowledged other than Craft degrees, and have not preserved even a shadow of a tradition that can in the remotest degree be held to identify Robert Bruce with the holding of Masonic Courts, or the Institution of a Secret Order at Kilwinning, the fraternity of the 'Herodim' must be attributed to another than the hero of Bannockburn, and a birthplace must be sought for it in a soil still more favorable to the growth of the high grades than Scotland has hitherto proved." He intimates that the legend was the invention of the Chevalier Ramsay, whose birthplace was in the vicinity of Kilwinning.

I confess that I look upon the legend and the documents that contain it with some favor, as at least furnishing the evidence that there has been among the Fraternity a general belief of the antiquity of the Kilwinning Lodge. Those, however, whose faith is of a more hesitating character, will find the most satisfactory testimonies of the existence of that Lodge in the beginning of the fifteenth century. At that period, when James II. was on the throne, the Barons of Roslin, as hereditary Patrons of Scotch Masonry, held their annual meetings at Kilwinning, and the Lodge at that place granted Warrants of Constitution for the formation of subordinate Lodges in other parts of the kingdom. The Lodges thus formed, in token of their respect for, and submission to, the mother Lodge whence they derived their existence, affixed the word Kilwinning to their own distinctive name; many instances of which are still to be found on the register of the Grand Lodge of Scotland—such as Canongate Kilwinning, Greenock Kilwinning, Cumberland Kilwinning, etc.

But, in process of time, this Grand Lodge at Kilwinning ceased to retain its supremacy, and finally its very existence. As in the case of the sister kingdom, where the Grand Lodge was removed from York, the birthplace of English Masonry, to London, so in Scotland, the supreme seat of the Order was at length transferred from Kilwinning to the metropolis; and hence, in the doubtful document entitled the "Charter of Cologne," which purports to have been written in 1542, we find, in a list of nineteen Grand Lodges in Europe, that that of Scotland is mentioned as sitting at Edinburgh, under the Grand Mastership of John Bruce. In 1736, when the Grand Lodge of Scotland was organized, the Kilwinning Lodge was one of its constituent bodies, and continued in its obedience until 1743. In that year it petitioned to be recognized as the oldest Lodge in Scotland; but as the records of the original Lodge had been lost, the present Lodge could not prove, says Lawrie, that it was the identical Lodge which had first practised Freemasonry in Scotland. The petition was therefore rejected, and, in consequence, the Kilwinning Lodge seceded from the Grand Lodge and established itself as an independent body. It organized Lodges in Scotland; and several instances are on record of its issuing charters as Mother Kilwinning Lodge to Lodges in foreign countries. Thus, it granted one to a Lodge in Virginia in 1758, and another in 1779 to some brethren in Ireland calling themselves the Lodge of High Knights Templar. But in 1807 the Mother Lodge of Kilwinning renounced all right of granting charters, and came once more into the bosom of the Grand Lodge, bringing with her all her daughter Lodges.

Here terminates the connection of Kilwinning as a place of any special importance with the Masonry of Scotland. As for the abbey, the stupendous fabric which was exe-

cuted by the Freemasons who first migrated into Scotland, its history, like that of the Lodge which they founded, is one of decline and decay. In 1560, it was in a great measure demolished by Alexander, Earl of Glencairne, in obedience to an Order from the States of Scotland, in the exercise of their usurped authority during the imprisonment of Mary Stuart. A few years afterward, a part of the abbey chapel was repaired and converted into the parish church, and was used as such until about the year 1775, when, in consequence of its ruinous and dangerous state, it was pulled down and an elegant church erected in the modern style. In 1789, so much of the ancient abbey remained as to enable Grose, the antiquary, to take a sketch of the ruins; but now not a vestige of the building is to be found, nor can its exact site be ascertained with any precision.

Kilwinning Manuscript. Also called the Edinburgh Kilwinning. This manuscript derives its name from its being written in a small quarto book, belonging to the celebrated "Mother Kilwinning Lodge" of Scotland. For its publication, the Masonic Fraternity is indebted to Bro. William James Hughan, who has inserted it in his *Unpublished Records of the Craft*, from a copy made for him from the original by Bro. D. Murray Lyon, of Ayr, Scotland. Bro. Lyon, "whilst glancing at the minutes of the Lodge of Edinburgh from December 27, 1675, till March 12, 1678, was struck with the similarity which the handwriting bore to that in which the Kilwinning copy of the *Narrative of the Founding of the Craft of Masonry* is written, and upon closer examination he was convinced that in both cases the caligraphy is the same." (*History of the Lodge of Edinburgh*, p. 107.) It was probably written in 1665. The Anglican phraseology, and the fact that one of the charges requires that Masons should be "liedgemen to the King of England," conclusively show that the manuscript was written in England and introduced into Scotland. It is so much like the text of the Grand Lodge MS., published by Bro. Hughan in his *Old Charges of British Freemasons*, that, to use the language of Bro. Woodford, "it would pass as an indifferent copy of that document."

Kilwinning, Mother Lodge. For an account of this body, which was for some time the rival of the Grand Lodge of Scotland, see *Kilwinning*.

Kilwinning System. The Masonry practised in Scotland, so called because it is supposed to have been instituted at the Abbey of Kilwinning. Oliver uses the term in his *Mirror for the Johannite Masons* (p. 120). (See *Saint John's Masonry*.)

King. The second officer in a Royal Arch Chapter in America. He is the representative of Zerubbabel, prince or governor of Judah. When the Chapter meets as a Lodge of Mark, Past, or Most Excellent Masters, the king acts as Senior Warden.

After the rebuilding of the second Temple, the government of the Jews was administered by the high priests as the vicegerents of the kings of Persia, to whom they paid tribute. This is the reason that the high priest is the presiding officer in a Chapter, and the king only a subordinate. But in the Chapters of England and Ireland, the king is made the presiding officer. The jewel of the king is a level surmounted by a crown suspended within a triangle.

King of the Sanctuary. A side degree formerly conferred in the presence of five Past Masters, now in disuse.

King of the World. A degree in the system of the Philosophical Rite.

Kings, The Five. The sacred code of the older Chinese. The word king signifies web of cloth, or the warp that keeps the threads in position, or upon which we may weave the somber and golden colors that make up this life's pictured history. This great light in Chinese secret societies contains the best sayings of the best sages on the ethico-political duties of life. They cannot be traced to a period beyond the tenth century B.C., although the religion is believed to be older.

Some of the superior classes of Chinese are believers in the great philosopher Lao-tse, and others in the doctrines of Confucius. The two religions appear to be twin in age, not strikingly dissimilar, and each has been given a personality in color in accordance with the character of ethics believed in by the two writers. Lao-tse and Confucius were the revivers of an older religion, the former of whom was born 604 B.C., and the latter fifty-four years subsequently.

The five kings are, the Yih-King, or Book of Changes; the Shi-King, or Book of Songs; the Shu-King, or Book of Annals; the Ch'un Ts'iu, or "Spring and Autumn"; and the Li-King, or Book of Rites. The fourth book was composed by Confucius himself, while the first three are supposed to have been compiled by him, and the fifth by his disciples from his teachings.

Dr. Legge, late Professor of Chinese at Oxford, England, and Dr. Medhurst assert that there are no authentic records in China earlier than 1100 B.C., and no alphabetical writing before 1500 B.C.

The grandeur of the utterances and brilliancy of the intellectual productions of Confucius and Mencius, as law-givers and expounders of the sacred code of the Chinese, called The Five Kings, are much to be admired, and are the trestle-board of fully 80,000,000 of the earth's population.

Kislev or **Chislev.** (כסלו.) The third month of the Hebrew civil year, and corresponding with the months November and December, beginning with the new moon of the former.

Kiss, Fraternal. The Germans call it *der bruder kuss;* the French, *le baiser fraternal.* It is the kiss given in the French and German Lodges by each brother to his right and left hand neighbor when the labors of the Lodge are closed. It is not adopted in the English or American systems of Ancient Craft Ma-

sonry, although practised in some of the high degrees.

Kiss of Peace. In the reception of an Ancient Knight Templar, it was the practise for the one who received him to greet him with a kiss upon the mouth. This, which was called the *osculum pacis,* or kiss of peace, was borrowed by the Templars from the religious orders, in all of which it was observed. It is not practised in the receptions of Masonic Templarism.

Kloss, Georg Burkh. Franz. A celebrated German Mason and Doctor of Medicine, who was born in 1788. Dr. Kloss was initiated into Masonry early in life. He reorganized the Eclectic Grand Lodge, of which he was several times Grand Master. He resided at Frankfort-on-the-Main, where he enjoyed a high reputation as a physician. He was the possessor of an extensive Masonic library, and devoted himself to the study of the antiquities and true character of the Masonic institution, insomuch that he was styled the "teacher of the German Freemasons." Kloss's theory was that the present Order of Freemasons found its origin in the stone-cutters and building corporations of the Middle Ages. He delivered, in the course of his life, many valuable historical discourses before the Lodge Zur Einigheit, several of which were printed and published: *Annals of the Lodge Zur Einigheit,* Frankfort, 1840; *Freemasonry in its true meaning, from the ancient and genuine documents of the Stonemasons,* Leipsic, 1846; *A History of Freemasonry in England, Scotland, and Ireland,* Leipsic, 1848; *A History of the Freemasons of France, from genuine documents,* Darmstadt, 1852; and a *Bibliography of Freemasonry,* Frankfort, 1844. This last is a most valuable contribution to Masonic literature. It contains a list of more than six thousand Masonic works in all languages, with critical remarks on many of them. Dr. Kloss died at Frankfort, February 10, 1854. Bro. Meisinger, who delivered his funeral eulogy, said of him: "He had a rare amount of learning, and was a distinguished linguist; his reputation as a physician was deservedly great; and he added to these a friendly, tender, amiable disposition, with great simplicity and uprightness of character."

Kneeling. Bending the knees has, in all ages of the world, been considered as an act of reverence and humility, and hence Pliny, the Roman naturalist, observes, that "a certain degree of religious reverence is attributed to the knees of man." Solomon placed himself in this position when he prayed at the consecration of the Temple; and Masons use the same posture in some portions of their ceremonies, as a token of solemn reverence. In the act of prayer, Masons in the lower degrees adopt the standing posture, which was the usage of the primitive Church, where it was symbolic of the resurrection; but Masons in the higher degrees generally kneel on one knee.

Knee to Knee. When, in his devotions to the G. A. O. T. U., he seeks forgiveness for the past and strength for the future, the Mason is taught that he should, in these offices of devotion, join his brother's name with his own. The prerogative that Job, in his blindness, thought was denied to him, when he exclaimed, "Oh that one might plead for a man with God, as a man pleadeth for his neighbor!" is here not only taught as a right, but inculcated as a duty; and the knee is directed to be bent in intercession, not for ourselves alone, but for the whole household of our brethren.

Knewt-neb-s. The Egyptian goddess personifying the West, facing the East.

Knife and Fork Degree. Those Masons who take more delight in the refreshments of the banquet than in the labors of the Lodge, and who admire Masonry only for its social aspect, are ironically said to be "Members of the Knife and Fork Degree."

The sarcasm was first uttered by Dermott, when he said in his *Ahiman Rezon* (p. 36), speaking of the Moderns, that "it was also thought expedient to abolish the old custom of studying geometry in the Lodge; and some of the young brethren made it appear that a good knife and fork in the hands of a dexterous brother, over proper materials, would give greater satisfaction and add more to the rotundity of the Lodge than the best scale and compass in Europe.

Knigge, Adolph Franz Friederich Ludwig, Baron von. He was at one time among the most distinguished Masons of Germany; for while Weishaupt was the ostensible inventor and leader of the system of Bavarian Illuminism, it was indebted for its real form and organization to the inventive genius of Knigge. He was born at Brendenbeck, near Hanover, October 16, 1752. He was initiated, January 20, 1772, in a Lodge of Strict Observance at Cassel, but does not appear at first to have been much impressed with the Institution, for, in a letter to Prince Charles of Hesse, he calls its ceremonies "absurd, juggling tricks." Subsequently his views became changed, at least for a time. When, in 1780, the Marquis de Costanzo was despatched by Weishaupt to Northern Germany to propagate the Order of the Illuminati, he made the acquaintance of Knigge, and succeeded in gaining him as a disciple. Knigge afterward entered into a correspondence with Weishaupt, in consequence of which his enthusiasm was greatly increased. After some time, in reply to the urgent entreaties of Knigge for more light, Weishaupt confessed that the Order was as yet in an unfinished state, and actually existed only in his own brain; the lower classes alone having been organized. Recognizing Knigge's abilities, he invited him to Bavaria, and promised to surrender to him all the manuscript materials in his possession, that Knigge might out of them, assisted by his own invention, construct the high degrees of the Rite.

Knigge accordingly repaired to Bavaria in 1781, and when he met Weishaupt, the latter consented that Knigge should elaborate the whole system up to the highest mysteries.

This task Knigge accomplished, and entered into correspondence with the Lodges, exerting all his talents, which were of no mean order, for the advancement of the Rite. He brought to its aid the invaluable labors of Bode, whom he prevailed upon to receive the degrees.

After Knigge had fully elaborated the system, and secured for it the approval of the Areopagites, he introduced it into his district, and began to labor with every prospect of success. But Weishaupt now interfered; and, notwithstanding his compact with Knigge, he made many alterations and additions, which he imperiously ordered the Provincial Directors to insert in the ritual. Knigge, becoming disgusted with this proceeding, withdrew from the Order and soon afterward entirely from Freemasonry, devoting the rest of his life to general literature. He died at Bremen, May 6, 1796.

Knigge was a man of considerable talents, and the author of many books, both Masonic and non-Masonic. Of these the following are the most important. A work published anonymously in 1781, entitled *Ueber Jesuiten, Freimaureren und deutsche Rosenkreuzer*, i. e., "On the Jesuits, Freemasons and Rosicrucians"; *Versuch über die Freimaurerei*, i. e., "Essay on Freemasonry," in 1784; *Beytrag zur neuesten Geschichte des Freimaurerordens*, i. e., "Contribution towards the latest History of the Order of Freemasons," in 1786; and, after he had retired from the Illuminati, a work entitled *Philo's endliche Erklärung*, or "Philo's final Declaration," 1788, which professed to be his answer to the numerous inquiries made of him in reference to his connection with the Order.

Among his most popular non-Masonic works was a treatise on Social Philosophy, with the title of *Ueber den Umgang mit Menschen*, or, "On Conversation with Men." This work, which was written toward the close of his life, was very favorably received throughout Germany, and translated into many languages. Although abounding in many admirable remarks on the various relations and duties of life, to the Mason it will be particularly interesting as furnishing a proof of the instability of the author's opinions, for, with all his abilities, Knigge evidently lacked a well-balanced judgment. Commencing life with an enthusiastic admiration for Freemasonry, in a few years he became disgusted with it; no long time elapsed before he was found one of its most zealous apostles; and again retiring from the Order, he spent his last days in writing against it. In his *Conversation with Men*, is a long chapter on Secret Societies, in which he is scarcely less denunciatory of them than Barruel or Robison.

Knighthood. The Saxon word *cniht*, from which we get the English *knight*, signified at first a youth, and then a servant, or one who did domestic service, or a soldier who did military service, which might either be on foot or on horseback; but the French word *chevalier* and the German *ritter* both refer to his equestrian character. Although Tacitus says that the German kings and chiefs were attended in war and peace by a select body of faithful servants, and although the Anglo-Saxon kings and thanes had their military attendants, who served them with a personal fealty, the knight, in the modern acceptation of the word, did not appear until the establishment in France of the order of chivalry. Thence knighthood rapidly passed into the other countries of Christendom; for it always was a Christian institution.

The stages through which a candidate passed until his full investiture with the rank of knighthood were three: the Page, the Squire or Esquire, and the Knight.

1. *The Page.* The child who was destined to knighthood continued until he was seven years old in the charge of women, who gave him that care which his tender age required. He was then taken from them and placed in the hands of a governor, who prepared him by a robust and manly education for the labors and dangers of war. He was afterward put into the household of some noble, where he first assumed the title of a Page. His employments were to perform the service of a domestic about the person of his master and mistress; to attend them in the chase, on their journeys, their visits, and their walks; to carry their messages, or even to wait on them at table. The first lessons given to him were in the love of God and attachment to and respect for females. His religious education was not neglected, and he was taught a veneration for all sacred things. His instructions in respect to manners, conversation, and virtuous habits were all intended to prepare him for his future condition as a knight.

2. *The Squire.* The youth, on emerging from the employment of a Page, took on him that of Squire, called in French *écuyer*. This promotion was not unaccompanied by an appropriate ceremony. The Page who was to be made a Squire was presented to the altar by his father and mother, or by those who represented them, each holding a lighted taper in his hand. The officiating priest took from the altar a sword and belt, on which he bestowed several benedictions, and then placed them on the youth, who from that time constantly wore them. The Squires were divided into various classes, each of whose employment was different. To some, as to the chamberlains, was committed the care of the gold and silver of the household; others, as the constable, had the charge of the table utensils; others were carvers, and others butlers. But the most honorable and the only one connected immediately with chivalry was the squire of Honor or the Body Squire. He was immediately attached to some knight, whose standard he carried. He helped to dress and undress him, and attended him morning and evening in his apartment. On a march, he led the war-horse of his master and carried his sword, his helmet, and his shield. In the hour of battle, the Squire, although he did not actually take a part in the combat, was not altogether an idle spectator of the contest. In the shock of battle, the two lines of knights, with their lances in rest, fell impetuously on each other; some, who were thrown from their horses, drew their swords or battle-axes to defend themselves and to make new attacks, while advantage was sought by their enemies over those who had been thrown. During all this time, the Squire was attentive to every motion of his master. In the one case, to give him new arms, or to supply him with another horse; to raise him up when he fell, and to ward off the strokes aimed at him; while in the other case, he seconded the knight by every means that his skill, his valor, and his zeal could suggest, always, however, within the strict bounds of the defensive, for the Squire was not permitted by the laws of chivalry to engage in offensive combat with a knight.

3. *The Knight.* These services merited and generally received from the knight the most grateful acknowledgment, and in time the high honor of the badge of knighthood bestowed by his own hand, for every knight possessed the prerogative of making other knights.

The age of twenty-one was that in which the youthful Squire, after so many proofs of zeal, fidelity, and valor, might be admitted to the honor of knighthood. The rule as to age was not, however, always observed. Sometimes the Squire was not knighted until he was further advanced in years, and in the case of princes the time was often anticipated. There are instances of infants, the sons of kings, receiving the dignity of knighthood.

The creation of a knight was accompanied by solemn ceremonies, which some writers have been pleased to compare to those of the Church in the administration of its sacraments, and there was, if not a close resemblance, a manifest allusion in the one to the other. The white habit and the bath of the knight corresponded to the form of baptism; the stroke on the neck and the embrace given to the new knight were compared to the ceremony of confirmation; and as the godfather made a present to the child whom he held at the font, so the lord who conferred knighthood was expected to make a gift or grant some peculiar favor to the knight whom he had dubbed.

The preliminary ceremonies which prepared the neophyte for the sword of chivalry were as follows: austere fasts; whole nights passed in prayers in a church or chapel; the sacraments of confession, penance, and the eucharist; bathings, which prefigured purity of manners and life; a white habit as a symbol of the same purity, and in imitation of the custom with new converts on their admission into the Church, and a serious attention to sermons, were all duties of preparation to be devoutly performed by the Squire previous to his being armed with the weapons and decorated with the honors of knighthood.

An old French chronicler thus succinctly details the ceremony of creation and investiture. The neophyte bathes; after which, clothed in white apparel, he is to watch all night in the church, and remain there in prayer until after the celebration of high mass. The communion being then received, the youth solemnly raises his joined hands and his eyes to heaven, when the priest who had administered the sacrament passes the sword over the neck of the youth and blesses it. The candidate then kneels at the feet of the lord or knight who is to arm him. The lord asks him with what intent he desires to enter into that sacred Order, and if his views tend only to the maintenance and honor of religion and of knighthood. The lord, having received from the candidate a satisfactory reply to these questions, administers the oath of reception, and gives him three strokes on the neck with the flat side of the sword, which he then girds upon him. This scene passes sometimes in a hall or in the court of a palace, or, in time of war, in the open field.

The girding on of the sword was accompanied with these or similar words: "In the name of God, of St. Michael, and of St. George, I make thee a knight: be brave, be hardy, and be loyal." And then the kneeling candidate is struck upon the shoulder or back of the neck by him who confers the dignity, with the flat of the sword, and directed to rise in words like these: "Arise, Sir Damian"; a formula still followed by the sovereigns of England when they confer the honor of knighthood. And hence the word "Sir," which is equivalent to the old French "Sire," is accounted, says Ashmole, "parcel of their style."

Sir William Segar, in his treatise on *Civil and Military Honor*, gives the following account of the ceremonies used in England in the sixth century:

"A stage was erected in some cathedral, or spacious place near it, to which the gentleman was conducted to receive the honor of knighthood. Being seated on a chair decorated with green silk, it was demanded of him if he were of a good constitution, and able to undergo the fatigue required in a soldier; also whether he were a man of good morals, and what credible witnesses he could produce to affirm the same.

"Then the Bishop or Chief Prelate of the Church administered the following oath: 'Sir, *you that desire to receive the honor of knighthood, swear before God and this holy book that you will not fight against his Majesty, that now bestoweth the order of knighthood upon you. You shall also swear to maintain and defend all Ladies, Gentlemen, Widows and Orphans; and you shall shun no adventure of your person in any war wherein you shall happen to be.*'

"The oath being taken, two Lords led him to the King, who drew his sword, and laid it upon his head, saying, *God and St. George* (or what other saint the King pleased to name,) *make thee a good knight;* after which seven Ladies dressed in white came and girt a sword to his side and four knights put on his spurs.

"These ceremonies being over, the Queen took him by the right hand, and a Duchess by the left, and leading him to a rich seat, placed him on an ascent, where they seated him, the King sitting on his right hand, and the Queen on his left.

"Then the Lords and Ladies also sat down upon other seats, three descents under the King; and being all thus seated, they were entertained with a delicate collation; and so the ceremony ended."

The manner of arming a newly made knight was first to put on the spurs, then the coat of mail, the cuirass, the brasset or casque, and the gauntlets. The lord or knight conferring the honor then girded on the sword, which last was considered as the most honorable badge of chivalry, and a symbol of the labor that the knight was in future to encounter. It was in fact deemed the real and essential part of the ceremony, and that which actually constituted the knight. Du Cange, in his *Glossarium*, defines the Latin word *militare*, in its medieval sense, as signifying "to make a knight," which was, he says, "balteo militari accingere," i. e., *to gird on him the knightly belt;* and it is worthy of remark, that *cingulus*, which in pure Latin signifies *a belt*, came in the later Latin of Justinian to denote the *military profession*. I need not refer to the common expression, "a belted knight," as indicating the close connection between knighthood and the *girding* of the belt. It was indeed the belt and sword that made the knight.

The oath taken by the knight at his reception devoted him to the defense of religion and the Church, and to the protection of widows, orphans, and all of either sex who were powerless, unhappy, or suffering under injustice and oppression; and to shrink from the performance of these duties whenever called upon, even at the sacrifice of his life, was to incur dishonor for the rest of his days.

Of all the laws of chivalry, none was maintained with more rigor than that which secured respect for the female sex. "If an honest and virtuous lady," says Brantome, "will maintain her firmness and constancy, her servant, that is to say, the knight who had devoted himself to her service, must not even spare his life to protect and defend her, if she runs the least risk either of her fortune, or her honor, or of any censorious word, for we are bound by the laws of Chivalry to be the champions of women's afflictions."

Nor did any human law insist with so much force as that of chivalry upon the necessity of an inviolable attachment to truth. Adherence to his word was esteemed the most honorable part of a knight's character. Hence to give the lie was considered the most mortal and irreparable affront, to be expiated only by blood.

An oath or solemn promise given in the name of a knight was of all oaths the most inviolable. Knights taken in battle engaged to come of their own accord to prison whenever it was required by their captors, and on their word of honor they were readily allowed liberty for the time for which they asked it; for no one ever doubted that they would fulfil their engagements. Sovereigns considered their oath of knighthood as the most solemn that they could give, and hence the Duke of Bretagne, having made a treaty of peace with Charles VI. of France, swore to its observance "by the faith of his body and the loyalty of his knighthood."

It is scarcely necessary to say that generous courage was an indispensable quality of a knight. An act of cowardice, of cruelty, or of dishonorable warfare in battle, would overwhelm the doer with deserved infamy. In one of the *tenzones*, or poetical contests of the Troubadours, it is said that to form a perfect knight all the tender offices of humanity should be united to the greatest valor, and pity and generosity to the conquered associated with the strictest justice and integrity. Whatever was contrary to the laws of war was inconsistent with the laws of chivalry.

The laws of chivalry also enforced with peculiar impressiveness sweetness and modesty of temper, with that politeness of demeanor which the word *courtesy* was meant perfectly to express. An uncourteous knight would have been an anomaly.

Almost all of these knightly qualities are well expressed by Chaucer in the Prologue to his *Knight's Tale* (l. 43–50; 67–72):

> "A knight there was, and that a worthy man,
> That from the time that he first began
> To riden out he loved chivalry,
> Truth and honor, freedom and courtesy.
> Full worthy was he in his lord's war
> And thereto had he ridden, no man farther;
> As well in Christendom as in Heatheness,
> And ever honored for his worthiness.

> . . . .

> "And ever more he had a sovereign price;
> And though that he was worthy, he was wise
> And of his port as meek as is a maid.
> He never yet no villainy not said
> In all his life unto no manner wight,
> He was a very perfect, gentle knight."

The most common and frequent occasions on which knights were created, independent of those which happened in war, were at the great feasts of the Church, and especially at the feast of Pentecost; also at the publications of peace or a truce, the coronations of kings, the birth or baptism of princes, and the days on which those princes had themselves received knighthood. But a knight could at any time confer the distinction on one whom he deemed deserving of it.

There was a distinction between the titles as well as the dress of a knight and a squire. The knight was called Don, Sire, Messire, or, in English, Sir—a title not bestowed upon a squire: and while the wife of the former was called a Lady, that of the latter was only a Gentlewoman. The wife of a knight was sometimes called *Militissa*, or female knight.

In their dresses and their harness, knights were entitled to wear gold and golden decorations, while the squires were confined to the use of silver. Knights alone had a right to wear, for the lining of their cloaks and mantles, ermine, sable, and meniver, which were the most valuable furs; while those of a less costly kind were for the squires. The long and trailing mantle, of a scarlet color, and lined with ermine or other precious furs, which was called the Mantle of Honor, was especially reserved for the knight. Such a mantle was always presented by the kings of France to knights whom they created. The mantle was considered the most august and noble decoration that a knight could wear, when he was not dressed in his armor. The official robes still worn by many magistrates in Europe are derived from the knightly Mantle of Honor.

It should be remarked that the order of knighthood, and the ceremonies accompanying the investiture of a knight, were of a symbolic character, and are well calculated to remind the Freemason of the symbolic character of his own Institution.

The sword which the knight received was called "the arms of mercy," and he was told to conquer his enemies by mercy rather than by force of arms. Its blade was two-edged, to remind him that he must maintain chivalry and justice, and contend only for the support of these *two chief pillars of the temple of honor*. The lance represented Truth, because truth, like the lance, is straight. The coat of mail was the symbol of a fortress erected against vice; for, as castles are surrounded by walls and ditches, the coat of mail is closed in all its parts, and defends the knight against treason, disloyalty, pride, and every other evil passion. The rowels of the spur were given to urge the possessor on to deeds of honor and virtue. The shield, which he places betwixt himself and his enemy, was to remind him that the knight is a shield interposed between the prince and the people, to preserve peace and tranquillity.

In a Latin manuscript of the thirteenth century, copied by Anstis (App., p. 95), will be found the following symbolical explanation of the ceremonial of knighthood. The *bath* was a symbol of the washing away of sin by the sacrament of baptism. The bed into which the novice entered and reposed after the bath, was a symbol of the peace of mind which would be acquired by the virtue of chivalry. The white garments with which he was afterward clothed, were a symbol of the purity which a knight should maintain. The scarlet robe put on the newly made knight was symbolic of the blood which he should be ready to shed for Christ and the Church. The dark boots are a sign of the earth, whence we all came, and to which we are all to return. The white belt is a symbol of chastity. The golden spur symbolizes promptitude of action. The sword is a symbol of severity against the attacks of Satan; its two edges are to teach the knight that he is to defend the poor against the rich, and the weak against the powerful. The white fillet around the head is a symbol of good works. The alapa or blow was in memorial of him who made him a knight.

There was one usage of knighthood which is peculiarly worthy of attention. The love of glory, which was so inspiring to the knights of chivalry, is apt to produce a spirit of rivalry and emulation that might elsewhere prove the fruitful source of division and discord. But this was prevented by the fraternities of arms so common among the knights. Two knights who had, perhaps, been engaged in the same expeditions, and had conceived for each other a mutual esteem and confidence, would enter into a solemn compact by which they became and were called "Brothers in arms." Under this compact, they swore to share equally the labors and the glory, the dangers and the profits of all enterprises, and never, under any circumstances, to abandon each other. The brother in arms was to be the enemy of those who were the enemies of his brother, and the friend of those who were his friends; both of them were to divide their present and future wealth, and to employ that and their lives for the deliverance of each other if taken prisoner. The claims of a brother in arms were paramount to all others, except those of the sovereign. If the services of a knight were demanded at the same time by a lady and by a brother in arms, the claim of the former gave way to that of the latter. But the duty which was owing to the prince or to the country was preferred to all others, and hence brothers in arms of different nations were only united together so long as their respective sovereigns were at peace, and a declaration of war between two princes dissolved all such confraternities between the subjects of each. But except in this particular case, the bond of brotherhood was indissoluble, and a violation of the oath which bound two brothers together was deemed an act of the greatest infamy. They could not challenge each other. They even wore in battle the same habits and armor, as if they desired that the enemy should mistake one for the other, and thus that both might incur an equal risk of the dangers with which each was threatened.

Knights were divided into two ranks, namely, Knights Bachelors and Knights Bannerets.

The *Knight Bachelor* was of the lower rank, and derived his title most probably from the French *bas chevalier*. In the days of chivalry, as well as in later times, this dignity was conferred without any reference to a qualification of property. Many Knights Bachelors were in fact mere adventurers, unconnected by feudal ties of any sort, who offered their services in war to any successful leader, and found in their sword a means of subsistence, not only by pay and plunder, but in the regularly established system of ransom, which every knight taken in action paid for his liberty. The Knight Bachelor bore instead of a square banner a pointed or triangular ensign, which was forked by being extended in two cornets or points, and which was called a pennon. The triangular banner, not forked, was called a pennoncel, and was carried by a squire.

The *Knight Banneret*, a name derived from *banneret*, a little banner, was one who possessed many fiefs, and who was obliged to serve in war with a large attendance of followers.

If a knight was rich and powerful enough to furnish the state or his sovereign with a certain number of armed men, and to entertain them at his own expense, permission was accorded to him to add to his simple designation of Knight or Knight Bachelor, the more noble and exalted title of Knight Banneret. This gave him the right to carry a square banner on the top of his lance. Knights Bachelors were sometimes made Bannerets on the field of battle, and as a reward of their prowess, by the simple ceremony of the sovereign cutting off with his sword the cornets or points of their pennons, thus transforming them into square banners. Clark, in his *History of Knighthood* (vol. i., p. 73), thus describes this ceremony in detail:

"The king or his general, at the head of his army drawn up in order of battle after a victory, under the royal standard displayed, attended by all the officers and nobility present, receives the knight led between two knights carrying his pennon of arms in his hand, the heralds walking before him, who proclaim his valiant achievements for which he has deserved to be made a Knight Banneret, and to display his banner in the field; then the king or general says to him, *Advancez toy banneret*, and causes the point of his pennon to be rent off; then the new knight, having the trumpets before him sounding, the nobility and officers bearing him company, is sent back to his tent, where they are all entertained."

But generally the same ceremonial was used in times of peace at the making of a Knight Banneret as at the institution of barons, viscounts, earls, and the other orders of nobility, with whom they claimed an almost equality of rank.

Not long after the institution of knighthood as an offshot of chivalry, we find, besides the individual Knights Bachelors and Knights Bannerets, associations of knights banded together for some common purpose, of which there were two classes. First: Fraternities possessing property and rights of their own as independent bodies into which knights were admitted as monks were into religious foundations. Of this class may be mentioned, as examples, the three great religious Orders—the Templars, the Hospitalers, and the Teutonic Knights.

The second class consisted of honorary associations established by sovereigns within their respective dominions, consisting of members whose only common tie is the possession of the same titular distinction. Such are most of the European orders of knighthood now existing, as the Knights of the Garter in England, the Knights of St. Andrew in Russia, and the Knights of the Golden Fleece in Spain. The institution of these titular orders of knighthood dates at a much more recent period than that of the Fraternities who constitute the first class, for not one of them can trace its birth to the time of the Crusades, at which time the Templars and similar orders sprang into existence.

Ragon, in his *Cours Philosophique*, attempts to draw a parallel between the institution of knighthood and that of Freemasonry, such as that there were three degrees in one as there are in the other, and that there was a close resemblance in the ceremonies of initiation into both orders. He thus intimates for them a common origin; but these parallels should rather be considered simply as coincidences. The theory first advanced by the Chevalier Ramsay, and adopted by Hund and the disciples of the Rite of Strict Observance, that all Freemasons are Templars, and that Freemasonry is a lineal successor of ancient knighthood, is now rejected as wholly untenable and unsupported by any authentic history. The only connection between knighthood and Freemasonry is that which was instituted after the martyrdom of James de Molay, when the Knights Templar sought concealment and security in the bosom of the Masonic Fraternity.

When one was made a knight, he was said to be *dubbed*. This is a word in constant use in the Medieval manuscripts. In the old Patavian statutes, "Miles adobatus," a *dubbed knight*, is defined to be "one who, by the usual ceremonies, acquires the dignity and profession of chivalry." The Provençal writers constantly employ the term *to dub*, "adouber," and designate a knight who has gone through the ceremony of investiture as "un chevalier adoubé," *a dubbed knight*. Thus, in the *Romaunt d'Auberi*, the Lady d'Auberi says to the king:

> "Sire, dit elle, par Dieu de Paradis
> Soit *adouber* mes frères auberis."

That is, "Sire, for the love of the God of Paradise, let my brothers be *dubbed*."

The meaning of the word then is plain: *to dub*, is to make or create a knight. But its derivation is not so easily settled amid the conflicting views of writers on the subject. The derivation by Menage from *duplex* is not worth consideration. Henschell's, from a Provençal word *adobare*, "to equip," although better, is scarcely tenable. The derivation from the Anglo-Saxon *dubban*, "to strike or give a blow," would be reasonable, were it not presumable that the Anglo-Saxons borrowed their word from the French and from the usages of chivalry. It is more likely that *dubban* came from *adouber*, than that *adouber* came from *dubban*. The Anglo-Saxons took their forms and technicalities of chivalry from the French. After all, the derivation proposed by Du Cange is the most plausible and the one most generally adopted, because it is supported by the best authorities. He says that it is derived from the Latin *adoptare*, to adopt, "quod qui aliquem armis instruit ac Militem facit, eum quodammodo adoptat in filium," i. e., "He who equips any one with arms, and makes him a knight, adopts him, as it were, as a son." To dub one as a knight is, then, to adopt him into the order of chivalry.

The idea was evidently taken from the Roman law of *adoptatio*, or adoption, where, as in conferring knighthood, a blow on the cheek was given.

The word *accolade* is another term of chivalry about which there is much misunderstanding. It is now supposed to mean the blow of the sword, given by the knight conferring the dignity, on the neck or shoulder of him who received it. But this is most probably an error. The word is derived, says Brewer (*Dict. Phr. and Fab.*), from the Latin *ad collum*, "around the neck," and signifies the embrace "given by the Grand Master when he receives a neophyte or new convert." It was an early custom to confer an embrace and the kiss of peace upon the newly made knight, which ceremony, Ashmole thinks, was called the *accolade*. Thus, in his *History of the Order of the Garter* (p. 15), he says: "The first Christian kings, at giving the belt, kissed the new knight on the left cheek, saying: *In the honor of the Father and the Son and the Holy Ghost, I make you a knight.* It was called the *osculum pacis*, the kiss of favor or of brotherhood [more correctly the kiss of peace], and is presumed to be the accolade or ceremony of embracing, which Charles the Great used when he knighted his son Louis the Débonnair." In the book of Johan de Vignay, which was written in the fourteenth century, this kiss of peace is mentioned together with the accolade: "Et le Seigneur leur doit donner une colée en signe de proeste et de hardement, et que il leur souveigne de celui noble homme qui la fait chevalier. Et donc les doit le Seigneur baisier en la bouche en signe de paix et d'amour"; i. e., "And the lord ought to give him [the newly-made knight] an accolade as a symbol of readiness and boldness, and in memory of the nobleman who has made him a knight; and then the lord ought to kiss him on the mouth as a sign of peace and love."

In an old manuscript in the Cottonian Library, entitled "The manner of makynge Knyghtes after the custome of Engelande," a copy of which is inserted in Anstis's *Historical Essay on the Knighthood of the Bath* (Append., p. 99), is this account of the embrace and kiss, accompanied with a blow on the neck: "Thanne shall the Squyere lift up his armes on high, and the Kynge shall put his armes about the nekke of the Squyer, and lyftynge up his right hande he shall smyte the Squyer in the nekke, seyeng thus: *Be ye a good Knyhte;* kissing hjm." Anstis himself is quite confused in his description of the ceremonial, and enumerates "the blow upon the neck, the accolade, with the embracing and kiss of peace," as if they were distinct and separate ceremonies; but in another part of his book he calls the accolade "the laying hands upon the shoulders." I am inclined to believe, after much research, that both the blow on the neck and the embrace constituted properly the accolade. This blow was sometimes given with the hand, but sometimes with the sword. Anstis says that "the action which fully and finally impresses the character of knighthood is the blow given with the hand upon the neck or shoulder." But he admits that there has been a controversy among writers whether the blow was heretofore given with a sword or by the bare hand upon the neck (p. 73).

The mystical signification which Caseneuve gives in his *Etymologies* (voc. Accollée) is ingenious and appropriate, namely, that the blow was given on the neck to remind him who received it that he ought never, by flight from battle, to give an enemy the opportunity of striking him on the same place.

But there was another blow, which was given in the earliest times of chivalry, and which has by some writers been confounded with the accolade, which at length came to be substituted for it. This was the blow on the cheek, or, in common language, the box on the ear, which was given to a knight at his investiture. This blow is never called the accolade by the old writers, but generally the *alapa*, rarely the *gautada*. Du Cange says that this blow was sometimes given on the neck, and that then it was called the *colaphus*, or by the French *colée*, from *col*, the neck. Duchesne says the blow was always given with the hand, and not with the sword.

Ashmole says: "It was in the time of Charles the Great the way of knighting by the *colaphum*, or blow on the ear, used in sign of sustaining future hardships, . . . a custom long after retained in Germany and France. Thus William, Earl of Holland, who was to be knighted before he could be emperor, at his being elected king of the Romans, received knighthood by the box of the ear, etc., from John, king of Bohemia, A. D. 1247."

Both the word *alapa* and the ceremony which it indicated were derived from the form of manumission among the Romans, where the slave on being freed received a blow called *alapa* on the cheek, characterized by Claudian as "*felix injuria*," a happy injury, to remind him that it was the last blow he was compelled to submit to: for thenceforth he was to be a freeman, capable of vindicating his honor from insult. The *alapa*, in conferring knighthood, was employed with a similar symbolism. Thus in an old register of 1260, which gives an account of the knighting of Hildebrand by the Lord Ridolfonus, we find this passage, which I give in the original, for the sake of the one word *gautata*, which is unusual: "Postea Ridolfonus de more dedit illi gautatam et dixit illi. Tu es miles nobilis militiæ equestris, et hæc gautata est in recordationem, illius qui te armavit militem, et hœc gautata debet esse ultima injuria, quam patienter acceperis." That is: "Afterwards Ridolfonus gave him in the customary way the blow, and said to him: Thou art a noble Knight of the Equestrian Order of Chivalry, and this blow is given in memory of him who hath armed thee as a knight, and it must be the last injury which thou shalt patiently endure." The first reason assigned for the blow refers to an old custom of cuffing the witnesses to a transaction, to

impress it on their memory. Thus, by the riparian law, when there was a sale of land, some twelve witnesses were collected to see the transfer of property and the payment of the price, and each received a box on the ear, that he might thus the better remember the occurrence. So the knight received the blow to make him remember the time of his receiving his knighthood and the person who conferred it.

For the commission of crime, more especially for disloyalty to his sovereign, a knight might be degraded from the Order; and this act of degradation was accompanied with many ceremonies, the chief of which was the hacking off his spurs. This was to be done for greater infamy, not by a knight, but by the master cook. Thus Stow says that, at the making of Knights of the Bath, the king's master cook stood at the door of the chapel, and said to each knight as he entered, "Sir Knight, look that you be true and loyal to the king my master, or else I must hew these spurs from your heels." His shield too was reversed, and the heralds had certain marks called *abatements*, which they placed on it to indicate his dishonor.

M. de St. Palaye concludes his learned and exhaustive *Memoires sur l'ancienne Chevalerie* with this truthful tribute to that spirit of chivalry in which ancient knighthood found its birth, and with it I may appropriately close this article:

"It is certain that chivalry, in its earliest period, tended to promote order and good morals; and although it was in some respects imperfect, yet it produced the most accomplished models of public valor and of those pacific and gentle virtues that are the ornaments of domestic life; and it is worthy of consideration, that in an age of darkness, most rude and unpolished, such examples were to be found as the results of an institution founded solely for the public welfare, as in the most enlightened times have never been surpassed and very seldom equalled."

Knight. 1. An order of chivalry. (See *Knighthood* and *Knight Masonic*.)

2. The Eleventh and last degree of the Order of African Architects.

Knight, Black. See *Black Brothers*.

Knight Commander. (*Chevalier Commandeur*.) 1. The Ninth Degree of the Rite of Elect Cohens. 2. A distinction conferred by the Supreme Council of the Ancient and Accepted Scottish Rite for the Southern Jurisdiction of the United States on deserving Honorary Thirty-thirds and Sublime Princes of the Royal Secret. It is conferred by a vote of the Supreme Council, and is unattended with any other ceremony than the presentation of a decoration and a patent.

Knight Commander of the Temple. See *Sovereign Commander of the Temple*.

Knight Commander of the White and Black Eagle. (*Chevalier Commandeur de l'Aigle blanc et noir*.) The Eightieth Degree of the collection of the Metropolitan Chapter of France.

Knight Crusader. (*Chevalier Croisé.*) Thory says (*Act. Lat.*, i., 303) that this is a chivalric degree, which was communicated to him by a member of the Grand Lodge of Copenhagen. He gives no further account of its character.

Knight Elect of Fifteen. 1. The Sixteenth Degree of the Ancient and Accepted Rite, more commonly called Illustrious Elect of the Fifteen. (See *Elect of Fifteen.*)

2. The Tenth Degree of the Chapter of Emperors of the East and West.

3. The Eleventh Degree of the Rite of Mizraim.

Knight Elect of Twelve, Sublime. The Eleventh Degree of the Ancient and Accepted Rite, sometimes called "Twelve Illustrious Knights." After vengeance had been taken upon the traitors mentioned in the degrees of Elected Knights of Nine and Illustrious Elected of Fifteen, Solomon, to reward those who had exhibited their zeal and fidelity in inflicting the required punishment, as well as to make room for the exaltation of others to the degree of Illustrious Elected of Fifteen, appointed twelve of these latter, chosen by ballot, to constitute a new degree, on which he bestowed the name of Sublime Knights Elected, and gave them the command over the twelve tribes of Israel. The Sublime Knights rendered an account each day to Solomon of the work that was done in the Temple by their respective tribes, and received their pay. The Lodge is called a Chapter. In the old rituals Solomon presides, with the title of Thrice Puissant, and instead of Wardens, there are a Grand Inspector and a Master of Ceremonies. In the modern ritual of the Southern Jurisdiction, the Master and Wardens represent Solomon, Hiram of Tyre, and Adoniram, and the style of the Master and Senior Warden is Thrice Illustrious. The room is hung with black, sprinkled with white and red tears.

The apron is white, lined and bordered with black, with black strings; on the flap, a flaming heart.

The sash is black, with a flaming heart on the breast, suspended from the right shoulder to the left hip.

The jewel is a sword of justice.

This is the last of the three Elus which are found in the Ancient Scottish Rite. In the French Rite they have been condensed into one, and make the Fourth Degree of that ritual, but not, as Ragon admits, with the happiest effect.

Knight Evangelist. A grade formerly in the archives of the Lodge of *St. Louis des Amis Réunis at Calais*. (Thory, *Acta Lat.*, i., 312.)

Knight Hospitaler. See *Knight of Malta.*

Knight, Illustrious or **Illustrious Elect.** (*Chevalier Illustre* or *Elu Illustre*.) The Thirteenth Degree of the Rite of Mizraim.

Knight Jupiter. (*Le Chevalier Jupiter*.) The Seventy-eighth Degree of the collection of Peuvret.

Knight Kadosh, formerly called Grand Elect Knight Kadosh. (*Grand Elu du Chevalier Kadosch*.) The Knight Kadosh is the Thirtieth Degree of the Ancient and Accepted Scottish Rite, called also Knight of the White and Black Eagle. While retaining the general Templar doctrine of the Kadosh system, it symbolizes and humanizes the old lesson of vengeance. It is the most popular of all the Kadoshes.

In the Knight Kadosh of the Ancient and Accepted Scottish Rite, the meetings are called Councils. The principal officers are, according to the recent rituals, a Commander, two Lieutenant Commanders, called also Prior and Preceptor; a Chancellor, Orator, Almoner, Recorder, and Treasurer. The jewel, as described in the ritual of the Southern Supreme Council, is a double-headed eagle, displayed resting on a teutonic cross, the eagle silver, the cross gold enameled red. The Northern Council uses instead of the eagle the letters J. B. M. The Kadoshes, as representatives of the Templars, adopt the Beauseant as their standard. In this degree, as in all the other Kadoshes, we find the mystical ladder of seven steps.

Knight Kadosh of Cromwell. Ragon says of this (*Tuileur*, p. 171), that it is a pretended degree, of which he has four copies, and that it appears to be a monstrosity invented by an enemy of the Order for the purposes of calumniation. The ritual says that the degree is conferred only in England and Prussia, which is undoubtedly untrue.

Knight Masonic. The word *knight*, prefixed to so many of the high degrees as a part of the title, has no reference whatever to the orders of chivalry, except in the case of Knights Templar and Knights of Malta. The word, in such titles as Knight of the Ninth Arch, Knight of the Brazen Serpent, etc., has a meaning totally unconnected with Medieval knighthood. In fact, although the English, German, and French words Knight, Ritter, and Chevalier, are applied to both, the Latin word for each is different. A Masonic knight is, in Latin, *eques;* while the Medieval writers always called a knight of chivalry *miles.* So constant is this distinction, that in the two instances of Masonic knighthood derived from the chivalric orders, the Knights Templar and the Knight of Malta, this word *miles* is used, instead of *eques,* to indicate that they are not really degrees of Masonic knighthood. Thus we say *Miles Templarius* and *Miles Melitæ.* If they had been inventions of a Masonic ritualist, the titles would have been *Eques Templarius* and *Eques Melitæ.*

The *eques*, or Masonic knight, is therefore not, in the heraldic sense, a knight at all. The word is used simply to denote a position higher than that of a mere Master; a position calling, like the "devoir" of knighthood, for the performance of especial duties. As the word "prince," in Masonic language, denotes not one of princely rank, but one invested with a share of Masonic sovereignty and command, so "knight" denotes one who is expected to be distinguished with peculiar fidelity to the cause in which he has enlisted. It is simply, as has been said, a point of rank above that of the Master Mason. It is, therefore, confined to the high degrees.

Knight Mahadon. (*Chevalier Mahadon.*) A degree in the Archives of the *Lodge of St. Louis des Amis Réunis at Calais.*

Knight of Asia, Initiated. See *Asia, Initiated Knights of.*

Knight of Athens. (*Chevalier d'Athènes.*) 1. The Fifty-second Degree of the Rite of Mizraim. 2. A degree in the nomenclature of Fustier. 3. A degree in the Archives of the Mother Lodge of the Philosophic Rite in France.

Knight of Aurora. (*Chevalier de l'Aurore.*) A degree belonging to the Rite of Palestine. It is a modification of the Kadosh, and is cited in the collection of Fustier. In the collection of M. Viany, it is also called *Knight of Palestine.*

Knight of Beneficence. (*Chevalier de la Bienfaisance.*) The Forty-ninth Degree of the collection of the Metropolitan Chapter of France. It is also called *Knight of Perfect Silence.*

Knight of Brightness. (*Chevalier de la Clarté.*) The Seventh and last degree of the system of the Clerks of Strict Observance, called also *Magus.*

Knight of Christ. After the dissolution of the Templars in the fourteenth century, those knights who resided in Portugal retained the possessions of the Order in that country, and perpetuated it under the name of the Knights of Christ. Their badge is a red cross pattée, charged with a plain white cross. (See *Christ, Order of.*)

Knight of Constantinople. A side degree; instituted, doubtless, by some lecturer; teaching, however, an excellent moral lesson of humility. Its history has no connection whatever with Masonry. The degree is not very extensively diffused; but several Masons, especially in the Western States, are in possession of it. It may be conferred by any Master Mason on another; although the proper performance of the ceremonies requires the assistance of several. When the degree is formally conferred, the body is called a Council, and consists of the following officers: Illustrious Sovereign, Chief of the Artisans, Seneschal, Conductor, Prefect of the Palace, and Captain of the Guards.

Knight of Hope. 1. A species of androgynous Masonry, formerly practised in France. The female members were called *Dames* or *Ladies of Hope.* 2. A synonym of *Knight of the Morning Star,* which see.

Knight of Iris. (*Chevalier de l'Iris.*) The Fourth Degree of the Hermetic Rite of Montpellier.

Knight of Jerusalem. (*Chevalier de Jerusalem.*) The Sixty-fifth Degree of the collection of the Metropolitan Chapter of France.

Knight of Justice. Knights Hospitalers of St. John of Jerusalem or Knights of Malta were called, in the technical language of the Order, Knights of Justice.

Knights of Malta. This Order, which at various times in the progress of its history received the names of Knights Hospitalers, Knights of St. John of Jerusalem, Knights of Rhodes, and, lastly, Knights of Malta, was one of the most important of the religious and military orders of knighthood which sprang into existence during the Crusades which were instituted for the recovery of the Holy Land. It owes its origin to the Hospitalers of Jerusalem, that wholly religious and charitable Order which was established at Jerusalem, in 1048, by pious merchants of Amalfi for the succor of poor and distressed Latin pilgrims. (See *Hospitalers of Jerusalem.*) This society, established when Jerusalem was in possession of the Mohammedans, passed through many vicissitudes, but lived to see the Holy City conquered by the Christian knights. It then received many accessions from the Crusaders, who, laying aside their arms, devoted themselves to the pious avocation of attending the sick. It was then that Gerard, the Rector of the Hospital, induced the brethren to take upon themselves the vows of poverty, obedience, and chastity, which they did at the hands of the Patriarch of Jerusalem, who clothed them in the habit selected for the Order, which was a plain, black robe bearing a white cross of eight points on the left breast. This was in the year 1099, and some writers here date the beginning of the Order of Knights of Malta. But this is an error. It was not until after the death of Gerard that the Order assumed that military character which it ever afterward maintained, or, in other words, that the peaceful Hospitalers of Jerusalem became the warlike Knights of St. John.

In 1118, Gerard, the Rector of the Hospital, died, and was succeeded by Raymond du Puy, whom Marulli, the old chronicler of the Order, in his *Vite de' Gran Maestri* (Napoli, 1636), calls "secondo Rettore e primo Maestro."

The peaceful habits and monastic seclusion of the Brethren of the Hospital, which had been fostered by Gerard, no longer suited the warlike genius of his successor. He therefore proposed a change in the character of the society, by which it should become a military Order, devoted to active labors in the field and the protection of Palestine from the encroachments of the infidels. This proposition was warmly approved by Baldwyn II., King of Jerusalem, who, harassed by a continual warfare, gladly accepted this addition to his forces. The Order having thus been organized on a military basis, the members took a new oath, at the hands of the Patriarch of Jerusalem, by which they bound themselves to defend the cause of Christianity against the infidels in the Holy Land to the last drop of their blood, but on no account to bear arms for any other purpose.

This act, done in 1118, is considered as the beginning of the establishment of the Order of Knights Hospitalers of St. John, of which Raymond du Puy is, by all historians, deemed the first Grand Master.

By the rule established by Du Puy for the government of the Order, it was divided into three classes, namely, 1. Knights, who were called Knights of Justice; 2. Chaplains; and 3. Serving Brothers; all of whom took the three vows of chastity, obedience, and poverty. There was also attached to the institution a body of men called Donats, who, without assuming the vows of the Order, were employed in the different offices of the hospital, and who wore what was called the demi-cross, as a badge of their connection.

The history of the Knights from this time until the middle of the sixteenth century is but a chronicle of continued warfare with the enemies of the Christian faith. When Jerusalem was captured by Saladin, in 1187, the Hospitalers retired to Margat, a town and fortress of Palestine which still acknowledged the Christian sway. In 1191, they made Acre, which in that year had been recaptured by the Christians, their principal place of residence. For just one hundred years the knights were engaged, with varying success, in sanguinary contests with the Saracens and other infidel hordes, until Acre, the last stronghold of the Christians in the Holy Land, having fallen beneath the blows of the victorious Moslems, Syria was abandoned by the Latin race, and the Hospitalers found refuge in the island of Cyprus, where they established their convent.

The Order had been much attenuated by its frequent losses in the field, and its treasury had been impoverished. But commands were at once issued by John de Villiers, the Grand Master, to the different Grand Priories in Europe, and large reinforcements in men and money were soon received, so that the Fraternity were enabled again to open their hospital and to recommence the practise of their religious duties. No longer able to continue their military exploits on land, the knights betook themselves to their galleys, and, while they protected the pilgrims who still flocked in vast numbers to Palestine, gave security to the Christian commerce of the Mediterranean. On sea, as on land, the Hospitalers still showed that they were the inexorable and terrible foes of the infidels, whose captured vessels soon filled the harbor of Cyprus.

But in time a residence in Cyprus became unpleasant. The king, by heavy taxes and other rigorous exactions, had so disgusted them, that they determined to seek some other residence. The neighboring island of Rhodes had long, under its independent princes, been the refuge of Turkish corsairs; a name equivalent to the more modern one of pirates. Fulk de Villaret, the Grand Master of the Hospital, having obtained the approval of Pope Clement and the assistance of several of the European States, made a descent upon the island, and, after months of hard fighting, on the 15th of August, 1310, planted the standard of the Order on the walls of the city of Rhodes; and the island thenceforth became the home of the Hospitalers, whence they were often called the Knights of Rhodes.

The Fraternity continued to reside at Rhodes for two hundred years, acting as the outpost and defense of Christendom from the encroachments of the Ottoman power. Of this long period, but few years were passed in peace, and the military reputation of the Order was still more firmly established by the prowess of the knights. These two centuries were marked by other events which had an important bearing on the fortunes of the institution. The rival brotherhood of the Templars was abolished by the machinations of a pope and a king of France, and what of its revenues and possessions was saved from the spoliation of its enemies was transferred to the Hospitalers.

There had always existed a bitter rivalry between the two Orders, marked by unhappy contentions, which on some occasions, while both were in Palestine, amounted to actual strife. Toward the Knights of St. John the Templars had never felt nor expressed a very kindly feeling; and now this acceptance of an unjust appropriation of their goods in the hour of their disaster, keenly added to the sentiment of ill-will, and the unhappy children of De Molay, as they passed away from the theater of knighthood, left behind them the bitterest imprecations on the disciples of the Hospital.

The Order, during its residence at Rhodes, also underwent several changes in its organization, by which the simpler system observed during its infancy in the Holy Land was rendered more perfect and more complicated. The greatest of all these changes was in the character of the European Commanderies. During the period that the Order was occupied in the defense of the holy places, and losing large numbers of its warriors in its almost continual battles, these Commanderies served as nurseries for the preparation and education of young knights who might be sent to Palestine to reinforce the exhausted ranks of their brethren. But now, secured in their island home, Jerusalem permanently in possession of the infidel, and the enthusiasm once inspired by Peter the Hermit forever dead, there was no longer need for new Crusaders. But the knights, engaged in strengthening and decorating their insular possession by erecting fortifications for defense, and palaces and convents for residence, now required large additions to their revenue to defray the expenses thus incurred. Hence the Commanderies were the sources whence this revenue was to be derived; and the Commanders, once the Principals, as it were, of military schools, became lords of the manor in their respective provinces. There, by a judicious and economical administration of the property which had been entrusted to them, by the cultivation of gardens and orchards, by the rent received from arable and meadow lands, of mills and fisheries appertaining to their estates, and even by the voluntary contributions of their neighbors, and by the raising of stock, they were enabled to add greatly to their income. Of this one-fifth was claimed, under the name of responsions, as a tribute to be sent annually to Rhodes for the recuperation of the always diminishing revenue of the Order.

Another important change in the organization of the Order was made at a General Chapter held about 1320 at Montpellier, under the Grand Mastership of Villanova. The Order was there divided into *languages*, a division unknown during its existence in Palestine. These languages were at first seven in number, but afterward increased to eight, by the subdivision of that of Aragon. The principal dignities of the Order were at the same time divided among these languages, so that a particular dignity should be always enjoyed by the same language. These languages, and the dignities respectively attached to them, were as follows:

1. Provence: Grand Commander.
2. Auvergne: Grand Marshal.
3. France: Grand Hospitaler.
4. Italy: Grand Admiral.
5. Aragon: Grand Conservator.
6. Germany: Grand Bailiff.
7. Castile: Grand Chancellor.
8. England: Grand Turcopolier.

But perhaps the greatest of all changes was that which took place in the personal character of the Knights. "The Order," says Taafe (*Hist.*, iv., 234), "had been above two hundred years old before it managed a boat, but was altogether equestrian during its two first, and perhaps most glorious, centuries." But on settling at Rhodes, the knights began to attack their old enemies by sea with the same prowess with which they had formerly met them on land, and the victorious contests of the galleys of St. John with the Turkish corsairs, who were infesting the Mediterranean, proved them well entitled to the epithet of naval warriors.

In the year 1480, Rhodes was unsuccessfully besieged by the Ottoman army of Mohammed II., under the command of Paleologus Pasha. After many contests, the Turks were repulsed with great slaughter. But the attack of the Sultan Solyman, forty-four years afterward, was attended with a different result, and Rhodes was surrendered to the Turkish forces on the 20th of December, 1522. The terms of the capitulation were liberal to the knights, who were permitted to retire with all their personal property; and thus, in the Grand Mastership of L'Isle Adam, Rhodes ceased forever to be the home of the Order, and six days afterward, on New Year's Day, 1523, the fleet, containing the knights and four thousand of the inhabitants, sailed for the island of Candia.

From Candia, where the Grand Master remained but a short time, he proceeded with his knights to Italy. Seven long years were passed in negotiations with the monarchs of Europe, and in the search for a home. At length, the Emperor Charles V., of Germany, vested in the Order the complete and perpetual sovereignty of the islands of Malta and Gozo, and the city of Tripoli; and in 1530,

the knights took formal possession of Malta, where, to borrow the language of Porter (*Hist.*, ii., 33), "for upwards of two centuries and a half, waved the banner of St. John, an honor to Christianity and a terror to the infidel of the East." From this time the Order received the designation of "Knights of Malta," a title often bestowed upon it, even in official documents, in the place of the original one of "Knights Hospitalers of St. John of Jerusalem."

For 268 years the Order retained possession of the island of Malta. But in 1798 it was surrendered without a struggle by Louis de Hompesch, the imbecile and pusillanimous Grand Master, to the French army and fleet under Bonaparte; and this event may be considered as the commencement of the suppression of the Order as an active power.

Hompesch, accompanied by a few knights, embarked in a few days for Trieste, and subsequently retired to Montpellier, where he resided in the strictest seclusion and poverty until May 12, 1805, when he died, leaving behind him not enough to remunerate the physicians who had attended him.

The great body of the knights proceeded to Russia, where the Emperor Paul had a few years before been proclaimed the protector of the Order. On the 27th of October, 1798, a Chapter of such of the knights as were in St. Petersburg was held, and the Emperor Paul I. was elected Grand Master. This election was made valid, so far as its irregularities would permit, by the abdication of Hompesch in July, 1799.

At the death of Paul in 1801, his successor on the throne, Alexander, appointed Count Soltikoff as Lieutenant of the Mastery, and directed him to convene a Council at St. Petersburg to deliberate on future action. This assembly adopted a new statute for the election of the Grand Master, which provided that each Grand Priory should in a Provincial Chapter nominate a candidate, and that out of the persons so nominated the Pope should make a selection. Accordingly, in 1802, the Pope appointed John de Tommasi, who was the last knight that bore the title of Grand Master.

On the death of Tommasi, the Pope declined to assume any longer the responsibility of nominating a Grand Master, and appointed the Bailiff Guevarr Luardo simply as Lieutenant of the Mastery, a title afterward held by his successors, Centelles, Busca, De Candida, and Collavedo. In 1826 and 1827, the first steps were taken for the revival of the English language, and Sir Joshua Meredith, Bart., who had been made a knight in 1798 by Hompesch, being appointed Lieutenant Prior of England, admitted many English gentlemen into the Order.

But the real history of the Order of St. John of Jerusalem ends with the disgraceful capitulation at Malta in 1798. All that has since remained of it, all that now remains—however imposing may be the titles assumed—is but the diluted shadow of its former existence.

The organization of the Order in its days of prosperity was very complicated, partaking both of a monarchial and a republican character. Over all presided a Grand Master, who, although invested with extensive powers, was still controlled by the legislative action of the General Chapter.

The Order was divided into eight languages, over each of which presided one of the Grand dignitaries with the title of Conventual Bailiff. These dignitaries were the Grand Commander, the Grand Marshal, the Grand Hospitaler, the Grand Conservator, the Grand Turcopolier, the Grand Bailiff, and the Grand Chancellor. Each of these dignitaries resided in the palace or inn at Malta which was appropriated to his language. In every province there were one or more Grand Priories presided over by Grand Priors, and beneath these were the Commanderies, over each of which was a Commander. There were scattered through the different countries of Europe 22 Grand Priories and 596 Commanderies.

Those who desired admission into the Order as members of the first class, or Knights of Justice, were required to produce proofs of noble descent. The ceremonies of initiation were public and exceedingly simple, consisting of little more than the taking of the necessary vow. In this the Hospitalers differed from the Templars, whose formula of admission was veiled in secrecy. Indeed, Porter (*Hist.,* i., 203) attributes the escape of the former Order from the accusations that were heaped upon the latter, and which led to its dissolution, to the fact that the Knights "abjured all secrecy in their forms and ceremonies."

The Order was dissolved in England by Henry VIII., and, although temporarily restored by Mary, was finally abolished in England. A decree of the Constituent Assembly abolished it in France in 1792. By a decree of Charles IV., of Spain, in 1802, the two languages of Aragon and Castile became the Royal Spanish Order of St. John, of which he declared himself the Grand Master.

Now, only the languages of Germany and Italy remain. The Order is, therefore, at this day in a state of abeyance, if not of disintegration, although it still maintains its vitality, and the functions of Grand Master are exercised by a Lieutenant of the Magistery, who resides at Rome. Attempts have also been made, from time to time, to revive the Order in different places, sometimes with and sometimes without the legal sanction of the recognized head of the Order. For instance, there are now in England two bodies—one Catholic, under Sir George Bowyer, and the other Protestant, at the head of which is the Duke of Manchester; but each repudiates the other. But the relic of the old and valiant Order of Knights Hospitalers claims no connection with the branch of Masonry which bears the title of Knights of Malta, and hence the investigation of its present condition is no part of the province of this work.

Knight of Malta, Masonic. The degree

26

of Knight of Malta is conferred in the United States as "an appendant Order" in a Commandery of Knights Templar. There is a ritual attached to the degree, but very few are in possession of it, and it is generally communicated after the candidate has been created a Knights Templar; the ceremony consisting generally only in the reading of the passage of Scripture prescribed in the Monitors, and the communication of the modes of recognition.

How anything so anomalous in history as the commingling in one body of Knights Templar and Knights of Malta, and making the same person a representative of both Orders, first arose, it is now difficult to determine. It was, most probably, a device of Thomas S. Webb, and was, it may be supposed, one of the results of a too great fondness for the accumulation of degrees. Mitchell, in his *History of Freemasonry* (ii., 83), says: "The degree, so called, of Malta, or St. John of Jerusalem, crept in, we suppose, by means of a bungler, who, not knowing enough of the ritual to confer it properly, satisfied himself by simply adding a few words in the ceremony of dubbing; and thus, by the addition of a few signs and words but imperfectly understood, constituted a Knights Templar also a Knight of Malta, and so the matter stands to this day." I am not generally inclined to place much confidence in Mitchell as an historian; yet I cannot help thinking that in this instance his guess is not very far from the truth, although, as usual with him, there is a tinge of exaggeration in his statement.

There is evidence that the degree was introduced at a very early period into the Masonry of this country. In the Constitution of the "United States Grand Encampment," adopted in 1805, one section enumerates "Encampments of Knights of Malta, Knights Templars, and Councils of Knights of the Red Cross," now Companions of the Red Cross. It will be observed that the Knight of Malta precedes the Knights Templar; whereas, in the present system, the former is made the ultimate degree of the series. Yet, in this Constitution, no further notice is taken of the degree; for while the fees for the Red Cross and the Templar degrees are prescribed, there is no reference to any to be paid for that of Malta. In the revised Constitution of 1816, the order of the series was changed to Red Cross, Templar, and Malta, which arrangement has ever since been maintained. The Knights of Malta are designated as one of the "Appendant Orders," a title and a subordinate position which the pride of the old Knights of Malta would hardly have permitted them to accept.

In 1856, the Knights Templar of the United States had become convinced that the incorporation of the Order of Malta with the Knights Templar, and making the same person the possessor of both Orders, was so absurd a violation of all historic truth, that at the session of the General Grand Encampment in that year, at Hartford, Connecticut, on the suggestion of the author, the degree was unanimously stricken from the Constitution; but at the session of 1862, in Columbus, Ohio, it was, I think, without due consideration, restored, and is now communicated in the Commanderies of Knights Templar.

There is no fact in history better known than that there existed from their very birth a rivalry between the two Orders of the Temple and of St. John of Jerusalem, which sometimes burst forth into open hostility. Porter says (*Hist. K. of Malta*, i., 107), speaking of the dissensions of the two Orders, "instead of confining their rivalry to a friendly emulation, whilst combating against their common foe, they appeared more intent upon thwarting and frustrating each other, than in opposing the Saracen."

To such an extent had the quarrels of the two Orders proceeded, that Pope Alexander III. found it necessary to interfere; and in 1179 a hollow truce was signed by the rival houses of the Temple and the Hospital; the terms of which were, however, never strictly observed by either side. On the dissolution of the Templars so much of their possessions as were not confiscated to public use were given by the sovereigns of Europe to the Knights of Malta, who accepted the gift without compunction. And there is a tradition that the surviving Templars, indignant at the spoliation and at the mercenary act of their old rivals in willingly becoming a party to the robbery, solemnly registered a vow never thereafter to recognize them as friends.

The attempt at this day to make a modern Knights Templar accept initiation into a hated and antagonistic Order is to display a lamentable ignorance of the facts of history.

Another reason why the degree of Knight of Malta should be rejected from the Masonic system is that the ancient Order never was a secret association. Its rites of reception were open and public, wholly unlike anything in Masonry. In fact, historians have believed that the favor shown to the Hospitalers, and the persecutions waged against the Templars, are to be attributed to the fact that the latter Order had a secret system of initiation which did not exist in the former. The ritual of reception, the signs and words as modes of recognition now practised in the modern Masonic ceremonial, are all a mere invention of a very recent date. The old Knights knew nothing of such a system.

A third, and perhaps the best, reason for rejecting the Knights of Malta as a Masonic degree is to be found in the fact that the Order still exists, although in a somewhat decayed condition; and that its members, claiming an uninterrupted descent from the Knights who, with Hompesch, left the island of Malta in 1797, and threw themselves under the protection of Paul of Russia, utterly disclaim any connection with the Freemasons, and almost contemptuously repudiate the so-called Masonic branch of the Order. In 1858, a manifesto was issued by the supreme authority of the Order, dated from "the Magisterial Palace of the Sacred Order" at Rome, which, after stating that the Order, as it then existed, consisted only of the Grand Priories in the Langues of Italy and Germany, the knights in Prussia, who trace descent from the Grand Bailiwick of Brandenburg, and a few other knights who had been legally received by the Mastership and Council, declares that:

"Beyond and out of the above-mentioned Langues and Priories, and excepting the knights created and constituted as aforesaid, all those who may so call or entitle themselves *are legally ignored* by our Sacred Order."

There is no room there provided for the so-called Masonic Knights of Malta. But a writer in *Notes and Queries* (3d Ser., iii., 413), who professes to be in possession of the degree, says, in reply to an inquiry, that the Masonic degree "has nothing whatever to do with the Knights Hospitalers of St. John of Jerusalem." This is most undoubtedly true in reference to the American degree. Neither in its form, its ritual, the objects it professes, its tradition, nor its historical relations, is it in the slightest degree assimilated to the ancient Order of Hospitalers, afterward called Knights of Rhodes, and, finally, Knights of Malta. To claim, therefore, to be the modern representatives of that Order, to wear its dress, to adopt its insignia, to flaunt its banners, and to leave the world to believe that the one is but the uninterrupted continuation of the other, are acts which must be regarded as a very ridiculous assumption, if not actually entitled to a less courteous appellation.

For all these reasons, I think that it is much to be regretted that the action of the Grand Encampment in repudiating the degree in 1856 was reversed in 1862. The degree has no historical or traditional connection with Masonry; holds no proper place in a Commandery of Templars, and ought to be wiped out of the catalogue of Masonic degrees.*

Knight of Masonry, Terrible. (*Chevalier Terrible de la Maçonnerie*.) A degree contained in the collection of Le Page.

Knight of Palestine. (*Chevalier de la Palestine*.) 1. The Sixty-third Degree of the Rite of Mizraim. 2. The Ninth Degree of the Reform of St. Martin. 3. One of the series of degrees formerly given in the Baldwyn Encampment of England, and said to have been introduced into Bristol, in 1800, by some French refugees under the authority of the Grand Orient of France.

---

* A different view is now generally held by Templars regarding the Knights of Malta, and a modified ritual has been adopted from the Canadian work where the Malta is the principal degree of their Priories. The adoption of this ritual among the Commanderies of America is optional, but when once adopted must be conformed to in their work. This change was brought about by the visiting influence from Canada and also the reasons for the Malta being a degree of chivalry. For a similar reason the Knights of the Red Cross has been justly changed to Companion of the Red Cross, and properly never deserved a place in the degrees of chivalry, as the ritual plainly shows. [E. E. C.]

Knight of Patmos. An apocalyptic degree mentioned by Oliver in his *Landmarks.* It refers, he says, to the banishment of St. John.

Knight of Perfumes. (*Chevalier des Parfums.*) The Eighth Degree of the Rite of the East (*Rite d'Orient*) according to the nomenclature of Fustier.

Knight of Pure Truth. (*Chevalier de la Pure Verité.*) Thory mentions this as a secret society instituted by the scholars of the Jesuitical college at Tulle. It could scarcely have been Masonic.

Knight of Purity and Light. (*Ritter der Klarheit und des Lichts.*) The Seventh and last degree of the Rite of the *Clerks of Strict Observance,* which see.

Knight of Rhodes. 1. One of the titles given to the Knights Hospitalers in consequence of their long residence on the island of Rhodes. 2. A degree formerly conferred in the Baldwyn Encampment at Bristol, England. It seems in some way to have been confounded with the Mediterranean Pass.

Knight of Rose Croix. See *Rose Croix.*

Knight of St. Andrew, Grand Scottish. (*Grand Ecossais de Saint André.*) Sometimes called "Patriarch of the Crusades." The Twenty-ninth Degree of the Ancient and Accepted Scottish Rite. Its ritual is founded on a legend, first promulgated by the Chevalier Ramsay, to this effect: that the Freemasons were originally a society of knights founded in Palestine for the purpose of building Christian churches; that the Saracens, to prevent the execution of this design, sent emissaries among them, who disguised themselves as Christians, and were continually throwing obstacles in their way; that on discovering the existence of these spies, the knights instituted certain modes of recognition to serve as the means of detection; that they also adopted symbolic ceremonies for the purpose of instructing the proselytes who had entered the society in the forms and principles of their new religion; and finally, that the Saracens, having become too powerful for the knights any longer to contend with them, they had accepted the invitation of a king of England, and had removed into his dominions, where they thenceforth devoted themselves to the cultivation of architecture and the fine arts. On this mythical legend, which in reality was only an application of Ramsay's theory of the origin of Freemasonry, the Baron de Tschoudy is said, about the middle of the last century, to have formed this degree, which Ragon says (*Orthod. Maçon.,* p. 138) at his death, in 1769, he bequeathed in manuscript to the Council of Emperors of the East and West. On the subsequent extension of the twenty-five degrees of the Rite of Perfection, instituted by that body, to the thirty-three degrees of the Ancient and Accepted Rite, this degree was adopted as the twenty-ninth, and as an appropriate introduction to the Knights of Kadosh, which it immediately precedes. Hence the jewel, a St. Andrew's cross, is said, by Ragon, to be only a concealed form of the Templar Cross. In allusion to the time of its supposed invention, it has been called "Patriarch of the Crusades." On account of the Masonic instruction which it contains, it also sometimes receives the title of "Grand Master of Light."

The Lodge is decorated with red hangings supported by white columns. There are eighty-one lights, arranged as follows: four in each corner before a St. Andrew's cross, two before the altar, and sixty-three arranged by nines in seven different parts of the room. There are three officers, a Venerable Grand Master and two Wardens. The jewel is a St. Andrew's cross, appropriately decorated, and suspended from a green collar bordered with red.

In the ritual of the Southern Jurisdiction, the leading idea of a communication between the Christian knights and the Saracens has been preserved; but the ceremonies and the legend have been altered. The lesson intended to be taught is toleration of religion.

This degree also constitutes the sixty-third of the collection of the Metropolitan Chapter of France; the fifth of the Rite of Clerks of Strict Observance; and the twenty-first of the Rite of Mizraim. It is also to be found in many other systems.

Knight of St. Andrew, Free. (*Chevalier libre de Saint-André.*) A degree found in the collection of Pyron.

Knight of St. Andrew of the Thistle. (*Chevalier Ecossais de S. André du Chardon.*) The Seventy-fifth Degree of the collection of the Metropolitan Chapter of France.

Knight of St. John of Jerusalem. 1. The original title of the Knights of Malta, and derived from the church and monastery built at Jerusalem in 1048 by the founders of the Order, and dedicated to St. John the Baptist. (See *Knight of Malta.*)

2. A mystical degree divided into three sections, which is found in the collection of Lemanceau.

Knight of St. John of Palestine. (*Chevalier de Sainte Jean de la Palestine.*) The Forty-eighth Degree of the Metropolitan Chapter of France.

Knight of the Altar. (*Chevalier de l'Autel.*) The Twelfth Degree of the Rite of the East according to the nomenclature of Fustier.

Knight of the American Eagle. An honorary degree invented many years ago in Texas or some other of the Western States. It was founded on incidents of the American Revolution, and gave an absurd legend of Hiram Abif's boyhood. It is believed to be now obsolete.

Knight of the Anchor. (*Chevalier de l'Ancre.*) 1. An androgynous degree. (See *Anchor, Order of Knights and Ladies of the.*) 2. The Twenty-first Degree of the collection of the Metropolitan Chapter of France.

Knight of the Ape and Lion. Gädicke says (*Freimaurer-Lex.*) that this Order appeared about the year 1780, but that its existence was only made known by its extinction. It adopted the lion sleeping with open eyes as a symbol of watchfulness, and the ape as a symbol of those who imitate without due penetration. The members boasted that they possessed all the secrets of the Ancient Templars, on which account they were persecuted by the modern Order. The lion and ape, as symbols of courage and address, are found in one of the degrees described in the *Franc-Maçons Ecrasés*.

Knight of the Arch. (*Chevalier de l'Arche.*) A degree found in the nomenclature of Fustier.

Knight of the Argonauts. (*Chevalier des Argonautes.*) The first point of the Sixth Degree, or Knight of the Golden Fleece of the Hermetic Rite of Montpellier.

Knight of the Banqueting Table of the Seven Sages. (*Chevalier de la Table du Banquet des Sept Sages.*) A degree in the Archives of the Mother Lodge of the Philosophic Scottish Rite.

Knight of the Black Eagle. (*Chevalier de l'Aigle noir.*) 1. The Seventy-sixth Degree of the collection of the Metropolitan Chapter of France; called also Grand Inquisitor, Grand Inspector, Grand Elu or Elect, in the collection of Le Rouge. 2. The Thirty-eighth Degree of the Rite of Mizraim.

Knight of the Brazen Serpent. (*Chevalier du Serpent d'Airain.*) The Twenty-fifth Degree of the Ancient and Accepted Scottish Rite. The history of this degree is founded upon the circumstances related in Numbers ch. xxi. ver. 6–9: "And the Lord sent fiery serpents among the people, and they bit the people; and much people of Israel died. Therefore the people came to Moses, and said, We have sinned; for we have spoken against the Lord, and against thee: pray unto the Lord that he take away the serpents from us. And Moses prayed for the people. And the Lord said unto Moses, Make thee a fiery serpent, and set it upon a pole: and it shall come to pass, that every one that is bitten, when he looketh upon it shall live. And Moses made a serpent of brass, and put it upon a pole; and it came to pass, that if a serpent had bitten any man, when he beheld the serpent of brass, he lived." In the old rituals the Lodge was called the Court of Sinai; the presiding officer was styled Most Puissant Grand Master, and represented Moses; while the two Wardens, or Ministers, represented Aaron and Joshua. The Orator was called Pontiff; the Secretary, Grand Graver; and the candidate, a Traveler. In the modern ritual adopted in this country, the Council represents the camp of the Israelites. The first three officers represent Moses, Joshua, and Caleb, and are respectively styled Most Puissant Leader, Valiant Captain of the Host, and Illustrious Chief of the Ten Tribes. The Orator represents Eleazar; the Secretary, Ithamar; the Treasurer, Phinchas; and the candidate an intercessor for the people. The jewel is a crux ansata, with a serpent entwined around it. On the upright of the cross is engraved חלתי, khalati, *I have suffered*, and on the arms נחושתן, nakhushtan, *a serpent*. The French ritualists would have done better to have substituted

for the first word חטאתי, khatati, *I have sinned;* the original in Numbers being חטאנו, Kathanu, *we have sinned*. The apron is white, lined with black, and symbolically decorated.

There is an old legend which says that this degree was founded in the time of the Crusades, by John Ralph, who established the Order in the Holy Land as a military and monastic society, and gave it the name of the Brazen Serpent, because it was a part of their obligation to receive and gratuitously nurse sick travelers, to protect them against the attacks of the Saracens, and escort them safely to Palestine; thus alluding to the healing and saving virtues of the Brazen Serpent among the Israelites in the wilderness.

Knight of the Burning Bush. (*Chevalier du Buisson ardent.*) A theosophic degree of the collection of the Mother Lodge of the Philosophic Scottish Rite.

Knight of the Chanuca. (*Chevalier de la Kanuka.*) The Sixty-ninth Degree of the Rite of Mizraim. The חנוכה, or *Chanuca*, is the feast of the dedication celebrated by the Jews in commemoration of the dedication of the Temple by Judas Maccabæus after its pollution by the Syrians. In the ritual of the degree, the Jewish lighting of seven lamps, one on each day, is imitated, and therefore the ceremony of initiation lasts for seven days.

Knight of the Christian Mark. Called also Guard of the Conclave. A degree formerly conferred in the United States on Knights Templar in a body called a Council of the Trinity. The legend of the Order is that it was organized by Pope Alexander for the defense of his person, and that its members were selected from the Knights of St. John of Jerusalem. In the ceremonies there is a reference to the tau cross or mark on the forehead, spoken of by the prophet Ezekiel, and hence the name of the degree. The motto of the Order is, "Christus regnat, vincit, triumphat. Rex regnantium, Dominus dominantium." Christ reigns, conquers, and triumphs. King of kings and Lord of lords.

Knight of the Columns. (*Chevalier des Colonnes.*) The Seventh Degree of the Rite of the East according to the nomenclature of Fustier.

Knight of the Comet. (*Chevalier de la Comète.*) A degree found in the collection of Hécart.

Knight of the Cork. (*Chevalier du Bouchon.*) An androgynous secret society established in Italy after the Papal bull excommunicating the Freemasons, and intended by its founders to take the place of the Masonic institution.

Knight of the Courts. (*Chevalier des Parvis.*) The Third Degree of the Rite of the East according to the nomenclature of Fustier.

Knight of the Crown. (*Chevalier de la Couronne.*) A degree in the collection of Pyron.

Knight of the Door. (*Chevalier de la Porte.*) The Fourth Degree of the Rite of the East according to the nomenclature of Fustier.

Knight of the Dove. The Knights and Ladies of the Dove (*Chevaliers et Chevalieres* *de la Colombe*) was an androgynous secret society framed on the model of Freemasonry, and instituted at Versailles in 1784. It had but an ephemeral existence.

Knight of the Eagle. (*Chevalier de l'Aigle.*) 1. The First Degree of the Chapter of Clermont. 2. The Third Degree of the Clerks of Strict Observance. 3. The Fifty-sixth Degree of the collection of the Metropolitan Chapter of France. 4. It was also one of the degrees of the Chapter of the Grand Lodge Royal York of Berlin. 5. The Thirty-seventh Degree of the Rite of Mizraim. Thory (*Acta Lat.*, i., 291) says it was also one of the appellations of the degree more commonly called *Perfect Master in Architecture*, which is the Fourteenth of the Primitive Scottish Rite, and is found also in some other systems.

Knight of the Eagle and Pelican. One of the appellations of the degree of Rose Croix, because the jewel has on one side an eagle and on the other a pelican, both at the foot of the cross, in allusion to the symbolism of the degree. (See *Rose Croix, Prince of.*)

Knight of the Eagle reversed. (*Chevalier de l'Aigle renversé.*) Thory (*Acta Lat.*, i., 292) records this as a degree to be found in the Archives of the Scottish Lodge *Saint Louis des Amis Réunis at Calais.* In heraldic phrase, an eagle reversed is an eagle with the wings drooping.

Knight of the East. (*Chevalier d'Orient.*) This is a degree which has been extensively diffused through the most important Rites, and it owes its popularity to the fact that it commemorates in its legend and its ceremonies the labors of the Masons in the construction of the second Temple.

1. It is the Fifteenth Degree of the Ancient and Accepted Scottish Rite, the description of which will apply with slight modifications to the same degree in all the other Rites. It is founded upon the history of the assistance rendered by Cyrus to the Jews, who permitted them to return to Jerusalem, and to commence the rebuilding of the house of the Lord. Zerubbabel, therefore, as the Prince of the Jews, and Cyrus the King of Persia, as his patron, are important personages in the drama of reception; which is conducted with great impressiveness even in the old and somewhat imperfect ritual of the last century, but which has been greatly improved in the modern rituals adopted by the Supreme Councils of the United States.

The cordon of a Knight of the East is a broad green watered ribbon, worn as a baldric from left to right. The sash or girdle is of white watered silk, edged above, and fringed below with gold. On it is embroidered a bridge, with the letters L. D. P. on the arch, and also on other parts of the girdle human heads, and mutilated limbs, and crowns, and swords. The apron is crimson, edged with green, a bleeding head and two swords crossed on the flap, and on the apron three triangles interlaced formed of triangular links of chains. The jewel is three triangles interlaced enclosing two naked swords.

Scripture and the traditions of the Order furnish us with many interesting facts in relation to this degree. The Knights of the East are said to derive their origin from the captivity of the Israelites in Babylon. After seventy-two years of servitude, they were restored to liberty by Cyrus, King of Persia, through the intercession of Zerubbabel, a prince of the tribe of Judah, and Nehemias, a holy man of a distinguished family, and permitted to return to Jerusalem and rebuild the Temple.

2. It is the Sixth Degree of the French Rite. It is substantially the same as the preceding degree.

3. The Sixth Degree of the old system of the Royal York Lodge of Berlin.

4. The Fifteenth Degree of the Chapter of the Emperors of the East and West, and this was most probably the original degree.

5. The Fifty-second Degree of the collection of the Metropolitan Chapter of France.

6. The Forty-first Degree of the Rite of Mizraim.

7. The Sixth Degree of the Rite of Philalethes.

8. The Eleventh Degree of the Adonhiramite Rite.

9. It is also substantially the Tenth Degree, or Knight of the Red Cross of the American Rite. Indeed, it is found in all the Rites and systems which refer to the second Temple.

Knight of the East and West. (*Chevalier d'Orient et d'Occident.*) 1. The Seventeenth Degree of the Ancient and Accepted Scottish Rite. The oldest rituals of the degree were very imperfect, and did not connect it with Freemasonry. They contained a legend that upon the return of the knights from the Holy Land, in the time of the Crusaders, they organized the Order, and that in the year 1118 the first knights, to the number of eleven, took their vows between the hands of Garinus, patriarch. The allusion, here, is evidently to the Knights Templar; and this legend would most probably indicate that the degree originated with the Templar system of Ramsay. This theory is further strengthened by the other legend, that the Knights of the East represented the Masons who remained in the East after the building of the first Temple, while the Knights of the East and West represented those who traveled West and disseminated the Order over Europe, but who returned during the Crusades and reunited with their ancient brethren, whence we get the name.

The modern ritual as used in the United States has been greatly enlarged. It still retains the apocalyptic character of the degree which always attached to it, as is evident from the old tracing-board, which is the figure described in the first chapter of the Revelation of St. John. The jewel is a heptagon inscribed with symbols derived from the Apocalypse, among which are the lamb and the book with seven seals. The apron is yellow, lined and edged with crimson. In the old ritual its device was a two-edged sword. In the new one it is a tetractys of ten dots. This is the first of the philosophical degrees of the Scottish Rite. 2. The Seventeenth Degree of the Chapter of Emperors of the East and West.

Knight of the Eastern Star. (*Chevalier de l'Etoile d'Orient.*) The Fifty-seventh Degree of the collection of the Metropolitan Chapter of France.

Knight of the East, Victorious. (*Chevalier victorieux de l'Orient.*) A degree found in the collection of Hécart.

Knight of the East, White. (*Chevalier d'Orient.*) The Fortieth Degree of the Rite of Mizraim.

Knight of the Election. (*Chevalier du Choix.*) The Thirty-third Degree of the Rite of Mizraim.

Knight of the Election, Sublime. (*Chevalier sublime du Choix.*) The Thirty-fourth Degree of the Rite of Mizraim.

Knight of the Golden Eagle. (*Chevalier de l'Aigle d'or.*) A degree in the collection of Pyron.

Knight of the Golden Fleece. (*Chevalier de la Toisson d'or.*) The Sixth Degree of the Hermetic Rite of Montpellier.

Knight of the Golden Key. (*Chevalier de la Clef d'or.*) The Third Degree of the Hermetic Rite of Montpellier.

Knight of the Golden Star. (*Chevalier de l'Etoile d'or.*) A degree contained in the collection of Peuvret.

Knight of the Grand Arch. (*Chevalier de la Grande Arche.*) A degree which Thory (*Acta Lat.*, i., 295) says is contained in the Archives of the Lodge of *Saint Louis des Amis Réunis at Calais*.

Knight of the Holy City, Beneficent. (*Chevalier bienfaisant de la Cité Sainte.*) The Order of Beneficent Knights of the Holy City of Jerusalem was created, according to Ragon, at Lyons, in France, in 1782, by the brethren of the Lodge of Chevaliers Bienfaisants. But Thory (*Acta Lat.*, i. 299) says it was rectified at the Congress of Wilhelmsbad. Both are perhaps right. It was probably first invented at Lyons, at one time a prolific field for the *hautes grades*, and afterward adopted at Wilhelmsbad, whence it began to exercise a great influence over the Lodges of Strict Observance. The Order professed the Rite of Martinism; but the members attempted to convert Freemasonry into Templarism, and transferred all the symbols of the former to the latter system. Thus, they interpreted the two pillars of the porch and their names as alluding to Jacobus Burgundus or James the Burgundian, meaning James de Molay, the last Grand Master of the Templars; the three gates of the Temple signified the three vows of the Knights Templar, obedience, poverty, and chastity; and the sprig of acacia referred to that which was planted over the ashes of De Molay when they were transferred to Heredom in Scotland. The Order and the doctrine sprang from the Templar system of Ramsay. The theory of its Jesuitic origin can scarcely be admitted.

Knight of the Holy Sepulcher. 1. As a Masonic degree, this was formerly given in what were called Councils of the Trinity, next after the Knight of the Christian Mark; but it is no longer conferred in America, and may now be considered as obsolete. The Masonic legend that it was instituted by St. Helena, the mother of Constantine, in 302, after she had visited Jerusalem and discovered the cross, and that, in 304, it was confirmed by Pope Marcellinus, is altogether apocryphal. The military Order of Knights of the Holy Sepulcher still exists; and Mr. Curzon, in his *Visits to the Monasteries in the Levant*, states that the Order is still conferred in Jerusalem, but only on Roman Catholics of noble birth, by the Reverendissimo or Superior of the Franciscans, and that the *accolade*, or blow of knighthood, is bestowed with the sword of Godfrey de Bouillon, which is preserved, with his spurs, in the sacristy of the Church of the Holy Sepulcher. Madame Pfeiffer, in her *Travels in the Holy Land*, confirms this account. Dr. Heylin says that the Order was instituted in 1099, when Jerusalem was regained from the Saracens by Philip of France. Faryn, in his *Theatre d' Honneur*, gives a different account of the institution. He says that while the Saracens possessed the city they permitted certain canons regular of St. Augustine to have the custody of the Holy Sepulcher. Afterward Baldwyn, King of Jerusalem, made them Men-of-Arms and Knights of the Holy Sepulcher, and ordained that they should continue to wear their white habits, and on the breast his own arms, which were a red cross potent between four Jerusalem crosses. Their rule was confirmed by Pope Innocent III. The Grand Master was the Patriarch of Jerusalem. They engaged to fight against infidels, to protect pilgrims, to redeem Christian captives, hear Mass every day, recite the hours of the cross, and bear the five red crosses in memory of our Savior's wounds. On the loss of the Holy Land, they retired to Perugia, in Italy, where they retained their white habit, but assumed a double red cross. In 1484, they were incorporated with the Knights Hospitalers, who were then at Rhodes, but in 1496, Alexander VI. assumed, for himself and the Popes his successors, the Grand Mastership, and empowered the Guardian of the Holy Sepulcher to bestow Knighthood of the Order upon pilgrims. Unsuccessful attempts were made by Philip II., of Spain, in 1558, and the Duke of Nevers, in 1625, to restore the Order. It is now found only in Jerusalem, where it is conferred, as has been already said, by the Superior of the Franciscans.

2. It is also the Fiftieth Degree of the Metropolitan Chapter of France.

Knight of the Interior. (*Chevalier de l'Intérieur.*) The Fifth Degree of the Rite of the East according to the nomenclature of Fustier.

Knight of the Kabbala. (*Chevalier de la Cabale.*) The Eighth Degree of the collection of the Metropolitan Chapter of France.

Knight of the Lilies of the Valley. This was a degree conferred by the Grand Orient of France as an appendage to Templarism. The

Knights Templar who received it were constituted Knights Commanders.

Knight of the Lion. (*Chevalier du Lion.*) The Twentieth Degree of the Metropolitan Chapter of France.

Knight of the Mediterranean Pass. An honorary degree that was formerly conferred in Encampments of Knights Templar, but is now disused. Its meetings were called Councils; and its ritual, which was very impressive, supplies the tradition that it was founded about the year 1367, in consequence of certain events which occurred to the Knights of Malta. In an excursion made by a party of these knights in search of forage and provisions, they were attacked while crossing the river Offanto (the ancient Aufidio) by a large body of Saracens, under the command of the renowned Amurath I. The Saracens had concealed themselves in ambush, and when the knights were on the middle of the bridge which spanned the river, they were attacked by a sudden charge of their enemies upon both extremities of the bridge. A long and sanguinary contest ensued; the knights fought with their usual valor, and were at length victorious. The Saracens were defeated with such immense slaughter that fifteen hundred of their dead bodies encumbered the bridge, and the river was literally stained with their blood. In commemoration of this event, and as a reward for their valor, the victorious knights had free permission to pass and repass in all the coasts of the Mediterranean Sea without danger of molestation, whence the name of the degree is derived. As the latter part of this legend has not been verified by voyagers in the Mediterranean, the degree has long been disused. Dr. Mackey says that he had a ritual of it, which was in the handwriting of Dr. Moses Holbrook, the Grand Commander of the Southern Supreme Council of the Ancient and Accepted Scottish Rite.

Knight of the Moon. A mock Masonic society, established in the last century in London. It ceased to exist in the year 1810.

Knight of the Morning Star. Called also Knight of Hope. A degree in the Archives of the Mother Lodge of the Philosophical Rite, which is said to be a modification of the Kadosh.

Knight of the Ninth Arch. The Thirteenth Degree of the Ancient and Accepted Scottish Rite, called also the "Royal Arch of Solomon," and sometimes the "Royal Arch of Enoch." It is one of the most interesting and impressive of what are called the Ineffable degrees. Its legend refers to Enoch and to the method by which, notwithstanding the destructive influence of the deluge and the lapse of time, he was enabled to preserve important secrets to be afterward communicated to the Craft. According to the present ritual, its principal officers are a Thrice Puissant Grand Master, representing King Solomon, and two Wardens, representing the King of Tyre and the Inspector Adoniram. Bodies of this degree are called Chapters. The color is black strewed with tears. The jewel is a

circular medal of gold, around which is inscribed the following letters: R. S. R. S. T. P. S. R. I. A. Y. E. S., with the date *Anno Enochi 2995*. On the reverse is a blazing triangle with the Tetragrammaton in the center in Samaritan letters.

This degree claims great importance in the history of Masonic ritualism. It is found, under various modifications, in almost all the Rites; and, indeed, without it, or something like it, the symbolism of Freemasonry cannot be considered as complete. Indebted for its origin to the inventive genius of the Chevalier Ramsay, it was adopted by the Council of the Emperors of the East and West, whence it passed into the Ancient and Accepted Rite. Though entirely different in its legend from the Royal Arch of the York and American Rites, its symbolic design is the same, for one common thought of a treasure lost and found pervades them all. Vassal, who is exceedingly flippant in much that he has written of Ecossism, says of this degree, that, "considered under its moral and religious aspects, it offers nothing either instructive or useful." It is evident that he understood nothing of its true symbolism.

Knight of the North. (*Chevalier du Nord.*) A degree in the Archives of the Lodge of *Saint Louis des Amis Réunis at Calais.* Thory (*Acta Lat.*, i., 328) mentions another degree called Sublime Knight of the North, which he says is the same as one in the collection of Peuvret, which has the singular title of Daybreak of the Rough Ashlar, *Point du Jour de la Pierre Brute.*

Knight of the Phenix. (*Chevalier du Phénix.*) The Fourth Degree of the Philosophic Scottish Rite.

Knight of the Prussian Eagle. (*Chevalier de l'Aigle Prussien.*) A degree in the collection of Hécart.

Knight of the Purificatory. (*Chevalier du Purificatoire.*) The Sixteenth Degree of the Rite of the East according to the nomenclature of Fustier.

Knight of the Pyramid. (*Chevalier de la Pyramide.*) The Seventh Degree of the Kabbalistic Rite.

Knight of the Rainbow. (*Chevalier de l'Arc-en-ciel.*) The Sixty-eighth Degree of the Rite of Mizraim.

Knight of the Red Cross. This degree, whose legend dates it far anterior to the Christian era, and in the reign of Darius, has no analogy with the chivalric orders of knighthood. It is purely Masonic, and intimately connected with the Royal Arch Degree, of which, in fact, it ought rightly to be considered as an appendage. It is, however, now always conferred in a Commandery of Knights Templar in this country, and is given as a preliminary to reception in that degree. Formerly, the degree was sometimes conferred in an independent council, which Webb (edit. 1812, p. 123) defines to be "a council that derives its authority immediately from the Grand Encampment unconnected with an Encampment of Knights Templars." The embassy of Zerubbabel and four other Jewish chiefs to the court of Darius to obtain the protection of that monarch from the encroachments of the Samaritans, who interrupted the labors in the reconstruction of the Temple, constitutes the legend of the Red Cross Degree. The history of this embassy is found in the eleventh book of the *Antiquities* of Josephus, whence the Masonic ritualists have undoubtedly taken it. The only authority of Josephus is the apocryphal record of Esdras, and the authenticity of the whole transaction is doubted or denied by modern historians. The legend is as follows: After the death of Cyrus, the Jews, who had been released by him from their captivity, and permitted to return to Jerusalem, for the purpose of rebuilding the Temple, found themselves obstructed in the undertaking by the neighboring nations, and especially by the Samaritans. Hereupon they sent an embassy, at the head of which was their prince, Zerubbabel, to Darius, the successor of Cyrus, to crave his interposition and protection. Zerubbabel, awaiting a favorable opportunity, succeeded not only in obtaining his request, but also in renewing the friendship which formerly existed between the king and himself. In commemoration of these events, Darius is said to have instituted a new order, and called it the Knights of the East. They afterward assumed their present name from the red cross borne in their banners. Webb, or whoever else introduced it into the American Templar system, undoubtedly took it from the Sixteenth Degree, or Prince of Jerusalem of the Ancient and Accepted Rite. It has, within a few years, been carried into England, under the title of the "Red Cross of Babylon." In New Brunswick, it has been connected with Cryptic Masonry. It is there as much out of place as it is in a Commandery of Knights Templar. Its only true connection is with the Royal Arch Degree.

Knight of the Red Eagle. (*Chevalier de l'Aigle rouge.*) The Thirty-ninth Degree of the Rite of Mizraim. The red eagle forms a part of the arms of the House of Brandenburg, and the Order of Knights of the Red Eagle was instituted, in 1705, by George William, hereditary Prince of Bayreuth. In 1792, it was placed among the Prussian orders. The Masonic degree has no connection with the political order. The Mizraimites appropriated all titles that they fancied.

Knight of the Rose. (*Chevalier de la Rose.*) The Order of the Knights and Ladies of the Rose (*Chevaliers et Chevalieres de la Rose*) was an order of adoptive or androgynous Masonry, invented in France toward the close of the eighteenth century. M. de Chaumont, the Masonic secretary of the Duc de Chartres, was its author. The principal seat of the order was at Paris. The hall of meeting was called the Temple of Love. It was ornamented with garlands of flowers, and hung round with escutcheons on which were painted various devices and emblems of gallantry. There were two presiding officers, a male and female, who were styled the Hierophant and the High Priestess. The former initiated men, and the latter, women. In the initiations, the Hierophant was assisted by a conductor or deacon called Sentiment, and the High Priestess by a conductress or deaconess called Discretion. The members received the title of Knights and Nymphs. The Knights wore a crown of myrtle, the Nymphs, a crown of roses. The Hierophant and High Priestess wore, in addition, a rose-colored scarf, on which were embroidered two doves within a wreath of myrtle. During the time of initiation, the hall was lit with a single dull taper, but afterward it was brilliantly illuminated by numerous wax candles.

When a candidate was to be initiated, he or she was taken in charge, according to the sex, by the conductor or conductress, divested of all weapons, jewels, or money, hoodwinked, loaded with chains, and in this condition conducted to the door of the Temple of Love, where admission was demanded by two knocks. Brother Sentiment then introduced the candidate by order of the Hierophant or High Priestess, and he or she was asked his or her name, country, condition of life, and, lastly, what he or she was seeking. To this the answer was, "Happiness."

The next question proposed was, "What is your age?" The candidate, if a male, replied, "The age to love"; if a female, "The age to please and to love."

The candidates were then interrogated concerning their private opinions and conduct in relation to matters of gallantry. The chains were then taken from them, and they were invested with garlands of flowers which were called "the chains of love." In this condition they were made to traverse the apartment from one extremity to another, and then back in a contrary direction, over a path inscribed with love-knots. The following obligation was then administered:

"I promise and swear by the Grand Master of the Universe never to reveal the secrets of the Order of the Rose; and should I fail in this my vow, may the mysteries I shall receive add nothing to my pleasures, and instead of the roses of happiness may I find nothing but the thorns of repentance."

The candidates were then conducted to the mysterious groves in the neighborhood of the Temple of Love, where the Knights received a crown of myrtle, and the Nymphs a simple rose. During this time a soft, melodious march was played by the orchestra. After this, the candidates were conducted to the altar of mystery, placed at the foot of the Hierophant's throne, and there incense was offered up to Venus and her son. If it was a Knight who had been initiated, he now exchanged his crown of myrtle for the rose of the last initiated Nymph; and if a Nymph, she exchanged her rose for the myrtle crown of Brother Sentiment. The Hierophant now read a copy of verses in honor of the god of Mystery, and the bandage was at length taken from the eyes of the candidate. Delicious music and brilliant lights now added to the charms of this enchanting scene, in the midst of which the Hierophant communicated to the candidate the modes of recognition peculiar to the Order. (Clavel, *Hist. Pitt.*, 115–7.)

The Order had but a brief existence. In 1784, F. B. von Grossing invented, in Germany, an Order bearing a similar name, but its duration was as ephemeral as that of the French one.

Knight of the Rosy and Triple Cross. (*Chevalier de la Rose et Triple Croix.*) A degree in the Archives of the Lodge of *Saint Louis des Amis Réunis at Calais.*

Knight of the Rosy Cross. See *Royal Order of Scotland.*

Knight of the Round Table. (*Chevalier de la Table ronde.*) A degree in the Archives of the Lodge of *Saint Louis des Amis Réunis at Calais.*

Knight of the Round Table of King Arthur. (*Chevalier de la Table ronde du Roi Arthur.*) 1. Thory (*Acta Lat. i.,* 341) says that this is a degree of the Primitive Rite; but neither Dr. Mackey nor the Rev. A. F. A. Woodford (*Kenning's Masonic Cyclopædia*) has been able to trace the degree. Dr. Mackey says that he has seen the manuscript of a degree of this name written many years ago, which was in the possession of Bro. C. W. Moore, of Boston. It was an honorary degree, and referred to the poetic legend of King Arthur and his knights.

Knight of the Royal Ax. (*Chevalier de la royale Hache.*) The Twenty-second Degree of the Ancient and Accepted Scottish Rite, called also Prince of Libanus, or Lebanon. It was instituted to record the memorable services rendered to Masonry by the "mighty cedars of Lebanon." The legend of the degree informs us that the Sidonians were employed in cutting cedars on Mount Libanus or Lebanon for the construction of Noah's ark. Their descendants subsequently cut cedars from the same place for the ark of the covenant; and the descendants of these were again employed in the same offices, and in the same place, in obtaining materials for building Solomon's Temple. Lastly, Zerubbabel employed them in cutting the cedars of Lebanon for the use of the second Temple. This celebrated nation formed colleges on Mount Lebanon, and in their labors always adored the Great Architect of the Universe. No doubt this last sentence refers to the Druses, that secret sect of Theists who still reside upon Mount Lebanon and in the adjacent parts of Syria and Palestine, and whose mysterious ceremonies have attracted so much of the curiosity of Eastern travelers.

The apron of the Knights of the Royal Ax is white, lined and bordered with purple. On it is painted a round table, on which are laid several architectural plans. On the flap is a three-headed serpent. The jewel is a golden ax, having on the handle and blade the initials of several personages illustrious in the history of Masonry. The places of meeting in this degree are called "Colleges." This de-

gree is especially interesting to the Masonic scholar in consequence of its evident reference to the mystical association of the Druses, whose connection with the Templars at the time of the Crusades forms a yet to be investigated episode in the history of Freemasonry.

Knight of the Sacred Mountain. (*Chevalier de la Montagne Sacrée.*) A degree in the Archives of the Lodge of *Saint Louis des Amis Réunis at Calais.*

Knight of the Sanctuary. (*Chevalier du Sanctuaire.*) The Eleventh Degree of the Rite of the East according to the collection of Fustier.

Knight of the Sepulcher. The Sixth Degree of the system of the Grand Lodge Royal York at Berlin.

Knight of the South. (*Chevalier du Sud.*) The Eighth Degree of the Swedish Rite, better known as the Favorite of St. John.

Knight of the Star. (*Chevalier de l'Etoile.*) A degree in the collection of Pyron.

Knight of the Sun. (*Chevalier du Soleil.*) The Twenty-eighth Degree of the Ancient and Accepted Scottish Rite, called also Prince of the Sun, Prince Adept, and Key of Masonry, or Chaos Disentangled. It is a Kabbalistic and Hermetic degree, and its instructions and symbols are full of the Kabbala and Alchemy. Thus, one of its favorite words is Stibium, which, with the Hermetic Philosophers, meant the primal matter of all things. The principal officers are Father Adam and Brother Truth, allegorizing in the old rituals the search of Man after Truth. The other officers are named after the seven chief angels, and the brethren are called Sylphs, or, in the American ritual, Aralim or Heroes. The jewel is a golden sun, having on its reverse a hemisphere with the six northern signs of the zodiac. There is but one light in the Lodge, which shines through a globe of glass.

This degree is not confined to the Scottish Rite, but is found sometimes with a different name, but with the same Hermetic design, more or less developed in other Rites. Ragon, with whom Delaunay and Chemin-Dupontès concur, says that it is not, like many of the high degrees, a mere modern invention, but that it is of the highest antiquity; and was, in fact, the last degree of the ancient initiations teaching, under an Hermetic appearance, the doctrines of natural religion, which formed an essential part of the Mysteries. But Ragon must here evidently refer to the general, philosophic design rather than to the particular organization of the degree. Thory (*Acta Lat.,* i., 339), with more plausibility, ascribes its invention as a Masonic degree to Pernetty, the founder of the Hermetic Rite. Of all the high degrees, it is, perhaps, the most important and the most interesting to the scholar who desires to investigate the true secret of the Order. Its old catechisms, now unfortunately too much neglected, are full of suggestive thoughts, and in its modern ritual, for which we are indebted to the inventive genius of Bro. Albert Pike, it is by far the most learned and philosophical of the Scottish degrees.

Knight of the Sword. (*Chevalier de l'Epée.*) One of the titles of the Scottish Rite degree of Knight of the East. So called in allusion to the legend that the Masons at the second Temple worked with the trowel in one hand and the sword in the other. Du Cange, on the authority of Arnoldus Lubeckius, describes an Order, in the Middle Ages, of Knights of the Sword (*Milites Gladii*), who, having vowed to wield the sword for God's service, wore a sword embroidered on their mantles as a sign of their profession, whence they took their name. But it was not connected with the Masonic degree.

Knight of the Tabernacle. In the Minute Book of the "Grand Lodge of all England," extracts from which are given by Bro. Hughan in his *Unpublished Records* (p. 146), we find the expression *Knight of the Tabernacle*, used in the year 1780, as synonymous with *Knight Templar*.

Knight of the Tabernacle of the Divine Truths. (*Chevalier du Tabernacle des Verités divines.*) A degree cited in the nomenclature of Fustier.

Knight of the Temple. (*Chevalier du Temple.*) This degree is common to all the systems of Masonry founded on the Templar doctrine.

1. It is a synonym of Knights Templar.
2. The Eighth Degree of the Rite of the Philalethes.
3. The Sixty-ninth Degree of the collection of the Metropolitan Chapter of France.
4. The Sixth Degree of the Clerks of Strict Observance.
5. The Ninth Degree of the Rite of the East according to the nomenclature of Fustier.
6. The Thirty-sixth Degree of the Rite of Mizraim.

Knight of the Three Kings. An American side degree of but little importance. Its history connects it with the dedication of the first Temple, the conferrer of the degree representing King Solomon. Its moral tendency appears to be the inculcation of reconciliation of grievances among Masons by friendly conference. It may be conferred by any Master Mason on another.

Knight of the Throne. (*Chevalier du Trône.*) The Second Degree of the Rite of the East according to the nomenclature of Fustier.

Knight of the Triple Cross. (*Chevalier de la Triple Croix.*) The Sixty-sixth Degree of the collection of the Metropolitan Chapter of France.

Knight of the Triple Period. (*Chevalier de la Triple Période.*) A degree in the Archives of the Lodge of *Saint Louis des Amis Réunis at Calais.*

Knight of the Triple Sword. (*Chevalier de la Triple Epée.*) A degree in the collection of Pyron.

Knight of the Two Crowned Eagles. (*Chevalier des deux Aigles Couronnées.*) The Twenty-second Degree of the collection of the Metropolitan Chapter of France.

Knight of the West. (*Chevalier d'Oc-cident.*) 1. The Sixty-fourth Degree of the collection of the Metropolitan Chapter of France. 2. The Forty-seventh Degree of the Rite of Mizraim.

Knight of the White and Black Eagle. (*Chevalier de l'Aigle blanc et noir.*) One of the titles of the Thirtieth Degree of the Ancient and Accepted Scottish Rite, or Knight Kadosh. In the Rite of Perfection of the Emperors of the East and West, it constituted the Twenty-fourth Degree, under the title of Knight Commander of the White and Black Eagle. The white eagle was the emblem of the eastern empire, and the black of the western. Hence we have the Knights of the White Eagle in Russia, and the Knights of the Black Eagle in Prussia, as orders of chivalry. The two combined were, therefore, appropriately (so far as the title is concerned) adopted by the Council which assumed Masonic jurisdiction over both empires.

Knight of the White Eagle. The Sixty-fourth Degree of the Rite of Mizraim. As a political order, that of the Knights of the White Eagle was instituted by Wladistas, King of Poland, in 1325. It is still conferred by the Czar of Russia.

Knight of Unction. (*Chevalier d'Onction.*) The Fifty-first Degree of the collection of the Metropolitan Chapter of France.

Knight, Perfect. (*Chevalier Parfait.*) A degree of the Ancient Chapter of Clermont, found in the Archives of the Mother Lodge of the Philosophic Rite.

Knight, Professed. See *Eques Professus.*

Knight, Prussian. See *Noachite.* Also the Thirty-fifth Degree of the Rite of Mizraim.

Knight Rower. (*Chevalier Rameur.*) The Order of the Knights and Ladies Rowers (*Ordre des Chevaliers Rameurs et Chevalieres Rameures*) was an androgynous and adoptive Rite, founded at the city of Rouen, in France, in 1738, and was therefore one of the earliest instances of the adoptive system. It met with very little success.

Knight, Royal Victorious. (*Chevalier royal Victorieux.*) A degree formerly conferred in the Chapter attached to the Grand Orient of Bologne.

Knight, Sacrificing. (*Chevalier Sacrifiant.*) A degree found in the Archives of the Lodge of *Saint Louis des Amis Réunis at Calais.*

Knight, Victorious. (*Chevalier Victorieux.*) A degree contained in the collection of Hécart.

Knights of the East, Council of. (*Conseil des Chevaliers d'Orient.*) A Chapter of High Degrees, under this name, was established at Paris, on July 22, 1762, by one Pirlet, a tailor, as the rival of the Council of Emperors of the East and West. Baron de Tschoudy became one of its members.

Knights Templar. The piety or the superstition of the age had induced multitudes of pilgrims in the eleventh and twelfth centuries to visit Jerusalem for the purpose of offering their devotions at the sepulcher of the Lord and the other holy place in that city. Many of these religious wanderers were weak or aged, almost all of them unarmed, and thousands of them were subjected to insult, to pillage, and often to death, inflicted by the hordes of Arabs who, even after the capture of Jerusalem by the Christians, continued to infest the sea coast of Palestine and the roads to the capital.

To protect the pious pilgrims thus exposed to plunder and bodily outrage, nine French knights, the followers of Baldwyn, united, in the year 1118, in a military confraternity or brotherhood in arms, and entered into a solemn compact to aid each other in clearing the roads, and in defending the pilgrims in their passage to the holy city.

Two of these knights were Hugh de Payens and Godfrey de St. Aldemar. Raynouard (*Les Templiers*) says that the names of the other seven have not been preserved in history, but Wilke (*Geschichte des T. H. Ordens*) gives them as Roral, Gundemar, Godfrey Bisol, Payens de Montidier, Archibald de St. Aman, André de Montbar, and the Count of Provence.

Uniting the monastic with the military character, they took, in the presence of the Patriarch of Jerusalem, the usual vows of poverty, chastity, and obedience, and with great humility assumed the title of "Poor Fellow Soldiers of Christ." Baldwyn, the King of Jerusalem, assigned for their residence a part of his palace which stood near the former site of the Temple; and the Abbot and Canons of the Temple gave them, as a place in which to store their arms and magazines, the street between the palace and the Temple, whence they derived the name of Templars; a title which they ever afterward retained.

Raynouard says that Baldwyn sent Hugh de Payens to Europe to solicit a new crusade, and that while there he presented his companions to Pope Honorius II., from whom he craved permission to form a religious military order in imitation of that of the Hospitalers. The pontiff referred them to the ecclesiastical council which was then in session at Troyes, in Champagne. Thither De Payens repaired, and represented to the fathers the vocation of himself and his companions as defenders of the pilgrim; the enterprise was approved, and St. Bernard was directed to prescribe a rule for the infant Order.

This rule, in which the knights of the Order are called *Pauperes commilitis Christi et Templi Salomonis*, or "The Poor Fellow Soldiers of Christ and of the Temple of Solomon," is still extant. It consists of seventy-two chapters, the details of which are remarkable for their ascetic character. It enjoined severe devotional exercises, self-mortification, fasting, and prayer. It prescribed for the professed knights white garments as a symbol of a pure life; esquires and retainers were to be clothed in black. To the white dress, Pope Eugenius II. subsequently added a red cross, to be worn on the left breast as a symbol of martyrdom.

Hugh de Payens, thus provided with a rule that gave permanence to his Order, and encouraged by the approval of the Church, returned to Jerusalem, carrying with him many recruits from among the noblest families of Europe.

The Templars soon became preeminently distinguished as warriors of the cross. St. Bernard, who visited them in their Temple retreat, speaks in the warmest terms of their self-denial, their frugality, their modesty, their piety, and their bravery. "Their arms," he says, "are their only finery, and they use them with courage, without dreading either the number or the strength of the barbarians. All their confidence is in the Lord of Hosts, and in fighting for his cause they seek a sure victory or a Christian and honorable death."

Their banner was the Beauseant, of divided white and black, indicative of peace to their friends, but destruction to their foes. At their reception each Templar swore never to turn his back on three enemies, but should he be alone, to fight them if they were infidels. It was their wont to say that a Templar ought either to vanquish or die, since he had nothing to give for his ransom but his girdle and his knife.

The Order of the Temple, at first exceedingly simple in its organization, became in a short time very complicated. In the twelfth century it was divided into three classes, which were Knights, Chaplains, and Serving Brethren.

1. *The Knights.* It was required that whoever presented himself for admission into the Order must prove that he was sprung from a knightly family, and was born in lawful wedlock; that he was free from all previous obligations; that he was neither married nor betrothed; that he had not made any vows of reception in another Order; that he was not involved in debt; and finally, that he was of a sound and healthy constitution of body.

2. *The Chaplains.* The Order of the Temple, unlike that of the Hospitalers, consisted at first only of laymen. But the bull of Pope Alexander III., issued in 1162, gave the Templars permission to receive into their houses spiritual persons who were not bound by previous vows, the technical name of whom was chaplains. They were required to serve a novitiate of a year. The reception was, except in a few points not applicable to the clergy, the same as that of the knights, and they were required to take only the three vows of poverty, chastity, and obedience. Their duties were to perform all religious offices, and to officiate at all the ceremonies of the Order, such as the admission of members at installations, etc. Their privileges were, however, unimportant, and consisted principally in sitting next to the Master, and being first served at table.

3. *The Serving Brethren.* The only qualification required of the serving brethren, was, that they should be free born and not slaves; yet it is not to be supposed that all the persons of this class were of mean condition. Many

men, not of noble birth, but of wealth and high position, were found among the serving brethren. They fought in the field under the knights, and performed at home the menial offices of the household. At first there was but one class of them, but afterward they were divided into two—the *Brethren-at-Arms* and the *Handicraft Brethren*. The former were the soldiers of the Order. The latter, who were the most esteemed, remained in the Preceptories, and exercised their various trades, such as those of farriers, armorers, etc. The reception of the serving brethren did not differ, except in some necessary particulars, from that of the knights. They were, however, by the accident of their birth, precluded from promotion out of their class.

Besides these three classes there was a fourth—not, however, living in the bosom of the Order—who were called *Affiliati* or the *Affiliated*. These were persons of various ranks and of both sexes, who were recognized by the Order, though not openly connected with it, as entitled to its protection, and admitted to a participation in some of its privileges, such as protection from the interdicts of the Church, which did not apply to the members of the Order.

There was also a class called *Donates* or *Donats*. These were either youths whom their parents destined for the service of the Order when they had attained the proper age, or adults who had bound themselves to aid and assist the Order so long as they lived, solely from their admiration of it, and a desire to share its honors.

Over these presided the Grand Master, more usually styled, in the early days of the Order, simply the Master of the Temple. In the treaty of peace executed in 1178, between the Templars and the Hospitalers, Odo de St. Armand calls himself "Humble Master of the Order of the Temple." But in after times this spirit of humility was lost sight of, and the title of Grand Master was generally accorded to him. His allowances were suitable to the distinguished rank he held, for in the best days of the Order the Grand Master was considered as the equal of a sovereign.

The Grand Master resided originally at Jerusalem; afterward, when that city was lost, at Acre, and finally at Cyprus. His duty always required him to be in the Holy Land; he consequently never resided in Europe. He was elected for life from among the knights in the following manner: On the death of the Grand Master, a Grand Prior was chosen to administer the affairs of the Order until a successor could be elected. When the day which had been appointed for the election arrived, the Chapter usually assembled at the chief seat of the Order; three or more of the most esteemed knights were then proposed; the Grand Prior collected the votes, and he who had received the greatest number was nominated to be the electing Prior. An Assistant was then associated with him, in the person of another knight. These two remained all night in the chapel, engaged in prayer. In the

morning, they chose two others, and these four, two more, and so on until the number of twelve (that of the apostles) had been selected. The twelve then selected a Chaplain. The thirteen then proceeded to vote for a Grand Master, who was elected by a majority of the votes. When the election was completed, it was announced to the assembled brethren; and when all had promised obedience, the Prior, if the person was present, said to him, "In the name of God the Father, the Son, and the Holy Ghost, we have chosen, and do choose thee, Brother N., to be our Master." Then, turning to the brethren, he said, "Beloved Sirs and Brethren, give thanks unto God; behold here our Master." The Chaplains then chanted the *Te Deum;* and the brethren, taking their new Master in their arms, carried him into the chapel and placed him before the altar, where he continued kneeling, while the brethren prayed, and the Chaplains repeated the *Kyrie Eleison*, the *Pater Noster*, and other devotional exercises.

Next in rank to the Grand Master was the *Seneschal*, who was his representative and lieutenant. Then came the *Marshal*, who was the General of the Order. Next was the *Treasurer*, an office that was always united with that of Grand Preceptor of Jerusalem. He was the Admiral of the Order. The *Draper*, the next officer in rank, had charge of the clothing of the Order. He was a kind of Commissary General. The *Turcopolier* was the Commander of the light-horse. There was also a class of officers called *Visitors*, whose duties, as their name imports, was to visit the different Provinces, and correct abuses. There were also some subordinate offices appropriated to the Serving Brethren, such as *Sub marshal*, *Standard-Bearer, Farrier*, etc.

These officers, with the Grand Preceptors of the Provinces and the most distinguished knights who could attend, constituted the General Chapter or great legislative assembly of the Order, where all laws and regulations were made and great officers elected. This assembly was not often convened, and in the intervals its powers were exercised by the Chapter of Jerusalem.

The Order thus organized, as it increased in prosperity and augmented its possessions in the East and in Europe, was divided into Provinces, each of which was governed by a Grand Preceptor or Grand Prior; for the titles were indiscriminately used. That, however, of Preceptor was peculiar to the Templars, while that of Prior was common both to them and to the Knights Hospitalers of St. John. These Provinces were fifteen in number, and were as follows: Jerusalem, Tripolis, Antioch, Cyprus, Portugal, Castile and Leon, Aragon, France and Auvergne, Normandy, Aquitaine, Provence, England, including Scotland and Ireland; Germany, Upper and Central Italy, and Apulia and Sicily. Hence it will be seen that there was no part of Europe, except the impoverished kingdoms of Denmark, Sweden, and Norway, where the Templars had not extended their possessions and their influence.

In all the Provinces there were numerous temple-houses called Preceptories, presided over by a Preceptor. In each of the larger Preceptories there was a Chapter, in which local regulations were made and members were received into the Order.

The reception of a knight into the Order was a very solemn ceremonial. It was secret, none but members of the Order being permitted to be present. In this it differed from that of the Knights of Malta, whose form of reception was open and public; and it is to this difference, between a public reception and a secret initiation, that may, perhaps, be attributed a portion of the spirit of persecution exhibited by the Church to the Order in its latter days.

Of this reception, the best and most authentic account is given by Münter in his *Statutenbuch des Ordens der Tempelherren* (pp. 29–42), and on that I shall principally rely.

On the day of the reception, the Master and the knights being in the Chapter, the Master said:

"Beloved Knights and Brethren, ye see that the majority are willing that this man shall be received as a brother. If there be among you any one who knows anything concerning him, wherefor he cannot rightfully become a brother, let him say so. For it is better that this should be made known beforehand than after he has been brought before us." All being silent, the candidate is conducted into an adjoining chamber. Two or three of the oldest knights are sent to him to warn him of the difficulties and hardships that he will have to encounter; or, as the Benedictine rule says, all the hard and rough ways that lead to God —"omnia dura et aspera, per quæ itur ad Deum."

They commenced by saying: "Brother, do you seek the fellowship of the Order?" If he replied affirmatively, they warned him of the rigorous services which would be demanded of him. Should he reply that he was willing to endure all for the sake of God and to become the slave of the Order, they further asked him if he were married or betrothed; if he had ever entered any other Order; if he owed more than he could pay; if he was of sound body; and if he was of free condition? If his replies were satisfactory, his examiners returned to the Chapter room and made report; whereupon the Master again inquired if any one present knew anything against the candidate. All being silent, he asked: "Are you willing that he should be received in God's name?" and all the knights answered: "Let him be received in God's name." His examiners then returned to him and asked him if he still persisted in his intention. If he replied that he did, they gave him the necessary instructions how he should act, and led him to the door of the Chapter room. There entering he cast himself on his knees before the Master, with folded hands, and said: "Sir, I am come before God, before you and the brethren, and pray and beseech you, for God and our dear Lady's sake, to admit me into your fellowship

and to the good deeds of the Order, as one who will for all his life long be the servant and slave of the Order."

The Master replied: "Beloved Brother, you are desirous of a great matter, for you see nothing but the outward shell of our Order. It is only the outward shell when you see that we have fine horses and rich caparisons, that we eat and drink well, and are splendidly clothed. From this you conclude that you will be well off with us. But you know not the rigorous maxims which are in our interior. For it is a hard matter for you, who are your own master, to become the servant of another. You will hardly be able to perform, in future, what you wish yourself. For when you wish to be on this side of the sea, you will be sent to the other side; when you will wish to be in Acre, you will be sent to the district of Antioch, to Tripolis, or to Armenia; or you will be sent to Apulia, to Sicily, or to Lombardy, or to Burgundy, France, England, or any other country where we have houses and possessions. When you will wish to sleep, you will be ordered to watch; when you will wish to watch, then you will be ordered to go to bed; when you will wish to eat, then you will be ordered to do something else. And as both we and you might suffer great inconvenience from what you have, mayhap, concealed from us, look here on the holy Evangelists and the word of God, and answer the truth to the questions which we shall put to you; for if you lie, you will be perjured, and may be expelled the Order, from which God keep you!"

The questions which had been before asked him by his examiners were then repeated more at large, with the additional one whether he had made any contract with a Templar or any other person to secure his admission.

His answers being satisfactory, the Master proceeded: "Beloved Brother, take good heed that you have spoken truth to us, for should you in any one point have spoken falsely, you would be put out of the Order, from which God preserve you. Now, beloved Brother, heed well what we shall say to you. Do you promise God and Mary, our dear Lady, that your life long you will be obedient to the Master of the Temple and the Prior who is set over you?"

"Yes, Sir, God willing."

"Do you promise God and Mary, our dear Lady, all your life long to live chaste in your body?"

"Yes, Sir, God willing."

"Do you promise God and Mary, our dear Lady, your life long to observe the laudable manners and customs of our Order, those which now are and those which the Master and knights may hereafter ordain?"

"Yes, Sir, God willing."

"Do you promise God and Mary, our dear Lady, that your life long you will, with the power and strength that God gives you, help to conquer the holy land of Jerusalem, and with your best power you will help to keep and guard that which the Christians possess?"

"Yes, Sir, God willing."

"Do you promise God and Mary, our dear Lady, never to hold this Order for stronger or weaker, for worse or for better, but with the permission of the Master or the convent which has the authority?"

"Yes, Sir, God willing."

"Finally, do you promise God and Mary, our dear Lady, that you will never be present when a Christian shall be unjustly and unlawfully despoiled of his heritage, and that you will never by counsel or act take part therein?"

"Yes, Sir, God willing."

Then the Master said: "Thus, in the name of God and Mary our dear Lady, and in the name of St. Peter of Rome, and our Father the Pope, and in the name of all the Brethren of the Temple, we receive you to all the good works of the Order which have been done from the beginning, and shall be done to the end, you, your father, your mother, and all your lineage, who you are willing shall have a share therein. In like manner do you receive us into all the good works which you have done or shall do. We assure you bread and water, and the poor clothing of the Order, and toil and labor in abundance."

The Chaplain then read the 133d Psalm and the prayer of the Holy Ghost, *Deus qui corda fidelium*, and the brethren repeated the Lord's prayer. The Prior and the Chaplain gave the recipient the fraternal kiss. He was then seated before the Master, who delivered to him a discourse on his duties and obligations as a member of the Order.

These duties may be thus summed up: He was never to assault a Christian, nor swear, nor receive any attendance from a woman without the permission of his superiors; not to kiss a woman, even his mother or sister; to hold no child to the baptismal font; and to abuse no man, but to be courteous to all. He was to sleep in a linen shirt, drawers and hose, and girded with a small girdle; to attend Divine service punctually, and to begin and end his meals with a prayer.

Such is the formula of reception, which has been collected by Münter from the most authentic sources. It is evident, however, that it is not complete. The secret parts of the ritual are omitted, so that the formula is here something like what a Freemason would call the monitorial part of the instruction. Münter does not even give the form of the oath taken by the candidate; although Raynouard says that it is preserved in the Archives of the Abbey of Alcobaza, in Aragon, and gives it in the following words, on the authority of Henriguez in his *Regula, etc., Ordinis Cisterniensis:*

"I swear to consecrate my discourse, my arms, my faculties, and my life, to the defence of the sacred mysteries of the faith, and to that of the unity of God. I also promise to be submissive and obedient to the Grand Master of the Order. . . . At all times that it may be necessary, I will cross the seas to go to battle; I will contribute succor against infidel kings and princes; I will not turn my back on three foes; and even if I be alone, I will fight them if they are infidels."

The fact that the Templars had a secret initiation is now generally conceded, although a few writers have denied it. But the circumstantial evidence in its favor is too great to be overcome by anything except positive proof to the contrary, which has never been adduced. It is known that at these receptions none but members of the Order were admitted; a prohibition which would have been unnecessary if the ceremonies had not been secret. In the meetings of the General Chapter of the Order, even the Pope's Legate was refused admission.

It would not be fair to quote the one hundred and twenty accusations preferred against the Templars by Clement, because they were undoubtedly malicious falsehoods invented by an unprincipled Pontiff pandering to the cupidity of an avaricious monarch; but yet some of them are of such a nature as to indicate what was the general belief of men at the time. Thus, Art. 32 says: "Quod receptiones istius clandestine faciebant"; i. e., *that they were wont to have their receptions in secret.* The 100th is in these words: "Quod sic se includunt ad tenenda capitula ut omnes januas domus et ecclesiæ in quibus tenent capitula ferment adeo firmiter quod nullus sit nec esse possit accessus ad eos nec juxta: ut possit quicunque videre vel audire de factis veldictis eorum"; i. e., *that when they held their Chapters, they shut all the doors of the house or church in which they met so closely that no one could approach near enough to see or hear what they were doing and saying.* And the next article is more particular, for it states that, to secure themselves against eavesdroppers, they were accustomed to place a watch, as we should now say a tiler, upon the roof of the house, "excubicum super tectum," who could give the necessary warning.

Of course it is impossible to obtain an accurate knowledge of all the details of this secret reception of the ancient Templars, since it must have been generally oral; but I have always been inclined to think, from allusions here and there scattered through the history of their customs, that many of its features have descended to us, and are to be found in the ritual of initiation practised by the Masonic Knights Templar.

The dress of the Templars was prescribed for them by St. Bernard, in the rule which he composed for the government of the Order, and is thus described in Chapter XX.

"To all the pro- 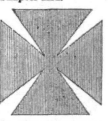 fessed knights, both in winter and summer, we give, if they can be procured, *white garments*, that those who have cast behind them a dark life, may know that they are to commend themselves to their Creator by a pure and white life." The white mantle was therefore the peculiar vestment of the Templars, as the black was of the Hospitalers.

The general direction of St. Bernard as to clothing was afterward expanded, so that the dress of a Templar consisted of a long, white tunic, nearly resembling that of a priest's in shape, with a red cross on the front and back; under this was his linen shirt clasped by a girdle. Over all was the white mantle with the red cross pattée. The head was covered by a cap or hood attached to the mantle. The arms were a sword, lance, mace, and shield. Although at first the Order adopted as a seal the representation of two knights riding on one horse, as a mark of their poverty, subsequently each knight was provided with three horses, and an esquire selected usually from the class of Serving Brethren.

To write the history of the Templar Order for the two centuries of its existence would, says Addison, be to write the Latin history of Palestine, and would occupy a volume. Its details would be accounts of glorious struggles with the infidel in defense of the Holy Land, and of Christian pilgrimage, sometimes successful and often disastrous; of arid sands well moistened with the blood of Christian and Saracen warriors; of disreputable contests with its rival of St. John; of final forced departure from the places which its prowess had conquered, but which it had not strength to hold, and of a few years of luxurious, and it may be of licentious indolence, terminated by a cruel martyrdom and dissolution.

The fall of Acre in 1292, under the vigorous assault of the Sultan Mansour, led at once to the evacuation of Palestine by the Christians. The Knights Hospitalers of St. John of Jerusalem, afterward called Knights of Rhodes, and then of Malta, betook themselves to Rhodes, where the former, assuming a naval character, resumed the warfare in their galleys against the Mohammedans. The Templars, after a brief stay in the island of Cyprus, retired to their different Preceptories in Europe.

Porter (*Hist. K. of Malta*, i., 174) has no panegyric for these recreant knights. After eulogizing the Hospitalers for the persevering energy with which, from their island home of Rhodes, they continued the war with the infidels, he says:

"The Templar, on the other hand, after a brief sojourn in Cyprus, instead of rendering the smallest assistance to his chivalrous and knightly brethren in their new undertaking, hurried with unseemly haste to his numerous wealthy European Preceptories, where the grossness of his licentiousness, the height of his luxury, and the arrogance of his pride, soon rendered him an object of the most invincible hatred among those who possessed ample power to accomplish his overthrow. During these last years of their existence little can be said in defense of the Order; and although the barbarous cruelty with which their extinction was accomplished has raised a feeling of compassion in their behalf, which bids fair to efface the memory of their crimes, still it cannot be denied that they had of late years so far deviated from the original purposes of their Institution as to render them highly unfit depositaries of that wealth which had been bequeathed to them for purposes so widely different from those to which they had appropriated it."

The act of cruelty and of injustice by which the Templar Order was dissolved in the fourteenth century, has bequeathed an inglorious memory on the names of the infamous king, and no less infamous pope, who accomplished it. In the beginning of the fourteenth century, the throne of France was filled by Philip the Fair, an ambitious, a vindictive, and an avaricious prince. In his celebrated controversy with Pope Boniface, the Templars had, as was usual with them, sided with the pontiff and opposed the king; this act excited his hatred: the Order was enormously wealthy; this aroused his avarice; their power interfered with his designs of political aggrandisement; and this alarmed his ambition. He, therefore, secretly concerted with Pope Clement V. a plan for their destruction, and the appropriation of their revenues. Clement, by his direction, wrote in June, 1306, to De Molay, the Grand Master, who was then at Cyprus, inviting him to come and consult with him on some matters of great importance to the Order. De Molay obeyed the summons, and arrived in the beginning of 1307 at Paris, with sixty knights and a large amount of treasure. He was immediately imprisoned, and, on the thirteenth of October following, every knight in France was, in consequence of the secret orders of the king, arrested on the pretended charge of idolatry, and other enormous crimes, of which Squin de Flexian, a renegade and expelled Prior of the Order, was said to have confessed that the knights were guilty in their secret Chapters.

What these charges were has not been left to conjecture. Pope Clement sent a list of the articles of accusation, amounting to one hundred and twenty in number, to all the archbishops, bishops, and Papal commissaries upon which to examine the knights who should be brought before them. This list is still in existence, and in it we find such charges as these: 1. That they required those who were received into the Order to abjure Christ, the Blessed Virgin, and all the saints. 7. That they denied that Christ had suffered for man's redemption. 9. That they made their recipient spit upon the cross or the crucifix. 14. That they worshiped a cat in their assemblies. 16. That they did not believe in the eucharistic sacrifice. 20. That they said that the Grand Master had the power of absolution. 26. That they practised obscene ceremonies in their receptions. 32. That their receptions were secret; a charge repeated in articles 97, 98, 99, 100, and 101, in different forms. 42. That they had an idol, which was a head with one or with three faces, and sometimes a human skull. 52, 53. That they exercised magic arts.

On such preposterous charges as these the

knights were tried, and of course, as a foregone conclusion, condemned. On the 12th of May, 1310, fifty-four of the knights were publicly burnt, and on the 18th of March, 1313, De Molay, the Grand Master, and the three principal dignitaries of the order, suffered the same fate. They died faithfully asserting their innocence of all the crimes imputed to them. The Order was now, by the energy of the King of France, assisted by the spiritual authority of the pope, suppressed throughout Europe. So much of its vast possessions as were not appropriated by the different sovereigns to their own use, or to that of their favorites, was bestowed upon the Order of the Knights of Malta, whose acceptance of the donation did not tend to diminish the ill feeling which had always existed between the members of the two Orders.

As to the story of the continuation of the Order, after the death of James de Molay, by Johannes Larmenius, under the authority of a charter of transmission given to him by De Molay a few days before his death, that subject is more appropriately treated in the history of the Order of the Temple, which claims, by virtue of this charter, to be the regular successor of the ancient Order.

From the establishment of the Order by Hugh de Payens, until its dissolution during the Mastership of De Molay, twenty-two Grand Masters presided over the Order, of whom the following is an accurate list, compiled on the authority of Addison. The roll of Grand Masters in the Rite of Strict Observance, and that in the Order of the Templar, differ in several names; but these rolls are destitute of authenticity.

1.	Hugh de Payens,	elected in	1118.
2.	Robert of Burgundy,	"	1136.
3.	Everard de Barri,	"	1146.
4.	Bernard de Tremellay,	"	1151.
5.	Bertrand de Blanquefort,	"	1154.
6.	Philip of Naplous,	"	1167.
7.	Odo de St. Amand,	"	1170.
8.	Arnold de Troye,	"	1180.
9.	Gerard de Ridefort,	"	1185.
10.	Brother Walter,	"	1189.
11.	Robert de Sablé,	"	1191.
12.	Gilbert Horal,	"	1195.
13.	Philip de Plessis,	"	1201.
14.	William de Chartres,	"	1217.
15.	Peter de Montaigu,	"	1218.
16.	Hermann de Perigord,	"	1236.
17.	William de Sonnac,	"	1245.
18.	Reginald de Vichier,	"	1252.
19.	Thomas Berard,	"	1256.
20.	William de Beaujeu,	"	1273.
21.	Theobald de Gaudini,	"	1291.
22.	James de Molay,	"	1297.

(See *Trans. Quar. Cor.*, vol. XX.)

Knights Templar, Masonic. The connection of the Knights Templar with the Freemasons may much more plausibly be traced than that of the Knights of Malta. Yet, unfortunately, the sources from which informa-

tion is to be derived are for the most part traditionary; authentic dates and documents are wanting. Tradition has always been inclined to trace the connection to an early period, and to give to the Templar system of secret reception a Masonic character, derived from their association during the Crusades with the mystical Society of the Assassins in Syria. Lawrie (*Hist.*, p. 87), or Sir David Brewster, the real author of the work which bears Lawrie's name, embodies the tradition in this form:

"Almost all the secret associations of the ancients either flourished or originated in Syria and the adjacent countries. It was here that the Dionysian artists, the Essenes and the Kasideans arose. From this country also came several members of that trading association of Masons which appeared in Europe during the dark ages; and we are assured, that, notwithstanding the unfavorable condition of that province, there exists at this day, on Mount Libanus, one of these Syriac fraternities. As the Order of the Templars, therefore, was originally formed in Syria, and existed there for a considerable time, it would be no improbable supposition that they received their Masonic knowledge from the Lodges in that quarter. But we are fortunately, in this case, not left to conjecture, for we are expressly informed by a foreign author [Adler, *de Drusis*], who was well acquainted with the history and customs of Syria, that the Knights Templar were actually members of the Syriac fraternities."

Even if this hypothesis were true, although it might probably suggest the origin of the secret reception of the Templars, it would not explain the connection of the modern Templars with the Freemasons, because there is no evidence that these Syriac fraternities were Masonic.

There are four sources from which the Masonic Templars are said to have derived their existence; making, therefore, as many different divisions of the Order.

1. The Templars who claim John Mark Larmenius as the successor of James de Molay.

2. Those who recognize Peter d'Aumont as the successor of De Molay.

3. Those who derive their Templarism from the Count Beaujeu, the nephew of Molay.

4. Those who claim an independent origin, and repudiate alike the authority of Larmenius, of Aumont, and of Beaujeu.

From the first class spring the Templars of France, who professed to have continued the Order by authority of a charter given by De Molay to Larmenius. This body of Templars designate themselves as the "Order of the Temple." Its seat is in Paris. The Duke of Sussex received from it the degree and the authority to establish a Grand Conclave in England. He did so; and convened that body once, but only once. During the remaining years of his life, Templarism had no activity in England, as he discountenanced all Christian and chivalric Masonry. (See *Temple, Order of the.*)

The second division of Templars is that which is founded on the theory that Peter d'Aumont fled with several knights into Scotland, and there united with the Freemasons. This legend is intimately connected with Ramsay's tradition—that Freemasonry sprang from Templarism, and that all Freemasons are Knights Templar. The Chapter of Clermont adopted this theory; and in establishing their high degrees asserted that they were derived from these Templars of Scotland. The Baron Hund carried the theory into Germany, and on it established his Rite of Strict Observance, which was a Templar system. Hence the Templars of Germany must be classed under the head of the followers of Aumont. (See *Strict Observance.*)

The third division is that which asserts that the Count Beaujeu, a nephew of the last Grand Master, De Molay, and a member of the Order of Knights of Christ—the name assumed by the Templars of Portugal—had received authority from that Order to disseminate the degree. He is said to have carried the degree and its ritual into Sweden, where he incorporated it with Freemasonry. The story is, too, that Beaujeu collected his uncle's ashes and interred them in Stockholm, where a monument was erected to his memory. Hence the Swedish Templar Masons claim their descent from Beaujeu, and the Swedish Rite is through this source a Templar system.

Of the last class, or the Templars who recognized the authority of neither of the leaders who have been mentioned, there were two subdivisions, the Scotch and the English; for it is only in Scotland and England that this independent Templarism found a foothold.

It was only in Scotland that the Templars endured no persecution. Long after the dissolution of the Order in every other country of Europe, the Scottish Preceptories continued to exist, and the knights lived undisturbed. One portion of the Scottish Templars entered the army of Robert Bruce, and, after the battle of Bannockburn, were merged in the "Royal Order of Scotland," then established by him. (See *Royal Order of Scotland.*)

Another portion of the Scottish Templars united with the Knights Hospitalers of St. John. They lived amicably in the same houses, and continued to do so until the Reformation. At this time many of them embraced Protestantism. Some of them united with the Freemasons, and established "the Ancient Lodge" at Stirling, where they conferred the degrees of Knight of the Sepulcher, Knight of Malta, and Knights Templar. It is to this division that we are to trace the Masonic Templars of Scotland.

The Roman Catholic knights remaining in the Order placed themselves under David Seaton. Lord Dundee afterward became their Grand Master. Charles Edward, the "Young Pretender," is said to have been admitted into the Order at Holyrood House, Edinburgh, on September 24, 1745, and made the Grand

Master. He is also said, but without any proof, to have established the Chapter of Arras and the high degrees.* To this branch, I think, there can be but little doubt that we are to attribute the Templar system of the Ancient and Accepted Scottish Rite as developed in its degree of Kadosh.

The English Masonic Templars are most probably derived from that body called the "Baldwyn Encampment," or from some one of the four coordinate Encampments of London, Bath, York, and Salisbury, which it is claimed were formed by the members of the Preceptory which had long existed at Bristol, and who, on the dissolution of their Order, are supposed to have united with the Masonic Fraternity. The Baldwyn Encampment claims to have existed from "time immemorial"—an indefinite period—but we can trace it back far enough to give it a priority over all other English Encampments. From this division of the Templars, repudiating all connection with Larmenius, with Aumont, or any other of the self-constituted leaders, but tracing its origin to the independent action of knights who fled for security and for perpetuity into the body of Masonry, we may be held justly entitled to derive the Templars of the United States.

Of this brief statement, we may make the following summary:

1. From Larmenius came the French Templars.

2. From Aumont, the German Templars of Strict Observance.

3. From Beaujeu, the Swedish Templars of the Rite of Zinnendorf.

4. From the Protestant Templars of Scotland and the Ancient Lodge of Stirling, the Scotch Templars.

5. From Prince Charles Edward and his adherents, the Templars of the Ancient and Accepted Scottish Rite.

6. From the Baldwyn Encampment and its coordinates, the old English and the American Templars.

The GOVERNMENT of Masonic Knights Templar in the United States is vested, first, in Commanderies, which confer the Red Cross and Templar degrees and instruct in the secrets of Malta.† The usual expression, that a candidate after being made a Knights Templar is also created a Knight of Malta, involves an absurdity. No man being a Knights Templar could, by the original statutes, be a member of any other Order; and it is to be regretted that the wise provision of the Grand Encampment in 1856, which struck the degree of Malta from the ritual of the Commanderies, should have been in 1862 unwisely repealed. The secrets in which the candidate is instructed are the modern inventions of the Masonic Knights of Malta. The original Order had no secrets.

---

* For a critical examination of this story see Hughan's *Jacobite Lodge at Rome*, ch. 3.

　　　　　　　　　　　　[E. L. H.]

† See foot-note after Knights of Malta.

Commanderies are under the control of Grand Commanderies in States in which those bodies exist. Where they do not, the Warrants are derived directly from the Grand Encampment.

The supreme authority of the Order is exercised by the Grand Encampment of the United States, which meets triennially. The presiding officer is a Grand Master.

The COSTUME of the Knights Templar of the United States is of two kinds. First, the original uniform, which was in general use until the year 1859, and is still used by Commanderies which were in existence before that time. It is thus described:

The suit is black, with black gloves. A black velvet sash, trimmed with silver lace, crosses the body from the left shoulder to right hip, having at its end a cross-hilted dagger, a black rose on the left shoulder, and a Maltese cross at the end. Where the sash crosses the left breast, is a nine-pointed star in silver, with a cross and serpent of gold in the center, within a circle, around which are the words, "*in hoc signo vinces.*" The apron is of black velvet, in triangular form, to represent the delta, and edged with silver lace. On its flap is placed a triangle of silver, perforated with twelve holes, with a cross and serpent in the center; on the center of the apron are a skull and crossbones, between three stars of seven points, having a red cross in the center of each. The belt is black, to which is attached a cross-hilted sword. The caps vary in form and decoration in different Encampments. The standard is black, bearing a nine-pointed cross of silver, having in its center a circle of green, with the cross and serpent in gold, and the motto around "*in hoc signo vinces.*"

In 1859 the Grand Encampment enacted a statute providing that all Commanderies which might be thereafter chartered should provide a new costume of an entirely different kind, which should also be adopted by the old Commanderies whenever they should change their uniform. This new costume was further altered in 1862, and is now of the following description, as detailed in the statute:

Full Dress.—Black frock coat, black pantaloons, scarf, sword, belt, shoulder straps, gauntlets, and chapeau, with appropriate trimmings.

Fatigue Dress.—Same as full dress, except for chapeau a black cloth cap, navy form, with appropriate cross in front, and for gauntlets, white gloves.

Scarf.—Five inches wide in the whole, of white, bordered with black one inch on either side, a strip of navy lace one-fourth of an inch wide, at the inner edge of the black. On the front center of the scarf a metal star of nine points, in allusion to the nine founders of the Temple Order, enclosing the Passion Cross, surrounded by the Latin motto, "*in hoc signo vinces*"; the star to be three and three-quarter inches in diameter. The scarf to be worn from the right shoulder to the left hip, with the ends extending six inches below the point of intersection.

Chapeau.—The military chapeau, trimmed with black binding, one white and two black plumes, and appropriate cross on the left side.

Gauntlets.—Of buff leather, the flap to extend four inches upward from the wrist, and to have the appropriate cross embroidered in gold, on the proper colored velvet, two inches in length.

Sword.—Thirty-four to forty inches, inclusive of scabbard; helmet head, cross handle, and metal scabbard.

Belt.—Red enameled or patent leather, two inches wide, fastened round the body with buckle or clasp.

From what has been said, it will appear that there are two modes of dress or costume in use among the Templars of the United States—one, the old or "black uniform," which was adopted at the first organization of the Order in this country, and which is still used by the old Commanderies which were in existence previous to the year 1859; and the new or "white uniform," which was adopted by the Grand Encampment in that year, and which has been prescribed for all Commanderies chartered since that year.

This difference of costume has recently been the occasion of much discussion in the Order. In 1872, Sir J. Q. A. Fellows, the Grand Master, thinking that it was his duty to enforce a uniform dress in the Order, issued his decree requiring all the Commanderies in the United States which were then using "the black uniform," to abandon it, and to adopt "the white uniform," which had been originally ordered in 1859, and subsequently amended in 1862. Much opposition has been manifested to this order in the Commanderies and Grand Commanderies where the black costume was in use. The Grand Master's interpretation of the statute of the Grand Encampment has been doubted or denied, and the order has been virtually disobeyed by most, if not by all of them. The question has assumed great importance in consequence of the feeling that has been created, and is therefore worthy of discussion. Dr. Mackey's views were against the correctness of the Grand Master's interpretation of the law, and so were those of the living Past Grand Masters of the Order. It is, however, but fair to say that some distinguished Templars have been of a different opinion. The following views advanced by Dr. Mackey in the *National Freemason* in December, 1872, express what he thought was the true condition of the question.

Previous to the year 1859 the costume of the Knights Templar of this country was determined only by a traditional rule, and consisted of a black dress, with the richly decorated baldric and apron; the latter intended to show the connection which existed between the Order and Ancient Craft Masonry.

In 1856, at Hartford, a new Constitution was proposed and adopted, with the exception of the part that referred to costume. Sir Knight Mackey, from the committee on the Constitution, made a report on the subject of dress, as a part of the Constitution; but the consideration of this report was postponed until the next triennial meeting. The changes in costume proposed by the committee were not very great; the baldric and the *essential* apron were preserved, and a white tunic, not hitherto used, was recommended.

At the session of 1859, at Chicago, the subject of dress was alluded to by the Grand Master in his address; and his remarks, together with the report of the committee made in 1856, were referred to a special committee of seven, of which the Grand Master was chairman, and Sir Knights Doyle, Pike, Simons, Mackey, Morris, and French were the members.

This committee reported a uniform which made material differences in the dress theretofore worn, and especially by the rejection of the apron and the introduction of a white tunic and a white cloak. These last were favorite notions of Grand Master Hubbard, and they were adopted by the committee mainly in deference to his high authority.

The proposed measure met at first with serious opposition, partly on account of the rejection of the apron, which many Templars then held, as they do now, to be an essential feature of Masonic Templarism, and a tangible record of the union at a specific period in history of the two Orders; but mainly, perhaps, on account of the very heavy expense and inconvenience which would devolve on the old Commanderies, if they were required at once to throw aside their old dress and provide a new one.

This opposition was only quelled by the agreement on a *compromise*, by which the old Commanderies were to be exempted from the operation of the law. The regulations for the new costume were then passed, and the *compromise* immediately after adopted in the words of the following resolution, which was proposed by Sir Knight Doyle, who was one of the committee:

"*Resolved*, That the costume this day adopted by the Grand Encampment be, and the same is hereby, ordered to be worn by all Commanderies chartered at this Communication, or that shall hereafter be established in this jurisdiction, and by all Commanderies heretofore existing, whenever they shall procure a new costume"; and all State Grand Commanderies were directed to enforce it in all subordinates that may hereafter be chartered in their respective jurisdictions.

This was a compromise, nothing more or less, and so understood at the time. The old Commanderies were then in the majority, and would not have consented to any change involving so much expenditure, unless they had been relieved from the burden themselves.

But the white tunic and cloak were never popular with the knights, who had been required by the regulations of 1859 to wear them. In consequence of this, at the session in 1862, on motion of Sir Knight Bailey, "the subject-matter of costume and the resolution relating thereto were referred to a Select Committee of Five."

This committee made a report, in which they "proposed" a uniform. The record says that "the report was agreed to, and the uniform was adopted." But there are some points in this report that are worthy of notice. In the first place, not a word is said about the compromise resolution adopted in 1859, although it was referred to the committee. That resolution was not repealed by any action taken at the session of 1862, and still must remain in force. It secured to the old Commanderies the right to wear the old black costume; a right which could not be taken from them, except by a repeal of the resolution conferring the right. Nothing need be said of the manifest injustice of repealing a resolution granted by the friends of a measure to its opponents to remove their opposition. In 1859, the promise was made to the old Commanderies, that if they would agree to a certain uniform, to be prescribed for new Commanderies, their own old, traditional costume should never be interfered with. *Might* could, it is true, repeal this compromise; but *Right* would, for that purpose, have to be sacrificed. But the fact is, that the sense of right in the Grand Encampment prevented such an act of discourtesy, "not to put too fine a point upon it," and no one can find in the proceedings of the Grand Encampment any act which repeals the compromise resolution of 1859; and this has been the opinion and the decision of all the Grand Masters who have wielded the baculus of office, except the present one.

But, in the second place, the report of 1862 shows clearly that the object of the committee was to recommend a change in the uniform that had been adopted for new Commanderies in 1859, and which had become objectionable on account of the tunic and cloak, and that they did not intend to refer at all to the old dress of the old Commanderies.

In the report the committee say: "The objections advanced to the costume adopted at the last Triennial Conclave of this Grand Body are want of adaptation to the requirements of our modern Templars, its liability to injury, and its expensiveness." Now, who advanced these objections? Clearly, not the old Commanderies. They were well satisfied with the mode of dress which they had received from their fathers; and which was dear to them for its solemn beauty and its traditional associations; and the right to wear which had been secured to them in 1859, with the understanding that if they ever desired, of their own accord, to lay it aside, they would then adopt, in its stead, the regulation dress of the Grand Encampment. But this was to be for their own free action.

It was very evident that the old Commanderies had never complained that the tunics and cloaks were from their material expensive, and from their color liable to injury. The old Commanderies did not use these expensive and easily soiled garments. It was the new Commanderies that had made the objection, and for them the legislation of 1862 was undertaken.

Dr. Mackey held, therefore, that the compromise resolution of 1859 still remains in force; that even if the Grand Encampment had the right to repeal it, which he did not admit, it never has enacted any such repeal; that the old Commanderies have the right to wear the old black uniform, and that the legislation of 1862 was intended only to affect the new Commanderies which had been established since the year 1859, when the first dress regulation was adopted.

It would scarcely be proper to close this article on Masonic Templarism without some reference to a philological controversy which has recently arisen among the members of the Order in the United States in reference to the question whether the proper title in the plural is "Knights Templars" or "Knights Templar." This subject was first brought to the attention of the Order by the introduction, in the session of the Grand Encampment in 1871, of the following resolutions by Sir Knight Charles F. Stansbury, of Washington City.

"*Resolved*, That the proper title of the Templar Order is 'Knights Templars,' and not 'Knights Templar,' as now commonly used under the sanction of the example of this Grand Encampment.

"*Resolved*, That the use of the term 'Knights Templar' is an innovation, in violation of historic truth, literary usage, and the philology and grammar of the English language."

This report was referred to a committee, who reported "that this Grand Encampment has no authority to determine questions of 'historic truth, literary usage, and the philology and grammar of the English language'"; and they asked to be discharged from the further consideration of the subject. This report is not very creditable to the committee, and puts a very low estimate on the character of the Grand Encampment. Certainly, it is the duty of every body of men to inquire whether the documents issued under their name are in violation of these principles, and if so, to correct the error. If a layman habitually writes bad English, it shows that he is illiterate; and the committee should have sought to preserve the Grand Encampment from a similar charge. It should have investigated the subject, which to scholars is of more importance than they seemed to consider it; they should have defended the Grand Encampment in the use of the term, or have recommended its abandonment. Moreover, the Grand Recorder reports that on examination he finds that the title *Knights Templars* was always used until 1856, when it was changed to *Knights Templar;* and the committee should have inquired by whose authority the change was made. But having failed to grapple with the question of good English, the Craft afterward took the subject up, and a long discussion ensued in the different Masonic journals, resulting at last in the expression, by the best scholars of the Order, of the opinion that *Knights Templars* was correct, because it was in accordance with

the rules of good English, and in unexceptional agreement with the usage of all literary men who have written on the subject.

Bro. Stansbury, in an article on this question which he published in Mackey's *National Freemason* (i., 191), has almost exhausted the subject of authority and grammatical usage. He says: " That it is an innovation in violation of historic truth is proved by reference to all historical authorities. I have made diligent researches in the Congressional Library, and have invoked the aid of all my friends who were likely to be able to assist me in such an investigation, and so far from finding any conflict of authority on the question, I have never been able to discover a single historical authority in favor of any other title than 'Knights Templars.'

"ı refer to the following list of authorities: *Encyclopedia Britannica, Encyclopedia Americana, Chambers's Encyclopedia, London Encyclopedia, Encyclopedia Metropolitana, Penny Cyclopedia, Cottage Cyclopedia, Rees's Cyclopedia,* Wade's *British Chronology,* Blair's *Chronological Tables, Chambers's Miscellany* (Crusades), *Chambers's Book of Days,* Addison's *Knights Templars, Pantalogia,* Boutelle's *Heraldry,* Hallam's *Middle Ages,* Lingard's *History of England; Glossographia Anglicana Nova,* 1707; Blackstone's *Commentaries,* vol. i., p. 406; *Appleton's Cyclopedia of Biography* (Molai); Townsend's *Calendar of Knights,* London, 1828; Mosheim's *Ecclesiastical History* (ed. 1832), vol. ii., p. 481; Dugdale's *Monasticon Anglicanum,* vol. vi., p. 813; Hayden's *Dictionary of Dates;* Beeton's *Dictionary of Universal Information;* Burne's *Sketch of the History of the Knights Templars;* Laurie's *History of Freemasonry;* Taffe's *History of Knights of Malta; London Freemasons' Magazine;* Sutherland's *Achievements of Knights of Malta;* Clark's *History of Knighthood;* Ashmole's *History of the Order of the Garter;* Turner's *England in the Middle Ages;* Brande's *Encyclopedia;* Tanner's *Notitia Monastica,* 1744, pp. 307–310.

"These will, perhaps, suffice to show what, in the opinion of historical authorities, is the proper title of the Order. In all of them, the term 'Knights Templars' is the only one employed.

"They might, perhaps, be sufficient also on the question of literary usage; but on that point I refer, in addition, to the following:

"*London Quarterly Review,* 1829, p. 608. Article: 'History of the Knights Templars.'

"*Edinburgh Review,* October, 1806, p. 196. Review of M. Renouard's work, *Les Templiers.*

"*Eclectic Review,* 1842, p. 189. Review of the *History of the Knights Templars, the Temple Church, and the Temple,* by Chas. G. Addison. The running title is *History of the Knights Templars.*

"*Retrospective Review,* 1821, vol. iv., p. 250. Review of the *History of the Templars,* by Nicholas Gaulterius, Amsterdam, 1703. The running title is *History of the Knights Templars.*

" In Dr. Mackey's various Masonic works both titles are occasionally used; but that fact is fully explained in the letter from that distinguished Masonic authority, with which I shall conclude this article."

On the philological and grammatical question, it mainly turns on the inquiry whether the word Templar is a noun or an adjective. I think it may be safely asserted that every dictionary of the English language in which the word occurs, gives it as a noun, and as a noun only. This is certainly the fact as to Johnson's Dictionary, Webster's Dictionary, Cole's Dictionary, Crabb's Dictionary (Technological), Imperial Dictionary, Craig's Dictionary (Universal), and Worcester's Dictionary.

If, then, the word " Templar" is a noun, we have in the combination—"Knights Templar"—two nouns, referring to the same person, one of which is in the plural, and the other in the singular. The well-known rule of apposition, which prevails in almost, if not quite all, languages, requires nouns under these circumstances to agree in number and case. This is, in fact, a principle of general grammar, founded in common sense. The combination "Knights Templar" is therefore false in grammar, if the word "Templar" is a noun. But some may say that it is a noun used as an adjective—a qualifying noun—a very common usage in the English tongue. If this were so, the combination " Knights Templar" would still be entirely out of harmony with the usage of the language in regard to qualifying nouns, the invariable practise being to place the adjective noun before the noun which it qualifies. A few familiar examples will show this. Take the following: mansion house, bird cage, sea fog, dog days, mouse trap, devil fish, ink stand, and beer cask. In every case the generic word follows the qualifying noun.

But if we even went to the length of admitting the word "Templar" to be an adjective, the combination "Knights Templar" would still be contrary to the genius of the language, which, except in rare cases, places the adjective before the noun which it qualifies. In poetry, and in some technical terms of foreign origin, the opposite practise prevails.

The analogy of the usage, in reference to the designations of other Orders of knighthood, is also against the use of " Knights Templar." We have Knights Commanders, Knights Bachelors, Knights Bannerets, Knights Baronets, and Knights Hospitalers.

Against all this, the only thing that can be pleaded is the present usage of the Grand Encampment of the United States, and of some Commanderies which have followed in its wake. The propriety of this usage is the very question at issue; and it would be curious reasoning, indeed, that would cite the fact of the usage in proof of its propriety. If the Templars of to-day are the successors of De Molay and Hugh de Payens, the preservation and restoration of the correct title of the Order cannot be a matter of indifference to them.

In coming to the consideration of the question, it appears that it must be examined in two ways, grammatically and traditionally: in other words, we must inquire, first, which of these two expressions better accords with the rules of English grammar; and, secondly, which of them has the support and authority of the best English writers.

1. If we examine the subject grammatically, we shall find that its proper decision depends simply on the question: Is " Templar" a noun or an adjective? If it is an adjective, then "Knights Templar" is correct, because adjectives in English have no plural form. It would, however, be an awkward and unusual phraseology, because it is the almost invariable rule of the English language that the adjective should precede and not follow the substantive which it qualifies.

But if "Templar" is a substantive or noun, then, clearly, " Knights Templar" is an ungrammatical phrase, because "Templar" would then be in apposition with " Knights," and should be in the same regimen; that is to say, two nouns coming together, and referring to the same person or thing, being thus said to be *in apposition*, must agree in number and case. Thus we say *King George* or *Duke William*, when *King* and *George*, and *Duke* and *William* are in apposition and in the singular; but speaking of Thackeray's " Four Georges," and intending to designate who they were by an explanatory noun in apposition, we should put both nouns in the plural, and say "the four *Georges, Kings* of England." So when we wish to designate a simple Knight, who is not only a Knight, but also belongs to that branch of the Order which is known as Templars, we should call him a "Knight Templar"; and if there be two or more of these Templars, we should call them "Knights Templars," just as we say "Knight Hospitaler" and "Knights Hospitalers."

Now there is abundant evidence, in the best works on the subject, of the use of the word " Templar" as a substantive, and none of its use as an adjective.

It would be tedious to cite authorities, but a reference to our best English writers will show the constant employment of "Templar" as a substantive only. The analogy of the Latin and French languages supports this view, for "Templarius" is a noun in Latin, as "Templier" is in French.

2. As to traditional authority, the usage of good writers, which is the "*jus et norma loquendi*," is altogether in favor of " *Knights Templars*," and not " *Knights Templar*."

In addition to the very numerous authorities collected by Bro. Stansbury from the shelves of the Congressional Library, Dr. Mackey collated all the authorities in his own library.

All the English and American writers, Masonic and unmasonic, except some recent American ones, use the plural of Templar to designate more than one Knight. In a few instances Dr. Mackey found "Knight Templars," but never "Knights Templar." The very recent

American use of this latter phrase is derived from the authority of the present Constitution of the Grand Encampment of the United States, and is therefore the very point in controversy. The former Constitution used the phrase 'Knights Templars.' "On the whole," Dr. Mackey concludes, "I am satisfied that the expression 'Knights Templar' is a violation both of the grammatical laws of our language and of the usage of our best writers on both sides of the Atlantic, and it should therefore, I think, be abandoned." *

Knights of St. John the Evangelist of Asia in Europe. Founded at Schleswig and Hamburg by Count of Ecker and Eckhoffen, in 1786, out of his Order of the "True Light," founded the previous year.

Knights of the True Light. A degree founded by Count of Ecker and Eckhoffen, in 1785.

Knocks, Three. When the Craft were to be called to labor in old North Germany, "the Master should give three knocks, a Pallirer two, consecutively; and in case the Craft at large were imperatively demanded, one blow must be struck, morning, midday, or at eventide." (*Ordnung der Steinmetzen*, 1462, Art. 28.) Fort, in his *Early History, etc.*, says, "three strokes by a Master convened all the members of that degree; two strokes by the Pallirer called the Fellows, and by a single blow each member was assembled in Lodge. In the opening and closing of Teutonic tribunals of justice, the judge carried a staff or mace, as an emblem of jurisdiction, and order was enjoined by a blow on the pedestal by the Arbiter."

An exposure of Masonry called *The Three Distinct Knocks*, was issued in 1760. Dermott (*Ahiman Rezon*, 1764, p. iii.) says Daniel Tadpole was the editor, but this is probably intended for a joke.

Knowledge. In the dualism of Masonry, knowledge is symbolized by light, as ignorance is by darkness. To be initiated, to receive light is to acquire knowledge; and the cry of the neophyte for light is the natural aspiration of the soul for knowledge.

Knowledge, Degrees of. See *Degrees of Knowledge*.

Kojiki. (*Book of Ancient Traditions*.) The oldest monument of Shintoism, the ancient religion of Japan. It is written in pure Japanese, and was composed by order of the Mikado Gemmio, A.D. 712, and first printed about 1625. The adherents of Shintoism number about 14,000,000.

Konx Ompax. There is hardly anything that has been more puzzling to the learned than the meaning and use of these two apparently barbarous words. Bishop Warburton says (*Div. Leg.*, I., ii., 4), but without giving his authority, that in the celebration of the Eleusinian mysteries, "the assembly was dismissed with these two barbarous words, ΚΟΓΞ ΟΜΠΑΞ"; and he thinks that this "shows the

Mysteries not to have been originally Greek." Le Clerc (*Bib. Univ.*, vi., 86) thinks that the words seem to be only an incorrect pronunciation of *kots* and *omphets*, which, he says, signify in the Phœnician language, "watch, and abstain from evil." Potter also (*Gr. Ant.*, 346) says that the words were used in the Eleusinian mysteries.

The words occur in none of the old Greek lexicons, except that of Hesychius, where they are thus defined:

"Κόγξ ομπαξ. An acclamation used by those who have finished anything. It is also the sound of the judge's ballots and of the clepsydra. The Athenians used the word *blops*."

The words were always deemed inexplicable until 1797, when Captain Wilford offered, in the *Asiatic Researches* (vol. v., p. 300), the following explanation. He there says that the real words are *Candsha Om Pacsha;* that they are pure Sanskrit; and are used to this day by the Brahmans at the conclusion of their religious rites. *Candsha* signifies the object of our most ardent wishes. *Om* is the famous monosyllable used both at the beginning and conclusion of a prayer or religious rite, like our word Amen. *Pacsha* exactly answers to the obsolete Latin word *vix;* it signifies change, course, stead, place, turn of work, duty, fortune, etc., and is particularly used in pouring water in honor of the gods.

Uwaroff (*Ess. sur les Myst. d'Eleus.*) calls this "the most important of modern discoveries." Creuzer, Schelling, and Münter also approve of it.

Not so with Lobeck, who, in his *Aglaophamus* (p. 775), denies not only that such words were used in the Eleusinian mysteries, but the very existence of the words themselves. He says that in the title of the article in Hesychius there is a misprint. Instead of κόγξ ὀμπάξ, it should be κόγξ ὀμ. πάξ, where ὀμ is the usual abbreviation of ὀμοίως, like or similar to; so that the true reading would be κογξ ὀμοίως παξ, or *konx*, like *pax;* and he confirms this by referring to παξ, to which Hesychius gives the same meaning as he does to κογξ. This is too simple for Godfrey Higgins, who calls it (*Anacal.*, i., 253) "a pretended emendation." It is nevertheless very ingenious, and is calculated to shake our belief that these words were ever used in the Eleusinian Rites, notwithstanding the learned authority of Meursius, Warburton, Lempriere, Creuzer, Uwaroff, and others.

Korah. The son of Izhar, uncle of Moses, who was famed for beauty and wealth. It is related that he refused to give alms, as Moses had commanded, and brought a villainous charge against Moses, who complained thereof to God; the answer was that the earth would obey whatever command he should give; and Moses said, "O earth, swallow them up"; then Korah and his confederates were sinking into the ground, when Korah pleaded for mercy, which Moses refused. Then God said, "Moses, thou hadst no mercy on Korah, though he asked pardon of thee four times; but I would have had compassion on him if he

---

* Knights Templar is the form now adopted.
[E. E. C.]

had asked pardon of me but once."—*Al Bei-dâwi*.

Koran. The sacred book of the Mohammedans, and believed by them to contain a record of the revelations made by God to Mohammed, and afterward dictated by him to an amanuensis, since the prophet could neither read nor write. In a Lodge consisting wholly of Mohammedans, the Koran would be esteemed as the Book of the Law, and take the place on the altar which is occupied in Christian Lodges by the Bible. It would thus become the symbol to them of the Tracing-Board of the Divine Architect. But, unlike the Old and New Testaments, the Koran has no connection with, and gives no support to, any of the Masonic legends or symbols, except in those parts which were plagiarized by the prophet from the Jewish and Christian Scriptures. Finch, however, in one of his apocryphal works, produced a system of Mohammedan Masonry, consisting of twelve degrees, founded on the teachings of the Koran, and the Hadeeses or traditions of the prophet. This system was a pure invention of Finch.

Krause, Carl Christian Friedrich. One of the most learned and laborious Masons of Germany, and one who received the smallest reward and the largest persecution for his learning and his labors. The record of his life reflects but little credit on his contemporaries who were high in office, but it would seem low in intellect. Findel (*Hist. of F. M.*, p. 628) calls them "the antiquated German Masonic world." Dr. Krause was born at Eisenberg, a small city of Altenberg, May 6, 1781. He was educated at Jena, where he enjoyed the instructions of Reinhold, Fichte, and Schelling. While making theology his chief study, he devoted his attention at the same time to philosophy and mathematics. In 1801, he obtained his degree as Doctor of Philosophy, and established himself at the University of Jena as an extraordinary professor. There he remained until 1805, marrying in the meantime a lady of the name of Fuchs, with whom he passed thirty years, leaving as the fruit of his union eight sons and five daughters.

In 1805, Krause removed to Dresden, and remained there until 1813. In April, 1805, he was initiated into Freemasonry in the Lodge "Archimedes." As soon as he had been initiated, he commenced the study of the Institution by the reading of every Masonic work that was accessible. It was at this time that Krause adopted his peculiar system of philosophy, which was founded on the theory that the collective life of man—that is to say, of humanity—was an organic and harmonious unity; and he conceived the scheme of a formal union of the whole race of mankind into one confederacy, embracing all partial unions of church organizations, of State government, and of private, social aggregations, into one general confederation, which should labor, irrespective of political, ecclesiastical, or personal influences, for the universal and uniform culture of mankind. Of such a confederation he supposed that he could see the

germ in the Order of Freemasonry, which, therefore, it was his object to elevate to that position.

He first submitted these views in a series of lectures delivered before the Lodge "Zu den drei Schwertern" in Dresden, of which he had been appointed the Orator. They were received with much approbation, and were published in 1811 under the title of the *Spiritualization of the Genuine Symbols of Freemasonry*. In these lectures, Krause has not confined himself to the received rituals and accustomed interpretations, but has adopted a system of his own. This is the course that was pursued by him in his greater work, the *Kunsturkunden;* and it was this which partly gave so much offense to his Masonic, but not his intellectual, superiors. In 1810, he published, as the result of all his labors and researches, his greatest work, the one on which his reputation principally depends, and which, notwithstanding its errors, is perhaps one of the most learned works that ever issued from the Masonic press. This is *Die drei ältesten Kunsturkunden der Freimaurerbrüderschaft*, or "The Three Oldest Professional Documents of the Brotherhood of Freemasons."

The announcement that this work was shortly to appear, produced the greatest excitement in the Masonic circles of Germany. The progressive members of the Craft looked with anxious expectation for the new discoveries which must result from the investigations of an enlightened mind. The antiquated and unprogressive Masons, who were opposed to all discussion of what they deemed esoteric subjects, dreaded the effects of such a work on the exclusiveness of the Order. Hence attempts were made by these latter to suppress the publication. So far were these efforts carried, that one of the German Grand Lodges offered the author a large amount of money for his book, which proposal was of course rejected. After the publication, the Grand Master of the three Grand Lodges sought every means of excommunicating Krause and Mossdorf, who had sustained him in his views. After much angry discussion, the Dresden Lodge, "Zu den drei Schwertern," was prevailed upon to act as executioner of this ignorant spirit of fanaticism, and Krause and Mossdorf, two of the greatest lights that ever burst upon the horizon of Masonic literature, were excommunicated. Nor did the persecution here cease. Krause experienced its effects through all the remaining years of his life. He was prevented on frequent occasions, by the machinations of his Masonic enemies, from advancement in his literary and professional pursuits, and failed through their influence to obtain professorships to which, from his learning and services, he was justly entitled. Findel (p. 629) has approvingly quoted Dr. Schauberg as calling this "the darkest page in the history of German Freemasonry."

In 1814 Krause removed to Berlin. In 1821 he traveled through Germany, Italy, and France, and in 1823 established himself at Göttingen, where he gave lectures on philosophy until 1830. He then removed to Munich, where he died September 27, 1832. Besides his contributions to Freemasonry, Krause was an extensive writer on philosophical subjects. His most important works are his *Lectures on the System of Philosophy*, 1828, and his *Lectures on the Fundamental Truths of Science*, 1829; both published at Göttingen.

His great work, however, to which he owes his Masonic fame, is his *Kunsturkunden*. He commences this work by a declaration of his design in writing it, which was twofold: first, to enlighten the brotherhood in reference to the three oldest documents in possession of the Craft, by a philological and philosophical examination of these records; and secondly, and with a higher purpose, to call their attention to a clear perception of the fundamental idea of a general union of mankind, to be accomplished by a reorganization of their own brotherhood. To the rituals of the present day he objected as wanting in scientific formula, and he thought that out of these old records they might well construct a better and more practical system.

But with all his learning, while his ideas of reform, if properly carried out, would undoubtedly advance and elevate the Masonic Institution, he committed grave errors in his estimation of the documents that he has made the groundwork of his system.

The three documents which he has presented as the oldest and most authentic records of the Fraternity are: 1. The well-known *Leland Manuscript*, a document of whose authenticity there are the gravest doubts; 2. The *Entered Apprentice's Lecture*, a document published early in the eighteenth century, to which, in his second edition, he has added what he calls the *New English Lecture;* but it is now known that Krause's Lecture is by no means the oldest catechism extant; and, 3. The *York Constitution*, which, claiming the date of 926, has been recently suspected to be not older than the early part of the eighteenth century.

Notwithstanding these assumptions of authenticity for documents not really authentic, the vast learning of the author is worthy of all admiration. His pages are filled with important facts and suggestive thoughts that cannot fail to exert an influence on all Masonic investigations. Krause cannot but be considered as one of the founders of a new Masonic literature, not for Germany alone, but for the whole world of Masonic students.

Krause Manuscript. A title sometimes given to the so-called York Constitutions, a German translation of which was published by Krause, in 1810, in his *Kunsturkunden*. (See *York Constitutions* and *Manuscripts, Apocryphal*.)

Krishna or **Christna**. One of the Trimurti in the Hindu religious system. The myth proceeds to state that Devanaguy, upon the appearance of Vishnu, fell in a profound ecstasy, and having been *overshadowed* (Sanskrit), the spirit was incarnated, and upon the birth of a child, the Virgin and Son were conducted to a sheepfold belonging to Nanda, on the confines of the territory of Madura. The newly born was named Krishna (in Sanskrit, sacred). The Rajah of Madura had been informed in a dream that this son of Devanaguy should dethrone and chastise him for all his crimes; he therefore sought the certain destruction of the child, and ordained the massacre, in all his states, of all the children of the male sex born during the night of the birth of Krishna. A troop of soldiers reached the sheepfold of Nanda, the lord of a small village on the banks of the Ganges, and celebrated for his virtues. The servants were about to arm in defense, when the child, who was at his mother's breast, suddenly grew to the appearance and size of a child ten years of age, and running, amused himself amidst the flock of sheep. The exploits of this wonder child, his preaching the new or reformed doctrine of India, his disciples and loved companion Ardjouna, the parables, philosophic teaching, the myth of his transfiguration, his ablutions in the Ganges before his death, and tragic end, together with the story of his revival after three days, and ascension, are graphically told by many authors, perhaps more brilliantly in *La Bible dans l'Inde*, as translated into English by Louis Jacolliot.

Kulma. The Hindustani Confession of Faith.

Kum, Kivi. These two words, pronounced *koom* and *keevy*, are found as ceremonial words in one of the high degrees. They are from the Hebrew, and are interpreted as meaning *arise!* and *kneel!* They are not significant words, having no symbolic allusion, and seem to have been introduced merely to mark the Jewish origin of the degree in which they are employed. In the modern rituals they are disused.

Kun. Arabic for *Be*, the creative fiat of God.

L

L. (Heb., ‫ל‬; Samaritan, 𝔏.) The shape of the twelfth English letter is borrowed from that of the Oriental *lomad*, coinciding with the Samaritan. The numerical value in Hebrew is thirty. The Roman numeral L is fifty. Hebrew name of Deity, as an equivalent, is ‫למד‬, Limmud, or Doctus. This letter also signifies a *stimulus*, generally female.

Laanah. (Heb., ‫לענה‬.) Wormwood, a word used in the Order of Ishmael.

Labady. A member of the G. Loge de France, banished, in 1766, for alleged libel. An exile to Blois, in October, 1767, for permitting Masonic assemblies at his residence contrary to the orders of the government.

Labarum. The monogram of the name of Christ, formed by the first two letters of that name, XPIΣTOΣ, in Greek. It is the celebrated sign which the legend says appeared in the sky at noonday to the Emperor Constantine, and which was afterward placed by him upon his standard. Hence it is sometimes called the Cross of Constantine. It was adopted as a symbol by the early Christians, and frequent instances of it are to be found in the catacombs. According to Eusebius, the Labarum was surrounded by the motto EN TOYTΩ NIKA, or "conquer by this," which has been Latinized into *in hoc signo vinces*, the motto assumed by the Masonic Knights Templar. The derivation of the word Labarum is uncertain. (See *In hoc signo vinces*.)

Labor. It is one of the most beautiful features of the Masonic Institution, that it teaches not only the necessity, but the nobility of labor. From the time of opening to that of closing, a Lodge is said to be at labor. This is but one of the numerous instances in which the terms of Operative Masonry are symbolically applied to Speculative; for, as the Operative Masons were engaged in the building of material edifices, so Free and Accepted Masons are supposed to be employed in the erection of a superstructure of virtue and morality upon the foundation of the Masonic principles which they were taught at their admission into the Order. When the Lodge is engaged in reading petitions, hearing reports, debating financial matters, etc., it is said to be occupied in *business;* but when it is engaged in the form and ceremony of initiation into any of the degrees, it is said to be at *work.* Initiation is Masonic labor. This phraseology at once suggests the connection of our speculative system with an operative art that preceded it, and upon which it has been founded.

"Labor," says Gädicke, "is an important word in Masonry; indeed, we might say the most important. For this, and this alone, does a man become a Freemason. Every other object is secondary or incidental. Labor is the accustomed design of every Lodge meeting. But do such meetings always furnish evidence of industry? The labor of an Operative Mason will be visible, and he will receive his reward for it, even though the building he has constructed may, in the next hour, be overthrown by a tempest. He knows that he has done his labor. And so must the Freemason labor. His labor must be visible to himself and to his brethren, or, at least, it must conduce to his own internal satisfaction. As we build neither a visible Solomonic Temple nor an Egyptian pyramid, our industry must become visible in works that are imperishable, so that when we vanish from the eyes of mortals it may be said of us that our labor was well done." As Masons, we labor in our Lodge to make ourselves a perfect building, without blemish, working hopefully for the consummation, when the house of our earthly tabernacle shall be finished, when the LOST WORD of Divine truth shall at last be discovered, and when we shall be found by our own efforts at perfection to have done God service.

Laborare est orare. *To labor is to pray;* or, in other words, *labor is worship*. This was a saying of the Medieval monks, which is well worth meditation. This doctrine, that labor is worship, has been advanced and maintained, from time immemorial, as a leading dogma of the Order of Freemasonry. There is no other human institution under the sun which has set forth this great principle in such bold relief. We hear constantly of Freemasonry as an institution that inculcates morality, that fosters the social feeling, that teaches brotherly love; and all this is well, because it is true; but we must never forget that from its foundation-stone to its pinnacle, all over its vast temple, is inscribed, in symbols of living light, the great truth that *labor is worship*.

Laboratory. The place where experiments in chemistry, pharmacy, etc., are performed; the workroom of the chemist. An important apartment in the conferring of the degrees of the Society of Rosicrucians.

Laborers, Statutes of. Toward the middle of the fourteenth century, a plague of excessive virulence, known in history as the Black Death, invaded Europe, and swept off fully one-half of the inhabitants. The death of so many workmen had the effect of advancing the price of all kinds of labor to double the former rate. In England, the Parliament, in 1350, enacted a statute, which was soon followed by others, the object of which was to regulate the rate of wages and the price of the necessaries of life. Against these enactments, which were called the Statutes of Laborers, the artisans of all kinds rebelled; but the most active opposition was found among the Masons, whose organization, being better regulated, was more effective.* In 1360, statutes were passed forbidding their "congregations, chapters, regulations, and oaths," which were

---

* See *Freemason*.

from time to time repeated, until the third year of the reign of Henry VI., A. D. 1425, when the celebrated statute entitled "Masons shall not confederate themselves in chapters and congregations," was enacted in the following words:

"Whereas, by yearly congregations and confederacies, made by the Masons in their General Assemblies, the good course and effect of the Statutes for Laborers be openly violated and broken, in subversion of the law, and to the great damage of all the Commons, our said sovereign lord the king, willing in this case to provide a remedy, by the advice and assent aforesaid, and at the special request of the Commons, hath ordained and established that such chapters and congregations shall not be hereafter holden; and if any such be made, they that cause such chapters and congregations to be assembled and holden, if they thereof be convict, shall be judged for felons, and that the other Masons that come to such chapters and congregations be punished by imprisonment of their bodies, and make fine and ransom at the king's will."

[Findel (*Hist. of F. M.*, p. 94), following Preston, says that this Statute was passed in the Parliament of Bats; but this is erroneous, for the Act forbidding Masons to meet in Chapters or Congregations was passed in 1425 by the Parliament at Westminster, while the Parliament of Bats met at Leicester in the following year. (See *Bats, Parliament of*.)—E. L. H.]

All the Statutes of Laborers were repealed in the fifth year of Elizabeth; and Lord Coke gave the opinion that this act of Henry VI. became, in consequence, "of no force or effect"; a decision which led Anderson, very absurdly, to suppose that "this most learned judge really belonged to the ancient Lodge, and was a faithful brother" (*Constitutions*, 1723, p. 57); as if it required a judge to be a Mason to give a just judgment concerning the interests of Masonry.

Labrum. From the Latin. A lip or edge, as of a dish or font; having reference to the vase at the entrance of places of worship for preliminary lustration.

Labyrinth. A place full of intricacies, with winding passages, as the Egyptian, Samian, and Cretan labyrinths. That of the Egyptians was near Lake Moeris, which contained twelve palaces under one roof, and was of polished stone, with many vaulted passages, and a court of 3,000 chambers, half under the earth and half above them. Pliny states it was 3,600 years old in his day. The labyrinth is symbolical of the vicissitudes and anxieties of life, and is thus metaphorically used in a number of the degrees of various Rites. Sage of the Labyrinth is the eighteenth grade, Rite of Memphis, in the Order of 1860. Sage Sublime of Labyrinth, the fifty-fifth grade of the same organization. (See *Catacombs*.)

Lacepède, B. G. E. de la Ville. A French savant and naturalist, born in 1756, died 1825. President of the Legislative Assembly in 1791.

Master of the Lodge "De St. Napoléon" in 1805. An account of his installation is recorded by Kloss.

Lacorne. The Count of Clermont, who was Grand Master of France, having abandoned all care of the French Lodges, left them to the direction of his Deputies. In 1761, he appointed one Lacorne, a dancing-master, his Deputy; but the Grand Lodge, indignant at the appointment, refused to sanction it or to recognize Lacorne as a presiding officer. He accordingly constituted another Grand Lodge, and was supported by adherents of his own character, who were designated by the more respectable Masons as the "Lacorne faction." In 1762, the Count of Clermont, influenced by the representations that were made to him, revoked the commission of Lacorne, and appointed M. Chaillou de Joinville his Substitute General. In consequence of this, the two rival Grand Lodges became reconciled, and a union was effected on the 24th of June, 1762. But the reconciliation did not prove altogether satisfactory. In 1765, at the annual election, neither Lacorne nor any of his associates were chosen to office. They became disgusted, and, retiring from the Grand Lodge, issued a scandalous protest, for which they were expelled; and subsequently they organized a spurious Grand Lodge and chartered several Lodges. But from this time Lacorne ceased to have a place in regular Masonry, although the dissensions first begun by him ultimately gave rise to the Grand Orient as the successor of the Grand Lodge.

Ladder. A symbol of progressive advancement from a lower to a higher sphere, which is common to Masonry and to many, if not all, of the Ancient Mysteries. In each, generally, as in Masonry, the number of steps was seven. (See *Jacob's Ladder*.)

Ladder, Brahmanical. The symbolic ladder used in the mysteries of Brahma. It had seven steps, symbolic of the seven worlds of the Indian universe. The lowest was the Earth; the second, the World of Reexistence; the third, Heaven; the fourth, the Middle World, or intermediate region between the lower and the upper worlds; the fifth, the World of Births, in which souls are born again; the sixth, the Mansion of the Blessed; and the seventh, or topmost round, the Sphere of Truth, the abode of Brahma, who was himself a symbol of the sun.

Ladder, Jacob's. See *Jacob's Ladder*.

Ladder, Kabbalistic. The ladder of the Kabbalists consisted of the ten Sephiroths or emanations of Deity. The steps were in an ascending series—the Kingdom, Foundation, Splendor, Firmness, Beauty, Justice, Mercy, Intelligence, Wisdom, and the Crown. This ladder formed the exception to the usual number of seven steps or rounds.

Ladder, Mithraitic. The symbolic ladder used in the Persian mysteries of Mithras. It had seven steps, symbolic of the seven planets and the seven metals. Thus, beginning at the bottom, we have Saturn represented by lead, Venus by tin, Jupiter by brass, Mercury by iron, Mars by a mixed metal, the Moon by silver, and the Sun by gold; the whole being a symbol of the sidereal progress of the sun through the universe.

Ladder of Kadosh. This ladder, belonging to the high degrees of Masonry, consists of the seven following steps, beginning at the bottom: Justice, Equity, Kindliness, Good Faith, Labor, Patience, and Intelligence or Wisdom. Its supports are love of God and love of our neighbor, and their totality constitute a symbolism of the devoir of Knighthood and Masonry, the fulfilment of which is necessary to make a Perfect Knight and Perfect Mason.

Ladder, Rosicrucian. Among the symbols of the Rosicrucians is a ladder of seven steps standing on a globe of the earth, with an open Bible, square, and compasses resting on the top. Between each of the steps is one of the following letters, beginning from the bottom: I. N. R. I. F. S. C., being the initials of Iesus, Nazarenus, Rex, Iudæorum, Fides, Spes, Caritas. But a more recondite meaning is sometimes given to the first four letters.

Ladder, Scandinavian. The symbolic ladder used in the Gothic mysteries. Dr. Oliver refers it to the Yggrasil, or sacred ash-tree. But the symbolism is either very abstruse or very doubtful. It retains, however, the idea of an ascent from a lower to a higher sphere, which was common to all the mystical ladder systems. At its root lies the dragon of death; at its top are the eagle and hawk, the symbols of life.

Ladder, Theological. The symbolic ladder of the Masonic mysteries. It refers to the ladder seen by Jacob in his vision, and consists, like all symbolical ladders, of seven rounds, alluding to the four cardinal and the three theological virtues. (See *Jacob's Ladder*.)

Lady. In the androgynous Lodges of Adoption, where the male members are called Knights, the female members are called Ladies; as, the Knights and Ladies of the Rose. The French use the word *Dame*.

Lakak Deror Pessah. (Hebrew, ררור פסה לקח.) The initials of these three words are found on the symbol of the Bridge in the Fifteenth Degree of the Scottish Rite, signifying liberty of passage and liberty of thought. (See *Bridge*, also *Liber*.)

Lalande. See *De la Lande*.

Lamaism. The name of the religion prevalent in Tibet and Mongolia. (Tibet, Llama, pronounced *lama*, a chief or high priest.) Buddhism, corrupted by Sivaism, an adoration of saints. At the summit of its hierarchy are two Lama popes, having equal rank and authority in spiritual and temporal affairs.

Lamb. In ancient Craft Masonry the lamb is the symbol of innocence; thus in the ritual of the First Degree: "In all ages the lamb has been deemed an emblem of innocence." Hence it is required that a Mason's apron should be made of lambskin. In the high degrees, and in the degrees of chivalry, as in Christian iconography, the lamb is a symbol of Jesus Christ. The introduction of this Christian symbolism of the lamb comes from the expression of St. John the Baptist, who exclaimed, on seeing Jesus, "Behold the Lamb of God"; which was undoubtedly derived from the prophetic writers, who compare the Messiah suffering on the cross to a lamb under the knife of a butcher. In the vision of St. John, in the Apocalypse, Christ is seen, under the form of a lamb, wounded in the throat, and opening the book with the seven seals. Hence, in one of the degrees of the Scottish Rite, the Seventeenth, or Knight of the East and West, the lamb lying on the book with the seven seals is a part of the jewel.

Lamb of God. See *Lamb, Paschal*.

Lamb, Paschal. The paschal lamb, sometimes called the Holy Lamb, was the lamb offered up by the Jews at the paschal feast. This has been transferred to Christian symbolism, and naturally to chivalric Masonry; and hence we find it among the symbols of modern Templarism. The paschal lamb, as a Christian and Masonic symbol, called also the *Agnus Dei*, or the Lamb of God, first appeared in Christian art after the sixth century. It is depicted as a lamb standing on the ground, holding by the left forefoot a banner, on which a cross is inscribed. This paschal lamb, or Lamb of God, has been adopted as a symbol by the Knights Templar, being borne in one of the banners of the Order, and constituting, with the square which it surmounts, the jewel of the Generalissimo of a Commandery. The lamb is a symbol of Christ; the cross, of his passion; and the banner, of his victory over death and hell. Mr. Barrington states (*Archæologia*, ix., 134) that in a deed of the English Knights Templar, granting lands in Cambridgeshire, the seal is a Holy Land, and the arms of the Master of the Temple at London were argent, a cross gules, and on the nombril point thereof a Holy Lamb, that is, a paschal or Holy Lamb on the center of a red cross in a white field.

Lamballe, The Princess of. Niece of Marie Antoinette, murdered in 1792 at Paris. The Grand Mistress of the so-called Mother Lodge of "La Maçonnerie d'Adoption."

Lambskin Apron. See *Apron*.

Lamma Sabactani. An expression used in the Masonic French Rite of Adoption.

Lamp, Knight of the Inextinguishable. A degree quoted in the nomenclature of Fustier. (Thory, *Acta Lat.*, i., 320.)

Lance. A weapon for thrusting at an enemy, usually adorned with a small flag, made of tough ash, weighted at one end and pointed at the other.

Landmarks. In ancient times, it was the custom to mark the boundaries of lands by means of stone pillars, the removal of which, by malicious persons, would be the occasion of much confusion, men having no other guide than these pillars by which to distinguish the limits of their property. To remove them, therefore, was considered a heinous crime. "Thou shalt not," says the Jewish law, "remove thy neighbor's landmark, which they of old time have set in thine inheritance." Hence those peculiar marks of distinction by which we are separated from the profane world, and by which we are enabled to designate our inheritance as the "sons of light," are called the landmarks of the Order. The *universal language* and the *universal laws* of Masonry are landmarks, but not so are the local ceremonies, laws, and usages, which vary in different countries. To attempt to alter or remove these sacred landmarks, by which we examine and prove a brother's claims to share in our privileges, is one of the most heinous offenses that a Mason can commit.

In the decision of the question what are and what are not the landmarks of Masonry, there has been much diversity of opinion among writers. Dr. Oliver says (*Dict. Symb. Mas.*) that "some restrict them to the O. B. signs, tokens, and words. Others include the ceremonies of initiation, passing, and raising; and the form, dimensions, and support; the ground, situation, and covering; the ornaments, furniture, and jewels of a Lodge, or their characteristic symbols. Some think that the Order has no landmarks beyond its peculiar secrets." But all of these are loose and unsatisfactory definitions, excluding things that are essential, and admitting others that are unessential.

Perhaps the safest method is to restrict them to those ancient, and therefore universal, customs of the Order, which either gradually grew into operation as rules of action, or, if at once enacted by any competent authority, were enacted at a period so remote, that no account of their origin is to be found in the records of history. Both the enactors and the time of the enactment have passed away from the record, and the landmarks are therefore "of higher antiquity than memory or history can reach."

The first requisite, therefore, of a custom or rule of action to constitute it a *landmark*, is, that it must have existed from "time whereof the memory of man runneth not to the contrary." Its antiquity is its essential element. Were it possible for all the Masonic authorities at the present day to unite in a universal congress, and with the most perfect unanimity to adopt any new regulation, although such regulation would, so long as it remained unrepealed, be obligatory on the whole Craft, yet it would not be a landmark. It would have the character of universality, it is true, but it would be wanting in that of antiquity.

Another peculiarity of these landmarks of Masonry is, that they are unrepealable. As the congress to which I have just alluded would not have the power to enact a landmark, so neither would it have the prerogative of abolishing one. The landmarks of the Order, like the laws of the Medes and the Persians, can suffer no change. What they were centuries ago, they still remain, and must so continue in force until Masonry itself shall cease to exist.

Until the year 1858, no attempt had been made by any Masonic writer to distinctly enumerate the landmarks of Freemasonry, and to give to them a comprehensible form. In October of that year, the author of this work published in the *American Quarterly Review of Freemasonry* (vol. ii., p. 230) an article on "The Foundations of Masonic Law," which contained a distinct enumeration of the landmarks, which was the first time that such a list had been presented to the Fraternity. This enumeration was subsequently incorporated by the author in his *Text Book of Masonic Jurisprudence.* It has since been very generally adopted by the Fraternity and republished by many writers on Masonic law; sometimes without any acknowledgment of the source whence they derived their information. According to this recapitulation, the result of much labor and research, the landmarks are twenty-five in number, and are as follows:

1. The modes of recognition are, of all the landmarks, the most legitimate and unquestioned. They admit of no variation; and if ever they have suffered alteration or addition, the evil of such a violation of the ancient law has always made itself subsequently manifest.

2. The division of symbolic Masonry into three degrees is a landmark that has been better preserved than almost any other; although even here the mischievous spirit of innovation has left its traces, and, by the disruption of its concluding portion from the Third Degree, a want of uniformity has been created in respect to the final teaching of the Master's Order; and the Royal Arch of England, Scotland, Ireland, and America, and the "high degrees" of France and Germany, are all made to differ in the mode in which they lead the neophyte to the great consummation of all symbolic Masonry. In 1813, the Grand Lodge of England vindicated the ancient landmark, by solemnly enacting that ancient Craft Masonry consisted of the three degrees of Entered Apprentice, Fellow-Craft, and Master Mason, including the Holy Royal Arch. But the disruption has never been healed, and the landmark, although acknowledged in its integrity by all, still continues to be violated.

3. The legend of the Third Degree is an important landmark, the integrity of which has been well preserved. There is no Rite of Masonry, practised in any country or language, in which the essential elements of this legend are not taught. The lectures may vary, and indeed are constantly changing, but the legend has ever remained substantially the same. And it is necessary that it should be so, for the legend of the Temple Builder constitutes the very essence and identity of Masonry. Any Rite which should exclude it, or materially alter it, would at once, by that exclusion or alteration, cease to be a Masonic Rite.

4. The government of the Fraternity by a presiding officer called a *Grand Master*, who is elected from the body of the Craft, is a fourth landmark of the Order. Many persons suppose that the election of the Grand Master is held in consequence of a law or regulation of

the Grand Lodge. Such, however, is not the case. The office is indebted for its existence to a landmark of the Order. Grand Masters, or persons performing the functions under a different but equivalent title, are to be found in the records of the Institution long before Grand Lodges were established; and if the present system of legislative government by Grand Lodges were to be abolished, a Grand Master would still be necessary.

5. The prerogative of the Grand Master to preside over every assembly of the Craft, wheresoever and whensoever held, is a fifth landmark. It is in consequence of this law, derived from ancient usage, and not from any special enactment, that the Grand Master assumes the chair, or as it is called in England, "the throne," at every communication of the Grand Lodge; and that he is also entitled to preside at the communication of every subordinate Lodge, where he may happen to be present.

6. The prerogative of the Grand Master to grant dispensations for conferring degrees at irregular times, is another and a very important landmark. The statutory law of Masonry requires a month, or other determinate period, to elapse between the presentation of a petition and the election of a candidate. But the Grand Master has the power to set aside or dispense with this probation, and to allow a candidate to be initiated at once. This prerogative he possessed before the enactment of the law requiring a probation, and as no statute can impair his prerogative, he still retains the power.

7. The prerogative of the Grand Master to give dispensations for opening and holding Lodges is another landmark. He may grant, in virtue of this, to a sufficient number of Masons, the privilege of meeting together and conferring degrees. The Lodges thus established are called "Lodges under dispensation." (See *Lodges*.)

8. The prerogative of the Grand Master to make Masons at sight is a landmark which is closely connected with the preceding one. There has been much misapprehension in relation to this landmark, which misapprehension has sometimes led to a denial of its existence in jurisdictions where the Grand Master was, perhaps, at the very time substantially exercising the prerogative, without the slightest remark or opposition. (See *Sight, Making Masons at.*)

9. The necessity for Masons to congregate in Lodges is another landmark. It is not to be understood by this that any ancient landmark has directed that permanent organization of subordinate Lodges which constitutes one of the features of the Masonic system as it now prevails. But the landmarks of the Order always prescribed that Masons should, from time to time, congregate together for the purpose of either Operative or Speculative labor, and that these congregations should be called Lodges. Formerly, these were extemporary meetings called together for special purposes, and then dissolved, the brethren departing to meet again at other times and other places, according to the necessity of circumstances. But Warrants of Constitution, by-laws, permanent officers, and annual arrears are modern innovations wholly outside the landmarks, and dependent entirely on the special enactments of a comparatively recent period.

10. The government of the Craft, when so congregated in a Lodge, by a Master and two Wardens, is also a landmark. A congregation of Masons meeting together under any other government, as that, for instance, of a president and vice-president, or a chairman and subchairman, would not be recognized as a Lodge. The presence of a Master and two Wardens is as essential to the valid organization of a Lodge as a Warrant of constitution is at the present day. The names, of course, vary in different languages; but the officers, their number, prerogatives, and duties are everywhere identical.

11. The necessity that every Lodge, when congregated, should be duly tiled, is an important landmark of the Institution which is never neglected. The necessity of this law arises from the esoteric character of Masonry. The duty of guarding the door, and keeping off cowans and eavesdroppers, is an ancient one, which therefore constitutes a landmark.

12. The right of every Mason to be represented in all general meetings of the Craft, and to instruct his representatives, is a twelfth landmark. Formerly, these general meetings, which were usually held once a year, were called "General Assemblies," and all the Fraternity, even to the youngest Entered Apprentice, were permitted to be present. Now they are called "Grand Lodges," and only the Masters and Wardens of the subordinate Lodges are summoned. But this is simply as the representatives of their members. Originally, each Mason represented himself; now he is represented by his officers. (See *Representatives of Lodges*.)

13. The right of every Mason to appeal from the decision of his brethren, in Lodge convened, to the Grand Lodge or General Assembly of Masons, is a landmark highly essential to the preservation of justice, and the prevention of oppression. A few modern Grand Lodges, in adopting a regulation that the decision of subordinate Lodges, in cases of expulsion, cannot be wholly set aside upon an appeal, have violated this unquestioned landmark, as well as the principles of just government.

14. The right of every Mason to visit and sit in every regular Lodge is an unquestionable landmark of the Order. This is called "the right of visitation." This right of visitation has always been recognized as an inherent right which inures to every Mason as he travels through the world. And this is because Lodges are justly considered as only divisions for convenience of the universal Masonic family. This right may, of course, be impaired or forfeited on special occasions by various circumstances; but when admission is refused to a Mason in good standing,

who knocks at the door of a Lodge as a visitor, it is to be expected that some good and sufficient reason shall be furnished for this violation of what is, in general, a Masonic right, founded on the landmarks of the Order.

15. It is a landmark of the Order, that no visitor unknown to the brethren present, or to some one of them as a Mason, can enter a Lodge without first passing an examination according to ancient usage. Of course, if the visitor is known to any brother present to be a Mason in good standing, and if that brother will vouch for his qualifications, the examination may be dispensed with, as the landmark refers only to the cases of strangers, who are not to be recognized unless after strict trial, due examination, or lawful information.

16. No Lodge can interfere in the business of another Lodge, nor give degrees to brethren who are members of other Lodges. This is undoubtedly an ancient landmark, founded on the great principles of courtesy and fraternal kindness, which are at the very foundation of our Institution. It has been repeatedly recognized by subsequent statutory enactments of all Grand Lodges.

17. It is a landmark that every Freemason is amenable to the laws and regulations of the Masonic jurisdiction in which he resides, and this although he may not be a member of any Lodge. Non-affiliation, which is, in fact, in itself a Masonic offense, does not exempt a Mason from Masonic jurisdiction.

18. Certain qualifications of candidates for initiation are derived from a landmark of the Order. These qualifications are that he shall be a man—unmutilated, free born, and of mature age. That is to say, a woman, a cripple, or a slave, or one born in slavery, is disqualified for initiation into the Rites of Masonry. Statutes, it is true, have from time to time been enacted, enforcing or explaining these principles; but the qualifications really arise from the very nature of the Masonic Institution, and from its symbolic teachings, and have always existed as landmarks.

19. A belief in the existence of God as the Grand Architect of the Universe, is one of the most important landmarks of the Order. It has been always admitted that a denial of the existence of a Supreme and Superintending Power is an absolute disqualification for initiation. The annals of the Order never yet have furnished or could furnish an instance in which an avowed Atheist was ever made a Mason. The very initiatory ceremonies of the First Degree forbid and prevent the possibility of such an occurrence.

20. Subsidiary to this belief in God, as a landmark of the Order, is the belief in a resurrection to a future life. This landmark is not so positively impressed on the candidate by exact words as the preceding; but the doctrine is taught by very plain implication, and runs through the whole symbolism of the Order. To believe in Masonry, and not to believe in a resurrection, would be an absurd anomaly, which could only be excused by the reflection, that he who thus confounded his belief and his

skepticism was so ignorant of the meaning of both theories as to have no rational foundation for his knowledge of either.

21. It is a landmark that a "Book of the Law" shall constitute an indispensable part of the furniture of every Lodge. I say, advisedly, *Book of the Law*, because it is not absolutely required that everywhere the Old and New Testaments shall be used. The "Book of the Law" is that volume which, by the religion of the country, is believed to contain the revealed will of the Grand Architect of the Universe. Hence, in all Lodges in Christian countries, the "Book of the Law" is composed of the Old and New Testaments; in a country where Judaism was the prevailing faith, the Old Testament alone would be sufficient; and in Mohammedan countries, and among Mohammedan Masons, the Koran might be substituted. Masonry does not attempt to interfere with the peculiar religious faith of its disciples, except so far as relates to the belief in the existence of God, and what necessarily results from that belief. The "Book of the Law" is to the Speculative Mason his spiritual trestle-board; without this he cannot labor; whatever he believes to be the revealed will of the Grand Architect constitutes for him this spiritual trestle-board, and must ever be before him in his hours of speculative labor, to be the rule and guide of his conduct. The landmark, therefore, requires that a "Book of the Law," a religious code of some kind, purporting to be an exemplar of the revealed will of God, shall form an essential part of the furniture of every Lodge.

22. The equality of all Masons is another landmark of the Order. This equality has no reference to any subversion of those gradations of rank which have been instituted by the usages of society. The monarch, the nobleman, or the gentleman is entitled to all the influence, and receives all the respect, which rightly belong to his position. But the doctrine of Masonic equality implies that, as children of one great Father, we meet in the Lodge upon the level—that on that level we are all traveling to one predestined goal—that in the Lodge genuine merit shall receive more respect than boundless wealth, and that virtue and knowledge alone should be the basis of all Masonic honors, and be rewarded with preferment. When the labors of the Lodge are over, and the brethren have retired from their peaceful retreat, to mingle once more with the world, each will then again resume that social position, and exercise the privileges of that rank, to which the customs of society entitle him.

23. The secrecy of the Institution is another and most important landmark. The form of secrecy is a form inherent in it, existing with it from its very foundation, and secured to it by its ancient landmarks. If divested of its secret character, it would lose its identity, and would cease to be Freemasonry. Whatever objections may, therefore, be made to the Institution on account of its secrecy, and however much some unskilful brethren have been

unwilling in times of trial, for the sake of expediency, to divest it of its secret character, it will be ever impossible to do so, even were the landmark not standing before us as an insurmountable obstacle; because such change of its character would be social suicide, and the death of the Order would follow its legalized exposure. Freemasonry, as a secret association, has lived unchanged for centuries; as an open society, it would not last for as many years.

24. The foundation of a speculative science upon an operative art, and the symbolic use and explanation of the terms of that art, for the purposes of religious or moral teaching, constitute another landmark of the Order. The Temple of Solomon was the symbolic cradle of the Institution, and, therefore, the reference to the Operative Masonry which constructed that magnificent edifice, to the materials and implements which were employed in its construction, and to the artists who were engaged in the building, are all component and essential parts of the body of Freemasonry, which could not be subtracted from it without an entire destruction of the whole identity of the Order. Hence, all the comparatively modern rites of Masonry, however they may differ in other respects, religiously preserve this Temple history and these operative elements, as the substratum of all their modifications of the Masonic system.

25. The last and crowning landmark of all is, that these landmarks can never be changed. Nothing can be subtracted from them—nothing can be added to them—not the slightest modification can be made in them. As they were received from our predecessors, we are bound by the most solemn obligations of duty to transmit them to our successors.

Langes, Savalette de. The Master of "Les Amis Réunis," who aided in founding the system of Philalethes in 1775.

Language, Universal. The invention of a universal language, which men of all nations could understand and through which they could communicate their thoughts, has always been one of the Utopian dreams of certain philologists. In the seventeenth century, Dalgarno had written his *Ars Signorum* to prove the possibility of a universal character and a philosophical language. About the same time Bishop Wilkins published his *Essay towards a Real Character and a Philosophical Language;* and even the mathematical Leibnitz entertained the project of a universal language for all the world. It is not, therefore, surprising, that when the so-called Leland Manuscript stated that the Masons concealed a "universelle longage," Mr. Locke, or whoever was the commentator on that document, should have been attracted by the statement. "A universal language," he says, "has been much desired by the learned of many ages. It is a thing rather to be wished than hoped for. But it seems the Masons pretend to have such

a thing among them. If it be true, I guess it must be something like the language of the Pantomimes among the ancient Romans, who are said to be able, by signs only, to express and deliver any oration intelligibly to men of all nations and languages."

The "guess" of the commentator was near the truth. A universal language founded on words is utterly impracticable. Even if once inaugurated by common consent, a thing itself impossible, the lapse of but a few years, and the continual innovation of new phrases, would soon destroy its universality. But there are signs and symbols which, by tacit consent, have always been recognized as the exponents of certain ideas, and these are everywhere understood. It is well known that such a system exists over the vast territory occupied by the North American savages, and that the Indians of two tribes, which totally differ in language, meeting on the prairie or in the forest, are enabled, by conventual signs of universal agreement, to hold long and intelligible intercourse. On such a basis the "universal language" of Freemasonry is founded. It is not universal to the world, but it is to the Craft; and a Mason of one country and language meeting a Mason of another can make himself understood for all practical purposes of the Craft, simply because the system of signs and symbols has been so perfected that in every language they convey the same meaning and make the same impression. This, and this only, is the extent to which the universal language of Masonry reaches. It would be an error to suppose that it meets the expectations of Dalgarno or Wilkins, or any other dreamer, and that it is so perfect as to supersede the necessity of any other method of intercommunication.

Lansdowne MS. This version of the *Old Charges* is of very early date, about the middle or latter half of the sixteenth century, as these *Free Masons Orders and Constitutions* are believed to have been part of the collection made by Lord Burghley (Sec. of State, *temp.* Edward VI.), who died A.D. 1598.

Bro. Gould, in his *History* (vol. i., p. 61), says the "MS. is contained on the inner side of three sheets and a half of stout paper, eleven by fifteen inches, making in all seven folios, many of the principal words being in large letters of an ornamental character. Mr. Sims (MS. Department of the British Museum) does not consider these 'Orders' ever formed a roll, though there are indications of the sheets having been stitched together at the top, and paper or vellum was used for additional protection. It has evidently 'seen service.' It was published in *Freemasons' Mag.*, February 24, 1858, and Hughan's *Old Charges* (p. 31), and since in facsimile by the Quatuor Coronati Lodge. The catalogue of the Lansdowne MSS.—which consisted of twelve hundred and forty-five volumes, bought by Parliament, in 1807, for £4925—has the following note on the contents of this document:

'No. 48. A very foolish legendary account of the original of the Order of Freemasonry '— in the handwriting, it is said, of Sir Henry Ellis.''

Lanturelus, Ordre des. Instituted, according to Clavel, in 1771, by the Marquis de Croismare. Its purposes or objects are not now understood.

Lapicida. A word sometimes used in Masonic documents to denote a Freemason. It is derived from *lapis*, a stone, and *cædo*, to cut, and is employed by Varro and Livy to signify "a stone-cutter." But in the low Latin of the Medieval age it took another meaning; and Du Cange defines it in his *Glossarium* as "Ædeficiorum structor; Gall. Maçon," i. e., "A builder of edifices; in French, a Mason"; and he quotes two authorities of 1304 and 1392, where *lapicidæ* evidently means *builders*. In the *Vocabularium* of Ugutio, Anno 1592, *Lapicedius* is defined "a cutter of stones." The Latin word now more commonly used by Masonic writers for *Freemason* is *Latomus;* but *Lapicida* is purer Latin. (See *Latomus.*)

Larmenius, Johannes Marcus. According to the tradition of the Order of the Temple—the credibility of which is, however, denied by most Masonic scholars—John Mark Larmenius was in 1314 appointed by James de Molay his successor as Grand Master of the Templars, which power was transmitted by Larmenius to his successors, in a document known as the "Charter of Transmission." (See *Temple, Order of the.*)

La Rochefoucault, Bayers, Le Marquis de. G. Master of the "Rite Ecossais Philosophique" in 1776. A Mason of considerable note.

Larudan, Abbe. The author of a work entitled *Les Franc-Maçons ecrasés. Suite du livre intitule l'Ordre des Franc-Maçons trahi, traduit du Latin.* The first edition was published at Amsterdam in 1746. In calling it the sequel of *L'Ordre des Franc-Maçons trahi*, by the Abbé Perau, Larudan has sought to attribute the authorship of his own libelous work to Perau, but without success, as the internal evidence of style and of tone sufficiently distinguishes the two works. Kloss says (*Bibliog.*, No. 1874) that this work is the armory from which all subsequent enemies of Masonry have derived their weapons. Larudan was the first to broach the theory that Oliver Cromwell was the inventor of Freemasonry.

Lasalle, Troubat de. One of the founders of the Mother Lodge of the "Rite Ecossais Philosophique."

Lateran Councils. They were five in number, regarded as ecumenical, and were held in the Church of St. John Lateran in Rome, in 1123, 1139, 1179, 1215, and 1512.

Latin Lodge. In the year 1785, the Grand Lodge of Scotland granted a Warrant for the establishment of Roman Eagle Lodge at Edinburgh; the whole of whose work was conducted in the Latin language. Of this Lodge, the celebrated and learned Dr. John Brown was the founder and Master. He had himself translated the ritual into the classical language of Rome, and the minutes were written in Latin. (Lyon's *Hist. of the Lodge of Edinburgh*, p. 257.) The Lodge is No. 160 on the Scotch Roll, but ceased to work in Latin in 1794.

Latomia. This word has sometimes been used in modern Masonic documents as the Latin translation of the word *Lodge*, with what correctness we will see. The Greek λατομεῖον, *latomeion* (or λατομία), from the roots *laas*, a stone, and *temno*, to cut, meant a place where stones were cut, a quarry. From this the Romans got their word *latomiæ*, more usually spelled *lautumiæ*, which also, in pure Latinity, meant a stone-quarry. But as slaves were confined and made to work in the quarries by way of punishment, the name was given to any prison excavated out of the living rock and below the surface of the earth, and was especially so applied to the prison excavated by Servius Tullius under the Capitoline hill at Rome, and to the state prison at Syracuse. Both λατομία and *lautumiæ* are seldom used by ancient writers in their primary sense of "a stone-quarry," but both are used in the secondary sense of "a prison," and therefore "Latomia" cannot be considered a good equivalent for "Lodge."

Latomus. By Masonic writers used as a translation of *Freemason* into Latin; thus, Thory entitles his valuable work, *Acta Latomorum*, i. e., "Transactions of the Freemasons." This word was not used in classical Latinity. In the low Latin of the Middle Ages it was used as equivalent to *lapicida*. Du Cange defines it, in the form of *lathomus*, as a cutter of stones, "Cæsor lapidum." He gives an example from one of the ecclesiastical Constitutions, where we find the expression "carpentarii ac Latomi," which may mean *Carpenters and Masons* or *Carpenters and Stone-Cutters.* Du Cange also gives Latomus as one of the definitions of *Maçonetus*, which he derives from the French *Maçon.* But *Maçonetus* and *Latomus* could not have had precisely the same meaning, for in one of the examples cited by Du Cange, we have "Joanne de Bareno, Maçoneto, Latonio de Gratianopolis," i. e., "John de Bareno, Mason and Stone-Cutter (?) of Grenoble." Latomus is here evidently an addition to Maçonetus, showing two different kinds of occupation. We have abundant evidence in Medieval documents that a Maçonetus was a builder, and a Latomus was most probably an inferior order, what the Masonic Constitutions call a "rough Mason." The propriety of applying it to a Freemason seems doubtful. The word is sometimes found as *Lathomus* and *Latomius.*

Latour d'Auvergne, Le Prince de. President of the Mother Lodge of the "Rite Ecossais Philosophique" in 1805, and member of the Grand Orient of France in 1814.

Latres. This word has given much unnecessary trouble to the commentators on the old Records of Masonry. In the legend of the Craft contained in all the old *Constitutions,* we are informed that the children of Lamech "knew that God would take vengeance for sinne, either by fire or water, wherefore they did write these sciences that they had found in twoe pillars of stone, that they might be found after that God had taken vengeance; the one was of marble and would not burne, the other was *Latres* and would not drowne in water." (Harleian MS. No. 1942.) It is the Latin word *later*, a brick. The legend is derived from Josephus (*Antiq.*, I., ii.), where the same story is told. Whiston properly translates the passage, "they made two pillars; the one of brick, the other of stone." The original Greek is πλίνθος, which has the same meaning. The word is variously corrupted in the manuscripts. Thus the Harleian MS. has *latres*, which comes nearest to the correct Latin plural *lateres;* the Cooke MS. has *lacerus;* the Dowland, *laterns;* the Lansdowne, *latherne;* and the Sloane MS., No. 3848, getting furthest from the truth, has *letera*. It is strange that Halliwell (*Early Hist. of F. M. in England*, 2d ed., p. 8) should have been ignorant of the true meaning, and that Hy. Phillips (*Freemasons' Quarterly Review*, 1836, p. 289) in commenting on the Harleian MS., should have supposed that it alluded "to some floating substance." The Latin word *later* and the passage in Josephus ought readily to have led to an explication.

Laurel Crown. A decoration used in some of the higher degrees of the Ancient and Accepted Scottish Rite. The laurel is an emblem of victory; and the *corona triumphalis* of the Romans, which was given to generals who had gained a triumph by their conquests, was made of laurel leaves. The laurel crown in Masonry is given to him who has made a conquest over his passions.

Laurens, J. L. A French Masonic writer, and the author of an *Essai historique et critique sur la Franche-Maçonnerie*, published at Paris in 1805. In this work he gives a critical examination of the principal works that have treated of the Institution. It contains also a refutation of the imputations of anti-Masonic writers. In 1808 he edited an edition of the *Vocabulaire des Franc-Maçons*, the first edition of which had been issued in 1805. In 1825 was published a *Histoire des Initiations de l'ancienne Egypt* with an essay by Laurens on the origin and aim of the Ancient Mysteries. (Kloss, *Bibliographie*, No. 3871.)

Laurie. See *Lawrie, Alexander*.

Laver, Brazen. A large brazen vessel for washing placed in the court of the Jewish tabernacle, where the officiating priest cleansed his hands and feet, and as well the entrails of victims. Constructed by command of Moses (Exod. xxxviii. 8). A similar vessel was symbolically used at the entrance, in the modern French and Scotch Rites, when conferring the Apprentice Degree. It is used in many of the degrees of the latter Rite.

Law, Moral. See *Moral Law*.

Law, Oral. See *Oral Law*.

Law, Parliamentary. See *Parliamentary Law*.

Law, Sacred. The Sacred Scriptures, the Bible, the Great Light in Masonry.

Lawful Information. See *Information, Lawful.*

Lawrie, Alexander. He was originally a stocking-weaver, and afterward became a bookseller and stationer in Parliament Square, Edinburgh, and printer of the *Edinburgh Gazette*. He was appointed bookseller and stationer to the Grand Lodge of Scotland, and afterward Grand Secretary. In 1804 he published a book entitled *The History of Freemasonry, drawn from authentic sources of information; with an Account of the Grand Lodge of Scotland, from its Institution in 1736 to the present time, compiled from the Records; and an Appendix of Original Papers*. Of this valuable and interesting work, Lawrie was at one time deemed the author, notwithstanding that the learning exhibited in the first part, and the numerous references to Greek and Latin authorities, furnished abundant internal evidence of his incapacity, from previous education, to have written it. The doubt which naturally arises, whether he was really the author, derives great support from the testimony of the late Dr. David Irving, Librarian to the Faculty of Advocates, Edinburgh. A writer in the *Notes and Queries* (3d Ser., iii., 366), on May 9, 1863, stated that at the sale of the library of Dr. Irving, on Saturday, March 28, 1862, a copy of Lawrie's *History of Freemasonry* was sold for £1. In that copy there was the following memorandum in the handwriting of Dr. Irving:

"The history of this book is somewhat curious, and perhaps there are only two individuals now living by whom it could be divulged. The late Alexander Lawrie, 'Grand Stationer,' wished to recommend himself to the Fraternity by the publication of such a work. Through Dr. Anderson, he requested me to undertake its compilation, and offered a suitable remuneration. As I did not relish the task, he made a similar offer to my old acquaintance David Brewster, by whom it was readily undertaken, and I can say was executed to the entire satisfaction of his employers. The title-page does not exhibit the name of the author, but the dedication bears the signature of *Alexander Lawrie*, and the volume is commonly described as Lawrie's *History of Freemasonry*."

There can be no doubt of the truth of this statement. It has never been unusual for publishers to avail themselves of the labors of literary men and affix their own names to books which they have written by proxy. Besides, the familiarity with abstruse learning that this work exhibits, although totally irreconcilable with the attainments of the stocking-weaver, can readily be assigned to Sir David Brewster the philosopher. (See Lyon's *Hist. of the Lodge of Edinburgh*, p. 55.)

Lawrie had a son, William Alexander Laurie (he had thus, for some unknown reason, changed the spelling of his name), who was for very many years the Grand Secretary of the

28

Grand Lodge of Scotland, and died in office in 1870, highly esteemed. In 1859 he published a new edition of the *History*, with many additions, under the title of *The History of Freemasonry and the Grand Lodge of Scotland, with chapters on the Knights Templar, Knights of St. John, Mark Masonry, and the R. A. Degree.*

Law, Sacred. See *Sacred Law.*

Laws, General. See *Laws of Masonry.*

Laws, Local. See *Laws of Masonry.*

Laws of Masonry. The laws of Masonry, or those rules of action by which the Institution is governed, are very properly divided into three classes: 1. Landmarks. 2. General Laws or Regulations. 3. Local Laws or Regulations.

1. *Landmarks.* These are the unwritten laws of the Order, derived from those ancient and universal customs which date at so remote a period that we have no record of their origin.

2. *General Laws.* These are all those Regulations that have been enacted by such bodies as had at the time universal jurisdiction. They operate, therefore, over the Craft wheresoever dispersed; and as the paramount bodies which enacted them have long ceased to exist, it would seem that they are unrepealable. It is generally agreed that these General or Universal Laws are to be found in the old Constitutions and Charges, so far as they were recognized and accepted by the Grand Lodge of England at the revival in 1717, and adopted previous to the year 1721.

3. *Local Laws.* These are the Regulations which, since 1721, have been and continue to be enacted by Grand Lodges. They are of force only in those jurisdictions which have adopted them, and are repealable by the bodies which have enacted them. They must, to be valid, be not repugnant to the Landmarks or the General Laws, which are of paramount authority.

Lawsuits. In the Old Charges which were approved in 1722, and published in 1723, by Anderson, in the *Book of Constitutions*, the regulations as to lawsuits are thus laid down: "And if any of them do you injury, you must apply to your own or his Lodge, and from thence you may appeal to the Grand Lodge, at the Quarterly Communication, and from thence to the Annual Grand Lodge, as has been the ancient laudable conduct of our forefathers in every nation; never taking a legal course but when the case cannot be otherwise decided, and patiently listening to the honest and friendly advice of Master and Fellows, when they would prevent you going to law with strangers, or would excite you to put a speedy period to all lawsuits, that so you may mind the affair of Masonry with the more alacrity and success; but with respect to Brothers or Fellows at law, the Master and Brethren should kindly offer their mediation, which ought to be thankfully submitted to by the contending brethren; and if that submission is impracticable, they must, however, carry on their process or lawsuit without

wrath and rancor, (not in the common way,) saying or doing nothing which may hinder brotherly love and good offices to be renewed and continued; that all may see the benign influence of Masonry, as all true Masons have done from the beginning of the world, and will do to the end of time." (*Constitutions*, 1723, p. 56.)

Lax Observance. (*Observantia Lata.*) When the Rite of Strict Observance was instituted in Germany by Von Hund, its disciples gave to all the other German Lodges which refused to submit to its obedience and adopt its innovations, but preferred to remain faithful to the English Rite, the title of "Lodges of Lax Observance." Ragon, in his *Orthodoxie Maçonnique* (p. 236), has committed the unaccountable error of calling it a schism, established at Vienna in 1767; thus evidently confounding it with Starck's Rite of the Clerks of Strict Observance.

Lay Brothers. A society founded in the eleventh century, consisting of two classes, who were skilled in architecture; also recognized as a degree in the Rite of Strict Observance.

Layer. A term used in the old Records to designate a workman inferior to an Operative Freemason. Thus: "Alsoe that no Mason make moulds, square or rule to any rough layers." (Harleian MS., No. 2054.) In Dr. Murray's new *English Dictionary* the word is said to mean "one who lays stones; a mason," and is described as obsolete in this sense. A quotation is given from Wyclif's Bible of 1382, 1 Chron. xxii. 15, "Many craftise men, masouns and leyers." [E. L. H.]

Lazarus, Order of. An order instituted in Palestine, termed the "United Order of St. Lazarus and of our Beloved Lady of Mount Carmel." It was a military order engaged against the Saracens, by whom it was nearly destroyed. In 1150 the knights assumed the vows of Obedience, Poverty, and Chastity, in the presence of William the Patriarch. In 1572, Gregory XII. united the Italian knights of the order with that of St. Maurice. Vincent de Paul, in 1617, founded a religious order, which was approved in 1626, and erected into a congregation in 1632, and so called from the priory of St. Lazarus in Paris, which was occupied by the order during the French Revolution. The members are called Priests of the Mission, and are employed in teaching and missionary labors.

Lebanon. A mountain, or rather a range of mountains in Syria, extending from beyond Sidon to Tyre, and forming the northern boundary of Palestine. Lebanon is celebrated for the cedars which it produces, many of which are from fifty to eighty feet in height, and cover with their branches a space of ground the diameter of which is still greater. Hiram, King of Tyre, in whose dominions Mount Lebanon was situated, furnished these trees for the building of the Temple of Solomon. In relation to Lebanon, Kitto, in his *Biblical Cyclopedia*, has these remarks: "The forests of the Lebanon mountains only could supply the timber for the Temple. Such of these forests as lay nearest the sea were in the possession of the Phœnicians, among whom timber was in such constant demand, that they had acquired great and acknowledged skill in the felling and transportation thereof; and hence it was of such importance that Hiram consented to employ large bodies of men in Lebanon to hew timber, as well as others to perform the service of bringing it down to the seaside, whence it was to be taken along the coasts in floats to the port of Joppa, from which place it could be easily taken across the country to Jerusalem."

The Ancient and Accepted Scottish Rite has dedicated to this mountain its Twenty-second Degree, or Prince of Lebanon. The Druses now inhabit Mount Lebanon, and still preserve there a secret organization. (See *Druses*.)

Lebanon, Prince of. See *Knight of the Royal Ax*.

Le Bauld de Nans, Claude Etienne. A distinguished Masonic writer, born at Besançon in 1736. He was by profession a highly respected actor, and a man of much learning, which he devoted to the cultivation of Freemasonry. He was for seven years Master of the Lodge St. Charles de l'Union, in Mannheim; and on his removal to Berlin, in 1771, became the Orator of the Lodge Royale York de l'Amitié, and editor of a Masonic journal. He delivered, while Orator of the Lodge—a position which he resigned in 1778—a large number of discourses, a collection of which was published at Berlin in 1788. He also composed many Masonic odes and songs, and published, in 1781, a collection of his songs for the use of the Lodge Royale York, and in 1786, his *Lyre Maçonnique*. He is described by his contemporaries as a man of great knowledge and talents, and Fessler has paid a warm tribute to his learning and to his labors in behalf of Masonry. He died at Berlin in 1789.

Lechangeur. An officer of one of the Lodges of Milan, Italy, of whom Rebold (*Hist. des Trois G. Loges*, p. 575) gives the following account. When, in 1805, a Supreme Council of the Ancient and Accepted Scottish Rite was established at Milan, Lechangeur became a candidate for membership. He received some of the degrees; but subsequently the founders of the Council, for satisfactory reasons, declined to confer upon him the superior grades. Incensed at this, Lechangeur announced to them that he would elevate himself above them by creating a rite of ninety degrees, into which they should not be admitted. He carried this project into effect, and the result was the Rite of Mizraim, of which he declared himself to be the Superior Grand Conservator. His energies seem to have been exhausted in the creation of his unwieldy rite, for no Chapters were established except in the city of Naples. But in 1810 a patent was granted by him to Michel Bedarride, by whom the Rite was propagated in France. Lechangeur's fame, as the founder of the Rite, was overshadowed by the greater zeal and impetuosity of Bedarride, by whom his self-assumed prerogatives were usurped. He died in 1812.

Lecture. Each degree of Masonry contains a course of instruction, in which the ceremonies, traditions, and moral instruction appertaining to the degree are set forth. This arrangement is called a lecture. Each lecture, for the sake of convenience, and for the purpose of conforming to certain divisions in the ceremonies, is divided into sections, the number of which have varied at different periods, although the substance remains the same. According to Preston, the lecture of the first degree contains six sections; that of the second, four; and that of the third, twelve. But according to the arrangement adopted in this country, commonly known as the "Webb lectures," there are three sections in the first degree, two in the second, and three in the third.

In the Entered Apprentices', the first section is almost entirely devoted to a recapitulation of the ceremonies of initiation. The initiatory portion, however, supplies certain modes of recognition. The second section is occupied with an explanation of the ceremonies that had been detailed in the first—the two together furnishing the interpretation of ritualistic symbolism. The third is exclusively occupied in explaining the signification of the symbols peculiar to the degree.

In the Fellow-Craft's Degree, the first section, like the first section of the Entered Apprentice, is merely a recapitulation of ceremonies, with a passing commentary on some of them. The second section introduces the neophyte for the first time to the differences between Operative and Speculative Masonry and to the Temple of King Solomon as a Masonic symbol, while the candidate is ingeniously deputed as a seeker after knowledge.

In the Master's Degree the first section is again only a detail of ceremonies. The second section is the most important and impressive portion of all the lectures, for it contains the legend on which the whole symbolic character of the Institution is founded. The third section is an interpretation of the symbols of the degree, and is, of all the sections, the one least creditable to the composer.

In fact, it must be confessed that many of the interpretations given in these lectures are unsatisfactory to the cultivated mind, and seem to have been adopted on the principle of the old Egyptians, who made use of symbols to conceal rather than to express their thoughts. Learned Masons have been, therefore, always disposed to go beyond the mere technicalities and stereotyped phrases of the lectures, and to look in the history and the philosophy of the ancient religions, and the organization of the ancient mysteries, for a true explanation of most of the symbols of Masonry, and there they have always been enabled to find this true interpretation. The lectures, however, serve as an introduction or preliminary essay, enabling the student, as he advances in his initiation, to become acquainted with the symbolic character of the Institution. But if he ever expects to become a learned Mason, he must seek in other sources for the true development of Masonic symbolism. The lectures alone are but the primer of the science.

Lecturer, Grand. An officer known only in the United States. He is appointed by the Grand Master or the Grand Lodge. His duty is to visit the subordinate Lodges, and instruct them in the ritual of the Order as practised in his jurisdiction, for which he receives compensation partly from the Grand Lodge and partly from the Lodges which he visits.

Lectures, History of the. To each of the degrees of Symbolic Masonry a catechetical instruction is appended, in which the ceremonies, traditions, and other esoteric instructions of the degree are contained. A knowledge of these lectures—which must, of course, be communicated by oral teaching—constitutes a very important part of a Masonic education; and, until the great progress made within the present century in Masonic literature, many "bright Masons," as they are technically styled, could claim no other foundation than such a knowledge for their high Masonic reputation. But some share of learning more difficult to attain, and more sublime in its character than anything to be found in these oral catechisms, is now considered necessary to form a Masonic scholar. Still, as the best commentary on the ritual observances is to be found in the lectures, and as they also furnish a large portion of that secret mode of recognition, or that universal language, which has always been the boast of the Institution, not only is a knowledge of them absolutely necessary to every practical Freemason, but a history of the changes which they have from time to time undergone constitutes an interesting part of the literature of the Order.

Comparatively speaking (comparatively in respect to the age of the Masonic Institution), the system of Lodge lectures is undoubtedly a modern invention. That is to say, we can find no traces of any forms of lectures like the present before the middle, or perhaps the close, of the seventeenth century. Examinations, however, of a technical nature, intended to test the claims of the person examined to the privileges of the Order, appear to have existed at an early period. They were used until at least the middle of the eighteenth century, but were perpetually changing, so that the tests of one generation of Masons constituted no tests for the succeeding one. Oliver very properly describes them as being "something like the conundrums of the present day—difficult of comprehension—admitting only of one answer, which appeared to have no direct correspondence with the question, and applicable only in consonance with the mysteries and symbols of the Institution." (*On the Masonic Tests of the Eighteenth Century. Golden Remains*, vol. iv., p. 16.) These tests were sometimes, at first, distinct from the lectures,

and sometimes, at a later period, incorporated with them. A specimen is the answer to the question, "How blows the wind?" which was, "Due east and west."

The "Examination of a German Stone-Mason," which is given by Findel in the appendix to his *History*, was most probably in use in the fourteenth century. Dr. Oliver was in possession of what purports to be a formula, which he supposes to have been used during the Grand Mastership of Archbishop Chichely, in the reign of Henry VI., and from which (*Rev. of a Sq.*, p. 11) he makes the following extracts:

"*Q*. Peace be here? *A*. I hope there is. *Q*. What o'clock is it? *A*. It is going to six, or going to twelve. *Q*. Are you very busy? *A*. No. *Q*. Will you give or take? *A*. Both; or which you please. *Q*. How go squares? *A*. Straight. *Q*. Are you rich or poor? *A*. Neither. *Q*. Change me that? *A*. I will. *Q*. In the name of the King and the Holy Church, are you a Mason? *A*. I am so taken to be. *Q*. What is a Mason? *A*. A man begot by a man, born of a woman, brother to a king. *Q*. What is a fellow? *A*. A companion of a prince, etc."

There are other questions and answers of a similar nature, conveying no instruction, and intended apparently to be used only as tests. Dr. Oliver attributes, it will be seen, the date of these questions to the beginning of the fifteenth century; but the correctness of this assumption is doubtful. They have no internal evidence in style of having been the invention of so early a period of the English tongue.

The earliest form of catechism that we have on record is that contained in the Sloane MS., No. 3329, now in the British Museum, which has been printed and published by the Rev. A. F. A. Woodford. One familiar with the catechisms of the eighteenth century will detect the origin of much that they contain in this early specimen. It is termed in the manuscript the Mason's "private discourse by way of question and answer," and is in these words:

"*Q*. Are you a mason? *A*. Yes, I am a Freemason. *Q*. How shall I know that? *A*. By perfect signes and tokens and the first poynts of my Entrance. *Q*. Which is the first signe or token, shew me the first and I will shew you the second. *A*. The first is heal and conceal or conceal and keep secrett by no less paine than cutting my tongue from my throat. *Q*. Where were you made a mason? *A*. In a just and perfect or just and lawfull lodge. *Q*. What is a just and perfect or just and lawfull lodge? *A*. A just and perfect lodge is two Interprintices two fellow craftes and two Mast'rs, more or fewer the more the merrier the fewer the better chear but if need require five will serve that is, two Interprintices, two fellow craftes and one Mast'r on the highest hill or lowest valley of the world without the crow of a cock or the bark of a dogg. *Q*. From whome do you derive your principalls? *A*. From a great'r than you. *Q*. Who is that on earth that is great'r than a freemason? *A*. He y't was caryed to y'e highest pinnicall of the temple of Jerusalem. *Q*. Whith'r is your lodge shut or open? *A*. It is shut. *Q*. Where lyes the keys of the lodge doore? *A*. They ley in a bound case or under a three cornered pavem't about a foote and halfe from the lodge door. *Q*. What is the key of your lodge doore made of? *A*. It is not made of wood stone iron or steel or any sort of mettle but the tongue of good report behind a Broth'rs back as well as before his face. *Q*. How many jewels belong to your lodge? *A*. There are three the square pavem't the blazing star and the Danty tassley. *Q*. How long is the cable rope of your lodge? *A*. As long as from the Lop of the liver to the root of the tongue. *Q*. How many lights are in your lodge? *A*. Three the sun the mast'r and the square. *Q*. How high is your lodge? *A*. Without foots yards or Inches, it reaches to heaven. *Q*. How stood your lodge? *A*. East and west as all holly Temples stand. *Q*. W'ch is the mast'rs place in the lodge? *A*. The east place is the mast'rs place in the lodge and the jewell resteth on him first and he setteth men to worke w't the m'rs have in the forenoon the wardens reap in the afternoon. *Q*. Where was the word first given? *A*. At the tower of Babylon. *Q*. Where did they first call their lodge? *A*. At the holy chapell of St. John. *Q*. How stood your lodge? *A*. As the said holy chapell and all other holy Temples stand (viz.) east and west. *Q*. How many lights are in your lodge? *A*. Two one to see to go in and another to see to work. *Q*. What were you sworne by? *A*. By God and the square. *Q*. Whither above the cloathes or und'r the cloathes? *A*. Und'r the cloathes. *Q*. Und'r what arme? *A*. Und'r the right arme. God is gratfull to all Worshipfull Mast'rs and fellows in that worshipfull lodge from whence we last came and to you good fellow w't is your name. *A*. J or B then giving the grip of the hand he will say Broth'r John greet you well you. *A*. God's good greeting to you dear Broth'r."

But when we speak of the lectures, in the modern sense, as containing an exposition of the symbolism of the Order, we may consider it as an established historical fact, that the Fraternity were without any such system until after the revival in 1717. Previous to that time, brief extemporary addresses and charges in addition to these test catechisms were used by the Masters of Lodges, which, of course, varied in excellence with the varied attainments and talents of the presiding officer. We know, however, that a series of charges were in use about the middle and end of the seventeenth century, which were ordered "to be read at the making of a Freemason." These "Charges and Covenants," as they were called, contained no instructions on the symbolism and ceremonies of the Order, but were confined to an explanation of the duties of Masons to each other. They were altogether exoteric in their character, and have accordingly been repeatedly printed in the authorized publications of the Fraternity.

Dr. Oliver, who had ampler opportunities than any other Masonic writer of investigating this subject, says that the earliest authorized lectures with which he has met were those of 1720. They were arranged by Drs. Anderson and Desaguliers, perhaps, at the same time that they were compiling the Charges and Regulations from the ancient Constitutions. They were written in a catechetical form, which form has ever since been retained in all subsequent Masonic lectures. Oliver says that "the questions and answers are short and comprehensive, and contain a brief digest of the general principles of the Craft as it was understood at that period." The "digest" must, indeed, have been brief, since the lecture of the Third Degree, or what was called "the Master's Part," contained only thirty-one questions, many of which are simply tests of recognition. Dr. Oliver says the number of questions was only seven; but he probably refers to the seven tests which conclude the lecture. There are, however, twenty-four other questions that precede these.

A comparison of these—the primitive lectures, as they may be called—with those in use in America at the present day, demonstrate that a great many changes have taken place. There are not only omissions of some things, and additions of others, but sometimes the explanations of the same points are entirely different in the two systems. Thus the Andersonian lectures describe the "furniture" of a Lodge as being the "Mosaic pavement, blazing star, and indented tassel," emblems which are now, perhaps more properly, designated as "ornaments." But the present furniture of a Lodge is also added to the pavement, star, and tassel, under the name of "other furniture." The "greater lights" of Masonry are entirely omitted, or, if we are to suppose them to be meant by the expression "fixed lights," then these are referred, differently from our system, to the three windows of the Lodge.

In the First Degree may be noticed, among others, the following points in the Andersonian lectures which are omitted in the American system: the place and duty of the Senior and Junior Entered Apprentices, the punishment of cowans, the bone bone-box, and all that refers to it; the clothing of the Master, the age of an Apprentice, the uses of the day and night, and the direction of the wind. These latter, however, are, strictly speaking, what the Masons of that time denominated "tests." In the same degree, the following, besides many other important points in the present system, are altogether omitted in the old lectures of Anderson: the place where Masons anciently met, the theological ladder, and the lines parallel. Important changes have been made in several particulars; as, for instance, in the "points of entrance," the ancient lecture giving an entirely different interpretation of the expression, and designating what are now called "points of entrance" by the term "principal signs"; the distinctions between Operative and Speculative Masonry, which are now referred to the Second Degree, are there given in the First; and the dedication of the Bible, compass, and square is differently explained.

In the Second Degree, the variations of the old from the modern lectures are still greater. The old lecture is, in the first place, very brief, and much instruction deemed important at the present day was then altogether omitted. There is no reference to the distinctions between Operative and Speculative Masonry (but this topic is adverted to in the former lecture); the approaches to the middle chamber are very differently arranged; and not a single word is said of the fords of the river Jordan. It must be confessed that the ancient lecture of the Fellow-Craft is immeasurably inferior to that contained in the modern system, and especially in that of Webb.

The Andersonian lecture of the Third Degree is brief, and therefore imperfect. The legend is, of course, referred to, and its explanation occupies nearly the whole of the lecture; but the details are meager, and many important facts are omitted, while there are in other points striking differences between the ancient and the present system.

But, after all, there is a general feature of similarity—a substratum of identity—pervading the two systems of lectures—the ancient and the modern—which shows that the one derives its parentage from the other. In fact, some of the answers given in the year 1730 are, word for word, the same as those used in America at the present time.

[Martin Clare and Dunckerley (*q. v.*) are often credited with being revisers of the English ritual and lectures, but as there is no proof whatever that they had anything to do with such revision it does not seem worth while to repeat the well-worn tale here. —E. L. H.]

[Nothing can be said with any certainty about the lectures in England until the last quarter of the eighteenth century, when William Preston took the matter in hand and revised or more probably rewrote them entirely.—E. L. H.]

He divided the lecture on the First Degree into six sections, the Second into four, and the third into twelve. But of the twelve sections of the third lecture, seven only strictly appertain to the Master's Degree, the remaining five referring to the ceremonies of the Order, which, in the American system, are contained in the Past Master's lecture. Preston has recapitulated the subjects of these several lectures in his *Illustrations of Masonry;* and if the book were not now so readily accessible, it would be worth while to copy his remarks. It is sufficient, however, to say that he has presented us with a philosophical system of Masonry, which, coming immediately after the unscientific and scanty details which up to his time had been the subjects of Lodge instructions, must have been like the bursting forth of a sun from the midst of midnight darkness. There was no twilight or dawn to warn the

unexpectant Fraternity of the light that was about to shine upon them. But at once, without preparation—without any gradual progress or growth from almost nothing to superfluity—the Prestonian lectures were given to the Order in all their fulness of illustration and richness of symbolism and science, as a substitute for the plain and almost unmeaning systems that had previously prevailed. Not that Freemasonry had not always been a science, but that for all that time, and longer, her science had been dormant—had been in abeyance. From 1717 the Craft had been engaged in something less profitable, but more congenial than the cultivation of Masonic science. The pleasant suppers, the modicums of punch, the harmony of song, the miserable puns, which would have provoked the ire of Johnson beyond anything that Boswell has recorded, left no time for inquiry into abstruser matters. The revelations of Dr. Oliver's square furnish us abundant positive evidence of the low state of Masonic literature in those days; and if we need negative proof, we will find it in the entire absence of any readable book on Scientific Masonry, until the appearance of Hutchinson's and Preston's works. Preston's lectures were, therefore, undoubtedly the inauguration of a new era in the esoteric system of Freemasonry.

These lectures continued for nearly half a century to be the authoritative text of the Order in England. But in 1813 the two Grand Lodges—the "Moderns" and the "Ancients," as they were called—after years of antagonism, were happily united, and then, as the first exercise of this newly combined authority, it was determined "to revise" the system of lectures.

This duty was entrusted to the Rev. Dr. Hemming, the Senior Grand Warden, and the result was the Union or Hemming lectures, which are now the authoritative standard of English Masonry. In these lectures many alterations of the Prestonian system were made, and some of the most cherished symbols of the Fraternity were abandoned, as, for instance, the *twelve grand points, the initiation of the free born,* and *the lines parallel.* Preston's lectures were rejected in consequence, it is said, of their Christian references; and Dr. Hemming, in attempting to avoid this error, fell into a greater one, of omitting in his new course some of the important ritualistic landmarks of the Order.

[Nothing definite can be stated about the lectures used in America until near the end of the eighteenth century, when a system of lectures was put forth by Thomas Smith Webb. —E. L. H.]

The lectures of Webb contained much that was almost a verbal copy of parts of Preston; but the whole system was briefer, and the paragraphs were framed with an evident view to facility in committing them to memory. It is an herculean task to acquire the whole system of Prestonian lectures, while that of Webb may be mastered in a comparatively short time, and by much inferior intellects. There have, in consequence, in former years, been many "bright Masons" and "skilful lecturers" whose brightness and skill consisted only in the easy repetition from memory of the set form of phrases established by Webb, and who were otherwise ignorant of all the science, the philosophy, and the history of Masonry. But in the later years, a perfect verbal knowledge of the lectures has not been esteemed so highly in America as in England, and the most erudite Masons have devoted themselves to the study of those illustrations and that symbolism of the Order which lie outside of the lectures. Book Masonry—that is, the study of the principles of the Institution as any other science is studied, by means of the various treatises which have been written on these subjects—has been, from year to year, getting more popular with the American Masonic public which is becoming emphatically a reading people.

The lecture on the Third Degree is eminently Hutchinsonian in its character, and contains the bud from which, by a little cultivation, we might bring forth a gorgeous blossom of symbolism. Hence, the Third Degree has always been the favorite of American Masons. But the lectures of the First and Second degrees, the latter particularly, are meager and unsatisfactory. The explanations, for instance, of the form and extent of the Lodge, of its covering, of the theological ladder, and especially of the point within the circle, will disappoint any intellectual student who is seeking, in a symbolical science, for some rational explanation of its symbols that promises to be worthy of his investigations.

Lefranc. The Abbé Lefranc, Superior of the House of the Eudistes at Caen, was a very bitter enemy of Freemasonry, and the author of two libelous works against Freemasonry, both published in Paris; the first and best known, entitled *Le Voile levé pour les curieux, ou le secret des révolutions, révélé à l'aide de la Franc-Maçonnerie*, 1791 (republished at Liege in 1827), and the other, *Conjuration contre la religion Catholique et les souverains, dont le projet, conçu eu France, doit s'éxécuter dans l'univers entier*, 1792. In these scandalous books, and especially in the former, Lefranc has, to use the language of Thory (*Acta Lat.*, i., 192), "vomited the most undeserved abuse of the Order." Of the *Veil Lifted*, the two great detractors of Masonry, Robison and Barruel, entertained different opinions. Robison made great use of it in his *Proofs of a Conspiracy;* but Barruel, while speaking highly of the Abbé's virtues, doubts his accuracy and declines to trust to his authority. Lefranc was slain in the massacre of September 2d, at the Convent of the Carmelites, in Paris, with one hundred and ninety-one other priests. Thory (*l. c.*) says that M. Ledhui, a Freemason, who was present at the sanguinary scene, attempted to save the life of Lefranc, and nearly lost his own in the effort. The Abbé says that, on the death of a friend, who was a zealous Mason and Master of a Lodge, he found among his papers a collection of Masonic writings containing the rituals of a great many degrees, and from these he obtained the information on which he has based his attacks upon the Order. Some idea may be formed of his accuracy and credibility, from the fact that he asserts that Faustus Socinus, the Father of Modern Unitarianism, was the contriver and inventor of the Masonic system—a theory so absurd that even Robison and Barruel both reject it.

Left Hand. Among the ancients the left hand was a symbol of equity and justice. Thus, Apuleius (*Met.*, l. xi.), when describing the procession in honor of Isis, says one of the ministers of the sacred rites "bore the symbol of equity, a left hand, fashioned with the palm extended; which seems to be more adapted to administering equity than the right, from its natural inertness, and its being endowed with no craft and no subtlety."

Left Side. In the symbolism of Masonry, the First Degree is represented by the left side, which is to indicate that as the left is the weaker part of the body, so is the Entered Apprentice's Degree the weakest part of Masonry. This doctrine, that the left is the weaker side of the body, is very ancient. Plato says it arises from the fact that the right is more used; but Aristotle contends that the organs of the right side are by nature more powerful than those of the left.

Legally Constituted. See *Constituted, Legally.*

Legate. In the Middle Ages, a legate, or *legatus*, was one who was, says Du Cange (*Glossar.*), "in provincias à Principe ad exercendas judicias mittebalur," sent by a prince into the provinces to exercise judicial functions. The word is now applied by the Supreme Council of the Ancient and Accepted Scottish Rite to designate certain persons who are sent into unoccupied territory to propagate the Rite. The word is, however, of recent origin, not having been used before 1866. A legate should be in possession of at least the Thirty-second Degree.

Legend. Strictly speaking, a legend, from the Latin, *legendus*, "to be read," should be restricted to a story that has been committed to writing; but by good usage the word has been applied more extensively, and now properly means a narrative, whether true or false, that has been traditionally preserved from the time of its first oral communication. Such is the definition of a Masonic legend. The authors of the *Conversations-Lexicon*, referring to the monkish lives of the saints which originated in the twelfth and thirteenth centuries, say that the title *legend* was given to all fictions which made pretensions to truth. Such a remark, however correct it may be in reference to these monkish narratives, which were often invented as ecclesiastical exercises, is by no means applicable to the legends of Freemasonry. These are not necessarily fictitious, but are either based on actual and historical facts which have been but slightly modified, or they are the offspring and expansion of some symbolic idea; in which latter respect they differ entirely from the monastic legends, which often have only the fertile imagination of some studious monk for the basis of their construction.

The instructions of Freemasonry are given to us in two modes: by the *symbol* and by the *legend*. The symbol is a material, and the legend a mental, representation of a truth. The sources of neither can be in every case authentically traced. Many of them come to us, undoubtedly, from the old Operative Masons of the Medieval gilds. But whence they got them is a question that naturally arises, and which still remains unanswered. Others have sprung from a far earlier source; perhaps, as Creuzer has suggested in his *Symbolik*, from an effort to engraft higher and purer knowledge on an imperfect religious idea. If so, then the myths of the Ancient Mysteries, and the legends or traditions of Freemasonry, would have the same remote and the same final cause. They would differ in construction, but they would agree in design. For instance, the myth of Adonis in the Syrian mysteries, and the legend of Hiram Abif in the Third Degree, would differ very widely in their details; but the object of each would be the same, namely, to teach the doctrine of the restoration from death to eternal life.

The legends of Freemasonry constitute a considerable and a very important part of its ritual. Without them, its most valuable portions as a scientific system would cease to exist. It is, in fact, in the traditions and legends of Freemasonry, more, even, than in its material symbols, that we are to find the deep religious instructions which the Institution is intended to inculcate. It must be remembered that Freemasonry has been defined to be "a system of morality, veiled in allegory and illustrated by symbols." Symbols, then, alone, do not constitute the whole of the system: allegory comes in for its share; and this allegory, which veils the Divine truths of Masonry, is presented to the neophyte in the various legends which have been traditionally preserved in the Order.

They may be divided into three classes: 1. The Mythical legend. 2. The Philosophical legend. 3. The Historical legend. And these three classes may be defined as follows:

1. The myth may be engaged in the transmission of a narrative of early deeds and events having a foundation in truth, which truth, however, has been greatly distorted and perverted by the omission or introduction of circumstances and personages, and then it constitutes the *mythical legend*.

2. Or it may have been invented and adopted as the medium of enunciating a particular thought, or of inculcating a certain doctrine, when it becomes a *philosophical legend*.

3. Or, lastly, the truthful elements of actual history may greatly predominate over the fictitious and invented materials of the myth; and the narrative may be, in the main, made up of facts, with a slight coloring of imagination, when it forms an *historical legend*.

Legend of Enoch. See *Enoch*.
Legend of Euclid. See *Euclid, Legend of.*
Legend of the Craft. The Old Records of the Fraternity of Operative Freemasons, under the general name of *Old Constitutions* or *Constitutions of Masonry*, or *Old Charges*, were written in the fourteenth, fifteenth, sixteenth, and seventeenth centuries. The loss of many of these by the indiscretion of overzealous brethren was deplored by Anderson; but a few of them have been long known to us, and many more have been recently recovered, by the labors of such men as Hughan, from the archives of old Lodges and from manuscript collections in the British Museum. In these is to be found a history of Freemasonry; full, it is true, of absurdities and anachronisms, and yet exceedingly interesting, as giving us the belief of our ancient brethren on the subject of the origin of the Order. This history has been called by Masonic writers the "Legend of the Craft," because it is really a legendary narrative, having little or no historic authenticity. In all these *Old Constitutions*, the legend is substantially the same; showing, evidently, a common origin; most probably an oral teaching which prevailed in the earliest ages of the confraternity. In giving it, the Dowland Manuscript, as reproduced in Hughan's *Old Charges* (1872), has been selected for the purpose, because it is believed to be a copy of an older one of the beginning of the sixteenth century, and because its rather modernized spelling makes it more intelligible to the general reader.

THE LEGEND OF THE CRAFT.

"Before Noyes floode there was a man called Lameche as it is written in the Byble, in the iiijth chapter of Genesis; and this Lameche had two wives, and the one height Ada and the other height Sella; by his first wife Ada he gott two sonns, and that one Jahell, and thother Tuball, And by that other wife Sella he gott a son and a daughter. And these four children founden the begining of all the sciences in the world. And this elder son Jahell found the science of Geometrie, and he departed flocks of sheepe and lambs in the field, and first wrought house of stone and tree, as is noted in the chapter above said. And his brother Tuball found the science of Musicke, songe of tonge, harpe, and orgaine. And the third brother Tuball Cain found smithcraft of gold, silver, copper, iron, and steele; and the daughter found the craft of Weavinge. And these children knew well that God would take vengeance for synn, either by fire or by water; wherefore they writt their science that they had found in two pillars of stone, that they might be found after Noyes flood. And that one stone was *marble*, for that would not bren with fire; and that other stone was clepped *laterns*, and would not drown in noe water.

"Our intent is to tell you trulie how and in what manner these stones were found, that thise sciences were written in. The great Hermarynes that was Cubys son, the which Cub was Sem's son, that was Noys son. This Hermarynes, afterwards was called Harmes the father of wise men: he found one of the two pillars of stone, and found the science written there, and he taught it to other men. And at the making of the Tower of Babylon there was Masonrye first made much of. And the Kinge of Babylon that height Nemrothe, was a mason himselfe, and loved well the science, as it is said with masters of histories. And when the City of Nyneve, and other citties of the East should be made, Nemrothe, the Kinge of Babilon, sent thither threescore Masons at the rogation of the Kinge of Nyneve his cosen. And when he sent them forth, he gave them a charge on this manner: That they should be true each of them to other, and that they should love truly together, and that they should serve their lord truly for their pay; soe that the master may have worshipp, and all that long to him. And other moe charges he gave them. And this was the first tyme that ever Masons had any charge of his science.

"Moreover, when Abraham and Sara his wife went into Egipt, there he taught the Seaven Scyences to the Egiptians; and he had a worthy Scoller that height Ewclyde, and he learned right well, and was a master of all the vij Sciences liberall. And in his dayes it befell that the lord and the estates of the realme had soe many sonns that they had gotten some by their wifes and some by other ladyes of the realme; for that land is a hott land and a plentious of generacion. And they had not competent livelode to find with their children; wherefore they made much care. And then the King of the land made a great Counsell and a parliament, to witt, how they might find their children honestly as gentlemen. And they could find noe manner of good way. And then they did crye through all the realme, if their were any man that could informe them, that he should come to them, and he should be soe rewarded for his travail, that he should hold him pleased.

"After that this cry was made, then came this worthy clarke Ewclyde, and said to the king and to all his great lords: 'If yee will, take me your children to governe, and to teache them one of the Seaven Scyences, wherewith they may live honestly as gentlemen should, under a condicion that yee will grant me and them a commission that I may have power to rule them after the manner that the science ought to be ruled.' And that the Kinge and all his Counsell granted to him anone, and sealed their commission. And then this worthy Doctor tooke to him these lords' sonns, and taught them the scyence of Geometrie in practice, for to work in stones all manner of worthy worke that belongeth to buildinge churches, temples, castells, towres, and mannors, and all other manner of buildings; and he gave them a charge on this manner:

"The first was, that they should be true to the Kinge, and to the lord that they owe. And that they should love well together, and

be true each one to other. And that they should call each other his fellowe, or else brother, and not by servant, nor his nave, nor none other foule name. And that the should deserve their paie of the lord, or of the master that they serve. And that they should ordaine the wisest of them to be master of the worke; and neither for love nor great lynneage, ne ritches ne for noe favour to lett another that hath little conning for to be master of the lord's worke, wherethrough the lord should be evill served and they ashamed. And also that they should call their governors of the worke, Master, in the time that they worke with him. And other many moe charges that longe to tell. And to all these charges he made them to sweare a great oath that men used in that time; and ordayned them for reasonable wages, that they might live honestly by. And also that they should come and semble together every yeare once, how they might worke best to serve the lord for his profitt, and to their own worshipp; and to correct within themselves him that had trespassed against the science. And thus was the scyence grounded there; and that worthy Mr. Ewclide gave it the name of Geometrie. And now it is called through all this land Masonrye.

"Sythen longe after, when the Children of Israell were coming into the Land of Beheast, that is now called amongst us the Country of Jhrlm, King David began the Temple that they called Templum D'ni and it is named with us the Temple of Jerusalem. And the same King David loved Masons well and cherished them much, and gave them good paie. And he gave the charges and the manners as he had learned of Egipt given by Ewclyde, and other charges moe that ye shall heare afterwards. And after the decease of Kinge David, Salamon, that was David's sonn, performed out the Temple that his father begonne; and sent after Masons into divers countries and of divers lands; and gathered them together, so that he had fourscore thousand workers of stone, and were all named Masons. And he chose out of them three thousand that were ordayned to be maisters and governors of his worke. And furthermore, there was a Kinge of another region that men called Iram, and he loved well Kinge Solomon, and he gave him tymber to his worke. And he had a son that height Aynon, and he was a Master of Geometrie, and was chiefe Maister of all his Masons, and was Master of all his gravings and carvinge, and of all other manner of Masonrye that longed to the Temple; and this is witnessed by the Bible *in libro Regum* the third chapter. And this Solomon confirmed both charges and the manners that his father had given to Masons. And thus was that worthy science of Masonrye confirmed in the country of Jerusalem, and in many other kingdomes.

"Curious craftsmen walked about full wide into divers countryes, some because of learninge more craft and cunninge, and some to teach them that had but little conynge. And soe it befell that there was one curious Mason that height Maymus Grecus, that had been at the making of Solomon's Temple, and he came into France, and there he taught the science of Masonrye to men of France. And there was one of the Regal lyne of France, that height Charles Martell; and he was a man that loved well such a science, and drew to this Maymus Grecus that is above said, and learned of him the science, and tooke upon him the charges and manners; and afterwards, by the grace of God, he was elect to be Kinge of France. And when he was in his estate he tooke Masons, and did helpe to make men Masons that were none; and set them to worke, and gave them both the charge and the manners and good paie, as he had learned of other Masons; and confirmed them a Chartor from yeare to yeare, to hold their semble wher they would; and cherished them right much; And thus came the science into France.

"England in all this season stood voyd as for any charge of Masonrye unto St. Albones tyme. And in his days the King of England that was a Pagan, he did wall the towne about that is called Sainct Albones. And Sainct Albones was a worthy Knight, and steward with the Kinge of his Household, and had governance of the realme, and also of the makinge of the town walls; and loved well Masons and cherished them much. And he made their paie right good, standinge as the realm did, for he gave them ijs. vjd. a weeke, and iijd. to their nonesynches. And before that time, through all this land, a Mason took but a penny a day and his meate, till Sainct Albone amended it, and gave them a chartour of the Kinge and his Counsell for to hold a general councell, and gave it the name of Assemble; and thereat he was himselfe, and helped to make Masons, and gave them charges as yee shall heare afterward.

"Right soone after the decease of Sainct Albone, there came divers warrs into the realme of England of divers Nations, soe that the good rule of Masonrye was destroyed unto the tyme of Kinge Athelstone days that was a worthy Kinge of England and brought this land into good rest and peace; and builded many great works of Abbyes and Towres, and other many divers buildings; and loved well Masons. And he had a son that height Edwinne, and he loved Masons much more than his father did. And he was a great practiser in Geometry; and he drew him much to talke and to commune with Masons, and to learne of them science; and afterward, for love that he had to Masons, and to the science, he was made a Mason, and he gatt of the Kinge his father a Chartour and Commission to hold every yeare once an Assemble, wher that ever they would within the realme of England; and to correct within themselves defaults and trespasses that were done within the science. And he held himself an Assemble at Yorke, and there he made Masons, and gave them charges, and taught them the manners, and commanded that rule to be kept ever after, and tooke then the Chartour and Commission to keepe, and

made ordinance that it should be renewed from Kinge to Kinge.

"And when the assemble was gathered he made a cry that all old Masons and young that had any writeinge or understanding of the charges and the manners that were made before in this land or in any other, that they should show them forth. And when it was proved, there were founden some in Frenche, and some in Greek, and some in English, and some in other languages; and the intent of them all was founden all one. And he did make a booke thereof, and how the science was founded. And he himselfe bad and commanded that it should be readd or tould, when that any Mason should be made, for to give him his Charge. And fro that day unto this tyme manners of Masons have beene kept in that forme as well as men might governe it. And furthermore divers Assembles have beene put and ordayned certaine charges by the best advice of Masters and fellowes."

If anyone carefully examines this legend, he will find that it is really a history of the rise and progress of architecture, with which is mixed allusions to the ancient gilds of the Operative Masons. Geometry also, as a science essentially necessary to the proper cultivation of architecture, receives a due share of attention. In thus confounding architecture, geometry, and Freemasonry, the workmen of the Middle Ages were but obeying a natural instinct which leads every man to seek to elevate the character of his profession, and to give to it an authentic claim to antiquity. It is this instinct which has given rise to so much of the mythical element in the modern history of Masonry. Anderson has thus written his records in the very spirit of the legend of the Craft, and Preston and Oliver have followed his example. Hence this legend derives its great importance from the fact that it has given a complexion to all subsequent Masonic history. In dissecting it with critical hands, we shall be enabled to dissever its historical from its mythical portions, and assign to it its true value as an exponent of the Masonic sentiment of the Middle Ages.

Legend of the Gild. A title by which the Legend of the Craft is sometimes designated in reference to the Gild of Operative Masons.

Legend of the Royal Arch Degree. Much of this legend is a myth, having very little foundation, and some of it none, in historical accuracy. But underneath it all there lies a profound stratum of philosophical symbolism. The destruction and the rebuilding of the Temple by the efforts of Zerubbabel and his compatriots, the captivity and the return of the captives, are matters of sacred history; but many of the details have been invented and introduced for the purpose of giving form to a symbolic idea. And this idea, expressed in the symbolism of the Royal Arch, is the very highest form of that which the ancient Mystagogues called the *euresis*, or the *discovery*. There are some portions of the legend which do not bear directly on the symbolism of the second Temple as a type of the second life, but which still have an indirect bearing on the general idea. Thus the particular legend of the *three weary sojourners* is undoubtedly a mere myth, there being no known historical testimony for its support; but it is evidently the enunciation symbolically of the religious and philosophical idea that Divine truth may be sought and won only by successful perseverance through all the dangers, trials, and tribulations of life, and that it is not in this, but in the next life, that it is fully attained.

The legend of the English and the American systems is identical; that of the Irish is very different as to the time and events; and the legend of the Royal Arch of the Scottish Rite is more usually called the *legend of Enoch*.

Legend of the Third Degree. The most important and significant of the legendary symbols of Freemasonry is, undoubtedly, that which relates to the fate of Hiram Abif, commonly called, "by way of excellence," the Legend of the Third Degree.

The first written record that I have been able to find of this legend is contained in the second edition of Anderson's *Constitutions*, published in 1738 (p. 14), and is in these words:

"It (the Temple) was finished in the short space of seven years and six months, to the amazement of all the world; when the cape-stone was celebrated by the Fraternity with great joy. But their joy was soon interrupted by the sudden death of their dear master, Hiram Abif, whom they decently interred in the Lodge near the Temple, according to ancient usage."

In the next edition of the same work, published in 1756 (p. 24), a few additional circumstances are related, such as the participation of King Solomon in the general grief, and the fact that the King of Israel "ordered his obsequies to be performed with great solemnity and decency." With these exceptions, and the citations of the same passages, made by subsequent authors, the narrative has always remained unwritten, and descended, from age to age, through the means of oral tradition.

The legend has been considered of so much importance that it has been preserved in the symbolism of every Masonic rite. No matter what modifications or alterations the general system may have undergone—no matter how much the ingenuity or the imagination of the founders of rites may have perverted or corrupted other symbols, abolishing the old and substituting new ones—the legend of the Temple Builder has ever been left untouched, to present itself in all the integrity of its ancient mythical form.

What, then, is the signification of this symbol so important and so extensively diffused? What interpretation can we give to it that will account for its universal adoption? How is it that it has thus become so intimately interwoven with Freemasonry as to make, to all appearances, a part of its very essence, and

to have been always deemed inseparable from it?

To answer these questions satisfactorily, it is necessary to trace, in a brief investigation, the remote origin of the institution of Freemasonry and its connection with the ancient systems of initiation.

It was, then, the object of all the rites and mysteries of antiquity to teach the doctrine of the immortality of the soul. This dogma, shining as an almost solitary beacon-light in the surrounding gloom of Pagan darkness, had undoubtedly been received from that ancient people or priesthood, among whom it probably existed only in the form of an abstract proposition or a simple and unembellished tradition. But in the more sensual minds of the Pagan philosophers and mystics, the idea, when presented to the initiates in their mysteries, was always conveyed in the form of a scenic representation. The influence, too, of the early Sabian worship of the sun and heavenly bodies, in which the solar orb was adored on its resurrection, each morning, from the apparent death of its evening setting, caused this rising sun to be adopted in the more ancient mysteries as a symbol of the regeneration of the soul.

Thus, in the Egyptian mysteries we find a representation of the death and subsequent regeneration of Osiris; in the Phœnician, of Adonis; in the Syrian, of Dionysus; in all of which the scenic apparatus of initiation was intended to indoctrinate the candidate into the dogma of a future life.

It will be sufficient here to refer to the theory of Oliver, that through the instrumentality of the Tyrian workmen at the Temple of King Solomon, what he calls the spurious and pure branches of the Masonic system were united at Jerusalem, and that the same method of scenic representation was adopted by the latter from the former, and the narrative of the Temple Builder substituted for that of Dionysus, which was the myth peculiar to the mysteries practised by the Tyrian workmen.

The idea, therefore, proposed to be communicated in the myth of the ancient mysteries was the same as that which is now conveyed in the Masonic Legend of the Third Degree.

Hence, then, Hiram Abif is, in the Masonic system, the symbol of human nature, as developed in the life here and the life to come; and so, while the Temple was the visible symbol of the world, its builder became the mythical symbol of man, the dweller and worker in that world.

Man, setting forth on the voyage of life, with faculties and powers fitting him for the due exercise of the high duties to whose performance he has been called, holds, if he be "a curious and cunning workman," skilled in all moral and intellectual purposes (and it is only of such men that the Temple Builder can be the symbol), within the grasp of his attainment, the knowledge of all that Divine truth imparted to him as the heirloom of his race—

that race to whom it has been granted to look, with exalted countenance, on high; which Divine truth is symbolized by the WORD.

Thus provided with the word of life, he occupies his time in the construction of a spiritual temple, and travels onward in the faithful discharge of all his duties, laying down his designs upon the trestle-board of the future, and invoking the assistance and direction of God.

But is his path always over flowery meads and through pleasant groves? Is there no hidden foe to obstruct his progress? Is all before him clear and calm, with joyous sunshine and refreshing zephyrs? Alas! not so. "Man is born to trouble, as the sparks fly upward." At every "gate of life"—as the Orientalists have beautifully called the different ages—he is beset by peril. Temptations allure his youth; misfortunes darken the pathway of his manhood, and his old age is encumbered with infirmity and disease. But clothed in the armor of virtue he may resist the temptation; he may cast misfortunes aside and rise triumphantly above them; but to the last —the direst, the most inexorable foe of his race—he must eventually yield, and, stricken down by death, he sinks prostrate into the grave, *and is buried in the rubbish* of his sin and human frailty.

Here then, in Masonry, is what was called the *aphanism*, concealment or disappearance in the Ancient Mysteries. The bitter, but necessary lesson of death has been imparted. The living soul, with the lifeless body which encased it, has disappeared, and *can nowhere be found*. All is darkness—confusion—despair. Divine truth—the WORD—for a time is lost, and the Master Mason may now say, in the language of Hutchinson, "I prepare my sepulchre. I make my grave in the pollution of the earth. I am under the shadow of death."

But if the mythic symbolism ended here, with this lesson of death, then were the lesson incomplete. That teaching would be vain and idle—nay more, it would be corrupt and pernicious—which should stop short of the conscious and innate instinct for another existence. And hence the succeeding portions of the legend are intended to convey the sublime symbolism of a resurrection from the grave and a new birth into a future life. The discovery of the body, which, in the initiations of the ancient mysteries, was called the *euresis*; and its removal, from the polluted grave into which it had been cast, to an honored and sacred place within the precincts of the temple, are all profoundly and beautifully symbolic of that great truth, the discovery of which was the object of all the ancient initiations, as it is almost the whole design of Freemasonry, namely, that when man shall have passed the gates of life and have yielded to the inexorable fiat of death, he shall then (not in the pictured ritual of an earthly Lodge, but in the realities of that eternal one, of which the former is but an antitype) be raised, at the omnific word of the Grand Master of the Universe, from time to eternity—from the tomb of corruption to the chambers of hope—from the darkness of death to the celestial beams of life—and that his disembodied spirit shall be conveyed as near to the holy of holies of the Divine presence as humanity can ever approach to deity.

Such I conceive to be the true interpretation of the symbolism of the Legend of the Third Degree.

I have said that this mythical history of the Temple Builder was universal in all nations and all rites, and that in no place and at no time had it, by alteration, diminution, or addition, acquired any essentially new or different form: the myth has always remained the same.

But it is not so with its interpretation. That which I have just given, and which I conceive to be the correct one, has been very generally adopted by the Masons of America. But elsewhere, and by various writers, other interpretations have been made, very different in their character, although always agreeing in retaining the general idea of a resurrection or regeneration, or a restoration of something from an inferior to a higher sphere or function.

Thus, some of the earlier continental writers have supposed the myth to have been a symbol of the destruction of the Order of the Templars, looking upon its restoration to its original wealth and dignities as being prophetically symbolized.

In some of the high philosophical degrees it is taught that the whole legend refers to the sufferings and death, with the subsequent resurrection of Christ.

Hutchinson, who has the honor of being the earliest philosophical writer on Freemasonry in England, supposes it to have been intended to embody the idea of the decadence of the Jewish religion and the substitution of the Christian in its place and on its ruins.

Dr. Oliver thinks that it is typical of the murder of Abel and Cain, and that it symbolically refers to the universal death of our race through Adam and its restoration to life in the Redeemer, according to the expression of the Apostle, "as in Adam we all died, so in Christ we all live."

Ragon makes Hiram a symbol of the sun shorn of its vivifying rays and fructifying power by the three winter months, and its restoration to prolific heat by the season of spring.

And, finally, Des Etangs, adopting, in part, the interpretation of Ragon, adds to it another which he calls the moral symbolism of the legend, and supposes that Hiram is no other than eternal reason, whose enemies are the vices that deprave and destroy humanity.

To each of these interpretations it seems to me that there are important objections, though perhaps to some less so than to others.

As to those who seek for an astronomical interpretation of the legend, in which the annual changes of the sun are symbolized, while the ingenuity with which they press their argument cannot but be admired, it is evident that, by such an interpretation, they yield all that Masonry has gained of religious development in past ages, and fall back upon that corruption and perversion of Sabaism from which it was the object, even of the Spurious Freemasonry of antiquity, to rescue its disciples.

The Templar interpretation of the myth must at once be discarded if we would avoid the difficulties of anachronism, unless we deny that the legend existed before the abolition of the Order of Knights Templar, and such denial would be fatal to the Antiquity of Freemasonry.

And as to the adoption of the Christian reference, Hutchinson and, after him, Oliver, profoundly philosophical as are the Masonic speculations of both, have, I am constrained to believe, fallen into a great error in calling the Master Mason's Degree a Christian institution. It is true that it embraces within its scheme the great truths of Christianity upon the subject of the immortality of the soul and the resurrection of the body; but this was to be presumed, because Freemasonry is truth, and Christianity is truth, and all truth must be identical. But the origin of each is different; their histories are dissimilar. The creed of Freemasonry is the primitive one of Noah and his immediate descendants. If Masonry were simply a Christian institution, the Jew and the Moslem, the Brahman and the Buddhist, could not conscientiously partake of its illumination; but its universality is its boast. In its language, citizens of every nation may converse; at its altar men of all religions may kneel; to its creed, disciples of every faith may subscribe.

But the true ancient interpretation of the legend—the universal, Masonic one—for all countries and all ages, undoubtedly, was that the fate of the Temple Builder is but figurative of the pilgrimage of man on earth, through trials and temptations, through sin and sorrow, until his eventual fall beneath the blow of death and his final and glorious resurrection to another and an eternal life.

And now, in conclusion, a word of historical criticism may not be misplaced. It is not at all essential to the value of the symbolism that the legend shall be proved to be historical. Whether considered as a truthful narrative of an event that actually transpired during the building of the Temple, or simply as a myth embodying the utterance of a religious sentiment, the symbolic lesson of life and death and immortality is still contained in its teachings, and commands our earnest attention.

Legislation. On the subject of that crying sin of the Order—over-legislation by Grand Lodges—Gov. Thomas Brown, formerly Grand Master of Florida, has wisely said: "Too much legislation is the vice of the present day, as well in *Masonic* as in civil government. The same thirst for change and innovation which has prompted tyros and demagogues to legislate upon constitutional law, and write expositions of the common law, has prompted uninformed and unscrupulous Masons to legislate upon the landmarks of Masonry."

Lehrling. German for an Entered Apprentice.

Leland, John. An eminent English antiquary, the chaplain of King Henry VIII., who appointed him "King's Antiquary," a title which he was the first and last to bear. The king also directed him to search after the antiquities of England, "and peruse the libraries of all cathedrals, abbies, priories, colleges, etc., as also all places wherein records, writings, and secrets of antiquity were deposited." Leland, accordingly, traveled over England for several years, and made many collections of manuscripts, which were afterward deposited in the Bodleian Library. He was a man of great learning and industry. He was born in London in the beginning of the sixteenth century (the exact year is uncertain), and died on the 18th of April, 1552. Anthony Wood says that he was by far the most eminent historian and antiquary ever born in England. His connection with Freemasonry arises from the manuscript containing the questions of King Henry VI., which he is said to have copied from the original. (See *Leland Manuscript.*)

Leland Manuscript. There is no one of the old Records of Freemasonry, except, perhaps, the Charter of Cologne, that has given rise to more controversy among the critics than the one generally known as the "Leland Manuscript." It derives this name from the statement made in its title, which is: "Certayne questyons with awnsweres to the same, concernynge the mystery of maconrye; wryttene by the hande of Kynge Henry the Sixthe of the name, and faythfullye copied by me, Johan Leylande Antiquarius, by the commaunde of His Highnesse." It first appeared in the *Gentleman's Magazine* for 1753 (p. 417), where it purports to be a reprint of a pamphlet published five years before at Frankfort. The title of the paper in the *Gentleman's Magazine* is: "Copy of a small pamphlet, consisting of twelve pages in 8vo, printed in Germany in 1748, entitled 'Ein Brief von dem berühmten Heren Johann Locke betreffend die Frey-Maurerein. So auf einem Schreib-Tisch eines verstorbnen Bruders ist gefunden worden.'" That is, "A Letter of the famous Mr. John Locke relating to Freemasonry. As found in the writing-desk of a deceased brother." Hearne copied it in his *Life of Leland* (p. 67), prefacing it with the remark that "it also appears that an ancient manuscript of Leland's has long remained in the Bodleian Library, unnoticed in any account of our author yet published." Hearne speaks of it thus:

"The original is said to be in the handwriting of King Henry VI., and copied by Leland by order of His Highness (King Henry VIII.). If the authenticity of this ancient monument of literature remains unquestioned, it demands particular notice in the present publication, on account of the singularity of the subject, and no less from a due regard to the royal writer, and our author, his transcriber, indefatigable in every part of literature: it will also be admitted, acknowledgment is due to the learned Mr. Locke, who, amidst the closest studies and the most strict attention to human understanding, could unbend his mind in search of this ancient treatise, which he first brought from obscurity in the year 1696."

The Manuscript purports to be a series of questions proposed by Henry VI. and answers given by the Masons. It is accompanied by an introductory letter and a commentary by Mr. Locke, together with a glossary of the archaic words. The best account of the Manuscript is contained in the letter of Locke to a nobleman, said to be the Earl of Pembroke, dated May 6, 1696, in which, after stating that he had procured a copy of it from the Bodleian Library, he adds:

"The Manuscript of which this is a copy appears to be about one hundred and sixty years old; yet (as your Lordship will observe by the title) it is itself a copy of one yet more ancient by about one hundred years. For the original is said to have been in the handwriting of King Henry the VI. Where that prince had it is an uncertainty; but it seems to me to be an examination (taken, perhaps, before the King) of some one of the Brotherhood of Masons, among whom he entered himself, as 'tis said, when he came out of his minority, and thenceforth put a stop to a persecution that had been raised against them."

After its appearance in the *Gentleman's Magazine*, which first introduced the knowledge of it to the world, and in Huddesford's *L. of Leland*, who evidently copied it from the *Magazine*, it next appeared, in 1764, in the *Pocket Companion*, and in 1769 in Calcott's *Candid Disquisition*. In 1775, Hutchinson introduced it into his *Spirit of Masonry*. Dermott published it in his *Ahiman Rezon*, and Preston in his *Illustrations*. Noorthouck, in 1784, embodied it in his edition of the *Constitutions;* and it has since been repeatedly published in England and America, so that the Craft have had every opportunity of becoming familiar with its contents. Translations of it have also been given in French by Thory, in his *Acta Latomorum;* in German by Lenning, in his *Encyclopädie;* by Krause, in his *Kunsturkunden*, and also by Fessler and several other French and German writers.

This document—so important, if true, as a record of the condition of Freemasonry in the beginning of the fifteenth century—has been from an early period attacked and defended with equal vehemence by those who have denied and those who have maintained its authenticity. As early as 1787, the Baron de Chefdebien, in a discourse entitled *Recherches Maçonniques à l'usage des Frères de Régime primif de Narbonne*, read before the Congress of the Philalethans, attacked the authenticity of the document. Thory also, although acknowledging that he wished that the Manuscript was true, presented his objections to its authenticity in a memoir read in

1806 before the Tribunal of the Philosophic Rite. His objections are eight in number, and are to this effect: 1. That it was not published in any of the early editions of the works of Locke. 2. That it was printed for the first time at Frankfort, in 1748. 3. That it was not known in England until 1753. 4. That Anderson makes no mention of it. 5. That it is not in any of the editions of Leland's works printed before 1772. 6. That Dr. Plot contends that Henry VI. was never made a Mason. 7. That the Manuscript says that Masonry was brought from the East by the Venetians. 8. That the troubles in the reign of Henry VI., and his incapacity, render it improbable that he would have occupied his mind with the subject of Freemasonry. The sixth and eighth of these objections merely beg the question; and the seventh is puerile, founded on ignorance of the meaning of the word "Venetian." But the other objections have much weight. Sloane, in his *New Curiosities of Literature* (1849, vol. ii., p. 80), attacks the document with the bitterness which he usually displays wherever Freemasonry is concerned.

Halliwell, in his *Early History of Freemasonry in England* (p. 40), has advanced the following arguments against its authenticity:

"It is singular that the circumstances attending its publication should have led no one to suspect its authenticity. I was at the pains of making a long search in the Bodleian Library last summer, in the hopes of finding the original, but without success. In fact, there can be but little doubt that this celebrated and well-known document is a forgery!

"In the first place, why should such a document have been printed abroad? Was it likely that it should have found its way to Frankfort, nearly half a century afterwards, and been published without any explanation of the source whence it was obtained? Again, the orthography is most grotesque, and too gross ever to have been penned either by Henry VI. or Leland, or both combined. For instance, we have Peter Gower, a Grecian, explained in a note by the fabricator—for who else could have solved it?—to be Pythagoras! As a whole, it is but a clumsy attempt at deception, and is quite a parallel to the recently discovered one of the *first Englishe Mercurie*."

Among the German opponents of the Manuscript are Lessing, Keller, and Findel; and more recently, the iconoclasts of England, who have been attacking so many of the ancient records of the Craft, have not left this one unspared.

On the other hand, it has ranked among its advocates some of the most learned Masons of England, Germany, and France, of whom may be named Krause, Fessler, Lenning, Reghellini, Preston, Hutchinson, Calcott (these three, perhaps, without critical examination), and Oliver. Of these the language of the last may be cited as a specimen of the arguments adduced in its favor.

"This famous Manuscript," says Dr. Oliver (*Freemasons' Quart. Rev.*, 1840, p. 10), "possesses the reputation of having converted the learned Locke, who was initiated after carefully perusing and analyzing it. Before any faith can be placed on this invaluable document, it will be necessary to say a word respecting its authenticity. I admit that there is some degree of mystery about it, and doubts have been entertained whether it be not a forgery. We have the strongest presumptive proofs that it was in existence about the middle of the last century, because the utmost publicity was given to it; and as at that time Freemasonry was beginning to excite a considerable share of public attention, the deception, had it been such, would have been publicly exposed by its opponents, who appear to have used the lash of ridicule very freely, as witness Hogarth's picture of *Night*, where the principal figures represent some brethren, decorated with aprons and jewels, returning from the Lodge in a state of intoxication; the broad sheet of the *Scald Miserables*, and other prints and publications in which Freemasonry is burlesqued. But no attempt was ever made to invalidate its claim to be a genuine document."

After enumerating the several books in which it had been published, he resumes his argument, as follows:

"Being thus universally diffused, had it been a suspected document, its exposure would certainly have been attempted; particularly about the close of the last century, when the progress of Masonry was sensibly checked by the publication of works which charged it with being the depository of principles fatal equally to the peace and religion of civil society; and if a forgery, it would have been unable to have endured the test of a critical examination. But no such attempt was made; and the presumption therefore is that the document is authentic.

"I should be inclined to pronounce, from internal evidence only, that the 'Letter and Annotations' were written by Locke; but there are corroborating facts which appear conclusive; for this great philosopher was actually residing at Oates, the country-seat of Sir Francis Masham, at the time when the paper is dated; and shortly afterwards he went up to town, where he was initiated into Masonry. These facts are fully proved by Locke's Letters to Mr. Molyneux, dated March 30 and July 2, 1696. For these reasons I entertain no doubt of the genuineness and authenticity of this valuable Manuscript."

If my own opinion is worth giving on this subject, I should say with much reluctance, and against my own wishes, that there is neither internal nor external evidence of the authenticity of this document to make it a sufficient foundation for historical evidence. [R. F. Gould (*Hist. of F. M.*, i., 489) styles the document "an impudent forgery."—E. L. H.]

Lemanceau. A zealous French Mason, and the possessor of a fine collection of degrees, the nomenclature of which is preserved by Thory in his *Acta Latomorum*. The most important are referred to in the present work.

Lemierre, A. M. Born in 1733, died in 1793. A writer of merit who belonged to the "Neuf Sœurs," and was present at the reception of Voltaire.

Length of the Lodge. See *Extent of the Lodge*.

Lenning, C. The assumed name of a learned German Mason, who resided at Paris in 1817, where Krause speaks of him as an estimable man and well-informed Freemason. He was the first projector of the *Encyclopädie der Freimaurerei*, which Findel justly calls "one of the most learned and remarkable works in Masonic literature." The manuscript coming into the possession of the Leipsic bookseller, Brockhaus, he engaged Friedrich Mossdorf to edit it. He added so much to the original, revising and amplifying all the most important articles and adding many new ones, that Kloss catalogues it in his *Bibliographie* as the work of Mossdorf. The *Encyclopädie* is in three volumes, of which the first was published in 1822, the second in 1824, and the third in 1828. A second edition, under the title of *Handbuch der Freimaurerei*, was published under the editorship of Schletter and Zille. A third edition in two volumes was published in 1900 (first vol.) and 1901 (second vol.).

Lenoir, Alexandre. A celebrated archeologist, who was born at Paris in 1761. Having studied at the Mazarin College, he entered the studio of Doyeu, and successfully cultivated painting. In 1790, the National Assembly having decreed that the treasures of art in the suppressed churches and convents should be collected at the Petits-Augustins, he was appointed the Conservator of the depot, which was subsequently called the Museum, of which he was then made the Director. He there collected more than five hundred monuments rescued from destruction, and classified them with great care. On the conversion of the garden of Moasseaux into a Museum of Monuments, he was appointed one of the administrators, and subsequently the administrator of the monuments of the Church of St. Denis. In all these appointments, Lenoir exhibited his taste and judgment as an archeologist. He was a member of the Society of Antiquaries of France, to whose *Transactions* he contributed several memoirs.

The Metropolitan Chapter of France had, from the year 1777, annually held philosophical conventions, at which lectures on Masonic subjects were delivered by such men as Court de Gebelin. In 1789 these conventions were discontinued in consequence of the political troubles of the times, but they were renewed in 1812 by M. Lenoir, who delivered before the Chapter a course of eight lectures on the relations which exist between the ancient mysteries of the Egyptians and the Greeks and those of Freemasonry. In 1814, he published the substance of these lectures in a work entitled *La Franche-Maçonnerie rendue à sa veritable origine, ou l'Antiquité de la Franche-Maçon-*

nerie prouvée par l'Explication des Mystères Anciens et Modernes (Paris, 4to, p. 304). The theory of the author being that the mysteries of Freemasonry are only a repetition of those of antiquity, he attempts to support it by investigations into the ancient initiations that are marked with profound learning, although the work was severely criticised in the *Journal de Débats*. He had previously published, in 1809, a work in three volumes, entitled *Nouvelle Explication des Hieroglyphes ou Anciens Allegories sacrées des Egiptiennes*. He died at Paris, June 12, 1839.

Leontica. Ancient sacrificial festivals in honor of the sun; the officiating priests being termed Leontes.

Leo XII., Pope. Born in 1760, died in 1829. On the 13th of March, 1825, he issued the well-remembered bull, beginning "Quo graviora mala," against the Freemasons.

Lepage. One of those French Masons who in the latter part of the last century occupied themselves in the accumulation of *cahiers* or rituals of Masonic degrees. Most of the degrees in his collection, which is said to have been a valuable one, are referred to by Thory in the nomenclature contained in his *Acta Latomorum*.

Lerouge, André Joseph Etienne. A man of letters and zealous Mason of Paris, born at Commercy, April 25, 1766. He made a large and valuable collection of manuscript and printed degrees. He died in 1834, and on the 7th of January, 1835, his collection was sold at public auction. Thory has made use of it in his *Nomenclature des Grades*. Lerouge was the author of several didactic writings on Masonic subjects, all of which, however, have had but an ephemeral existence. He was one of the editors of the French Masonic journal *Hermes*, published in 1819, and of the *Melanges de Philosophic, d'Histoire et de Literature Maçonnique*. He was a man of much learning, and is said to have supplied several of his Masonic contemporaries with assistance in the preparation of their works.

Lesser Lights. In the lecture of the First Degree we are told that a Lodge has three symbolic lesser lights; one of these is in the East, one in the West, and one in the South. There is no light in the North, because King Solomon's Temple, of which every Lodge is a representation, was placed so far north of the ecliptic that the sun and moon, at their meridian height, could dart no rays into the northern part thereof. The North we therefore Masonically call a place of darkness.

This symbolic use of the three lesser lights is very old, being found in the earliest lectures of the last century.

The three lights, like the three principal officers and the three principal supports, refer, undoubtedly, to the three stations of the sun —its rising in the East, its meridian in the South, and its setting in the West; and thus the symbolism of the Lodge, as typical of the world, continues to be preserved.

The use of lights in all religious ceremonies is an ancient custom. There was a seven-branched candlestick in the tabernacle, and in the Temple "were the golden candlesticks, five on the right hand and five on the left." They were always typical of moral, spiritual, or intellectual light.

The custom prevalent in some localities, of placing the burning tapers, or three symbolic lesser lights, East, West, and South, near the altar, is sometimes changed so that these respective lights are burning on or beside the pedestals of the Master and his two Wardens at their several stations. In the old Teutonic mythology, and in accordance with Medieval court usage, flaming lights or fires burned before each column, similarly situated, on which rested the image of Odin, Thor, and Frey. These columns are further represented as Wisdom, Strength, and Beauty, sustaining the "Starry-decked Heaven," roof or ceiling colored blue, with stars.

Lessing, Gottfried Ephraim. A learned litterateur of Germany, who was born at Kaumitz, in the Neiderlausetz, January 22, 1729, and died on the 15th of February, 1781, at Woefenbutal, where he was librarian to the Duke of Brunswick. Lessing was initiated in a Lodge at Hamburg, and took great interest in the Institution. His theory, that it sprang out of a secret association of Templars which had long existed in London, and was modified in form by Sir Christopher Wren, has long been rejected, if it was ever admitted by any; but in his two works *Ernst und Falk* and *Nathan der Weise*, he has given profound and comprehensive views on the genius and spirit of Freemasonry. Lessing was the most eminent litterateur of his age, and has been styled "the man who was the forerunner of the philosophers, and whose criticisms supplied the place of poetry." (See *Ernest and Falk*.)

Lessons. The passages of Scripture recited by the Prelate in the ceremony of inducting a candidate into the Masonic Order of Knights Templar. It is an ecclesiastical term, and is used by the Templars because these passages are intended to instruct the candidate in reference to the incidents of our Savior's life which are referred to in the ritual.

Letter of Application. More properly called a *Petition*, which see.

Letters Patent. See *Patents*.

Lettuce. A sacred plant used in the mysteries of Adonis, and therefore the analogue of the Acacia in the mysteries of Freemasonry.

Leucht. A Masonic charlatan of the eighteenth century, better known by his assumed name of *Johnson*, which see.

Level. In Freemasonry, the level is a symbol of equality; not of that social equality which would destroy all distinctions of rank and position, and beget confusion, insubordination, and anarchy; but of that fraternal equality which, recognising the fatherhood of God, admits as a necessary corollary the brotherhood of man. It, therefore, teaches us that, in the sight of the Great Architect of the Universe, his creatures, who are at an immeasurable distance from him, move upon the same plane; as the far-moving stars, which though millions of miles apart, yet seem to shine upon the same canopy of the sky. In this view, the level teaches us that all men are equal, subject to the same infirmities, hastening to the same goal, and preparing to be judged by the same immutable law.

The level is deemed, like the square and the plumb, of so much importance as a symbol, that it is repeated in many different relations. First, it is one of the jewels of the Lodge; in the English system a movable, in the American an immovable, one. This leads to its being adopted as the proper official ensign of the Senior Warden, because the Craft when at labor, at which time he presides over them, are on a common level of subordination. And then it is one of the working-tools of a Fellow-Craft, still retaining its symbolism of equality.

Levi, Eliphas. The pseudonym of Louis Alphonse Constance, a prolific writer on Magical Masonry, or of works in which he seeks to connect the symbols of Masonry with the dogmas of the High Magic. His principal works, which abound in dreamy speculations, are *Dogme et Rituel de la Haute Magie*, Paris, 1860; *Histoire de la Magie*, same place and year; and *Le Clef des Grand Mystères*, published a year afterward.

Levit, Der. The Levite was the fourth grade of the Order of the Knights of the True Light.

Levite, Knight. The Knight Levite was the fourth section of the Seventh Degree of the Rite of Clerks of Strict Observance.

Levite of the External Guard. The lowest of the nine Orders of the Priesthood, or highest of the Masonic degrees in the Order of the Temple as modified by Fabré-Palaprat. It was equivalent to Kadosh.

Levites. Those descendants of Levi who were employed in the lowest ministerial duties of the Temple, and were thus subordinate to the priests, who were the lineal descendants of Aaron. They are represented in some of the high degrees.

Levite, Sacrificer. A degree in the collection of the Mother Lodge of the Philosophic Scottish Rite.

Levitikon. There is a spurious Gospel of St. John, supposed to have been forged in the fifteenth century, which contradicts the genuine Gospel in many particulars. It contains an introduction and a commentary, said to have been written by Nicephorus, a Greek monk of Athens. This commentary is called the "Levitikon." Out of this Gospel and its commentary, Fabré-Palaprat, about the year 1814, composed a liturgy for the sect of Johannites, which he had established and attached to the Order of the Temple at Paris.

Levy. A collection of men raised for a particular purpose. The lectures tell us that the timbers for building the Temple at Jerusalem were felled in the forests of Lebanon, where a *levy* of thirty thousand men of Jerusalem were employed by monthly courses of ten thousand. Adoniram was placed over this levy. The facts are derived from the statement in 1 Kings v. 13, 14: "And King Solomon raised a levy out of all Israel; and the levy was thirty thousand men. And he sent them to Lebanon ten thousand a month by courses; a month they were in Lebanon and two months at home: and Adoniram was over the levy." These wood-cutters were not Tyrians, but all Israelites.

Lewis. 1. An instrument in Operative Masonry. It is an iron cramp which is inserted in a cavity prepared for that purpose in any large stone, so as to give attachment to a pulley and hook whereby the stone may be conveniently raised to any height and deposited in its proper position. It is well described by Mr. Gibson, in the *British Archæologia* (vol. x., p. 127); but he is in error in attributing its invention to a French architect in the time of Louis XIV., and its name to that monarch. The contrivance was known to the Romans, and several taken from old ruins are now in the Vatican. In the ruins of Whitby Abbey, in England, which was founded by Oswy, King of Northumberland, in 658, large stones were discovered, with the necessary excavation for the insertion of a lewis. The word is most probably derived from the old French *lévis*, any contrivance for lifting. The modern French call the instrument a *louve*.

2. In the English system, the lewis is found on the tracing-board of the Entered Apprentice, where it is used as a symbol of strength, because, by its assistance, the Operative Mason is enabled to lift the heaviest stones with a comparatively trifling exertion of physical power. It has not been adopted as a symbol by the American Masons, except in Pennsylvania, where, of course, it receives the English interpretation.

3. The son of a Mason is, in England, called a lewis, because it is his duty to support the sinking powers and aid the failing strength of his father; or, as Oliver has expressed it, "to bear the burden and heat of the day, that his parents may rest in their old age; thus rendering the evening of their lives peaceful and happy." In the rituals of the middle of the last century he was called a *louffton*. From this the French derived their word *lufton*, which they apply in the same way. They also employ the word *louveteau*, and call the daughter of a Mason *louvetine*. Louveteau is probably derived directly from the louve, the French name of the implement; but it is a singular coincidence that louveteau also means a young wolf, and that in the Egyptian mysteries of Isis the candidate was made to wear the mask of a wolf's head. Hence, a wolf and a candidate in these mysteries were often used as synonymous terms. Macrobius, in his *Saturnalia*, says, in reference to this custom, that the ancients perceived a relationship between the sun, the great symbol in these mysteries, and a wolf, which the candidate represented at his initiation. For, he remarks, as the flocks of sheep and cattle fly and disperse at the sight of the wolf, so the flocks of

stars disappear at the approach of the sun's light. The learned reader will also recollect that in the Greek language *lukos* signifies both the sun and a wolf. Hence some etymologists have sought to derive *louveteau*, the son of a Mason, from *louveteau*, a young wolf. But the more direct derivation from *louve*, the operative instrument is preferable.

In Browne's *Master Key*, which is supposed to represent the Prestonian lecture, we find the following definition:

"What do we call the son of a Freemason?

"A lewis.

"What does that denote?

"Strength.

"How is a lewis depicted in a Mason's Lodge?

"As a cramp of metal, by which, when fixed into a stone, great and ponderous weights are raised to a certain height and fixed upon their proper basis, without which Operative Masons could not so conveniently do.

"What is the duty of a lewis, the son of a Mason, to his aged parents?

"To bear the heavy burden in the heat of the day and help them in time of need, which, by reason of their great age, they ought to be exempted from, so as to render the close of their days happy and comfortable.

"His privilege for so doing?

"To be made a Mason before any other person, however dignified by birth, rank, or riches, unless he, through complaisance, waives this privilege."

[The term occurs in this sense in the *Constitutions* of 1738 at the end of the Deputy Grand Master's song—in allusion to the expected birth of George III., son of Frederick, Prince of Wales:

"May a Lewis be born, whom the World shall admire, Serene as his Mother, August as his Sire."

It is sometimes stated that a Lewis may be initiated before he has reached the age of twenty-one; but this is not so under the English Constitution, by which a dispensation is required in all cases of initiation under age, as was distinctly stated at the meeting of the Grand Lodge of England held on December 2, 1874. The Scotch Constitution, however, does allow a Lewis to be entered at eighteen years of age. (Rule 180.)

No such right is recognized in America, where the symbolism of the Lewis is unknown, though it has been suggested, not without some probability, that the initiation of Washington when he was only twenty years and eight months old, may be explained by a reference to this supposed privilege of Lewis.—E. L. H.]

Lexington, Congress of. This Congress was convoked in 1853, at Lexington, Kentucky, for the purpose of attempting to form a General Grand Lodge.* A plan of constitution was proposed, but a sufficient number of Grand Lodges did not accede to the proposition to give it efficacy.

---

* See *General Grand Lodge*.

Libanus. The Latin name of *Lebanon*, which see.

Libation. Among the Greeks and Romans the libation was a religious ceremony, consisting of the pouring of wine or other liquid upon the ground, or, in a sacrifice, upon the head of the victim after it had been first tasted by the priest and by those who stood next to him. The libations were usually of unmixed wine, but were sometimes of mingled wine and water. Libations are used in some of the chivalric and the high degrees of Masonry.

Libavius, Andreas. A learned German physician, who was born at Halle, in Saxony, and died at Coburg, where he was rector of the Gymnasium in 1616. He was a vehement opponent of Paracelsus and of the Rosicrucians. In 1613 he published at Frankfort his *Syntagma selectorum alchimia arcanorum*, in two folio volumes, and two years after, an *Appendix*, in which he attacks the Society of the Rosicrucians, and analyzes the *Confessio* of Valentine Andreä. De Quincey has used the works of Libavius in his article on Secret Societies.

Liber. Liberty. Of which the eagle, in the Rose Croix Degree, is symbolical. Liberty of thought, speech, and action, within the bounds of civil, political, and conscientious law, without license. A book, and hence the word library, or collection of books. It was also one of the names of the god Bacchus. The freedom which knowledge confers. Liber, the bark, or inner rind of a tree, on which books were originally written; hence, leaves

of a book and leaves of a tree; or, similarly in Latin, folio of a book, the foliage of a tree. Thus, the "tree of knowledge" becomes the "book of wisdom"; the "tree of life" becomes the "book of life." (See *Lakak Deror Pessah* and *Libertas*.) The Bridge mentioned in the Sixteenth Degree, Scottish Rite, has the initials of Liberty of Passage over its arches.

Liberal Arts and Sciences. We are indebted to the Scholastic philosophers of the Middle Ages for the nomenclature by which they distinguished the seven sciences then best known to them. With the metaphorical spirit of the age in which they lived, they called the two classes into which they divided them the *trivium*, or meeting of three roads, and the *quadrivium*, or meeting of four roads; calling grammar, logic, and rhetoric the trivium, and arithmetic, geometry, music, and astronomy the quadrivium. These they styled the seven liberal arts and sciences, to separate them from the mechanical arts which were practised by the handicraftsmen. The liberal man, *liberalis homo*, meant, in the Middle Ages, the man who was his own master—free, independent, and often a nobleman.

Mosheim, speaking of the state of literature in the eleventh century, uses the following language: "The seven liberal arts, as they were now styled, were taught in the greatest part of the schools that were erected in this century for the education of youth. The first stage of these sciences was grammar, which was followed successively by rhetoric and logic. When the disciple, having learned these branches, which were generally known by the name of *trivium*, extended his ambition further, and was desirous of new improvement in the sciences, he was conducted slowly through the *quadrivium* (arithmetic, music, geometry, and astronomy) to the very summit of literary fame."

The Freemasons of the Middle Ages, always anxious to elevate their profession above the position of a mere operative art, readily assumed these liberal arts and sciences as a part of their course of knowledge, thus seeking to assimilate themselves rather to the scholars who were above them than to the workmen who were below them.* Hence in all the Old Constitutions we find these liberal arts and sciences introduced at the beginning as forming an essential part of the body of Masonry. Thus, in the Lansdowne MS., whose date is about 1560 (and it may be taken as a fair specimen of all the others), these sciences are thus referred to:

"Wee minde to shew you the charge that belongs to every trew Mason to keep, for in good and ffaith if you take good heed it is well worthy to be kept for A worthy Craft and curious science,—Sirs, there be Seaven Liberall Sciencies of the which the Noble Craft of Masonry is one." And then the writer proceeds to define them in the order which they still retain. It is noteworthy, however, that that order must have been changed; for in what is probably the earliest of the manuscripts—the Regius MS.—geometry appears as the last, instead of the fifth of the sciences, and arithmetic as the sixth. (Lines 557–563.)

It is not therefore surprising that, on the revival of Masonry in 1717, these seven liberal arts and sciences were made a part of the system of instruction. At first, of course, they were placed in the Entered Apprentice's Degree, that being the most important degree of the period, and they were made to refer to the seven Masons who composed a Lodge. Afterward, on the more methodical division of the degrees, they were transferred to the Fellow-Craft, because that was the degree symbolic of science, and were made to refer to seven of the steps of the winding stairs, that being itself, when properly interpreted, a symbol of the progress of knowledge. And there they still remain.

Libertas. (Latin) Liberty. A significant

* The claim has been made that Charlemagne, in his castle at Aix-la-Chapelle, set apart a separate place where the Seven Liberal Arts and Sciences were taught. [E. E. C.]

word in the Red Cross Degree. It refers to the "liberty of passage" gained by the returning Jews over their opponents at the river Euphrates, as described in the Scottish Rite degree of Knight of the East, where the old French rituals have "liberté du passer."

Liberte, Ordre de la. (*Order of Liberty.*) A French androgyn Order existing in Paris in 1740, and the precursor of "La Maçonnerie d'Adoption." (Thory, *Acta Lat.*, i., 320.)

Libertine. The Charges of 1722 commence by saying that "a Mason is obliged by his tenure to obey the moral law; and if he rightly understands the art, he will never be a stupid Atheist, nor an *irreligious libertine*." (*Constitutions*, 1723, p. 50.) The word "libertine" there used conveyed a meaning different from that which it now bears. In the present usage of language it signifies a profligate and licentious person, but originally it meant a freethinker, or Deist. Derived from the Latin "libertinus," a man that was once a bondsman but who has been made free, it was metaphorically used to designate one who had been released, or who had released himself from the bonds of religious belief, and become in matters of faith a doubter or denier. Hence "a stupid Atheist" denoted, to use the language of the Psalmist, "the fool who has said in his heart there is no God," while an "irreligious libertine" designated the man who, with a degree less of unbelief, denies the distinctive doctrines of revealed religion. And this meaning of the expression connects itself very appropriately with the succeeding paragraph of the Charge. "But though in ancient times, Masons were charged in every country to be of the religion of that country or nation, whatever it was, yet 'tis now thought more expedient only to oblige them to that religion in which all men agree, leaving their particular opinions to themselves."

The expression "irreligious libertine," alluding, as it does, to a scoffer at religious truths, is eminently suggestive of the religious character of our Institution, which, founded as it is on the great doctrines of religion, cannot be properly appreciated by anyone who doubts or denies their truth.

"Liberty, Equality, Fraternity." The motto of the French Freemasons.

Liberty of Passage. A significant phrase in the high degrees. (See *Libertas*.) The French rituals designate it by the letters L∴ D∴ P∴ as the initials of *liberté de passer*, or liberty of passage. But Bro. Pike proposes to interpret these letters as *liberté de penser*, liberty of thought; the prerogative of a freeman and a Freemason.

Library. It is the duty as well as the interest of Lodges to facilitate the efforts of the members in the acquisition of Masonic knowledge, and no method is more appropriate than the formation of Masonic libraries. The establishment of a Grand Lodge library is of course not objectionable, but it is of far less value and importance than a Lodge library. The original outlay of a few dollars in the beginning for its establishment, and of a few more annually for its maintenance and increase, would secure to every Lodge in the land a rich treasury of Masonic reading for the information and improvement of its members. The very fact that Masonic books were within their reach, showing themselves on the well-filled shelves at every meeting, and ready at their hands for the mere asking or the trouble of taking them down, would induce many brethren to read who never yet have read a page or even a line upon the subject of Masonic history and science.

Considering the immense number of books that have been published on the subject of Speculative Masonry, many of which would be rendered accessible to every one by the establishment of Lodge libraries, the Mason who would then be ignorant of the true genius of his art would be worthy of all shame and reproach.

As thoughtful municipalities place public fountains in their parks and at the corners of streets, that the famished wayfarer may allay his thirst and receive physical refreshment, so should Masonic Lodges place such intellectual fountains in reach of their members, that they might enjoy mental refreshment. Such fountains are libraries; and the Lodge which spends fifty dollars, more or less, upon a banquet, and yet does without a library, commits a grave Masonic offense; for it refuses, or at least neglects, to diffuse that light among its children which its obligation requires it to do.

Of two Lodges—the one without and the other with a library—the difference is this, that the one will have more ignorance in it than the other. If a Lodge takes delight in an ignorant membership, let it forego a library. If it thinks there is honor and reputation and pleasure in having its members well informed, it will give them means of instruction.*

Libyan or **Lybic Chain.** The eighty-fifth grade of the Rite of Memphis; old style.

Licht, Ritter von Wahren. Knight of the True Light, presumed to have been founded in Austria, in 1780, by Hans Heinrich Freiherr von Ecker and Eckhoffen. It consisted of five grades.

Lichtseher, Oder Erleuchtete. (*The Enlightened.*) A mystical sect established at Schlettstadt by Küper Martin Steinbach, in the sixteenth century. Mentioned in the *Handbuch*, in 1566, by Pastor Reinhard Lutz. It delved in Scriptural interpretation.

Lieutenant Grand Commander. The title of the second and third officers of a Grand Consistory in the Ancient and Accepted Scot-

---

* The three most important Masonic libraries in America are: The Grand Lodge Library of Iowa, at Cedar Rapids, it having a separate building devoted entirely to its uses, and containing a large number of books and collections, many of which are rare. The Grand Lodges of both Pennsylvania and Massachusetts have been ardent collectors of Masonic literature. The Grand Lodge of Massachusetts has lately acquired by gift of the late Samuel R. Lawrence his own library and that of Enoch T. Carson, which he had purchased.   [E. E. C.]

tish Rite, and the second officer in a Supreme Council.

Life. The three stages of human life are said in the lectures to be symbolized by the three degrees of Ancient Craft Masonry, and the doctrine is illustrated in the Third Degree by the emblem of the *Steps on the Master's Carpet*, which see.

Life, Eternal. See *Eternal Life*.

Life Member. It is the custom in some Lodges to permit a member to become a life member by paying dues for some number of years (21 to 25) determined by the By-Laws of the Lodge or the immediate payment of a sum of money, after which he is released from any subsequent payment of quarterly or yearly dues. Such a system is of advantage in a pecuniary sense to the Lodge, if the money paid for life membership is invested in profitable stock, because the interest continues to accrue to the Lodge even after the death of a member. A Lodge consisting entirely of life members would be a Lodge the number of whose members might increase, but could never decrease. Life members are subject to all the discipline of the Lodge, such as suspension or expulsion, just as the other members. [Such Life Membership is, however, not recognized by the Grand Lodge of England, which restricts the privileges of the Craft to those who continue to be subscribing members of some Lodge. (*Report of G. L. of England for June, 1873.*)—E. L. H.]

Light. Light is an important word in the Masonic system. It conveys a far more recondite meaning than it is believed to possess by the generality of readers. It is in fact the first of all the symbols presented to the neophyte, and continues to be presented to him in various modifications throughout all his future progress in his Masonic career. It does not simply mean, as might be supposed, *truth* or *wisdom*, but it contains within itself a far more abstruse allusion to the very essence of Speculative Masonry, and embraces within its capacious signification all the other symbols of the Order. Freemasons are emphatically called the "sons of light," because they are, or at least are entitled to be, in possession of the true meaning of the symbol; while the profane or uninitiated who have not received this knowledge are, by a parity of expression, said to be in darkness.

The connection of material light with this emblematic and mental illumination, was prominently exhibited in all the ancient systems of religion and esoteric mysteries.

Among the Egyptians, the hare was the hieroglyphic of eyes that are open, because that animal was supposed to have his eyes always open. The priests afterward adopted the hare as the symbol of the moral illumination revealed to the neophytes in the contemplation of the Divine truth, and hence, according to Champollion, it was also the symbol of Osiris, their principal divinity, and the chief object of their mystic rites—thus showing the intimate connection that they maintained in their symbolic language between the process of initiation and the contemplation of divinity. On this subject a remarkable coincidence has been pointed out by M. Portal (*Symb. des Egypt*, 69), in the Hebrew language. There the word for "hare" is *arnebet*, which seems to be compounded of *aur*, "light," and *nabat*, "to see"; so that the word which among the Egyptians was used to designate an initiation, among the Hebrews meant to see the light.

If we proceed to an examination of the other systems of religion which were practised by the nations of antiquity, we shall find that light always constituted a principal object of adoration, as the primordial source of knowledge and goodness, and that darkness was with them synonymous with ignorance and evil. Dr. Beard (*Encyc. Bib. Lit.*) attributes this view of the Divine origin of light among the Eastern nations, to the fact that "light in the East has a clearness and brilliancy, is accompanied by an intensity of heat, and is followed in its influence by a largeness of good, of which the inhabitants of less genial climates have no conception. Light easily and naturally became, in consequence, with Orientals, a representative of the highest human good. All the more joyous emotions of the mind, all the pleasing sensations of the frame, all the happy hours of domestic intercourse, were described under imagery derived from light. The transition was natural—from earthly to heavenly, from corporeal to spiritual things; and so light came to typify true religion and the felicity which it imparts. But as light not only came from God, but also makes man's way clear before him, so it was employed to signify moral truth, and preeminently that divine system of truth which is set forth in the Bible, from its earliest gleamings onward to the perfect day of the Great Sun of Righteousness."

As light was thus adored as the source of goodness, darkness, which is the negation of light, was abhorred as the cause of evil, and hence arose that doctrine which prevailed among the ancients, that there were two antagonistic principles continually contending for the government of the world.

"Light," says Duncan (*Relig. of Prof. Ant.*, 187), "is a source of positive happiness: without it man could barely exist. And since all religious opinion is based on the ideas of pleasure and pain, and the corresponding sensations of hope and fear, it is not to be wondered if the heathen reverenced light. Darkness, on the contrary, by replunging nature, as it were, into a state of nothingness, and depriving man of the pleasurable emotions conveyed through the organ of sight, was ever held in abhorrence, as a source of misery and fear. The two opposite conditions in which man thus found himself placed, occasioned by the enjoyment or the banishment of light, induced him to imagine the existence of two antagonistic principles in nature, to whose dominion he was alternately subjected."

Such was the dogma of Zoroaster, the great Persian philosopher, who, under the names of Ormusd and Ahriman, symbolized these two principles of light and darkness.

Such was also the doctrine, though somewhat modified, of Manes, the founder of the sect of Manichees, who describes God the Father as ruling over the kingdom of light and contending with the powers of darkness.

Pythagoras also maintained this doctrine of two antagonistic principles. He called the one, unity, *light*, the right hand, equality, stability, and a straight line; the other he named binary, *darkness*, the left hand, inequality, instability, and a curved line. Of the colors, he attributed white to the good principle, and black to the evil one.

The Jewish Kabbalists believed that, before the creation of the world, all space was filled with the Infinite Intellectual Light, which afterward withdrew itself to an equal distance from a central point in space, and afterward by its emanation produced future worlds. The first emanation of this surrounding light into the abyss of darkness produced what they called the "Adam Kadmon," the first man, or the first production of the Divine energy.

In the Bhagvat Geeta (one of the religious books of the Brahmans), it is said: "Light and darkness are esteemed the world's eternal ways; he who walketh in the former path returneth not—that is, he goeth immediately to bliss; whilst he who walketh in the latter cometh back again upon the earth."

In fact, in all the ancient systems, this reverence for light, as an emblematic representation of the Eternal Principle of Good, is predominant. In the mysteries, the candidate passed, during his initiation, through scenes of utter darkness, and at length terminated his trials by an admission to the splendidly illuminated sacellum, where he was said to have attained pure and perfect light, and where he received the necessary instructions which were to invest him with that knowledge of the Divine truth which had been the object of all his labors.

Lights, Fixed. According to the old rituals of the last century, every Lodge room was furnished, or supposed to be furnished, with three windows, situated in the East, West, and South. They were called the *Fixed Lights*, and their uses were said to be "to light the men to, at, and from their work."

Lights, Greater. The *Bible*, and the *Square and Compasses*, which see. In the Persian initiations, the Archimagus informed the candidate, at the moment of illumination, that the *Divine Lights* were displayed before him.

Light, To Bring to. A technical expression in Masonry meaning to initiate; as, "He was brought to light in such a Lodge," that is, he was initiated in it.

Ligure. לֶשֶׁם. The first stone in the third row of the high priest's breastplate. Commentators have been divided in opinion as to the nature of this stone; but it is now supposed by the best authorities to have been the rubellite, which is a red variety of the tourmaline. The ligure in the breastplate was referred to the tribe of Dan.

Lilis or **Lilith.** In the popular belief of the Hebrews, a female specter, in elegant attire, who secretly destroys children. The fabled wife of Adam, before he married Eve, by whom he begat devils.

Lily. The plant so frequently mentioned in the Old Testament under the name of lily, as an emblem of purity and peace, was the lotus lily of Egypt and India. It occupied a conspicuous place among the ornaments of the Temple furniture. The brim of the molten sea was wrought with flowers of the lotus; the chapiters on the tops of the pillars at the porch, and the tops of the pillars themselves, were adorned with the same plant. Sir Robert Ker Porter, describing a piece of sculpture which he found at Persepolis, says, "Almost every one in this procession holds in his hand a figure like the lotus. This flower was full of meaning among the ancients, and occurs all over the East. Egypt, Persia, Palestine, and India present it everywhere over their architecture, in the hands and on the heads of their sculptured figures, whether in statue or in bas-relief. We also find it in the sacred vestments and architecture of the tabernacle and Temple of the Israelites. The lily which is mentioned by our Savior, as an image of peculiar beauty and glory, when comparing the works of nature with the decorations of art, was a different flower; probably a species of *lilium*. This is also represented in all pictures of the salutation of Gabriel to the Virgin Mary; and, in fact, has been held in mysterious veneration by people of all nations and times. 'It is the symbol of divinity, of purity, and abundance, and of a love most complete in perfection, charity, and benediction; as in Holy Scripture, that mirror of purity, Susanna is defined *Susa*, which signified the lily flower, the chief city of the Persians, bearing that name for excellency. Hence, the lily's three leaves in the arms of France meaneth Piety, Justice, and Charity.' So far, the general impression of a peculiar regard to this beautiful and fragrant flower; but the early Persians attached to it a peculiar sanctity." We must not, however, forget the difference between the lotus of the Old Testament and the lily of the New. The former is a Masonic plant; the latter is scarcely referred to. Nevertheless, through the ignorance of the early translators as to sacred plants, the lotus is constantly used for the lily; and hence the same error has crept into the Masonic rituals. (See *Lotus*.)

Lily-of-the-Valley. A side degree in the Templar system of France.

Lily Work. The lily work which is described as a part of the ornamentation of the two pillars in the porch of Solomon's Temple is said to be, from the whiteness of the plant, symbolic of purity and peace. Properly, it is lotus work. (See *Lily, Lotus,* and *Pillars of the Porch*.)

Limbs. See *Qualifications, Physical*.

Lindner, Friederich Wilhelm. A professor of philosophy in Leipsic, who published in 1818–19 an attack on Freemasonry under the title of *Mac Benac; Er lebet im Sohne; oder das Positive der Freimaurerei*. This work contains some good ideas, although taken from an adverse point of view; but, as Lenning has observed, these bear little fruit because of the fanatical spirit of knight errantry with which he attacks the Institution.

Line. One of the working-tools of a Past Master, and presented to the Master of a Lodge at his installation. (See *Plumb Line*.)

Linear Triad. Oliver says that the Linear Triad is a figure which appears in some old Royal Arch floor-cloths. It bore a reference to the sojourners, who represented the three stones on which prayers and thanksgivings were offered on the discovery of the lost Word; thereby affording an example that it is our duty in every undertaking to offer up our prayers and thanksgivings to the God of our salvation.

Lines, Parallel. See *Parallel Lines*.

Lingam. The lingam and the youi of the Indian mysteries were the same as the phallus and cteis of the Grecian. (See *Phallic Worship*.)

Link. A degree formerly conferred in England, in connection with the Mark Degree, under the title of the "Mark and Link or Wrestle." It is now obsolete.

Linnecar, Richard. The author of the celebrated Masonic anthem beginning

"Let there be Light! th' Almighty spoke;
Refulgent beams from chaos broke,
T' illume the rising earth."

Little is known of his personal history except that he was the Coroner of Wakefield, England, and for many years the Master of the Lodge of Unanimity, No. 238, in that town. He was a zealous and studious Mason. In 1789 he published, at Leeds, a volume of plays, poems, and miscellaneous writings, among which was an essay entitled *Strictures on Freemasonry*, and the anthem already referred to. He appears to have been a man of respectable abilities.

Lion, Chevalier du. (*Knight of the Lion*.) The twentieth grade of the third series of the Metropolitan Chapter of France.

Lion of the Tribe of Judah. See *Tribe of Judah, Lion of the*.

Lion's Paw. A mode of recognition so called because of the rude resemblance made by the hand and fingers to a lion's paw. It refers to the "Lion of the tribe of Judah."

Literature of Masonry. Freemasonry has its literature, which has been rapidly developed in the last few decades of the present century, far more than in any preceding ones. This literature is not to be found in the working of its degrees, in the institution of its Lodges, in the diffusion of its charities, or in the extension of its fraternal ties. Of all these, although necessary and important ingredients of the Order, its literature is wholly independent. This is connected with its ethics as a science of moral, social, and religious philosophy; with its history and archeology, as springing up out of the past times; with its biography as the field in which men of intellect have delighted to labor; and with its bibliography as the record of the results of that labor. It is connected, too, incidentally, with many other arts and sciences. Mythology affords an ample field for discussion in the effort to collate the analogies of classic myths and symbols with its own. Philology submits its laws for application to the origin of its mystic words, all of which are connected with its history. It has, in fine, its science and its philosophy, its poetry and romance. No one who has not studied the literature of Masonry can even dream of its beauty and extent; no one who has studied it can have failed to receive the reward that it bestows.

Litigation. See *Lawsuits.*

Livery. The word *livery* is supposed to be derived from the clothing *delivered* by masters to their servants. The trading companies or gilds of England began about the time of Edward I. to wear a suit of clothing of a form, color, and material peculiar to each company, which was called its livery, and also its clothing. To be admitted into the membership and privileges of the company was called "to have the clothing." The Grocers' Company, for instance, were ordered "to be *clothed* once a year in a suit of livery"; and there is an order in the reign of Henry V. to purchase cloth "for the *clothing* of the brethren of the brewers' craft." There can be no doubt that the usage of speaking of a Mason's clothing, or of his being clothed, is derived from the custom of the gilds. A Mason's clothing, "black dress and white gloves and apron," is, in fact, his livery. (See *Clothed.*)

Livre d'Architecture. The French designation of the book of minutes.

Livre d'Eloquence. A French expression for a collection of minutes of addresses made in a Lodge.

Livre d'Or. French. The *Book of Gold,* which see.

Local Laws. See *Laws of Masonry.*

Locke's Letter. The letter of John Locke which is said to have accompanied the Leland MS., and which contains his comments on it. (See *Leland Manuscript.*)

Lodge. There are three definitions which, in the technical language of Masonry, apply to the word *Lodge.*

1. It is a place in which Freemasons meet. In this sense the words more generally used are *Lodge Room,* which see.

2. It is the assembly or organized body of Freemasons duly congregated for labor or for business. These two distinctions are precisely the same as those to be found in the word "church," which is expressive both of the building in which a congregation meets to worship and the congregation of worshipers themselves. This second definition is what distinguishes a meeting of Symbolic Masons, who constitute a Lodge, from one of Royal Arch Masons, whose meeting would be called a Chapter, or of Cryptic Masons, whose assembly would be a Council.

The word appears in French as *loge;* German, *loge;* Spanish, *logia;* Portuguese, *loja;* and Italian, *loggia.* This is irrefragible evidence that the word was, with the Institution, derived by the Continent of Europe from England.

The derivation of the word is, I think, plain. Ragon says that it comes from the Sanskrit *loga,* signifying the world. There would, at first sight, seem to be a connection between this etymology and the symbolic meaning of a Lodge, which represents the world; but yet it is evidently far-fetched, since we have a much simpler root immediately at hand. Mr. Hope says, speaking of the Freemasons of the Middle Ages (and Wren had previously said the same thing), that wherever they were engaged to work, they "set themselves to building temporary huts, for their habitation, around the spot where the work was to be carried on." These huts the German Masons called *hutten;* the English, *lodges,* which is from the Anglo-Saxon, *logian,* to dwell. Lodge, therefore, meant the dwelling-place or lodging of the Masons; and this is undoubtedly the origin of the modern use of the word. To corroborate this, we find Du Cange (*Gloss.*) defining the Medieval Latin, *logia* or *logium,* as "a house or habitation." He refers to the Italian, *loggia,* and quotes Lambertus Ardensis as saying that "*logia* is a place next to the house, where persons were accustomed to hold pleasant conversation." Hence Lambertus thinks that it comes from the Greek, *logos,* a discourse. Du Cange asserts that there is no doubt that in the Middle Ages *logia* or *logium* was commonly used for an apartment or dwelling connected with the main building. Thus, the smallest apartments occupied by the cardinals when meeting in conclave were called *logiæ* or Lodges. All of which sustains the idea that the Lodges of the old Operative Masons were small dwellings attached, or at least contiguous, to the main edifice on which they were at work.

In the Old Charges, the word is not generally met with. The meeting of the Craft is there usually called *the Assembly.* But there are instances of its employment in those documents. Thus in the *Lodge of Antiquity MS.* whose date is 1686, the word occurs several times. There is also abundant documentary evidence to show that the word Lodge was long before the eighteenth century, applied to their meeting by the Freemasons of England and Scotland.

Before the restoration of the Grand Lodge of England in 1717, Preston tells us that any number of brethren might assemble at any place for the performance of work, and, when so assembled, were authorized to receive into the Order brothers and fellows, and to practise the rites of Masonry. The ancient charges were the only standard for the regulation of their conduct. The Master of the Lodge was elected *pro tempore,* and his authority terminated with the dissolution of the meeting over which he had presided, unless the Lodge was permanently established at any particular place. To the general assembly of the Craft, held once or twice a year, all the brethren indiscriminately were amenable, and to that power alone. But on the formation of Grand Lodges, this inherent right of assembling was voluntarily surrendered by the brethren and the Lodges, and vested in the Grand Lodge. And from this time Warrants of Constitution date their existence.

The mode of bringing a Lodge into existence under the present system in America is as follows: Seven Master Masons, being desirous of establishing a Lodge, apply by petition to the Grand Master, who will, if he thinks proper, issue his dispensation authorizing them to congregate as Masons in a Lodge, and therein to confer the three degrees of Ancient Craft Masonry. This instrument is of force during the pleasure of the Grand Master. At the next meeting of the Grand Lodge it expires, and is surrendered to the Grand Lodge, which, if there be no objection, will issue a Charter, technically called a Warrant of Constitution, whereby the body is permanently established as a Lodge, and as one of the constituents of the Grand Lodge.

The power of granting Warrants of Constitution is vested in the Grand Lodges of Scotland, Ireland, Germany, and France, as it is in America; but in England the rule is different, and there the prerogative is vested in the Grand Master.

A Lodge thus constituted consists, in the American system, of the following officers: Worshipful Master, Senior and Junior Wardens, Treasurer, Secretary, Senior and Junior Deacons, two Stewards, and a Tiler.

Under the English Constitution the officers are, in addition to these, a Director of Ceremonies, a Chaplain, an Inner Guard, an Organist and an Almoner.

In a Lodge of the French Rite, the officers are still more numerous. They are Le Venerable or Worshipful Master, Premier and Second Surveillants or Senior and Junior Wardens, Orator, Treasurer, Secretary, Hospitaler or Collector of Alms, the Expert, combining the duties of the Senior Deacon and an examining committee, Master of Ceremonies, Architecte, who attends to the decoration of the Lodge, and superintends the financial department, Archiviste or Librarian, Keeper of the Seal, Master of the Banquets or Steward, and Guardian of the Temple or Tiler.

The officers in a Lodge of the Ancient and Accepted Scottish Rite are a Master, two Wardens, Orator, Treasurer, Secretary, Almoner, Expert, Assistant Expert, Master of Ceremonies, Almoner Steward, Tiler, and sometimes a few others as Pursuivant, and Keeper of the Seals.

In other Rites and countries the officers vary to a slight extent, but everywhere there are four officers who always are found, and who may therefore be considered as indispensable, namely, the Master, two Wardens and Tiler.

A Lodge thus constituted is a Lodge of Master Masons. Strictly and legally speaking, such a body as a Lodge of Entered Apprentices or of Fellow-Crafts is not known under the present Masonic system. No Warrant is ever granted for an Apprentices' or Fellow-Crafts' Lodge, and without a Warrant a Lodge cannot exist. The Warrant granted is always for a Masters' Lodge, and the members composing it are all Master Masons. The Lodges mentioned by Wren and Hope, to which allusion has been made, and which were congregated, in the Middle Ages, around the edifices which the Masons were constructing, were properly Fellow-Crafts' Lodge, because all the members were Fellow-Crafts; even the Master being merely a gradation of rank, not a degree of knowledge. So at the revival of Masonry in 1717, the Lodges were Entered Apprentices' Lodges, because in them nothing but the First Degree was conferred, and nearly all the members were Entered Apprentices. But when the Grand Lodge, where only at first the Fellow-Craft and Master's Degree were conferred, permitted them to be conferred in the subordinate Lodges, then the degree of Master Mason was sought for by all the Craft, and became the object of every Mason's ambition. From that time the Craft became master Masons, and the First and Second degrees were considered only as preliminary steps. So it has remained to this day; and all modern Lodges, wherever Masonry has extended, are Masters' Lodges, and nothing less.

Sometimes secretaries, ignorant of these facts, will record in their minutes that "the Lodge of Master Masons was closed and a Lodge of Entered Apprentices was opened." Neither written nor unwritten law sanctions any such phraseology. If the Lodge of Master Masons is closed, there is an end of the Masonic congregation. Where is the Warrant under which a Lodge of Entered Apprentices is opened, and how can a Lodge, in which there is not, probably, a single Apprentice, but where all the officers and all the members are Master Masons, be called a Lodge of Apprentices?" The ritual has wisely provided for the avoidance of such an anomaly, and, seeing that the Warrant says that the Lodge of Master Masons is empowered to make Apprentices and Fellow-Crafts, it says "the Lodge was opened on the first degree." That is to say, the Lodge of Masters still retaining its character as a Masters' Lodge, without which it would lose its legality, and not venturing to open a kind of Lodge for which its members had no Warrant nor authority, simply placed itself on the points of a degree in which it was about to give instruction.

Some of the rituals speak, it is true, of Lodges composed in ancient times of Masters and Fellow-Crafts or Masters and Apprentices; and the Webb lectures tell us that at the Temple of Solomon the Lodges of Entered Apprentices consisted of one Master and six Apprentices, and the Lodges of Fellow-Crafts of two Masters and three Fellow-Crafts. But all this is purely symbolic, and has no real existence in the practical working of the Order. No one in these days has seen a Lodge of one Master Mason and six Apprentices. The Masons working in the First Degree are as much Master Masons as the same Masons are when they are working in the Third. The Lodge legally is the same, though it may vary the subjects of its instruction so as to have them in the First, Second, or Third Degree.

So important a feature in Masonry as a Lodge, the congregations of Masons for work or worship, cannot be without its appropriate symbolism. Hence a Lodge when duly opened becomes a symbol of the world. Its covering is like the world's, a sky or clouded canopy, to reach which, as the abode of those who do the will of the Great Architect, it is furnished with the theological ladder, which reaches from earth to heaven; and it is illuminated as is the world, by the refulgent rays of the sun, symbolically represented in his rising in the East, his meridian height in the South, and his setting in the West; and lastly, its very form, a long quadrangle or oblong square, is in reference to the early tradition that such was the shape of the inhabited world.

3. The Lodge, technically speaking, is a piece of furniture made in imitation of the Ark of the Covenant, which was constructed by Bezaleel (Exodus xxxvii. 1) according to the form prescribed by God himself, and which, after the erection of the Temple, was kept in the Holy of Holies. As that contained the table of the laws, the Lodge contains the Book of Constitutions and the Warrant of Constitution granted by the Grand Lodge. It is used only in certain ceremonies, such as the constitution and consecration of new Lodges, but its use is obsolete in England.

Lodge, Chartered. See *Chartered Lodge.*

Lodge, Clandestine. See *Clandestine Lodge.*

Lodge, Constituted. See *Constituted Legally.*

Lodge, Dormant. See *Dormant Lodge.*

Lodge, Emergent. See *Emergent Lodge.*

Lodge, Extinct. See *Extinct Lodge.*

Lodge, Holy. See *Holy Lodge.*

Lodge Hours. Dermott says (*Ahim. Rez.*, p. xxiii.) "that Lodge hours, that is, the time in which it is lawful for a Lodge to work or do business, are from March 25th to September 25th, between the hours of seven and ten; and from September 25th to March 25th, between the hours of six and nine." Whence he derived the law is unknown; but it is certain that it has never been rigidly observed even by the "ancient Lodges," for whom his *Ahiman Rezon* was written.

Lodge, Just. See *Just Lodge.*

Lodge Master, English. (*Maître de Lodge Anglais.*) A degree in the nomenclature of Thory, inserted on the authority of Lemanceau.

Lodge Master, French. (*Maître de Loge Français.*) The Twenty-sixth Degree of the collection of the Metropolitan Chapter of France.

Lodge, Occasional. See *Occasional Lodge.*

Lodge of Instruction. These are assemblies of brethren congregated without a Warrant of Constitution, under the direction of a lecturer or skilful brother, for the purpose of improvement in Masonry, which is accomplished by the frequent rehearsal of the work and lectures of each degree. These bodies should consist exclusively of Master Masons; and though they possess no Masonic power, it is evident to every Mason that they are extremely useful as schools of preparation for the duties that are afterward to be performed in the regular Lodge. In England, these Lodges of Instruction are attached to regularly Warranted Lodges, or are specially licensed by the Grand Master. But they have an independent set of officers, who are elected at no stated periods—sometimes for a year, sometimes for six or three months, and sometimes changed at every night of meeting. They of course have no power of initiation, but simply meet for purposes of practise in the ritual. They are, however, bound to keep a record of their transactions, subject to the inspection of the superior powers.

Lodge of St. John. The Masonic tradition is that the primitive or mother Lodge was held at Jerusalem, and dedicated to St. John, first the Baptist, then the Evangelist, and finally to both. Hence this Lodge was called "The Lodge of the Holy St. John of Jerusalem." From this Lodge all other Lodges are supposed figuratively to descend, and they therefore receive the same general name, accompanied by another local and distinctive one. In all Masonic documents the words ran formerly as follows: "From the Lodge of the holy St. John of Jerusalem, under the distinctive appellation of Solomon's Lodge, No. 1," or whatever might be the local name. In this style foreign documents still run; and it is but a few years since it has been at all disused in America. Hence we say that every Mason hails from such a Lodge, that is to say, from a just and legally constituted Lodge. In the earliest catechisms of the eighteenth century we find this formula: "*Q.* What Lodge are you of? *A.* The Lodge of St. John." And another question is, "How many angles in St. John's Lodge?" In one of the high degrees it is stated that Lodges receive this title "because, in the time of the Crusades, the Perfect Masons communicated a knowledge of their Mysteries to the Knights of St. John of Jerusalem," and as both were thus under the same law, the Lodges were called St. John's Lodges. But this was only one of the attempts to connect Freemasonry with the Templar system.

Lodge, Perfect. See *Just Lodge.*

Lodge, Regular. See *Regular Lodge.*

Lodge Room. The Masons on the Continent of Europe have a prescribed form or ritual of building, according to whose directions it is absolutely necessary that every hall for Masonic purposes shall be erected. No such regulation exists among the Fraternity of America or Great Britain. Still, the usages of the Craft, and the objects of convenience in the administration of our rites, require that certain general rules should be followed in the construction of a Lodge room. These rules, as generally observed in America, are as follows:

A Lodge room should always, if possible, be situated due East and West. This position is not absolutely necessary; and yet it is so far so as to demand that some sacrifices should be

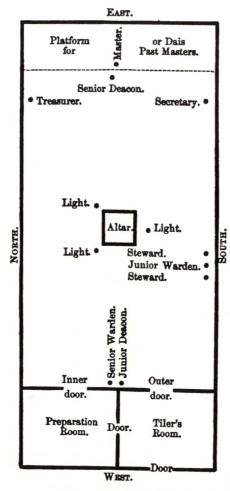

made, if possible, to obtain so desirable a position. It should also be isolated, where it is practicable, from all surrounding buildings, and should always be placed in an upper story. No Lodge should ever be held on the ground floor.

The form of a Lodge room should be that of a parallelogram or oblong square, at least one-third larger from East to West than it is from North to South. The ceiling should be lofty, to give dignity to the appearance of the hall, as well as for the purposes of health, by compensating, in some degree, for the inconvenience of closed windows, which necessarily will deteriorate the quality of the air in a very

short time in a low room. The approaches to the Lodge room from without should be angular, for, as Oliver says, "A straight entrance is unmasonic, and cannot be tolerated." There should be two entrances to the room, which should be situated in the West, and on each side of the Senior Warden's station. The one on his right hand is for the introduction of visitors and members, and leading from the Tiler's room, is called the Tiler's, or the outer door; the other, on his left, leading from the preparation room, is known as the "inner door," and sometimes called the "northwest door." The situation of these two doors, as well as the rooms with which they are connected, and which are essentially necessary in a well-constructed Lodge room, may be seen from the diagram in opposite column, which also exhibits the seats of the officers and the arrangement of the altar and lights. For further observations, see *Hall, Masonic*.

Lodge, Royal. See *Royal Lodge*.

Lodge, Sacred. See *Sacred Lodge*.

Lodge, Symbol of the. The modern symbol or hieroglyphic of the word Lodge is the figure ▭, which undoubtedly refers to the form of the Lodge as an "oblong square." But in the old rituals of the early part of the last century we find this symbol: The cross here, as Krause (*Kunsturk.*, i., 37) suggests, refers to the "four angles" of the Lodge, as in the question: "How many angles in St. John's Lodge? *A.* Four, bordering on squares"; and the delta is the Pythagorean symbol of Divine Providence watching over the Lodge. This symbol has long since become obsolete.

Loge. The French word for Lodge.

Logic. The art of reasoning, and one of the seven liberal arts and sciences, whose uses are inculcated in the Second Degree. The power of right reasoning, which distinguishes the man of sane mind from the madman and the idiot, is deemed essential to the Mason, that he may comprehend both his rights and his duties. And hence the unfortunate beings just named, who are without this necessary mental quality, are denied admission into the Order. The Old Charges define logic to be the art "that teacheth to discern truth from falsehood."

Loki. See *Balder*.

Lombardy. At the close of the dark ages, Lombardy and the adjacent Italian States were the first which awakened to industry. New cities arose, and the kings, lords, and municipalities began to encourage the artificers of different professions. Among the arts exercised and improved in Lombardy, the art of building held a preeminent rank, and from that kingdom, as from a center, the Comacine Masters were dispersed over all Europe. (See *Traveling Freemasons: Comacine*.)

London. With the city of London, the modern history of Freemasonry is intimately connected. A congress of Masons, as it may properly be called, was convened there by the four old Lodges, at the Apple-Tree Tavern, in 1717. Its results were the formation of the Grand Lodge of England, and a modification of the Masonic system, whence the Freemasonry of the present day has descended. Anderson, in his second edition of the *Book of Constitutions* (1738), gives the account of this, as it is now called, *Revival of Masonry*, which see.

Lost Word. The mythical history of Freemasonry informs us that there once existed a WORD of surpassing value, and claiming a profound veneration; that this Word was known to but few; that it was at length lost; and that a temporary substitute for it was adopted. But as the very philosophy of Masonry teaches us that there can be no death without a resurrection—no decay without a subsequent restoration—on the same principle it follows that the loss of the Word must suppose its eventual recovery.

Now, this it is, precisely, that constitutes the myth of the Lost Word and the search for it. No matter what was the word, no matter how it was lost, nor why a substitute was provided, nor when nor where it was recovered. These are all points of subsidiary importance, necessary, it is true, for knowing the legendary history, but not necessary for understanding the symbolism. The only term of the myth that is to be regarded in the study of its interpretation, is the abstract idea of a word lost and afterward recovered.

The WORD, therefore, may be conceived to be the symbol of *Divine Truth;* and all its modifications—the loss, the substitution, and the recovery—are but component parts of the mythical symbol which represents a search after truth. In a general sense, the *Word* itself being then the symbol of *Divine Truth,* the narrative of its loss and the search for its recovery becomes a mythical symbol of the decay and loss of the true religion among the ancient nations, at and after the dispersion on the plains of Shinar, and of the attempts of the wise men, the philosophers, and priests, to find and retain it in their secret mysteries and initiations, which have hence been designated as the Spurious Freemasonry of Antiquity.

But there is a special or individual, as well as a general interpretation, and in this special or individual interpretation the Word, with its accompanying myth of a loss, a substitute, and a recovery, becomes a symbol of the personal progress of a candidate from his first initiation to the completion of his course, when he receives a full development of the mysteries.

Lotus. The lotus plant, so celebrated in the religions of Egypt and Asia, is a species of Nymphæa, or water-lily, which grows abundantly on the banks of streams in warm climates. Although more familiarly known as the lotus of the Nile, it was not indigenous to Egypt, but was probably introduced into that country from the East, among whose people it was everywhere consecrated as a sacred symbol. The Brahmanical deities were almost always represented as either decorated with its flowers, or holding it as a scepter, or seated on it as a throne. Coleman says (*Mythol.*

Hindus, p. 388) that to the Hindu poets the lotus was what the rose was to the Persians. Floating on the water it is the emblem of the world, and the type also of the mountain Meru, the residence of the gods. Among the Egyptians, the lotus was the symbol of Osiris and Isis. It was esteemed a sacred ornament by the priests, and was placed as a coronet upon the heads of many of the gods. It was also much used in the sacred architecture of the Egyptians, being placed as an entablature upon the columns of their temples. Thence it was introduced by Solomon into Jewish architecture, being found, under the name of "lily work," as a part of the ornaments of the two pillars at the porch of the Temple. (See *Lily* and *Pillars of the Porch.*)

Louis Napoleon. Second Adjoint of the Grand Master of the G. Orient of France. Nominated, in 1806, King of Holland. Louis Napoleon III. was widely known as an interested Mason.

Louisiana. Masonry was introduced into Louisiana in 1793 by the organization of Perfect Union Lodge, under a Charter issued by the Grand Lodge of South Carolina. A second Lodge was established by the Mother Lodge of Marseilles, in France; and three others were subsequently chartered by the Grand Lodge of Pennsylvania. These five Lodges instituted a Grand Lodge on July 11, 1812, and Francis du Bourg was elected the first Grand Master. A difference of nationality and of Masonic rites have been a fertile source of controversy in Louisiana, the results of which it would be tedious to follow in detail. In 1848, there were two Grand Lodges, which were united in 1850 to constitute the present Grand Lodge.

The Grand Chapter of Louisiana was instituted on March 5, 1813; a Grand Council of Royal and Select Masters on February 16, 1856; and a Grand Commandery of Knights Templar on February 4, 1864. The Ancient and Accepted Scottish Rite has always held a prominent position in the Masonry of Louisiana, and it has a Grand Consistory and many subordinate bodies of the Rite in active and successful operation.

Louveteau. See *Lewis.*

Lowen. In the Lansdowne Manuscript we meet with this charge: "that a Master or ffellow make not a moulde stone square, nor rule to no *Lowen,* nor sett no *Lowen* worke within the Lodge." [This has been said to be an error for "*Cowan,*" but it is more probably intended for "*Layer*" (*q. v.*), which is the word used in the parallel passage in other MSS.—E. L. H.]

Low Twelve. In Masonic language midnight is so called. The reference is to the sun, which is then below the earth. Low twelve in Masonic symbolism is an unpropitious hour.

Loyalty. Notwithstanding the calumnies of Barruel, Robison, and a host of other anti-Masonic writers who assert that Masonry is ever engaged in efforts to uproot the governments within which it may exist, there is nothing more evident than that Freemasonry is a loyal institution, and that it inculcates, in all its public instructions, obedience to government. Thus, in the Prestonian charge given in the last century to the Entered Apprentice, and continued to this day in the same words in English Lodges, we find the following words:

"In the State, you are to be a quiet and peaceable subject, true to your sovereign, and just to your country; you are not to countenance disloyalty or rebellion, but patiently submit to legal authority, and conform with cheerfulness to the government under which you live, yielding obedience to the laws which afford you protection, but never forgetting the attachment you owe to the place of your nativity, or the allegiance due to the sovereign or protectors of that spot."

The charge given in American Lodges is of the same import, and varies but slightly in its language.

"In the State, you are to be a quiet and peaceful subject, true to your government, and just to your country; you are not to countenance disloyalty or rebellion, but patiently submit to legal authority, and conform with cheerfulness to the government of the country in which you live."

The charge given in French Lodges, though somewhat differing in form from both of these, is couched in the same spirit and teaches the same lesson. It is to this effect:

"Obedience to the laws and submission to the authorities are among the most imperious duties of the Mason, and he is forbidden at all times from engaging in plots and conspiracies."

Hence it is evident that the true Mason must be a true patriot.

Luchet, Jean Pierre Louis, Marquis de. A French historical writer, who was born at Saintes in 1740, and died in 1791. He was the writer of many works of but little reputation, but is principally distinguished in Masonic literature as the author of an attack upon Illuminism under the title of *Essai sur la Secte des Illuminés.* It first appeared anonymously in 1789. Four editions of it were published. The third and fourth with augmentations and revisions, which were attributed to Mirabeau, were printed with the outer title of *Histoire secret de la Cour de Berlin (par Mirabeau).* This work was published, it is known, without his consent, and was burned by the common executioner in consequence of its libelous character. Luchet's essay has become very scarce, and is now valued rather on account of its rarity than for its intrinsic excellence.

Ludewig, H. E. An energetic Mason, born in 1810, in Germany; died in 1856, in America. By "powers from home" this ardent brother attempted to set up an independent authority to the existing Grand Lodge system in the United States; but, like many such attempts, it flashed brilliantly for a season, but proved of ephemeral nature.

Lufton. One of the French terms for Louveteau, or *Lewis,* which see.

Lully, Raymond. A celebrated chemist and philosopher, the seneschal of Majorca, surnamed *le docteur illuminé.* His discoveries are most noted, such as the mode of rectifying spirits, the refining of silver, etc. He was born about 1234. In 1276 he founded a college of Franciscans at Palma, for instruction in Eastern lore, and especially the study of the Arabic language, for which purpose he instituted several colleges between the years 1293 and 1311. He died in 1314. He is known as an eminent Rosicrucian, and many fables as to his longevity are related of him.

Lumiere, La Grande. (*The Grand Light.*) A grade in the collection of Brother Viany.

Lumiere, La Vraie. (*The True Light, or Perfect Mason.*) A degree in the Chapter of the Grand Lodge of Royal York of Berlin. (Thory, *Acta Lat.,* i., 321.)

Luminaries. The first five officers in a French Lodge, namely, the Master, two Wardens, Orator, and Secretary, are called *luminaires* or luminaries, because it is by them that light is dispensed to the Lodge.

Lunus. An Egyptian deity, known as Khons Lunus, and represented as hawk-headed, surmounted by the crescent and disk. When appearing with the head of an ibis, he is called Thoth-Lunus. His worship was very extensive through ancient Egypt, where he was known as Aah, who presides over rejuvenation and resurrection. Champollion mentions in his *Pantheon* a Lunus bifrons.

Lustration. A religious rite practised by the ancients, and performed before any act of devotion. It consisted in washing the hands, and sometimes the whole body, in lustral or consecrated water. It was intended as a symbol of the internal purification of the heart. It was a ceremony preparatory to initiation in all the Ancient Mysteries. The ceremony is practised with the same symbolic import in some of the high degrees of Masonry. So strong was the idea of a connection between lustration and initiation, that in the low Latin of the Middle Ages *lustrare* meant to initiate. Thus Du Cange (*Glossarium*) cites the expression "lustrare religione Christianorum" as signifying "to initiate into the Christian religion."

Lux. Latin for *light,* which see. Freemasonry anciently received, among other names, that of "Lux," because it is that sublime doctrine of truth by which the pathway of him who has attained it is to be illumined in the pilgrimage of life. Among the Rosicrucians, light was the knowledge of the philosopher's stone; and Mosheim says that in chemical language the cross was an emblem of light, because it contains within its figure the forms of the three figures of which LVX, or light, is composed.

Lux e tenebris. *Light out of darkness.* A motto very commonly used in the caption of Masonic documents as expressive of the object of Masonry, and of what the true Mason supposes himself to have attained. It has a recondite meaning. In the primeval ages and in the early mythology, darkness preceded light. "In the thought," says Cox, "of these early ages, the sun was the child of night or darkness." (*Aryan Myth.*, i., 43.) So *lux* being truth or Masonry, and *tenebræ*, or darkness, the symbol of initiation, *lux e tenebris* is Masonic truth proceeding from initiation.

Lux Fiat et Lux Fit. Latin. "Let there be light, and there was light." A motto sometimes prefixed to Masonic documents.

Luz. An ever-living power, according to the old Jewish Rabbis, residing in a small joint-bone existing at the base of the spinal column. To this undying principle, watered by the dew of heaven, is ascribed the immortality in man.

"R. Joshua Ben Hananiah replied to Hadrian, as to how man revived in the world to come, 'From *Luz*, in the back-bone.' When asked to demonstrate this, he took Luz, a little bone out of the back-bone, and put it in water, and it was not steeped; he put it in the fire, and it was not burned; he brought it to the mill, and that could not grind it; he laid it on the anvil, and knocked it with a hammer, but the anvil was cleft, and the hammer broken."

L. V. C. Letters inscribed on the rings of profession, worn by the Knights of Baron von Hund's Templar system. They are the initials of the sentence *Labor Viris Convenit. Labor is suitable for men.* It was also engraved on their seals.

Lyon, David Murray. This well-known writer and historian of Freemasonry in Scotland was initiated in 1856 in Lodge Ayr St. Paul, No. 204, on the roll of the Grand Lodge of Scotland. He was a printer by trade and was at one time employed by the Ayrshire Express Company. In 1877 he was appointed Grand Secretary of the Grand Lodge of Scotland and held the post until 1900. He died on January 30, 1903.

He was, without doubt, the foremost Masonic student of Scotland, either of this or any other period; and the results of his continuous and arduous researches are to be found in all the books and periodicals of the Craft for the last twenty years, both at home and abroad. It is simply impossible to furnish anything like an accurate and complete list of his many valuable contributions to Masonic magazines. . . . His chief works have been the *History of the Mother Lodge Kilwinning*, Scotland, the *History of the Old Lodge at Thornhill*, and, finally, the *History of the Ancient Lodge at Edinburgh* (Mary's Chapel), from the sixteenth century. This grand work, which was published in 1873, has placed its author in the front rank of Masonic authors.

[E. L. H.]

Lyons, Congress of. A Masonic congress was convoked in 1778, at the city of Lyons, France, by the Lodge of Chevaliers Bienfaisants. It was opened on the 26th of November, and continued in session until the 27th of December, under the presidency of M. Villermoz. Its ostensible object was to procure a reformation in Masonry by the abjuration of the Templar theory; but it wasted its time in the correction of rituals and in Masonic intrigues, and does not appear to have been either sagacious in its methods, or successful in its results. Even its abjuration of the Strict Observance doctrine that Templarism was the true origin of Freemasonry, is said to have been insincere, and forced upon it by the injunctions of the political authorities, who were opposed to the propagation of any system which might tend to restore the Order of Knights Templar.

Thank you for buying this Cornerstone book!

For over 25 years now, I've tried to provide the Masonic community with quality books on Masonic education, philosophy, and general interest. Your support means everything to us and keeps us afloat. Cornerstone is by no means a large company. We are a small family owned operation that depends on your support.

Please visit our website and have a look at the many books we offer as well as the different categories of books.

If your lodge, Grand Lodge, research lodge, book club, or other body would like to have quality Cornerstone books to sell or distribute, write us. We can give you outstanding books, prices, and service.

Thanks again!

Michael R. Poll
Publisher
Cornerstone Book Publishers
1cornerstonebooks@gmail.com
http://cornerstonepublishers.com

New Orleans Scottish Rite College
http://www.youtube.com/c/NewOrleansScottishRiteCollege

Clear, Easy to Watch
Scottish Rite and Craft Lodge
Video Education

Made in the USA
Las Vegas, NV
04 October 2021